11/98

3000 800030 39417

WITHDRAWN

D1212477

FRAME BY FRAME II

FRAME BY FRAME II

A FILMOGRAPHY
OF THE AFRICAN AMERICAN IMAGE,
1978-1994

Phyllis R. Klotman and Gloria J. Gibson

Indiana University Press
Bloomington & Indianapolis

The paper used in this publication meets the minimum requirements of American National Standard for Information Sciences—Permanence of Paper for Printed Library Materials, ANSI Z39.48-1984.

Manufactured in the United States of America

Library of Congress Cataloging-in-Publication Data

Klotman, Phyllis Rauch.
    Frame by frame II : a filmography of the African American image, 1978-1994 / Phyllis R. Klotman and Gloria J. Gibson.
        p. cm.
    Includes bibliographical references and indexes.
    ISBN 0-253-33280-X (cl : alk. paper). — ISBN 0-253-21120-4 (pa : alk. paper)
    1. Afro-Americans in the motion picture industry—Dictionaries. 2. Afro-American motion picture actors and actresses—Biography—Dictionaries. 3. Motion pictures—United States—Catalogs. I. Gibson, Gloria J.   II. Title.
PN 1995.9.N4K56   1997
791.43'08996073—dc21   96-29770

1 2 3 4 5 02 01 00 99 98 97

Contents

Acknowledgments   vii

Introduction   ix

How to Use This Volume   xiii

Alphabetical Listing of Films   1

Index of Black Cast *performer*   535

Index of Black Directors   688

Index of Black Executive Producers   701

Index of Black Music Performers   704

Index of Black Producers   723

Index of Black Screenwriters   735

Index of Distributors *appendix in volume I*   744

Selected Archives   760

Selected Bibliography   762

African American Oscar Award Winners
  and Nominees   768

The two people most responsible for getting this book into print are Monique Threatt and Ronald Edge. Monique has lived through every permutation of design, learned every new database program, suffered over power outages and the sometimes inexplicable loss of data. She has continued to enter data into the computer, always believing that this work would ultimately find its way into print. Ron has given countless (pro bono) hours to saving our data, moving us from one program to another and finally designing the special features that allowed the transition to FOXPRO Windows to be successful. There is no way to thank them enough.

Professor Ronald Smith of the Folklore Institute, an early member of the BFC/A's Advisory Council, helped with the conceptual development of this second volume. His knowledge and insight into the database world pointed us in the right direction. In addition, we have had funding assistance from a Ford Foundation grant, under the direction of Professor Portia Maultsby, to the Department of Afro-American Studies.

Over time a number of graduate and undergraduate students have worked at the BFC/A more than one semester and assisted with the research or the early program development: Nick Baham, Michelle Brown, Richara Jennings, Julie Lalwani, Leslie Lewis, Kelly Megnin, Jill Moniz, Andrea Morehead. Their work has been invaluable to the project.

We have also sought the help of those knowledgeable in the field with the numerous problems that arise when compiling such a work: Tanya Kersey-Henley, Sergio Mims, Jesse Rhines, Floyd Webb, as well as Madeline Matz in the Motion Picture, Broadcasting, and Recorded Sound Division of the Library of Congress and Indiana University librarians Kristine Brancolini and Colleen Talty. And certainly there are countless others who have responded to our queries or volunteered information about their own work or the work of others, e.g. Carroll Blue, St. Clair Bourne, Tony Brown, Zeinabu Davis, Louise Greaves, Dr. Roland Jefferson, Iverson White.

We also wish to acknowledge the use of such sources as the California Newsreel, Third World Newsreel and Women Make Movies catalogs; "Film Index International" issued by the British Film Institute, Library and Information Service (Paris: Chadwyck-Healy, 1995); "The Motion Picture Guide" (New York: Cinebooks, 1995) both on CD-ROM; and the "Academy Award Nominations and Winners Binder," published by the Academy of Motion Picture Arts and Sciences.

Finally, our thanks go to Professor John McCluskey, chair of the Department of Afro-American Studies, to Dean Mort Lowengrub of the College of Arts and Sciences and to Vice President and Chancellor Kenneth R. R Gros Louis for their continuing support of the Black Film Center/Archive and their expressions of confidence in the unique contributions of the BFC/A to the intellectual and cultural life of the university.

This publication is a project of the Black Film Center/Archive in the Department of Afro-American Studies at Indiana University. It is an addition to the original Frame by Frame--A Black Filmography, edited by Phyllis Klotman and published by Indiana University Press in 1979. We have backtracked to 1978 in order to complete entries for that year, but the cut-off date unfortunately excludes a number of earlier films that have since been found and are now accessible; for example, Oscar Micheaux's Within our Gates (1920) and Veiled Aristocrats (1932), and the epic--reduced to one reel--The Birth of a Race (1918), conceived by Emmett J. Scott as an answer to the racial calumny in D. C. Griffith's The Birth of a Nation.

The concept of Frame by Frame is still the same: to give credit to African Americans who have contributed their talents to a film industry that has scarcely recognized their contributions, and to acknowledge those independents who have set their own course in direct opposition to Hollywood. If the vast majority of the entries in the "Alphabetical Listing of Films" are Hollywood films (many of them "B" films), produced and directed by whites, it is because African Americans have had limited opportunities to control the means of production.

The objective here is not to judge the "worthiness" of inclusion, but to strive to present the totality of African Americans' contributions. We see it as important, then, to acknowledge those whose appearance in feature films may be brief and may be token because their minimal presence also illuminates the larger picture of American society in which conscious or unconscious racism still operates at every level. Therefore, inclusion allows readers/audiences to investigate how films with African American images both inform and misinform. Scholars can investigate how films are imbued with historical accuracy or how they deviate from it. At one end of the spectrum are films that heighten our sensitivity to historical, social, political and cultural issues involving African Americans--films that evoke questions; at the other end are films that are primarily formulaic. There exist many gradations between these two points. It is only from an inclusive framework that the totality of cultural imagery and societal dynamics can be discussed and evaluated.

To identify this reference volume as a filmography of the black image further reflects an inclusive perspective. However, some films documented do not include visual images. For example, several films, like The Addams Family, are included yet there is no African American image in this film. There is, however, an African American imprint because the title song was written and performed by M. C. Hammer, an African American. The contribution of black musicians to mainstream film, especially during the last two decades, has been extraordinary. Many films have included black performers, others have proved to be popular and financial successes because of the soundtrack. Therefore, image refers not only to the visual but also to the aural dimension.

There have been several other salutary developments in independent

African American film since the seventies. First, the number of productions by independents has increased dramatically. Some of these occurred when ethnic studies arrived at UCLA, along with Charles Burnett, Haile Gerima, Larry Clark, Billy Woodberry and somewhat later Julie Dash, Alile Sharon Larkin and Barbara McCullough. On the east coast, film departments and schools produced the Hudlin brothers, Charles Lane, Spike Lee, Matty Rich, whose independent works attracted mainstream funding and wider audiences. The box office success of Lee's films led to financial support of USC's John Singleton (Boyz N the Hood, 1991), the Hughes brothers (Menace II Society, 1991) and Mario Van Peebles (New Jack City). In fact, in 1991 more black-oriented films were released than in the previous decade. Not surprisingly, Hollywood financial support meant less independence, less control of the image. Yet women were usually absent from the picture. Most of the articles acclaiming the new phenomenon of the nineties scarcely mentioned black women filmmakers. The struggle for inclusion continues to take place on both coasts and in both genres, feature film and documentaries.

Second, despite the fact that images of black women have improved very little in mainstream cinema, strides have been made in the number of productions by black women independent filmmakers. Their films and videos span most genres; they produce and experiment in short and feature length formats, and in everything from high 8 video to 35mm film. Sometimes they explore issues and themes germane to women (Zeinabu irene Davis, Cycles), and other times they are commissioned or selected to write, produce or direct films on various topics (Carroll Blue, Nigerian Art: Kindred Spirits). While many black women filmmakers suffer from a shortage of funding, they continue to seek innovative filmic formats and resourceful funding strategies.

Finally, the documentary has presented African Americans an entre into the business and art of the image. However, because there are so few theaters that show documentaries, they have either been screened in schools/colleges or on television. Black Journal (1968-71), America's first broadcast television news program to focus exclusively on African American concerns, was guided by Executive Producer William Greaves. He and his staffers, Madeline Anderson, St. Clair Bourne, Charles Hobson, Stan Lathan, and others went on to form a "first wave" of social documentarians with their subsequent independently produced and commissioned works. Tony Brown's Journal, Say Brother and Like It Is were also important in changing the way Black Americans saw themselves and the way others saw them on screen. Two decades later Henry Hampton brought the Civil Rights Movement into American homes with two Eyes on the Prize series. While it is impossible to include every production in this volume, we have included ground-breaking television documentaries that fit the period 1978-1994, for example, William Miles' I Remember Harlem series, and Marlon Riggs' Tongues Untied, which first aired on Public Television's P.O.V. Many of these programs are now available on videotape from some distributors.

Technology has brought about many extraordinary changes since 1979: 16mm films for teaching purposes or community screenings are difficult to get; film distributors have gone out of business, and 16mm projectors are going the way of the covered wagon. Video players now occupy space in almost every home, community center, school and even some theaters. With the advent of video cameras and playback, and digital and satellite technology, it is possible to record and disseminate thousands of programs a day. New technology also contributes to the explosion of video works produced on a local level through community workshops or access television. Video installations are also becoming more and more common place in museums. These formats are significant because they examine and give priority to community-based issues. This volume does not document these expanding formats. An all-encompassing database is needed to record these works so that communities can take advantage of each others' work and struggles. Unfortunately, we also have not been able to include an exhaustive listing of television features or documentaries in this volume or works available on laser disc.

Frame by Frame II represents only a portion of a larger database on African Americans and cinema. Over the past ten years, technology has allowed us to develop a more sophisticated means of information management and retrieval. Included in the larger database are additional fields, such as key word, geographic location, genre, historical era and gender specification. The database also includes positions such as cinematographer, editor, associate and co-producer. These detailed categories allow scholars, teachers and programmers to locate examples needed for research, teaching and community programming. Because computer technology has expanded since the first volume, the sophistication of the present system allows not only greater flexibility to document African American contributions, but also numerous ways to query and retrieve data.

With an undertaking this exhaustive, there are bound to be errors and omissions. The editors would be grateful for readers' comments and corrections. Please direct them to the Black Film Center/Archive at Indiana University (bfca@indiana.edu).

Frame by Frame II is a compendium of films and videos which credits the work of African American actors, screenwriters, musicians, directors and producers. It extends the original volume to include the years from 1978-1994. However, this publication does not include television features or television documentaries unless they have African Americans in front of, as well as behind, the camera, i.e. as producer, director, writer, and/or can be considered to have broken new ground, as did the Eyes on the Prize series (1987, 1990), Henry Hampton, Executive Producer. Original videos by African American videomakers are included although complete information was not always available for those entries.

African American(s), Black(s) and Black American(s) are used interchangeably; the letter b is capitalized when used as a noun; it is not capitalized when used as an adjective. African American and Black American are never hyphenated. All are used as denotations of respect.

Each one of the entries was researched for the following data:

Film Title
Series Title/Alternate Title
Cast/Narrator/Speaker
Director
Executive Producer
Music By
Music Performer
Producer
Screenwriter
Storywriter
Technical Information: color/sound/time
Type
Date/Country of Origin
Studio/Company
Distributor/Archive
Annotation

African Americans are identified by an asterisk following the name. Black Africans are designated in the same way.[1] In the cast/narrator/speaker categories, they are listed first regardless of whether or not they play leading roles in the film. We have attempted to validate ethnicity by using a number of different sources. If there are mistakes, we would appreciate corrections from our readers

---

[1]

Although the sub-title of Frame by Frame II makes it clear that African Americans are the focus of this volume, we have chosen to acknowledge the important contributions of Black Africans to the independent as well as the Hollywood films listed here by using the same designation for both.

1. Film Title/Series Title/Alternate Title

Film entries are listed alphabetically according to the first word of the title, exclusive of the article. Series titles follow. Foreign films are listed by the title used when the film was released in the United States. Its original title in the language of the country in which it was produced is listed as the **Alternate Title.**

2. Cast

The term **Cast** applies to fiction films, narrator and speaker to documentaries. As much as possible, the cast and crew were taken directly from the film, supplemented by secondary sources, e.g."Film Index International" and "Motion Picture Guide" on CD-ROM; print sources such as, Black Film Review, Ebony, New York Times Film Reviews, Premiere, Variety; catalogs, such as those from California Newsreel, Third World Newsreel and Women Make Movies. Because of space constraints, most cast lists have been limited to six actors; in those rare instances, e. g.Daughters of the Dust, in which over 40 African American actors appear, we have limited the list to 20 names.

3. Director

4. Executive Producer

5. Music By/ Music Performer

The **Music By** category credits the composer or arranger of the film music; the **Music Performer** may or may not be an actor in the film.

6. Producer

This category does not include co-producers or associate producers.

7. Screenwriter/Storywriter

African American writers whose work has been adapted to film are referenced in the annotations as well as in the **Storywriter** category.

8. Technical Info: Color/Sound/Time

Feature films are usually 90 minutes or more. Documentaries have traditionally been shorter. For consistency, we have arbitrarily designated **Documentary Feature** as 51 minutes or more, **Documentary Short** as 50 minutes or less.

9. Type

Animated Feature
Animated Short
Comedy Feature
Comedy Short
Concert Feature
Concert Short

Docudrama
Documentary Feature
Documentary Short
Dramatic Feature
Dramatized Documentary
Experimental Feature
Experimental Short
Musical Feature
Musical Short
Television Documentary
Television Feature
Television Miniseries

10. Date/Country of Origin

We have attempted to be consistent in the use of the release date of films that have had a theatrical release. In the case of original videos, we have used the date on the video itself.

11. Studio/Company

Since the demise of the studio system, the term Studio is rarely used. Company is the more appropriate term.

12. Distributor

Film distributors are listed if the film has been located; they can be found in the **Index of Distributors** if addresses and/or phone numbers were available. There are many more outlets for the rental or purchase of films on video now than there are for the rental and purchase of films in 16mm. (For the Main Distributor Sources see **Selected Bibliography**.) In fact, renting 16mm or 35mm films for teaching purposes (and purchasing, or even servicing, the equipment to project them) has become extremely problematic for schools and universities. Libraries are now using video almost exclusively. Certainly the availability of films on video has been a boon to the intensive study of individual films, but nothing can replace the experience of viewing a film in its original format. Original videos do not present the same problem; however, those without large distributors--the case with many independent African American videomakers who often do their own distributing--may be more difficult to locate.

13. Archives

Films available for screening on site at the Black Film Center/Archive and the Archives of African American Music and Culture at Indiana University are listed in the entries. **Neither archive distributes films or videos.** Inquiries regarding the holdings of other archives should be directed to the research facilities in the **Selected Archives** listing.

14. Annotation

As in the original <u>Frame by Frame</u>, descriptive annotations emphasize the presence and participation of African Americans. Each is identified and full cast lists have been assembled wherever possible. Main plots are secondary to the action in the film that is either participated in or initiated by the black actor(s), even if the role played is a minor one. Some films were excluded if only one uncredited black actor, or a single black actor with a generic designation, i. e. the Maid, the Driver, rather than a character name, appeared.

FRAME BY FRAME II

'ROUND MIDNIGHT
Cast: Herbie Hancock*, Dexter Gordon*, Sandra Reaves-Phillips*, Lonette McKee*, Bobby Hutcherson*, Victoria Gabriella Platt*, Jimmy Slyde*, Marpessa Dawn*, Francois Cluzet, Martin Scorsese, Arthur French
Director: Bertrand Tavernier
Music Performer: Dexter Gordon*, Sandra Reaves-Phillips*, Lonette McKee*, Billy Higgins*, Freddie Hubbard*, Ron Carter*
Music by: Herbie Hancock*
Producer: Irwin Winkler
Screenwriter: Bertrand Tavernier, David Rayfiel
Tech Info: color/sound/132 min.   Type: Dramatic Feature
Date: 1986   Origin: France, USA
Company: PECF, Little Bear
Distributors/Format: Warner Bros. Home Video, Inc. (1/2")
Archives/Format: IUB - BFC/A (1/2")
Annotation: The film follows the last days of sax great Dale Turner (Gordon) in Paris and New York. Hancock plays Eddie Wayne whose group Turner joins in Paris; McKee is singer Darcey Leigh, a lover from Turner's past; Reaves-Phillips plays Buttercup, a singer in Paris who looks out for Turner before that job is assumed by Francois (Cluzet). Platt plays Turner's daughter, Chan; Hutcherson, Ace; French, a drug dealer.

...AND JUSTICE FOR ALL
Cast: Robert Christian*, Joe Morton*, Jack Warden, Al Pacino, Lee Strasberg, Christine Lahti
Director: Norman Jewison
Music by: Dave Grusin
Producer: Patrick Palmer, Norman Jewison
Screenwriter: Barry Levinson, Valerie Curtin
Tech Info: color/sound/120 min.   Type: Dramatic Feature
Date: 1979   Origin: USA
Company: Columbia
Distributors/Format: Columbia Pictures Home Video (1/2")
Annotation: Kirkland (Pacino) is an idealistic defense attorney who is disillusioned by what he sees happening to his clients in an often cruel and unfair judicial system. Morton plays a prison doctor and Christian plays Agee, a transvestite.

...BUT THEN, SHE'S BETTY CARTER
Director: Michelle Parkerson*
Music Performer: Betty Carter*
Producer: Michelle Parkerson*
Screenwriter: Michelle Parkerson*
Speaker: Betty Carter*
Storywriter: Michelle Parkerson*
Tech Info: color/sound/53 min.   Type: Documentary Feature
Date: 1980   Origin: USA
Company: Eye of the Storm Productions
Distributors/Format: Women Make Movies, Inc. (16mm; 1/2")
Annotation: Parkerson juxtaposes the life of Carter as a jazz performer to the social and political issues involved for women in non-traditional roles.

1941
Cast: Frank McRae*, Dan Aykroyd, Ned Beatty, Samuel Fuller, John Belushi, Toshiro Mifune
Director: Steven Spielberg
Executive Producer: John Milius
Music by: John Williams
Producer: John Milius, Buzz Feitshans
Screenwriter: Robert Zemeckis, Bob Gale
Storywriter: Robert Zemeckis, John Milius
Tech Info: color/sound/118 min.   Type: Comedy Feature
Date: 1979   Origin: USA
Company: A-Team, Universal, Columbia
Distributors/Format: Universal Home Video (1/2")
Annotation: There are seven different story lines in this comedy that is loosely based on "The Great Los Angeles Air Raid." McRae plays Ogden Johnson Jones.

1990: THE BRONX WARRIORS

Alternate: 1990: I Guerrieri Del Bronx or Bronx Warriors
Cast: Fred Williamson*, Vic Morrow, George Eastman, Christopher Connelly, Stefani Girolami
Director: Enzo G. Castellari, Dardana Sachetti, Elisa Livia Brighanti
Music by: Walter Rizzati
Producer: Fabrizio De Angelis
Screenwriter: Dardano Sacchetti
Storywriter: Dardano Sacchetti
Tech Info: color/sound/84 min.   Type: Dramatic Feature
Date: 1983   Origin: Italy
Company: Deaf
Distributors/Format: United (16mm)
Annotation: Hammer (Morrow) is hired to find an heiress being used as a pawn in a war between two rival gangs who have control of the Bronx. Williamson portrays The Ogre.

24 HOURS TO MIDNIGHT
Cast: Stack Pierce*, Myra J. *, Leo Fong, Cynthia Rothrock, Bernie Pock
Director: Leo Fong
Screenwriter: Leo Fong
Tech Info: color/sound/91 min.   Type: Dramatic Feature
Date: 1992   Origin: USA
Company: AIP
Distributors/Format: AIP Home Video (1/2")
Annotation: When local gangster "White Powder" Chan (Pierce) kills government witnesses prepared to convict him, Devon Grady (Rothrock), wife of one of the slain witnesses, dons her martial arts gear and seeks revenge. Lee Ann Jackson (Myra) is one of the cops on the case.

38TH PARALLEL
Director: Reginald Woolery*
Tech Info: color/sound/16 min.   Type: Experimental Short

Date: 1992   Origin: USA
Studio: Independent
Distributors/Format: Third World Newsreel (1/2")
Annotation: This autobiographical video uses a mixture of visual media, images and sounds to present the alienation of an African American Korean War veteran from his adult son.

3:15, THE MOMENT OF TRUTH
Cast: Rusty Cundieff*, Mario Van Peebles*, Deborah Foreman, Adam Baldwin, Danny De La Paz
Director: Larry Gross
Music by: Gary Chang
Producer: Robert Kenner, Dennis Brody
Screenwriter: Sam Bernard, Michael Jacobs
Tech Info: color/sound/85 min.   Type: Dramatic Feature
Date: 1986   Origin: USA
Company: Romax, Jones Kenner, Brody
Distributors/Format: Dakota (1/2")
Annotation: Jeff Hannah (Baldwin) leaves behind his street gang to return to a normal high school life, but Cinco (De La Paz) suspects he has become a police informant. Van Peebles is Whisperer and Cundieff's role is uncredited.

48 HOURS
Cast: Eddie Murphy*, Frank McRae*, Nick Nolte, Annette O'Toole, James Remar
Director: Walter Hill
Executive Producer: Lawrence Gordon, D. Constantine Conte
Music Performer: The Bus Boys *
Music by: James Horner
Producer: Lawrence Gordon, Joel Silver, D. Constantine Conte
Screenwriter: Larry Gross, Walter Hill, Roger Spottiswoode, Steven E. DeSouza
Tech Info: color/sound/97 min.   Type: Comedy Feature
Date: 1983   Origin: USA
Company: Paramount
Distributors/Format: Paramount Home Video (1/2")
Archives/Format: IUB - BFC/A (1/2")
Annotation: Reggie Hammond (Murphy), who is doing time in prison for robbery, gets 48 hours out of jail, courtesy of policeman Jack Cates (Nolte) who wants Reggie's help in apprehending a vicious escaped criminal with whom Reggie has unfinished business. The Bus Boys perform "The Boys are Back in Town."

52 PICK-UP
Cast: Vanity *, Clarence Williams III*, Roy Scheider, Ann-Margret
Director: John Frankenheimer
Executive Producer: Henry T. Weinstein
Music by: Gary Chang
Producer: Yoram Globus, Menahem Golan, Henry T. Weinstein
Screenwriter: John Steppling
Storywriter: Elmore Leonard
Tech Info: color/sound/114 min.   Type: Dramatic Feature

Date: 1986   Origin: USA
Company: Cannon
Distributors/Format: Cannon Home Video (1/2")
Annotation: Williams plays Bobby Shy, one of three blackmailers who make life difficult for prosperous Los Angeles businessman Harry Mitchell (Scheider). Vanity plays Doreen.

8 MILLION WAYS TO DIE
Cast: Tom "Tiny" Lister Jr.*, James Avery*, Rosanna Arquette, Jeff Bridges, Randy Brooks, Andy Garcia
Director: Hal Ashby
Music by: James Newton Howard*
Producer: Stephen J. Roth, Charles Mulvehill
Screenwriter: Oliver Stone, David Lee Henry
Storywriter: Lawrence Block
Tech Info: color/sound/115 min.   Type: Dramatic Feature
Date: 1986   Origin: USA
Company: Producers Sales Organization
Distributors/Format: TriStar Pictures Inc. (1/2")
Annotation: Ex-detective Matt Scudder (Bridges) and Chance (Brooks), who was once busted by Scudder but is now a semi-legitimate business man, join forces to get Angel (Garcia) the real drug kingpin and rescue Sarah (Arquette) from Angel's clutches. Lister plays Nosegard, Chance's bodyguard.

84 CHARLIE MOPIC
Cast: Richard Brooks*, Jonathan Emerson, Nicholas Cascone, Jason Tomlins, Christopher Burgard, Glenn Morshower
Director: Patrick Duncan
Producer: Michael Nolin
Screenwriter: Patrick Duncan
Tech Info: color/sound/95 min.   Type: Dramatic Feature
Date: 1989   Origin: USA
Company: Charlie Mopic Company
Distributors/Format: New Century/Vista Film Corp (1/2")
Annotation: The experiences of a seven man unit stationed in Vietnam during the war are seen through the eyes of a cameraman who accompanies them on the front line. Brooks plays O.D., the sergeant who is the most experienced man in the unit and one of the three who survives.

ABOVE THE LAW
Cast: Pam Grier*, Thalmus Rasulala*, Gregory Alan-Williams*, Steven Seagal, Sharon Stone
Director: Andrew Davis
Producer: Steven Seagal, John T. Wilson, Andrew Davis
Screenwriter: Ronald Shusett, Andrew Davis, Steven Pressfield
Storywriter: Steven Seagal, Andrew Davis
Tech Info: color/sound/99 min.   Type: Dramatic Feature

Date: 1988　Origin: USA
Company: Warner Bros.
Annotation: Delores "Jax" Jackson (Grier) is a detective about to become a city prosecutor. Before her departure from the police force, she and her partner (Seagal) "bust" the biggest drug dealer in Chicago, but he is released by an FBI agent (Williams). Deputy Superintendent Crowder (Rasulala) removes Jax and her partner from the case to prevent their interference in a federal investigation.

ABOVE THE RIM

Cast: Tonya Pinkins*, Tupac Shakur*, Duane Martin*, Marlon Wayans*, Bernie Mac*
Director: Jeff Pollack, Tom Priestly
Executive Producer: James D. Brubaker
Music by: Marcus Miller*
Producer: Benny Medina*, James D. Brubaker, Jeff Pollack
Screenwriter: Barry Michael Cooper*, Jeff Pollack
Storywriter: Benny Medina*, Jeff Pollack
Tech Info: color/sound/96 min.　　　　Type: Dramatic Feature
Date: 1994　Origin: USA
Company: New Line Cinema
Annotation: Kyle Lee Watson (Martin) is an inner-city high school basketball star torn between college and the love of the streets. During an important championship play-off game, Kyle tries to catch the attention of a Georgetown University scout. Instead, he impresses Birdie (Shakur), a powerful gang leader who is assembling a team to compete in the neighborhood shoot-out contest.

ABYSS, THE

Cast: Michael Beach*, Kimberly Scott*, Mary Elizabeth Mastrantonio, Ed Harris
Director: James Cameron
Music by: Alan Silvestri
Producer: Gale Anne Hurd
Screenwriter: James Cameron
Tech Info: color/sound/140 min.　　　　Type: Dramatic Feature
Date: 1989　Origin: USA
Company: Fox
Distributors/Format: Fox Home Video (1/2")
Annotation: Lisa (Scott) is one of Bud Brigman's (Harris) oil-rig crew called in to help rescue a U.S. submarine carrying nuclear warheads that sank under strange circumstances. Beach plays a radioman on the sub.

ACE VENTURA: PET DETECTIVE

Cast: Tone-Loc *, Jim Carrey, Sean Young, Courteney Cox, Dan Marino
Director: Tom Shadyac
Executive Producer: Gary Barber
Music by: Ira Newborn
Producer: James G. Robinson, Gary Barber
Screenwriter: Jim Carrey, Tom Shadyac, Jack Bernstein
Storywriter: Jack Bernstein
Tech Info: color/sound/85 min.　　　　Type: Comedy Feature

Date: 1994   Origin: USA
Company: Ace Productions, Morgan Creek
Distributors/Format: Warner Bros. Home Video, Inc. (1/2")
Annotation: Ace Ventura (Carrey), a pet detective, is hired to find Snowflake, the abducted mascot of the Miami Dolphins. When a suspect is murdered, Ace is put on the trail of the psychotic kicker Ray Finkle who, through a sex change, has become Lieutenant Lois Einhorn (Young). Tone Loc appears as Emilio.

ACES: IRON EAGLE III

Alternate: Iron Eagle III: Aces
Cast: Louis Gossett Jr.*, Phill Lewis*, Rachel McLish, Paul Freeman
Director: John Glenn, Alec Mius
Music by: Harry Man Fredini
Producer: Ron Samuels
Screenwriter: Kevin Elders
Tech Info: color/sound/98 min.   Type: Dramatic Feature
Date: 1992   Origin: USA
Company: Seven Arts Productions
Distributors/Format: Columbia/TriStar Pictures (35mm; 1/2")
Annotation: Col. "Chappy" Sinclair (Gossett) leads a band of international war Aces in this conclusion to the IRON EAGLE series. Chappy and his Aces team up with Anna (McLish) to save her Peruvian village held hostage by a Latin American drug cartel led by a German madman (Freeman). Lewis plays Tee Vee, a street-smart ghetto kid.

ACTION JACKSON

Cast: Carl Weathers*, Vanity *, Thomas F. Wilson*, Bill Duke*, Armelia McQueen*, Chino "Fats" Williams*, Alonzo Brown*, Miguel Nunez*, Craig T. Nelson
Director: Craig R. Baxley
Music Performer: Vanity *
Music by: Herbie Hancock*, Michael Kamen, Jackie Krost
Producer: Joel Silver
Screenwriter: Robert Reneau
Tech Info: color/sound/96 min.   Type: Dramatic Feature
Date: 1988   Origin: USA
Company: Lorimar Film Entertainment Company
Distributors/Format: Lorimar Home Video (1/2")
Archives/Format: IUB - BFC/A (1/2")
Annotation: Detroit police sergeant Jericho "Action" Jackson (Weathers) has to outwit a vicious auto tycoon (Nelson) which he eventually does after much bloodshed and muscle display. He also ends up with beautiful damsel-in-distress Sydney Ash (Vanity).

ADAM CLAYTON POWELL

Series: The American Experience
Director: Richard Kilberg
Music by: Michael Sahl
Narrator: Julian Bond*, David McCollough
Producer: Yvonne Smith*, Richard Kilberg
Speaker: Dr. John Henrik Clarke*, Rev. Wyatt Tee Walker*, Rev. Wyatt Tee Walker*, Shirley Chisholm*, Stokely Carmichael*, Adam Clayton Powell Jr.*, Marian

Logan*, Isabel Washington Powell*, Dr. Lenworth Gunther*, J. Raymond Jones*, Reverend Calvin Butts*, Hattie Dodson*, Dr. Charles Hamilton*, Roger Wilkins*, Julius Lester*, Adam Clayton Powell III.*, James Farmer*, John Brademus
Tech Info: mixed/sound/53 min.   Type: Documentary Feature
Date: 1989   Origin: USA
Company: RKB Productions
Distributors/Format: Direct Cinema Limited (16mm; 1/2"), Filmic Archives (1/2")
Archives/Format: IUB - AAAMC (1/2")
Annotation: Bond is the narrator of this documentary on the rise and fall of Powell, who was elected to 12 terms in the House. Archival footage of Powell and interviews of major black figures establish the period and illuminate the personality of the controversial figure whom Congress expelled but was forced to reseat.

ADDAMS FAMILY, THE
Cast: Christopher Lloyd, Anjelica Huston, Raul Julia, Christina Ricci, Jimmy Workman
Director: Barry Sonnenfeld
Music Performer: M.C. Hammer *
Music by: Marc Shaiman
Producer: Scott Rudin
Screenwriter: Caroline Thompson, Larry Wilson
Tech Info: color/sound/102 min.   Type: Comedy Feature
Date: 1991   Origin: USA
Company: Paramount
Distributors/Format: Paramount Home Video (1/2")
Annotation: M.C. Hammer provides the soundtrack for this adaptation of the Charles Addams characters with such tunes as, "The Addams Groove," "Too Legit to Quit," "This is the Way We Roll," and "Burn It Up."

ADVENTURES IN ASSIMILATION
Director: Richard Dean Moss*
Tech Info: color/sound/8 min.   Type: Experimental Short
Date: 1992   Origin: USA
Company: Third World Newsreel
Distributors/Format: Third World Newsreel (1/2")
Annotation: Moss experiments with his own choreography, using movement within a fixed frame to express self-discovery.

ADVENTURES OF BUCKAROO BANZAI: ACROSS THE 8TH DIMENSION, THE
Cast: Rosalind Cash*, Carl Lumbly*, Bill Henderson*, Damon Hines*, Peter Weller, Ellen Barkin, Jeff Goldblum, John Lithgow
Director: W.D. Richter
Executive Producer: Sidney Beckerman
Music by: Michael Roddicker
Producer: Sidney Beckerman, Neil Canton, W.D. Richter
Screenwriter: Earl Mac Rauch
Tech Info: color/sound/103 min.   Type: Comedy Feature

Date: 1984   Origin: USA
Company: Sherwood
Distributors/Format: Fox Home Video (1/2")
Annotation: John Parker (Lumbly), Black Electroid from the 8th Dimension, arrives on earth with an urgent message for Buckaroo Banzai (Weller) in this sci-fi parody. The message, which will save the earth from the Hitler-like madman (Lithgow), is delivered by the leader of Plant 10 (Cash). Henderson plays Casper Lindley, helicopter pilot; Hines plays his son Scooter.

ADVENTURES OF FORD FAIRLANE, THE

Cast: Morris Day*, Tone-Loc *, Steve White*, Sheila E. *, , Wayne Newton
Director: Renny Harlin
Executive Producer: Michael I. Levy
Music Performer: Jimi Hendrix*, Sheila E. *
Music by: Yello
Producer: Joel Silver, Steve Perry, Michael I. Levy
Screenwriter: Daniel Waters, David Arnott, James Cappe
Storywriter: David Arnott, James Cappe
Tech Info: color/sound/100 min.   Type: Comedy Feature
Date: 1990   Origin: USA
Company: Silver Pictures
Distributors/Format: Fox Home Video (1/2")
Annotation: Rock and Roll detective Ford Fairlane (Clay) exposes bad guy Julian Grendl (Newton) who is stealing from his own musicians by bootlegging their music in South Africa. Day plays Ford's good friend, producer Don Cleveland; Sheila E. is a club singer; Loc is Slam the Rapper; White plays a detective.

ADVENTURES OF HUCK FINN

Cast: Brock Peters*, Forrest Tucker, Larry Storch
Director: Jack B. Hively
Producer: Bill Cornford
Screenwriter: Tom Chapman
Tech Info: color/sound/97 min.   Type: Dramatic Feature
Date: 1980   Origin: USA
Company: Vidamerica
Distributors/Format: Vidamerica (1/2")
Annotation: In this adaptation of the novel by Mark Twain, Peters plays Jim the runaway slave. Jim is at the center of this version of Huck Finn's adventures down the river in which Huck learns that freedom for Jim is not an adventure but a matter of life or death. Lynn and Roy (uncredited black actors) are plantation children who give food to the two hungry travelers.

ADVENTURES OF HUCK FINN

Cast: Courtney B. Vance*, Robbie Coltrane, Jason Robards, Elijah Wood
Director: Stephen Sommers
Executive Producer: Steve White*, Berry Bernardi
Music by: Bill Conti
Producer: Steve White*, Lawrence Mark, Berry Bernardi
Screenwriter: Stephen Sommers
Tech Info: color/sound/108 min.   Type: Dramatic Feature

Date: 1993   Origin: USA
Company: Walt Disney
Distributors/Format: Filmic Archives (1/2")
Annotation: Wood plays Huck Finn in this 1990s adaptation of the Mark Twain novel. Vance is the runaway slave Jim.

AFFIRMATIONS

Director: Marlon T. Riggs*
Producer: Marlon T. Riggs*
Screenwriter: Marlon T. Riggs*
Speaker: Essex Hemphill*, Wayson Jones*, Reginald Jackson*, Michael Bell*, Gay Men of African Descent*, R. Battle*, Blackberri *, David Kirkland
Tech Info: color/sound/10 min.   Type: Television Documentary
Date: 1990   Origin: USA
Company: Signifyin' Productions
Distributors/Format: Frameline Distribution (1/2"), Signifyin' Works (1/2")
Archives/Format: IUB - BFC/A (1/2")
Annotation: The film affirms the homosexual/black community as a vital part of society. While marching, many black gay men confront hatred and stand together.

AFTER WINTER: STERLING BROWN

Director: Haile Gerima*
Producer: Haile Gerima*
Speaker: Sterling Brown*
Tech Info: color/sound/60 min.   Type: Documentary Feature
Date: 1985   Origin: USA
Company: Howard University School of Communications
Distributors/Format: Mypheduh Films, Inc. (16mm; 1/2")
Annotation: Howard University students were involved in the production of this film which takes its title from one of Brown's poems. It documents the life and work of one of the pivotal figures in African American literature. Brown speaks throughout most of the film on the issues that most concern and interest him.

AGAINST ALL ODDS

Cast: Dorian Harewood*, Sam Scarber*, Rachel Ward, James Woods, Jeff Bridges
Director: Taylor Hackford
Music Performer: Kid Creole*
Music by: Michael Colombier, Larry Carlton
Producer: Taylor Hackford, William F. Gilmore
Screenwriter: Eric Hughes
Storywriter: Daniel Mainwarning
Tech Info: color/sound/128 min.   Type: Dramatic Feature
Date: 1984   Origin: USA
Company: New Visions
Distributors/Format: RCA/Columbia Pictures Home Video (1/2")
Annotation: Tommy (Harewood) is a retired football player from the Outlaws, a Los Angeles team where Sam (Scarber) is a trainer. Tommy works for Jake (Woods) running numbers at Jake's nightclub where Kid Creole and the Coconuts perform.

AIN'T GONNA SHUFFLE NO MORE (1964-1972)
Series: Eyes on the Prize II
Director: Sam Pollard*, Shelia Bernard
Executive Producer: Henry Hampton*
Screenwriter: Sam Pollard*, Shelia Bernard
Speaker: Harry Belafonte*, Imamu Amiri Baraka*, Kareem Abdul-Jabbar*, Stokely Carmichael*, Jackie Robinson*, Paula Giddings*, Charles Diggs*, Cassius Clay*, Black Poets *, Sonia Sanchez*, Malcolm X *, Jabir Herbert Muhammad*, Floyd Patterson*, Tony Gittens*, Adrienne Manns*, Robert Byrd*, Gloster Current*, Fred Black*, Kenneth Clark*, Ewart Brown*, Arthur Eves*, Benjamin Chavis*, Mary Hightower*, Queen Mother Moore*, Dick Gregory*, Coleman Young*, Jessie Jackson*, Richard Hatcher*, Willie Felder*, Edwin Pope, Angelo Dundee, Edwin McKee, Richard Nixon
Tech Info: mixed/sound/60 min.   Type: Television Documentary
Date: 1989   Origin: USA
Company: Blackside, Inc.
Distributors/Format: PBS Video (16mm; 1/2")
Archives/Format: IUB - AAAMC (1/2")
Annotation: This segment focuses on the Black Consciousness Movement that re-defined the black image. It includes the religious stand of Muhammad Ali (aka Cassius Clay) against induction into the armed services; the demand of Howard University students for recognition of the school as a black university; and the Black National Political Convention held in Gary (IN) after the deaths of Martin Luther King, Jr. and Malcolm X.

AIN'T SCARED OF YOUR JAILS (1960-61) - EPISODE 3
Series: Eyes on the Prize: America's Civil Rights Years
Executive Producer: Henry Hampton*
Narrator: Julian Bond*
Producer: Orlando Bagwell*, Henry Hampton*
Speaker: Adam Clayton Powell*, James Farmer*, C.T. Vivian*, John Lewis*, Coretta Scott King*, Fred L. Shuttlesworth*, Jim Lawson*, Leo Lillard*, Diane Nash*, Fredrick Leonard*, Martin Luther King Jr.*, Burke Marshall, Robert Kennedy, Ben West, Harris Wofford, Bernie Schweid, John Patterson, John Seigenthaler, Floyd Maun, Jim Zwerg
Tech Info: mixed/sound/56 min.   Type: Television Documentary
Date: 1986   Origin: USA
Company: Blackside, Inc.
Distributors/Format: PBS Video (16mm; 1/2")
Archives/Format: IUB - AAAMC (1/2")
Annotation: This segment focuses on the growing involvement of young people in the Civil Rights Movement. SNCC (Student Nonviolent Coordinating Corps) organizes sit-ins as well as Freedom Rides. Despite the violence they suffer, the youth refuse to back down, forcing confrontation between state and federal governments.

AIR UP THERE, THE
Cast: Nigel Miguel*, Winston Ntshona*, Charles Gitonga Maina*, Mabutho "Kid" Sithole*, Ili Mutombo*, Miriam Owiti*, Kevin Bacon
Director: Paul Michael Glaser
Executive Producer: Lance Hool, Scott Kroopf

Music by: David Newman
Producer: Ted Field, Robert Cort, Lance Hool, Scott Kroopf, Rosalie Swedlin
Screenwriter: Max Apple
Tech Info: color/sound/107 min.   Type: Comedy Feature
Date: 1994   Origin: USA
Company: Interscope, Polygram, et al.
Distributors/Format: Buena Vista Home Video (1/2")
Annotation: Jimmy Dolan (Bacon), a coach at St. Joseph's, travels to Africa to recruit a young Winabi man, Jimmy Saleh (Maina), he saw playing basketball on a video about the college's missionary work. Dolan learns the ways of the Winabi who are in a power struggle with the Mingori. The two tribes decide to settle their differences on the basketball court.

AIRHEADS

Cast: Ernie Hudson*, Judd Nelson, Steve Buscemi, Brendan Fraser, Adam Sandler
Director: Michael Lehmann
Executive Producer: Todd Baker
Music by: Carter Burwell*
Producer: Mark Burg, Todd Baker, Robert Simonds
Screenwriter: Rich Wilkes
Tech Info: color/sound/91 min.   Type: Comedy Feature
Date: 1994   Origin: USA
Company: Fox, Island World, Robert Simonds
Distributors/Format: Fox Home Video (1/2")
Annotation: Three aging heavy-metal rockers storm a radio station and demand air time. Hudson plays Sgt. O'Malley.

AIRPLANE II

Cast: James A. Watson Jr.*, Al White*, William Shatner, Robert Hays, Julie Hagerty, Peter Graves, Clint Smith, Lloyd Bridges
Director: Ken Finkleman
Music by: Richard Hazard, Elmer Bernstein
Producer: Howard W. Koch
Screenwriter: Ken Finkleman
Storywriter: Ken Finkleman
Tech Info: color/sound/84 min.   Type: Comedy Feature
Date: 1983   Origin: USA
Company: Paramount
Distributors/Format: Paramount Home Video (1/2")
Annotation: In this sequel, Watson joins the cast as co-pilot. An explosion forces him out of the door of the Mayflower I space shuttle into his own lunar orbit. White repeats his performance as the "jive dude"; Smith appears as a ticket scalper.

AIRPLANE!

Cast: Kareem Abdul-Jabbar*, Jimmy/Jimmie Walker*, Norman Alexander Gibbs*, Al White*, Lloyd Bridges, Leslie Nielson, Robert Stack, Robert Hays, Julie Hagerty, Peter Graves
Director: Jerry Zucker, David Zucker, Jim Abrahams
Executive Producer: Jerry Zucker, David Zucker, Jim Abrahams
Music Performer: Elmer Bernstein
Music by: Elmer Bernstein
Producer: Jerry Zucker, David Zucker, Jim Abrahams, Jon Davison

Screenwriter: David Zucker, Jim Abrahams
Storywriter: Jerry Zucker, David Zucker, Jim Abrahams
Tech Info: color/sound/88 min.   Type: Comedy Feature
Date: 1980   Origin: USA
Company: Paramount
Distributors/Format: Paramount Home Video (1/2")
Annotation: When bad weather and a failed crew threaten the safety of the passengers, hero and heroine (Hays, Hagerty) save the day. Abdul-Jabbar appears as co-pilot Roger Murdock; Gibbs and White portray two "jive dudes" whose speech is translated by subtitles; Walker plays an airplane windshield wiper man.

ALHAJI BAI KONTE

Cast: Alhaji Bai Konte*
Director: Oliver Franklin*
Producer: Oliver Franklin*
Tech Info: color/sound/12 min.   Type: Documentary Short
Date: 1978   Origin: Gambia, Senegal
Studio: Independent
Annotation: This film offers a glimpse into the world of Alhaji Bai Konte, a renown Kora musician and griot. He is shown performing and talking with other musicians, and a sense of the lives of the Mandinka people of Gambia and Senegal is conveyed.

ALIEN

Cast: Yaphet Kotto*, John Hurt, Tom Skerritt, Harry Dean Stanton, Sigourney Weaver
Director: Ridley Scott
Executive Producer: Ronald Shusett
Music Performer: Jerry Smith
Music by: Jerry Smith
Producer: Walter Hill, Ronald Shusett, Gordon Carroll, David Giler
Screenwriter: Dan O'Bannon
Storywriter: Dan O'Bannon, Ronald Shusett
Tech Info: color/sound/116 min.   Type: Dramatic Feature
Date: 1979   Origin: USA
Company: Fox
Annotation: Parker (Kotto), is one of the unfortunate crew members of the commercial towing vehicle "Nostromo." When the ship receives transmitter signals from Saturn, it lands on a planet carrying aboard an alien that feeds off the ship's oxygen lines. Parker struggles with the alien in order to rescue another crew member, but Ripley (Weaver) is the sole survivor.

ALIEN 3

Cast: Charles S. Dutton*, Lance Henriksen, Sigourney Weaver, Charles Dance
Director: Ridley Scott, Alex Thompson
Music by: Elliot Goldenthal
Producer: Walter Hill, Gordon Carroll, David Giler
Screenwriter: Walter Hill, David Giler
Tech Info: color/sound/115 min.   Type: Dramatic Feature

Date: 1992   Origin: USA
Company: Fox
Distributors/Format: Fox Home Video (1/2")
Annotation: Lt. Ripley (Weaver), the lone survivor of a spaceship crash on
Weyland-Yutan Work Prison Fury 161, destroys an alien presence with the help of
ex-cons, especially Dillon (Dutton), the only convict who knows how to lead the other
men.

ALIEN INTRUDER
Cast: Billy Dee Williams*, Maxwell Caulfield, Tracy Scoggins, Gary Roberts
Director: Ricardo Jacques Gale
Music by: Miriam Cutler
Producer: Richard Pepin, Joseph Merhi
Screenwriter: Nick Stone
Tech Info: color/sound/90 min.   Type: Dramatic Feature
Date: 1993   Origin: USA
Company: PM Entertainment
Distributors/Format: PM Home Video (1/2")
Annotation: Determined to stop the slaughter in space, Commander Skyler
(Williams), survivor of a mutiny in the cosmos, recruits four convicts to follow him
into deep space to solve the mystery of lost exploratory vessels and their crews.

ALIENS
Cast: Al Matthews*, Lance Henriksen, Michael Biehn, Sigourney Weaver, Paul
Reiser, Carrie Henn
Director: James Cameron
Executive Producer: Walter Hill, Gordon Carroll, David Giler
Music by: James Horner
Producer: Gale Anne Hurd, Walter Hill, Gordon Carroll, David Giler
Screenwriter: David Giler, James Cameron, David Cameron
Storywriter: Walter Hill, James Cameron
Tech Info: color/sound/137 min.   Type: Dramatic Feature
Date: 1986   Origin: USA
Company: Brandywine
Distributors/Format: Fox Home Video (1/2")
Annotation: Ripley (Weaver) is found in suspended animation 57 years after
surviving the original Alien. She joins a group of Marines sent to rescue colonists
who have disappeared, and takes over the battle against the egg-laying queen of the
aliens. Matthews plays Apone, the tough, competent Marine sergeant.

ALL DOGS GO TO HEAVEN
Cast: Melba Moore*, Burt Reynolds, Loni Anderson, Dom DeLuise, Charles Nelson
Reilly
Director: Don Bluth
Music Performer: Freddie Jackson*, Irene Cara*
Music by: Ralph Burns
Producer: Don Bluth, Gary Goldman, John Pomeroy
Screenwriter: Gary Goldman, David N. Weiss, David Steinberg
Storywriter: Don Bluth, John Pomeroy, David N. Weiss, Ken Cromar, Larry Leker,
Linda Miller, Monica Parker, Guy Schulman
Tech Info: color/sound/87 min.   Type: Animated Feature

Date: 1989   Origin: USA
Company: Sullivan Bluth, Goldcrest
Distributors/Format: United Artists Home Video (1/2")
Annotation: Charlie, a wayward dog, is killed but escapes from heaven and returns to earth. Moore is the voice of the angel. Cara and Jackson sing the title song, "Love Survives."

ALL THAT JAZZ
Cast: Ben Vereen*, Roy Scheider, Jessica Lang, Ann Reinking, Leland Palmer, Cliff Gorman
Director: Bob Fosse
Executive Producer: Daniel Melnick
Producer: Robert Alan, Arthur Fosse, Daniel Melnick
Screenwriter: Robert Alan, Arthur Fosse, Bob Fosse
Tech Info: color/sound/123 min.   Type: Musical Feature
Date: 1979   Origin: USA
Company: Fox, Columbia
Distributors/Format: Facets Multimedia, Inc. (1/2")
Annotation: As he nears death, Broadway producer Joey Gideon (Scheider) re-lives his past as a womanizer, father, husband and teenage vaudeville actor. Vereen plays as televised benefit host, O'Connor Flood, in this musical biography loosely based on the life of choreographer/dancer Bob Fosse.

ALLAN QUARTERMAIN AND THE LOST CITY OF GOLD
Cast: James Earl Jones*, Brown Aldango*, Richard Chamberlain
Director: Gary Nelson
Music by: Jerry Goldsmith, Michael Linn
Producer: Yoram Globus, Menahem Golan
Screenwriter: Gene Quintano, Lee Reynolds
Storywriter: Eddie Hodges
Tech Info: color/sound/103 min.   Type: Dramatic Feature
Date: 1986   Origin: USA
Company: Cannon
Annotation: Jones is the lone native who leads Alan Quartermain (Chamberlin) into the depths of Africa in search of Quartermain's lost brother.

ALLIGATOR II: THE MUTATION
Cast: Brock Peters*, Joseph Bologna, Dee Wallace Stone, Woody Brown
Director: Jon Hess
Executive Producer: Walter Manley
Music by: Jack Tillar
Producer: Brandon Chase, Walter Manley
Screenwriter: Curt Allen
Tech Info: color/sound/92 min.   Type: Dramatic Feature
Date: 1991   Origin: USA
Company: Group 1
Distributors/Format: New Line Cinema Home Video (1/2")
Annotation: A greedy developer has been pouring toxic waste into a lake, and the resulting giant alligator begins terrorizing a resort town. Investigating Officer Hodges (Bologna) must first convince his superiors the mutant reptile exists and then destroy it. Peters plays Chief Speed.

ALLNIGHTER, THE
Cast: Pam Grier*, Meshach Taylor*, Dedee Pfeiffer, Michael Ontkean, Joan Cusack, Susanna Hoffs
Director: Tamar Simon Hoffs
Executive Producer: James L. Stewart
Music by: Charles Bernstein
Producer: James L. Stewart, Nancy Israel, Tamar Simon Hoffs
Screenwriter: Tamar Simon Hoffs
Tech Info: color/sound/108 min.   Type: Comedy Feature
Date: 1987   Origin: USA
Company: Universal
Distributors/Format: Universal Pictures (16mm; 1/2")
Annotation: Three college roommates who share a beach house become involved in misadventures when one of them (Hoffs) attempts to find romance with a fading rock star (Ontkean). Grier plays Sgt. MacLeish and Taylor appears as Philip, the House detective.

ALMA'S RAINBOW
Cast: Victoria Gabriella Platt*, Kim Weston-Moran*, Mizan Nunes
Director: Ayoka Chenzira*, Ronald K. Gray*
Music by: Jean-Paul Bourelly
Producer: Ayoka Chenzira*, Charles Lane*, Howard M. Brickner
Screenwriter: Ayoka Chenzira*
Tech Info: color/sound/85 min.   Type: Dramatic Feature
Date: 1993   Origin: USA
Company: Crossgrain Pictures, Rhinoceros Productions
Distributors/Format: Red Carnelian Films/Video (16mm; 1/2")
Annotation: Alma Gold (Weston-Moran) is the owner of a popular beauty parlor. Her daughter Rainbow (Platt), is struggling to find her own identity and deal with her awakening sexuality. Alma and her sister, Ruby (Nunes), a free-spirited chanteuse, present the alternatives which Rainbow must come to terms with in order to find her own way. Ronald Gray is director of photography.

ALMOST BLUE
Cast: Yaphet Kotto*, Garrett Morris*, Michael Madsen, Lynette Walden, Gale Mayron
Director: Keoni Waxman
Executive Producer: A.B. Goldberg
Music by: John Venzon
Producer: Douglas Olson, Anthony Parker, Keoni Waxman, A.B. Goldberg
Screenwriter: Keoni Waxman
Tech Info: color/sound/99 min.   Type: Dramatic Feature
Date: 1993   Origin: USA
Company: Almost Blue Productions, First Films, et al.
Distributors/Format: LIVE Home Video (1/2")
Annotation: Morris Poole (Madsen) is a jazz saxophonist who is unable to play after his wife dies in an accident. Morris plays Charles, his philosophical and encouraging agent. Kotto plays Terry, a bar habitue.

ALMOST PERFECT AFFAIR, AN

Cast: Dick Anthony Williams*, Anna Maria Horsford*, Keith Carradine, Monica Vitti, Raf Vallone, Christian De Sica
Director: Michael Ritchie
Producer: Terry Carr
Screenwriter: Walter Bernstein
Storywriter: Michael Ritchie, Don Petersen
Tech Info: color/sound/93 min.   Type: Dramatic Feature
Date: 1979   Origin: USA
Company: Paramount
Distributors/Format: Paramount Home Video (1/2")
Annotation: Hal (Carradine), an ambitious film director, determined to get his film into the Cannes film festival, seduces the producer's wife (Vitti). Horsford plays Amy Zon and Williams plays Jackson.

ALPHABET CITY

Cast: Michael Winslow*, Vincent Spano, Jami Gertz, Zohra Lampert, Kenny Marino, Kate Vernon
Director: Amos Poe
Executive Producer: Thomas Coleman, Michael Rosenblatt
Music Performer: Nile Rodgers*
Music by: Nile Rodgers*
Producer: Andrew Braunsberg, Thomas Coleman, Michael Rosenblatt
Screenwriter: Gregory K. Heller, Amos Poe
Storywriter: Gregory K. Heller
Tech Info: color/sound/85 min.   Type: Dramatic Feature
Date: 1984   Origin: USA
Company: Fox
Distributors/Format: Atlantic Home Video (1/2")
Annotation: Johnny (Spano) is a successful drug dealer who wants to go straight but his crime bosses threaten him and his loved ones with death if he quits working the streets. Ultimately, Johnny's friend and co-dealer Lippy (Winslow) rescues Johnny and his girlfriend from Mafia hitmen.

ALWAYS

Cast: Keith David*, John Goodman, Richard Dreyfuss, Brad Johnson, Holly Hunter
Director: Steven Spielberg
Executive Producer: Kathleen Kennedy
Music by: John Williams
Producer: Steven Spielberg, Frank Marshall, Kathleen Kennedy, Kathleen Kennedy
Screenwriter: Jerry Belson
Storywriter: Frederick Hazlitt Brennan, Chandler Sprague, David Boehm
Tech Info: color/sound/121 min.   Type: Dramatic Feature
Date: 1989   Origin: USA
Company: United Artists
Distributors/Format: Universal Home Video (1/2")
Annotation: Flying firefighter Pete Sandich (Dreyfuss) is killed on the job and returns to Earth as an angel. David plays Powerhouse.

ALWAYS FOR PLEASURE
Director: Les Blank
Producer: Les Blank
Tech Info: color/sound/58 min.   Type: Documentary Feature
Date: 1978 Origin: USA
Company: Flower Films
Distributors/Format: Facets Multimedia, Inc. (1/2"), Flower Films (16mm; 1/2")
Annotation: Blank documents the neighborhood revelry of New Orleans. He focuses on African Americans with Indian tribal affiliation who pay homage to the Louisiana Indians who harbored escaped slaves.

AMAZING GRACE, AN
Series: Black History
Director: Gil Noble*, Frank Olivo
Executive Producer: Miskit Airth*
Speaker: Stokely Carmichael*, Jesse Jackson*
Tech Info: mixed/sound/60 min.   Type: Television Documentary
Date: 1978 Origin: USA
Studio: WABC-TV (New York)
Archives/Format: IUB - BFC/A (1/2")
Annotation: Broadcast on public affairs program "Like It Is," this documentary profiles Dr. Martin Luther King, Jr., eminent leader of the Montgomery Boycott movement which gave birth to other anti-racial movements across the U.S. Before his assassination in 1968, King organized people to act to achieve racial integration in interstate travel and public accommodations.

AMAZON
Cast: Rae Dawn Chong*, Robert Davi, Kari Vaananen
Director: Mika Kaurismaki
Executive Producer: Klaus Heydemann, Bruce Marchfelder
Music by: Nana Vasconcelos
Producer: Mika Kaurismaki, Klaus Heydemann, Bruce Marchfelder
Storywriter: Mika Kaurismaki, Richard Reitinger
Tech Info: color/sound/125 min.   Type: Dramatic Feature
Date: 1991 Origin: USA, Finland, Switzerland, France
Company: Villealfa Films Production, Noema Pictures, et al.
Distributors/Format: Cabriolet Films, Inc. (16mm)
Annotation: Finnish businessman Kari (Vaananen) is on the run in Brazil with his two daughters. He meets Paola (Chong), an environmental activist, and Dan (Davi), who gets him involved in a scheme to stripmine for diamonds.

AMAZON WOMEN ON THE MOON
Cast: William Marshall*, B.B. King*, Arsenio Hall*, T.K. Carter*, Steve Guttenberg, Rosanna Arquette, Ralph Bellamy, Howard Hessman
Director: John Landis, Robert K. Weiss, Carl Gottlieb, Joe Dante, Peter Horton
Executive Producer: George Folsey Jr., John Landis
Producer: George Folsey Jr., John Landis, Robert K. Weiss
Screenwriter: Michael Barrie, Jim Mulholland
Tech Info: color/sound/85 min.   Type: Comedy Feature

Date: 1987   Origin: USA
Company: Universal
Distributors/Format: MCA/Universal Home Video (1/2"), Universal Home Video (1/2")
Annotation: This satiric view of contemporary life and the mass media revolves around a television channel that entertains its viewers with a 1950's style sci-fi movie by intercutting a series of far out commercials, silly shorts and weird specials. Hall is one of many performers in the skits.

AMBUSHED

Director: Jared Katsiane*
Tech Info: bw/sound/12 min.   Type: Experimental Short
Date: 1993   Origin: USA
Studio: Independent
Distributors/Format: Third World Newsreel (1/2")
Annotation: Using experimental techniques, the film explores the life of an inner-city black youth, depicting the brutality and violence he experiences at the hands of the police.

AMERICAN BOYFRIENDS

Cast: Jason Blicker*, Troy Mallory*, Margaret Langrick, John Wildman, Liisa Repo Martell
Director: Sandy Wilson
Executive Producer: Robert Lantos
Music by: Terry Frewer
Producer: Robert Lantos, Sandy Wilson, Steven Denure
Screenwriter: Sandy Wilson
Tech Info: color/sound/90 min.   Type: Comedy Feature
Date: 1989   Origin: Canada
Company: Telefilm Canada, First Choice, et al.
Annotation: Marty (Blicker), a UC-Berkeley radical, and his friend Spider (Mallory) are rescued from aggressive beach boys in Santa Cruz by Sandy (Langrick) and Julie (Martell), two Canadian coeds, in this exploration of middle class attitudes in the 60s. Sandy temporarily pairs off with Spider.

AMERICAN FLYERS

Cast: Robert Townsend*, Rae Dawn Chong*, John Amos*, Kevin Costner, David Grant, Janice Rule, Mel Torme, Doi Johnson
Director: John Badham
Music by: Lee Ritenour, Greg Mathieson
Producer: Paula Weinstein, Garth Wigan
Storywriter: Steve Tesich
Tech Info: color/sound/113 min.   Type: Dramatic Feature
Date: 1985   Origin: USA
Company: WW Production
Annotation: Dennis (Amos) is a doctor helping his friend (Costner) who is dying of a brain disease to mend his relationship with his mother and brother. Chong plays Sarah, Costner's love interest. Together they take his brother camping and to a bike race. Jerome (Townsend) is Sarah's old boyfriend's biking teammate.

AMERICAN GAME, THE
Cast: Stretch Graham*, Brian Walker, Gil Ferschtman, Dave Tawil
Director: Jay Freund, David Wolfe
Producer: Anthony Jones
Screenwriter: Jay Freund, David Wolfe
Tech Info: color/sound/89 min.   Type: Documentary Feature
Date: 1979   Origin: USA
Company: World Northal Corporation, Anthony Jones
Distributors/Format: Corinth Films (1/2")
Annotation: The pressures inflicted upon star high school athletes are depicted in
this documentary which focuses on a white basketball player from Lebanon, Indiana,
and a black basketball player (Graham) from Brooklyn, New York.

AMERICAN GIGOLO
Cast: Bill Duke*, Richard Gere, Hector Elizondo, Lauren Hutton
Director: Paul Schrader
Executive Producer: Freddie Fields
Music by: Giorgio Moroder
Producer: Freddie Fields, Jerry Bruckheimer
Screenwriter: Paul Schrader
Tech Info: color/sound/117 min.   Type: Dramatic Feature
Date: 1980   Origin: USA
Company: Paramount
Distributors/Format: Paramount (1/2")
Annotation: Julian (Gere), a Beverly Hills gigolo, is set up to take the blame for a
murder and hopes his lover, a politician's wife (Hutton), will provide an alibi. Duke
plays Leon James.

AMERICAN HOT WAX
Cast: Chuck Berry*, Sam Harkness*, Arnold McCuller*, Al Chalk*, Maurice Starr*,
Screamin' Jay Hawkins*, Jerry Lee Lewis, Tim McIntire, Jeff Altman, Fran Drescher,
Jay Leno, Laraine Newman
Director: Floyd Mutrux
Music by: Kenny Vance
Producer: Art Linson
Screenwriter: John Kaye
Tech Info: color/sound/91 min.   Type: Musical Feature
Date: 1978   Origin: USA
Company: Paramount
Distributors/Format: Paramount Home Video (1/2")
Annotation: The film depicts the early days of rock 'n' roll focussing on the disk
jockey Alan Freed (McIntire) who helped to popularize the new music. Berry,
Hawkins and others perform.

AMITYVILLE II: THE POSSESSION
Cast: Moses Gunn*, Burt Young, James Olson, Diane Franklin, Rutanya Alda, Jack
Magner
Director: Damiano Damiani
Executive Producer: Bernard Williams
Music by: Lalo Schifrin
Producer: Bernard Williams, Ira N. Smith, Stephen R. Greenwald

Screenwriter: Tommy Lee Wallace
Tech Info: color/sound/104 min.   Type: Dramatic Feature
Date: 1982   Origin: USA
Company: DEG
Distributors/Format: Orion Home Video (1/2")
Annotation: Sonny Montelli (Franklin) is a troubled teenager who becomes possessed by the evil lurking in the basement and hacks his family to pieces. Gunn plays Detective Turner.

AMONG GOOD CHRISTIAN PEOPLES

Director: Jacqueline Woodson*, Catherine Saalfield
Music Performer: Lavender Light*, Choir Lesbian and Gay Gospel*, Black People of All Color
Producer: Jacqueline Woodson*, Catherine Saalfield
Speaker: Thomas Allen Harris*, Jocelyn Taylor*, Linda Villarosa*, Michelle Adams*, Lidell Jackson*, Tony Teal*, Michael Mewborn*, Dionne Freeney
Tech Info: mixed/sound/30 min.   Type: Documentary Short
Date: 1991   Origin: USA
Company: A Cold Hard Dis' Production
Distributors/Format: Third World Newsreel (1/2"), Frameline Distribution (1/2")
Annotation: Co-director Woodson documents her story as a black lesbian raised as a Jehovah Witness.

AMOS AND ANDREW

Cast: Samuel L. Jackson*, Giancarlo Esposito*, Dabney Coleman, Michael Lerner, Nicolas Cage, Margaret Colin
Director: E. Max Frye, Walt Lloyd
Music by: Richard Gibbs
Producer: Gary Goetzman
Screenwriter: E. Max Frye
Tech Info: color/sound/95 min.   Type: Comedy Feature
Date: 1993   Origin: USA
Company: Castle Rock Entertainment
Distributors/Format: Columbia/New Line Home Video (1/2")
Annotation: When affluent Andrew Sterling (Jackson) buys a home on an exclusive New England resort island, the local police mistake him for a thief and almost kill him. To get rid of Sterling, the police give Amos Odell (Cage), a career criminal and incorrigible wiseguy, a chance to get out of jail if he breaks into Sterling's home and takes him hostage.

ANANSI, THE SPIDER

Tech Info: color/sound/11 min.   Type: Animated Short
Date: 1985   Origin: USA
Studio: Independent
Distributors/Format: Media Arts Center (16mm)
Archives/Format: IUB - BFC/A (16mm)
Annotation: Anansi the spider is a folk hero of the Ashanti of Ghana. Anansi is depicted as a lovable mischief maker who protects his people.

AND GOD CREATED WOMAN
Cast: Gail Boggs*, Thelma Houston*, Rebecca De Mornay, Benjamin Mouton, Jaime McEnnan
Director: Roger Vadim
Executive Producer: Steven Reuther, Ruth Vitale, Mitchell Cannold
Music Performer: Giuseppe Verdi, Wolfgang Amadeus Mozart
Music by: Thomas Chase, Steve Rucker, Christoph Willibald von Gluck
Producer: Ron Hamady, Steven Reuther, Ruth Vitale, George G. Braunstein, Mitchell Cannold
Screenwriter: R.J. Stewart
Tech Info: color/sound/98 min.   Type: Dramatic Feature
Date: 1988   Origin: USA
Company: Crow
Distributors/Format: Vestron Home Video (1/2")
Annotation: A remake of the successful 1956 French film, this version focuses on a wrongly imprisoned woman who eventually becomes a successful rock 'n roll performer. Houston appears as a prison singer.

ANGEL 3: THE FINAL CHAPTER
Cast: Richard Roundtree*, Paunita Nichols*, Maud Adams, Mitzi Kapture, Anna Navarro
Director: Tom DeSimone
Music by: Berlin Game , Don Great, Alan Ett, Chris Spedding
Producer: Arnold Orgolini
Screenwriter: Tom DeSimone
Tech Info: color/sound/99 min.   Type: Dramatic Feature
Date: 1988   Origin: USA
Company: New World
Annotation: Freelance photographer Molly (Kapture) is reunited with her mother while on a shoot. After her mother is murdered, Molly goes on a search for her missing half-sister and her mother's killer. Roundtree plays police Lt. Doniger and Nichols plays a hooker.

ANGEL 4: UNDERCOVER
Cast: Stone/Stoney Jackson*, Sam Phillips, Darlene Vogel, Shane Fraser, Mark DeCarlo
Director: George Axmith
Executive Producer: Jim Begg
Music by: Kevin Gilbert
Producer: Jim Begg, Brad Southwick, Gary Depew
Screenwriter: Dode B. Levenson, Frank Chance
Tech Info: color/sound/94 min.   Type: Dramatic Feature
Date: 1994   Origin: USA
Company: Park Avenue Productions
Distributors/Format: LIVE Home Video (1/2")
Annotation: Once a prostitute known on the street as Angel, Molly (Vogel) has become a police photographer. Working undercover, she infiltrates the rock 'n roll scene to solve a murder. Jackson plays Mojo Clark.

ANGEL HEART

Alternate: Falling Angel
Cast: Lisa Bonet*, Brownie McGhee*, Peggy Severe*, Jarrett Narcisse*, Gerald
Orange*, Yvonne Bywaters*, Mickey Rourke, Robert De Niro
Director: Alan Parker
Executive Producer: Mario Kassar, Andrew Vajna
Music Performer: Trevor Jones
Music by: Trevor Jones
Producer: Alan Marshall, Elliot Kastner, Mario Kassar, Andrew Vajna
Screenwriter: Alan Parker
Storywriter: William Hjortsberg
Tech Info: color/sound/112 min.   Type: Dramatic Feature
Date: 1987   Origin: USA
Company: Carolco, TriStar
Annotation: Harry Angel (Rourke) is caught up in a New Orleans network of voodoo,
murder, and horror that leads to a revelation of his true identity. Epiphany Proudfoot
(Bonnet) is a young mother who has an affair with Angel. Narcisse plays Epiphany's
son; Severe is Mammy Carter, owner of an herb shop; Bywaters plays a maid;
Orange is Pastor John, a corrupt church leader.

ANGELS IN THE OUTFIELD

Cast: Danny Glover*, Christopher Lloyd, Ben Johnson, Tony Danza, Brenda Fricker
Director: William Dean
Executive Producer: Gary Stutman
Music by: Randy Edelman
Producer: Joe Roth, Irby Smith, Roger Birnbaum, Gary Stutman
Screenwriter: Dorothy Kingsley, George Wells, Holly Goldberg Sloan
Tech Info: color/sound/103 min.   Type: Dramatic Feature
Date: 1994   Origin: USA
Company: Walt Disney
Annotation: Glover plays George Knox in this story about a little boy who prays for a
father and winning the baseball pennant.

ANGIE

Cast: Charlaine Woodard*, John Toles-Bey*, Geena Davis, Stephen Rea, James
Gandolfini, Aida Turturro, Philip Bosco
Director: Martha Coolidge
Executive Producer: Joe Roth, Roger Birnbaum
Music by: Jerry Goldsmith
Producer: Joe Roth, Larry Brezner, Patrick McCormick, Roger Birnbaum
Screenwriter: Todd Graff*
Tech Info: color/sound/108 min.   Type: Dramatic Feature
Date: 1994   Origin: USA
Company: Caravan Pictures, Scapa Via Productions
Distributors/Format: Buena Vista Home Video (1/2")
Annotation: Unmarried and pregnant, Angie (Davis) begins a romance with Noel
(Rea) who abandons her after the baby is born. Toles-Bey plays a guard and
Woodard, a floor nurse in the psychiatric hospital where Angie finds her mother.

ANGKOR-CAMBODIA EXPRESS
Cast: Woody Strode*, Nancy Kwan, Robert Walker Jr., Christopher George, Lui Leung Wai
Director: Lek Kitiparaporn
Executive Producer: Chari Amartyakul
Music by: Stelvio Cipriani
Producer: Lek Kitiparaporn, Richard Randall, Chari Amartyakul
Screenwriter: Roger Crutchley, Kailan
Tech Info: color/sound/96 min.   Type: Dramatic Feature
Date: 1981   Origin: Thailand, Italy
Company: Network, Spectacular Trading
Distributors/Format: Monarex (16mm)
Annotation: Strode plays Woody in this story about the ongoing struggle in Cambodia two years after the United States' withdrawal from Vietnam. The film was unavailable to American audiences until its 1986 release on video.

ANITA BAKER - ONE NIGHT OF RAPTURE
Executive Producer: Robin Sloane
Music Performer: Anita Baker*
Producer: Robin Sloane, Jon Small
Tech Info: color/sound/46 min.   Type: Concert Short
Date: 1987   Origin: USA
Company: Elektra Entertainment
Distributors/Format: Warner Bros. Home Video, Inc. (1/2")
Annotation: The Grammy-winning performer sings many of her top hits, including: "Mystery," "You've Changed," "Sweet Love," "Caught Up in the Rapture," "Been So Long," "No One in the World," "Watch Your Step," "You Bring Me Joy," and "Same Ole Love."

ANNIE
Cast: Geoffrey Holder*, Ann Reinking, Albert Finney, Tim Curry, Carol Burnett, Bernadette Peters, Aileen Quinn
Director: John Huston
Music by: Charles Strouse
Producer: Ray Stark
Screenwriter: Carol Sobieski
Storywriter: Thomas Meehan
Tech Info: color/sound/128 min.   Type: Musical Feature
Date: 1981   Origin: USA
Company: Rastar Films, Columbia
Distributors/Format: Columbia Pictures Home Video (1/2")
Annotation: Orphan Annie (Quinn) is brought to live with Oliver Warbucks (Finney) as part of a publicity stunt arranged by his secretary, Grace (Reinking). Warbucks and his staff, including Punjab (Holder), come to love Annie, but when she says she wants her real parents, Warbucks attempts to find them. When things go awry, Punjab saves Annie and reunites her with Warbucks and Grace.

ANOTHER 48 HOURS

Cast: Eddie Murphy*, Bernie Casey*, Tisha Campbell*, Francis Ward*, Brent Jennings*, Laurie Morrison*, Bar Band *, Nick Nolte
Director: Walter Hill
Executive Producer: Mark Lipsky, Ralph S. Singleton
Music Performer: Fred Braughton
Music by: James Horner
Producer: Eddie Murphy*, Mark Lipsky, Ralph S. Singleton, Lawrence Gordon, Robert D. Wachs
Screenwriter: John Fasano, Jeb Stuart, Larry Gross
Storywriter: Fred Braughton
Tech Info: color/sound/98 min.   Type: Comedy Feature
Date: 1990   Origin: USA
Company: Eddie Murphy* Productions w/Lawrence Gordon Prod.
Distributors/Format: Paramount Home Video (1/2")
Annotation: When Reggie Hammond (Murphy) gets out of jail, he must give $75,000 to Kirkland Smith's (Casey) daughter Amy (Campbell) as a debt for protection while he was in prison. Trouble begins when Hammond's money is held by Jack (Nolte), a policeman who needs Reggie's help to catch a drug dealer. Jennings plays the front man for the drug dealer; Morrison plays a pickpocket.

ANOTHER KIND OF MUSIC

Cast: Tommy Sans*, Patrick Monize
Director: Gene Salzman
Music Performer: Fruits & Roots
Producer: Rebecca Yates, Gene Salzman
Tech Info: color/sound/25 min.   Type: Documentary Short
Date: 1978   Origin: USA
Company: Phoenix Films
Annotation: Two young rock musicians from different cultures are drawn together by the powerful beat of reggae.

ANOTHER STAKEOUT

Cast: Larry B. Scott*, Blu Mankuma*, Emilio Estevez, Richard Dreyfuss, Rosie O'Donnell
Director: John Badham
Executive Producer: John Badham
Music by: Arthur B. Rubinstein
Producer: Cathleen Summers, John Badham, Jim Kouf, Lynn Bigelow
Screenwriter: Joseph Loeb III, Matthew Weisman, Jim Kouf
Tech Info: color/sound/109 min.   Type: Comedy Feature
Date: 1993   Origin: USA
Company: Kouf/Bigelow Productions, Touchstone
Distributors/Format: Buena Vista Home Video (1/2")
Annotation: Chris Lecce (Dryfuss) and Bill Reimers (Estevez) are joined by federal prosecutor Garret (O'Donnell), in an attempt to locate a witness, and rescue her from a mob attack. Scott plays a garage attendant and Mankuma plays Detective Wills.

ANOTHER YOU
Cast: Richard Pryor*, Tammy Hanson*, Vanessa Williams*, Gene Wilder, Stephen Lang
Director: Maurice Phillips
Executive Producer: Ted Zachary
Music by: Charles Gross
Producer: Ziggy Steinberg, Ted Zachary
Screenwriter: Ziggy Steinberg
Tech Info: color/sound/110 min.   Type: Comedy Feature
Date: 1991   Origin: USA
Company: TriStar/Columbia, New Man Productions
Distributors/Format: Columbia/TriStar Home Video (1/2")
Annotation: Eddie Dash (Pryor), a convicted con man, must fulfill 100 hours of community service by taking a recently released mental patient (Wilder) to cultural sites. Hanson plays the hat check girl.

ANSWER, THE
Director: Spike Lee*
Producer: Spike Lee*
Screenwriter: Spike Lee*
Storywriter: Spike Lee*
Tech Info: bw/sound/20 min.   Type: Dramatic Short
Date: 1980   Origin: USA
Studio: Independent
Annotation: A struggling black screenplay writer, Miles Toomer (Lee), is hired by a major motion picture studio to direct a $50 million remake of BIRTH OF A NATION. Toomer mistakenly believes he will have creative impact but his rebellion is met with harassment by the Klu Klux Klan.

ANTHEM
Director: Marlon T. Riggs*
Producer: Marlon T. Riggs*
Speaker: Marlon T. Riggs*, Bernard Branner*, Brian Freeman*, Jesse Harris*, Willi Ninja, The Bella Boys , David Kirkland
Tech Info: color/sound/9 min.   Type: Documentary Short
Date: 1991   Origin: USA
Company: Signifyin' Productions
Distributors/Format: Frameline Distribution (1/2"), Signifyin' Works (1/2")
Archives/Format: IUB - BFC/A (1/2")
Annotation: This short film explores how the homosexual community is depicted in society and serves as a weapon of empowerment for its members.

APOCALYPSE NOW
Cast: Albert Hall*, Laurence/Larry Fishburne*, Robert Duvall, Harrison Ford, Martin Sheen, Marlon Brando, Frederic Forrest, Dennis Hopper
Director: Francis Ford Coppola
Music Performer: Francis Ford Coppola, Carmine Coppola
Music by: Francis Ford Coppola, Carmine Coppola
Narrator: Martin Sheen
Producer: Francis Ford Coppola
Screenwriter: John Milius, Michael Herr, Francis Ford Coppola
Storywriter: Joseph Conrad

Tech Info: color/sound/139 min.   Type: Dramatic Feature
Date: 1979   Origin: USA
Company: United Artists
Distributors/Format: Facets Multimedia, Inc. (1/2"), Paramount Home Video (1/2"),
United Artists Home Video (1/2")
Annotation: Captain Benjamin Willard (Sheen) is accompanied through the Vietnam
jungle by Chief Boat Commander (Hall), Clean (Fishburne), Chef (Forrest), and
Lance (Bottoms). All are subordinates unaware of Willard's mission, the
assassination of American Colonel Kurtz (Brando). Other uncredited black
performers appear.

APPLE, THE

Cast: George Clinton*, Catherine Mary Stewart, George Gilmour, Vladek Sheybal
Director: Menahem Golan
Music by: Coby Recht, Iris Recht
Producer: Yoram Globus, Menahem Golan
Screenwriter: Menahem Golan
Tech Info: color/sound/90 min.   Type: Musical Feature
Date: 1980   Origin: USA, West Germany
Company: N.F. Geria III
Distributors/Format: Cannon Home Video (1/2")
Annotation: In this musical sci-fi, folk singers Bibi (Stewart) and Alphie (Gilmour)
sign a recording contract with devilish producer Boogalow (Sheybal). Clinton plays
Joe.

APPOINTMENT WITH FEAR

Cast: James Avery*, Michele Little, Michael Wyle, Kerry Remsen, Garrick Dowhen
Director: Ramzi Thomas
Executive Producer: Moustapha Akkad
Music by: Andrea Saparoff
Producer: Moustapha Akkad, Tom Boutross
Screenwriter: Ramzi Thomas, Bruce Meade
Tech Info: color/sound/98 min.   Type: Dramatic Feature
Date: 1985   Origin: USA
Company: Galaxy
Annotation: Avery plays Conners in this film about a crazed killer (Dowhen) who
uses the Egyptian god Attis as his role model.

APPRENTICE TO MURDER

Cast: Tiger Haynes*, Donald Sutherland, Mia Sara, Chad Lowe, Knut Husebo
Director: Ralph L. Thomas
Executive Producer: Michael Rauch
Music by: Charles Gross
Producer: Howard Grossman, Michael Rauch
Screenwriter: Allan Scott, Wesley Moore
Tech Info: color/sound/94 min.   Type: Dramatic Feature
Date: 1988   Origin: USA
Company: Hot
Distributors/Format: New World Home Video (1/2")
Annotation: Billy Kelly (Lowe) travels with faith healer John Reese (Sutherland) after
Reese cures Kelly's father of alcoholism. Haynes plays Rufus.

APRIL FOOL'S DAY
Cast: Thomas F. Wilson*, Deborah Foreman, Jay Baker, Pat Barlow, Lloyd Berry
Director: Fred Walton
Executive Producer: Dick Randall, Steve Minasian
Music by: Charles Bernstein
Producer: Dick Randall, Frank Mancuso Jr., Steve Minasian
Screenwriter: Danilo Bach
Tech Info: color/sound/88 min.   Type: Dramatic Feature
Date: 1986   Origin: USA
Company: Hometown
Distributors/Format: Paramount Home Video (1/2")
Annotation: Eight college friends join a classmate (Foreman) at her island mansion for a weekend of practical jokes and murder in this spoof of slasher movies. Wilson plays Arch, one of the visiting friends.

ARE WE DIFFERENT?
Producer: John Arthos
Speaker: Cornel West*
Tech Info: color/sound/27 min.   Type: Documentary Short
Date: 1993   Origin: USA
Studio: Independent
Distributors/Format: Filmakers Library, Inc. (16mm; 1/2")
Annotation: The film gives voice to African American students as they discuss issues of race, racism and race relations as well as the causes and nature of anger and frustration in the black community.

ARMED AND DANGEROUS
Cast: Tony Burton*, Larry "Flash" Jenkins*, John Candy, Eugene Levy, Meg Ryan
Director: Mark L. Lester
Executive Producer: Bernie Brillstein, Harold Ramis
Music by: Bill Meyers, James DiPasquale
Producer: Bernie Brillstein, Harold Ramis, James Keach, Brian Grazer
Screenwriter: Harold Ramis, Peter Torokvei
Storywriter: Harold Ramis, James Keach, Brian Grazer
Tech Info: color/sound/88 min.   Type: Comedy Feature
Date: 1986   Origin: USA
Company: Frostbacks
Distributors/Format: Columbia Pictures Home Video (1/2")
Annotation: An unemployed policeman and a disbarred attorney, Frank Dooley (Candy) and Norman Kane (Levy), take jobs as security guards. Burton plays Cappy.

ARTICLE 99
Cast: Keith David*, Forest Whitaker*, Lynn Thigpen*, Lea Thompson, Ray Liotta, Keifer Sutherland
Director: Howard Deutch, Richard Bowen
Producer: Michael Gruskoff, Michael I. Levy
Screenwriter: Ron Cutler
Tech Info: color/sound/99 min.   Type: Dramatic Feature

Date: 1992   Origin: USA
Company: Orion
Annotation: Dr. Sid Handleman (Whitaker) is on the staff of a Veteran's
Administration Hospital where doctors must hide patients in hallways, steal
pacemakers, hijack supplies and schedule unauthorized operations because needy
patients are being denied treatment. All this is a result of bureaucratic red tape and
a corrupt hospital administration, led by maverick head surgeon, Dr. Sturgen
(Liotta).

AS I REMEMBER IT: A PORTRAIT OF DOROTHY WEST

Director: Salem Mekuria*
Speaker: Dorothy West*
Tech Info: color/sound/56 min.   Type: Documentary Feature
Date: 1991   Origin: USA
Studio: Independent
Distributors/Format: Women Make Movies, Inc. (16mm; 1/2")
Archives/Format: IUB - BFC/A (1/2")
Annotation: This intimate portrait of writer West explores the forgotten role of women
in the Harlem Renaissance. From the perspective of her 83 years, West relates her
memories of growing up African American, privileged and enchanted by literature.

ASHANTI

Alternate: Ashanti: Land of No Mercy
Cast: Johnny Sekka*, Akosua Busia*, Beverly Johnson*, Olu Jacobs*, Tyrone
Jackson*, Winston Ntshona*, Peter Ustinov, Kabir Bedi, Michael Caine
Director: Richard Fleischer
Music Performer: Jimmy Chambers*
Music by: Don Black*, Michael Melvion
Producer: Monty Irvin
Screenwriter: Stephen Geller
Tech Info: color/sound/102 min.   Type: Dramatic Feature
Date: 1979   Origin: Switzerland
Company: GAV, Beverly Films
Distributors/Format: Trans World Entertainment (1/2")
Annotation: A modern-day version of the slave trade, young men and beautiful
women are kidnapped from their African homeland and sold to the highest bidder.
Anansa Linderby (Johnson), a beautiful doctor, is kidnapped to become the lover of
an Arab king. Dr. David Linderby (Caine), her husband, rescues her.

ASHES AND EMBERS

Cast: Kathy Flewellen*, Uwezo Flewellen*, Evelyn Blackwell*, John Anderson*,
Norman Blalock*, Dr. Charles Cobb Sr.*, Barry Wiggins*, Vantile Whitfield*, Robert
Kemp*
Director: Haile Gerima*
Music by: Brother Ah *
Producer: Haile Gerima*
Screenwriter: Haile Gerima*
Storywriter: Haile Gerima*
Tech Info: mixed/sound/120 min.   Type: Dramatic Feature

Date: 1985 Origin: USA
Company: Mypheduh Films, Inc.
Archives/Format: IUB - BFC/A (1/2")
Annotation: Charles (Anderson), a Vietnam veteran, struggles with his transition from ex-soldier to civilian. He must also deal with his status as an African American in a racist society. His grandmother (Blackwell) and his friends aid in his psychological transformation.

ASSASSINATION OF MARTIN LUTHER KING, JR.

Director: Denis Mueller
Screenwriter: Warren Leming
Speaker: Dick Gregory*, James Lawson*, Reverend Kyles*
Tech Info: mixed/sound/85 min.   Type: Documentary Feature
Date: 1993 Origin: USA
Distributors/Format: MPI Home Video (1/2"), Filmic Archives (1/2")
Annotation: An investigative report of assassination, the documentary includes interviews with people who were with Martin Luther King during his last hours.

ASSAULT ON PRECINCT 13

Cast: Austin Stoker*, Tony Burton*, Len Whitaker*, Darwin Joston, Laurie Zimmer
Director: John Carpenter
Music by: John Carpenter
Producer: Irwin Yablans
Screenwriter: John Carpenter
Tech Info: color/sound/91 min.   Type: Dramatic Feature
Date: 1981 Origin: USA
Company: CKK Corporation, Turtle Releasing Organization
Distributors/Format: Media Home Entertainment, Inc. (1/2")
Annotation: When two convicts (Joston and Burton) are transferred to Los Angeles' Precinct 13, a local gang attempts to assassinate them. Stoker plays Lt. Bishop, head of the 13th precinct's police force; Whitaker plays a hoodlum.

AT THE RIVER I STAND

Series: African American Perspectives
Director: David Appleby, Allison Graham, Steven Ross
Tech Info: mixed/sound/56 min.   Type: Documentary Feature
Date: 1993 Origin: USA
Studio: Independent
Distributors/Format: California Newsreel (1/2")
Annotation: The film reconstructs the two eventful months in 1968 which led to the tragic death of Dr. Martin Luther King, Jr. and the climax of the Civil Rights Movement.

AVA'S MAGICAL ADVENTURE

Cast: Georg Stanford Brown*, Timothy Bottoms, Patrick Dempsey, Remy Ryan
Director: Patrick Dempsey, Rocky Parker
Executive Producer: Barbara Javitz, Gary Binkow
Music by: Mark Holden
Producer: Steven Paul, Barry Collier, Barbara Javitz, Gary Binkow
Screenwriter: Susan D. Nimm
Storywriter: Mark Twain
Tech Info: color/sound/94 min.   Type: Comedy Feature

Date: 1994   Origin: USA
Company: Stolen Elephant Inc.
Distributors/Format: Prism Entertainment (1/2")
Annotation: Clayton (Brown), an escaped convict who was framed for embezzlement by Slayton (Bottoms), has returned to confront him. Meanwhile, Slayton plans to kill an elephant to collect the insurance money. Edwina (Ryan) overhears the plot, steals the elephant and meets up with Clayton, and the two of them force Slayton to reveal his crimes.

AVENGING ANGEL

Cast: Ossie Davis*, Susan Tyrrell, Rory "The Texan" Calhoun, Betsy Russell
Director: Robert Vincent O'Neil
Executive Producer: Mel Pearl, Don Levin
Music by: Christopher Young
Producer: Sandy Howard, Mel Pearl, Don Levin, Keith Rubinstein
Screenwriter: Robert Vincent O'Neil, Joseph M. Cala
Tech Info: color/sound/93 min.   Type: Dramatic Feature
Date: 1985   Origin: USA
Company: Republic
Distributors/Format: New World Home Video (1/2")
Annotation: Molly/Angel (Russell), a former Hollywood hooker turned law student, avenges the death of the detective who got her off the streets. Davis is Capt. Moradian.

AVENGING DISCO GODFATHER

Alternate: Avenging Godfather
Cast: Rudy Ray Moore*, Carol Speed*, Jimmy Lynch*
Director: J. Robert Wagoner
Producer: Rudy Ray Moore*, Theodore Toney
Tech Info: color/sound/93 min.   Type: Dramatic Feature
Date: 1986   Origin: USA
Company: Active
Distributors/Format: Active Home Video (1/2")
Annotation: Moore takes on the "bad guys" with martial arts, and heroics.

AWAKENINGS

Cast: Dexter Gordon*, Mary Alice*, Keith Diamond*, Robin Williams, Robert De Niro
Director: Penny Marshall
Music by: Randy Newman
Producer: Penny Marshall, Arne Schmidt, Elliot Abbott
Screenwriter: Steven Zaillian
Storywriter: Oliver Sacks, MD
Tech Info: color/sound/120 min.   Type: Dramatic Feature
Date: 1990   Origin: USA
Company: Columbia, TriStar
Distributors/Format: Columbia/TriStar Pictures (35mm; 1/2"), Facets Multimedia, Inc. (1/2")
Annotation: Aiding Dr. Malcolm Sayers (Williams) in his work with post-encephalitic patients are Nurse Margaret (Alice) and Anthony (Diamond) whose long hours and devotion are rewarded with the awakenings of their patients. Rolando (Gordon) is one of the patients who awakens to music running through his head.

AWAKENINGS (1954-56) - EPISODE 1
Series: Eyes On The Prize: America's Civil Rights Years
Cast: J.W. Milum
Director: Judith Vecchione
Executive Producer: Henry Hampton*
Narrator: Julian Bond*
Producer: Henry Hampton*, Judith Vecchione, Judith Vecchione
Speaker: Reverend Ralph Abernathy*, Amzie Moore*, Virginia Durr*, Constance Baker Motley*, Mose Wright*, Roy Wilkins*, Mamie Till Bradley*, Curtis Jones*, Charles Diggs*, Rev. Fred Shuttlesworth*, Rosa Parks*, E.D. Nixon*, Jo Ann Robinson*, Frances Belser*, Dr. Martin Luther King Jr.*, Coretta Scott King*, Rufus Lewis*, Georgia Gilmore*, Donie Jones*, James Hicks, Thomas Waring, H.C. Strider, William Bradford Huie, Joe Azbell, Sen. James Eastland, Sam Engelhardt, Clyde Sellers
Tech Info: color/sound/55 min.   Type: Television Documentary
Date: 1986   Origin: USA
Company: Blackside, Inc.
Distributors/Format: PBS Video (16mm; 1/2")
Archives/Format: IUB - AAAMC (1/2")
Annotation: This segment documents the awakening of the Civil Rights Movement reflected in acts of personal courage: Wright risks his life by testifying against the killers of his nephew Emmet Till in a white courtroom; Parks refuses to move from her seat on a Montgomery bus; King, along with SCLC, begin the challenge to desegregate the South.

BABIES MAKING BABIES
Director: Carl Clay*
Producer: Black Spectrum Theater *
Screenwriter: Carl Clay*
Storywriter: Carl Clay*
Tech Info: color/sound/25 min.   Type: Documentary Short
Date: 1990   Origin: USA
Studio: Independent
Distributors/Format: AM Home Video (1/2")
Annotation: Fifteeen year old Yolanda recalls the events preceding her pregnancy and offers insight into the increasing problem of babies making babies.

BACHELOR PARTY
Cast: Ji-Tu Cumbuka*, Tom Hanks, George Grizzard, Tawny Kitaen, Adrian Zmed
Director: Neal Israel
Executive Producer: Joe Roth
Music by: Robert Folk, Tom Jenkins, Barry Schleifer
Producer: Joe Roth, Ron Moler, Bob Israel
Screenwriter: Neal Israel, Pat Proft
Storywriter: Bob Israel
Tech Info: color/sound/106 min.   Type: Comedy Feature
Date: 1984   Origin: USA
Company: Aspect Ratio, Twin Continental, Bachelor Party
Distributors/Format: Fox Home Video (1/2")
Annotation: To celebrate the wedding of Rick Gasko (Hanks), his friends throw him a bachelor party to end all bachelor parties. Cumbuka plays the Alley Pimp.

BACK INSIDE HERSELF
Cast: Barbara O *, Makini Gena Jones*, Michael Petit, Henry Farrell
Director: Saundra Sharp*
Producer: Saundra Sharp*
Speaker: Saundra Sharp*, Arabella Chavers*, Gamy L. Tyler*, Henry A. Saunders*, Al Lorenzo*
Storywriter: Saundra Sharp*
Tech Info: bw/sound/5 min.   Type: Experimental Short
Date: 1984   Origin: USA
Company: A Sharp* Show
Archives/Format: IUB - BFC/A (1/2")
Annotation: Voice-overs by Tyler, Saunders, Lorenzo, Chavers, and Sharp describe the interior journey of a black woman who represents the collective identity of African American women.

BACK ROADS
Cast: Nell Carter*, David Keith, Alex Colon, Sally Field, Tommy Lee Jones, Miriam Colon
Director: Martin Ritt
Music by: Henry Mancini
Producer: Ronald Shedlo
Screenwriter: Gary Devore
Tech Info: color/sound/94 min.   Type: Comedy Feature
Date: 1981   Origin: USA
Company: Warner Bros.
Distributors/Format: Warner Bros. Home Video, Inc. (1/2")
Annotation: Amy Post (Field), a hooker, falls in love with boxer Elmore Pratt (Jones). Carter plays a waitress.

BACK TO THE FUTURE
Cast: Harry Waters Jr.*, Donald Fullilove*, Christopher Lloyd, Michael J. Fox, Lea Thompson
Director: Robert Zemeckis
Executive Producer: Steven Spielberg, Frank Marshall, Kathleen Kennedy
Music Performer: Alan Silvestri
Producer: Steven Spielberg, Frank Marshall, Kathleen Kennedy, Rob Gale, Neil Canton
Screenwriter: Robert Zemeckis
Tech Info: color/sound/117 min.   Type: Comedy Feature
Date: 1985   Origin: USA
Company: Universal
Distributors/Format: MCA Home Video (1/2")
Annotation: Goldie Wilson (Fullilove) is the Mayor of Hill Valley, where as Marty McFly (Fox) finds out in his fantastic visit to the past, he was once a waiter at a local soda shop. Marvin Berry (Waters) is the leader of a band called the Starlighters, who play at the climactic high school dance. The Starlighters are not identified in the credits.

BACK TO THE MOVEMENT (1979-MID 1980S)
Series: Eyes On The Prize II
Director: Madison Davis Lacey Jr.*, James A. DeVinney
Executive Producer: Henry Hampton*
Narrator: Julian Bond*
Producer: Henry Hampton*, Madison Davis Lacey Jr.*, James A. DeVinney
Screenwriter: Madison Davis Lacey Jr.*, James A. DeVinney
Speaker: C.T. Vivian*, John Brown*, Dorothy Graham*, Georgia Jones Ayres*, Dewey Knight Sr.*, Lonnie Lawrence*, Clyde Killens*, Jessie McCrary*, Frank Legree*, Frederica Watts McDuffie*, Louis McDuffie*, Eula McDuffie*, Otis Pitts*, Walter Fauntroy*, Renault Robinson*, Nancy Jefferson*, Marion Stamps*, Clifford Kelly*, Lu Palmer*, Harold Washington*, Edward Gardner*, Joseph Gardner*, Rosie Mars*, Fannie Lou Hammer*, Unita Blackwell*, Eleanor Holmes Norton*, George Clemants*, Dale Bowlin, Ronald Wright, Janet Reno, Charles Veverka, Mark Meier, Phillip Carlton, Maurice Ferre, Jimmy Carter, Ronald Reagan, Jane Byrne, Slim Coleman
Tech Info: mixed/sound/60 min.   Type: Television Documentary
Date: 1989   Origin: USA
Company: Blackside, Inc.
Distributors/Format: PBS Video (16mm; 1/2")
Archives/Format: IUB - AAAMC (1/2")
Annotation: This segment concludes the series by examining two racially explosive cities. One is Miami where, in the late 70s, early 80s, 20,000 Blacks are displaced, unemployment skyrockets, and a three day riot ensues. The film concludes with a brief survey of Civil Rights through the lives of five important figures of the movement.

BACKFIRE
Cast: Bernie Casey*, Virginia Capers*, Keith Carradine, Jeff Fahey, Karen Allen
Director: Gilbert Cates
Executive Producer: Dennis Brown
Music by: David Shire
Producer: Danton Rissner, Dennis Brown
Screenwriter: Larry Brand, Rebecca Reynolds
Tech Info: color/sound/90 min.   Type: Dramatic Feature
Date: 1989   Origin: USA
Company: ITC
Distributors/Format: Vidmark Entertainment Home Video (1/2")
Annotation: Everyone on St. James Island envies rich, young and attractive Donnie (Fahey) and Mara (Allen), but they don't realize Donnie suffers nightmares about his Vietnam experience. Casey plays Clint; Capers plays Maxine.

BACKTRACK
Cast: Grand L. Bush*, Sy Richardson*, Sarina Grant*, Dennis Hopper, Dean Stockwell, Jodie Foster
Director: Dennis Hopper
Executive Producer: Steven Reuther, Mitchell Cannold
Music by: Curt Sobel
Producer: Steven Reuther, Dan Paulson, Mitchell Cannold, Dick Clark
Screenwriter: Rachel Kronstadt-Mann, Stephen L. Cotler, Lanny Cotler
Storywriter: Rachel Kronstadt-Mann

Tech Info: color/sound/98 min.   Type: Dramatic Feature
Date: 1992   Origin: USA
Company: Vestron Pictures, Precision Films, et al.
Distributors/Format: Vestron Home Video (1/2")
Annotation: Artist Anne Benton (Foster) accidentally witnesses a Mafia murder and is placed in the witness protection program. Milo (Hopper), the hitman, manages to track her down. Bush plays the bank teller.

BAD BOYS
Cast: Jim Moody*, Robert Lee Rush*, Eric Barefield*, Donald James*, Sean Penn, Ally Sheedy, Esai Morales
Director: Richard Rosenthal
Music Performer: Bill Conti
Music by: Bill Conti
Producer: Robert H. Solo
Screenwriter: Richard Di Lello
Storywriter: Richard Di Lello
Tech Info: color/sound/123 min.   Type: Dramatic Feature
Date: 1982   Origin: USA
Company: EMI Films
Distributors/Format: Universal Home Video (1/2"), Associated Film (16mm)
Annotation: Mick O'Brien (Penn) is sentenced to the Rainford Correctional facility for juveniles after his plot to sabotage a drug transaction fails. Gene Daniels, (Moody) a corrections supervisor, tries to reform the young boys; Rush plays Tweety.   Many young black men are cast as prisoners or gang members including Barefield and James.

BAD JIM
Cast: Richard Roundtree*, John Clark Gable*, James Brolin, Ty "Bronco Lane" Hardin, Henry Casey Jr.
Director: Clyde Ware, David Golia
Music by: Jamie Sheriff
Producer: Joseph Wouk
Storywriter: Clyde Ware
Tech Info: color/sound/90 min.   Type: Comedy Feature
Date: 1989   Origin: USA
Company: RCA, Columbia
Annotation: An identity transformation takes place when a cowpoke buys and rides Billy the Kid's horse. He finds himself behaving like the deceased outlaw.

BAD LIEUTENANT
Cast: Minnie Gentry*, John Steven Jones*, Shawn McLean*, Harvey Keitel
Director: Abel Ferrara
Executive Producer: Patrick Wachsberger, Ronna B. Wallace
Music by: Joe Delia
Producer: Patrick Wachsberger, Edward R. Pressman, Ronna B. Wallace, Mary Kane
Screenwriter: Abel Ferrara, Zoe Tamarlaine Lund
Tech Info: color/sound/96 min.   Type: Dramatic Feature

Date: 1992   Origin: USA
Company: Lt. Productions, Edward R. Pressman Film Corp.
Distributors/Format: Aries Film Releasing (16mm)
Annotation: A New York City Lieutenant's (Keitel) happy family life stands in stark contrast to the drug-addicted, gambling extortionist path he takes on the job. The Lieutenant tries to mend his ways by solving the rape of a nun. McLean is black kid #1; Jones is black kid #2; and Gentry plays an elderly woman.

BAGDAD CAFE
Cast: CCH Pounder*, Monica Calhoun*, Darron Flagg*, G. Smokey Campbell*, Marriane Sagebrecht, Jack Palance
Director: Percy Aldon
Producer: Percy Aldon
Screenwriter: Percy Aldon, Christopher Doherty
Storywriter: Percy Aldon
Tech Info: color/sound/91 min.   Type: Dramatic Feature
Date: 1987   Origin: USA
Company: Pelemele Films, Island
Distributors/Format: Virgin Visions Home Video (1/2")
Annotation: Brenda (Pounder), the angry owner of Bagdad Cafe, gets little help from her lazy husband Sal (Campbell), her son Sal Jr. (Flagg) who does nothing but play the piano, or her daughter Phyllis (Calhoun) who thumbs a ride with any man who passes through Bagdad. When Jasmin (Sagebrecht), a German woman, abandons her husband for a single room at the local motel, she brings about changes at the cafe.

BALTIMORE BULLET, THE
Cast: Calvin Lockhart*, James Coburn, Omar Shariff, Bruce Boxleitner, Ronee Blakley
Director: Robert Ellis Miller
Executive Producer: William D. Jekel, Norman G. Rudman
Music Performer: Johnny Mandel
Music by: Johnny Mandel
Producer: John Brascia, William D. Jekel, Norman G. Rudman
Screenwriter: Robert Vincent O'Neil, John Brascia
Storywriter: John Brascia
Tech Info: color/sound/103 min.   Type: Dramatic Feature
Date: 1980   Origin: USA
Company: Filmfair, Inc., Embassy
Distributors/Format: Embassy Home Video (1/2")
Annotation: Pool players Nick Casey (Coburn) and Billy Joe (Boxleitner) arrange a match with "The Deacon" (Shariff) who is rumored to be the world's greatest pool shark. Lockhart plays Snow White, a poker player from whom Casey and Billy Joe steal thousands of dollars.

BAND OF THE HAND
Cast: Laurence/Larry Fishburne*, Leon (credited as Leon) Robinson*, James Remar, Stephen Lang, Daniele Quinn
Director: Paul Michael Glaser
Executive Producer: Michael Mann
Music Performer: Bob Dylan
Music by: Michel Rubini

Producer: Michael Mann, Michael Rauch
Screenwriter: Leo Garen, Jack Baran
Tech Info: color/sound/110 min.   Type: Dramatic Feature
Date: 1986   Origin: USA
Company: Delphi IV & V, TriStar
Annotation: A group of criminals are taken in hand by a tough survivalist who teaches them how to survive in the wild. At first afraid of wildlife, they come to respect it and each other. They finally return to their neighborhood and swear to clean it up. Fishburne plays Cream.

BANK ROBBER

Cast: Forest Whitaker*, Paula Kelly*, Lisa Bonet*, Judge Reinhold, Olivia D'abo, Patrick Dempsey
Director: Nick Mead
Executive Producer: Miles A. Copeland III, Paul Colichman, Jean Cazes
Music by: Stewart Copeland
Producer: Miles A. Copeland III, Paul Colichman, Lila Cazes, Jean Cazes
Screenwriter: Nick Mead
Tech Info: color/sound/91 min.   Type: Comedy Feature
Date: 1993   Origin: USA
Company: IRS Media, Initial Groupe
Distributors/Format: IRS Releasing (16mm)
Annotation: A call girl, Priscilla (Bonet), shows sympathy for Billy (Dempsey), the object of an intense manhunt. Robbing a bank, Billy is shot by police officers Battle (Whitaker) and Gross (Reinhold) who deliver him back to Priscilla. Kelly plays Mother.

BARON, THE

Cast: Calvin Lockhart*, Marlene Clark*, Leonard Jackson*, Beverly Johnson*, George Farley*, Samm-Art Williams*, Larry Marshall*, Node Clarke*, Joan Blondell, Charles McGregor, Richard Lynch
Director: Philip Fently
Music Performer: Gil Scott Heron*, Brian Jackson, Barnett Williams
Producer: Chiz Schultz*, Thomas Tatham
Tech Info: color/sound/90 min.   Type: Dramatic Feature
Date: 1987   Origin: USA
Company: King of Video, Paragon
Distributors/Format: Paragon Video Productions (1/2")
Annotation: Jason (Lockhart) is an independent filmmaker trying to pay off his debts to "Cokeman" (McGregor), a drug pusher. Bruce Brown (Farley) is a corporate executive who lends Jason money. Junebug (Jackson) is a mechanic who helps Jason evade the drug kings and Caroline (Clark) is Jason's girlfriend.

BAT 21

Cast: Danny Glover*, Gene Hackman, Jerry Reed
Director: Peter Markle
Music by: Christopher Young
Producer: David Fisher, Gary A. Neil, Michael Balson
Storywriter: William C. Anderson, Norman Mare
Tech Info: color/sound/105 min.   Type: Dramatic Feature

Date: 1988   Origin: USA
Company: Vision P.D.G., Eagle Films, Bat 21 Productions
Distributors/Format: TriStar Pictures Inc. (1/2")
Annotation: Based on a true story, this Vietnam war tale centers on the relationship between a downed aerial officer (Hackman) and his pilot (Glover) who is determined to rescue him.

BATMAN

Cast: Billy Dee Williams*, Kim Basinger, Jack Nicholson, Michael Keaton, Pat Hingle, Jack Palance
Director: Tim Burton
Executive Producer: Benjamin Meeniker, Michael Uslan
Music Performer: Prince (Rogers Nelson) *
Music by: Danny Elfman
Producer: Peter Guber, Jon Peters, Benjamin Meeniker, Michael Uslan
Screenwriter: Warren Skaaren, Sam Hamm
Storywriter: Sam Hamm
Tech Info: color/sound/126 min.   Type: Dramatic Feature
Date: 1989   Origin: USA
Company: Warner Bros.
Annotation: Williams plays District Attorney Harvey Dent in crime ridden Gotham City who must be saved by Batman, aka Bruce Wayne (Keaton).

BATTERIES NOT INCLUDED

Cast: Frank McRae*, Jessica Tandy, Elizabeth Pena, Hume Cronyn, Michael Carmine
Director: Matthew Robbins
Executive Producer: Steven Spielberg, Frank Marshall, Kathleen Kennedy
Music by: James Horner
Producer: Steven Spielberg, Frank Marshall, Kathleen Kennedy, Ronald L. Schwary
Screenwriter: Matthew Robbins, Brent Maddock, S.S. Wilson, Brad Bird
Storywriter: Steven Spielberg, Mick Garris
Tech Info: color/sound/105 min.   Type: Comedy Feature
Date: 1987   Origin: USA
Company: Amblin
Distributors/Format: Universal Home Video (1/2")
Annotation: Harry (McRae) is evicted from his apartment along with all the other tenants as the building is being torn down to make room for skyscrapers. Refusing to leave, Harry and a few other persistent tenants meet up with some other-worldly flying creatures that aid in the rescue of the historic site.

BATTLESTAR GALLACTICA

Cast: Terry Carter*, Dirk Benedict, Lorne Greene, Richard Hatch, Jane Seymour
Director: Richard A. Colla
Executive Producer: Glen A. Larsen
Music Performer: Stu Phillips
Music by: Stu Phillips
Producer: Glen A. Larsen, John Dykstra
Screenwriter: Glen A. Larsen
Tech Info: color/sound/125 min.   Type: Dramatic Feature

Date: 1979   Origin: USA
Company: Universal
Annotation: Colonel Tigh (Carter) is second in command to Battlestar Galactica's Captain Adama (Greene). When Cylon warriors attempt to exterminate humanity, the Galactica's crew must gather the survivors and colonize a new planet.

BEAST WITHIN, THE
Cast: Meshach Taylor*, Ronny Cox, Bibi Besch, Paul Clemens
Director: Philippe Mora
Executive Producer: Jack B. Bernstein
Music by: Les Baxter
Producer: Gabriel Katzka, Harvey Bernhard, Jack B. Bernstein
Screenwriter: Tom Holland
Tech Info: color/sound/90 min.   Type: Dramatic Feature
Date: 1982   Origin: USA
Company: MGM
Distributors/Format: United Artists Home Video (1/2")
Annotation: Meshach Taylor plays a deputy who must investigate horrifying events which involve giant creatures with hairy legs.

BEASTMASTER, THE
Cast: John Amos*, Tanya Roberts, Rip Torn, Marc Singer
Director: Don Coscarelli
Executive Producer: Sylvio Tabet, Nader Atassi
Music by: Lee Holdridge
Producer: Paul Pepperman, Sylvio Tabet, Sylvio Tabet, Nader Atassi
Screenwriter: Paul Pepperman, Don Coscarelli
Tech Info: color/sound/118 min.   Type: Dramatic Feature
Date: 1982   Origin: USA
Company: MGM
Distributors/Format: United Artists Home Video (1/2")
Annotation: As the beastmaster, Dar (Singer) has the power to make animals conform to his will. Amos plays Seth in this sci-fi/fantasy.

BEAT STREET
Cast: Kadeem Hardison*, Rae Dawn Chong*, Leon W. Grant*, Guy Davis*, Robert Taylor*, Mary Alice*, Jazzy Jay *, Duane Jones*, Kool Herc *, Gina Belafonte*, Richard Sisco*
Director: Stan Lathan*
Music Performer: Rock Steady Crew *, Grandmaster Melle Mel*, The Furious Five *, Fantastic Duo *, N.Y.City Breakers *, African Bambataa and The Soul Sonic Force*, Shango *, The System*, The Treacherous Three *, US Girls *, Bernard Fowler
Producer: Harry Belafonte*, David V. Picker
Screenwriter: Andy Davis, David Gilbert, Paul Golding
Storywriter: Steven Hager
Tech Info: color/sound/106 min.   Type: Musical Feature
Date: 1984   Origin: USA
Company: Orion
Distributors/Format: Orion Home Video (1/2")
Annotation: Brothers Kenny (Davis) and Lee (Taylor) are street artists dreaming of fame. Fantasy becomes reality when they meet New York University student Tracy (Chong) who has close connections with Robert (Jones), a record producer. Alice

plays the boys' worried mother, Cora.

BEAUTY IN THE BRICKS
Director: Allen Mondell, Cynthia Salzman Mondell
Producer: Allen Mondell, Cynthia Salzman Mondell
Speaker: Teresa Evans*, Karen Morgan*, Michelle Wells*, Tina Williams*, Audrey Hinton*
Tech Info: color/sound/33 min.   Type: Documentary Short
Date: 1981   Origin: USA
Company: Bette Clair McMurray Foundation, Media Projects
Distributors/Format: New Day Films (16mm; 1/2")
Archives/Format: IUB - BFC/A (16mm)
Annotation: Baba (Morgan) is a young determined black woman who excels in spite of her poor background. She gives her best in everything she does and is an inspiration for young black girls in the community in Dallas.

BEBE'S KIDS
Cast: Nell Carter*, Reynaldo Rey*, John Witherspoon*, Chino "Fats" Williams*, Tone-Loc *, Brad Sanders*, Bebe Drake-Massey*, DeVaughn Nixon*, Rodney Winfield*, Vanessa Bell Calloway*, Faison Love*, George Wallace*, Wayne Collins Jr.*, Jonell Greene*, Marques Huston*, Myra J. *
Director: Bruce Smith
Executive Producer: Reginald Hudlin*, Warrington Hudlin*
Music by: John Barnes*
Producer: Reginald Hudlin*, Warrington Hudlin*, Willard Carroll, Thomas Wilhite
Screenwriter: Reginald Hudlin*
Tech Info: color/sound/74 min.   Type: Animated Feature
Date: 1992   Origin: USA
Company: Hyperion Animation Company, Paramount
Distributors/Format: Facets Multimedia, Inc. (1/2"), Paramount Home Video (1/2")
Archives/Format: IUB - BFC/A (1/2")
Annotation: Harris (Love) takes Jamika (Calloway) and her son Leon (Collins) to Fun World for a date. Jamika insists on bringing the children she babysits, LaShawn (Greene), Kahlil (Huston), Pee-Wee (Tone-Loc), and the kids eventually take over the park and the disagreements begin. Myra J. plays Dorothea, Harris' ex-wife; Carter plays Vivian, her friend; Sanders portrays the bartender; Rey plays Lush; and Drake-Massey plays a barfly. Witherspoon, Williams, Winfield and Wallace are the voices of the card players.

BEER
Cast: Charles Barnett*, David Alan Grier*, Rip Torn, Loretta Swit, Kenneth Mars
Director: Patrick Kelly
Executive Producer: James D. Brubaker
Music by: Bill Conti
Producer: Robert Chartoff, James D. Brubaker
Screenwriter: Allan Weisbecker
Tech Info: color/sound/82 min.   Type: Comedy Feature

Date: 1986   Origin: USA
Company: Orion
Annotation: Elliot Morrison (Grier), a well-dressed black lawyer, becomes entrapped with a group of other people in a bar after psychotic hoodlums attempt a robbery.

BEETHOVEN'S 2ND

Cast: Virginia Capers*, Charles Grodin, Bonnie Hunt, Nicholle Tom, Christopher Castile
Director: Rod Daniel
Executive Producer: Ivan Reitman
Music by: Randy Edelman
Producer: Ivan Reitman, Michael Gross, Joe Medjuck
Screenwriter: Len Blum
Tech Info: color/sound/86 min.   Type: Comedy Feature
Date: 1993   Origin: USA
Company: Northern Lights
Distributors/Format: Universal Home Video (1/2")
Annotation: When Beethoven and the St. Bernard of his dreams have puppies, the Newton family (Grodin, Hunt, Tom, Castile) must protect mother and newborns from ruthless owners. Capers is the chemistry teacher.

BEETLEJUICE

Cast: Duane Davis*, Geena Davis, Michael Keaton, Winona Ryder, Alec Baldwin
Director: Tim Burton
Music by: Danny Elfman
Producer: Larry Wilson, Richard Hashimoto, Michael Bender
Screenwriter: Warren Skaaren, Michael McDowell
Storywriter: Larry Wilson, Michael McDowell
Tech Info: color/sound/92 min.   Type: Comedy Feature
Date: 1988   Origin: USA
Company: Geffen
Distributors/Format: Warner Bros. Home Video, Inc. (1/2")
Annotation: After they're killed in a car accident, Adam (Baldwin) and Barbara Maitland (Davis) return to their perfect country home as ghosts. When a New York couple move in and decide to redecorate, the ghosts get haunting help from Betelgeuse (Keaton). Davis plays a dumb football player.

BEING THERE

Cast: Ruth Attaway*, Richard Basehart, Jack Warden, Melvyn Douglas, Peter Sellers, Shirley MacLaine, Richard Dysart
Director: Hal Ashby
Executive Producer: Jack Schartzman
Music Performer: Johnny Mandel
Music by: Johnny Mandel
Producer: Jack Schartzman, Andrew Braunsberg
Screenwriter: Jerry Kosinski
Storywriter: Jerry Kosinski
Tech Info: color/sound/124 min.   Type: Dramatic Feature

Date: 1980   Origin: USA
Company: Northstar International, Lorimar
Annotation: Chance (Sellers) has lived a sheltered life as a gardener for a rich old man. When the old man dies, Chance is thrust out into the real world. Louise (Attaway) is the old man's devoted maid.

BEN WEBSTER: THE BRUTE AND THE BEAUTIFUL
Director: John Jeremy
Music Performer: Ben Webster*
Producer: John Jeremy
Speaker: Ben Webster*
Tech Info: mixed/sound/60 min.   Type: Documentary Feature
Date: 1992   Origin: USA
Company: Shanachie
Annotation: This portrait of Webster, one of the great jazz saxophonists, traces the evolution of his style from his origins in Kansas City in the 1920s to his last professional engagement in Holland in September 1973. The film includes performance clips featuring Webster with a whole range of collaborators as well as recollections of friends and associates.

BENJAMIN BANNEKER: THE MAN WHO LOVED THE STARS
Cast: Ossie Davis*
Director: Bob Walsh, Leroy Morais
Producer: Jochen Breitenstein
Tech Info: color/sound/58 min.   Type: Documentary Feature
Date: 1981   Origin: USA
Company: Phoenix Films
Distributors/Format: Phoenix Film and Video (16mm; 1/2")
Annotation: The film documents the life and accomplishments of Banneker who, in the 1700s, overcame racial barriers to become a noted surveyor, mathematician and astronomer.

BENNY & JOON
Cast: CCH Pounder*, Johnny Depp, Mary Stuart Masterson, Julianna Moore, Aidan Quinn
Director: Jeremiah Chechik
Music Performer: Rachel Portman
Music by: J.A.C. Redford
Producer: Susan Arnold, Donna Roth
Screenwriter: Barry Berman
Storywriter: Barry Berman, Leslie McNeil
Tech Info: color/sound/98 min.   Type: Dramatic Feature
Date: 1990   Origin: USA
Company: MGM
Annotation: Joon (Masterson) is a smart and pretty young girl who is also a little unbalanced. A romance develops between her and a whimsical misfit Sam (Depp). Her overprotective brother Benny (Quinn) and her psychiatrist, Dr. Garvey (Pounder), with all good intention, threaten the relationship.

BERKELEY IN THE SIXTIES

Director: Mark Kitchell
Producer: Mark Kitchell
Screenwriter: Mark Kitchell
Speaker: Huey Newton*, Martin Luther King Jr.*, Joan Baez, Ronald Reagan, Allen Ginsberg
Storywriter: Stephen Most, Susan Griffin
Tech Info: mixed/sound/110 min.   Type: Documentary Feature
Date: 1990   Origin: USA
Company: Kitchell Films w/P.O.V. Films
Distributors/Format: California Newsreel (1/2")
Annotation: The film documents the student protests of the 1960s. It includes archival footage of Civil Rights demonstrations and the actions of the Black Panther Party which fought for political power and economic freedom.

BEST DEFENSE

Cast: Eddie Murphy*, Kate Capshaw, Dudley Moore
Director: Willard Huyck
Music Performer: Patrick Williams
Producer: Gloria Katz
Screenwriter: Gloria Katz, Willard Huyck
Storywriter: Robert Grossbach
Tech Info: color/sound/94 min.   Type: Comedy Feature
Date: 1984   Origin: USA
Company: Paramount
Distributors/Format: Films Inc. (1/2")
Annotation: Lieutenant Landry (Murphy), commander of an army tank in Kuwait, is needed to save some American military personnel trapped in a war-torn city. He succeeds in rescuing the Americans with the help of an inventor (Moore) and the tank he constructs.

BEST LITTLE WHOREHOUSE IN TEXAS, THE

Cast: Theresa Merritt*, Burt Reynolds, Dom DeLuise, Dolly Parton
Director: Colin Higgins
Producer: Thomas Miller, Edward Milkis, Robert Boyett
Screenwriter: Colin Higgins, Larry L. King, Peter Masterson
Storywriter: Larry L. King, Peter Masterson
Tech Info: color/sound/114 min.   Type: Musical Feature
Date: 1982   Origin: USA
Company: Universal
Distributors/Format: Universal Home Video (1/2")
Annotation: Mona Strangely (Parton) runs a bordello which is forced to close due to public pressure. Merritt portrays Jewel, one of the prostitutes at the bordello.

BETRAYED

Alternate: Sundown, Summer Lightning
Cast: Albert Hall*, Kevin C. White*, Debra Winger, Tom Berenger, John Heard, Jeffrey DeMunn, John Mahoney
Director: Constantin Costa-Gavras
Music by: Bill Conti
Producer: Irwin Wrinkler

Screenwriter: Joe Eszterhas
Tech Info: color/sound/128 min.　　Type: Dramatic Feature
Date: 1988　Origin: USA
Company: United Artists
Annotation: Al Sanders (Hall) is an FBI agent who is investigating the Klu Klux Klan murder of a D.J., Jeff (White). Jeff was given a gun and told to run into the woods and defend himself from the hunters. Sanders becomes more involved in the case when he shoots one of the klansmen who is jeopardizing the case.

BETSY'S WEDDING
Cast: Samuel L. Jackson*, Frankie Faison*, Alan Alda, Madeline Kahn, Joey Bishop
Director: Alan Alda
Music by: Bruce Broughton
Producer: Martin Bregman, Louis A. Stroller
Screenwriter: Alan Alda
Tech Info: color/sound/97 min.　　Type: Comedy Feature
Date: 1990　Origin: USA
Company: Silver Screen Partners IV, Touchstone
Distributors/Format: Buena Vista Home Video (1/2")
Annotation: Eddie Hopper (Alda) is determined to give his daughter Betsy (Ringwald) the best wedding ever, but his plans go awry. Faison plays Zack Monroe and Jackson appears as a taxi dispatcher.

BETSY, THE
Alternate: Harold Robbin's The Betsy
Cast: Roy Poole*, Robert Duvall, Jane Alexander, Katharine Ross, Laurence Olivier
Director: Daniel Petrie
Music by: John Barry
Producer: Robert R. Weston
Screenwriter: Walter Bernstein, William Bast
Storywriter: Harold Robbins
Tech Info: color/sound/120 min.　　Type: Dramatic Feature
Date: 1978　Origin: USA
Company: Allied Artists
Annotation: An auto mogul (Olivier) attempts to launch a new automobile, and faces opposition because it lacks built-in obsolescence. Poole plays Duncan.

BETWEEN BLACK & WHITE
Producer: Giannella Garrett
Tech Info: color/sound/26 min.　　Type: Documentary Short
Date: 1994　Origin: USA
Studio: Independent
Distributors/Format: Filmakers Library, Inc. (16mm; 1/2")
Annotation: The film explores the dilemma faced by people of mixed racial background as society attempts to classify them. Sensitive issues of personal and social identities are examined through interviews, family photos and live-action footage.

BEVERLY HILLS COP

Cast: Eddie Murphy*, Damon Wayans*, Gilbert R. Hill*, Art Kimbro*, Ronny Cox, Lisa Eilbacher, Judge Reinhold, John Ashton
Director: Martin Brest
Executive Producer: Mike Moder
Music Performer: Harold Faltermeyer
Music by: Harold Faltermeyer
Producer: Don Simpson, Jerry Bruckheimer, Mike Moder
Screenwriter: Daniel Petrie Jr.
Storywriter: Daniel Petrie Jr., Danilo Bach
Tech Info: color/sound/105 min.   Type: Comedy Feature
Date: 1984   Origin: USA
Company: Paramount
Distributors/Format: Films Inc. (1/2"), Paramount Home Video (1/2")
Archives/Format: IUB - BFC/A (1/2")
Annotation: Murphy plays Axel Foley, a street smart Detroit detective, who goes to Beverly Hills to search for his friend's murderer. Foley's unorthodox methods lead to his success in resolving a drug smuggling plot. Hill is Inspector Todd, Foley's Detroit Chief; Kimbro is a Beverly Hills detective.

BEVERLY HILLS COP II

Cast: Eddie Murphy*, Chris Rock*, Dean Stockwell, Judge Reinhold, Jurgen Prochnow, Brigitte Nielsen
Director: Tony Scott
Executive Producer: Robert D. Wachs, Richard Tienken
Music by: Harold Faltermeyer
Producer: Jerry Bruckheimer, Robert D. Wachs, Richard Tienken, Don Simpson
Screenwriter: Eddie Murphy*, Larry Ferguson, Skaaren Warren
Storywriter: Robert D. Wachs
Tech Info: color/sound/103 min.   Type: Comedy Feature
Date: 1987   Origin: USA
Company: Paramount
Distributors/Format: Paramount Home Video (1/2")
Archives/Format: IUB - BFC/A (1/2")
Annotation: Murphy reprises his role as Axel Foley of the Detroit Police Department and is reunited with his Beverly Hills buddies. Together they solve the "alphabet" thefts masterminded by munitions dealers (Prochnow, Nielsen and Stockwell). Rock makes a cameo appearance as a valet at Hugh Hefner's Mansion.

BEVERLY HILLS COPS III

Cast: Eddie Murphy*, Helen Martin*, Gilbert R. Hill*, Theresa Randle*, Hattie Winston*, Judge Reinhold, Hector Elizondo, Bronson Pinchot
Director: John Landis, Mac Ahlberg
Executive Producer: Mark Lipsky
Music by: Nile Rodgers*
Producer: Mark Lipsky, Mace Neufeld, Robert Rehme
Screenwriter: Steven E. DeSouza
Tech Info: color/sound/104 min.   Type: Comedy Feature

Date: 1994   Origin: USA
Company: Paramount, Eddie Murphy* Productions, et al.
Distributors/Format: Paramount Home Video (1/2")
Annotation: Murphy returns as Detroit cop Axel Foley, this time, in pursuit of ruthless killers with a little help from Serge (Pinchot) and Billy (Reinhold). Randle plays Janice; Hill is Todd and Winston, Mrs. Todd. Martin plays Grandma.

BEYOND THE FOREST
Director: William Greaves*
Narrator: William Greaves*
Producer: William Greaves*
Screenwriter: William Greaves*
Tech Info: color/sound/40 min.   Type: Documentary Short
Date: 1985   Origin: USA, India
Company: William Greaves* Production
Annotation: Greaves' film shot in India, is a candid camera look at the lives and culture of the Adivasis people (the so-called tribals) of Dadra and Nagar Haveli and their transition to a modern society in India. It shows the work done by the Indian Red Cross and the Indian government to improve the educational, health and economic status of the people.

BEYOND THE LAW
Cast: Courtney B. Vance*, Charlie Sheen, Larry Ferguson, Linda Fiorentino, Michael Madsen
Director: Larry Furguson
Executive Producer: Ronna B. Wallace, Richard Gladstein
Music by: Cory Lerios
Producer: Mark Tarlov, Ronna B. Wallace, Richard Gladstein, John Fiedler
Screenwriter: Larry Furguson
Tech Info: color/sound/105 min.   Type: Dramatic Feature
Date: 1994   Origin: USA
Company: Polar Entertainment
Distributors/Format: LIVE Home Video (1/2")
Annotation: A psychologically disturbed cop (Sheen) goes undercover to infiltrate a biker group. While trying to set up a sting, he becomes even more unbalanced. Vance plays Conroy Price, an investigator from the Arizona Attorney General's office responsible for the sting operation.

BIG SCORE, THE
Cast: Richard Roundtree*, D'Urville Martin*, Nancy Wilson*, Fred Williamson*, Jimmy/James Spinks*, Tony King*, John Saxon
Director: Fred Williamson*
Executive Producer: Harry Hurwitz, David Forbes
Music by: Jay Chattaway
Producer: Harry Hurwitz, David Forbes, Michael S. Landes, Albert Schwartz
Screenwriter: Gail Morgan Hickman*
Tech Info: color/sound/82 min.   Type: Dramatic Feature

Date: 1983   Origin: USA
Company: ALMI Pictures, Po' Boy Productions
Distributors/Format: Almi Home Video (1/2")
Annotation: Officer Frank Hooks (Williamson) is fired from the Chicago police force when he is accused of stealing a large amount of money, so he goes after the real criminals on his own. Wilson plays his wife Angie; Roundtree plays Gordon; Martin is Easy; Spinks appears as Cheech.

BIG SHOTS

Cast: Olivia Cole*, Beah Richards*, Joe Seneca*, Darius McCrary*, Paul Winfield*, Janet MacLachlan*, Jimmy/James Spinks*, Cedric Young*, Maria McCrary*, Robert Prosky, Jerzy Skolimowsky, Ricky Busker
Director: Robert Mandel
Executive Producer: Ivan Reitman
Music Performer: Little Richard (Penniman) *
Music by: Bruce Broughton
Producer: Ivan Reitman, Michael Gross, Joe Medjuck
Screenwriter: Joe Eszterhas
Tech Info: color/sound/91 min.   Type: Dramatic Feature
Date: 1987   Origin: USA
Company: Lorimar
Distributors/Format: Fox Home Video (1/2")
Annotation: Scam (Darius McCrary) is a streetwise, car driving pre-teen who helps a lost boy named Obie (Busker) find his recently deceased father's Rolex watch. Johnny Red (Winfield) is a big league con artist who is befriended by the boys and ultimately helps reunite Scam with his real father. Richards plays Miss Hanks, a hotel lobby manager; Cole plays Mrs. Newton, a school teacher.

BIG TOP PEE-WEE

Cast: Kevin Peter Hall*, Penelope Ann Miller, Kris Kristofferson, Valeria Golino, Pee-Wee Herman
Director: Randal Kleiser
Executive Producer: William McEuen, Richard Gilbert Abramson
Music by: Danny Elfman
Producer: William McEuen, Paul Reubens, Richard Gilbert Abramson, Debra Hill
Screenwriter: Paul Reubens, George McGrath
Tech Info: color/sound/86 min.   Type: Comedy Feature
Date: 1988   Origin: USA
Company: Paramount
Distributors/Format: Paramount Home Video (1/2")
Annotation: Pee-Wee Herman, playing himself, runs a farm and romances local school teacher Winnie (Miller) when a lusty Italian acrobat (Golino) comes through town and attracts Pee-Wee's love. Hall plays Big John.

BILL AND TED'S BOGUS JOURNEY

Alternate: Bill and Ted Go to Hell
Cast: Pam Grier*, Terry Finn*, Taj Mahal *, Ed Cambridge*, Keanu Reeves, Alex Winter
Director: Pete Hewitt
Music by: David Newman
Producer: Scott Kroopf

Screenwriter: Chris Matheson, Ed Solomon
Tech Info: color/sound/98 min.   Type: Comedy Feature
Date: 1991   Origin: USA
Company: Interscope, Nelson Entertainment, Elsboy Entertain
Distributors/Format: Orion Home Video (1/2")
Annotation: Bill (Winter) and Ted (Reeves) go to hell and heaven in order to combat their evil clones who jeopordize the state of the universe. Grier plays Mrs. Wardroe, the agent who allows Bill and Ted to play in the "Battle of the Bands," a performance that will insure their success. Finn is the heavenly greeter who allows Bill and Ted to see God.

BILL AND TED'S EXCELLENT ADVENTURE
Cast: Bernie Casey*, George Carlin, Keanu Reeves, Alex Winter
Director: Stephen Herek
Executive Producer: Ted Field, Robert Cort
Music by: David Newman
Producer: Ted Field, Michael Murphey, Joel Soisson, Robert Cort, Scott Kroopf
Screenwriter: Chris Matheson, Ed Solomon
Tech Info: color/sound/90 min.   Type: Comedy Feature
Date: 1989   Origin: USA
Company: Nelson, Interscope, Nelson-Murphey
Distributors/Format: Orion Home Video (1/2")
Annotation: Bill (Winter) and Ted (Reeves) are high school seniors who won't graduate unless they pass a history exam. Rufus (Carlin), an emissary from the future, takes them on a trek through time to help them prepare. Casey plays Mr. Ryan.

BILL COSBY--HIMSELF
Cast: Bill Cosby*
Director: Bill Cosby*
Executive Producer: William (Bill) H. Cosby Jr.*
Music Performer: Bill Cosby*, Stu Gardner*
Music by: Ann Gardner
Screenwriter: Bill Cosby*
Tech Info: color/sound/104 min.   Type: Comedy Feature
Date: 1981   Origin: USA
Company: Jemmin, Inc., Fox
Distributors/Format: Fox Home Video (1/2")
Annotation: Comedian Cosby performs an extended stand-up routine, drawing upon much of his own experience. The presentation covers drug and alcohol use, a visit to the dentist, the trauma of childbirth and childrearing, as well as relationships between the generations.

BILL COSBY: 49
Cast: Bill Cosby*
Director: Camille O. Cosby*, David Lewis
Executive Producer: Camille O. Cosby*
Music Performer: Stu Gardner*, Eddie "Lockjaw" Davis*, Tommy Flanagan, Cameron Brown, Rodney Jones, Grady Tate
Music by: Stu Gardner*
Producer: Camille O. Cosby*, Susan Adams-Houston
Screenwriter: Bill Cosby*

Tech Info: color/sound/69 min.   Type: Comedy Feature
Date: 1987   Origin: USA
Company: C.O.C Productions Inc.
Distributors/Format: Kodak Video Programs (1/2")
Annotation: Cosby dedicates his solo performance to the memory of Marcus
Hemphill (1930-86). He philosophizes about the mysterious ways the body ages
physically, and discusses his parents, his childhood and his life as a youth in the
United States Army.

BIRD

Cast: Forest Whitaker*, Damon Whitaker*, Samuel E. Wright*, Jason Bernard*, Tim
Russ*, Diane Venora
Director: Clint Eastwood
Music by: Lennie Niehaus
Producer: Clint Eastwood
Screenwriter: Joel Oliansky
Tech Info: color/sound/160 min.   Type: Dramatic Feature
Date: 1988   Origin: USA
Company: Warner Bros.
Distributors/Format: Warner Bros. Home Video, Inc. (1/2")
Archives/Format: IUB - BFC/A (1/2")
Annotation: A dramatic version of the life and times of saxophone great Charlie
Parker who died in 1955 at the age of 34. Forest Whitaker plays Charlie Parker;
Damon Whitaker is the young Charlie Parker; Wright plays Dizzy Gillespie.

BIRD ON A WIRE

Cast: Bill Duke*, Blu Mankuma*, Harry Caesar*, David Carradine, Mel Gibson,
Goldie Hawn
Director: John Badham
Music by: Hans Zimmer, Shirley Walker
Producer: Rob Cohen
Screenwriter: Louis Venosta, Eric Lerner, David Seltzer
Storywriter: Louis Venosta, Eric Lerner
Tech Info: color/sound/110 min.   Type: Comedy Feature
Date: 1990   Origin: USA
Company: Badham-Cohen-Interscope Communications
Distributors/Format: MCA/Universal Home Video (1/2")
Annotation: After Nick Jarmin (Gibson) puts Albert Diggs (Duke) and Eugene
Serasco (Carradine) behind bars with his incriminating testimony, the FBI gives him
a new identity. Years later, Diggs and Serasco, now on parole, attempt to exact
revenge.

BIRDY

Cast: Danny Glover*, Sandy Baron, Matthew Modine, Nicolas Cage, John Harkins
Tech Info: color/sound/120 min.   Type: Dramatic Feature
Date: 1984   Origin: USA
Studio: Independent
Annotation: Bird (Glover), a Vietnam veteran, sits in a catatonic state where he has
come to believe he is one of the feathered creatures of his dreams. Al, his best
friend, tries to reach the disturbed Birdy and bring him back to reality.

BIRTH OF A NATION: 4*29*1992

Director: Matthew McDaniel*
Producer: Matthew McDaniel*
Tech Info: color/sound/60 min.   Type: Documentary Feature
Date: 1993   Origin: USA
Studio: Independent
Distributors/Format: Third World Newsreel (1/2")
Archives/Format: IUB - BFC/A (1/2")
Annotation: After the Rodney King verdict, residents of Los Angeles express their outrage; businesses burn, and tensions between neighbors escalate. The film includes a rap soundtrack and interviews with rappers, Ice T, Ice Cube, Public Enemy.

BLACK AND BLUE

Director: Hugh King*, Lamar Williams*
Tech Info: color/sound/58 min.   Type: Documentary Feature
Date: 1987   Origin: USA
Studio: Independent
Distributors/Format: Third World Newsreel (1/2")
Annotation: This documentary is testimony to the long-standing tensions between the Philadelphia police force and people of color. Using archival material, news clips and documentary footage, the film depicts the history of the use of deadly force by the police.

BLACK AND THE GREEN, THE

Director: St. Clair Bourne*
Producer: St. Clair Bourne*
Tech Info: color/sound/45 min.   Type: Documentary Short
Date: 1982
Company: The Chamba Organization
Annotation: African Americans travel to Belfast to find commonalities between the struggle for human rights, religious freedom and social change in the U.S. and in Northern Ireland.

BLACK BODY

Director: Thomas Allen Harris*
Tech Info: color/sound/7 min.   Type: Experimental Short
Date: 1992   Origin: USA
Studio: Independent
Distributors/Format: Third World Newsreel (1/2")
Annotation: Harris uses text, special effects, and a shackled male nude to underscore the humanity underlying the various definitions of black identity and subjectivity.

BLACK BRIGADE

Cast: Billy Dee Williams*, Richard Pryor*, Moses Gunn*, Robert Hooks*, Roosevelt "Rosey" Grier*, Stephen Boyd, Susan Oliver
Director: George McCowan
Producer: Aaron Spelling
Screenwriter: Aaron Spelling, David Kidd
Tech Info: color/sound/75 min.   Type: Dramatic Feature

Date: 1989   Origin: USA
Company: Gemstone Entertainment
Distributors/Format: Armchair Cinema Home Video (1/2")
Annotation: An untested black Army unit is the only hope for saving a strategic dam from the Nazis during World War II. Racial tension erupts when a prejudiced white commando officer is sent to mold the soldiers into an effective combat force.

BLACK CHAMPIONS

Producer: William Miles*
Tech Info: mixed/sound/60 min.   Type: Documentary Feature
Date: 1986   Origin: USA
Company: Miles* Educational Film Production, Inc.
Distributors/Format: Miles Educational Film Production, Inc. (1/2")
Annotation: Miles' three-part documentary explores the accomplishments of black athletes in the 20th century.

BLACK COBRA

Cast: Fred Williamson*, Adlo Menegolino, Sabrina Gaddi, Laura Lancia
Director: Stelvio Massi
Tech Info: color/sound/87 min.   Type: Dramatic Feature
Date: 1986   Origin: Italy
Company: Po' Boy Productions
Annotation: This international film stars Williamson as Black Cobra. It was released theatrically in Europe, but only on video in the United States. BLACK COBRA II and III followed in 1989 and 1990.

BLACK ELIMINATOR

Alternate: Death Dimension
Cast: Aldo Ray*, Jim Kelly*, George Lazenby, Bob Minor, Myron Bruce Lee
Director: Al Adamson
Music by: Chuck Ransdell
Producer: Harry Hope
Screenwriter: Harry Hope
Storywriter: Harry Hope
Tech Info: color/sound/91 min.   Type: Dramatic Feature
Date: 1978   Origin: USA
Company: Spectacular Film Productions, Nichols Comm.
Annotation: A police lieutenant (Kelly) must stop a sadistic madman from gaining control over a freeze bomb that will instantly kill all living things.

BLACK HISTORY DOCUMENTARIES

Producer: Tony Brown*
Tech Info: mixed/sound   Type: Documentary Feature
Date: 1994   Origin: USA
Company: Tony Brown* Productions, Inc.
Distributors/Format: Tony Brown Productions (1/2")
Annotation: These films are approximately one to two hours in length and cover a range of Black History: AMERICA'S BLACK EAGLES (94 minutes); BLACK HOLLYWOOD: THE WAY IT WAS (104 minutes); BOOKER T. WASHINGTON FREEDOM TRAIL (80 minutes); THE COLOR OF FREEDOM (108 minutes); THE LONGEST STRUGGLE (96 minutes); RED AND BLACK: THE FIRST WORLD (53

minutes); THANK GOD! (94 minutes).

BLACK IMAGES FROM THE SCREEN
Cast: Bodacious Buggerrilla*
Director: John Rier
Narrator: Barbara O *
Producer: John Rier
Tech Info: mixed/sound/60 min.   Type: Documentary Feature
Date: 1978   Origin: USA
Studio: Independent
Annotation: From 1972 to 1975 Hollywood produced an unprecedented number of films and television programs which purported to portray the black experience. This film, narrated by Barbara O and featuring performances by black theatre group Bodacious Buggerrilla, examines the impact of these media images on young Blacks.

BLACK MAGIC
Director: Kirk Wolfinger
Music Performer: Lorez Alexandria
Music by: Michael Masser, Linda Creed
Narrator: Sahara Nej*
Producer: David Hoffman
Tech Info: color/sound/43 min.   Type: Documentary Short
Date: 1984   Origin: USA
Company: Sunburst Communications
Distributors/Format: United Technologies (35mm)
Annotation: The film focuses on a prize winning double dutch team, a group of young girls from inner-city Hartford, Connecticut, who excel at jumping rope. It depicts the sport, the girls, and their contest victory prize--a trip to England.

BLACK MAGIC WOMAN
Cast: Apollonia Kotero*, Mark Hamill, Amanda Wyss, Abadah Viera
Director: Deryn Warren
Executive Producer: Joan Baribeault, Mark Armin
Music by: Randy Miller
Producer: Deryn Warren, Marc Springer, Joan Baribeault, Mark Armin
Screenwriter: Gerry Daly
Storywriter: Deryn Warren, Marc Springer
Tech Info: color/sound/91 min.   Type: Dramatic Feature
Date: 1991   Origin: USA
Company: The Bewitched Company, Vidmark Entertainment
Annotation: Art gallery owner Brad Travis (Hamill) has a tempestuous affair with Cassandra Perry (Apollonia) who has an interest in lucky charms and talismans, but she leaves when he hesitates to give up Diane (Wyss) his long time girlfriend. Cassandra's departure is only the beginning of his troubles.

BLACK MUSIC IN AMERICA: THE 70'S
Executive Producer: Naima Fuller*
Narrator: Isaac Hayes*, Dionne Warwick*
Screenwriter: Orde Coombs*
Tech Info: mixed/sound/32 min.   Type: Documentary Short

Date: 1979   Origin: USA
Company: Learning Corporation of America
Archives/Format: IUB - BFC/A (16mm)
Annotation: The film is a musical excursion through the world of black music in the 1970s from the Motown sound of Diana Ross to the disco beat of Donna Summer. It includes film clips of over 75 groups showing the growth and influence of black music and black performers.

BLACK OLYMPIANS 1904-1984: ATHLETICS AND SOCIAL
Series: America: A Cultural Mosaic
Tech Info: color/sound/28 min.   Type: Documentary Short
Date: 1986   Origin: USA
Company: Modern Educational Video, Churchill Films
Distributors/Format: Modern Educational Video Network/Churchill Films (1/2")
Annotation: The film chronicles the experience of African American athletes in the Olympic Games against the background of 20th century United States history.

BLACK PATHS OF LEADERSHIP
Director: Pam Hughes
Producer: Donald Coughlin
Tech Info: bw/sound/28 min.   Type: Documentary Short
Date: 1985   Origin: USA
Company: Tellens, Inc., Churchill Films
Distributors/Format: Churchill Films (16mm), Filmic Archives (1/2")
Archives/Format: IUB - BFC/A (16mm)
Annotation: The film shows how three historically important black men took different paths in fighting for the rights of African Americans. It uses rare archival footage to document the lives of Booker T. Washington (1856-1915), Marcus Garvey (1887-1940), and W.E.B. DuBois (1868-1963).

BLACK POWER IN AMERICA: MYTH OR REALITY?
Director: William Greaves*
Narrator: William Greaves*
Producer: William Greaves*, Louise Archambault
Screenwriter: William Greaves*
Storywriter: William Greaves*, Lou Potter*
Tech Info: color/sound/60 min.   Type: Television Documentary
Date: 1986   Origin: USA
Company: William Greaves* Productions Inc.
Annotation: The film surveys some of the changes in American society since the Civil Rights Movement of the 1960s. It looks at African American men and women who have achieved power and influence.

BLACK STALLION RETURNS, THE
Cast: Woody Strode*, Vincent Spano, Kelly Reno, Teri Garr, Ferdinand Mayne
Director: Robert Dalva
Executive Producer: Francis Coppola
Music Performer: Georges Delerue
Music by: Georges Delerue
Producer: Fred Roos, Doug Claybourne, Tom Sternberg, Francis Coppola
Screenwriter: Richard Kletter, Jerome Kass
Storywriter: Walter Farley

Tech Info: color/sound/103 min.   Type: Dramatic Feature
Date: 1983   Origin: USA
Company: Zoetrope
Distributors/Format: United Artists Home Video (1/2")
Annotation: In this sequel, Alex Ramsey (Reno) pursues the kidnappers of his horse to Morocco where he meets a young prince, Raj (Spano) and his protector Meslar (Strode). Meslar defends both Raj and Alex from murderers at the expense of being taken captive himself.

BLACK STALLION, THE

Cast: Clarence Muse*, Mickey Rooney, Kelly Reno, Teri Garr, Hoyt Axton
Director: Carroll Ballard
Executive Producer: Francis Ford Coppola
Music Performer: Carmine Coppola
Music by: Carmine Coppola
Producer: Francis Ford Coppola, Fred Roos
Screenwriter: Melissa Mathison, Jeanne Rosenberg, William D. Wittliff
Storywriter: Walter Farley
Tech Info: color/sound/118 min.   Type: Dramatic Feature
Date: 1979   Origin: USA
Company: Zoetrope
Distributors/Format: Magnetic Video/20th Century-Fox Home Video (1/2"), United Artists Home Video (1/2")
Annotation: In this adaptation of the novel, Muse plays Snoe, one of Alex Ramsey's (Reno) training team. While preparing the black stallion for racing, Snoe warns Ramsey to remember that the horse is wild and eventually must have his freedom.

BLACK STARS IN ORBIT

Director: William Miles*
Music Performer: Andrew Halbreich, Michael Case Kissel
Music by: Andrew Halbreich, Michael Case Kissel
Producer: William Miles*
Speaker: Nichelle Nichols*, Guion S. Bluford Jr.*, Ronald E. McNair*, Frederick D. Gregory*, Mae C. Jemison*, Charles F. Bolden*, Edward J. Dwight Jr.*, Robert H. Lawrence Jr.*, Robert E. Shurney*, George R. Carruthers*
Tech Info: mixed/sound/60 min.   Type: Television Documentary
Date: 1989   Origin: USA
Company: Miles* Educational Film Productions, Inc.
Distributors/Format: Direct Cinema Limited (16mm; 1/2")
Annotation: The film documents the contributions that black astronauts, astrophysicists, and engineers have made to NASA and the American space exploration program, and the obstacles the first black astronauts encountered, including racism and discrimination within the space program. Five black astronauts, talk about their backgrounds, their achievements, and their aspirations.

BLACK THEATRE MOVEMENT: FROM A RAISIN IN THE SUN TO THE PRESENT

Director: Woodie King Jr.*
Producer: Woodie King Jr.*
Speaker: Lorraine Hansberry*, Imamu Amiri Baraka*, Ed Bullins*, Ron Milner*, Shauneille Perry*, Lonne Elder*, Negro Ensemble Company Players*, Douglas Turner*

Tech Info: mixed/sound/130 min.   Type: Documentary Feature
Date: 1978   Origin: USA
Company: Woodie King Jr.* Production
Annotation: Through interviews, footage of plays in production at the time of filming and stock footage dating back to 1962, the film documents the history of black theatre from 1959 to 1978.

BLACK THEATRE: THE MAKING OF A MOVEMENT
Series: African American Perspectives
Director: Woodie King Jr.*
Producer: Woodie King Jr.*
Speaker: James Earl Jones*, Imamu Amiri Baraka*, Ed Bullins*, Ntozake Shange*
Tech Info: sound/114 min.   Type: Documentary Feature
Date: 1978   Origin: USA
Studio: Independent
Distributors/Format: California Newsreel (1/2")
Annotation: This film recaptures the rise of a new kind of theatre out of the Civil Rights activism of the 1950s, 60s and 70s. Interviews with James Earl Jones, Ntozake Shange are interspesed with excerpts from A RAISIN IN THE SUN, BLACK GIRL, and FOR COLORED GIRLS to reveal how these playwrights used theatre as a tool for social change.

BLACK WALLSTREET
Music by: Rosalind Holloway*
Narrator: Teressa Williams-Thompson*
Producer: Latressa Wallace*, Annette Wilson*
Tech Info: mixed/sound/60 min.   Type: Documentary Feature
Date: 1991   Origin: USA
Studio: Independent
Distributors/Format: Dularon, Inc. (1/2")
Archives/Format: IUB - BFC/A (1/2")
Annotation: The film traces the demise of a prosperous African American community in Tulsa, Oklahoma, in 1921.

BLACK WATER
Cast: Stacey Dash*, Rod Steiger, Julian Sands, Denise Crosby
Director: Allen Moore
Music by: Orlando Haddad
Producer: Allen Moore, Charlotte Cerf
Screenwriter: Charlotte Cerf
Tech Info: color/sound/88 min.   Type: Dramatic Feature
Date: 1994   Origin: USA
Company: First Run Features
Distributors/Format: Icarus Films (16mm; 1/2")
Annotation: After overhearing the murder of a criminal in the neighboring hotel room, Wolfgang Leighton (Sands) picks up Minnie (Dash), a hitchhiker who guides him though the back roads of the deep South.

BLACK WEST, THE
Narrator: Danny Glover*
Producer: William Miles*
Tech Info: color/sound/60 min.   Type: Television Documentary
Date: 1994   Origin: USA
Company: Miles* Educational Film Production, Inc.
Distributors/Format: Movie Unlimited (35mm)
Annotation: Miles' film depicts the contributions of the African American experience in the building of the American West. It is one part of the series THE UNTOLD WEST.

BLACK WOMEN, SEXUAL POLITICS & THE REVOLUTION
Series: Not Channel Zero
Director: Cyrille Phipps*
Music Performer: James Brown*, Public Enemy *, Shabba Ranks*, The Last Poets*, L.L. Cool J. *, Bell Biv Devoe*
Producer: Cyrille Phipps*, Michelle McKenzie
Speaker: Michelle Wallace*, LaRose Parris*, Vernice D. Miller*, Carletta Joy Walker*, Reena Walker*, Sam Anderson*, Karen Daughtry*
Tech Info: mixed/sound/30 min.   Type: Documentary Short
Date: 1991   Origin: USA
Company: Black Planet Productions
Distributors/Format: Third World Newsreel (1/2")
Archives/Format: IUB - AAAMC (1/2")
Annotation: Using interviews, archival footage and music, this video explores the effects of sexism within the black community during the Civil Rights Movement.

BLAME IT ON THE NIGHT
Cast: Billy Preston*, Merry Clayton*, Ollie E. Brown*, Byron Thames, Nick Mancuso, Leslie Ackerman
Director: Gene Taft
Executive Producer: Tony Wade
Music by: Ted Neeley
Producer: Gene Taft, Tony Wade
Screenwriter: Len Jenkin, Michael Philip
Storywriter: Mick Jagger, Gene Taft
Tech Info: color/sound/85 min.   Type: Dramatic Feature
Date: 1984   Origin: USA
Company: Pentimento
Distributors/Format: TriStar Pictures Inc. (1/2")
Annotation: Rock-n-roller Chris Dalton (Mancuso) takes the son he's never seen on the road with him after the boy's mother dies. Clayton, Preston and Brown appear as themselves.

BLANK CHECK
Cast: Tone-Loc *, Miguel Ferrer, Karen Duffy, Brian Bonsall, James Rebhorn
Director: Rupert Wainwright
Executive Producer: Blake Snyder, Hilary Wayne
Music by: Nicholas Pike
Producer: Gary Adelson, Craig Baumgarten, Blake Snyder, Hilary Wayne
Screenwriter: Blake Snyder, Colby Carr

Tech Info: color/sound/93 min.   Type: Comedy Feature
Date: 1994   Origin: USA
Company: Check Less Productions, Disney Productions, et al.
Distributors/Format: Buena Vista Home Video (1/2")
Annotation: Eleven-year-old Preston (Bonsall) is given a blank check by gangster Quigley (Ferrer) when Quigley runs over his bike. Preston cashes the check for a million dollars. Eventually, he spends all the money and helps to catch the gangsters. Tone Loc plays Juice, Quiqley's muscleman.

BLANKMAN

Cast: Robin Givens*, Arsenio Hall*, Damon Wayans*, David Alan Grier*, Lynn Thigpen*, Yvette Wilson*, Michael Wayans*, Cara Mia Wayans*, Jon Polito, Jason Alexander
Director: Mike Binder, Tom Sigel
Executive Producer: Damon Wayans*
Music by: Miles Goodman
Producer: Damon Wayans*, Eric L. Gold, C.O. Erickson
Screenwriter: Damon Wayans*, J.F. Lawton*
Storywriter: Damon Wayans*
Tech Info: color/sound/96 min.   Type: Comedy Feature
Date: 1994   Origin: USA
Company: Wife N' Kids Production, Columbia
Distributors/Format: Columbia/TriStar Pictures (35mm; 1/2"), Films Inc. (1/2")
Annotation: A crime-fighting comedy about two slapstick heroes who triumph over evil. Clad in bullet-proof underwear and his grandma's housecoat, Darryl Walker (Damon Wayans) takes to the streets in pursuit of truth, justice and his first romance.

BLESS THEIR LITTLE HEARTS

Cast: Nate Hardman*, Kaycee Moore*, Angela Burnett*, Ronald Burnett*, Kimberly Burnett*, Eugene Cherry*, Lawrence Pierott*, Ernest Knight*, Ellis Griffin*
Director: Billy Woodberry*
Music by: Archie Shepp*, Little Esther Phillips*
Producer: Billy Woodberry*
Screenwriter: Charles Burnett*
Tech Info: bw/sound/80 min.   Type: Dramatic Feature
Date: 1983   Origin: USA
Company: Black Independent Features
Distributors/Format: Billy Woodberry (16mm; 3/4"; 1/2")
Archives/Format: IUB - BFC/A (16mm)
Annotation: Charlie Banks (Hardman), an unemployed factory worker in south central Los Angeles, struggles to find a job and take care of his family. His wife Andais, (Moore) works exhaustedly as a domestic to help make ends meet. Their marriage and their children (Angela, Ronald, Kimberly Burnett) are affected by the bleak economic privation of their lives.

BLIND DATE

Cast: Stanley Jordan*, Bruce Willis, Kim Basinger, John Larroquette
Director: Blake Edwards
Executive Producer: Gary Hendler, Jonathan D. Krane
Music Performer: Stanley Jordan*
Music by: Henry Mancini

Producer: Tony Adams, Gary Hendler, Jonathan D. Krane
Screenwriter: Dale Launer
Tech Info: color/sound/95 min.   Type: Comedy Feature
Date: 1987   Origin: USA
Company: TriStar
Distributors/Format: RCA/Columbia Pictures Home Video (1/2")
Annotation: A blind date turns into a long term love affair in this comedy film starring Basinger and Willis. Jordan appears as himself in a recording session scene; he also wrote and performed the song "Treasures."

BLIND RAGE

Cast: D'Urville Martin*, Fred Williamson*, Dick Adair, Leo Fong, Tony Ferrer
Director: Efren Pinon
Tech Info: color/sound/80 min.   Type: Dramatic Feature
Date: 1978   Origin: Philippines, USA
Company: Cannon Films, MGM
Distributors/Format: MGM (35mm)
Annotation: Five blind martial arts masters help protect 15 million dollars being transported from the United States to the Phillipines.

BLIND TOM: THE STORY OF THOMAS BETHUNE

Cast: Fran Bennett*, Vaughn Tyree Jelks*, Jessie Ferguson*, Darius Lawrence*, Missy Gold, Ben Piazza, Bonnie Bartlett
Director: Mark Travis
Music Performer: Gerald Fried
Music by: Thomas Bethune*, Gerald Fried
Producer: Bette Cox*
Screenwriter: Kathleen McGhee-Anderson
Storywriter: Kathleen McGhee-Anderson
Tech Info: color/sound/29 min.   Type: Dramatic Short
Date: 1987   Origin: USA
Studio: KCET
Company: Beem Foundation
Distributors/Format: KCET Home Video (1/2")
Archives/Format: IUB - BFC/A (1/2")
Annotation: A dramatized version of the extraordinary true story of a young blind slave, Tom Bethune (Jelks), whose natural ability to play the piano earns money for his master who continues to control Tom's life and earnings even after emancipation.

BLIND VISION

Cast: Stone/Stoney Jackson*, Ned Beatty, Robert Vaughn, Deborah Shelton, Lenny Von Dohlen
Director: Shuki Levy
Music by: Shuki Levy
Producer: Jonathon Braun
Screenwriter: Shuki Levy, Winston Rickard
Tech Info: color/sound/1992 min.   Type: Dramatic Feature

Date: 1992   Origin: USA
Company: Saban Pictures, Vertigo Pictures
Distributors/Format: World Vision Home Video (1/2")
Annotation: William Dalton (Van Dohlen) and Tony David (Jackson) are mailroom workers and friends. Dalton, obsessed with an unattainable co-worker, starts to spy on her through a camera with a telephoto lens. As it turns out, William is not the only one watching.

BLOOD AND CONCRETE - A LOVE STORY
Cast: Jennifer Beals*, Darren McGavin, Billy Zane, James LeGros, Nicholas Worth
Director: Jeffrey Reiner
Executive Producer: Miles A. Copeland III, Paul Colichman, Harold Welb
Music by: Vinny Golia
Producer: Miles A. Copeland III, Paul Colichman, Harold Welb, Richard LaBrie
Screenwriter: Richard LaBrie, Jeffrey Reiner
Tech Info: color/sound/99 min.   Type: Dramatic Feature
Date: 1991   Origin: USA
Company: IRS Media
Distributors/Format: IRS Releasing (16mm)
Annotation: In a twisted turn of fate, Joey (Zane) and Mona (Beals) meet in a cemetery. He has been shot by mobsters and she is preparing to commit suicide. He helps to change her mind and they then join forces to evade the mob.

BLOOD SAVAGE
Cast: Evander Holyfield*, Ray Walston, John Saxon, Danny Nelson, Lori Birdsong
Director: Tucker Johnston
Executive Producer: Ken C. Sanders
Music by: Tim Temple
Producer: Martin J. Fischer, Ken C. Sanders, Ken C. Sanders
Screenwriter: Ken C. Sanders, Tucker Johnston
Tech Info: color/sound/98 min.   Type: Comedy Feature
Date: 1990   Origin: USA
Company: Ken C. Sanders, High Five Productions
Distributors/Format: Magnum Entertainment (1/2"), Paragon Video Productions (1/2")
Annotation: Jake Pruitt (Nelson), upset that his wife was refused an organ transplant that could have saved her, opens a "body" shop where he crudely extracts organs and sells them to a black market broker. Heavyweight boxer Holyfield makes a cameo appearance as himself.

BLOOD SIMPLE
Cast: Samm-Art Williams*, M. Emmet Walsh, Frances McDormand, John Getz, Dan Hedaya
Director: Joel Coen
Executive Producer: Daniel F. Bacaner
Music by: Carter Burwell*
Producer: Ethan Coen, Daniel F. Bacaner
Screenwriter: Ethan Coen, Joel Coen
Tech Info: color/sound/97 min.   Type: Dramatic Feature

Date: 1984   Origin: USA
Company: River Road
Distributors/Format: Circle (1/2")
Annotation: Visser (Walsh) is a private detective who is hired by Julian (Hedaya) to kill his wife Abby (McDormand) and her lover. Visser instead kills Julian. The lover (Getz), thinking Abby has committed the crime, tries to keep her from becoming a suspect. Williams plays Maurice.

BLOOD TIDE

Alternate: Red Tide, The
Cast: James Earl Jones*, Jose Ferrer, Lila Kedrova, Mary Louise Weller
Director: Richard Jeffries
Executive Producer: John D. Schofield
Music by: Jerry Moseley
Producer: Niko Mastorakis, John D. Schofield, Donald Langdon
Screenwriter: Niko Mastorakis, Donald Langdon, Richard Jeffries
Tech Info: color/sound/82 min.   Type: Dramatic Feature
Date: 1982   Origin: USA
Company: 21st Century
Distributors/Format: Continental Video (1/2")
Annotation: American treasure hunter Frye (Jones) sets off an explosion that awakens a mythical sea monster, asleep in an underwater grotto for centuries, with devastating consequences.

BLOODFIST

Cast: Billy Blanks*, Don "The Dragon" Wilson, Michael Shaner, Riley Bowman
Director: Terence H. Winkless
Music by: Sasha Matson
Producer: Roger Corman
Screenwriter: Robert King
Tech Info: color/sound/85 min.   Type: Dramatic Feature
Date: 1989   Origin: USA
Company: Concorde, New Horizons
Distributors/Format: Concorde Home Video (1/2")
Annotation: Blanks plays Black Rose in this martial arts action film centered around Jake (Wilson) who travels to Manila to investigate his brother's murder.

BLOWN AWAY

Cast: Forest Whitaker*, Jeff Bridges, Tommy Lee Jones, Suzy Amis
Director: Stephen Hopkins
Executive Producer: Lloyd Segan
Music by: Alan Silvestri
Producer: John Watson, Pen Densham, Richard B. Lewis, Lloyd Segan
Screenwriter: Joe Batteer, John Rice
Storywriter: Joe Batteer, John Rice, M. Jay Roach
Tech Info: color/sound/121 min.   Type: Dramatic Feature
Date: 1994   Origin: USA
Company: Trilogy Entertainment Group
Distributors/Format: MGM Home Video (1/2")
Annotation: Franklin (Whitaker) and Dave (Bridges) become partners on Boston's bomb squad to stop psychopathic bomber Gaerity (Jones).

BLUE CHIPS
Cast: Louis Gossett Jr.*, Alfre Woodard*, Cylk Cozart*, Shaquille O'Neal*, Marques Johnson*, Anfernee "Penny" Hardaway*, George Raveling*, Dorothy McCann*, Qiana Petty*, Alicia N. Jones*, Britney Mitchell*, Anthony C. Hall*, Nick Nolte, Mary McDonnell, Matt Nover
Director: William Friedkin, Tom Priestly
Executive Producer: Ron Shelton, Wolfgang Glattes
Music by: Nile Rodgers*, Jeff Beck, Jed Leiber
Producer: Ron Shelton, Michele Rappaport, Wolfgang Glattes
Screenwriter: Ron Shelton
Tech Info: color/sound/107 min.   Type: Dramatic Feature
Date: 1994   Origin: USA
Company: Paramount
Distributors/Format: Paramount Home Video (1/2")
Annotation: Championship winning coach Pete Bell (Nolte) finds himself in conflict with his own code of ethics when he gets caught up in the politics of big-time college athletics. His team includes assistant coaches Mel (Johnson) and Slick (Cozart) and "blue chips" Butch McRae (Hardaway) and Neon Bodeaux (O'Neal) a seven-foot center. Gossett plays Butch's high school coach; Woodard is his mother, Lavada; McCann, his grandmother; Petty, Jones and Mitchell, his sisters. Raveling plays the Coach of rival team Coast.

BLUE CITY
Cast: Paul Winfield*, Felix Nelson*, Vaughn Tyree Jelks*, Tom "Tiny" Lister Jr.*, Joe Eszterhas, Judd Nelson, Ally Sheedy
Director: Michelle Manning
Executive Producer: Robert Kenner, Anthony Jones
Music Performer: Ry Cooder
Music by: Ry Cooder
Producer: Walter Hill, William Hayward, Robert Kenner, Anthony Jones
Screenwriter: Walter Hill, Lukas Heller
Storywriter: Ross MacDonald
Tech Info: color/sound/83 min.   Type: Dramatic Feature
Date: 1986   Origin: USA
Company: Paramount
Distributors/Format: Paramount Home Video (1/2")
Annotation: A young man (Judd Nelson) attempts to avenge his father's murder by killing his stepmother's new husband, only to find the true culprit is the new Police Chief (Winfield).

BLUE COLLAR
Cast: Richard Pryor*, Yaphet Kotto*, Chip Fields*, Harvey Keitel, Cliff DeYoung
Director: Paul Schrader
Executive Producer: Robin French
Music by: Jack Nitzsche
Producer: Robin French, Don Gulst
Screenwriter: Paul Schrader
Storywriter: Paul Schrader, Leonard Schrader
Tech Info: color/sound/114 min.   Type: Dramatic Feature

Date: 1978   Origin: USA
Company: TAT Communications, Universal
Distributors/Format: Universal Home Video (1/2")
Archives/Format: IUB - BFC/A (1/2")
Annotation: Three Detroit auto workers, Zeke (Pryor), Smokey (Kotto), and Jerry (Keitel) decide to take action against their corrupt union and senior company officials, but violence perpetrated against them and disunity foil their efforts to undermine the company.

BLUE THUNDER

Cast: Jason Bernard*, Candy Clark, Roy Scheider, Malcolm McDowell, Ed Bernard
Director: John Badham
Executive Producer: Phil Feldman, Andrew Fogelson
Music by: Arthur B. Rubinstein
Producer: Phil Feldman, Gordon Carroll, Andrew Fogelson
Screenwriter: Dan O'Bannon, Don Jakoby
Tech Info: color/sound/108 min.   Type: Dramatic Feature
Date: 1983   Origin: USA
Company: Columbia
Distributors/Format: Columbia Pictures Home Video (1/2")
Annotation: A special chopper, "Blue Thunder," is used to help combat terrorist activities during the 1984 Los Angeles Olympics. Bernard plays the mayor.

BLUES BROTHERS, THE

Cast: Cab Calloway*, Ray Charles*, Aretha Franklin*, James Brown*, Jesse Johnson*, Reggie Johnson*, Steven Williams*, Devoreaux White*, Chaka Khan*, Willie Hall*, Matt Murphy*, John Lee Hooker*, James Cleveland's South. CA Community Choir*, Walter Horton*, Luther Jackson*, Willie "Big Eyes" Smith*, Luther "Guitar Jr." Johnson*, Dan Aykroyd, John Belushi
Director: John Landis
Executive Producer: Bernie Brillstein
Music Performer: John Lee Hooker*
Music by: Ira Newborn
Producer: Robert K. Weiss, Bernie Brillstein
Screenwriter: Dan Aykroyd, John Landis, John Belushi
Tech Info: color/sound/133 min.   Type: Musical Feature
Date: 1980   Origin: USA
Company: Universal
Distributors/Format: H.E.D. (1/2"), Universal Home Video (1/2")
Annotation: Brothers Jake (Belushi) and Elwood (Akroyd) set out on a mission from God to rescue a nun and the orphanage they grew up in from debt. Williams plays state trooper Mount; Calloway is Curtis, the brothers' best friend at the orphanage; Charles runs Ray's Music Exchange; Franklin owns the Soul Food Cafe; Murphy is her husband. Brown is Reverend Cleophus James, his singers are James Cleveland's Southern California Community choir; Hooker is the choirmaster; Khan, a choir soloist. White plays a young guitar thief. The Maxwell Street musicians include Horton as Tampa Pete, Jackson as "Pinetop" Perkins; Smith on drums, Johnson on guitar, Jones on bass.

BOB MARLEY: LEGEND

Alternate: Best of Bob Marley and the Wailers, The
Music Performer: Bob Marley*
Speaker: Bob Marley*
Tech Info: color/sound/55 min.   Type: Concert Feature
Date: 1984   Origin: USA
Company: Island Records, Inc.
Distributors/Format: Music Vision (16mm), RCA/Columbia Pictures Home Video
(1/2")
Archives/Format: IUB - AAAMC (1/2")
Annotation: Marley, a legendary figure who revolutionized the world of music with his
reggae compositions, sings about every day life, politics, injustice, unity, love, peace
and freedom.

BOB ROBERTS

Cast: Giancarlo Esposito*, Lynn Thigpen*, Harry J. Lennix*, Jim West*, Angela
Hall*, Gore Vidal, Susan Sarandon, Helen Hunt, Tim Robbins, Ray Wise
Director: Tim Robbins
Executive Producer: Tim Bevan, Paul Webster, Ronna B. Wallace
Music by: David Robbins
Producer: Forrest Murray, Tim Bevan, Paul Webster, Ronna B. Wallace
Screenwriter: Tim Robbins
Tech Info: color/sound/1021 min.   Type: Comedy Feature
Date: 1992   Origin: USA
Company: Paramount
Distributors/Format: Paramount Home Video (1/2")
Annotation: Bugs Raplin (Esposito) editor of "Troubled Times," an alternative
newspaper in Philadelphia, attempts to expose Bob Roberts (Robbins), senatorial
candidate whose charming facade hides a hate mongering, self-serving agenda that
includes murder. Thigpen plays Kelly Noble, a TV journalist who challenges
Roberts. Lennix plays Franklin Dockett, token black member of Roberts' campaign
team; West is his bus driver. Hall is the gospel choir soloist at the church Roberts
visits.

BODY AND SOUL

Cast: Leon Isaac Kennedy*, Jayne Kennedy*, Muhammad Ali*
Director: George Bowers
Producer: Yoram Globus, Menahem Golan
Screenwriter: Leon Isaac Kennedy*
Tech Info: color/sound/100 min.   Type: Dramatic Feature
Date: 1981   Origin: USA
Studio: Independent
Distributors/Format: Facets Multimedia, Inc. (1/2")
Annotation: Corruption threatens a young black boxer (Leon Kennedy) as he
attempts to resist destructive influences and to succeed in the professional boxing
world. Ali makes a cameo appearance.

BODY DOUBLE
Cast: Larry "Flash" Jenkins*, Melanie Griffith, Craig Wasson, Dennis Franz, Deborah Shelton
Director: Brian De Palma
Executive Producer: Howard Gottfried
Music by: Pino Donaggio
Producer: Brian De Palma, Howard Gottfried
Screenwriter: Brian De Palma, Robert J. Avrech
Storywriter: Brian De Palma
Tech Info: color/sound/109 min.   Type: Dramatic Feature
Date: 1984   Origin: USA
Company: Delphi II, Columbia
Distributors/Format: Columbia Pictures Home Video (1/2")
Annotation: Jake (Wasson), an actor between films, takes a housesitting job in the Hollywood hills. Every night he watches a woman across the way through a telescope as she undresses and one night he witnesses her murder. Jenkins plays the assistant director of the horror film that Jake is fired from.

BODY HEAT
Cast: J.A. Preston*, Richard Crenna, William Hurt, Kathleen Turner
Director: Lawrence Kasdan
Music by: John Barry
Producer: Fred T. Gallo
Screenwriter: Lawrence Kasdan
Tech Info: color/sound/113 min.   Type: Dramatic Feature
Date: 1981   Origin: USA
Company: Ladd Company
Distributors/Format: Warner Bros. Home Video, Inc. (1/2")
Annotation: Preston plays investigator Oscar Grace whose friend Ned Racine (Hurt) has a steamy affair with Matty Walker (Turner). When Racine conspires with Walker to murder her husband, Grace pursues the culprits.

BODY OF EVIDENCE
Cast: Stan Shaw*, Lillian Lehman*, Willem Dafoe, Madonna , Joe Mantegna
Director: Uli Edel
Executive Producer: Stephen Deutsch, Melinda Jason
Producer: Dino de Laurentis, Stephen Deutsch, Melinda Jason
Screenwriter: Brad Mirman, Alison Cross
Tech Info: color/sound/99 min.   Type: Dramatic Feature
Date: 1993   Origin: USA
Company: Dino De Laurentis Communications
Distributors/Format: MGM Home Video (1/2")
Annotation: Rebecca Carlson (Madonna) is accused of having murdered her wealthy older lover by using her sexual abilities to over excite him, causing a fatal heart attack. Dafoe plays Dulaney, her defense attorney; Shaw is Charles Biggs.

BODY SNATCHERS
Cast: Forest Whitaker*, Tonea Stewart*, Meg Tilly, Terry Kinney, Gabrielle Anwar
Director: Abel Ferrara
Music by: Joe Delia
Producer: Robert H. Solo

Screenwriter: Dennis Paoli, Stuart Gordon, Nicholas St. John
Storywriter: Larry Cohen, Raymond Cistheri
Tech Info: color/sound/87 min.   Type: Dramatic Feature
Date: 1994   Origin: USA
Company: Dorset Productions, Solofilm
Distributors/Format: Warner Bros. Home Video, Inc. (1/2")
Annotation: This third version of the horror film classic is told from the point-of-view of teenager Marti Malone (Anwar) whose widowed father has just married and uprooted Marty from her Washington, D.C. home. Whitaker plays Doctor Malone, Marine Camp physician who commits suicide to save his soul from the still powerful pods.

BODYGUARD, THE

Cast: Bill Cobbs*, Whitney Houston*, DeVaughn Nixon*, Kevin Costner, Ralph Waite
Director: Mick Jackson, Andrew Dunn
Music by: Alan Silvestri
Producer: Kevin Costner, Lawrence Kasdan, Jim Wilson
Storywriter: Lawrence Kasdan
Tech Info: color/sound/130 min.   Type: Dramatic Feature
Date: 1992   Origin: USA
Company: TIG Productions w/Kasdan Pictures
Distributors/Format: Warner Bros. Home Video, Inc. (1/2")
Annotation: In her film debut, Houston plays Rachel Marron, a music/movie superstar at the peak of her career. Fans want to see, hear and touch her, but one wants to kill her. Security expert Frank Farmer (Costner) is hired to protect her.

BOILING POINT

Cast: Wesley Snipes*, Dennis Hopper, Lolita Davidovich, Dan Hedaya
Director: James B. Harris, King Baggot
Executive Producer: Rene Bonnell, Olivier Granier
Producer: Rene Bonnell, Olivier Granier, Marc Frydman, Leonard De La Fuente
Screenwriter: James B. Harris
Tech Info: color/sound/93 min.   Type: Dramatic Feature
Date: 1993   Origin: USA
Company: Warner Bros.
Distributors/Format: Warner Bros. Home Video, Inc. (1/2")
Annotation: Snipes portrays Meuer, an FBI agent who is tough, proud, and willing to bend the law to apprehend his partner's killers.

BOMBING OF OSAGE AVENUE, THE

Director: Louis J. Massiah*
Narrator: Toni Cade Bambara*
Producer: Louis J. Massiah*
Screenwriter: Toni Cade Bambara*
Tech Info: color/sound/56 min.   Type: Documentary Feature
Date: 1986   Origin: USA
Company: WHYY Philadelphia
Distributors/Format: Scribe Video Center (1/2")
Annotation: The film is a reconstruction of the 1985 Philadelphia police bombing and burning of a black neighborhood from the perspective of the community residents.

BONFIRE OF THE VANITIES
Cast: Morgan Freeman*, Novella Nelson*, Mary Alice*, John Hancock*, Patrick
Malone*, Sheik Mahmud-Bey*, Staci Francis*, Barbara Gooding*, Lorraine Moore*,
Paul Bates*, Doris Leggett*, Kathleen Murphy Palmer*, Tom Hanks, Melanie Griffith
Director: Brian De Palma
Music by: Dave Grusin
Producer: Brian De Palma
Screenwriter: Michael Cristofer
Storywriter: Tom Wolfe
Tech Info: color/sound/126 min.   Type: Dramatic Feature
Date: 1990   Origin: USA
Company: De Palma
Distributors/Format: Warner Bros. Home Video, Inc. (1/2")
Annotation: Judge White (Freeman) presides over a case involving the hit-and-run
accident that puts young Henry Lamb (Malone) into a coma. McCoy (Hanks) and
his illicit friend Maria Ruskin (Griffith), blame each other. A media frenzy sets off
Reverend Bacon (Hancock) who brings out demonstrators against McCoy and
pushes Henry's mother Annie (Alice) to sue the hospital. Francis, Gooding, Moore,
Leggett and Palmer are gospel singers in Bacon's church; Nelson is one of the
media vultures.

BOOKER T. WASHINGTON
Series: Black Americans of Achievement Video Collection
Director: Rhonda Fabian, Jerry Baber, Keith Smith
Executive Producer: Andrew Schlessinger
Narrator: Michael Logan
Producer: Rhonda Fabian, Jerry Baber, Andrew Schlessinger
Tech Info: mixed/sound/30 min.   Type: Documentary Short
Date: 1992   Origin: USA
Studio: Independent
Company: Schlessinger Video Productions
Distributors/Format: Filmic Archives (1/2")
Annotation: The film chronicles Washington's life as a free man in West Virginia, his
education at the Hampton Institute, his job as a teacher, and finally his struggle to
build and finance Tuskegee Institute. His contributions to black education are
highlighted.

BOOKER T. WASHINGTON: THE LIFE & THE LEGACY
Cast: Barbara Montgomery*, Maurice Woods*, Al Freeman Jr.*, Count Stovall*,
Director: William Greaves*
Narrator: Gil Noble*
Producer: William Greaves*, Billy Jackson*
Screenwriter: Lou Potter*
Tech Info: mixed/sound/30 min.   Type: Docudrama
Date: 1982   Origin: USA
Studio: Independent
Company: William Greaves* Productions Inc.
Distributors/Format: Facets Multimedia, Inc. (1/2")
Archives/Format: IUB - BFC/A (16mm)
Annotation: Using historic photographs for authenticity, this dramatized documentary
focuses on Washington's career as the most influential educator of his time. Woods

plays Washington, Freeman is W.E.B. DuBois.

BOOMERANG
Cast: Eddie Murphy*, Reginald Hudlin*, Warrington Hudlin*, Robin Givens*, Grace Jones*, Eartha Kitt*, Geoffrey Holder*, Tisha Campbell*, Martin Lawrence*, John Witherspoon*, Leonard Jackson*, John Canada Terrell*, Chris Rock*, Bebe Drake-Massey*, Halle Berry*, Melvin Van Peebles*, David Alan Grier*, Lela Rochon*, Louise Vyent*, Jonathan P. Hicks*, Irv Dotten*
Director: Reginald Hudlin*, Woody Omens
Executive Producer: Mark Lipsky
Music by: Marcus Miller*, Kenny "Babyface" Edmonds*
Producer: Warrington Hudlin*, Mark Lipsky, Brian Grazer
Screenwriter: Barry W. Blaustein, David Sheffield
Storywriter: Eddie Murphy*
Tech Info: color/sound/118 min.   Type: Comedy Feature
Date: 1992   Origin: USA
Company: Imagine Films Ent., Hudlin Bros.*, Paramount
Distributors/Format: Films Inc. (1/2"), Paramount Home Video (1/2")
Annotation: Marcus Graham (Murphy), marketing director for a cosmetics firm, is demoted after his company is taken over by Lady Eloise (Kitt) and headed by his new boss Jacqueline (Givens). Supermodel Strange (Jones) and the other two women are more interested in Marcus' body than his mind. Neither he nor his friends (Grier, Lawrence) seem to understand the concept of "boomerang," but Angela (Berry) who cares for Marcus does. Holder plays Nelson who devises a disastrous ad campaign for the firm. Both Hudlins appear as street hustlers.

BOPHA!
Cast: Danny Glover*, Alfre Woodard*, Malcolm McDowell, Marius Weyers
Director: Morgan Freeman*
Executive Producer: Arsenio Hall*
Music by: James Horner
Producer: Arsenio Hall*, Lawrance Taubman
Screenwriter: John Wierick, Brian Bird
Tech Info: color/sound/120 min.   Type: Dramatic Feature
Date: 1992   Origin: South Africa
Company: Paramount
Distributors/Format: Filmic Archives (1/2")
Annotation: Freeman makes his directorial debut with this drama, shot on location in Zimbabwe, about a South African policeman, Micah Mangena (Glover), who must choose between duty and family when he learns that his son is involved in a violent anti-apartheid rebellion. Woodard plays Mangena's wife Rosie. They are supported by a largely black South African cast.

BORN IN FLAMES
Cast: Jeanne Satterfield*, D.J. Honey*, Flo Kennedy*, Bill Tatum*, Adele Bertier, Becky Johnston, Pat Murphy, Kathryn Bigelow, Hillary Hurst
Director: Lizzie Borden
Music Performer: The Bloods, The Red Crayola, Ibis
Producer: Lizzie Borden
Screenwriter: Lizzie Borden
Tech Info: mixed/sound/90 min.   Type: Experimental Feature

Date: 1983   Origin: USA
Studio: Independent
Distributors/Format: First Run/Icarus Films (16mm), Women Make Movies, Inc. (16mm; 1/2")
Annotation: Set ten years after the Social Democratic cultural revolution, the film takes a futuristic look at the women's movement. An underground women's liberation army emerges in New York with Adeline Norris (Satterfield) its leader. Zella Wylie (Kennedy) is Adeline's mentor and inspiration. When Norris is murdered by the government and the Radical Phoenix Free Radio Station is destroyed by an arsonist, the women band together and go to war against their oppressors.

BORN ON THE FOURTH OF JULY

Cast: Rocky Carroll*, Tom Cruise, Kyra Sedgwick, Raymond J. Barry, Jerry Levine, Willem Dafoe
Director: Oliver Stone
Music by: John Williams
Producer: Oliver Stone, A. Kitman Ho
Screenwriter: Oliver Stone, Ron Kovic
Tech Info: color/sound/140 min.   Type: Dramatic Feature
Date: 1989   Origin: USA
Company: Fourth of July
Distributors/Format: Universal Home Video (1/2")
Annotation: After Ron Kovic (Cruise) loses the use of his legs in Vietnam, his idealism deserts him. Willie (Carroll), one of his nurses in a Bronx veterans hospital, tells Kovic that he has essentially missed the big picture. "It's about Detroit and Newark, it's about racism" Willie says. The film is adapted from Kovic's autobiography.

BORROWER, THE

Cast: Antonio Fargas*, Rae Dawn Chong*, Sam Scarber*, Tom Towles, Don Gordon
Director: John McNaughton
Executive Producer: William H. Coleman
Music by: Steven A. Jones, Robert McNaughton
Producer: Steven A. Jones, R.P. Sekon, William H. Coleman
Screenwriter: Richard Fire, Mason Nage
Storywriter: Mason Nage
Tech Info: color/sound/88 min.   Type: Dramatic Feature
Date: 1991   Origin: USA
Company: Atlantic Entertainment Group
Distributors/Format: Cannon Home Video (1/2")
Annotation: Detective Diana Pierce (Chong) and her partner are on the trail of a serial killer from space who decapitates his victims and attaches their heads to his headless body.

BOUND BY HONOR

Alternate: Blood In, Blood Out
Cast: Ving Rhames*, Delroy Lindo*, Jesse Borrego, Damian Chapa, Benjamin Bratt
Director: Taylor Hackford
Executive Producer: Stratton Leopold, Jimmy Santiago Baca
Producer: Taylor Hackford, Jerry Gershwin, Stratton Leopold, Jimmy Santiago Baca
Screenwriter: Floyd Mutrux, Jimmy Santiago Baca, Jeremy Iacone

Storywriter: Ross Thomas
Tech Info: color/sound/180 min.   Type: Dramatic Feature
Date: 1993   Origin: USA
Company: Vata De Atole Productions Inc, et al.
Distributors/Format: Buena Vista Home Video (1/2")
Annotation: The film follows three young Latinos (Borrego, Bratt, Chapa) through gang life and its aftermath in east Los Angeles. Rhames portrays Ivan and Lindo is Bonafide.

BOUNTY HUNTER, THE

Cast: Bo Hopkins, Robert Ginty, Loreta Waterdown
Director: Bill Duke*, Robert Ginty
Executive Producer: David Winters
Music by: Tim James, Steve McClintock, Mark Mancina
Producer: Fritz Mathews, David Winters, Bruce Lewin, Peter Lefcourt
Screenwriter: Robert Ginty, Thomas Baldwin, Steve Brown
Storywriter: Steve Brown
Tech Info: color/sound/91 min.   Type: Dramatic Feature
Date: 1989   Origin: USA
Studio: A.I.P. Studios
Company: Mace Neufeld in assoc. with Orion Television
Distributors/Format: A.I.P. Home Video (1/2"; 3/4")
Annotation: Duke Evans is a bounty hunter who always gets his man. When his best friend is killed, he sets out on a mission of vengeance.

BOY WHO COULD FLY, THE

Cast: Janet MacLachlan*, Lucy Deakins, Bonnie Bedelia, Jay Underwood, Fred Savage
Director: Nick Castle
Music by: Bruce Broughton
Producer: Gary Adelson
Screenwriter: Nick Castle
Tech Info: color/sound/114 min.   Type: Dramatic Feature
Date: 1986   Origin: USA
Company: Gary Adelson, Fox
Distributors/Format: Fox Home Video (1/2")
Annotation: When Charlene (Bedelia), a recent widow, moves into a new home with her 15-year-old daughter, Milly (Deakens), and eight-year-old son Louis (Savage), Milly soon notices their neighbor Eric (Underwood), an autistic boy her age who believes he can fly. Their many adventures together include a magical flight. MacLachlan plays Mrs. D'Gregario.

BOYS IN COMPANY C, THE

Cast: Stan Shaw*, Michael Lembeck, Andrew Stevens, James Canning, Craig Wasson, Scott Hylands, James Whitmore Jr., Noble Willingham
Director: Sidney J. Furie
Executive Producer: Raymond Chow
Producer: Raymond Chow, Andre Morgan
Screenwriter: Sidney J. Furie, Rick Natkin
Tech Info: color/sound/127 min.   Type: Dramatic Feature

Date: 1978   Origin: USA
Company: Golden Harvest
Distributors/Format: Columbia Pictures Home Video (1/2")
Annotation: The film follows the training of a group of men entering Marine boot camp and their subsequent battles in Vietnam. Tyrone Washington (Shaw) is the only black recruit in Company C. He uses his street smarts to help him deal with the racist attitudes of his fellow soldiers and to survive the horrors of war.

BOYZ N THE HOOD

Cast: Laurence/Larry Fishburne*, Tammy Hanson*, Whitman Mayo*, Tyra Ferrell*, Angela Bassett*, Ice Cube *, Cuba Gooding Jr.*, Morris Chestnut*, Dedrick D. Gobert*, Redge Green*, Nia Long*, Yolanda ("Yo-Yo") Whitaker*, Regina King*, Alysia Rodgers*, Meta King*, Desi Arnez Hines III*, Baha Jackson*, Donovan McCrary*
Director: John Singleton*, Charles Nills
Music Performer: Kool Moe Dee *, 2 Live Crew *, Ice Cube *, Run-D.M.C. *, Hi Five *, Monie Love*, Al B. Sure *, Tony! Toni! Tone! *
Music by: Quincy Jones*, Stanley Clarke*
Producer: Steve Nicolaides
Screenwriter: John Singleton*
Tech Info: color/sound/107 min.   Type: Dramatic Feature
Date: 1991   Origin: USA
Company: Both Inc., Columbia
Distributors/Format: Columbia/TriStar Pictures (35mm; 1/2"), Films Inc. (1/2")
Archives/Format: IUB - BFC/A (1/2")
Annotation: The film focuses on the lives of three young men in south central Los Angeles: Ricky (Chestnut), a high school father who hopes to go to USC; his brother Doughboy (Ice Cube), an unemployed drug dealer on parole; and their neighbor, Tre Styles (Gooding) whose father (Fishburne) gives his son the necessary guidance to survive in the 'hood. Bassett plays Tre's mother; Farrell is Ricky's and Doughboy's mother.

BRAINWAVES

Cast: Percy Rodriguez*, Vera Miles, Tony Curtis, Keir Dullea, Suzanna Love
Director: Ulli Lommel
Executive Producer: Gary Gillingham, Charles Aperia, Tim Nielsen
Music by: Robert O. Ragland
Producer: Gary Gillingham, Ulli Lommel, Charles Aperia, Tim Nielsen
Screenwriter: Suzanna Love, Ulli Lommel
Tech Info: color/sound/81 min.   Type: Dramatic Feature
Date: 1983   Origin: USA
Company: MPM
Annotation: Kaylie (Love) is in a coma and receives a donor brain from a murdered woman. The operation is a success, but Kaylie must now deal with memories of the murder and her knowledge of the identity of the killer. Rodriguez plays Dr. Robinson.

BREAKIN'

Cast: Michael Boogaloo Shrimp Chambers*, Phineas Newborn III*, Ice-T *, Lucinda Dickey, Adolfo "Shabba-Doo" Quinones, Ben Lokey, Christopher McDonald
Director: Joel Silberg
Executive Producer: Yoram Globus, Menahem Golan
Music Performer: Al Jarreau*, Ice-T *, Timothy "Poppin' Pete" Solomon*, Art Of Noise
Producer: Yoram Globus, Menahem Golan, Allen DeBevoise, David Zito
Screenwriter: Allen DeBevoise, Gerald Scaife, Charles Parker
Storywriter: Allen DeBevoise, Charles Parker
Tech Info: color/sound/87 min.   Type: Musical Feature
Date: 1984   Origin: USA
Company: Golan/Globus Production, Cannon Films
Distributors/Format: Cannon Home Video (1/2")
Annotation: A trained dance performer, Kelly (Dickey) meets two naturally talented street dancers, Ozone (Quinones) and Turbo (Chambers)and they join their acts together in order to "break into the business." Their mutual friend, Adam (Newborn) manages the trio.

BREAKIN' 2: ELECTRIC BOOGALOO

Alternate: Breakdance 2: Electric Boogaloo
Cast: Michael Boogaloo Shrimp Chambers*, Ice-T *, Harry Caesar*, Lucinda Dickey, Adolfo "Shabba-Doo" Quinones
Director: Peter Yates
Music Performer: Ice-T *, Russ Regan
Music by: Russ Regan
Producer: Yoram Globus, Menahem Golan
Screenwriter: Steve Tesich
Storywriter: Jan Ventura, Julie Reichert
Tech Info: color/sound/94 min.   Type: Musical Feature
Date: 1984   Origin: USA
Company: Cannon
Distributors/Format: TriStar Pictures Inc. (1/2")
Annotation: Ozone (Quinones), Turbo (Chambers) and Kelly (Dickey) team up again to save a neighborhood recreation site from being turned into a supermarket. Caesar appears as Byron, the manager of Miralles, the recreation site. Ice-T performs "Reckless Rivalry" and "Go Off."

BREAKING IN

Cast: Lorraine Toussaint*, Burt Reynolds, Sheila Kelley, Casey Siemaszko, Albert Salmi
Director: Bill Forsyth
Executive Producer: Andrew Meyer, Sarah Ryan Black
Music by: Michael Gibbs
Producer: Harry Gittes, Andrew Meyer, Sarah Ryan Black
Screenwriter: John Sayles
Tech Info: color/sound/91 min.   Type: Comedy Feature

Date: 1989   Origin: USA
Company: Act III
Distributors/Format: Goldwyn Home Video (1/2")
Annotation: Mullins (Reynolds), an aging professional burglar, decides to take a young thief, Lefebb (Siemaszko) under his wing. He finds the younger man to be adept at picking up his professional techniques, but that he is interested only in material gain. Toussaint plays Delphine.

BREAKING POINT
Cast: Blu Mankuma*, Deryl Hayes*, Gary Busey, Kim Cattrall, Darlanne Fluegel, Jeff Griggs
Director: Paul Ziller
Executive Producer: Michael Strange
Music by: Graeme Coleman
Producer: Robert Vince, William Vince, Michael Strange
Screenwriter: Michael Berlin, Eric Estrin
Tech Info: color/sound/96 min.   Type: Dramatic Feature
Date: 1994   Origin: USA
Company: Entertainment Securities Ltd., Nu Image
Distributors/Format: World Vision Home Video (1/2")
Annotation: Retired police detective Meadows (Busey) is asked by Lt. Lockhart (Mankuma) to return to the force to catch the serial killer who eluded him once before. Meadows is teamed up with Detective Dana Preston (Fluegel) the sister of one of the victims.

BREEDING OF IMPOTENCE, THE
Director: John Arthos
Speaker: Cornel West*, Luis Rodriguez, Valerie Polakow
Tech Info: color/sound/55 min.   Type: Documentary Feature
Date: 1993   Origin: USA
Studio: Independent
Distributors/Format: Cinema Guild (1/2")
Annotation: Educators and parents discuss educational institutions that hold children of color and in poverty in lesser regard.

BRER RABBIT AND THE WONDERFUL TAR BABY
Music by: Taj Mahal *
Narrator: Danny Glover*
Tech Info: color/sound/30 min.   Type: Animated Short
Date: 1991   Origin: USA
Annotation: The comic adventures of Brer Rabbit are bawdy and exuberant in this animated version.

BREWSTER'S MILLIONS
Cast: Richard Pryor*, Grand L. Bush*, Lonette McKee*, Tichina Arnold*, Rosetta La Noire*, Brad Sanders*, Ji-Tu Cumbuka*, Frank Slaten*, John Candy, Pat Hingle, Dolores Hawkins, Dean Stanton, Jerome Moross
Director: Walter Hill
Producer: Lawrence Gordon, Joel Silver
Screenwriter: Timothy Harris, Herschel Weingrod
Storywriter: Royal Dawe
Tech Info: color/sound/97 min.   Type: Comedy Feature

Date: 1985   Origin: USA
Company: Universal
Distributors/Format: Universal Home Video (1/2")
Annotation: Montgomery Brewster (Pryor) is a minor league baseball player who stands to inherit 300 million dollars, if he can spend $30 million in 30 days. Angela Drake (McKee) is his accountant and romantic interest. Melvin (Cumbuka) plays a security guard; Bush is Rudy, a minor leaguer who gets in a fight with Brewster over his girlfriend; La Noir plays Judge R. Woods who presides over the battery case; and Slaten appears as court bailiff.

BRIDE OF RE-ANIMATOR, THE
Cast: Mel Stewart*, David Bynum*, Jeffrey Combs, Bruce Abbott, Claude Earl Jones
Director: Brian Yuzna
Executive Producer: Keith Walley, Paul White, Hidetaka Konno
Music by: Richard Band
Producer: Brian Yuzna, Keith Walley, Paul White, Hidetaka Konno
Screenwriter: Keith Woody, Rick Fry
Storywriter: Brian Yuzna, Keith Woody, Rick Fry
Tech Info: color/sound/97 min.   Type: Comedy Feature
Date: 1991   Origin: USA
Company: Wild Street Pictures, Re-Animator 2 Productions
Distributors/Format: 50th St. Films (16mm)
Annotation: Dr. Wilbur Graves (Stewart) discovers some leftover re-animating fluid and performs his own experiments of bringing the dead back to life, while the medical students who developed the formula continue to try to refine it. Bynum plays a corpse.

BRIDE, THE
Cast: Jennifer Beals*, David Rappaport, Sting , Clancy Brown, Anthony Higgins
Director: Franc Roddam
Executive Producer: Keith Addis
Music by: Maurice Jarre
Producer: Victor Drai, Keith Addis
Screenwriter: Lloyd Fonvielle
Storywriter: Mary Shelley
Tech Info: color/sound/119 min.   Type: Dramatic Feature
Date: 1985 . Origin: USA
Company: Columbia
Distributors/Format: Columbia Pictures Home Video (1/2")
Annotation: Two parallel stories unfold. The first is about the friendship between Frankenstein (Sting), Viktor (Brown) and the dwarf (Rappaport). The second story concerns a love affair between Frankenstein and Eva (Beals).

BRIDGE TO FREEDOM (1965) - EPISODE 6
Series: Eyes On The Prize: America's Civil Right Years
Director: Callie Crossley*, James A. DeVinney
Executive Producer: Henry Hampton*
Narrator: Julian Bond*
Producer: Henry Hampton*, Callie Crossley*, James A. DeVinney
Screenwriter: Callie Crossley*, James A. DeVinney
Speaker: James Forman*, Stokely Carmichael*, Dr. Martin Luther King Jr.*,
Frederick D. Reese*, Sheyann Webb*, Rachel West Nelson*, C.T. Vivian*, Marion

Torner*, John Lewis*, James Bevel*, Andrew Young*, Ralph Abernathy*, Jimmy Webb*, Coretta Scott King*, Lyndon B. Johnson, Nicholas Katzenbach, Joe Clark, Richard Valeriani, George C. Wallace, Ralph W. Yarborough, Orioff Miller, L.C. Crocker, Wilson Baker
Tech Info: mixed/sound/57 min. Type: Television Documentary
Date: 1986 Origin: USA
Company: Blackside, Inc.
Distributors/Format: PBS Video (16mm; 1/2")
Archives/Format: IUB - AAAMC (1/2")
Annotation: In the final segment of EYES ON THE PRIZE (I), events culminate in the Selma to Montgomery march where, after Joe Clark's abusive police tactics, the marchers are granted federal sanction. SNCC and the SCLC split into factions, and President Johnson approves the Voting Rights Act.

BRIGHT LIGHTS, BIG CITY
Cast: Gina Belafonte*, Teresa Yvon Farley*, Michael J. Fox, Keifer Sutherland
Director: James Bridges
Executive Producer: Gerald R. Molen
Music by: Donald Fagen
Producer: Sydney Pollack, Mark Rosenberg, Gerald R. Molen
Screenwriter: Jay McInerney
Storywriter: Jay McInerney
Tech Info: color/sound/110 min. Type: Dramatic Feature
Date: 1988 Origin: USA
Company: Mirage
Distributors/Format: MGM/UA Home Video (1/2")
Annotation: Belafonte plays Kathy in this story about Jamie Conway (Fox), a mild-mannered would-be novelist by day and an uncontrollable fun-seeking bachelor by night.

BRIGHTON BEACH MEMOIRS
Cast: Alan Weeks*, Judith Ivey, Blythe Danner, Bob Dishy, Jonathan Silverman
Director: Gene Saks
Music Performer: Michael Small
Producer: Ray Stark
Screenwriter: Neil Simon
Storywriter: Neil Simon
Tech Info: color/sound/110 min. Type: Dramatic Feature
Date: 1986 Origin: USA
Company: Rastar Production, Universal
Distributors/Format: MCA Home Video (1/2")
Annotation: This coming-of-age story follows a Jewish boy growing up in Brighton Beach during the Depression. Andrew (Weeks), who also lives in Brooklyn, sweeps the floor in a hat shop.

BRONCO BILLY
Cast: Scatman Crothers*, Clint Eastwood, Sondra Locke
Director: Clint Eastwood
Producer: Dennis Hackin, Neal Dobrousky
Screenwriter: Dennis Hackin
Storywriter: Dennis Hackin
Tech Info: color/sound/117 min. Type: Dramatic Feature

Date: 1980   Origin: USA
Company: Warner Bros.
Distributors/Format: Warner Bros. Home Video, Inc. (1/2")
Annotation: Doc Lynch (Crothers) is ringleader and personal advisor to Bronco Billy McCoy's (Eastwood) Touring Wild West Show. Doc also functions as intermediary between Billy and the show members who, for reasons Billy can't understand, threaten to quit when they don't get paid.

BRONX: A CRY FOR HELP, THE
Producer: Brent Owens*
Tech Info: color/sound/52 min.   Type: Documentary Feature
Date: 1989   Origin: USA
Studio: Independent
Company: Brent Owens Productions
Annotation: Owens provides an insiders view of the south Bronx. Over a 12-year period, he filmed everyday people as they struggle to survive.

BROTHER FROM ANOTHER PLANET, THE
Cast: Joe Morton*, Darryl Edwards*, Leonard Jackson*, Bill Cobbs*, Reggie Rock Bythewood*, Minnie Gentry*, Steve James, John Sayles, Rosanna Carter
Director: John Sayles
Music Performer: Mason Daring*
Music by: Mason Daring*
Producer: Peggy Rajski, Maggie Renzi
Screenwriter: John Sayles
Tech Info: color/sound/109 min.   Type: Comedy Feature
Date: 1984   Origin: USA
Company: Cinecom International Films, Inc., A-Train Films
Distributors/Format: Facets Multimedia, Inc. (1/2"), October Films (16mm; 35mm)
Archives/Format: IUB - BFC/A (1/2")
Annotation: Morton is the fugitive brother on the run from another planet who arrives in Harlem and is helped by his new acquaintances (Edwards, James, Jackson, Gentry) to escape from his planet's slave catchers. A number of African Americans serve on the film's production crew: Ernest R. Dickerson (Director of Photography), Fronza Woods (Boom), and Marco Williams (Continuity).

BROTHER FUTURE
Series: Wonderworks Family Movie
Cast: Moses Gunn*, Akosua Busia*, Vonetta McGee*, Carl Lumbly*, Phill Lewis*, Frank Converse*
Director: Roy Campanella Jr.*
Producer: Wayne Morris*, Eric Laneuville*
Screenwriter: Anne E. Eskridge
Tech Info: color/sound/116 min.   Type: Television Feature
Date: 1991   Origin: USA
Distributors/Format: Public Media Video (1/2"), Filmic Archives (1/2")
Annotation: While running from police, an inner-city youngster is knocked unconscious and wakes up to find that he has been transported back in time to Charleston, 1822, where he is taken captive and enslaved.

BRUBAKER

Cast: Morgan Freeman*, Richard Ward*, Yaphet Kotto*, Roy Poole*, Robert Redford, David Keith, Jane Alexander
Director: Stuart Rosenberg
Executive Producer: Ted Mann
Music by: Lalo Schifrin
Producer: Ron Silverman, Ted Mann
Screenwriter: W.D. Richter
Storywriter: W.D. Richter, Arthur Ross
Tech Info: color/sound/132 min.   Type: Dramatic Feature
Date: 1980   Origin: USA
Company: Fox
Distributors/Format: Fox Home Video (1/2")
Annotation: New prison warden Brubaker (Redford) has himself incarcerated before he takes over in order to see the prison from the inmate's point of view. He finds horrifying conditions and terrible corruption, and as warden attempts to make changes. Kotto is featured as "Dickie" Coombes, Freeman portrays Walter, Ward is Abraham and Poole plays Dr. Gregory.

BUFFY THE VAMPIRE SLAYER

Cast: Paris Vaughan*, Rutger Hauer, Donald Sutherland, Kristy Swanson, Paul Reubens, Luke Perry
Director: Fran Rubel Kuzui
Executive Producer: Sandy Gallin, Carol Baum, Fran Rubel Kuzui
Music by: Carter Burwell*
Producer: Howard Rosenman, Sandy Gallin, Carol Baum, Fran Rubel Kuzui, Kaz Kuzui
Screenwriter: Joss Whedon
Tech Info: color/sound/86 min.   Type: Comedy Feature
Date: 1992   Origin: USA
Company: Buffy Films, Kazui Enterprises, Sandollar Prod.
Distributors/Format: Fox Home Video (1/2")
Annotation: Buffy (Swanson), a Valley girl cheerleader, discovers that she is the latest descendant in a race of vampire slayers, and that her skills will be needed again. Vaughn plays Nicole, one of Buffy's fellow cheerleaders.

BURBS, THE

Cast: Franklin Ajaye*, Tom Hanks, Bruce Dern, Wendy Schaal
Director: Joe Dante
Music by: Jerry Goldsmith
Producer: Larry Brezner, Michael Finnell, Dana Olsen
Screenwriter: Dana Olsen
Tech Info: color/sound/102 min.   Type: Comedy Feature
Date: 1989   Origin: USA
Company: Rollins-Morra-Brezner, Imagine
Distributors/Format: Universal Home Video (1/2")
Annotation: Ray Peterson (Hanks) and his family decide to spend their vacation at home in the suburbs. Their peaceful vacation is disrupted when they hear allegations that their new neighbors from Eastern Europe are Satanists conducting grisly rituals in their new home.

BURGLAR
Cast: Whoopi Goldberg*, G.W. Bailey, Bobcat Goldthwait, Lesley Ann Warren
Director: Hugh Wilson
Executive Producer: Michael Hirsh, Tom Jacobson
Music by: Sylvester Levay
Producer: Kevin McCormick, Michael Hirsh, Tom Jacobson
Screenwriter: Hugh Wilson, Joseph Loeb III, Matthew Weisman
Storywriter: Lawrence Block
Tech Info: color/sound/103 min.　　Type: Comedy Feature
Date: 1987　Origin: USA
Company: Nelvana Entertainment
Distributors/Format: Warner Bros. Home Video, Inc. (1/2")
Annotation: Bernice Rhodenbarr (Goldberg) is a burglar who also owns a book store. Hired by her dentist (Warren) to steal jewels from the dentist's ex-husband, Bernice becomes a prime suspect when he is murdered.

BURKINA FASO: LAND OF THE PEOPLE OF DIGNITY
Director: Abraham Ford*
Narrator: Yosef Ford*
Screenwriter: Abraham Ford*
Tech Info: color/sound/45 min.　　Type: Documentary Short
Date: 1988　Origin: Africa; USA
Studio: Independent
Distributors/Format: Abraham Ford (16mm; 3/4"; 1/2")
Annotation: The film is about the African country of eight million people which achieved its freedom from colonial rule in 1960. The camera pans the landscape, architecture and the people; narration fills in the history of the "land of the upright people."

BURN HEADS
Producer: Bart Mallard
Speaker: Warren Lewis*
Tech Info: color/sound/22 min.　　Type: Documentary Short
Date: 1993　Origin: USA
Distributors/Format: Filmakers Library, Inc. (16mm; 1/2")
Annotation: Set in a black neighborhood of Memphis, the film shows a slice of ghetto life different from that which shows on the evening news. Lewis may be the only barber in America who uses a lit candle instead of scissors to style his clients' hair.

BUSTIN' LOOSE
Cast: Richard Pryor*, Robert Christian*, Cicely Tyson*, George Coe
Director: Oz Scott
Executive Producer: William Greaves*
Music Performer: Roberta Flack*
Music by: Roberta Flack*
Producer: Richard Pryor*, William Greaves*, Michael S. Glick
Screenwriter: Roger L. Simon
Storywriter: Richard Pryor*
Tech Info: color/sound/94 min.　　Type: Dramatic Feature

Date: 1981   Origin: USA
Company: Richard Pryor* Production
Distributors/Format: MCA Home Video (1/2")
Annotation: Joe Braxton (Pryor) has led a life of crime. To avoid further incarceration, he must drive Miss Perry (Tyson) and eight special education students from their present facility in Philadelphia to a farm in Seattle. Reluctantly, he takes the assignment and is changed by the journey.

BUY & CELL

Cast: Michael Winslow*, Ben Vereen*, Robert Carradine, Malcolm McDowell, Lise Cutter
Director: Robert Boris
Executive Producer: Charles Band
Music by: Mark Shreeve
Producer: Charles Band, Frank Yablans
Screenwriter: Neal Israel, Larry Siegel
Tech Info: color/sound/91 min.   Type: Comedy Feature
Date: 1989   Origin: USA
Company: Altar
Distributors/Format: Empire (16mm)
Annotation: Altman (Carradine) is framed by a senior partner for insider trading and sent to prison. While there, he refuses an offer by the warden for special treatment in return for financial advice and is forced to live with the general prison population to which Sly (Winslow) and Shaka (Vereen) belong.

BY DAWN'S EARLY LIGHT

Cast: James Earl Jones*, Powers Boothe, Rebecca De Mornay, Martin Landau
Director: Jack Sholder
Music by: Trevor Jones
Producer: Bruce Gilbert, Thomas M. Hammel
Screenwriter: Bruce Gilbert
Storywriter: William Prochnau
Tech Info: color/sound/100 min.   Type: Dramatic Feature
Date: 1990   Origin: USA
Studio: Independent
Company: Paravision International, S.A.
Annotation: Political and military debate is carried on in this cold war thriller as "the button" is about to be pushed initiating World War III.

BY THE SWORD

Cast: Stone/Stoney Jackson*, Eric Roberts, Mia Sara, F. Murray Abraham, Christopher Rydell
Director: Jeremy Paul Kagan
Executive Producer: Philip Rose, Robert H. Straight, Frank Giustra
Music by: Bill Conti
Producer: Philip Rose, Peter E. Strauss, Marlon Staggs, Robert H. Straight, Frank Giustra
Screenwriter: John McDonald, James Donadio
Tech Info: color/sound/91 min.   Type: Dramatic Feature

Date: 1994   Origin: USA
Company: Foil Productions, Film Horizon
Distributors/Format: Hansen Entertainment (1/2")
Annotation: Fencing maestro Alexander Villard (Roberts) instructs Olympic hopefuls. When Max Suba (Abraham), an older man, comes to be coached, Villard is suspicious of his motives. Jackson plays Johnson.

C.H.U.D.

Alternate: Cannibalistic Humanoid Underground Dwellers
Cast: Frankie Faison*, John Heard, Laure Mattos, Kim Geist, Brenda Currin
Director: Douglas Cheek
Executive Producer: Larry Abrams
Music by: Cooper Hughes
Producer: Andrew Bonime, Larry Abrams
Screenwriter: Parnell Hall
Tech Info: color/sound/110 min.   Type: Dramatic Feature
Date: 1984   Origin: USA
Company: New World
Distributors/Format: New World Home Video (1/2")
Annotation: After toxic waste is dumped into city sewers, the homeless inhabitants of the underground turn cannibalistic and wreak havoc in the community. Faison plays Parker.

CADENCE

Cast: Laurence/Larry Fishburne*, Blu Mankuma*, Eugenia Wright*, Michael Beach*, Harry Stewart*, Deryl Hayes*, Douglas Judge*, John Toles-Bey*, Charlie Sheen, Martin Sheen
Director: Martin Sheen
Music Performer: Sam Cook*, Harry Stewart*, Rick Gibsee
Music by: Georges Delerue
Producer: Richard Davis*, Glennis Liberty
Screenwriter: Dennis Shryack
Storywriter: Glynn Turman*, Gordon Weaver
Tech Info: color/sound/97 min.   Type: Dramatic Feature
Date: 1990   Origin: USA
Studio: Independent
Company: The Movie Group With Northern Lights Media Corp.
Distributors/Format: Republic Pictures Home Video (1/2")
Annotation: Private Bean (Charlie Sheen) finds himself in the stockade with Roosevelt Stokes (Fishburne) and several other black soldiers. At first their relationship is antagonistic, but they eventually grow to trust one another. However, problems surface again when Sgt. McKinney (Martin Sheen) kills one of the prisoners while in a drunken rage.

CAGED IN PARADISO

Cast: Irene Cara*, Paula Bond*, Peter Kowanko, Joseph Culp, Beverly Purcell
Director: Mike Snyder
Music by: Bob Mamet, Kevin Klingler
Producer: John G. Thomas
Screenwriter: Michele Thyne
Tech Info: color/sound/84 min.   Type: Dramatic Feature

Date: 1990   Origin: USA
Company: Vidmark
Annotation: Eva (Cara) decides to accompany her husband Eric (Kowanko) to Paradiso Island, a penal colony where he's been sentenced for bombing a federal building. The island is divided into several contingents including bikers, a black-power faction headed by Josh (Cumbuka) and a feminist group.

CAJUN COUNTRY: DON'T DROP THE POTATO
Series: American Patchwork: Songs & Stories about America
Host: Alan Lomax
Tech Info: color/sound/60 min.   Type: Documentary Feature
Date: 1991
Company: Cultural Equity, Inc.
Annotation: The cultural roots of Mardi Gras celebrations are explored in this documentary.

CALIFORNIA SUITE
Cast: Richard Pryor*, Bill Cosby*, Sheila Frazier*, Gloria Gifford*, Jane Fonda, Alan Alda, Michael Caine, Walter Matthau, Elaine May, Maggie Smith
Director: Herbert Ross
Music Performer: Claude Bolling
Music by: Claude Bolling
Producer: Ray Stark
Screenwriter: Neil Simon
Tech Info: color/sound/103 min.   Type: Comedy Feature
Date: 1978   Origin: USA
Company: Rastar Films, Inc., Columbia
Annotation: In one of four segments of the film, Chicago residents and friends Dr. & Mrs. Chauncey Gump (Pryor and Gifford) and Dr. & Mrs. Willis Panama (Cosby and Frazier) visit Los Angeles and occupy the elegant hotel suite. After a series of mishaps, their hopes of relaxation are shattered and their friendship is in tatters.

CALL OF THE JITTERBUG, THE
Cast: John "Dizzy" Gillespie*, Margaret Batiuchok, Bill Dillard, Sandra Gibson, Delilah Jackson, George Lloyd, Frank Manning, Norma Miller, Mama Lu Potts
Music Performer: Cab Calloway*, Chick Webb*, Earl Hines*, Jimmy Lungeford, Harlem Blues and Jazz Band, The Swing Now Trio , Harry James
Producer: Tana Ross, Jesper Sorensen, Vibeke Winding
Tech Info: mixed/sound/30 min.   Type: Documentary Short
Date: 1988   Origin: USA
Company: Green Room Productions
Distributors/Format: Filmakers Library, Inc. (16mm; 1/2")
Annotation: Swing musicians from the 1930s discuss the artistic development and cultural implications of the Jitterbug.

CAN'T JAIL THE REVOLUTION & BREAK THE WALLS DOWN
Director: Kenyatta Tyehimba*, Ada Griffin
Speaker: Huey Newton*, Fred Hampton*, Kwame Toure*, Geronimo Ji-Jaga Pratt*, Jalil Muntaqin*, Ahmed Obafemi*, Safiya Bukhari-Alston*, Alejandrina Torres
Tech Info: mixed/sound/60 min.   Type: Documentary Short

Date: 1991   Origin: USA
Studio: Independent
Distributors/Format: Third World Newsreel (1/2")
Annotation: These two 30-minute videos use footage compiled from over 40 social justice media productions to chronicle the perspectives of African American, Puerto Rican, Native American and white political prisoners of war within the United States.

CANDYMAN

Cast: Vanessa Williams*, Tony Todd*, Kasi Lemmons*, Virginia Madsen, Xander Berkeley
Director: Bernard Rose, Anthony B. Richmond
Executive Producer: Clive Barker
Music by: Phillip Glass
Producer: Bernard Rose, Steve Golin, Sigurjon Sighvatsson, Alan Paul, Clive Barker
Screenwriter: Bernard Rose
Tech Info: color/sound/98 min.   Type: Dramatic Feature
Date: 1992   Origin: USA
Company: Columbia, TriStar
Distributors/Format: Columbia/TriStar Pictures (35mm; 1/2"), Facets Multimedia, Inc. (1/2")
Annotation: Todd plays Candyman, a murdered slave who haunts the Cabrini housing project in Chicago. His spirit comes alive when a graduate student, Helen (Madsen), does research about modern folklore and repeats his name three times. Williams is a tenant.

CANNERY ROW

Cast: Frank McRae*, Nick Nolte, Debra Winger, Audra Lindley
Director: David S. Ward
Music by: Jack Nitzsche
Producer: Michael Phillips
Screenwriter: David S. Ward
Storywriter: John Steinbeck
Tech Info: color/sound/120 min.   Type: Comedy Feature
Date: 1982   Origin: USA
Company: United Artists
Distributors/Format: MGM Home Video (1/2"), Filmic Archives (1/2")
Annotation: On the Monterey waterfront that once harbored a thriving fishing industry, a marine biologist (Nolte) and a young prostitute (Winger) find romance amid an assortment of hapless characters. McRae plays Hazel.

CANNONBALL RUN II

Cast: Sammy Davis Jr.*, Burt Reynolds, Dom DeLuise, Shirley MacLaine, Dean Martin
Director: Hal Needham
Executive Producer: Raymond Chow, Andre Morgan
Music by: Snuff Garrett, Al Capps
Producer: Albert S. Ruddy, Raymond Chow, Andre Morgan
Screenwriter: Albert S. Ruddy, Hal Needham
Storywriter: Harvey Miller
Tech Info: color/sound/109 min.   Type: Comedy Feature

Date: 1983   Origin: USA
Company: Albert S. Ruddy Production, et al.
Annotation: Fenderbaum (Davis) and Blake (Martin) reunite as driving partners in this sequel to the original Trans-America Cannonball Run Contest. Reynolds, Deluise, and others return as well, but the race's completion is muddled this time by Mafia bosses.

CANNONBALL RUN, THE

Cast: Sammy Davis Jr.*, Roger Moore, Burt Reynolds, Dom DeLuise, Dean Martin, Jackie Chan, Farrah Fawcett
Director: Hal Needham
Executive Producer: Raymond Chow
Music Conductor: Al Capps
Music by: Snuff Garrett, Al Capps
Producer: Albert S. Ruddy, Raymond Chow
Screenwriter: Brock Yates
Tech Info: color/sound/96 min.   Type: Comedy Feature
Date: 1981   Origin: USA
Company: Fox, Golden Harvest, Eurasia Investments Ltd.
Annotation: An assortment of Hollywood stars set out in the automobile of their choice to be the first to complete the cross-country Cannonball Run race. Fenderbaum (Davis) and Jamie Blake (Martin) pose as Catholic priests who sidetrack rival drivers by convincing them to pull off the race route and receive prayer and blessings.

CANTA FOR OUR SISTERS

Cast: Lois *
Director: Zeinabu irene Davis*
Producer: Zeinabu irene Davis*
Tech Info: color/sound/10 min.   Type: Experimental Short
Date: 1987   Origin: USA
Company: Wimmin with a Mission Productions
Annotation: Originally conceived as a long form documentary, the video is an experimental rendition of a poem "Black Woman" by Cuban feminist poet, Nancy Morejon.

CAPOEIRA OF BRAZIL

Cast: Jelom Vieira, J.C. Andradre (Apollo), Timothy Moe, Herbert Kerr, Clifton Murdock, Wilbert Murdock, Kevin Winnick, Loremil Machado, Eus Ebio Da Silva
Director: Warrington Hudlin*
Producer: Warrington Hudlin*
Screenwriter: Warrington Hudlin*
Tech Info: color/sound/10 min.   Type: Television Documentary
Date: 1980   Origin: USA
Studio: WGBH New Television Workshop with BFF
Company: Independent
Distributors/Format: Independent (16mm)
Archives/Format: IUB - BFC/A (16mm)
Annotation: Hudlin's film features a dance performance of Capoeira which was originally devised by Brazilian slaves as a fighting art of revolt and escape. When the Portuguese slave owners outlawed the practice, the slaves disguised Capoeira as a dance in order to continue its practice.

CAPRICORN ONE
Cast: O.J. Simpson*, Denise Nicholas*, James Brolin, Sam Waterston, Elliot Gould
Director: Peter Hyams
Music by: Jerry Goldsmith
Producer: Paul N. Lazarus III
Storywriter: Peter Hyams
Tech Info: color/sound/123 min.   Type: Dramatic Feature
Date: 1978   Origin: USA
Company: Capricorn One Associates
Annotation: Simpson, Brolin, and Waterson play three Astronauts whose mission to
Mars is aborted seconds before take-off. The Government threatens the men with
the murders of their families if they expose the plot to fake a landing. Nicholas plays
the Simpson character's wife.

CAPTAIN RON
Cast: J.A. Preston*, Kurt Russell, Mary Kay Place, Martin Short, Emmanuel Logrono
Director: Thom Eberhardt
Executive Producer: Ralph Winter
Music by: Nicholas Pike
Producer: Ralph Winter, David Permut, Paige Simpson
Screenwriter: Thom Eberhardt, John Dwyer
Storywriter: John Dwyer
Tech Info: color/sound/104 min.   Type: Comedy Feature
Date: 1992   Origin: USA
Company: Hybrid Productions, Touchstone, et al.
Distributors/Format: Buena Vista Home Video (1/2")
Annotation: Captain Ron (Russell) is a dry-docked bum hired to sail a family and the
boat they have inherited from the Caribbean to Miami. Tension builds between the
conservative father and his family, as they find Captain Ron's way of life more fun.
Preston portrays a magistrate.

CAR 54, WHERE ARE YOU?
Cast: Nipsey Russell*, Tone-Loc *, Fran Drescher, John C. McGinley, David
Johansen
Director: Bill Fishman
Music by: Pray for Rain , Bernie Worrell
Producer: Robert H. Solo
Screenwriter: Erik Tarloff, Peter McCarthy, Ebbe Roe Smith, Peter Crabbe
Storywriter: Erik Tarloff
Tech Info: color/sound/89 min.   Type: Comedy Feature
Date: 1994   Origin: USA
Company: Robert Solo Productions, Haymarket Prod., Orion
Distributors/Format: Orion Home Video (1/2")
Annotation: Captain Dave Anderson (Russell) returns with Officer Toody (Johansen)
and Muldoon (McGinley) in this movie version of the 1960s sitcom. Tone Loc
appears as Hackman.

CARBON COPY
Cast: Denzel Washington*, Paul Winfield*, Joe Eszterhas, Jack Warden, George Segal, Dick Martin, Susan St. James
Director: Michael Schultz*
Executive Producer: John Daly
Music Performer: England Dan Seals
Producer: John Daly, Stanley Shapiro, Carter DeHaven
Screenwriter: Stanley Shapiro
Tech Info: color/sound/91 min.   Type: Comedy Feature
Date: 1981   Origin: USA
Company: Hemdale, First City, RKO Pictures
Distributors/Format: Embassy Home Video (1/2")
Annotation: Roger (Washington) locates his white father Walter (Segal) after the death of his mother. Roger's arrival precipitates problems between Walter and his wife (Saint James), but father and son decide to stay together.

CARNIVAL '78
Director: Reggie Life*
Producer: Reggie Life*
Tech Info: color/sound/10 min.   Type: Documentary Short
Date: 1978   Origin: Trinidad-Tobago
Studio: Independent
Annotation: CARNIVAL '78 offers a look at both the preparation for and celebration of the annual Carnival in Trinidad-Tobago.

CARNY
Cast: Robert DoQui*, Theodore "Teddy" Wilson*, Gary Busey, Jodie Foster, Robbie Robertson, Meg Foster
Director: Robert Kaylor
Executive Producer: Jonathan Taplin
Music by: Alex North
Producer: Robbie Robertson, Jonathan Taplin
Screenwriter: Thomas Baum
Storywriter: Robbie Robertson, Robert Kaylor, Phoebe Taylor
Tech Info: color/sound/105 min.   Type: Dramatic Feature
Date: 1980   Origin: USA
Company: United Artists
Distributors/Format: United Artists Home Video (1/2")
Annotation: Donna (Foster) is a teenager who runs away with a carnival. Her romances with two of the carnival's mainstays is played out against the backdrop of daily carnival life. Wilson plays Nails; DoQui is uncredited.

CARO DIARIO
Cast: Jennifer Beals*, Alexandre Rockwell, Nanni Moretti, Giovanna Bozzolo, Sebastiano Nardone
Director: Nanni Moretti
Producer: Nanni Moretti, Angelo Barbagallo, Nella Banfi
Screenwriter: Nanni Moretti
Tech Info: color/sound/100 min.   Type: Comedy Feature

Date: 1994   Origin: Italy, France
Company: Sacher Film, Banfilm, La Sept, Studio Canal Plus
Distributors/Format: Fine Line Home Video (1/2")
Annotation: Beals plays herself in this three part comedy drama. Nanni Moretti uses
the cinematic diary format to examine his homeland and philosophize about his own
mortality.

CASUALTIES OF WAR
Cast: Ving Rhames*, Sean Penn, Michael J. Fox, John Leguizamo, Don Harvey,
John C. Reilly
Director: Brian De Palma
Music by: Ennio Morricone
Producer: Fred Caruso, Art Linson
Screenwriter: David Rabe
Tech Info: color/sound/120 min.   Type: Dramatic Feature
Date: 1989   Origin: USA
Company: Columbia
Distributors/Format: Paramount Home Video (1/2")
Annotation: Eriksson (Fox), a recent enlistee, is horrified by the treatment of civilians
during the Vietnam War. After seeing members of his platoon rape and murder a
young Vietnamese girl, he fights to have the incident reported, and those who took
part in it punished. Rhames plays Lt. Reilly.

CAT PEOPLE
Cast: Ruby Dee*, Frankie Faison*, Annette O'Toole, Nastassia Kinski, John Heard,
Malcolm McDowell
Director: Paul Schrader
Executive Producer: Jerry Bruckheimer
Music by: Giorgio Moroder, David Bowie
Producer: Jerry Bruckheimer, Charles Fries
Screenwriter: Alan Ormsby
Storywriter: DeWitt Bodeen
Tech Info: color/sound/118 min.   Type: Dramatic Feature
Date: 1982   Origin: USA
Company: Universal
Distributors/Format: RKO Radio Pictures (16mm)
Annotation: The Cat People, Irena and Paul Gallier (Kinski and McDowell),
descendants of an African Shaman who mated with leopards, look normal but turn
into ravenous beasts during moments of stress. Dee is the landlady who rents to
Irena and Paul and seems to be aware of their transformation. Faison plays
Detective Brandt.

CB4: THE MOVIE
Alternate: Cell Block IV
Cast: Khandi Alexander*, Arthur/Art Evans*, Chris Rock*, Ice-T *, Ice Cube *, Allen
Payne*, Charles Q. Murphy*, Otis O. Otis*, Phil Hartman, Chris Elliot
Director: Tamra Davis
Producer: Nelson George*
Storywriter: Chris Rock*, Nelson George*
Tech Info: color/sound/89 min.   Type: Comedy Feature

Date: 1993   Origin: USA
Annotation: Three middle-class teenagers turn themselves into a hard-core gangster rap group called CB4 (Cell Block 4).

CELEBRATING BIRD: THE TRIUMPH OF CHARLIE PARKER

Director: Gary Giddins, Kendrick Simmons, Steve Alpert
Music Performer: Thelonious Monk*, Charlie Parker*, Harry "Sweets" Edison*, Don Byas*, Lucky Thompson*, Charles Mingus*, John "Dizzy" Gillespie*
Music by: Charlie Parker*
Narrator: Ted Ross*
Producer: Gary Giddins, Toby Byron
Screenwriter: Gary Giddins
Speaker: Jay McShann*, John "Dizzy" Gillespie*, Frank Morgan*, Rebecca Parker-Davis*, Roy Haynes*, Roy Porter*, Chan Parker, Leonard Feather
Tech Info: mixed/sound/60 min.   Type: Documentary Feature
Date: 1987   Origin: USA
Company: Pioneer Artists, Sony Video Software Co., et al.
Distributors/Format: Sony Home Video (1/2")
Archives/Format: IUB - BFC/A (1/2")
Annotation: This documentary on the life of Charlie Parker (1920-1955) is dedicated to his memory. It covers his early years in Kansas City through his career, two marriages, addictions and death in New York. Based on the book, "Celebrating Bird: The Triumph of Charlie Parker," it includes interviews with major figures in his life.

CEMETERY CLUB, THE

Cast: Bernie Casey*, Etta Cox*, Danny Aiello, Diane Ladd, Olympia Dukakis, Ellen Burstyn
Director: Bill Duke*
Executive Producer: David Manson, Howard Hurst, Philip Rose
Music by: Elmer Bernstein
Producer: David Brown, Bonnie Palef, Sophie Hurst, David Manson, Howard Hurst, Philip Rose
Screenwriter: Ivan Menchell
Tech Info: color/sound/100 min.   Type: Comedy Feature
Date: 1993   Origin: USA
Company: Down to Earth Productions, Touchstone
Distributors/Format: Buena Vista Home Video (1/2")
Annotation: Three Jewish widows regularly visit their late husbands' graves together and then swap stories in a local deli. Casey plays John.

CENSUS TAKER, THE

Cast: Garrett Morris*, Timothy Bottoms, Greg Mullavey, Meredith MacRae, Austen Taylor
Director: Bruce Cook
Executive Producer: Gordon Smith
Music by: Jay Seagrave
Producer: Robart Bealmer, Gordon Smith
Screenwriter: Gordon Smith, Bruce Cook
Tech Info: color/sound/95 min.   Type: Comedy Feature

Date: 1984   Origin: USA
Company: Argentum
Distributors/Format: Seymour Borde (16mm)
Annotation: Harvey McGraw (Morris) is an extremely nosey census taker who is shot
by a couple, George (Mullavey) and Martha (MacRae), out of annoyance. They then
hide the corpse from a strange detective (Bottoms).

CERTAIN FURY

Cast: Moses Gunn*, Irene Cara*, Nicholas Campbell, Tatum O'Neal, George
Murdock
Director: Stephen Gyllenhaal
Executive Producer: Lawrence Vanger
Music by: Bill Payne, Russell Kunkel, George Massenburg
Producer: Gil Adler, Lawrence Vanger
Screenwriter: Michael Jacobs
Tech Info: color/sound/87 min.   Type: Dramatic Feature
Date: 1985   Origin: USA
Company: New World
Annotation: Street smart Scarlet (O'Neal) and affluent Tracy (Cara) are in court for
unrelated warrants when two hookers steal a gun and shoot up the courtroom.
Scarlet and Tracy escape, but are mistakenly assumed to be in cahoots with the
shooters.

CHAINED HEAT

Cast: Tamara Dobson*, Henry Silva, Linda Blair, John Vernon, Sybil Danning, Stella
Stevens, Sharon Hughes, Jennifer Ashley, Kendall Kaldwell, Dee Biederbeck
Director: Paul Nicholas
Executive Producer: Ernst von Theumer, Louis Paciocco, Louis Paciocco
Music by: Joseph Conlan
Producer: Billy Fine, Ernst von Theumer, Louis Paciocco, Louis Paciocco
Screenwriter: Paul Nicholas, Vincent Mongol
Tech Info: color/sound/97 min.   Type: Dramatic Feature
Date: 1983   Origin: USA
Studio: Independent
Company: Heat GBR/TAT-film/Intercontinental films
Annotation: The drama is centered around an innocent inmate Carol (Blair) who is
overwhelmed by prison corruption. In an attempt to expose the prison's power
hungry warden, Carol teams up with Duchess (Dobson), black prison cell leader who
is seeking vengeance for the death of another black inmate, Brenda Mansfield
(uncredited).

CHAINS OF GOLD

Cast: Bernie Casey*, John Travolta, Joey Lawrence, Marilu Henner
Director: Rod Holcomb
Music by: Trevor Jones
Producer: Jonathan D. Krane
Screenwriter: John Travolta, John Petz, Linda Favila, Anson Downes
Tech Info: color/sound/95 min.   Type: Dramatic Feature

Date: 1992   Origin: USA
Company: Management Company Entertainment Group
Distributors/Format: Academy Home Entertainment Video (1/2")
Annotation: Recovering alcoholic social worker Scott Barnes (Travolta) tries to infiltrate a drug ring that has his young client Tommy (Lawrence) working for them. Casey is Sergeant Palco.

CHAMELEON STREET
Cast: Wendell B. Harris Jr.*, Angela Leslie*, Amina Fakir*, Paula McGee*, Richard David Kiley Jr.*, Anthony Ennis*
Director: Wendell B. Harris Jr.*, Daniel S. Noga
Executive Producer: Helen B. Harris*
Music by: Peter Moore*
Producer: Helen B. Harris*, Dan Lawton
Screenwriter: Wendell B. Harris Jr.*
Tech Info: color/sound/98 min.   Type: Dramatic Feature
Date: 1992   Origin: USA
Company: Filmworld International Productions, Inc., et al.
Archives/Format: IUB - BFC/A (1/2")
Annotation: Based on the true story of William Douglas Street, who impersonated a Time Magazine reporter, a surgeon, a Yale student and a lawyer before winding up behind bars, the film stars Harris as the chameleon-like Street. Leslie plays his girlfriend. The film won the Grand Jury Prize at the 1990 Sundance Film Festival.

CHASING THE MOON
Director: Dawn Suggs*
Tech Info: bw/sound/4 min.   Type: Experimental Short
Date: 1991   Origin: USA
Studio: Independent
Distributors/Format: Third World Newsreel (1/2")
Annotation: A black lesbian woman comes to grips with memories of abuse and struggles to overcome her fears.

CHEAP DETECTIVE, THE
Cast: Scatman Crothers*, Sid Caesar, Ann-Margret , Eileen Brennan, Peter Falk
Director: Robert Moore
Music by: Patrick Williams
Producer: Ray Stark
Screenwriter: Neil Simon
Tech Info: color/sound/92 min.   Type: Comedy Feature
Date: 1978   Origin: USA
Company: Columbia
Distributors/Format: Columbia Pictures Home Video (1/2")
Annotation: Lou Peckinpaugh (Falk), a Bogart-style detective, solves crimes remarkably similar to those in the MALTESE FALCON and CASABLANCA. Crothers plays Tinker.

CHECKING OUT
Cast: Felton Perry*, Jeff Daniels, Michael Tucker, Melanie Mayron, Kathleen York
Director: David Leland
Executive Producer: George Harrison, Denis O'Brien
Music by: Carter Burwell*
Producer: George Harrison, Denis O'Brien, Ben Myron, Garth Thomas
Screenwriter: Joe Eszterhas
Tech Info: color/sound/93 min.   Type: Comedy Feature
Date: 1989   Origin: USA
Company: HandMade
Distributors/Format: Warner Bros. Home Video, Inc. (1/2")
Annotation: Ray Machlin (Daniels) becomes obsessed with the idea that he is dying after his boss suffers a fatal heart attack at a company barbeque. His hypochondria complicates his life, as well as the lives of those around him. Perry portrays Dr. Duffin.

CHEECH AND CHONG'S NICE DREAMS
Cast: Michael Winslow*, Stacy Keach, Richard "Cheech" Marin, Thomas Chong, Evelyn Guerreo, Dr. Timothy Leary
Director: Thomas Chong
Music by: Harry Betts, Harry Bates
Producer: Howard Brown
Screenwriter: Richard "Cheech" Marin, Thomas Chong
Storywriter: Richard "Cheech" Marin, Thomas Chong
Tech Info: color/sound/90 min.   Type: Comedy Feature
Date: 1981   Origin: USA
Company: Columbia
Distributors/Format: Columbia Pictures Home Video (1/2")
Annotation: Another drug infused Cheech and Chong adventure, this one is with Dr. Timothy Leary himself. Winslow plays "Superspade," who performs in a surreal sequence in which he becomes a figment of Cheech and Chong's marijuana imaginings.

CHEECH AND CHONG: CORSICAN BROTHERS
Cast: Rae Dawn Chong*, Robbi Chong*, Richard "Cheech" Marin, Thomas Chong
Director: Thomas Chong
Executive Producer: Joseph Mannis, Stan Coleman
Music Performer: GEO
Music by: GEO
Producer: Peter MacGregor-Scott, Joseph Mannis, Stan Coleman
Screenwriter: Richard "Cheech" Marin, Thomas Chong
Storywriter: Alexander Dumas*
Tech Info: color/sound/91 min.   Type: Comedy Feature
Date: 1984   Origin: USA
Company: Orion
Distributors/Format: Lightning Home Video (1/2")
Annotation: Cheech and Chong satirize Alexander Dumas' historical novel as the Corsican Brothers of pre-revolutionary France. Robbi Chong plays the illegitimate child of a local baroness and Rae Dawn Chong is a gypsy whose mystical powers allow her to see into the brother's past.

CHEECH AND CHONG: STILL SMOKIN'

Cast: Richard "Cheech" Marin, Thomas Chong, Carol Van Herwijhen, Susan Hahn
Director: Thomas Chong
Executive Producer: Joseph Mannis
Music Performer: George Clinton*
Music by: George Clinton*
Producer: Peter MacGregor-Scott, Joseph Mannis
Screenwriter: Richard "Cheech" Marin, Thomas Chong
Tech Info: color/sound/91 min.   Type: Comedy Feature
Date: 1983   Origin: USA
Company: Paramount
Distributors/Format: Paramount Home Video (1/2")
Annotation: Cheech and Chong visit Holland for a film festival where Cheech is mistaken for Burt Reynolds. Most of the film is taken from their stand-up comic routines. Clinton performs soundtrack music. Songs include "Delirious" by Prince.

CHEECH AND CHONG: UP IN SMOKE

Cast: Christopher Joy*, Ray Vite*, Tommy Chong, Cheech Marin, Edie Adams, Tom Skerritt, Strother Martin, Stacy Keach
Director: Lou Adler
Music Performer: War *, Herb Alpert
Producer: Lou Adler, Lou Lombardo
Screenwriter: Tommy Chong, Cheech Marin
Tech Info: color/sound/87 min.   Type: Comedy Feature
Date: 1980   Origin: USA
Company: Paramount
Distributors/Format: Paramount Home Video (1/2")
Annotation: Joy and Vite appear momentarily, as members of Chong's rock band. They are two of the many faces that Cheech and Chong encounter on their psychedelic drug journey.

CHILD'S PLAY 3

Cast: Jeremy Sylvers*, Justin Whalen, Perry Reaves
Director: Jack Bender
Executive Producer: David Kirschner
Music by: Cory Lerios, John D'Andrea
Producer: Laura Moscowitz, David Kirschner, Robert Latham Brown
Screenwriter: Don Mancini
Tech Info: color/sound/90 min.   Type: Dramatic Feature
Date: 1991   Origin: USA
Company: Universal
Annotation: In this sequel, the possessed, foul-mouthed "Good Guy" doll, Chucky, returns to the scene. This time he tries to switch bodies with an eight year-old military academy student named Tyler (Sylvers). Although youthfully naive and trusting, Tyler is successful in escaping the evils of Chucky.

CHILDREN OF THE NIGHT

Cast: Garrett Morris*, Karen Black, Peter DeLuise, Ami Dolenz
Director: Tony Randel
Executive Producer: Steven Jacobs, Norman Jacobs
Music by: Daniel Licht
Producer: Christopher Webster, Steven Jacobs, Norman Jacobs

Screenwriter: Nicolas Falacci, Tom Holliday, William Hopkins
Storywriter: Christopher Webster, Tony Randel, Nicolas Falacci, William Hopkins
Tech Info: color/sound/91 min.   Type: Dramatic Feature
Date: 1992   Origin: USA
Company: Fangoria Films
Distributors/Format: Columbia/TriStar Home Video (1/2")
Annotation: Mark Gardener (DeLuise) and Lucy Barrett (Dolenz) team up with town drunk Matty (Morris) to rid Allburg of the re-awakened band of vampires who threaten to kill or vampirize all of the small town's inhabitants. A sobered Matty, driving a religious van, puts an end to the evil one.

CHINA MOON

Cast: Roger Aaron Brown*, Charles Dance, Ed Harris, Madeleine Stowe, Patricia Healy
Director: John Bailey
Music by: George Fenton
Producer: Barrie M. Osborne
Screenwriter: Roy Carlson
Tech Info: color/sound/99 min.   Type: Dramatic Feature
Date: 1994   Origin: USA
Company: TIG Productions
Distributors/Format: Orion Home Video (1/2")
Annotation: Kyle Bodine (Harris) is a cop who falls in love with a beautiful, but crafty woman. After she kills her husband, she enlists his help to cover up the crime. Brown plays a police captain.

CHOOSE ME

Cast: Rae Dawn Chong*, Lesley Ann Warren, Keith Carradine, Genevieve Bujold, John Larroquette, Patrick Bauchau
Director: Alan Rudolph
Music Performer: Teddy Pendergrass*
Producer: David Blocker, Carolyn Pfeiffer
Screenwriter: Alan Rudolph
Tech Info: color/sound/114 min.   Type: Dramatic Feature
Date: 1984   Origin: USA
Company: Island Alive
Distributors/Format: Kino International Corp. (1/2"), Video Treasures (1/2")
Annotation: Chong plays Pearl Antoine in this comedy drama about a maladjusted radio psychologist (Bujold) who tries to solve the problems of frightened people.

CHORUS LINE, A

Cast: Sharon Brown*, Gregg Burge*, Mansoor Najeeullah*, Michael Douglas, Vicki Frederick
Director: Richard Attenborough
Executive Producer: Gordon Stulberg
Music by: Marvin Hamlisch, Ralph Burns
Producer: Cy Feuer, Ernest H. Martin, Gordon Stulberg
Screenwriter: Arnold Schulman
Storywriter: James Kirkwood, Nicholas Dante
Tech Info: color/sound/113 min.   Type: Musical Feature

Date: 1985   Origin: USA
Company: Polygram Pictures
Distributors/Format: Columbia Pictures Home Video (1/2"), Embassy Home Video (1/2")
Annotation: Richie Walters (Burge) survives the massive cuts to be a finalist in the Broadway production of "A Chorus Line." Brown plays Kim, personal secretary to choreographer Zach (Douglas), in this film version of the long running Broadway musical.

CHU CHU AND THE PHILLY FLASH

Cast: Danny Glover*, Jack Warden, Danny Aiello, Carol Burnett, Alan Arkin
Director: David Lowell Rich
Executive Producer: Melvin Simon
Music by: Pete Rugolo
Producer: Jay Weston, Melvin Simon
Screenwriter: Barbara Dana
Storywriter: Henry Barrow
Tech Info: color/sound/100 min.   Type: Comedy Feature
Date: 1981   Origin: USA
Company: Fox
Distributors/Format: Fox Home Video (1/2")
Annotation: Flash (Arkin), an ex-baseball player and alcoholic, meets Emily (Burnett), a failed entertainer, when both spot a briefcase on the street and lay claim to it. Glover plays Morgan.

CHUCK BERRY: HAIL! HAIL! ROCK 'N' ROLL!

Alternate: Hail! Hail! Rock 'n' Roll!
Cast: Chuck Berry*, Etta James*
Director: Taylor Hackford
Music Performer: Robert Cray*, Keith Richards, Julian Lennon
Producer: Chuck Berry*, Stephanie Bennett, Keith Richards
Speaker: Little Richard (Penniman) *, Bo Diddley*, Robert Cray*, Johnnie Johnson*, Willie Dixon*, Henry William Berry, Sr.*, Themetta Berry*, Thelma Smith*, Paul Berry*, Bruce Springsteen, Jerry Lee Lewis, Eric Clapton, Keith Richards, Dick Alen, Roy Orbison, Francine Gillium, Phil Everly, Don Everly
Tech Info: color/sound/121 min.   Type: Musical Feature
Date: 1987   Origin: USA
Company: Delilah Films, Universal
Distributors/Format: MCA Home Video (1/2")
Archives/Format: IUB - BFC/A (1/2")
Annotation: An array of rock 'n' roll musicians perform hits and discuss the musical contributions of Chuck Berry. Berry performs many of his works including: "Maybelline" and Johnny B. Good."

CHUCK DAVIS, DANCING THROUGH WEST AFRICA

Director: Gorham Kindem
Host: Chuck Davis*, John Danzell*
Music by: Khalid Saleem*
Producer: Gorham Kindem, Jane Desmond
Tech Info: color/sound/28 min.   Type: Documentary Short

Date: 1986   Origin: Africa
Distributors/Format: Filmakers Library, Inc. (16mm; 1/2")
Archives/Format: IUB - AAAMC (1/2")
Annotation: Chuck Davis and his dance company are filmed as they travel and dance through Senegal and the Gambia.

CIA II TARGET: ALEXA

Cast: Daryl Roach*, Lorenzo Lamas, Kathleen Kinmont
Director: Lorenzo Lamas
Music by: Louis Febre
Producer: Richard Pepin, Joseph Merhi
Screenwriter: Michael January
Storywriter: Kathleen Kinmont, Michael January
Tech Info: color/sound/88 min.   Type: Dramatic Feature
Date: 1994   Origin: USA
Company: PM Entertainment Group
Distributors/Format: PM Home Video (1/2")
Annotation: With the help of Wilson (Roach), a CIA mole, terrorist Ralph Straker (Ryan) steals the U.S. nuclear guidance actuator module and plans to sell it to the North Koreans. In this sequel Graver (Lamas) and Alexa (Kinmont) again overcome all odds.

CIA--CODE NAME ALEXA

Cast: O.J. Simpson*, Dan Tullis Jr.*, Lorenzo Lamas, Kathleen Kinmont, Michael Bailey Smith, Alex Cord
Director: Joseph Merhi
Music by: Louis Febre
Producer: Richard Pepin, Joseph Merhi
Screenwriter: John Weidner, Ken Lamplugh
Tech Info: color/sound/93 min.   Type: Dramatic Feature
Date: 1993   Origin: USA
Company: PM Entertainment
Distributors/Format: PM Home Video (1/2")
Annotation: Alexa (Kinmont) and Graver (Lamas), secret agents on opposite sides, first battle each other over the recovery of a micro-chip, then work together to save the life of Alexa's daughter. Simpson is featured as Nick Murphy, a police detective.

CINEMATIC JAZZ OF JULIE DASH, THE

Director: Yvonne Welbon*
Speaker: Julie Dash*
Tech Info: color/sound/26 min.   Type: Experimental Short
Date: 1992   Origin: USA
Studio: Independent
Distributors/Format: Third World Newsreel (1/2")
Archives/Format: IUB - BFC/A (1/2")
Annotation: In an in-depth interview with Julie Dash, whose first feature film, DAUGHTERS OF THE DUST, has become a critical sensation since its release in 1992, the filmmaker discusses the making of DAUGHTERS and the trials and triumphs of two decades of filmmaking by African American women.

CISSY HOUSTON: SWEET INSPIRATION

Director: Dave Davidson
Music Performer: Aretha Franklin*, Cissy Houston*, Whitney Houston*, Ann Drinkard Moss*, Nicholas Drinkard*
Music by: Cissy Houston*
Producer: Dave Davidson
Speaker: Aretha Franklin*, Dionne Warwick*, Luther Vandross*, Whitney Houston*, Reverend C.E. Thomas*, Joe Bostick*, Arif Mardin, Jerry Wexler, Tom Dowd
Tech Info: mixed/sound/58 min.   Type: Documentary Feature
Date: 1987   Origin: USA
Company: Hudson West Productions, Cinema Guild
Distributors/Format: Xenon Entertainment Group (1/2")
Annotation: Cissy Houston is the architect of the group Sweet Inspiration. Teacher, mother and entertainer, she combines gospel and secular music to reach out to her audience.

CITY HEAT

Cast: Richard Roundtree*, Irene Cara*, Harry Caesar*, Tab Thacker*, John Hancock*, Clint Eastwood, Burt Reynolds, Rip Torn, Jane Alexander, Madeline Kahn
Director: Richard Benjamin
Music Performer: Irene Cara*, Al Jarreau*, Lennie Niehaus
Music by: Lennie Niehaus
Producer: Fritz Manes
Screenwriter: Joseph Stinson, Blake Edwards
Storywriter: Blake Edwards
Tech Info: color/sound/98 min.   Type: Dramatic Feature
Date: 1984   Origin: USA
Company: Malpaso, Deliverance
Distributors/Format: Warner Bros. Home Video, Inc. (1/2")
Annotation: Dehl Swift (Roundtree) and Mike Murphy (Reynolds) run a detective agency. Ginny Lee (Cara), Swift's girlfriend, sings in Fat Freddie's (Hancock) nightclub and when she is kidnapped, attempts to save her. Caesar plays a boxing gym attendant.

CITY LIMITS

Cast: James Earl Jones*, Rae Dawn Chong*, Kim Cattrall, Darrell Larson, John Stockwell, Bobby Benson
Director: Aaron Lipstadt
Executive Producer: Warren Goldberg
Music by: Mitchell Froom
Narrator: James Earl Jones*
Producer: Warren Goldberg, Rupert Harvey, Barry Opper
Screenwriter: Don Opper
Storywriter: James Reigle, Aaron Lipstadt
Tech Info: color/sound/85 min.   Type: Dramatic Feature
Date: 1985   Origin: USA
Company: Skouras Pictures, Shofilms Ltd. w/ Videoform
Annotation: Albert (Jones) lives in the mountains and raises Leland (Stockwell) who came to live with him after the plague killed most of the adults in the early 21st century. Later, Leland goes off to the city to become a member of the Clippers motorcycle gang. Yogi (Chong) is the gang's mechanic.

CITY OF HOPE
Cast: Joe Morton*, Darryl Edwards*, Gloria Foster*, Thomas Lee Wright*, Frankie
Faison*, Angela Bassett*, JoJo Smollett*, Edward Jay Townsend Jr.*, Vincent
Spano, John Sayles, Tony Lo Bianco
Director: John Sayles
Music Performer: Neville Brothers *
Music by: Mason Daring*
Producer: Maggie Renzi, Sarah Green
Screenwriter: John Sayles
Storywriter: John Sayles
Tech Info: color/sound/130 min.   Type: Dramatic Feature
Date: 1991   Origin: USA
Studio: Independent
Company: Samuel Goldwyn
Archives/Format: IUB - BFC/A (1/2")
Annotation: Morton plays Wynn, Hudson City's newly elected black councilman.
When two young black boys, (Smollett and Townsend) are harassed by white police
officers and they retaliate, Wynn and the minority community openly confront the
city hierarchy seeking change, recognition and representation.

CITY SLICKERS
Cast: Bill Henderson*, Phill Lewis*, Daniel Stern, Billy Crystal, Jack Palance, Bruno
Kirby
Director: Ron Underwood
Executive Producer: Billy Crystal
Producer: Billy Crystal, Irby Smith
Screenwriter: Babaloo Mandel, Lowell Canz
Tech Info: color/sound/114 min.   Type: Comedy Feature
Date: 1991   Origin: USA
Company: Nelson Entertainment Face Production, Castle Rock
Annotation: When Mitch Robbins (Crystal), Ed Furillo (Kirby), and Phil Burquist
(Stern) experience a middle-age crisis, they head for a cattle drive in the American
Southwest to reaffirm their manhood. Other members of the drive include father and
son, Ben and Steve Jessup (Henderson and Lewis) who leave the drive early in
order to transport a wounded member back to civilization.

CLARA'S HEART
Cast: Whoopi Goldberg*, Beverly Todd*, Wanda Christine*, Maria Broom*, Maryce
Carter*, Angel Harper*, Hattie Winston*, Kathleen Quinlan, Michael Ontkean, Neil
Patrick Harris
Director: Robert Mulligan
Music Performer: Dave Grusin
Music by: Dave Grusin
Producer: Martin Elfand
Screenwriter: Mark Medoff, Doug Claybourne
Storywriter: Joseph Olshan
Tech Info: color/sound/107 min.   Type: Dramatic Feature

Date: 1988   Origin: USA
Company: Warner Bros.
Distributors/Format: Swank Motion Pictures, Inc. (16mm; 1/2"), Warner Bros. Home Video, Inc. (1/2")
Archives/Format: IUB - BFC/A (1/2")
Annotation: Clara Mayfield (Goldberg) is the housekeeper for a family whose 13-year-old son, David Hart (Harris), cannot cope with his parents' divorce. Clara's history is slowly unraveled as David becomes acquainted with figures from her world: close friend Blanche Lowden (Winston) and Clara's nemesis, Dora Cambridge (Todd). Others in her circle are four hairdressers: Felicia (Broom), Lydia (Christine), Bobs (Carter), and Rita (Harper).

CLARENCE AND ANGEL
Cast: Darren Brown*, Cynthia McPherson*, Janice Jenkins*, Ellwoodson Williams*, Louise Mike*, Mark Cardova, Robert Middleton
Director: Robert Gardner*
Music Performer: Sheila Jordon*
Producer: Robert Gardner*
Tech Info: color/sound/75 min.   Type: Dramatic Feature
Date: 1981   Origin: USA
Company: Gardner
Distributors/Format: Tapeworm Video Distributors (1/2")
Archives/Format: IUB - BFC/A (1/2")
Annotation: Two 12-year-old boys, one African American, Clarence (Brown), and one Hispanic, Angel (Cardova), are constantly in trouble in a New York public school. Clarence, a child of migrant workers, has not been in one place long enough to learn how to read. Angel helps him learn outside of class what the teacher is too impatient and insensitive to teach in the classroom.

CLASS
Cast: Anna Maria Horsford*, Andrew McCarthy, Jacqueline Bisset, Cliff Robertson, Rob Lowe, John Cusack
Director: Lewis John Carlino
Executive Producer: Cathleen Summers
Music by: Elmer Bernstein
Producer: Cathleen Summers, Martin Ransohoff
Screenwriter: Jim Kouf, David Greenwalt
Tech Info: color/sound/100 min.   Type: Dramatic Feature
Date: 1983   Origin: USA
Company: Orion
Distributors/Format: Orion Home Video (1/2")
Annotation: Jonathan (McCarthy), a naive prep school student, has an affair with Ellen (Bisset), an older woman, only to find that she's the mother of his roommate Skip (Lowe). Horsford plays Maggie.

CLASS ACT
Cast: Christopher Reid*, Christopher Martin*, Doug E. Doug*, Meshach Taylor*, Karyn Parsons*, Alysia Rodgers*, Rhea Pearlman, Pauly Shore
Director: Francis Kenny, Randall Miller
Executive Producer: Suzanne DePasse*, Joe Wizan
Music by: Vassal Benford*
Producer: Suzanne DePasse*, Maynell Thomas*, Joe Wizan, Todd Black

Screenwriter: John Semper, Cynthia Friedlob
Storywriter: Michael Swerdlick, Wayne Rice, Richard Brenne
Tech Info: color/sound/98 min.　　　Type: Comedy Feature
Date: 1992　Origin: USA
Company: Warner Bros.
Distributors/Format: Warner Bros. Home Video, Inc. (1/2")
Annotation: The film shows what happens when the school records of a "braniac dweeb" (Reid) and a "got-attitude" street tough (Martin) get accidently switched.

CLASS ACTION

Cast: Laurence/Larry Fishburne*, Hanna D. Moss*, Gene Hackman, Mary Elizabeth Mastrantonio
Director: Michael Apted
Music by: James Horner
Producer: Ted Field, Robert Cort, Scott Kroopf, Christopher Ames
Screenwriter: Carolyn Shelby, Christopher Ames
Tech Info: color/sound　　　　Type: Dramatic Feature
Date: 1991　Origin: USA
Company: Fox, Interscope Communications
Distributors/Format: Fox Home Video (1/2")
Annotation: Fishburne plays Nick Holbrook, a law partner to Jed Ward (Hackman). Together they take on a case defended by Ward's long time adversary Maggie (Mastrantonio), who is also his daughter. Laura (Moss) and Nick help Jed and Maggie through her mother's untimely death and Nick helps bring about a reconciliation between father and daughter.

CLASS OF 1999

Cast: Pam Grier*, Stacy Keach, Malcolm McDowell, Patrick Kilpatrick, Bradley Gregg, Traci Lin
Director: Mark L. Lester
Executive Producer: Lawrence Kasanoff, Ellen Steloff
Music by: Michael Hoenig, Derek Power, Seth Kaplan
Producer: Mark L. Lester, Lawrence Kasanoff, Ellen Steloff
Screenwriter: Courtney Joyner
Storywriter: Mark L. Lester
Tech Info: color/sound/98 min.　　　Type: Dramatic Feature
Date: 1990　Origin: USA
Company: Lightning, Original
Distributors/Format: Taurus Home Video (1/2")
Annotation: When gang activity virtually closes the nation's schools, the government employs three discipline-happy androids to teach in an experimental classroom. Grier plays Ms. Conners.

CLASS OF 1999 II: THE SUBSTITUTE

Cast: John Cothran Jr.*, Nick Cassavetes, Caitlin Dulany, Sasha Mitchell, Rick Hill
Director: Spiro Razatos
Executive Producer: Catalaine Knell
Music by: Andrew Keresztes
Producer: Russell D. Markowitz, Catalaine Knell
Screenwriter: Mark Sevi
Tech Info: color/sound/91 min.　　　Type: Dramatic Feature

Date: 1994   Origin: USA
Company: CineTel Films
Distributors/Format: Vidmark Entertainment Home Video (1/2")
Annotation: CIA agent Gordon Ash (Hill) trails "android" high school teacher Bolen (Mitchell) after he kills four punks. Bolen turns up at Monroeville High School where the killings continue. Cothran plays the high school principal.

CLASS OF MISS MAC MICHAEL, THE
Cast: Rosalind Cash*, Oliver Reed, Michael Murphy, Glenda Jackson
Director: Silvio Narizzano
Music by: Stanley Myers
Producer: Judd Bernard
Screenwriter: Judd Bernard
Tech Info: color/sound/100 min.   Type: Dramatic Feature
Date: 1978   Origin: Great Britain, USA
Company: Brut
Distributors/Format: Brut (16mm)
Annotation: A dedicated high school English teacher (Jackson) remains with her foul-mouthed students rather than accept a marriage proposal. Cash plays Una Ferrer.

CLEAN AND SOBER
Cast: Morgan Freeman*, Veronica Redd*, Kathy Baker, Michael Keaton
Director: Jan Kiesser, Glenn Gordon Caron
Executive Producer: Don Howard
Music by: Gabriel Yared
Producer: Tony Ganz, Deborah Blum, Don Howard
Screenwriter: Todd Carroll
Tech Info: color/sound/124 min.   Type: Dramatic Feature
Date: 1989   Origin: USA
Company: Image, Warner Bros.
Distributors/Format: Facets Multimedia, Inc. (1/2"), Warner Bros. Home Video, Inc. (1/2")
Annotation: Daryl Poynter (Keaton), a young successful real estate broker, has a drug abuse problem he refuses to acknowledge. When he gets into trouble with his company and the law, he decides to hide out in a de-toxication program. Freeman plays Craig, a recovering addict who oversees Poynter's group and forces him to follow the rules and face his addiction.

CLEAR AND PRESENT DANGER
Cast: James Earl Jones*, Willem Dafoe, Anne Archer, Harrison Ford
Director: Phillip Noyce
Music by: James Horner, Tim Sexton
Producer: Mace Neufeld, Robert Rehme
Screenwriter: John Milius, Steven Zaillian, Donald Stewart
Storywriter: Tom Clancy
Tech Info: color/sound/114 min.   Type: Dramatic Feature

Date: 1994   Origin: USA
Company: Paramount
Distributors/Format: Facets Multimedia, Inc. (1/2"), Films Inc. (1/2"), Paramount
Home Video (1/2")
Annotation: When his mentor Admiral James Greer (Jones) becomes gradually ill,
Jack Ryan (Ford), an intrepid CIA agent, is appointed acting CIA Deputy Director of
Intelligence. His first assignment is to investigate the murder of one of the
President's friends, a prominent U.S. businessman with secret ties to Columbian
drug cartels.

CLIENT, THE
Cast: Ossie Davis*, Kimberly Scott*, Mary Louise Parker, Susan Sarandon, Tommy
Lee Jones, Brad Renfro, David Speck
Director: Joel Schumacher
Music by: Howard Shore
Producer: Arnon Milchan, Steven Reuther
Screenwriter: Akiva Goldsman, Robert Getchell
Tech Info: color/sound/124 min.   Type: Dramatic Feature
Date: 1994   Origin: USA
Company: Client Productions Inc., New Regency, Alcor Films
Distributors/Format: Warner Bros. Home Video, Inc. (1/2")
Annotation: A young boy (Renfro) and his brother (Speck) learn mob secrets from a
man about to kill himself in the woods. Lawyer Reggie Love (Sarandon) agrees to
help the boys. Davis plays Judge Harry Roosevelt.

CLIFFHANGER
Cast: Paul Winfield*, Leon (credited as Leon) Robinson*, Michael Rooker, Sylvester
Stallone, John Lithgow, Janine Turner
Director: Renny Harlin
Executive Producer: Mario Kassar
Music by: Trevor Jones
Producer: Alan Marshall, Renny Harlin, Mario Kassar
Screenwriter: Sylvester Stallone, Michael France
Storywriter: Michael France
Tech Info: color/sound/112 min.   Type: Dramatic Feature
Date: 1993   Origin: USA, Netherlands
Company: Carolco International N.V.
Distributors/Format: TriStar Pictures Inc. (1/2")
Annotation: Walker (Stallone) is a forest ranger who battles hijackers and the
wilderness to retrieve three bins of stolen money and save his partner who is being
held by the hijackers. Robinson plays Kynette, a hijacker who fights Walker to the
death. Winfield plays Walter Wright.

CLIFTON CHENIER
Cast: Clifton Chenier*
Director: Carl Colby
Producer: Carl Colby
Tech Info: color/sound/58 min.   Type: Concert Feature

Date: 1978   Origin: USA
Company: Thiermann Finch Productions, Phoenix Films
Annotation: Chenier is one of the best known performers of Zydeco, a folk-blues music performed primarily by French-speaking Blacks in southern Louisiana and southern Texas.

CLOSER, THE

Cast: Michael Colyar*, Michael Pare, Danny Aiello, Joe Cortese, Justine Bateman, Rick Aiello
Director: Dimitri Logothetis
Executive Producer: Tony Conforti, George Pappas
Music by: Al Kasha, Joel Hirschhorn
Producer: Nabeel Zahid, Joseph Madawar, F. Daniel Somrack, Michel Kossak, Tony Conforti, George Pappas
Screenwriter: Robert Keats, Louis LaRusso II
Tech Info: color/sound/86 min.   Type: Dramatic Feature
Date: 1991   Origin: USA
Company: ION Pictures
Distributors/Format: ION Pictures (16mm)
Annotation: Chester Grant (Danny Aiello), a ruthless businessman with a knack for closing deals, must retire after a series of heart attacks compromises his health. He invites his three possible successors to Thanksgiving dinner. Colyar plays the hustler.

CLUB EXTINCTION

Alternate: Docteur M.
Cast: Jennifer Beals*, Alan Bates, Jan Niklas, Hanns Zischler
Director: Claude Chabrol
Executive Producer: Hans Brockmann, Francois Duplat
Music by: Paul Hindemith
Producer: Hans Brockmann, Adolphe Viezzi, Ingrid Windisch, Francois Duplat
Screenwriter: Claude Chabrol, Sollace Mitchell
Storywriter: Thomas Bauermeister, Norbert Jacques
Tech Info: color/sound/116 min.   Type: Dramatic Feature
Date: 1990   Origin: France
Company: Clea Productions, FR3 Films Productions, et al.
Distributors/Format: Prism Entertainment (1/2")
Annotation: A remake of Fritz Lang's 1922 classic, DR. MABUSE, this version stars Beals as Sonja. The story revolves around the exploits of a media genius who commits mass murder.

CLUB FED

Cast: Sherman Hemsley*, Lance Kinsey, Burt Young, Karen Black, Judy Landers
Director: Nathaniel Christian
Executive Producer: Ruth Landers, Mark Polan
Music by: Rod McBrien, Questar Welsh
Screenwriter: Jordan Rush
Storywriter: Ruth Landers
Tech Info: color/sound/91 min.   Type: Comedy Feature

Date: 1991   Origin: USA
Company: Rumar Films
Distributors/Format: Prism Entertainment (1/2")
Annotation: Wealthy and prominent convicts are sentenced to Club Fed, an experimental minimum security prison with condo-style cells. Hemsley plays Reverend Tessler, a corrupt TV evangelist now at Club Fed.

CLUB PARADISE

Cast: Adolph Caesar*, Jimmy Cliff*, Robin Williams, Rick Moranis, Peter O'Toole, Twiggy , Eugene Levy, Joanna Cassidy
Director: Harold Ramis
Executive Producer: Alan Greisman
Producer: Alan Greisman, Michael Shamberg
Screenwriter: Harold Ramis, Brian Doyle-Murray
Storywriter: Ed Roberto, Tom Leopold, Chris Miller
Tech Info: color/sound/96 min.   Type: Comedy Feature
Date: 1986   Origin: USA
Company: Warner Bros.
Distributors/Format: Warner Bros. Home Video, Inc. (1/2")
Annotation: Jack (Williams), a retired fireman from Chicago and Ernest (Cliff), an owner of property in the Caribbean, team up to turn Ernest's place into a night club. They run into problems when the prime minister (Caesar) joins forces with a real estate tycoon to take the property for their own corrupt purposes.

COLIN POWELL

Series: Black Americans of Achievement Video Collection
Director: Rhonda Fabian, Jerry Baber, Keith Smith
Executive Producer: Andrew Schlessinger
Narrator: Michael Logan
Producer: Rhonda Fabian, Jerry Baber, Andrew Schlessinger
Tech Info: mixed/sound/30 min.   Type: Documentary Short
Date: 1992   Origin: USA
Studio: Independent
Company: Schlessinger Video Productions
Distributors/Format: Filmic Archives (1/2")
Annotation: Several prominent African Americans discuss the contributions of General Colin Powell, Joint Chiefs of Staff.

COLLISION COURSE

Cast: Ernie Hudson*, John Hancock*, Chris Sarandon, Jay Leno, Pat Morita
Director: Lewis Teague
Executive Producer: Rene Dupont
Music by: Ira Newborn
Producer: Rene Dupont, Ted Field, Robert Cort, Howard W. Koch Jr.
Screenwriter: Robert Resnikoff, Frank Darius Namei
Tech Info: color/sound/96 min.   Type: Comedy Feature
Date: 1992   Origin: USA
Company: Interscope, DeLaurentiis Ent., Sign of the Ram
Distributors/Format: HBO Home Video (1/2")
Annotation: Detroit Detective Tony Costas (Leno), angered when an old pal is murdered in a junkyard, uncovers a partnership between the auto industry, the underworld, and a Japanese auto-part smuggler. Hudson plays Shortcut.

COLOR ADJUSTMENT
Director: Marlon T. Riggs*
Music by: Mary Watkins
Producer: Marlon T. Riggs*, Vivian Kleinman
Speaker: Esther Rolle*, Ruby Dee*, Tim Reid*, Diahann Carroll*, Henry Louis Gates Jr.*, Alvin Poussaint*, Herman Gray*, Daphne Reid*
Tech Info: color/sound/88 min.   Type: Documentary Feature
Date: 1991   Origin: USA
Studio: Independent
Company: Signifyin' Works
Distributors/Format: California Newsreel (1/2"), Signifyin' Works (1/2")
Archives/Format: IUB - BFC/A (1/2")
Annotation: Riggs brings his compelling study of racial prejudice begun in ETHNIC NOTIONS into the Television Age, examining the roles of African Americans on TV from Amos n' Andy to the Cosby Show.

COLOR OF MONEY, THE
Cast: Forest Whitaker*, Bill Cobbs*, Tom Cruise, Paul Newman, Mary Elizabeth Mastrantonio, Helen Shaver
Director: Martin Scorsese, Michael Ballhaus
Music by: Robbie Robertson
Producer: Paul Newman, Irvin Axelrad, Barbara De Fina
Screenwriter: Richard Price
Storywriter: Walter Trevis
Tech Info: color/sound/119 min.   Type: Dramatic Feature
Date: 1986   Origin: USA
Company: Touchstone
Distributors/Format: Buena Vista Home Video (1/2")
Annotation: Aging pool shark "Fast Eddie" Felsen (Newman) forms a profitable yet uneasy relationship with a young pool hustler (Cruise) whom he teaches the tricks of the game. But Eddie, finding it difficult to stay away from the bottle, allows himself to be humiliated by Amos (Whitaker), a seemingly dimwitted youth who is a real pro.

COLOR PURPLE, THE
Cast: Whoopi Goldberg*, Danny Glover*, Adolph Caesar*, Oprah Winfrey*, Rae Dawn Chong*, Margaret Avery*, Akosua Busia*, Willard Pugh*
Director: Steven Spielberg
Executive Producer: Quincy Jones*, Peter Guber, Jon Peters
Music by: Quincy Jones*
Producer: Quincy Jones*, Steven Spielberg, Peter Guber, Jon Peters, Kathleen Kennedy
Screenwriter: Menno Meyjes
Storywriter: Alice Walker*
Tech Info: color/sound/154 min.   Type: Dramatic Feature
Date: 1985   Origin: USA
Company: Warner Bros.
Distributors/Format: Warner Bros. Home Video, Inc. (1/2"), Filmic Archives (1/2")
Archives/Format: IUB-BFC/A (1/2")
Annotation: Seen through the eyes of shy, withdrawn Celie (Goldberg), who secretly writes to God and her sister Nettie (Busia) after her husband Mr. (Glover), separates her from Nettie (Busia), the film is based on the novel by Alice Walker. It is the story

of a woman's emergence from an abusive childhood and marriage into a loving, nurturing lesbian relationship with blues singer Shug (Avery). Ceasar plays Mr's father; Winfrey is Sophia.

COLORS
Cast: Damon Wayans*, Don Cheadle*, Sy Richardson*, Glenn Plummer*, Grand L. Bush*, Leon (credited as Leon) Robinson*, Sean Penn, Robert Duvall, Maria Alonso Conchita
Director: Dennis Hopper
Music Performer: Herbie Hancock*
Music by: Herbie Hancock*
Producer: Robert H. Solo
Screenwriter: Michael Schiffer
Storywriter: Michael Schiffer, Richard Di Lello
Tech Info: color/sound/127 min.   Type: Dramatic Feature
Date: 1988   Origin: USA
Company: Orion
Distributors/Format: Orion Home Video (1/2")
Archives/Format: IUB - BFC/A (1/2")
Annotation: Rocket (Cheadle), a "Crips" gang member is on the run after committing a drive-by shooting. Danny (Penn) and Bob (Duvall) are police officers trying to solve the murder. The story focuses on east Los Angeles gangs the "Crips" and the "Bloods." Bush, Plummer and Wayans play gangsters.

COLOUR
Cast: Ayoka Chenzira*, Carol-Jean Lewis*, Pat Matthew*, Linda Thomas Wright*, Andrea Thompson*, Virginia McKinzie*, Lola Holman*, Yvette Hawkins*, Don Charles Manning*
Director: Warrington Hudlin*
Music Performer: Jacob Slighter, Ronald Bell
Music by: Jacob Slighter
Producer: Warrington Hudlin*
Screenwriter: Denise Oliver
Tech Info: color/sound/30 min.   Type: Dramatic Short
Date: 1983   Origin: USA
Studio: Independent
Company: Black Filmmaker Foundation, PBS, WNET-TV
Distributors/Format: Independent (16mm)
Annotation: In simulated interview style, the film focuses on the experiences of two black women in search of identity and acceptance. One is dark-skinned and straightens her hair, the other is light-skinned with Caucasian features. Both are objects of prejudice within the African American community, ironically for the same reasons, hair style, degree of blackness and facial features.

COMING HOME
Cast: Olivia Cole*, Jane Fonda, Bruce Dern, Jon Voight
Director: Hal Ashby
Producer: Jerome Hellman
Screenwriter: Waldo Salt, Robert C. Jones
Storywriter: Nancy Dowd
Tech Info: color/sound/126 min.   Type: Dramatic Feature

Date: 1978   Origin: USA
Company: United Artists
Distributors/Format: United Artists Home Video (1/2")
Annotation: When her husband is sent to Vietnam, Sally Hyde (Fonda) volunteers at a veteran's hospital where she meets paraplegic Luke Martin (Voight) and eventually has an affair with him. Cole plays Corrine.

COMING TO AMERICA
Cast: Eddie Murphy*, James Earl Jones*, Arsenio Hall*, John Amos*, Madge Sinclair*, Shari Headley*, Eriq LaSalle*, Vanessa Bell*
Director: John Landis
Producer: George Folsey Jr., Robert D. Wachs
Screenwriter: Barry W. Blaustein, David Sheffield
Storywriter: Eddie Murphy*
Tech Info: color/sound/116 min.   Type: Comedy Feature
Date: 1988   Origin: USA
Company: Gulf & Western
Distributors/Format: Films Inc. (1/2"), Paramount Home Video (1/2")
Annotation: When the Prince of Zamunda, Akeem Joffer (Murphy) reaches twenty-one, the King (Jones) and Queen (Sinclair) introduce him to his bride-to-be (Bell). Wishing to control his own future, Akeem comes to America and ends up working for restauranteur Leo McDowell (Amos). Akeem falls in love with McDowell's daughter Lisa (Headley) who is dating Soul-Glo ad model, Darrel (LaSalle). All is resolved Hollywood style.

COMMANDO
Cast: Rae Dawn Chong*, Bill Duke*, Arnold Schwarzenegger, Alyssa Milano
Director: Mark L. Lester
Music by: James Horner
Producer: Joel Silver
Screenwriter: Steven E. DeSouza
Storywriter: Matthew Weisman, Joseph Lieb
Tech Info: color/sound/88 min.   Type: Dramatic Feature
Date: 1985   Origin: USA
Studio: Independent
Annotation: Chong plays Cindy, a flight stewardess, who is caught up in Matrix's (Schwarzenegger) rescue mission when his daughter is abducted by a South American terrorist group. One of his more formidable henchmen is a green beret named Cooke (Duke).

COMMISSIONED IN CONCERT
Music Performer: Fred Hammond, Michael Brooks, Mitchell Jones, Keith Staten, Michael Williams, Karl Reid
Music by: Fred Hammond, Michael Brooks, Mitchell Jones, Keith Staten, Michael Williams, Karl Reid
Producer: Ron Scott*
Tech Info: color/sound/90 min.   Type: Concert Feature

Date: 1989   Origin: USA
Company: CHE III Productions
Distributors/Format: Xenon Entertainment Group (1/2")
Annotation: Various gospel groups that have been commissioned to deliver the gospel through song give a live performance at Detroit's State Theatre.

COMMITMENTS, THE

Cast: Winston Dennis*, Robert Arkins, Michael Aherne, Angeline Hall, Maria Doyle, Dave Finnegan
Director: Alan Parker
Producer: Roger Randall-Cutler, Lynda Myles
Screenwriter: Roddy Doyle, Dick Clement, Ian La Frenais
Storywriter: Roddy Doyle
Tech Info: color/sound/116 min.   Type: Musical Feature
Date: 1992   Origin: Ireland
Company: Beacon Communications Corp., Fox
Distributors/Format: Fox Home Video (1/2")
Annotation: The Commitments, a group of Dublin working class youths who play black soul music, re-work hits by Redding, Pickett, Franklin, and others. The film includes archival footage of James Brown in concert.

COMMON BONDS

Alternate: Chaindance
Cast: Rae Dawn Chong*, Bruce Glover, Brad Dourif, Michael Ironside
Director: Allan Goldstein
Music by: Graeme Coleman
Producer: Richard Davis*
Screenwriter: Michael Ironside, Alan Aylward
Tech Info: color/sound/108 min.   Type: Dramatic Feature
Date: 1992   Origin: Canada
Company: R&R, The Movie Group, Chaindance Productions
Distributors/Format: Academy Entertainment (35mm; 1/2")
Annotation: Because of a lack of social workers, work-released prisoner J.T. Blake (Ironside) is handcuffed to a patient at a home for the severely disabled and told to take care of him. Chong plays Ilene.

COMMUNITY PLOT

Director: J.T. Takagi
Tech Info: color/sound/20 min.   Type: Experimental Short
Date: 1984   Origin: USA
Studio: Independent
Distributors/Format: Third World Newsreel (1/2")
Annotation: The film takes place in a building on New York's multi-ethnic lower east side. It uses humor to depict the life of the urban poor, and to show people of varying ethnic backgrounds working and living side by side.

COMPLEX WORLD

Cast: Ray Parker Jr.*, Stanley Matis, Margot Dionne, Allen Oliver, Daniel Von Bargen, Dan Welch, Bob Owczarek
Director: James Wolpaw
Executive Producer: Rich Lupo
Music by: Steven Snyder

Producer: Rich Lupo, Rich Lupo, Geoff Adams, Denis Maloney
Screenwriter: James Wolpaw
Tech Info: color/sound/81 min.   Type: Musical Feature
Date: 1992   Origin: USA
Company: Heartbreak Hits
Distributors/Format: Hemdale Home Video (1/2")
Annotation: Angry folk songwriter and small time terrorist, Morris Brock (Matis) aims to eliminate his only venue, The Heartbreak Hotel, a lively but deteriorating bar managed by Jeff Burgess (Welch). As a doorman to the establishment, Parker is an observer.

COMPROMISING POSITIONS
Cast: Bill Cobbs*, Paul Butler*, Raul Julia, Susan Sarandon, Edward Herrmann
Director: Frank Perry
Executive Producer: Salah M. Hassanein
Music by: Brad Fiedel
Producer: Frank Perry, Salah M. Hassanein
Screenwriter: Susan Isaacs
Tech Info: color/sound/98 min.   Type: Comedy Feature
Date: 1985   Origin: USA
Company: Blackhawk, C.P.
Distributors/Format: Paramount Home Video (1/2")
Annotation: When her periodontist is murdered, Judith Singer (Sarandon) launches an investigation and discovers her doctor was sleeping with all his female patients except her. Cobbs is Sgt. Williams and Butler is another policeman.

CONAN THE BARBARIAN
Cast: James Earl Jones*, William Smith, Arnold Schwarzenegger, Mako , Max Von Sydow, Sandahl Bergman
Director: John Milius
Executive Producer: D. Constantine Conte, Edward R. Pressman
Music Performer: Basil Poledouris
Music by: Basil Poledouris
Producer: Buzz Feitshans, Raffaella DeLaurentiis, D. Constantine Conte, Edward R. Pressman
Screenwriter: Oliver Stone, John Milius
Storywriter: Oliver Stone, John Milius
Tech Info: color/sound/128 min.   Type: Dramatic Feature
Date: 1981   Origin: USA
Company: Universal
Distributors/Format: MCA Home Video (1/2")
Annotation: Conan (Schwarzenegger) sets out to avenge his parents' death and return a princess to her father by killing an evil warlord, Thulsa Doom, (Jones) who has usurped the throne.

CONAN THE DESTROYER
Cast: Grace Jones*, Wilt Chamberlain*, Arnold Schwarzenegger, Olivia D'abo, Sarah Douglas, Mako
Director: Richard Fleischer
Executive Producer: Stephen Kesten
Music Performer: Basil Poledouris
Music by: Basil Poledouris

Producer: Dino de Laurentis, Raffaella DeLaurentiis, Stephen Kesten
Screenwriter: Stanley Mann
Storywriter: Roy Thomas
Tech Info: color/sound/101 min.   Type: Dramatic Feature
Date: 1984   Origin: USA
Company: Universal
Distributors/Format: MCA Home Video (1/2")
Annotation: Conan (Schwarzenegger) swears to aid a young princess (D'abo) in the fulfillment of her destiny. He must rely on the help of Bombata (Chamberlain), her assigned protector who is secretly plotting the princess' sacrifice, and Zula, a female warrior and bandit (Jones) whose loyalty to Conan is unmatched.

CONCORDE, THE--AIRPORT '79

Alternate: Airport '79/Airport '80: The Concorde
Cast: Jimmy/Jimmie Walker*, Cicely Tyson*, Susan Blakely, George Kennedy, Alain Delon, Robert Wagner
Director: David Lowell Rich
Music by: Lalo Schifrin
Producer: Jennings Lang
Screenwriter: Eric Roth, Jennings Lang
Storywriter: Arthur Hailey
Tech Info: color/sound/123 min.   Type: Dramatic Feature
Date: 1979   Origin: USA
Company: Universal
Distributors/Format: Universal Home Video (1/2")
Annotation: Joseph Patroni (Kennedy) is a pilot who rescues the Concorde's passengers from several catastrophes including electronic missile attacks, loss of the cargo door, and a landing without brakes. Tyson plays Elaine, a woman on her way to Paris with a donor organ for her husband; Walker plays Boise, a jazz musician who carries his saxophone with him wherever he goes.

CONEHEADS

Cast: Sinbad *, Garrett Morris*, Eddie Griffin*, Dan Aykroyd, Laraine Newman, Jane Curtin
Director: Steven Barron
Executive Producer: Michael Rachmil
Music by: David Newman
Producer: Michael Rachmil, Lorne Michaels
Screenwriter: Dan Aykroyd, Tom Davis, Bonnie Turner, Terry Turner
Tech Info: color/sound/86 min.   Type: Comedy Feature
Date: 1993   Origin: USA
Company: Broadway Video, Paramount
Distributors/Format: Paramount Home Video (1/2")
Annotation: Beldar and Prymaat Conehead (Aykroyd and Curtin) are stranded on Earth for 18 years. They fit into the New Jersey suburbs, raise their daughter there, and thwart a later conehead invasion. Sinbad plays Otto and Morris portrays Captain Orecruiser.

CONSENTING ADULTS
Cast: Forest Whitaker*, Michael L. Nesbitt*, Kevin Kline, Mary Elizabeth Mastrantonio, Kevin Spacey, Rebecca Miller
Director: Alan J. Pakula, Stephen Goldblat
Executive Producer: Pieter Jan Brugge
Music by: Michael Small
Producer: Pieter Jan Brugge, Alan J. Pakula, David Permut
Screenwriter: Matthew Chapman
Tech Info: color/sound/95 min.   Type: Dramatic Feature
Date: 1992   Origin: USA
Company: Hollywood Pictures, et al.
Distributors/Format: Buena Vista Home Video (1/2")
Annotation: Eddy Otis (Spacey) frames Richard Parker (Kline) for the murder of Eddy's wife, Kay (Miller) in order to collect a $1.5 insurance policy. With the help of insurance investigator David Duttonville (Whitaker), Parker discovers that his own wife Priscilla (Mastrantonio) has moved in with Otis, and also discovers that Kay is still alive. Nesbitt portrays a Charleston deputy.

CONVERSATION WITH MAGIC, A
Alternate: Magic Talks to Kids About HIV and AIDS
Director: Robert Hersh
Host: Earvin "Magic" Johnson*, Linda Ellerbee
Producer: Bob Brienza
Screenwriter: Linda Ellerbee
Tech Info: color/sound/30 min.   Type: Experimental Short
Date: 1992   Origin: USA
Studio: Independent
Company: Magic Johnson Foundation, et al.
Distributors/Format: Barr Films (1/2")
Annotation: This educational program provides children a format for addressing their questions about HIV and AIDS with Los Angeles Lakers basketball star Earvin "Magic" Johnson, who contracted the HIV virus.

CONVERSATIONS WITH ROY DECARAVA
Director: Carroll Parrott Blue*
Music Performer: Jimmy Owens*
Music by: Jimmy Owens*
Narrator: Alex Haley*
Producer: Carroll Parrott Blue*
Screenwriter: Carroll Parrott Blue*
Tech Info: color/sound/28 min.   Type: Documentary Short
Date: 1983   Origin: USA
Studio: Independent
Distributors/Format: First Run/Icarus Films (16mm)
Archives/Format: IUB - BFC/A (1/2")
Annotation: Narrated by Haley, Blue's documentary provides an overview of the artistic contributions of Roy DeCarava, a photographer who captured the Jazz Age. It features many of DeCarava's popular works.

CONVERSE

Director: Reginald Woolery*
Music Performer: Miles Davis*
Tech Info: color/sound/6 min.   Type: Experimental Short
Date: 1992   Origin: USA
Studio: Independent
Distributors/Format: Third World Newsreel (1/2")
Annotation: A jazzy, poetic choreography-for-camera starring a pair of hightops.

CONVICTS

Cast: James Earl Jones*, Starletta DuPois*, Mel Winkler*, Robert Duvall, Lukas Haas
Director: Peter Masterson
Music by: Peter Melnick
Producer: Jonathan D. Krane, Sterling Van Wagenen
Screenwriter: Horton Foote
Tech Info: color/sound/92 min.   Type: Dramatic Feature
Date: 1991   Origin: USA
Company: Management Company Entertainment Group, Sterling
Distributors/Format: Management Company Entertainment Group (16mm)
Annotation: Plantation owner Soll Gautier (Duvall) oversees the black convicts who work his land. Jones is Ben Johnson and DuPois plays his wife Martha; Winkler is a convict named Jackson.

CONVOY

Cast: Franklin Ajaye*, Madge Sinclair*, Burt Young, Kris Kristofferson, Ernest Borgnine, Ali MacGraw
Director: Sam Peckinpah
Executive Producer: Michael Deeley, Barry Spikings
Music by: Chip Davis
Producer: Robert M. Sherman, Michael Deeley, Barry Spikings
Screenwriter: B.W.L. Norton
Tech Info: color/sound/110 min.   Type: Comedy Feature
Date: 1978   Origin: USA
Company: United Artists
Distributors/Format: United Artists Home Video (1/2")
Annotation: Truck driver Rubber Duck (Kristofferson) clashes with a corrupt sheriff. Ajaye is trucker Spider Mike; Sinclair plays the Widow Woman.

COOL AS ICE

Cast: Allison Dean*, Kevin Hicks*, Deezer D. *, Naomi Campbell*, Vanilla Ice , Kristin Minter
Director: David Kellogg
Music by: Stanley Clarke*
Producer: Carolyn Pfeiffer, Lionel Wigram
Storywriter: David Stenn
Tech Info: color/sound/92 min.   Type: Musical Feature

Date: 1991   Origin: USA
Company: Universal
Distributors/Format: MCA/Universal Home Video (1/2")
Annotation: Vanilla Ice plays Johnny, a band leader whose "homies," Sir D. (Hicks), Jazz (Deezer D.), and Princess (Dean) are part of the backdrop, while Johnny takes the forefront and meets the girl of his dreams, Kathy (Minter). Campbell is featured as a nightclub singer.

COOL RUNNINGS

Cast: Doug E. Doug*, Malik Yoba*, Rawle D. Lewis*, Leon (credited as Leon) Robinson*, Charles Hyatt*, Bertina Macauley*, Pauline Stone Myrie*, Kristoffer Cooper*, John Candy
Director: Jon Turteltaub
Executive Producer: Christopher Meledandri, Susan B. Landau
Music by: Hans Zimmer
Producer: Dawn Steel, Christopher Meledandri, Susan B. Landau
Screenwriter: Lynn Siefert, Tommy Swerdlow
Storywriter: Michael Ritchie, Lynn Siefert
Tech Info: color/sound/98 min.   Type: Comedy Feature
Date: 1993   Origin: USA
Company: Steel Pictures, Touchstone
Distributors/Format: Buena Vista Home Video (1/2")
Annotation: With the help of Irv Blitzer (Candy) as their coach, four Jamaicans: Derice Bannock (Robinson), Sanka Coffie (Doug), Yul Brenner (Yoba) and Junior Bevel (Lewis) leave their Jamaican island home to enter the chilly winter Olympics. They compete for the gold in a sport they know nothing about, bobsled racing, and soon become heroes.

COP AND A HALF

Cast: Ruby Dee*, Norman D. Golden II*, Ray Sharkey, Burt Reynolds
Director: Henry Winkler
Music by: Alan Silvestri
Producer: Paul Maslansky
Screenwriter: Arne Olson
Tech Info: color/sound/93 min.   Type: Comedy Feature
Date: 1993   Origin: USA
Company: MCA, Universal
Distributors/Format: MCA/Universal Home Video (1/2")
Annotation: A streetwise youngster (Golden) teams up with a hard-edged detective (Reynolds) to catch murderers.

CORRINA, CORRINA

Cast: Whoopi Goldberg*, Harold Sylvester*, Jenifer Lewis*, Jevetta Steele*, Don Ameche, Ray Liotta, Tina Majorino
Director: Bruce Surtees, Jesse Nelson
Executive Producer: Ruth Vitale, Bernie Goldmann
Music by: Thomas Newman, Fred Kaz
Producer: Ruth Vitale, Bernie Goldmann, Steve Tisch, Jessie Nelson, Paula Mazur
Screenwriter: Jesse Nelson
Tech Info: color/sound/115 min.   Type: Dramatic Feature

Date: 1994   Origin: USA
Company: Hughes Ave Films, Tisch Company
Distributors/Format: Films Inc. (1/2"), New Line Cinema Home Video (1/2")
Annotation: After his wife's death, advertising writer Marty Singer (Liotta) and his young, withdrawn daughter Molly (Majorino) are alone. Marty hires Corrina Washington (Goldberg) as the new housekeeper. She's funny, smart, educated and overqualified for the job, but needs the money. Lewis plays Corrina's sister.

COSMIC DEMONSTRATION OF SEXUALITY, A
Director: Shari Frilot*
Producer: Shari Frilot*
Screenwriter: Shari Frilot*
Tech Info: color/sound/20 min.   Type: Experimental Short
Date: 1992   Origin: USA
Studio: Independent
Distributors/Format: Third World Newsreel (1/2")
Annotation: A humorous comparison between women's sexuality and the cosmic structure, this experimental video interviews five different women on such topics as menstruation, masturbation, and ejaculation.

COSMIC SLOP: SPACE TRADERS
Cast: Brock Peters*, Robert Guillaume*, Jason Bernard*, Jedda Jones*, George Wallace*, Roger Guenveur Smith*, Myra J. *, Michelle Lamar Richards*, Bertice Berry*, Roxie Roker*, Ann Walker*, Ebonie Smith*, Craig Kirkwood*, Lamont Johnson
Director: Reginald Hudlin*
Music by: John Barnes*
Narrator: George Clinton*
Producer: Ernest Johnson*
Screenwriter: Trey Ellis*
Storywriter: Derrick Bell*
Tech Info: color/sound/25 min.   Type: Television Feature
Date: 1994   Origin: USA
Company: HBO
Distributors/Format: HBO Home Video (1/2")
Annotation: Based on the short story by Derrick Bell, the first segment of this African American "Twilight Zone" focuses on Space Traders (aliens in the form of Ronald Reagan). In exchange for the U.S. black population, they will provide unlimited treasures to eliminate the budget deficit and clean the environment. Guillaume plays Professor Gleason Golightly; Richards is Gail Golightly; Bernard plays TV announcer Bernard Shields; Peters appears as Minister Coombs.

COSMIC SLOP: TANG
Cast: Paula Jai Parker*, Chi McBride*, Reno Wilson*
Director: Kevin Rodney Sullivan*
Music by: John Barnes*
Producer: Ernest Johnson*
Storywriter: Chester Himes*
Tech Info: color/sound/25 min.   Type: Television Feature

Date: 1994   Origin: USA
Company: HBO
Distributors/Format: HBO Home Video (1/2")
Annotation: In this last segment, based on a short story by Chester Himes, Tang (Parker) and her abusive, illiterate husband, T-Bone (McBride) receive a package from a mysterious visitor (Wilson) whose contents make for a surprise finale.

COSMIC SLOP: THE FIRST COMMANDANT

Cast: John Witherspoon*, Kelly Jo Minter*, Chino "Fats" Williams*, Eugene Allen*, Bowlegged Lou *, B. Fine *, Paul Anthony*, Daryl "Chill" Mitchell*, George Logan*, Bob Wisdom*, Irma Williams*, Nicholas Turturro, Efran Figueroa, Richard Herd
Director: Warrington Hudlin*
Music by: John Barnes*
Producer: Ernest Johnson*
Screenwriter: Warrington Hudlin*
Tech Info: color/sound/25 min.   Type: Television Feature
Date: 1994   Origin: USA
Company: HBO
Distributors/Format: HBO Home Video (1/2")
Annotation: In this second segment, a small community in the Bronx that practices the Santeria religion becomes the economic target for the Catholic Church. The Church dismisses the religion and sells the Santeria sacred statue to a local museum. Mitchell and Allen are delivery men; Witherspoon, Chino "Fats" Williams and Bowlegged Lou play homeless men; Wisdom appears as a police detective and Irma Williams is Oshun.

COTTON CLUB, THE

Cast: Giancarlo Esposito*, Gregory Hines*, Lonette McKee*, Mario Van Peebles*, Maurice Hines*, Laurence/Larry Fishburne*, Novella Nelson*, Thelma Carpenter*, Larry Marshall*, Wynonna Smith*, Diane Lane, Richard Gere, Bob Hoskins
Director: Francis Ford Coppola
Music by: John Barry
Producer: Robert Evans
Screenwriter: Francis Ford Coppola, William Kennedy
Storywriter: William Kennedy, Mario Puzo, Francis Coppola
Tech Info: color/sound/128 min.   Type: Dramatic Feature
Date: 1984   Origin: USA
Company: Zoetrope
Distributors/Format: Orion Home Video (1/2")
Annotation: The Harlem Cotton Club promotes musical talent but also functions as a setting for a powerful Mafia underground. Gregory Hines plays Sandman Williams, the club's finest tap dancer, who stays clear of the mob as does most of the club's black community. McKee is his love interest. There are minor appearances by Fishburne, Esposito, Van Peebles and Maurice Hines.

COUNTERFEIT COMMANDOS

Alternate: Inglorious Bastards
Cast: Fred Williamson*, Bo Svenson, Peter Hooten, Michel Constantin
Director: Enzo G. Castellari
Music by: Francesci do Masi
Screenwriter: Sergio Grieco

Tech Info: color/sound/99 min.   Type: Dramatic Feature
Date: 1978   Origin: Italy
Company: Aquarius
Annotation: Williamson is one of five soldiers who attempt to escape into Switzerland in order to avoid a court-martial in France.

COUNTERFORCE

Cast: Isaac Hayes*, George Kennedy, George Rivero, Hugo Stiglitz, Andrew Stevens, Louis Jourdan
Director: J. Anthony Loma
Producer: Carlos Vasallo
Screenwriter: Douglass Borton
Tech Info: color/sound/98 min.   Type: Dramatic Feature
Date: 1987   Origin: USA
Company: Soltar Corporation, Golden Son, ESME Productions
Distributors/Format: MCA Distributing Corp (1/2")
Annotation: Mercenaries are hired to protect a Middle Eastern leader sought by an opposing political party.

COVER-UP

Cast: Louis Gossett Jr.*, Dolph Lundgren, John Finn, Lisa Berkley, Sharon Brandon-Hacohen
Director: Manny Coto
Executive Producer: Bob Misiorowski, Jane Barclay
Music by: Bruno Louchouarn
Producer: Jacob Kotzky, Sharon Harel, Bob Misiorowski, Jane Barclay
Screenwriter: William Tannen
Tech Info: color/sound/89 min.   Type: Dramatic Feature
Date: 1991   Origin: USA
Company: Electra Films Ltd.
Distributors/Format: LIVE Home Video (1/2")
Annotation: American reporter Mike Anderson (Lundgren) investigates a terrorist robbery on a U.S. base in Israel, run by Jackson (Gossett). He discovers that a renegade soldier is behind the robbery and that nerve gas that could destroy all of Iraq was stolen.

COWBOY WAY, THE

Cast: Ernie Hudson*, Keifer Sutherland, Woody Harrelson, Dylan McDermott, Cara Buono, Marg Helgenberger, Joaquin Martinez
Executive Producer: William D. Wittliff, G. Mac Brown, Karen Kehela
Producer: William D. Wittliff, Brian Grazer, G. Mac Brown, Karen Kehela
Tech Info: color/sound/102 min.   Type: Comedy Feature
Date: 1994   Origin: USA
Company: Imagine
Distributors/Format: Universal Home Video (1/2")
Annotation: Pepper (Harrelson) and Sonny (Sutherland) are a champion rodeo team who part ways only to reunite in a search for their friend Nacho (Martinez). They head to New York and, with the help of Officer Sam Shaw (Hudson), they track their friend to the morgue.

CRACK HOUSE

Cast: Jim Brown*, Richard Roundtree*, Cheryl Kay, Anthony Geary, Angel Tompkins, Gregg Gomez Thomsen, Clyde R. Jones
Director: Michael Fischa
Producer: Jim Silverman
Screenwriter: Blake Shaefer
Storywriter: Jack Silverman
Tech Info: color/sound/91 min.   Type: Dramatic Feature
Date: 1989   Origin: USA
Company: Silverman
Distributors/Format: 20th Century-Fox Home Video (1/2")
Annotation: The film revolves around Rick Morales (Thomsen) and Melissa (Kay) Los Angeles high school kids who want to avoid gang and drug violence and go to college. Brown plays Steadman and Roundtree is Lt. Johnson.

CRACKERS

Cast: Larry Riley*, Charlaine Woodard*, Anna Maria Horsford*, Sean Penn, Jack Warden, Donald Sutherland
Director: Louis Malle
Music by: Paul Chihara
Producer: Edward Lewis, Robert Cortes
Screenwriter: Jeffrey Alan Fiskin
Storywriter: Suso Cecchi D'Amico, Mario Monicelli, Agenore Incrocci, Furio Scarpelli
Tech Info: color/sound/92 min.   Type: Comedy Feature
Date: 1984   Origin: USA
Company: Universal
Distributors/Format: Universal Home Video (1/2")
Annotation: Westlake (Sutherland), an unemployed security guard hangs around the Mission district of San Francisco. Slam Dunk (Horsford), Boardwalk (Riley) and Dillard (Penn), among others of the Mission crowd, plot to rob the safe of the local pawnshop.

CRAZY PEOPLE

Cast: Paul Bates*, Dudley Moore, Paul Reiser, Daryl Hannah
Director: Tony Bill
Executive Producer: Robert K. Weiss
Music by: Cliff Eidelman
Producer: Robert K. Weiss, Tom Barad
Screenwriter: Mitch Markowitz
Tech Info: color/sound/92 min.   Type: Comedy Feature
Date: 1990   Origin: USA
Company: Paramount
Distributors/Format: Paramount Home Video (1/2")
Annotation: Emory Leeson (Moore) is a top advertising executive who decides to be honest about his products. His boss fires him and has him committed. Bates plays Manuel Robles.

CRITICAL CONDITION
Cast: Richard Pryor*, Garrett Morris*, Ruben Blades, Bob Dishy, Rachel Ticotin, Joe Mantegna
Director: Michael Apted
Executive Producer: Bob Larson
Music Performer: Alan Silvestri
Music by: Alan Silvestri
Producer: Ted Field, Robert Cort, Bob Larson
Screenwriter: Dennis Hamill, John Hamill
Storywriter: Dennis Hamill, John Hamill, Alan Swyer
Tech Info: color/sound/99 min.   Type: Comedy Feature
Date: 1986   Origin: USA
Company: Paramount
Distributors/Format: Paramount Home Video (1/2")
Annotation: During a hospital black-out, Eddie (Pryor) escapes from the mental ward and is mistaken for hospital director, Chambers (Mantegna). Eddie reorganizes the chaotic situation into an efficient unit, while Chambers is held hostage by Eddie's friends back in the mental ward. A junkie (Morris) is recruited by Eddie to aid in the hospital's volunteer force.

CRITTERS 4
Cast: Angela Bassett*, Terrence Mann, Paul Witthorne, Anders Hove
Director: Rupert Harvey
Music by: Peter Manning Robinson
Producer: Rupert Harvey, Barry Opper
Screenwriter: Joseph Lyle, David J. Schow
Tech Info: color/sound/94 min.   Type: Dramatic Feature
Date: 1992   Origin: USA
Company: Nicolas Entertainment, New Line
Distributors/Format: New Line Cinema Home Video (1/2")
Annotation: Fran (Bassett), a level-headed space pilot, is part of a group that finds unhatched critter eggs in this sci-fi adventure.

CROCODILE CONSPIRACY
Director: Zeinabu irene Davis*
Speaker: Willa Ledbetter*
Tech Info: color/sound/13 min.   Type: Experimental Short
Date: 1986   Origin: USA
Studio: Independent
Distributors/Format: Third World Newsreel (1/2")
Annotation: Ledbetter, a black middle-aged school teacher in Watts, grapples with a longing to visit Cuba, her parent's homeland.

CROCODILE DUNDEE 2
Cast: Charles S. Dutton*, Paul Hogan, Ernie Dingo, Mark Saunders
Director: John Cornell
Executive Producer: Paul Hogan
Screenwriter: Paul Hogan, Brett Hogan
Tech Info: color/sound/110 min.   Type: Comedy Feature

Date: 1988   Origin: USA, Australia
Company: Rimfire Films
Distributors/Format: Paramount Home Video (1/2")
Annotation: When South American drug lords kidnap Mick Dundee's (Hogan) girlfriend (Kozlowski), Mick must use all the tricks of the Australian outback to outmaneuver them. The first half of the film is based in New York where Dutton plays Leroy Brown, Mick's friend who aids him in the pursuit of the mobsters.

CROOKLYN

Cast: Spike Lee*, Alfre Woodard*, Frances Foster*, Delroy Lindo*, Isaiah Washington*, Zelda Harris*, Carlton Williams*, Patriece Nelson*, RuPaul *
Director: Spike Lee*, Arthur Jafa*
Executive Producer: Jon Kilik
Music by: Terence Blanchard*
Producer: Spike Lee*, Jon Kilik
Screenwriter: Spike Lee*, Joie Lee*, Cinque Lee*
Storywriter: Joie Lee*
Tech Info: color/sound/114 min.   Type: Dramatic Feature
Date: 1994   Origin: USA
Company: 40 Acres and a Mule Filmworks
Distributors/Format: Universal Pictures (16mm; 1/2")
Archives/Format: IUB - BFC/A (1/2")
Annotation: Carolyn Carmichael (Woodard) is a loving, devoted and fiercely independent mother who, along with her musician husband Woody (Lindo), struggles to raise her family in difficult circumstances. The film covers one special summer in their Brooklyn neighborhood and is loosely based on storywriter Joie Lee's childhood.

CROSS CREEK

Cast: Alfre Woodard*, Bo Rucker*, Mary Steenburgen, Rip Torn, Peter Coyote, Dana Hill
Director: Martin Ritt
Music Performer: Leonard Rosenman
Music by: Leonard Rosenman
Producer: Robert A. Radnitz
Screenwriter: Dalene Young
Storywriter: Majorie Kinnan Rawlings
Tech Info: color/sound/115 min.   Type: Dramatic Feature
Date: 1983   Origin: USA
Company: Thorn EMI Films, Inc.
Annotation: The film chronicles the life of author Majorie Kinnan Rawlings (Steenburgen). Woodard portrays Geechee, Rawlings' hired help who becomes one of the writer's closest companions. Leroy (Ruckner) is Geechee's love interest.

CROSSROADS

Cast: Akosua Busia*, Joe Seneca*, Joe Morton*, Al Fann*, Gretchen F. Palmer*, Robert Judd*, John Hancock*, Tim Russ*, Guy Killum*, J.W. Smith*, Natasha Peacock*, Jami Gertz, Ralph Macchio,
Director: Walter Hill
Executive Producer: Tim Zinnemann
Music Performer: Sonny Terry*, John "Juke" Logan*, Ry Cooder
Producer: Mark Carliner, Tim Zinnemann

Screenwriter: John Fusco
Tech Info: mixed/sound/100 min.   Type: Dramatic Feature
Date: 1986   Origin: USA
Company: Columbia
Distributors/Format: Columbia Pictures Home Video (1/2")
Annotation: Young guitarist Eugene Martone (Macchio) tracks down blues legend Willie Brown (Seneca), who is now hospitalized. Martone helps him escape in the hope of finding a legendary lost song that Robert Johnson (Russ), another blues icon, had supposedly given to Brown. Judd plays the devil at the crossroad.

CROW, THE

Cast: Ernie Hudson*, Tony Todd*, Michael Wincott, Brandon Lee, Rochelle Davis
Director: Alex Proyas
Executive Producer: Robert L. Rosen, Mark M. Galvin, Shermin L. Baldin
Music by: Graeme Revell
Producer: Edward R. Pressman, Robert L. Rosen, Jeff Most, Mark M. Galvin, Shermin L. Baldin
Screenwriter: David J. Schow, John Shirley
Tech Info: color/sound/100 min.   Type: Dramatic Feature
Date: 1994   Origin: USA
Company: Crowvision Inc., Pressman Film Corp., et al.
Distributors/Format: Miramax Home Video (1/2")
Annotation: Eric Draven (Lee) returns from the dead and, with the help of a mystical crow, avenges his murder and that of his girlfriend. He works with good cop Albrecht (Hudson) and neighborhood waif Sarah (Davis).

CRUZ BROTHERS AND MISS MALLOY, THE

Director: Kathleen Collins*
Producer: Kathleen Collins*
Storywriter: Henry Roth
Tech Info: color/sound/54 min.   Type: Dramatic Feature
Date: 1980   Origin: USA
Studio: Independent
Annotation: Based on "The Cruz Chronicle: A Novel" by Henry Roth, Collins' film depicts the times and troubles of three Puerto Rican brothers living in a small town. This episode focuses on the hiring of the brothers by an elderly Irish woman, Miss Malloy. The boys' dead father occasionally appears as a meddling ghost.

CRY FREEDOM

Cast: Denzel Washington*, Zakes Mokae*, Josette Simeon*, John Matshikiza*, Juanita Waterman*, Patricia Gumede*, Angela Gavaza*, Kevin Kline
Director: Richard Attenborough
Executive Producer: Terence Clegg
Music by: Jonas Gwangwa*, George Fenton
Producer: Richard Attenborough, Norman Spencer, John Briley, Terence Clegg
Screenwriter: John Briley
Storywriter: Donald Woods
Tech Info: color/sound/154 min.   Type: Dramatic Feature

Date: 1987   Origin: Great Britain
Company: Universal
Distributors/Format: Facets Multimedia, Inc. (1/2"), Filmic Archives (1/2"), Universal Home Video (1/2")
Archives/Format: IUB - BFC/A (1/2")
Annotation: Based on the books "Biko" and "Asking For Trouble" by Donald Woods, the film depicts the moral awakening of a liberal white newspaper publisher, Woods (Kline), to the real horrors of apartheid through his friendship with "banned" activist Steve Biko (Washington). Biko, along with thousands of other black South Africans, was tortured and murdered by the Afrikaans government.

CRYING GAME, THE
Cast: Forest Whitaker*, Jaye Davidson*, Stephen Rea, Miranda Richardson
Director: Neil Jordan, Ian Wilson
Executive Producer: Nik Powell
Music by: Anne Dudley
Producer: Stephen Woolley, Elizabeth Karlsen, Nik Powell
Screenwriter: Neil Jordan
Tech Info: color/sound/108 min.   Type: Dramatic Feature
Date: 1992   Origin: Ireland
Company: AdPak, Miramax
Distributors/Format: LIVE Home Video (1/2")
Archives/Format: IUB - BFC/A (1/2")
Annotation: Jordie (Whitaker) is a British soldier held hostage by Irish terrorists, one of whom, Fergus (Rea) treats him humanely. Chared by Jordie to seek out his lover (Davidson), Fergus is drawn into a London scene of love and betrayal that shocks and mesmerizes him.

CUBA
Cast: Lonette McKee*, Sean Connery, Alejandro Rey, Brooke Adams, Chris Sarandon
Director: Richard Lester
Executive Producer: Denis O'Dell
Music by: Patrick Williams
Producer: Arlene Sellers, Alex Winitsky, Denis O'Dell
Screenwriter: Charles Wood
Tech Info: color/sound/122 min.   Type: Dramatic Feature
Date: 1979   Origin: USA
Company: MGM, United Artists
Distributors/Format: MGM/UA Home Video (1/2")
Annotation: The Cuban Revolution of 1959 is seen from the perspective of American Major Dapes (Connery). Dapes runs into his former lover, now a factory owner, Alexandre Pulido (Adams), whose lazy and unfaithful husband Juan (Sarandon) is sleeping with factory worker Therese Mederos (McKee).

CUBA CROSSING
Alternate: Kill Castro
Cast: Woody Strode*, Raymond St. Jacques*, Stuart Whitman, Robert Vaughn, Caren Kaye
Director: Chuck Workman
Producer: Peter J. Barton

Screenwriter: Chuck Workman
Tech Info: color/sound/90 min.   Type: Dramatic Feature
Date: 1980   Origin: USA
Company: Key West
Distributors/Format: Key West (16mm)
Annotation: A plot to kill Cuban dictator Fidel Castro is at the center of the film which uses stock footage of Castro and the Bay of Pigs for authenticity. Capt. Tony Terracino (Whitman) is pressured by the CIA to become involved in the assassination plot. St. Jacques plays Bell, Strode is Titi.

CURLY SUE

Cast: Gail Boggs*, James Belushi, Kelly Lynch, John Getz, Alisan Porter
Director: John Hughes
Executive Producer: Tarquin Gotch
Music by: Georges Delerue
Producer: John Hughes, Tarquin Gotch
Screenwriter: John Hughes
Tech Info: color/sound/102 min.   Type: Dramatic Feature
Date: 1991   Origin: USA
Company: Hughes Entertainment, Warner Bros.
Distributors/Format: Warner Bros. Home Video, Inc. (1/2")
Annotation: Street person Bill Dancer (Belushi) and his daughter Curly Sue (Porter) con rich people out of their money. When Bill pretends to be injured by Grey Ellison's (Lynch) car, father and daughter find themselves "recuperating" in style. Boggs plays Anise Hall.

CUT AND RUN

Alternate: Inferno in Diretta
Cast: Willie Aames*, Karen Black, Richard Lynch, Lisa Blount, Leonard Mann
Director: Ruggero Deodato
Music by: Claudio Simonetti
Producer: Alessandro Fracassi
Screenwriter: Cesare Frugoni, Dardano Sacchetti
Tech Info: color/sound/87 min.   Type: Dramatic Feature
Date: 1986   Origin: Italy
Company: Racing
Distributors/Format: New World Pictures (1/2")
Annotation: Journalist Fran Hudson (Blount) finds a photo showing a colonel, believed to be dead, beside an airplane loaded with cocaine. She and her cameraman take off for South America to investigate. In the jungle, they find hostile Amazonian Indians and reluctant drug dealers. Aames plays Tommy.

CYCLES

Cast: Zeinabu irene Davis*, Doris Owanda Johnson*, Stephanie Ingram*, Darryl Munyungo Jackson*, Marc Chery*
Director: Zeinabu irene Davis*
Music by: Miriam Makeba*, Clora Bryant*
Producer: Zeinabu irene Davis*
Storywriter: Doris Owanda Johnson*
Tech Info: bw/sound/15 min.   Type: Experimental Short

Date: 1989   Origin: USA
Studio: Independent
Company: Mosaic Films
Distributors/Format: Women Make Movies, Inc. (16mm; 1/2")
Archives/Format: IUB - BFC/A (16mm)
Annotation: Davis experiments with various cinematic techniques-- pixillation, voice overs and silences, special sound effects and music--in this brief narrative about a woman waiting for her period. Miriam Makeba's music compliments the African elements.

D.C. CAB

Alternate: Street Fleet
Cast: Denise Gordy*, Charles Barnett*, Marsha Warfield*, Irene Cara*, Mr. T. *, Whitman Mayo*, Michael Bland*, Phillip C. *, Rosie Gaines*, DeWayne Jessie*, Gloria Gifford*, J.W. Smith*, Jim Moody*, Michael E. Hill*, Paula Davis*, Alfredine Brown*, Gary Busey, Paul Rodriguez
Director: Joel Schumacher
Executive Producer: Peter Guber
Music Performer: Irene Cara*, Giorgio Moroder
Producer: Topper Carew*, Cassius Vernon Weathersby*, Peter Guber
Screenwriter: Joel Schumacher
Storywriter: Topper Carew*, Joel Schumacher
Tech Info: color/sound/100 min.   Type: Comedy Feature
Date: 1984   Origin: USA
Company: Guber/Peters Company
Distributors/Format: MCA Home Video (1/2"), RKO Radio Pictures (16mm)
Annotation: Ophelia (Warfield), Bonco Lennie (Jessie), Sampson (Mr. T.), and Tyrone (Barnett) are drivers for D.C. Cab Company. Miss Floyd (Gifford) is the dispatcher; Mr. Rhythm (Mayo), a homeless man who lives in an old D.C. cab. Alex (Moody) works for a competing cab company. Matty (Brown) and Denise (Gordy) take care of two children. When the children are kidnapped, the cab company hunts down the kidnappers.

D2: THE MIGHTY DUCKS

Cast: Kareem Abdul-Jabbar*, Brandon Adams*, Emilio Estevez, Jan Rubes, Kathryn Erbe, Joshua Jackson
Director: Sam Weisman
Executive Producer: Doug Claybourne, Salli Newman
Music by: J.A.C. Redford
Producer: Jon Avnet, Jordan Kerner, Doug Claybourne, Salli Newman
Screenwriter: Steven Brill
Tech Info: color/sound/107 min.   Type: Comedy Feature
Date: 1994   Origin: USA
Company: Bombay Films, Avnet/Kerner Company, Walt Disney
Distributors/Format: Buena Vista Home Video (1/2")
Annotation: Gordon Bombay (Estevez) and the Mighty Ducks return in this sequel. The Ducks welcome two new members to battle a European team for the world championship cup. Abdul-Jabbar has a cameo appearance as a superstar pitchman.

DAMIEN--OMEN II

Cast: Meshach Taylor*, Jimmy/James Spinks*, Lance Henriksen, William Holden, Lee Grant, Jonathan Scott-Taylor
Director: Don Taylor
Music by: Jerry Goldsmith
Producer: Harvey Bernhard
Screenwriter: Stanley Mann, Mike Hodges
Tech Info: color/sound/109 min.   Type: Dramatic Feature
Date: 1978   Origin: USA
Company: Fox
Distributors/Format: Fox Home Video (1/2")
Annotation: Everyone who is suspicious of Damien (Scott-Taylor), age 13 in this sequel, dies mysteriously. Spinks plays a technician at Thorn Industries, part of the industrial empire that Damien inherits.

DANCE BLACK AMERICA

Cast: Chuck Green*, The Magnificent Force *, The Jazzy Jumpers *, Al Perryman*, Leon Jackson*, Halifu Osumare*, Louis Johnson*, Charles Moore Dance Company*, Alvin Ailey American Dance Theater*, The Bucket Dance Company *, Mama Lu Parks Jazz Dancers*, Dejan's Olympia Brass Band of New Orleans, Rudy Stevenson Band, Ruth Brisbane, Biss Harmonisers, Chuck Davis Dance Company
Director: Chris Hegedus, D.A. Pennebaker
Narrator: Geoffrey Holder*, Ellen Haag
Producer: Frazer Pennebaker
Tech Info: mixed/sound/90 min.   Type: Documentary Feature
Date: 1985   Origin: USA
Studio: Independent
Company: Pennebaker Associates Productions
Distributors/Format: Kino International Corp. (1/2")
Annotation: The film documents traditional black folk dances as well as innovative modern choreography. Performers include some of the black community's most talented dance companies.

DANGEROUS GAME

Cast: Glenn Plummer*, Harvey Keitel, James Russo, Madonna , Nancy Ferrara
Director: Abel Ferrara
Executive Producer: Freddy DeMann, Ron Rotholz
Music by: Joe Delia
Producer: Mary Kane, Freddy DeMann, Ron Rotholz
Screenwriter: Nicholas St. John, Abel Ferrara
Tech Info: color/sound/107 min.   Type: Dramatic Feature
Date: 1993   Origin: USA
Company: Maverick Pict., Eye Films, Cecchi Gori Group, MGM
Distributors/Format: MGM Home Video (1/2")
Annotation: Director Eddie Israel (Keitel) drives his stars Sarah Jennings (Madonna) and Francis Burns (Russo) to dangerous extremes during filmming. Plummer plays a friend of Burns.

DANGEROUS HEART

Cast: Bill Nunn*, Alice Carter*, Tim Daly, Lauren Holly, Jeffrey Nordling
Director: Michael Scott
Executive Producer: Janet Meyers
Music by: Philip Giffin
Producer: Harvey Frand, Janet Meyers
Screenwriter: Patrick Cirillo
Tech Info: color/sound/120 min.   Type: Dramatic Feature
Date: 1994   Origin: USA
Company: Point of View Productions, MCA Television Ent.
Distributors/Format: MCA/Universal Home Video (1/2")
Annotation: Mulkey (Nunn) is the partner of an undercover cop (Nordling) who is murdered when he absconds with the money from a drug operation he was trying to expose. Although Mulkey is put off by Lee's wife Carol (Holly), who unwittingly falls in love with her husband's murderer, Angel Perno (Daly), he helps to bring Perno's henchmen to justice.

DARK EXODUS

Cast: Starletta DuPois*, Geraldine Dunston*, John Jelks*, Harold House*, Jeff Dixon*
Director: Iverson White*
Producer: Iverson White*
Screenwriter: Iverson White*
Tech Info: color/sound/28 min.   Type: Dramatic Short
Date: 1985   Origin: USA
Studio: Independent
Distributors/Format: Oracy Productions (16mm)
Annotation: The film looks at the migration of Blacks from the South to the North in early 1900s and shows the impact of a lynching on one proud black family.

DARKER SIDE OF BLACK

Director: Isaac Julien
Music Performer: Shabba Ranks*, Ice Cube *, Monie Love*, Buju Banton*, Michael Franti*
Speaker: Shabba Ranks*, Ice Cube *, Cornel West*, Michael Manly*
Tech Info: color/sound/60 min.   Type: Documentary Feature
Date: 1993   Origin: USA, Jamaica, Great Britain
Company: Arts Council Films
Distributors/Format: Filmakers Library, Inc. (16mm; 1/2")
Annotation: Filmed in dance halls, hip hop clubs, and using interviews and music video clips, the film takes the audience to London, Jamaica and the United States to hear and see the hard edge of Rap and Reggae.

DARKMAN

Cast: Julius Harris*, Frances McDormand, Colin Friels, Liam Neeson, Larry Drake, Nelson Mashita
Director: Sam Raimi
Music by: Danny Elfman
Producer: Robert Tapert
Screenwriter: Sam Raimi, Chuck Pfarrer, Daniel Goldin, Joshua Goldin
Storywriter: Sam Raimi

Tech Info: color/sound/96 min.   Type: Dramatic Feature
Date: 1990   Origin: USA
Company: Robert Tapert
Distributors/Format: Universal Home Video (1/2")
Annotation: Payton (Neeson) is a "scientist" trying to replicate human skin. Although his lab is blown up with him in it, Peyton survives. Harris plays a gravedigger.

DAUGHTERS OF THE DUST

Cast: Verta Mae Grosvenor*, Kaycee Moore*, Umar Abdurrahman*, Cheryl Lynn Bruce*, Cora Lee Day*, Geraldine Dunston*, Tommy Hicks*, Trula Hoosier*, Ertha D. Robinson*, Alva Rodgers*, Cornell Royal*, Catherine Tarver*, Bahni Turpin*, Kai-Lynne Warren*, Malik Farrakhan*, Althea Long*, Ron Daise*, Barbara O *, Adisa Anderson*, M. Cochise Anderson
Director: Julie Dash*
Executive Producer: Lindsay Law
Music by: John Barnes*
Producer: Julie Dash*, Floyd Webb*, Arthur Jafa*, Pam R. Jackson*, J. Bernard Nicholas*, Lindsay Law
Screenwriter: Julie Dash*
Tech Info: color/sound/113 min.   Type: Dramatic Feature
Date: 1991   Origin: USA
Studio: Independent
Company: Geechee Girls Productions
Distributors/Format: Third World Newsreel (1/2")
Archives/Format: IUB - BFC/A (1/2")
Annotation: From their Sea Island home, matriarch Nana Peazant (Day) has taught her family the cultural values of their African heritage, but fears these values will be lost when the family migrates North to the mainland. The pregnancy of Eula Peazant (Rodgers) leaves her husband Eli (Anderson) in turmoil as to his relationship to the unborn child (Warren). The return of Yellow Mary (Barbara O) from the mainland with her friend Trula (Hoosier) leads to additional family tensions. Arthur Jaffa is the cinematographer. The film was awarded Best Cinematography at the Sundance Film Festival.

DAWN OF THE DEAD

Cast: Ken Foree*, David Emge, Scott Reiniger, Gaylen Ross
Director: George A. Romero
Music by: Dario Argento
Producer: Richard Rubinstein
Screenwriter: George A. Romero
Tech Info: color/sound/125 min.   Type: Dramatic Feature
Date: 1979   Origin: USA
Company: United Film
Distributors/Format: United Film Distribution (16mm, 1/2")
Annotation: Francine (Ross), a TV station employee, and her boyfriend Stephen (Emge), the station helicopter pilot, fly to a suburban shopping mall to escape flesh-eating zombies. The mall is already infested with the monsters and the two fight them off. Foree plays Peter.

DAY OF ATONEMENT
Alternate: Le Grand Pardon II
Cast: Jennifer Beals*, Jim Moody*, Christopher Walken, Jill Clayburgh, Richard Berry, Roger Hanin
Director: Alexandre Arcady
Executive Producer: Robert Benmussa
Music by: Romano Musumarra
Producer: Alexandre Arcady, Robert Benmussa
Screenwriter: Alexandre Arcady, Daniel Saint-Hamont, Marc Angelo
Tech Info: color/sound/124 min.   Type: Dramatic Feature
Date: 1993   Origin: France
Distributors/Format: Vidmark Entertainment Home Video (1/2")
Annotation: In this sequel to LE GRANDE PARDON, aging patriarch Raymond Bettoun (Hanin) now out of prison joins his family in Miami for his grandson's bar mitzvah. The Bettoun family like the Corleones are involved in drugs, money, power and revenge. The women, Sally White (Clayburgh) and Joyce Feranti (Beals) are purely secondary. Moody plays Etienne Williams.

DAY TO REMEMBER: AUGUST 28, 1963, A
Speaker: John Lewis*, Walter Fauntroy*, Moe Tandler
Tech Info: mixed/sound/29 min.   Type: Documentary Short
Date: 1978   Origin: USA
Studio: Independent
Distributors/Format: Filmic Archives (1/2")
Annotation: The documentary includes interviews with principle participants in march and Dr. Martin Luther King's "I Have a Dream" speech.

DEAD AIM
Cast: Lynn Whitfield*, Randal Patrick*, Darrell Larson, Ed Marinaro, Cassandra Gavas
Director: William Van Der Kloot
Executive Producer: Stan Wakefield, Jerry Silva, Kirk Smith
Music by: James Oliverio
Producer: Michael A. Simpson, William Van Der Kloot, Stan Wakefield, Jerry Silva, Kirk Smith
Screenwriter: Michael A. Simpson
Tech Info: color/sound/88 min.   Type: Dramatic Feature
Date: 1990   Origin: USA
Company: Double Helix
Annotation: Reporter Shiela Freeman (Whitfield) figures prominently in unraveling the mystery surrounding the drug overdose deaths of topless dancers by furnishing the name of a hooker who knew some of the dead strippers. Douglas (Marinaro) and Cain (Larson) are the two cops caught between an undercover investigation of prostitution and subplots of drugs and foreign intrigue. Patrick plays Stephens.

DEAD AIR
Cast: Gregory Hines*, Debrah Farentino
Director: Fred Walton
Executive Producer: Alan Barnette
Producer: Alan Barnette, Oscar L. Costo
Screenwriter: David Amann

Tech Info: color/sound/91 min.   Type: Dramatic Feature
Date: 1994   Origin: USA
Company: MCA, Universal
Distributors/Format: MCA/Universal Home Video (1/2")
Annotation: Hines plays Mack Jannek a disc jockey who finds himself in the middle
of a murderous adventure when one of his fans calls with a terrifying message.

DEAD CONNECTION

Cast: Lisa Bonet*, Tim Russ*, Michael Madsen, Parker Posey, Gary Stretch,
Clarence Landry
Director: Nigel Dick
Music by: Rolfe Kent
Producer: Steve Golin, Sigurjon Sighvatsson, Gregg Fienberg, Gary Milkis
Screenwriter: Larry Golin
Storywriter: Jonathan Tydor
Tech Info: color/sound/93 min.   Type: Dramatic Feature
Date: 1994   Origin: USA
Company: Propaganda Films
Distributors/Format: Gramercy Pictures Home Video (1/2")
Annotation: Catherine Briggs (Bonet), the sister of a murder victim, goes undercover
to apprehend the serial killer.

DEAD HEAT

Cast: Mel Stewart*, Darren McGavin, Joe Piscopo, Treat Williams, Lindsay Frost
Director: Mark Goldblatt
Music by: Ernest Troost
Producer: Michael Meltzer, David Helpern
Screenwriter: Terry Black
Tech Info: color/sound/86 min.   Type: Dramatic Feature
Date: 1988   Origin: USA
Company: New World
Distributors/Format: New World Home Video (1/2")
Annotation: Police detectives Roger Mortis (Williams) and Doug Bigelow (Piscopo)
attempt to crack a crime ring that brings the dead back to life through the use of a
mysterious machine. Stewart plays Captain Mayberry.

DEAD MAN'S REVENGE

Alternate: You Only Die Once
Cast: Vondie Curtis-Hall*, Bruce Dern, Michael Ironside, Tobin Bell, Keith Coulouris
Director: Alan J. Levi
Executive Producer: Charmaine Balian
Music by: David Shwartz
Producer: Sheldon Pinchuk, William Finnegan, Ed Lahti, Charmaine Balian
Screenwriter: David Chisholm, Jim Byrnes
Tech Info: color/sound/120 min.   Type: Dramatic Feature
Date: 1994   Origin: USA
Company: Finnegan/Pinchuck Company, MCA Television
Distributors/Format: MCA/Universal Home Video (1/2")
Annotation: Luck Hatcher (Ironside) seeks revenge on Payton McCay (Dern) who
killed his family in 1876. Hatcher enlists the help of others in the New Mexico
territory and McCay faces frontier justice. Curtis-Hall plays Jessup Bush.

DEAD ON SIGHT
Cast: Jennifer Beals*, Daniel Baldwin, William H. Macy, Kirkwood Smith, Kent
Williams
Director: Ruben Preuss
Executive Producer: Kathryn Cass
Music by: Harry Manfredini
Producer: Roxanne Messina Captor, Kathryn Cass
Screenwriter: Lewis Green
Tech Info: color/sound/90 min.   Type: Dramatic Feature
Date: 1994   Origin: USA
Company: MCEG
Distributors/Format: Summa Video (1/2")
Annotation: Caleb O'Dell (Baldwin) is obsessed with the unsolved murder of his wife.
Rebecca (Beals), begins to experience murders of the past and future. O'Dell and
Rebecca team up after she begins experiencing visions of his wife's death.

DEAD-BANG
Cast: Tim Reid*, Sam Scarber*, Penelope Ann Miller, Don Johnson, William
Forsythe
Director: John Frankenheimer
Executive Producer: Robert L. Rosen
Music by: Gary Chang, Michael Kamen
Producer: Robert L. Rosen, Stephen J. Roth
Screenwriter: Robert Foster
Tech Info: color/sound/105 min.   Type: Dramatic Feature
Date: 1989   Origin: USA
Company: Lorimar
Distributors/Format: Warner Bros. Home Video, Inc. (1/2")
Annotation: Jerry Beck (Johnson) is a homocide detective who must contend with
the separate murders of a shopkeeper and a police officer, as well as his own
divorce. Reid is featured as Chief Dixon and Scarber portrays Detective Bilson.

DEADLY BLESSING
Cast: Sharon Stone, Maren Jensen, Susan Buckner, Jeff East
Director: Wes Craven
Executive Producer: William S. Gilmore
Music by: James Horner
Narrator: Percy Rodriguez*
Producer: William S. Gilmore, Patricia Herskovic, Micheline Keller, Max Keller
Screenwriter: Wes Craven, Glenn M. Benest, Matthew Barr
Tech Info: color/sound/102 min.   Type: Dramatic Feature
Date: 1981   Origin: USA
Company: Polygram
Distributors/Format: United Artists Home Video (1/2")
Annotation: Martha's (Jensen) husband dies mysteriously after leaving a religious
cult. After two friends (Buckner and Stone) arrive to comfort her, all three are
harassed by the cult, and more murders occur. Rodriguez narrates the film.

DEADLY EXPOSURE

Cast: Isaac Hayes*, Laura Johnson, Andrew Prine, Robby Benson, Bentley Mitchum
Director: Lawrence Mortorff, Russel Brandt
Executive Producer: Steven Paul
Music by: Gary Thomas Griffin, Taso Kotsos
Producer: Steven Paul, Lawrence Mortorff
Screenwriter: Asher Brauner
Tech Info: color/sound/100 min.   Type: Dramatic Feature
Date: 1993   Origin: USA
Company: Crystal Sky Communications, Kushner-Locke
Distributors/Format: Atlantic Home Video (1/2")
Annotation: Max (Benson) and Rita (Johnson) are targeted for death when their
investigation uncovers an assassination conspiracy that reaches into the highest
levels of the government. Hayes plays Lt. Johanson.

DEADLY EYES

Cast: Scatman Crothers*, Kareem Abdul Jabaar*
Director: Robert Clouse
Music by: Anthony Guefen
Producer: Charles Egilee, Jeffrey Schechtman, Paul Kahnert
Screenwriter: Charles Egilee, London Smith
Storywriter: James Herbert
Tech Info: color/sound/87 min.   Type: Dramatic Feature
Date: 1982   Origin: Canada, USA
Company: Filmtrust, Golden Harvest
Annotation: George Hoskins (Crothers) is an exterminator for the city of Toronto who
is sent to investigate disturbances in the underwater sewer tunnels. He is attacked
by mutated rats that overtake the city, attacking people in a movie theatre that is
showing a film starring Bruce Lee and Kareem Abdul Jabbar.

DEADLY ILLUSION

Alternate: Love You to Death
Cast: Billy Dee Williams*, Vanity *, Morgan Fairchild, John Beck, Joe Cortese
Director: Larry Cohen, William Tannen
Executive Producer: Michael Shapiro, Rodney Sheldon
Producer: Irwin Meyer, Michael Shapiro, Rodney Sheldon
Screenwriter: Larry Cohen
Tech Info: color/sound/90 min.   Type: Dramatic Feature
Date: 1987   Origin: USA
Studio: Independent
Company: Pound Ridge Films
Archives/Format: IUB - BFC/A (1/2")
Annotation: Williams portrays a private detective who tries to solve a crime, but ends
up framed for the murder.

DEADLY VENGEANCE

Cast: Grace Jones*, Arthur Roberts, Alan Marlowe
Director: A.C. Qamar
Producer: Amin Q. Chaudhri
Tech Info: color/sound/84 min.   Type: Dramatic Feature

Date: 1985   Origin: USA
Studio: Independent
Distributors/Format: Active Home Video (1/2")
Annotation: Jones must avenge her boyfriend's death, but she meets her match when she comes up against the leaders of a crime syndicate.

DEAL OF THE CENTURY
Cast: Gregory Hines*, J.W. Smith*, Sigourney Weaver, Chevy Chase
Director: William Friedkin
Executive Producer: Michael Melvion
Music Performer: Arthur B. Rubinstein
Music by: Arthur B. Rubinstein
Producer: Bud Yorkin, Michael Melvion
Screenwriter: Paul Brickman
Tech Info: color/sound/99 min.   Type: Comedy Feature
Date: 1983   Origin: USA
Company: Warner Bros.
Distributors/Format: Warner Bros. Home Video, Inc. (1/2"), Universal Home Video (1/2")
Annotation: Eddie Muntz (Chase), Mrs. Devoto (Weaver), and Ray Kasternak (Hines) band together in an attempt to unload defective United States military equipment on naive South American countries. Conscience-stricken Kasternak eventually foils the plan.

DEATH BEFORE DISHONOR
Cast: Paul Winfield*, Brian Keith, Sasha Mitchell, Fred Dryer, Joey Gian
Director: Terry J. Leonard
Executive Producer: Frank Capra Jr., Arthur H. Maslanksy, William Braunstein
Music by: Brian May
Producer: Frank Capra Jr., Lawrence Kubik, Arthur H. Maslanksy, William Braunstein
Screenwriter: Lawrence Kubik, John Gatliff
Storywriter: Lawrence Kubik, John Gatliff
Tech Info: color/sound/95 min.   Type: Dramatic Feature
Date: 1987   Origin: USA
Company: Lawrence Kubik, M.P.I., Bima, New World
Distributors/Format: Balcor Film Investors (1/2"), New World Pictures (1/2")
Annotation: Sgt. Jack Burns (Dryer) runs security at the U.S. Embassy in the Middle Eastern country of Jamal. When a friend is kidnapped, Burns wants to go after him, but the Ambassador (Winfield) insists on strict observance of the rules.

DEATH OF A PROPHET
Alternate: The Last Days of Malcolm X
Series: Independent Treasure's Collection
Cast: Morgan Freeman*, Yolanda King*, Mansoor Najeeullah*, Sam Singleton*, Tommy Hicks*, Yuri Kochiyama
Director: Woodie King Jr.*
Music Performer: Max Roach*
Music by: Max Roach*
Narrator: Ossie Davis*
Producer: Woodie King Jr.*

Screenwriter: Woodie King Jr.*
Speaker: Imamu Amiri Baraka*, Ossie Davis*, Yuri Kochiyama
Tech Info: mixed/sound/59 min.   Type: Docudrama
Date: 1981   Origin: USA
Studio: Independent
Company: Woodie King* Productions
Distributors/Format: Essenay Entertainment Corporation (1/2"), Xenon
Entertainment Group (1/2"), Filmic Archives (1/2")
Archives/Format: IUB - BFC/A (1/2")
Annotation: This docudrama follows the last hours of Malcolm X (Freeman) by
weaving documentary footage with dramatic reenactment. The film emphasizes the
mysterious circumstances surrounding the assassination. Davis, Kochiyama, and
Baraka discuss the impact Malcolm had on their lives.

DEATH WARRANT
Cast: Robert Guillaume*, Jean-Claude Van Damme, Cynthia Gibb, George
Dickerson, Patrick Kilpatrick
Director: Deran Sarafian, Mark DiSalle, Russell Carpenter
Music by: Gary Chang
Producer: Mark DiSalle
Screenwriter: David S. Goyer
Tech Info: color/sound/90 min.   Type: Dramatic Feature
Date: 1990   Origin: USA
Company: MGM, United Artists
Distributors/Format: MGM/UA Home Video (1/2")
Annotation: There are a series of unexplained, brutal murders at Harrison
Penitentiary and Detective Louis Burke (Van Damme) is assigned to go undercover
as an inmate to break the case. Burke befriends a fellow inmate (Guillaume) who
puts his neck on the line to help a new friend.

DEATH WISH II
Cast: Laurence/Larry Fishburne*, Stuart K. Robinson*, Charles Bronson, Vincent
Gardenia, Jill Ireland, J.D. Cannon
Director: Michael Winner
Executive Producer: Bob Roberts, Hal Landers
Music by: Jimmy Page
Producer: Yoram Globus, Menahem Golan, Bob Roberts, Hal Landers
Screenwriter: David Engelbach
Tech Info: color/sound/93 min.   Type: Dramatic Feature
Date: 1982   Origin: USA
Company: Columbia
Distributors/Format: Warner Bros. Home Video, Inc. (1/2"), EMI Home Video (1/2")
Annotation: In this sequel businessman Paul Kersey (Bronson) becomes a part-time
vigilante seeking revenge on the killer thugs who rape and murder his maid and his
daughter.   Fishburne plays Cutter; Robinson Jiver; Johnson appears as Punk-Cut,
all members of the gang that commits the crimes.

DEEP COVER

Cast: Laurence/Larry Fishburne*, Glynn Turman*, Clarence Williams III*, Paunita Nichols*, Cory Curtis*, Victoria Dillard*, Roger Guenveur Smith*, Jeff Goldblum, , Gregory Sierra
Director: Bill Duke*
Executive Producer: David Streit
Music by: Michel Colombier
Producer: Debra Moore*, Henry Bean, David Streit, Pierre David
Screenwriter: Henry Bean, Michael Tolkin
Storywriter: Michael Tolkin
Tech Info: color/sound/112 min.   Type: Dramatic Feature
Date: 1992   Origin: USA
Company: New Line, Image Organization
Distributors/Format: New Line Cinema Home Video (1/2"), Turner Home Entertainment (1/2")
Archives/Format: IUB - BFC/A (1/2")
Annotation: Police detective Russell Stevens (Fishburne) goes undercover to bring down a major drug supplier with the help of a drug dealing attorney (Goldblum). Turman plays Russell's junkie father who comes to a bad end as does Williams who plays Ken Taft, a sympathetic cop. Dillard plays Betty McCutcheon; Smith appears as Eddie.

DEEP NORTH, THE

Director: William Greaves*
Producer: William Greaves*
Screenwriter: William Greaves*
Speaker: Mike Schneider
Tech Info: color/sound/48 min.   Type: Documentary Short
Date: 1989   Origin: USA
Studio: Independent
Company: William Greaves* Productions Inc.
Annotation: Three groups discuss problems of racial and ethnic prejudice in their New York communities.

DEEPSTAR SIX

Cast: Taurean Blacque*, Nia Peeples*, Nancy Everhard, Greg Evigan
Director: Sean S. Cunningham
Executive Producer: Mario Kassar, Andrew Vajna
Music by: Harry Manfredini
Producer: Mario Kassar, Andrew Vajna, Sean S. Cunningham, Patrick Markey
Screenwriter: Lewis Abernathy, Geof Miller
Storywriter: Lewis Abernathy
Tech Info: color/sound/100 min.   Type: Dramatic Feature
Date: 1989   Origin: USA
Company: Carolco
Annotation: Laidlaw (Blacque) is a member of a naval mission to install an underwater missile base that accidentally unleashes a huge, fast-moving sea-monster. Peeples appears as Scarpelli.

DEF BY TEMPTATION

Cast: Kadeem Hardison*, Bill Nunn*, Melba Moore*, Samuel L. Jackson*, Rony Clanton*, James Bond III*, Guy Davis*, John Canada Terrell*, Jason Bernard*, Minnie Gentry*, Cynthia Bond*, Michael Zelniker
Director: James Bond III*
Executive Producer: James Bond III*
Music Performer: Melba Moore*, Freddie Jackson*, Najee *
Music by: Freddie Jackson*, Ashford & Simpson *, Eric Gable*, Paul Lawrence
Producer: James Bond III*, Nelson George*, Charles Huggins, Kevin Harewood
Screenwriter: James Bond III*
Tech Info: color/sound/95 min.   Type: Comedy Feature
Date: 1990   Origin: USA
Studio: Independent
Company: Orpheus Pictures, Bonded Filmworks
Distributors/Format: A Troma Team Release/Orpheus Picture (1/2")
Annotation: Joel (James Bond) is a Divinity student who is beguiled by a sultry temptress (Cynthia Bond) of "devilish" origins. Moore plays Madame Sonja, a fortune teller.

DEFENDING YOUR LIFE

Cast: Lillian Lehman*, Meryl Streep, Albert Brooks
Director: Albert Brooks
Screenwriter: Albert Brooks
Tech Info: color/sound/112 min.   Type: Comedy Feature
Date: 1991   Origin: USA
Company: Geffen Pictures
Annotation: Daniel Miller (Brooks) dies and must come face to face with his past actions. Lehman plays one of Daniel's judges forcing him to defend his behavior in court.

DEFENSELESS

Cast: Barbara Hershey, Randy Brooks, Sam Shepard, J.T. Walsh, Mary Beth Hurt
Director: Martin Campbell
Executive Producer: Taylor Hackford, Stuart Benjamin
Music by: Curt Sobel
Producer: Taylor Hackford, Stuart Benjamin, Renee Missel, David Bombyk
Screenwriter: James Hicks
Storywriter: James Hicks, Jeff Burkhart
Tech Info: color/sound/104 min.   Type: Dramatic Feature
Date: 1991   Origin: USA
Company: GFN Productions, New Visions Pictures
Distributors/Format: Seven Arts (16mm)
Annotation: Brooks plays Monroe, a politically ambitious prosecuting attorney, who tries to convict Ellie Seldes (Hurt) of murdering her husband Steven (Walsh) who turns out to be a child pornographer and worse. Detective Beutel (Shepard) and defense attorney T.K. (Hershey) solve the case.

DEFT CHANGES: AN IMPROVISED EXPERIENCE
Director: Alonzo Speight*
Music Performer: Mark Whitfield*, Frederick Waits*
Tech Info: color/sound/10 min.　　Type: Experimental Short
Date: 1991　Origin: USA
Studio: Independent
Distributors/Format: Third World Newsreel (1/2")
Annotation: Music and dance function as tools to explore the relationship between a father and son. The film features performances by guitarist Whittfield, and master drummer, Waits.

DELTA FORCE COMMANDO 2
Cast: Fred Williamson*, Van Johnson, Richard Hatch, Giannina Facio
Director: Frank Valenti
Executive Producer: Alfred Nicolaj
Music by: Elio Polizzi
Screenwriter: Lewis Cole
Storywriter: Frank Valenti
Tech Info: color/sound/100 min.　　Type: Dramatic Feature
Date: 1991　Origin: Italy
Company: Surf Film, Realta Cinematografica
Distributors/Format: LIVE Home Video (1/2")
Annotation: Captain Sam Beck (Williamson) is caught in a web of intrigue when he is accused of negligence because clandestine information has leaked from his base. Piecing together information from several sources, Beck learns that General McCailland (Johnson) has stolen nuclear weapons and confronts him.

DELUSION
Cast: Tommy Hicks*, Jennifer Rubin, Jerry Orbach, Jim Metzler, Kyle Secor
Director: Carl Colpaert
Executive Producer: Seth M. Willenson, Christoph Henkel
Music by: Barry Adamson
Producer: Daniel Hassid, Seth M. Willenson, Christoph Henkel
Screenwriter: Kurt Voss, Carl Colpaert
Tech Info: color/sound/100 min.　　Type: Dramatic Feature
Date: 1991　Origin: USA
Company: Cineville
Distributors/Format: IRS Releasing (16mm)
Annotation: George O'Brien (Metzler) leaves his Silicon Valley executive position but not before embezzling $250,000. He goes on the road to avoid capture but makes the error of picking up gun-crazy hitchhikers. Hicks plays Redmond.

DEMARCATIONS
Director: Kym Ragusa*
Tech Info: color/sound/5 min.　　Type: Experimental Short
Date: 1992　Origin: USA
Studio: Independent
Company: Third World Newsreel Production
Distributors/Format: Third World Newsreel (1/2")
Annotation: The film uses the female body as a landscape to explore memories of a rape. Ragusa focuses on ways in which identity and exoticism are played out on the

level of the body.

DEMOLITION MAN
Cast: Wesley Snipes*, Sylvester Stallone, Sandra Bullock, Nigel Hawthorne
Director: Alex Thompson, Marco Brambilla
Executive Producer: Steven Bratter, Faye Schwab
Music by: Elliot Goldenthal
Producer: Joel Silver, Michael I. Levy, Howard Karanjian, Steven Bratter, Faye Schwab
Screenwriter: Robert Reneau, Daniel Waters, Peter Lenkov
Storywriter: Robert Reneau, Peter Lenkov
Tech Info: color/sound/115 min.   Type: Dramatic Feature
Date: 1993   Origin: USA
Company: Warner Bros.
Distributors/Format: Warner Bros. Home Video, Inc. (1/2")
Annotation: The year is 2032 and archcriminal Simon Phoenix (Snipes) has emerged from a 35-year deep freeze in Cryo Prison to find a serene, non-violent southern California, is ready for the taking. Ill-equipped to deal with Phoenix's psychopathic 1990s style, city officials decide they need Spartan (Stallone), an old-fashioned cop to fight old-fashioned crime.

DENIAL
Cast: Rae Dawn Chong*, Barry Primus, Robin Wright, Jason Patric, Christina Harnos
Director: Erin Dignam
Executive Producer: Johnny Mercer, Rick Hyde, Mamadi Diane, Ibrahi Keita
Music by: Harold Budd
Producer: Johnny Mercer, Loretha C. Jones, Christina Schmidlin, Rick Hyde, Mamadi Diane, Ibrahi Keita
Screenwriter: Erin Dignam
Tech Info: color/sound/103 min.   Type: Dramatic Feature
Date: 1991   Origin: USA
Company: One World Productions, Sculptor Films
Distributors/Format: Republic Pictures Home Video (1/2")
Annotation: Julie (Chong), a friend of Sarah's when they were both young and free-spirited, turns up many years later. She unwittingly reminds Sarah of her tempestuous relationship with an artist (Patric) which she has tried to forget in order to live a balanced life and raise her now teen-aged daughter (Harnos).

DENNIS THE MENACE
Cast: Paul Winfield*, Christopher Lloyd, Walter Matthau, Joan Plowright, Mason Gamble
Director: Nick Castle
Executive Producer: Ernest Chambers
Music by: Jerry Goldsmith
Producer: John Hughes, Richard Vane, Ernest Chambers
Screenwriter: John Hughes, Hank Ketcham
Tech Info: color/sound/94 min.   Type: Comedy Feature

Date: 1993 Origin: USA
Company: Hughes Entertainment, Warner Bros.
Distributors/Format: Family Home Entertainment (1/2")
Annotation: Dennis (Gamble) and Mr. Wilson (Matthau) battle it out in this adaptation of the comic strip. When Dennis tries to warn Mr. Wilson that switchblade Sam (Lloyd) has stolen his coin collection, he is rebuked, runs away from home and falls into the clutches of Sam. Winfield plays the Chief of Police.

DESPERATE MOVES

Cast: Isabel Sanford*, Christopher Lee, Steve Tracey, Eddie Deezen, Paul Benedict
Director: Oliver Hellman
Music Performer: Patti Gallant, Dwayne Ford
Music by: Steve Power
Producer: Ovidio G. Assonitis
Screenwriter: Allan Berger
Tech Info: color/sound/106 min.   Type: Dramatic Feature
Date: 1986 Origin: USA
Studio: Independent
Company: Transworld Entertainment
Annotation: Dottie Butts (Sanford) is a woman who rents out her spare room to a young boy who has trouble with love. She assists his initiation into manhood with both advice and money.

DEVIL AND MAX DEVLIN, THE

Cast: Bill Cosby*, Elliot Gould, Adam Rich, Julie Budd, Susan Anspach
Director: Steven Hillard Stern
Producer: Jerome Courtland
Screenwriter: Mary Rodgers
Storywriter: Mary Rodgers, Jimmy Sangster
Tech Info: color/sound/95 min.   Type: Comedy Feature
Date: 1981 Origin: USA
Company: Walt Disney
Annotation: When Max Devlin (Gould) dies and goes to hell, he is given a chance at redemption if he obtains the souls of three children. Cosby is the devilish assistant to Gould's mission.

DEXTER GORDON QUARTET

Director: John Beyer
Music Performer: Dexter Gordon*, Rufus Reid*, Eddie Gladden
Tech Info: color/sound/58 min.   Type: Musical Feature
Date: 1979 Origin: USA
Distributors/Format: Facets Multimedia, Inc. (1/2")
Annotation: Gordon, star of 'ROUND MIDNIGHT, plays alongside his companions Cables, Reid and Gladden.

DIALOGUE BETWEEN A BLACK AND A JEW, A

Speaker: Ishmael Reed*, Zev Putterman
Tech Info: color/sound/64 min.   Type: Documentary Feature

Date: 1989   Origin: USA
Studio: Independent
Company: Invision Productions
Distributors/Format: Black Heritage Reference Center (1/2")
Archives/Format: IUB - BFC/A (1/2")
Annotation: Writers Reed and Putterman engage each other in a Black-Jewish dialogue. Reed perceives all minority groups to have a common history that is indicative of their experience. He is an advocate for a strong minority alliance to ensure survival in the U.S.

DIARY OF A HITMAN

Cast: Forest Whitaker*, James Belushi, Sharon Stone, Sherilyn Fenn
Director: Roy London, Yuri Sokol
Executive Producer: Mark Damon
Music by: Michel Colombier
Producer: Amin Q. Chaudhri, Mark Damon
Screenwriter: Kenneth Pressman
Storywriter: Kenneth Pressman
Tech Info: color/sound/90 min.   Type: Dramatic Feature
Date: 1991   Origin: USA
Company: Continental Film Group, LTD., Vision International
Annotation: Dekker (Whitaker) is a professional killer. Now on the eve of his retirement, he must decide if he will kill a young wife (Fenn) and her baby for $40,000. Belushi and Stone co-star in this psychological thriller.

DICE RULES

Cast: Eddie Griffin*, Sylvia Harman, Lee Lawrence, Maria Parkinson, Johnny West, Andrew "Dice" Clay
Director: Jay Dubin
Executive Producer: J.R. Guterman, Jana Sue Memel
Producer: Fred Silverstein, J.R. Guterman, Jana Sue Memel
Screenwriter: Lenny Shulman
Storywriter:
Tech Info: color/sound/87 min.   Type: Comedy Feature
Date: 1991   Origin: USA
Company: Fox
Distributors/Format: Seven Arts (16mm)
Annotation: Clay traces his comedic path from the past to the present. A pivotal encounter with a gas station attendant (Griffin) who insults him and destroys his car helps mold Clay into the obscene comedian he is today.

DIDN'T WE RAMBLE ON: THE BLACK MARCHING BAND

Narrator: John "Dizzy" Gillespie*
Producer: Billy Jackson*
Tech Info: color/sound/14 min.   Type: Documentary Short
Date: 1989   Origin: USA
Studio: Independent
Distributors/Format: Filmakers Library, Inc. (16mm; 1/2")
Annotation: The film shows how the spirit and soul of the West African people has been passed down from generation to generation to the black marching band. Gillespie introduces the orchestrated maneuvers of the Florida A&M Marching Band, as well as scenes of a jazz procession in New Orleans.

DIE HARD

Cast: Grand L. Bush*, Reginald Veljohnson*, Devoreaux White*, Clarence Gilyard Jr.*, Bruce Willis, Bonnie Bedelia
Director: John McTiernan
Executive Producer: Charles Gordon
Music by: Michael Kamen
Producer: Lawrence Gordon, Joel Silver, Charles Gordon
Screenwriter: Jeb Stuart, Steven E. DeSouza
Storywriter: Ivan Mogul, Roderick Thorp
Tech Info: color/sound/132 min.   Type: Dramatic Feature
Date: 1988   Origin: USA
Company: Gordon Company, Silver Pictures
Distributors/Format: Films Inc. (1/2"), Fox Home Video (1/2")
Annotation: Argyle (White), a chauffeur, is trapped in a building when terrorists attack. He prevents their escape by crashing his limousine into their truck. Theo (Gilyard) is the terrorist who breaks into a vault containing 640 million dollars. Johnson (Bush) is an FBI agent killed while trying to stop the terrorists. Al Powell (Veljohnson), a Los Angeles cop, saves McLane (Willis) from the terrorists.

DIE HARD 2: DIE HARDER

Cast: Arthur/Art Evans*, John Amos*, Bill Smillie*, Dominique Jennings*, Reginald Veljohnson*, Bruce Willis, Paul Bollen
Director: Renny Harlin
Music by: Michael Kamen
Producer: Lawrence Gordon, Joel Silver, Charles Gordon, Steve Perry
Screenwriter: Doug Richardson
Storywriter: Walter Wanger
Tech Info: color/sound/96 min.   Type: Dramatic Feature
Date: 1990   Origin: USA
Company: Gordon Company, Silver Pictures, Fox
Distributors/Format: Films Inc. (1/2"), Fox Home Video (1/2")
Annotation: While waiting for his wife's plane to arrive at Dulles Airport in Washington, D.C., police officer John McClane (Willis) encounters a terrorist take-over. He saves Leslie Barnes (Evans), the control tower chief engineer who restores radio contact so that the pilots can be informed of the terrorist situation. Major Grant (Amos) is in charge of a special anti-terrorist unit.

DIE HARD WITH A VENGEANCE

Cast: Samuel L. Jackson*, Bruce Willis, Colleen Camp, Jeremy Irons, Graham Green, Sam Phillips
Director: John McTiernan, Peter Menzies Jr.
Executive Producer: Buzz Feitshans, Andrew Vajna, Robert Lawrence
Music by: Michael Kamen
Producer: Buzz Feitshans, Andrew Vajna, Robert Lawrence, Michael Tadross
Screenwriter: Jonathan Hensleigh
Tech Info: color/sound/131 min.   Type: Dramatic Feature

Date: 1994   Origin: USA
Company: Fox
Distributors/Format: Films Inc. (1/2"), Fox Home Video (1/2")
Annotation: John McClane (Willis) teams up with an unwilling African American civilian and activist (Jackson) to pursue a mad man (Irons) who is literally blowing up Manhattan.

DIFFERENT DRUMMER: BLACKS IN THE MILITARY, THE

Producer: William Miles*
Tech Info: color/sound/180 min.   Type: Television Documentary
Date: 1983   Origin: USA
Company: Miles* Educational Film Production, Inc.
Distributors/Format: Miles Educational Film Production, Inc. (1/2")
Annotation: Miles' three-part series illuminates the often neglected history of Blacks' patriotism and involvement in America's military conflicts from colonial times to the present.

DIFFERENT IMAGE, A

Cast: Margot Saxon-Federalla*, Michael Anderson*, Leslie Speights*, A. Rucker*, Mandisa Olivier*, Michael Bruce*
Director: Charles Burnett*, Alile Sharon Larkin*
Producer: Alile Sharon Larkin*
Screenwriter: Alile Sharon Larkin*
Tech Info: color/sound/52 min.   Type: Dramatic Feature
Date: 1982   Origin: USA
Studio: Independent
Distributors/Format: Women Make Movies, Inc. (16mm; 1/2")
Archives/Format: IUB - BFC/A (16mm)
Annotation: The film focusses on a beautiful young black woman Alana (Saxon-Federella), who insists on defining herself and her relationship with her friend Vincent (Anderson). The film confronts the sexism of black men who have adopted western attitudes towards women as sex objects.

DIGGSTOWN

Alternate: Midnight Sting
Cast: Louis Gossett Jr.*, Duane Davis*, James Woods, Bruce Dern, Oliver Platt
Director: Michael Ritchie
Music by: James Newton Howard*
Producer: Robert Schaffel
Screenwriter: Steven McKay
Tech Info: color/sound/97 min.   Type: Comedy Feature
Date: 1992   Origin: USA
Company: Schaffel/Eclectic Films Production, et al.
Distributors/Format: MGM Home Video (1/2")
Annotation: After being convicted for peddling phony art, con man Gabriel Caine (Woods) organizes small town boxing matches. He bets that his boxer, "Honey" Roy Palmer (Gossett), can beat any challenger. Davis plays Hambone Busby.

DIRT, GROUND, EARTH, AND LAND
Director: Alonzo Crawford*
Tech Info: color/sound/120 min.   Type: Documentary Feature
Date: 1983   Origin: USA
Studio: Independent
Annotation: This four-segment film develops a parallel between a people's growing awareness of their collective strength and of the symbolic value of their homes. The battle over land is fought by adults, yet it is a battle which scars the children. The film mirrors their confusion and frustration, but also suggests their sense of hope.

DISORDERLIES
Cast: The Fat Boys *, Ralph Bellamy, Anthony Geary, Tony Plana
Director: Michael Schultz*
Executive Producer: Charles Stettler, Joseph E. Zynczak
Producer: Michael Schultz*, George Jackson*, Michael Jaffe, Charles Stettler, Joseph E. Zynczak
Screenwriter: Mark Feldberg, Mitchell Klebanoff
Tech Info: color/sound/86 min.   Type: Comedy Feature
Date: 1987   Origin: USA
Company: Warner Bros.
Distributors/Format: Warner Bros. Home Video, Inc. (1/2")
Annotation: The Fat Boys, Mark "Prince Markie Dee" Morales, Damon "Kool Rock-Ski" Wimbley and Darren "The Human Beat Box" Robinson, are taken to Palm Beach, Florida's richest community, to care for an irascible, bedridden old millionaire played by Bellamy. What the Fat Boys don't know is they are being set-up for a con.

DISTINGUISHED GENTLEMAN, THE
Cast: Eddie Murphy*, Sheryl Lee Ralph*, Della Reese*, Victoria Rowell*, Charles S. Dutton*, Sonny Jim Gaines*, Joe Don Baker
Director: Jonathan Lynn, Gabriel Beristain
Executive Producer: Marty Kaplan
Music Performer: Randy Edelman
Producer: Marty Kaplan, Leonard Goldberg, Michael Peyser
Screenwriter: Marty Kaplan
Storywriter: Johnathan Reynolds, Marty Kaplan
Tech Info: color/sound/112 min.   Type: Comedy Feature
Date: 1992   Origin: USA
Company: Hollywood Pictures
Distributors/Format: Hollywood Pictures Home Video (1/2")
Annotation: A small time con man, Thomas Jefferson (Murphy), wins a Congressional seat and uses the perks and power of his new position to con for cash without breaking the law. Ralph plays Jefferson's secretary; Rowell, his love interest.

DIVINE ENFORCER, THE
Cast: Jim Brown*, Erik Estrada, Judy Landers, Don Stroud, Jan-Michael Vincent
Director: Robert Rundle
Tech Info: color/sound/90 min.   Type: Dramatic Feature

Date: 1991   Origin: USA
Distributors/Format: Prism Entertainment (1/2")
Annotation: A monsignor in a crime ridden Los Angeles neighborhood tries to stave off perpetrators of injustice. Fortunately, help arrives in the form of a mysterious priest (Brown) who is handy with prayers, fists and guns.

DIZZY GILLESPIE: A MUSICAL PORTRAIT
Director: Bryan Elsom
Music by: John "Dizzy" Gillespie*
Narrator: Leonard Feather
Producer: Bryan Elsom
Tech Info: color/sound/28 min.   Type: Documentary Short
Date: 1990   Origin: USA
Company: View Video, Kingfisher Films
Distributors/Format: Educational Video Network (1/2")
Annotation: This film presents rehearsal scenes, interviews, commentary by Feather, and a live performance by Gillespie.

DIZZY GILLESPIE: JAZZ IN AMERICA
Director: Les Blank
Music Performer: John "Dizzy" Gillespie*
Producer: Michael Vidor
Tech Info: color/sound/90 min.   Type: Concert Feature
Date: 1980   Origin: USA
Annotation: The concert functions as a historical tribute to be-bop. Musical performances by Dizzy Gillespie and his Dream Band at Lincoln Center are featured.

DO THE RIGHT THING
Cast: Bill Nunn*, Spike Lee*, Joie Lee*, Giancarlo Esposito*, Ruby Dee*, Ossie Davis*, Martin Lawrence*, Danny Aiello, Richard Edson, John Savage, John Turturro
Director: Spike Lee*, Ernest Dickerson*
Music by: Bill Lee*
Producer: Spike Lee*, Monty Ross
Storywriter: Spike Lee*
Tech Info: color/sound/120 min.   Type: Dramatic Feature
Date: 1989   Origin: USA
Company: 40 Acres and a Mule Film Works, Universal
Distributors/Format: Facets Multimedia, Inc. (1/2"), MCA Home Video (1/2")
Archives/Format: IUB - BFC/A (1/2")
Annotation: The film traces a single day on a block in the Bedford-Stuyvesant area of Brooklyn. On the hottest day of the year, the lives of the residents: Mookie (Lee) a delivery man for Sal's (Aiello) pizzeria; da Mayor (Davis); Radio Rayheem (Nunn); and Buggin' Out (Esposito) will change forever.

DOC HOLLYWOOD
Cast: Helen Martin*, Edye Byrde*, Mel Winkler*, Michael J. Fox, David Ogden Stiers, Woody Harrelson, Julie Warner, Barnard Hughes
Director: Michael Caton-Jones
Executive Producer: Marc Merson
Music by: Carter Burwell*
Producer: Deborah Johnson*, Susan Solt, Marc Merson
Screenwriter: Daniel Pyne, Jeffrey Price, Peter S. Seaman

Storywriter: Laurian Leggett
Tech Info: color/sound/114 min.   Type: Comedy Feature
Date: 1991   Origin: USA
Company: Warner Bros.
Distributors/Format: Warner Bros. Home Video, Inc. (1/2")
Annotation: On his way to Hollywood, plastic surgeon Ben Stone (Fox) crashes his car into the fence of small town Southern judge Nick Nicholson (Stiers). Forced to perform community service, he falls in love with the town and Lou (Warner). Martin portrays Maddie, one of the women quilters; Winkler is Melvin, an auto mechanic who disassembles Stone's car; and Byrde is Nurse Packer who runs the hospital.

DOCTOR DETROIT

Cast: James Brown*, T.K. Carter*, Lynn Whitfield*, Pershing P. Anderson*, Jimmy/James Spinks*, Dan Aykroyd, Fran Drescher, Howard Hessman, George Furth, Donna Dixon
Director: Michael Pressman
Executive Producer: Bernie Brillstein
Music Performer: James Brown*, Lalo Schifrin, Devo
Music by: James Brown*, Lalo Schifrin, Devo
Producer: Robert K. Weiss, Bernie Brillstein
Screenwriter: Robert Boris, Carl Gottlieb, Bruce Jay Friedman
Storywriter: Bruce Jay Friedman
Tech Info: color/sound/91 min.   Type: Comedy Feature
Date: 1983   Origin: USA
Company: Black Rhino, Brillstein Company
Distributors/Format: MCA Home Video (1/2")
Annotation: Mild-mannered college professor Clifford Skridlow (Aykroyd) takes on the identity of a pimp, Dr. Detroit, in order to protect four prostitutes from a rival mob boss. Whitfield plays one of the call girls, Thelma Cleland. Carter plays Diavolo Washington, the girls' limousine driver. Anderson appears momentarily as a bodyguard. Brown plays himself, performing at a concert in honor of Dr. Detroit.

DOIN' TIME

Cast: Muhammad Ali*, Jimmy/Jimmie Walker*, John Vernon, Jeff Altman, Dey Young, Richard Mulligan, Judy Landers
Director: George Mendeluk
Producer: Bruce Mallen, George Mendeluk
Screenwriter: Franelle Silver, Ron Zwang, Dee Caruso, Peter Wilson
Storywriter: Ron Zwang
Tech Info: color/sound/80 min.   Type: Comedy Feature
Date: 1986   Origin: USA
Company: The Ladd Company
Distributors/Format: Warner Bros. Home Video, Inc. (1/2")
Annotation: Door-to-door salesman Duke Jarrett (Altman) knocks on the wrong door (the governor's wife) and ends up serving time at the John Dillinger Memorial Penitentiary. Walker plays Shaker and Ali plays himself.

DOMINICK AND EUGENE
Cast: Bill Cobbs*, Jamie Lee Curtis, Ray Liotta, Tom Hulce
Director: Robert M. Young
Music by: Trevor Jones
Producer: Marvin Minoff, Mike Farrell
Screenwriter: Alvin Sargent, Corey Blechman
Storywriter: Danny Porfirio
Tech Info: color/sound/111 min.   Type: Dramatic Feature
Date: 1988   Origin: USA
Company: Orion
Annotation: Medical student Gino Luciano (Liotta) is supported by his mildly retarded twin brother Nicky (Hulce) and must decide whether to accept an internship at Stanford that would lead to a two year separation. Cobbs plays Jesse Johnson.

DOMINOES: AN UNCENSORED JOURNEY THROUGH THE SIXTIES
Producer: John Lawrence Re, Barry A. Brown
Tech Info: mixed/sound/60 min.   Type: Documentary Feature
Date: 1988   Origin: USA
Studio: Independent
Company: Red Dawn Productions
Annotation: Jimi Hendrix, Janis Joplin, and The Dead are among the many groups represented in this portrait of the 1960s. The film includes documentary film footage and rock music from the era.

DON'T CRY, IT'S ONLY THUNDER
Cast: Roger Aaron Brown*, Tom Joyner*, Susan Saint James, Dennis Christopher
Director: Peter Werner
Executive Producer: Tsuji Shintaro, Ogisu Teruyuki, Ken Kawarai
Music by: Maurice Jarre
Producer: Walt deFaria, Tsuji Shintaro, Ogisu Teruyuki, Ken Kawarai
Screenwriter: Paul Hensler
Tech Info: color/sound/108 min.   Type: Dramatic Feature
Date: 1982   Origin: USA
Company: Sanrio
Annotation: Brian (Christopher) opposes Katherine's (Saint James) efforts to assist a group of Vietnamese war orphans, and so does the U.S. government. Brown plays Moses.

DOPPELGANGER
Cast: Sarina Grant*, Scott Lawrence*, Leslie Hope, Sally Kellerman, Drew Barrymore, Dennis Christopher, George Newbern
Director: Avi Nesher
Producer: Donald P. Borchers
Screenwriter: Avi Nesher
Tech Info: color/sound/120 min.   Type: Dramatic Feature
Date: 1993   Origin: USA
Company: Planet Productions Corporation, ITC Entertainment
Distributors/Format: Fox Home Video (1/2")
Annotation: Holly Gooding (Barrymore) has what appears to be a murderous double who is attacking her loved ones. She seduces Patrick (Newbern) who works to solve the murders. Grant plays Detective Pouget of the Los Angeles Police Department

and Lawrence is a male nurse at the sanitarium where Holly's brother is a patient.

DOUBLE MCGUFFIN, THE

Cast: Dion Pride*, Ed "Too Tall" Jones*, George Kennedy, Ernest Borgnine, Elke Sommer
Director: Joe Camp
Music Performer: Dion Pride*
Music by: Eucl Box, Eucl Box, Betty Box, Betty Box
Producer: Joe Camp
Screenwriter: Joe Camp
Storywriter: Joe Camp, Richard Baker
Tech Info: color/sound/100 min.   Type: Dramatic Feature
Date: 1979   Origin: USA
Company: Mulberry Square Productions, Inc.
Annotation: Pride leads a group of junior sleuths as they unravel a plot to assassinate the Prime Minister of Kabour. Jones is one of the terrorists planning the murder. Pride is also featured on the soundtrack.

DOUBLE TROUBLE

Cast: Adrienne-Joi Johnson*, Willie C. Carpenter*, Roddy McDowall, Peter Paul, David Paul
Director: John Paragon
Producer: Brad Krevoy, Steven Stabler
Screenwriter: Jeffrey Kerns, Kurt Wimmer, Chuck Osborne
Storywriter: Kurt Wimmer, Chuck Osborne
Tech Info: color/sound/87 min.   Type: Comedy Feature
Date: 1992   Origin: USA
Company: Motion Picture Corporation of America
Distributors/Format: Motion Picture Marketing (16mm)
Annotation: A hardworking policeman (David Paul) and his black-sheep twin (Peter Paul) are pursued by a man who plans to steal diamonds with the help of a key the "evil" twin pocketed during a burglary. Carpenter plays Michaelson.

DOWN AND OUT IN BEVERLY HILLS

Cast: Little Richard (Penniman) *, Nick Nolte, Bette Midler, Richard Dreyfuss
Director: Paul Mazursky
Producer: Paul Mazursky
Screenwriter: Paul Mazursky, Leon Capetanos
Storywriter: Rene Fauchois
Tech Info: color/sound/103 min.   Type: Comedy Feature
Date: 1986   Origin: USA
Company: Silver Screen Partners II, Touchstone
Distributors/Format: Touchstone Home Video (1/2")
Annotation: Rescued from drowning in the swimming pool of a Beverly Hills couple (Dreyfuss and Midler), a disconsolate bum (Nolte) brings startling changes to the entire household including the family dog. Little Richard performs a song, within the movie, for a birthday party.

DOWN FOR THE 'HOOD: FIVE UNFINISHED STORIES
Producer: Terry Halberg, Lisa Plendl
Tech Info: color/sound/45 min.   Type: Documentary Feature
Date: 1994   Origin: USA
Studio: Independent
Company: Continental Cablevision
Annotation: This documentary profiles five former Los Angeles gang members who were shot and permanently injured by street gang violence, and shows how living in wheelchairs has changed them.

DOWN THE DRAIN
Cast: Ken Foree*, Andrew Stevens, Don Stroud, Teri Copley, Nick DeMauro
Director: Robert C. Hughes
Music by: Rick Krizman
Producer: Ronnie Hadar
Screenwriter: Moshe Hadar
Tech Info: color/sound/106 min.   Type: Comedy Feature
Date: 1990   Origin: USA
Company: Ronnie Hadar
Distributors/Format: Trans World Entertainment (1/2")
Annotation: Vic Scalia (Stevens), a defense attorney and criminal mastermind, organizes a $20 million bank robbery. The thugs he hires attempt to double cross him but Vic outshoots them. Foree plays Buckley.

DOWNTOWN
Cast: Forest Whitaker*, Arthur/Art Evans*, Roger Aaron Brown*, Glenn Plummer*, Kimberly Scott*, Laura Williams*, Marc Robinson*, Tony T. Johnson*, Candace Mack*, David Lennon*, Ella Mae Evans*, Anthony Edwards, Penelope Ann Miller
Director: Richard Benjamin
Executive Producer: Gale Anne Hurd
Music by: Alan Silvestri
Producer: Nat Mauldin, Gale Anne Hurd, Charles H. MaGuire
Screenwriter: Nat Mauldin
Tech Info: color/sound/96 min.   Type: Comedy Feature
Date: 1990   Origin: USA
Company: Gale Anne Hurd Productions
Distributors/Format: Fox Home Video (1/2")
Archives/Format: IUB - BFC/A (1/2")
Annotation: Sgt. Dennis Curren (Whitaker) reluctantly becomes the partner of Alex Kearney (Edwards), a naive suburban cop who gets demoted to Philadelphia's roughest precinct. Jerome Sweet (Lennon) is District Commissioner. Christine Curren (Scott) is Dennis' devoted wife; Robert (Robinson), Adam (Johnson), and Amy (Mack) are the Curren children. Valentine (Plummer) is a minor criminal; Williams plays a small girl held at gunpoint.

DR. GIGGLES
Cast: Doug E. Doug*, Cliff DeYoung, Larry Drake, Holly Marie Combs, Glenn Quinn
Director: Manny Coto
Executive Producer: Jack Roe
Music by: Brian May
Producer: Stuart M. Besser, Jack Roe

Screenwriter: Manny Coto, Graeme Whifler
Tech Info: color/sound/93 min.   Type: Dramatic Feature
Date: 1992   Origin: USA
Company: Largo Entertainment, Dark Horse Entertainment
Distributors/Format: Universal Home Video (1/2")
Annotation: Dr. Evan Rendell (Drake) escapes from an insane asylum after murdering a couple of workers and proceeds to perform his maniacal operations on unsuspecting victims. Doug plays Trotter.

DRAGON: THE BRUCE LEE STORY

Cast: Forry Smith*, Nancy Kwan, Lauren Holly, Robert Wagner, Jason Scott Lee, Michael Learned
Director: Rob Cohen
Executive Producer: John Badham, Dan York
Music by: Randy Edelman
Producer: John Badham, Raffaella De Laurentiis, Charles Wang, Dan York
Screenwriter: Rob Cohen, Edward Khmara, John Raffo
Tech Info: color/sound/114 min.   Type: Dramatic Feature
Date: 1993   Origin: USA
Company: Old Code Productions Ltd.
Distributors/Format: Universal Home Video (1/2")
Annotation: Bruce Lee (Lee) is trained rigorously in Kung-Fu as a boy. In the U.S., he becomes the owner of a chain of Kung-Fu schools, and also appears on television and in movies. Smith plays the "Green Hornet."

DREAM ONE

Alternate: Nemo
Cast: Nipsey Russell*, Jason Connery, Seth Kibel, Mathilda May
Director: Arnaud Selignac
Music by: Gabriel Yared
Producer: John Boorman, Claude Nedjar
Screenwriter: Arnaud Selignac, Jean-Pierre Esquenazi, Telshe Boorman
Tech Info: color/sound/97 min.   Type: Dramatic Feature
Date: 1984   Origin: Great Britain, France
Company: NEF Diffusion, Christel, A2, Channel 4
Distributors/Format: Columbia Pictures Home Video (1/2")
Annotation: When his parents go out for the night, teenage Nemo (Connery) fantasizes travel to another planet by means of an elevator, that burrows underground. There he has a series of adventures on The Nautilus, a submarine. Russell is featured as Mr. Rip/Benjamin.

DREI LIEDER

Cast: Harry Belafonte*, Dianne Reeves*
Director: Jurgen Bottcher
Music Performer: Harry Belafonte*, Dianne Reeves*
Music by: Harry Belafonte*
Producer: Bernd Nuva
Tech Info: color/sound/28 min.   Type: Musical Short

Date: 1983   Origin: West Germany
Company: DEFA Studio Fur Documentarfilme
Annotation: Harry Belafonte and Dianne Reeves prepare for and sing three songs: "Martin Luther King," "Mathilda" and "Peace on Earth."

DRESSED TO KILL

Cast: Robert Lee Rush*, Nancy Allen, Angie Dickinson, Michael Caine, Keith Gordon
Director: Brian De Palma
Executive Producer: Samuel Z. Arkoff
Music by: Pino Donaggio
Producer: George Litto, Samuel Z. Arkoff
Screenwriter: Brian De Palma
Tech Info: color/sound/105 min.   Type: Dramatic Feature
Date: 1980   Origin: USA
Company: Samuel Z. Arkoff
Distributors/Format: Filmways Home Video (1/2")
Annotation: Kate (Dickinson), a bored, middle-aged housewife, is dissatisfied with her sex life, and at the urging of her psychiatrist (Caine) has an affair. After Kate is murdered, her son and the prostitute who discover her body track down the killer. Rush plays a hood.

DRIVE BY SHOOT

Director: Portia Cobb*
Tech Info: color/sound/12 min.   Type: Experimental Short
Date: 1993   Origin: USA
Studio: Independent
Annotation: Footage of urban America and West Africa is visually layered to create a montage of the shifting histories of the African diaspora.

DRIVING ME CRAZY

Cast: Billy Dee Williams*, Tom "Tiny" Lister Jr.*, Michelle Johnson*, Dom DeLuise, Thomas Gottschalk
Director: Jon Turteltaub
Executive Producer: Tarquin Gotch
Music by: Christophe Franke
Producer: Brad Krevoy, Steven Stabler, Tarquin Gotch
Screenwriter: Jon Turteltaub, Johnny London, David Tausik
Tech Info: color/sound/89 min.   Type: Comedy Feature
Date: 1991   Origin: USA
Company: Motion Picture Corporation of America
Distributors/Format: Motion Picture Marketing (16mm)
Annotation: Gunther (Gottschalk), an eccentric East German inventor, teams up with a parking lot attendant at his hotel, ex-car-thief Max (Williams), to help him sell his invention, a car that runs on vegetable fuel without polluting the atmosphere.

DRIVING MISS DAISY

Cast: Morgan Freeman*, Esther Rolle*, Jessica Tandy, Patti LuPone, Dan Aykroyd
Director: Bruce Beresford
Executive Producer: Jake Eberts, David Brown
Music by: Hans Zimmer
Producer: Jake Eberts, David Brown, Richard D. Zanuck, Lili Fini Zanuck
Screenwriter: Alfred Uhry

Tech Info: color/sound/99 min.   Type: Dramatic Feature
Date: 1989   Origin: USA
Company: Zanuck Company
Distributors/Format: Warner Bros. Home Video, Inc. (1/2")
Archives/Format: IUB - BFC/A (1/2")
Annotation: Hoke Colburn (Freeman) is hired by Miss Daisy's son (Aykroyd) to drive for his aging mother after she wrecks the car. Colburn and Miss Daisy (Tandy) have a tense relationship at first, but eventually build the friendship of a lifetime. Rolle plays the dedicated housekeeper.

DROP SQUAD
Cast: Spike Lee*, Paula Kelly*, Eric Payne*, Vanessa Williams*, Michael Ralph*, Afemo Omilani*, Kasi Lemmons*, Vondie Curtis-Hall*, Ving Rhames*, Charnele Brown*, Eriq LaSalle*, Nicole Powell*, Crystal Fox*, Maggie Rush*, Tico Wells*, Bill/Billy Williams*, Ray Aranha*, Fran Carter*, Donna Biscoe*, Ed Wheeler*, Leonard Thomas
Director: David C. Johnson*, Ken Kelsch
Executive Producer: Spike Lee*
Music by: Michael Bearden*
Producer: Spike Lee*, Butch Robinson*, Shelby Stone
Screenwriter: David C. Johnson*, Butch Robinson*, David Taylor*
Storywriter: David Taylor*
Tech Info: color/sound/86 min.   Type: Dramatic Feature
Date: 1994   Origin: USA
Company: 40 Acres and a Mule Filmworks
Distributors/Format: Gramercy Pictures Home Video (1/2")
Annotation: Drop Squad is an extra-legal group organized by Rocky (Curtis-Hall) to de-program black people who have committed black-on-black crime or sold out the community in some way like executive Jamison (LaSalle). Lee makes a cameo appearance.

DROP ZONE
Cast: Wesley Snipes*, Gary Busey, Yancy Butler
Director: John Badham, Roy Wagner
Executive Producer: John Badham
Music by: Hans Zimmer
Producer: John Badham, D.J. Caruso, Wallis Nicita, Lauren Lloyd
Screenwriter: John Bishop, Peter Barsocchini
Storywriter: Peter Barsocchini, Tony Griffin, Guy Manos
Tech Info: color/sound/101 min.   Type: Dramatic Feature
Date: 1994   Origin: USA
Company: Paramount
Distributors/Format: Facets Multimedia, Inc. (1/2"), Films Inc. (1/2"), Paramount Home Video (1/2")
Annotation: Snipes plays U.S. Marshal Pete Nessip, who seeks revenge after sky-diving terrorists kill his brother and kidnap a government witness.

DRUGSTORE COWBOY
Cast: Beah Richards*, Matt Dillon, Kelly Lynch, William S. Burroughs
Director: Gus Van Sant
Music by: Elliot Goldenthal
Producer: Nick Wechsler, Karen Murphy
Screenwriter: Gus Van Sant, Daniel Yost
Storywriter: James Fogle
Tech Info: color/sound/104 min.   Type: Adaptation
Date: 1989   Origin: USA
Company: Avenue Pictures
Distributors/Format: IVE Home Video (1/2")
Annotation: Richards has a cameo role as a drug counselor to Bob (Dillon) after he
goes on methadone treatment in his hometown of Portland. The story focuses on
the '70s drug scene.

DRY WHITE SEASON, A
Cast: Zakes Mokae*, Winston Ntshona*, Thoko Ntshinga*, Donald Sutherland,
Marlon Brando, Jurgen Prochnow, Janet Suzman, Susan Sarandon
Director: Euzhan Palcy
Producer: Paula Weinstein
Tech Info: color/sound/107 min.   Type: Dramatic Feature
Date: 1990   Origin: USA, Africa
Company: MGM
Distributors/Format: Facets Multimedia, Inc. (1/2"), MGM Home Video (1/2")
Archives/Format: IUB - BFC/A (1/2")
Annotation: The politics of apartheid are put into human terms in this film about a
prominent white schoolteacher (Sutherland) who is awakened to the reality of South
African justice partly through his relationship with an underground activist (Mokae).

DUKE ELLINGTON: REMINISCING IN TEMPO
Director: Robert Levi
Music Performer: Duke Ellington*
Speaker: Duke Ellington*
Tech Info: mixed/sound/89 min.   Type: Documentary Feature
Date: 1991   Origin: USA
Studio: Independent
Archives/Format: IUB - AAAMC (1/2")
Annotation: Documentary portrait examines the life of Ellington, who for 50 years led
a dance band around the world and created a lasting body of music.

DUMB AND DUMBER
Cast: Felton Perry*, Victoria Rowell*, Jim Carrey, Jeff Daniels, Lauren Holly, Karen
Duffy
Director: Peter Farrelly
Executive Producer: Gerald T. Olson, Aaron Meyerson
Music by: Todd Rundgren
Producer: Gerald T. Olson, Brad Krevoy, Steven Stabler, Charles B. Wessler, Aaron
Meyerson
Screenwriter: Bob Farrelly, Bennett Yellin
Tech Info: color/sound/106 min.   Type: Comedy Feature

Date: 1994 Origin: USA
Company: New Line, Motion Picture Corporation of America
Distributors/Format: New Line Cinema Home Video (1/2")
Annotation: Two "mentally challenged" buddies (Carrey and Daniels) put the life of a young woman's (Holly) kidnapped husband in jeopardy by unwittingly interfering with the ransom transaction to his captors. Perry plays Detective Dale and Rowell, an athletic beauty.

DYING YOUNG
Cast: Adrienne-Joi Johnson*, Campbell Scott, Colleen Dewhurst, Vincent D'Onofrio, Julia Roberts
Director: Joel Schumacher
Producer: Kevin McCormick, Sally Field
Screenwriter: Richard Friedenberg
Tech Info: color/sound/100 min.   Type: Dramatic Feature
Date: 1991 Origin: USA
Company: Fox, Fogwood Films
Distributors/Format: Fox Home Video (1/2")
Annotation: Hillary O'Neil (Roberts) lands a job as a caretaker for Victor Geddes (Scott), a young man with leukemia. Although their personalities are completely mismatched, they fall in love. Johnson plays Shauna.

EARTH DAY SPECIAL, THE
Cast: Quincy Jones*, Morgan Freeman*, Fresh Prince *, Bill Cosby*, Dan Aykroyd, Bette Midler
Director: Dwight Hemion
Executive Producer: Armyan Bernstein
Producer: Armyan Bernstein, Richard Baskin, Paul Witt
Speaker: Earvin "Magic" Johnson*
Tech Info: color/sound/95 min.   Type: Documentary Feature
Date: 1990 Origin: USA
Company: Warner Bros.
Distributors/Format: Warner Bros. Home Video, Inc. (1/2")
Annotation: In celebration of Earth Day, celebrities perform in environmentally-aware vignettes.

EARTH GIRLS ARE EASY
Cast: Damon Wayans*, T.C. Diamond*, Tita Omeze*, Geena Davis, Jeff Goldblum, Jim Carrey
Director: Julien Temple
Music by: Nile Rodgers*
Producer: Tony Garnett
Screenwriter: Julie Brown
Tech Info: mixed/sound/100 min.   Type: Comedy Feature
Date: 1988 Origin: USA
Company: Kestrel Films, Vestron Pictures
Annotation: Manicurist Valerie (Davis) befriends three aliens whose UFO crash lands in her backyard pool. Mac (Goldblum), Zeebo (Wayans), and Wiploc (Carrey) are the adventurous aliens whose main interests are Earth women.

EARTH, WIND AND FIRE IN CONCERT

Director: Michael Schultz*
Producer: Michael Schultz*, Maurice White*, Gloria Schultz*
Tech Info: color/sound/58 min.   Type: Concert Feature
Date: 1982   Origin: USA
Company: Crystallite Productions
Annotation: Earth, Wind and Fire perform their most memorable hits including "Shining Star" and "Sing a Song."

EDDIE AND THE CRUISERS

Cast: Harry Caesar*, Howard Johnson*, Rufus Harley*, Ellen Barkin, Tom Berenger
Director: Martin Davidson
Executive Producer: Rich Irvine, James L. Stewart
Music Performer: Bill Goodson
Music by: Kenny Vance, John Cafferty
Producer: Joseph Brooks, Robert K. Lifton, Rich Irvine, James L. Stewart
Screenwriter: Martin Davidson, Arlene Davidson
Storywriter: P.F. Kluge
Tech Info: color/sound/95 min.   Type: Dramatic Feature
Date: 1983   Origin: USA
Company: Aurora, Embassy Pictures
Distributors/Format: Aurora/Embassy Home Video (1/2")
Annotation: Johnson and Harley are both featured as sax players and members of a legendary 1960s rock band whose leader reportedly died in a car accident. A television reporter tries to determine if he is actually still alive as rumors suggest.

EDDIE MURPHY DELIRIOUS

Director: Ron Taylor*, Bruce Gowers
Music Performer: Kendall McCarthy*, Bus Boys *
Producer: Eddie Murphy*, Robert D. Wachs, Richard Tienken
Speaker: Eddie Murphy*
Tech Info: color/sound/70 min.   Type: Concert Feature
Date: 1983   Origin: USA
Company: Gulf & Western
Distributors/Format: Paramount Home Video (1/2")
Archives/Format: IUB - BFC/A (1/2")
Annotation: Murphy appears in person at Constitution Hall in Washington, D.C., on his 18-cities tour. His stand-up comedy act contains impersonations, vignettes and adult-oriented material.

EDDIE MURPHY RAW

Director: Robert Townsend*
Producer: Keenen Ivory Wayans*, Robert D. Wachs
Screenwriter: Eddie Murphy*, Keenen Ivory Wayans*
Speaker: Eddie Murphy*
Tech Info: color/sound/90 min.   Type: Concert Feature
Date: 1987   Origin: USA
Company: Eddie Murphy* Production
Distributors/Format: Paramount Home Video (1/2")
Archives/Format: IU BFC/A (1/2")
Annotation: A controversial comedian, Murphy entertains his audience with unique

impersonations and language often as raw as the title.

ELLIOT FAUMAN, PH.D.
Cast: John Canada Terrell*, Shelley Berman, Randy Dreyfuss, Jean Kasem, Támara Williams
Director: Ric Klass
Music by: Roger Trefousse
Producer: Ric Klass
Screenwriter: Ric Klass
Tech Info: color/sound/86 min.　　　Type: Comedy Feature
Date: 1990　Origin: USA
Company: Ventcap, Double Helix
Distributors/Format: Taurus Home Video (1/2")
Annotation: Elliot Fauman (Dreyfuss), a psychologist studying human sexuality, becomes the manager of an escort service through a bizarre set of circumstances. Terrell plays Gene.

EMANON
Cast: Jay Scorpio*, Stuart Paul, Cheryl M. Lynn, Patrick Wright, Jeremy Miller
Director: Stuart Paul
Music by: Lennie Niehaus
Producer: Hank Paul, Dorothy Koster-Paul
Screenwriter: Stuart Paul
Tech Info: color/sound/94 min.　　　Type: 'Dramatic Feature
Date: 1987　Origin: USA
Company: Paul
Annotation: Jason Ballentine (Miller) is a wealthy child who meets a skid-row bum (Paul) in New York City who has no name and who may be Christ returned to earth. Scorpio plays Single Wing.

EMPIRE STRIKES BACK, THE
Cast: James Earl Jones*, Billy Dee Williams*, Mark Hamill, Harrison Ford,
Director: Irvin Kershner
Executive Producer: George Lucas
Music Performer: John Williams
Music by: John Williams
Producer: George Lucas, Gary Kurtz
Screenwriter: Lawrence Kasdan, Leigh Brackett
Storywriter: George Lucas
Tech Info: color/sound/124 min.　　　Type: Dramatic Feature
Date: 1980　Origin: USA
Company: Lucas Films, Ltd.
Distributors/Format: CBS/Fox Home Video (1/2")
Annotation: Williams is Lando Calrissian who leaves the comfort and security of his station as a governing administrator to help Luke Skywalker (Hamill) and his old flying buddy Hans Solo (Ford) triumph over Darth Vader. Jones is again Vader's voice in this sequel to STAR WARS.

END OF AUGUST, THE
Cast: Roy Poole*, Lilia Skala, Sally Sharp, David Marshall Grant, Kathleen Widdoes
Director: Bob Graham
Executive Producer: Martin Jurow
Music by: Shirley Walker
Producer: Sally Sharp, Warren Jacobson, Martin Jurow
Screenwriter: Eula Seaton, Leon Heller, Anna Thomas, Gregory Nava
Storywriter: Kate Chopin
Tech Info: color/sound/105 min.   Type: Dramatic Feature
Date: 1982   Origin: USA
Company: Quartet
Annotation: Edna (Sharp) is a married woman trying to become her own person in turn-of-the-century New Orleans, in this adaptation of Kate Chopin's "The Awakening." Poole plays Dr. Mandalet.

END OF INNOCENCE, THE
Cast: Madge Sinclair*, Dyan Cannon
Tech Info: color/sound/102 min.   Type: Dramatic Feature
Date: 1991   Origin: USA
Company: OPV Productions
Distributors/Format: Skouras (1/2")
Annotation: Stephanie Lewis (Cannon) grows up with overbearing parents, and as an adult enters a series of bad relationships, until she has a breakdown, enters therapy in a sanatorium, and learns to live her own life. Sinclair plays Dora Bowlin, psychiatric nurse in the sanitarium.

END OF THE LINE
Cast: Michael Beach*, Mary Steenburgen, Wilford Brimley, Levon Helm
Director: Jay Russell
Executive Producer: Mary Steenburgen
Music by: Andy Summers
Producer: Mary Steenburgen, Peter Newman, Lewis Allen, Walker Stuart
Screenwriter: Jay Russell, John Wohlbruck
Tech Info: color/sound/105 min.   Type: Dramatic Feature
Date: 1988   Origin: USA
Company: Guadalupe-Hudson, Sundance Institute
Distributors/Format: Orion Home Video (1/2")
Annotation: Set in Clifford, Arkansas, a quiet rural area, the film examines the consequences when Southland Railroad Yard, the major company in town, is taken over by the larger company and everyone is fired. Beach plays Alvin.

END, THE
Cast: Frank McRae*, Harry Caesar*, Queenie Smith*, Burt Reynolds, Dom DeLuise, Sally Field
Director: Burt Reynolds
Executive Producer: Hank Moonjean
Music by: Paul Williams
Producer: Lawrence Gordon, Hank Moonjean
Screenwriter: Jerry Belson
Tech Info: color/sound/100 min.   Type: Comedy Feature

Date: 1978   Origin: USA
Company: United Artists
Distributors/Format: United Artists Home Video (1/2")
Annotation: Sonny Lawson (Reynolds) learns he will die in three months and tries to commit suicide. Caesar plays a hospital orderly.

ENDLESS LOVE

Cast: Don Murray, Shirley Knight, Brooke Shields, Martin Hewitt
Director: Franco Zeffirelli
Executive Producer: Keith Barish
Music Performer: Lionel Ritchie*
Music by: Jonathan Tunick
Producer: Keith Barish, Dyson Lovell
Screenwriter: Judith Rascoe
Storywriter: Scott Spencer
Tech Info: color/sound/115 min.   Type: Dramatic Feature
Date: 1981   Origin: USA
Company: Universal
Distributors/Format: Universal Home Video (1/2")
Annotation: Lionel Richie wrote the Oscar nominated title song for this teenage love gone bad movie.

ENEMY MINE

Cast: Louis Gossett Jr.*, Bumper Robinson*, Dennis Quaid, Brion James, Carolyn McCormick
Director: Wolfgang Peterson
Executive Producer: Stanley O'Toole
Music Performer: Maurice Jarre
Music by: Maurice Jarre
Producer: Stanley O'Toole, Stephen Friedman
Screenwriter: Edward Khmara
Storywriter: Barry Longyear
Tech Info: color/sound/108 min.   Type: Dramatic Feature
Date: 1985   Origin: USA
Company: King's Road Entertainment
Distributors/Format: Fox Home Video (1/2")
Annotation: Alien space traveler Jerry Dracman (Gossett) is stranded on a planet with Willis A. Davidge (Quaid). Although they are enemies, they must work together to survive. As time passes they become friends and when Jerry "becomes pregnant" and dies, Davidge assumes responsibility for the baby, Zammis (Robinson).

ENEMY TERRITORY

Cast: Ray Parker Jr.*, Frances Foster*, Stacey Dash*, Tiger Haynes*, Tony Todd*, Robert Lee Rush*, Deon Richmond*, Gary Frank, Jan-Michael Vincent
Director: Peter Manoogian
Music Performer: Boogie Boys *
Music by: Sam Winans*, Richard Koz Kosinski
Producer: Cynthia DePaula, Tim Kincaid
Screenwriter: Stuart M. Kaminsky, Bobby Liddell
Tech Info: color/sound/89 min.   Type: Dramatic Feature

Date: 1987   Origin: USA
Company: Millennial Films Production
Distributors/Format: Empire (16mm)
Annotation: A violent street gang, the Vampires, focus their criminal activities on a small group of citizens trapped in a New York City project. Todd plays "The Count"; Rush the "psycho"; Foster is Elva Briggs; Dash, Toni Briggs; Parker is Jackson and Haynes is Barton.

ENEMY UNSEEN

Cast: Stack Pierce*, Ken Gampu*, Sam Ntsinyi*, Vernon G. Wells, Angela O'Neill
Director: Elmo DeWitt
Screenwriter: Greg Latter
Tech Info: color/sound/90 min.   Type: Dramatic Feature
Date: 1991   Origin: USA
Company: AIP
Distributors/Format: AIP Home Video (1/2")
Annotation: Josh (Pierce) and Malanga (Gampu) are members of a team which rescues a young woman from an African tribe that sacrifices young virgins to crocodiles. Ntsinyi plays the tribe's Shaman.

ENEMY WITHIN, THE

Cast: Forest Whitaker*, Lisa Summerour*, Willie Norwood Jr.*, Sam Waterston, Jason Robards
Tech Info: color/sound   Type: Dramatic Feature
Date: 1994   Origin: USA
Annotation: Colonel MacKenzie Casey (Whitaker) uncovers a home-grown plot to remove the President (Waterston) and take over the U.S. government. At great risk to his family, wife Jean (Summerour) and son Todd (Norwood), Casey exposes his former boss (Robards) and outwits the traitorous politicians.

ENTERTAINERS, THE

Series: Ebony/Jet Guide to Black Excellence
Speaker: Bill Cosby*, Maya Angelou*, Charles S. Dutton*
Tech Info: color/sound/38 min.   Type: Documentary Short
Date: 1991   Origin: USA
Distributors/Format: Filmic Archives (1/2")
Annotation: African Americans in the entertainment industry are profiled, e.g. Bill Cosby, Maya Angelou and actor Charles Dutton.

ENTREPRENEURS, THE

Series: Ebony/Jet Guide to Black Excellence
Speaker: Oprah Winfrey*, John H. Johnson*, Joshua I. Smith*
Tech Info: color/sound/35 min.   Type: Documentary Short
Date: 1991   Origin: USA
Distributors/Format: Facets Multimedia, Inc. (1/2"), Public Media Video (1/2")
Annotation: African Americans who built their own businesses are profiled.

EQUINOX

Cast: Tyra Ferrell*, Fred Ward, Marisa Tomei, Matthew Modine, Lara Flynn Boyle
Director: Alan Rudolph
Executive Producer: Nicolas Stiliadis, Syd Cappe, Sandy Stern
Producer: David Blocker, Nicolas Stiliadis, Syd Cappe, Sandy Stern
Screenwriter: Alan Rudolph
Tech Info: color/sound/108 min.   Type: Dramatic Feature
Date: 1993   Origin: USA
Company: Rain City, Inc.
Distributors/Format: IRS Releasing (16mm)
Annotation: Freddy and Henry are twins separated at birth (both characters played by Modine). They stand to inherent $1 million from their natural mother after she dies. Instead, Freddy gets shot and Henry's whole life changes. Ferrell plays Sonya Kirk the morgue worker and aspiring writer who discovers the inheritance letter in the dead woman's pocket.

ERIK THE VIKING

Cast: Eartha Kitt*, John Cleese, Mickey Rooney, Tim Robbins, Gary Cady, Imogen Stubbs
Director: Terry Jones
Executive Producer: Terry Glinwood
Music by: Neil Innes
Producer: Terry Glinwood, John Goldstone
Screenwriter: Terry Jones
Storywriter: Terry Jones
Tech Info: color/sound/103 min.   Type: Dramatic Feature
Date: 1989   Origin: Great Britain
Studio: Independent
Company: John Goldstone, Prominent, Svensk
Annotation: Erik the Viking (Robbins), tired of raping and pillaging, visits the soothsayer Freya (Kitt) and she tells him how to stop the destruction of the dark, war-plagued Age of Ragnarok.

ESCAPE ARTIST, THE

Cast: Harry Caesar*, Hal Williams*, Teri Garr, Raul Julia, Griffin O'Neal, Desiderio Arnaz
Director: Caleb Deschanel
Executive Producer: Francis Ford Coppola, Fred Roos
Music by: Georges Delerue
Producer: Francis Ford Coppola, Fred Roos, Doug Claybourne, Buck Houghton
Screenwriter: Melissa Mathison, Stephen Zito
Tech Info: color/sound/93 min.   Type: Dramatic Feature
Date: 1982   Origin: USA
Company: Zoetrope
Distributors/Format: Orion Home Video (1/2"), Warner Bros. Home Video, Inc. (1/2")
Annotation: Danny Masters (O'Neal), the son of a great escape artist, steals the wallet of Stu Quinones (Julia), the corrupt mayor's son, and is set upon by thugs. Caesar plays the sax player.

ESCAPE FROM ALCATRAZ
Cast: Danny Glover*, Paul Benjamin*, Clint Eastwood, Fred Ward, Jack Thibeau, Patrick McGoohan, Roberts Blossom
Director: Don Siegel
Executive Producer: Robert Daley
Producer: Don Siegel, Robert Daley
Screenwriter: Richard Tuggle
Tech Info: color/sound/112 min.   Type: Dramatic Feature
Date: 1979   Origin: USA
Company: Paramount
Distributors/Format: Paramount Home Video (1/2")
Annotation: Frank Morris (Eastwood), an Alcatraz inmate, plans the impossible escape. With the Anglin Brothers (Thibeau and Ward) English (Benjamin), who's doing time for murder, and others, Morris exits Alcatraz Island and is never seen again. Glover has an uncredited role.

ESCAPE FROM NEW YORK
Cast: Isaac Hayes*, Donald Pleasence, Kurt Russell, Season Hubley, Ernest Borgnine, Adrienne Barbeau, Lee Van Cleef
Director: John Carpenter
Music by: John Carpenter, Alan Howarth
Producer: Debra Hill, Larry Franco
Screenwriter: John Carpenter, Nick Castle
Tech Info: color/sound/99 min.   Type: Dramatic Feature
Date: 1981   Origin: USA
Company: Avco Embassy
Annotation: In this futuristic thriller, Snake Plissken (Russell), an ex-war hero now a convict, is sent to rescue the President (Pleasence) from a plane crash in New York City. The city has become a fortress of criminals and madmen. Hayes is cast as the "Duke of New York."

ESCAPE FROM...SURVIVAL ZONE
Cast: Ivan Rogers*, Terence Ford, Paris Jefferson, Raymond Johnson, Truce Mitchell
Tech Info: color/sound/85 min.   Type: Dramatic Feature
Date: 1992   Origin: USA
Company: Living Spirit Pictures
Distributors/Format: AIP Home Video (1/2")
Annotation: In this science fiction drama, Lewis T. Holden (Rogers) and Sean McBain (Mitchell) are paranoid ex-marines who run a survival camp. McBain goes insane, kills Holden and two of the people attending the camp before being killed himself.

ESCAPE TO ATHENA
Cast: Richard Roundtree*, Roger Moore, Telly Savalas
Director: George P. Cosmatos
Music by: Lalo Schifrin
Producer: Jack Wiener, David Niven Jr.
Screenwriter: Richard S. Lochte, Edward Anhalt
Storywriter: George P. Cosmatos, Richard S. Lochte
Tech Info: color/sound/125 min.   Type: Dramatic Feature

Date: 1979   Origin: USA
Company: Grade
Distributors/Format: CBS/Fox Home Video (1/2"), Associated Film (16mm)
Annotation: Maj. Otto Hecht (Moore) is a German officer running a Greek POW camp during WWII. He helps a group of Allied soldiers including Nat (Roundtree) escape.

ETHNIC NOTIONS

Director: Marlon T. Riggs*
Music Performer: Mary Watkins
Music by: Mary Watkins
Narrator: Esther Rolle*
Producer: Marlon T. Riggs*
Speaker: Barbara Christian*, Leni Sloan*, Pat Turner*, Erskine Peters*, Carlton Moss*, Jan Faulkner*, Larry Levine, George Fredrickson
Tech Info: mixed/sound/56 min.   Type: Television Documentary
Date: 1986   Origin: USA
Studio: Independent
Company: KOED TV
Distributors/Format: California Newsreel (1/2"), Signifyin' Works (1/2")
Archives/Format: IUB - BFC/A (1/2")
Annotation: The film documents 100 years of racist media caricatures: "Mammy," "Sambo," "Picaninny," "Coon," "Jim Crow," and "Uncle Tom," are all depicted in a historical survey covering the pre-civil war origins of many popular caricatures to manifestations in the 1980s. The Aunt Jemima image of the 1980s challenges any assumption that racist stereotypes have disappeared.

EUBIE

Cast: Gregory Hines*, Leslie Doolkery*, Maurice Hines*, Lynnie Godfrey*, David Jackson*, Donna Ingram*, Mel Johnson Jr.*, Alaina Reed*, Terri Barrell*, Jeffrey Vithenson
Director: Julianne Boyd
Tech Info: color/sound/85 min.   Type: Musical Feature
Date: 1981   Origin: USA
Studio: Independent
Company: Group W Cable Productions/Warner Communications
Annotation: A video transfer of the popular Broadway musical showcases many of Eubie Blake's best known songs including "The Charleston Rag" and "In Honeysuckle Time."

EVE OF DESTRUCTION

Cast: Gregory Hines*, Tim Russ*, Renee Soutendijk, Kurt Fuller, Michael Greene
Director: Duncan Gibbins
Executive Producer: Robert Cort, Rick Finkelstein, Melinda Jason
Music by: Phillipe Sadde
Producer: Robert Cort, David Madden, Rick Finkelstein, Melinda Jason
Screenwriter: Duncan Gibbins, Yale Udoff
Tech Info: color/sound/101 min.   Type: Dramatic Feature

Date: 1991   Origin: USA
Company: Interscope, Nelson Entertainment Group
Distributors/Format: Orion Home Video (1/2")
Annotation: An anti-terrorist expert Jim McQuade (Hines) is assigned by the Pentagon to help a female scientist track down her android double, which has blown a fuse and is now uncovering her secret past.

EVENING WITH RAY CHARLES, AN

Music Conductor: Sid Feller
Music Performer: Ray Charles*, ITV Concert Orchestra
Tech Info: color/sound/50 min.   Type: Concert Short
Date: 1981   Origin: Canada
Company: MCA, Universal
Distributors/Format: MCA/Universal Home Video (1/2")
Annotation: Ray Charles performs many of his favorite hits at the Jubilee Auditorium in Edmonton, Canada.

EVIL THAT MEN DO, THE

Cast: Joe Seneca*, Raymond St. Jacques*, Jose Ferrer, Charles Bronson, Theresa Saldana
Director: J. Lee Thompson
Music by: Ken Thorne
Producer: Pancho Kohner
Screenwriter: David Lee Henry, John Crowther
Storywriter: R. Lance Hill
Tech Info: color/sound/90 min.   Type: Dramatic Feature
Date: 1984   Origin: USA
Company: TriStar
Distributors/Format: TriStar Pictures Inc. (1/2")
Annotation: Bronson plays Holland, an assassin who exterminates the masterminds of a South American fascist regime supported by the U.S. Government. St. Jacques plays Randolph, one of the fascist henchmen; Seneca is Santiago, a friend of Holland.

EXIT TO EDEN

Cast: Iman *, Tanya Reed*, Dan Aykroyd, Stuart Wilson, Dana Delaney, Rosie O'Donnell, Paul Mercurio
Director: Garry Marshall
Executive Producer: Edward Milkis, Nick Abdo
Music by: Patrick Doyle
Producer: Garry Marshall, Edward Milkis, Alexandra Rose, Nick Abdo
Screenwriter: Deborah Amelon, Bob Brunner
Tech Info: color/sound/116 min.   Type: Comedy Feature
Date: 1994   Origin: USA
Company: Savoy Pictures
Distributors/Format: Savoy Home Video (1/2")
Annotation: Diamond smugglers Nina (Iman) and Omar (Wilson) are accidentally caught on film by Elliot Slater (Mercurio), a photo journalist. They follow him to a hedonistic resort run by Lisa Emerson (Delany) where the guests pay lots of money to act out their sexual fantasies. Reid plays Naomi, one of the resort's barely clad staff.

EXORICIST III: THE LEGION
Cast: Grand L. Bush*, Patrick Ewing*, George C. Scott, Ryan Paul Amick, Nicol Williamson
Director: William Peter Blatty
Executive Producer: Joe Roth, James Robinson
Music by: Barry Devorzon
Producer: Joe Roth, Carter DeHaven, James Robinson
Screenwriter: William Peter Blatty
Storywriter: William Peter Blatty
Tech Info: color/sound/105 min.   Type: Dramatic Feature
Date: 1990   Origin: USA
Company: Moretan Creek
Distributors/Format: Fox Home Video (1/2")
Annotation: Police Lieutenant Kinderman (Scott) has been haunted by the death of his friend, Father Damien, coupled with nightmares that his friend is in an asylum of dead people. Ewing plays the Angel of Death in the asylum.

EXPLORERS
Cast: Meshach Taylor*, River Phoenix, Ethan Hawke, Jason Presson
Director: Joe Dante
Executive Producer: Michael Finnell
Music by: Jerry Goldsmith
Producer: Edward S. Feldman, Michael Finnell, David Bombyk
Screenwriter: Eric Luke
Tech Info: color/sound/109 min.   Type: Dramatic Feature
Date: 1985   Origin: USA
Company: Paramount
Distributors/Format: Paramount Home Video (1/2")
Annotation: Two children, Ben (Hawke) and Wolfgang (Phoenix), create a spaceship and visit aliens who have been communicating with them. Taylor plays Gordon Miller.

EXTERMINATOR II
Cast: Reggie Rock Bythewood*, Thomas Lee Wright*, Paul Bates*, Frankie Faison*, Mario Van Peebles*, Robert Ginty, John Turturro
Director: Mark Buntzman, William Sachs
Music by: David Spear
Producer: Mark Buntzman, William Sachs
Screenwriter: Mark Buntzman, William Sachs
Tech Info: color/sound/89 min.   Type: Dramatic Feature
Date: 1984   Origin: USA
Company: Cannon
Distributors/Format: Cannon Home Video (1/2")
Annotation: A sequel to THE EXTERMINATOR (1980) sees Ginty return as the Vietnam veteran, Johnny Eastland, who has gotten fed up with the "sickos" in society. A gang leader with delusions of grandeur, "X" (Van Peebles), leads his sadistic followers through the streets of New York City randomly torturing and murdering.

EXTERMINATOR, THE
Cast: Michele Harrell*, Antonia French*, Dwouane Wilson*, Robert Ginty, Steve
James
Director: James Glickenhaus
Music by: Joe Renzetti
Producer: Mark Buntzman
Screenwriter: James Glickenhaus
Tech Info: color/sound/101 min.   Type: Dramatic Feature
Date: 1982   Origin: USA
Company: Avco Embassy
Annotation: Best friends John (Ginty) and Michael (James) survive the days of
Vietnam only to return to crime and violence on the streets of New York City. After a
mugging paralyzes Michael, John decides to "exterminate" criminals. Harrell appears
as Michael's wife.

EXTRA CHANGE
Cast: Amini Nuru-Jeter*, Pernell King*
Director: Carmen Coustaut*
Music by: Sais Kamulidiin*
Screenwriter: Carmen Coustaut*
Storywriter: Carmen Coustaut*
Tech Info: color/sound/28 min.   Type: Dramatic Short
Date: 1987   Origin: USA
Studio: Independent
Distributors/Format: Third World Newsreel (1/2")
Annotation: The film explores the consequences of peer pressure and low
self-esteem on a 12 year old girl. The film is based on a short story written by
Coustaut in 1972.

EXTREME PREJUDICE
Cast: Larry B. Scott*, Dan Tullis Jr.*, Tom "Tiny" Lister Jr.*, Nick Nolte, Powers
Boothe, Maria Conchita Alonso
Director: Walter Hill
Executive Producer: Mario Kassar, Andrew Vajna
Music by: Jerry Goldsmith
Producer: Buzz Feitshans, Mario Kassar, Andrew Vajna
Screenwriter: Deric Washburn, Harry Kleiner
Storywriter: John Milius, Fred Rexer
Tech Info: color/sound/104 min.   Type: Dramatic Feature
Date: 1987   Origin: USA
Company: Carolco, TriStar
Distributors/Format: International Video Entertainment (35mm; 1/2")
Annotation: Scott plays Sgt. Charles Biddle and Tullis is Sgt. Luther Fry in this
border drama with Nolte as Texas Ranger Jack Benteen attempting to thwart a
para-military group backed by the C.I.A. Lister appears as Monday, Bailey's (Boothe)
bodyguard.

EXTREMITIES

Cast: Alfre Woodard*, Farrah Fawcett, James Russo, Diana Scarwid
Director: Robert M. Young
Producer: Bert Sugarman
Screenwriter: William Mastrosimone
Tech Info: color/sound/89 min.   Type: Dramatic Feature
Date: 1986   Origin: USA
Company: Atlantic Entertainment Group
Distributors/Format: Paramount Home Video (1/2")
Annotation: Marjorie (Fawcett) is sexually assaulted by a stranger (Russo); however, the tables are turned when she plots to get revenge. Woodard plays Marjorie's lawyer.

EYEWITNESS

Alternate: Janitor, The
Cast: Morgan Freeman*, Christopher Plummer, James Woods, Sigourney Weaver, William Hurt, Pamela Reed
Director: Peter Yates
Music by: Stanley Silverman
Producer: Peter Yates
Screenwriter: Steve Tesich
Tech Info: color/sound/108 min.   Type: Dramatic Feature
Date: 1981   Origin: USA
Company: Fox
Distributors/Format: Fox Home Video (1/2")
Annotation: Daryll Deever (Hurt) is a janitor who is so infatuated with television newscaster Tony Sokolow (Weaver) that he pretends to know something about a murder in his building so she'll interview him. Freeman plays Lt. Black.

F/X

Cast: Roscoe Orman*, Angela Bassett*, Brian Dennehy, Diane Venora, Bryan Brown, Jerry Orbach
Director: Robert Mandel
Executive Producer: Michael Peyser
Music by: Bill Conti, Harry Rabinowitz
Producer: Michael Peyser, Dodi Fayed, Jack Wiener
Screenwriter: Robert T. Megginson, Gregory Fleeman
Tech Info: color/sound/107 min.   Type: Dramatic Feature
Date: 1986   Origin: USA
Company: Orion
Annotation: Bassett appears as a television reporter in this suspense thriller about a movie special effects man (Brown) who is hired by government agents to fake the death of a mafia kingpin scheduled to testify against the "family." Orman plays Captain Wallenger.

FABULOUS BAKER BOYS, THE

Cast: Albert Hall*, Beau Bridges, Jeff Bridges, Xander Berkeley, Michelle Pfeiffer, Ellie Raab
Director: Steve Kloves
Executive Producer: Sydney Pollack
Music by: Dave Grusin

Producer: Sydney Pollack, Paula Weinstein, Mark Rosenberg, William Finnegan
Screenwriter: Steve Kloves
Tech Info: color/sound/114 min.   Type: Dramatic Feature
Date: 1989   Origin: USA
Company: Gladden, Mirage
Distributors/Format: Fox Home Video (1/2")
Annotation: Jack (Jeff Bridges) and Frank (Beau Bridges) Baker are lounge pianists who decide to liven up the act with a female vocalist, Susie Diamond (Pfeiffer). Hall plays Henry.

FACES IN A FAMINE
Producer: Robert Lieberman
Tech Info: color/sound/51 min.   Type: Documentary Feature
Date: 1985   Origin: USA
Studio: Independent
Company: Ithaca Filmworks
Annotation: The film documents the Ethiopian drought through a visual survey of the main characters in the tragedy: starving citizens, relief workers, journalists and disaster groupies.

FACING THE FACADE
Director: Jerald B. Harkness*
Narrator: Avery Brooks*
Tech Info: color/sound/55 min.   Type: Documentary Feature
Date: 1994   Origin: USA
Studio: Independent
Distributors/Format: Cinema Guild (1/2")
Annotation: Harkness documents the experiences of black students on a predominately white campus at Indiana University in Bloomington, Indiana.

FADE TO BLACK
Director: Tony Cokes*, Donald Trammel
Producer: Tony Cokes*
Screenwriter: Tony Cokes*
Speaker: Malcolm X *
Storywriter: Donald Bogle*, Donald Trammel
Tech Info: color/sound/33 min.   Type: Experimental Short
Date: 1991   Origin: USA
Studio: Independent
Distributors/Format: Third World Newsreel (1/2")
Annotation: The film re-examines racism in every day life. Juxtaposing archival movie footage with quotations in the form of text and voice-overs, the filmmakers explore the ideological implications of the rhetoric between blacks and whites.

FALCON AND THE SNOWMAN, THE
Cast: Dorian Harewood*, Sean Penn, Timothy Hutton, Lori Singer, David Suchet, Pat Hingle
Director: John G. Schlesinger
Music by: Pat Methany
Producer: Gabriel Katzka, John Daly, John G. Schlesinger
Screenwriter: Steven Zaillian
Storywriter: Robert Lindsey

Tech Info: color/sound/131 min.   Type: Dramatic Feature
Date: 1984   Origin: USA
Company: Orion
Distributors/Format: Vestron/Orion Home Video (1/2")
Annotation: Based on a true story, the film is about Gene (Harewood) and Chris (Hutton), co-workers at a high security federal office. The pair eventually become disillusioned by the United States' involvement in the Vietnamese War and decide to sell secrets to the Soviet Union.

FALLING DOWN

Cast: Kimberly Scott*, Vondie Curtis-Hall*, Robert Duvall, Rachel Ticotin, Barbara Hershey, Michael Douglas
Director: Joel Schumacher
Executive Producer: Arnon Milchan
Music by: James Newton Howard*
Producer: Timothy Harris, Herschel Weingrod, Arnold Kopelson, Arnon Milchan
Screenwriter: Ebbe Roe Smith
Tech Info: color/sound/115 min.   Type: Dramatic Feature
Date: 1993   Origin: USA
Company: Arnold Kopelson Productions
Distributors/Format: Warner Bros. Home Video, Inc. (1/2")
Annotation: A man (Douglas) pushed to the edge of sanity after losing his defense industry job goes on a killing spree in Los Angeles. Curtis-Hall plays the "Not Economically Viable Man."

FAME

Cast: Irene Cara*, Debbie Allen*, Gene Anthony Ray*, Laura Dean, Anne Meara, Barry Miller
Director: Alan Parker
Music by: Michael Gore
Producer: Alan Marshall, David DeSilva
Screenwriter: Christopher Gore
Tech Info: color/sound/133 min.   Type: Musical Feature
Date: 1980   Origin: USA
Company: MGM
Distributors/Format: MGM Home Video (1/2")
Annotation: Leroy Johnson (Ray) is a talented dancer at New York's High School of Performing Arts whose English teacher (Meara) refuses to allow him to graduate an illiterate. Cara plays Coco, a singer struggling to become a Broadway success. Several unidentified black performers appear but are not credited.

FAMILY ACROSS THE SEA

Series: African American Perspectives
Director: Domino Boulware*
Producer: Tim Carrier
Screenwriter: Tim Carrier
Tech Info: color/sound/56 min.   Type: Television Documentary

Date: 1990   Origin: USA
Studio: South Carolina ETV
Distributors/Format: California Newsreel (1/2"), Modern Educational Video
Network/Churchill Films (1/2")
Archives/Format: IUB - AAAMC (1/2")
Annotation: The film traces the connection between the Gullah people of South
Carolina's Sea Islands and the people of Sierra Leone, Africa.

FAMILY BUSINESS
Cast: Willie C. Carpenter*, Matthew Broderick, Dustin Hoffman, Sean Connery,
Rosana DeSoto
Director: Sidney Lumet
Executive Producer: Burtt Harris, Jennifer Ogden
Music by: Cy Coleman, Sonny Kompanek
Producer: Lawrence Gordon, Burtt Harris, Jennifer Ogden
Screenwriter: Vincent Patrick
Tech Info: color/sound/114 min.   Type: Comedy Feature
Date: 1989   Origin: USA
Company: TriStar, Regency, Gordon
Distributors/Format: TriStar Pictures Inc. (1/2")
Annotation: Three generations (Connery, Hoffman, Broderick) of a thieving family
plot to steal test tubes containing gene-splicing plasma. The youngest bungles the
job and the older two take the fall. Carpenter plays "Caper" cop.

FANNIE'S FILM
Series: Invisible Women
Director: Fronza Woods*
Producer: Fronza Woods*, Women's Interart Center *
Speaker: Fannie Drayton*
Tech Info: color/sound/15 min.   Type: Experimental Short
Date: 1981   Origin: USA
Studio: Independent
Company: Smith-Woods Productions
Annotation: Woods profiles a lower-income black woman, Mrs. Fannie Drayton, and
her life as a maid for a primarily white establishment.

FAR OUT MAN
Cast: Rae Dawn Chong*, Michael Winslow*, Reynaldo Rey*, Tina Fava*, Tommy
Chong, Martin Mull, Judd Nelson
Director: Tommy Chong
Executive Producer: Paul Hertzberg
Music Performer: Kool Moe Dee *, Tommy Chong, Samantha Fox
Music by: Jay Chattaway
Producer: Lisa Hansen, Paul Hertzberg
Screenwriter: Tommy Chong
Tech Info: color/sound/85 min.   Type: Comedy Feature
Date: 1990   Origin: USA
Company: Paul Hertzberg-Lisa Hansen
Distributors/Format: CineTel Home Video (1/2")
Annotation: Rae Dawn Chong appears as herself, a film star whose burnt-out father,
Far Out Man (Tommy Chong), keeps interrupting the set on her most recent film.
Winslow plays an airport cop; Fava plays a woman who sleeps with Lou (Rey), an

oversexed drug addict.

FAREWELL TO THE KING
Cast: Frank McRae*, Nick Nolte, Gerry Lopez, Nigel Havers, Marilyn Tokuda
Director: John Milius
Music by: Basil Poledouris
Producer: Albert S. Ruddy, Andre Morgan
Screenwriter: John Milius
Storywriter: Pierre Schoendoerffer
Tech Info: color/sound/117 min.　　　Type: Dramatic Feature
Date: 1989　 Origin: USA
Company: Vestron
Distributors/Format: Orion Home Video (1/2")
Annotation: Learoyd (Nolte) is an American soldier who deserts at the height of
WWII, and becomes the leader of a tribe of head hunters in Borneo. Capt.
Fairbourne (Havers) and Sgt. Tenga (McRae) are British soldiers who convince
Learoyd to help in fighting the Japanese.

FAST BREAK
Cast: Harold Sylvester*, Michael Warren*, Bernard King*, Mavis Washington*,
Gabriel Kaplan, Reb Brown
Director: Jack Smight
Executive Producer: Jerry Frankel
Music Performer: David Shire, James Di Pasquale
Music by: David Shire, James Di Pasquale
Producer: Stephen Friedman, Jerry Frankel
Screenwriter: Sandor Stern
Storywriter: Marc Kaplan
Tech Info: color/sound/107 min.　　　Type: Dramatic Feature
Date: 1979　 Origin: USA
Company: Regal Productions
Distributors/Format: Columbia Pictures Home Video (1/2")
Annotation: David Greene (Kaplan) risks his marriage and career in order to fulfill a
life-long dream to coach a college basketball team. In his relocation from New York
to Nevada, Greene brings along four local basketball legends, D.C. (Sylvester),
Preacher (Warren), Hustler (King), and Swish (Washington).

FAST FOOD
Cast: Randal Patrick*, Michael Pollard, Clark Brandon, Tracy Griffith
Director: Michael A. Simpson
Executive Producer: Jerry Silva
Music by: Iris Gillon
Producer: Michael A. Simpson, Stan Wakefield, Jerry Silva
Screenwriter: Randal Patrick*, Clark Brandon, Lanny Horn, Jim Bastille
Storywriter: Scott B. Sowers
Tech Info: color/sound/92 min.　　　Type: Comedy Feature
Date: 1989　 Origin: USA
Company: Double Helix
Distributors/Format: Fries Home Video (1/2")
Annotation: Drew (Patrick) and Auggie (Brandon) are college seniors who get thrown
out of school for petty illegal activities. Later they attempt to create a fast food
business at a friend's gas station in order to save it from being taken over by a

hamburger joint.

FAST FORWARD

Cast: Robert DoQui*, Don Franklin*, Cindy McGee*, Gretchen F. Palmer*, Monique Cintron*, Tracy Silver*, Debra Varnado, John Scott Clough, Michael DeLorenzo
Director: Sidney Poitier*
Music by: Jack Hayes*, Tom Scott
Producer: John Patrick Veitch
Screenwriter: Richard Wesley*
Storywriter: Timothy March
Tech Info: color/sound/109 min.   Type: Musical Feature
Date: 1985   Origin: USA
Company: Verdon, Cedric
Distributors/Format: Columbia Pictures Home Video (1/2")
Archives/Format: IUB - BFC/A (1/2")
Annotation: Michael (Franklin), Francine (McGee), Valerie (Palmer), Ruth (Clinton), and Debbie (Varnado) all leave a small town in the Midwest to find dance fame in New York.

FAST TIMES AT RIDGEMONT HIGH

Cast: Forest Whitaker*, Stanley Davis Jr.*, Sean Penn, Judge Reinhold, Jennifer Jason Leigh
Director: Amy Heckerling
Executive Producer: C.O. Erickson
Music by: Joe Walsh
Producer: Irving Azoff, Art Linson, C.O. Erickson
Screenwriter: Cameron Crowe
Tech Info: color/sound/92 min.   Type: Comedy Feature
Date: 1982   Origin: USA
Company: Universal
Distributors/Format: Universal Home Video (1/2")
Annotation: Reinhold, Leigh and Penn star in this comedy about a group of California teenagers that became a cult favorite. Whitaker makes his film debut as Charles Jefferson; Davis plays his brother.

FATAL BEAUTY

Cast: Whoopi Goldberg*, Ruben Blades, Sam Elliott, Harris Yulin, Jennifer Warren
Director: Tom Holland
Music Performer: Harold Faltermeyer
Music by: Harold Faltermeyer
Producer: Leonard Kroll
Screenwriter: Hilary Henkin, Dean Riesner
Storywriter: Bill Svande
Tech Info: color/sound/103 min.   Type: Dramatic Feature
Date: 1987   Origin: USA
Company: MGM
Distributors/Format: MGM Home Video (1/2")
Annotation: Rita Rizzoli (Goldberg) and her partner (Blades) are police detectives who have a personal vendetta against drug dealers and the lethal drug they are distributing, "fatal beauty."

FATAL INSTINCT
Cast: Eartha Kitt*, John Witherspoon*, James Remar, Sherilyn Fenn, Armand Assante
Director: Carl Reiner
Executive Producer: Pieter Jan Brugge
Music by: Richard Gibbs
Producer: Pieter Jan Brugge, , Pierce Gardner
Screenwriter: David O'Malley
Tech Info: color/sound/89 min.   Type: Comedy Feature
Date: 1993   Origin: USA
Company: MGM, Jacobs/Gardner Productions
Distributors/Format: MGM Home Video (1/2")
Annotation: Ned Ravine (Assante) is a lawyer-detective who becomes involved with a series of murderous women in this spoof of BASIC INSTINCT and FATAL ATTRACTION. Witherspoon plays Arch; Kitt portrays the first trial judge.

FATAL INSTINCT
Cast: Tommy Hicks*, Laura Johnson, Michael Madsen, Richard Foronjy, Tony Hamilton
Director: John Dirlam
Executive Producer: Mark Polan
Music by: Stephen Allen, Bobby Crew
Producer: Mark Polan, Stacy Codikow
Screenwriter: George Putnam
Tech Info: color/sound/93 min.   Type: Dramatic Feature
Date: 1992   Origin: USA
Company: Baby Dica Productions, Nucleus Entertainment
Distributors/Format: New Line Cinema Home Video (1/2")
Annotation: Pressured by Captain Merrihew (Hicks), Cliff Burden (Madsen) tries to solve the murder of two guests in a hotel. Since there were only two other people in the hotel, the manager (Foronjy) and sultry owner Catherine (Johnson), the list of suspects is short.

FATHER AND SON: DANGEROUS RELATIONS
Cast: Rae Dawn Chong*, Louis Gossett Jr.*, Clarence Williams III*, Blair Underwood*
Director: Georg Stanford Brown*
Tech Info: color/sound/120 min.   Type: Television Feature
Date: 1993   Origin: USA
Studio: NBC-TV
Annotation: A father (Gossett) and son (Underwood) try to build a relationship after the father is released from prison. Chong plays a parole officer.

FATHER HOOD
Cast: Halle Berry*, Patrick Swayze, Diane Ladd, Michael Ironside, Sabrina Lloyd
Director: Darrell James Roodt
Executive Producer: Jeffrey Chernov, Richard H. Prince
Music by: Patrick O'Hearn
Producer: Jeffrey Chernov, Nicholas Pileggi, Anant Singh, Gillian Gorfil, Richard H. Prince
Screenwriter: Scott Spencer

Tech Info: color/sound/84 min.   Type: Comedy Feature
Date: 1993   Origin: USA
Company: Rare Touch Productions
Distributors/Format: Buena Vista Home Video (1/2")
Annotation: Jack Charles (Swayze) is an irresponsible father who abandons his children. Kathleen Mercer (Berry) is a reporter who develops a relationship with him. The twosome eventually team up to fight gangsters and reform the child welfare system.

FATHERS AND SONS

Cast: Samuel L. Jackson*, Joie Lee*, Rocky Carroll*, Mitchell Marchand*, Jeff Goldblum, Rory Cochrane
Director: Paul Mones
Executive Producer: Nick Wechsler, Keith Addis
Music by: Mason Daring*
Producer: Jon Kilik, Nick Wechsler, Keith Addis
Screenwriter: Paul Mones
Tech Info: color/sound/99 min.   Type: Dramatic Feature
Date: 1992   Origin: USA
Company: Asbury Park Productions, Columbia TriStar, et al.
Distributors/Format: Pacific Pictures Distribution Company (16mm)
Annotation: Max Fish (Goldblum) and his son Ed (Cochrane) are growing apart as Ed discovers drugs and women. With high school friend Smiley (Marchand), Ed tries a new psychedelic drug sold by Smiley's brother Flo (Carroll). Jackson plays Marshall and Lee plays Lois.

FBI'S WAR ON BLACK AMERICA

Director: Denis Mueller, Deb Ellis
Tech Info: mixed/sound/50 min.   Type: Documentary Short
Date: 1990   Origin: USA
Distributors/Format: Facets Multimedia, Inc. (1/2"), Filmic Archives (1/2")
Annotation: J. Edgar Hoover and the FBI were concerned over the threat to internal security from Black Americans and organized a campaign to discredit organizations and individuals.

FEAR CITY

Cast: Billy Dee Williams*, Rae Dawn Chong*, Melanie Griffith, Tom Berenger, Rossano Brazzi, Michael V. Gazzo
Director: Abel Ferrara
Executive Producer: Stanley R. Zupnik, Tom Curtis, Tom Curtis
Music by: Richard Halligan
Producer: Bruce Cohn Curtis, Stanley R. Zupnik, Tom Curtis, Tom Curtis
Storywriter: Nicholas St. John
Tech Info: color/sound/93 min.   Type: Dramatic Feature
Date: 1984   Origin: USA
Company: Zupnik Curtis Enterprises
Distributors/Format: Thorn/EMI Home Video (1/2")
Annotation: Wheeler (Williams), a homicide investigator in New York City, and Ross (Berenger), a talent agent for topless dancers, team up to go after a killer who is stalking Ross's dancers (Chong, et al).

FEAR OF A BLACK HAT
Cast: Larry B. Scott*, George Jackson*, Doug McHenry*, Brad Sanders*, Don Reed*, Kasi Lemmons*, Rosemarie Jackson*, Rusty Cundieff*, Eric Laneuville*, Mark Christopher Lawrence*, Shabaka*, Faizon *
Director: Rusty Cundieff*, John Demps Jr.*
Executive Producer: William Christopher Girog
Music by: Larry Robinson*
Producer: Darin Scott*, William Christopher Girog
Screenwriter: Rusty Cundieff*
Tech Info: color/sound/85 min.   Type: Comedy Feature
Date: 1994   Origin: USA
Company: Oakwood Films
Distributors/Format: Samuel Goldwyn Home Video (1/2")
Annotation: Filmmaker Nina Blackburn (Lemmons) infiltrates Rap's most controversial and well-armed band. She follows NWH on their final tour as Ice Cold (Cundieff), Tasty-Taste (Scott) and Tone Def (Lawrence) confront their biggest career challenges.

FERNGULLY: THE LAST RAINFOREST
Cast: Tone-Loc *, Tim Curry, Christian Slater, Samantha Mathis, Jonathan Ward
Director: Bill Kroyer
Executive Producer: Ted Field, Robert Cort
Music by: Alan Silvestri
Producer: Ted Field, Robert Cort, Wayne Young, Peter Faiman
Screenwriter: Jim Cox
Storywriter: Diana Young
Tech Info: color/sound/72 min.   Type: Animated Feature
Date: 1992   Origin: Australia, USA
Company: FAI Films, Youngheart Productions, Interscope
Distributors/Format: Fox Home Video (1/2")
Annotation: In this animated fantasy, Hexxus (Curry), an evil force who was trapped in a tree, is released by a logging machine which he then takes over, threatening to chop down all of Ferngully. Tone Loc appears as the Goanna, a singing monitor lizard.

FERRIS BUELLER'S DAY OFF
Cast: Virginia Capers*, Larry "Flash" Jenkins*, Matthew Broderick, Jennifer Grey, Mia Sara, Alan Ruck
Director: John Hughes
Executive Producer: Michael Chinich
Music by: Arthur Baker*, Ira Newborn, John Robie
Producer: John Hughes, Tom Jacobson, Michael Chinich
Screenwriter: John Hughes
Tech Info: color/sound/103 min.   Type: Comedy Feature
Date: 1986   Origin: USA
Company: Paramount
Distributors/Format: Paramount (1/2")
Annotation: Ferris Bueller (Broderick) and friends celebrate a day away from school by taking his father's Ferrari through downtown Chicago. Capers plays Florence Sparrow.

FEW GOOD MEN, A
Cast: J.A. Preston*, Cuba Gooding Jr.*, Wolfgang Bodison*, Tom Cruise, Jack Nicholson, Demi Moore
Director: Rob Reiner, Robert Richardson
Executive Producer: William F. Gilmore, Rachel Pheffer
Music by: Marc Shaiman
Producer: David Brown, William F. Gilmore, Steve Nicolaides, Rob Reiner, Andrew Scheinman, Rachel Pheffer, Jeffrey Stott
Screenwriter: Aaron Sorkin
Storywriter: Aaron Sorkin
Tech Info: color/sound/138 min.   Type: Dramatic Feature
Date: 1992   Origin: USA
Company: Castle Rock, Manhattan Project
Distributors/Format: Columbia/TriStar Pictures (35mm; 1/2")
Annotation: Lance Cpl. Harold Dawson (Bodison) is one of two Marines accused of killing a fellow soldier. Lt. J.G. Daniel Kaffee (Cruise) is the Navy lawyer who's teamed up with litigator Lt. Cmdr. JoAnne Galloway (Moore) in the politically explosive murder case. Gooding is Cpl. Carl Hammaker; Preston plays Judge Randolph.

FIELD OF DREAMS
Cast: James Earl Jones*, Kevin Costner, Burt Lancaster, Amy Madigan, Ray Liotta
Director: Phil Alden Robinson
Music Performer: James Horner
Music by: James Horner
Producer: Lawrence Gordon, Charles Gordon
Screenwriter: Phil Alden Robinson
Storywriter: W.P. Kinsella
Tech Info: color/sound/106 min.   Type: Dramatic Feature
Date: 1989   Origin: USA
Company: Gordon Company, Universal
Distributors/Format: Facets Multimedia, Inc. (1/2"), Universal Home Video (1/2")
Annotation: When Ray Kinsella (Costner) hears a voice whispering in his cornfield, he builds a baseball diamond where greats from baseball's past emerge to play. Ray is also told by the voice to track down 1960s sage author Terrence Mann (Jones) and bring him back to Iowa. The ballplayers allow Mann to venture into the part of the cornfield where only they are allowed to be.

FIGHT BLACK: URBAN MARTIAL ARTS
Producer: Third World Newsreel
Tech Info: color/sound/15 min.   Type: Documentary Short
Date: 1991   Origin: USA
Studio: Independent
Distributors/Format: Third World Newsreel (1/2")
Annotation: Salgado is a young martial artist from the south Bronx who leads the viewer through an array of community martial arts activity in New York City.

FIGHT, THE
Director: Narcel Reedus*
Tech Info: color/sound   Type: Dramatic Short
Date: 1993   Origin: USA
Studio: Independent
Distributors/Format: Southwest Alternate Media Project (1/2"), Image Film & Video Center (1/2")
Annotation: The film is a visual poem describing the last thoughts of a black man preparing for the fight of his life.

FIGHTER FOR FREEDOM
Director: William Greaves*
Producer: William Greaves*
Screenwriter: William Greaves*, Lou Potter*
Tech Info: color/sound/18 min.   Type: Docudrama
Date: 1985   Origin: USA
Company: William Greaves* Productions
Distributors/Format: Williams Greaves Productions, Inc. (16mm)
Annotation: A child's biography of the famous abolitionist leader Frederick Douglass interweaves short dramatic re-creations of scenes from his life with archival graphics and narration.

FIGHTING BACK
Alternate: Death Vengeance
Cast: Yaphet Kotto*, Patti LuPone, Tom Skerritt, Michael Sarrazin
Director: Lewis Teague
Music by: Piero Piccioni
Producer: D. Constantine Conte
Screenwriter: Tom Hedley, David Z. Goodman
Tech Info: color/sound/96 min.   Type: Dramatic Feature
Date: 1982   Origin: USA
Company: DEG
Distributors/Format: Paramount Home Video (1/2"), EMI Home Video (1/2")
Annotation: Kotto plays a black leader who voices concern over a racial backlash that may be created by urban vigilantism.

FIGHTING BACK (1957-62), EPISODE 2
Series: Eyes On The Prize: America's Civil Rights Years
Director: Judith Vecchione
Executive Producer: Henry Hampton*
Narrator: Julian Bond*
Producer: Henry Hampton*, Judith Vecchione
Speaker: Constance Baker Motley*, Autherine Lucy*, Thurgood Marshall*, Ernest Green*, L.C. Bates*, Melba Patilld Beals*, Terrence Roberts*, Minnie Jean Brown*, James Meredith*, Myrlie Evers*, Medgar Evers*, James Hicks, Sen. James Eastland, Pres. Dwight D. Eisenhower, Sheriff Mel Bailey, Craig Rains, Harold Engstrom, Gov. Orval Faubus, Herbert Brownell, Lindsay Almond Jr., John F. Kennedy, Ross Barnett, Judge John Minor Wisdom, Burke Marshall, Robert Ellis, Nicholas Katzenbach, Jan Robertson
Tech Info: mixed/sound/60 min.   Type: Television Documentary

Date: 1986   Origin: USA
Company: Blackside, Inc.
Distributors/Format: PBS Video (16mm; 1/2")
Archives/Format: IUB - AAAMC (1/2")
Annotation: This segment takes a look at integration in southern schools focussing on Arkansas' Little Rock Central High School and the University of Mississippi. Nine Blacks enroll at Little Rock and in 1962, James Meredith enters "Ole Miss" with the aid of federal enforcement.

FIGHTING MAD

Cast: Leon Isaac Kennedy*, Jayne Kennedy*, Carmen Argenziano, James Iglemart
Producer: Robert E. Waters*
Tech Info: color/sound/83 min.   Type: Dramatic Feature
Date: 1979   Origin: USA
Company: Cosa Nueva Production
Distributors/Format: Continental Video (1/2")
Annotation: McGee (Leon Isaac Kennedy) and Russell (Iglemart) serve in Vietnam together. After collecting a pay-off for smuggled gold bullions they head back to California. McGee and his friend stab Russell and throw him overboard. He is swept ashore a deserted island where two Japanese soldiers, stranded since W.W.II, nurse him back to health and teach him the art of the Samurai. Eventually, Russell returns to Los Angeles to save his wife (Jayne Kennedy) and son from McGee.

FILMSTATEMENT

Cast: Afua Amowa Hassan*, Kenny Elmore*, Michael Clarke*, Dagbe Nagbe Bropleh*, Tom Holloway*, Khari Moore*
Director: Zeinabu irene Davis*
Producer: Zeinabu irene Davis*
Screenwriter: Zeinabu irene Davis*
Tech Info: mixed/sound/10 min.   Type: Experimental Short
Date: 1982   Origin: USA
Company: Wimmin with a Mission Productions
Annotation: Davis' first film is the depiction of a woman's experience from slavery to the present in Providence, Rhode Island. It features traditional drumming from Ghana, West Africa.

FINAL CONFLICT, THE

Cast: Al Matthews*, Louis Mahoney*, Rossano Brazzi, Sam Neill, Don Gordon
Director: Graham Baker
Executive Producer: Richard Donner
Music by: Jerry Goldsmith
Producer: Richard Donner, Harvey Bernhard
Screenwriter: Andrew Birkin
Tech Info: color/sound/108 min.   Type: Dramatic Feature
Date: 1981   Origin: USA
Company: Fox
Distributors/Format: Fox Home Video (1/2")
Annotation: In this final installment of THE OMEN saga, Damien the Antichrist (Neill) is now a successful industrial leader who is about to take over the world. Under the leadership of Father DeCarlo (Brazzi), six priests, among them Brother Paulo (Mahoney), vow to destroy Damien.

FINAL COUNTDOWN, THE
Cast: Ron O'Neal*, Kirk Douglas, Martin Sheen, Katharine Ross, James Farentino
Director: Don Taylor
Executive Producer: Richard R. St. Johns
Music by: John Scott
Producer: Peter Douglas, Richard R. St. Johns
Screenwriter: David Ambrose, Gerry Davis, Thomas Hunter, Peter Powell
Tech Info: color/sound/104 min.   Type: Dramatic Feature
Date: 1980   Origin: USA
Company: United Artists
Distributors/Format: United Artists Home Video (1/2")
Annotation: O'Neal plays Commander Dan Thurman in this sci-fi look back to the tragedy at Pearl Harbor. The action takes place aboard the USS Nimitz captained by Douglas.

FINAL EXECUTIONER, THE
Cast: Woody Strode*, William Mang, Marina Costa, Harrison Muller, Margi Newton
Director: Romolo Guerrieri
Music by: Carlo De Nonno
Producer: Luciano Appignani
Screenwriter: Roberto Leoni
Tech Info: color/sound/94 min.   Type: Dramatic Feature
Date: 1986   Origin: Italy
Company: Immagine
Distributors/Format: Cannon Home Video (1/2")
Annotation: In a post-nuclear holocaust future, Sam (Strode) is an ex-cop who teaches Alan (Mang) how to fight so that he can revenge himself on those who hunted him for sport. The two men decide to team up to fight for justice.

FINAL TERROR, THE
Alternate: Bump in the Night; Campsite Massacre
Cast: Akosua Busia*, Rachel Ward, John Friedrich, Adrian Zmed
Director: Andrew Davis
Executive Producer: Samuel Z. Arkoff
Music by: Susan Justin
Producer: Joe Roth, Samuel Z. Arkoff
Screenwriter: Ronald Shusett, Jon George, Neill Hicks
Tech Info: color/sound/84 min.   Type: Dramatic Feature
Date: 1983   Origin: USA
Company: Comworld, Watershed, Roth
Distributors/Format: Comworld Home Video (1/2")
Annotation: A bevy of teenage campers die one by one in the redwood forest at the hands of a deranged woman. Busia plays Vanessa.

FINDERS KEEPERS
Cast: Louis Gossett Jr.*, Blu Mankuma*, Pamela Stephenson, Michael O'Keefe, Ed Lauter, Beverly D'Angelo
Director: Richard Lester
Executive Producer: Richard Lester
Music by: Ken Thorne
Producer: Terence Marsh, Richard Lester, Sandra Marsh

Screenwriter: Terence Marsh, Ronny Graham, Charles Dennis
Storywriter: Charles Dennis
Tech Info: color/sound/96 min.   Type: Comedy Feature
Date: 1984   Origin: USA
Company: CBS
Distributors/Format: Warner Bros. Home Video, Inc. (1/2")
Annotation: Georgiana Latimer (Stephenson) and Josef Sirola (Lauter) steal five million dollars from Georgiana's father and set off on a cross-country trip by train with the money hidden in a coffin. Gossett plays Century, and Mankuma portrays Wade Eichorn.

FINDING CHRISTA

Director: Camille Billops*, James Hatch, Dion Hatch
Music Performer: Christa Victoria*
Producer: Camille Billops*, James Hatch
Screenwriter: Camille Billops*, James Hatch
Speaker: Camille Billops*, Christa Victoria*
Storywriter: Camille Billops*, James Hatch
Tech Info: color/sound/55 min.   Type: Documentary Feature
Date: 1991   Origin: USA
Company: Hatch-Billops Production, Cinnamon
Distributors/Format: Third World Newsreel (1/2")
Archives/Format: IUB - BFC/A (1/2")
Annotation: Hatch and Billops document her personal story, an artist who leaves her three-year old daughter Christa Victoria at a children's home. Later, at the urging of her adoptive mother, Victoria, now a performing artist, seeks Billops out.

FINE MESS, A

Cast: Theodore "Teddy" Wilson*, Maria Conchita Alonso, Ted Danson, Paul Sorvino, Richard Mulligan, Howie Mandel, Stuart Margolin
Director: Blake Edwards
Executive Producer: Jonathan D. Krane
Music by: Henry Mancini
Producer: Tony Adams, Jonathan D. Krane
Tech Info: color/sound/88 min.   Type: Comedy Feature
Date: 1986   Origin: USA
Company: B.E.E., Delphi V, Columbia
Distributors/Format: Columbia Pictures Home Video (1/2")
Annotation: While working on location at a racetrack, Hollywood extra Spence Holden (Danson) overhears two crooks (Mulligan and Margolin) plotting to dope a horse and persuades his friend Dennis (Mandel) to bet his savings on the sure winner. When the crooks' boss Tony Pazzo (Sorvino) hears that someone else knows about the plot, he sends his hoods out to get them. Wilson plays Covington, Pazzo's snobbish valet-doorman- chauffeur who also takes part in the one of the chase scenes.

FIRE BIRDS

Alternate: Wings of the Apache
Cast: J.A. Preston*, Cylk Cozart*, Nicolas Cage, Tommy Lee Jones, Sean Young
Executive Producer: Arnold Kopelson, Keith Barish
Producer: Arnold Kopelson, Keith Barish, Bill Badalato

Tech Info: color/sound/85 min.   Type: Experimental Feature
Date: 1990   Origin: USA
Company: Nova International Films-Arnold Kopelson, et al.
Distributors/Format: Buena Vista Home Video (1/2")
Annotation: On an observation mission in South America, ace pilot Jake Preston
(Cage) spots narco-terrorists shooting down military airplanes. The U.S. sends an
elite team of pilots in response. Cozart plays Dewar Proctor.

FIRE THIS TIME, THE
Director: Randy Holland*
Tech Info: color/sound/90 min.   Type: Documentary Feature
Date: 1994   Origin: USA
Studio: Independent
Annotation: A controversial documentary about the 1922 Los Angeles riots. Traces
the events leading up to the conflict, including the federal government's bungling of
the Watts riot decades earlier.

FIRE WITH FIRE
Cast: Tim Russ*, Virginia Madsen, Craig Sheffer, Jon Polito, Jeffrey Jay Cohen
Director: Duncan Gibbins
Executive Producer: Tova Laiter
Music by: Howard Shore
Producer: Gary Nardino, Tova Laiter
Screenwriter: Warren Skaaren, Paul Boorstin, Sharon Boorstin, Bill Phillips
Tech Info: color/sound/103 min.   Type: Dramatic Feature
Date: 1986   Origin: USA
Company: Paramount
Distributors/Format: Paramount Home Video (1/2")
Annotation: Joe Fish (Sheffer) is a juvenile delinquent who falls in love with Lisa
Taylor (Madsen), a student at a Catholic girl's high school. Russ portrays Jerry.

FIREPOWER
Cast: O.J. Simpson*, Conrad Roberts*, James Coburn, Eli Wallach, Sophia Loren
Director: Michael Winner
Music by: Gato Barbieri
Producer: Michael Winner
Screenwriter: Gerald Wilson
Tech Info: color/sound/104 min.   Type: Dramatic Feature
Date: 1979   Origin: Great Britain
Company: Associated Film Distribution
Annotation: Believing her husband was killed by order of an industrialist, Adele
Tasca (Loren) seeks help from the U.S. Government. The Justice Department
involves a crime leader (Wallach) who recruits a former assassin (Coburn) to kill the
industrialist, with assistance from Catlett (Simpson). Roberts is featured as Lestor.

FIRESTARTER
Cast: Moses Gunn*, Antonio Fargas*, Drew Barrymore, Louise Fletcher, Martin
Sheen, George C. Scott
Director: Mark L. Lester
Music Performer: Tangerine Dream
Music by: Tangerine Dream
Producer: Frank Capra Jr.

Screenwriter: Stanley Mann
Storywriter: Stephen King
Tech Info: color/sound/113 min.   Type: Dramatic Feature
Date: 1984   Origin: USA
Company: Universal
Distributors/Format: MCA Home Video (1/2")
Annotation: Dr. Pynchot (Gunn) is a scientist who tests and documents the mental powers of Charlene McGee (Barrymore) who has the ability to start fires. He and Captain Hollister (Sheen) hope to provide evidence to Congress that through drugs, mental processes can control and manipulate physical elements.

FIREWALKER

Cast: Louis Gossett Jr.*, Sonny Landham, Chuck Norris
Director: J. Lee Thompson
Music Performer: Gary Chang
Music by: Gary Chang
Producer: Yoram Globus, Menahem Golan
Screenwriter: Robert Gosnell
Storywriter: Robert Gosnell, Jeffrey M. Rosenbaum, Norman Alad Jem
Tech Info: color/sound/106 min.   Type: Dramatic Feature
Date: 1986   Origin: USA
Company: Cannon Group, Inc.
Distributors/Format: Cannon Home Video (1/2")
Annotation: Max Donigan (Norris) and his sidekick (Gossett) set out to find a fabulous treasure. Instead they encounter everything from hostile Indians to man-eating crocodiles.

FIRST FAMILY

Cast: Julius Harris*, John Hancock*, Sylvia Anderson*, Gilda Radner, Madeline Kahn, Bob Newhart
Director: Buck Henry
Music Performer: Ralph Burns, John Philip Sousa
Music by: John Philip Sousa
Producer: Daniel Melnick
Screenwriter: Buck Henry
Tech Info: color/sound/100 min.   Type: Comedy Feature
Date: 1980   Origin: USA
Company: Iniprod Productions
Distributors/Format: Warner Bros. Home Video, Inc. (1/2")
Annotation: Newhart, Radner, and Kahn make up the incompetent "First Family" in this satirical look at American politics and foreign policy. The family travels to the African island of "Upper Gorm", where Harris, Hancock, and Anderson are cast as primitive tribal leaders who wish to buy some middle-class white Americans in order to have a repressed minority in their country.

FIRST POWER, THE

Cast: Dan Tullis Jr.*, Grand L. Bush*, Mykelti Williamson*, Lou Diamond Phillips, Tracy Griffith, Jeff Kober
Director: Robert Resnikoff
Executive Producer: Ted Field, Robert Cort, Melinda Jason
Music by: Stewart Copeland, Laura J. Perlman, Jeff Levi
Producer: Ted Field, Robert Cort, David Madden, Melinda Jason

Screenwriter: Robert Resnikoff
Tech Info: color/sound/99 min.　　　Type: Dramatic Feature
Date: 1990　Origin: USA
Company: Nelson-Interscope
Distributors/Format: Orion Home Video (1/2")
Annotation: Police detectives Russell Logan (Phillips) and Oliver Franklin (Williamson) capture a serial killer who carves pentagrams in his victim's bodies. Although the killer is executed, his spirit returns to commit more murders. Bush is the reservoir worker.

FISH THAT SAVED PITTSBURGH, THE
Cast: James Bond III*, Kareem Abdul-Jabbar*, Julius Erving*, Meadowlark Lemon*, Margaret Avery*, Flip Wilson*, Debbie Allen*, Jonathan Winters
Director: Gilbert Moses
Producer: David Dashev, Gary Stromberg
Tech Info: color/sound/104 min.　　　Type: Comedy Feature
Date: 1979　Origin: USA
Company: Lorimar Pictures
Distributors/Format: Karl-Lorimar Home Video (1/2")
Annotation: Astrological charts are consulted to help a doomed Pittsburgh basketball team. Changing their name to Pisces improves their game. Numerous NBA players, including Erving and Nixon, appear on the teams. Allen is a cheerleader; Avery falls for Irving.

FIVE HEARTBEATS, THE
Cast: Robert Townsend*, Diahann Carroll*, John Witherspoon*, Anne-Marie Johnson*, Arnold Johnson*, John Canada Terrell*, Michael Wright*, Roy Fegan*, Harold Nicholas*, Theresa Randle*, Kasi Lemmons*, Veronica Redd*, Troy Beyer*, Leon (credited as Leon) Robinson*, Tico Wells*, Tressa Thomas*, Harry J. Lennix*, Chuck Patterson*, Carla Brothers*, Hawthorne James*, Monique Mannen
Director: Robert Townsend*
Executive Producer: Robert Townsend*
Music by: Stanley Clarke*
Producer: Robert Townsend*, Loretha C. Jones
Screenwriter: Robert Townsend*, Keenen Ivory Wayans*
Tech Info: color/sound/121 min.　　　Type: Musical Feature
Date: 1991　Origin: USA
Company: Quest Productions, Tinsel Townsend Talkies
Distributors/Format: Fox Home Video (1/2")
Archives/Format: IUB - BFC/A (1/2")
Annotation: Five young, highly talented men (Townsend, Leon, Wright, Lennix, Wells) form a music group in the 1960s. With the help of a seasoned choreographer (Nicholas) and astute manager (Patterson), the Five Heartbeats rise to fame. Problems occur when the manager is killed, one of the Heartbeats turns to drugs, and two brothers want the same girl (Brothers).

FIVE OUT OF FIVE
Director: Ayoka Chenzira*
Tech Info: color/sound/7 min.　　　Type: Musical Short

Date: 1987   Origin: USA
Studio: Independent
Distributors/Format: Women Make Movies, Inc. (16mm; 1/2")
Annotation: This Rap-Rock music video features New York Women Against Rape's Acting Out Teen Theatre in a serious look at the problem of child and teen sexual abuse.

FLAG

Director: Linda Gibson*
Narrator: Linda Gibson*, Maggie Glynn*
Tech Info: color/sound/24 min.   Type: Experimental Short
Date: 1989   Origin: USA
Studio: Independent
Distributors/Format: Women Make Movies, Inc. (16mm; 1/2")
Archives/Format: IUB - BFC/A (1/2")
Annotation: After having grown up believing that the freedom and opportunity symbolized by the flag are equally available to everyone, a young black woman becomes disillusioned by injustice.

FLAMINGO KID, THE

Cast: Novella Nelson*, Leon (credited as Leon) Robinson*, Hector Elizondo, Matt Dillon, Molly McCarthy, Martha Gehman
Director: Garry Marshall
Producer: Maurice Phillips
Screenwriter: Garry Marshall, Neal Marshall
Storywriter: Neal Marshall
Tech Info: color/sound/100 min.   Type: Comedy Feature
Date: 1984   Origin: USA
Company: Mercury, ABC
Distributors/Format: Fox Home Video (1/2")
Annotation: Jeffrey Willis (Dillon) is a kid from the wrong side of the tracks who gets a summer job at a ritzy beach club in the 1950s. Nelson plays Lizzy, the housekeeper.

FLASHDANCE

Cast: Jennifer Beals*, Michael Nouri, Belinda Bauer, Lilia Skala
Director: Adrian Lyne
Executive Producer: Peter Guber, Jon Peters
Music Performer: Irene Cara*, Michael Stembello, Giorgio Moroder
Music by: Giorgio Moroder
Producer: Don Simpson, Jerry Bruckheimer, Peter Guber, Jon Peters
Screenwriter: Joe Eszterhas, Tom Hedley
Storywriter: Tom Hedley
Tech Info: color/sound/95 min.   Type: Musical Feature
Date: 1983   Origin: USA
Company: Polygram
Distributors/Format: Paramount Home Video (1/2")
Annotation: The film follows the trials and rewards of Alex (Beals) as she struggles for success in the middle of Pittsburg's steel industry, by following her two great loves (Nouri) and dancing.

FLATLINERS
Cast: Kimberly Scott*, Kesha Reed*, Keifer Sutherland, Julia Roberts, William Baldwin, Kevin Bacon
Director: Joel Schumacher
Executive Producer: Scott Rudin, Michael Rachmil, Peter Filardi
Music by: James Newton Howard*
Producer: Scott Rudin, Michael Rachmil, Michael Douglas, Rick Bieber, Peter Filardi
Screenwriter: Peter Filardi
Tech Info: color/sound/111 min.   Type: Dramatic Feature
Date: 1990   Origin: USA
Company: Stonebridge
Distributors/Format: Columbia Pictures Home Video (1/2")
Annotation: Five medical students decide to learn about death by inducing clinical death in each other, then using CPR to bring each back to life. Scott plays Winnie Hicks; Reed plays Winnie as a young girl.

FLESH, METAL, WOOD
Director: Floyd Webb*
Music Performer: Floyd Webb*, Edward Wilkerson Jr.*
Music by: Floyd Webb*, Edward Wilkerson Jr.*
Producer: Floyd Webb*
Screenwriter: Floyd Webb*
Tech Info: bw/sound/10 min.   Type: Experimental Short
Date: 1982   Origin: USA
Studio: Independent
Annotation: The film explores the spiritual nature of musical creativity while paying homage to black music.

FLETCH
Cast: Kareem Abdul-Jabbar*, James Avery*, Larry Fischer Jenkins*, Chevy Chase, Joe Don Baker, Dana Wheeler-Nicholson
Director: Michael Ritchie
Music Performer: Harold Faltermeyer
Music by: Harold Faltermeyer
Producer: Alan Greisman, Peter Douglas
Screenwriter: Andrew Bergman
Storywriter: Gregory McDonald
Tech Info: color/sound/98 min.   Type: Comedy Feature
Date: 1985   Origin: USA
Company: Douglas/Greisman Production, Universal
Distributors/Format: MCA Home Video (1/2")
Annotation: Avery is a crooked cop who helps to plant heroin on Fletch (Chase) to stop him from printing a story about police involvement in the selling of drugs in Los Angeles. Jenkins plays Gummy, a drug runner for the police who works with Fletch. Abdul-Jabbar has a cameo role appearing as a Los Angeles Laker.

FLETCH LIVES
Cast: Cleavon Little*, Chevy Chase, Julianne Phillips
Director: Michael Ritchie
Music by: Harold Faltermeyer
Producer: Peter Douglas, Alan Creisman
Storywriter: Leon Capetanos

Tech Info: color/sound/95 min.   Type: Comedy Feature
Date: 1989   Origin: USA
Company: Universal
Distributors/Format: MCA Home Video (1/2")
Annotation: When Fletch (Chase) journeys into the deep South, he is confronted with murder, a phony evangelist, a beautiful woman, and Calculus (Little), the caretaker of Fletch's inherited Southern plantation. Calculus aids Fletch in uncovering a land-snatching scheme.

FLIGHT OF THE INTRUDER
Cast: Danny Glover*, Ving Rhames*, Willem Dafoe, Rosanna Arquette, Brad Johnson, Tom Sizemore
Director: John Milius
Executive Producer: Brian Frankish
Music by: Basil Poledouris
Producer: Brian Frankish, Mace Neufeld
Screenwriter: David Shaber, Robert Dillon
Storywriter: Stephen Coonts
Tech Info: color/sound/115 min.   Type: Dramatic Feature
Date: 1991   Origin: USA
Company: Paramount
Distributors/Format: Paramount Home Video (1/2")
Annotation: When two A-6 Navy bomber pilots Cole (Dafoe) and Grafton (Johnson) attempt an unassigned mission, their superior officer, Campanelli (Glover) turns them in for Court Martial. The proceedings are dropped when they are ordered on a offensive against Vietnam sites. When Campanelli's plane goes down, the pilots attempt an unassigned mission to rescue him.

FLINTSTONES, THE
Cast: Sheryl Lee Ralph*, Halle Berry*, Messiri Freeman*, Elizabeth Perkins, John Goodman, Rick Moranis, Kyle MacLachlan, Rosie O'Donnell
Director: Brian Levant
Executive Producer: Kathleen Kennedy, David Kirschner, William Hanna, Gerald R. Molen, Joseph Barbera
Music by: David Newman
Producer: Kathleen Kennedy, David Kirschner, Bruce Cohen, William Hanna, Gerald R. Molen, Joseph Barbera
Screenwriter: Tom Parker, Jim Jennewein, Steven E. de Souza
Tech Info: color/sound/92 min.   Type: Comedy Feature
Date: 1994   Origin: USA
Company: Amblin
Distributors/Format: Universal Home Video (1/2")
Annotation: Berry portrays Miss Rosetta Stone, assistant to Cliff Vandercave (MacLachlan). They plan to embezzle funds from the Slate Gravel Company in this transition from cartoon to live-action film.

FLIRTING
Cast: Thandie Newton*, Freddie Paris*, Femi Taylor*, Nicole Kidman, Noah Taylor
Director: John Duigan
Producer: George Miller, Terry Hayes, Doug Mitchell
Screenwriter: John Duigan
Tech Info: color/sound/96 min.   Type: Dramatic Feature

Date: 1992   Origin: Australia
Company: Kennedy-Miller Productions
Distributors/Format: Samuel Goldwyn Home Video (1/2")
Annotation: In 1960s Australia, boarding school student Danny Embling (Taylor) meets Thandiwe Adjewa (Newton), a girl from Africa who is at a neighboring girls school. The two fall in love, but are separated when Adjewa's father (Paris) returns with his family to Uganda, and is killed in the civil strife there. Taylor plays Letitia Adjewa.

FLOUNDERING

Cast: Sy Richardson*, Kim Wayans*, Maritza Rivera, Ethan Hawke, John Cusack, James LeGros
Director: Peter McCarthy
Music by: Pray for Rain
Producer: Peter McCarthy
Screenwriter: Peter McCarthy
Tech Info: color/sound/97 min.   Type: Comedy Feature
Date: 1994   Origin: USA
Company: Front Films
Distributors/Format: Strand Releasing Company (16mm)
Annotation: John Boyz (LeGros), an unemployed resident of Los Angeles who, in the months following the Rodney King riots, goes in search of $3,000 to try to help his brother. Richardson appears as Commander K; Wayans an EDD clerk.

FLY BY NIGHT

Cast: M.C. Lyte *, Leo Burmester*, Jeffery Sams*, Ron Brice*, Kid Capri *, DJ Scratch *, Maura Tierney*, Christopher Michael Gerrard*, Todd Graff*, Lawrence/Larry Gilliard Jr.*, Soulfood *, Special Ed *, Omar Carter*, Ebony Jo-Ann*, Sharon Angela*, Michael Harris Austin*, Daryl "Chill" Mitchell*, Yul Vazquez
Director: Steve Gomer
Executive Producer: Clarence Jones*, Christopher Meledandri, Mark Gordon
Music by: Sidney Mills*
Producer: Calvin Skaggs*, Clarence Jones*, Christopher Meledandri, Mark Gordon
Screenwriter: Todd Graff*
Tech Info: color/sound/94 min.   Type: Dramatic Feature
Date: 1994   Origin: USA
Company: Lumiere, Fly by Night Films, Inc. et al.
Distributors/Format: Arrow Releasing (16mm)
Annotation: Rich (Sams) dreams of rapping his way to stardom. Abandoning his wife and child, he takes up with a quick-tempered gangster rapper Cletus (Brice) who becomes as violent as his lyrics. Although the duo is successful, Rich begins to doubt the choice he has made. Mitchell is featured as Kayam, Rich's cousin; Graff plays Naji and Burmester plays Ricky Tick.

FLYIN' CUT SLEEVES

Producer: Henry Chalfant, Rita Fecher
Tech Info: color/sound/60 min.   Type: Documentary Feature

Date: 1993   Origin: USA
Studio: Independent
Distributors/Format: Cinema Guild (1/2")
Annotation: The film documents the history of black and Latino street gangs in New York City.

FM

Cast: Cleavon Little*, Martin Mull, Michael Brandon, Eileen Brennan, Alex Karras
Director: Lamont Johnson
Music Performer: Steely Dan
Producer: Rand Houston
Screenwriter: Ezra Sacks
Tech Info: color/sound/104 min.   Type: Dramatic Feature
Date: 1978   Origin: USA
Company: Universal
Distributors/Format: MCA/Universal Home Video (1/2")
Annotation: The film chronicles life at a radio network station, whose talented disc jockeys unite in a strike when corporate executives fire their boss, Jeff Dugan (Mull). Little is the airwave's "Prince of Darkness," who announces the strike and enlists the support of his listeners.

FOLKS!

Cast: Wanda Christine*, Don Ameche, Tom Selleck, Anne Jackson, Christine Ebersole
Director: Ted Kotcheff
Executive Producer: Mario Cecchi Gori, Vittorio Cecchi Gori
Music by: Michel Colombier
Producer: Victor Drai, Malcolm R. Harding, Mario Cecchi Gori, Vittorio Cecchi Gori
Screenwriter: Robert Klane
Tech Info: color/sound/109 min.   Type: Comedy Feature
Date: 1992   Origin: USA
Company: Penta Pictures, Victor Drai Productions
Distributors/Format: Fox Home Video (1/2")
Annotation: Successful Chicago stock trader Jon Aldrich (Selleck) decides to take his ill mother and demented father into his home. A string of bad luck leaves him jobless, abandoned by wife and kids, and physically injured. Christine plays the County Nurse.

FOR KEEPS

Alternate: Maybe Baby
Cast: Sharon Brown*, Miriam Flynn, Kenneth Mars, Molly Ringwald, Randall Batinkoff
Director: John G. Avildsen
Music by: Bill Conti
Producer: Walter Coblenz, Jerry Belson
Screenwriter: Tim Kazurinsky, Denise DeClue
Tech Info: color/sound/98 min.   Type: Comedy Feature

Date: 1988   Origin: USA
Company: ML Delphi Premier
Distributors/Format: TriStar Pictures Inc. (1/2")
Annotation: Brown plays Lila in this coming-of-age film that examines how pregnancy disrupts the lives of Darcy (Ringwald) and Stan (Batinkoff), two aspiring professionals.

FOR QUEEN AND COUNTRY
Cast: Denzel Washington*, Dorian Healy*
Director: Martin Stellman
Producer: Tim Bevan
Storywriter: Martin Stellman, Trix Worrell
Tech Info: color/sound   Type: Dramatic Feature
Date: 1989   Origin: Great Britain
Studio: Independent
Annotation: Rueben (Washington) is a man who has devoted the better part of his youth serving his country in Northern Ireland and the Falklands. With a chestful of medals, he returns home to a country that eventually turns its back on him.

FORCE 10 FROM NAVARONE
Cast: Carl Weathers*, Barbara Bach, Edward Fox, Harrison Ford, Robert Shaw
Director: Guy Hamilton
Music by: Ron Goodwin
Producer: Paul Winfield*, Oliver A. Unger
Screenwriter: Carl Foreman, Robin Chapman
Storywriter: Alistair MacLean
Tech Info: color/sound/118 min.   Type: Dramatic Feature
Date: 1978   Origin: Yugoslavia
Company: American International Pictures, Inc.
Annotation: Weathers plays Weaver, a member of the United States Medical Corps who becomes a vital part of the commando mission led by Barnsby (Ford) and Miller (Fox). Together they blow up a bridge that is essential to German defense.

FOREIGN STUDENT
Cast: Robin Givens*, Cliff McMullen*, Charles S. Dutton*, Jon Hendricks*, Philip Branch*, Harold Lighty*, Clement Burnette*, Robert Pointdexter*, Hinton Battle*, Linita Corbett*, Marco Hofschneider, Rick Johnson, Charlotte Ross
Director: Eva Sereny
Executive Producer: Tarak Ben Ammar, Mark Lombardo, Peter Hoffman
Music by: Jean-Claude Petit
Producer: Tarak Ben Ammar, Tarak Ben Ammar, Mark Lombardo, Mark Lombardo, Peter Hoffman
Screenwriter: Menno Meyjes
Tech Info: color/sound/93 min.   Type: Dramatic Feature
Date: 1994   Origin: USA
Company: Carthago Films, Libra UK, Holland, Featherstone
Distributors/Format: Facets Multimedia, Inc. (1/2"), Gramercy Pictures Home Video (1/2")
Archives/Format: IUB - BFC/A (1/2")
Annotation: Philippe Le Clerc (Hofschneider), a French foreign exchange student, falls for black school teacher April (Givens) despite the fact that interracial relationships are taboo in 1955 Virginia. Dutton plays Howlin' Wolf; Battle is Sonny

Boy Williams.

FOREVER YOUNG

Cast: Joe Morton*, Jamie Lee Curtis, Mel Gibson, Elijah Wood
Director: Steve Miner
Executive Producer: Edward S. Feldman, Jeffrey Abrams
Music by: Jerry Goldsmith
Producer: Edward S. Feldman, Jeffrey Abrams, Bruce Davey
Screenwriter: Jeffrey Abrams
Tech Info: color/sound/102 min.   Type: Dramatic Feature
Date: 1992   Origin: USA
Company: Warner Bros., Icon Productions
Distributors/Format: Warner Bros. Home Video, Inc. (1/2")
Annotation: Daniel (Gibson) agrees to be the subject of a cryogenic experiment in
the 1940s. He wakes up in the present day, and must adjust to late 20th century
culture as well as find out what went wrong with the experiment. Morton plays
Cameron, a scientist working with the government, who is interested in the
experiment because of its potential for space travel.

FORREST GUMP

Cast: Mykelti Williamson*, Tom Hanks, Robin Wright, Sally Field, Gary Sinise
Director: Robert Zemeckis, Peyton Reed
Producer: William Rus
Screenwriter: Eric Roth
Tech Info: mixed/sound/142 min.   Type: Dramatic Feature
Date: 1994   Origin: USA
Company: Paramount
Distributors/Format: Films Inc. (1/2"), Paramount Home Video (1/2")
Annotation: A man with a subnormal IQ, Forrest Gump (Hanks) sits on a bus-stop
bench and tells his incredible life-long story to strangers waiting for the bus. While
stationed in Vietnam, Forrest meets Bubba (Williamson), a man with similar
characteristics, who invites Forrest to go into the shrimp canning industry with him.

FORT APACHE THE BRONX

Cast: Pam Grier*, Paul Newman, Edward Asner, Ken Wahl, Danny Aiello
Director: Daniel Petrie Jr.
Executive Producer: David Susskind, David Susskind
Music by: Jonathan Tunick
Producer: David Susskind, David Susskind, Martin Richards, Tom Fiorello, Gill
Champion
Screenwriter: Heywood Gould
Tech Info: color/sound/120 min.   Type: Dramatic Feature
Date: 1981   Origin: USA
Company: Producer Circle Co., Fox
Distributors/Format: Vestron Home Video (1/2")
Annotation: When two policemen are murdered in the 41st precinct of New York,
otherwise known as Fort Apache, the Bronx, the Chief (Asner) enlists the entire force
including Murphy (Newman) and Corelli (Wahl) in an attempt to track down the
murderer. Grier plays Charlotte a prostitute/addict who not only kills the two
policemen, but also commits murders all over the Bronx in a drugged stupor.

FORT MOSE
Alternate: A New Chapter in American History
Director: Bill Suchy
Narrator: Russ Wheeler*, Wayne Fields*
Producer: Bill Suchy
Screenwriter: Bill Suchy
Storywriter: G. Denise Stripling
Tech Info: color/sound/25 min.   Type: Documentary Short
Date: 1991   Origin: USA
Studio: Independent
Company: Ironwood Productions
Annotation: The film tells the story of the first legally sanctioned settlement for free Africans in America, providing evidence that African American colonial history extended far beyond slavery and oppression.

FORTUNE DANE
Cast: Carl Weathers*, Adolph Caesar*, Sonny Landham, Daphne Ashbrook, Joe Dallesandro
Director: Nicholas Sgarro
Music by: David Kurtz, Ron Ramin, Stewart Levin
Producer: Thomas Kane
Screenwriter: Charles Correll
Storywriter: Charles Correll
Tech Info: color/sound/83 min.   Type: Dramatic Feature
Date: 1986   Origin: USA
Company: Vidmark Entertainment, Stormy Weather Production
Distributors/Format: Vidmark Entertainment Home Video (1/2")
Archives/Format: IUB - BFC/A (1/2")
Annotation: When a hit man brutally massacres nine people including a personal friend, Fortune Dane (Weathers) demands justice.

FOURTH WAR, THE
Cast: Tim Reid*, Roy Scheider, Jurgen Prochnow, Harry Dean Staton, Lara Harris
Director: John Frankenheimer, Gerry Fisher
Executive Producer: William Stuart, Sam Perlmutter
Music by: Bill Conti
Producer: William Stuart, Wolf Schmidt, Robert L. Rosen, Sam Perlmutter
Screenwriter: Stephen Peters, Kenneth Ross
Tech Info: color/sound/95 min.   Type: Dramatic Feature
Date: 1990   Origin: USA
Company: Kodiak Films
Distributors/Format: HBO Home Video (1/2")
Annotation: Col. Jack Knowles (Scheider) and Col. N.A. Valachev (Prochnow) are American and Soviet officers who vent their frustrations over not being able to fight in a private war played out on the West German-Czech border. Reid portrays Lt. Col. Timothy Clark, Knowles' second-in-command, who tries to stop the battle.

FRAGMENTS
Director: Barbara McCullough*
Tech Info: color/sound/10 min.   Type: Experimental Short
Date: 1980   Origin: USA
Studio: Independent
Distributors/Format: Third World Newsreel (1/2")
Archives/Format: IUB - BFC/A (1/2")
Annotation: A montage of magic centered imagery, this work contains some of the
footage from McCullough's SHOPPING BAGS SPIRITS plus new material.

FRANKIE & JOCIE
Director: Jocelyn Taylor*
Speaker: Jocelyn Taylor*, Frankie Taylor*
Tech Info: mixed/sound/20 min.   Type: Experimental Short
Date: 1994   Origin: USA
Studio: Independent
Distributors/Format: Third World Newsreel (1/2")
Annotation: Taylor's video presents a provocative discussion between a black
lesbian and her straight brother.

FRANKIE AND JOHNNY
Cast: Al Fann*, Glenn Plummer*, Hector Elizondo, Al Pacino, Michelle Pfeiffer
Director: Garry Marshall
Music by: Marvin Hamlisch
Producer: Garry Marshall
Screenwriter: Terrance McNally
Storywriter: Terrance McNally
Tech Info: color/sound/118 min.   Type: Dramatic Feature
Date: 1991   Origin: USA
Company: Paramount
Distributors/Format: Paramount Home Video (1/2")
Annotation: Johnny (Pacino) is an ex-con who falls in love with Frankie (Pfeiffer) a
waitress in a New York diner, and woos her with Shakespeare. Plummer appears as
Peter.

FRATERNITY VACATION
Cast: Franklin Ajaye*, Tim Robbins, Stephen Geoffreys, Sheree J. Wilson
Director: James Frawley
Executive Producer: Larry Thompson
Music by: Brad Fiedel
Producer: Robert C. Peters, Larry Thompson
Screenwriter: Lindsay Harrison
Tech Info: color/sound/95 min.   Type: Comedy Feature
Date: 1985   Origin: USA
Company: New World
Annotation: Tvedt (Geoffreys), a nerdish college freshman, joins two of his frat
brothers on a vacation trip to Palm Springs. They agree to take him because Tvedt's
father has promised the frat house a new hot tub if they show his son a good time.
Ajaye plays Harry.

FREDERICK DOUGLASS: AN AMERICAN LIFE
Director: William Greaves*
Producer: William Greaves*
Screenwriter: William Greaves*, Lou Potter*
Tech Info: color/sound/31 min.   Type: Docudrama
Date: 1984   Origin: USA
Studio: Independent
Company: William Greaves* Productions
Distributors/Format: Academic Industries Video Division (1/2"), Williams Greaves
Productions, Inc. (16mm)
Annotation: This dramatization of the life of Douglass focuses on the person behind
the public figure. Born a slave and entirely self-educated, Douglass played a critical
role, as orator, writer, newspaper publisher, editor and political leader, in the struggle
for the emancipation of the slaves, and also in the early women's rights movement.

FREE AT LAST
Executive Producer: Don Jackson
Music Performer: Ella Jenkins*
Narrator: LeVar Burton*
Producer: Barbara L. Wilson, Don Jackson, Carolyn D. Sartar
Tech Info: color/sound/17 min.   Type: Documentary Short
Date: 1990   Origin: USA
Company: Central City Productions
Distributors/Format: Filmic Archives (1/2"), Encyclopedia Britannica Educational
Corporation (1/2")
Annotation: The film pays tribute to Dr. Martin Luther King, Jr. by Jenkins and school
children around the country.

FREEDOM BAGS
Producer: Stanley Nelson*, Elizabeth Clark-Lewis*
Tech Info: mixed/sound/32 min.   Type: Documentary Short
Date: 1980   Origin: USA
Studio: Independent
Company: Diversity Video Project
Distributors/Format: Filmakers Library, Inc. (16mm; 1/2")
Annotation: This is the story of African American women who migrated from the
rural South during the first three decades of the 20th century. Hoping to escape
from the racism and poverty of the post-Civil War South, they boarded segregated
trains for an uncertain future up North.

FREEDOM ON MY MIND
Director: Marilyn Mulford, Connie Field
Producer: Marilyn Mulford, Connie Field
Tech Info: mixed/sound/115 min.   Type: Documentary Feature
Date: 1994   Origin: USA
Studio: Independent
Distributors/Format: California Newsreel (1/2"), Clarity Educational Productions, Inc.
(16mm; 1/2")
Annotation: Focussing on the freedom summer and voter registration drives, the film
includes interviews and historical footage. It won the 1994 Sundance Grand Jury
Prize for Documentary.

FREEDOM RINGS
Producer: Wendy Scott-Penson, Mike Grundmann
Speaker: Erika Alexander*
Tech Info: color/sound/29 min.   Type: Documentary Short
Date: 1992   Origin: USA
Studio: Independent
Distributors/Format: Cinema Guild (1/2")
Annotation: The film documents black children, who during the summer, learn self-discipline and build self-confidence while attending Philadelphia's Freedom Theatre.

FREEDOM ROAD
Cast: Muhammad Ali*, Alfre Woodard*, Ron O'Neal*, Barbara O *, Rooney King Athens*, Veronica Ali*, Kennedy Dixon*, Kris Kristofferson
Director: Jan Kadar
Producer: Zen Braun
Screenwriter: David Zelag Goodman
Storywriter: Howard Fast
Tech Info: mixed/sound/190 min.   Type: Television Feature
Date: 1978   Origin: USA
Company: Zev Braun, Inc.
Distributors/Format: World Vision Home Video (1/2")
Annotation: The film tells of one newly freed black man, Gideon Jackson (Ali), who during the chaos of reconstruction is able to educate himself and his family, as well as initiate legislative action. Eventually Jackson becomes a South Carolina Senator, but his vigorous strides toward democracy are not received well by bitter southerners who resort to violence.

FREEDOM STATION, THE
Cast: Jada Pinkett*, Christine Cunningham*, Friday Nelson*
Director: Scott Hilton Davis*
Executive Producer: Frank Batarick
Music by: Mark Roumelis
Narrator: Nigel Reed
Producer: Scott Hilton Davis*, Cheryl Magill, Frank Batarick
Screenwriter: Scott Hilton Davis*, Cheryl Magill
Tech Info: color/sound/28 min.   Type: Dramatic Short
Date: 1988   Origin: USA
Studio: Independent
Company: Maryland Instructional Television
Distributors/Format: Filmic Archives (1/2")
Annotation: This drama is set in 1850 in the root cellar of a safehouse along Maryland's Underground Railroad. The shared experiences of a young escaped slave girl and a farm girl from an abolitionist family help define the hardships of slavery, the legal and moral dilemmas facing abolition, and the complexities of freedom.

FREEJACK

Cast: Grand L. Bush*, Emilio Estevez, Anthony Hopkins, Rene Russo, Mick Jagger
Director: Geoff Murphy
Executive Producer: James G. Robinson, David Nicksay, Gary Barber
Music by: Trevor Jones
Producer: Ronald Shusett, James G. Robinson, David Nicksay, Gary Barber, Stuart Oken
Screenwriter: Ronald Shusett, Steven Pressfield, Dan Gilroy
Tech Info: color/sound/108 min.   Type: Dramatic Feature
Date: 1992   Origin: USA
Company: Morgan Creek, Freejack Productions
Distributors/Format: Warner Bros. Home Video, Inc. (1/2")
Annotation: Because strapping young race car driver Alex Furlong (Estevez) is about to die on the track, a body builder (Jagger) from the future transports Alex so that a physically decrepit human can have his body. Bush plays Boone.

FRESH

Cast: Samuel L. Jackson*, Giancarlo Esposito*, N'Bushe Wright*, Sean Nelson*
Director: Boaz Yakin, Adam Holender
Executive Producer: Dorian Harris
Music by: Stewart Copeland
Producer: Lawrence Bender, Randy Ostrow, Dorian Harris
Screenwriter: Boaz Yakin
Tech Info: color/sound/112 min.   Type: Dramatic Feature
Date: 1994   Origin: USA
Company: Fresh Productions, A Band Apart Productions, et al
Distributors/Format: Miramax Home Video (1/2")
Annotation: Twelve-year-old Fresh (Nelson) is an intelligent and perceptive boy growing up in a world of poverty and violence, being raised by his Aunt, but still in contact with his father, Sam (Jackson). Fresh goes to work for Esteban (Esposito) a drug dealer, who also gets Fresh's sister Nicole (Wright) addicted to drugs. Fresh hatches a complex and audacious scheme to get himself and his sister out of their seemingly hopeless situation. McClarin plays Darryl; Whitfield is Smokey; Smith plays Tarleak.

FRIED GREEN TOMATOES

Cast: Stan Shaw*, Cicely Tyson*, Lashondra Phillips*, Suzi Bass*, Enjolik Oree*, Jessica Tandy, Mary Louise Parker, Kathy Bates, Mary Stuart Masterson
Director: Jon Avnet, Geoffrey Simpson
Executive Producer: Norman Lear, Andrew Meyer
Music by: Thomas Newman
Producer: Jon Avnet, Jordan Kerner, Norman Lear, Andrew Meyer
Screenwriter: Carol Sobieski, Fannie Flagg
Tech Info: color/sound/130 min.   Type: Dramatic Feature
Date: 1991   Origin: USA
Company: Avent/Kerner, Electric Shadow, Act III Comm.
Distributors/Format: Facets Multimedia, Inc. (1/2"), MCA/Universal Home Video (1/2")
Annotation: A spry octagenerian (Tandy) in a nursing home tells a dowdy housewife (Bates) the story of a fiercely independent woman, Idgie Threadgoode (Masterston) half a century ago inspires the housewife to change her life. Sipsey (Tyson), a

seamstress, and her handyman son, Big George (Shaw), not only help Idgie at the Whistlestop Cafe during segregation, but also protect her friend Ruth's (Parker) baby from Ruth's abusive husband.

FROM BEYOND
Cast: Ken Foree*, Jeffrey Combs, Barbara Crampton, Ted Sorel, Carolyn Purdy-Gordon
Director: Stuart Gordon
Executive Producer: Charles Band
Music Performer: Richard Band
Music by: Richard Band
Producer: Brian Yuzna, Charles Band
Screenwriter: Dennis Paoli
Storywriter: H.P. Lovecraft
Tech Info: color/sound/85 min.   Type: Dramatic Feature
Date: 1986   Origin: USA
Company: Taryn Productions, Empire Pictures
Annotation: Foree, Crampton, and Combs struggle to destroy a demonic machine that can stimulate the pineal (third eye) gland in the victim's body.

FROM HARLEM TO HARVARD
Director: Marco Williams*
Producer: Marco Williams*, David Gifford*, Carole Markin*, David Lewis
Tech Info: color/sound/30 min.   Type: Documentary Short
Date: 1982   Origin: USA
Company: Foursquare Productions
Distributors/Format: Third World Newsreel (1/2")
Annotation: The film offers a unique perspective of the difficulties of life at an Ivy League school for college freshman George, the first African American student from his high school to be admitted to Harvard.

FROM THE HIP
Cast: David Alan Grier*, Meshach Taylor*, Beatrice Winde*, Judd Nelson, Elizabeth Perkins, John Hurt
Director: Bob Clark
Executive Producer: Howard Baldwin, Bill Minot, Brian Russell
Music by: Paul Zaza
Producer: Bob Clark, Rene Dupont, Howard Baldwin, Bill Minot, Brian Russell
Screenwriter: David E. Kelly, Bob Clark
Storywriter: David E. Kelly
Tech Info: color/sound/112 min.   Type: Dramatic Feature
Date: 1987   Origin: USA
Studio: Independent
Company: De Laurentis Entertainment Group (DEG)
Distributors/Format: Lorimar Home Video (1/2")
Annotation: Steve Hadley (Grier) is the comical assistant to attorney Robin "Stormy" Weathers (Nelson), as they attempt to defend an accused murderer. Winde plays the presiding judge over their case. Taylor plays an uncontrollable black "Queen."

FULL METAL JACKET
Cast: Dorian Harewood*, Adam Baldwin, Matthew Modine, Vincent D'Onofrio, Lee Ermey
Director: Stanley Kubrick
Music by: Abigail Mead
Producer: Stanley Kubrick
Screenwriter: Stanley Kubrick, Michael Herr, Gustav Hasford
Storywriter: Gustav Hasford
Tech Info: color/sound/116 min.   Type: Dramatic Feature
Date: 1987   Origin: USA
Company: Warner Bros.
Distributors/Format: Warner Bros. Home Video, Inc. (1/2")
Annotation: Harewood plays a non-commisioned officer in his platoon during the Vietnam War. When the platoon is moving through parts of a wartorn city, Harewood is sent out to find a safe path through the buildings.

FUNDI: THE STORY OF ELLA BAKER
Director: Joanne Grant
Music by: Bernice Johnson Reagon*
Producer: Joanne Grant
Speaker: Ella Baker*, James Forman*, Julian Bond*, Eleanor Holmes Norton*, Bob Moses*, Stokely Carmichael*, Gloster Current*, C.T. Vivian*, Victoria J. Gray*, Fred L. Shuttlesworth*, Wyatt Tee Walker*, Ralph D. Abernathy*, Grace Hamilton*, Dorothy Cotton*, Dorie Ladner*, Charles Cobb*, Marion Berry*, Conrad Lynn*, June Johnson*, Annie Devine*, Hazel Palmer*, Vincent Harding*, Anne Braden, Robert Zellner
Storywriter: Joanne Grant
Tech Info: mixed/sound/60 min.   Type: Documentary Feature
Date: 1981   Origin: USA
Company: Fundi Productions
Distributors/Format: First Run/Icarus Films (16mm), New Day Films (16mm; 1/2")
Archives/Format: IUB - BFC/A (16mm)
Annotation: "Fundi," Swahili for "Master of her Craft,"is a title bestowed upon Baker by her admirers to honor her efforts as one of the leading female activists of the Civil Rights Movement. Through interviews with former SNCC and SCLC members, the story of her remarkable career is depicted. The film includes archival footage of the movement.

FUNKY BEAT
Series: 1987 CEBA Awards
Director: Melvin Van Peebles*
Music Performer: Whodini *
Tech Info: color/sound/4 min.   Type: Musical Short
Date: 1986   Origin: USA
Studio: Independent
Company: World Institute of Black Communications
Annotation: This is one of 17 music videos targeting the African American community. The CEBA Awards is an annual competition sponsored by The World Institute of Black Communications. Inc.

FUNLAND

Cast: Randal Patrick*, David L. Lander, Bruce Mahler, William Windom, Mary McDonough
Director: Michael A. Simpson
Music by: James Oliverio
Producer: Michael A. Simpson, William Van Der Kloot
Screenwriter: Bonnie Turner, Terry Turner, Michael A. Simpson
Tech Info: color/sound/86 min.   Type: Comedy Feature
Date: 1987   Origin: USA
Company: Double Helix-Hyacinth
Distributors/Format: RMC Films-Vestron Video (16mm, 1/2")
Annotation: When the amusement park where he works is taken over and he is fired, the park's clown, Brace Burger (Lander), goes insane, moves into the wax museum, and attempts to assassinate his replacement. Patrick plays Chip Cox.

FUNNY FARM

Cast: Glenn Plummer*, Chevy Chase, Madolyn Smith, Joseph Maher, Brad Sullivan
Director: George Roy Hill
Executive Producer: Patrick Kelley, Bruce Bodner
Music by: Elmer Bernstein
Producer: Robert L. Crawford, Patrick Kelley, Bruce Bodner
Screenwriter: Jeffrey Boam
Storywriter: Jay Cronley
Tech Info: color/sound/101 min.   Type: Comedy Feature
Date: 1988   Origin: USA
Company: Cornelius, Pan Arts
Distributors/Format: Warner Bros. Home Video, Inc. (1/2")
Annotation: Andy and Elizabeth Farmer (Chase and Smith) are yuppies who move to the country but have a hard time fitting in. Plummer appears as Mickey.

GAME FOR VULTURES

Cast: Richard Roundtree*, Richard Harris, Joan Collins, Ray Milland
Director: James Fargo
Music by: John Field, Tony Duhig, Wilf Gibson
Producer: Hazel Adair
Screenwriter: Phillip Baird
Storywriter: Michael Hartman
Tech Info: color/sound/113 min.   Type: Dramatic Feature
Date: 1979   Origin: Great Britain
Company: Pyramid Films
Distributors/Format: Trans World Entertainment (1/2")
Annotation: A black man fighting against racist laws and policies in Rhodesia turns into an angry revolutionary.

GAME OF DEATH

Cast: Kareem Abdul Jabaar*, Colleen Camp, Bruce Lee, Dean Jagger
Director: Robert Clouse
Music by: John Barry
Producer: Raymond Chow
Screenwriter: Jan Spears
Tech Info: color/sound/102 min.   Type: Dramatic Feature

Date: 1979   Origin: USA
Company: Golden Harvest & Paragon Films
Annotation: Hakim (Abdul-Jabaar) is Billy Lo's (Lee) towering nemesis. In the choreographed fight sequence, Hakim is twice the height of Billy who defeats Hakim in the end.

GAME, THE
Cast: Richard Ross*, Curtis Brown*, Vanessa Shaw*, Bill/Billy Williams*, Damon Clark*, Dick Biel, Carolina Beaumont
Director: Curtis Brown*
Executive Producer: Julia Wilson
Music by: Julia Wilson
Producer: Curtis Brown*, Julia Wilson
Screenwriter: Curtis Brown*, Julia Wilson
Storywriter: Curtis Brown*
Tech Info: color/sound/116 min.   Type: Dramatic Feature
Date: 1990   Origin: USA
Studio: Independent
Company: Curtis
Distributors/Format: Visual Perspectives (1/2")
Annotation: Leon Hunter (Brown), an ambitious black executive, is campaign manager for Carl Rydell (Biel), a white candidate. Rydell's chief opponent is Bill Arrington (Clark), an intelligent, committed politician who has a chance to become New York's first black mayor. Hunter finds an opportunity to defeat Arrington after the arrest of black bicycle messenger Vail Yearwood (Williams) and his apparent death. Shaw plays Yearwood's wife Sylvia. The film is based on a short story by Curtis Brown.

GANDY DANCERS
Director: Barry Dornfeld, Maggie Holtzberg-Call
Tech Info: color/sound/30 min.   Type: Documentary Short
Date: 1994   Origin: USA
Studio: Independent
Distributors/Format: Cinema Guild (1/2")
Annotation: The film documents the musical and verbal orations of retired African American railroad track laborers.

GARDENS OF STONE
Cast: James Earl Jones*, Lonette Mckee*, Laurence/Larry Fishburne*, Dick Anthony Williams*, James Caan, Anjelica Huston, D.B. Sweeney
Director: Francis Ford Coppola
Music by: Carmine Coppola
Producer: Francis Ford Coppola, Michael I. Levy
Screenwriter: Nicholas Proffitt, Ronald Bass
Tech Info: color/sound/112 min.   Type: Dramatic Feature
Date: 1987   Origin: USA
Company: ML Delphi Premier Productions, TriStar
Distributors/Format: Facets Multimedia, Inc. (1/2"), TriStar Pictures Inc. (1/2")
Annotation: "Goody" Nelson (Jones) and Cecil Hazard (Caan) take devoted, but inexperienced Private Willow (Sweeney) under their wing only to see him die in Vietnam. Betty Rae (McKee) is Nelson's wife. Slasher Williams (Williams) is a hard-core superior officer. Fishburne appears as Flanigan, a vindictive fellow soldier

who is called down for threatening a weaker soldier.

GENUINE RISK
Cast: Theodore "Teddy" Wilson*, Michelle Johnson*, Peter Berg, Terence Stamp, M.K. Harris
Director: Kurt Voss
Executive Producer: Miles A. Copeland III, Paul Colichman
Music by: Deborah Holland
Producer: Miles A. Copeland III, Paul Colichman, Larry J. Rattner, William Ewart, Guy J. Louthan
Screenwriter: Kurt Voss
Storywriter: Larry J. Rattner
Tech Info: color/sound/89 min.   Type: Dramatic Feature
Date: 1991   Origin: USA
Company: IRS Media
Distributors/Format: RCA/Columbia Pictures Home Video (1/2")
Annotation: Henry (Berg), a parolee, takes a job with a gangster (Stamp) at the urging of his old friend Jack (Harris). Wilson plays Billy.

GEORGE WASHINGTON CARVER
Series: Black Americans of Achievement Video Collection
Director: Rhonda Fabian, Jerry Baber, Keith Smith
Executive Producer: Andrew Schlessinger
Narrator: Michael Logan
Producer: Rhonda Fabian, Jerry Baber, Andrew Schlessinger
Tech Info: mixed/sound/30 min.   Type: Documentary Short
Date: 1992   Origin: USA
Studio: Independent
Company: Schlessinger Video Productions
Distributors/Format: Filmic Archives (1/2")
Annotation: The film documents the story of Carver, the famous botanist whose research with peanuts was finally recognized for its importance.

GEORGIA MASS CHOIR
Music Performer: Georgia Mass Choir *
Tech Info: color/sound/120 min.   Type: Concert Feature
Date: 1989   Origin: USA
Studio: Independent
Annotation: The Georgia Mass Choir sings 14 of their all-time Gospel favorites.

GET A JOB
Series: Trying Times
Director: Hugh Thompson*
Producer: Hugh Thompson*
Screenwriter: Hugh Thompson*
Storywriter: Hugh Thompson*
Tech Info: color/sound/16 min.   Type: Dramatic Short

Date: 1978   Origin: USA
Studio: Independent
Annotation: The film shows job applicants of various backgrounds being interviewed for jobs illustrating the proper way to make a favorable impression in an interview.

GETTING OVER

Cast: Floyd Chatman*, John R. Daniels*, Mabel King*, Renee Gentry*, Donniece Jackson*, Aurelia Sweeny*, Gwen Brisco, Mary Hopkins, Bernice Givens, Sheila Dean, Sandra Sully, Paulette Gibson
Director: Bernie Rollins
Music by: Johnny Rodgers
Producer: John R. Daniels*, Cassius Vernon Weathersby*
Screenwriter: Bernie Rollins
Storywriter: John R. Daniels*, Bernie Rollins
Tech Info: color/sound/108 min.   Type: Dramatic Feature
Date: 1981   Origin: USA
Company: Maverick
Distributors/Format: Continental Video (1/2")
Annotation: An unscrupulous record producer, Stone (Goff), hires promoter Mike Barnett (Daniels) and the all-female rock group Love Machine to comply with affirmative action employment policies. Sweeney plays Zulu; King plays Mabel Queen; Chatman appears as Noble; Jackson is Penny.

GHETTOBLASTER

Cast: Harry Caesar*, R.G. Armstrong*, Richard Hatch, Rosemarie
Director: Alan L. Stewart
Executive Producer: Marco Columbo
Music by: Sam Winans*, Reg Powell*
Producer: David DeCoteau, John Schouweiler, Marco Columbo
Screenwriter: Clay McBride
Tech Info: color/sound/86 min.   Type: Dramatic Feature
Date: 1989   Origin: USA
Company: Prism
Distributors/Format: Prism Entertainment (1/2")
Annotation: Travis (Hatch) becomes a vigilante when he discovers his childhood neighborhood has become a war zone. Caesar plays Mr. Dobson.

GHOST

Cast: Whoopi Goldberg*, Armelia McQueen*, Gail Boggs*, Augie Blunt*, Vivian Bonnel*, Patrick Swayze, Demi Moore, Tony Goldwyn, Rick Aviles
Director: Jerry Zucker
Producer: Wade Davis, Lisa Weinstein
Screenwriter: Bruce Joel Rubin
Tech Info: color/sound/128 min.   Type: Dramatic Feature
Date: 1990   Origin: USA
Company: Howard Koch Production
Distributors/Format: Paramount Home Video (1/2")
Annotation: Oda Mae Brown (Goldberg) is able to hear voices of the deceased. Aided by her sisters (McQueen and Boggs), she helps Sam Wheat (Swayze), a ghost, prevent his girlfriend from being harmed by the men that killed him.

GHOST DAD

Cast: Bill Cosby*, Denise Nicholas*, Kimberly Russell*, Ian Bannen, Raynor Scheine
Director: Sidney Poitier*
Music Performer: Henry Mancini
Music by: Henry Mancini
Producer: Terry Nelson
Screenwriter: Chris Reese, Brent Maddock, S.S. Wilson
Storywriter: Brent Maddock, S.S. Wilson
Tech Info: color/sound/84 min.   Type: Comedy Feature
Date: 1990   Origin: USA
Company: SAH Enterprises
Distributors/Format: MCA/Universal Home Video (1/2")
Annotation: When a looney taxi driver (Scheine) drives off a bridge, Elliot (Cosby), his passenger, is killed. Elliot returns as a ghost who still is attempting to control his family's life, especially that of his daughter Diane (Russell) and his girlfriend Joan (Nicholas).

GHOST FEVER

Cast: Joe Frazier*, Sherman Hemsley*, Luis Avalos, Jennifer Rhodes, Deborah Benson, Diana Brookes
Director: Lee Madden
Executive Producer: Wolf Schmidt, Kenneth Johnston
Music by: James V. Hart
Producer: Wolf Schmidt, Edward Coe, Ron Rich, Kenneth Johnston
Screenwriter: Oscar Brodney, Ron Rich, Richard Egan
Tech Info: color/sound/86 min.   Type: Comedy Feature
Date: 1987   Origin: USA
Company: Infinite
Distributors/Format: Charter Entertainment (1/2"), Miramax Home Video (1/2")
Annotation: Buford (Hemsley) and Benny (Avalos) are two detectives assigned to evict the residents of a plantation due for demolition. In the process, they encounter the ghost of Beauregard Lee (Martin) the home's original owner. Frazier plays fighter Terrible Tucker.

GHOST IN THE MACHINE

Cast: Brandon Adams*, Nigel Gibbs*, Karen Allen, Chris Mulkey, Ted Marcoux, Jessica Walter
Director: Rachel Talalay
Producer: Paul Schiff
Screenwriter: William Davies, William Osbourne
Tech Info: color/sound/104 min.   Type: Dramatic Feature
Date: 1993   Origin: USA
Company: Fox
Distributors/Format: Fox Home Video (1/2")
Annotation: When Terry Munroe (Allen) buys her boss an electronic address book, she gets more than she bargained for. During a storm, Karl (Marcoux), the Address Book Killer, is struck by lightning and his soul gets zapped into the computer mainframe. He then wreaks havoc on everyone. Frazer (Adams) is a friend to Terry's son.

GHOSTBUSTERS
Cast: Ernie Hudson*, Dan Aykroyd, Bill Murray, Harold Ramis, Sigourney Weaver,
Rick Moranis
Director: Ivan Reitman
Music Performer: Ray Parker Jr.*
Music by: Ray Parker Jr.*
Producer: Ivan Reitman
Screenwriter: Dan Aykroyd, Harold Ramis
Tech Info: color/sound/103 min.   Type: Comedy Feature
Date: 1984   Origin: USA
Company: Delphi Productions; Black Rhino Productions
Distributors/Format: RCA/Columbia Pictures Home Video (1/2")
Annotation: Winston Zeddmore (Hudson) is hired by Peter Venkman (Murray),
Raymond Stantz (Aykroyd), and Elon Spengler (Ramis), as the fourth ghostbuster.
Zeddmore senses the apocalyptic nature of the sudden rush of ghosts in New York
City.

GHOSTBUSTERS II
Cast: Ernie Hudson*, Bobby Brown*, Dan Aykroyd, Bill Murray, Harold Ramis,
Sigourney Weaver
Director: Ivan Reitman
Music Performer: Run-D.M.C. *, Bobby Brown*, Ray Parker Jr.*, Dougie Fresh and
The Get Fresh Crew*, Randy Edelman
Producer: Ivan Reitman
Screenwriter: Dan Aykroyd, Harold Ramis
Storywriter: Dan Aykroyd, Harold Ramis
Tech Info: color/sound/102 min.   Type: Comedy Feature
Date: 1989   Origin: USA
Company: Columbia
Distributors/Format: Columbia Pictures Home Video (1/2")
Annotation: Winston Zeddmore (Hudson) is still one of the Ghostbusters, this time
fighting the evil slime running beneath the city and creating major paranormal
disturbances. When the Ghostbusters go to see the Mayor, whose doorman
(Brown) asks for their autographs, they are committed to a psychiatric ward.

GIFT OF THE BLACK FOLK, THE
Director: Carlton Moss*, William Hurtz
Music by: Robert Holmes*
Producer: David Driskell*
Screenwriter: Carlton Moss*
Tech Info: color/sound/20 min.   Type: Documentary Short
Date: 1978   Origin: USA
Studio: Independent
Archives/Format: IUB - BFC/A (1/2")
Annotation: Moss uses W.E.B. Du Bois' title to explore the lives and
accomplishments of Frederick Douglass, Harriet Tubman and Denmark Vesey. The
film employs on-screen graphics instead of narration and has a full orchestral
accompaniment.

GIFTED, THE
Cast: Dick Anthony Williams*, J.A. Preston*, Bianca Ferguson*, Cassandra Johnson*
Director: Scott Zakarin
Music by: Fred Shehadi
Producer: Charles Zakarin, Scott Zakarin
Screenwriter: Scott Zakarin
Tech Info: color/sound/90 min.   Type: Dramatic Feature
Date: 1994   Origin: USA
Company: Merazel Productions
Distributors/Format: Myriad Enterprises, Inc. (16mm)
Annotation: Daniel (Williams), Jacob (Preston) and Lisa (Ferguson) are descendants of a West African tribe with the power to thwart Ogo, the evil force from the star Sirius in this science fiction adventure.

GIG, THE
Cast: Cleavon Little*, Joel Silver, Wayne Rogers, Jay Thomas, Andrew Duncan, Daniel Nalbach
Director: Frank D. Gilroy
Music by: Warren Vache
Producer: Norman I. Cohen
Screenwriter: Frank D. Gilroy
Storywriter: Frank D. Gilroy
Tech Info: color/sound/92 min.   Type: Comedy Feature
Date: 1985   Origin: USA
Company: The Gig Company, Castle Hill
Distributors/Format: Karl-Lorimar Home Video (1/2")
Annotation: Little plays the "goody two shoes" replacement in a jazz quintet who are given the opportunity to play professionally at a Catskills Mountain resort.

GIRLS JUST WANT TO HAVE FUN
Cast: Phineas Newborn III*, Helen Hunt, Sarah Jessica Parker, Lee H. Montgomery
Director: Alan Metter
Executive Producer: Stuart Cornfeld, James G. Robinson
Music by: Thomas Newman
Producer: Stuart Cornfeld, James G. Robinson, Chuck Russell
Screenwriter: Amy Spies
Tech Info: color/sound/87 min.   Type: Comedy Feature
Date: 1985   Origin: USA
Company: New World
Annotation: Two high school girls (Parker and Hunt) hope to appear on "Dance Television." Newborn plays Quarterback Dancer.

GLADIATOR
Cast: Ossie Davis*, Cuba Gooding Jr.*, Vonte Sweet*, Brian Dennehy
Director: Rowdy Herrington
Executive Producer: Kenneth Utt
Music by: Brad Fiedel
Producer: Kenneth Utt, Steve Roth, Frank Price
Screenwriter: Robert Mark Kamen, Lyle Kessler
Storywriter: Djordje Milicevic, Robert Mark Kamen

Tech Info: color/sound/88 min.   Type: Dramatic Feature
Date: 1992   Origin: USA
Company: Columbia, Price Entertainment
Distributors/Format: Columbia Pictures Home Video (1/2")
Annotation: Riley (Marshall), a white suburbanite, becomes a boxer in inner-city Chicago and befriends two fellow-fighters, including Lincoln (Gooding). Lincoln and Reily refuse to fight each other and team up against a common enemy. Davis plays Noah and Sweet plays Tidbits.

GLENGARRY GLEN ROSS

Cast: Paul Butler*, Jack Lemmon, Al Pacino, Alec Baldwin, Ed Harris
Director: James Foley
Executive Producer: Joe Caracciolo Jr.
Music by: James Newton Howard*
Producer: Stanley R. Zupnik, Joe Caracciolo Jr., Jerry Tokofsky
Screenwriter: David Mamet
Tech Info: color/sound/100 min.   Type: Dramatic Feature
Date: 1992   Origin: USA
Company: Zupnik Enterprises Inc.
Distributors/Format: New Line Cinema Home Video (1/2")
Annotation: Veteran salesman Shelley Levine (Lemmon) and his colleagues offer investment scams to potential buyers. Butler plays the policeman who investigates an incriminating office theft.

GLITCH

Cast: Ted Lange*, Julia Nickson, Teri Weigel, Will Egan, Dick Gautier, Steve Donmeyer
Director: Niko Mastorakis
Music by: Tom Marolda
Producer: Niko Mastorakis
Screenwriter: Niko Mastorakis
Tech Info: color/sound/90 min.   Type: Comedy Feature
Date: 1989   Origin: USA
Company: Omega Pictures
Distributors/Format: Academy Entertainment (35mm; 1/2")
Annotation: Lange plays mob collector DuBois who shows up at the estate of Hollywood producer Julius Lazar (Gautier) looking for money while the estate is in the hands of Todd (Egan) and Bo (Donmyer), would be burglars, pretending to be Lazar and his director.

GLORIA: A CASE OF ALLEGED POLICE BRUTALITY

Producer: Oren Rudavsky
Speaker: Gloria *
Tech Info: color/sound/27 min.   Type: Documentary Short
Date: 1984   Origin: USA
Studio: Independent
Annotation: An entire Ohio community divides along racial lines after seven white policemen shoot and wound a black, ex-mental patient in her home.

GLORY
Cast: Morgan Freeman*, Denzel Washington*, Jihmi Kennedy*, Andre Braugher*, Raymond St. Jacques*, Saundra Franks*, Matthew Broderick, Cary Elwes
Director: Edward Zwick
Music by: Boys Choir of Harlem *, James Horner
Producer: Pieter Jan Brugge, Freddie Fields
Screenwriter: Kevin Jarre
Storywriter: Lincoln Kirstein, Peter Burchard
Tech Info: color/sound/122 min.   Type: Dramatic Feature
Date: 1989   Origin: USA
Company: TriStar
Distributors/Format: RCA/Columbia Pictures Home Video (1/2"), Filmic Archives (1/2")
Archives/Format: IUB-BFC/A (1/2")
Annotation: In this fictionalized version of the 54th Regiment of Massachusetts Volunteer Infantry and the battle of Fort Wagner, Thomas Searles (Braugher) John Rawlins (Freeman) and Trip (Washington) are among the members of the first "unit of colored troops" organized during the Civil War. St. Jacques appears as Frederick Douglass.

GLOVE, THE
Cast: Aldo Ray*, Roosevelt "Rosey" Grier*, Joan Blondell, John Saxon
Director: Ross Hagen
Music by: Robert O. Ragland
Producer: Julian Roffman
Tech Info: color/sound/93 min.   Type: Dramatic Feature
Date: 1980   Origin: USA
Studio: Independent
Company: Tommy J. Production
Annotation: Ex-cop Sam Killough (Saxon), a bounty hunter, faces the challenge of his life. He must bring in a 250-pound ex-con, Victor Hale (Grier), who is wreaking havoc with a glove made of leather and steel.

GO TELL IT ON THE MOUNTAIN
Cast: James Bond III*, Giancarlo Esposito*, Olivia Cole*, Ruby Dee*, Alfre Woodard*, Rosalind Cash*, Linda Hopkins*, Paul Winfield*, Douglas Turner Ward*, CCH Pounder*, Ving Rhames*, Roderic Wimberly*
Director: Stan Lathan*
Music by: W. Michael Lewis*
Producer: Calvin Skaggs*
Screenwriter: Leslie Lee*, Gus Edwards
Storywriter: James Baldwin*
Tech Info: color/sound/96 min.   Type: Dramatic Feature
Date: 1984   Origin: USA
Company: Learning in Focus
Distributors/Format: Facets Multimedia, Inc. (1/2"), Filmic Archives (1/2")
Annotation: Adapted from James Baldwin's novel, the film follows the journey of a black family from the rural South to Harlem in the 1930s. It focuses on the struggle of a young boy (Bond) seeking salvation and understanding, as well as the approval of a self-righteous and often unloving stepfather (Winfield). Cole is the boy's mother; Cash is the understanding Aunt; Esposito, Elijah; Pounder plays Deborah,

Gabriel's first wife.

GOBOTS: BATTLE OF THE ROCK LORDS
Cast: Leslie Speights*, Margot Kidder, Telly Savalas, Roddy McDowall
Director: Ray Patterson
Executive Producer: William Hanna, Joseph Barbera, Stephen G. Shank
Music by: Larry Curtin
Producer: William Hanna, Joseph Barbera, Kay Wright, Stephen G. Shank
Screenwriter: Jeff Segal
Tech Info: color/sound/75 min.   Type: Animated Feature
Date: 1986   Origin: USA
Company: Hanna, Barbera, Tonka
Distributors/Format: Clubhouse, Atlantic (1/2")
Annotation: An animated feature about GoBots, robots that can transform themselves into other devices, this film pits Rock People against Rock Lords. Speights provides one of the voices.

GOD'S ALCATRAZ: RENEWING A COMMUNITY IN DESPAIR
Director: Boris Stout
Speaker: Dr. Johnny Ray Youngblood*
Tech Info: bw/sound/36 min.   Type: Documentary Short
Date: 1993   Origin: USA
Distributors/Format: Filmakers Library, Inc. (16mm; 1/2")
Annotation: Youngblood arrived in New Lots, north Howard Beach in east Brooklyn, 18 years ago to infuse new life into a community plagued with unemployment, drug abuse and violence.

GOING BERSERK
Cast: Ernie Hudson*, Julius Harris*, Gloria Gifford*, Murphy Dunne*, John Candy, Eugene Levy, Joe Flaherty, Alley Mills
Director: David Steinberg
Executive Producer: Pierre David
Music by: Tom Scott
Producer: Pierre David, Claude Heroux
Screenwriter: Dana Olsen, David Steinberg
Tech Info: color/sound/85 min.   Type: Comedy Feature
Date: 1983   Origin: USA
Company: Universal
Distributors/Format: Universal Home Video (1/2")
Annotation: Limousine driver John Bourgignon (Candy) falls in love with a congressman's daughter (Mills) and is brainwashed by a bizarre religious sect into killing her father. Hudson plays Muhammed; Dunne is the public defender.

GOLDEN CHILD, THE
Cast: Eddie Murphy*, Charlotte Lewis, Charles Dance, Victor Wong, J.L. Reate
Director: Michael Ritchie
Executive Producer: Richard Tienken, Charles R. Meeker
Producer: Edward S. Feldman, Robert D. Wachs, Richard Tienken, Charles R. Meeker
Screenwriter: Dennis Feldman
Tech Info: color/sound/93 min.   Type: Dramatic Feature

Date: 1986   Origin: USA
Company: Eddie Murphy* Production, FM
Distributors/Format: Paramount Home Video (1/2")
Archives/Format: IUB - BFC/A (1/2")
Annotation: Chandler Jarrell (Murphy) a "child finder" from Los Angeles, is selected
to rescue Tibetan Golden Child (Reate) from the hands of evildoers, led by Sardo
Numspa (Dance), a representative of the underworld.

GOLDENGIRL
Cast: James A. Watson Jr.*, James Coburn, Susan Anton, Curt Jurgens, Leslie
Caron
Director: Joseph Sargent
Executive Producer: Elliot Kastner
Music by: Bill Conti
Producer: Elliot Kastner, Danny O'Donovan
Screenwriter: John Kohn
Tech Info: color/sound/104 min.   Type: Dramatic Feature
Date: 1979   Origin: USA
Company: Avco Embassy
Annotation: A Supermodel (Anton) prepares for the 1980 Olympics and thinks that
winning three gold medals will also earn her true love. Watson plays Winters.

GONG SHOW MOVIE, THE
Cast: Roosevelt "Rosey" Grier*, Mabel King*, Chuck Barris, Robin Altman, Lillie
Shelton, Jaye P. Morgan
Director: Chuck Barris
Music by: Milton De Lugg
Producer: Budd Granoff
Screenwriter: Robert Downey, Chuck Barris
Tech Info: color/sound/89 min.   Type: Comedy Feature
Date: 1980   Origin: USA
Company: Universal
Distributors/Format: Universal Home Video (1/2")
Annotation: Chuck Barris, host of the television GONG SHOW, portrays himself as a
sensitive television personality driven to madness by the crazy show. King plays
Mabel and Grier appears in an uncredited role.

GOOD MAN IN AFRICA, A
Cast: Louis Gossett Jr.*, Sean Connery, John Lithgow, Joanne Whalley-Kilmer,
Diane Riggs
Director: Bruce Beresford, Andrzej Bartkowiak
Executive Producer: Joe Caracciolo Jr., Avi Lerner
Music by: John Du Prez
Producer: Mark Tarlov, John Fielder, Joe Caracciolo Jr., Avi Lerner
Screenwriter: William Boyd
Tech Info: color/sound   Type: Dramatic Feature
Date: 1994   Origin: USA
Company: Southern Sun
Distributors/Format: MCA/Universal Home Video (1/2")
Annotation: Gossett plays husband to Whalley-Kilmer in this fictional Kinjanja, West
African mystery.

GOOD MORNING VIETNAM
Cast: Forest Whitaker*, Juney Smith*, Robin Williams, Tung Thanh Tran, Chintara Sukapatana
Director: Barry Levinson
Music by: Alex North
Producer: Mark Johnson, Larry Brezner, Ben Moses, Harry Benn
Screenwriter: Mitch Markowitz
Tech Info: color/sound/121 min.   Type: Dramatic Feature
Date: 1987   Origin: USA
Company: Silver Partners III
Distributors/Format: Touchstone Home Video (1/2")
Annotation: Edward Garlick (Whitaker) is assigned to aid the new Air Force disc jockey Adrian Cronauer (Williams) whose task is to build troop morale in Vietnam. Phil McPherson (Smith) is the radio technician.

GOOD MOTHER, THE
Cast: Joe Morton*, Liam Neeson, Diane Keaton, Jason Robards Jr., James Naughton
Director: Leonard Nimoy
Music by: Elmer Bernstein
Producer: Arnold Glimcher
Screenwriter: Michael Bortman
Tech Info: color/sound/103 min.   Type: Dramatic Feature
Date: 1988   Origin: USA
Company: Touchstone-Silver Screen Part. IV-Arnold Glimcher
Distributors/Format: Buena Vista Home Video (1/2")
Annotation: Anna Dunlap (Keaton), divorced mother of six-year-old Molly, begins a passionate affair with an Irish sculptor (Neeson). Because of her ex-husband's misperception of the relationship, he (Naughton) sues for custody of the child. Lawyer Frank Williams (Morton) helps him win the case.

GOODFELLAS
Cast: Samuel L. Jackson*, Paul Sorvino, Joe Pesci, Ray Liotta, Robert De Niro, Lorraine Bracco
Director: Martin Scorsese
Executive Producer: Barbara DeFina
Music by: Jerry Ross, Hoagy Carmichael, Richard Adler, Morris Levy
Producer: Irwin Winkler, Barbara DeFina
Screenwriter: Martin Scorsese, Nicholas Pileggi
Tech Info: color/sound/148 min.   Type: Dramatic Feature
Date: 1990   Origin: USA
Company: Irwin Winkler
Distributors/Format: Warner Bros. Home Video, Inc. (1/2")
Annotation: Henry Hill (Liotta), a member of the federal witness protection program, prepares to testify against his former partners James Conway (De Niro) and Tommy DeVito (Pesci) who killed everyone involved during a $6 million cargo robbery at an airport. Jackson plays Stacks Edwards.

GORDON PARKS' VISIONS
Director: Gordon Parks*
Music by: Gordon Parks*
Producer: Shep Morgan
Screenwriter: Gordon Parks*
Speaker: Avery Brooks*, Joe Seneca*
Tech Info: color/sound/60 min.   Type: Documentary Feature
Date: 1986   Origin: USA
Company: Post America Inc.
Distributors/Format: Xenon Entertainment Group (1/2")
Archives/Format: IUB - BFC/A (1/2")
Annotation: Photo-Journalist Parks, (also composer, director, writer and musician) recapitulates his experiences in documenting African American life in Harlem and the struggle for Civil Rights in the South. The film is an expression of Parks' unique vision.

GORP
Cast: Julius Harris*, Michael Lembeck, Rosanna Arquette, Dennis Quaid, Fran Drescher, Philip Casnoff
Director: Joseph Ruben
Producer: Louis S. Arkoff, Jeffrey Konvitz
Screenwriter: Jeffrey Konvitz
Storywriter: Jeffrey Konvitz, Martin Zweiback
Tech Info: color/sound/90 min.   Type: Comedy Feature
Date: 1980   Origin: USA
Company: AIP
Distributors/Format: Filmways Home Video (1/2")
Annotation: Jokes about drugs, sex, and racism pervade this summer camp comedy. Harris plays Fred the Chef.

GOSPEL
Cast: Reverend James Cleveland*, Shirley Caesar*, Walter Hawkins*, The Hawkins Family *, The Mighty Clouds of Joy *, The Clark Sisters *
Director: David Leiveck, Frederick Ritzengerg
Music Performer: Reverend James Cleveland*, Shirley Caesar*, Walter Hawkins*, The Hawkins Family *, The Mighty Clouds of Joy *, The Clark Sisters *
Producer: David Leiveck, Frederick Ritzengerg
Tech Info: color/sound/92 min.   Type: Musical Feature
Date: 1987   Origin: USA
Company: Golden Door, Ritzenberg, Monterey
Annotation: The leading performers of gospel music come together to pay tribute to the history and development of Gospel.

GOSPEL ACCORDING TO AL GREEN
Director: Robert Mugge
Music Performer: Al Green*
Speaker: Al Green*
Tech Info: color/sound/94 min.   Type: Documentary Feature

Date: 1984   Origin: USA
Studio: Independent
Distributors/Format: Facets Multimedia, Inc. (1/2")
Annotation: Al Green is credited with such 1970s hits as "Lay Your Head on My Pillow" and "Let's Stay Together," but today Green is committed to gospel music.

GOTTA MAKE THIS JOURNEY: SWEET HONEY IN THE ROCK
Director: Michelle Parkerson*
Music Performer: Sweet Honey in the Rock *
Producer: Michelle Parkerson*
Tech Info: color/sound/58 min.   Type: Documentary Feature
Date: 1983   Origin: USA
Studio: Independent
Company: Eye of the Storm Productions
Distributors/Format: Women Make Movies, Inc. (16mm; 1/2")
Annotation: The members of the vocal group Sweet Honey in the Rock discuss the development of their group, the political and social significance of the music they perform, and their desire as black artists to make a creative contribution to their musical heritage. The film shows Sweet Honey in performance at their 9th Anniversary concert at Gallaudet College and at the Sisterfire Festival '82.

GRAFITTI BRIDGE
Cast: Morris Day*, Prince (Rogers Nelson) *, Jerome Benton*, The Time *, Jill Jones*, Mavis Staples*, Tevin Campbell*, Levi Seacer Jr.*, Tony Mosley*, George Clinton*, Ingrid Chavez, Rocky Santo, Jonathan Webb
Director: Prince (Rogers Nelson) *
Music Performer: Prince (Rogers Nelson) *, Mavis Staples*, Michael Bland*, Phillip C. *, Rosie Gaines*
Music by: Prince (Rogers Nelson) *
Producer: Arnold Steifel, Randy Phillips
Screenwriter: Prince (Rogers Nelson) *
Tech Info: color/sound/90 min.   Type: Musical Feature
Date: 1990   Origin: USA
Company: A Paisley Park Production
Distributors/Format: Warner Bros. Home Video, Inc. (1/2")
Archives/Format: IUB - AAAMC (1/2")
Annotation: Prince plays "The Kid" in this sequel to PURPLE RAIN. Day is The Kid's rival club owner, whose band is The Time. Benton is Day's conspiratorial sidekick. Day and The Kid compete for Aura (Chavez), but her death resolves the feud between them.

GRAND CANYON
Cast: Danny Glover*, Henry King*, Alfre Woodard*, Basil Wallace*, Patrick Malone*, Gregg Dandridge*, Deon Sams*, Willie C. Carpenter*, Destinee DeWalt*, Tina Lifford*, Shaun Baker*, K. Todd Freeman*, Christopher K. Brown*, Steven Keith Davis*, Kevin Kline, Steve Martin, Mary McDonnell
Director: Lawrence Kasdan
Music by: James Newton Howard*
Producer: Lawrence Kasdan, Charles Okun, Michael Grillo
Screenwriter: Lawrence Kasdan, Meg Kasdan
Storywriter: Lawrence Kasdan, Meg Kasdan
Tech Info: color/sound/134 min.   Type: Dramatic Feature

Date: 1991   Origin: USA
Company: Fox
Distributors/Format: Fox Home Video (1/2")
Annotation: When an affluent Los Angeles suburbanite (Kline) gets lost and his car breaks down in south central Los Angeles, tow-truck driver (Glover) rescues him from local gang members. As their lives coincide, they become friends. Woodard is cast as Glover's romantic interest, and Malone plays Glover's nephew, a youth who is being sucked into gang life.

GRANDVIEW, U.S.A.
Cast: Michael Winslow*, C. Thomas Howell, Jamie Lee Curtis, Patrick Swayze, Jennifer Jason Leigh, Troy Donahue
Director: Randal Kleiser
Executive Producer: Jonathan Taplin, Andrew Gellis
Music by: Thomas Newman
Producer: Jonathan Taplin, William Warren Blaylock, Peter W. Rea, Andrew Gellis
Screenwriter: Ken Hixon
Tech Info: color/sound/97 min.   Type: Dramatic Feature
Date: 1984   Origin: USA
Company: CBS
Distributors/Format: Warner Bros. Home Video, Inc. (1/2")
Annotation: Tim (Howell), a graduate from a rural high school, meets Michelle "Mike" Cody (Curtis), a young woman trying to keep her demolition derby from bankruptcy. Winslow plays Spencer.

GRAY LADY DOWN
Cast: Dorian Harewood*, Charlton Heston, Stacy Keach, David Carradine, Rosemary Forsyth
Director: David Greene
Music by: Jerry Fielding
Producer: Walter Mirisch
Screenwriter: Howard Sackler, James Whittaker
Tech Info: color/sound/111 min.   Type: Dramatic Feature
Date: 1978   Origin: USA
Company: Mirisch
Distributors/Format: Universal Home Video (1/2")
Annotation: Capt. Paul Blanchard (Heston) runs a nuclear submarine that's teetering on a precipice on the ocean floor. Capt. Bennett (Keach) is put in charge of the rescue operation. Harewood plays Fowler, the ship's second officer, who goes berserk from the pressure.

GREAT DAY IN HARLEM, A
Director: Steve Petropoulos, Jean Bach
Music Performer: Maxine Sullivan
Narrator: Quincy Jones*
Producer: Jean Bach
Speaker: John "Dizzy" Gillespie*, Sonny Rollins*, Artie Kane, Art Blakely, Marian McPartland
Storywriter: Matthew Seig, Jean Bach, Susan Peehl
Tech Info: mixed/sound/60 min.   Type: Documentary Feature

Date: 1994   Origin: USA
Company: Castle Hill Productions
Distributors/Format: Facets Multimedia, Inc. (1/2"), Castle Hill Home Video (1/2")
Annotation: The film is ostensibly about the shooting of a famous photograph for the January 1959 issue of Esquire magazine composed of 57 jazz musicians, spanning three generations.

GREAT SANTINI, THE

Alternate: The Ace
Cast: Stan Shaw*, Theresa Merritt*, Robert Duvall, Blythe Danner, Michael O'Keefe
Director: Lewis John Carlino
Executive Producer: John E. Pommer
Music Performer: Elmer Bernstein
Music by: Elmer Bernstein
Producer: Charles A. Pratt, John E. Pommer
Screenwriter: Lewis John Carlino
Storywriter: Pat Conroy
Tech Info: color/sound/115 min.   Type: Dramatic Feature
Date: 1979   Origin: USA
Company: Orion
Distributors/Format: Warner Bros. Home Video, Inc. (1/2")
Annotation: Shaw befriends O'Keefe who is undergoing a frustrating and violent relationship with his father (Duvall). O'Keefe's friendship with Shaw gives him insight into black-white relations and his problems with his father. Merritt plays Shaw's mother.

GREATEST WEEK IN GOSPEL, THE

Tech Info: color/sound/80 min.   Type: Concert Feature
Date: 1989   Origin: USA
Company: Xenon Entertainment
Distributors/Format: Xenon Entertainment Group (1/2")
Archives/Format: IUB - AAAMC (1/2")
Annotation: A rare gathering filmed in Los Angeles with 28 of today's hottest gospel acts. This four volume set is one of the most successful collections of live gospel music performance ever filmed.

GREEN CARD

Cast: Novella Nelson*, Conrad Roberts*, Gerard Depardieu, Andie MacDowell, Gregg Edelman
Director: Peter Weir
Executive Producer: Edward S. Feldman
Music by: Hans Zimmer
Producer: Edward S. Feldman, Peter Weir, Duncan Henderson, Jean Gontier
Screenwriter: Peter Weir
Tech Info: color/sound/108 min.   Type: Comedy Feature
Date: 1990   Origin: Australia, France
Company: Touchstone, Green Card
Distributors/Format: Buena Vista Home Video (1/2")
Annotation: A Frenchman (Depardieu) marries an American (MacDowell) to get his green card. Nelson, a Marriage Celebrant, performs the ceremony.

GREMLINS
Cast: Glynn Turman*, Hoyt Axton, Phoebe Cates, Zach Galligan
Director: Joe Dante
Executive Producer: Steven Spielberg, Frank Marshall, Kathleen Kennedy
Music by: Jerry Goldsmith
Producer: Steven Spielberg, Frank Marshall, Kathleen Kennedy, Michael Finnell
Screenwriter: Chris Columbus
Tech Info: color/sound/111 min.   Type: Dramatic Feature
Date: 1984   Origin: USA
Company: Warner Bros.
Distributors/Format: Warner Bros. Home Video, Inc. (1/2")
Annotation: Gremlins, lizardlike creatures, multiply and destroy an entire town.
Turman plays a science teacher who is killed by the gremlins.

GREMLINS 2: THE NEW BATCH
Cast: Bubba Smith*, Phoebe Cates, Zach Galligan, John Glover, Howie Mandel
Director: Joe Dante
Executive Producer: Steven Spielberg, Frank Marshall, Kathleen Kennedy
Music by: Jerry Goldsmith
Producer: Steven Spielberg, Frank Marshall, Kathleen Kennedy, Michael Finnell
Screenwriter: Charlie Haas
Tech Info: color/sound/105 min.   Type: Dramatic Feature
Date: 1990   Origin: USA
Company: Mike Finnell, Amblin
Distributors/Format: Warner Bros. Home Video, Inc. (1/2")
Annotation: Gizzmo, a furry pet, is rescued and spawns more destructive gremlins
that overtake the Chinatown Center. Smith appears as himself.

GRIM PRAIRIE TALES
Cast: James Earl Jones*, Brad Dourif
Director: Wayne Coe
Music by: Steve Dancz
Producer: Richard Hahn
Storywriter: Wayne Coe
Tech Info: color/sound/87 min.   Type: Dramatic Feature
Date: 1990   Origin: USA
Company: East West Film Partners, Academy Entertainment
Distributors/Format: Academy Entertainment (35mm; 1/2")
Annotation: A city slicker (Dourif) and a frontier bounty hunter (Jones) meet in the
middle of the desert one night and set up camp together. The two pass the entire
evening seeing who can tell the most effective story.

GROSS ANATOMY
Cast: Zakes Mokae*, Alice Carter*, Christine Lahti, Matthew Modine, Todd Field,
Daphne Zuniga, John Scott Clough
Director: Thom Eberhardt
Executive Producer: Sandy Gallin, Carol Baum
Music by: David Newman
Producer: Howard Rosenman, Sandy Gallin, Carol Baum, Debra Hill
Screenwriter: Ron Nyswaner, Mark Spragg
Storywriter: Howard Rosenman, Alan Jay Glueckman, Mark Spragg, Stanley Isaacs

Tech Info: color/sound/107 min.   Type: Dramatic Feature
Date: 1989   Origin: USA
Company: Silver Screen Part. IV, Hill-Rosenman, Touchstone
Distributors/Format: Buena Vista Home Video (1/2")
Annotation: Gross Anatomy is the gate-keeping course at a high powered medical school which Joe Slovak (Modine) attends with an assortment of other students (Zuniga, Field, Clough, Carter). Lahti plays the exacting, humorless professor; Mokae is her slightly more humane colleague, Dr. Banumbra.

GRUMPY OLD MEN

Cast: Ossie Davis*, Jack Lemmon, Walter Matthau, Ann-Margret
Director: Donald Petrie
Executive Producer: Dan Kolsrud
Music by: Alan Silvestri
Producer: John Davis, Richard C. Berman, Dan Kolsrud
Screenwriter: Mark Steven Johnson
Tech Info: color/sound/104 min.   Type: Comedy Feature
Date: 1993   Origin: USA
Company: Warner Bros., Davis Entertainment
Distributors/Format: Warner Bros. Home Video, Inc. (1/2")
Annotation: Two old friends (Lemmon and Matthau) spend time ice fishing and goading each other in Minnesota. Davis is Chuck, the proprietor of the fishing grounds' canteen, whose death prompts the men to confront their mortality.

GUARDIAN, THE

Cast: Theresa Randle*, Carey Lowell, Jenny Seagrove, Dwier Brown
Director: William Friedkin
Executive Producer: David Salven
Music by: Jack Hues
Producer: Joe Wizan, David Salven
Screenwriter: William Friedkin, Stephen Volk, Dan Greenburg
Tech Info: color/sound/98 min.   Type: Dramatic Feature
Date: 1990   Origin: USA
Company: Joe Wizan
Distributors/Format: Universal Home Video (1/2")
Annotation: Phil (Brown), an advertising artist, and his wife Kate (Lowell) move to an idyllic area near Los Angeles. After their baby is born, they begin interviewing nannies, one of whom is Arlene Russell (Randle) who comes to a violent end when Camilla (Seagrove), who feeds babies to trees, wants her out of the way so that she can get the job.

GUN IN BETTY LOU'S HANDBAG, THE

Cast: Alfre Woodard*, Paul Bates*, Penelope Ann Miller, Julianna Moore, Eric Thal
Director: Alan Moyle
Executive Producer: Ted Field, Robert Cort
Music by: Richard Gibbs
Producer: Ted Field, Robert Cort, Scott Kroopf
Screenwriter: Grace Cary Bickley
Tech Info: color/sound/89 min.   Type: Comedy Feature

Date: 1992   Origin: USA
Company: In the Bag Prod. Inc., Interscope, Touchstone
Distributors/Format: Buena Vista Home Video (1/2")
Annotation: Betty Lou Perkins (Miller) is an assistant librarian in the quiet little town
of Tettley, Missouri, but after a murder occurs, the town explodes. Ann (Woodard),
an attorney and Betty Lou's friend is caught in the middle of the action as Officer
Finney (Bates) tries to solve the crime.

GUNMEN

Cast: Kadeem Hardison*, Mario Van Peebles*, Sally Kirkland, Christopher Lambert,
Denis Leary, Patrick Stewart
Director: Deran Sarafian, Hiro Narita
Executive Producer: Lance Hool, Conrad Hool
Music by: John Debney
Producer: John Davis, Lance Hool, Lawrence Mark, John Flock, Conrad Hool
Screenwriter: Stephen Sommers
Tech Info: color/sound/97 min.   Type: Dramatic Feature
Date: 1994   Origin: USA
Company: Grey Gunmen Productions
Distributors/Format: LIVE Home Video (1/2"), Dimension (16mm)
Annotation: A bounty hunter (Van Peebles) and a con man (Lambert) each have half
the clues to the whereabouts of a $400 million treasure of stolen drug money.
Against their will, they are forced to team up to battle an elite squad of mafia
assassins.   Hardison plays Iggy.

GUY FROM HARLEM, THE

Cast: Loye Hawkins*, Cathy Davis*, Patricia Fulton*
Director: Rene Martinez Jr.
Producer: International Cinema, Inc.
Tech Info: color/sound/86 min.   Type: Dramatic Feature
Date: 1989   Origin: USA
Studio: Independent
Company: Blaction Productions
Distributors/Format: Xenon Entertainment Group (1/2")
Annotation: When the CIA calls on him to guard a beautiful African princess, a tough
private investigator (Hawkins) encounters treachery, greed, and revenge.

GUYVER, THE

Cast: Jimmy/Jimmie Walker*, Willard Pugh*, Mark Hamill, Vivian Wu, Jack
Armstrong
Director: Screaming Mad George , Steve Wang
Executive Producer: Yutaka Wada, Aki Komine
Music by: Matthew Morse
Producer: Brian Yuzna, Yutaka Wada, Aki Komine
Screenwriter: Jon Purdy
Tech Info: color/sound/92 min.   Type: Dramatic Feature
Date: 1992   Origin: USA
Company: Guyver Productions
Distributors/Format: New Line Cinema Home Video (1/2")
Annotation: Max (Hamill) investigates Chronos Corporation where ancient alien
power has been used to transform humans into Zoanoid henchmen. Walker plays
Striker, one of the monstrous goons and Pugh plays Castle.

H-2 WORKER
Director: Stephanie Black
Music Performer: Mutabaruka *
Music by: Mutabaruka *
Producer: Stephanie Black
Tech Info: color/sound/70 min. Type: Documentary Feature
Date: 1990 Origin: USA
Company: Valley Filmworks, Inc.
Distributors/Format: First Run/Icarus Films (16mm)
Annotation: H-2 guest worker visas allow Jamaican immigrant laborers to work in Florida's sugar cane field, albeit for "slave wages."

HAIR
Cast: Nell Carter*, Melba Moore*, Dorsey Wright*, Cheryl Barnes*, Rahsaan Curry*, John Savage, Beverly D'Angelo, Treat Williams
Director: Milos Forman
Music by: Galt MacDermot
Producer: Michael Butler, Lester Persky
Screenwriter: Michael Weller
Storywriter: Gerome Ragni, James Rado, Galt MacDermot
Tech Info: color/sound/118 min. Type: Musical Feature
Date: 1979 Origin: USA
Company: United Artists
Distributors/Format: United Artists Home Video (1/2")
Annotation: An Oklahoma Vietnam draftee (Savage) is adopted by a group of New York flower children including Berger (Williams) and Hud/Lafayette (Wright). Barnes plays Hud's fiancee and Curry their child Lafayette, Jr. Carter performs in several numbers, Moore in one, in this adaptation of the popular Broadway musical.

HAIR PIECE: A FILM FOR NAPPY-HEADED PEOPLE
Director: Ayoka Chenzira*
Narrator: Carol-Jean Lewis*
Producer: Ayoka Chenzira*
Screenwriter: Ayoka Chenzira*
Tech Info: color/sound/10 min. Type: Animated Short
Date: 1984 Origin: USA
Studio: Independent
Distributors/Format: Third World Newsreel (1/2"), Women Make Movies, Inc. (16mm; 1/2"), Red Carnelian Films/Video (16mm; 1/2")
Archives/Format: IUB - BFC/A (16mm)
Annotation: Chenzira's animated satire explores the "hair problem" among African Americans. This historical overview examines the various techniques black men and women have used to change the texture of their hair.

HAIRSPRAY
Cast: Ruth Brown*, Sonny Bono, Divine , Pia Zadora, Rikki Lake, Debbie Harry, Jerry Stiller
Director: John Waters
Executive Producer: Robert Shaye, Sara Risher
Music Performer: Ruth Brown*
Producer: Rachel Talalay, Robert Shaye, Sara Risher

Screenwriter: John Waters
Tech Info: color/sound/92 min.　　　Type: Comedy Feature
Date: 1987　Origin: USA
Company: New Line Cinema
Distributors/Format: Facets Multimedia, Inc. (1/2"), New Line Cinema Home Video (1/2")
Annotation: Tracy Tunblad (Lake) has the biggest bouffant and all the right moves to be a star on Baltimore's "The Corny Collins Show." Brown is a music performer during a "Blacks only" party when whites are not using the sound stage.

HALF SLAVE, HALF FREE

Alternate: Part One: Solomon Northup's Odyssey
Cast: Rhetta Green*, Avery Brooks*, Joe Seneca*, Janet League*, Jay McMillian*, Arthur/Art Evans*, Lee Bryant, John Saxon, Michael Tolan
Director: Gordon Parks*
Music by: Gordon Parks*
Producer: Yanna Kroyt Brandt
Screenwriter: Lou Potter*, Samm-Art Williams*
Tech Info: color/sound/118 min.　　　Type: Dramatic Feature
Date: 1984　Origin: USA
Company: The Fremantle Corporation, Past America Inc.
Distributors/Format: Facets Multimedia, Inc. (1/2"), Xenon Entertainment Group (1/2"), Filmic Archives (1/2")
Archives/Format: IUB - BFC/A (1/2")
Annotation: Adapted from the 19th century autobiographical "Narrative of the Life of Solomon Northup," the film dramatizes Northup's (Brooks) experiences as a free man sold into slavery by two kidnappers. After 12 years as a slave in Louisiana, he is finally returned to Saratoga, New York, where his wife and three children, now grown, await him.

HALLELUJAH!: A GOSPEL CELEBRATION

Cast: Five Blind Boys *
Tech Info: color/sound/60 min.　　　Type: Concert Feature
Date: 1991　Origin: USA
Company: Xenon Video
Distributors/Format: Xenon Entertainment Group (1/2")
Archives/Format: IUB - AAAMC (1/2")
Annotation: The film includes exquisite vintage performances by the legendary Five Blind Boys and others. This tape has found great appeal among lovers of many musical styles from Gospel to Jazz to Blues.

HALLOWEEN II

Cast: Gloria Gifford*, Jamie Lee Curtis, Donald Pleasence, Lance Guest, Charles Cyphers, Jeffrey Kramer
Director: Rick Rosenthal
Executive Producer: Irwin Yablans, Joseph Wolf
Music by: John Carpenter, Alan Howarth
Producer: Irwin Yablans, John Carpenter, Debra Hill, Joseph Wolf
Screenwriter: John Carpenter, Debra Hill
Tech Info: color/sound/92 min.　　　Type: Dramatic Feature

Date: 1981   Origin: USA
Company: DEG
Distributors/Format: Universal Home Video (1/2")
Annotation: Laurie (Curtis), the lone survivor of the first film, is chased and terrorized in a hospital by the killer. Gifford plays Mrs. Alves.

HAMBONE AND HILLIE

Cast: O.J. Simpson*, Lillian Gish, Candy Clark, Timothy Bottoms, Alan Hale, Hambone
Director: Roy Watts
Executive Producer: Mel Pearl, Don Levin
Music Performer: George Garvarentz
Music by: George Garvarentz
Producer: Sandy Howard, Gary Gillingham, Mel Pearl, Don Levin
Screenwriter: Sandra K. Bailey, Michael Murphey, Joel Soisson
Tech Info: color/sound/97 min.   Type: Dramatic Feature
Date: 1984   Origin: USA
Company: Adams Apple Film Company, New World Pictures
Distributors/Format: Thorn/EMI Home Video (1/2")
Archives/Format: IUB - AAAMC (1/2")
Annotation: When Hambone is separated from his owner Hillie (Gish) at a New York airport terminal, the dog must trek 3,000 miles in order to find her again. Along the way, several individuals aid him in his journey, including a friendly semi-truck driver named Tucker (Simpson).

HAMBURGER HILL

Cast: Michael P. Boatman*, Don Cheadle*, Don James*, Courtney B. Vance*, Mitchell Donlan, Steven Weber
Director: John Irving
Music by: Phillip Glass
Producer: Marcia Nasatir, Larry De Waay
Screenwriter: Jim Carabatsos
Tech Info: color/sound/94 min.   Type: Dramatic Feature
Date: 1987   Origin: USA
Company: Paramount, RKO
Distributors/Format: Paramount Home Video (1/2")
Annotation: In this bloody operation during the Vietnam War, Doc (Vance) is the medic who instructs the platoon about hygiene. His best friends are McDaniel (James), Motown (Boatman) and Washburn (Cheadle). Washburn and two white soldiers are the only survivors after finally taking Hamburger Hill.

HAMMER TIME

Cast: M.C. Hammer *
Director: Rupert Wainwright, Susan Friedman, David Florimbi, Jules Lichtman
Music Performer: M.C. Hammer *
Producer: John E. Oetjen, Susan Friedman, Tracy Lee Wong, Terrance Power
Tech Info: mixed/sound/60 min.   Type: Concert Feature

Date: 1990   Origin: USA
Company: Fragile Films, Capitol Video
Distributors/Format: Capitol Home Video (1/2")
Archives/Format: IUB - AAAMC (1/2")
Annotation: The film presents Hammer in eight of his most successful video performances: "Let's Get it Started," "Turn this Mutha Out," "Pump it Up," "They Put Me in the Mix," "Please Hammer Don't Hurt 'Em," "U Can't Touch This," "Have You Seen Her," and "Pray." The program also includes a seven-minute documentary on PLEASE HAMMER DON'T HURT 'EM--THE MOVIE, where Hammer comments on his youth in Oakland.

HAND THAT ROCKS THE CRADLE, THE
Cast: Ernie Hudson*, Rebecca De Mornay, Annabella Sciorra, Matt McCoy
Director: Curtis Hanson
Music by: Graeme Revell
Producer: David Madden
Screenwriter: Amanda Silver
Tech Info: color/sound/110 min.   Type: Dramatic Feature
Date: 1992   Origin: USA
Company: Interscope Communications, Hollywood Pictures
Distributors/Format: Hollywood Pictures Home Video (1/2")
Annotation: Solomon (Hudson) portrays a mentally disabled man employed by a handicap agency to do light outdoor work for a family being subtlety taunted by a mentally disturbed nanny (De Mornay).

HANGFIRE
Cast: Ken Foree*, Yaphet Kotto*, Jan-Michael Vincent, Kim Delaney, Brad Davis, Lee DeBroux, James Tolkan
Director: Peter Maris
Music by: Jim Price
Producer: Brad Krevoy, Steven Stabler
Screenwriter: Brian D. Jeffries
Tech Info: color/sound/89 min.   Type: Dramatic Feature
Date: 1991   Origin: USA
Company: Krevoy/Stabler Productions
Distributors/Format: MPCA (1/2")
Annotation: When a cloud of toxic gas is released, a group of prisoners escape during the evacuation of the penitentiary. A state police lieutenant (Kotto) attempts to handle the crisis when several of the escapees hold hostages in Sonora. Foree plays Billy, an Army buddy of Sonora's sheriff (Davis), and the two work together to save the hostages.

HANGIN' WITH THE HOMEBOYS
Cast: Rony Clanton*, Danitra Vance*, Doug E. Doug*, Mario Joyner*, Kimberly Russell*, LaTanya Richardson*, Reggie Montgomery*, Rosemarie Jackson*, Jonathan Solomon*, Victor L. Cook*, Ellis Williams*, John Leguizamo, Nestor Serrano
Director: Joseph B. Vasquez
Music Performer: Snap *, 2 Live Crew *, T-Bone Walker*, TripleXXX , Poison Clan , Stevie B.
Producer: Richard Brick
Screenwriter: Joseph B. Vasquez

Tech Info: color/sound/88 min.   Type: Dramatic Feature
Date: 1991   Origin: USA
Company: New Line Cinema
Distributors/Format: New Line Cinema Home Video (1/2")
Archives/Format: IUB - BFC/A (1/2")
Annotation: The film depicts one night in the life of four South Bronx youths, a night in which alcohol, women, nightclubs, and boredom force each to examine the reality of his harsh urban existence. Willie (Doug) is the phony militant; Tommy (Joyner), an aspiring actor; Vinny (Serrano), a Puerto-Rican who attempts to disguise his ethnicity; Johnny (Leguizamo), a naive innocent.

HANNAH AND HER SISTERS
Cast: Paul Bates*, Woody Allen, Michael Caine, Barbara Hershey, Dianne Wiest, Carrie Fisher, Mia Farrow
Director: Woody Allen
Executive Producer: Charles H. Joffe, Jack Rollins
Producer: Charles H. Joffe, Robert Greenhut, Jack Rollins
Screenwriter: Woody Allen
Tech Info: color/sound/106 min.   Type: Comedy Feature
Date: 1986   Origin: USA
Company: Orion
Distributors/Format: Orion Home Video (1/2")
Annotation: Bates plays a theater manager in this Woody Allen film that revolves around the lives of three sisters (Farrow, Hershey, Wiest) in New York.

HAPPILY EVER AFTER
Cast: Irene Cara*, Dom DeLuise, Malcolm McDowell, Michael Horton, Phyllis Diller, Zsa Zsa Gabor
Director: John Howley
Music by: Frank W. Becker
Producer: Lou Scheimer
Screenwriter: Martha Moran, Robby London
Tech Info: color/sound/74 min.   Type: Animated Feature
Date: 1993   Origin: USA
Company: Lou Scheimer Productions, Kel-Air Entertainment
Distributors/Format: First National Film Corporation (16mm)
Annotation: While en route to the home of the seven dwarfs to deliver a wedding invitation, Snow White and her Prince (Horton) encounter the evil Lord Maliss (McDowell) who tries to stop them. Cara provides the voice of Snow White.

HAPPY HOUR
Cast: Beverly Todd*, Jamie Farr, Richard Gilliland, Tawny Kitaen
Director: John De Bello
Executive Producer: J. Stephen Peace
Music by: Neal Fox, Rick Patterson
Producer: J. Stephen Peace, J. Stephen Peace, John De Bello
Screenwriter: J. Stephen Peace, John De Bello, Constantine Dillon
Tech Info: color/sound/88 min.   Type: Comedy Feature

Date: 1987   Origin: USA
Company: Four Square
Distributors/Format: The Movie Store (16mm)
Annotation: A beer company loses the formula that makes the public love its product. Todd plays Laura.

HARD TARGET

Cast: Kasi Lemmons*, Willie C. Carpenter*, Lance Henriksen, Yancy Butler, Jean-Claude Van Damme
Director: John Woo
Executive Producer: Moshe Diamant, Sam Raimi, Robert Tapert
Music by: Kodo
Producer: Moshe Diamant, Sean Daniel, Sam Raimi, Robert Tapert, James Jacks
Screenwriter: Chuck Pfarrer
Tech Info: color/sound/92 min.   Type: Dramatic Feature
Date: 1993   Origin: USA
Company: Alphaville Productions, S&R Productions, Universal
Distributors/Format: Universal Home Video (1/2")
Annotation: Natasha Binder (Butler) hires out-of-work merchant marine Chance Boudreaux (Van Damme) to hunt her father's killer. Elijah Roper (Carpenter), a friend of the deceased and a fellow homeless Vietnam veteran, is the next target of Fouchon (Henriksen) who makes a game of killing. Lemmons plays Carmine Mitchell.

HARD WAY, THE

Cast: Bill Cobbs*, Conrad Roberts*, L.L. Cool J. *, Bryant Gumbel*, James Woods, Penny Marshall, Michael J. Fox
Director: John Badham
Music Performer: L.L. Cool J. *
Music by: Arthur B. Rubinstein
Producer: Rob Cohen, William Sackheim
Screenwriter: Daniel Pyne, Lem Dobbs
Storywriter: Lem Dobbs, Michael Kozoll
Tech Info: color/sound/111 min.   Type: Comedy Feature
Date: 1991   Origin: USA
Company: Badham/Cohen Group
Distributors/Format: MCA/Universal Home Video (1/2")
Annotation: L.L. Cool J plays Billy, a New York City cop who helps John Moss (Woods) catch a psychotic murderer. Cobbs plays "Raggedy Man" who confronts Nick Lang (Fox) with the reality of stench and filth in the ghettos of New York.

HARDCORE

Alternate: Hardcore Life, The
Cast: Hal Williams*, Peter Boyle, Season Hubley, George C. Scott
Director: Paul Schrader
Executive Producer: John Milius
Music by: Jack Nitzsche
Producer: John Milius, Buzz Feitshans
Screenwriter: Paul Schrader
Tech Info: color/sound/105 min.   Type: Dramatic Feature

Date: 1979   Origin: USA
Company: Columbia
Distributors/Format: Columbia Pictures Home Video (1/2")
Annotation: Niki (Hubley), the daughter of religious man Jake Van Dorn (Scott), disappears only to reappear in a pornographic film. Van Dorn's search leads him to porn houses and pimps. Williams plays Big Dick Blaque.

HARDWOOD DREAMS

Director: Michael Tollin*
Narrator: Wesley Snipes*
Tech Info: color/sound/47 min.   Type: Documentary Short
Date: 1993   Origin: USA
Studio: Independent
Distributors/Format: Cinema Guild (1/2")
Annotation: Wesley Snipes narrates this film about inner-city Los Angeles youths who play for Morningside High School basketball's team and their determination to make it as professionals.

HARLEM NIGHTS

Cast: Richard Pryor*, Eddie Murphy*, Stan Shaw*, Howard "Sandman" Sims*, Redd Foxx*, Arsenio Hall*, Jasmine Guy*, Della Reese*, Charles Q. Murphy*, Lela Rochon*, Danny Aiello, Michael Lerner
Director: Eddie Murphy*
Music Performer: Herbie Hancock*
Music by: Herbie Hancock*
Producer: Mark Lipsky, Robert D. Wachs
Screenwriter: Eddie Murphy*
Storywriter: Eddie Murphy*
Tech Info: color/sound/118 min.   Type: Comedy Feature
Date: 1989   Origin: USA
Company: Eddie Murphy* Production
Distributors/Format: Paramount Home Video (1/2")
Archives/Format: IUB - BFC/A (1/2")
Annotation: Quick (Murphy) and Sugar (Pryor) are two Harlem nightclub owners who outsmart both the mob and corrupt police. Rochon plays Sunshine; Guy is Dominique; Reese, a madame. The film is set during the 1930s.

HARLEY DAVIDSON AND THE MARLBORO MAN

Cast: Giancarlo Esposito*, Vanessa Williams*, Julius Harris*, Marlin Darton*, Don Johnson, Mickey Rourke
Director: Simon Wincer
Music by: Basil Poledouris
Producer: Don Michael Paul, Jere Henshaw
Screenwriter: Don Michael Paul
Storywriter: Don Michael Paul
Tech Info: color/sound/98 min.   Type: Dramatic Feature
Date: 1991   Origin: USA
Company: MGM-Pathe Communications Co.
Distributors/Format: MGM Home Video (1/2")
Annotation: Harley Davidson (Rourke) and the Marlboro Man (Johnson) battle corporate Mafia when they rob an armored truck carrying an expensive new drug. The robbery is performed in the hope of helping the owner (Harris) of a Burbank

landmark bar and grill. Lulu Daniels (Williams) is the club's singer and Jimmy Jiles (Esposito) is one of the bar's frequent customers.

HARRY AND SON

Cast: Ossie Davis*, Ellen Barkin, Paul Newman, Wilford Brimley, Robby Benson
Director: Paul Newman
Music by: Henry Mancini
Producer: Paul Newman, Ronald L. Buck
Screenwriter: Paul Newman, Ronald L. Buck
Tech Info: color/sound/117 min.   Type: Dramatic Feature
Date: 1984   Origin: USA
Company: Orion
Annotation: Harry (Newman), a middle-aged construction worker, is laid off when he temporarily loses his sight. His son Howard (Benson) bears the brunt of Harry's self-pity. Davis plays Raymond and Freeman is Siemanowski.

HARRY AND THE HENDERSONS

Cast: Kevin Peter Hall*, John Lithgow, David Suchet, Margaret Langrick, Melinda Dillon, Joshua Rudoy
Director: William Dear
Music by: Bruce Broughton
Producer: Richard Vane, William Dear
Screenwriter: William Dear, William E. Martin, Ezra D. Rappaport
Tech Info: color/sound/110 min.   Type: Comedy Feature
Date: 1987   Origin: USA
Company: Amblin
Distributors/Format: Universal Home Video (1/2")
Annotation: George Henderson (Lithgow) and his family are heading home in the family station wagon when they hit what they think is a huge creature. Thinking it is dead, they strap it onto the roof, but Harry (Hall), the legendary Big Foot, is only stunned and the family decides to keep him.

HE WHO WALKS ALONE

Cast: Louis Gossett Jr.*, Mary Alice*, Clu Gulager
Director: Jerrold Freedman
Producer: Harry Sherman
Screenwriter: Jerrold Freedman
Storywriter: Jerrold Freedman
Tech Info: color/sound/90 min.   Type: Dramatic Feature
Date: 1978   Origin: USA
Studio: Independent
Company: VCL Communications, Inc.
Annotation: Gossett portrays Thomas E. Gilmore, who was elected sheriff in the 1960s, becoming the South's first black law enforcement official.

HE'S MY GIRL

Cast: T.K. Carter*, Misha McK*, David Hallyday, Jennifer Tilly
Director: Gabrielle Beaumont
Executive Producer: Tony Scotti, Ben Scotti, Fred Scotti
Producer: Lawrence Mortorff, Angela P. Schapiro, Tony Scotti, Ben Scotti, Fred Scotti
Screenwriter: Taylor Ames, Charles F. Bohl

Tech Info: color/sound/104 min.   Type: Comedy Feature
Date: 1987   Origin: USA
Company: Scotti Bros.
Distributors/Format: Scotti Bros. Productions (16mm)
Annotation: When singer-songwriter Bryan Peters (Hallyday) wins a trip to Los Angeles with his non-existent girlfriend, his best friend Reggie (Carter) dons a wig and becomes Regina.

HEAR NO EVIL

Cast: Greg Elam*, George Rankins*, Martin Sheen, D.B. Sweeney, Marlee Matlin, John C. McGinley
Director: Robert Greenwald
Music Performer: A-Zaya Acappella Band *, Graeme Revell
Music by: Graeme Revell
Storywriter: R.M. Badat, Danny Rubin
Tech Info: color/sound/98 min.   Type: Comedy Feature
Date: 1993   Origin: USA
Company: Fox
Distributors/Format: Fox Home Video (1/2")
Annotation: An athletic trainer, Jillian (Matlin) is stalked by a killer, who knows she cannot hear, after her client Mickey O'Malley (McGinley) a journalist, appears to be killed for a stolen museum coin. Sheen plays Brock, a corrupt policeman; Elam plays Cooper, one of his lieutenants.

HEART AND SOULS

Cast: Ernie Hudson*, B.B. King*, Alfre Woodard*, Janet MacLachlan*, Wanya Green*, Chasiti Hampton*, Tony Coleman*, Javar David Levingston*, Kyra Sedgwick, Charles Grodin, Tom Sizemore, Robert Downey Jr., Elisabeth Shue, David Paymer
Director: Ron Underwood
Tech Info: color/sound/104 min.   Type: Comedy Feature
Date: 1993   Origin: USA
Company: Alphaville/Stampede Entertainment
Distributors/Format: Universal Home Video (1/2")
Annotation: Woodard plays Penny, a single mother who, on her way to work, dies in a bus accident with three other people (Sedgwick, Grodin and Sizemore). They all become ghosts and are transformed into the soul of Thomas Reilly (Downey). King appears as himself; MacLachlan, Green, Hampton, Coleman, and Levingston have minor roles as Woodard's family members.

HEART CONDITION

Cast: Denzel Washington*, Ja'net DuBois*, Ron Taylor*, Kendall McCarthy*, Dasanea Johnson*, Jonquaette Johnson*, Shauntae Johnson*, Theresa Randle*, Roger E. Mosley*, Bob Hoskins, Chloe Webb, Ray Baker
Director: James D. Parriott
Executive Producer: Robert Shaye
Music Performer: Bonnie Raitt
Music by: Patrick Leonard
Producer: Robert Shaye, Steve Tisch
Screenwriter: James D. Parriott
Tech Info: color/sound/100 min.   Type: Dramatic Feature

Date: 1990   Origin: USA
Company: Steve Tisch, James D. Parriott
Distributors/Format: New Line Cinema Home Video (1/2")
Annotation: Napoleon Stone (Washington), a lawyer, dies and his heart is donated to racist policeman Jack Moony (Hoskins). Stone also leaves a pregnant girlfriend (Webb) behind, the same girl Moony is in love with. DuBois plays Stone's mother; McCarthy is Archimedes, Stone's brother; Mosley plays Moony's boss.

HEARTBREAK RIDGE

Cast: Moses Gunn*, Mario Van Peebles*, Clint Eastwood, Everett McGill, Marsha Mason, Arlen Dean Snyder, Boyd Gaines
Director: Clint Eastwood
Executive Producer: Fritz Manes
Producer: Clint Eastwood, Fritz Manes
Screenwriter: James Carabatsos
Storywriter: James Carabatsos
Tech Info: color/sound/129 min.   Type: Dramatic Feature
Date: 1986   Origin: USA
Company: Malpaso/Jay Weston Productions
Distributors/Format: Warner Bros. Home Video, Inc. (1/2")
Annotation: An aging sergeant (Eastwood) is charged with getting a Marine platoon in shape for the Grenada invasion. Van Peebles is one of the recruits, Gunn, a hardened trainer.

HEARTBURN

Cast: Anna Maria Horsford*, Meryl Streep, Maureen Stapleton, Jack Nicholson, Jeff Daniels
Director: Mike Nichols
Music by: Carly Simon
Producer: Mike Nichols, Robert Greenhut
Screenwriter: Nora Ephron
Tech Info: color/sound/108 min.   Type: Comedy Feature
Date: 1986   Origin: USA
Company: Paramount
Distributors/Format: Paramount Home Video (1/2")
Annotation: Rachel (Streep), a divorced magazine writer, and Mark (Nicholson), a D.C. columnist, meet and marry but gradually Mark starts to feel stifled by the marriage. Horsford plays Della.

HEAVEN IS A PLAYGROUND

Cast: Victor Love*, Michael Warren*, Nigel Miguel*, Cylk Cozart*, Hakeem Olajuwon*, Bo Kimble*, D.B. Sweeney, Richard Jordan, Janet Julian
Director: Randall Fried
Executive Producer: William Stuart, Larry Edwards, Douglas S. Cook
Music by: Patrick O'Hearn
Producer: Billy Higgins*, Keith Bank, William Stuart, Larry Edwards, Douglas S. Cook
Screenwriter: Randall Fried
Tech Info: color/sound/111 min.   Type: Dramatic Feature

Date: 1992   Origin: USA
Company: Aurora Productions, Heaven Corporation
Distributors/Format: Columbia/TriStar Home Video (1/2")
Annotation: Based on the novel by Rick Telander, freelance talent scout Byron Harper (Warren) uses a ghetto basketball court as a recruitment center for college and pro basketball. When Truth Harrison (Love), one of Harper's most talented players destined for a professional career, cracks under pressure, Harper re-evaluates with his friend Zack's (Sweeney) aid their approach to helping young players. Kimble is Matthew Lockhart, one of the players; Olajuwon plays himself.

HEAVEN, EARTH & HELL
Cast: Thomas Allen Harris*, Ayisha Abraham*, Andrea Fatona*, Alain Pistolozzi, Patrick Fernier
Director: Thomas Allen Harris*
Tech Info: color/sound/26 min.   Type: Experimental Short
Date: 1994   Origin: USA
Studio: Independent
Distributors/Format: Third World Newsreel (1/2")
Annotation: Reflecting on the "trickster" figure in African and Native American cultures, while recounting the story of his first love, Harris laments the loss of innocence in a world without magic.

HELP SAVE PLANET EARTH
Series: Easy Ways To Make A Big Difference
Director: Chuck Vinson
Narrator: Ted Danson
Producer: George Paige
Speaker: Whoopi Goldberg*, Sinbad *, Beau Bridges, Lloyd Bridges, Max Casella, Jamie Lee Curtis, Sally Kellerman, Cheech Marin, John Ritter
Tech Info: color/sound/71 min.   Type: Documentary Feature
Date: 1990   Origin: USA
Company: George Paige Associates, Inc.
Distributors/Format: MCA/Universal Home Video (1/2"), Filmic Archives (1/2")
Annotation: The film examines the state of our environment and what needs to be done to improve it. The celebrities speak to the issue of conservation/preservation.

HENRY: PORTRAIT OF A SERIAL KILLER
Cast: Michael Rooker, Tom Towles, Tracy Arnold
Director: John McNaughton
Executive Producer: Waleed B. Ali*, Malik B. Ali*
Music by: Steven A. Jones, Ken Hale
Producer: Waleed B. Ali*, Malik B. Ali*, John McNaughton, Steven A. Jones, Lisa Dedmond
Screenwriter: Richard Fire, John McNaughton
Tech Info: color/sound/90 min.   Type: Documentary Feature
Date: 1989   Origin: USA
Company: Maljack Productions
Distributors/Format: Maljack Productions (MPI Home Video) (1/2")
Annotation: Rated "X," the film is based on the life story of serial killer Henry Lee Lucas. Graphic murder scenes illustrate the severity of Henry's madness.

HERO AND THE TERROR
Cast: Ron O'Neal*, Murphy Dunne*, Chuck Norris, Steve James, Jack O'Halloran
Director: William Tannen
Executive Producer: Yoram Globus, Menahem Golan
Music by: David Michael Frank
Producer: Yoram Globus, Menahem Golan, Raymond Wagner
Screenwriter: Dennis Shryack, Michael Blodgett
Storywriter: Michael Blodgett
Tech Info: color/sound/96 min.   Type: Dramatic Feature
Date: 1988   Origin: USA
Company: Golan-Globus
Distributors/Format: Cannon Home Video (1/2")
Annotation: A police detective (Norris) is plagued by a brutalizing criminal (O'Halloran). O'Neal plays the Mayor who congratulates the city's hero.

HIDDEN HERITAGE: THE ROOTS OF BLACK AMERICAN PAINTING
Producer: David Driskell*
Speaker: David Driskell*
Tech Info: color/sound/52 min.   Type: Documentary Feature
Date: 1990   Origin: USA
Studio: Independent
Distributors/Format: Landmark Films Inc. (1/2")
Annotation: Professor Driskell traces the history of African American artists from the American Revolution to the Second World War, placing artist's individual achievements in the context of social change.

HIDE IN PLAIN SIGHT
Cast: Beatrice Winde*, Danny Aiello, James Caan, Jill Eikenberry
Director: James Caan
Music by: Leonard Rosenman
Producer: Robert Christiansen, Rick Rosenberg
Screenwriter: Spencer Eastman
Tech Info: color/sound/92 min.   Type: Dramatic Feature
Date: 1980   Origin: USA
Company: MGM
Distributors/Format: United Artists Home Video (1/2")
Annotation: Thomas Hacklin (Caan) goes to the home of his ex-wife to visit his children, only to find them vanished into the federal witness relocation program. Winde plays the unemployment clerk.

HIGHER LEARNING
Cast: Laurence/Larry Fishburne*, Omar Epps*, Ice Cube *, Regina King*, Tyra Banks*, Busta Rhymez *, John Walton Smith Jr.*, D-Knowledge *, Kristy Swanson, Jennifer Connelly
Director: John Singleton*, Peter Lyons Collister
Music by: Stanley Clarke*
Producer: John Singleton*, Paul Hall, Dwight Alonzo Williams
Screenwriter: John Singleton*
Tech Info: color/sound/126 min.   Type: Dramatic Feature

Date: 1994   Origin: USA
Company: A New Deal Production
Distributors/Format: Columbia/TriStar Pictures (35mm; 1/2"), Facets Multimedia,
Inc. (1/2"), Films Inc. (1/2")
Archives/Format: IUB - BFC/A (1/2")
Annotation: Violence erupts on the campus of fictional Columbus University when
neo-Nazis attack students celebrating diversity. Epps is featured as Malik Williams,
an athletic scholarship student who learns in and out of the classroom from political
science professor Maurice Phipps (Fishburne), Fudge (Ice Cube), a sixth year
policized student, his girlfriend Deja (Banks), and his coach (Smith).

HIGHLANDER III: THE SORCERER
Cast: Mario Van Peebles*, Christopher Lambert
Director: Andrew Morahan
Storywriter: Paul Ohl
Tech Info: color/sound/98 min.   Type: Dramatic Feature
Date: 1994   Origin: USA
Company: Miramax
Distributors/Format: Miramax Home Video (1/2")
Annotation: Conner Macleod (Lambert), the Highlander, is blessed with immortality
and cursed with immortal enemies. Kane (Van Peebles), a sorcerer unearthed after
300 years, begins his quest for ultimate power and the two ageless enemies wage
war again.

HIGHLIGHTS OF AMERICA'S BLACK EAGLES
Alternate: The Story of America's All-Black Air Force
Producer: Tony Brown*
Tech Info: color/sound/30 min.   Type: Television Documentary
Date: 1985   Origin: USA
Company: Tony Brown* Productions
Annotation: The film discusses the black experience in the military, focussing on the
training and participation of black airmen in the United States Air Force during W.W.
II.

HIGHWAY TO HELL
Cast: Kevin Peter Hall*, Kristy Swanson, Gilbert Gottfried, Chad Lowe, Patrick
Bergin, C.J. Graham
Director: Ate De Jong
Executive Producer: Derek Gibson, John Daly
Music by: Hidden Faces
Producer: Derek Gibson, John Daly, Mary Anne Page, John Byers
Screenwriter: Brian Helgeland
Tech Info: color/sound/92 min.   Type: Dramatic Feature
Date: 1992   Origin: USA
Company: Goodman-Rosen Production, Josa Productions, et al.
Distributors/Format: Hemdale Home Video (1/2")
Annotation: Charlie Sykes (Lowe) and girlfriend Rachel (Swanson) are heading to
Las Vegas to elope when "Hellcop" (Graham) kidnaps Rachel. With the help of a
mechanic named Beelzebub (Bergin), Charlie searches for Rachel. Hall plays
Charon.

HILLS HAVE EYES II, THE
Cast: Willard Pugh*, Michael Berryman, Janus Blythe, Robert Houston
Director: Wes Craven
Music by: Harry Manfredini
Producer: Barry Cahn, Peter Locke
Screenwriter: Wes Craven
Tech Info: color/sound/86 min.   Type: Dramatic Feature
Date: 1985   Origin: USA
Company: New Realm
Distributors/Format: VTC Home Video (1/2")
Annotation: Ruby (Blythe) and Bobby (Houston), who re-entered "normal" society as partners in a motorcycle shop, find themselves confronting uncivilized desert dwellers. Pugh plays Foster.

HISTORY OF THE WORLD, PART 1
Cast: Gregory Hines*, Dom DeLuise, Madeline Kahn, Harvey Korman, Mel Brooks
Director: Mel Brooks
Music Performer: John Morris
Music by: John Morris
Narrator: Orson Welles
Producer: Mel Brooks
Screenwriter: Mel Brooks
Storywriter: Mel Brooks
Tech Info: color/sound/93 min.   Type: Comedy Feature
Date: 1981   Origin: USA
Company: CBS, Fox
Distributors/Format: CBS/Fox Home Video (1/2")
Archives/Format: IUB - BFC/A (16mm)
Annotation: In Brooks' satire, Josephus (Hines) is a slave who claims he cannot be thrown to the lions because he is Jewish, not Christian. When this does not save his life he tap dances the Ethiopian Slim Slam and is consequently hired as a palace wine steward.

HIT LIST
Cast: Harold Sylvester*, Rip Torn, Jan-Michael Vincent, Leo Rossi
Director: William Lustig
Executive Producer: Lisa Hansen
Music by: Gary Schyman
Producer: Lisa Hansen, Paul Hertzberg, Jef Richard
Screenwriter: John Goff, Peter Brosnan
Storywriter: Aubrey K. Rattan
Tech Info: color/sound/87 min.   Type: Dramatic Feature
Date: 1990   Origin: USA
Company: Cinetel
Distributors/Format: New Line Cinema Home Video (1/2")
Annotation: DaSalvo (Rossi), a witness to a Mafia kingpin's (Torn) crimes, and his family are guarded by FBI agent Collins (Vincent). While the DeSalvos barbeque with Armstrong (Sylvester), the Mafia kidnaps the wrong child.

HOLLYWOOD CHRONICLES: STEREOTYPES AND MINORITIES
Alternate: Familiar Faces, Unknown Names
Director: James Forsher
Host: Jackie Cooper
Music by: Andrew Belling
Producer: Gailya Melchior
Screenwriter: Bruce Bailey, Laurie Jacobson
Tech Info: color/sound/50 min.   Type: Documentary Feature
Date: 1991   Origin: USA
Company: Facets Entertainment Group
Distributors/Format: MPI Home Video (1/2")
Archives/Format: IUB - BFC/A (1/2")
Annotation: The film looks at the use of stereotypes in early Hollywood films focussing on the black experience.

HOLLYWOOD SHUFFLE
Cast: Grand L. Bush*, Robert Townsend*, Keenen Ivory Wayans*, Franklin Ajaye*, John Witherspoon*, Helen Martin*, Ludie Washington*, Damon Wayans*, Anne-Marie Johnson*, Craigus R. Johnson*, Starletta DuPois*, Brad Sanders*, David McKnight*, Don Reed*, Kim Wayans*, Roy Fegan*, Rusty Cundieff*, Sarah Katie Coughlin*, Angela Teek*, Paul Mooney
Director: Robert Townsend*
Executive Producer: Carl Craig*
Music Performer: Gregory Alexander*, Roy Fegan*
Music by: Patrice Rushen*, Udi Harpaz
Producer: Robert Townsend*, Carl Craig*
Screenwriter: Robert Townsend*, Keenen Ivory Wayans*
Tech Info: color/sound/82 min.   Type: Comedy Feature
Date: 1987   Origin: USA
Company: A Conquering Unicorn Production
Distributors/Format: Facets Multimedia, Inc. (1/2"), Virgin Visions Video (35mm; 1/2"), Goldwyn Home Video (1/2")
Archives/Format: IUB - BFC/A (1/2")
Annotation: Bobby Taylor's (Townsend) greatest dream is to make it as a Hollywood superstar. However, the studios insist on his being "Hollywood black"--clown, pimp, drug pusher. He finally makes a decision about his future. Ann Marie Johnson plays his love interest; Witherspoon and Keenan Ivory Wayans his co-workers; Martin his grandmother.

HOLLYWOOD VICE SQUAD
Cast: Leon Isaac Kennedy*, Julius Harris*, Ronny Cox, Frank Gorshin, Trish Van Devere
Director: Penelope Spheeris
Executive Producer: Mel Pearl, William Fay
Music by: Michael Convertino, Chris Spedding, Keith Levine
Producer: Sandy Howard, Mel Pearl, Arnold Orgolini, William Fay
Screenwriter: James J. Docherty
Tech Info: color/sound/101 min.   Type: Dramatic Feature

Date: 1986   Origin: USA
Company: Cinema Group
Distributors/Format: Concorde Home Video (1/2")
Annotation: Capt. Jensen (Cox) is a Los Angeles police squad chief who helps Pauline Stanton (Van Devere) find her runaway daughter, investigates an S&M porn operation, and cracks down on a New York mobster. Kennedy plays Hawkins and Harris plays Jesse.

HOLY MATRIMONY

Cast: Bubba Smith*, Courtney B. Vance*, Tate Donovan, Patricia Arquette, John Shuck
Director: Leonard Nimoy
Executive Producer: Ted Field, Robert Cort
Music by: Bruce Broughton
Producer: Ted Field, Robert Cort, David Madden, William Stuart, Diane Nabatoff
Screenwriter: David Weisberg, Douglas S. Cook
Tech Info: color/sound/93 min.   Type: Comedy Feature
Date: 1994   Origin: USA
Company: Colony Productions, Interscope, et al.
Distributors/Format: Buena Vista Home Video (1/2")
Annotation: A carnival showgirl (Arquette) escapes to a religious sect in Canada with her boyfriend (Donovan) and the carnival's receipts. An FBI agent (Shuck) tracks them down. Vance plays Cooper and Smith appears as a Hutterite boy.

HOME OF ANGELS

Cast: Joe Frazier*, Sherman Hemsley*, Abe Vigoda, Lance Robinson, Craig Sechler, Karen Wolfe
Director: Nick Stagliano
Executive Producer: Nicolas L. DePace
Music by: George Small
Producer: James Oliva, Nicolas L. DePace
Screenwriter: James Oliva, Nicolas L. DePace
Tech Info: color/sound/90 min.   Type: Dramatic Feature
Date: 1994   Origin: USA
Company: Cloverlay Productions
Distributors/Format: Cloverlay Entertainment (1/2")
Annotation: Little Billy (Robinson) decides to rescue his Grandfather (Vigoda) from a nursing home where he's confined with Alzheimer's. Once on the streets, Billy and his Grandfather are taunted by gang members but escape into a homeless shantytown with the help of Buzzard Bracken (Hemsley), a former prize fighter. Frazier appears as himself.

HOMEBOYS

Cast: Todd Bridges*, David Garrison, Ron Odriozola, Keo Michaels, Sigrid Salazar
Director: Lindsay Norgard
Executive Producer: Vito DiBari, Riccardo DiBari
Music by: Peter Foldy
Producer: James A. Holt, Lindsay Norgard, Vito DiBari, Riccardo DiBari
Tech Info: color/sound/91 min.   Type: Dramatic Feature

Date: 1992   Origin: USA
Company: JWP Production, DB Films
Distributors/Format: AIP Home Video (1/2")
Annotation: Rivalry between Black and Hispanic gangs escalates as Los Angeles police plan a drug sting. Bridges plays Johnny Davis, a kid from the projects who shunned crime and became an advertisement executive.

HOMEBOYZ II: CRACK CITY

Cast: Brian Paul Stuart*, McKinley Winston*, Yvonne Kersey*, Quetzal Castro, Blas Hernandez
Director: Daniel Matmor
Producer: Joe Paradise, Richard Garcia, Karen Burns
Screenwriter: Daniel Matmor
Tech Info: color/sound/90 min.   Type: Dramatic Feature
Date: 1993   Origin: USA
Company: A.I.P.
Distributors/Format: A.I.P. Home Video (1/2"; 3/4")
Annotation: Survival means dealing crack for David and Spider (Stuart and Winston) two homeboys from the hood who work for Spanish Harlem's most feared godfather.

HOMECOMIN'

Director: Sati Jamal*
Producer: Sati Jamal*, Reginald Brown*
Screenwriter: Sati Jamal*, Reginald Brown*
Storywriter: Sati Jamal*, Reginald Brown*
Tech Info: color/sound/28 min.   Type: Dramatic Short
Date: 1980   Origin: USA
Company: Phoenix Films
Annotation: Jason, a black father, tries to assume his responsibilities to his son while separated from his wife, but the estrangement takes its toll on the whole family.

HOMER & EDDIE

Cast: Whoopi Goldberg*, Beah Richards*, Ernestine McClendon*, James Belushi,
Director: Andrei Konchalovsky
Music by: Eduard Artemyev
Producer: Moritz Borman, James Cady
Screenwriter: Patrick Cirillo
Tech Info: color/sound/100 min.   Type: Dramatic Feature
Date: 1990   Origin: USA
Company: Kings Road Entertainment Inc., Skouras
Annotation: Eddie (Goldberg), a terminally ill, cynical wanderer, teams up with Homer (Belushi), a brain-damaged innocent in search of his parents. They develop a deep friendship that ends tragically. Richards plays Linda Cervi, Eddie's mother.

HOMOCIDE

Cast: Paul Butler*, Ving Rhames*, Joe Mantegna, William H. Macy, J.J. Johnston, Natalija Nogulich
Director: David Mamet
Executive Producer: Ron Rotholz
Music by: Alaric Jans
Producer: Michael Hausman, Edward R. Pressman, Ron Rotholz

Screenwriter: David Mamet
Tech Info: color/sound/102 min.   Type: Dramatic Feature
Date: 1991   Origin: USA
Company: Cinehaus Inc., Edward R. Pressman Corporation
Distributors/Format: Triumph Releasing (16mm)
Annotation: While tracking down Randolph (Rhames), an escaped drug dealer, homocide detective Bobby Gold (Mantegna) stumbles onto a crime scene. An elderly Jewish woman has been murdered as part of an anti-Semitic plot. Butler is Deputy Mayor Walker.

HOOK

Cast: Tony Burton*, Dustin Hoffman, Robin Williams, Julia Roberts
Director: Steven Spielberg
Executive Producer: James V. Hart
Music by: John Williams
Producer: Frank Marshall, Kathleen Kennedy, Gerald R. Molen, James V. Hart
Screenwriter: James V. Hart, Malia Scotch Marmo
Storywriter: Nick Castle, James V. Hart
Tech Info: color/sound/144 min.   Type: Dramatic Feature
Date: 1991   Origin: USA
Company: Hook Productions, Amblin
Distributors/Format: TriStar Pictures Inc. (1/2")
Annotation: After his children disappear, Peter Banning (Williams) realizes that he is Peter Pan and that his kids have been kidnapped by Captain Hook (Hoffman). Burton plays Bill Jukes.

HOOP DREAMS

Director: Steve James, Frederick Marx, Peter Gilbert, Peter Gilbert
Executive Producer: Gordon Quinn, Catherine Allan
Producer: Steve James, Gordon Quinn, Frederick Marx, Peter Gilbert, Catherine Allan
Speaker: Arthur Agee*, William Gates*, Mrs. Agee*
Tech Info: color/sound/174 min.   Type: Documentary Feature
Date: 1994   Origin: USA
Company: New Line Cinema
Distributors/Format: Facets Multimedia, Inc. (1/2"), Films Inc. (1/2")
Annotation: The documentary explores five years in the lives of two young African American basketball players, Agee and Gates, from inner-city Chicago.

HOT RESORT

Cast: Samm-Art Williams*, Tom Parsekian, Debra Kelly, Marcy Walker, Daniel Schneider
Director: John Robins
Music by: Dave Powell, Ken Brown
Producer: Yoram Globus, Menahem Golan
Screenwriter: Boaz Davidson, John Robins
Storywriter: Paul Max Rubenstein
Tech Info: color/sound/93 min.   Type: Comedy Feature

Date: 1985   Origin: USA
Company: Cannon
Distributors/Format: Cannon Home Video (1/2")
Annotation: The student employees at a posh summer resort hotel in the islands are trained by the tough and exacting manager of Royal St. Kitts Hotel, Bill Martin (Williams). He whips them into line so that they best their snobbish rivals at rowing and women.

HOT SHOT
Cast: Mario Van Peebles*, Derek Lewis*, Pele , Jim Youngs, Rutanya Alda, Billy Warlock, David Groh, Leon Russom
Director: Rick King
Music by: William Orbit
Producer: Steve Pappas
Screenwriter: Rick King, Joe Sauter, Ray Errol Fox, Bill Guttentag
Tech Info: color/sound/101 min.   Type: Dramatic Feature
Date: 1987   Origin: USA
Company: Intl. Film Marketing, Arista
Distributors/Format: Arista Home Video (1/2")
Annotation: Jimmy Kristidis (Youngs), an aspiring New York Rockers soccer star, travels to Brazil to learn how to succeed from Santos (Pele), the greatest, now retired, soccer player in the world. Van Peebles plays Winston, an eccentric Jamaican, and Lewis plays Derek Johnson, both of whom are Jimmy's teammates on the Rockers.

HOT SHOTS! PART DEUX
Cast: Michael Colyar*, Ron Pitts*, Charlie Sheen, Lloyd Bridges, Valeria Golino, Jerry Haleva
Director: Jim Abrahams
Executive Producer: Pat Proft
Music by: Basil Poledouris
Producer: Pat Proft, Bill Badalato
Screenwriter: Jim Abrahams, Pat Proft
Tech Info: color/sound/89 min.   Type: Comedy Feature
Date: 1993   Origin: USA
Company: Fox
Distributors/Format: Fox Home Video (1/2")
Annotation: Colyar plays Williams and Pitts is a black kick boxing sportscaster in this comedy sequel in which Topper (Sheen) abjures violence and joins an order of monks.

HOT STUFF
Cast: Ossie Davis*, Matthew Burch*, Dom DeLuise, Suzanne Pleshette
Director: Dom DeLuise
Music Performer: Patrick Williams
Producer: Mort Engelberg
Screenwriter: Michael Keaton, Donald E. Westlake
Tech Info: color/sound/92 min.   Type: Dramatic Feature

Date: 1979   Origin: USA
Company: Rastar-Mort Engelberg
Distributors/Format: Columbia Pictures Home Video (1/2")
Annotation: Davis is Captain of the Miami Police Department. He and his officers take over a fencing operation frequented by such small-time crooks as Clifford (Burch) in an attempt to catch mobsters in the act of fencing stolen goods.

HOT TO TROT
Cast: Chino "Fats" Williams*, Harry Caesar*, Bobcat Goldthwait, Virginia Madsen, Dabney Coleman, John Candy
Director: Michael Dinner
Music by: Danny Elfman
Producer: Wendy Finerman, Steve Tisch
Screenwriter: Stephen Neigher, Hugo Gilbert, Charlie Peters
Storywriter: Stephen Neigher, Hugh Gilbert
Tech Info: color/sound/83 min.   Type: Comedy Feature
Date: 1988   Origin: USA
Company: Warner Bros.
Distributors/Format: Warner Bros. Home Video, Inc. (1/2")
Annotation: Fred Chaney (Goldthwait) and his rotten stepfather each inherit half of a business but neither wants to work with the other. Caesar plays Gideon Cole.

HOTEL NEW HAMPSHIRE
Cast: Dorsey Wright*, Beau Bridges, Jodie Foster, Rob Lowe, Nastassia Kinski
Director: Tony Richardson
Executive Producer: George Yaneff, Kent Walwin, Grahame Jennings
Music by: Jacques Offenbach
Producer: Neil Hartley, George Yaneff, Kent Walwin, Grahame Jennings, James Beach
Screenwriter: Tony Richardson
Storywriter: John Irving
Tech Info: color/sound/110 min.   Type: Dramatic Feature
Date: 1984   Origin: USA
Company: Orion, Woodfall Films
Distributors/Format: Orion Home Video (1/2")
Annotation: Junior Jones (Wright) is a black football player who rescues Franny (Foster) from a gang rape in high school. They eventually marry after Jones' career ends due to bad knees.

HOUSE OF CARDS
Cast: Esther Rolle*, Kathleen Turner, Tommy Lee Jones, Asha Menina
Director: Michael Lessac
Executive Producer: Mario Cecchi Gori, Vittorio Cecchi Gori
Music by: James Horner
Producer: Wolfgang Glattes, Mario Cecchi Gori, Vittorio Cecchi Gori, Dale Pollack, Lianne Halfon
Screenwriter: Michael Lessac
Storywriter: Robert Litz, Michael Lessac
Tech Info: color/sound/109 min.   Type: Dramatic Feature

Date: 1993   Origin: USA
Company: House of Cards Productions Inc, et al.
Distributors/Format: Miramax Home Video (1/2")
Annotation: A young girl (Menina) retreats into a world of silence due to the death of her father. Rolle plays Adelle, assistant to a psychiatrist (Jones) who tries to help.

HOUSE OF GAMES

Cast: Meshach Taylor*, Lilia Skala, Lindsay Crouse, Joe Mantegna
Director: David Mamet
Music by: Alaric Jans
Producer: Michael Hausman
Screenwriter: David Mamet
Tech Info: color/sound/102 min.   Type: Dramatic Feature
Date: 1987   Origin: USA
Company: Filmhaus
Distributors/Format: Orion Home Video (1/2")
Annotation: A psychologist (Crouse) becomes captivated by the confidence games of a patient (Mantegna). Taylor plays Mr. Dean.

HOUSE OF GOD, THE

Cast: Ossie Davis*, Howard E. Rollins Jr.*, Charles Haid, Tim Matheson, Michael Sacks
Director: Donald Wrye
Music by: Basil Poledouris
Producer: Charles H. Joffe, Harold Schneider
Screenwriter: Donald Wrye
Tech Info: color/sound/108 min.   Type: Dramatic Feature
Date: 1984   Origin: USA
Company: United Artists
Distributors/Format: United Artists Home Video (1/2")
Annotation: A group of young interns try to survive their high-pressure hospital jobs. Davis plays Dr. Sanders.

HOUSE PARTY

Cast: Christopher Reid*, Robin Harris*, Christopher Martin*, Tisha Campbell*, Martin Lawrence*, John Witherspoon*, Kelly Jo Minter*, Adrienne-Joi Johnson*, Bebe Drake-Massey*, Shaun Baker*, Eugene Allen*, George Clinton*, Bowlegged Lou *, Desi Arnez Hines III*, B. Fine *, Paul Anthony*, Daryl "Chill" Mitchell*, Leah Aldridge*, Val Gamble*, Barry Diamond, Michael Pniewski
Director: Reginald Hudlin*, Peter Deming
Executive Producer: Gerald T. Olson, Gerald T. Jolson
Music Performer: Christopher Reid*
Music by: Marcus Miller*, Lenny White*
Producer: Warrington Hudlin*, Earl Watson*, Gerald T. Olson, Gerald T. Jolson
Screenwriter: Reginald Hudlin*
Tech Info: color/sound/100 min.   Type: Comedy Feature
Date: 1990   Origin: USA
Company: New Line Cinema
Distributors/Format: Films Inc. (1/2"), New Line Cinema Home Video (1/2")
Archives/Format: IUB - BFC/A (1/2")
Annotation: Kid (Reid) and his father (Harris) represent the problems all teenagers encounter with their parents. Kid wants to show his peers that he can be "cool" and

instead gets himself into trouble at home, school, and parties. Play (Martin) is his competition and best friend; Sidney (Campbell) his love interest; Johnson plays a Projects girl.

HOUSE PARTY 2: THE PAJAMA JAM

Cast: Whoopi Goldberg*, Christopher Reid*, Robin Harris*, Christopher Martin*, Tisha Campbell*, Martin Lawrence*, Helen Martin*, Tony Burton*, Queen Latifah*, Iman *, Georg Stanford Brown*, D. Christopher Judge*, George Anthony Bell*, Eugene Allen*, Bowlegged Lou *, B. Fine *, Paul Anthony*, Daryl "Chill" Mitchell*, Alice Carter*, Mark "Whiz" Eastmond*, Barry Diamond, Kamron
Director: George Jackson*, Doug McHenry*
Executive Producer: Janet Grillo
Music by: Vassal Benford*
Producer: George Jackson*, Doug McHenry*, Janet Grillo
Screenwriter: Rusty Cundieff*, Daryl G. Nickens*
Tech Info: color/sound/94 min.   Type: Comedy Feature
Date: 1991   Origin: USA
Company: New Line Cinema
Distributors/Format: New Line Cinema Home Video (1/2")
Archives/Format: IUB - BFC/A (1/2")
Annotation: Kid (Reid) is off to college and Play (Martin) remains behind, hoping to launch his musical career. When con artist Sheila Landrau (Iman) poses as a big record producer, Play falls for her scheme. To save Kid from being expelled, the boys plan the biggest house party on campus. Brown plays a college professor; Queen Latifah plays Sydney's (Campbell) roommate. Goldberg plays a satan-like character.

HOUSE PARTY 3

Cast: Christopher Reid*, Reynaldo Rey*, Christopher Martin*, Tisha Campbell*, Jimmy Woodard*, Khandi Alexander*, Roy Fegan*, Joe Torry*, Daniel Gardner*, Chris Tucker*, Bernie Mac*, Angela Means*, TLC *, Immature *, Michael Colyar*, David Edwards*, Anthony S. Johnson*, Luv Freeze*, Yvette Wilson*, Simply Marvelous *, Bigga Don*, Soul Gee *, Ketty Lester
Director: Eric Meza, Anghel Decca
Executive Producer: George Jackson*, Doug McHenry*, Janet Grillo
Music Performer: Bigga Don*, Soul Gee *
Music by: David Allen Jones*
Producer: Carl Craig*, George Jackson*, Doug McHenry*, Janet Grillo
Screenwriter: Takashi Bufford*, David Toney*
Storywriter: David Toney*
Tech Info: color/sound/94 min.   Type: Comedy Feature
Date: 1994   Origin: USA
Company: New Line Cinema
Distributors/Format: New Line Cinema Home Video (1/2")
Annotation: Kid (Reid) is making plans to get married while Play (Martin) is trying to persuade local rap promoter Showboat (Colyar) to sign an all-girl group called Sex as a Weapon (TLC). Play throws Kid the bachelor party of all time. Mac plays Uncle Vester, the original lady killer; Veda (Means) plays Kid's fiance who accuses her groom-to-be of hanky panky with his former girlfriend Sydney (Campbell).

HOUSEGUEST

Cast: Sinbad *, Phil Hartman, Jeffrey Jones, Kim Greist
Director: Randy Miller, Jerry Zielinski
Executive Producer: Dennis Bishop
Music by: John Debney
Screenwriter: Lawrence Gay
Tech Info: color/sound/109 min.   Type: Comedy Feature
Date: 1994   Origin: USA
Company: Hollywood Pictures, Caravan Pictures
Distributors/Format: Hollywood Pictures Home Video (1/2")
Annotation: Kevin Franklin (Sinbad) impersonates a dentist and cons a rich
suburbanite (Hartman), but his scam gets him into more trouble than he ever
imagined.

HOUSEKEEPING

Cast: Bill Smillie*, Christine Lahti, Sara Walker, Andrea Burchill, Anne Pitoniak
Director: Bill Forsyth
Music by: Michael Gibbs
Producer: Robert F. Colesberry
Screenwriter: Bill Forsyth
Tech Info: color/sound/116 min.   Type: Dramatic Feature
Date: 1987   Origin: USA
Company: Columbia
Distributors/Format: Columbia Pictures Home Video (1/2")
Annotation: An eccentric great-aunt (Lahti) takes care of her two orphaned nieces
(Walker and Burchill). Smillie plays the sheriff who intervenes in the household on
behalf of a concerned teacher.

HOW I GOT INTO COLLEGE

Cast: Tichina Arnold*, Duane Davis*, Marlene Warfield*, Anthony Edwards, Richard
Jenkins, Lara Flynn Boyle, Corey Parker
Director: Savage Steve Holland
Music by: Joseph Vitarelli
Producer: Michael Shamberg, Elizabeth Cantillon
Screenwriter: Terrel Seltzer
Tech Info: color/sound/87 min.   Type: Comedy Feature
Date: 1989   Origin: USA
Company: Fox
Distributors/Format: Fox Home Video (1/2")
Annotation: Marlon Browne (Parker), whose G.P.A. is too low to get into his college
of choice, teams up with over-achiever Jessica Kailo (Boyle), a marketing firm, and
an elephant to gain admission. Davis plays Ronny Paulson.

HOW TO BEAT THE HIGH COST OF LIVING

Cast: Garrett Morris*, Susan Saint James, Jessica Lange, Jane Curtin, Robert
Benjamin
Director: Robert Scheerer
Executive Producer: Samuel Z. Arkoff
Music by: Patrick Williams
Producer: Jerome M. Zeitman, Robert Kaufman, Samuel Z. Arkoff
Screenwriter: Robert Kaufman

Storywriter: Leonora Thuna
Tech Info: color/sound/110 min.   Type: Comedy Feature
Date: 1980   Origin: USA
Company: Filmways
Distributors/Format: AIP Home Video (1/2")
Annotation: Jane (Saint James), a divorcee who needs money for her kids, Elaine (Curtin) who's been left by her husband; and Louise (Lange), who needs money for her business, all turn to a life of crime to solve their financial troubles. Morris plays the Power and Light man.

HOW U LIKE ME NOW

Cast: Darryl Roberts*, Darnell Williams*, Salli Richardson*, Daniel Gardner*, Charnele Brown*, Raymond Whitefield*, Debra Crable*, Byron Stewart*, Jonelle Kennedy*
Director: Darryl Roberts*, Michael Goi
Executive Producer: Robert Woolf
Music by: Khalil El Zabar*, Chuck Webb*
Producer: Darryl Roberts*, Robert Woolf
Screenwriter: Darryl Roberts*
Tech Info: color/sound/109 min.   Type: Dramatic Feature
Date: 1992   Origin: USA
Studio: Independent
Distributors/Format: Facets Multimedia, Inc. (1/2"), MCA/Universal Home Video (1/2")
Annotation: The film explores the life and loves of four young black men: Thomas (Williams), Spoony (Gardner), Alex (Whitefield) and B.J. (Roberts). Richardson plays Thomas' frustrated girlfriend Valerie; Crable is his superior, Michelle; Kennedy plays Sharon.

HOWLING VI--THE FREAKS

Cast: Antonio Fargas*, Sean Sullivan, Bruce Payne, Carol Lynley, Brendan Hughes, Michele Matheson, Jered Barclay
Director: Hope Perello
Executive Producer: Ronna B. Wallace, Steven Lane, Edward Simons
Music by: Patrick Gleeson
Producer: Ronna B. Wallace, Robert Pringle, Steven Lane, Edward Simons
Screenwriter: Kevin Rock
Tech Info: color/sound/102 min.   Type: Dramatic Feature
Date: 1991   Origin: USA
Company: Allied Vision, Lane & Pringle Productions
Distributors/Format: LIVE Home Video (1/2")
Annotation: Ian (Hughes) drifts into Canton Bluff and finds work restoring a church. When a traveling carnival comes through town, its owner (Payne), a vampire, recognizes that Ian is a werewolf and asks him to join his freak show. Fargas is a geek in the show.

HUDSON HAWK

Cast: Lorraine Toussaint*, Bruce Willis, Danny Aiello, Andie MacDowell
Director: Michael Lehmann
Executive Producer: Robert Kraft
Music by: Michael Kamen
Producer: Joel Silver, Robert Kraft

Screenwriter: Daniel Waters, Steven E. de Souza
Storywriter: Bruce Willis, Robert Kraft
Tech Info: color/sound/95 min.   Type: Comedy Feature
Date: 1991   Origin: USA
Company: Silver Pictures, Ace Bone Productions
Distributors/Format: TriStar Pictures Inc. (1/2")
Annotation: Hawk (Willis), a reformed cat burglar, is kidnapped and forced to steal three Da Vinci works of art from the Vatican. Toussaint plays Almond Joy.

HUNT FOR RED OCTOBER, THE
Cast: James Earl Jones*, Courtney B. Vance*, Sean Connery, Alec Baldwin
Director: John McTiernan
Producer: Mace Neufeld
Screenwriter: Larry Ferguson, Donald Stewart
Storywriter: Tom Clancy
Tech Info: color/sound/135 min.   Type: Dramatic Feature
Date: 1990   Origin: USA
Company: Paramount
Distributors/Format: Paramount Home Video (1/2")
Annotation: Admiral Greer (Jones) calls in submarine expert and old friend Jack Ryan (Baldwin), to assess the capabilities of a newly developed Soviet underwater vessel, captained by Markos Ramius (Connery). Seaman Jones (Vance) is the perceptive radar/sonar control officer.

HUNTER, THE
Cast: LeVar Burton*, Theodore "Teddy" Wilson*, Dea St. La Mount*, Jimmy/James Spinks*, Taurean Blacque*, Steve McQueen
Director: Buzz Kulik
Music Performer: Michel Legrand, Pamela Hicks
Music by: Michel Legrand, Pamela Hicks
Producer: Mort Engelberg
Screenwriter: Peter Hyams, Richard Levinson, William Link, Ted Leighton
Storywriter: Christopher Keane
Tech Info: color/sound/97 min.   Type: Dramatic Feature
Date: 1980   Origin: USA
Company: Rastar/Mort Engelberg
Distributors/Format: Paramount Home Video (1/2")
Annotation: The real-life experiences of modern day bounty hunter Ralph "Papa" Thorson (McQueen) are chronicled. Burton plays Tommy Price, an electronics whiz who befriends Thorson. St. Lamount is Annie, a bar owner; Wilson appears as Winston, another offender; Spinks, a Cadillac owner whose vehicle is being continually wrecked by Thorson; Blacque, a hustler.

HYSTERICAL
Cast: Franklin Ajaye*, Pat Colbert*, Maurice Sneed*, Julie Newmar, Bill Hudson, Mark Hudson, Brett Hudson
Director: Chris Bearde
Executive Producer: William J. Immerman
Music by: Bob Alcivar
Producer: Gene Levy, William J. Immerman
Screenwriter: Mark Hudson, Brett Hudson, William Hudson, Trace Johnston
Tech Info: color/sound/86 min.   Type: Comedy Feature

Date: 1983   Origin: USA
Company: H&W, Cinema Group
Distributors/Format: EMB (1/2")
Annotation: Ajaye plays Leroy in this horror film parody in which Frederick (Bill Hudson), a writer vacationing in an old lighthouse on the Oregon coast, is visited by ghosts and zombies. Colbert and Sneed's roles are unidentified.

I AM YOUR SISTER

Series: Forging Global Connections Across Differences
Director: Jennifer Abod*, Catherine Russo
Producer: Jennifer Abod*, Catherine Russo
Speaker: Jacqui Alexander*
Tech Info: color/sound/60 min.   Type: Experimental Feature
Date: 1991   Origin: USA
Studio: Independent
Company: Third World Newsreel
Distributors/Format: Third World Newsreel (1/2")
Annotation: In October, 1990, over 1,000 women from 22 countries came to Boston to celebrate and honor poet Audre Lorde at this conference.

I BE DONE WAS IS

Director: Debra J. Robinson*
Narrator: Rhonda Hansome*
Producer: Debra J. Robinson*, Leslie Holder
Speaker: Marsha Warfield*, Alice Arthur*, Rhonda Hansome*, Jane Galvin-Lewis*
Storywriter: Terry L. McMillan*
Tech Info: color/sound/60 min.   Type: Documentary Feature
Date: 1984   Origin: USA
Company: CBS, Movielab Video
Distributors/Format: Independent (16mm)
Archives/Format: IUB - BFC/A (1/2")
Annotation: A documentary on black comediennes, it includes clips of their performances and interviews designed to reveal their unique experiences in a profession that is not hospitable to Blacks or women.

I KNOW WHY THE CAGED BIRD SINGS

Cast: Esther Rolle*, Paul Benjamin*, Ruby Dee*, Diahann Carroll*, Arthur/Art Evans*, Madge Sinclair*, Sonny Jim Gaines*, Roger E. Mosley*, Constance Good*, John M. Driver*
Director: Fielder Cook
Producer: Jean Moore Edwards
Screenwriter: Maya Angelou*, Leonora Thona
Storywriter: Maya Angelou*
Tech Info: color/sound/96 min.   Type: Dramatic Feature
Date: 1978   Origin: USA
Studio: Independent
Company: Tomorrow Entertainment Inc.
Distributors/Format: USA Home Video (1/2"), Filmic Archives (1/2")
Annotation: Adapted from Angelou's autobiography, the story is about a spirited and gifted, but poor, black girl growing up in the South in the 1930s. It shows how she grew up experiencing prejudice, family difficulties, and a relationship with a teacher who taught her to respect books, learning, and herself.

I LIKE IT LIKE THAT
Cast: Toukie A. Smith*, Lauren Velez, Jon Seda, Rita Moreno, Jesse Borrego
Director: Darnell Martin*, Alexander Gruszynski
Executive Producer: Wendy Finerman
Music by: Sergio George
Producer: Ann Carli, Lane Janger, Diane Phillips, Wendy Finerman
Screenwriter: Darnell Martin*
Tech Info: color/sound/108 min.   Type: Comedy Feature
Date: 1994   Origin: USA
Company: A Think Again Production
Distributors/Format: Columbia/TriStar Pictures (35mm; 1/2"), Films Inc. (1/2")
Annotation: Lisette (Velez), and her husband Chino (Seda) are a young hispanic couple with three children. Chino goes to jail for looting during a blackout and Lisette takes a job with a music company. Smith plays a model search agent who recommends Lisette to a big music producer.

I NEVER DANCED THE WAY GIRLS WERE SUPPOSED TO
Director: Dawn Suggs*
Music Performer: Chaka Kahn*, Lil' Louis & The World *
Screenwriter: Dawn Suggs*
Speaker: Juana Diaz*, Shari Frilot*, Charlein Preston*, Angela Weaver*, Linda Jo Allen*, Karen Gaddis*, Dina Suggs*
Storywriter: Dawn Suggs*
Tech Info: mixed/sound/8 min.   Type: Experimental Short
Date: 1992   Origin: USA
Company: Third World Newsreel Production
Distributors/Format: Third World Newsreel (1/2")
Archives/Format: IUB - BFC/A (1/2")
Annotation: An intimate portrait revealing the life experiences of an African American lesbian.

I PROMISE TO REMEMBER
Alternate: The Story of Frankie Lymon and the Teenagers
Director: Steve Fisher, Joel Sucher
Music Performer: Frankie Lymon*, The Teenagers *
Producer: Steve Fisher, Joel Sucher, Jane Praeger
Tech Info: color/sound/27 min.   Type: Documentary Short
Date: 1983   Origin: USA
Annotation: The film documents the rise and fall of Frankie Lymon and the Teenagers in the 1950s. The Teenagers were one of the first black rock and roll groups to cross the color barrier and to achieve general popularity.

I REMEMBER HARLEM: THE DEPRESSION YEARS, 1930-1940
Director: William Miles*
Narrator: Adolph Caesar*
Producer: William Miles*, Clayton Riley
Storywriter: William Miles*
Tech Info: color/sound/60 min.   Type: Television Documentary

Date: 1980   Origin: USA
Company: Miles* Educational Film Production, Inc.
Distributors/Format: Films for the Humanities (1/2")
Archives/Format: IUB - BFC/A (16mm)
Annotation: The second program in the series that traces the early history of Harlem over three centuries covers the depression years.

I REMEMBER HARLEM: THE EARLY YEARS (1600-1930)

Director: William Miles*
Narrator: Adolph Caesar*
Producer: William Miles*, Clayton Riley
Storywriter: William Miles*
Tech Info: color/sound/60 min.   Type: Television Documentary
Date: 1980   Origin: USA
Company: Miles* Educational Film Production, Inc.
Distributors/Format: Films for the Humanities (1/2")
Archives/Format: IUB - BFC/A (16mm)
Annotation: The first of four programs traces the history of African Americans and other ethnic groups arriving and surviving over three centuries in Harlem.

I REMEMBER HARLEM: TOWARD A NEW DAY, 1965-1980

Director: William Miles*
Narrator: Adolph Caesar*
Producer: William Miles*, Clayton Riley
Storywriter: William Miles*
Tech Info: color/sound/60 min.   Type: Television Documentary
Date: 1980   Origin: USA
Company: Miles* Educational Film Production, Inc.
Distributors/Format: Films for the Humanities (1/2")
Archives/Format: IUB - BFC/A (16mm)
Annotation: The last program in the series that traces the rise, decline and regeneration of Harlem over three centuries.

I REMEMBER HARLEM: TOWARD FREEDOM, 1940-1965

Director: William Miles*
Narrator: Adolph Caesar*
Producer: William Miles*, Clayton Riley
Storywriter: William Miles*
Tech Info: color/sound/60 min.   Type: Television Documentary
Date: 1980   Origin: USA
Company: Miles* Educational Film Production, Inc.
Distributors/Format: Films for the Humanities (1/2")
Archives/Format: IUB - BFC/A (16mm)
Annotation: The third program in the series that traces the early history of Harlem over three centuries, covers the 1940s to 1965.

I SHALL MOULDER BEFORE I SHALL BE TAKEN

Narrator: James Earl Jones*
Producer: S. Allen Counter*
Storywriter: S. Allen Counter*, David L. Evans*
Tech Info: color/sound/58 min.   Type: Documentary Feature

Date: 1978   Origin: USA
Studio: Independent
Distributors/Format: Education Development Center, Inc (1/2")
Annotation: The film documents authors S. Allen Counter's and David L. Evans' expedition to the jungles of Surinam to study the Djuka tribe, a society peopled by runaway African slaves from the Caribbean and the United States, who created a culture comprising of traditions from many nations.

I'LL DO ANYTHING
Cast: Ken Page*, Suzzanne Douglas*, Nick Nolte, Albert Brooks, Whittni Wright, Julie Kavner, Tracey Ullman
Director: James L. Brooks
Executive Producer: Penney Finkelman Cox
Music by: Hans Zimmer
Producer: James L. Brooks, Polly Platt, Penney Finkelman Cox
Screenwriter: James L. Brooks
Tech Info: color/sound/115 min.   Type: Dramatic Feature
Date: 1994   Origin: USA
Company: Gracie Films, Columbia
Distributors/Format: Columbia Pictures (16mm)
Annotation: Matt (Nolte), a struggling Hollywood actor, is suddenly given sole custody of his six-year-old daughter Jeannie (Wright) when his ex-wife (Ullman) is imprisoned. Douglas is a Rainbow House star; Page has a bit part as a "hair person."

I'M DANCING AS FAST AS I CAN
Cast: Robert DoQui*, CCH Pounder*, Roger Etienne*, Jill Clayburgh, Dianne Weist
Director: Jack Hofsiss
Executive Producer: David Rabe
Music by: Stanley Silverman
Producer: Scott Rudin, Edgar J. Scherick, David Rabe
Screenwriter: David Rabe
Storywriter: Barbara Gordon
Tech Info: color/sound/106 min.   Type: Dramatic Feature
Date: 1982   Origin: USA
Company: Paramount
Distributors/Format: Paramount Home Video (1/2")
Annotation: A valium-addicted, TV documentary filmmaker (Clayburgh) goes to therapist Julie Addison (Wiest) for rehabilitation. Etienne is a waiter, DoQui plays Teddy and Pounder plays Anne.

I'M GONNA GIT YOU SUCKA
Cast: Keenen Ivory Wayans*, Bernie Casey*, Antonio Fargas*, Isaac Hayes*, Jim Brown*, Ja'net DuBois*, Clarence Williams III*, Anne-Marie Johnson*, Dawnn Lewis*, Chris Rock*, John Vernon, Steve James
Director: Keenen Ivory Wayans*
Executive Producer: Raymond Katz, Eric L. Gold
Music by: David Michael Frank
Producer: Carl Craig*, Peter McCarthy, Raymond Katz, Eric L. Gold
Screenwriter: Keenen Ivory Wayans*
Tech Info: color/sound/88 min.   Type: Comedy Feature

Date: 1988   Origin: USA
Company: Ivory Way
Distributors/Format: MGM/UA Home Video (1/2")
Archives/Format: IUB - BFC/A (1/2")
Annotation: In this satire of 1970s blaxploitation films, Wayans plays Jack Spade, an Army veteran who returns home to avenge the death of his brother, who died because he wore too many gold chains. Jack Slade (Casey), Spade's childhood hero, helps shut down gold-chain pusher Mr. Big (Vernon). Fargas plays Flyguy; James is Kung Fu Joe; Hays is Hammer; Brown is Slammer; and DuBois plays Ma Bell.

ICE PIRATES, THE

Cast: Max Roach*, John Carradine, Ron Perlman, Anjelica Huston, Michael D. Roberts, Robert Urich, Mary Crosby
Director: Stewart Raffill
Music by: Bruce Broughton
Producer: John Foreman
Screenwriter: Stewart Raffill
Tech Info: color/sound/96 min.   Type: Comedy Feature
Date: 1984   Origin: USA
Company: MGM
Distributors/Format: United Artists Home Video (1/2")
Annotation: In this science fiction comedy, Roscoe (Roberts) and Jason (Urich) are partners as they attempt to steal water in ice form from the evil Templar fleets. Roach has a cameo role.

ICE-T: OG, ORIGINAL GANGSTER

Cast: Ice-T *
Director: Ice-T *
Executive Producer: Ice-T *
Music by: Ice-T *, DaeBoe *,
Producer: Ice-T *, Doug Friedman, Julia Robertson, David Naylor
Tech Info: mixed/sound/70 min.   Type: Concert Feature
Date: 1991   Origin: USA
Studio: Independent
Company: Fragile Films (Bust It Productions)
Distributors/Format: Warner Reprise Home Video (1/2")
Archives/Format: IUB - AAAMC (1/2")
Annotation: The video is composed of 24 segments featuring rapper Ice-T. Songs include the title track as well as "New Jack Hustler," from the film NEW JACK CITY and others.

ICEMAN

Cast: Danny Glover*, Timothy Hutton, Lindsay Crouse, John Lone
Director: Fred Schepisi
Music Performer: Bruce Smeaton
Music by: Bruce Smeaton
Producer: Patrick Palmer, Norman Jewison
Screenwriter: Chip Proser, John Drimmer
Storywriter: John Drimmer
Tech Info: color/sound/101 min.   Type: Dramatic Feature

Date: 1984   Origin: USA
Company: Universal
Distributors/Format: MCA Home Video (1/2")
Annotation: Glover plays a minor role as a lab technician who is part of a team that finds a prehistoric man encased in ice and successfully revives him, only to face the ethical questions that are raised by his resuscitation.

IDA B. WELLS: A PASSION FOR JUSTICE

Series: The American Experience
Director: William Greaves*
Music Performer: Tuskeegee Institute Choir, Virginia State Choir
Music by: Kermit Moore
Narrator:
Producer: William Greaves*, Louise Archambault
Screenwriter: William Greaves*
Speaker: Toni Morrison*, Paula Giddings*, Troy Duster*, Rosalyn Terborg-Penn*, John Demott, David Tucker
Tech Info: mixed/sound/58 min.   Type: Documentary Feature
Date: 1989   Origin: USA
Studio: Public Broadcasting System
Company: William Greaves* Productions
Distributors/Format: Williams Greaves Productions, Inc. (16mm)
Archives/Format: IUB - AAAMC (1/2")
Annotation: This documentary provides an in-depth examination of the life of journalist Ida B. Wells from her birth in the South to her life as a successful journalist in Chicago. Rare photos and readings from her autobiography help to document her rise as a prominent civil rights leader.

IDENTIFIABLE QUALITIES

Alternate: A Conversation with Toni Morrison
Tech Info: color/sound/30 min.   Type: Documentary Short
Date: 1989   Origin: USA
Company: Corentyne Productions
Archives/Format: IUB - AAAMC (1/2")
Annotation: Novelist Toni Morrison, addresses the events of the 1960s which led her to write her first novel "The Bluest Eye"; the use of personal experience as a sources for her strong, black female characters; and the advantage to publishers of placing black writers in the mainstream.

IDENTITY CRISIS

Cast: Mario Van Peebles*, Shelly Burch, Ilan Mitchell-Smith, Richard Fancy
Director: Melvin Van Peebles*
Music by: Dunn E. Pearson
Producer: Melvin Van Peebles*
Screenwriter: Mario Van Peebles*
Tech Info: color/sound/90 min.   Type: Comedy Feature
Date: 1991   Origin: USA
Company: Block & Chip Productions
Annotation: Chilly D. (Van Peebles) constantly switches personalities: sometimes he's a rapper and sometimes he's a famous clothing designer. Both identities prove to be problematic for him.

IF YOU COULD SEE WHAT I HEAR
Cast: Shari Belafonte Harper*, Marc Singer, R.H. Thomson, Sarah Torgov, Douglas Campbell
Director: Eric Till
Executive Producer: Gene Corman, Gene Corman, Dale Falconer
Music Performer: Helen Reddy
Music by: Eric Robertson
Producer: Gene Corman, Gene Corman, Dale Falconer, Eric Till
Screenwriter: Stuart Gillard
Storywriter: Tom Sullivan, Derek Gill
Tech Info: color/sound/100 min.　　　Type: Dramatic Feature
Date: 1981　Origin: USA
Company: Cypress Grove Films, Ltd., Till, Gillard
Annotation: Tom (Singer) is blind and Heather (Belafonte) is black. They fall in love while attending the same university however, Heather decides a love affair between them is too difficult.

ILLUSIONS
Cast: Lonette McKee*, Rosanne Katon*, Ned Bellamy, Jack Radar
Director: Julie Dash*
Music by: Chick Webb*
Producer: Julie Dash*
Screenwriter: Julie Dash*
Storywriter: Julie Dash*
Tech Info: bw/sound/34 min.　　　Type: Dramatic Short
Date: 1983　Origin: USA
Studio: Independent
Distributors/Format: Third World Newsreel (1/2"), Women Make Movies, Inc. (16mm; 1/2")
Archives/Format: IUB - BFC/A (16mm)
Annotation: Dash's film is set in Hollywood in 1942. Mignon (Mckee) works in that illusory world where she is mistaken for white and knows that if her race were known, she would never have been hired at National Pictures. What she learns about herself and how she deals with the power behind the illusion is the essence of the film. Katon plays the black singer Ester Jeeter who dubs for the white star.

IMAGEMAKER, THE
Cast: Will Smith*, Michael Nouri, Jerry Orbach, Anne Twomey, Jessica Harper
Director: Hal Weiner
Executive Producer: Melvyn J. Estrin
Music by: Fred Karns
Producer: Marilyn Weiner, Melvyn J. Estrin, Hal Weiner
Screenwriter: Hal Weiner, Dick Goldberg
Tech Info: color/sound/93 min.　　　Type: Dramatic Feature
Date: 1986　Origin: USA
Company: Screenscope
Distributors/Format: Castle Hill Home Video (1/2")
Annotation: A Washington insider (Nouri) plans a feature film that will expose government corruption and the manipulative media. Smith plays a pollster.

IMPORTANCE OF BEING ERNEST, THE
Cast: Brock Peters*, CCH Pounder*, Daryl Roach*, Obba Babatunde*, Lanei Chapman*, Wren T. Brown*, Chris Calloway*, Barbara Isaacs*, Ann Weldon*, Sylvester Hayes*
Director: Kurt Baker
Executive Producer: Peter A. Andrews
Music by: Roger Hamilton Spotts
Producer: Nancy Carter Crow, Peter A. Andrews
Screenwriter: Peter A. Andrews, Kurt Baker
Storywriter: Oscar Wilde
Tech Info: color/sound/123 min.   Type: Comedy Feature
Date: 1992   Origin: USA
Company: Eclectic Concepts Limited, Paco Global Inc.
Distributors/Format: Eclectic Concepts/Paco Global Inc. Home Video (1/2")
Annotation: Wilde's classic play is filmed with an African American cast. Algernon (Brown) and Jack (Roach) take the name Ernest to attract Cecily (Chapman) and Gwendolyn (Calloway). Algernon's aunt (Weldon) cautiously observes. Peters plays Doctor Chausible who marries Miss Prism (Pounder); Babatunde appears as Lane; Isaacs as Merriman; Hayes as the Butler.

IMPRESSIONS OF JOYCE
Director: Roy Campanella Jr.*
Producer: Roy Campanella Jr.*
Screenwriter: Roy Campanella Jr.*
Storywriter: Roy Campanella Jr.*
Tech Info: color/sound/28 min.   Type: Experimental Short
Date: 1979   Origin: USA
Studio: Independent
Annotation: The film is about Joyce, a recovering drug addict who struggles to adjust to a new job and a new marriage.

IMPULSE
Cast: Lynn Thigpen*, Theresa Russell, Jeff Fahey, George Dzundza, Shawn Elliott
Director: Sondra Locke
Executive Producer: Dan Kolsrud
Music by: Michel Colombier, Joe Isgro
Producer: Albert S. Ruddy, Andre Morgan, Dan Kolsrud
Screenwriter: Leigh Chapman, John De Marco
Storywriter: John De Marco
Tech Info: color/sound/108 min.   Type: Dramatic Feature
Date: 1990   Origin: USA
Company: Ruddy Morgan
Distributors/Format: Warner Bros. Home Video, Inc. (1/2")
Annotation: An undercover policewoman (Russell) builds a case against underworld kingpin Tony Peron (Elliott). Thigpen plays Dr. Gardner.

IN GOD WE TRUST
Cast: Richard Pryor*, Peter Boyle, Wilfred Hyde-White, Marty Feldman, Andy Kaufman, Louise Lasser
Director: Marty Feldman
Executive Producer: Norman T. Herman
Music by: John Morris

Producer: Howard West, George Shapiro, Norman T. Herman
Screenwriter: Marty Feldman, Chris Allen
Tech Info: color/sound/97 min.   Type: Comedy Feature
Date: 1980   Origin: USA
Company: Universal
Distributors/Format: Universal Home Video (1/2")
Annotation: Feldman plays Brother Ambrose, a naive monk who tries to raise money
for his monastery. In robe and sandals, Ambrose solicits funds from Armageddon T.
Thunderbird (Kaufman), TV evangelist, who makes Ambrose a partner in his Church
of Divine Profit. Pryor, as God, is the target of Ambrose's prayers for assistance.

IN MOTION: AMIRI BARAKA

Director: St. Clair Bourne*
Producer: St. Clair Bourne*
Screenwriter: Lou Potter*
Speaker: Imamu Amiri Baraka*
Tech Info: mixed/sound/58 min.   Type: Documentary Feature
Date: 1982   Origin: USA
Studio: Independent
Company: The Chamba Organization
Distributors/Format: Facets Multimedia, Inc. (1/2"), First Run/Icarus Films (16mm)
Annotation: Amiri Baraka talks about his early days in Greenwich Village and his
present literary and political activities. The film focuses on the final two weeks
before his sentencing at federal court on the charges of resisting arrest.

IN REMEMBRANCE OF MARTIN

Speaker: Desmond Tutu*, Julian Bond*, Coretta Scott King*, Ralph Abernathy*,
Jesse Jackson*, Jimmy Carter, Edward Kennedy
Tech Info: mixed/sound/60 min.   Type: Documentary Feature
Date: 1986   Origin: USA
Distributors/Format: Filmic Archives (1/2")
Annotation: Dr. King is memorialized in interviews and archival footage of his
leadership in the Civil Rights Movement.

IN SEARCH OF OUR FATHERS

Director: Marco Williams*
Executive Producer: Nick Paleologos, Frederick Zello
Music by: Billy Childs*
Narrator: Marco Williams*
Producer: Marco Williams*, Nick Paleologos, Frederick Zello
Screenwriter: Marco Williams*
Tech Info: color/sound/60 min.   Type: Documentary Feature
Date: 1992   Origin: USA
Studio: Independent
Company: Conjare Films
Distributors/Format: Filmakers Library, Inc. (16mm; 1/2")
Annotation: The film documents filmmaker Williams' seven-year search for the
father he never knew and his coming to terms with the truth of his origins.

IN THE ARMY NOW

Cast: Ernie Hudson*, Lynn Whitfield*, David Alan Grier*, Esai Morales, Pauly Shore, Andy Dick
Director: Daniel Petrie Jr.
Executive Producer: Nicholas Hassitt, Cyrus Yavneh
Music by: Robert Folk
Producer: Michael Rotenberg, Nicholas Hassitt, Cyrus Yavneh
Screenwriter: Daniel Petrie Jr., Kenneth Kaufman, Fax Bahr, Adam Small
Storywriter: Steve Zacharias, Jeff Buhai, Robbie Fox
Tech Info: color/sound/91 min.   Type: Comedy Feature
Date: 1994   Origin: USA
Company: Hollywood Pictures
Distributors/Format: Buena Vista Home Video (1/2")
Annotation: Bones Conway (Shore) and his friend Jack Kaufman (Dick) join the Army Reserves hoping to earn enough money to open a stereo store. During basic training, Sgt. Ladd, the drill instructor (Whitfield) takes a dislike to Conway. He and Kaufman befriend Fred Ostroff (Grier), a dentist, and they all go on active duty which includes fighting in Libya. Hudson has a minor role.

IN THE HANDS OF THE ENEMY

Cast: Joe Morton*, Glenn Plummer*, Maidie Norman*, Sam Waterston, Robert Davi, Ron Leibman
Director: Jeff Bleckner
Executive Producer: George Englund
Music by: Jimmie Haskell
Producer: Robert A. Papazian, George Englund
Screenwriter: Richard Levinson, William Link
Tech Info: color/sound/100 min.   Type: Dramatic Feature
Date: 1994   Origin: USA
Company: Robert Papazani Productions
Distributors/Format: Vidmark Entertainment Home Video (1/2")
Annotation: An Arab terrorist (Davi) is captured and imprisoned by U.S. Marines. Morton plays an assistant D.A. at the terrorist's trial. Plummer is a Marine M.P. and Norman plays Edna.

IN THE LINE OF FIRE

Cast: Gregory Alan-Williams*, Clint Eastwood, John Malkovich, Rene Russo
Director: Wolfgang Petersen
Executive Producer: David Valdes, Wolfgang Petersen, Gail Katz
Music by: Ennio Morricone
Producer: Jeffrey D. Apple, David Valdes, Wolfgang Petersen, Gail Katz
Screenwriter: Jeff Maguire
Tech Info: color/sound/123 min.   Type: Dramatic Feature
Date: 1993   Origin: USA
Company: Apple/Rose Productions, Castle Rock
Distributors/Format: Columbia Pictures Home Video (1/2")
Annotation: Secret Service agent Frank Horrigan (Eastwood) tracks down a psychopath (Malkovich) who is determined to kill the president of the United States. Alan-Williams plays Matt Wilder.

IN THE SOUP
Cast: Jennifer Beals*, Seymour Cassel, Will Patton, Carol Kane, Steve Buscemi, Stanley Tucci
Director: Alexandre Rockwell, Phil Parmet
Music by: Mader
Producer: Jim Stark, Hank Blumenthal
Screenwriter: Alexandre Rockwell, Tim Kissell
Tech Info: color/sound/96 min.   Type: Comedy Feature
Date: 1992   Origin: USA
Company: Academy Entertainment
Distributors/Format: Triton Home Video (1/2")
Annotation: Before Adolfo Rollo (Buscemi) met Joe (Cassel), his excitement focused on spying on his neighbor Angelica (Beals). Joe helped Aldolfo with his spying and now he wants Adolfo to help him with car theft, burglary and romancing women.

IN YOUR FACE
Cast: Tobar Mayo*, J.W. Smith*, Roxy Young, Robert Williams, Lonnie James
Director: Frank Packard
Producer: J.P. Joshua
Tech Info: color/sound/90 min.   Type: Dramatic Feature
Date: 1990   Origin: USA
Company: Stellar Films
Distributors/Format: Xenon Entertainment Group (1/2")
Annotation: When a courageous black doctor and his family take up residence in a white neighborhood, the welcoming party quickly turns racist. A black motorcycle gang eventually helps them out.

INCHON
Cast: Richard Roundtree*, Ben Gazzara, Jacqueline Bisset, Laurence Olivier, Nam Goon Won
Director: Terence Young
Music by: Jerry Goldsmith, Sun Myung Moon
Producer: Mitsuharu Ishii
Screenwriter: Robin Moore, Laird Koenig
Storywriter: Robin Moore, Paul Savage
Tech Info: color/sound/140 min.   Type: Dramatic Feature
Date: 1981   Origin: USA, South Korea
Company: One Way
Distributors/Format: MGM/UA Home Video (1/2")
Annotation: The film recounts the Inchon landing during the Korean war. Roundtree plays Sgt. August Henderson.

INKWELL
Cast: Glynn Turman*, Joe Morton*, Mary Alice*, Phyllis Yvonne Stickney*, Suzzanne Douglas*, Morris Chestnut*, Vanessa Bell Calloway*, Jada Pinkett*, Larenz Tate*, Duane Martin*, Adrienne-Joi Johnson*, Markus Redmond*, Perry Moore*, Tonya Kelly*, Joi Marshall*, Di Reed*, Jade *, Akia Victor*
Director: Matty Rich*
Executive Producer: Jon Jashni
Music by: Terence Blanchard*
Producer: Irving Azoff, Guy Riedel, Jon Jashni

Screenwriter: Paris Qualles*, Trey Ellis*
Tech Info: color/sound/112 min.   Type: Dramatic Feature
Date: 1994   Origin: USA
Company: Touchstone, Vineyard Inc., Giant Pictures
Distributors/Format: Touchstone Home Video (1/2")
Annotation: The film focuses on a young teenager, Drew (Tate), who after setting fire to his parents' (Morton and Douglas) garage in Brooklyn, is taken to spend time with relatives (Alice, Bell Calloway, Turman, Martin) on Inkwell Beach at Martha's Vineyard. Stickney plays an island psychiatrist who allows Drew to learn about himself.

INNERSPACE
Cast: Harold Sylvester*, Kevin Hooks*, Dennis Quaid, Martin Short, Meg Ryan
Director: Joe Dante
Executive Producer: Steven Spielberg, Peter Guber, Jon Peters
Music by: Jerry Goldsmith
Producer: Steven Spielberg, Peter Guber, Jon Peters, Chip Proser, Michael Finnell
Screenwriter: Chip Proser, Jeffrey Boam
Storywriter: Chip Proser
Tech Info: color/sound/120 min.   Type: Comedy Feature
Date: 1987   Origin: USA
Company: Amblin, Guber, Peters
Distributors/Format: Warner Bros. Home Video, Inc. (1/2")
Annotation: Lt. Tuck Pendleton (Quaid) is an American pilot who is miniaturized as part of a government experiment, then accidentally injected into Jack Putter (Short), a weak-willed nobody. They work together to battle the villains who are after the miniaturization formula. Sylvester plays Pete Blanchard; Hooks plays Duane.

INNOCENT BLOOD
Cast: Angela Bassett*, Robert Loggia, Anthony LaPaglia, Anne Parillaud
Director: John Landis
Executive Producer: Jonathan Sheinberg
Music by: Ira Newborn
Producer: Lee Rich, Jonathan Sheinberg, Leslie Belzberg
Screenwriter: Michael Wolk
Tech Info: color/sound/115 min.   Type: Dramatic Feature
Date: 1992   Origin: USA
Company: Lee Rich Productions, Landis/Belzberg
Distributors/Format: Warner Bros. Home Video, Inc. (1/2")
Annotation: Marie (Parillaud) is a bloodsucking vampire who only preys on evil people. As a mob war erupts, she senses this is the perfect cover for her activities. Bassett plays U.S. Attorney Sinclair.

INNOCENT MAN, AN
Cast: Badja Djola*, Tom Selleck, F. Murray Abraham, Laila Robins
Director: Peter Yates
Executive Producer: Scott Kroopf
Music by: Howard Shore
Producer: Ted Field, Robert Cort, Scott Kroopf, Neil Machlis
Screenwriter: Larry Brothers
Tech Info: color/sound/113 min.   Type: Dramatic Feature

Date: 1989   Origin: USA
Company: Touchstone, Silver Screen Partners IV, Interscope
Distributors/Format: Buena Vista Home Video (1/2")
Annotation: After mistakenly bursting into Jimmie Rainwood's (Selleck) house and shooting him, two corrupt cops frame him on narcotics charges to cover up. Djola plays John Fitzgerald.

INSIDE MOVES
Cast: Harold Sylvester*, Tony Burton*, Bill Henderson*, Diana Scarwid, John Savage, David Morse
Director: Richard Donner
Executive Producer: David Salven
Music by: John Barry
Producer: R.W. Goodwin, Mark M. Tanz, David Salven
Screenwriter: Barry Levinson, Valerie Curtin
Tech Info: color/sound/113 min.   Type: Dramatic Feature
Date: 1980   Origin: USA
Company: Goodmark
Distributors/Format: Associated Film (16mm)
Annotation: Roary (Savage) attempts suicide but ends up paralyzed. He befriends other handicapped people at a bar. Burton plays Lucius Porter and Sylvester is Alvin Martin.

INTERNATIONAL SWEETHEARTS OF RHYTHM, THE
Speaker: Anna Mae Winburn*, Tiny Davis*, Helen Jones*, Helen Saine*, Evelyn McGee*, Jessie Stone*, Mr. Kirkland*, Al Cobbs*, Panama Francis*, Tina *, Rosalind "Roz" Cron
Tech Info: color/sound/30 min.   Type: Documentary Short
Date: 1986   Origin: USA
Company: Channel Four Television, Ltd., et al.
Distributors/Format: Cinema Guild (1/2")
Archives/Format: IUB - BFC/A (1/2")
Annotation: Through interviews with surviving members of the "Sweethearts" and their fans, as well as clips of their performances, this documentary tells the story of a unique group of multi-racial female musicians. Their experiences reflect the social attitudes of the 1940s toward gender and race.

INTERVIEW WITH THE VAMPIRE
Cast: Thandie Newton*, Nicole DuBois*, Tom Cruise, Brad Pitt, Kirsten Dunst
Director: Neil Jordan
Music by: Elliot Goldenthal
Producer: David Geffen, Stephen Woolley
Screenwriter: Anne Rice
Storywriter: Anne Rice
Tech Info: color/sound/122 min.   Type: Dramatic Feature
Date: 1994   Origin: USA, Great Britain
Company: Geffen Pictures
Distributors/Format: Warner Bros. Home Video, Inc. (1/2")
Annotation: Louis (Pitt) is given eternal life by the Vampire Lestat (Cruise) in 18th-century Louisiana. Newton is Yvette, who is initiated into the fraternity of the living dead; DuBois plays a creole woman.

INTO THE NIGHT
Cast: Andrew Marton*, Arthur/Art Evans*, Hope Clarke*, Jeff Goldblum, Michelle Pfeiffer, Stacey Pickren
Director: John Landis
Executive Producer: Dan Allingham
Music by: Ira Newborn
Producer: George Folsey Jr., Ron Koslow, Dan Allingham
Screenwriter: Ron Koslow
Tech Info: color/sound/115 min.   Type: Comedy Feature
Date: 1985   Origin: USA
Company: Universal
Distributors/Format: Universal Home Video (1/2")
Annotation: Ed Okin (Goldblum) an unhappily married aerospace engineer with insomnia, meets Diana (Pfeiffer) at the Los Angeles Airport when she falls on the hood of his car while trying to escape from four Iranian hoods who want to retrieve the six emeralds of the Shah's that she has smuggled into the country. Clarke is an "Airport Cop"; Evans is Jimmy, doorman at one of the swank apartment buildings in Beverly Hills.

INTRO TO CULTURAL SKIT-ZO-FRENIA
Director: Jamika Ajalon*
Producer: Jamika Ajalon*
Tech Info: color/sound/10 min.   Type: Experimental Short
Date: 1993   Origin: USA
Studio: Independent
Distributors/Format: Third World Newsreel (1/2")
Annotation: The film challenges homophobia within the African American community, and graphically depicts the "homo-hate," sexism and classism that divides the community today.

IRON EAGLE
Cast: Louis Gossett Jr.*, Larry B. Scott*, Jason Gedrick, Tim Thomerson, Caroline Lagerfelt, David Suchet
Director: Sidney J. Furie
Executive Producer: Kevin Elders
Music Performer: Basil Poledouris
Music by: Basil Poledouris
Producer: Kevin Elders, Ron Samuels, Joe Wizan
Screenwriter: Sidney J. Furie, Kevin Elders
Tech Info: color/sound/108 min.   Type: Dramatic Feature
Date: 1986   Origin: USA
Company: Joe Wizan/Ron Samuels Production
Distributors/Format: TriStar Pictures Inc. (1/2")
Annotation: Chappy Sinclair (Gossett), a retired Air Force pilot, undertakes an impossible mission to save an 18-year-old pilot, Masters (Gedrick) whose father's plane crashes in the Middle East. They are aided by Reggie (Scott), Masters' best friend from high school.

IRON EAGLE II

Cast: Louis Gossett Jr.*, Clark Johnson*, Mark Humphrey, Maury Chaykin
Director: Sidney J. Furie
Executive Producer: Mario Kassar, Andrew Vajna, Andras Hamori
Music by: Amin Bhatia, Sam Feldman, Bruce Allen, Steve Love
Producer: John Kemeny, Mario Kassar, Andrew Vajna, Jacob Kotzky, Sharon Harel, Andras Hamori
Screenwriter: Sidney J. Furie
Storywriter: Kevin Elders
Tech Info: color/sound/105 min.   Type: Dramatic Feature
Date: 1988   Origin: USA
Company: Alliance-Harkot
Distributors/Format: IVE Home Video (1/2")
Annotation: Colonel Chappy Sinclair's (Gossett) assignment in this sequel involves an outcast squad of United States fighter pilots and an elite group of Soviet pilots who band together in order to destroy a nuclear facility in the Middle East. Graves (Johnson) is one of Sinclair's underlings who attempts to benefit from the Soviet pilots' unfamiliarity with American ways.

IT COULD HAPPEN TO YOU

Cast: Isaac Hayes*, Beatrice Winde*, Rosie Perez, Nicolas Cage, Victor Rojas, Bridget Fonda
Director: Andrew Bergman
Executive Producer: Gary Adelson, Craig Baumgarten
Music by: Carter Burwell*
Producer: Gary Adelson, Mike Lobell, Craig Baumgarten
Screenwriter: Jane Anderson
Tech Info: color/sound/101 min.   Type: Comedy Feature
Date: 1994   Origin: USA
Company: Lobell/Bergman Prod., Adelson/Baumgarten Prod.
Distributors/Format: TriStar Pictures Inc. (1/2")
Annotation: Originally called COPS TIPS WAITRESS $2M, the film is loosely based on a real incident in which a New York policeman, in this case Officer Charlie Lang (Cage), and a waitress, Yvonne Biasi (Fonda), share a winning lottery ticket. Perez plays Charlie's wife Muriel and Hayes plays Angel.

JACKIE ROBINSON

Series: Black Americans of Achievement Video Collection
Director: Rhonda Fabian, Jerry Baber, Keith Smith
Executive Producer: Andrew Schlessinger
Narrator: Michael Logan
Producer: Rhonda Fabian, Jerry Baber, Andrew Schlessinger
Tech Info: mixed/sound/30 min.   Type: Documentary Short
Date: 1992   Origin: USA
Studio: Independent
Company: Schlessinger Video Productions
Annotation: The documentary is adapted from the biography, "Jackie Robinson Baseball Great" by Richard Scott.

JACKSONS: AN AMERICAN DREAM, THE
Cast: Billy Dee Williams*, Lawrence-Hilton Jacobs*, Vanessa Williams*, Angela Bassett*, Kelli M. Martin*, Alex Burrall*, Holly Robinson*, Jermaine Jackson II*
Executive Producer: Suzanne DePasse*
Producer: Suzanne DePasse*, Margaret Jackson
Screenwriter: Joyce Elliason
Tech Info: color/sound/225 min.   Type: Television Miniseries
Date: 1992   Origin: USA
Studio: ABC-TV
Annotation: The series is based on the true story of Michael Jackson and his family spanning five decades--beginning with the family's rise from Gary, Indiana to the premier stages of the world.

JACOB'S LADDER
Cast: S. Epatha Merkerson*, Ving Rhames*, Eriq LaSalle*, Bryon Minns*, Danny Aiello, Elizabeth Pena, Suzanne Shepherd, Tim Robbins
Director: Adrian Lyne
Executive Producer: Mario Kassar, Andrew Vajna
Music Performer: James Brown*, Marvin Gaye*, K. Nolan, Al Jolson
Music by: Maurice Jarre
Producer: Alan Marshall, Mario Kassar, Andrew Vajna
Screenwriter: Bruce Joel Rubin
Tech Info: color/sound/115 min.   Type: Dramatic Feature
Date: 1990   Origin: USA
Company: Carolco
Distributors/Format: TriStar Pictures Inc. (1/2")
Annotation: Jacob (Robbins), a Vietnam veteran, experiences bizarre hallucinations and discovers he was part of a secret experimental drug test during the war. La Salle plays Frank, Rhames is George and Merkerson is Elsa.

JAGGED EDGE
Cast: William Allen Young*, Phyllis Applegate*, Michael Dorn*, Peter Coyote, Robert Loggia, Glenn Close, Jeff Bridges
Director: Richard Marquand
Music by: John Barry
Producer: Martin Ranshoff
Screenwriter: Joe Eszterhas
Tech Info: color/sound/108 min.   Type: Dramatic Feature
Date: 1985   Origin: USA
Company: Columbia
Distributors/Format: Columbia Pictures Home Video (1/2")
Annotation: Attorney Barnes (Close) takes a case to defend Forrester (Bridges) who alleges his innocence, knowing she let Stiles, an innocent man go to prison where he later hanged himself. In Forrester's case, Attorneys Krasny (Coyote) and Arnold (Young) bury pertinent evidence; however, Barnes wins the case with the help of Investigators Ransom (Loggia) and Hislan (Dorn). She then confesses to withholding evidence in the Stiles' case in front of the young man's mother (Applegate).

JAGUAR LIVES!
Cast: Woody Strode*, Joe Lewis*, Christopher Lee, Donald Pleasence, Barbara Bach, Joseph Wiseman, John Huston
Director: Ernest Pintoff
Executive Producer: Sandy Howard
Music by: Robert O. Ragland
Producer: Derek Gibson, Sandy Howard
Storywriter: Yabo Yablonsky
Tech Info: color/sound/90 min.   Type: Dramatic Feature
Date: 1979   Origin: USA/Europe
Studio: Independent
Company: AIP
Distributors/Format: InterGlobal Video Promotions Ltd. (1/2")
Annotation: Jaguar (Lewis) is a karate champ who is determined to restore tranquility after an international drug cartel wreaks havoc. Strode is the Jaguar's sensei.

JAMES BALDWIN: THE PRICE OF THE TICKET
Series: American Masters
Executive Producer: Albert Maysles
Producer: William Miles*, Albert Maysles, Douglas K. Dempsey
Screenwriter: Ishmael Reed*, Karen Thorsen
Speaker: Maya Angelou*, Imamu Amiri Baraka*, David Baldwin*, Mrs. Berdis Baldwin*, Bernard Hassel*, James Briggs Murray*, Frances Foster*, El-Hajj Malik El-Shabazz*, Eldridge Cleaver*, Reverend Martin Luther King*, Reverend Martin Luther King*, William Styron, David Leeming, Lucien Happersberger, Engin Cezzar, Yashar Kemal, Bobby Short
Storywriter: Karen Thorsen, Douglas K. Dempsey
Tech Info: mixed/sound/90 min.   Type: Documentary Feature
Date: 1988   Origin: USA
Company: Maysles Film, Inc
Distributors/Format: California Newsreel (1/2")
Annotation: Opening with Baldwin's funeral in December, 1987, in the Cathedral of St. John the Divine, the film traces his life history and accomplishments. It includes interviews with friends, family members and colleagues.

JAMES BROWN LIVE IN CONCERT
Director: Barrie McLean
Music Performer: James Brown*
Producer: Wendell Wilkes
Tech Info: color/sound/48 min.   Type: Concert Short
Date: 1979   Origin: Canada, USA
Studio: Independent
Company: Heron Communications, Inc.
Annotation: Performing for over 30 years, Brown paved the way for other soul shouters, as well as the resurgence of funk. It is a concert by the man generally acknowledged to be the father of funk and soul. (The film was shot at the 1979 Summer Festival in Toronto, Canada.)

JANINE
Director: Cheryl Dunye*
Producer: Cheryl Dunye*
Tech Info: bw/sound/9 min.   Type: Documentary Short
Date: 1990   Origin: USA
Studio: Independent
Distributors/Format: Third World Newsreel (1/2")
Annotation: A black woman tells of her relationship with an white upper- middle class friend and their subsequent struggle for mutual acceptance despite racial and sexual differences.

JANUARY MAN, THE
Cast: Bill Cobbs*, Kevin Kline, Harvey Keitel, Mary Elizabeth Mastrantonio, Susan Sarandon
Director: Pat O'Conner
Music by: Marvin Hamlisch, Moe Koffman
Producer: Norman Jewison, Ezra Swerdlow
Screenwriter: John Patrick Shanley
Tech Info: color/sound/97 min.   Type: Dramatic Feature
Date: 1989   Origin: USA
Company: MGM/United Artists
Annotation: Maverick New York police detective Nick Starkey (Kline) tries to catch a serial killer and, in the meantime, falls in love with Bernadette Flynn (Mastrantonio), the mayor's daughter. Cobbs is Detective Reilly.

JASON'S LYRIC
Cast: Forest Whitaker*, Suzzanne Douglas*, Jada Pinkett*, Bokeem Woodbine*, Allen Payne*, Eddie Griffin*, Treach (Anthony Criss) *, Lahmard Tate*, Lisa Carson*, Sean Hutchinson*, Burleigh Moore*, Clarence Whitemore*, Asheamu Earl Randle*, Rushion McDonald*, Bebe Drake*, Kenneth Randle*, Wayne DeHart*, Olivia Gatewood*, Michon Benson*
Director: Doug McHenry*, Francis Kenny
Music by: Afrika *, Matt Noble*
Producer: George Jackson*, Doug McHenry*
Screenwriter: Bobby L. Smith Jr.*
Tech Info: color/sound/106 min.   Type: Dramatic Feature
Date: 1994   Origin: USA
Company: Jackson-McHenry* Company, Propaganda Films
Annotation: Jason (Payne) and Joshua Alexander (Woodbine) are bound together by the terrible death of their father, Maddog (Whitaker). Jason has put the past behind him, but his younger brother Joshua has memories that lead him into a life of drugs and violence. Douglas plays Gloria, their abused mother; Pinkett is Jason's love interest, Lyric Greer; Treach plays her gangster brother Alonzo.

JAWS III
Cast: Louis Gossett Jr.*, Alonzo Ward*, Dennis Quaid, Bess Armstrong
Director: Joe Alves
Executive Producer: Alan Landsburg, Howard Lipstone
Music Performer: John Williams, Alan Parker
Producer: Alan Landsburg, Rupert Hitzig, Howard Lipstone, Howard Lipstone
Screenwriter: Richard Matheson, Carl Gottlieb
Storywriter: Guerdon Trueblood

Tech Info: color/sound/98 min.   Type: Dramatic Feature
Date: 1983   Origin: USA
Company: Alan Landsburg Productions
Distributors/Format: MCA Home Video (1/2")
Annotation: Calvin Bouchard (Gossett) runs a sea life park which is about to celebrate its grand opening. Bouchard has foreseen all problems except a 35-foot shark. Fred (Ward), Bouchard's nephew, is the engineer in the control room who regulates the underwater tunnels.

JAWS: THE REVENGE
Cast: Lynn Whitfield*, Melvin Van Peebles*, Mario Van Peebles*, Lorraine Gary, Lance Guest, Karen Young
Director: Joseph Sargent
Music by: John Williams, Michael Small
Producer: Joseph Sargent
Screenwriter: Michael de Guzman
Tech Info: color/sound/89 min.   Type: Dramatic Feature
Date: 1987   Origin: USA
Company: Universal
Distributors/Format: Universal Home Video (1/2")
Annotation: In this fourth of the JAWS series, the police chief's widow becomes the target of the Sharks's revenge. Mario Van Peebles plays Jake, her son's partner, Melvin Van Peebles plays Mr. Witherspoon and Whitfield is Louisa.

JAZZ SINGER, THE
Cast: Franklin Ajaye*, John Witherspoon*, Neil Diamond, Laurence Oliver, Lucie Arnaz
Director: Richard Fleischer
Music Performer: Leonard Rosenman, Neil Diamond
Music by: Neil Diamond
Producer: Jerry Leider
Screenwriter: Herbert Baker, Stephen H. Foreman
Storywriter: Samson Raphaelson
Tech Info: color/sound/115 min.   Type: Musical Feature
Date: 1980   Origin: USA
Company: Paramount
Distributors/Format: Paramount/EMI Home Video (1/2")
Annotation: Jess Robin (Diamond) dreams of being a successful musician until his friend Bubba (Ajaye) provides him with connections to the "big time" through a music producer's recording studio. Bubba supports Jess through his turbulent dealings with love, family, and fame.

JEKYLL AND HYDE...TOGETHER AGAIN
Cast: Jesse Goins*, Tim Thomerson, Bess Armstrong, Mark Blankfield, Krista Errickson, Michael McGuire
Director: Jerry Belson
Music by: Barry Devorzon
Producer: Lawrence Gordon
Screenwriter: Harvey Miller, Monica Johnson, Jerry Belson, Michael Lesson
Tech Info: color/sound/87 min.   Type: Comedy Feature

Date: 1982   Origin: USA
Company: Paramount
Distributors/Format: Paramount Home Video (1/2")
Annotation: Dr. Jekyll (Blankfield) is a surgeon who accidentally snorts a cocaine-like substance and turns into Hyde, a hip alter-ego sporting disco clothes and jewelry. Goins plays Dutch.

JENNIFER EIGHT
Cast: Paul Bates*, John Malkovich, Kathy Baker, Lance Henriksen, Uma Thurman, Andy Garcia
Director: Bruce Robinson
Executive Producer: Scott Rudin
Music by: Christopher Young
Producer: Scott Rudin, David Wimbury, Gary Lucchesi
Screenwriter: Bruce Robinson
Tech Info: color/sound/127 min.   Type: Dramatic Feature
Date: 1992   Origin: USA
Company: Scott Rudin Productions
Distributors/Format: Paramount (1/2")
Annotation: Bates plays Venables in this thriller about the unsolved murders of seven blind girls in rural California.

JERK, THE
Cast: Richard Ward*, Olivia Frances Williams*, Mabel King*, Dick Anthony Williams*, Sonny Terry*, Brownie McGhee*, Shawn Harris*, Niles Harris*, Niko Denise Holmes*, Susan Denise Harison*, Steve Martin, Bernadette Peters
Director: Carl Reiner
Music by: Jack Elliott
Producer: David V. Picker, William McEuen
Screenwriter: Steve Martin, Carl Gottlieb, Michael Elias
Storywriter: Steve Martin, Carl Gottlieb
Tech Info: color/sound/95 min.   Type: Comedy Feature
Date: 1979   Origin: USA
Company: David Picker, William McEven
Distributors/Format: Universal Home Video (1/2")
Annotation: Navin Johnson (Martin), who is raised by a black family in the South, becomes distraught because his life is going nowhere. When his foster parents (King and Ward) tell him he is not really their child, he decides to venture out to California to see the world.

JESSE JACKSON
Alternate: Civil Rights Leader and Politician
Series: Black Americans of Achievement Video Collection
Director: Rhonda Fabian, Jerry Baber, Keith Smith
Executive Producer: Andrew Schlessinger
Producer: Rhonda Fabian, Jerry Baber, Andrew Schlessinger
Speaker: Jesse Jackson*
Tech Info: mixed/sound/30 min.   Type: Documentary Short

Date: 1992   Origin: USA
Studio: Independent
Company: Schlessinger Video Productions
Annotation: The documentary is adapted from the book "Jesse Jackson, Civil Rights Leader and Politician" by Robert Jakovbek.

JIMI HENDRIX: EXPERIENCE
Music Performer: Jimi Hendrix*
Tech Info: color/sound/102 min.   Type: Documentary Feature
Date: 1992   Origin: USA
Company: Warner Bros.
Distributors/Format: Warner Bros. Home Video, Inc. (1/2")
Annotation: The Master guitarist Hendrix electrifies his audience on- stage and educates his followers off-stage in this 1967 program. Other performance videos include: JIMI HENDRIX: BERKELEY--MAY, 1970 (1991), JIMI HENDRIX: RAINBOW BRIDGE (1989) and JIMI HENDRIX CONCERTS VIDEOGRAM (1983).

JIMMY THE KID
Cast: Cleavon Little*, Gary Coleman*, Fay Hauser*, Sarina Grant*, Ruth Gordon, Don Adams, Pat Morita
Director: Gary Nelson
Music Performer: John Cameron, Jackie English
Producer: Ronald Jacobs
Screenwriter: Sam Bobrick
Storywriter: Donald E. Westlake
Tech Info: color/sound/125 min.   Type: Comedy Feature
Date: 1982   Origin: USA
Company: Zephyr Productions
Distributors/Format: New World Pictures (1/2"), Sight & Sound (1/2")
Annotation: Jimmy (Coleman) is the 12-year-old son of a famous country/western duo Herb (Little) and Nina Lovejoy (Hauser). Kidnapped by four societal rejects, Jimmy ends up helping them negotiate his own release with his parents.

JO JO DANCER, YOUR LIFE IS CALLING
Cast: Richard Pryor*, Paula Kelly*, Ken Foree*, Tanya Boyd*, Debbie Allen*, Arthur/Art Evans*, Fay Hauser*, Scoey Mitchell*, Ludie Washington*, Bebe Drake-Massey*, Carmen McRae*, Marlene Warfield*, Diahnne Abbott*, E'Lon Cox*, Barbara Williams
Director: Richard Pryor*
Music by: Herbie Hancock*
Producer: Richard Pryor*
Screenwriter: Richard Pryor*, Rocco Urbisci, Paul Mooney
Tech Info: color/sound/97 min.   Type: Dramatic Feature
Date: 1986   Origin: USA
Company: Columbia
Distributors/Format: Columbia Pictures Home Video (1/2")
Archives/Format: IUB - BFC/A (1/2")
Annotation: Pryor portrays Jo Jo Dancer, a comedian at the peak of his career and the bottom rung of his self-esteem. After a drug-related accident that leaves him near death, Jo Jo looks back on his life, from his upbringing in a brothel, through his early comedic performances in cellar nightclubs, to his eventual stardom. Kelly plays a stripper who gets Jo Jo a gig at the nightclub where she performs.

JOCKS

Alternate: Road Trip
Cast: Richard Roundtree*, Stone/Stoney Jackson*, Scott Strader, Perry Lang, Mariska Hargitay
Director: Steve Carver
Music by: David McHugh
Producer: Ahmet Yasa
Screenwriter: David Obst, Jeff Buhai
Tech Info: color/sound/90 min.   Type: Comedy Feature
Date: 1987   Origin: USA
Company: Mt. Olympus
Distributors/Format: Crown Home Video (1/2")
Annotation: Athletic director Beetlebom (Armstrong) wants to cut the high school tennis program. Coach Chip Williams (Roundtree) and his star player, "The Kid" (Strader) are forced to take extreme measures to save the program. Jackson plays Andy.

JOE VERSUS THE VOLCANO

Cast: Ossie Davis*, Tom Hanks, Lloyd Bridges, Abe Vigoda, Meg Ryan
Director: John Patrick Shanley
Executive Producer: Steven Spielberg, Frank Marshall, Kathleen Kennedy
Music by: Georges Delerue
Producer: Steven Spielberg, Frank Marshall, Kathleen Kennedy, Teri Schwartz
Screenwriter: John Patrick Shanley
Tech Info: color/sound/94 min.   Type: Comedy Feature
Date: 1990   Origin: USA
Company: Amblin
Distributors/Format: Warner Bros. Home Video, Inc. (1/2")
Annotation: Hypochondriac Joe Banks (Hanks) is convinced he's going to die and volunteers to jump into an active volcano. Davis plays Marshall.

JOE'S BED-STUY BARBERSHOP: WE CUT HEADS

Cast: Leon Errol*, Elyse Knox*, Morris Carnovsky
Director: Spike Lee*
Producer: Spike Lee*
Tech Info: bw/sound/60 min.   Type: Experimental Feature
Date: 1983   Origin: USA
Studio: Independent
Company: 40 Acres and a Mule Film Works
Distributors/Format: First Run/Icarus Films (16mm)
Annotation: Joe's barbershop in Bedford-Stuyvesant is a central meeting place in the neighborhood. Clients discuss and debate personal and political issues, as well as bet their number(s).

JOEY BREAKER

Cast: Erik King*, Cedella Marley*, Richard Edson, Gina Gershon
Director: Steven Starr, Joe De Salvo
Music by: Paul Aston
Producer: Amos Poe, Steven Starr
Screenwriter: Steven Starr
Tech Info: color/sound/92 min.   Type: Dramatic Feature

Date: 1993   Origin: USA
Company: Paramount
Distributors/Format: Paramount Home Video (1/2")
Annotation: Joey Breaker (Edson) is a high-pressure talent agent in New York whose life is making deals. But things change for him when he meets a remarkable young Jamaican woman Cyan Worthington (Marley) who is a friend of a young comedian, Hip Hop Hank (King) whom Joey wants to sign.

JOHN COLTRANE: THE COLTRANE LEGACY

Series: History of Jazz
Director: Burrill Crohn
Music Performer: Miles Davis*, Reggie Workman*, John Coltrane*, Wynton Kelly*, Paul Chambers*, Eric Dolphy*, McCoy Tyner*, Jimmy Garrison*
Music by: John Coltrane*
Producer: Burrill Crohn
Speaker: Reggie Workman*, Elvin Jones*, Jimmy Cobb*, John Coltrane*
Tech Info: mixed/sound/61 min.   Type: Musical Feature
Date: 1985   Origin: USA
Company: Jazz Images, Inc., Video Artists International
Distributors/Format: ACA/Ariola International (35mm)
Archives/Format: IUB - BFC/A (1/2")
Annotation: Coltrane performs a number of the works for which he is famous, e.g., "So What" (1959) with the Miles Davis Quartet; and "Alabama" (1964) which was composed after four children died in an Alabama church bombing.

JOHNNY BE GOOD

Cast: Michael Colyar*, Robert Downey Jr., Anthony Michael Hall, Paul Gleason
Director: Bud Smith
Executive Producer: David Obst, Steve Zacharias, Jeff Buhai
Music by: Dick Rudolph
Producer: David Obst, Steve Zacharias, Jeff Buhai, Adam Fields
Screenwriter: David Obst, Steve Zacharias, Jeff Buhai
Tech Info: color/sound/98 min.   Type: Comedy Feature
Date: 1988   Origin: USA
Company: Orion
Distributors/Format: Orion Home Video (1/2")
Annotation: High-school quarterback Johnny Walker (Hall) is recruited by all the top college football programs, but he has promised his girlfriend, that he'd go to nearby State University. Colyar plays Mike, a recruiter.

JOHNNY DANGEROUSLY

Cast: Frank Slaten*, Maureen Stapleton, Michael Keaton, Joe Piscopo, Marilu Henner
Director: Amy Heckerling
Executive Producer: Harry Colomby, Bud Austin
Music by: John Morris
Producer: Harry Colomby, Michael Hertzberg, Bud Austin
Screenwriter: Harry Colomby, Norman Steinberg, Bernie Kukoff, Jeff Harris
Tech Info: color/sound/89 min.   Type: Comedy Feature

Date: 1984   Origin: USA
Company: Fox
Distributors/Format: Fox Home Video (1/2")
Annotation: In this spoof of Warner Bros. crime movies, Keaton plays Johnny Dangerously, a boy forced into a life of crime to pay his mother's medical bills. Slaten appears as a henchman.

JOHNNY HANDSOME
Cast: Morgan Freeman*, Forest Whitaker*, J.W. Smith*, Mickey Rourke, Ellen Barkin, Elizabeth McGovern
Director: Walter Hill
Producer: Charles Roven
Screenwriter: Ken Friedman
Storywriter: John Godey
Tech Info: mixed/sound/96 min.   Type: Dramatic Feature
Date: 1989   Origin: USA
Company: Carolco
Distributors/Format: International Video Entertainment (35mm; 1/2")
Archives/Format: IUB - BFC/A (1/2")
Annotation: When severely deformed criminal John Sedley (Rourke) is set up by his partners, he is sent to prison where Dr. Steven Resher (Whitaker) restructures his face and gives him a new identity. Smith plays Larry, one of the co-conspirators in the failed robbery. Freeman is Lt. A.Z. Drones.

JOHNNY SUEDE
Cast: Samuel L. Jackson*, Brad Pitt, Richard Boes, Cheryl Costa
Director: Tom DiCillo
Executive Producer: Steven Starr, Ruth Waldburger
Music by: Jim Farmer
Producer: Yoram Mandel, Steven Starr, Ruth Waldburger, Ruth Waldburger
Screenwriter: Tom DiCillo
Tech Info: color/sound/95 min.   Type: Comedy Feature
Date: 1992   Origin: USA
Company: Vegas Films, Balthazar Pictures, et al.
Distributors/Format: Miramax Home Video (1/2")
Annotation: Johnny Suede (Pitt) aspires to be a rock 'n roll star like his idol, Ricky Nelson. He has the right attitude and a big pompadour, but no shoes. When a pair of black suede shoes appear before him, his luck changes. Jackson plays B-Bop.

JOSEPHINE BAKER STORY, THE
Cast: Louis Gossett Jr.*, Lynn Whitfield*, Ruben Blades, Craig T. Nelson, David Dukes
Director: Brian Gibson
Executive Producer: Robert Halmi Sr.
Music by: Ralph Burns, Georges Delerue
Producer: Robert Halmi Sr., John Kemeny
Storywriter: Ron Hutchinson, Michael Zagor
Tech Info: color/sound/129 min.   Type: Dramatic Feature

Date: 1991   Origin: USA
Company: HBO
Distributors/Format: HBO Home Video (1/2"), Warner Bros. Home Video, Inc. (1/2")
Annotation: The film is a dramatic account of the real life story of Josephine Baker who achieved fame through her performances on the American vaudeville circuit and on the stages of Paris. The narrative also reveals Baker's fight against racism and her contributions to France during World War II.

JOURNEY OF NATTY GANN, THE
Cast: Scatman Crothers*, Ray Wise, John Cusack, Meredith Salenger, Lainie Kazan
Director: Jeremy Paul Kagan
Music by: James Horner
Producer: Mike Lobell
Screenwriter: Jeanne Rosenberg
Tech Info: color/sound/100 min.   Type: Dramatic Feature
Date: 1985   Origin: USA
Company: Walt Disney, Silver Screen Partners
Distributors/Format: Buena Vista Home Video (1/2")
Annotation: After her father leaves Chicago for a job in the Northwest, young Natty Gann (Salenger) decides to make her way across country to join him. A wolf becomes her traveling companion. Crothers plays Sherman.

JOY OF SEX
Cast: Ernie Hudson*, Miguel Nunez*, Colleen Camp, Cameron Dye, Michelle Meyrink, Lisa Langlois
Director: Martha Coolidge
Music by: Bishop Holiday, Scott Lipsker, Harold Payne
Producer: Frank Konigsberg
Screenwriter: Kathleen Rowell, J.J. Salter
Tech Info: color/sound/93 min.   Type: Comedy Feature
Date: 1984   Origin: USA
Company: Paramount
Distributors/Format: Paramount Home Video (1/2")
Annotation: Alan Holt (Dye), a student at Richard Nixon High, can only think of sex. He has his eye on Leslie (Meyrink), who happens to be the daughter of a forbidding gym teacher. Hudson plays Mr. Porter and Nunez is a jock.

JUDGEMENT NIGHT
Cast: Cuba Gooding Jr.*, Emilio Estevez, Stephen Dorff, Denis Leary, Jeremy Piven
Director: Stephen Hopkins, Peter Levy
Executive Producer: Lloyd Segan, Marilyn Vance
Music by: Alan Silvestri
Producer: Gene Levy, Lloyd Segan, Marilyn Vance
Screenwriter: Kevin Jarre, Lewis Colick, Jere Cunningham
Storywriter: Jere Cunningham
Tech Info: color/sound/110 min.   Type: Dramatic Feature
Date: 1993   Origin: USA
Company: Universal
Distributors/Format: Universal Home Video (1/2")
Annotation: Frank (Estevez), Mike (Gooding), John (Dorff) and Ray (Piven) are four suburbanites who inadvertently find themselves in a Chicago underworld nightmare.

JUICE
Cast: Samuel L. Jackson*, Eric Payne*, Grace Garland*, Jermaine Hopkins*, Queen Latifah*, LaTanya Richardson*, Omar Epps*, Khalil Kain*, Tupac Shakur*, Cindy Herron*, Dr. Dre *, Donald Adeosun Faison*, Maggie Rush*, Fab 5 Freddy *, Idina Harris*, Sharon Cook*, Darien Berry*, Lauren Jones*, George Gore*, Oran "Juice" Jones*, Jacqui Dickerson, Vincent Laresca
Director: Ernest Dickerson*, Larry Banks*
Music by: Hank Shocklee*, The Bomb Squad *
Producer: David Heyman, Neal H. Moritz, Peter Frankfurt
Screenwriter: Ernest Dickerson*, Gerard Brown*
Storywriter: Ernest Dickerson*
Tech Info: color/sound/94 min.   Type: Dramatic Feature
Date: 1992   Origin: USA
Company: IMPix Inc, Island World, Moritz/Heyman Productions
Distributors/Format: Paramount Home Video (1/2")
Archives/Format: IUB - BFC/A (1/2")
Annotation: Q (Epps), Steel (Hopkins), Bishop (Shakur) and Raheem (Kain) are a group of Harlem youths who commit a robbery which ends with a double murder and the young men turning against one another as the police close in. Jackson plays the owner of a local video arcade which students frequent instead of attending school.

JUMPIN' AT THE BONEYARD
Cast: Samuel L. Jackson*, Danitra Vance*, Jeffrey Wright*, Alexis Arquette, Elizabeth Bracco, Tim Roth
Director: Jeff Stanzler
Music by: Steve Postel
Producer: Nina R. Sadowsky, Lloyd Goldfine
Screenwriter: Jeff Stanzler
Tech Info: color/sound/107 min.   Type: Dramatic Feature
Date: 1992   Origin: USA
Company: Boneyard Productions, Kasdan Pictures
Distributors/Format: Fox Home Video (1/2")
Annotation: Manny (Roth) catches Danny (Arquette), his drug-addicted brother, and Danny's girlfriend Jeanette (Vance) breaking into his house for drug money. Manny forces Danny to seek help. The two brothers visit a community center where the director, Mr. Simpson (Jackson) offers Danny assistance.

JUMPIN' JACK FLASH
Cast: Whoopi Goldberg*, Roscoe Lee Browne*, James Belushi, Shephen Collins
Director: Penny Marshall
Music Performer: Aretha Franklin*, Thomas Newman
Music by: Thomas Newman
Producer: Lawrence Gordon, Joel Silver
Screenwriter: J.W. Melville, Patricia Irving, Christopher Thompson
Storywriter: David H. Franzoni
Tech Info: color/sound/100 min.   Type: Dramatic Feature
Date: 1986   Origin: USA
Company: Fox
Distributors/Format: Fox Home Video (1/2")
Annotation: Terri Dolittle (Goldberg) becomes involved with the KGB and British Intelligence when she begins a computer correspondence with a British agent, code

name "Jumpin' Jack Flash." Agent Lincoln (Brown) works for the C.I.A.

JUNGLE FEVER
Cast: Samuel L. Jackson*, Spike Lee*, Wesley Snipes*, Ruby Dee*, Lonette
McKee*, Ossie Davis*, Phyllis Yvonne Stickney*, Doug E. Doug*, Queen Latifah*,
Veronica Webb*, Tyra Ferrell*, Halle Berry*, Veronica Timbers*, Charles Q.
Murphy*, Theresa Randle*, Averell Curtle*, Melvin Bethea*, Randolph May*, El-Shah
Muhammad*, Suzanna White*, Danielle Coleman*, Marilyn Nelson*, Bob Adrian*,
Scott Anthony Robinson*, Curtis Atkins*, Yvette Brooks*, Mamie Louise Anderson*,
Anthony Quinn, John Turturro, Annabella Sciorra
Director: Spike Lee*
Music Performer: Stevie Wonder*, Boys Choir of Harlem *
Music by: Stevie Wonder*
Producer: Spike Lee*
Screenwriter: Spike Lee*
Tech Info: color/sound/132 min.   Type: Dramatic Feature
Date: 1991   Origin: USA
Company: 40 Acres and a Mule Film Works
Distributors/Format: Universal Home Video (1/2")
Archives/Format: IUB - BFC/A (1/2")
Annotation: When Flipper Purley (Snipes) sleeps with Italian secretary Angie Tucci
(Sciorra), violence breaks out on all sides. Neither Flipper's nor Angie's family can
cope with the relationship, nor apparently can most of society. Lee plays Flipper's
buddy; McKee plays Drew, Flipper's wife; Jackson plays Gator, Flipper's
drug-addicted brother; Berry plays Vivian, Gator's girlfriend; Dee and Davis are
Gator's and Flipper's parents; Latifah plays a waitress.

JUNGLE WARRIORS
Cast: Woody Strode*, Paul L. Smith, John Vernon, Alex Cord, Nina Van Pallandt
Director: Ernst von Theumer
Executive Producer: Monika Teuber, Francisco Araiz-Condoy
Music by: Roland Baumgartner
Producer: Ernst von Theumer, Monika Teuber, Francisco Araiz-Condoy
Screenwriter: Ernst von Theumer, Robert Collector
Tech Info: color/sound/93 min.   Type: Dramatic Feature
Date: 1984   Origin: USA, Mexico, West Germany
Company: TAT, Jungle Warriors, International, Araiz, Condoy
Distributors/Format: Aquarius Home Video (1/2")
Annotation: The crew and models for a fashion school arrive in South America at the
same time as a mafioso (Vernon) arrives to make a cocaine deal with Cesar (Smith).
Strode plays Luther, the leader of Cesar's private army who is in charge of capturing
the models who stray.

JURASSIC PARK
Cast: Samuel L. Jackson*, Jeff Goldblum, Richard Attenborough, Sam Neill, Laura
Dern, Bob Peck
Director: Steven Spielberg
Music by: John Williams
Producer: Kathleen Kennedy, Gerald R. Molen
Screenwriter: Michael Crichton, Malia Scotch Marmo, David Koepp
Tech Info: color/sound/127 min.   Type: Dramatic Feature

Date: 1993   Origin: USA
Company: Universal, Amblin
Distributors/Format: Universal Home Video (1/2")
Annotation: Amusement entrepreneur John Hammond (Attenborough) genetically engineers dinosaurs to populate an island theme park. A disgruntled employee sabotages the operation and the dinosaurs hunt the people on the island. Jackson plays Arnold, the park operations supervisor.

JURY OF HER PEERS, A

Cast: Gloria Davis-Hill*, Lloyd Davis*, Jannine Shaw*
Director: Edgar Patterson Davis*
Music by: Nathaniel Brown*
Producer: Edgar Patterson Davis*
Screenwriter: Edgar Patterson Davis*
Tech Info: color/sound/45 min.   Type: Dramatic Short
Date: 1994   Origin: USA
Annotation: Filmmaker Davis focuses on a mother (Davis-Hill) from an affluent community whose son is murdered due to street violence.

JUST AN OVERNIGHT GUEST

Cast: Richard Roundtree*, Rosalind Cash*, Tiffany Hill*, Fran Robinson, Eleanor Donahue
Director: Gina Blumenfeld
Producer: Joanna Mallas
Screenwriter: Gina Blumenfeld
Storywriter: Gina Blumenfeld
Tech Info: color/sound/38 min.   Type: Dramatic Short
Date: 1983   Origin: USA
Studio: Independent
Company: Phoenix Films
Archives/Format: IUB - BFC/A (16mm)
Annotation: Based on the novel by Eleanora Tate, the film is about a ten-year old who has trouble adjusting when a disruptive and neglected six-year-old moves in with her family. Roundtree and Cash are the parents.

JUST ANOTHER GIRL ON THE I.R.T.

Cast: Ariyan Johnson*, Ebony Jerido*, Kevin Thigpen*, Jerard Washington*
Director: Leslie Harris*, Richard Conners
Executive Producer: Leslie Harris*
Music by: Eric "Vietnam" Sadler*
Producer: Leslie Harris*, Erwin Wilson
Screenwriter: Leslie Harris*
Tech Info: color/sound/96 min.   Type: Dramatic Feature
Date: 1993   Origin: USA
Company: Miramax
Distributors/Format: Facets Multimedia, Inc. (1/2"), LIVE Home Video (1/2"), Miramax Home Video (1/2")
Annotation: A spirited Brooklyn teenager (Johnson) copes with life in the projects and sustains her fierce desire to go to college and become a doctor.

JUST LIKE IN THE MOVIES
Cast: Paul Bates*, Katherine Borowitz, Alan Ruck, Jay O. Sanders, Michael Jeter
Director: Bram Towbin, Mark Halliday
Music by: John Hill
Producer: Alon Kasha
Screenwriter: Bram Towbin
Tech Info: color/sound/90 min.   Type: Comedy Feature
Date: 1992   Origin: USA
Company: Alon Kasha Productions
Distributors/Format: Cabriolet Films, Inc. (16mm)
Annotation: Ryan Legrand (Sanders) is a private eye who specializes in recording marital infidelities for his clients who need evidence for pending divorces. He is joined by an odd lot of assistants. Bates plays "Don."

JUSTIFIABLE HOMICIDE
Director: Eric Thiermann
Storywriter: Eric Thiermann
Tech Info: bw/sound/5 min.   Type: Docudrama
Date: 1978   Origin: USA
Studio: Independent
Company: Thiermann-Finch Productions
Archives/Format: IUB - BFC/A (16mm)
Annotation: Set in a black neighborhood, the film focuses on a murder which at first appears to be justifiable homocide. It reconstructs the circumstances preceding the crime in order to show the true nature of the incident.

K-9
Cast: J.W. Smith*, Kevin Tighe*, James Belushi, Ed O'Neill, Mel Harris, Jerry Lee the Dog
Director: Rod Daniel
Executive Producer: Donna Smith
Music by: Miles Goodman
Producer: Lawrence Gordon, Charles Gordon, Donna Smith
Screenwriter: Steven Siegel, Scott Myers
Tech Info: color/sound/105 min.   Type: Comedy Feature
Date: 1989   Origin: USA
Company: Universal
Distributors/Format: Universal Home Video (1/2")
Annotation: Officer Dooley (Belushi) teams with drug-sniffing dog K-9 to catch cocaine dealer Lyman (Tighe). Smith appears as a pimp.

K2
Cast: Blu Mankuma*, Christopher K. Brown*, Michael Biehn, Patricia Charbonneau, Matt Craven, Hiroshi Fujioka
Director: Franc Roddam
Executive Producer: Melvyn J. Estrin, Hal Weiner
Music by: Chaz Jankel
Producer: Jonathan Taplin, Marilyn Weiner, Tim Van Rellim, Melvyn J. Estrin, Hal Weiner
Screenwriter: Scott Roberts, Patrick Meyers
Storywriter: Patrick Meyers

Tech Info: color/sound/111 min.   Type: Dramatic Feature
Date: 1992   Origin: Great Britain
Company: Trans Pacific Films, Majestic Film Intnl., et al.
Distributors/Format: Paramount Home Video (1/2")
Annotation: A team of hopeful climbers attempts to reach the summit of K2, the second-highest mountain in the world. Mankuma is the man in the wheelchair.

KEYS TO THE KINGDOM, THE (1974-1980)
Series: Eyes on the Prize II
Director: Jacqueline Shearer*, Paul Steckler
Executive Producer: Henry Hampton*
Music by: Bernice Johnson Reagon*
Narrator: Julian Bond*
Producer: Henry Hampton*, Jacqueline Shearer*, Paul Steckler
Screenwriter: Jacqueline Shearer*, Paul Steckler
Speaker: Eleanor Holmes Norton*, Thomas Atkins*, Juanita Wade*, Mary Francis Perry*, Ruth Batson*, Jean McGuire*, Kevin C. White*, Ellen Jackson*, Alexzandrina Young*, Phyllis Ellison*, Maynard Jackson*, Ethel Mae Matthews*, Walter Huntley*, Maggie Thomas*, Emma Darnell*, Willie Bolden*, Toni Johnson-Chavis*, Louis Day Hicks, Alan Lupo
Tech Info: mixed/sound/60 min.   Type: Television Documentary
Date: 1989   Origin: USA
Company: Blackside, Inc.
Distributors/Format: PBS Video (16mm; 1/2")
Archives/Format: IUB - AAAMC (1/2")
Annotation: The series continues with an examination of the struggle to enforce integration laws in the educational system as well as the workplace. In Boston, Blacks attempt to improve their children's education through court-ordered bussing, resulting in angry white reaction. In Atlanta, Mayor Maynard Jackson enforces affirmative action.

KID THOMAS AND THE PRESERVATION HALL BAND
Music by: Kid Thomas and the Preservation Hall Band
Producer: Carl Colby
Speaker: Kid Thomas Valentine*
Tech Info: color/sound/58 min.   Type: Documentary Feature
Date: 1980   Origin: USA
Studio: Independent
Company: Videovision Productions
Distributors/Format: Time/Life Home Video (1/2")
Annotation: A live performance featuring Kid Thomas and the Preservation Hall Band. Selections include: "Bourbon Street Parade" and "Rum and Coca Cola."

KID WITH THE 200 I.Q., THE
Cast: Gary Coleman*, Robert Guillaume*, Mel Stewart*, Kari Michaelson, Darian Mathias, Charles Bloom
Director: Leslie Martinson
Executive Producer: Robert Guillaume*, Phil Margo
Producer: Robert Guillaume*, Jim Begg, Phil Margo
Tech Info: color/sound/96 min.   Type: Comedy Feature

Date: 1982   Origin: USA
Company: Zephyr Productions, Guillaume-Margo Productions
Distributors/Format: USA Home Video (1/2")
Annotation: Coleman plays a brilliant 13-year-old who ends up at a university where he and his fellow students have problems adjusting.

KID WITH THE BROKEN HALO, THE

Cast: Gary Coleman*, Robert Guillaume*, Mason Adams, Ray Walston, June Allyson
Director: Leslie Martinson
Producer: Jim Begg
Tech Info: color/sound/96 min.   Type: Comedy Feature
Date: 1981   Origin: USA
Company: Satellite Productions
Distributors/Format: Family Home Entertainment (1/2")
Annotation: A 12-year-old angel (Coleman) faces many trials and tribulations as he tries to earn his wings.

KILLING FLOOR, THE

Cast: Moses Gunn*, Alfre Woodard*, Damien Leake*, Mary Alice*, Jimmy/James Spinks*, Art Kimbro*, Stanley Jordan*, Ernest Rayford*, Jason Green*, Jamarr Johnson*, Micaeh Johnson*, Paul Eaton*, Zaid Farid*
Director: Bill Duke*
Music by: Ruth Attaway*, Elizabeth Swados
Producer: Bill Lancaster, George Manasse
Screenwriter: Leslie Lee*
Storywriter: Elsa Rassbach
Tech Info: mixed/sound/118 min.   Type: Dramatic Feature
Date: 1984   Origin: USA
Company: Public Forum Productions, Ltd.
Distributors/Format: New Line Cinema Home Video (1/2")
Archives/Format: IUB - BFC/A (1/2")
Annotation: Frank Custer (Leake) relocates his family during World War I from the rural South to Chicago, anticipating better living and working conditions. He is soon involved in the massive union rallies and organized strikes against the meat packers who use black workers as scabs to break the union. Woodard plays his wife Mattie; Rayford his friend Thomas, a World War I veteran; Gunn, Heavy Williams, an anti-union worker; Alice, Lilah Dean, who helps Frank write letters home. Based on actual events, the film uses newsreel footage (including Chicago Race Riot, 1919, clips) to authenticate the period.

KILLING TIME

Director: Fronza Woods*
Producer: Fronza Woods*, Women's Interart Center *
Screenwriter: Fronza Woods*, Women's Interart Center *
Tech Info: color/sound/9 min.   Type: Experimental Short
Date: 1979   Origin: USA
Studio: Independent
Distributors/Format: BFDS (16mm)
Annotation: The central character in the film, Sage Brush, is determined to kill herself but not until she finds the right outfit for the occasion.

KILLPOINT
Cast: Richard Roundtree*, Stack Pierce*, Danene Pyant*, Leo Fong
Director: Frank Harris
Music by: Daryl Stevenett*, Herman Jeffreys
Producer: Frank Harris, Diane Stevenett
Screenwriter: Frank Harris
Tech Info: color/sound/89 min.   Type: Dramatic Feature
Date: 1984   Origin: USA
Company: Killpoint Productions, Crown International
Annotation: Police officers Long (Fong) and Bryant (Roundtree) attempt to track down gun-running mob members, controlled by an unconscionable murderer called Nighthawk (Pierce). Pyant is Nighthawk's chauffeur. Several unidentified black performers play chauffeurs, gang members and criminals.

KING JAMES VERSION
Director: Robert Gardner*
Tech Info: color/sound/91 min.   Type: Dramatic Feature
Date: 1988   Origin: USA
Studio: Independent
Distributors/Format: First Run/Icarus Films (16mm)
Annotation: The film depicts the experience of a young black girl who is caught between the conflicting religious values of her parents.

KING OF KICKBOXERS, THE
Cast: Billy Blanks*, Richard Jaeckel, Don Stroud, Loren Avedon, Sherrie Rose
Director: Lucas Lowe
Executive Producer: Ne See Yuen
Music by: Richard Yuen
Producer: Keith W. Strandberg, Ne See Yuen
Screenwriter: Keith W. Strandberg
Tech Info: color/sound/90 min.   Type: Dramatic Feature
Date: 1991   Origin: Hong Kong
Company: Seasonal Film Corporation
Distributors/Format: Imperial Entertainment Home Video (1/2")
Annotation: Khan (Blanks) is a ruthless martial arts killer who is eventually stopped by New York police officer Jack Donahue (Avedon).

KING OF NEW YORK
Cast: Freddie Jackson*, Giancarlo Esposito*, Wesley Snipes*, Laurence/Larry Fishburne*, Theresa Randle*, Roger Guenveur Smith*, Christopher Walken, David Caruso
Director: Abel Ferrara
Executive Producer: Augusto Camintino, Jay Julien, Vittorio Squillante
Music by: Joe Delia
Producer: Mary Kane, Augusto Camintino, Jay Julien, Vittorio Squillante
Screenwriter: Nicholas St. John
Tech Info: color/sound/103 min.   Type: Dramatic Feature

Date: 1990   Origin: Italy, USA
Company: Augusto Caminito
Distributors/Format: New Line Cinema Home Video (1/2")
Annotation: Frank White (Walken), just released from prison, decides to help save a
struggling neighborhood hospital. Old enemies try to stop White and his sidekick,
Jimmy Jump (Fishburne) and both are killed. Snipes plays Thomas Flannigan and
Esposito is Lance. Randle has an uncredited role.

KINJITE: FORBIDDEN SUBJECTS
Cast: Sy Richardson*, Charles Bronson, Peggy Lipton, Perry Lopez, Juan Fernandez
Director: J. Lee Thompson
Music by: Greg DeBelles
Producer: Pancho Kohner
Screenwriter: Harold Nebenzal
Tech Info: color/sound/97 min.   Type: Dramatic Feature
Date: 1989   Origin: USA
Company: Golan-Globus
Distributors/Format: Cannon Home Video (1/2")
Annotation: Lt. Crowe (Bronson) goes after Duke (Fernandez), a pimp who is into
child prostitution. Richardson plays Lavonne.

KISS GRANDMAMA GOODBYE
Cast: Nicole Donielle*, Mary Watts*, Clarence Young III*
Producer: Debra J. Robinson*
Storywriter: Terry L. McMillan*
Tech Info: bw/sound/72 min.   Type: Dramatic Feature
Date: 1991   Origin: USA
Studio: Independent
Company: Purple Flower Films, Inc.
Distributors/Format: Women Make Movies, Inc. (16mm; 1/2")
Archives/Format: IUB - BFC/A (1/2")
Annotation: The love between Gail (Donielle) and her widowed grandmother (Watts),
and their relationship to family and neighbors are the central themes of the film.
Strong family values help the family survive the death of grandmother. Based on the
short story by Terry McMillan, the film is set in a black, middle-class neighborhood
during the 1960s.

KKK BOUTIQUE AIN'T JUST REDNECKS, THE
Director: Camille Billops*
Tech Info: color   Type: Experimental Feature
Date: 1994   Origin: USA
Studio: Independent
Company: Hatch-Billops Production
Annotation: Based loosely on Dante's vision of hell, this docu/fantasy is a journey
into everyone's racism. Billops leads the "Boutikeers" through levels of hell, where
the punishment fits the crime. Some of the "boutiques" include: The Room of Asian
Fantasies, The Wall of the Greats, the Men's room at the Metropolitan, the Tick-Tock
Room for lynchers and the Stump room where people are frozen in their hatred.

KNEEGRAYS IN RUSSIA
Director: Zeinabu irene Davis*
Music Performer: Clora Bryant*, Kevin Milton*, Darrin Milton*
Producer: Zeinabu irene Davis*
Tech Info: color/sound/5 min.   Type: Documentary Short
Date: 1990   Origin: USA
Company: Wimmin with a Mission Productions
Archives/Format: IUB - BFC/A (1/2")
Annotation: Davis' video is a portrait of a black jazz family, Clora Bryant and her sons Kevin and Darrin, and their visit to the Soviet Union in 1989.

KNIGHT MOVES
Cast: Blu Mankuma*, Diane Lane, Tom Skerritt, Christopher Lambert
Producer: Ziad El Khoury
Tech Info: color/sound/116 min.   Type: Dramatic Feature
Date: 1993   Origin: Germany
Company: CineVox Filmproduktion, Knight Moves Prod., et al.
Annotation: Paul Sanderson (Lambert) is a chess master who solves a series of murders that he's accused of committing. Mankuma plays Steve Nolan.

KNIGHT MOVES
Alternate: Schachzuge
Tech Info: color/sound/116 min.   Type: Dramatic Feature
Date: 1993   Origin: Germany
Company: CineVox Filmproduktion, Knight Moves Prod., et al.
Distributors/Format: InterStar Releasing (16mm)
Annotation: Paul Sanderson (Lambert) is a chess master who solves a series of murders that he's accused of committing. Mankuma plays Steve Nolan.

KNIGHTRIDERS
Cast: Ken Foree*, Ed Harris, Tom Savini, Gary Lahti, Amy Ingersoll
Director: George A. Romero
Executive Producer: Salah M. Hassanein
Music by: Donald Rubinstein
Producer: Richard Rubinstein, Salah M. Hassanein
Screenwriter: George A. Romero
Tech Info: color/sound/145 min.   Type: Dramatic Feature
Date: 1981   Origin: USA
Company: Laurel
Distributors/Format: United (16mm)
Annotation: A troupe of Arthurian motorcyclists led by Billy (Harris) travel around selling crafts and staging motorcycle jousts. Billy's adversary Morgan (Savini) wants fame in his own right and divides up the group. Foree plays Little John.

KNIGHTS OF THE CITY
Cast: Leon Isaac Kennedy*, Kurtis Blow*, Stone/Stoney Jackson*, Mark Morales*, Smokey Robinson*, Darren Robinson*, Damon Wimbley*, Janine Turner, Nicholas Campbell
Executive Producer: Robert E. Schultz, Michael Franzese, Dominic Orlando
Music by: Misha Segal, Paul Gilreath
Producer: Leon Isaac Kennedy*, John C. Strong III, Robert E. Schultz, Michael

Franzese, Dominic Orlando
Screenwriter: Leon Isaac Kennedy*
Storywriter: Leon Isaac Kennedy*, David Wilder
Tech Info: color/sound/87 min.   Type: Dramatic Feature
Date: 1985   Origin: USA
Company: New World
Distributors/Format: New World Home Video (1/2")
Annotation: Troy (Kennedy), the leader of a Miami street gang, forms a rock band in order to get off the streets. Jackson plays Eddie, the drummer; Robinson, Wimbley and Morales (The Fat Boys) perform a number in jail with Troy and his gang; Smokey Robinson plays himself as M.C. of the contest for prize money and a record contract.

KNOW YOUR ENEMY
Director: Art Jones*
Tech Info: color/sound/27 min.   Type: Documentary Short
Date: 1990   Origin: USA
Studio: Independent
Distributors/Format: Third World Newsreel (1/2")
Annotation: Using the controversy surrounding Rap group Public Enemy, the film critiques the mass media's bias against Rap music and culture.

KNOWLEDGE REIGNS SUPREME
Director: Art Jones*
Tech Info: color/sound/8 min.   Type: Experimental Short
Date: 1991   Origin: USA
Studio: Independent
Distributors/Format: Third World Newsreel (1/2")
Annotation: Using the words and music of rapper KRS-1, this video questions the current wave of multiculturalism in the educational system based on the myths of societal homogeneity and assumed cultural and intellectual supremacy.

KRUSH GROOVE
Cast: Rae Dawn Chong*, Leon W. Grant*, Blair Underwood*, The Fat Boys*, Kurtis Blow*, New Edition*, Guy Davis*, Robert Taylor*, Sheila E. *, Mary Alice Smith*, Run-D.M.C. *, Russell Simmons*, Saundra Santiago
Director: Michael Schultz*
Executive Producer: Michael Schultz*, George Jackson*, Robert O. Kaplan
Music Performer: The Fat Boys*, Kurtis Blow*, New Edition*, Sheila E. *, Run-D.M.C. *
Producer: Michael Schultz*, George Jackson*, Doug McHenry*, Robert O. Kaplan, Robert O. Kaplan
Screenwriter: Ralph Farquhar*
Tech Info: color/sound/185 min.   Type: Musical Feature
Date: 1985   Origin: USA
Company: Dough McHenry, Crystalite
Distributors/Format: Warner Bros. Home Video, Inc. (1/2")
Annotation: Russell (Simmons) is the manager for a group of artists. Although he does not succeed in getting a loan to start his music industry, friends help him establish one. Russell falls apart when his brother Ron signs with Galaxy music company. Russell later reconciles with Ron and becomes a manager for Warner Bros.--a major music company.

L.A. STORY
Cast: Iman *, Wesley Thompson*, Steve Martin, Marilu Henner, Richard E. Grant, Victoria Tennant
Director: Mick Jackson
Executive Producer: Steve Martin, Mario Kassar
Music by: Peter Melnick
Producer: Steve Martin, Daniel Melnick, Mario Kassar, Michael Rachmil
Screenwriter: Steve Martin
Storywriter: Steve Martin
Tech Info: color/sound/95 min.   Type: Comedy Feature
Date: 1991   Origin: USA
Company: Carolco, IndieProd Company, L.A. Films
Distributors/Format: TriStar Pictures Inc. (1/2")
Annotation: Harris Telemacher (Martin) is a Los Angeles weatherman who falls for British reporter Sara (Tennant) and captures her love with the aid of a neon signpost on the freeway. Iman appears as Cynthia and Thompson plays Jesse.

L.A. VICE
Cast: Jim Brown*, Lawrence-Hilton Jacobs*, William Smith
Director: Joseph Merhi
Tech Info: color/sound/90 min.   Type: Dramatic Feature
Date: 1989   Origin: USA
Distributors/Format: Paramount Home Video (1/2")
Annotation: In this sequel to L.A. HEAT, a detective (Brown) is transferred to the vice squad, where he must investigate a series of murders.

LA BAMBA
Cast: Howard Huntsberry*, Lou Diamond Phillips, Elizabeth Pena, Danielle von Zerneck
Director: Luis Valdez
Executive Producer: Stuart Benjamin
Music Performer: Los Lobos, Buddy Holly
Music by: Chuck Berry*, Little Richard (Penniman) *, Miles Goodman, Carlos Santana
Producer: Taylor Hackford, Stuart Benjamin
Screenwriter: Luis Valdez
Tech Info: color/sound/103 min.   Type: Musical Feature
Date: 1987   Origin: USA
Company: New Visions
Distributors/Format: RCA/Columbia Pictures Home Video (1/2")
Archives/Format: IUB - BFC/A (1/2")
Annotation: Jackie Wilson (Huntsberry) performs at a major Rock n' Roll festival in Brooklyn, Allan Freed's 1st Anniversary of Rock n' Roll Show. He helps Richie Valens (Phillips) overcome nerves before the performance that makes Valens an overnight sensation.

LADIES CLUB, THE
Cast: Beverly Todd*, Diana Scarwid, Karen Austin, Christine Belford
Director: Janet Greek
Music by: Lalo Schifrin
Producer: Paul Mason, Nick J. Mileti
Screenwriter: Paul Mason, Fran Lewis Ebeling
Storywriter: Betty Black, Casey Bishop
Tech Info: color/sound/90 min.   Type: Dramatic Feature
Date: 1986   Origin: USA
Company: Media, Heron
Distributors/Format: New Line Cinema (16mm; 3/4"; 1/2")
Annotation: Joan Taylor (Austin), a police officer, is attacked by a gang of vicious
rapists. She and Dr. Lewis (Belford) start a support group. Todd plays Georgiane.

LADY DAY AT EMERSON'S BAR & GRILL
Cast: Kimberly Hebert*, William Knowles*
Director: Rochelle Calhoun*
Screenwriter: Lanie Robertson*
Storywriter: Lanie Robertson*
Tech Info: color/sound/60 min.   Type: Docudrama
Date: 1994   Origin: USA
Studio: Independent
Company: Mount Holyoke College Psychology and Theatre Arts
Annotation: Billie Holiday (Herbert) performs at Emerson's Bar & Grill in Philadelphia
accompanied by her pianist. In the last year of her life, she sings and talks about
music, racism, her loves, her drinking and her life as a black performer.

LADY DAY: THE MANY FACES OF BILLIE HOLIDAY
Series: Masters of American Music Series
Director: Matthew Seig
Narrator: David Smyrl
Producer: Toby Byron, Richard Saylor
Screenwriter: Robert O'Meally
Speaker: Ruby Dee*, Harry "Sweets" Edison*, Buck Clayton*, Carmen McRae*,
Albert Murray*, Mal Waldron*, Annie Ross, Milt Gabler
Tech Info: mixed/sound/60 min.   Type: Documentary Feature
Date: 1991   Origin: USA
Company: Toby Byron/Mutiprises
Distributors/Format: Koltor International Films (1/2")
Archives/Format: IUB - AAAMC (1/2")
Annotation: This documentary takes a close, intimate look at the controversial life of
Holiday. Included are interviews with Clayton, Edison, vocalists McRae and Ross,
pianist Waldron, and producer Gabler, as well as, rare musical footage of Smith,
Webster, Young and Eldridge. A film clip from NEW ORLEANS (1946) depicts
Holiday in her role as maid.

LADYBUGS
Cast: Jackee Harry*, Rodney Dangerfield, Jonathan Brandis, Ilene Graff, Jeannetta
Arnette, Black Clark
Director: Sidney J. Furie
Executive Producer: Gray Frederickson, Lloyd Bloom

Music by: Richard Gibbs
Producer: Albert S. Ruddy, Andre E. Morgan, Gray Frederickson, Lloyd Bloom
Screenwriter: Curtis Burch
Tech Info: color/sound/88 min.   Type: Comedy Feature
Date: 1992   Origin: USA
Company: Paramount
Distributors/Format: Paramount Home Video (1/2")
Annotation: A salesman who volunteers to coach the company-sponsored girls' soccer team, finds himself with a lineup of clutzy newcomers. He decides to turn his fiancee's son, Matthew, into Martha, the newest member of the Ladybugs. Harry plays Julie Benson.

LAND OF LOOK BEHIND
Director: Alan Greenberg
Music by: Bob Marley*, The Wailers *, Gregory Isaacs*, K. Leimer*, Lui Lepki
Producer: Alan Greenberg
Tech Info: color/sound/88 min.   Type: Documentary Feature
Date: 1982   Origin: USA/Jamaica
Studio: Independent
Company: Solo Man, Inc.
Distributors/Format: Kino International Corp. (1/2")
Annotation: The documentary is about Reggae music and the Rastafarian Sect from which it springs. The film begins with Bob Marley's funeral and also surveys Jamaican oppression and poverty.

LAND WHERE MY FATHERS DIED
Cast: Daresha Kyi*, Isaiah Washington*
Director: Daresha Kyi*
Music by: Robin Eubanks*
Producer: Daresha Kyi*
Tech Info: color/sound/25 min.   Type: Dramatic Short
Date: 1991   Origin: USA
Studio: Independent
Company: Dare She Productions
Distributors/Format: Third World Newsreel (1/2"), Women Make Movies, Inc. (16mm; 1/2")
Annotation: Kyi's film explores the emotionally charged dynamics between a young black woman, her alcoholic father, and her dogmatic boyfriend. It is a commentary on black masculinity, family, and self-respect.

LAND WHERE THE BLUES BEGAN
Director: Alan Lomax
Narrator: Alan Lomax
Producer: Alan Lomax
Screenwriter: Alan Lomax
Speaker: Napoleon Strickland*, Sam Chatmon*, Wilbert Puckett*, J.T. Tucker*, George Johnson*, Joe Savage*, William S. Hart*, Belton Sutherland*
Tech Info: mixed/sound/60 min.   Type: Television Documentary

Date: 1979 Origin: USA
Studio: Mississippi Authority for Educational Television
Archives/Format: IUB - AAAMC (1/2")
Annotation: Lomax journeys into the heart of the Mississippi Delta region, origin of the Blues. The film chronicles men and women of the area at work on the railroads and in the fields, singing the songs of labor.

LANGSTON HUGHES: THE DREAM KEEPER

Series: Voices and Visions
Cast: Roscoe Orman*, David Langston Smyrl*, Robert Macbeth*, D. Stevens*
Director: St. Clair Bourne*
Executive Producer: Lawrence Pitkethly
Music Performer: Max Roach*, Novella Nelson*, Olu Dara*, Abdul Waddoud*, Ed Cherry*
Music by: Stanley Cowell
Producer: Robert Chapman, Lawrence Pitkethly
Screenwriter: Leslie Lee*
Speaker: Imamu Amiri Baraka*, James Baldwin*, Novella Nelson*, Gwendolyn Brooks*, Hon. Leopold Senghor*
Tech Info: mixed/sound/56 min.   Type: Television Documentary
Date: 1988 Origin: USA
Studio: Independent
Company: New York Center for Visual Hearing
Distributors/Format: Facets Multimedia, Inc. (1/2"), Filmic Archives (1/2"), Intellimation (1/2")
Archives/Format: IUB - BFC/A (1/2")
Annotation: A cinematic biography of poet and novelist Hughes was filmed in Paris, France and Dakar, Senegal. The film features appearances by Baldwin, Baraka, Senghor, and Brooks. Jazz drummer Roach performs.

LAST BOY SCOUT, THE

Cast: Damon Wayans*, Halle Berry*, Lynn Swann*, Billy Blanks*, Bruce Willis, Chelsea Field
Director: Tony Scott
Music by: Michael Kamen
Producer: Joel Silver, Michael I. Levy, Steve Perry
Screenwriter: Shane Black
Storywriter: Shane Black, Greg Hicks
Tech Info: color/sound   Type: Dramatic Feature
Date: 1991 Origin: USA
Company: Geffen Pictures, Silver Partners
Distributors/Format: Warner Bros. Home Video, Inc. (1/2")
Annotation: When Private Investigator Joe Hallenback (Willis) is given a surveillance assignment on adult dancer Cory (Berry), he meets her boyfriend, one time pro football great, Jimmy Dix (Wayans). After Cory is brutally murdered, Jimmy and Joe team up in order to track down her killer. Swann cameos as himself, a football game announcer; Blanks plays football player Billy Cole.

LAST DRAGON, THE

Alternate: Berry Gordy's The Last Dragon
Cast: Vanity *, Jim Moody*, Taimak *, Julius J. Carry III*, Keshia Knight-Pulliam*,
Ernie Reyes Sr., Ernie Reyes Jr., Thomas Ikeda
Director: Michael Schultz*, James A. Coutner
Executive Producer: Berry Gordy Jr.*
Music by: Misha Segal
Producer: Berry Gordy Jr.*, Rupert Hitzig
Screenwriter: Louis Venosta
Tech Info: color/sound/109 min.   Type: Musical Feature
Date: 1985   Origin: USA
Company: Motown
Distributors/Format: Columbia/TriStar Pictures (35mm; 1/2")
Annotation: Leroy Green (Taimak), a black youth, strives to reach the highest level
of enlightenment through Kung Fu. His martial arts instructor (Ikeda) sends him into
the exciting streets of New York to find the meaning of life. There he encounters a
real life villain, Sho 'Nuff (Carry), a self-proclaimed Shogun of Harlem who wants
domination over the neighborhood, and the lovely video disc jockey, Laura (Vanity).

LAST FIGHT, THE

Cast: Don King*, Fred Williamson*, Ruben Blades, Joe Spinell, Willie Colon,
Nereida Mercado, Darlanne Fluegel
Director: Fred Williamson*
Music by: Jay Chattaway
Producer: Jerry Masucci
Screenwriter: Fred Williamson*
Storywriter: Jerry Masucci
Tech Info: color/sound/85 min.   Type: Dramatic Feature
Date: 1983   Origin: USA
Company: Movie and Pictures
Distributors/Format: Best Films (16mm)
Annotation: The story of a singer turned boxer and the underworld's attempt to
control the fight game are the themes explored in this suspense drama.

LAST OF THE BLUE DEVILS, THE

Cast: Count Basie and his Orchestra*, Jay McShann*, Big Joe Turner
Director: Bruce Ricker
Executive Producer: Mitchell Donlan
Producer: Bruce Ricker, Mitchell Donlan
Tech Info: mixed/sound/90 min.   Type: Documentary Feature
Date: 1980   Origin: USA
Studio: Independent
Company: Rhapsody Films, Inc.
Distributors/Format: Kino International Corp. (1/2")
Annotation: A documentary recollection of music and musicians associated with
Kansas City, in the 1930s features Count Basie and his orchestra, Turner, and
McShann.

LAST RESORT
Cast: Mario Van Peebles*, Charles Grodin, Robin Pearson Rose, Megan Mullally
Director: Zane Buzby
Executive Producer: Nessa Cooper
Music Performer: Steve Nelson, Thom Sharp
Music by: Steve Nelson, Thom Sharp
Producer: Julie Corman, Nessa Cooper
Screenwriter: Steve Zacharias, Jeff Buhai
Tech Info: color/sound/80 min.   Type: Comedy Feature
Date: 1985   Origin: USA
Company: Vestron, Concorde, Trinity, Silver Screen II
Distributors/Format: Touchstone Home Video (1/2")
Annotation: Van Peebles plays host to a furniture executive (Grodin) who takes his family on vacation and ends up in a sleazy singles hotel. The hotel becomes an outing intermixed with sex and guerilla warfare.

LAST SEDUCTION, THE
Cast: Bill Nunn*, Bill Pullman, Linda Fiorentino, J.T. Walsh, Peter Berg
Director: John Dahl
Music by: Joseph Vitarelli
Producer: Jonathan Shestak
Screenwriter: Steve Barancik
Tech Info: color/sound/110 min.   Type: Dramatic Feature
Date: 1994   Origin: USA
Company: Oakwood Films Inc., DBA Kroy Pictures Inc.
Distributors/Format: October Films (16mm; 35mm)
Annotation: Bridget Gregory (Fiorentino) and her husband Clay (Pullman) pull off a $700,000 drug deal that leaves them in debt to mobsters. Bridget runs away with the money; Nunn plays Harlan, the detective hired by Clay to find her.

LAST TIME OUT
Cast: Larry Riley*, Gail Strickland, Michael Beck, Christopher Conrad
Director: Don Fox Greene
Executive Producer: David Z. McMahon
Music by: Larry Riley*
Producer: Don Fox Greene, David Z. McMahon
Screenwriter: Don Fox Greene
Tech Info: color/sound/92 min.   Type: Dramatic Feature
Date: 1994   Origin: USA
Company: Strong-McMahon
Distributors/Format: Greene Film Ventures 1 (1/2")
Annotation: Danny Dolan (Conrad) and father Joe Dolan (Beck) exorcize past and present personal demons on the college football field with the help of Coach Washington (Riley).

LAUGH, A TEAR, A
Cast: Frank Ferguson
Host: Whoopi Goldberg*
Producer: Whoopi Goldberg*, Beverly Todd*, Percey Helton, Kelly Flynn
Speaker: Richard Pryor*, Bill Cosby*, Robert Townsend*, Keenen Ivory Wayans*, Tim Reid*, Sinbad *, Redd Foxx*, Arsenio Hall*, Marsha Warfield*, Jimmy/Jimmie

Walker*, George Kirby*, Dick Gregory*, William Campbell*
Tech Info: mixed/sound/92 min.   Type: Documentary Feature
Date: 1990   Origin: USA
Studio: Independent
Company: S.I. Communications Inc.
Distributors/Format: International Broadcasting Systems, LTD. (1/2")
Archives/Format: IUB - BFC/A (1/2")
Annotation: A documentary, narrated by Goldberg, delineates the history of African American comedians and black comedy/humor in America from Bert Williams to the present. It includes clips from stand up comedy routines, television sitcoms, and movies.

LEADERS, THE
Series: Ebony/Jet Guide to Excellence
Tech Info: color/sound/35 min.   Type: Documentary Short
Date: 1991   Origin: USA
Distributors/Format: Filmic Archives (1/2")
Annotation: African American leaders are profiled, e.g. L. Douglas Wilder, Governor of Virginia; Marian Wright Edelman, President of the Children's Defense Fund, and Dr. James P. Comer, Director of Yale University's Child Study Center.

LEAN ON ME
Cast: Morgan Freeman*, Robert Guillaume*, Sandra Reaves-Phillips*, Beverly Todd*, Michael Beach*, Jermaine Hopkins*, Karen Malina White*, Tony Todd*, Lynn Thigpen*, Regina Taylor*
Director: John G. Avildsen
Executive Producer: John G. Avildsen
Music by: Bill Conti
Producer: John G. Avildsen, Norman Twain
Screenwriter: Michael Schiffer
Tech Info: color/sound/104 min.   Type: Dramatic Feature
Date: 1989   Origin: USA
Company: Warner Bros.
Distributors/Format: Warner Bros. Home Video, Inc. (1/2")
Archives/Format: IUB - BFC/A (1/2")
Annotation: A fictional depiction of Joe Clark (Freeman), the controversial principal of Eastside High School in Patterson, New Jersey, shows him standing against parents, teachers, and the state for his approach to the betterment of Eastside's students.

LEAP OF FAITH
Cast: Black Gospel Choir *, Debra Winger, Steve Martin
Music Performer: The Angels of Mercy *
Tech Info: color/sound   Type: Comedy Feature
Date: 1992   Origin: USA
Annotation: A phony faith healer (Martin) filches money out of unsuspecting believers in town after town until he finally sees the light. His road show has the benefit of "the Angels of Mercy" gospel choir.

LEATHERFACE: THE TEXAS CHAINSAW MASSACRE III
Cast: Ken Foree*, Duane Whitaker*, Viggo Mortensen, William Butler, Kate Hodge, R.A. Mihailoff
Director: Jeff Burr
Executive Producer: Robert Shaye
Music by: Jim Manzie, Pat Regan
Producer: Robert Shaye, Robert Engelman
Screenwriter: David J. Schow
Tech Info: color/sound/87 min.   Type: Dramatic Feature
Date: 1990   Origin: USA
Company: New Line
Distributors/Format: New Line Cinema Home Video (1/2")
Annotation: A couple driving through Texas on the way to Florida encounter a murder scene and are warned by police not to stop for anything. They pick up Tex (Mortensen) a hitchhiker and encounter Benny (Foree) a survivalist with a trunk full of guns, both of whom help the couple stave off a chainsaw wielding monster. Whitaker plays Kim.

LEGACY OF MALCOLM X
Speaker: Dr. John Henrik Clarke*
Tech Info: color/sound/46 min.   Type: Experimental Short
Date: 1988   Origin: USA
Studio: Independent
Distributors/Format: Trans Atlantic Productions (1/2")
Archives/Format: IUB - AAAMC (1/2")
Annotation: Dr. John Henrik Clark, an activist influenced by the works of Malcolm X, believes Malcolm was killed by Blacks who acted for whites. Promoting the cause of black people and their liberation, Dr. Clark applauds both violence and non-violence as strategies for change contending that both are necessary.

LEGACY OF MARCUS GARVEY
Cast: Clinton Black*
Speaker: Dr. John Henrik Clarke*, Walter Wilson*
Tech Info: color/sound/101 min.   Type: Experimental Feature
Date: 1988   Origin: USA
Studio: Independent
Company: Transatlantic Productions
Archives/Format: IUB - AAAMC (1/2")
Annotation: Dr. John Henrik Clark of African Studies at Hunter College gives his perspective on the Garvey legacy in light of the present conditions of black society. Chronicling the life of Garvey, he cites Garvey's ability to politically inspire the spirit of revolution in America.

LEGAL EAGLES
Cast: Roscoe Lee Browne*, Debra Winger, Robert Redford, Brian Dennehy, Daryl Hannah
Director: Ivan Reitman
Executive Producer: Michael Gross, Joe Medjuck
Music by: Elmer Bernstein
Producer: Ivan Reitman, Michael Gross, Joe Medjuck
Screenwriter: Jim Cash, Jack Epps Jr.

Storywriter: Ivan Reitman, Jim Cash, Jack Epps
Tech Info: color/sound/114 min.   Type: Dramatic Feature
Date: 1986   Origin: USA
Company: Northern Lights
Distributors/Format: Universal Home Video (1/2")
Annotation: Brown plays Judge Dawkins in this courtroom drama concerning the daughter of a famous artist who steals her deceased father's painting that has been dedicated to her.

LEONARD PART 6

Cast: Moses Gunn*, Bill Cosby*, Victoria Rowell*, Pat Colbert*, Gloria Foster*, Tom Courtenay
Director: Paul Weiland
Music by: Elmer Bernstein
Producer: Bill Cosby*, Steve Sohmer
Screenwriter: Johnathan Reynolds
Storywriter: Bill Cosby*
Tech Info: color/sound/83 min.   Type: Comedy Feature
Date: 1987   Origin: USA
Company: Columbia
Distributors/Format: Columbia Pictures Home Video (1/2")
Annotation: Leonard Parker (Cosby) is a wealthy super-agent who must battle the evil Medusa (Foster), a maniacal woman with plans to take over the world by turning all the animals into man-eating monsters. Leonard's wife, Alice (Colbert) aids him in his mission. Gunn appears as a director named Georgio who seduces Leonard's daughter Joan (Rowell).

LESLIE

Alternate: A Portrait of Schizophrenia
Director: Chiz Schultz*
Producer: Chiz Schultz*
Speaker: Leslie Cooper*
Tech Info: color/sound/57 min.   Type: Documentary Feature
Date: 1988   Origin: USA
Studio: Independent
Annotation: In this portrait of Cooper, he recounts his life as a sufferer of paranoid schizophrenia.

LET'S GET HARRY

Cast: J.W. Smith*, Gary Busey, Mark Harmon, Michael Schoeffling, Tom Wilson, Glenn Frey, Bruce Gray
Director: Stuart Rosenberg
Music by: Brad Fiedel
Producer: Daniel H. Blatt, Robert Singer
Screenwriter: Charles Robert Carner
Storywriter: Samuel Fuller, Mark Feldberg
Tech Info: color/sound/107 min.   Type: Dramatic Feature

Date: 1987   Origin: USA
Company: TriStar, Delphi IV & V
Distributors/Format: TriStar Pictures Inc. (1/2")
Annotation: Harry Burk (Harmon) and Ambassador Douglas (Gray) are kidnapped by Colombian drug dealers. After the U.S. government declines to get involved, a crew of mercenaries led by Norman Shrike (Duvall) "get Harry." Smith is one of the mercenaries.

LETHAL WEAPON

Cast: Danny Glover*, Ebonie Smith*, Damon Hines*, Darlene Love*, Traci Wolfe*, Gary Busey, Mel Gibson, Joe Pesci
Director: Richard Donner
Music Performer: Eric Clapton, Michael Kamen
Music by: Eric Clapton, Michael Kamen
Producer: Joel Silver, Richard Donner
Screenwriter: Shane Black
Storywriter: Shane Black
Tech Info: color/sound/110 min.   Type: Dramatic Feature
Date: 1987   Origin: USA
Company: Warner Bros.
Distributors/Format: Warner Bros. Home Video, Inc. (1/2")
Annotation: Roger Murtaugh (Glover) is a stable family man and police officer who is about to retire. However, a few days before he can retire, he is forced to work with a mentally disturbed but courageous partner Martin Riggs (Gibson) who is the real "lethal weapon." Love, Wolfe, Hines and Smith appear as Murtaugh's family.

LETHAL WEAPON 2

Cast: Danny Glover*, Olu Jacobs*, Ebonie Smith*, Damon Hines*, Darlene Love*, Traci Wolfe*, Mel Gibson, Joe Pesci, Joss Ackland, Derrick O'Conner, Garth Wigan
Director: Richard Donner
Music Performer: Eric Clapton, Michael Kamen, David Sanborn
Producer: Joel Silver, Richard Donner
Screenwriter: Jeffrey Boam
Storywriter: Shane Black, Warren Murphy
Tech Info: color/sound/114 min.   Type: Dramatic Feature
Date: 1989   Origin: USA
Company: Warner Bros.
Distributors/Format: Warner Bros. Home Video, Inc. (1/2")
Annotation: In this sequel, the same actors reprise their roles as Roger Murtaugh (Glover) and Martin Riggs (Gibson). This time the plot centers around apartheid in South Africa and the crimes committed by international operatives.

LETHAL WEAPON 3

Cast: Danny Glover*, Mel Gibson, Joe Pesci, Rene Russo, Stuart Wilson
Director: Richard Donner
Music by: Eric Clapton, Michael Kamen, David Sanborn
Producer: Joel Silver, Richard Donner, Steve Perry, Jennie Lew Tugend
Screenwriter: Jeffrey Boam, Robert Mark Kamen
Storywriter: Jeffrey Boam
Tech Info: color/sound/118 min.   Type: Dramatic Feature

Date: 1992   Origin: USA
Company: Warner Bros.
Distributors/Format: Warner Bros. Home Video, Inc. (1/2")
Annotation: Riggs (Gibson) and Murtaugh (Glover) return as Los Angeles police detectives whose work routine is anything but routine. They are joined by an Internal Affairs investigator (Russo) who loves taking risks as much as Riggs does.

LEVIATHAN

Cast: Ernie Hudson*, Richard Crenna, Peter Weller, Amanda Pays, Daniel Stern
Director: George P. Cosmatos
Music Performer: Jerry Goldsmith
Music by: Jerry Goldsmith
Producer: Luigi DeLaurentis, Aurelio DeLaurentis
Screenwriter: Jeb Stuart, David Peoples
Storywriter: David Peoples
Tech Info: color/sound/98 min.   Type: Dramatic Feature
Date: 1989   Origin: USA
Company: Gordon Company
Distributors/Format: MGM Home Video (1/2")
Annotation: When a mysterious virus infects deep-sea miners, Beck (Weller), Willie (Pays), and Jones (Hudson) are the only members who escape their underwater home and reach the ocean surface. Jones escapes the Leviathan only to find another disaster waiting for him.

LIBERATORS: FIGHTING ON TWO FRONTS IN WORLD WAR II

Narrator: Denzel Washington*, Louis Gossett Jr.*
Producer: William Miles*, Nina Rosenblum
Screenwriter: Lou Potter*, John Crowley, Daniel Allentuck
Tech Info: mixed/sound/90 min.   Type: Television Documentary
Date: 1992   Origin: USA
Company: Miles* Educational Film Production, Inc.
Distributors/Format: Miles Educational Film Production, Inc. (1/2")
Archives/Format: IUB - BFC/A (1/2")
Annotation: The documentary tells the story of African American battalions focussing on the 761st, which spearheaded General Patton's Third Army and helped to liberate the concentration camps at Buchenwald, Dachau and Lambach.

LICENCE TO KILL

Cast: Frank McRae*, Anthony Zerbe, Timothy Dalton, Carey Lowell, Robert Davi, Talisa Soto
Director: John Glen
Music Performer: Patti Labelle*, Gladys Knight*, Narada Michael Walden*, Walter Afanasieff*
Producer: Albert R. Broccoli, Michael G. Wilson
Storywriter: Richard Maibaum, Michael G. Wilson
Tech Info: color/sound/133 min.   Type: Dramatic Feature
Date: 1989   Origin: Great Britain
Company: Eon
Distributors/Format: MGM/UA Home Video (1/2")
Annotation: James Bond (Dalton) heads to South America to avenge the deaths of two friends at the hands of international drug trafficker Sanchez (Davi). McRae plays Bond's friend Sharkey.

LIFE IS A SAXOPHONE
Cast: Billy Higgins*, Dadisi Sanyika*, Lula Washington*, Gale Fulton-Ross*, Dadisi Wells Komolafe*, Kamaau Da'oud*, Nirankar Singh Khalsa, Roberto Miguel Miranda
Director: Saundra Sharp*, Orlando Bagwell*
Music Performer: Dadisi Wells Komolafe*, Nirankar Singh Khalsa, Roberto Miguel Miranda
Tech Info: mixed/sound/54 min.   Type: Experimental Feature
Date: 1985   Origin: USA
Company: A Sharp Show
Distributors/Format: A Sharp Show (1/2")
Archives/Format: IUB - BFC/A (1/2")
Annotation: The film focuses on the oral interpretations of poet, Kamau Da'oud, recipient of Black American Cinema Society's 1985 Award of Special Merit, whose works are translated into several other mediums. Sanyika interprets the poet's works through the martial arts, Washington through dance, Fulton-Ross through sketching, and Miranda, Komolate, and Khalsa through music.

LIFE STINKS
Cast: Theodore "Teddy" Wilson*, James Mapp*, Terrence Williams*, Mel Brooks, Lesley Ann Warren, Howard Morris
Director: Mel Brooks
Music by: John Morris
Producer: Mel Brooks
Screenwriter: Mel Brooks, Rudy De Luca, Steve Haberman
Storywriter: Mel Brooks, Ron Clark, Rudy De Luca, Steve Haberman
Tech Info: mixed/sound/93 min.   Type: Comedy Feature
Date: 1991   Origin: USA
Company: Brooks Films
Distributors/Format: MGM Home Video (1/2")
Annotation: Corporate tycoon Goddard Bolt (Brooks) accepts a bet to live on the slum streets of Los Angeles for 30 days without a penny. Fumes (Wilson), Molly (Warren), and Shilor (Morris) are homeless people whom Bolt befriends.

LIFE WITH BABY: HOW DO THE PARENTS FEEL?
Director: Grania Gurievitch
Producer: Grania Gurievitch
Tech Info: color/sound/27 min.   Type: Documentary Short
Date: 1984   Origin: USA
Studio: New England Children's Mental Health Task Force
Company: TOGG Films Incorporated
Annotation: The film shows three families, one black and two white adjusting to the emotional and physical demands of raising a baby.

LIGHTNING JACK
Cast: Frank McRae*, Cuba Gooding Jr.*, Kamala Dawson*, Beverly D'Angelo, Paul Hogan
Director: Simon Wincer
Executive Producer: Anthony Stewart, Graham Brukent
Music by: Bruce Romland
Producer: Simon Wincer, Paul Hogan, Anthony Stewart, Graham Brukent, Greg Coote

Screenwriter: Paul Hogan
Tech Info: color/sound/93 min.   Type: Comedy Feature
Date: 1994   Origin: Australia
Company: Lightning Ridge Prod., Village Roadshow Pictures
Distributors/Format: Savoy Home Video (1/2")
Annotation: Outlaw Lightning Jack (Hogan) picks up Ben Doyle (Gooding) in an abortive bank robbery. Ben, who has been mute all his life, rebels against the strictness of his adoptive father Mr. Doyle (McRae) and the racist customers in Doyle's general store. He joins Jack who gives him an education in the outlaw's profession and arranges Ben's first sexual encounter with Pilar (Dawson).

LIGHTSHIP, THE
Cast: Badja Djola*, Robert Duvall, Klaus Maria Brandauer, Tom Bower
Director: Jerzy Skolimowsky
Executive Producer: Rainer Soehnlein
Music by: Stanley Myers
Producer: Moritz Borman, Bill Benenson, Rainer Soehnlein
Screenwriter: David Taylor*, William Mai
Tech Info: color/sound/89 min.   Type: Dramatic Feature
Date: 1986   Origin: USA
Company: CBS, Castle Hill
Distributors/Format: CBS/Castle Hill (16mm)
Annotation: Capt. Miller (Brandauer) is a German-born American citizen who operates a lightship off the Virginia shore. After rescuing the passengers of a stranded speedboat, Miller is torn when asked to leave his watch. Djola plays Nate.

LIMIT UP
Cast: Danitra Vance*, Ray Charles*, Nancy Allen, Dean Stockwell, Brad Hall
Director: Richard Martini
Producer: Jonathan D. Krane
Screenwriter: Richard Martini, Lu Anders
Storywriter: Richard Martini
Tech Info: color/sound/88 min.   Type: Dramatic Feature
Date: 1990   Origin: USA
Studio: Independent
Company: M.C.E.G.
Distributors/Format: M.C.E.G. Release (1/2")
Annotation: A talented girl with a dream makes a deal with the devil, to become a trader in the fast-moving, high-stakes commodities market. Charles appears as God.

LION KING, THE
Cast: Whoopi Goldberg*, James Earl Jones*, Robert Guillaume*, Madge Sinclair*, Matthew Broderick, Jeremy Irons, Moira Kelly, Jonathan Taylor Thomas
Director: Roger Allers, Robert Minkoff
Executive Producer: Thomas Schumacher, Sarah McArthur
Music by: Hans Zimmer
Producer: Don Hahn, Thomas Schumacher, Sarah McArthur
Screenwriter: Irene Mecchi, Jonathan Roberts, Linda Woolverton
Tech Info: color/sound/87 min.   Type: Animated Feature

Date: 1994   Origin: USA
Company: Walt Disney Productions
Distributors/Format: Buena Vista Home Video (1/2")
Annotation: Lion King Mufasa (voice by Jones) proudly displays his new cub Simba, future King of Prideland. Mufasa's jealous brother Scar convinces Simba to stray with the help of hyenas, including Shenzi (voice of Goldberg), and when Scar's connivings lead to the death of Mufasa, Scar manipulates Simba so he can take the throne. Guillaume provides the voice of Rafiki; Sinclair provides the voice for Sarabi.

LIONHEART

Cast: Billy Blanks*, Christopher K. Brown*, Jean-Claude Van Damme, Harrison Page, Deborah Rennard
Director: Sheldon Lettich
Executive Producer: Anders P. Jensen, Sundip R. Shah, Sunil R. Shah
Producer: Ash R. Shah, Eric Karson, Anders P. Jensen, Sundip R. Shah, Sunil R. Shah
Screenwriter: Sheldon Lettich, Jean-Claude Van Damme, R.N. Warren
Storywriter: Jean-Claude Van Damme
Tech Info: color/sound/105 min.   Type: Dramatic Feature
Date: 1991   Origin: USA
Company: Imperial Entertainment, Wrong Bet Productions
Distributors/Format: Universal Home Video (1/2")
Annotation: Lyon Gaultier (Van Damme) must avenge his brother's death even though he has been instructed to leave matters to the authorities. Blanks is cast as an African Legionnaire.

LISTEN UP: THE LIVES OF QUINCY JONES

Director: Ellen Weissbrod
Music by: Quincy Jones*, Arthur Baker*
Producer: Courtney Sales Ross
Speaker: Herbie Hancock*, Quincy Jones*, Kool Moe Dee *, Ella Fitzgerald*, Ray Charles*, John "Dizzy" Gillespie*, Ice-T *, Jesse Jackson*, Big Daddy Kane*
Tech Info: mixed/sound/116 min.   Type: Documentary Feature
Date: 1990   Origin: USA
Company: Warner Bros., Courtney Sale Ross
Distributors/Format: Warner Bros. Home Video, Inc. (1/2")
Archives/Format: IUB - AAAMC (1/2")
Annotation: The film captures the musical genius of the mega-hit producer Jones, through interviews with him, his family, and celebrity friends, as well as clips from movie soundtracks and artistic performances.

LITTLE BIG LEAGUE

Cast: Duane Davis*, Wolfgang Bodison*, John Ashton, Timothy Busfield, Luke Edwards, Ashley Crow
Director: Andrew Scheinman
Executive Producer: Andrew Bergman, Steve Nicolaides
Music by: Stanley Clarke*
Producer: Andrew Bergman, Steve Nicolaides, Mike Lobell
Screenwriter: Gregory K. Pincus, Adam Scheinman
Storywriter: Gregory K. Pincus
Tech Info: color/sound/119 min.   Type: Dramatic Feature

Date: 1994   Origin: USA
Company: Lobell/Bergman Productions, Castle Rock
Distributors/Format: Columbia Pictures (16mm)
Annotation: Twelve-year-old baseball enthusiast Billy Heywood (Edwards) inherits the Minnesota Twins from his grandfather and decides to work in the main office during his summer vacation. Bodison plays Spencer Hamilton and Davis plays Jerry Johnson.

LITTLE MAN TATE

Cast: Danitra Vance*, John Bell*, Jodie Foster, Dianne Wiest, Harry Connick Jr., Adam Hann-Byrd
Director: Jodie Foster
Executive Producer: Randy Stone
Music by: Mark Isham
Producer: Peggy Rajski, Scott Rudin, Randy Stone
Screenwriter: Scott Frank
Tech Info: color/sound/95 min.   Type: Dramatic Feature
Date: 1991   Origin: USA
Company: Little Man Inc., Orion
Distributors/Format: Orion Home Video (1/2")
Annotation: Child genius Fred Tate (Hann-Byrd) leaves his working-class mother (Foster) to develop his extraordinary intellectual skills at Dr. Grierson's (Wiest) educational center. Vance plays a clinic doctor in this drama which ultimately suggests that a child needs both emotional support and exposure to a stimulating environment.

LITTLE NIKITA

Cast: Sidney Poitier*, Loretta Devine*, Caroline Kava, River Phoenix, Richard Jenkins
Director: Richard Benjamin
Music by: Marvin Hamlisch
Producer: Stanley R. Jaffe, Harry Gittes
Screenwriter: Eric Barefield*, Donald James*, Bo Goldman, John Hill
Storywriter: Erin Blunt, Jerry Fielding, Tom Musca, Teri Schwartz
Tech Info: color/sound/98 min.   Type: Dramatic Feature
Date: 1988   Origin: USA
Company: Columbia
Distributors/Format: Swank/RCA/Columbia Pictures (16mm; 1/2")
Annotation: FBI agent Roy Parmenter (Poitier) must protect an American teenager, Jeff Grant (Phoenix), from knowledge of his parents' Russian heritage as well as their KGB involvement. Verna McLaughlin (Devine) is a staff member at Grant's high school who becomes romantically involved with Parmenter.

LITTLE RASCALS, THE

Cast: Whoopi Goldberg*, John Wesley*, Kevin Jamal Woods*, Ross Elliot Bagley*, Raven-Symone *, Travis Tedford, Bug Hall
Director: Penelope Spheeris
Executive Producer: Deborah J. Newmyer, Gerald R. Molen
Music by: William Ross
Producer: Deborah J. Newmyer, Michael King, Bill Oakes, Gerald R. Molen
Storywriter: Penelope Spheeris, Robert Wolterstorff, Mike Scott
Tech Info: color/sound/72 min.   Type: Comedy Feature

Date: 1994   Origin: USA
Company: King World Entertainment
Distributors/Format: MCA/Universal Home Video (1/2")
Annotation: The first motion picture based on Hal Roach's lovable gang begins at an emergency meeting of the "He-Man, Woman Haters Club." Trouble ensues when their clubhouse is destroyed, and their prized go-cart is stolen by neighborhood bullies. Woods plays Stymie; Bagley plays Buckwheat, and Goldberg is featured as Buckwheat's mom.

LITTLE SHOP OF HORRORS

Cast: Tisha Campbell*, Tichina Arnold*, Michelle Weeks*, Levi Stubbs*, Bertice Reading*, Steve Martin, Rick Moranis, Ellen Greene
Director: Frank Oz
Music by: Alan Menken
Producer: David Geffen
Screenwriter: Howard Ashman
Tech Info: color/sound/94 min.   Type: Musical Feature
Date: 1986   Origin: USA
Company: Geffen Company
Distributors/Format: Warner Bros. Home Video, Inc. (1/2")
Annotation: Mushnik's Flower Shop houses an exotic potted plant called The Audrey II that survives by drinking fresh human blood. Stubbs is the voice of Audrey II. Campbell, Arnold and Weeks are a trio of vocalists who comment on the narrative.

LIVE THE JAZZ

Alternate: Music Revitalizes the Ederly
Director: Evelyn Navarro
Executive Producer: Bobbie R. Szyller
Producer: Bobbie R. Szyller, Evelyn Navarro, Donald R. Perry
Tech Info: color/sound/30 min.   Type: Documentary Short
Date: 1991   Origin: USA
Studio: Independent
Annotation: New Orleans jazz musicians, no youngsters themselves, perform at a nursing home. Caught up in the rhythm, the residents twirl their parasols New Orleans style as they dance together.

LIVIN' LARGE!

Cast: Terence "T.C." Carson*, Lisa Arrindell*, Nathaniel "Afrika" Hall*, Gerard Brown*, Loretta Devine*, Randal Patrick*, Tonea Stewart*, Eloise Whitman*, Harrison Avery*, Arlena Starr*, George Allen*, Tony Franciscus*, Joe Washington*, Blanche Baker
Director: Michael Schultz*
Executive Producer: Justin Ackerman
Music Performer: Terminator X *, John Valadez
Music by: Herbie Hancock*
Producer: David V. Picker, Justin Ackerman
Screenwriter: William Mosley Payne*
Tech Info: color/sound/95 min.   Type: Comedy Feature

Date: 1991   Origin: USA
Company: Samuel Goldwyn Company, WGM Productions
Distributors/Format: MGM Home Video (1/2")
Annotation: When Dexter Jackson (Carson) happens into the news reporting job of his dreams, he compromises his black identity to survive the ratings. Best friend Baker Moon (Hall) and girlfriend Toynelle Davis (Arrindell) are alienated from Dexter's new "white" life, that involves exploiting the black community. Eventually, he returns to his original value system and is promoted to co-anchor for his honesty.

LOCK UP
Cast: Frank McRae*, William Allen Young*, John Amos*, Troy Curvey*, Sylvester Stallone, Donald Sutherland
Director: John Flynn
Music by: Bill Conti
Producer: Lawrence Gordon, Charles Gordon
Screenwriter: Richard Smith, Henry Rosenbaum, Jeff Stuart
Tech Info: color/sound/115 min.   Type: Dramatic Feature
Date: 1990   Origin: USA
Company: Gordon Co., White Eagle, Carol Company
Distributors/Format: Carolco (1/2"), TriStar Pictures Inc. (1/2")
Annotation: Captain Meissner (Amos) is the captain of the guards in Gateway prison. Braden (Young) is also a guard who is critical of the poor treatment of the inmates. Meissner tapes the warden (Sutherland) after he confesses to conspiracy to commit murder. Eclipse (McRae) is the inmate in charge of the garage; Curvey is the prison receptionist.

LOIS MAILOU JONES: FIFTY YEARS OF PAINTING
Director: Alonzo Crawford*, Abraham Ford*
Narrator: Lois Mailou Jones*
Producer: Abraham Ford*
Screenwriter: Abraham Ford*
Tech Info: color/sound/55 min.   Type: Documentary Feature
Date: 1983   Origin: USA
Studio: Independent
Distributors/Format: Abraham Ford (16mm; 3/4"; 1/2")
Annotation: The film shows the work of Jones who has been making art for 50 years and has taught at Howard University for 47. Her marriage to graphic artist Pierre-Noel of Haiti in 1953 leads to Haitian/African influences in her art. Music is used to emphasize particular themes, e.g. Billie Holiday's "Strange Fruit" when Jones's painting of a lynching is on screen.

LONG TRAIN RUNNING: THE STORY OF THE OAKLAND BLUES
Director: Marlon T. Riggs*
Producer: Marlon T. Riggs*
Tech Info: color/sound/30 min.   Type: Documentary Short
Date: 1983   Origin: USA
Annotation: Riggs' film explores the development of the blues in Oakland, California.

LONG WALK HOME, THE
Cast: Whoopi Goldberg*, Ving Rhames*, Erika Alexander*, Richard Habersham*, Jason Weaver*, Sissy Spacek, Dwight Schultz, Crystral Robbins, Dylan Baker
Director: Richard Pearce
Executive Producer: Taylor Hackford, Stuart Benjamin
Music by: George Fenton
Producer: Taylor Hackford, Stuart Benjamin, Dave Bell, Howard W. Koch Jr.
Screenwriter: John Cork
Tech Info: color/sound/98 min.   Type: Dramatic Feature
Date: 1991   Origin: USA
Company: New Visions Pictures
Distributors/Format: Image Entertainment (35mm), Filmic Archives (1/2")
Archives/Format: IUB - BFC/A (1/2")
Annotation: Odessa Carter (Goldberg), a maid for the white Thompson family, is caught in the middle of the Montgomery bus boycott. Mrs. Thompson (Spacek) stands up to white racists and her husband (Schultz) when they discover she is helping car pool "Negroes" to work.

LOOK WHO'S TALKING
Cast: Blu Mankuma*, Bruce Willis, Kirstie Alley, John Travolta, Olympia Dukakis
Director: Amy Heckerling
Music by: David Kitay
Producer: Jonathan D. Krane
Screenwriter: Amy Heckerling
Tech Info: color/sound/93 min.   Type: Comedy Feature
Date: 1989   Origin: USA
Company: TriStar
Annotation: Mollie (Alley) meets James (Travolta), a cab driver, as she's going into labor. A voiceover (Willis) offers the baby's impressions of the events. Mankuma plays the Director.

LOOKER
Cast: Dorian Harewood*, James Coburn, Albert Finney, Susan Dey, Leigh Taylor-Young
Director: Michael Crichton
Music by: Barry Devorzon
Producer: Howard Jeffrey
Screenwriter: Michael Crichton
Tech Info: color/sound/94 min.   Type: Dramatic Feature
Date: 1981   Origin: USA
Company: Ladd
Distributors/Format: Warner Bros. Home Video, Inc. (1/2")
Annotation: Plastic surgeon Larry Roberts (Finney) discovers his patients are being killed and replicated for subliminal TV ads. Harewood plays Lt. Masters.

LOOSE CANNONS
Cast: David Alan Grier*, S. Epatha Merkerson*, Dan Aykroyd, Gene Hackman, Dom DeLuise, Nancy Travis
Director: Bob Clark
Executive Producer: Rene Dupont
Music by: Paul Zaza
Producer: Rene Dupont, Aaron Spelling, Alan Greisman

Screenwriter: Bob Clark, Richard Matheson, Richard Christian Matheson
Tech Info: color/sound/94 min.   Type: Comedy Feature
Date: 1990   Origin: USA
Company: Aaron Spelling-Alan Greisman
Distributors/Format: TriStar Pictures Inc. (1/2")
Annotation: Mac Stern (Hackman) and Ellis Fielding (Aykroyd) are D.C. policemen fighting for possession of a porn video supposedly depicting Hitler with a prominent German politician. Merkerson plays Rachel.

LOOSE SHOES

Alternate: Coming Attractions
Cast: Murphy Dunne*, Lewis Arquette, Danny Dayton, Buddy Hackett
Director: Ira Miller
Executive Producer: Byron Lasky, Lee Weisel
Music by: Murphy Dunne*
Producer: Joel Chernoff, Byron Lasky, Lee Weisel
Screenwriter: Ira Miller, Varley Smith, Ian Paiser, Royce D. Applegate
Tech Info: color/sound/74 min.   Type: Comedy Feature
Date: 1980   Origin: USA
Company: Brooksfilm
Distributors/Format: Atlantic Home Video (1/2")
Annotation: Spoofs of movie trailers comprise the entire film. Dunne plays the tough G.I. in one trailer.

LORDS OF DISCIPLINE, THE

Cast: Mark Breland*, David Keith, Robert Prosky, G.D. Spradlin, Barbara Babcock, Michael Biehn
Director: Franc Roddam
Music Performer: Howard Blake
Producer: Herb Jaffe, Gabriel Katzka
Screenwriter: Thomas Pope, Lloyd Fonvielle
Tech Info: color/sound/103 min.   Type: Dramatic Feature
Date: 1983   Origin: USA
Company: Paramount
Distributors/Format: Paramount Home Video (1/2"), Sight & Sound (1/2")
Annotation: Will (Keith) is assigned to look after Pearce (Breland), a young dedicated cadet. As the first black cadet at a Southern military academy, Pearce finds other soldiers are callous and racist.

LOSING GROUND

Cast: Bill Gunn*, Seret Scott*, Duane Jones*, Billie Allen*, Gary Bolling*, Norberto Kerner*, Maritza Rivera
Director: Kathleen Collins*
Music Performer: Frank Diaz, Los Patines
Music by: Michael D. Minard
Producer: Kathleen Collins*, Ronald K. Gray*, Eleanor Charles
Screenwriter: Kathleen Collins*
Tech Info: color/sound/86 min.   Type: Dramatic Feature

Date: 1982   Origin: USA
Studio: Independent
Company: Losing Ground Productions
Distributors/Format: Mypheduh Films, Inc. (16mm; 1/2")
Archives/Format: IUB - BFC/A (16mm)
Annotation: Professor Sarah Rogers (Scott) and her artist husband (Gunn) come to an impasse in their marriage. In her research on and pursuit of ecstasy, Sarah meets Duke Richards (Jones) who changes her life. Allen plays her mother; Bolling is one of her students who involves Sarah in his film.

LOSING ISAIAH

Cast: Samuel L. Jackson*, LaTanya Richardson*, Halle Berry*, Cuba Gooding Jr.*, David Strathairn, Jessica Lange, Marc John Jeffries
Director: Andrzej Bartkowiak, Stephen Gyllenhaal
Music by: Mark Isham
Producer: Howard W. Koch Jr., Naomi Foner
Screenwriter: Naomi Foner
Storywriter: Seth Margolis
Tech Info: color/sound/108 min.   Type: Dramatic Feature
Date: 1994   Origin: USA
Company: Paramount
Distributors/Format: Facets Multimedia, Inc. (1/2"), Films Inc. (1/2"), Paramount Home Video (1/2")
Annotation: Lange plays an adoptive mother who gives an abandoned child a new chance at life. Berry is the birth mother who cleans up her life and sets out to reclaim the child; Jackson portrays her attorney.

LOUIE BLUIE

Director: Terry Zwigoff
Music Performer: Howard "Louie Bluie" Armstrong*
Producer: Terry Zwigoff
Speaker: Howard "Louie Bluie" Armstrong*, Ted Bogon
Tech Info: mixed/sound/60 min.   Type: Documentary Feature
Date: 1985   Origin: USA
Company: Superior Pictures
Distributors/Format: Kino International Corp. (1/2")
Annotation: A combination of interviews, reminiscences, comments and performances, are arranged to form a character study of Armstrong, a versatile musician and artist, as well as one of the last of the old time "lusty" storytellers. The film includes interesting historical clips of black musicians in Tennessee.

LOVE AFFAIR

Cast: Ray Charles*, Cylk Cozart*, Warren Beatty, Annette Bening, Katharine Hepburn
Director: Glenn Gordon Caron
Executive Producer: Andrew Davis
Music by: Ennio Morricone
Producer: Andrew Davis, Warren Beatty
Screenwriter: Robert Towne, Warren Beatty
Tech Info: color/sound/107 min.   Type: Dramatic Feature

Date: 1994   Origin: USA
Company: Warner Bros., Mullholland
Distributors/Format: Warner Bros. Home Video, Inc. (1/2")
Annotation: Los Angeles football star turned TV journalist Mike Gambril (Beatty) meets Terry McKay (Bening) on a plane to Australia. After a brief affair, the two decide to meet in three months, but a car accident leaves Terry paralyzed and Mike feeling rejected. Cozart plays Dr. Punch.

LOVE AT FIRST BITE
Cast: Isabel Sanford*, Sherman Hemsley*, George Hamilton, Susan St. James
Director: Stan Dragoti
Producer: Joel Freeman
Tech Info: color/sound/96 min.   Type: Comedy Feature
Date: 1979   Origin: USA
Company: American International Pictures
Annotation: Count Dracula (Hamilton) searches New York night life for the girl of his dreams. Along the way, he encounters Reverend Mike (Hemsley).

LOVE AT LARGE
Cast: Ruby Dee*, Tom Berenger, Elizabeth Perkins, Neil Young
Director: Alan Rudolph
Music by: Mark Isham
Producer: David Blocker
Screenwriter: Alan Rudolph
Tech Info: color/sound/97 min.   Type: Dramatic Feature
Date: 1990   Origin: USA
Company: David Blocker
Distributors/Format: Orion Home Video (1/2")
Annotation: Dee makes a brief appearance as Corrine Dart, the owner of a detective agency who fires her new employee, Stella (Perkins), for not doing her job correctly. Stella then falls in love with another detective, Harry Dobbs (Berenger) and solves her case.

LOVE FIELD
Cast: Dennis Haysbert*, Stephanie McFadden*, Michelle Pfeiffer, Brian Kerwin, Louise Latham, Peggy Rea
Director: Jonathan Kaplan
Executive Producer: George Goodman, Kate Guinzburg
Music by: Jerry Goldsmith
Producer: Sarah Pillsbury, Midge Sanford, George Goodman, Kate Guinzburg
Screenwriter: Don Roos
Tech Info: color/sound/104 min.   Type: Dramatic Feature
Date: 1992   Origin: USA
Company: Sanford/Pillsbury Prod., Jacqueline Prod., Orion
Distributors/Format: Orion Home Video (1/2")
Annotation: Lurene Hallett (Pfeiffer) emulates Jackie Kennedy and travels to Washington, D.C., to attend John F. Kennedy's funeral. En route, she meets Paul Cater (Haysbert) and his daughter Jonell (McFadden), whom he has rescued from an abusive state home where she has been since her mother's death.

LOVE POTION
Director: Ayoka Chenzira*
Producer: Ayoka Chenzira*
Tech Info: color/sound   Type: Television Documentary
Date: 1993   Origin: USA
Company: ITVS
Annotation: A bittersweet story of a couple trying to have children while dealing with the turmoils of their New York neighborhood.

LOVELINES
Cast: Michael Winslow*, Greg Bradford, Don Michael Paul, Mary Beth Evans
Director: Rod Amateau
Producer: Michael Lloyd, Hal Taines
Screenwriter: Chip Hand, William Hillman
Storywriter: Michael Lloyd, Chip Hand, William Hillman
Tech Info: color/sound/93 min.   Type: Comedy Feature
Date: 1984   Origin: USA
Company: Taines, Lloyd, TriStar, Delphi II
Distributors/Format: TriStar Pictures Inc. (1/2")
Annotation: Two rival high school bands in Los Angeles battle for stature. Winslow plays J.D.

LOW BLOW
Cast: Akosua Busia*, Stack Pierce*, Cameron Mitchell, Leo Fong, Diane Stevenett, Troy Donahue
Director: Frank Harris
Executive Producer: Bertrand Ungar, Mark Moldenhauer
Music by: Steve Amundsen
Producer: Leo Fong, Bertrand Ungar, Mark Moldenhauer
Screenwriter: Leo Fong
Tech Info: color/sound/85 min.   Type: Dramatic Feature
Date: 1986   Origin: USA
Company: Action
Distributors/Format: Crown Home Video (1/2")
Annotation: Joe Wong (Fong) is a policeman-turned-private detective who is hired by a wealthy industrialist (Donahue) to rescue his daughter from a cult. Busia plays Karma and Pierce plays Duke.

LOW DOWN DIRTY SHAME
Cast: Keenen Ivory Wayans*, Kim Wayans*, Charles S. Dutton*, Jada Pinkett*, Salli Richardson*, Andrew Divoff
Director: Keenen Ivory Wayans*
Executive Producer: Eric L. Gold, Lee R. Mayes
Music by: Marcus Miller*
Producer: Eric L. Gold, Joe Roth, Lee R. Mayes, Roger Birnbaum
Screenwriter: Keenen Ivory Wayans*
Tech Info: color/sound/104 min.   Type: Comedy Feature

Date: 1994   Origin: USA
Company: Caravan Pictures
Distributors/Format: Caravan Pictures Home Video (1/2")
Annotation: Keenan Ivory Wayans plays Shame, a down-on-his luck ex-policeman turned private investigator. He's hired by Sonny (Dutton), a drug enforcement official, to track down his former girlfriend and $20 million in stolen drug money. With his trusty sidekick Peaches (Pinkett), Shame aims to make money and clear his name in what becomes his wildest and most dangerous assignment.

LUNCH WAGON

Alternate: Lunch Wagon Girls
Cast: Rosanne Katon*, Maurice Sneed*, Pamela Bryant, Candy Moore
Director: Ernest Pintoff
Executive Producer: Seymour Borde
Music by: Richard Band
Producer: Mark Borde, Seymour Borde
Screenwriter: Leon Phillips, Marshall Harvey, Terrie Frankle
Tech Info: color/sound/88 min.   Type: Comedy Feature
Date: 1981   Origin: USA
Company: Seymour Borde
Distributors/Format: Bordeaux Home Video (1/2")
Annotation: Marcy (Bryant), Shannon (Katon), and Diedra (Moore), three unemployed young women, set up a lunch wagon near construction sites. Sneed plays Ben.

LURE AND THE LORE, THE

Director: Ayoka Chenzira*
Producer: Ayoka Chenzira*
Speaker: Thomas Osha Pinnock*
Tech Info: color/sound/15 min.   Type: Documentary Short
Date: 1989   Origin: USA
Studio: Independent
Distributors/Format: Third World Newsreel (1/2"), Red Carnelian Films/Video (16mm; 1/2")
Annotation: This video is a collaboration between film/video artist Chenzira and performance artist Pinnock. Pinnock performs his "immigrant folktales," using traditional lore of his native Jamaica to dramatize his migration to New York in the 1960s. His earlier views of the U.S. are contrasted with the realities of his life in America.

LUST IN THE DUST

Cast: Woody Strode*, Geoffry Lewis, Divine , Lainie Kazan, Tab Hunter
Director: Paul Bartel
Executive Producer: James C. Katz, Robert E.M. Raymond
Music by: Peter Matz
Producer: James C. Katz, Tab Hunter, Allan Glaser, Robert E.M. Raymond
Screenwriter: Philip John Taylor
Tech Info: color/sound/87 min.   Type: Comedy Feature

Date: 1985   Origin: USA
Company: Fox Run
Distributors/Format: New World Home Video (1/2")
Annotation: In this western spoof, 300-pound female impersonator Rosie Velez (Divine) is saved from a gang of brutal desperadoes by Abel Wood (Hunter). Strode plays Blackman.

LUTHER VANDROSS LIVE AT WEMBLEY

Music Performer: Luther Vandross*
Music by: Nat Adderley Jr.*
Producer: John Smith
Tech Info: color/sound/90 min.   Type: Concert Feature
Date: 1989   Origin: Great Britain
Studio: Independent
Company: White Rabbit Productions
Distributors/Format: Proud To Be... (1/2"), Sony Music Video Enterprises (1/2")
Annotation: Recorded at the Wembley Arena in London, the concert include: "Never Too Much," "Any Love," "Come Back," "Love Won't Let Me Wait," "Give Me the Reason," "Searching," "For You to Love," "Superstar," "A House is Not a Home," "She Won't Talk to Me," and "Stop to Love."

M.C. HAMMER: PLEASE HAMMER DON'T HURT 'EM

Cast: M.C. Hammer *, Julie Sneed*, Davina H'Ollier*, Joe Mack*, Ho Frat Hoo!! *, Torture *, Special Generation*, One Cause One Effect*
Director: Rupert Wainwright
Executive Producer: M.C. Hammer *
Music Performer: M.C. Hammer *
Music by: M.C. Hammer *
Producer: M.C. Hammer *, John E. Oetjen
Screenwriter: M.C. Hammer *
Tech Info: color/sound/60 min.   Type: Musical Feature
Date: 1990   Origin: USA
Company: Fragile Films, Bustin Productions, Capitol Records
Distributors/Format: Capitol Home Video (1/2")
Annotation: This feature length video includes five individual videos from Hammer's quadruple platinum album, "Please Hammer, Don't Hurt 'Em." Some videos are: "Here Comes The Hammer," "Pray," and "Help The Children." Hammer's message of a drug-free youth is reinforced by his dual role as Reverend Pressure. Cast members appear as themselves.

M.C. LYTE: LYTE YEARS

Cast: Sinbad *, Michelle Webb*, Lath Berclaz*, Lanier Long*, Mad Man Jay *, Ed Lover*, Kroc *, Master T. *, King of Chill *, Kadeem Hardison*, Dana Dane*, Positive K *, Ron Norsworthy, Emilo Sosa Jr., Flea
Director: Nancy Bennett
Executive Producer: Lori Weintraub
Producer: Lori Weintraub, Nancy Bennett
Tech Info: color/sound/65 min.   Type: Documentary Feature

Date: 1991   Origin: USA
Company: A*Vision Entertainment
Archives/Format: IUB - AAAMC (1/2")
Annotation: The film includes interviews, videos, concert footage, and other film clips that highlight the musical career of M.C. Lyte, one of Rap's most successful female stars. Friends and co-workers comment on her work, and excerpts from YO MTV RAPS and "Musicians For Life" public service announcements add a political dimension to her lyrics and performances.

MAC

Cast: John Amos*, Ellen Barkin, John Turturro, Michael Badalucco, Carl Capotorto, Katherine Borowitz
Director: John Turturro, Ron Fortunato
Music by: Richard Termini, Vin Tese
Producer: Nancy Tenenbaum, Brenda Goodman
Screenwriter: John Turturro, Brandon Cole
Tech Info: color/sound/118 min.   Type: Dramatic Feature
Date: 1992   Origin: USA
Company: Columbia, TriStar
Distributors/Format: Columbia/TriStar Pictures (35mm; 1/2")
Annotation: Mac, Vico and Bruno Vittelli, three brothers in an Italian American family, struggle to scrape together enough money to start their own construction company in Queens in the 1950s. Amos plays Nat, one of the laborers who works for the Vitellis and is seriously injured on the job.

MAD MAX BEYOND THUNDERDOME

Cast: Tina Turner*, Mel Gibson, Bruce Spence, Helen Buday
Director: George Miller, George Ogilvie
Music by: Maurice Jarre
Producer: George Miller
Screenwriter: George Miller, Terry Hayes
Storywriter: George Miller, Terry Hayes
Tech Info: color/sound/109 min.   Type: Dramatic Feature
Date: 1985   Origin: Australia
Company: Kennedy Miller
Distributors/Format: Warner Bros. Home Video, Inc. (1/2")
Annotation: Aunty Entity (Turner) runs Barter Town which makes methylene gas from pig manure. She hires Mad Max (Gibson) to kill the man who is the brains behind the process. He agrees, but when he finds himself about to kill a mentally impaired man, Max refuses.

MADAM C.J. WALKER

Series: Black Americans of Achievement Video Collection
Director: Rhonda Fabian, Jerry Baber, Keith Smith
Executive Producer: Andrew Schlessinger
Narrator: Michael Logan
Producer: Rhonda Fabian, Jerry Baber, Andrew Schlessinger
Tech Info: mixed/sound/30 min.   Type: Documentary Short

Date: 1992   Origin: USA
Studio: Independent
Company: Schlessinger Video Productions
Distributors/Format: Filmic Archives (1/2")
Annotation: Born just after the Civil War, Walker grew up in poverty, but was able to develop a formula for restoring hair and build a successful business from it, expanding from the United States to Central America and the Caribbean and becoming a positive role model for black women across the country.

MADE IN AMERICA

Cast: Whoopi Goldberg*, Mel Stewart*, Nia Long*, Will Smith*, Ted Danson
Director: Richard Benjamin, Ralf Bode
Executive Producer: Carol Burnett, Nadine Schiff, Marcia Brandywine
Music by: Mark Isham
Producer: Carol Burnett, Arnon Milchan, Nadine Schiff, Marcia Brandywine, Michael Douglas, Rick Bieber
Screenwriter: Holly Goldberg Sloan
Storywriter: Nadine Schiff, Marcia Brandywine, Holly Goldberg Sloan
Tech Info: color/sound/109 min.   Type: Comedy Feature
Date: 1993   Origin: USA
Company: New Regency Prod., Le Studio Canal Plus, Alcor
Annotation: Sarah (Goldberg) is the parent of bright, college-bound Zora (Long). Inquisitive Zora and her pal Tea Cake (Smith) discover that her biological father is an anonymous sperm-bank donor, used car salesman Hal (Danson), whose cornball commercials blanket cable television.

MADONNA: TRUTH OR DARE

Alternate: In Bed with Madonna
Cast: Donna Delory*, Niki Harris*, Oliver Crumes*, Gabriel Trupin*, Carlton Wilborn*, Madonna
Director: Alex Keshishian
Executive Producer: Madonna
Producer: Jay Roewe, Madonna
Tech Info: mixed/sound/118 min.   Type: Musical Feature
Date: 1991   Origin: USA
Company: Boy Toy Inc., Propaganda Films
Distributors/Format: LIVE Home Video (1/2"), Miramax Home Video (1/2")
Annotation: The film follows Madonna and her entourage backstage on the 1990 international "Blonde Ambition" tour. Madonna's dance troupes are predominantly black men with one black woman. Concert sequences are done in color; documentary footage is in a grainy black and white.

MAGIC LOVE

Cast: Laura Williams*, John Jelks*
Director: Iverson White*
Producer: Iverson White*
Screenwriter: Iverson White*
Tech Info: color/sound/97 min.   Type: Dramatic Feature

Date: 1993   Origin: USA
Studio: Independent
Distributors/Format: Oracy Productions (16mm)
Annotation: The film intermingles contemporary and period sequences to tell the story of Jelks and Williams as the 20th century reincarnations of an 18th century African shaman and his pre-destined bride who are separated by the African slave trade.

MAID TO ORDER

Cast: Theodore "Teddy" Wilson*, Mary Claxton*, Vince Monroe Townsend Jr.*, Kevin Clayton*, Reina King*, Kim Silver*, Khandi Alexander*, Bennet Guillory*, Ally Sheedy, Beverly D'Angelo
Director: Amy Jones
Music by: Georges Delerue
Producer: Herb Jaffe, Mort Engelberg
Screenwriter: Perry Howze, Randy Howze
Tech Info: color/sound/93 min.   Type: Comedy Feature
Date: 1987   Origin: USA
Company: The Vista Organization
Distributors/Format: New Century/Vista Film Corp (1/2")
Annotation: When a rich man's daughter is out of control, his wish that he never had a daughter comes true. Jessica (Sheedy) is forced to work as a maid with Audrey James (Claxton). Audrey has three children: Jomo (Clayton), Tiffany (King), and Jeanine (Silver); Townsend plays their father. Wilson plays a chauffeur and Alexander has a minor role as a prostitute.

MAIDS: A DOCUMENTARY, THE

Director: Muriel Jackson*
Tech Info: color/sound/28 min.   Type: Documentary Short
Date: 1985   Origin: USA
Studio: Independent
Company: Atlanta Media Project
Distributors/Format: Women Make Movies, Inc. (16mm; 1/2")
Annotation: Jackson's film takes a historical look at the work, circumstances, and attitudes surrounding female dayworkers. The film considers their personal views, the organizing efforts of Dorothy Bolden, president of the National Domestic Workers Union and the disappearance of the one-household maid as franchised services become more popular.

MAIN EVENT, THE

Cast: Richard Lawson*, Ernie Hudson*, Arthur/Art Evans*, Whitman Mayo*, Badja Djola*, Maurice Sneed*, Alvin Childress*, Barbra Streisand, Ryan O'Neal
Director: Howard Zieff
Executive Producer: Howard Rosenman, Renee Missel
Music by: Gary LeMel
Producer: Barbra Streisand, Howard Rosenman, Jon Peters, Renee Missel
Screenwriter: Gail Parent, Andrew Smith
Tech Info: color/sound/112 min.   Type: Comedy Feature

Date: 1979   Origin: USA
Company: Barwood
Distributors/Format: Warner Bros. Home Video, Inc. (1/2")
Annotation: Mayo is Percy Washington, trainer for Kid Natural (O'Neal) a boxer who Hillary Kramer (Streisand) hires to fight Hector Mantilla (Lawson) in order to win money.

MAJOR LEAGUE

Cast: Wesley Snipes*, Dennis Haysbert*, Charlie Sheen, Tom Berenger, Margaret Whitton, Corbin Bernsen
Director: David S. Ward
Music by: James Newton Howard*
Producer: Chris Chesser, Irby Smith
Screenwriter: David S. Ward
Tech Info: color/sound/107 min.   Type: Comedy Feature
Date: 1989   Origin: USA
Company: Paramount
Distributors/Format: Paramount Home Video (1/2")
Annotation: Willie Mays Hayes (Snipes) and Pedro Cerrano (Haysbert) are both part of the rejuvenation attempt of the Cleveland Indians that have not won a pennant in nearly 30 years. Hayes shows up at try-outs uninvited but proves his speed and determination, eventually becoming the league's most valuable base stealer. Cerrano is a defector from Cuba in search of religious freedom for his voodoo practices.

MAJOR LEAGUE II

Cast: Dennis Haysbert*, Omar Epps*, Charlie Sheen, Tom Berenger, Corbin Bernsen, Bob Uecker
Director: David S. Ward, Victor Hammer
Executive Producer: Gary Barber
Music by: Michel Colombier
Producer: David S. Ward, James Robinson, Gary Barber
Screenwriter: R.J. Stewart
Storywriter: R.J. Stewart, Tom Parker, Jim Jennewein
Tech Info: color/sound/105 min.   Type: Comedy Feature
Date: 1994   Origin: USA
Company: Warner Bros.
Distributors/Format: Warner Bros. Home Video, Inc. (1/2")
Annotation: The diehard Cleveland Indians who went from worst to first in an amazing Major League season now cope with fame and its perquisites as the team tries to repeat the performance. Reckless thrower Rick Vaughn (Sheen), catcher Jake Taylor (Berenger), self-adoring infielder Roger Dorn (Bernsen), slugger Pedro Cerano (Haysbert) and more are in for a whole new season.

MAKING "DO THE RIGHT THING"

Director: St. Clair Bourne*
Narrator: St. Clair Bourne*
Producer: St. Clair Bourne*
Screenwriter: St. Clair Bourne*
Speaker: Spike Lee*
Tech Info: color/sound/60 min.   Type: Documentary Feature

Date: 1988   Origin: USA
Company: The Chamba Organization
Distributors/Format: First Run/Icarus Films (16mm), Williams Greaves Productions, Inc. (16mm)
Annotation: Bourne chronicles the making of Lee's major motion picture, DO THE RIGHT THING, surveying actors, people in the neighborhood and Lee himself.

MALCOLM X

Cast: Denzel Washington*, Spike Lee*, Lonette McKee*, Albert Hall*, Joe Seneca*, Frances Foster*, Phyllis Yvonne Stickney*, Michael Ralph*, Ertha D. Robinson*, Al Freeman Jr.*, LaTanya Richardson*, Theresa Randle*, James McDaniel*, Angela Bassett*, Delroy Lindo*, Tommy Hollis*, Ernest Thomas*, Jean LaMarre*, James E. Gaines*, O.L. Duke*
Director: Spike Lee*, Ernest Dickerson*
Music by: Terence Blanchard*
Producer: Spike Lee*, Marvin Worth
Screenwriter: Spike Lee*, Arnold Perl
Storywriter: Alex Haley*, James Baldwin*
Tech Info: color/sound/201 min.   Type: Dramatic Feature
Date: 1992   Origin: USA
Company: 40 Acres and a Mule Film Works, Marvin Worth Prod.
Distributors/Format: Facets Multimedia, Inc. (1/2"), Warner Bros. Home Video, Inc. (1/2"), Filmic Archives (1/2")
Archives/Format: IUB - BFC/A (1/2")
Annotation: Adapted from "The Autobiography of Malcolm X" (as told to Alex Haley), Lee's film dramatizes the life of Malcolm X (Washington). Filmed on locations ranging from New York to Egypt, the film follows Malcolm through the criminal activities of his early years to his rise within and his break with the Nation of Islam. Bassett portrays his wife Betty Shabazz, and Freeman plays the Honorable Elijah Muhammad.

MALCOLM X

Series: Black Americans of Achievement Video Collection
Director: Rhonda Fabian, Jerry Baber, Keith Smith
Executive Producer: Andrew Schlessinger
Narrator: Michael Logan
Producer: Rhonda Fabian, Jerry Baber, Andrew Schlessinger
Tech Info: mixed/sound/30 min.   Type: Documentary Short
Date: 1992   Origin: USA
Studio: Independent
Company: Schlessinger Video Productions
Distributors/Format: Filmic Archives (1/2")
Annotation: Black historians and leaders comment on the life of Malcolm X, who experienced violence from the Klu Klux Klan as a child and grew up to become a leader of the black Muslims and a spokesperson for black nationalism.

MALONE

Cast: Blu Mankuma*, Burt Reynolds, Cliff Robertson, Cynthia Gibb
Director: Harley Cokliss
Music by: David Newman
Producer: Leo L. Fuchs
Screenwriter: Christopher Frank

Storywriter: William Wingate
Tech Info: color/sound/93 min.   Type: Dramatic Feature
Date: 1987   Origin: USA
Company: Orion
Annotation: Malone (Reynolds) is a CIA assassin who is tired of the business. He takes off across the country in his Mustang, but discovers a right-wing plan for a "patriotic" revolution when he has to stop for car repairs. Mankuma plays Reverend Danby.

MAMA'S PUSHCART

Director: Demetria Royals*, Louise Diamond
Speaker: Ellen Stewart*
Tech Info: color/sound/54 min.   Type: Documentary Feature
Date: 1988   Origin: USA
Studio: Independent
Distributors/Format: Women Make Movies, Inc. (16mm; 1/2")
Annotation: The film is a tribute to Ellen Stewart, founder of New York's La MaMa Experimental Theatre Company.

MAMBO KINGS, THE

Cast: Roscoe Lee Browne*, Vondie Curtis-Hall*, Celia Cruz*, Cathy Moriarty, Antonio Banderas, Armand Assante
Director: Arne Glimcher
Executive Producer: Steven Reuther
Producer: Arnon Milchan, Steven Reuther, Arne Glimcher
Screenwriter: Cynthia Cidre
Tech Info: color/sound/101 min.   Type: Musical Feature
Date: 1992   Origin: France, USA
Company: King Mambo Inc., Alcor Films, et al.
Distributors/Format: Warner Bros. Home Video, Inc. (1/2")
Annotation: Based on the novel, "The Mambo Kings Play Songs of Love," the story centers around two brothers who leave Cuba to pursue their music careers in New York. Brown portrays Fernando Perez. Curtis-Hall plays Miguel Montoya; Cruz portrays Evalina, his wife.

MAN WHO LOVED WOMEN, THE

Cast: Ben Powers*, Kim Basinger, Burt Reynolds, Julie Andrews
Director: Blake Edwards
Executive Producer: Jonathan D. Krane
Music by: Henry Mancini
Producer: Blake Edwards, Tony Adams, Jonathan D. Krane
Screenwriter: Blake Edwards, Milton Wexler, Geoffrey Edwards
Storywriter: Francois Truffaut
Tech Info: color/sound/118 min.   Type: Comedy Feature
Date: 1983   Origin: USA
Company: Columbia
Distributors/Format: Columbia Pictures Home Video (1/2")
Annotation: David (Reynolds) is a sculptor who seeks out therapy to overcome a creative block, but instead falls in love with the psychiatrist (Andrews). Powers plays Al.

MANDELA

Executive Producer: Mabel Haddock*
Narrator: Max Robinson*
Producer: Mabel Haddock*, Peter Davis
Speaker: Winnie Mandela*, Nelson Mandela*, Adelaide Tambo*, Zindziswa Mandela*, Adelaide Joseph*, Paul Joseph*, Fatima Meer
Tech Info: color/sound/58 min.   Type: Documentary Feature
Date: 1986   Origin: South Africa
Company: NBPC & Villon Films
Distributors/Format: California Newsreel (1/2")
Archives/Format: IUB - BFC/A (1/2")
Annotation: The human rights struggle in South Africa by Nelson Mandela is told from the perspective of his former wife, Winnie. The film includes archival footage of the marches, protests, and political speeches of the Mandela family and the ANC, as well as interviews with Paul Joseph, Famita Meer, Adelaide Tambo, Adelaide Joseph, and daughter Zindziswa Mandela. The focus on the South African women's struggle is epitomized in the strength and endurance of Winnie Mandela.

MANDELA IN AMERICA

Director: Danny Schechter
Music by: Aretha Franklin*, Stevie Wonder*, Tracy Chapman*
Producer: Danny Schechter
Speaker: Nelson Mandela*
Tech Info: color/sound/90 min.   Type: Documentary Feature
Date: 1990   Origin: USA
Studio: Independent
Distributors/Format: Facets Multimedia, Inc. (1/2")
Annotation: The authorized, behind-the-scenes look at Mandela's triumphant visit to the United States provides an insider's view of the most memorable public and private moments of his trip and his message against apartheid.

MANHUNTER

Cast: Frankie Faison*, Garcelle Beauvais*, William Petersen, Kim Greist, Joan Allen, Brian Cox
Director: Michael Mann
Executive Producer: Richard A. Roth, Bernard Williams
Music by: Michel Rubini, The Reds
Producer: Richard A. Roth, Richard A. Roth, Bernard Williams
Screenwriter: Michael Mann
Tech Info: color/sound/119 min.   Type: Dramatic Feature
Date: 1986   Origin: USA
Company: DEG
Annotation: Will Graham (Petersen) tracks serial killers for the F.B.I.'s Behavioral Science Unit. He visits his last catch, Hannibal Lektor (Cox), to help him get inside the mind of a new killer. Faison plays Lt. Fisk and Beauvais is the young woman housebuyer.

MANIAC COP 2

Cast: Clarence Williams III*, Robert Earl Jones*, Michael Lerner, Robert Davi, Leo Rossi, Robert Z'Dar
Director: William Lustig
Executive Producer: David Hodgins, Frank D'Alessio
Music by: Jay Chattaway
Producer: Larry Cohen, David Hodgins, Frank D'Alessio
Screenwriter: Larry Cohen
Tech Info: color/sound/88 min.   Type: Dramatic Feature
Date: 1991   Origin: USA
Company: Fadd Enterprises, Cordell Productions Inc.
Distributors/Format: LIVE Home Video (1/2")
Annotation: Turkell (Rossi), a stripper killer, teams up with an "unkillable" maniac cop (Z'Dar) and the two wreck havoc in New York. Williams plays Blum and Jones appears as Harry.

MANIAC COP 3: BADGE OF SILENCE

Cast: Grand L. Bush*, Gretchen Becker, Robert Davi, Robert Z'Dar, Caitlin Dulany, Paul Gleason
Director: William Lustig
Music by: Joel Goldsmith
Producer: Joel Soisson, Michael Leahy
Screenwriter: Larry Cohen
Tech Info: color/sound/85 min.   Type: Dramatic Feature
Date: 1993   Origin: USA
Company: Footstone, Inc., Neo Motion Pictures
Distributors/Format: Academy Home Entertainment Video (1/2")
Annotation: Zombie cop Matt Cordell (Z'Dar) is brought back to life, terrorizing young officer Kate Sullivan (Becker). Bush plays Willie.

MANNEQUIN

Cast: Olivia Frances Williams*, Meshach Taylor*, Andrew McCarthy, Kim Cattrall, Estelle Getty, G.W. Bailey
Director: Michael Gottlieb
Executive Producer: Edward Rugoff, Joel Sill
Music Performer: Sylvester Levay
Music by: Sylvester Levay
Producer: Edward Rugoff, Art Levinson, Joseph Farrell, Joel Sill
Screenwriter: Edward Rugoff, Michael Gottlieb
Tech Info: color/sound/90 min.   Type: Comedy Feature
Date: 1987   Origin: USA
Company: Gladden Entertainment
Distributors/Format: Fox Home Video (1/2"), Media Home Entertainment, Inc. (1/2")
Annotation: Hollywood (Taylor), a gay window-dresser, helps his best friend Jonathan (McCarthy) save the woman he loves (Cattrall). In the climactic scene, Hollywood holds off security so that Jonathan can rescue her.

MANNEQUIN 2: ON THE MOVE
Cast: Meshach Taylor*, Kristy Swanson, William Ragsdale
Director: Stewart Raffill
Producer: Edward Rugoff
Screenwriter: Edward Rugoff, David Isaacs, Ken Levine, Betsy Israel
Tech Info: color/sound/95 min.   Type: Comedy Feature
Date: 1991   Origin: USA
Company: Gladden Entertainment
Distributors/Format: Fox Home Video (1/2"), LIVE Home Video (1/2")
Annotation: In this sequel, Hollywood (Taylor), a flashy fashion designer who drives a pink cadillac convertible, desires to try on the mannequin's (Swanson) jeweled necklace. In the process, Hollywood becomes a mannequin himself for a short period.

MARCH ON WASHINGTON REMEMBERED, THE
Speaker: Martin Luther King Jr.*
Tech Info: mixed/sound/20 min.   Type: Documentary Short
Date: 1990   Origin: USA
Distributors/Format: Filmic Archives (1/2"), Encyclopedia Britannica Educational Corporation (1/2")
Annotation: The story of the march on August 28, 1963, includes King's "I Have A Dream" speech.

MARDI GRAS FOR THE DEVIL
Cast: Margaret Avery*, John Amos*, Lesley-Anne Down, Robert Davi, Michael Ironside
Director: David A. Prior
Executive Producer: David Winters
Music by: Christopher Farrell
Producer: David Winters, Jill Silverthorne
Screenwriter: David A. Prior, John Cianetti
Tech Info: color/sound/95 min.   Type: Dramatic Feature
Date: 1993   Origin: USA
Company: West Side Studios
Distributors/Format: Prism Entertainment (1/2")
Annotation: Bishop (Ironside) is a demonic spirit on the rampage killing everyone in his path. Policeman Mike Turner (Davi) does not realize he is dealing with the supernatural until he confers with Miss Sadie (Avery) who is an occultist.

MARIAN ANDERSON
Narrator: Avery Brooks*
Tech Info: color/sound/60 min.   Type: Television Documentary
Date: 1991
Company: WETA
Annotation: The life of legendary black opera singer Anderson is chronicled from her early appearances in Philadelphia to concerts in America and Europe.

MARIE

Alternate: Marie, A True Story
Cast: Morgan Freeman*, Sissy Spacek, Jeff Daniels, Keith Szarabajka, Lisa Banes, Fred Thompson
Director: Roger Donaldson
Executive Producer: Elliot Schick
Music by: Francis Lai
Producer: Frank Capra Jr., Elliot Schick
Screenwriter: John Briley
Tech Info: color/sound/112 min.   Type: Dramatic Feature
Date: 1985   Origin: USA
Company: DEG
Distributors/Format: MGM/UA Home Video (1/2")
Annotation: Based on real events, Marie Ragghianti (Spacek) becomes Chair of the Tennessee Parole Board, only to be pressured by the Governor and other officials to release certain well-paying criminals. Marie is fired and goes to court to get her job and dignity back. Freeman plays Charles Traughber.

MARKED FOR DEATH

Cast: Keith David*, Basil Wallace*, Thomas Lee Wright*, Victor Romero Evans*, Michael Ralph*, Noel L. Walcott III*, Prince I. Joe*, Jeffrey Anderson*, Rita Verreds*, Steven Seagal, Jeanna Pacula
Director: Dwight H. Little
Music Performer: Jimmy Cliff*, Peter Tosh*, James Newton Howard*, Shabba Ranks*, Papa Juggs *, Tone-Loc *,
Screenwriter: Mark Victor, Michael Grais
Tech Info: color/sound/93 min.   Type: Dramatic Feature
Date: 1990   Origin: USA
Company: Victor and Grais
Distributors/Format: Fox Home Video (1/2")
Annotation: Hatcher (Seagal) quits the DEA and comes home to a Chicago suburb to find the town overrun with Jamaican drug dealers. He looks up his Vietnam buddy, Max (David), whose family is suffering from the influx of crack. Together they go after the drug posse led by Screwface (Wallace). Evans plays Nesta, Ralph is Monkey (posse members), and Wright is Charles, a Jamaican DEA agent.

MARTHA AND ETHEL

Director: Joseph Friedman, Jyll Johnstone
Narrator: Jyll Johnstone, Barbara Ettinger
Producer: Jyll Johnstone, Barbara Ettinger
Speaker: Ethel Edwards*, Martha Kneifel
Tech Info: mixed/sound/80 min.   Type: Documentary Feature
Date: 1994   Origin: USA
Company: Sony Picture Classics
Distributors/Format: Facets Multimedia, Inc. (1/2")
Annotation: Two invincible, 80-year-old nannies offer a portrait of American life in this documentary. Spanning four decades and crossing the barriers of race, class and sex, the film celebrates the legacies of love and discipline these women have created, as seen through the eyes of the filmmaker, who herself was brought up by the two nannies profiled.

MARTIN LUTHER KING - SPEECHES
Speaker: Martin Luther King Jr.*
Tech Info: bw/sound/60 min.   Type: Documentary Feature
Date: 1988   Origin: USA
Studio: Independent
Distributors/Format: Evergreen (1/2")
Annotation: The film follows King from his early days as a young pastor in Montgomery, to the march on Washington, to the final prophetic speech in Memphis just before his assassination.

MARTIN LUTHER KING COMMEMORATIVE COLLECTION
Music Performer: Bernice Johnson Reagon*, Martin Luther King Coalition Chorale
Speaker: Nathaniel R. Jones*, K.Z. Smith*, Orlando B. Yates*, Paula Jackson*, Frank Allison, David Howard, Arthur S. Green, William H. Cross, Dwight Tillery
Tech Info: mixed/sound/115 min.   Type: Documentary Feature
Date: 1993   Origin: USA
Studio: Independent
Distributors/Format: Facets Multimedia, Inc. (1/2"), Filmic Archives (1/2")
Annotation: The film presents the Martin Luther King, Jr. commemorative program held in Cincinnati, on January 18, 1993, and featuring speaker Nathaniel R. Jones.

MARTIN LUTHER KING, JR.
Series: Black Americans of Achievement Video Collection
Director: Rhonda Fabian, Jerry Baber, Keith Smith
Executive Producer: Andrew Schlessinger
Narrator: Michael Logan
Producer: Rhonda Fabian, Jerry Baber, Andrew Schlessinger
Tech Info: mixed/sound/30 min.   Type: Documentary Short
Date: 1992   Origin: USA
Studio: Independent
Company: Schlessinger Video Productions
Distributors/Format: Filmic Archives (1/2")
Annotation: The documentary examines the life of the Civil Rights leader who helped American Blacks win many battles for equal rights.

MARTIN LUTHER KING: "I HAVE A DREAM"
Speaker: Martin Luther King Jr.*
Tech Info: bw/sound/25 min.   Type: Documentary Short
Date: 1986   Origin: USA
Studio: Independent
Distributors/Format: Third World Newsreel (1/2"), Filmic Archives (1/2")
Archives/Format: IUB - BFC/A (1/2")
Annotation: King delivers his powerful, "I Have A Dream" speech to 200,000 civil rights marchers at the Lincoln Memorial in August of 1963.

MARVIN AND TIGE
Cast: Billy Dee Williams*, Fay Hauser*, Denise Nicholas-Hill*, Gibran Brown*, John Cassavetes
Director: Eric Weston
Executive Producer: Wanda Dell, Frank Menke
Music by: Patrick Williams
Producer: Wanda Dell, Wanda Dell, Frank Menke

Screenwriter: Wanda Dell, Eric Weston
Storywriter: Frankcina Glass
Tech Info: color/sound/104 min.   Type: Dramatic Feature
Date: 1983   Origin: USA
Company: Marvin
Distributors/Format: Major Video Concepts, Inc. (1/2")
Annotation: Tige Jackson (Brown) is an 11-year-old street kid, left alone after his
mother (Nicholas-Hill) dies. The child is rescued from suicide by a middle-aged
white man, Marvin Stewart (Cassavetes) and a bond gradually forms between them.
When Tige becomes ill, Marvin discovers that the boy's father (Williams) is unwilling
to assume responsibility for his son.

MARY LOU WILLIAMS: MUSIC ON MY MIND
Director: Joanne Burke*
Narrator: Roberta Flack*
Speaker: Mary Lou Williams*, John "Dizzy" Gillespie*, Buddy Tate
Tech Info: color/sound/60 min.   Type: Documentary Feature
Date: 1990   Origin: USA
Studio: Independent
Distributors/Format: Media Artists/New Works (1/2"), Women Make Movies, Inc.
(16mm; 1/2")
Annotation: Pioneering African American composer-arranger-pianist Williams is one
of the most remarkable figures in the history of jazz. At the height of her career, she
dropped out of music to help drug-addicted musicians in Harlem, making a
triumphant comeback 15 years later.

MASK
Cast: Marsha Warfield*, Estelle Getty, Eric Stoltz, Richard Dysart, Sam Elliott, Cher
Director: Peter Bogdanovich
Producer: Martin Starger, Howard Alston
Screenwriter: Anna Hamilton Phelan
Storywriter: Rocky Dennis
Tech Info: color/sound/120 min.   Type: Dramatic Feature
Date: 1985   Origin: USA
Company: Universal
Distributors/Format: Universal Home Video (1/2")
Annotation: Rocky Dennis (Stoltz) has an incurable disease that causes calcium to
amass in his head. His mother, Rusty (Cher), turns to drugs to deal with her son's
imminent death. Warfield is Rocky's homeroom teacher.

MASSACHUSETTS 54TH COLORED INFANTRY, THE
Director: Jacqueline Shearer*
Narrator: Morgan Freeman*, David G. McCullough
Producer: Jacqueline Shearer*
Tech Info: mixed/sound/58 min.   Type: Documentary Feature
Date: 1991   Origin: USA
Company: WGBH, Boston
Distributors/Format: Filmic Archives (1/2")
Archives/Format: IUB - BFC/A; IUB - AAAMC (1/2")
Annotation: Shearer documents the story of the first officially sanctioned regiment of
Northern black soldiers formed in Boston during the Civil War. Their heroism is
obvious in the details she depicts about their battle at Fort Wagner.

MATEWAN
Cast: James Earl Jones*, Mary McDonnell, Chris Cooper, Will Oldham
Director: John Sayles
Producer: Peggy Rajski, Maggie Renzi
Screenwriter: John Sayles
Tech Info: color/sound/132 min.   Type: Dramatic Feature
Date: 1987   Origin: USA
Company: Cinecom, Goldcrest, Red Dog Films
Annotation: A union organizer arrives in the coal mining town of Matewan entirely owned by an exploitative coal company. When white miners strike for improved working conditions and pay, black men and Italian immigrants are brought in as scabs. Jones plays Fewclothes, the unofficial leader of the black miners.

MAUSOLEUM
Cast: La Wanda Page*, Marjoe Gortner, Bobbie Bresee, Norman Burton
Director: Michael Dugan
Executive Producer: Jerry Zimmerman, Jerry Franzese
Music by: Jaime Mendoza-Nava
Producer: Robert Barich, Robert Madero, Jerry Zimmerman, Jerry Franzese
Screenwriter: Robert Barich, Robert Madero
Storywriter: Katherine Rosenwink
Tech Info: color/sound/96 min.   Type: Dramatic Feature
Date: 1983   Origin: USA
Company: Western
Distributors/Format: Motion Picture Marketing (16mm)
Annotation: Susan (Bresee) is the eldest daughter in a bloodline afflicted with an ancient curse. She takes a series of lovers and kills them in a variety of gory ways. Page is featured as Elsie.

MAXIMUM OVERDRIVE
Cast: Giancarlo Esposito*, Frankie Faison*, Emilio Estevez, Pat Hingle, Laura Harrington
Director: Stephen King
Executive Producer: Mel Pearl, Don Levin
Music by: AC/DC , Richard Wagner
Producer: Mel Pearl, Don Levin, Martha Schumacher
Screenwriter: Stephen King
Tech Info: color/sound/97 min.   Type: Dramatic Feature
Date: 1986   Origin: USA
Company: DEG
Distributors/Format: DEG (16mm)
Annotation: A comet passes near Earth and causes machines to turn into mad killers. Faison plays Handy and Esposito is the video player.

MAXINE SULLIVAN: LOVE TO BE IN LOVE
Director: Greta Schiller
Music Performer: Louis Armstrong*, Maxine Sullivan
Producer: The Cinema Guild
Speaker: Maxine Sullivan
Tech Info: color/sound/48 min.   Type: Documentary Short

Date: 1990
Studio: Independent
Annotation: Sullivan, legendary black vocalist, rose from poverty to become one of the foremost female performers in America. Vintage clips of performances with Armstrong and other musicians accompany photographs and testimonies.

ME AND HIM

Alternate: Ich und Er
Cast: Charlaine Woodard*, David Alan Grier*, Samuel E. Wright*, Toukie A. Smith*, Craig T. Nelson, Ellen Greene, Griffin Dunne
Director: Doris Dorrie
Music by: Klaus Doldinger
Producer: Bernd Eichinger
Screenwriter: Warren Leight, Doris Dorrie, Michael Juncker
Tech Info: color/sound/90 min.   Type: Comedy Feature
Date: 1990   Origin: West Germany
Company: Neue Constantin
Distributors/Format: Columbia Pictures (16mm)
Annotation: Bert Uttanzi (Dunne) is an architect plagued by his talking penis. Smith plays Deli-Delilah; Grier plays Peter Conklin; Wright and Woodard have unacknowledged roles.

MEAN DOG BLUES

Cast: Scatman Crothers*, Felton Perry*, George Kennedy, Kay Lenz, Gregg Henry
Director: Mel Stuart
Music by: Fred Karlin
Producer: Charles A. Pratt, George Lefferts
Screenwriter: George Lefferts
Tech Info: color/sound/108 min.   Type: Dramatic Feature
Date: 1978   Origin: USA
Company: Crosby
Distributors/Format: AIP Home Video (1/2")
Annotation: Paul Ramsey (Henry), a country-western musician, is mistakenly implicated in a crime and sentenced to five years on the chain gang. Crothers plays Mudcat and Perry is Jake Turner.

MEDIA ASSASSIN

Director: Art Jones*
Tech Info: color/sound/17 min.   Type: Experimental Short
Date: 1989   Origin: USA
Studio: Independent
Distributors/Format: Third World Newsreel (1/2")
Annotation: Adopting a politically analysis of hip-hop culture, Jones combines rap riffs, interviews with writers, and multilayered images of street culture.

MEET THE APPLEGATES

Cast: Roger Aaron Brown*, Stockard Channing, Dabney Coleman, Ed Begley Jr., Cami Cooper
Director: Michael Lehmann
Executive Producer: Steve White*, Christopher Webster
Music by: David Newman
Producer: Steve White*, Christopher Webster, Denise DiNovi

Screenwriter: Michael Lehmann, Redbeard Simmons
Tech Info: color/sound/82 min.   Type: Comedy Feature
Date: 1991   Origin: USA
Company: New World/Trans Atlantic Pictures, Cinemarque Ent.
Distributors/Format: Triton Home Video (1/2")
Annotation: The Applegate family came from the Brazilian rain forest. They are actually giant Cocorada bugs who transform themselves into human to try to annihilate mankind and save the earth for bugs. Brown plays Sheriff Heidegger.

MEMORIES OF DUKE

Director: Gary Keys
Music Performer: Duke Ellington*, Cootie Williams*, Russell Procope*, Duke Ellington Band *
Producer: Gary Keys
Speaker: Cootie Williams*, Russell Procope*
Tech Info: color/sound/85 min.   Type: Musical Feature
Date: 1984   Origin: Mexico
Company: Warner Bros., A*Vision Entertainment, Atlantic
Annotation: Shot at Mexico City's Palacio de Belles Artes as well as in Guadalajara, the film features interviews with Williams and Procope and captures Ellington and his band on a 1968 Mexican tour. Some of the songs included are: "Satin Doll," "Creole Love Call," "Black and Tan Fantasy," "Mexican Suite," "I Got it Bad and that Ain't Good," "Mood Indigo," "Take the A train," "Sophisticated Lady," and "Do Nothing 'til You Hear from Me."

MEN AT WORK

Cast: Keith David*, Sy Richardson*, Leslie Hope, Charlie Sheen, Darrell Larson, Emilio Estevez, Sean Cameron, John Getz
Director: Emilio Estevez
Executive Producer: Irwin Yablans, Moshe Diamant
Music by: Stewart Copeland
Producer: Irwin Yablans, Barbara Sterdahl, Moshe Diamant, Cassian Elwes
Screenwriter: Emilio Estevez
Tech Info: color/sound/98 min.   Type: Comedy Feature
Date: 1990   Origin: USA
Company: Epic-Elwes-Euphoria
Distributors/Format: Epic Home Video (1/2"), RCA/Columbia Pictures Home Video (1/2")
Annotation: When Louis Freuders (David) is hired on the job to supervise two garbage collectors, Carl Taylor (Sheen) and James St. James (Estevez), the friction among the three results in explosive action, until they find a dead politician in the garbage. Then the three unite against police and criminals to solve the murder.

MENACE II SOCIETY

Cast: Samuel L. Jackson*, Bill Duke*, Marilyn Coleman*, Arnold Johnson*, Khandi Alexander*, Glenn Plummer*, Charles S. Dutton*, Tyrin Turner*, Jada Pinkett*, Larenz Tate*, M.C. Eight *, Vonte Sweet*
Director: Allen Hughes*, Albert Hughes*, Lisa Rinzler
Executive Producer: Kevin Morton
Music by: QD III
Producer: Darin Scott*, Allen Hughes*, Albert Hughes*, Tyger Williams*, Kevin Morton

Screenwriter: Tyger Williams*
Storywriter: Allen Hughes*, Albert Hughes*, Tyger Williams*
Tech Info: color/sound/104 min.   Type: Dramatic Feature
Date: 1993   Origin: USA
Company: New Line Cinema
Distributors/Format: Facets Multimedia, Inc. (1/2"), New Line Cinema Home Video
(1/2")
Archives/Format: IUB - BFC/A (1/2")
Annotation: The big-screen debut of the 21-year-old Hughes brothers captures the
lives of black teens, Caine (Turner), O-Dog (Tate) and Sherrif (Sweet) trying to
survive inner-city life. Plummer plays Purnell; Jackson and Alexander play Turner's
drug addicted parents.

MESSENGER, THE
Cast: Sandy Cummings*, Val Avery*, Fred Williamson*, Jimmy/James Spinks*,
Magic Wand*, Vince Townsend*, Cameron Mitchell, Jerry Jones, Joe Spinell,
Michael Dante
Director: Fred Williamson*, Jerry Jones
Executive Producer: Fred Williamson*, Pier Luigi Ciriali
Music by: William Stuckey
Producer: Fred Williamson*, Jerry Jones, Pier Luigi Ciriali
Screenwriter: Brian Johnson, Conghita Lee, Anthony Wisdom
Storywriter: Fred Williamson*
Tech Info: color/sound/95 min.   Type: Dramatic Feature
Date: 1986   Origin: USA
Studio: Realta Cinematografia
Company: Management Group Associates (MGA) and Hugh Pike Jr
Distributors/Format: Orion Home Video (1/2")
Annotation: Sabastian "Jake" Turner (Williamson), a famous catburglar just released
from prison in Italy, finds out that his wife, Sabrina (Cummings), is addicted to
cocaine. When she is gunned down in front of him, he vows to find her killers and
he starts by going back to his roots in Chicago. He enlists Benny (Spinks), a cook,
to supply him with weapons and transportation. Wand plays Sweet Louie, a drug
dealer connected to Sabrina.

METEOR MAN, THE
Cast: Samuel L. Jackson*, James Earl Jones*, Bill Cosby*, Robert Townsend*,
Sinbad *, Robert Guillaume*, Charlaine Woodard*, Marilyn Coleman*, John
Witherspoon*, Don Cheadle*, Roy Fegan*, Luther Vandross*, Marla Gibbs*, Tommy
Hicks*, Big Daddy Kane*, Eddie Griffin*, Another Bad Creation *, Jenifer Lewis*, Stu
Gilliam*, Cynthia Belgrave*, Bobby McGee*, Asia Dosreis*, Wallace Shawn
Director: Robert Townsend*
Music Performer: Luther Vandross*, Another Bad Creation *, Naughty by Nature *,
Big Daddy Kane *, Cypress Hill
Music by: Cliff Eidelman
Producer: Loretha C. Jones
Storywriter: Robert Townsend*
Tech Info: color/sound/100 min.   Type: Comedy Feature

Date: 1993   Origin: USA
Company: Tinsel Townsend Productions, MGM
Distributors/Format: MGM Home Video (1/2")
Annotation: Jefferson Reed (Townsend), a substitute teacher, finds himself with supernatural powers after he is hit by a meteor. As the Meteor Man, he uses his new found power to bring peace to his crime ridden neighborhood and to learn a few valuable life lessons along the way. Gibbs and Guillaume play Reed's parents; Jones is Mr. Moses; Jackson is Dre, and Cosby plays Marvin, a local bum.

MIDNIGHT EDITION
Cast: Ji-Tu Cumbuka*, Will Patton, Clare Wren, Michael DeLuise, Judson Vaughn
Director: Howard Libov
Music by: Murray Attaway
Producer: Jonathan Cordish, Ehud Epstein, Howard Libov
Screenwriter: Yuri Zeltser, Howard Libov, Michael Stewart
Tech Info: color/sound/98 min.   Type: Dramatic Feature
Date: 1994   Origin: USA
Company: Libov Epstein Productions
Distributors/Format: Shapiro Glickenhaus Entertainment (16mm)
Annotation: Small-town journalist Jack Travers (Patton) gets the story of a lifetime when a young drifter slaughters an entire local farm family and grants Travers the only interviews. Cumbuka plays Reginald Brown.

MIDNIGHT RAMBLE
Cast: Paul Robeson*
Director: Pearl Bowser*, Bestor Cram*
Music by: Caleb Sampson*
Producer: Pamela A. Thomas*, Bestor Cram*
Screenwriter: Clyde Taylor*
Speaker: Pearl Bowser*, Toni Cade Bambara*
Tech Info: color/sound/60 min.   Type: Documentary Feature
Date: 1994   Origin: USA
Company: WGBH-TV Boston
Annotation: The documentary traces the history of race movies, between WWI and WWII, when black producers, directors and actors turned out hundreds of films whose characters departed from the eye-ball rolling, shuffling and comically black. Clips include works from Oscar Micheaux.

MIDNIGHT RUN
Cast: Yaphet Kotto*, Charles Grodin, Robert De Niro
Director: Martin Brest, John Alonzo
Producer: Martin Brest
Storywriter: George Gallo
Tech Info: color/sound/125 min.   Type: Dramatic Feature
Date: 1988   Origin: USA
Company: Universal
Distributors/Format: MCA Home Video (1/2")
Annotation: Jack Walsh (De Niro) is a tough ex-policeman turned bounty hunter. Jonathan "Duke" (Grodin) is a sensitive accountant who embezzled $15 million from the Mob, gave it to charity and then jumped bail. Jack will get $100,000 if he can deliver "Duke" from New York to Los Angeles on time and alive. Kotto plays F.B.I. agent Alonzo Mosley.

MIGHTY DUCKS, THE
Cast: Brandon Adams*, Emilio Estevez, Joss Ackland, Lane Smith, Heidi Kling, Josef Sommer
Director: Stephen Herek
Music by: David Newman
Producer: Jon Avnet, Jordan Kerner
Screenwriter: Steven Brill, Brian Hohlfield
Tech Info: color/sound/104 min.   Type: Comedy Feature
Date: 1992   Origin: USA
Company: Bombay Films, Avent/Kerner Company, Walt Disney
Distributors/Format: Buena Vista Home Video (1/2"), Filmic Archives (1/2")
Annotation: Gordon Bombay (Estevez) is forced to coach a kid's hockey team as part of his community service following his driving under the influence conviction. Even though he initially hates kids and hockey, Bombay trains the team well and they are eventually victorious. Adams portrays Jesse Hall, the African American Duck.

MIGHTY QUINN, THE
Cast: Denzel Washington*, Esther Rolle*, Robert Townsend*, Sheryl Lee Ralph*, Arthur/Art Evans*, Tyra Ferrell*, Cedella Marley*, Marie McDonald*, Dave Ellis*, Ronald Goshop*, Kenneth Casey*, Sharon Marley Prendergast*, Dallas Anderson*, Calvin Mitchell*, Dennis Titus*, Alex Colon
Director: Carl Schenkel
Executive Producer: Dale Pollock, Gil Friesen
Music by: Anne Dudley, David Anderle
Producer: Dale Pollock, Gil Friesen, Sandy Lieberson, Marion Hunt, Ed Elbert
Screenwriter: Hampton Fancher
Storywriter: A.H.Z. Carr*
Tech Info: color/sound/98 min.   Type: Dramatic Feature
Date: 1989   Origin: USA
Company: A&M
Distributors/Format: MGM/UA Home Video (1/2")
Annotation: Xavier Quinn (Washington) is the police chief of a small island nation. En route to investigate the murder of a prominent businessman, he encounters boyhood friend Maubee (Townsend). At the murder scene, Quinn learns Maubee is the prime suspect. Film also features Ralph as Quinn's wife, Rolle as Ubu Pearl and Evans as Jump.

MIKE'S MURDER
Cast: Paul Winfield*, Darrell Larson, Debra Winger, Mark Keyloun
Director: James Bridges
Executive Producer: Kim Kurumada
Music Performer: John Barry
Music by: John Barry
Screenwriter: James Bridges
Storywriter: James Bridges
Tech Info: color/sound/110 min.   Type: Dramatic Feature

Date: 1984   Origin: USA
Company: Ladd Company
Distributors/Format: Warner Bros. Home Video, Inc. (1/2")
Annotation: Phillip (Winfield) is a famous musician who was once in love with Mike (Keyloun). After Mike is murdered, Betty (Winger), who was also in love with Mike, enlists Phillip's help in order to solve the mystery of Mike's death.

MILES OF SMILES, YEARS OF STRUGGLES
Alternate: The Untold Story of the Black Pullman Porter
Director: Paul Wagner, Jack Santino, John Hiller, John Hiller
Narrator: Rosina Tucker*
Producer: Paul Wagner, Jack Santino
Speaker: A. Philip Randolph*
Tech Info: mixed/sound/60 min.   Type: Documentary Feature
Date: 1982   Origin: USA
Studio: Independent
Company: California Newsreel
Distributors/Format: California Newsreel (1/2")
Archives/Format: IUB - BFC/A; IUB - AV (16mm; 16mm, 1/2")
Annotation: The film chronicles the organizing of the first black trade union, the Brotherhood of Sleeping Car Porters. It provides an in-depth account of African American working life between the Civil War and World War II.

MILLION DOLLAR MYSTERY
Cast: Gail Neely*, Eddie Deezen, Wendy Sherman, Rick Overton, Mona Lyden
Executive Producer: Richard Fleischer
Music by: Al Gorgoni
Producer: Richard Fleischer, Stephen Kesten
Screenwriter: Miguel Tejada-Flores, Tim Metcalfe, Rudy DeLuca
Tech Info: color/sound/95 min.   Type: Comedy Feature
Date: 1987   Origin: USA
Company: DEG
Annotation: Sidney Preston (Bosley), a government official, scammed $4 million from Libya and hid the money in four places. Preston has a heart attack, but before he dies, he divulges clues to the money's whereabouts. Neely plays Officer Gretchen.

MINNIE THE MOOCHER & MANY MANY MORE
Director: Manny Pittson
Host: Cab Calloway*
Music Performer: Cab Calloway*
Music by: Cab Calloway*
Producer: Manny Pittson
Tech Info: mixed/sound/55 min.   Type: Documentary Feature
Date: 1981   Origin: USA
Archives/Format: IUB - BFC/A; IUB - AAAMC (16mm; 1/2")
Annotation: Narrated by Calloway, the film tours Harlem night clubs of the 1930s and 1940s, where the careers of such stars as Duke Ellington, Louis Armstrong, Fats Waller, Count Basie and Bill Robinson were developed. It includes clips of their performances.

MISS FIRECRACKER
Cast: Alfre Woodard*, Mary Steenburgen, Tim Robbins, Holly Hunter
Director: Thomas Schlamme
Executive Producer: Lewis M. Allen, Ross Milloy
Music by: David Mansfield, Homer Denison
Producer: Fred Berner, Lewis M. Allen, Ross Milloy
Screenwriter: Beth Henley
Storywriter: Beth Henley
Tech Info: color/sound/102 min.   Type: Comedy Feature
Date: 1989   Origin: USA
Company: Corsair
Annotation: Carnelle Scott (Hunter) hopes to win the Miss Firecracker Contest in Yazoo City, Mississippi. Woodard plays Popeye Jackson.

MISS FLUCI MOSES
Director: Alile Sharon Larkin*
Music by: Darryl Munyungo Jackson*
Narrator: Peter Miller
Producer: Alile Sharon Larkin*
Speaker: Olivia Frances Williams*, Beryl Jones*, Lillian Lehman*, Julia *, Norman Alexander Gibbs*, Peter Miller
Tech Info: mixed/sound/22 min.   Type: Documentary Short
Date: 1987   Origin: USA
Company: Alile Productions
Distributors/Format: Women Make Movies, Inc. (16mm; 1/2")
Archives/Format: IUB - BFC/A (1/2")
Annotation: The film uses interviews and photographs to tell the story of librarian and poet Moses, who is herself on-camera most of the time. She and other readers relate the story of black life in America through her and other readers' poems.

MISSION OF JUSTICE
Cast: Tony Burton*, Jeff Wincott, Brigitte Nielsen
Director: Steve Barnett
Executive Producer: Robert W. Mann
Producer: Pierre David, Kurt Anderson, Robert W. Mann
Screenwriter: George Saunders, John Bryant Hedberg
Storywriter: David Pierre
Tech Info: color/sound/95 min.   Type: Dramatic Feature
Date: 1992   Origin: USA
Company: Image Organization, Westwind Productions
Distributors/Format: Republic Pictures Home Video (1/2")
Annotation: Tough cop Kurt Harris (Wincott) seeks the murderer of his friend Cedric Williams (Burton), a former boxing champ.

MISSISSIPPI BLUES
Director: Bertrand Tavernier, Robert Parrish
Speaker: Reverend Moore*, Roosevelt Barnes, Joe Cooper, Hayward Mills
Tech Info: mixed/sound/92 min.   Type: Documentary Feature

Date: 1983   Origin: France, USA
Studio: Independent
Company: Corinth Films
Distributors/Format: Kino International Corp. (1/2"), MPI Home Video (1/2")
Archives/Format: IUB - BFC/A (1/2")
Annotation: The unique folk music of the deep South and the difficult lifestyle that cultivated it are explored in this film by two famous directors.

MISSISSIPPI BURNING

Cast: Badja Djola*, Darius McCrary*, Frankie Faison*, Ralnardo Davis*, Kevin Dunn*, Lou Walker*, Billie Jean Young*, Lannie Spann McBride*, Bernice Poindexter*, James Lloyd*, Barbara Gibson*, Willem Dafoe, Gene Hackman, Frederick Zollo, Robert F. Colesberry
Director: Alan Parker
Music Performer: Mahalia Jackson*, Ray Parker Jr.*
Music by: Trevor Jones
Producer: Frederick Zollo, Robert F. Colesberry
Screenwriter: Chris Gerolmo
Tech Info: color/sound/125 min.   Type: Dramatic Feature
Date: 1988   Origin: USA
Company: Frederick Zollo
Distributors/Format: Orion Home Video (1/2"), Filmic Archives (1/2")
Archives/Format: IUB - BFC/A (1/2")
Annotation: Inspired by the actual event of three murdered civil rights workers, the film focuses on FBI agents Anderson (Hackman) and Ward (Dafoe) as they investigate the murders. Police officers are actually KKK members who burn black property, harass and kill black citizens. Djola plays Agent Bird; Faison, the church pastor.

MISSISSIPPI MASALA

Cast: Denzel Washington*, Joe Seneca*, Charles S. Dutton*, Sarita Choudhury, Roshan Seth
Director: Mira Nair, Ed Lachman
Executive Producer: Cherie Rodgers
Music by: L. Subramaniam
Producer: Michael Nozik, Mira Nair, Cherie Rodgers
Screenwriter: Sooni Taraporevala
Tech Info: color/sound/117 min.   Type: Dramatic Feature
Date: 1991   Origin: USA
Company: Samuel Goldwyn
Distributors/Format: Columbia/TriStar Pictures (35mm; 1/2")
Annotation: Demetrius (Washington), a southern businessman falls in love with Mina (Choudhury), an Indian immigrant whose family was expelled from Uganda during the reign of dictator Idi Amin. Like the colorful Indian dish "Masala," Mina is a mix of cultures. When she and Demetrius fall in love, nothing in her past prepares them for the family outrage they face.

MISSISSIPPI MASS CHOIR, THE

Music Performer: Mississippi Mass Choir *
Tech Info: color/sound/120 min.   Type: Concert Feature
Date: 1989   Origin: USA
Studio: Independent
Annotation: The choir performs such hits at: "All in His Hands," "Call Him Up," "I Just Can't Tell You (How Good He's Been)," "I'm Pressing On," "Having You There," "Lord, We Thank You," "Until He Comes," "The Birds," "We Shall Meet Again" and "Near the Cross."

MISSISSIPPI TRIANGLE

Director: Christine Choy, Worth Long, Allen Siegel
Music by: Lee Ray*
Producer: Worth Long
Tech Info: color/sound/110 min.   Type: Documentary Feature
Date: 1984   Origin: USA
Company: Allan Siegel, Film News Now Foundation
Distributors/Format: Third World Newsreel (1/2")
Annotation: The film explores ethnic relations among Chinese, African Americans, and whites in the Mississippi Delta. It focuses on the little known history of the Chinese community in this area using historical footage and interviews with Delta residents.

MISSISSIPPI: IS THIS AMERICA? - EPISODE 5

Series: Eyes On The Prize
Executive Producer: Henry Hampton*
Narrator: Julian Bond*
Producer: Orlando Bagwell*, Henry Hampton*
Speaker: Ella Baker*, Bob Moses*, Roy Wilkins*, Myrlie Evers*, Medgar Evers*, Fannie Lou Hammer*, Unita Blackwell*, Lawrence Guyot*, Robert L.T. Smith*, Dave Dennis*, Jim Forman*, Victoria J. Gray*, Victoria Gray-Adams*, William J. Simmons, Hodding Carter III, Allard Lowenstein, Peter Orris, Tom P. Brady, J. Edgar Hoover, Joseph L. Raugh Jr., Hubert Humphrey, Walter Mondale
Tech Info: mixed/sound/57 min.   Type: Television Documentary
Date: 1986   Origin: USA
Company: Blackside, Inc.
Distributors/Format: PBS Video (16mm; 1/2")
Archives/Format: IUB - AAAMC (1/2")
Annotation: This segment records the rampant white violence that prevailed throughout the Civil Rights Movement. When Blacks demonstrated for voting rights in Mississippi, Medgar Evers was murdered. As a result the movement declared the hot months of 1964 as Freedom Summer, concentrating on integration in Mississippi. The summer climaxed in one triple murder of Chaney, Goodman, and Schwerner.

MISTRESS

Cast: Sheryl Lee Ralph*, Danny Aiello, Eli Wallach, Robert De Niro, Robert Wuhl, Laurie Metcalf
Director: Barry Primus
Executive Producer: Ruth Charny
Music by: Galt MacDermot

Producer: Robert De Niro, Meir Teper, Ruth Charny
Screenwriter: J.F. Lawton*, Barry Primus
Storywriter: Barry Primus
Tech Info: color/sound/108 min.   Type: Dramatic Feature
Date: 1992   Origin: USA
Company: Mistress Productions, et al.
Distributors/Format: Rainbow Releasing/Tribeca Productions (1/2")
Annotation: A struggling director (Wuhl) has the opportunity to shoot his screenplay but only if he agrees to find parts for the girlfriends of his financial backers (Wallach, Aiello and De Niro). Ralph plays De Niro's girlfriend, Beverly Dumont.

MO' BETTER BLUES

Cast: Bill Nunn*, Denzel Washington*, Robin Harris*, Spike Lee*, Cynda Williams*, Joie Lee*, Giancarlo Esposito*, Rev. Herbert Daughtry*, Wesley Snipes*, Dick Anthony Williams*, Charles Q. Murphy*, John Turturro, Nicholas Turturro
Director: Spike Lee*
Music Performer: Terence Blanchard*, Branford Marsalis*
Music by: Bill Lee*
Producer: Spike Lee*, Monty Ross
Screenwriter: Spike Lee*
Tech Info: color/sound/120 min.   Type: Musical Feature
Date: 1990   Origin: USA
Company: 40 Acres and a Mule Film Works, Universal
Distributors/Format: Universal Home Video (1/2")
Archives/Format: IUB - BFC/A (1/2")
Annotation: The first fiction film on black music by a black director since Gordon Parks, Sr.'s LEADBELLY (1976). Lee's film stars Washington as Bleak, a rising New York trumpeter trapped between the affections of two women, played by Joie Lee and Williams. He resists a commitment to either. Ernest Dickerson is the cinematographer.

MO' MONEY

Cast: Damon Wayans*, Stacey Dash*, Jimmy/James Spinks*, Salli Richardson*, Marlon Wayans*, Bernie Mac*, Almayvonne Wayans*, Evan Lionel Smith*, Gordon McClure*, Joe Santos, John Diehl
Director: Peter MacDonald, Don Burgess
Executive Producer: Damon Wayans*, Eric L. Gold
Music by: Jay Gruska
Producer: Damon Wayans*, Eric L. Gold, Michael Rachmil
Screenwriter: Damon Wayans*
Tech Info: color/sound/98 min.   Type: Comedy Feature
Date: 1992   Origin: USA
Company: Wife and Kids Productions, Columbia
Distributors/Format: Columbia Pictures Home Video (1/2")
Annotation: Johnny and Seymour Stewart (Damon and Marlon Wayans) are streetwise Brooklynites looking to make an illegal buck. Johnny decides to go straight and meets Amber Evans (Dash), an employee at Dynasty Credit Card Services. However, he and Seymour eventually get involved in a shopping spree with a stolen credit card. Smith plays Lt. Mills.

MODERN PROBLEMS

Cast: Nell Carter*, Chevy Chase, Dabney Coleman, Patti D'Arbanville, Mary Kay
Place, Brian Doyle-Murray
Director: Ken Shapiro
Executive Producer: Douglas C. Kenney
Music Performer: Dominic Fortiere
Music by: Dominic Fortiere
Producer: Alan Greisman, Michael Shamberg, Douglas C. Kenney
Screenwriter: Ken Shapiro, Tom Sherohman, Arthur Sellers
Tech Info: color/sound/93 min.   Type: Comedy Feature
Date: 1981   Origin: USA
Company: Shamberg-Greisman
Distributors/Format: Fox Home Video (1/2")
Annotation: Carter plays Dorita, a Haitian woman working as a maid for Max's
(Chase) friend Brian (Doyle-Murray). Supposedly an expert in Voodoo, Dorita tries
to help Max who has been endowed with magical power after nuclear waste spills on
him. When Max loses his power through a bolt of lightning which also hits Dorita,
she is content because she can do her job without lifting a finger.

MONA LISA

Cast: Cathy Tyson*, Stephen Persaud*, Michael Caine, Bob Hoskins, Kate Hardie
Director: Neil Jordan
Executive Producer: George Harrison, Denis O'Brien
Music by: Michael Kamen
Producer: Patrick Cassavetti, George Harrison, Denis O'Brien, Stephen Woolley
Screenwriter: Neil Jordan, David Leland
Tech Info: color/sound/104 min.   Type: Dramatic Feature
Date: 1986   Origin: Great Britain
Company: Palace
Distributors/Format: Island Home Video (1/2"), Handmade Home Video (1/2")
Annotation: George (Hoskins) has recently been released from prison only to find
that his mob boss wants him to chauffeur high-class call girl Simone (Tyson) around
London. Despite his initial dislike, George falls in love with Simone only to find out
she has a lover, Cathy (Hardie). Persaud is the "black youth."

MONEY FOR NOTHING

Cast: Frankie Faison*, Michael Rapaport, Debi Mazar, Michael Madsen, John
Cusack, Benicio Del Toro
Director: Ramon Menendez
Executive Producer: David Permut, Gordon Freedman, Matthew Tolmach
Music by: Craig Safan
Producer: Tom Musca, David Permut, Gordon Freedman, Matthew Tolmach
Screenwriter: Carol Sobieski, Tom Musca, Ramon Menendez
Tech Info: color/sound/100 min.   Type: Dramatic Feature
Date: 1993   Origin: USA
Company: Set for Life Productions
Distributors/Format: Buena Vista Home Video (1/2")
Annotation: Joey Coyle (Cusack) finds a bag of cash that has fallen off an armored
car. Instead of returning it, Joey entrusts the money to a small-time hood (Del Toro)
who launders it through the Mafia. Faison plays Madigan.

MONEY PIT, THE
Cast: Afemo Omilani*, Frankie Faison*, Tom Hanks, Maureen Stapleton, Shelley Long, Alexander Godunov
Director: Richard Benjamin
Executive Producer: Steven Spielberg, David Giler, Kathleen Kennedy
Music by: Michel Colombier, Johann Sebastian Bach
Producer: Art Levinson, Steven Spielberg, David Giler, Frank Marshall, Kathleen Kennedy, Kathleen Kennedy
Screenwriter: David Giler
Tech Info: color/sound/91 min.   Type: Comedy Feature
Date: 1986   Origin: USA
Company: Amblin
Distributors/Format: Universal Home Video (1/2")
Annotation: Walter Fielding (Hanks) and Anna Crowley (Long) must quickly find a new home when Anna's ex-husband returns and claims the apartment. They buy a huge dilapidated house and try to renovate it. Faison plays James and Omilani is part of the construction crew.

MONIQUE
Director: Yvonne Welbon*
Tech Info: bw/sound/3 min.   Type: Experimental Short
Date: 1990   Origin: USA
Studio: Independent
Distributors/Format: Third World Newsreel (1/2")
Archives/Format: IUB - BFC/A (1/2")
Annotation: Using a childhood experience of racial bigotry at school, Welbon looks at the ways in which racism is ingrained in American society, even in the play of children. Her film is an exploration of identity and memory.

MONSTER IN THE CLOSET
Cast: Kevin Peter Hall*, Henry Gibson, Donald Moffat, Donald Grant, Denise DuBarry, Howard Duff
Director: Bob Dahlin
Executive Producer: Lloyd Kaufman Jr., Michael Herz
Music by: Barrie Guard
Producer: David Levy, Peter L. Bergquist, Lloyd Kaufman Jr., Michael Herz
Screenwriter: Bob Dahlin
Storywriter: Peter L. Bergquist, Bob Dahlin
Tech Info: color/sound/87 min.   Type: Dramatic Feature
Date: 1987   Origin: USA
Company: Closet
Distributors/Format: Troma (16mm)
Annotation: All over San Francisco people are being lured into their closets, never to be seen again. Hall plays the monster who is shot at by the Army when he emerges from a closet. The authorities urge citizens to "destroy all closets."

MOON 44
Cast: Roscoe Lee Browne*, Michael Pare, Malcolm McDowell, Lisa Eichhorn, Dean Devlin
Director: Roland Emmerich
Executive Producer: Michael A.P. Scording

Music by: Joel Goldsmith
Producer: Dean Heyde, Roland Emmerich, Michael A.P. Scording
Screenwriter: Dean Heyde, Oliver Eberle, P.J. Mitchell
Storywriter: Dean Heyde, Roland Emmerich, Oliver Eberle
Tech Info: color/sound/99 min.　　　　Type: Dramatic Feature
Date: 1991　Origin: USA
Company: Centropolis Film Prod., Spectrum Ent., et al.
Distributors/Format: LIVE Home Video (1/2")
Annotation: Set in the year 2038, the Earth's resources are nearly depleted. Rival companies, Galactic and Pyrite, vie for resources on other planets. Galactic's chairman (Brown) sends out his best security agents to infiltrate and overcome the evil Pyrite company officials.

MOON IN THE GUTTER

Alternate: La Lune Dans Le Caniveau
Cast: Bertice Reading*, Nastassia Kinski, Gerard Depardieu, Victoria Abril
Director: Jean-Jacques Beineix
Music by: Gabriel Yared
Producer: Lise Fayolle
Screenwriter: Jean-Jacques Beineix, Olivier Mergault
Storywriter: David Goodis
Tech Info: color/sound/126 min.　　　　Type: Dramatic Feature
Date: 1983　Origin: France, Italy
Company: TF-1, Opera, SFPC, Gaumont
Distributors/Format: Columbia Pictures Home Video (1/2"), Triumph Releasing (16mm)
Annotation: Gerard (Depardieu), a dock worker, tries to find out who raped his sister, the crime which led to her suicide. Reading plays Lola.

MOON OVER PARADOR

Cast: Roger Aaron Brown*, Sammy Davis Jr.*, Richard Dreyfuss, Raul Julia, Sonia Braga
Director: Paul Mazursky
Music by: Maurice Jarre
Producer: Paul Mazursky, Pato Guzman, Geoffrey Taylor
Screenwriter: Paul Mazursky, Leon Capetanos
Storywriter: Charles G. Boothe
Tech Info: color/sound/105 min.　　　　Type: Comedy Feature
Date: 1988　Origin: USA
Company: Universal
Distributors/Format: Universal Home Video (1/2")
Annotation: Jack Noah is a second-class American actor who finds himself standing in for Parador's ruler after he is killed. Davis plays himself; Brown plays Desmond, a loyalist to the corrupt government.

MORTUARY ACADEMY

Cast: Stone/Stoney Jackson*, Tracey Walter, Paul Bartel, Perry Lang, Mary Woronov
Director: Michael Schroeder
Executive Producer: Kim Jorgensen
Music by: David Spear

Producer: Kim Jorgensen, Dennis Winfrey, Chip Miller
Screenwriter: William Kelman
Tech Info: color/sound/85 min.   Type: Comedy Feature
Date: 1992   Origin: USA
Company: Landmark Films, Priority Films
Distributors/Format: RCA/Columbia Pictures Home Video (1/2")
Annotation: Two boys stand to inherit the family business, a mortician school, but must first pass its courses taught by Mary Purcell (Woronov) and Dr. Paul Truscott (Bartel), a necrophiliac. Jackson plays James Dandridge.

MOSCOW ON THE HUDSON
Cast: Cleavant Derricks*, Robert Macbeth*, Barbara Montgomery*, Edye Byrde*, Tiger Haynes*, Donna Ingram-Young*, Rosetta La Noire*, Joy Todd*, James Prendergast*, Robin Williams, Alejandro Rey, Maria Alonso Conchita
Director: Paul Mazursky
Music Performer: David McHugh
Music by: David McHugh
Producer: Paul Mazursky
Screenwriter: Paul Mazursky, Leon Capetanos
Tech Info: color/sound/115 min.   Type: Dramatic Feature
Date: 1984   Origin: USA
Company: Columbia
Distributors/Format: RCA/Columbia Pictures Home Video (1/2")
Annotation: Lionel Witherspoon (Derricks), a Bloomingdale's security guard in New York, helps Vladimir (Williams) enter the country as a Russian defector. Vladimir moves to Witherspoon's house where Mamma (Byrde), Fletcher (Macbeth), and Lionel's grandmother (Haynes) nurture him and help him become a true American.

MOSQUITO COAST, THE
Cast: Butterfly McQueen*, Conrad Roberts*, Harrison Ford, Helen Mirren, River Phoenix
Director: Peter Weir
Executive Producer: Saul Zaentz
Music by: Maurice Jarre
Producer: Jerome Hellman, Saul Zaentz
Screenwriter: Paul Schrader
Storywriter: Paul Theroux
Tech Info: color/sound/117 min.   Type: Dramatic Feature
Date: 1986   Origin: USA
Company: Warner Bros.
Distributors/Format: Warner Bros. Home Video, Inc. (1/2")
Annotation: Allie Fox (Ford), an eccentric inventor who is disgusted with America, takes his wife (Mirren) and four children to an unsettled area near Honduras called the Mosquito Coast. Fox mercilessly pushes his family, the locals, and himself to recreate society along Utopian lines. Roberts as Mr. Haddy and McQueen as Ma Kennywick are also featured.

MOTHER IS A MOTHER, A
Producer: Lyn Blum, Cynthia Ealey, Child Care Resource Center/Southside, Elizabeth Berardo, Kathleen Laughlin
Tech Info: color/sound/27 min.   Type: Documentary Short
Date: 1981   Origin: USA
Studio: Independent
Annotation: Seven black, teenage mothers discuss the dreams they have and obstacles they face.

MOTHER'S BOYS
Cast: Lorraine Toussaint*, Jamie Lee Curtis, Peter Gallagher, Joanne Whalley-Kilmer, Venessa Redgrave
Director: Yves Simoneau
Executive Producer: Bob Weinstein, Harvey Weinstein, Randall Poster
Music by: George Clinton*
Producer: Bob Weinstein, Harvey Weinstein, Patricia Herskovic, Jack E. Freedman, Wayne S. Williams, Randall Poster
Screenwriter: Barry Schneider, Richard Hawley
Tech Info: color/sound/114 min.   Type: Dramatic Feature
Date: 1994   Origin: USA
Company: Jack Freedman Productions, Wayne Williams, et al.
Distributors/Format: Dimension (16mm)
Annotation: Jude (Curtis) returns to her family whom she abandoned three years earlier only to find her kids don't remember her and her husband Robert (Gallagher) wants to marry someone else. Toussaint is Robert's associate.

MOTHER'S HANDS
Cast: Cenen *, Candace Churchill*
Director: Vejan Lee Smith*
Screenwriter: Vejan Lee Smith*
Storywriter: Vejan Lee Smith*
Tech Info: color/sound/10 min.   Type: Experimental Short
Date: 1992   Origin: USA
Studio: Independent
Company: Third World Newsreel Production
Distributors/Format: Third World Newsreel (1/2")
Annotation: This experimental narrative explores the memories of an adult haunted by a childhood of sexual and physical abuse. Using music and chants we experience a darker connection between a poverty-stricken mother and her daughter.

MOTORAMA
Cast: Garrett Morris*, John Diehl, Jordan Christopher Michael, Martha Quinn, Susan Tyrell
Director: Barry Shils
Executive Producer: Steven Bratter, Lauren Graybow, Barry Shils, Barbara Ligeti
Music by: Andy Summers
Producer: Donald P. Borchers, Steven Bratter, Lauren Graybow, Barry Shils, Barbara Ligeti
Screenwriter: Joseph Minion
Tech Info: color/sound/90 min.   Type: Comedy Feature

Date: 1993   Origin: USA
Company: Planet Productions, Goldstreet Pictures
Distributors/Format: Two Moon Releasing (16mm)
Annotation: Ten-year-old Gus (Michael) steals a classic Mustang and drives across a fictional country to collect Motorama game pieces at gas stations. Morris plays Andy in a cameo role.

MOTV (MY OWN TV)

Director: Ayoka Chenzira*, Herman Lew
Producer: Ayoka Chenzira*
Screenwriter: Thomas Osha Pinnock*
Tech Info: color/sound   Type: Television Feature
Date: 1993   Origin: USA
Company: Red Carnelian Productions
Distributors/Format: Red Carnelian Films/Video (16mm; 1/2")
Annotation: Produced for the Independent Television Service (ITS) for its five hour dramatic series, "TV Families," this story is about the love between a no-nonsense African American woman and her Jamaican husband whose fantasies about American life end in tragedy.

MOVING

Cast: Richard Pryor*, Beverly Todd*, Stacey Dash*, Raphael Harris*, Ishmael Harris*, John Wesley*, Randy Quaid, Dave Thomas, Dana Carvey
Director: Alan Metter
Music by: Howard Shore
Producer: Stuart Cornfeld
Screenwriter: Andy Breckman
Tech Info: color/sound/89 min.   Type: Comedy Feature
Date: 1988   Origin: USA
Company: Warner Bros.
Distributors/Format: Warner Bros. Home Video, Inc. (1/2")
Annotation: After Roy Henderson (Wesley) fires his transportation engineer, Arlo Pear (Pryor), the Pear family is thrown into chaos. When Arlo accepts a job in Boise, Idaho, his teenage daughter Casey (Dash) refuses to leave New Jersey. His wife, Monica (Todd) suggests he work instead at her father's mustard factory, and his twin sons Marshall (Raphael Harris) and Randy (Ishmael Harris) reject the idea as vehemently as the others.

MOVING VIOLATIONS

Cast: Don Cheadle*, Willard Pugh*, James Keach, Jennifer Tilly, John Murray, Lisa Hart Carroll
Director: Neal Israel
Executive Producer: Pat Proft, Doug Draizin
Music by: Ralph Burns
Producer: Joe Roth, Harry Ufland, Pat Proft, Robert Israel, Doug Draizin
Screenwriter: Neal Israel, Pat Proft
Storywriter: Paul Boorstin, Sharon Boorstin
Tech Info: color/sound/90 min.   Type: Comedy Feature

Date: 1985   Origin: USA
Company: Ufland, Roght, IPI
Distributors/Format: Fox Home Video (1/2")
Annotation: Dana Cannon (Murray) and other students pit themselves against traffic
school police who are determined to keep them off the streets. Cheadle plays the
Juicy Burger worker.

MR. AND MRS. BRIDGE
Cast: Saundra McClain*, Paul Newman, Blythe Danner, Joanne Woodward
Director: James Ivory
Music Performer: Charles Perkins*, Allen Monroe*, Richard Ross*, Milton Abel*
Music by: Richard Robbins
Producer: Ismail Merchant
Screenwriter: Ruth Prawer Jhabvala
Storywriter: Evan S. Connell
Tech Info: color/sound/127 min.   Type: Dramatic Feature
Date: 1990   Origin: USA
Company: Cineplex Oden Films
Distributors/Format: Miramax Home Video (1/2")
Annotation: Harriet (McClain) is the maid in this well-to-do traditional household in
Kansas City, with patriarchal Mr. Bridge (Newman), his wife Mrs. Bridge
(Woodward) and their three children. Change does not come easily to either of the
adults. One scene features a black jazz group.

MR. BASEBALL
Cast: Dennis Haysbert*, Tom Selleck, Ken Takakura, Aya Takanashi, Toshi Shioya,
Kohsuke Toyohara
Director: Fred Schepisi
Executive Producer: Jeffrey Silver, Susumu Kondoh, John Kao
Music by: Jerry Goldsmith
Producer: Fred Schepisi, Doug Claybourne, Robert Newmyer, Jeffrey Silver,
Susumu Kondoh, John Kao
Screenwriter: Kevin Wade, Gary Ross, Monte Merrick
Storywriter: Theo Pelletier, John Junkerman
Tech Info: color/sound/109 min.   Type: Comedy Feature
Date: 1992   Origin: USA
Company: Sogo Produce, Outlaw Productions, Universal
Distributors/Format: Universal Home Video (1/2")
Annotation: Jack Elliot (Selleck), an American baseball player on the wane, is traded
to a Japanese team where he's expected to win them a pennant. He also falls in
love with Hiroko Uchiyama (Takanashi), the team manager's daughter. Haysbert
plays Max "Hammer" Dubois, the other American on the Japanese team.

MR. JONES
Cast: Anna Maria Horsford*, Delroy Lindo*, Richard Gere, Anne Bancroft, Lena Olin,
Tom Irwin
Director: Mike Figgis
Executive Producer: Richard Gere, Jerry A. Baerwitz
Music by: Maurice Jarre
Producer: Richard Gere, Alan Greisman, Debra Greenfield, Jerry A. Baerwitz
Screenwriter: Michael Cristofer, Eric Roth
Storywriter: Eric Roth

Tech Info: color/sound/114 min.　　　Type: Dramatic Feature
Date: 1993　Origin: USA
Company: Rastar Productions
Distributors/Format: TriStar Pictures Inc. (1/2")
Annotation: Mr. Jones (Gere), an unstable construction worker, has a psychotic episode on the job and is sent to see Dr. Elizabeth "Libbie" Bowen (Olin) who suggests treatment. Jones is nevertheless released and continues to behave erratically, despite the love and support Libbie offers him. Lindo plays Howard and Horsford plays Judge Harris who presides over Jones' competency hearing.

MR. NANNY
Cast: Sherman Hemsley*, Mother Love*, Austin Pendleton, Hulk Hogan, Robert Gorman, Madeline Zima
Director: Michael Gottlieb, Peter Stein
Executive Producer: Benni Korzen, Michael Harpster
Music by: David Johansen, Brian Koonin
Producer: Bob Engelman, Benni Korzen, Michael Harpster
Screenwriter: Edward Rugoff, Michael Gottlieb
Tech Info: color/sound/84 min.　　　Type: Comedy Feature
Date: 1993　Origin: USA
Company: New Line Cinema
Distributors/Format: Columbia/TriStar Pictures (35mm; 1/2")
Annotation: Thinking his manager (Hemsley) has found a job as a bodyguard for him, former pro-wrestler Sean Armstrong (Hogan) is horrified to learn that he's been hired to watch over two nanny-hating kids.

MR. SATURDAY NIGHT
Cast: Tim Russ*, Slappy White*, Billy Crystal, David Paymer, Julie Warner
Director: Billy Crystal
Executive Producer: Lowell Ganz, Babaloo Mandel
Music by: Marc Shaiman
Producer: Billy Crystal, Lowell Ganz, Babaloo Mandel
Screenwriter: Billy Crystal, Lowell Ganz, Babaloo Mandel
Tech Info: color/sound/119 min.　　　Type: Comedy Feature
Date: 1992　Origin: USA
Company: Face Productions, Castle Rock
Distributors/Format: Columbia Pictures (16mm)
Annotation: The film follows the life of Buddy Young (Crystal), a stand-up comic whose life also has its serious moments. White plays Joey and Russ is A.D.

MR. WONDERFUL
Cast: Paul Bates*, Matt Dillon, William Hurt, Annabella Sciorra, Mary Louise Parker
Director: Anthony Minghella
Music by: Michael Gore
Producer: Marianne Moloney
Screenwriter: Anthony Minghella, Amy Schor, Vicki Polon
Tech Info: color/sound/109 min.　　　Type: Comedy Feature

Date: 1993   Origin: USA
Company: Nightlife Films, Samuel Goldwyn Company
Distributors/Format: Warner Bros. Home Video, Inc. (1/2")
Annotation: Gus (Dillon), tired of making alimony payments, decides to find his
ex-wife a new husband. Through his antics, he realizes he still loves his wife. Bates
plays Marlon.

MRS. PARKER AND THE VICIOUS CIRCLE
Cast: Jennifer Beals*, Matthew Broderick, Campbell Scott, Andrew McCarthy, Peter
Gallagher, Jennifer Jason Leigh
Director: Alan Rudolph
Executive Producer: Ira Deutchman, Scott Bushnell
Music by: Mark Isham
Producer: Robert Altman, Ira Deutchman, Scott Bushnell
Screenwriter: Alan Rudolph, Randy Sue Coburn
Tech Info: color/sound/125 min.   Type: Dramatic Feature
Date: 1994   Origin: USA
Company: Sandcastle 5, Odyssey Entertainment, et al.
Distributors/Format: Fine Line Home Video (1/2")
Annotation: Dorothy Parker (Leigh) is remembered as both a writer of short stories
and a member of the "New Yorker" circle. The film examines her life and loves
including an affair with Robert Benchley (Scott). Beals portrays his demanding wife
Gertrude.

MUCH ADO ABOUT NOTHING
Cast: Denzel Washington*, Michael Keaton, Keanu Reeves, Kenneth Branagh,
Emma Thompson, Richard Briers
Director: Kenneth Branagh, Roger Lanser
Music by: Patrick Doyle
Producer: Kenneth Branagh, Stephen Evans, David Parfitt
Screenwriter: Kenneth Branagh
Tech Info: color/sound/110 min.   Type: Comedy Feature
Date: 1993   Origin: Italy
Company: Columbia, TriStar
Distributors/Format: Columbia/TriStar Pictures (35mm; 1/2"), Facets Multimedia,
Inc. (1/2"), Filmic Archives (1/2")
Annotation: Branagh adapts William Shakespeare's comedy and plays Benedick to
Thompson's Beatrice. Washington plays the Duke.

MUPPET MOVIE, THE
Cast: Richard Pryor*, Milton Berle, Telly Savalas, Jim Henson, Frank Oz, Jerry
Nelson, Mel Brooks, Paul Williams
Director: James Frawley
Executive Producer: Martin Starger
Music Performer: Paul Williams
Music by: Paul Williams
Producer: Jim Henson, Martin Starger
Screenwriter: Jerry Juhl, Jack Burns
Tech Info: color/sound/96 min.   Type: Comedy Feature

Date: 1979   Origin: USA
Company: ITC Films, Jim Henson Productions
Annotation: Pryor is a balloon vendor who sells muppets Gonzo and Camille a massive bunch of balloons resulting in a high altitude experience that Gonzo won't soon forget. Pryor's is one of the many special star appearances on the Muppets' road trip to Hollywood.

MURDER BY NUMBERS
Cast: Cleavon Little*, Shari Belafonte Harper*, Ronee Blakley, Sam Behrens, Dick Sargent, Wlad Cembrowicz, Robert Hosea
Director: Paul Leder
Music by: Bob Summers
Producer: Ralph Tornberg, Paul Leder
Screenwriter: Paul Leder
Tech Info: color/sound/91 min.   Type: Dramatic Feature
Date: 1990   Origin: USA
Company: Burnhill
Distributors/Format: Cobra Entertainment Group, Magnum (16mm)
Annotation: David Shelby (Little), an ex-con with a talent for breaking and entering, tries to assist amateur detective Lee Bolger (Behrens) in solving the murder/suicide of Walter (Cembrowicz), a wealthy homosexual. Lisa (Belafonte) faithful assistant to Richard (Hosea), Walter's lover, helps put together a transfer deed on one of Walter's buildings.

MURPHY'S LAW
Cast: Bill Henderson*, Charles Bronson, Carrie Snodgress, Kathleen Wilhoite, Robert F. Lyons, Richard Romanus
Director: J. Lee Thompson
Executive Producer: Yoram Globus, Menahem Golan
Music by: Marc Donahue, Valentine McCallum
Producer: Yoram Globus, Menahem Golan, Pancho Kohner
Screenwriter: Gail Morgan Hickman*
Tech Info: color/sound/97 min.   Type: Dramatic Feature
Date: 1986   Origin: USA
Company: Golan-Globus
Distributors/Format: Cannon Home Video (1/2")
Annotation: Jack Murphy (Bronson) is a detective who is framed for the murder of his ex-wife, a stripper, and her husband. Henderson plays Ben Wilcove.

MUSIC BOX
Cast: Albert Hall*, Ellis Williams*, Kevin C. White*, Cheryl Lynn Bruce*, Jessica Lange, Armin Mueller-Stahl
Director: Constantin Costa-Gavras
Executive Producer: Joe Eszterhas, Hal Polaire
Music by: Philippe Sarde, Harry Rabinowitz
Producer: Joe Eszterhas, Irwin Winkler, Hal Polaire
Screenwriter: Joe Eszterhas
Tech Info: color/sound/124 min.   Type: Dramatic Feature

Date: 1989   Origin: USA
Company: Carolco
Distributors/Format: TriStar Pictures Inc. (1/2")
Annotation: Ann Talbot (Lange), a defense lawyer, defends her father Michael Laszlo (Mueller-Stahl) against charges of Nazi war atrocities until she discovers the truth. Bruce is Georgine Wheeler, a colleague and friend of Talbot's; Hall is Mack Jones; White, a court clerk at the trial of Laszlo.

MY BROTHER'S WEDDING

Cast: Sy Richardson*, Everett Silas*, Jessie Holmes*, Gaye Shannon-Burnett*, Ronnie Bell*, Dennis Kemper*, Frances Nealy*
Director: Charles Burnett*
Executive Producer: Gaye Shannon-Burnett*
Producer: Charles Burnett*, Gaye Shannon-Burnett*, Gaye Shannon-Burnett*
Screenwriter: Charles Burnett*
Tech Info: color/sound/116 min.   Type: Dramatic Feature
Date: 1983   Origin: USA
Company: Charles Burnett* Production
Distributors/Format: Charles Burnett Production (1/2")
Annotation: Pierce Monday (Silas) works in his family's dry cleaning business in Watts (Los Angeles). His family loyalty is tested when he has to decide whether to attend the funeral of his best friend (Bell) or his brother Wendell's (Kemper) wedding. Shannon-Burnett plays Wendell's fiancee Sonia; Nealy and Richardson play Sonia's mother and father.

MY HEROES HAVE ALWAYS BEEN COWBOYS

Cast: Clarence Williams III*, Gary Busey, Scott Glenn, Ben Johnson, Mickey Rooney, Kate Capshaw
Director: Stuart Rosenberg
Music by: James Horner
Producer: Martin Poll, E.K. Gaylord II
Screenwriter: Joel Don Humphreys
Tech Info: color/sound/106 min.   Type: Dramatic Feature
Date: 1991   Origin: USA
Company: Martin Poll Productions
Distributors/Format: MGM/UA Home Video (1/2")
Annotation: Rodeo star H.D. Dalton (Glenn) returns home to his father and childhood sweetheart after a severe riding accident. Williams plays Virgil, Dalton's old friend who is also the local sheriff.

MY LIFE

Cast: Queen Latifah*, Michael Keaton, Nicole Kidman, Haing S. Ngor
Director: Bruce Joel Rubin, Peter James
Executive Producer: Gil Netter
Producer: Bruce Joel Rubin, Jerry Zueker, Gil Netter
Screenwriter: Bruce Joel Rubin
Storywriter: Bruce Joel Rubin, Hunt Loury
Tech Info: color/sound/117 min.   Type: Dramatic Feature

Date: 1993   Origin: USA
Company: Columbia
Annotation: A high-powered executive, diagnosed with terminal cancer, is forced to make plans for his unborn son. He begins filming a home video, in which he teaches his son all the things a man must know--how to shave, how to slam dunk and how to fall in love. Latifah is the dying man's (Keaton) home nurse.

MY MAN ADAM

Cast: Denise Gordy*, Charles Barnett*, Sam Scarber*, Veronica Cartwright, Dave Thomas, Raphael Sbarge
Director: Roger L. Simon
Executive Producer: Thom Mount
Music by: Sylvester Levay
Producer: Paul Aratow, Renee Missel, Gail Stayden, Thom Mount
Screenwriter: Roger L. Simon, Renee Missel
Tech Info: color/sound/84 min.   Type: Comedy Feature
Date: 1986   Origin: USA
Company: TriStar, Delphi III, Mount
Distributors/Format: TriStar Pictures Inc. (1/2")
Annotation: Teenager Adam Swit (Sbarge) spends his time looking for the girl and career of his dreams. Barnett plays Leroy.

MYSTERY TRAIN

Cast: Sy Richardson*, Rufus Thomas*, Vondie Curtis-Hall*, Cinque Lee*, Screamin' Jay Hawkins*, Masatoshi Nagase, Youki Kudoh, Nicoletta Braschi, Elizabeth Bracco
Director: Jim Jarmusch
Executive Producer: Kunjiro Harata, Hideaki Suda
Music by: John Lurie
Producer: Jim Stark, Kunjiro Harata, Hideaki Suda
Screenwriter: Jim Jarmusch
Tech Info: color/sound/113 min.   Type: Comedy Feature
Date: 1989   Origin: USA
Company: MTI
Distributors/Format: Orion Home Video (1/2")
Annotation: Japanese tourists, an Italian woman who has come to collect her dead husband, and a girl cutting out on her British boyfriend all come together in Memphis' rundown Arcade Hotel. Curtis-Hall plays Ed.

MYSTIQUE

Alternate: Circle of Power
Cast: Wally Taylor*, Yvette Mimieux, Christopher Allport, Cindy Pickett, John Considine
Director: Bobby Roth
Executive Producer: Anthony Quinn
Music by: Richard Markowitz
Producer: Anthony Quinn, Gary L. Mehlman, Jeffrey White
Screenwriter: Beth Sullivan, Stephen Bello
Tech Info: color/sound/97 min.   Type: Dramatic Feature

Date: 1981   Origin: USA
Company: Mehlman
Annotation: A homosexual, a drunkard, and a transvestite meet at an Executive Development Training session run by Bianca Ray (Mimieux). Taylor appears as Charlie Carter.

N.Y. LAW
Director: Dick Fontaine
Speaker: Bruce Wright*
Tech Info: color/sound/52 min.   Type: Documentary Feature
Date: 1990   Origin: USA
Annotation: The film follows a group of bright minority students in a journey through our legal system.

NAKED GUN 2 1/2: THE SMELL OF FEAR
Cast: O.J. Simpson*, Gail Neely*, Al Fann*, James Gilstrap*, Leslie Nielson, George Kennedy, Prisilla Presley
Director: David Zucker
Music Performer: E. Y. Harburg
Music by: Duke Ellington*, Billy Strayhorn*, Ira Newborn, Harold Arlen, Johnny Mercer
Producer: Robert K. Weiss
Screenwriter: David Zucker
Tech Info: color/sound/85 min.   Type: Comedy Feature
Date: 1991   Origin: USA
Company: Paramount
Distributors/Format: Paramount Home Video (1/2")
Annotation: Lt. Frank Drebin (Nielson) returns in this sequel in order to protect the President of the United States. Nordberg (Simpson) is his faithful, bumbling fellow officer. Fann portrays a security officer and Gilstrap is Sam, the piano player.

NAKED GUN 33 1/3: THE FINAL INSULT
Cast: James Earl Jones*, O.J. Simpson*, Leslie Nielson, Fred Ward, George Kennedy, Prisilla Presley, Pia Zadora, Anna-Nicole Smith
Director: Robert Stevens, Peter Segal
Executive Producer: Jerry Zucker, Jim Abrahams, Gil Netter
Music by: Ira Newborn
Producer: Jerry Zucker, David Zucker, Robert K. Weiss, Jim Abrahams, Gil Netter
Screenwriter: David Zucker, Pat Proft, Robert Lolash
Tech Info: color/sound/83 min.   Type: Comedy Feature
Date: 1994   Origin: USA
Company: Paramount
Distributors/Format: Paramount Home Video (1/2")
Annotation: Simpson returns with bumbling Lt. Frank Drebin (Nielsen) crashing the Oscar night ceremonies to stop a terrorist plot. Jones makes a cameo appearance.

NAKED GUN, THE: FROM THE FILES OF POLICE SQUAD
Cast: O.J. Simpson*, Reggie Jackson*, Prince Hughes*, Susan Beaubian*, Leslie Nielson, George Kennedy, Prisilla Presley
Director: David Zucker
Music by: Ira Newborn
Producer: Jerry Zucker, David Zucker, Robert K. Weiss, Jim Abrahams, Pat Proft

Screenwriter: David Zucker
Storywriter: Jerry Zucker, David Zucker, Pat Proft, Jim Abrahams
Tech Info: color/sound/85 min. Type: Comedy Feature
Date: 1988 Origin: USA
Company: Paramount
Distributors/Format: Paramount Home Video (1/2")
Annotation: Nielson continues his comic role as Lt. Frank Drebin who is assisted by his fellow officer, Nordberg (Simpson). Accident-prone Nordberg is placed in intensive care after an unsuccessful drug bust, and by the end of the film has substantially recovered, only to be catapulted from the California Angels' Baseball Stadium. Nordberg's wife, Wilma, is played by Beaubian. Hughes appears as Idi Amin and Jackson cameos as an Angels' right fielder.

NAKED IN NEW YORK

Cast: Whoopi Goldberg*, Roscoe Lee Browne*, Lynn Thigpen*, Eric Stoltz, Mary Louise Parker
Director: Dan Algrant
Executive Producer: Martin Scorsese
Music by: Angelo Badalamenti
Producer: Martin Scorsese, Frederick Zollo
Screenwriter: Dan Algrant, John Warren
Tech Info: color/sound/91 min. Type: Comedy Feature
Date: 1994 Origin: USA
Company: Some Film Inc., Zollo Productions, Red Shoes Co.
Distributors/Format: Fine Line Home Video (1/2")
Annotation: Jake Briggs (Stoltz), a playwright who just graduated from Harvard, decides to stay in Cambridge rather than try to make it on Broadway. After a friend persuades him to come to New York, his personal and professional life begin to intensify.

NARROW MARGIN

Cast: J.A. Preston*, Anne Archer, James B. Sikking, Gene Hackman, Harris Yulin
Director: Peter Hyams
Executive Producer: Mario Kassar, Andrew Vajna
Music by: Bruce Broughton
Producer: Mario Kassar, Andrew Vajna, Jonathan A. Zimbert
Screenwriter: Peter Hyams
Storywriter: Martin Goldsmith, Jack Leonard
Tech Info: color/sound/97 min. Type: Dramatic Feature
Date: 1990 Origin: USA
Company: Carolco, Jonathan A. Zimbert
Distributors/Format: TriStar Pictures Inc. (1/2")
Annotation: Caulfield (Hackman), an L.A. Deputy D.A., wants gangster Leo Watts (Yulin) behind bars. Convinced that his boss Martin Larner (Preston) is undermining his efforts, Caulfield tracks down a possible witness.

NAT KING COLE - UNFORGETTABLE

Director: Alan Lewens
Music Performer: Nat King Cole*
Narrator: Ricco Ross*
Producer: Maria Cole*, Jo Lustig
Speaker: Quincy Jones*, Ella Fitzgerald*, Harry Belafonte*, Oscar Peterson*, Don

Newcombe*, Eartha Kitt*, Natalie Cole*, Maria Cole*, Freddy Cole*, Rev. James Cole*, Coles*, Dempsey Travis*, Spanky Tavares*, Carol Cole*, Lee Young*, Frank Sinatra
Tech Info: mixed/sound/90 min.   Type: Documentary Feature
Date: 1989   Origin: USA
Company: A Jo Lustig Ltd. Production, et al.
Distributors/Format: MPI Home Video (1/2")
Archives/Format: IUB - BFC/A (1/2")
Annotation: The film documents the biography of Nat King Cole with clips from his television show, early film footage, and interviews with family, fellow musicians, and friends.

NATION ERUPTS, THE (PART 1 & 2)
Director: Caryn Rogoff
Music Performer: James Brown*, Public Enemy *, Prince (Rogers Nelson) *, John Coltrane*, Ice-T *, Ice Cube *
Producer: Donna Golden*, Art Jones*, Thomas Poole
Screenwriter: George Sosa*
Speaker: Bongo *, Nabil Antoine*, Chris Nicholsen*
Tech Info: mixed/sound/60 min.   Type: Television Documentary
Date: 1992   Origin: USA
Studio: Independent
Company: Black Planet Productions/Deep Dish TV Network
Distributors/Format: Third World Newsreel (1/2")
Archives/Format: IUB - AAAMC (1/2")
Annotation: Deep Dish T.V. discusses the motivations behind the violent aftermath of the Rodney King verdict, emphasizing the long standing history of confrontation between Black America and police.

NATION OF LAW?, A (1968-1971)
Series: Eyes On The Prize II
Director: Thomas Ott
Executive Producer: Henry Hampton*
Narrator: Julian Bond*
Producer: Henry Hampton*, Louis J. Massiah*, Terry Kay Rockefeller, Thomas Ott
Screenwriter: Louis J. Massiah*, Thomas Ott
Speaker: Imamu Amiri Baraka*, Arthur Eves*, C.T. Vivian*, Elaine Brown*, Nancy Jefferson*, Marion Stamps*, George Clemants*, Bobby Seale*, William O'Neal*, Jerris Leonard*, Fred Hampton*, Howard Saffold*, Deborah Johnson*, Bobby Rush*, Angela Davis*, Frank Smith*, Herbert Blyden*, John Johnson*, Laverne Barkley*, Richard Nixon, Edward Hanraham, Tom Wicker, Nelson Rockefeller
Tech Info: mixed/sound/60 min.   Type: Television Documentary
Date: 1989   Origin: USA
Company: Blackside Inc.
Distributors/Format: PBS Video (16mm; 1/2")
Archives/Format: IUB - AAAMC (1/2")
Annotation: This segment looks at the terrorist tactics that were used by police and F.B.I. in order to contain the Black Power Movement from 1968-1971. In Chicago, Fred Hampton, local Black Panther Party leader, and Black Panther Member, Mark Clark are murdered in a police assault. Similar violence appears at New York's Attica prison when inmates attempt to gain reforms by a prison take over.

NATION, THE

Alternate: A Story of the Nation of Islam
Director: Juney Smith*
Producer: Juney Smith*
Speaker: Bennet Guillory*, Reed McCants*, Michael Whaley*, Smoky Campbell*
Tech Info: 120 min.   Type: Documentary Feature
Date: 1992   Origin: USA
Annotation: The film tells the story of Master Fard Muhammad, Elijah Muhammad, Malcolm X and Louis Farrakhan, the men who helped to shape the Nation of Islam.

NATIONAL LAMPOON'S CLASS REUNION

Cast: Chuck Berry*, Arthur/Art Evans*, Gerrit Graham, Fred McCarren, Miriam Flynn, Blackie Dammett
Director: Michael Miller
Music Performer: Peter Bernstein, Mark Goldenberg
Music by: Peter Bernstein, Mark Goldenberg
Producer: Matty Simmons
Screenwriter: John Hughes
Tech Info: color/sound/86 min.   Type: Comedy Feature
Date: 1982   Origin: USA
Company: ABC Motion Pictures, Fox
Distributors/Format: ABC Home Video (1/2")
Annotation: The Lizzie Borden High School class reunion is terrorized by a classmate (Dammett) who was the butt of a foul joke ten years before. Berry guest stars as himself performing "It Wasn't Me," "My Dingaling," and "Festival." Evans plays Carl Clapton who was stoned all the way through high school and still is at the reunion.

NATIONAL LAMPOON'S LOADED WEAPON I

Cast: Bill Nunn*, Samuel L. Jackson*, Whoopi Goldberg*, Frank McRae*, Emilio Estevez, William Shatner
Director: Gene Quintano, Peter Deming
Executive Producer: Michael Roy, Howard Klein, Erwin Stoff
Producer: Suzanne Todd, David Willis, Michael Roy, Howard Klein, Erwin Stoff
Screenwriter: Gene Quintano, Don Holley
Storywriter: Don Holley, Tori Tellen
Tech Info: color/sound/83 min.   Type: Comedy Feature
Date: 1993   Origin: USA
Company: 3 Arts Ent., Todd/Williams Prod., New Line Cinema
Distributors/Format: New Line Cinema Home Video (1/2")
Annotation: Jackson plays Wes Luguar, a dangerous over-the-edge detective who uncovers a plot to rot American's brains and teeth with drug-laced wilderness girl scout cookies.

NATIONAL LAMPOON'S VACATION

Cast: Frank McRae*, Christopher Jackson*, Chevy Chase, Beverly D'Angelo, Imogene Coca
Director: Harold Ramis
Music by: Ralph Burns
Producer: Matty Simmons
Screenwriter: John Hughes

Tech Info: color/sound/98 min.   Type: Comedy Feature
Date: 1983   Origin: USA
Company: Warner Bros.
Distributors/Format: Warner Bros. Home Video, Inc. (1/2")
Annotation: Clark Griswold (Chase) takes his family on a cross-country trip to an
amusement park called Wally World. McRae plays Frank and Jackson appears as a
pimp.

NATIVE SON

Cast: Oprah Winfrey*, Akosua Busia*, Victor Love*, Arthur/Art Evans*, Willard
Pugh*, Elizabeth McGovern, Matt Dillon, Carroll Baker, Geraldine Page
Director: Terrold Freedman
Executive Producer: Lindsay Law
Music Performer: James Mtume*
Music by: James Mtume*
Producer: Diane Silver, Lindsay Law
Screenwriter: Richard Wesley*
Storywriter: Richard Wright*
Tech Info: color/sound/112 min.   Type: Dramatic Feature
Date: 1986   Origin: USA
Company: Diane Silver, American Playhouse, Cinetudes
Distributors/Format: Facets Multimedia, Inc. (1/2")
Annotation: Richard Wright's novel is adapted to the screen for a second time. In
this version, a frustrated and angry young black man confined with his family to the
Chicago ghetto of the 1930s, Bigger Thomas (Love), accidentally kills the daughter
of his employer. After he is sentence to death, he begins to understand his fate and
that of all black people who live without opportunity or hope. Winfrey plays Bigger's
mother; Busia is Bessie, his girlfriend; Evans is Doc; Pugh, Gus.

NAVY SEALS

Cast: Dennis Haysbert*, S. Epatha Merkerson*, Charlie Sheen, Michael Biehn, Bill
Paxton, Joanne Whalley-Kilmer, Rick Rossovich
Director: Lewis Teague, John A. Alonzo
Music by: Sylvester Levay, Michael Dilbeck
Producer: Bernard Williams, Brenda Feigen
Screenwriter: Gary Goldman, Chuck Pfarrer
Tech Info: color/sound/104 min.   Type: Dramatic Feature
Date: 1990   Origin: USA
Company: Brenda Feigen
Distributors/Format: Orion Home Video (1/2")
Annotation: A Navy Seal team tries to stop a dictator from starting World War III in
the Middle East. Lt. Hawkins (Sheen) wants to destroy the missiles but SEAL team
member Lt. Cuman (Biehn) knows that would be suicide and leads their escape.
Haysbert plays Graham and Merkerson is Jolena.

NEAR DARK

Cast: Roger Aaron Brown*, Theresa Randle*, Lance Henriksen, Adrian Pasdar,
Jenny Wright, Troy Evans
Director: Kathryn Bigelow
Executive Producer: Edward S. Feldman, Charles R. Meeker
Music by: Tangerine Dream
Producer: Edward S. Feldman, Charles R. Meeker, Steven-Charles Jaffe, Eric Red

Screenwriter: Kathryn Bigelow, Eric Red
Tech Info: color/sound/95 min.   Type: Dramatic Feature
Date: 1987   Origin: USA
Company: F/M
Distributors/Format: DEG (16mm)
Annotation: Many twists and turns frame this film about vampires who slay victims for blood and avoid daylight and the authorities. Brown plays a cajun truck driver; Randle is one of the "Ladies in the car."

NECESSARY ROUGHNESS
Cast: Sinbad *, Jim Kelly*, Duane Davis*, Tony Dorsett*, Evander Holyfield*, Ed "Too Tall" Jones*, Jerry Rice*, Herschel Walker*, Randy White*, Scott Bakula
Director: Stan Dragoti
Producer: Mace Neufeld, Robert Rehme
Screenwriter: Rick Natkin, David Fuller
Tech Info: color/sound/108 min.   Type: Comedy Feature
Date: 1991   Origin: USA
Company: Paramount
Distributors/Format: Paramount Home Video (1/2")
Annotation: When University of Texas State attempts to revitalize its football team, the coaching staff recruits farmboy Paul Blake (Bakula) who convinces Andre Krimm (Sinbad) to join the Texas Armadillos also. The team is beset by many problems, not the least of which is their running back, Featherstone (Davis), who can't catch a pass. Sports star cameos include: Dorsett, Holyfield, Jones, Rice, Walker, Davidson, Kelly, and White.

NERVOUS TICKS
Cast: Brent Jennings*, Peter Boyle, Bill Pullman, Julie Brown, James Le Gros
Director: Rocky Lang
Executive Producer: Harold Welb
Music by: Jay Ferguson
Producer: Harold Welb, Arthur Goldblatt
Screenwriter: David Frankel
Tech Info: color/sound/95 min.   Type: Comedy Feature
Date: 1993   Origin: USA
Company: Nervous Ticks, Grandview Ave., Columbia/TriStar
Distributors/Format: Columbia/TriStar Home Video (1/2")
Annotation: York Daley (Pullman), a luggage handler for Grandview Airlines, tries to leave for Rio with his girlfriend but people keep getting in his way. Jennings plays Cole, a courier who has stolen a suitcase full of money and is being chased by "Iceman's" henchmen.

NETHERWORLD
Cast: Alex Datcher*, Michael Bendetti, Holly Floria, Denise Gentile, Anjanette Comer
Director: David Schmoeller
Executive Producer: Charles Band
Music by: David Bryan
Producer: Charles Band, Thomas Bradford
Screenwriter: Billy Chicago
Storywriter: Charles Band
Tech Info: color/sound/91 min.   Type: Dramatic Feature

Date: 1992   Origin: USA
Company: Full Moon Entertainment
Distributors/Format: Paramount (1/2")
Annotation: Corey Thornton (Bendetti) inherits a Louisiana mansion from the father
that abandoned him years ago. Down the road, at a brothel full of strange creatures
and succubi, Corey realizes that his father was heavily involved in black magic and
hopes to return from the dead. Datcher plays Mary Magdalene.

NEVER SAY NEVER AGAIN
Cast: Bernie Casey*, Klaus Maria Brandauer, Sean Connery, Max Von Sydow,
Barbara Carrera, Kim Basinger
Director: Irvin Kershner
Music Performer: Michel Legrand
Music by: Michel Legrand
Producer: Jack Schartzman
Screenwriter: Lorenzo Semple Jr.
Storywriter: Gus Fleming*, Kevin McClory, Jack Wittingham
Tech Info: color/sound/134 min.   Type: Dramatic Feature
Date: 1983   Origin: USA
Company: Warner Bros.
Distributors/Format: Warner Bros. Home Video, Inc. (1/2")
Annotation: Felix Leitner (Casey) is James Bond's (Connery) old buddy. Together
they follow the 007 routine of sex, violence and good guys eliminating bad guys.
The arch villain of this adventure is Emilio Largo (Brandauer).

NEVER TOO YOUNG TO DIE
Cast: Vanity *, John Stamos, John Anderson, Robert Englund, George Lazenby,
Gene Simmons
Director: Gil Bettman
Executive Producer: Hank Paul, Dorothy Koster-Paul
Music by: Lennie Niehaus, Chip Taylor, Ralph Lane, Michael Kingsley, Iren Koster,
Ralph Kingsley
Producer: Steven Paul, Hank Paul, Dorothy Koster-Paul
Screenwriter: Anton Fritz
Storywriter: Steven Paul
Tech Info: color/sound/97 min.   Type: Dramatic Feature
Date: 1986   Origin: USA
Company: Paul Entertainment, Inc.
Distributors/Format: Paul Releasing, Inc. (16mm, 1/2")
Annotation: Lance Stargrove (Stamos) and Danja Deering (Vanity) are secret agents
who must stop the Hermaphrodite Velvet Von Ranger (Simmons) in his maniacal
plans to take over the world.

NEVERENDING STORY, THE
Alternate: Die Unendliche Geschichte
Cast: Moses Gunn*, Barret Oliver, Gerald McRaney, Patricia Hayes, Tami Stronach
Director: Wolfgang Petersen
Executive Producer: Mark Damon, John W. Hyde
Music by: Giorgio Moroder, Klaus Doldinger
Producer: Mark Damon, Bernd Eichinger, John W. Hyde, Dieter Geissler
Screenwriter: Herman Weigel

Tech Info: color/sound/94 min.   Type: Dramatic Feature
Date: 1984   Origin: West Germany
Company: Neve Constantin, WDR
Distributors/Format: Warner Bros. Home Video, Inc. (1/2")
Annotation: Bastian (Oliver), troubled by the death of his mother and school bullies, wanders into a bookstore one day and soon finds himself moving through "Fantasia," a magical land he discovers in a book he borrows. Gunn plays Cairon, one of the characters in the book.

NEW AGE, THE
Cast: Samuel L. Jackson*, Peter Weller, Patrick Bauchau, Judy Davis, Rachel Rosenthal, Adam West
Director: Michael Tolkin
Executive Producer: Oliver Stone, Arnon Milchan
Music by: Mark Mothersbaugh
Producer: Oliver Stone, Arnon Milchan, Nick Wechsler, Keith Addis
Screenwriter: Michael Tolkin
Tech Info: color/sound/110 min.   Type: Comedy Feature
Date: 1994   Origin: USA
Company: Ixtlan Productions, Addis-Wechsler, Regency, Alcor
Distributors/Format: Warner Bros. Home Video, Inc. (1/2")
Annotation: In the midst of a recession, Los Angeles literary agent Peter Witner (Weller) decides to quit his job. He womanizes while Katherine (Davis), his graphic designer wife, tries to adapt to his wanderings. Jackson plays Dale Deveaux, a trainer for a sleazy telemarketing outfit where Peter seeks employment.

NEW BARBARIANS, THE
Alternate: I Nuovi Barbari
Cast: Fred Williamson*, George Eastman, Anna Kanakis, Enzo G. Castellari, Giancarlo Prete
Director: Enzo G. Castellari
Music by: Claudio Simonetti
Producer: Fabrizio De Angelis
Screenwriter: Tito Carpi, Enzo G. Castellari
Tech Info: color/sound/91 min.   Type: Dramatic Feature
Date: 1983   Origin: Italy
Company: Deaf
Annotation: Skorpion (Prete) and Nadir (Williamson) fend off gay bikers in the desert after a nuclear holocaust.

NEW EDEN
Cast: Lisa Bonet*, Janet Hubert-Whitten*, Adam Verduzco*, Stephen Baldwin, Michael Bowen, Tobin Bell
Director: Alan Metzger
Executive Producer: Jordan Davis
Producer: Harvey Frand, Jordan Davis
Screenwriter: Dan Gordon
Tech Info: color/sound/89 min.   Type: Dramatic Feature

Date: 1994   Origin: USA
Company: Davis Entertainment
Distributors/Format: MCA/Universal Home Video (1/2")
Annotation: The year is 2237 and all criminals are remanded to a prison colony in outer space. One of the prisoners befriends Lily (Bonet) and tries to help her improve her existence. Meanwhile, opposing factions fight for resources on the devastated planet.

NEW JACK CITY
Cast: Bill Nunn*, Wesley Snipes*, Kelly Jo Minter*, Phyllis Yvonne Stickney*, Bill Cobbs*, Tracy Camilla Johns*, Vanessa Williams*, Chris Rock*, Ice-T *, Flavor Flav*, Thalmus Rasulala*, Mario Van Peebles*, Teddy Riley*, Aaron Hall*, Damien Hall*, Allen Payne*, Fab 5 Freddy *, Michael Michele*, Christopher Williams*, Nick Ashford*, Laverne Hart*, Eek-A-Mouse *, Keith Sweat*, Marcella Lowery*, Tiger Frederick*, Rynel Johnson*, Judd Nelson, Russell Wong
Director: Mario Van Peebles*
Music by: Michel Colombier
Producer: George Jackson*, Doug McHenry*
Screenwriter: Thomas Lee Wright*, Barry Michael Cooper*
Tech Info: color/sound/97 min.   Type: Dramatic Feature
Date: 1991   Origin: USA
Company: Jacmac Films Inc.
Distributors/Format: Warner Bros. Home Video, Inc. (1/2")
Archives/Format: IUB - BFC/A (1/2")
Annotation: Detective Stone (Van Peebles), determined to arrest drug dealer Nino Brown (Snipes) and his sidekick Gee Money (Payne), brings unorthodox policeman Appleton (Ice-T) and Officer Peretti (Nelson) together. Appleton convinces ex-junkie Pookie (Rock) to inform on Brown. When finally brought to trial, Brown blames society and gets a light sentence only to be killed by the Old Man (Cobbs). Michele plays Selina; Nunn is Duh Duh Duh Man; Christopher Williams is Kareem Akbar; Vanessa Williams plays Keisha; Johns is Uniqua; Ashford is Rev. Oates; Stickney is Hawkins; Rasulala plays the Police Commissioner.

NIGERIAN ART: KINDRED SPIRITS
Series: Smithsonian World
Executive Producer: Adrian Malone*
Music by: Akin Euba*, Randy Weston
Narrator: Ruby Dee*
Producer: Carroll Parrott Blue*, Adrian Malone*
Screenwriter: Michael Olmert*
Tech Info: color/sound/60 min.   Type: Television Documentary
Date: 1990   Origin: USA
Company: WETA-TV/Smithsonian Institution
Distributors/Format: PBS Video (16mm; 1/2"), Smithsonian Institute (35mm)
Annotation: This documentary surveys contemporary Nigerian art and examines its roots in traditional African art and society; profiles eleven of Nigeria's painters, sculptors, textile artists, et. al.

NIGHT ANGEL

Cast: Helen Martin*, Debra Feuer, Karen Black, Isa Anderson, Linden Ashby, Sam Hennings
Director: Dominique Othenin-Girard
Executive Producer: Walter Josten
Music by: Cory Lerios
Producer: Joe Augustyn, Jeff Geoffray, Walter Josten
Screenwriter: Joe Augustyn, Walter Josten
Tech Info: color/sound/90 min.   Type: Dramatic Feature
Date: 1990   Origin: USA
Company: Paragon Arts
Distributors/Format: Paragon Video Productions (1/2")
Annotation: Lilith (Anderson), the demoness of Jewish folklore, rises from her grave and hopes to become a cover model for "Siren" magazine. She unsuccessfully seduces then kills its owner (Hennings) and crashes an office party to try to get her way. Lilith is finally contained by Sadie (Martin), a witch doctor who skewers the demon.

NIGHT EYES 2

Cast: Tim Russ*, Andrew Stevens, Shannon Tweed, Richard Chaves, Geno Silva
Director: Rodney McDonald
Executive Producer: Howard Baldwin, Barry Barnholtz
Producer: Howard Baldwin, Ashok Amritraj, Barry Barnholtz
Screenwriter: Simon Louis Ward
Storywriter: Andrew Stevens
Tech Info: color/sound/97 min.   Type: Dramatic Feature
Date: 1992   Origin: USA
Company: Two Eyes Productions, Amritraj Entertainment
Distributors/Format: Prism Entertainment (1/2")
Annotation: Will Griffith (Stevens) is a security expert protecting a dictator-in-exile (Chaves) and Marilyn (Tweed), his wife, until the dictator's bodyguard (Silva) catches Griffith's affair with Marilyn on tape. Russ appears as Jesse, Griffith's partner.

NIGHT OF THE LIVING DEAD

Cast: Tony Todd*, Tom Towles, Patricia Tallman, McKee Anderson, William Butler
Director: Tom Savini
Executive Producer: Menahem Golan, George A. Romero
Music by: Paul McCollough, Chris Pangikas
Producer: Menahem Golan, George A. Romero, John Russo, Russ Streiner
Screenwriter: George A. Romero
Tech Info: color/sound/96 min.   Type: Dramatic Feature
Date: 1990   Origin: USA
Company: John Russo-21st Century
Distributors/Format: Columbia Pictures Home Video (1/2")
Annotation: In this color remake of the 1968 classic, Ben (Todd) and Barbara (Tallman) join forces in a farm house besieged by zombies. Unlike the original, Barbara is the most rational of those trapped in the house.

NIGHT OF THE WARRIOR

Cast: Ken Foree*, Anthony Geary, Lorenzo Lamas, Kathleen Kinmont, Felicity Waterman
Director: Rafal Zielinski
Music by: Ed Tomney
Producer: Thomas Ian Griffith, Mike Erwin
Screenwriter: Thomas Ian Griffith
Tech Info: color/sound/100 min.   Type: Dramatic Feature
Date: 1991   Origin: USA
Company: Little Bear/Kodiak Films, A Place to Hide, et al.
Distributors/Format: Trimark Pictures (1/2")
Annotation: Miles Keane (Lamas), a Kung Fu master, borrows money from Lynch (Geary) to open a dance club and is forced to participate in illegal martial arts matches as repayment. Foree plays Oliver.

NIGHT ON EARTH

Cast: Giancarlo Esposito*, Rosie Perez, Winona Ryder, Gena Rowlands, Armin Mueller-Stahl
Director: Jim Jarmusch, Frederick Elmes
Executive Producer: Jim Stark
Music by: Kathleen Brennan, Tom Waits
Producer: Jim Jarmusch, Jim Stark
Storywriter: Jim Jarmusch
Tech Info: color/sound/128 min.   Type: Dramatic Feature
Date: 1992   Origin: USA
Company: Fine Line Features
Distributors/Format: New Line Cinema Home Video (1/2"), Turner Home Entertainment (1/2")
Annotation: Occupants of five taxi cabs in Los Angeles, New York, Paris, Rome and Helsinki are headed for some unexpected destinations. Esposito plays a New York cab driver.

NIGHT VISITOR

Alternate: Never Cry Devil
Cast: Richard Roundtree*, Elliot Gould, Henry Gibson, Allen Garfield, Shannon Tweed, Derek Rydall
Director: Rupert Hitzig
Executive Producer: Tom Broadbridge, Shelley E. Reid
Music by: Parmer Fuller
Producer: Alain Silver, Tom Broadbridge, Shelley E. Reid
Screenwriter: Randal Visovich
Tech Info: color/sound/93 min.   Type: Dramatic Feature
Date: 1990   Origin: USA
Company: Premiere
Distributors/Format: MGM/UA Home Video (1/2")
Annotation: Billy (Rydell) discovers that his high school history teacher Zachary Willard (Garfield) is responsible for a series of prostitute kidnappings. Police Captain Crane (Roundtree) doesn't believe Billy's story, so the boy calls upon retired policeman Devereaux (Gould), a friend of his dead father, to help.

NIGHT WE NEVER MET, THE
Cast: Naomi Campbell*, Matthew Broderick, Annabella Sciorra, Kevin Anderson, Justine Bateman
Director: Warren Leight
Executive Producer: Bob Weinstein, Harvey Weinstein, Sidney Kimmell
Music by: Evan Lurie
Producer: Bob Weinstein, Harvey Weinstein, Michael Peyser, Sidney Kimmell
Screenwriter: Warren Leight
Tech Info: color/sound/99 min.   Type: Comedy Feature
Date: 1993   Origin: USA
Company: Never Met Productions, Mike's Movies, TriBeCa
Distributors/Format: Miramax Home Video (1/2")
Annotation: Three strangers rent a time share in Manhattan and two of them fall in love. Campbell plays the French Cheese Shopper.

NIGHTHAWKS
Cast: Billy Dee Williams*, Sylvester Stallone, Rutger Hauer, Nigel Davenport, Lindsay Wagner
Director: Bruce Malmuth
Music Performer: Keith Emerson
Music by: Keith Emerson
Producer: Martin Poll
Screenwriter: David Shaber
Storywriter: David Shaber, Paul Sylbert
Tech Info: color/sound/99 min.   Type: Dramatic Feature
Date: 1981   Origin: USA
Company: Martin Poll, The Production Company
Distributors/Format: MCA Home Video (1/2")
Annotation: Police partners DaSilva (Stallone) and Fox (Williams) must catch an international terrorist, Wulfgar (Hauer), who has been bombing public places of business in London, Paris and New York. When Fox is wounded and DaSilva's girlfriend (Wagner) is threatened by Wulfgar, the assassination of the terrorist becomes a personal vendetta for DaSilva.

NIGHTMARE ON ELM STREET 3: DREAM WARRIORS, A
Cast: Laurence/Larry Fishburne*, Craig Wasson, Patricia Arquette, Heather Langenkamp, Priscilla Pointer
Director: Chuck Russell
Music by: Angelo Badalamenti
Producer: Robert Shaye, Sara Risher
Screenwriter: Wes Craven, Frank Darabont, Chuck Russell, Bruce Wagner
Storywriter: Wes Craven, Bruce Wagner
Tech Info: color/sound/96 min.   Type: Dramatic Feature
Date: 1987   Origin: USA
Company: New Line, Heron, Smart Egg
Distributors/Format: New Line Cinema Home Video (1/2")
Annotation: Teenagers in a small town have nightmares about Freddy Krueger which bring them to suicide. Fishburne plays Max.

NINA SIMONE

Alternate: Nina Simone at Ronnie Scott's London
Director: Steve Cleary, Rob Lemkin
Music Performer: Nina Simone*, Paul Robinson*
Producer: Steve Cleary, Rob Lemkin
Tech Info: color/sound/57 min.   Type: Concert Feature
Date: 1985   Origin: Great Britain
Annotation: Legendary African American blues singer and supporter during the Civil
Rights movement, Simone sings "Mr. Smith," "Fodder in her wings," "Be my
husband," "I loves you," "Porgy," "The other woman," among other songs.

NINTH CONFIGURATION, THE

Alternate: Twinkle Twinkle Killer Kane
Cast: Moses Gunn*, Scott Wilson, Jason Miller, Stacy Keach, Ed Flanders, George
Dicenzo
Director: William Peter Blatty
Music Performer: Barry Devorzon
Producer: William Peter Blatty
Screenwriter: William Peter Blatty
Tech Info: color/sound/115 min.   Type: Dramatic Feature
Date: 1980   Origin: USA
Company: Ninth Configuration, Co.
Distributors/Format: New World Home Video (1/2"), Warner Bros. Home Video, Inc.
(1/2")
Annotation: The film was one of the first to examine traumatized veterans and their
mental disorders. Isolated in a remote sanitarium, patients, one of whom is played
by Gunn, are treated by a doctor (Keach) who is also a victim.

NO EASY WALK (1962-66) - EPISODE 4

Series: Eyes On The Prize: America's Civil Rights Years
Director: Callie Crossley*, James A. DeVinney
Executive Producer: Henry Hampton*
Narrator: Julian Bond*
Producer: Henry Hampton*, Callie Crossley*, James A. DeVinney
Screenwriter: Callie Crossley*, James A. DeVinney
Speaker: A. Philip Randolph*, James Forman*, Bernice Johnson Reagon*, John
Lewis*, James Bevel*, Andrew Young*, Ralph Abernathy*, Fred L. Shuttlesworth*,
Charles Sherrod*, William G. Anderson*, John F. Kennedy, Burke Marshall, George
C. Wallace, Robert Kennedy, Eugene "Bull" Connor, David Vann, Phillipe Sadde,
Joe Medtuck, Michael Gross, Jerry Bick, Sterling Hayden, Jim Bouton
Tech Info: mixed/sound/56 min.   Type: Television Documentary
Date: 1986   Origin: USA
Company: Blackside, Inc.
Distributors/Format: PBS Video (16mm; 1/2")
Archives/Format: IUB - AAAMC (1/2")
Annotation: This segment chronicles the mass confrontations between white
authority and civil rights demonstrators. Sheriff Pritchett successfully stops the
marches led by King in Albany, Georgia, when the U.S. Government refuses to send
federal troops. In Birmingham, Bull Connor uses police dogs and fire hoses to stop
marches. The episode culminates in the climactic march on Washington, D.C.

NO ESCAPE

Cast: Ernie Hudson*, Lance Henriksen, Kevin J. O'Connor, Ray Liotta, Stuart Wilson, Kevin Dillon
Director: Martin Campbell
Executive Producer: Jake Eberts
Music by: Graeme Revell
Producer: Gale Anne Hurd, Jake Eberts
Screenwriter: Michael Gaylin, Joel Gross
Tech Info: color/sound/118 min.   Type: Dramatic Feature
Date: 1994   Origin: USA
Company: Platinum Pictures, Pacific Western
Distributors/Format: Savoy Home Video (1/2")
Annotation: In the year 2002, military killer Robbins (Liotta) faces life imprisonment for murdering his commanding officer. Unable to adapt to life in prison, Robbins is remanded to Absalom, an isolated island for hard-core criminals. Hudson plays Hawkins.

NO HOLDS BARRED

Cast: Armelia McQueen*, Bill Henderson*, Tom "Tiny" Lister Jr.*, Hulk Hogan, Kurt Fuller
Director: Thomas J. Wright
Executive Producer: Hulk Hogan, Vince McMahon
Music by: Jim Johnston, Richard Stone
Producer: Hulk Hogan, Michael Rachmil, Vince McMahon
Screenwriter: Dennis Hackin
Tech Info: color/sound/93 min.   Type: Dramatic Feature
Date: 1989   Origin: USA
Company: Shane
Distributors/Format: New Line Cinema Home Video (1/2")
Annotation: Rip (Hogan), a pro-wrestler, refuses to appear on World Television Network so Brell (Fuller), the network boss, comes up with a new idea inspired by drunken bar brawls. Lister plays Zeus, Henderson is Charlie and McQueen plays Sadie.

NO MAN'S LAND

Cast: Bill Duke*, Charlie Sheen, D.B. Sweeney, Lara Harris
Director: Peter Werner
Executive Producer: Ron Howard, Tony Ganz
Music by: Basil Poledouris
Producer: Ron Howard, Joseph Stern, Tony Ganz, Dick Wolf
Screenwriter: Dick Wolf, Jack Behr, Sandy Kroopf
Tech Info: color/sound/107 min.   Type: Dramatic Feature
Date: 1987   Origin: USA
Company: Orion
Distributors/Format: Orion Home Video (1/2")
Annotation: Officer Benjy Taylor (Sweeney) goes undercover at a Porshe dealership to solve a murder and expose a ring of car thieves. Duke plays Malcolm.

NO MAPS ON MY TAPS
Cast: Howard "Sandman" Sims*, Chuck Green*, Bunny Briggs*, Bill "Bojangles" Robinson*
Director: George T. Nierenberg
Tech Info: color/sound/58 min.   Type: Documentary Feature
Date: 1979   Origin: USA
Studio: Independent
Distributors/Format: Direct Cinema Limited (16mm; 1/2")
Archives/Format: IUB - BFC/A (16mm)
Annotation: Nierenberg's film is a portrait of three surviving hoofers, Sandman Sims, Chuck Green, and Bunny Briggs. Rare film footage and personal interviews provide insight into the social history and performance development of jazz tap dancing.

NO REGRET (NON, JE NE REGRETTE RIEN)
Director: Marlon T. Riggs*
Producer: Marlon T. Riggs*
Tech Info: color/sound/38 min.   Type: Documentary Feature
Date: 1992   Origin: USA
Studio: Independent
Company: Signifyin' Productions
Distributors/Format: Frameline Distribution (1/2"), Signifyin' Works (1/2")
Archives/Format: IUB - BFC/A (1/2")
Annotation: Riggs film portrays the strength of HIV victims. It forces the audience to confront the stigma and shame that surrounds AIDS.

NO TIME TO LOSE
Director: Allen Siegel, Patricia Benoit
Tech Info: color/sound/28 min.   Type: Documentary Short
Date: 1988   Origin: USA
Studio: Independent
Distributors/Format: Third World Newsreel (1/2")
Annotation: 40% of all black children and 50% of all hispanic children live below the national poverty line. Seven bright children describe the day-to-day conditions behind the statistics.

NO WAY OUT
Cast: Jason Bernard*, Iman *, Kevin Costner, Gene Hackman, Sean Young
Director: Roger Donaldson
Executive Producer: Mace Neufeld
Music by: Maurice Jarre
Producer: Mace Neufeld, Laura Ziskin, Robert Garland
Screenwriter: Robert Garland
Tech Info: color/sound/114 min.   Type: Dramatic Feature
Date: 1987   Origin: USA
Company: Neufeld, Ziskin, Garland
Distributors/Format: Orion Home Video (1/2")
Annotation: Susan Atwell (Young), who is Tom Farrell's (Costner) lover and mistress to his boss (Hackman) is murdered. Bernard plays Major Donovan in this military mystery, a remake of the 1948 film noir classic THE BIG CLOCK.

NOBODY'S FOOL
Cast: Charles Barnett*, Rosanna Arquette, Louise Fletcher, Eric Roberts, Mare Winningham, Jim Youngs
Director: Evelyn Purcell
Executive Producer: Cary Brokaw
Music by: James Newton Howard*
Producer: Cary Brokaw, James C. Katz, Jon S. Denny
Screenwriter: Beth Henley
Tech Info: color/sound/107 min.   Type: Dramatic Feature
Date: 1986   Origin: USA
Company: Katz, Denny
Distributors/Format: Island Home Video (1/2")
Annotation: Cassie (Arquette), a young pregnant woman, assaults her baby's father after he reneges on his promise to marry her. She then decides to follow her dream of becoming a member of a traveling theater troupe. Barnett plays Nick.

NOCTURNA
Alternate: Nocturna, Granddaughter of Dracula
Cast: Sy Richardson*, Nai Bonet*, John Carradine, Yvonne De Carlo, Tony Hamilton
Director: Harry Hurwitz
Executive Producer: Nai Bonet*
Producer: Nai Bonet*, Vernon Becker
Screenwriter: Harry Hurwitz
Tech Info: color/sound/85 min.   Type: Dramatic Feature
Date: 1979   Origin: USA
Company: Compass
Annotation: Nocturna (Bonet), granddaughter of Count Dracula (Carradine), runs away with a disco musician (Hamilton). Richardson appears as RH Factor.

NORMA RAE
Cast: Frank McRae*, Beau Bridges, Sally Field, Ron Leibman
Tech Info: color/sound/110 min.   Type: Dramatic Feature
Date: 1979   Origin: USA
Company: Fox
Distributors/Format: Fox Home Video (1/2")
Annotation: Norma Rae (Field), a cotton mill worker in the South, decides to help Reuben (Liebman), a New York labor organizer, establish a union. Despite her husband's (Bridges) jealousy of the relationship between Norma Rae and Reuben, she disrupts production by organizing a workers' strike. McRae appears as James Brown.

NORTH AVENUE IRREGULARS, THE
Cast: Virginia Capers*, Barbara Harris, Edward Herrmann, Susan Clark
Director: Bruce Bilson
Music by: Robert F. Brunner
Producer: Ron Miller, Tom Leetch
Screenwriter: Don Tait
Tech Info: color/sound/99 min.   Type: Comedy Feature

Date: 1979   Origin: USA
Company: Walt Disney Productions
Annotation: Priest Michael Hill (Herrmann) delegates church authority to the women of his parish. After one woman (Kelly) squanders church money at the races, the group bands together to recover their loss and expose the organized crime ring that runs the track. Capers plays Cleo.

NORTH DALLAS FORTY
Cast: Carlos Brown*, Nick Nolte, Charles Durning, Bo Svenson, Mac Davis, Dayle Haddon
Director: Ted Kotcheff
Executive Producer: Jack B. Bernstein
Music by: John Scott
Producer: Frank Yablans, Jack B. Bernstein
Screenwriter: Ted Kotcheff, Frank Yablans, Peter Gent
Tech Info: color/sound/119 min.   Type: Dramatic Feature
Date: 1979   Origin: USA
Distributors/Format: Paramount Home Video (1/2")
Annotation: Phillip Elliott (Nolte) is a veteran pass-receiver for the North Dallas Bulls, whose injuries suffered in the game leave him in constant pain. The coaches and team owner have little or no regard for the health of Balford (Brown) whose career is ended by a permanent injury on the field.

NOTHING LASTS FOREVER
Cast: Clarice Taylor*, Dan Aykroyd, Lauren Tom, Zach Galligan, Appollonia van Ravenstein
Producer: Lorne Michaels
Tech Info: color/sound/82 min.   Type: Comedy Feature
Date: 1984   Origin: USA
Company: Broadway
Distributors/Format: MGM/UA Home Video (1/2")
Annotation: Beckett (Galligan), a New York City artist, is not permitted to make his art but is told by the Port Authority which rules the city to work the Holland Tunnel. After taking an unexpected trip to the moon, he finds true love and performs at Carnegie Hall. Taylor appears as Lu.

NOTHING PERSONAL
Cast: Roscoe Lee Browne*, Donald Sutherland, Suzanne Somers, Lawrence Dane
Director: George Bloomfield
Executive Producer: Alan Hamel, Jay Bernstein, Norman Hirschfield
Producer: David Perlmutter, Alan Hamel, Jay Bernstein, Norman Hirschfield
Screenwriter: Robert Kaufman
Tech Info: color/sound/97 min.   Type: Comedy Feature
Date: 1980   Origin: Canada
Company: AIP, Filmways
Annotation: Keller (Sutherland) is a professor who objects to the killing of baby seals. He teams up with others, like Mr. Paxton (Browne), who try to stop the senseless slaughter.

NOW PRETEND

Director: Leah Gilliam*
Speaker: David *, Leah *, Lisa *, Sonya *, Tanya *
Storywriter: John Howard Griffin
Tech Info: bw/sound/11 min.   Type: Experimental Short
Date: 1992   Origin: USA
Studio: Independent
Distributors/Format: Third World Newsreel (1/2")
Annotation: This experimental film uses language, personal memories and the 1959 text, "Black Like Me," to investigate the use of race as an arbitrary signifier.

NUMBER ONE WITH A BULLET

Cast: Billy Dee Williams*, Mykelti Williamson*, Robert Carradine, Valerie Bertinelli
Director: Jack Smight
Music by: Alf Clausen
Producer: Yoram Globus, Menahem Golan
Screenwriter: Gail Morgan Hickman*, James Belushi, Andrew Kurtzman, Rob Riley
Storywriter: Gail Morgan Hickman*
Tech Info: color/sound/101 min.   Type: Dramatic Feature
Date: 1987   Origin: USA
Company: Golan-Globus
Distributors/Format: Cannon Home Video (1/2")
Annotation: Nick Berzak (Carradine) and Frank Hazeltine (Williams) are policemen who will bend the law to make an arrest. Berzak is separated from his wife Teresa (Bertinelli) and jealous of her whereabouts, while Hazeltine is a womanizer. Williamson plays Casey.

ODD JOBS

Cast: Robert Townsend*, Starletta DuPois*, Paul Reiser, Rick Overton, Scott McGinnis
Director: Mark Story
Music by: Robert Folk
Producer: Keith Rubinstein
Screenwriter: Robert Conte, Peter Martin Wortmann
Tech Info: color/sound/89 min.   Type: Comedy Feature
Date: 1986   Origin: USA
Company: HBO, Silver Screen
Distributors/Format: TriStar Pictures Inc. (1/2")
Annotation: After their summer jobs fall through, five college roommates decide to form their own moving company. Townsend is Dwight, who works as a caddy before becoming a mover. DuPois plays his mother.

ODDS & ENDS: A NEW-AGE AMAZON FABLE

Cast: Cora Lee Day*, Latanya West*, Cyndi Gossett*, Kenya Williams*, Juliette Jeffers*, Jacquelyn Levy*, Larry Marks, Al Calabrese
Director: Michelle Parkerson*
Music by: Wayson Jones*
Producer: Gail Choice
Screenwriter: Michelle Parkerson*
Tech Info: color/sound/30 min.   Type: Dramatic Short

Date: 1993   Origin: USA
Studio: Independent
Company: Eye of the Storm Productions
Distributors/Format: American Film Institute (16mm; 1/2"), Third World Newsreel (1/2")
Annotation: Parkerson's allegory explores the struggle of the sexes and races. Loz (West) is a commander for mother power trying to bring unity among all women in the hope of defeating the evil, ultra-right clones.

OFF BEAT
Cast: Cleavant Derricks*, Judge Reinhold, Meg Tilly, Jacques D'Amboise, Harvey Keitel
Director: Michael Dinner
Producer: Joe Roth, Harry Ufland
Screenwriter: Mark Medoff
Storywriter: Mark Medoff
Tech Info: color/sound/92 min.   Type: Comedy Feature
Date: 1986   Origin: USA
Company: Silver Screen Partners II
Distributors/Format: Touchstone Home Video (1/2")
Annotation: Reinhold plays Joe Gower, a librarian who agrees to impersonate a police officer as a favor for his friend Abe Washington (Derricks) whose cover Gower accidentally blows. The impersonation goes awry when Joe falls in love with one of "New York's finest," policewoman Rachel Wareham (Tilly).

OFF LIMITS
Cast: Gregory Hines*, Willem Dafoe, Amanda Pays, Scott Glenn, Fred Ward, Kai Tong Lim
Director: Christopher Crowe
Tech Info: color/sound/102 min.   Type: Dramatic Feature
Date: 1988   Origin: USA
Company: American Entertainment Partners, Fox
Distributors/Format: Fox Home Video (1/2")
Annotation: Albaby Perkins (Hines) is ordered to keep the peace in a city slowly being strangled by the effects of war. In plainclothes, he finds that crimes of war are not only on the front lines, but also on the battlefields of Khe Sanh.

OFFICER AND A GENTLEMAN, AN
Cast: Louis Gossett Jr.*, Harold Sylvester*, Debra Winger, Richard Gere, David Keith, Robert Loggia
Director: Taylor Hackford
Music Performer: Jack Nitzsche
Music by: Jack Nitzsche
Producer: Martin Elfand
Screenwriter: Douglas Day Stewart
Tech Info: color/sound/126 min.   Type: Dramatic Feature
Date: 1982   Origin: USA
Company: Lorimar
Distributors/Format: Paramount Home Video (1/2")
Archives/Format: IUB - BFC/A (1/2")
Annotation: Gossett is Zack Mayo's (Gere) hard core drill sergeant, Emil Foley, who pushes him and all his Naval Officer candidates to peak potential. Sylvester

appears as Perryman, a fellow candidate who has difficulty shining his belt buckles.

OFFSPRING, THE

Alternate: From a Whisper to a Scream
Cast: Rosalind Cash*, Harry Caesar*, Clu Gulager, Vincent Price, Terry Kiser
Director: Jeff Burr
Executive Producer: Bubba Truckadaro, David Shaheen
Music by: Jim Manzie, Pat Regan
Producer: Darin Scott*, William Burr, Bubba Truckadaro, David Shaheen
Screenwriter: Darin Scott*, Jeff Burr, Courtney Joyner
Tech Info: color/sound/96 min.   Type: Dramatic Feature
Date: 1987   Origin: USA
Company: Conquest
Distributors/Format: TMS (16mm)
Annotation: Julian White (Price) relates four terrifying tales about small Oldfield, Tennessee, to a news reporter. Caesar plays Felder Evans, an eccentric man who rescues a wounded hood from the swamp in one tale. Cash plays the snake woman and voodoo priestess who owns a circus sideshow.

OLDER WOMEN AND LOVE

Director: Camille Billops*, James Hatch
Producer: Camille Billops*, James Hatch
Tech Info: color/sound/26 min.   Type: Experimental Short
Date: 1987   Origin: USA
Studio: Independent
Company: Hatch-Billops Production
Distributors/Format: Third World Newsreel (1/2")
Annotation: Using interviews and dramatizations, Billops and Hatch explore social attitudes towards relationships between older women and younger men.

OLIVER & COMPANY

Cast: Roscoe Lee Browne*, Sheryl Lee Ralph*, William Glover*, Bette Midler, Joey Lawrence, Billy Joel
Music by: J.A.C. Redford
Producer: George Scribner
Screenwriter: Gerrit Graham, Jim Cox, Timothy J. Disney, James Mangold, Roger Allers, Chris Bailey, Michael Cedeno, Kirk Wise, Pete Young, Dave Michener, Leon Joosen, Samuel Graham, Chris Hubbell, Steve Hulet, Danny Mann
Storywriter: Vance Gerry, Mike Gabriel, Joe Ranft, Gary Trousdale, Jim Mitchell, Kevin Lima
Tech Info: color/sound/72 min.   Type: Animated Feature
Date: 1988   Origin: USA
Company: Walt Disney Prod., Silver Screen Partners III
Distributors/Format: Buena Vista Home Video (1/2")
Annotation: Loosely based on Dickens' "Oliver Twist," the film is set in contemporary New York. Oliver (Lawrence) tries to avoid trouble as he learns to fend for himself. Browne plays Francis.

OLIVER'S STORY
Cast: Cynthia McPherson*, Beatrice Winde*, Candice Bergen, Ryan O'Neal, Nicola Pagett
Director: John Korty
Music by: Lee Holdridge
Producer: David V. Picker
Screenwriter: John Korty, Erich Segal
Storywriter: Erich Segal
Tech Info: color/sound/92 min.   Type: Dramatic Feature
Date: 1978   Origin: USA
Company: Paramount
Distributors/Format: Paramount Home Video (1/2")
Annotation: In this sequel to LOVE STORY, Oliver Barrett IV (O'Neal) mourns his young wife's death, but manages to find success and love again. McPherson plays Anita.

ON BECOMING A WOMAN: MOTHERS AND DAUGHTERS TALKING TOGETHER
Director: Cheryl Chisholm*
Executive Producer: Byllye Avery*
Music by: Bernice Johnson Reagon*, Tashi Reagon*
Producer: Byllye Avery*, Cheryl Chisholm*
Speaker: Byllye Avery*, Melba Hill*, Leslie P. Allen*, Rashaunda Allen*, Sonja Avery*, Cheryl Chisholm*, Hallie Hobson*, Margaret Cole*, Crystal Cole*, Cecelia Caines*, Mellissa Caines*, Daphne Hoyt*, Eleanor Hinton-Hoyt*, Ama Saran*, Imania Saran-Coleman*, Janice Whatley*, Daria Whatley*
Tech Info: color/sound/95 min.   Type: Documentary Feature
Date: 1987   Origin: USA
Company: Black Women's Health Project
Distributors/Format: National Black Women's Health Project (16mm)
Archives/Format: IUB - BFC/A (16mm)
Annotation: Mothers and daughters share their experiences about their first menstrual period; discuss sex and birth control, love and desire; and bare their innermost feelings about their relationships. Workshop leaders: Byllye Avery, Melba Hill, Leslie P. Allen; Shirikiana Gerima is the cinematographer.

ON MY OWN: THE TRADITIONS OF DAISY TURNER
Speaker: Daisy Turner*
Tech Info: color/sound/28 min.   Type: Documentary Short
Date: 1987   Origin: USA
Company: The Vermont Folklife Center, University of VT
Distributors/Format: Filmakers Library, Inc. (16mm; 1/2")
Annotation: In the Vermont hills, 102-year-old Daisy Turner's memories go back to the Civil War. Daughter of a slave, Daisy was one of 13 children whose days were spent on farm chores and evenings were spent story-telling and singing.

ON THE BLOCK
Cast: Howard E. Rollins Jr.*, Blaze Starr, Marilyn Jones, Jerry Whiddon, Michael Gabel
Director: Steve Yeager
Music by: Charles Barnett*

Producer: Steve Yeager, Manuel Cabrera-Santos
Screenwriter: Steve Yeager, Linda Chambers
Tech Info: color/sound/95 min.   Type: Dramatic Feature
Date: 1991   Origin: USA
Company: Snakeskin Pictures
Distributors/Format: Vidmark Entertainment Home Video (1/2")
Annotation: Rollins is city developer Clay Beasley who wants to tear down the Block (Baltimore's red-light district) and construct office buildings. The district attracts Libby (Jones) to its lucrative markets.

ON THE EDGE

Cast: Pam Grier*, Bruce Dern, Bill Bailey, Jim Haynie, John Marley
Director: Rob Nilsson
Music by: Herb Philhofer
Producer: Jeffrey Hayes, Rob Nilsson
Screenwriter: Rob Nilsson
Tech Info: color/sound/92 min.   Type: Dramatic Feature
Date: 1985   Origin: USA
Company: Alliance
Distributors/Format: Skouras (1/2")
Annotation: Wes Holman (Dern) is a long-distance runner banned from the sport 20 years ago who is determined to win the Cielo-Sea race as an "outlaw" runner. Grier plays Cora, Holman's lover.

ON THE NICKEL

Cast: Hal Williams*, Ralph Waite, Donald Moffat, Penelope Allen
Director: Ralph Waite
Music by: Fred Myrow
Producer: Ralph Waite
Screenwriter: Ralph Waite
Tech Info: color/sound/96 min.   Type: Dramatic Feature
Date: 1980   Origin: USA
Company: Rose's Park
Annotation: Sam (Moffat) recovered from alcoholism and pulled himself out of the gutter only to find himself facing addiction again when his friend C.G. (Waite) is in trouble. Williams plays Paul.

ON THE RIGHT TRACK

Cast: Gary Coleman*, Maureen Stapleton, Michael Lembeck, Lisa Eilbacher, Norman Fell
Director: Lee Philips
Executive Producer: Harry Evans Sloan
Producer: Ronald Jacobs, Harry Evans Sloan
Tech Info: color/sound/97 min.   Type: Dramatic Feature
Date: 1981
Company: Zephyr Productions
Distributors/Format: CBS/Fox Video (Canada) LTD. (1/2")
Annotation: A 10-year-old orphan shoe shine boy (Coleman) lives in a train station and discovers that he has a talent for picking racetrack horse winners.

ON THE RUN
Cast: Paul Winfield*, Rod Taylor, Beau Cox, Shirley Cameron
Director: Mende Brown
Executive Producer: Bill Anderson
Music by: Laurie Lewis
Producer: Bill Anderson, Mende Brown
Screenwriter: Michael Fisher
Tech Info: color/sound/101 min.   Type: Dramatic Feature
Date: 1983   Origin: Australia
Company: Pigelu
Distributors/Format: Cineworld (1/2")
Annotation: Harry (Winfield), an American ex-convict in Sydney, befriends a
French-speaking youngster who's witnessed a murder.

ONCE UPON A FOREST
Cast: Ben Vereen*, Angel Harper*, Rickey Collins*, Michael Crawford, Ellen Blain,
Ben Gregory
Director: Charles Grosvenor
Executive Producer: William Hanna, Paul Gertz
Music by: James Horner
Producer: David Kirschner, Jerry Mills, William Hanna, Paul Gertz
Screenwriter: Mark Young, Kelly Ward
Tech Info: color/sound/72 min.   Type: Animated Feature
Date: 1993   Origin: USA
Company: Hanna-Barbera Productions
Distributors/Format: Fox Home Video (1/2")
Annotation: Forest creatures seek herbs to save their friend who's been poisoned by
gas fumes. Vereen provides the voice of Phineas, a preacher bird who navigates the
creatures past dangerous construction and into the meadows.

ONE DARK NIGHT
Cast: Leslie Speights*, Meg Tilly, Melissa Newman, Robin Evans, Donald Hotton
Director: Tom McLoughlin
Executive Producer: Thomas P. Johnson
Music by: Bob Summers
Producer: Michael Schroeder, Thomas P. Johnson
Screenwriter: Tom McLoughlin
Tech Info: color/sound/89 min.   Type: Dramatic Feature
Date: 1983   Origin: USA
Company: ComWorld
Annotation: Julie (Tilly), desperate to be accepted by her peers, agrees to spend the
night in a mausoleum. A dead man with telekinetic powers saves her from her
friends' planned pranks. Speights plays Kitty.

ONE DOWN, TWO TO GO
Cast: Jim Brown*, Jim Kelly*, Richard Roundtree*, Fred Williamson*, Paula Sills*,
Jerry Jones
Director: Fred Williamson*, Jerry Jones
Music by: Joe Trunzo, Herb Hetzer, Rodney Franklin
Producer: Fred Williamson*, Jerry Jones
Tech Info: color/sound/84 min.   Type: Dramatic Feature

Date: 1983
Studio: Almi Cinema 5 Films Release
Company: Po' Boy Productions & Camelot Films
Annotation: When a martial arts match is rigged and the winners don't get paid, Ralph (Roundtree) and Chuck (Kelly), the actual match winner, take matters into their own hands. Their friends, J (Brown) and Cal (Williamson) appear on the scene and seek justice.

ONE FALSE MOVE
Cast: Cynda Williams*, Michael Beach*, Phyllis Kirklin*, Kevin Hunter*, Robert Anthony Bell*, B.L. Brister*, Bill Paxton, Billy Bob Thornton
Director: Carl Franklin*
Music Performer: Brenda Sutton*, Reverend Julian Turner*, Michael Sutton*, Eric Gale*, Charles Meeks*, Peter Haycock, Terry Plumeri
Music by: Peter Haycock, Derek Holt, Terry Plumeri
Producer: Jesse Beaton, Ben Myron, Miles A. Copeland III, Paul Colichman, Harold Welb
Screenwriter: Billy Bob Thornton, Tom Epperson
Tech Info: color/sound/106 min.   Type: Dramatic Feature
Date: 1991   Origin: USA
Company: I.R.S. Media Inc.
Distributors/Format: Kino International Corp. (1/2"), Columbia/TriStar Home Video (1/2")
Annotation: After brutally murdering a black family in Los Angeles, Fantasia (Williams), her lover Ray (Thornton), and the knife wielding Pluto (Beach) become fugitives from the law. Hunter plays Fantasia's brother; Kirklin, Fantasia's mother; and Bell, Fantasia's five-year-old son. Brister briefly appears as the blues harmonic player.

ONE GOOD COP
Cast: Lisa Arrindell*, Vondie Curtis-Hall*, Michael Keaton, Anthony LaPaglia, Rene Russo, Kevin Conway
Director: Heywood Gould
Executive Producer: Harry Colomby
Music by: William Ross
Producer: Harry Colomby, Lawrence Mark
Screenwriter: Heywood Gould
Tech Info: color/sound/107 min.   Type: Dramatic Feature
Date: 1991   Origin: USA
Company: Hollywood Pictures
Distributors/Format: Buena Vista Home Video (1/2")
Annotation: Artie Lewis (Keaton), a police officer and his wife decide to adopt three children after their mother is killed. The added stress and pressure forces him to become involved in illegal activities. Despite the momentary indiscretions, all is worked out in the end. Arrindell portrays the character Raisa.

ONE MORE SATURDAY NIGHT
Cast: Meshach Taylor*, Dianne B. Shaw*, Wynetta Harris*, Wynton Harris*, Tom Davis, Al Franken, Moira Harris
Director: Dennis Klein
Executive Producer: Dan Aykroyd
Music by: David McHugh

Producer: Dan Aykroyd, Tova Laiter, Robert Kosberg, Jonathan Bernstein
Screenwriter: Tom Davis, Al Franken
Tech Info: color/sound/95 min.　　　Type: Comedy Feature
Date: 1986　Origin: USA
Company: AAR, Tova Laiter
Distributors/Format: Columbia Pictures Home Video (1/2")
Annotation: Residents of a small, Minnesota town prepare to go out on Saturday night. Bill Neal (Taylor) and his wife Lynn (Shaw) leave their kids (Wynton and Wynetta Harris) with a babysitter.

ONLIEST ONE ALIVE, THE
Director: Dustin Teel
Music Performer: Val Ward*
Narrator: Val Ward*
Producer: Sara Buchwald
Screenwriter: Sara Buchwald
Speaker: Hyazinth Thrash*
Storywriter: Marion Torner*
Tech Info: color/sound/58 min.　　　Type: Dramatized Documentary
Date: 1989　Origin: USA
Company: Indiana Community for the Humanities, Filmusik Inc
Archives/Format: IUB - BFC/A (1/2")
Annotation: A survivor of the Jamestown massacre, Hyazinth, expresses the agony and frustration that are characteristic of disaster survivors.

OPPORTUNITY KNOCKS
Cast: John Cothran Jr.*, Todd Graff*, Robert Loggia, Julia Campbell, Dana Carvey
Director: Donald Petrie
Executive Producer: Brad Grey
Music by: Miles Goodman, Tim Sexton, Becky Mancuso
Producer: Christopher Meledandri, Mark Gordon, Brad Grey
Screenwriter: Mitchel Katlin, Nat Bernstein
Tech Info: color/sound/105 min.　　　Type: Comedy Feature
Date: 1990　Origin: USA
Company: Imagine Entertainment
Distributors/Format: Universal Home Video (1/2")
Annotation: Eddie Farrell (Carvey), a small-time Chicago con man, gets involved in a complicated scam that gets him into trouble with the mob then he falls in love with the sister of his latest victim. Cothran plays the building commissioner.

ORIGINAL INTENT
Cast: Robert DoQui*, Patrick Malone*, Virginia Capers*, Leslie DoQui*, Kris Kristofferson, Jay Richardson
Director: Rob Marcarelli
Music by: Ernie Rettino, Debby Kerner Rettino, C. Barny Robertson
Producer: Rob Marcarelli
Screenwriter: Rob Marcarelli, Joyce Marcarelli
Tech Info: color/sound/97 min.　　　Type: Dramatic Feature

Date: 1992   Origin: USA
Company: Mission of Hope Productions, Marcarelli Production
Distributors/Format: Paramount Home Video (1/2")
Annotation: Matthew Cameron (Richardson) recruits his yuppie friends to aid a Los Angeles homeless shelter run by Ben Reid (Robert DoQui). Cameron has a change of heart when Ben (Malone), a homeless boy who is staying with him, steals his appliances. Leslie DoQui also appears.

ORNETTE: MADE IN AMERICA
Director: Shirley Clarke
Producer: Kathelin Hoffman
Tech Info: color/sound/80 min.   Type: Documentary Feature
Date: 1985   Origin: USA
Studio: Independent
Company: Caravan of Dreams
Distributors/Format: Facets Multimedia, Inc. (1/2"), Caravan Pictures Home Video (1/2")
Annotation: An in-depth documentary tracing the rhythms, images and myths of America through the eyes of saxophonist Coleman, whose radical music defied the conventions of modern jazz.

ORPHANS
Cast: Novella Nelson*, Albert Finney, Matthew Modine, Kevin Anderson
Director: Alan J. Pakula
Music by: Michael Small
Producer: Alan J. Pakula, Susan Solt
Screenwriter: Lyle Kessler
Storywriter: Lyle Kessler
Tech Info: color/sound/115 min.   Type: Dramatic Feature
Date: 1987   Origin: USA
Company: Lorimar
Annotation: Treat (Modine) and Phillip (Anderson), two orphaned brothers, unintentionally befriend a Chicago gangster on the run. Harold (Finney) hires the boys as bodyguards and treats them lavishly. When Harold dies, the two are devastated. Nelson plays Mattie.

OTIS REDDING AT MONTEREY
Director: Chris Hegedus, D.A. Pennebaker, Stuart Cornfeld
Tech Info: mixed/sound/30 min.   Type: Concert Short
Date: 1986   Origin: USA
Company: Douglas Corporation, Pennebraker Associates
Archives/Format: IUB - BFC/A (1/2")
Annotation: Black and white footage of Redding's performance at the Monterey Pop Festival (1967) a few months before his death in a plane crash. It includes a live performance from his "Stay Volt" tour the same year and on camera interview with fellow musicians, Jones and Cropper from the band, Booker T. Jones and the M.G.'s.

OUR HOUSE: GAYS AND LESBIANS IN THE HOOD
Series: Not Channel Zero
Director: Cyrille Phipps*
Producer: Cyrille Phipps*, Donna Golden*
Speaker: Reverend Calvin Butts*, Jerome Wright*, LaRose Parris*, Jocelyn Taylor*, George Sosa*, Aarin Burch*, Candace Boyce*, Rev. Zachary Jones*
Tech Info: color/sound/28 min.   Type: Documentary Short
Date: 1993   Origin: USA
Studio: Independent
Company: Black Planet Productions
Distributors/Format: Third World Newsreel (1/2")
Archives/Format: IUB - AAAMC (1/2")
Annotation: The film examines black gay/lesbian perspectives, highlighting media images of gay bashing and how these attitudes reflect mainstream notions about homosexuality.

OUR OLYMPIC HERO: JESSE OWENS STORY, THE
Cast: Dorian Harewood*, Debbi Morgan*, Georg Stanford Brown*, George Kennedy, Barry Corbin, Kai Wulff
Director: Richard Irving
Producer: Harold Gast
Screenwriter: Harold Gast
Tech Info: color/sound/160 min.   Type: Docudrama
Date: 1984   Origin: USA
Company: Paramount
Distributors/Format: Magnum Entertainment (1/2"), Paramount Home Video (1/2")
Annotation: Spanning more than 40 years, this film traces Owen's life from his days as a sharecropper's son, through his record-breaking college years, his marriage to his high school sweetheart, his victories in the 1936 Olympics, and his 30 year struggle to survive in a prejudiced country that he deeply loved.

OUT OF BOUNDS
Cast: Glynn Turman*, Ji-Tu Cumbuka*, Anthony Michael Hall, Jenny Wright, Jeff Kober
Director: Richard Tuggle
Executive Producer: John Tarnoff, Ray Hartwick
Music by: Stewart Copeland
Producer: Charles Fries, Mike Rosenfeld, John Tarnoff, Ray Hartwick
Screenwriter: Tony Kayden
Tech Info: color/sound/93 min.   Type: Dramatic Feature
Date: 1986   Origin: USA
Company: Fries, Delphi V
Distributors/Format: Columbia Pictures (16mm)
Annotation: Iowa farmboy Daryl Cage (Hall) goes to visit his older brother in Los Angeles while his parents attempt a trial separation. When his duffel bag is switched with that of a heroin smuggler, his visit becomes complicated. Turman is Lt. Delgado and Cumbuka plays Lamar.

OUTRAGEOUS FORTUNE
Cast: J.W. Smith*, Ji-Tu Cumbuka*, Eyan Williams*, Bette Midler, Peter Coyote, Shelley Long
Director: Arthur Hiller
Music by: Alan Silvestri
Producer: Ted Field, Robert Cort, Scott Kroopf, Peter V. Herald, Martin Mickelson
Screenwriter: Leslie Dixon
Tech Info: color/sound/100 min.   Type: Comedy Feature
Date: 1987   Origin: USA
Company: Interscope, Touchstone
Distributors/Format: Buena Vista Home Video (1/2")
Annotation: Sandy (Midler) and Lauren (Long) vie for the perfect man (Coyote) who seems to elude them both. Cumbuka plays a cab driver; Williams is listed as "Black Girl Dancer"; Smith's role is uncredited.

OVER THE TOP
Cast: Sam Scarber*, Tyrone Jackson*, Winston Ntshona*, Rose Dursey*, Sylvester Stallone, Susan Blakely, Robert Loggia, David Mendenhall
Director: Menahem Golan
Music by: Giorgio Moroder
Producer: Yoram Globus, Menahem Golan
Screenwriter: Sylvester Stallone, Stirling Silliphant
Storywriter: Don Black*, Jimmy Chambers*, Sylvester Stallone
Tech Info: color/sound/94 min.   Type: Dramatic Feature
Date: 1987   Origin: USA
Company: Cannon Films
Distributors/Format: Warner Bros. Home Video, Inc. (1/2")
Annotation: In order to keep his son (Mendenhall) and his trucking rig, Lincoln Hawk (Stallone) must compete in the truckers' national arm wrestling championship. Harry Bosco (Scarber) is his semi-final opponent. Dursey appears as a clerk at the hospital where Hawk's wife (Blakely) is admitted.

PACIFIC HEIGHTS
Cast: Dorian Harewood*, Carl Lumbly*, Melanie Griffith, Michael Keaton, Matthew Modine
Director: John G. Schlesinger
Executive Producer: Joe Roth, James G. Robinson
Music by: Hans Zimmer
Producer: Joe Roth, James G. Robinson, Scott Rudin, William Sackheim
Screenwriter: Daniel Pyne
Tech Info: color/sound/103 min.   Type: Dramatic Feature
Date: 1990   Origin: USA
Company: Morgan Creek, Fox
Distributors/Format: Fox Home Video (1/2")
Annotation: When Patty Parker (Griffith) and Drake Goodman (Modine) consider buying an apartment complex, friend Dennis Reed (Harewood) warns them against it, but they decide to become landlords anyway. Lou Baker (Lumbly) is one of their rent applicants whose credit references are lost.

PACKAGE, THE
Cast: Pam Grier*, Thalmus Rasulala*, Gene Hackman, Joanna Cassidy, Miguel Nino
Director: Andrew Davis
Executive Producer: Arne Schmidt
Music by: James Newton Howard*
Producer: Arne Schmidt, Beverly J. Camhe, Tobie Haggerty
Screenwriter: John Bishop
Storywriter: John Bishop, Dennis Haggerty
Tech Info: color/sound/108 min.   Type: Dramatic Feature
Date: 1989   Origin: USA
Company: Orion
Distributors/Format: Orion Home Video (1/2")
Annotation: On the eve of a U.S.-Soviet nuclear disarmament treaty, military leaders from both nations plot to undermine the treaty and preserve the military-industrial complex. Grier plays Ruth Butler and Rasulala is the Secret Service Commander.

PAGEMASTER, THE
Cast: Whoopi Goldberg*, Christopher Lloyd, Patrick Stewart, Macaulay Culkin
Director: Joe Johnston
Music by: James Horner
Producer: David Kirschner, Paul Geetz
Screenwriter: David Kirschner, David Casci, Ernie Contreas
Storywriter: David Kirschner, David Casci
Tech Info: color/sound/82 min.   Type: Animated Feature
Date: 1994   Origin: USA
Company: Fox
Distributors/Format: Films Inc. (1/2"), Fox Home Video (1/2")
Annotation: Seeking refuge from a storm, timid Richard Tyler (Culkin) enters an empty library only to be swept away into the magical animated world of the Pagemaster.

PAINT IT BLACK
Cast: Jason Bernard*, Rick Rossovich, George Savant, Julie Carmen
Director: Tim Hunter
Executive Producer: Dan Ireland, William J. Quigley
Music by: Jurgen Knieper
Producer: Dan Ireland, Anne Kimmel, Mark Forstater, William J. Quigley
Screenwriter: Herschel Weingrod, Tim Harris
Tech Info: color/sound/102 min.   Type: Dramatic Feature
Date: 1990   Origin: USA
Company: Vestron
Distributors/Format: Vestron Home Video (1/2")
Annotation: Johnathan Dunbar is a struggling artist; Marion (Kirkland), a gallery owner who wants to exploit him and Eric (Savant), a psychotic art collector who wants to control him. Complications arise when Marion ends up dead. Bernard plays police Lt. Wilder.

PANIC IS THE ENEMY

Producer: Third World Newsreel
Tech Info: color/sound/10 min.   Type: Documentary Short
Date: 1986   Origin: USA
Studio: Independent
Company: Third World Newsreel Workshop
Distributors/Format: Third World Newsreel (1/2")
Annotation: In 1984, Bernhard Goetz, shot four young men in a New York City subway car, because he thought they were dangerous. The video focuses on the panic which followed, its origin and implications.

PAPER, THE

Cast: Lynn Thigpen*, Robert Duvall, Marisa Tomei, Randy Quaid, Michael Keaton, Glenn Close
Director: Ron Howard
Executive Producer: Dylan Sellers, Todd Hallowell
Music by: Randy Newman
Producer: Brian Grazer, Frederick Zollo, Dylan Sellers, Todd Hallowell
Screenwriter: David Koepp, Stephen Koepp
Tech Info: color/sound/112 min.   Type: Dramatic Feature
Date: 1994   Origin: USA
Company: Imagine
Distributors/Format: Universal Home Video (1/2")
Annotation: Henry Hackett (Keaton), city editor at the New York Sun, argues with managing Editor Alicia Clark (Close) about whether to print details of a story he steals from a rival newspaper. Thigpen plays Janet.

PARADISE ALLEY

Cast: Frank McRae*, Anne Archer, Sylvester Stallone, Lee Canalito, Armand Assante
Director: Sylvester Stallone
Executive Producer: Edward R. Pressman
Music by: Bill Conti
Producer: Edward R. Pressman, John F. Roach, Ronald A. Suppa
Screenwriter: Sylvester Stallone
Tech Info: color/sound/107 min.   Type: Comedy Feature
Date: 1978   Origin: USA
Company: Force Ten
Distributors/Format: Universal Home Video (1/2")
Annotation: Cosmo Carboni (Stallone) encourages his younger brother Lenny (Assante) to wrestle at Paradise Alley where illegal matches are staged, so that their family will have enough money to leave New York's Hell's Kitchen. McRae plays Big Glory, the aging resident champ at Paradise's Alley.

PARASITE

Cast: Al Fann*, Luca Bercovici, Demi Moore, Robert Glaudini, James Davidson
Director: Charles Band
Executive Producer: Irwin Yablans
Music by: Richard Band
Producer: Irwin Yablans, Charles Band
Screenwriter: Alan J. Adler, Michael Shoob, Frank Levering

Tech Info: color/sound/85 min.   Type: Dramatic Feature
Date: 1982   Origin: USA
Company: Parasite Venture
Distributors/Format: Embassy Home Video (1/2")
Annotation: Dr. Dean (Glaudini) creates creatures that grow on the insides of their victims and then burst out. Fann plays Collins.

PASS/FAIL
Cast: Arabella Chavers*, Gamy L. Tyler*, Ilunga Adell*, Stephen Geller, Robbie McCauley
Director: Roy Campanella Jr.*
Producer: Roy Campanella Jr.*
Screenwriter: Roy Campanella Jr.*
Tech Info: color/sound/36 min.   Type: Docudrama
Date: 1978   Origin: USA
Annotation: A struggling filmmaker, Brian Wells (Adell), is seeking funding for his documentary on Harlem's Hale House Drug Rehabilitation Center. Wells' wife (Campbell) and daughter (Neal) are affected by Wells' struggle. Wells' experiences closely parallel that of Campanella.

PASSENGER 57
Cast: Wesley Snipes*, Robert Hooks*, Alex Datcher*, Tom Sizemore, Bruce Payne, Elizabeth Hurley, Michael Horse
Director: Kevin Hooks*
Executive Producer: Jonathan Sheinberg
Music by: Stanley Clarke*
Producer: Lee Rich, Dan Paulson, Jonathan Sheinberg
Screenwriter: Dan Gordon, David Loughery
Storywriter: Stewart Raffill, Dan Gordon
Tech Info: color/sound/84 min.   Type: Dramatic Feature
Date: 1992   Origin: USA
Company: Warner Bros.
Distributors/Format: Warner Bros. Home Video, Inc. (1/2")
Annotation: Cutter (Snipes) is an undercover airline security operative who steps into the lavatory and re-emerges to discover the plane is being hijacked. Charles "The Rane of Terror" Rane (Payne), the man behind recent terrorist attacks targets passenger flight 57. Datcher plays Marti, airline attendant and Cutter's love interest. Robert Hooks plays Dwight Henderson.

PASSIN' IT ON
Director: John Valadez
Music by: David Earle Johnson*
Producer: Peter Miller
Speaker: Dhoruba Bin Wahad*
Tech Info: mixed/sound/87 min.   Type: Documentary Feature
Date: 1992   Origin: USA
Company: Tapestry International
Distributors/Format: First Run/Icarus Films (16mm)
Annotation: The film examines urban African American life in the story of Black Panther leader Dhoruba Bin Wahad formerly known as Richard Moore.

PASSION AND MEMORY

Director: Roy Campanella Jr.*
Narrator: Robert Guillaume*
Producer: Roy Campanella Jr.*
Screenwriter: Roy Campanella Jr.*
Storywriter: Donald Bogle*
Tech Info: mixed/sound/60 min.　　Type: Documentary Feature
Date: 1986　Origin: USA
Studio: Independent
Company: Morningstar Production
Annotation: Campanella adapts Donald Bogle's book, "Toms, Coons, Mulattoes, Mammies, and Bucks," which focuses on black stars Stepin Fetchit, Hattie McDaniel, Bill Robinson, and Sidney Poitier. It includes rare stills and clips including one of Dorothy Dandridge at the Academy Awards.

PASSION FISH

Cast: Alfre Woodard*, Leo Burmester*, Mary McDonnell, Vondie Curtis-Hall, David Strathairn
Director: John Sayles, Roger Deakins
Executive Producer: John Sloss
Music by: Mason Paring
Producer: Maggie Renzi, Sarah Green, John Sloss
Screenwriter: John Sayles
Storywriter: John Sayles
Tech Info: color/sound/135 min.　　Type: Dramatic Feature
Date: 1993　Origin: USA
Company: Miramax
Distributors/Format: Columbia/TriStar Pictures (35mm; 1/2")
Annotation: Mary Alice Culhane (McDonnell), a television soap opera star, is paralyzed in a car accident. She returns to her deserted family home in Louisiana and spends her days drinking and watching television until Chantelle (Woodard), the only nurse who will stay with her, forces her to shape up. Chantelle is recovering from drug addiction brought on by her father who took her daughter away. The two learn that they need each other.

PASTIME

Alternate: One Cup of Coffee
Cast: Ernie Banks*, Glenn Plummer*, William Russ, Scott Plank, Reed Rudy, Ricky Paull Goldin
Director: Robin B. Armstrong
Music by: Lee Holdridge
Producer: Eric Tynan Young, Robin B. Armstrong
Screenwriter: David M. Eyre Jr.
Tech Info: color/sound/94 min.　　Type: Dramatic Feature
Date: 1991　Origin: USA
Company: Bullpen Ltd., Open Road Productions
Distributors/Format: Miramax Home Video (1/2")
Annotation: Roy Dean (Russ), an aging baseball player, befriends team newcomer Tyrone Debray (Plummer). Despite Dean's mentor status, he's fired to make room for younger players.

PATERNITY

Cast: Murphy Dunne*, Juanita Moore*, Norman Fell, Burt Reynolds, Beverly D'Angelo
Director: David Steinberg
Executive Producer: Jerry Tokofsky
Music by: David Shire
Producer: Lawrence Gordon, Jerry Tokofsky, Hank Moonjean
Screenwriter: Charlie Peters
Tech Info: color/sound/94 min.   Type: Comedy Feature
Date: 1981   Origin: USA
Company: Paramount
Distributors/Format: Paramount (1/2")
Annotation: Buddy Evans (Reynolds), the manager of Madison Square Garden, wants to enrich his life by having a baby but doesn't want to get married. Moore plays Celia; Dunne is the singing telegram man.

PATRIOT GAMES

Cast: Samuel L. Jackson*, James Earl Jones*, Anne Archer, Harrison Ford, Patrick Beign, Thora Birch
Director: Phillip Noyce
Music by: James Horner
Producer: Mace Neufeld, Robert Rehme
Screenwriter: Donald Stewart, W. Peter Iliff
Storywriter: Tom Clancy
Tech Info: color/sound/117 min.   Type: Dramatic Feature
Date: 1992   Origin: USA
Company: Paramount
Distributors/Format: Paramount Home Video (1/2")
Annotation: A former CIA analyst Jack Ryan (Ford), vacationing with his family in London, helps thwart a terrorist attack on a member of the Royal family and becomes the target of the terrorist whose brother he killed. Jones plays Admiral James Greer and Jackson plays Robby Jackson.

PATRIOT, THE

Cast: Stack Pierce*, Diane Stevenett, Michael Pollard, Gregg Henry, Simone Griffeth
Director: Frank Harris
Executive Producer: Mark Tenser
Music by: Jay Ferguson
Producer: Michael Bennett, Mark Tenser
Screenwriter: Andy Ruben, Katt Shea Ruben
Tech Info: color/sound/88 min.   Type: Dramatic Feature
Date: 1986   Origin: USA
Company: Patriot
Distributors/Format: Crown Home Video (1/2")
Annotation: A group of Ninja-clad bad guys led by Atkins (Pierce) steal two atomic bombs. Matt Ryder (Henry), a Vietnam veteran, is summoned to help recover them.

PAUL ROBESON: A TRIBUTE TO AN ARTIST
Cast: Paul Robeson*
Director: Saul Turell, Saul J. Turell
Narrator: Sidney Poitier*
Screenwriter: Saul J. Turell
Tech Info: bw/sound/29 min.   Type: Documentary Short
Date: 1979   Origin: USA
Company: Janus Films, Turell
Archives/Format: IUB - BFC/A (1/2")
Annotation: This Academy Award winning documentary records the career experiences of actor Robeson. From Broadway performances in OTHELLO to his work in films like PROUD VALLEY, KING SOLOMON'S MINES, and the EMPEROR JONES, Robeson was a pioneer in the visual arts. The film chronicles his increasing political activism, as captured through the evolution of the lyrics of "Ol' Man River."

PAUL ROBESON: MAN OF CONSCIENCE
Producer: William Miles*
Tech Info: color/sound/60 min.   Type: Television Documentary
Date: 1987   Origin: USA
Company: Miles* Educational Film Production, Inc.
Distributors/Format: Miles Educational Film Production, Inc. (1/2")
Annotation: Miles' documentary examines the life and points out the milestones in the career of Paul Robeson, scholar, athlete, singer, actor and activist.

PCU
Cast: Kevin Thigpen*, Sarah Trigger, Christopher Young, Jeremy Piven
Director: Hart Bochner
Music Performer: George Clinton*, Greg Boyer*, Gary Cooper*, Bennie Cowan*, Belita Woods*, Nichole Tindall*, Williams Michael Payne*, Louis Kabbabie*, Greg Thomas*, Tracy Lewis*, Ray Davis*, Dewayne McKnight*, Cardell Mosson*, Gary Shider*
Music by: Steve Vai
Producer: Paul Schiff
Screenwriter: Zak Penn, Adam Leff
Tech Info: color/sound/79 min.   Type: Comedy Feature
Date: 1994   Origin: USA
Company: Hilltop Enterprises, Fox
Distributors/Format: Fox Home Video (1/2")
Annotation: Prospective Freshman Tom Lawrence (Young) visits politically correct PCU and is hosted by Droz (Piven), leader of the only non-PC faction on campus. To raise money for their group, Droz organizes a keg party. Clinton and the P-Funk Allstars provide music for the party. Thigpen plays an Afrocentrist.

PEACEMAKER
Cast: Wally Taylor*, Robert Forster, Robert Davi, Lance Edwards, Hilary Shepard
Director: Kevin Tenney
Executive Producer: Charles Fries
Producer: Charles Fries, Wayne Crawford, Andrew Lane
Screenwriter: Kevin Tenney
Tech Info: color/sound/90 min.   Type: Dramatic Feature

Date: 1990   Origin: USA
Company: Crawford/Lane
Distributors/Format: Fries Home Video (1/2")
Annotation: Yates (Forster) and Townsend (Edwards), two aliens that look like humans, land on earth and antagonize the Los Angeles Police Department. Townsend, the peacemaker, is on earth to capture Yates, the criminal. Taylor plays Moses.

PEE WEE'S BIG ADVENTURE
Cast: Starletta DuPois*, Daryl Roach*, Paul Reubens, Elizabeth Daily, Mark Holton, Jan Hooks, Phil Hartmann
Director: Tim Burton
Music by: Danny Elfman
Producer: Robert Shapiro, Richard Gilbert Abramson
Screenwriter: Paul Reubens, Phil Hartmann, Michael Varhol
Tech Info: color/sound/92 min.   Type: Comedy Feature
Date: 1985   Origin: USA
Company: Aspen Film
Distributors/Format: Warner Bros. Home Video, Inc. (1/2")
Annotation: When his bike is stolen, Pee Wee Herman (Reubens) sets out on a journey to recover his most prized possession. Chuck (Roach) is a bike store owner who offers Pee Wee a new bike, and Sergeant Hunter (DuPois) is the officer who files Pee Wee's stolen bike report.

PELICAN BRIEF, THE
Cast: Denzel Washington*, Tony Goldwyn, John Heard, Julia Roberts, Sam Shepard, Robert Culp
Director: Alan J. Pakula, Stephen Goldblatt
Producer: Pieter Jan Brugge, Alan J. Pakula
Screenwriter: Alan J. Pakula
Storywriter: John Grisham
Tech Info: color/sound/141 min.   Type: Adaptation
Date: 1993   Origin: USA
Company: Warner Bros.
Distributors/Format: Warner Bros. Home Video, Inc. (1/2")
Annotation: Two Supreme Court Justices have been assassinated, and a young law student (Roberts) stumbles upon the truth. An investigative journalist (Washington) wants her story, but everybody else wants them dead.

PENITENTIARY
Cast: Leon Isaac Kennedy*, Thommy Pollard*, Hazel Spears*, Floyd Chatman*, Badja Djola*, Donovan Womack*, Wilbur "HiFi" White*, Gloria Delaney
Director: Jamaa Fanaka*
Executive Producer: Robert Edelen, Robert Gordon Sr., Beatrice Gordon
Music by: Frankie Gaye*
Producer: Jamaa Fanaka*, Robert Edelen, Robert Gordon Sr., Beatrice Gordon
Screenwriter: Jamaa Fanaka*
Tech Info: color/sound/99 min.   Type: Dramatic Feature

Date: 1979   Origin: USA
Company: Jerry Gross
Distributors/Format: Xenon Entertainment Group (1/2")
Archives/Format: IUB - BFC/A (1/2")
Annotation: The film depicts violence in a state penitentiary where the strongest survive. Martel Gordon (Kennedy), nicknamed "Too Sweet" has boxing skills that get him out of prison. But the fear of starting a new life on the outside is frightening to inmates like "Seldom Seen" (Chatman).

PENITENTIARY II
Cast: Leon Isaac Kennedy*, Ernie Hudson*, Mr. T. *, Donovan Womack*, Glynn Turman*, Sephton Moody*, Malick Carter*, Eugenia Wright*, Cepheus Jaxon*, Peggy Blow*
Director: Jamaa Fanaka*
Music Performer: Jack Wheaton, Gordon Banks
Music by: Jack Wheaton, Gordon Banks
Producer: Jamaa Fanaka*
Screenwriter: Jamaa Fanaka*
Tech Info: color/sound/108 min.   Type: Dramatic Feature
Date: 1982   Origin: USA
Company: Bob-Bea Productions
Distributors/Format: United Artists Home Video (1/2"), Xenon Entertainment Group (1/2")
Archives/Format: IUB - BFC/A (1/2")
Annotation: When Martel "Too Sweet" Gordon's (Kennedy) girlfriend (Wright) is murdered by "Half Dead" (Hudson), a former fellow prisoner, Gordon goes back into the ring with Mr. T and old pal "Seldom Seen" (Carter) as trainers. "Half Dead" continues to harass Gordon and his family (Blow, Turman, Moody), culminating in a parallel boxing sequence where Gordon defeats Jesse Amos (Womak) and Mr. T does the same to "Half Dead."

PENITENTIARY III
Cast: Leon Isaac Kennedy*, Anthony Geary, Renny Harlin, Ric Mancinx, The Maiti Kid
Director: Jamaa Fanaka*
Music by: Gary Schyman
Producer: Leon Isaac Kennedy*, Jamaa Fanaka*
Screenwriter: Jamaa Fanaka*
Tech Info: color/sound/91 min.   Type: Dramatic Feature
Date: 1987   Origin: USA
Company: Jamaa-Leon
Distributors/Format: Cannon Home Video (1/2")
Annotation: Another sequel follows the triumph and struggles of Martel "Too Sweet" Gordon (Kennedy), a black ex-con trying to make it as a boxer.

PEOPLE UNDER THE STAIRS, THE
Cast: Kelly Jo Minter*, Bill Cobbs*, Brandon Adams*, Ving Rhames*, Everett McGill, Wendy Robie, Jeremy Roberts
Director: Wes Craven
Music by: Don Peake
Producer: Marianne Maddalena, Stuart M. Besser
Screenwriter: Wes Craven

Storywriter: Wes Craven
Tech Info: color/sound/102 min.   Type: Dramatic Feature
Date: 1991   Origin: USA
Company: Alive Films, Under the Stairs Inc, Wes Craven Film
Distributors/Format: Facets Multimedia, Inc. (1/2"), Universal Home Video (1/2")
Annotation: Adams plays a young boy nicknamed "Fool" whose poverty- stricken
urban life forces him to aid two burglars (Rhames, Roberts) when they rob the local
landlord's mysterious mansion. "Fool" is trapped inside the estate when the robbery
fails and is exposed to the terrible secrets of its inhabitants.

PEOPLE UNITED, THE

Director: Alonzo Speight*
Music by: John Hicks*
Narrator: Abbey Lincoln*
Producer: Alonzo Speight*
Screenwriter: Alonzo Speight*, Martha Golden, Elizabeth Phillips
Speaker: Aminata Moseka*
Tech Info: color/sound/60 min.   Type: Documentary Feature
Date: 1985   Origin: USA
Studio: Independent
Distributors/Format: Third World Newsreel (1/2")
Annotation: Within the span of one year, 12 black women were murdered in Boston.
Lincoln's narration focuses on the community's coming together in the face of
governmental indifference. The film examines racial unrest, discrimination and
violence against women during the 1980s.

PERFECT MODEL, THE

Cast: Tatiana Tumbtzen*, Reggie Theus*, Anthony Norman McKay*, Catero
Colbert*, Darryl Roberts*, Stone/Stoney Jackson*, Lisa Cruzat*, Denise Simon*,
Tony Smith*, Nadiera Bost, Morgan Proctor
Director: Darryl Roberts*
Executive Producer: Darryl Roberts*, Theresa McDade*, Kari A. Coken
Music by: Joe Thomas, Steve Grissette
Producer: Darryl Roberts*, Darryl Roberts*, Theresa McDade*, Kari A. Coken
Screenwriter: Darryl Roberts*, Theresa McDade*, Ivory Ocean
Tech Info: color/sound/89 min.   Type: Dramatic Feature
Date: 1989   Origin: USA
Company: Chicago Cinema
Distributors/Format: Chicago Cinema Home Video (1/2")
Annotation: Mario Sims (McKay), a Hollywood actor with ghetto roots, returns to
Chicago for a project and agrees to help childhood friend Stedman Austin (Jackson)
by judging a beauty pageant. Colbert plays 12-year-old David Johnson who breaks
into Sims' car; Cruzat is David's sister Linda with whom Sims falls in love; and
Theus plays Sims' brother Dexter who encourages him to follow his heart.

PERFORMED WORD, THE

Cast: Infinity *, Burkhalter Elementary *, Rhythm Rockers Blues Band*
Narrator: Gerald Davis*
Speaker: Bishop E.E. Cleveland*, Harvell D. Guiton*, Sylvia L. Guiton*, Iola Parker
Jackson*, Sheila Robinson*, Edward Givans*, Dorothy Curry*, Pastor Ernestine
Cleveland Reems*, Lakeside Roliers*, Ephesian Church Of God In Christ
Congregation*, Center Of Hope Congregation And Choirs*

Tech Info: mixed/sound/58 min.   Type: Documentary Feature
Date: 1982   Origin: USA
Company: Red Taurus Films Production
Distributors/Format: Center for Southern Folklore (35mm; 16mm)
Archives/Format: IUB - AAAMC (1/2")
Annotation: Davis' film explores black expressive language, the spoken word dynamically performed in clubs, on playgrounds, and in churches. Berkeley's Bishop E.E. Cleveland of Ephesian Church of God in Christ, and his daughter Pastor Ernestine Cleveland Reems of Oakland's Center of Hope, are among those who exemplify this rich and vital tradition.

PERFUME

Cast: Ted Lange*, Felton Perry*, Nancy Cheryll Davis*, John Johnson*, Eugenia Wright*, Kathleen Bradley*, Cheryl Francis Harrington*, Shy Jefferson*, Lynn Marlin*, Don Mitchell*, Cal Wilson*, J.D. Hall*, Melvin Howard Taylor*, Carmen Hayward*, Renee Gentry-Lord*, Lynn Griffith*, Arnold Turner*, Peter Moret*, Tony McLaughlin*, Arthur Fuller*, Alonzo Roberto*, Shannon Jefferson*
Director: Roland S. Jefferson*
Executive Producer: Roland S. Jefferson*, James Mays, M.D.*, Linda Garhan
Music by: Willie Hutch*
Producer: Roland S. Jefferson*, Shirley M. Calloway*, James Mays, M.D.*, Miriam Holder Jacobs*, Linda Garhan
Screenwriter: Roland S. Jefferson*
Tech Info: color/sound/105 min.   Type: Dramatic Feature
Date: 1990   Origin: USA
Studio: Independent
Company: Triumph Realty
Distributors/Format: Triumph-Realty (16mm, 1/2")
Annotation: The story centers around the lifelong friendship of five contemporary black women who are both attractive and rich. And like all friendships, theirs is tested by events that shape their respective lives as well as the men with whom they are involved.

PERIOD PIECE, A

Director: Zeinabu irene Davis*
Tech Info: bw/sound/4 min.   Type: Experimental Short
Date: 1991   Origin: USA
Studio: Independent
Distributors/Format: Women Make Movies, Inc. (16mm; 1/2")
Annotation: The film is a riff on menstruation. It follows Davis' film CYCLES.

PERMANENT WAVE

Cast: Anna Maria Horsford*, Lisette Smith*, Lauren Tom, Tony Head, Fiddle Viracola
Director: Christine Choy
Producer: Renee Tajima
Tech Info: color/sound/20 min.   Type: Dramatic Short

Date: 1986   Origin: USA
Studio: Independent
Distributors/Format: Third World Newsreel (1/2")
Annotation: The life and tribulations of the workers in a beauty parlor at Christmas time are seen through the eyes of the owner's daughter.

PERSONAL BEST
Cast: Jim Moody*, Linda Hightower*, Desiree Gauthier*, Scott Glenn, Mariel Hemingway, Patrice Donnelly, Kenny Moore
Director: Robert Towne
Music Performer: Jack Nitzsche, Jill Fraser
Music by: Jack Nitzsche, Jill Fraser
Producer: Robert Towne, David Geffen
Screenwriter: Robert Towne
Tech Info: color/sound/129 min.   Type: Dramatic Feature
Date: 1982   Origin: USA
Company: Geffen Film Co.
Distributors/Format: Warner Bros. Home Video, Inc. (1/2")
Annotation: Chris Cahill (Hemingway) and Tory Skinner (Donnelly) are women athletes on the 1976 U.S. Olympic team who fall in love despite their coach's admonitions. Moody plays Roscoe Travis.

PETER TOSH LIVE
Director: Michael C. Collins
Music Performer: Peter Tosh*, Word, Sound, and Power
Producer: Michael C. Collins
Tech Info: color/sound/55 min.   Type: Concert Feature
Date: 1984   Origin: USA
Studio: Independent
Company: Sony Video
Annotation: Filmed at the Greek Theatre, August 23, 1983, the concert includes: "Start All Over," "Africa," "Comin' in Hot," "Not Gonna Give It Up," "Rastafari Is," "Where You Gonna Run," "Equal Rights/Downpresser Man," "Get Up, Stand Up," among others.

PETEY WHEATSTRAW
Cast: Rudy Ray Moore*, Jimmy Lynch*, Wildman Steve *, Lady Reed*, Leroy & Skillet *, Eboni Wryte*, G. Tito Shaw*, Doc Watson*
Director: Cliff Roquemore*
Executive Producer: Burt Steiger
Producer: Theodore Toney, Burt Steiger
Screenwriter: Cliff Roquemore*
Tech Info: color/sound/93 min.   Type: Comedy Feature
Date: 1978   Origin: USA
Company: Tronsue
Distributors/Format: Generation Home Video (1/2")
Annotation: Moore plays an obnoxious comedian who becomes embroiled in a gang war when a rival comedy team tries to eliminate him. Satan appears and agrees to resurrect everyone who's been killed if Moore marries and impregnates his hideous daughter.

PHILADELPHIA

Cast: Denzel Washington*, Obba Babatunde*, Anna Deavere Smith*, Tom Hanks, Mary Steenburgen, Jason Robards, Joanne Woodward
Director: Jonathan Demme
Executive Producer: Ron Bozman, Gary Goetzman, Kenneth Off
Music by: Howard Shore
Producer: Jonathan Demme, Edward Saxon, Ron Bozman, Gary Goetzman, Kenneth Off
Screenwriter: Ron Nyswaner
Tech Info: color/sound/125 min.   Type: Dramatic Feature
Date: 1993   Origin: USA
Company: Columbia/TriStar, Tripod Pictures
Distributors/Format: Columbia/TriStar Pictures (35mm; 1/2"), Facets Multimedia, Inc. (1/2")
Annotation: Two lawyers, Joe Miller (Washington) and Andrew Beckett (Hanks), join together to sue a prestigious Philadelphia law firm when the firm fires Beckett because he has AIDS. Smith plays paralegal Anthea Brown; Babatunde is Jerome Green.

PHILADELPHIA EXPERIMENT, THE

Cast: Bill Smillie*, Kene Holliday*, Nancy Allen, Michael Pare, Bobby di Cicco, Eric Christmas
Director: Stewart Raffill
Music Performer: Nat'l Philharmonic Orchestra of London
Music by: Joel Fein
Producer: Joel B. Michaels, Douglas Curtis
Screenwriter: William Gray, Michael Janover
Storywriter: Wallace Bennett, Don Jakoby
Tech Info: color/sound/102 min.   Type: Dramatic Feature
Date: 1984   Origin: USA
Company: New World Pictures
Distributors/Format: New World Home Video (1/2")
Annotation: The film is loosely based on the rumored World War II anti-radar experiment that misfired and caused a battleship to disappear and reappear later. Major Clark (Holliday) aids the military in tracking down two sailors, David Herdeg (Pare) and Jim Parker (di Cicco), who were teleported from the 1943 battleship to the present.

PHILADELPHIA, MISSISSIPPI

Director: Garth Stein
Tech Info: color/sound/60 min.   Type:- Documentary Feature
Date: 1994   Origin: USA
Studio: Independent
Distributors/Format: Cinema Guild (1/2")
Annotation: The film documents the social and racial attitudes in Philadelphia since three young civil rights activists were murdered there in June 1964, 30 years earlier.

PICK-UP ARTIST, THE
Cast: Vanessa Williams*, Dennis Hopper, Robert Downey Jr., Molly Ringwald
Director: James Toback
Executive Producer: Warren Beatty
Music by: Georges Delerue
Producer: Warren Beatty, Warren Beatty
Screenwriter: James Toback
Tech Info: color/sound/81 min.   Type: Dramatic Feature
Date: 1987   Origin: USA
Company: Amercent, American Entertainment Partners, Fox
Distributors/Format: Fox Home Video (1/2")
Annotation: Jack Jericho (Downey), a womanizer and pick-up artist, falls for Randy
Jensen (Ringwald) who has a response for all of his lines. Her father Flash (Hopper)
complicates the affair. Williams plays Rae.

PICKING TRIBES
Director: Saundra Sharp*
Tech Info: color/sound/7 min.   Type: Animated Short
Date: 1988   Origin: USA
Studio: Independent
Distributors/Format: A Sharp Show (1/2"), Women Make Movies, Inc. (16mm; 1/2")
Annotation: The struggle between African American and Native American heritages
is the thematic issue explored in this short animation. Sharp uses vintage
photographs and watercolor animation.

PICKLE, THE
Cast: Little Richard (Penniman) *, Ally Sheedy, Danny Aiello, Dyan Cannon, Shelly
Winters, Griffin Dunne
Director: Paul Mazursky, Fred Murphy
Executive Producer: Patrick McCormick
Music by: Michel Legrand
Producer: Paul Mazursky, Patrick McCormick
Screenwriter: Paul Mazursky
Tech Info: color/sound/103 min.   Type: Comedy Feature
Date: 1993   Origin: USA
Company: Columbia, Doze Inc.
Distributors/Format: Columbia Pictures Home Video (1/2")
Annotation: Director Harry Stone (Aiello) attempts to get out of debt from three flops
in a row by directing a teen-age science fiction movie about a flying pickle. Sheedy
plays Molly, heroine of THE PICKLE, who flies to Cleveland in a giant cucumber and
meets with the president (Little Richard).

PIPPIN': HIS LIFE AND TIMES
Cast: Ben Vereen*, William Katt, Martha Raye, Chita Rivera, Leslie Denniston, Ben
Rayson
Director: David Sheehan
Executive Producer: Hillard Elkins, Susan Haymer
Music by: Steven Schwartz
Producer: Hillard Elkins, Susan Haymer, Carol Scott, David Sheehan
Screenwriter: Bob Fosse
Tech Info: color/sound/120 min.   Type: Musical Feature

Date: 1981   Origin: USA
Company: David Sheehan Productions, Tele, Scenes
Distributors/Format: Facets Multimedia, Inc. (1/2")
Annotation: Vereen is "The Leader Player" who narrates the tale of Pippin (Katt), the son of King Charlemagne (Rayson). Through song and dance, the Leader Player influences Pippin and helps him become King.

PIRATES
Cast: Olu Jacobs*, Walter Matthau, Charlotte Lewis, Cris Campion, Damien Thomas, Richard Pearson
Director: Roman Polanski
Executive Producer: Thom Mount, Mark Lombardo, Umberto Sambuco
Music by: Philippe Sarde
Producer: Thom Mount, Tarak Ben Ammar, Mark Lombardo, Umberto Sambuco
Screenwriter: Roman Polanski, Gerard Brach, John Brownjohn
Tech Info: color/sound/124 min.   Type: Dramatic Feature
Date: 1986   Origin: France, Tunisia
Company: Carthago, Accent, Cominco
Distributors/Format: Cannon Home Video (1/2")
Annotation: Captain Thomas Red (Matthau) a pirate, hears about a golden throne from Boumako (Jacobs), a fellow prisoner on a ship, and plots to steal it.

PIZZA MAN
Cast: David McKnight*, Bob Delegall*, Bill Maher, Annabelle Gurwitch, Andy Roano, Bryan Clark, Cathy Shambly
Director: J.D. Athens
Executive Producer: Teresa Lawton
Music by: Daniel May
Screenwriter: J.D. Athens
Tech Info: color/sound/90 min.   Type: Comedy Feature
Date: 1991   Origin: USA
Company: Megalomania Productions
Distributors/Format: Jonathan F. Lawton (16mm)
Annotation: Elmo Bunn (Maher), a Los Angeles pizza delivery man, gets a call for a pizza in a dangerous part of town. The gang of thugs who ordered the pizza refuse to pay and when Elmo insists, Mayor Tom Bradley (Delegall) tries to gun him down. Other prominent figures e.g. Ronald Reagan (Clark) and Geraldine Ferraro (Shambly), impede his attempts to collect payment. McKnight plays Vince.

PLACE OF RAGE, A
Director: Pratiba Parmar
Music Performer: Prince (Rogers Nelson) *, Neville Brothers *, Janet Jackson*, Staple Singers *
Speaker: Angela Davis*, Alice Walker*, June Jordan*
Tech Info: color/sound/52 min.   Type: Documentary Feature
Date: 1991   Origin: USA
Studio: Independent
Distributors/Format: Women Make Movies, Inc. (16mm; 1/2")
Annotation: Parmar's celebration of African American women and their achievements features interviews with Davis, Jordan and Walker.

PLACES IN THE HEART
Cast: Danny Glover*, Devoreaux White*, John Malkovich, Ray Baker, Sally Field, Amy Madigan, Ed Harris
Director: Robert Benton
Producer: Arlene Donovan
Screenwriter: Robert Benton
Tech Info: color/sound/110 min.　　　Type: Dramatic Feature
Date: 1984　Origin: USA
Company: Delphi Productions
Distributors/Format: Films Inc. (1/2"), TriStar Pictures Inc. (1/2")
Annotation: After Wylie (White), a young drunk black boy, accidentally shoots and kills his friend Sheriff Spaulding (Baker), the sheriff's widow Edna (Field) is confronted with losing her farm. Edna (Field) takes on hired hand Mose (Glover) and together they successfully plant, harvest and sell the cotton crop to meet the payment.

PLATOON
Cast: Keith David*, Forest Whitaker*, Reggie Johnson*, Corey Glover*, Corkey Ford*, Charlie Sheen, Willem Dafoe, Tom Berenger
Director: Oliver Stone
Executive Producer: Derek Gibson, John Daly
Music Performer: Georges Delerue
Music by: Georges Delerue
Producer: Derek Gibson, Arnold Kopelson, John Daly
Screenwriter: Oliver Stone
Tech Info: color/sound/120 min.　　　Type: Dramatic Feature
Date: 1986　Origin: USA
Company: Hemdale Film, Co.
Distributors/Format: HBO Home Video (1/2"), Orion Home Video (1/2")
Annotation: Chris (Sheen) has just begun his tour of duty in Vietnam and is faced with a platoon conflict between his commanders Elias (Dafoe) and Barnes (Berenger). Chris befriends fellow soldiers, Big Harold (Whitaker), Manny (Ford), Junior (Johnson), Francis (Glover), and King (David). The film examines the relationships of officers to "grunts", rich politicians to poor soldiers and conflict within the military.

PLAYER, THE
Cast: Whoopi Goldberg*, Fred Ward, Peter Gallagher, Cynthia Stevenson, Greta Scacchi, Tim Robbins
Director: Robert Altman, Jean Lepine
Executive Producer: Cary Brokaw
Music by: Thomas Newman
Producer: David Brown, Nick Wechsler, Michael Tolkin, Cary Brokaw
Screenwriter: Michael Tolkin
Tech Info: color/sound/124 min.　　　Type: Dramatic Feature
Date: 1992　Origin: USA
Company: Fine Line Features, Avenue Pictures
Distributors/Format: Columbia/TriStar Pictures (35mm; 1/2")
Annotation: Altman's film satirizes the Hollywood studio system when a studio executive receives anonymous death threats from a rejected screenwriter. A celebrity studded thriller of murderous obsession among Hollywood's glamourous

elite.

PLAYING FOR KEEPS
Cast: Leon W. Grant*, Daniel Jordan, Matthew Penn, Jimmy Baio, Harold Gould
Director: Bob Weinstein, Harvey Weinstein
Executive Producer: Julia Palau, Michael Ryan, Patrick Wachsberger
Music Performer: Sister Sledge *, Loose Ends *, Eugene Wilde
Producer: Bob Weinstein, Harvey Weinstein, Alan Brewer, Julia Palau, Michael Ryan, Patrick Wachsberger
Screenwriter: Bob Weinstein, Harvey Weinstein, Jeremy Leven
Tech Info: color/sound/103 min.   Type: Dramatic Feature
Date: 1986   Origin: USA
Company: Miramax
Distributors/Format: MCA Home Video (1/2")
Annotation: Silk (Grant), a dancer, is best friends with Danny (Jordano) and Spikes (Penn). Together the three, with the aid of Steinberg (Baio), restore an old hotel. Silk's club act helps to make the hotel a success.

PLAYING IT SAFE: TRUTH ABOUT HIV, AIDS AND YOU, THE
Director: Malcolm Jamaal Warner*
Executive Producer: Arsenio Hall*
Host: Arsenio Hall*, Earvin "Magic" Johnson*
Producer: Arsenio Hall*, Kim Swain
Screenwriter: Thad Mumford
Speaker: Sinbad *, Jasmine Guy*, Jaleel White*, Tom Cruise, Kirstie Alley, Paula Abdul, Mayim Bialik, Luke Perry
Tech Info: color/sound/42 min.   Type: Documentary Short
Date: 1992   Origin: USA
Company: Paramount
Distributors/Format: Facets Multimedia, Inc. (1/2"), Paramount Home Video (1/2"), Filmic Archives (1/2")
Annotation: A cast of celebrities help Hall and Johnson educate teens and adults about the HIV virus.

POETIC JUSTICE
Cast: Maya Angelou*, Khandi Alexander*, Tone-Loc *, Tupac Shakur*, Joe Torry*, Janet Jackson*, Regina King*, Tyra Farrell*, Jenifer Lewis*, Roger Guenveur Smith*, Michael Colyar*, Special K McCray*, Rose Weaver*, Billy Zane, Lori Petty
Director: John Singleton*
Music by: Stanley Clarke*
Producer: John Singleton*, Steve Nicolaides
Screenwriter: John Singleton*
Tech Info: color/sound/109 min.   Type: Dramatic Feature
Date: 1993   Origin: USA
Company: New Deal Productions, Nickel Productions
Distributors/Format: Columbia/TriStar Pictures (35mm; 1/2"), Facets Multimedia, Inc. (1/2"), Films Inc. (1/2")
Archives/Format: IUB - BFC/A (1/2")
Annotation: Lucky (Shakur), a street-wise mailman, and Justice (Jackson) are a mismatched pair pushed together on a road trip from south central Los Angeles to Oakland. Torry plays Chicago; King appears as Iesha, Chicago's girlfriend.

POINT OF NO RETURN

Alternate: Assassin, The
Cast: Lorraine Toussaint*, Dermot Mulroney, Anne Bancroft, Bridget Fonda, Gabriel Byrne
Director: John Badham
Music by: Hans Zimmer
Producer: Art Linson
Screenwriter: Robert Getchell, Alexandra Seros
Tech Info: color/sound/109 min.   Type: Dramatic Feature
Date: 1993   Origin: USA
Company: Art Linson Productions, Warner Bros.
Distributors/Format: Warner Bros. Home Video, Inc. (1/2")
Annotation: After a drug store robbery lands her on death row, Maggie (Fonda) opts to become an undercover government assassin in exchange for her life. Toussaint plays Beth.

POLICE ACADEMY

Cast: Marion Ramsey*, Michael Winslow*, Ted Ross*, Kim Cattrall, Steve Guttenberg, David Graf
Director: Hugh Wilson
Music by: Robert Folk
Producer: Paul Maslansky
Screenwriter: Neal Israel, Pat Proft, Hugh Wilson
Storywriter: Neal Israel, Pat Proft
Tech Info: color/sound/96 min.   Type: Comedy Feature
Date: 1984   Origin: USA
Company: Paul Maslanky Production, Ladd Company
Annotation: Larvel Jones (Winslow) is a police cadet who is a genius at making sounds. Tackleberry (Graf) is an enormous cadet who is befriended by Laverne Hooks (Ramsey), a quiet passive cadet. The three help Mahony (Guttenberg) and each other to graduate from the academy and become effective police officers.

POLICE ACADEMY 2: THEIR FIRST ASSIGNMENT

Cast: Marion Ramsey*, Michael Winslow*, Bubba Smith*, Christopher Jackson*, Church Ortiz*, Steve Guttenberg, David Graf
Director: Jerry Paris
Executive Producer: John Goldwyn
Music Performer: Michael Chapman
Music by: Robert Folk
Producer: Paul Maslansky, Leonard Kroll, John Goldwyn
Screenwriter: Barry W. Blaustein, David Sheffield
Tech Info: color/sound/87 min.   Type: Comedy Feature
Date: 1985   Origin: USA
Company: Warner Bros.
Distributors/Format: Warner Bros. Home Video, Inc. (1/2")
Annotation: Hooks (Ramsey), Hightower (Smith), and Jones (Winslow) are fresh from the academy and are placed on duty. Hooks is a dispatcher, Hightower has foot patrol, and Jones, with his noisemaking antics, is placed with an old racist policeman. Despite the odds, the trio manages to save the city from people like Mojo (Jackson), who belongs to the Skullians gang.

POLICE ACADEMY 3: BACK IN TRAINING
Cast: Marion Ramsey*, Michael Winslow*, Bubba Smith*, Steve Guttenberg, David
Graf, Leslie Easterbrook, Bobcat Goldthwait, George Gaynes
Director: Jerry Paris
Music by: Robert Folk
Producer: Paul Maslansky
Tech Info: color/sound/83 min.   Type: Comedy Feature
Date: 1990   Origin: USA
Company: Warner Bros.
Distributors/Format: Warner Bros. Home Video, Inc. (1/2")
Annotation: Determined to save their alma mater from extinction during a statewide
budget slash, the original Police Academy graduates return.

POLICE ACADEMY 4: CITIZENS ON PATROL
Cast: Brown Aldango*, Marion Ramsey*, Michael Winslow*, Tab Thacker*, Steve
Guttenberg, David Graf, Lance Kinsey, Bobcat Goldthwait, George Gaynes
Director: Jim Drake
Music Performer: Michael Winslow*
Music by: Robert Folk
Producer: Paul Maslansky
Screenwriter: Gene Quintano
Storywriter: Neal Israel, Pat Proft
Tech Info: color/sound/88 min.   Type: Comedy Feature
Date: 1987   Origin: USA
Company: Warner Bros.
Distributors/Format: Warner Bros. Home Video, Inc. (1/2")
Annotation: The academy decides to open the police force to volunteers in their new
program, linked to neighborhood watch group, Citizens on Patrol. Mahoney
(Guttenberg) and partner Jones (Winslow) are reunited with Hooks (Ramsey) and
Hightower (Smith). The newest recruit is Hefty House (Thacker).

POLICE ACADEMY 5: ASSIGNMENT MIAMI BEACH
Cast: Bubba Smith*, Marion Ramsey*, Michael Winslow*, Tab Thacker*, Beryl
Jones*, Leslie Easter Brook, Janet Jones
Director: Alan Myerson
Music by: Robert Folk
Producer: Paul Maslansky
Screenwriter: Steven Lurwick
Tech Info: color/sound/90 min.   Type: Comedy Feature
Date: 1988   Origin: USA
Company: Warner Bros.
Distributors/Format: Warner Bros. Home Video, Inc. (1/2")
Annotation: In this sequel, newly graduated Officer Thomas Conklin (Thacker),
better known as House because of his size, is working side by side with the more
seasoned officers: Hightower (Smith), Hooks (Ramsey), and Jones (Winslow).

POLICE ACADEMY 6: CITY UNDER SIEGE
Cast: Marion Ramsey*, Michael Winslow*, Bubba Smith*, David Graf, Lance Kinsey,
Leslie Easterbrook, Gerrit Graham
Director: Peter Bonerz
Music by: Robert Folk

Producer: Paul Maslansky
Screenwriter: Stephen J. Curwick
Tech Info: color/sound/83 min.   Type: Comedy Feature
Date: 1989   Origin: USA
Company: Paul Maslansky
Distributors/Format: Warner Bros. Home Video, Inc. (1/2")
Annotation: Hightower (Smith), Jones (Winslow), and Hooks (Ramsey) return with the rest of the Police Academy gang in an attempt to bring a band of thieves on a robbery spree to justice.

PORTRAIT OF MAX
Director: Sam Pollard*
Executive Producer: St. Clair Bourne*
Producer: St. Clair Bourne*, Sam Pollard*, Dolores Elliott*
Tech Info: color/sound   Type: Documentary Feature
Date: 1988   Origin: USA
Studio: Independent
Annotation: Filmed in California, New York and Milan, Italy, this musical documentary examines the life of percussionist and composer Max Roach.

POSSE
Cast: Reginald Hudlin*, Warrington Hudlin*, Isaac Hayes*, Pam Grier*, Robert Hooks*, Nipsey Russell*, Blair Underwood*, Reginald Veljohnson*, Tom "Tiny" Lister Jr.*, Melvin Van Peebles*, Mario Van Peebles*, Charles Lane*, Big Daddy Kane*, Tone-Loc *, Salli Richardson*, Tracy Lee Chavis*, Richard Jordan, Stephen Baldwin
Director: Mario Van Peebles*, Peter Menzies Jr.
Executive Producer: Tim Bevan, Eric Fellner, Bill Fishman, Paul Webster
Music by: Michel Colombier
Producer: Tim Bevan, Eric Fellner, Bill Fishman, Paul Webster, Preston Holmes, Jim Steele, Jim Fishman
Screenwriter: Sy Richardson*, Dario Scardapane
Tech Info: color/sound/113 min.   Type: Dramatic Feature
Date: 1993   Origin: USA
Company: PolyGram Pictures
Distributors/Format: Facets Multimedia, Inc. (1/2")
Archives/Format: IUB - BFC/A (1/2")
Annotation: Mario Van Peebles stars as Jessie Lee in this Western about a mostly black posse who battle a pompous, racist colonel, and a vicious white sheriff who want to take over Freemanville, a peaceful black frontier settlement. Hooks plays King David, Jessie's preacher father who is murdered by klansmen; Melvin Van Peebles is Papa Joe, Jessie's mentor; Lane is Weezie; Tone-Loc, Angel; Kane, Father Time; Grier, Phoebe; Richardson, Lana; and the Hudlin brothers play reporters.

POSTCARDS FROM THE EDGE
Cast: CCH Pounder*, Meryl Streep, Gene Hackman, Shirley MacLaine, Dennis Quaid
Director: Mike Nichols
Executive Producer: Robert Greenhut, Neil Machlis
Music by: Howard Shore, Carly Simon
Producer: Mike Nichols, Robert Greenhut, John Calley, Neil Machlis
Screenwriter:

Storywriter:
Tech Info: color/sound/101 min.   Type: Comedy Feature
Date: 1990   Origin: USA
Company: Columbia
Distributors/Format: Columbia Pictures Home Video (1/2")
Annotation: In this adaptation of Carrie Fisher's novel, "Postcards from the Edge,"
Streep plays cocaine addicted actress Suzanne Vale. During her rehabilitation,
Suzanne has to contend with therapist Julie Marsden (Pounder) whose methods are
difficult for her to contend with.

POTLUCK AND THE PASSION, THE
Director: Cheryl Dunye*
Tech Info: color/sound/30 min.   Type: Dramatic Short
Date: 1993   Origin: USA
Studio: Independent
Distributors/Format: Third World Newsreel (1/2"), Frameline Distribution (1/2")
Annotation: An anniversary feast is the backdrop for this focus on contemporary
lesbian relationships.

POWER
Cast: Denzel Washington*, Darryl Edwards*, Richard Gere, Julie Christie, Gene
Hackman
Director: Sidney Lumet
Music by: Cy Coleman
Producer: Reene Schisgal, Mark Tarlov
Screenwriter: David Himmelstein
Tech Info: color/sound/111 min.   Type: Dramatic Feature
Date: 1986   Origin: USA
Company: Lorimar, Polar
Distributors/Format: Fox Home Video (1/2")
Annotation: Arnold Billing (Washington) and his company, Aerabia Petroleum, hire
Pete St. John (Gere), a noted propaganda expert, to insure the election of Jerome
Cade (Walsh) in the race for senator of New Mexico. The film exposes the corrupt
political maneuvers utilized in the campaign which Billing finds somewhat
distasteful, yet necessary, to win the game.

POWER OF ONE, THE
Cast: Morgan Freeman*, Winston Ntshona*, Alois Moyo*, Nomadlozi Kubheka*,
Cecil Zilla Mamanzi*, Tonderai Masenda*, Winston Mangwarara*, Faith Edwards*,
John Gielgud, Armin Mueller-Stahl, Fay Masterson
Director: John G. Avildsen, Dean Semler
Executive Producer: Steven Reuther, Greg Coote, Graham Burke
Music by: Hans Zimmer
Producer: Arnon Milchan, Steven Reuther, Greg Coote, Graham Burke
Screenwriter: Robert Mark Kamen
Tech Info: color/sound/111 min.   Type: Dramatic Feature
Date: 1992   Origin: USA, Germany, France
Company: Regency Enterprises, Le Studio Canal Plus, et al.
Annotation: Freeman is Geel Piet, a prison inmate who teaches a young English
boy, orphaned in a foreign land and terrorized for his political beliefs, how to box. As
he grows up, he fights the social injustices around him finding that one person can
make a difference.

POWER! (1966-68)
Series: Eyes On The Prizes II
Director: Louis J. Massiah*, Terry Kay Rockefeller
Executive Producer: Henry Hampton*
Narrator: Julian Bond*
Producer: Henry Hampton*, Louis J. Massiah*, Terry Kay Rockefeller
Screenwriter: Louis J. Massiah*, Terry Kay Rockefeller
Speaker: Stokely Carmichael*, Geraldine Williams*, Floyd McKissick*, Carl Stokes*, Thompson Gaines*, Huey Newton*, Emory Douglas*, Elaine Brown*, H. Rap Brown*, Herbert Oliver*, Rhody McCoy*, Karriema Jordan*, Dolores Torres*, Elaine Rooke*, Edgar Morris*, Les Campbell*, Sonny Carson*, Ralph Locher, Charles Butts, Seth Taft, Richard Jensen, Charles O'Brien, John Lindsay, Fred Nauman, Sandra Feldman, Albert Shanker, John Powis, Bernard Donovan
Tech Info: mixed/sound/60 min.   Type: Television Documentary
Date: 1989   Origin: USA
Company: Blackside, Inc
Distributors/Format: PBS Video (16mm; 1/2")
Archives/Format: IUB - AAAMC (1/2")
Annotation: In this segment, Carl Stokes becomes the first black mayor of Cleveland. On the West Coast, formation of the Black Panther Party begins with founders, Huey Newton and Bobby Seale. Parents of minority school children attempt to form community boards that influence how their children are educated in the Ocean Hill-Brownsville struggle in Brooklyn.

POWERFUL THANG, A
Cast: Asha Feyitinmi Sinki*, Craig Watkins*, James S. Davis*, Barbara O *, Cuong Rhodis*, Edwina L. Tyler*, Akim Feyijinmi*, John Jeeks*
Director: Zeinabu irene Davis*
Music Performer: The Ohio Players *, Lakeside *, Zapp *, Rufus *
Producer: Zeinabu irene Davis*
Screenwriter: Zeinabu irene Davis*, Marc Arthur Chery
Storywriter: Doris Owanda Johnson*
Tech Info: color/sound/57 min.   Type: Experimental Feature
Date: 1991   Origin: USA
Studio: Independent
Company: Wimmin With A Mission Production
Distributors/Format: Women Make Movies, Inc. (16mm; 1/2")
Archives/Format: IUB - BFC/A (1/2")
Annotation: Davis's film takes an intimate look at love and its risks as experienced by Yasmine Allen (Feyijinmi) and her "Ebony Prince" Craig Watkins (Jeeks). Poetry readings from the works of Alice Dunbar Nelson, Paul Laurence Dunbar and Rita Dove are interwoven in the story.

PRAISE HOUSE
Cast: Urban Bush Women *
Director: Julie Dash*
Tech Info: color/sound/30 min.   Type: Experimental Short

Date: 1991   Origin: USA
Studio: Independent
Distributors/Format: Third World Newsreel (1/2"), Women Make Movies, Inc. (16mm; 1/2")
Archives/Format: IUB - BFC/A (1/2")
Annotation: Dash's video made originally for television, features the dance troupe Urban Bush Women. It uses dance, chants and field hollers to tell the story of a young black woman whose drive to express herself artistically is limited by the 'workaday' world.

PRAYER OF THE ROLLERBOYS
Cast: Julius Harris*, G. Smokey Campbell*, J.C. Quinn, Corey Haim, Patricia Arquette, Christopher Collet
Director: Rick King
Executive Producer: Tetsu Fujimura, Martin F. Gold, Richard Lorber, Robert Baruc
Music by: Stacy Widelitz
Producer: Robert Mickelson, Tetsu Fujimura, Martin F. Gold, Richard Lorber, Robert Baruc
Screenwriter: W. Peter Iliff
Tech Info: color/sound/94 min.   Type: Dramatic Feature
Date: 1992   Origin: USA
Company: Academy Home Entertainment, Fox/Lorber Ass., et al
Distributors/Format: Academy Entertainment (35mm; 1/2")
Annotation: Economic disasters have plunged America into a hopeless recession and foreigners are taking over the country. A gang of Aryan rollerbladers, hoping to take advantage of the situation, plots an overthrow. Campbell plays Watt.

PREACHING THE WORD
Producer: William Miles*
Tech Info: color/sound/30 min.   Type: Television Documentary
Date: 1987   Origin: USA
Studio: Independent
Company: Miles* Educational Film Productions, Inc.
Distributors/Format: Miles Educational Film Production, Inc. (1/2")
Annotation: Miles' film explores the history and invaluable tradition of the African American Church, it's architects, keepers and congregation.

PRECIOUS MEMORIES: STROLLING 47TH STREET
Director: Dick Carter
Music Performer: Colette , Earl Crossley, Roland Faulkner, Carl "Kansas" Fields, Duke Groner, Dickie Harris, Sonny Turner
Producer: Glenn Duboose
Speaker: George Dixon*, Harriet Jackson*, Ed Gardner*, Finis Henderson Jr.*, Ron Boyd*, Scotty Piper*, Gerri Oliver*, Theresa Needham*, Lonnie Simmons*
Storywriter: Val Gray Ward*, Francis Ward*
Tech Info: color/sound/58 min.   Type: Television Documentary
Date: 1987   Origin: USA
Studio: WTTW/Chicago
Company: The Kuumba Theatre
Distributors/Format: WTTW/Chicago (1/2")
Archives/Format: IUB - BFC/A (1/2")

Annotation: Made originally for television, the film is a tribute to the artists, musicians, and entertainers in the culturally rich 47th Street neighborhood on the south side of Chicago.

PREDATOR
Cast: Carl Weathers*, Bill Duke*, Kevin Peter Hall*, Arnold Schwarzenegger
Director: John McTiernan
Music by: Alan Silvestri
Producer: Lawrence Gordon, Joel Silver, John Davis
Screenwriter: John Thomas, Jim Thomas
Tech Info: color/sound/107 min.   Type: Dramatic Feature
Date: 1987   Origin: USA
Company: Fox
Distributors/Format: CBS/Fox Home Video (1/2")
Annotation: Dillon (Weathers) and Dutch (Schwarzenegger) are old friends who are called in by the CIA to free American hostages in Central America. Events are complicated when the rescue team meets up with an alien predator (Hall). One of Dutch's group, Mac (Duke), perceives that the creature is visible even when camouflaged, but not in enough time to save his own life.

PREDATOR 2
Cast: Danny Glover*, Calvin Lockhart*, Kevin Peter Hall*, Gerard Williams*, Michael Mark Edmonson*, Vonte Sweet*, Jeffrey Reed*, Paul Abascal*, Ruben Blades, Gary Busey, Maria Conchita Alonso
Director: Stephen Hopkins
Music Performer: Papa Dee*
Music by: Alan Silvestri
Producer: Lawrence Gordon, Joel Silver, John Davis
Screenwriter: James Thomas, John Thomas
Tech Info: color/sound/110 min.   Type: Dramatic Feature
Date: 1990   Origin: USA
Company: Gordon, Silver, Davis
Distributors/Format: CBS/Fox Home Video (1/2")
Annotation: Glover is Harrigan, a San Francisco policeman investigating a serial cult killer who strips people of skin and skeleton. Harringan assumes the murders are part of the Jamaican drug war led by Goldtooth (Edmonson) and King Willie (Lockhart). When both are found dead, Harrigan meets face to face, with the Predator (Hall), an alien who comes to earth to hunt for skulls.

PRELUDE TO A KISS
Cast: Rocky Carroll*, Salli Richardson*, Ned Beatty, Alec Baldwin, Kathy Bates, Meg Ryan
Director: Norman Rene
Executive Producer: Jennifer Ogden
Music by: Howard Shore
Producer: Michael Gruskoff, Michael I. Levy, Jennifer Ogden
Screenwriter: Craig Lucas
Tech Info: color/sound/110 min.   Type: Dramatic Feature

Date: 1992   Origin: USA
Company: East 22nd Company Productions, Gruskoff/Levy, Fox
Distributors/Format: Fox Home Video (1/2")
Annotation: After a whirlwind courtship, Peter Hoskins (Baldwin) marries bartender Rita Boyle (Ryan) but her soul is transferred into the body of a loitering wedding guest after a congratulatory kiss. Carroll plays Tom; Richardson is the second bridesmaid.

PRESUMED INNOCENT

Cast: Anna Maria Horsford*, Paul Winfield*, Leland Gantt*, Brian Dennehy, Harrison Ford, Bonnie Bedelia, Raul Julia, Greta Sacchi
Director: Alan J. Pakula
Music by: John Williams
Producer: Sydney Pollack, Mark Rosenberg
Screenwriter: Frank Pierson, Alan J. Pakula
Storywriter: Scott Turow
Tech Info: color/sound/127 min.   Type: Dramatic Feature
Date: 1990   Origin: USA
Company: Mirage Production
Distributors/Format: Warner Bros. Home Video, Inc. (1/2")
Annotation: Judge Larren Lyttle (Winfield) is picked to preside over Rusty Savage's (Ford) trial for the murder of a district attorney. But Lyttle is compromised by his own relationship with the victim. Gantt plays Leon Wells, a criminal arrested for soliciting a police officer; Horsford plays Eugina, Savage's secretary.

PRETTY BABY

Cast: Antonio Fargas*, Seret Scott*, Gerrit Graham, Keith Carradine, Susan Sarandon, Brooke Shields, Frances Fay
Director: Louis Malle
Music by: Jerry Wexler
Producer: Louis Malle
Screenwriter: Polly Platt
Storywriter: Polly Platt, Louis Malle
Tech Info: color/sound/109 min.   Type: Dramatic Feature
Date: 1978   Origin: USA
Company: Paramount
Distributors/Format: Paramount (1/2")
Annotation: In Storyville (turn of the century New Orleans), a photographer, E.J. Bellocq (Carradine) takes up with 12-year-old prostitute Violet (Shields), daughter of Hattie (Sarandon) who has raised her child in Madam Nell's brothel. Fargas portrays Professor, the brothel's piano player, and Scott plays Flora, one of Madam Nell's "girls."

PRETTY SMART

Cast: Paris Vaughan*, Patricia Arquette, Tricia Leigh Fisher, Lisa Lorient, Dennis Cole
Director: Dimitri Logothetis
Executive Producer: Joseph Medawar
Music by: Jay Levy
Producer: Jeff Begun, Ken Solomon, Melanie J. Alschuler, Joseph Medawar
Screenwriter: Dan Hoskins
Storywriter: Jeff Begun, Melanie J. Alschuler

Tech Info: color/sound/84 min.   Type: Comedy Feature
Date: 1987   Origin: USA
Company: Balcor, Chroma III, First American
Distributors/Format: New World Home Video (1/2")
Annotation: Two sisters, Daphne (Fisher) and Jennifer (Lorient), are sent to finishing school in Greece where girls are split into groups based on haircolor and social class. The headmaster exploits the girls by having them perform in secret porno videos. Jennifer, a brunette, is in a group with Torch (Vaughan).

PRIME RISK
Cast: Caron Tate*, Sam Bottoms, Clu Gulager, Lee H. Montgomery, Toni Hudson
Director: Michael Farkas, Tom Schiller
Executive Producer: Bernard Farkas
Music by: Phil Marshall
Producer: Herman Grigsby, Bernard Farkas, John Head
Screenwriter: Michael Farkas, Tom Schiller
Tech Info: color/sound/100 min.   Type: Dramatic Feature
Date: 1985   Origin: USA
Company: Mikas I
Distributors/Format: Almi Home Video (1/2")
Annotation: Julie Collins (Hudson), a recent college graduate looking for a job in the computer department of a bank, is angered to learn the bank stole ideas she discussed in her interview. She dreams up a scheme to drain all the automatic teller machines of cash. Tate plays a bank teller.

PRIME TARGET
Cast: Isaac Hayes*, David Heavener, Robert Reed, Tony Curtis, Andrew Robinson, Jenilee Harrison
Director: David Heavener
Executive Producer: Gerald Milton
Music by: Robert Garrett
Producer: David Heavener, Gerald Milton, Merlin Miller
Screenwriter: David Heavener
Tech Info: color/sound/84 min.   Type: Dramatic Feature
Date: 1991   Origin: USA
Company: Hero Films
Distributors/Format: Hemdale Home Video (1/2")
Annotation: John Bloodstone (Heavener) is suspended from the police force for having used excessive force dealing with bank robbers. His bosses order him to transport Mafioso Marrietta Copella (Curtis) to another prison. They expect both Bloodstone and Copella to meet with disaster, but the plan backfires. Hayes plays Thompkins, a desk-bound police captain.

PRINCE JACK
Cast: Robert Guillaume*, Lloyd Nolan, Kenneth Mars, Robert Hogan, James F. Kelly
Director: Bert Lovitt
Executive Producer: Jim Milio
Music by: Elmer Bernstein
Producer: Jim Milio, Jim Milio
Screenwriter: Bert Lovitt
Tech Info: color/sound/100 min.   Type: Docudrama

Date: 1985   Origin: USA
Company: LMF
Distributors/Format: Castle Hill Home Video (1/2")
Annotation: In the 1960s, President Kennedy (Hogan) debates the Cuban missile crisis and Southern desegregation with his brother Bobby (Kelly) and Martin Luther King (Guillaume), among others, in the Oval Office.

PRINCE OF THE CITY

Cast: Robert Christian*, Jerry Orbach, Treat Williams, Richard Foronjy, Don Billett
Director: Sidney Lumet
Executive Producer: Jay Presson Allen
Music by: Paul Chihara
Producer: Burtt Harris, Jay Presson Allen
Screenwriter: Sidney Lumet, Jay Presson Allen
Tech Info: color/sound/167 min.   Type: Dramatic Feature
Date: 1981   Origin: USA
Company: Orion
Distributors/Format: Warner Bros. Home Video, Inc. (1/2")
Annotation: Daniel Ciello (Williams), a New York police officer recruited by the Department of Justice to inform on corrupt cops, uncovers many abuses of power. Christian plays "The King."

PRINCE: SIGN O' THE TIMES

Director: Prince (Rogers Nelson) *
Music Performer: Prince (Rogers Nelson) *, Sheila E. *, Dr. Fink *, Levi Seacer Jr.*, Atlanta Bliss *, Sheena Easton, Miko Weaver, Boni Boyer
Producer: Joseph Ruffalo, Steven Fargnoli, Simon Fields, Robert Carallo
Tech Info: color/sound/90 min.   Type: Concert Feature
Date: 1987   Origin: USA
Company: Cineplex Odeon Films
Distributors/Format: MCA Home Video (1/2")
Annotation: A concert film headlined by Prince, Sheila E. on drums, Boni Boyer on keyboards, Miko Weaver on guitar, Atlanta Bliss on sax and horn. Songs include: "U Got the Look," "Sign O' the Times," "Play in the Sunshine," "Little Red Corvette," "Housequake," "Slow Love," "I Could Never Take the Place of Your Man," "Hot Thing," "Now's the Time," "If I Was Your Girlfriend," "Forever in My Life," "It's Gonna Be a Beautiful Night," and "The Cross."

PRINCIPAL, THE

Cast: Rae Dawn Chong*, Louis Gossett Jr.*, Michael Wright*, Troy Winbush*, James Belushi, Esai Morales, J.J. Cohen
Director: Christopher Cain
Music by: Jay Gruska
Producer: Thomas H. Brodek
Screenwriter: Frank Deese
Tech Info: color/sound/112 min.   Type: Dramatic Feature
Date: 1987   Origin: USA
Company: TriStar
Distributors/Format: TriStar Pictures Inc. (1/2")
Annotation: When Rick Latimer (Belushi) is appointed as principal of Brandel High School, he is confronted by a drug mafia that controls the school. Jake Phillips (Gossett) is a school security officer who helps Latimer tighten discipline and Malary

Orozco (Chong) is a teacher who is assaulted by a student. Wright plays Victor Duncan, the drug king who controls Brandel through burglary and violence.

PRISON

Cast: Tom "Tiny" Lister Jr.*, Larry "Flash" Jenkins*, Lincoln Kilpatrick*, Lane Smith, Chelsea Field, Viggo Mortensen
Director: Renny Harlin
Executive Producer: Charles Band
Music by: Richard Band, Christopher L. Stone
Producer: Irwin Yablans, Charles Band
Screenwriter: Courtney Joyner
Storywriter: Irwin Yablans
Tech Info: color/sound/102 min.   Type: Dramatic Feature
Date: 1988   Origin: USA
Company: Empire
Distributors/Format: Empire (16mm)
Annotation: An innocent man is executed for the murder of another prisoner which was committed by prison guard Ethan Sharpe (Smith). Twenty years later, Sharpe is appointed as Warden of the same prison, and the vengeful ghost of the executed man seeks revenge. Lister plays Tiny and Jenkins portrays Hershey.

PRIVATE BENJAMIN

Cast: Hal Williams*, Damita Jo Freeman*, Goldie Hawn, Eileen Brennan, Armand Assante
Director: Howard Zieff
Executive Producer: Goldie Hawn
Music by: Bill Conti
Producer: Goldie Hawn, Harvey Miller, Nancy Meyers, Charles Shyer
Screenwriter: Harvey Miller, Nancy Meyers, Charles Shyer
Tech Info: color/sound/109 min.   Type: Comedy Feature
Date: 1980   Origin: USA
Company: Warner Bros.
Distributors/Format: Warner Bros. Home Video, Inc. (1/2")
Annotation: Judy Benjamin (Hawn), a well-to-do socialite, enlists in the Army and endures rigorous drills and encounters with strict commanding officers. Williams plays a non-commissioned officer; Freeman has an uncredited role.

PRIVATE WARS

Cast: Dan Tullis Jr.*, Stuart Whitman, Steven Railsback, Holly Floria, Michael Champion
Director: John Weidner
Music by: Louis Febre
Producer: Richard Pepin, Joseph Merhi
Screenwriter: John Weidner, Ken Lamplugh
Tech Info: color/sound/94 min.   Type: Dramatic Feature
Date: 1993   Origin: USA
Company: PM Entertainment
Distributors/Format: PM Home Video (1/2")
Annotation: Alexander Winters (Whitman), a powerful businessman who wants to excavate Los Angeles' Jackson Heights neighborhood and build an office complex, engineers local gang activity to harass the residents. Community leader Mo Williams (Tullis) hires a mercenary (Railsback) when he sees the police won't stop

the violence.

PRIVILEGE
Cast: Novella Nelson*, Faith Ringgold*, Tyrone Wilson*, Alice Spivak, Blair Baron, Rico Elias
Director: Yvonne Rainer
Producer: Yvonne Rainer, Kathryn Colbert
Screenwriter: Yvonne Rainer
Tech Info: color/sound/100 min.   Type: Docudrama
Date: 1991   Origin: USA
Company: Zeitgeist Films
Distributors/Format: Media Artists/New Works (1/2")
Annotation: Yvonne Washington (Nelson), a documentary filmmaker, interviews Jenny (Spivak) about menopause and aging. Jenny shares memories of her youth as a dancer on New York's lower east side. They also discuss issues of race, gender, and sexuality. Ringgold has an uncredited role.

PRIZZI'S HONOR
Cast: CCH Pounder*, Jack Nicholson, Robert Loggia, Anjelica Huston, Kathleen Turner
Director: John Huston
Music by: Alex North
Producer: John Foreman
Screenwriter: Richard Condon, Janet Roach
Storywriter: Richard Condon
Tech Info: color/sound/129 min.   Type: Comedy Feature
Date: 1985   Origin: USA
Company: ABC
Distributors/Format: Fox Home Video (1/2")
Annotation: Charley Partanna (Nicholson) is an aging hit man who works for a powerful New York Mafia family. He falls in love with Irene Walker (Turner) at a mafia wedding, but he discovers she is really a hit woman for the mob and she's out to get him. Pounder plays Peaches Altamont.

PROGRAM, THE
Cast: Halle Berry*, Duane Davis*, Lynn Swann*, Omar Epps*, Alfred Wiggins*, Kristy Swanson, James Caan
Director: David S. Ward
Executive Producer: Duncan Henderson, Tom Rothman
Producer: Samuel Goldwyn Jr., Duncan Henderson, Tom Rothman
Screenwriter: David S. Ward, Aaron Latham
Tech Info: color/sound/112 min.   Type: Dramatic Feature
Date: 1993   Origin: USA
Company: Samuel Goldwyn Company, Wolf Den Productions
Distributors/Format: Touchstone Home Video (1/2")
Annotation: Darnell Jefferson (Epps) is one of the young athletes who survive intercollegiate football with the help of their demanding coach (Caan). Berry plays Autumn, a high society girl; Wiggins appears as Autumn's father.

PROJECT X
Cast: Randal Patrick*, Matthew Broderick, Bob Minor, Helen Hunt, William Sadler, Johnny Ray McGhee
Director: Jonathan Kaplan
Executive Producer: C.O. Erickson
Music by: James Horner
Producer: C.O. Erickson, Walter Parkes, Lawrence Lasker
Screenwriter: Stanley Weiser
Storywriter: Lawrence Lasker, Stanley Weiser
Tech Info: color/sound/108 min.   Type: Comedy Feature
Date: 1987   Origin: USA
Company: Parkes, Lasker, Amercent, American Ent. Partners
Distributors/Format: Fox Home Video (1/2")
Annotation: Graduate student Teri McDonald (Hunt) learns that funding for her research is being discontinued. Her chimp Virgil becomes part of a top-secret project where chimps are taught to work a flight simulator. Patrick plays Mackler.

PROMISED LAND, THE (1967-68)
Series: Eyes On The Prize II
Director: Jacqueline Shearer*, Paul Steckler
Executive Producer: Henry Hampton*
Narrator: Julian Bond*
Producer: Henry Hampton*, Jacqueline Shearer*, Paul Steckler
Screenwriter: Jacqueline Shearer*, Paul Steckler
Speaker: Harry Belafonte*, Stokely Carmichael*, Marian Logan*, Coretta Scott King*, Jessie Jackson*, Andrew Young*, H. Rap Brown*, Edward Brooke*, Marian Wright*, Taylor Rogers*, James Smith*, William Rutherford*, Hosea Williams*, James Lawson*, Juanita Abernathy*, Barry Goldwater, Harry McPherson, Robert Kennedy, Henry Loeb, Michael Harrington
Tech Info: mixed/sound/60 min.   Type: Television Documentary
Date: 1989   Origin: USA
Company: Blackside, Inc.
Distributors/Format: PBS Video (16mm; 1/2")
Archives/Format: IUB - AAAMC (1/2")
Annotation: This segment chronicles the last days of Reverend Martin Luther King, Jr. as he attempts to organize a Poor People's Campaign. He is sidetracked by violence in Memphis as black sanitation workers go on strike, and is assassinated there on April 4, 1968. The Civil Rights Movement begins to fall into disarray, as lack of direction permeates the vacuum left by King's death.

PUBLIC ENEMY: TOUR OF A BLACK PLANET
Cast: Hank Shocklee*, Chuck D. *, Flavor Flav*, Terminator X *, Brother James 1*, Brother Roger*, Brother Mike*, James Bomb*, Carl Ryder*, Keith Shocklee*, Eric "Vietnam" Sadler*, Gary G-Wiz*, Sister Souljah *, Harry Allen*, T. Money *, Pop Diezel*, Krunch *, The Drew*, Rhondu *
Director: Moses Edinborough
Music Performer: Public Enemy *
Music by: Public Enemy *
Producer: Deborah Bolling*
Screenwriter: Moses Edinborough
Tech Info: mixed/sound/65 min.   Type: Concert Feature

Date: 1991   Origin: USA
Company: Def Jam Films, Sony Music Entertainment, Inc.
Distributors/Format: Sony Music Video Enterprises (1/2")
Archives/Format: IUB - AAAMC (1/2")
Annotation: Concert footage of Public Enemy's 1990 World tour ranges from American cities (Oakland, New York, Houston and Los Angeles) to European locales (Brussels, Paris and London). Lyrics by Chuck D, Flavor Flav, and Terminator X attempt to expose the myths of racial freedom and justice in American political and social structures.

PULL YOUR HEAD TO THE MOON: STORIES OF CREOLE WOMEN

Director: Ayoka Chenzira*, Ronald K. Gray*
Screenwriter: Ayoka Chenzira*
Storywriter: David Rousseve*
Tech Info: color/sound   Type: Television Feature
Date: 1992   Origin: USA
Company: Alive TV
Distributors/Format: Red Carnelian Films/Video (16mm; 1/2")
Annotation: Produced for Alive TV and in collaboration with performance artist David Rousseve, the story makes connections between a young man's mortal loss and the experiences of his Creole grandmother in the early 1900s Louisiana. Ronald K. Gray is Director of Photography.

PULP FICTION

Cast: Samuel L. Jackson*, Ving Rhames*, Bruce Willis, John Travolta, Harvey Keitel, Uma Thurman, Amanda Plummer
Director: Quentin Tarantino, Andrzej Sekala
Executive Producer: Danny Devito, Bob Weinstein, Harvey Weinstein, Stacy Sher
Producer: Danny Devito, Bob Weinstein, Harvey Weinstein, Lawrence Bender, Stacy Sher
Screenwriter: Quentin Tarantino
Storywriter: Quentin Tarantino
Tech Info: color/sound/154 min.   Type: Dramatic Feature
Date: 1994   Origin: USA
Company: Miramax
Distributors/Format: Facets Multimedia, Inc. (1/2"), Miramax Home Video (1/2")
Annotation: Tongue-in-cheek Tarantino tells three overlapping stories about robbery, treachery, drugs, sex of various kinds, and murder in Los Angeles. They are held together by two characters, Jules Winnfield (Jackson) and Vincent Vega (Travolta), hit men in the employ of gang boss Marcellus Wallace (Rhames).

PUNCHLINE

Cast: Damon Wayans*, George Wallace*, Tom Hanks, John Goodman, Sally Field, Mark Rydell
Director: David Seltzer
Music by: Charles Gross, Daniel Allan Carlin
Producer: Daniel Melnick, Michael Rachmil
Screenwriter: David Seltzer
Tech Info: color/sound/128 min.   Type: Comedy Feature

Date: 1988   Origin: USA
Company: Columbia
Distributors/Format: Columbia Pictures Home Video (1/2")
Annotation: Lilah Krytsick (Field), a suburban housewife and Steven Gold (Hanks), a med-school drop out, become friends after meeting at a comedy club where they both perform. Wayans plays Percy and Wallace is the man with his arm in a cast.

PUNISHER, THE

Cast: Louis Gossett Jr.*, Dolph Lundgren, Kim Miyori, Jerden Krabbe
Director: Mark Goldblatt
Producer: Robert Mark Kamen
Screenwriter: Boaz Yakin
Tech Info: color/sound/93 min.   Type: Adaptation
Date: 1989   Origin: Australia
Company: New World Pictures
Distributors/Format: LIVE Home Video (1/2")
Annotation: Based on the comic book serial about a policeman, Frank Castle (Lundgren), who after the murder of his family, appoints himself "The Punisher." Castle is watched and followed by Lt. Jake Berkowitz (Gossett) who attempts to save Castle from himself and a conscience that has confused ethics and morality.

PUPPET MASTER 4

Cast: Felton Perry*, Guy Rolfe, Teresa Hill, Chandra West, Gordon Currie
Director: Jeff Burr
Executive Producer: Charles Band
Music by: Richard Band
Producer: Charles Band, Charles Band
Screenwriter: Todd Henschell, Steven E. Carr, Jo Duffy, Doug Aarniokoski, Keith Payson
Tech Info: color/sound/80 min.   Type: Dramatic Feature
Date: 1993   Origin: USA
Company: Full Moon Entertainment
Distributors/Format: Paramount Home Video (1/2")
Annotation: Monster-children from the earth's center absorb the brains of Dr. Carl Baker (Perry) and Dr. Leslie Piper (Randall), scientists studying artificial intelligence. A third scientist discovers an animating serum that brings monster- fighting puppets to life.

PURE LUCK

Cast: Danny Glover*, Martin Short
Director: Nadia Tass
Executive Producer: Francis Veber
Music by: Danny Elfman, Jonathan Sheffer
Producer: Francis Veber, Lance Hool, Sean Daniel
Screenwriter: Timothy Harris, Herschel Weingrod
Tech Info: color/sound/96 min.   Type: Comedy Feature
Date: 1991   Origin: France
Company: Sean Daniel Company
Distributors/Format: Universal Home Video (1/2")
Annotation: In this remake of LA CHEVRE (1985), Raymond Campanolla (Glover) is a professional investigator hired as an assistant to Proctor (Short) to go to Mexico in search of a missing woman. Raymond does the bulk of the investigation and

spends most of his time cleaning up Proctor's mess.

PURPLE HEARTS
Cast: David Harris*, Bruce Guilchard*, Ken Wahl, Donald Barry, Paul Williams, Cheryl Ladd
Director: Sidney J. Furie
Music Performer: Robert Folk
Music by: Robert Folk
Producer: Sidney J. Furie
Storywriter: Sidney J. Furie, Rick Natkin
Tech Info: color/sound/115 min.   Type: Dramatic Feature
Date: 1984   Origin: USA
Company: Ladd Company
Distributors/Format: Warner Bros. Home Video, Inc. (1/2")
Annotation: Navy surgeon Don Jardian (Wahl) is in Vietnam attempting to perform his duties without a conscience. While trying to save Corporal Jackson (Guilchard), he meets a volunteer nurse (Ladd) whose devotion inspires him and with whom he falls in love. Harris plays Hanes, a serviceman.

PURPLE RAIN
Cast: Apollonia Kotero*, Morris Day*, Clarence Williams III*, Prince (Rogers Nelson) *, Olga Karlatos
Director: Albert Magnoli
Music Performer: Prince (Rogers Nelson) *, Mark Cardenas
Music by: Prince (Rogers Nelson) *, Michael Colombier
Producer: Robert Cavallo, Joseph Ruffalo, Steven Fargnoli
Screenwriter: William Blinn, Albert Magnoli
Tech Info: color/sound/113 min.   Type: Musical Feature
Date: 1984   Origin: USA
Company: Purple Rain Company
Distributors/Format: Warner Bros. Home Video, Inc. (1/2")
Archives/Format: IUB - BFC/A (1/2")
Annotation: A young musician, The Kid (Prince), experiences tumultuous times in his career, his home life, and his relationship with Apollonia (Kotero). Day plays himself as the impeccable competitor complicating the Kid's rise to fame and his love life.

Q
Alternate: The Winged Serpent
Cast: Richard Roundtree*, Candy Clark, David Carradine, Michael Moriarty
Director: Larry Cohen
Music by: Robert O. Ragland
Producer: Larry Cohen
Screenwriter: Larry Cohen
Tech Info: color/sound/100 min.   Type: Dramatic Feature
Date: 1982   Origin: USA
Company: United Film Distribution, Larco Productions
Distributors/Format: MCA Home Video (1/2")
Annotation: Detectives Powell (Roundtree) and Shepard (Carradine) link several mysterious, brutal deaths to a prehistoric, winged beast-god living atop New York's Empire State Building.

QUEST FOR FIRE
Cast: Rae Dawn Chong*, Ron Perlman, Nameer El-Kadi, Everett McGill
Director: Jean-Jacques Annaud
Executive Producer: Michael Gruskoff
Music Performer: Philippe Sarde
Music by: Philippe Sarde
Producer: John Kemeny, Denis Heraix, Michael Gruskoff
Screenwriter: Gerard Brach
Tech Info: color/sound/100 min.   Type: Dramatic Feature
Date: 1981   Origin: USA
Company: Fox, United Artists
Distributors/Format: CBS/Fox Home Video (1/2")
Annotation: Three cavemen go in search of fire after their tribe's flame is doused
during an attack. Chong is a cavewoman the men encounter during their quest for
fire.

QUESTION OF COLOR, A
Series: African American Perspectives
Director: Kathe Sandler*
Executive Producer: St. Clair Bourne*
Music by: Jason Hwang
Screenwriter: Kathe Sandler*, Luke Charles Harris*
Speaker: Verta Mae Grosvenor*, Malcolm X *, Johnny Ford*, Curtis James*, Esther
Lloyd*, Wiley Woodard*, Kim Mayner*, Harold Mayner*, Annie Cadwell*, Bobby
Davis*, Benjamin Payton*, Baylies Davis*, Keyonn Sheppard*, Keith Brown*, Dianne
Houston*, Patricia Williams*, Melba Tolliver*, Kathleen Cleaver*, Karen Halliburton*,
Robin Peagles*, Kayin Sheppard*, Ferdinand Ofodile*, Mrs. Howard*
Tech Info: mixed/sound/57 min.   Type: Documentary Feature
Date: 1992   Origin: USA
Studio: Independent
Company: Film Two Productions
Distributors/Format: California Newsreel (1/2")
Archives/Format: IUB - BFC/A (1/2")
Annotation: Sandler examines the issue of color consciousness within the black
community, a caste system based on how closely skin color, hair texture and facial
features conform to a European ideal. She interviews a number of African
Americans who provide testimony of their experiences and attitudes regarding color.

QUICKSILVER
Cast: Laurence/Larry Fishburne*, Jami Gertz, Paul Rodriguez, Kevin Bacon, Rudy
Ramos
Director: Tom Donnelly
Music by: Becky Mancuso, Tony Banks
Producer: Daniel Melnick, Michael Rachmil
Screenwriter: Thomas Michael Donnelly
Tech Info: color/sound/101 min.   Type: Dramatic Feature
Date: 1986   Origin: USA
Company: Indie
Distributors/Format: Columbia Pictures Home Video (1/2")
Annotation: Jack Casey (Bacon) is a yuppie stockbroker who loses a fortune and
decides to join the working class as a bicycle courier. Fishburne plays "Voodoo."

RABBIT TEST
Cast: Jimmy/Jimmie Walker*, Roosevelt "Rosey" Grier*, Billy Crystal, Alex Rocco, Joan Prather, Doris Roberts
Director: Joan Rivers
Executive Producer: Melvin Simon
Music by: Mike Post, Peter Carpenter
Producer: Melvin Simon, Edgar Rosenberg
Screenwriter: Joan Rivers, Jay Redack
Tech Info: color/sound/84 min.   Type: Comedy Feature
Date: 1978   Origin: USA
Company: Laugh or Die
Distributors/Format: Avco Embassy (16mm)
Annotation: Lionel (Crystal) who is engaged to Segoynia (Prather), becomes the world's first pregnant man. Grier plays a taxi driver, and Walker portrays Umbuto.

RACE AGAINST PRIME TIME
Director: David Shulman
Narrator: Pola Rapaport*, Norm Fruchter
Producer: David Shulman
Screenwriter: David Shulman
Tech Info: color/sound/58 min.   Type: Documentary Feature
Date: 1984   Origin: USA
Company: New Decade Productions
Distributors/Format: California Newsreel (1/2")
Annotation: In 1980, Arthur McDuffie, an African American community worker was brutally kicked, beaten and clubbed to death by Miami police. His murder mobilized protests in two black neighborhoods troubled with economic underdevelopment, high unemployment and numerous previous incidents of police brutality.

RACISM 101
Series: Frontline
Director: Orlando Bagwell*
Producer: Orlando Bagwell*, Thomas Lennon
Tech Info: color/sound/58 min.   Type: Television Documentary
Date: 1988   Origin: USA
Company: PBS
Annotation: Bagwell examines the problem of racial conflict on American college campuses focusing on instances of racism at the University of Michigan and Dartmouth college.

RAGE AND HONOR
Cast: Alex Datcher*, Cynthia Rothrock, Peter Cunningham, Richard Norton, Terri Treas
Director: Terence H. Winkless
Executive Producer: Miles A. Copeland III, Paul Colichman
Music by: Darryl Way
Producer: Miles A. Copeland III, Paul Colichman, Donald Paul Pemrick
Screenwriter: Terence H. Winkless
Tech Info: color/sound/90 min.   Type: Dramatic Feature

Date: 1993   Origin: USA
Company: IRS Media
Distributors/Format: Columbia/TriStar Home Video (1/2")
Annotation: A high school student catches a drug deal on videotape and is chased by the criminals. One of the villains he encounter is Hannah the Hun (Datcher), leader of an all-girl group.

RAGE IN HARLEM, A

Cast: Forest Whitaker*, Danny Glover*, Robin Givens*, Samm-Art Williams*, Gregory Hines*, Zakes Mokae*, Reynaldo Rey*, T.K. Carter*, Stack Pierce*, Helen Martin*, Badja Djola*, Leonard Jackson*, Ron Taylor*, Willard Pugh*, Jimmy/James Spinks*, John Toles-Bey*, Wendell Pierce*, George Wallace*, Tasha O'Bryant*, Tyler Collins*, Anthonia Dotson*
Director: Bill Duke*
Executive Producer: Bob Weinstein, Harvey Weinstein, Nik Powell, William Horberg, Terry Glinwood
Music by: Elmer Bernstein
Producer: Bob Weinstein, Harvey Weinstein, Stephen Woolley, Nik Powell, William Horberg, Terry Glinwood, John Nicolella, Kerry Boyle
Screenwriter: John Toles-Bey*, Bobby Crawford
Storywriter: Chester Himes*
Tech Info: color/sound/115 min.   Type: Comedy Feature
Date: 1991   Origin: Great Britain
Company: Palace Pictures, Miramax
Distributors/Format: Miramax Home Video (1/2")
Archives/Format: IUB - BFC/A (1/2")
Annotation: When Immabelle (Givens) arrives from Mississippi with a chest of stolen gold, everybody wants a part of the scam, including mobster Easy Money (Glover) and street-wise con-man Goldy (Hines). All Jackson (Whitaker) wants is Immabelle. However, they must all face Slim (Djola), deadliest crook among them. The film is adapted from the novel by Chester Himes.

RAGTIME

Cast: Moses Gunn*, Debbie Allen*, Howard E. Rollins Jr.*, Elizabeth McGovern, James Cagney, Mandy Patinkin
Director: Milos Forman
Executive Producer: Michael Hausman, Bernard Williams
Music Performer: Randy Newman
Music by: Brad Dourif, Randy Newman
Producer: Dino de Laurentis, Michael Hausman, Bernard Williams
Screenwriter: Michael Weller
Storywriter: E.L. Doctorow
Tech Info: mixed/sound/155 min.   Type: Dramatic Feature
Date: 1981   Origin: USA
Company: Dino De Laurentis Production
Distributors/Format: Paramount Home Video (1/2")
Annotation: "Coalhouse" Walker, Jr. (Rollins) is a ragtime pianist who begins his career as an accompanist for silent films. When his career takes off, he finds his love Sarah (Allen) and proposes marriage. Trouble erupts when racist firemen deface his new car and he insists they clean it.

RAIN WITHOUT THUNDER
Cast: Bahni Turpin*, Linda Hunt, Frederic Forrest, Carolyn McCormick, Ali Thomas, Betty Buckley
Director: Gary Bennett
Executive Producer: Mike Mihalich, Rick Callahan
Music by: Randall Lynch, Allen Lynch
Producer: Nanette Sorensen, Gary Sorensen, Mike Mihalich, Rick Callahan
Screenwriter: Gary Bennett
Tech Info: color/sound/99 min.   Type: Dramatic Feature
Date: 1993   Origin: USA
Company: TAZ Pictures
Distributors/Format: Orion Home Video (1/2")
Annotation: The rise of religious fanaticism in the 21st century leads to the incarceration of women for having abortions. Alison (Thomas) finds herself in jail on this charge. Turpin plays the "Baby Bomb" prisoner.

RALLY OR IF BEALE STREET COULDN'T TALK, THE
Director: Cal Ward Jr.*
Tech Info: color/20 min.   Type: Experimental Short
Date: 1994   Origin: USA
Studio: Independent
Distributors/Format: Cal Ward Jr. (35mm)
Annotation: This satirical silent film attacks racism and montebank preachers. Moses (Ward) is a self serving minister who addresses his congregation via videotape and receives kickbacks from local white politicians. Agreeing to appear at a fundraising rally, Moses gets his addresses mixed up and winds up at a KKK rally instead.

RAP'S MOST WANTED
Director: Tas Salini
Executive Producer: Luther Campbell*
Host: Luther Campbell*
Producer: Luther Campbell*, Luther Campbell*, Tas Salini
Speaker: Ice-T *, 2 Live Crew *, Luther Campbell*, Geto Boys *, Chuck D. *, H.W.A. *, Too Short *
Tech Info: mixed/sound/90 min.   Type: Concert Feature
Date: 1991   Origin: USA
Company: Stepping Stone Productions, et al.
Distributors/Format: A*Vision Home Entertainment (1/2")
Archives/Format: IUB - AAAMC (1/2")
Annotation: Campbell, of the rap music group 2 Live Crew, interviews some of Rap's most controversial performers, including other crew members, the Geto Boys, H.W.A., Chuck D of Public Enemy, Too Short, and Ice-T. The musicians discuss the motivations behind their explicit lyrics, defining them as social commentary on the sex, racism, violence, and politics that dominate America.

RAP, RACE & EQUALITY
Music Performer: Ice-T *, Ice Cube *, Naughty by Nature *
Producer: Ewan Burnett*
Speaker: Ice-T *, Ice Cube *, Naughty by Nature *, Dr. Tricia Rose*, Jon Pareles
Tech Info: color/sound/58 min.   Type: Documentary Feature

Date: 1994   Origin: USA
Company: Burberry Productions
Distributors/Format: Filmakers Library, Inc. (16mm; 1/2")
Annotation: The documentary demystifies controversial artists who speak for many of today's African American youth. It looks at the issues in Rap music, such as racism, economic and social inequality, and race relations.

RAPID FIRE
Cast: Basil Wallace*, Powers Boothe, Nick Mancuso, Brandon Lee, Kate Hodge, Tzi Ma
Director: Dwight H. Little
Executive Producer: John Fasano, Gerald T. Olson
Music by: Christopher Young
Producer: John Fasano, Gerald T. Olson, Robert Lawrence
Screenwriter: Alan B. McElroy, Cindy Cirile, Paul Attanasio
Storywriter: Alan B. McElroy, Cindy Cirile
Tech Info: color/sound/96 min.   Type: Dramatic Feature
Date: 1992   Origin: USA
Company: Robert Lawrence Productions, Fox
Distributors/Format: Fox Home Video (1/2")
Annotation: After witnessing a murder, Jake Lo (Lee) is placed in protective custody and brought to Chicago to testify against the killer, drug kingpin Serrano (Mancuso). Lo barely escapes an attempt on his life by crooked agents. Wallace plays Agent Wesley.

RAPPIN'
Cast: Kadeem Hardison*, Rony Clanton*, Edye Byrde*, Ice-T *, Mario Van Peebles*, Eriq LaSalle*, Melvin Plowden*, Tasia Valenza, Charles Flohe
Director: Joel Silberg
Music by: Michael Linn
Producer: Yoram Globus, Menahem Golan
Screenwriter: Robert Litz, Adam Friedman
Tech Info: color/sound/92 min.   Type: Musical Feature
Date: 1985   Origin: USA
Company: Cannon
Annotation: John Hood (Van Peebles), a rapping ex-con determined to go straight, finds that his girlfriend Dixie (Valenza) has taken up with Duane (Flohe), a member of a rival gang. LaSalle is Ice; Hardison is Moon; Plowden is Fats; Clanton plays Cedric; and Ice-T appears as himself.

RATBOY
Cast: Robert Townsend*, Tiger Haynes*, Damita Jo Freeman*, Sondra Locke, Christopher Hewitt, S.L. Baird
Director: Sondra Locke
Music by: Lennie Niehaus
Producer: Fritz Manes
Screenwriter: Rob Thompson
Tech Info: color/sound/104 min.   Type: Dramatic Feature

Date: 1986   Origin: USA
Company: Malpaso
Distributors/Format: Warner Bros. Home Video, Inc. (1/2")
Annotation: Nikki Morrison (Locke) is a Los Angeles window dresser looking for her big break. While scanning the local garbage dump for display worthy items, she discovers Ratboy (Baird), a boy who looks like a rat. With the help of Manny (Townsend), a street hustler, Nikki exploits her find.

RAVAGERS, THE

Cast: Woody Strode*, Richard Harris, Art Carney, Ernest Borgnine, Ann Turkel
Director: Richard Compton
Music by: Fred Karlin
Producer: John W. Hyde
Screenwriter: David S. Sanford
Tech Info: color/sound/91 min.   Type: Dramatic Feature
Date: 1979   Origin: USA
Company: Columbia
Distributors/Format: Columbia Pictures Home Video (1/2")
Annotation: In post-nuclear war America, Falk (Harris) seeks revenge after his wife is raped and murdered by motorcycle hoods. He meets a group of people who live in a cave and together they fight off the hoods. Strode plays Brown.

READING READINESS - VOLUME 5

Series: Bill Cosby's Picture Pages
Cast: Bill Cosby*
Tech Info: color/sound/30 min.   Type: Dramatic Short
Date: 1988   Origin: USA
Company: Walt Disney
Distributors/Format: Walt Disney Home Video (1/2")
Annotation: Cosby helps young children to learn the skills necessary for reading. Colorful activity books help students learn along with Cosby's teaching techniques which are simple, easy to understand, and effective.

READY TO WEAR

Alternate: Pret a Porter
Cast: Forest Whitaker*, Kim Basinger, Sophia Loren, Marcello Mastroianni, Julia Roberts
Director: Robert Altman, Jean Lepine, Pierre Mignot
Executive Producer: Bob Weinstein, Harvey Weinstein, Ian Jessel
Producer: Bob Weinstein, Harvey Weinstein, Robert Altman, Ian Jessel
Screenwriter: Robert Altman, Barbara Shulgasser
Tech Info: color/sound/133 min.   Type: Comedy Feature
Date: 1994   Origin: France
Company: Miramax
Distributors/Format: Miramax Home Video (1/2")
Annotation: Whitaker is one of many fashion designers at the most important Spring fashion show in Paris. He is also involved in a three-way love affair. Unfortunately, a murder has been committed and everyone is suspect. Unidentified top black women models are featured.

REAL LIFE
Cast: J.A. Preston*, Charles Grodin, Albert Brooks, Dick Haynes
Director: Albert Brooks
Executive Producer: Norman Epstein, Jonathan Kovler
Music by: Mort Lindsey
Producer: Penelope Spheeris, Norman Epstein, Jonathan Kovler
Screenwriter: Albert Brooks, Monica Johnson, Harry Shearer
Tech Info: color/sound/99 min.   Type: Comedy Feature
Date: 1979   Origin: USA
Company: Paramount
Distributors/Format: Paramount Home Video (1/2")
Annotation: Albert Brooks appears as himself, a documentary filmmaker in search of a typical American family to film. The family he finds cracks under the pressure of the camera's intrusive eye. Preston plays Dr. Ted Cleary.

RECRUITS
Cast: John Canada Terrell*, Steve Osmond, Doug Annear, Alan Deveau, Lolita David
Director: Rafal Zielinski
Music by: Steve Parsons
Producer: Maurice Smith
Screenwriter: Charles Wiener, B.K. Roderick
Tech Info: color/sound/82 min.   Type: Comedy Feature
Date: 1986   Origin: USA
Company: Concorde
Annotation: A crooked police captain is out to publicly disgrace the mayor. He hires a new group of bumbling recruits and stages a phony assassination when the governor is in town. Terrell plays Winston, one of the recruits who is individualized by his spoofs of Eddie Murphy's role in the 48 HOURS films.

RED DAWN
Cast: Ron O'Neal*, Frank McRae*, Charlie Sheen, Powers Boothe, Harry Dean Stanton, Lea Thompson, Patrick Swayze
Director: John Milius
Executive Producer: Sidney Beckerman
Music Performer: Basil Poledouris
Music by: Basil Poledouris
Producer: Sidney Beckerman, Buzz Feitshans, Barry Beckerman
Screenwriter: John Milius, Kevin Reynolds
Storywriter: Kevin Reynolds
Tech Info: color/sound/100 min.   Type: Dramatic Feature
Date: 1984   Origin: USA
Company: MGM
Distributors/Format: United Artists Home Video (1/2")
Annotation: Bella (O'Neal) is a Cuban colonel fighting in the Russian overthrow of America. He befriends some of the rebels (Swayze and Thompson) who eventually succeed in regaining American soil and allows them to win because he loves his country. McRae plays a school teacher who is shot and killed during the onslaught of the invasion.

RED HEAT
Cast: Laurence/Larry Fishburne*, Gretchen F. Palmer*, James Belushi, Arnold Schwarzenegger, Gina Gershon, Ed O'Ross, Richard Bright
Director: Walter Hill
Executive Producer: Mario Kassar, Andrew Vajna
Music by: James Horner
Producer: Walter Hill, Gordon Carroll, Mario Kassar, Andrew Vajna
Screenwriter: Walter Hill, Harry Kleiner, Troy Kennedy Martin
Storywriter: Walter Hill
Tech Info: color/sound/103 min.   Type: Dramatic Feature
Date: 1988   Origin: USA
Company: Carolco, Lone Wolf, Oak
Distributors/Format: TriStar Pictures Inc. (1/2")
Annotation: Soviet Police Captain Ivan Danko (Schwarzenegger) pursues drug kingpin Viktor Rostavili (O'Ross) to the U.S. Chicago detectives Ridzik and Gallagher (Belushi and Bright) are assigned to work with Danko. Fishburne is Lt. Stobbs; Palmer has a small role.

REFLECTIONS
Director: Kim Watson*, Caleb Oglesby*
Tech Info: mixed/sound/6 min.   Type: Experimental Short
Date: 1987   Origin: USA
Studio: Independent
Distributors/Format: Third World Newsreel (1/2")
Annotation: The voice and vision of civil rights activist Dr. Martin Luther King, Jr. provide the foundation for this short experimental video.

REFORM SCHOOL GIRLS
Cast: Denise Gordy*, Sybil Danning, Linda Carol, Wendy O. Williams, Pat Ast, Charlotte McGinnis
Director: Tom DeSimone
Executive Producer: Leo Angelos, Gregory Hinton
Music by: Tedra Gabriel, Martin Schwartz
Producer: Jack Cummins, Leo Angelos, Gregory Hinton
Screenwriter: Tom DeSimone
Tech Info: color/sound/94 min.   Type: Dramatic Feature
Date: 1986   Origin: USA
Company: Balcor, New World
Distributors/Format: New World Home Video (1/2")
Annotation: In this parody of women-in-prison films, Jenny (Carol) is sent to reform school after helping her boyfriend rob a convenience store. There she must defend herself from attacks by the other inmates. Gordy plays Claudie.

REGARDING HENRY
Cast: Bill Nunn*, Harrison Ford, Annette Benning
Director: Mike Nichols
Executive Producer: Robert Greenhut
Music by: Hans Zimmer
Producer: Mike Nichols, Scott Rudin, Robert Greenhut
Storywriter: Jeffrey Abrams
Tech Info: color/sound/107 min.   Type: Dramatic Feature

Date: 1991   Origin: USA
Company: Paramount
Distributors/Format: Paramount Home Video (1/2")
Annotation: Henry (Ford), an upwardly mobile trial lawyer is completely changed when he is shot in a burglary. Nunn plays the physical therapist who helps him back to recovery.

REGGAE SUNSPLASH II

Director: Stefan Paul
Music Performer: Bob Marley*, Peter Tosh*, Burning Spear*, Third World *, The Wailers *, Clancy Eccles*
Producer: Stefan Paul
Screenwriter: Stefan Paul
Tech Info: color/sound/109 min.   Type: Concert Feature
Date: 1979   Origin: Jamaica/Germany
Company: New Line Cinema
Distributors/Format: New Line Cinema Home Video (1/2")
Annotation: Recorded at the Reggae Sunsplash Festival in Jamaica, the film highlights Reggae's musical performers.

RELENTLESS III

Cast: Felton Perry*, William Forsythe, Leo Rossi, Signy Coleman
Director: James Lemmo
Music by: Scott Grusin
Producer: Lisa Hansen, Paul Hertzberg
Screenwriter: James Lemmo
Tech Info: color/sound/85 min.   Type: Dramatic Feature
Date: 1993   Origin: USA
Company: New Line Cinema
Distributors/Format: New Line Cinema (16mm; 3/4"; 1/2")
Annotation: Walter (Forsythe) is a psychopathic killer who murders his victims and then has sex with the corpses for days before dumping them. Detective Sam Dietz (Rossi) is the policeman who tracks the killer. Perry is Detective Ziskie.

REMEMBER MY NAME

Cast: Moses Gunn*, Alfre Woodard*, Marilyn Coleman*, Carlos Brown*, Jeff Goldblum, Geraldine Chaplin, Anthony Perkins, Berry Berenson
Director: Alan Rudolph
Music by: Alberta Hunter*
Producer: Robert Altman
Screenwriter: Alan Rudolph
Tech Info: color/sound/94 min.   Type: Documentary Feature
Date: 1978   Origin: USA
Company: Lion's Gate Films
Distributors/Format: Columbia Pictures (16mm)
Annotation: Neil Curry (Perkins), a construction worker, and his wife Barbara (Berenson) live quietly until his ex-wife (Chaplin) out of prison after serving a jail term for murder, begins to harass Barbara. Woodard plays Rita; Gunn, Pike; Coleman, Teresa; Brown, Rusty.

REMEMBERING THELMA
Director: Kathe Sandler*
Producer: Kathe Sandler*
Screenwriter: Kathe Sandler*
Storywriter: Kathe Sandler*
Tech Info: color/sound/15 min.   Type: Documentary Short
Date: 1981   Origin: USA
Studio: Independent
Distributors/Format: Women Make Movies, Inc. (16mm; 1/2")
Archives/Format: IUB - BFC/A (1/2")
Annotation: Sandler uses photographs, rare film footage, and interviews as a tribute to the late Thelma Hill, an influential dancer and instructor.

RENAISSANCE MAN
Cast: Kadeem Hardison*, Gregory Hines*, Stacey Dash*, Khalil Kain*, Jenifer Lewis*, Richard Timothy Jones*, Danny Devito, Mark Walberg
Tech Info: color/sound/128 min.   Type: Comedy Feature
Date: 1994   Origin: USA
Company: Touchstone
Annotation: A down-on-his-luck businessman takes the only job offered, a teacher in the US Army. His mission is to keep a bunch of misfits from flunking out of basic training. Hines plays a touch drill sergeant; Hardison, Dash and Kain are trainees.

RENEGADES
Cast: Paul Butler*, Jami Gertz, Lou Diamond Phillips, Keifer Sutherland
Director: Jack Sholder
Executive Producer: Joe Roth, Ted Field, Robert Cort, James G. Robinson
Music by: Michael Kamen
Producer: Joe Roth, Ted Field, Robert Cort, James G. Robinson, David Madden, Paul Schiff
Screenwriter: David Rich
Tech Info: color/sound/105 min.   Type: Dramatic Feature
Date: 1989   Origin: USA
Company: Morgan Creek, Interscope
Distributors/Format: Universal Home Video (1/2")
Annotation: Undercover cop Buster McHenry (Sutherland) becomes involved in a diamond theft that gets out of hand due to the sadism of its mastermind. Butler plays Capt. Blalock.

RENT-A-COP
Cast: Bernie Casey*, Dionne Warwick*, Burt Reynolds, James Remar, Liza Minnelli
Director: Jerry London
Music by: Jerry Goldsmith
Producer: Raymond Wagner
Screenwriter: Dennis Shryack, Michael Blodgett
Tech Info: color/sound/95 min.   Type: Dramatic Feature
Date: 1988   Origin: USA
Company: Kings Road
Annotation: The sole survivor of a botched drug bust, former Chicago cop Tony Church (Reynolds) protects the only witness to the shooting, hooker Della Roberts (Minnelli). Casey plays Lemar, Church's former partner, and Warwick plays Beth.

REPO MAN
Cast: Helen Martin*, Vonetta McGee*, Sy Richardson*, Emilio Estevez, Harry Dean Stanton, Tracey Walter
Director: Alex Cox
Executive Producer: Michael Nesmith
Music Performer: Iggy Pop
Music by: Steven Huesteter, Humberto Larriva
Producer: Peter McCarthy, Jonathan Wacks, Michael Nesmith
Screenwriter: Alex Cox
Tech Info: color/sound/93 min.   Type: Comedy Feature
Date: 1983   Origin: USA
Company: Edge City Productions
Distributors/Format: MCA Home Video (1/2")
Annotation: Lite (Richardson) is a repo man who teaches Otto (Estevez) the tricks of repossessing cars. Marleen (McGee) is the secretary for the repossession business for which Lite and Otto work. Otto saves Marleen from being killed and she in turn helps him get a car that has aliens in the trunk.

RESPECT IS DUE
Producer: Cyrille Phipps*
Speaker: Sister Souljah *, Ralph McDaniels*, Dream Hampton*
Tech Info: color/sound/10 min.   Type: Experimental Short
Date: 1992   Origin: USA
Studio: Independent
Company: Third World Newsreel Production
Distributors/Format: Third World Newsreel (1/2")
Archives/Format: IUB - AAAMC (1/2")
Annotation: The film demonstrates the way women, especially black women, are portrayed in the media. It details the negative ways in which women are thought of and suggests how those sexist beliefs can be changed into positive ones.

RESTING PLACE
Cast: Morgan Freeman*, CCH Pounder*, John Lithgow
Director: John Korty
Music by: Eugene Marks
Producer: Robert Huddleston
Screenwriter: Walter Halsey Davis
Tech Info: color/sound/95 min.   Type: Television Feature
Date: 1986   Origin: USA
Studio: Hallmark Picture
Company: Marian Rees Associates, Inc.
Annotation: John Korty, maker of the AUTOBIOGRAPHY OF MISS JANE PITTMAN, directs this T.V. feature which explores racial tensions of the post-Vietnam era. When a southern town refuses to grant burial rights to the parents (Pounder and Freeman) of a black soldier, John Lithgow is the officer who must enforce the family's civil rights. In order to do this, he must reunite the dead soldier's army unit while prejudice surfaces as well.

RESURGENCE
Alternate: The Movement for Equality vs. the KKK
Director: T. Siegal, Tom Siegel
Producer: P. Yates, T. Siegal
Tech Info: color/sound/54 min.   Type: Documentary Feature
Date: 1981   Origin: USA
Company: Skylight Pictures, Emancipation Arts
Distributors/Format: First Run/Icarus Films (16mm)
Annotation: The film contrasts the build up in right wing racist organizations and the efforts of union and civil rights activists in the South to protect civil rights and improve working conditions.

RESURRECTIONS: PAUL ROBESON
Cast: Moses Gunn*
Director: William Greaves*
Producer: William Greaves*
Screenwriter: William Greaves*
Tech Info: Type: Television Feature
Date: 1990
Studio: Independent
Company: William Greaves* Productions
Distributors/Format: Williams Greaves Productions, Inc. (16mm)

RETRIBUTION
Cast: Harry Caesar*, Dennis Lipscomb, Leslie Wing, Suzanne Snyder
Director: Guy Magar
Executive Producer: Scott Lavin, Brian Christian
Music by: Alan Howarth
Producer: Guy Magar, Scott Lavin, Brian Christian
Screenwriter: Guy Magar, Lee Wasserman
Tech Info: color/sound/107 min.   Type: Dramatic Feature
Date: 1988   Origin: USA
Company: Renegade
Distributors/Format: United (16mm)
Annotation: George Miller (Lipscomb) survives a suicide attempt but is possessed by an evil spirit that causes him to murder people while dreaming. Caesar plays Charlie.

RETURN OF SUPERFLY, THE
Cast: Samuel L. Jackson*, Rony Clanton*, Eric Payne*, Margaret Avery*, John Canada Terrell*, Tico Wells*, Nathan Purdee*, Kirk Taylor*, Timothy Stickney*, O.L. Duke*, Leonard Thomas, Luis Ramos
Director: Sig Shore
Music by: Curtis Mayfield*
Producer: Sig Shore, Anthony Wisdom
Screenwriter: Anthony Wisdom
Tech Info: color/sound/95 min.   Type: Dramatic Feature

Date: 1990   Origin: USA
Company: Crash, Littoral
Distributors/Format: Vidmark Entertainment Home Video (1/2"), Triton Home Video (1/2")
Annotation: Upon his return to the U.S. from Europe, Superfly (Purdee) is nabbed by the government. Even though he has been clean for two decades, they threaten to arrest him if he doesn't help them apprehend the current drug lords. Nate (Jackson) warns Superfly of the danger that awaits him and Francine (Avery) helps him in every way she can. In this belated sequel to SUPERFLY (1972), Superfly once again is victorious.

RETURN OF THE JEDI
Cast: Billy Dee Williams*, James Earl Jones*, Mark Hamill, Harrison Ford, Kenny Baker, Anthony Daniels, David Prowse, Carrie Fisher
Director: Richard Marquand
Executive Producer: George Lucas
Music by: John Williams
Producer: George Lucas, Howard Kazanjian, Robert Watts, Jim Bloom
Screenwriter: Lawrence Kasdan, George Lucas
Storywriter: George Lucas
Tech Info: color/sound/133 min.   Type: Dramatic Feature
Date: 1983   Origin: USA
Company: Lucasfilm
Distributors/Format: Fox Home Video (1/2")
Annotation: In the final segment of the STAR WARS trilogy, Darth Vader (acted by Prowse, voice by Jones) is building a new Death Star that cannot be destroyed. Han Solo (Ford) has been imprisoned in carbonite. Luke Skywalker (Hamill) sends C-3P0 (Daniels) and R2-D2 (Baker) to rescue Solo. Princess Leia (Fisher), masquerading as a bounty hunter, is victorious when she and the robots team up with Lando Calrissian (Williams).

RETURN TO HORROR HIGH
Cast: Al Fann*, Alex Rocco, Lori Lethin, Brendan Hughes, Scott Jacoby, Andy Romano
Director: Bill Froehlich
Executive Producer: Greg H. Sims
Music by: Stacy Widelitz
Producer: Mark Lisson, Greg H. Sims
Screenwriter: Mark Lisson, Greg H. Sims, Bill Froehlich, Dana Escalante
Tech Info: color/sound/95 min.   Type: Comedy Feature
Date: 1987   Origin: USA
Company: New World
Distributors/Format: Balcor Film Investors (1/2"), New World Home Video (1/2")
Annotation: The crew filming a horror movie is massacred while shooting scenes of a massacre at a school where a real life massacre took place several years before. Fann appears as Amos.

REVENGE OF THE NERDS

Cast: Bernie Casey*, Larry B. Scott*, Curtis Armstrong, Brian Tochi, John Goodman
Director: Jeff Kanew
Executive Producer: David Obst, Peter Bart
Music by: Thomas Newman
Producer: Ted Field, Peter Samuelson, David Obst, Peter Bart
Storywriter: Steve Zacharias, Jeff Buhai, Miguel Tejada-Flores, Tim Metcalfe
Tech Info: color/sound/89 min.   Type: Comedy Feature
Date: 1984   Origin: USA
Company: Interscope Communications, Fox
Distributors/Format: CBS/Fox Home Video (1/2")
Annotation: Lamar (Scott) is a black homosexual who, with a group of nerds, tries to join a fraternity. The chapter president, U.N. Jefferson (Casey), is at first hesitant, then supports the nerds by getting big black frat brothers from the mean football fraternity to protect them.

REVENGE OF THE NERDS II: NERDS IN PARADISE

Cast: Larry B. Scott*, Donald Gibb, Timothy Busfield, Robert Carradine, Bradley Whitford
Director: Joe Roth
Executive Producer: Joe Roth
Music Performer: Devo
Music by: Mark Mother Baugh
Producer: Ted Field, Peter Bart, Robert Cort, Joe Roth
Screenwriter: Dan Guntzelman, Steve Marshall
Tech Info: color/sound/89 min.   Type: Comedy Feature
Date: 1987   Origin: USA
Company: Interscope Communications, Fox
Distributors/Format: CBS/Fox Home Video (1/2")
Annotation: In this sequel, Lamar (Scott), is a member of Lambda, Lambda, Lambda fraternity. The frat boys of tri-Lambda are harassed by the members of another fraternity at the meeting of the brotherhood of fraternities in Florida. Eventually, Lamar and his frat brothers get revenge on the Alphas and become heroes.

RHYTHM AND BLUES PART 1

Series: America's Music (Volume 5)
Director: Kip Walton
Host: Billy Eckstine*
Music Performer: Scatman Crothers*, Billy Preston*, Billy Eckstine*, Ruth Brown*, Gloria Lynne*, Sheer Delight *, Amos Milburn*, Louis Jordan*
Producer: Sandra Turbow
Tech Info: mixed/sound/57 min.   Type: Documentary Feature
Date: 1982   Origin: USA
Studio: Independent
Company: Skylark/Savoy
Distributors/Format: Century Home Video (1/2")
Archives/Format: IUB - BFC/A (1/2")
Annotation: Eckstine provides insight into the origin of Rhythm and Blues while top performing artists perform a variety of rhythm and blues songs.

RHYTHM AND BLUES PART 2
Series: America's Music (Volume 6)
Director: Kip Walton
Host: Brock Peters*
Music Performer: Scatman Crothers*, O.C. Smith*, Sam Moore*, Brook Benton*, Sam Gaillard*, Mary Wells*
Producer: Sandra Turbow
Tech Info: mixed/sound/57 min.   Type: Documentary Feature
Date: 1982   Origin: USA
Studio: Independent
Company: Skylark/Savoy Productions
Distributors/Format: Century Home Video (1/2")
Archives/Format: IUB - BFC/A (1/2")
Annotation: Another in the America's Music series presents live performances by original performers of Rhythm and Blues. Included in the program are Brooke Benton, Scatman Crothers, Mary Wells, O.C. Smith, and Sam Moore. Host Peters provides a black & white clip of Sam Gilliard playing with Scatman Crothers on drums.

RICH GIRL
Cast: Gail Neely*, Don Michael Paul, Bentley Mitchum, Jill Schoelen, Sean Kanan
Director: Joel Bender
Executive Producer: Mark Hoffman, Steven H. Parker
Music by: Jay Chattaway
Producer: Mark Hoffman, Michael B. London, Steven H. Parker
Screenwriter: Robert Elliot
Tech Info: color/sound/96 min.   Type: Dramatic Feature
Date: 1991   Origin: USA
Company: Rich Girl, Film West
Distributors/Format: Studio Three Film Corporation (16mm)
Annotation: Rich Courtney Wells (Schoelen) rebels against her wealthy father, rejects her snobbish fiance, and becomes part of Los Angeles' rock and roll club scene where she meets Rick (Paul), a musician with a checkered past. Neely is the Cook.

RICH IN LOVE
Cast: Alfre Woodard*, Albert Finney, Jill Clayburgh, Piper Laurie, Ethan Hawke, Kyle MacLachlan
Director: Bruce Beresford, Peter James
Music by: Georges Delerue
Producer: Richard D. Zanuck, Lili Fini Zanuck
Screenwriter: Alfred Uhry
Tech Info: color/sound/105 min.   Type: Dramatic Feature
Date: 1993   Origin: USA
Company: MGM, United Artists
Distributors/Format: MGM/UA Home Video (1/2")
Annotation: Helen Odom (Clayburgh) leaves her husband Warren (Finney) and two young daughters, Lucille (Erbe) and Rae (Amis), without warning. The father and daughters begin a new life until Helen shows up unexpectedly. Woodard plays Rhody Poole, a family friend.

RICH KIDS
Cast: Beatrice Winde*, Trini Alvarado, Jeremy Levy, Kathryn Walker
Director: Robert M. Young
Music by: Craig Doerge
Producer: Michael Hausman, George W. George
Screenwriter: Judith Ross
Tech Info: color/sound/96 min.   Type: Dramatic Feature
Date: 1979   Origin: USA
Company: Lion's Gate
Distributors/Format: United Artists Home Video (1/2")
Annotation: Franny (Alvarado) knows her parents are about to divorce and is helped by her friend Jamie (Levy) who has been through it already with his family. Winde plays Corine.

RICHARD PRYOR: HERE AND NOW
Director: Richard Pryor*
Executive Producer: Jim Brown*
Producer: Jim Brown*, Bob Parkinson, Andy Friendly
Screenwriter: Richard Pryor*
Speaker: Richard Pryor*
Tech Info: color/sound/94 min.   Type: Comedy Feature
Date: 1983   Origin: USA
Company: Columbia
Distributors/Format: Columbia Pictures (16mm)
Annotation: Pryor muses on drugs, sex and politics in this performance shot in New Orleans's Saenger Theatre.

RICHARD PRYOR: LIVE IN CONCERT
Cast: Richard Pryor*
Director: Jeff Margolis
Executive Producer: Saul Barnett
Music by: Harry Betts
Producer: Del Jack, J. Mark Travis, Saul Barnett
Tech Info: color/sound/78 min.   Type: Comedy Feature
Date: 1979   Origin: USA
Company: Special Event Entertainment
Distributors/Format: Facets Multimedia, Inc. (1/2")
Annotation: This Pryor one-man show, with all his infamous routines, was filmed at the Hollywood Palladium.

RICHARD PRYOR: LIVE ON THE SUNSET STRIP
Cast: Richard Pryor*
Director: Joe Layton
Music by: Harry Betts
Producer: Richard Pryor*
Screenwriter: Richard Pryor*
Tech Info: color/sound/82 min.   Type: Comedy Feature

Date: 1982   Origin: USA
Company: Rastar Films, Inc.
Distributors/Format: Columbia Pictures (16mm)
Annotation: Pryor talks about his trip to Africa, one-night acts in Mafia-owned clubs and his near-fatal burning accident.

RICOCHET

Cast: Denzel Washington*, John Amos*, Ice-T *, Victoria Dillard*, John Cothran Jr.*, Lydell W. Chesher*, Lindsay Wagner, John Lithgow
Director: Russell Mulcahy
Music Performer: Ice-T *, Pointer Sisters *
Music by: Alan Silvestri
Producer: Joel Silver, Michael I. Levy
Screenwriter: Steven E. DeSouza
Storywriter: Fred Dekker
Tech Info: color/sound/104 min.   Type: Dramatic Feature
Date: 1991   Origin: USA
Company: Silver Pictures
Distributors/Format: Warner Bros. Home Video, Inc. (1/2")
Annotation: When Nick Stiles (Washington) is promoted from police officer to Assistant District Attorney, a psychotic inmate, Blake (Lithgow), whom Stiles had imprisoned, escapes and plots Stiles' public humiliation and personal demise. When the media and City Council turn against him, Stiles joins with drug lord Odessa (Ice-T) to regain his personal dignity and entrap Blake. Amos plays Nick's father; Dillard, his wife, and Cothran plays City Councilman Ferris.

RIDERS OF THE STORM

Alternate: American Way, The
Cast: Al Matthews*, Dennis Hopper, Michael Pollard, Eugene Lipinski
Director: Maurice Phillips
Executive Producer: Maqbool Hameed
Music by: Brian Bennett
Producer: Laurie Keller, Paul Cowan, Maqbool Hameed
Screenwriter: Scott Roberts
Tech Info: color/sound/92 min.   Type: Comedy Feature
Date: 1988   Origin: Great Britain
Company: Miramax
Annotation: "Captain" (Hopper) and his crew of Vietnam veterans fly their B-29s across the country monitoring the media for lies and jamming network signals with anti-conservative telecasts. Matthews plays Ben.

RIGHT ON

Speaker: Gylan Kain*, David Nelson*, Felipe Luciano*
Tech Info: color/sound/80 min.   Type: Documentary Feature
Date: 1985   Origin: USA
Distributors/Format: Filmic Archives (1/2")
Annotation: The documentary explores the work of 1960s jazz poets Kain, Luciano and Nelson.

RING OF FIRE II: BLOOD AND STEEL
Cast: Sy Richardson*, Don "The Dragon" Wilson, Ian Jacklin, Maria Ford
Director: Richard W. Munchkin
Music by: John Gonzalez
Producer: Richard Pepin, Joseph Mehri
Screenwriter: Steve Tymon, Paul Mazlak
Storywriter: Richard W. Munchkin, Steve Tymon
Tech Info: color/sound/94 min.   Type: Dramatic Feature
Date: 1993   Origin: USA
Company: PM Productions
Distributors/Format: PM Entertainment Video (1/2")
Annotation: Johnny (Wilson) seeks the robbers who kidnapped his fiancee. With the guidance of Ernest (Richardson), a homeless Vietnam veteran, Johnny traverses the access tunnels under Los Angeles where the robbers have their lair.

RISING SUN
Cast: Wesley Snipes*, Sean Connery, Harvey Keitel, Mako , Tia Carrere, Kevin Anderson
Director: Philip Kaufman, Michael Chapman
Executive Producer: Sean Connery
Music by: Toru Takemitsu
Producer: Sean Connery, Peter Kaufman
Screenwriter: Philip Kaufman, Michael Crichton, Michael Backes
Tech Info: color/sound/129 min.   Type: Adaptation
Date: 1993   Origin: USA
Company: Fox
Distributors/Format: Fox Home Video (1/2")
Annotation: When a Los Angeles policeman (Snipes) is called in to investigate the murder of a prostitute in the boardroom of a Japanese-owned company, he discovers a "shadow world" of futuristic technology, ancient-ways and confusing loyalties.

RIVER NIGER, THE
Cast: James Earl Jones*, Louis Gossett Jr.*, Glynn Turman*
Director: Krishna Shab
Producer: Sidney Beckerman, Ike Jones
Tech Info: color/sound/104 min.   Type: Dramatic Feature
Date: 1978   Origin: USA
Distributors/Format: Continental Video (1/2")
Annotation: Adaptation based on the play by Joseph A. Walker.

RIVERBEND
Cast: Margaret Avery*, Tyrees Allen*, Vanessa Tate*, Julius Tennon*, Alex Morris*, Keith Kirk*, Steve James, Tony Frank
Director: Sam Firstenberg
Executive Producer: Regina Dale, Troy Dale
Music by: Paul Loomis
Producer: Samuel Vance, Valerie Vance, Regina Dale, Troy Dale
Screenwriter: Samuel Vance
Tech Info: color/sound/106 min.   Type: Dramatic Feature

Date: 1990   Origin: USA
Company: Vandale
Distributors/Format: Prism Entertainment (1/2")
Annotation: During the Vietnma War, three African American officers, Gus (Allen), Tony (Tennon) and Butch (Morris), refuse to massacre Vietnamese women and children and are sent to Georgia for their court martial. Once home, the soldiers escape and find refuge in the home of Bell Coleman (Avery). Forces clash when African American citizens who are tired of this and other injustices join forces and rebel. Tate appears as Pauline; Kirk plays Mike.

ROAD HOUSE
Cast: Keith David*, Chino "Fats" Williams*, Patrick Swayze, Ben Gazzara, Kelly Lynch, Sam Elliott
Director: Rowdy Herrington
Executive Producer: Steven H. Perry, Tim Moore
Music by: Michael Kamen
Producer: Joel Silver, Steven H. Perry, Tim Moore
Screenwriter: David Lee Henry, Hilary Henkin
Storywriter: David Lee Henry
Tech Info: color/sound/114 min.   Type: Dramatic Feature
Date: 1989   Origin: USA
Company: Silver
Distributors/Format: MGM/UA Home Video (1/2")
Annotation: Dalton (Swayze) rides into town to restore law and order to the saloons. When he crosses Brad Wesley (Elliott) in Jasper, Missouri, a showdown is inevitable. David plays Ernie Bass and Williams plays a derelict.

ROADSIDE PROPHETS
Cast: Bill Cobbs*, Don Cheadle*, Harry Caesar*, John Doe, Adam Horovitz, Dr. Timothy Leary, Arlo Guthrie
Director: Abbe Wool
Executive Producer: Nancy Israel
Music by: Pray for Rain
Producer: Peter McCarthy, David Swinson, Nancy Israel
Screenwriter: Abbe Wool
Tech Info: color/sound/96 min.   Type: Comedy Feature
Date: 1992   Origin: USA
Company: New Line Cinema, Swinson/Stankey Productions
Distributors/Format: Fine Line Home Video (1/2")
Annotation: Joe (Doe) and Sam (Horowitz) travel to Eldorado, Nevada, to scatter the ashes of a friend and meet a number of insightful strangers on the way. Caesar plays Jesse.

ROBIN HOOD: MEN IN TIGHTS
Cast: Isaac Hayes*, Dave Chappelle*, Cary Elwes, Richard Lewis, Roger Rees, Mark Blankfield
Director: Mel Brooks
Executive Producer: Peter Schindler
Music by: Hummie Mann
Producer: Mel Brooks, Peter Schindler
Screenwriter: Mel Brooks, J. David Shapiro
Storywriter: J. David Shapiro

Tech Info: color/sound/102 min.   Type: Comedy Feature
Date: 1993   Origin: USA
Company: Brooksfilms, Ltd., Gaumont
Distributors/Format: Fox Home Video (1/2")
Annotation: The Robin Hood legend has Robin (Elwes) returning from the Crusades to find King Richard usurped by evil King John (Lewis) and his henchman, the Sheriff of Rottingham (Rees). After Robin defeats the Sheriff in a fight, he vows revenge against Robin and his band of merry men that includes Achoo (Chappelle), Asneeze (Hayes) and his family's blind servant, Blinken (Blankfield).

ROBIN HOOD: PRINCE OF THIEVES

Cast: Morgan Freeman*, Kevin Costner, Alan Rickman, Mary Elizabeth Mastrantonio, Christian Slater
Director: Kevin Reynolds, Doug Milsome
Executive Producer: James G. Robinson, David Nicksay
Music by: Michael Kamen
Producer: John Watson, Pen Densham, Richard B. Lewis, James G. Robinson, David Nicksay
Screenwriter: John Watson, Pen Densham
Storywriter: Pen Densham
Tech Info: color/sound/144 min.   Type: Dramatic Feature
Date: 1991   Origin: USA
Company: Warner Bros., Morgan Creek
Distributors/Format: Spotlight Video (1/2"), Warner Bros. Home Video, Inc. (1/2"), Filmic Archives (1/2")
Annotation: When Robin of Locksley (Costner) saves Azeem's life (Freeman) while on a crusade in Jerusalem, Azeem swears to return the favor and follows Robin to England. There, both become protectors of the throne as they attempt to subvert the Sheriff of Nottingham's (Rickman) evil plan to crown himself.

ROBOCOP

Cast: Robert DoQui*, Ken Page*, Felton Perry*, Jesse Goins*, Nancy Allen, Peter Weller
Director: Paul Verhoeven
Executive Producer: Jon Davison
Music by: Basil Poledouris
Producer: Jon Davison, Arne Schmidt
Screenwriter: Michael Miner, Edward Neumeier
Tech Info: color/sound/103 min.   Type: Dramatic Feature
Date: 1987   Origin: USA
Company: Jon Davison Production
Distributors/Format: Orion Home Video (1/2")
Annotation: Murphy (Weller), is a Detroit policeman who is rebuilt into a cyborg after being declared dead. He is killed by a sadistic "cop killer" and leader of a murderous, and equal opportunity gang which includes Goins. DoQui plays Sergeant Reed who heads Murphy's precinct; Johnson (Perry) is a corporate executive who is in on the take-over of the city police department.

ROBOCOP II

Cast: Robert DoQui*, Felton Perry*, Willard Pugh*, Roger Aaron Brown*, Nancy Allen, Peter Weller
Director: Irvin Kershner
Music Performer: Leonard Rosenman
Music by: Leonard Rosenman
Producer: Jon Davison
Screenwriter: Frank Miller, Walon Green
Storywriter: Frank Miller
Tech Info: color/sound/117 min.   Type: Dramatic Feature
Date: 1990   Origin: USA
Company: Jon Davison Production
Distributors/Format: Orion Home Video (1/2")
Annotation: Weller returns as Sergeant Murphy (Robocop) in this sequel. Precinct officer Reed (DoQui) plays Murphy's superior; Donald Johnson (Perry) continues in his role as an O.C.P. executive who is controlled by a corrupt industrialist. Pugh plays Detroit Mayor Kuzak who owes O.C.P. thirty-eight million dollars in city debt. Whitaker (Brown) is one of the many police officers who is angry at corporate control of city police.

ROBOCOP III

Cast: Robert DoQui*, Felton Perry*, CCH Pounder*, Nancy Allen, Rip Torn, Robert Burke
Director: Fred Dekker
Executive Producer: Jon Davison
Music by: Basil Poledouris
Producer: Jon Davison, Patrick Crowley
Screenwriter: Frank Miller, Fred Dekker
Storywriter: Frank Miller
Tech Info: color/sound/105 min.   Type: Dramatic Feature
Date: 1993   Origin: USA
Company: OCP Pictures, Orion
Distributors/Format: Orion Home Video (1/2")
Annotation: Robocop (Burke), now programmed by a ruthless Japanese conglomerate that is buying up Detroit, must help evict working class neighborhoods so futuristic Delta City can be built. He rebels and joins forces with the Homeless Underground led by Bertha (Pounder). DoQui is Sgt. Reed and Perry plays Johnson.

ROBOT JOX

Cast: Anne-Marie Johnson*, Danny Kamekona, Gary Graham, Paul Koslo, Robert Sampson
Director: Stuart Gordon
Executive Producer: Charles Band
Music by: Frederic Talgorn
Producer: Charles Band, Charles Band, Albert Band
Screenwriter: Joe Haldeman
Storywriter: Stuart Gordon
Tech Info: color/sound/96 min.   Type: Dramatic Feature

Date: 1990   Origin: USA
Company: Epic, Empire
Distributors/Format: Triumph Releasing (16mm)
Annotation: Achilles (Graham) is the robot "jock" for the U.S., a man who inhabits a heavily armed robot to do battle with representatives from other nations. Athena (Johnson) is the cyborg who replaces Achilles but needs his help in a battle with the Soviet Union.

ROCKULA

Cast: Bo Diddley*, Tony Cox*, Dean Cameron, Tawny Fere, Susan Tyrrell, Thomas Dolby
Director: Luca Bercovici
Music Performer: Bo Diddley*
Music by: Hilary Berkovich
Producer: Yoram Globus, Christopher Pearce, Jeffrey Levy
Screenwriter: Christopher Verwiel
Tech Info: color/sound/87 min.   Type: Comedy Feature
Date: 1990   Origin: USA
Company: Pathe Communication Corporation
Distributors/Format: Cannon Home Video (1/2")
Annotation: When young vampire Ralph (Cameron) falls for beautiful rock star Mona (Fere), he must form a band to attract her attention. Axman (Diddley) is a local bar guitarist whom Ralph recruits as part of the band.

ROCKY II

Cast: Carl Weathers*, Frank McRae*, Tony Burton*, Sylvia Meals*, Taurean Blacque*, Sylvester Stallone, Talia Shire, Burgess Meredith
Director: Sylvester Stallone
Music Performer: Bill Conti
Producer: Irwin Wrinkler, Robert Chartoff
Screenwriter: Sylvester Stallone
Tech Info: color/sound/119 min.   Type: Dramatic Feature
Date: 1979   Origin: USA
Company: United Artists
Distributors/Format: United Artists Home Video (1/2")
Annotation: Apollo Creed (Weathers) wants a rematch with Rocky, but his coach (Burton), doesn't think Rocky is worth it, and Apollo's wife (Meals) wants him to retire. After their first fight, Rocky worked at a meat company under a foreman (McRae) who had to lay him off. The rematch is ROCKY I revisited.

ROCKY III

Cast: Carl Weathers*, Mr. T. *, Wally Taylor*, Tony Burton*, Sylvester Stallone, Talia Shire, Burgess Meredith
Director: Sylvester Stallone
Music Performer: Bill Conti
Music by: Bill Conti
Producer: Irwin Wrinkler, Robert Chartoff
Screenwriter: Sylvester Stallone
Tech Info: color/sound/100 min.   Type: Dramatic Feature

Date: 1982   Origin: USA
Company: Robert Chartoff - Irwin Wrinkler
Distributors/Format: United Artists Home Video (1/2")
Annotation: Apollo Creed (Weathers) quits his job as a boxing commentator in order to train Rocky (Stallone) in his fight against Clubber Lang (Mr. T). Apollo introduces Rocky to Duke (Burton), his old coach, and together they teach Rocky the right moves. Taylor plays Clubber's coach.

ROCKY IV
Cast: Carl Weathers*, James Brown*, Tony Burton*, Sylvia Meals*, Sylvester Stallone, Talia Shire, Burt Young, Brigitte Nelsen, Dolph Lundgren, James Newton
Director: Sylvester Stallone
Executive Producer: James D. Brubaker, Arthur Chobanian
Music Performer: James Brown*, Gladys Knight*, Tina Fava*, Shabba Ranks*
Music by: Vince Di Cola, Vince Di Cola
Producer: Irwin Wrinkler, Robert Chartoff, James D. Brubaker, Arthur Chobanian
Screenwriter: Sylvester Stallone
Storywriter: Sylvester Stallone
Tech Info: color/sound/93 min.   Type: Dramatic Feature
Date: 1985   Origin: USA
Company: The New United Artists
Distributors/Format: MGM/CBS Home Video (1/2")
Annotation: When Apollo Creed (Weathers) is killed in the ring by Russian superman Drago (Lundgren), Rocky (Stallone) seeks vengeance and returns to the ring. The Godfather of Soul (Brown) performs "Living in America" as part of the media-hyped festivities surrounding Apollo's fatal match. Meals plays Creed's wife, and Tony Burton plays Duke, Apollo's former trainer, now working with Rocky.

ROCKY V
Cast: Tony Burton*, Sylvester Stallone, Talia Shire, Burt Young, Tommy "Duke" Morrison
Director: John G. Avildsen
Executive Producer: Michael S. Glick
Music by: Bill Conti
Producer: Robert Chartoff, Michael S. Glick, Irwin Winkler
Screenwriter: Sylvester Stallone
Tech Info: color/sound/104 min.   Type: Dramatic Feature
Date: 1990   Origin: USA
Company: MGM-UA, Chartoff-Winkler, Star Partners III
Distributors/Format: MGM/UA Home Video (1/2")
Annotation: Rocky Balboa (Stallone) gives up his boxing career when he learns he has irreparable brain damage. He helps young athlete Tommy Gunn (Morrison) train. Burton plays Tony.

ROLL OF THUNDER, HEAR MY CRY, BY MILDRED D. TAYLOR
Director: Greg Lanning
Producer: Peter Griffiths
Speaker: Mildred D. Taylor*
Tech Info: mixed/sound/26 min.   Type: Documentary Short

Date: 1992   Origin: USA
Studio: Independent
Distributors/Format: Films for the Humanities (1/2")
Annotation: Filmed in Mississippi, where her Newberry Medal winning novel is set, Mildred Taylor talks about the origins of the story and characters from which the 1986 TV feature was made, her family's experience, and the more general experience of Blacks in the American South.

ROMEO IS BLEEDING
Cast: Paul Butler*, Annabella Sciorra, Juliette Lewis, Gary Oldman, Lena Olin
Director: Peter Medak
Executive Producer: Tim Bevan, Eric Fellner
Music by: Mark Isham
Producer: Hilary Henkin, Tim Bevan, Eric Fellner, Paul Webster
Screenwriter: Hilary Henkin
Tech Info: color/sound/108 min.   Type: Dramatic Feature
Date: 1994   Origin: USA
Company: Working Title, DDF Films
Distributors/Format: Gramercy Pictures Home Video (1/2")
Annotation: New York policeman Jack Grimaldi (Oldman) must guard hit woman and femme fatale Mona Demarkov (Olin) for the feds but is seduced by her and helps her fake her own death. Butler plays Federal Agent Skouras.

ROOFTOPS
Cast: John Canada Terrell*, Tisha Campbell*, Troy Beyer*, Allen Payne*, Jason Gedrick, Eddie Velez, Alexis Cruz
Director: Robert Wise
Executive Producer: Taylor Hackford, Stuart Benjamin
Music by: Michael Kamen, David A. Stewart
Producer: Taylor Hackford, Stuart Benjamin, Howard W. Koch Jr.
Screenwriter: Terence Brennan
Storywriter: Allan Goldstein, Tony Mark
Tech Info: color/sound/95 min.   Type: Dramatic Feature
Date: 1989   Origin: USA
Company: Koch, Mark-Jett
Distributors/Format: New Visions Home Video (1/2")
Annotation: The rooftop "home" of T (Gedrick) and Squeak (Cruz) is threatened by Lobo (Velez) a crack dealer who has moved his operation to their building. Beyer plays Elana and Campbell is Amber.

ROOKIE OF THE YEAR
Cast: Albert Hall*, Gary Busey, Daniel Stern, Dan Hedaya, Thomas Ian Nicholas, Amy Morton
Director: Daniel Stern
Executive Producer: Irby Smith, Jack Brodsky
Music by: Bill Conti
Producer: Irby Smith, Robert Harper, Jack Brodsky
Screenwriter: Sam Harper
Tech Info: color/sound/105 min.   Type: Comedy Feature

Date: 1993   Origin: USA
Company: Featherstone Productions, Fox
Distributors/Format: Fox Home Video (1/2")
Annotation: Little-leaguer Henry Rowengartner (Nicholas) breaks his arm, and when it heals finds he has a major-league pitching arm which gets him a job with the Chicago Cubs. Hall plays Martinella.

ROOTS OF RESISTANCE: A STORY OF THE UNDERGROUND RAILROAD

Series: American Experience
Host: David McCollough
Narrator: Ruby Dee*
Producer: Orlando Bagwell*, Susan Bellows
Screenwriter: Theodore Thomas*
Storywriter: Theodore Thomas*
Tech Info: mixed/sound/58 min.   Type: Television Documentary
Date: 1989   Origin: USA
Studio: Independent
Company: Roja Film Prod. & WGBH Boston, WNET NY, KCET, L.A.
Distributors/Format: Filmic Archives (1/2")
Archives/Format: IUB - AAAMC (1/2")
Annotation: The story of Black America's secret railroad to freedom is recounted through narratives of escaped black slaves.

ROUGH CUT

Cast: Al Matthews*, Burt Reynolds, Lesley-Anne Down, David Niven
Director: Don Siegel
Producer: David Merrick
Screenwriter: Francis Burns
Storywriter: Derek Lambert
Tech Info: color/sound/112 min.   Type: Dramatic Feature
Date: 1980   Origin: USA
Company: Paramount
Distributors/Format: Paramount Home Video (1/2")
Annotation: Ferguson (Matthews) is talked into conspiring in the crime of the century, theft of thirty million dollars in diamonds, by old friend Jack Rhodes (Reynolds). Fergie flies the get-away plane and also plays piano and sings at a Paris night club.

ROXANNE

Cast: Damon Wayans*, Steve Martin, Rick Rossovich, Daryl Hannah
Director: Fred Schepisi
Executive Producer: Steve Martin
Music by: Bruce Smeaton
Producer: Steve Martin, Daniel Melnick, Michael Rachmil
Screenwriter: Steve Martin
Storywriter: Edmond Rostand
Tech Info: color/sound/107 min.   Type: Comedy Feature

Date: 1987   Origin: USA
Company: Columbia
Distributors/Format: Columbia Pictures Home Video (1/2")
Annotation: In this comic version of CYRANO DE BERGERAC, Charlie Bales (Martin), a fire chief with a big nose, falls for astronomer Roxanne (Hannah) but she's interested in brainless Chris (Rossovich), another firefighter. Chris uses Charlie's poetic words to woo Roxanne. Wayans plays Jerry.

ROYAL FEDERAL BLUES

Alternate: Story Of The African American Civil War Soldier
Director: Greg McCampbell
Music by: Bill Watson*
Producer: Greg McCampbell
Screenwriter: Greg McCampbell
Tech Info: color/sound/45 min.   Type: Documentary Feature
Date: 1991   Origin: USA
Company: Video F/X Productions
Distributors/Format: PPI Entertainment (1/2"), Filmic Archives (1/2")
Annotation: The film documents the history of African American soldiers in the Union Army during the Civil War.

RUBY IN PARADISE

Cast: Allison Dean*, Bentley Mitchum, Ashley Judd, Todd Field, Dorothy Lyman
Director: Victor Nunez
Executive Producer: Sam Gowan
Music by: Charles Engstrom
Producer: Keith Crofford, Sam Gowan
Screenwriter: Victor Nunez
Tech Info: color/sound/115 min.   Type: Dramatic Feature
Date: 1993   Origin: USA
Company: Republic
Distributors/Format: Republic Pictures Home Video (1/2")
Annotation: The film portrays a young woman's developing sense of identity after she escapes small-town West Virginia and experiences life in Panama City, Florida. Dean plays Rochelle Bridges.

RUDY

Cast: Charles S. Dutton*, Ned Beatty, Robert Prosky, Sean Astin, Lili Taylor
Director: David Anspaugh, Oliver Wood
Executive Producer: Lee R. Mayes
Music by: Jerry Goldsmith
Producer: Robert N. Fried, Cary Woods, Lee R. Mayes
Screenwriter: Angelo Pizzo
Tech Info: color/sound/112 min.   Type: Dramatic Feature
Date: 1993   Origin: USA
Company: TriStar
Distributors/Format: TriStar Pictures Inc. (1/2")
Annotation: The true story of a young man, Rudy (Astin) who dreams of playing football for Notre Dame University. Because of his blue-collar background and small stature, nobody believes he can do it, but he confounds them all by gaining admission and becoming a walk-on player for the team. Dutton plays a caretaker of

the football field who encourages Rudy.

RUMBLE FISH

Cast: Laurence/Larry Fishburne*, Dennis Hopper, Mickey Rourke, Diane Lane, Matt
Dillon, Nicolas Cage
Director: Francis Ford Coppola
Executive Producer: Francis Ford Coppola
Music by: Stewart Copeland
Producer: Francis Ford Coppola, Fred Roos, Doug Claybourne
Screenwriter: Francis Ford Coppola, S.E. Hinton
Tech Info: color/sound/105 min.   Type: Dramatic Feature
Date: 1983   Origin: USA
Company: Zoetrope
Distributors/Format: Universal Home Video (1/2")
Annotation: Rusty James (Dillon) idolizes his older brother Motorcycle Boy (Rourke),
who has repudiated his gang-leader past, but can't think of anything better to offer
his younger brother. Fishburne portrays "Midget."

RUN FOR THE ROSES

Alternate: Thoroughbred
Cast: Theodore "Teddy" Wilson*, Stuart Whitman, Lisa Eilbacher, Vera Miles, Sam
Groom, Panchito Gomez
Director: Henry Levin
Executive Producer: Arnold Pessin
Music by: Raul Lavista
Producer: Wolf Schmidt, Mario Crespo Jr., Arnold Pessin
Screenwriter: Joseph Prieto, Mimi Avins
Tech Info: color/sound/93 min.   Type: Dramatic Feature
Date: 1978   Origin: USA
Company: Pan-American
Distributors/Format: Kodiak (1/2")
Annotation: Young Juanito (Gomez) wants a horse of his own to race in the
Kentucky Derby. When a thoroughbred gives birth to a deformed colt, he gets his
chance. Wilson plays Flash.

RUNAWAY

Cast: Stan Shaw*, Gene Simmons, Kirstie Alley, Tom Selleck, Cynthia Rhodes
Director: Michael Crichton
Executive Producer: Kurt Villadsen
Music by: Jerry Goldsmith
Producer: Michael Rachmil, Kurt Villadsen
Screenwriter: Michael Crichton
Tech Info: color/sound/100 min.   Type: Dramatic Feature
Date: 1984   Origin: USA
Company: TriStar, Delphi III
Distributors/Format: TriStar Pictures Inc. (1/2")
Annotation: Sgt. Jack Ramsey (Sellek) a policeman raising his kid with the help of a
robot maid, must terminate a group of killer robots programmed by evil genius
Luther (Simmons). Shaw plays Marvin.

RUNAWAY TRAIN

Cast: T.K. Carter*, Tom "Tiny" Lister Jr.*, Rebecca De Mornay, Eric Roberts, Jon Voight
Director: Andrei Konchalovsky
Executive Producer: Henry T. Weinstein, Robert A. Goldston, Roger Whitmore
Music by: Trevor Jones
Producer: Yoram Globus, Menahem Golan, Henry T. Weinstein, Robert A. Goldston, Roger Whitmore
Screenwriter: Djordje Milicevic, Paul Zindel, Edward Bunker
Tech Info: color/sound/111 min.   Type: Dramatic Feature
Date: 1985   Origin: USA
Company: Northbrook
Distributors/Format: Cannon Home Video (1/2")
Annotation: Two escaped convicts (Voight and Roberts) hop a passenger train but find themselves at its helm when the engineer suffers a fatal heart attack. Carter plays Dave Prince and Lister is the black Prison Guard.

RUNNING

Cast: Giancarlo Esposito*, Susan Anspach, Eugene Levy, Michael Douglas, Lawrence Dane
Director: Steven Hillard Stern
Executive Producer: Michael Douglas
Music by: Andre Gagnon
Producer: Robert Cooper, Michael Douglas, Ronald I. Cohen
Screenwriter: Steven Hillard Stern
Tech Info: color/sound/102 min.   Type: Dramatic Feature
Date: 1979   Origin: USA
Company: Universal
Distributors/Format: Universal Home Video (1/2")
Annotation: Michael Andropolis (Douglas) is determined to run in the Montreal Olympic Marathon in order to make up for his past failures. Esposito appears as a teenager.

RUNNING ON EMPTY

Cast: Lynn Thigpen*, Michael P. Boatman*, Christine Lahti, Judd Hirsch, River Phoenix
Director: Sidney Lumet
Executive Producer: Burtt Harris, Naomi Foner
Music by: Tony Mottola
Producer: Burtt Harris, Griffin Dunne, Naomi Foner, Amy Robinson
Screenwriter: Naomi Foner
Tech Info: color/sound/116 min.   Type: Dramatic Feature
Date: 1988   Origin: USA
Company: Lorimar, Double Play
Distributors/Format: Warner Bros. Home Video, Inc. (1/2")
Annotation: Danny Pope (Phoenix) is encouraged by his music teacher to apply to Julliard, but because his parents are former student radicals wanted by the FBI, he hesitates. Thigpen is their contact at Eldridge Street and Boatman plays Spaulding.

RUNNING OUT OF LUCK
Cast: Rae Dawn Chong*, Dennis Hopper, Mick Jagger, Jerry Hall, Angelo Di Biase, Raul Gazzola
Director: Julien Temple
Music by: Luis Jardim
Screenwriter: Julien Temple, Mick Jagger
Tech Info: color/sound/80 min.   Type: Dramatic Feature
Date: 1986   Origin: USA
Company: Nitrate
Distributors/Format: CBS Records Group (16mm)
Annotation: Jaggar goes to Rio to film a rock video but is kidnapped by extras and forced to serve as a sex slave on a banana plantation. Chong plays a slave girl on the plantation with whom he falls in love.

RUNNING SCARED
Cast: Gregory Hines*, Felton Perry*, Tracy Reed*, Billy Crystal, Jimmy Smits
Director: Peter Hyams
Executive Producer: Peter Hyams, Peter Hyams
Producer: Peter Hyams, Peter Hyams, David Foster, Lawrence Turman
Screenwriter: Gary Devore, Jimmy Huston
Storywriter: Gary Devore
Tech Info: color/sound/108 min.   Type: Comedy Feature
Date: 1986   Origin: USA
Company: Turman-Foster Co.
Distributors/Format: MGM/UA Home Video (1/2")
Annotation: Ray Hughes (Hines) and his partner Danny Costanzo (Crystal) are Chicago detectives who are ready to retire to Florida and open their own bar, but become obsessed with destroying the criminal empire of drug dealer Julio Gonzales (Smits). Along the way, Hughes meets Mary Ann Thomas (Reed) and falls in love with her. However, Mary Ann is involved with Adam Robertson (Perry). Hughes has Adam arrested so he and Mary Ann can be together.

RUNNING WITH JESSE
Series: Frontline
Host: Judy Woodruff
Producer: Orlando Bagwell*, Jeanne Jordan
Speaker: Jesse Jackson*, Lary Lewman
Tech Info: color/sound/60 min.   Type: Television Documentary
Date: 1989   Origin: USA
Studio: PBS
Company: The Documentary Consortium
Annotation: Bagwell is a producer of this documentary which chronicles Jesse Jackson's 1988 presidential campaign through the eyes of reporters who accompanied him, his supporters and detractors.

RUSSIA HOUSE, THE
Cast: Blu Mankuma*, Sean Connery, Roy Scheider, Michelle Pfeiffer
Director: Fred Schepisi
Executive Producer: Alan Ladd Jr.
Music by: Jerry Goldsmith
Producer: Paul Maslansky, Fred Schepisi, Alan Ladd Jr.

Screenwriter: Tom Stoppard
Storywriter: Tom Le Carre
Tech Info: color/sound/123 min.   Type: Dramatic Feature
Date: 1990   Origin: USA
Company: Pathe
Distributors/Format: MGM/UA Home Video (1/2")
Annotation: Katya (Pfeiffer), a Russian woman, tries to get a manuscript to British publisher Barley Blair (Connery). The document is intercepted by British Intelligence who determine it contains a detailed analysis of the Russian defense system. Mankuma plays Merv.

RUTHLESS PEOPLE
Cast: Arthur/Art Evans*, Bette Midler, Danny Devito, Judge Reinhold, Helen Slater
Director: Jerry Zucker, David Zucker, Jim Abrahams
Executive Producer: Richard Wagner, Joanna Lancaster, Walter Yetnikoff
Music by: Michel Colombier
Producer: Michael Peyser, Richard Wagner, Joanna Lancaster, Walter Yetnikoff
Screenwriter: Dale Launer
Tech Info: color/sound/93 min.   Type: Comedy Feature
Date: 1986   Origin: USA
Company: Touchstone, Silver Screen Partners II
Distributors/Format: Buena Vista Home Video (1/2")
Annotation: The Kesslers (Reinhold and Slater) kidnap Barbara Stone (Midler) to avenge themselves on her husband Sam (DeVito) who refuses to pay the ransom, hoping they will kill her. Evans appears as Lt. Bender.

SAINT OF FORT WASHINGTON, THE
Cast: Danny Glover*, Joe Seneca*, Bahni Turpin*, Ving Rhames*, Matt Dillon, Nina Siemaszko
Director: Frederick Elmes, Tim Hunter
Executive Producer: Lyle Kessler, Carl Clifford
Music by: James Newton Howard*
Producer: David V. Picker, Lyle Kessler, Carl Clifford, Nessa Hyams
Screenwriter: Lyle Kessler
Tech Info: color/sound/103 min.   Type: Dramatic Feature
Date: 1992   Origin: USA
Company: Fort Washington Productions, J&M Ent., Carrie Prod
Distributors/Format: Warner Bros. Home Video, Inc. (1/2")
Annotation: Jerry (Glover) is a street person who did everything right in life but was blindsided by fate. Jerry befriends Matthew (Dillon) who also lives on the streets. The friendship of two men coping with life on New York City's streets gives them the heart to work toward their dream of getting back in the mainstream.

SANDLOT, THE
Cast: James Earl Jones*, Brandon Adams*, Tom Guiry, Karen Allen, Mike Vitar, Patrick Renna
Director: David Mickey Evans
Executive Producer: Cathleen Summers, Mark Burg, Chris Zarpas
Music by: David Newman
Producer: Cathleen Summers, Mark Burg, William S. Gilmore, Dale De La Torre, Chris Zarpas
Screenwriter: David Mickey Evans, Robert Gunter

Tech Info: color/sound/109 min.   Type: Comedy Feature
Date: 1993   Origin: USA
Company: Island World, Evans/De La Torre Productions
Distributors/Format: Fox Home Video (1/2")
Annotation: Set during the late 1950s or early 60s, the film traces the friendships in a children's baseball team. Mr. Mertle (Jones) is a pleasant old man who use to play baseball before going blind. He trades the team's old ball for his autographed 1927 ball. In exchange the team must visit him weekly to discuss baseball. Adams plays Kenny DeNunez.

SANKOFA

Cast: Afemo Omilani*, Mutabaruka *, Kofi Ghanaba*, Oyafunmike Ogunlano*, Alexandra Duah*, Nick Medley*, Mzuri *, Jimmy Lee Savage*, Maxwell Parris*, Hasinatu Camara*, Jim Faircloth*, Reginald Carter
Director: Haile Gerima*
Music by: David J. White*
Producer: Haile Gerima*, Shirikiana Aina Gerima*
Screenwriter: Haile Gerima*
Tech Info: color/sound/124 min.   Type: Dramatic Feature
Date: 1994   Origin: Burkina Faso, Ghana, German, USA
Company: Negod Gwad Productions, et al.
Distributors/Format: Mypheduh Films, Inc. (16mm; 1/2")
Archives/Format: IUB - BFC/A (1/2")
Annotation: Mona (Ogunlano), an African American model is on a shoot at the site of a dungeon where Africans were imprisoned until slave ships hauled them away. Sankofa (Ghanaba), guardian of the dungeon site, admonishes Mona to return to her past. Haunted by his command, she enters the dungeon and does not emerge until she experiences the pain and degradation of plantation slavery. Other slaves include Shango (Mutabaruka), Nunu (Duah) and Joe (Medley).

SARAFINA!

Cast: Whoopi Goldberg*, Miriam Makeba*, Leleti Khumalo*, Dumisani Dlamini*, Mbongeni Ngema*, Sipho Kunene*, Nonhlanhla Sithole*, Mary Twala*, James Mthoba*, John Kani
Director: Darrell James Roodt
Executive Producer: Kirk D'Amico, Sudhir Pragjee, Helena Spring, Sanjeev Singh
Music by: Stanley Myers
Producer: Anant Singh, David M. Thompson, Kirk D'Amico, Sudhir Pragjee, Helena Spring, Sanjeev Singh
Screenwriter: Mbongeni Ngema*, William Nicholson
Tech Info: color/sound/96 min.   Type: Dramatic Feature
Date: 1992   Origin: France, Great Britain, South Africa, USA
Company: Distant Horizon, Ideal Films, BBC, et al.
Distributors/Format: Buena Vista Home Video (1/2"), Facets Multimedia, Inc. (1/2")
Annotation: Sarafina (Khumalo) is a student in 1970s apartheid South Africa. One of her teachers, Mary Masembuko (Goldberg) attempts to teach the students about their own culture. She is arrested and Sarafina and the other students rebel, sparking an uprising which engulfs the entire township.

SARAH
Director: Spike Lee*
Producer: Spike Lee*
Tech Info: color/sound/27 min.　　Type: Experimental Short
Date: 1981　Origin: USA
Studio: Independent
Annotation: Forty-year-old Sarah is hurt when her family is abusive toward her new male friend at Thanksgiving dinner, and she discovers the impact her family has on her.

SARAH VAUGHAN: THE DIVINE ONE
Director: Matthew Seig
Music Performer: Sarah Vaughan*
Speaker: Roy Haynes*, Billy Eckstine*, Joe Williams*
Tech Info: color/sound/60 min.　　Type: Documentary Feature
Date: 1991　Origin: USA
Distributors/Format: Facets Multimedia, Inc. (1/2")
Annotation: Friends, family and fellow musicians, including Eckstein, Haynes, Williams and others, talk about Vaughan's artistry. Her performances include: "Misty," "Someone to Watch over Me," "I've Got a Crush on You," and "Send in the Clowns."

SATURDAY NIGHT, SUNDAY MORNING: THE TRAVELS OF GATEMOUTH MOORE
Series: African American Perspectives
Director: Louis Guida
Producer: Louis Guida
Speaker: B.B. King*, Rufus Thomas*, Arnold D. "Gatemouth" Moore*, Benjamin Hooks*, Andrew Chaplin Jr.*
Tech Info: color/sound/70 min.　　Type: Documentary Feature
Date: 1992　Origin: USA
Studio: Independent
Company: Co-Media Productions
Distributors/Format: California Newsreel (1/2")
Archives/Format: IUB - BFC/A (1/2")
Annotation: Guida documents, through interviews and early photos, the life of Arnold Dwight "Gatemouth" Moore, a prominent blues singer who left the stage at the height of his career to preach and sing gospel.

SAVE ME
Cast: Bill Nunn*, Michael Ironside, Harry Hamlin, Lysette Anthony, Steven Railsback
Director: Alan Roberts
Music by: Rick Marvin
Producer: Alan Amiel, Alexander Tabrizi
Screenwriter: Neil Ronco
Tech Info: color/sound/99 min.　　Type: Dramatic Feature
Date: 1994　Origin: USA
Company: Mark Damon Productions
Distributors/Format: Spark Film (16mm)
Annotation: Jim Stevens (Hamlin), newly separated from his wife, meets Ellie (Anthony) and finds himself implicated in the murder of her live-in lover. Nunn plays

Detective Vincent.

SAXO
Cast: Akosua Busia*, Richard Brooks*, Gerard Lanvin, Laure Killing, Clement Harari
Director: Ariel Zeitoun
Executive Producer: Ariel Zeitoun
Producer: Ariel Zeitoun, Ariel Zeitoun
Screenwriter: Ariel Zeitoun, Gilbert Tanugi, Jacques Audiard
Tech Info: color/sound/116 min.   Type: Dramatic Feature
Date: 1988   Origin: France
Company: Canal Plus, Partner's, A2
Distributors/Format: UGC (16mm)
Annotation: Parisian record producer Sam Friedman (Lanvin) signs American blues artists Puppet (Busia) and Joe Bennet (Brooks) to a contract and finds himself taking the rap for a murder Joe committed.

SAY AMEN, SOMEBODY
Cast: Billy Smith*, Jackie Jackson*
Director: George T. Nierenberg, Karen Nierenberg
Music Performer: Willie Mae Ford Smith*, Thomas A. Dorsey*, Eddie and Edgar O'Neal*, Mahalia Jackson*, Sallie Martin*, Bertha Smith*, Lee Cochron*, Charles Pikes*, Lee G. Scott*
Music by: Thomas A. Dorsey*, Sallie Martin*
Producer: George T. Nierenberg, Karen Nierenberg
Speaker: Willie Mae Ford Smith*, Thomas A. Dorsey*, Eddie and Edgar O'Neal*, Sallie Martin*
Tech Info: color/sound/86 min.   Type: Documentary Feature
Date: 1982   Origin: USA
Company: A George T. Nierenberg Production
Distributors/Format: United Artists Home Video (1/2"), October Films (16mm; 35mm)
Archives/Format: IUB - BFC/A; IUB - AAAMC (16mm; 1/2")
Annotation: The film is an exploration of gospel music with performances by and interviews with gospel greats. It focuses on Thomas Dorsey, the "father of gospel," Willie Mae Ford Smith, the O'Neal twins, and the Barrett Sisters.

SCAVENGER HUNT
Cast: Cleavon Little*, Scatman Crothers*, Willie Aames*, Ruth Gordon, Cloris Leachman, Roddy McDowall, Robert Morley, Tony Randall, Richard Benjamin
Director: Michael Schultz*
Music by: Billy Goldenberg
Producer: Steven A. Vail
Screenwriter: John Thompson*, Steven A. Vail, Henry Harper
Storywriter: Steven A. Vail
Tech Info: color/sound/116 min.   Type: Comedy Feature
Date: 1979   Origin: USA
Company: Simon Film Productions
Distributors/Format: Fox Home Video (1/2")
Annotation: Jackson (Little) is a chauffeur who, with three other staff members, tries to win their boss' fortune through a scavenger hunt. Sam (Crothers) is a security guard at a bridal shop who is recruited by another fortune hunter (McDowell) to help win the hunt.

SCENES FROM THE NEW WORLD

Cast: Michael Ralph*, Christine Clementson*, David Chan
Director: Heather Johnston*, Gordon Eriksen
Music by: Tony Silbert, Laurie Fitzgerald
Producer: Heather Johnston*, Gordon Eriksen, Karol Martesko
Screenwriter: Heather Johnston*, Gordon Eriksen
Tech Info: color/sound/103 min.   Type: Dramatic Feature
Date: 1994   Origin: USA
Annotation: Alex (Chan) runs an illegal boarding house in Queens, New York. He rents to three African Americans. In retaliation, Alex's grandfather rents the house to three Hong Kong architecture students. Issues of race, stereotyping, identity and cross-cultural relationships arise.

SCHOOL DAZE

Cast: Kadeem Hardison*, Bill Nunn*, James Bond III*, Spike Lee*, Joie Lee*, Giancarlo Esposito*, Branford Marsalis*, Eric Payne*, Laurence/Larry Fishburne*, Joe Seneca*, Ossie Davis*, Arthur/Art Evans*, Tisha Campbell*, Ellen Holly*, Jasmine Guy*, Adrienne-Joi Johnson*, Ertha D. Robinson*, Alva Rodgers*, Kyme *, Kasi Lemmons*, Cylk Cozart*, Rusty Cundieff*, Darryl M. Bell*, Monique Mannen
Director: Spike Lee*
Executive Producer: Grace Blake*
Music Performer: Phyllis Hyman*
Music by: Bill Lee*
Producer: Spike Lee*, Grace Blake*
Screenwriter: Spike Lee*
Tech Info: color/sound/114 min.   Type: Comedy Feature
Date: 1988   Origin: USA
Company: 40 Acres and a Mule Film Works
Distributors/Format: Columbia Pictures Home Video (1/2")
Archives/Format: IUB - BFC/A (1/2")
Annotation: Dap Dunlap (Fishburne) tries to rally students of Mission College to protest the college's investments in South Africa. He is challenged by Julian (Esposito), "Big Brother Almighty" of the Gamma Fraternity, who disagrees with Dap's ideas. Half-pint (Lee) is a new recruit to the Gamma Fraternity. Jane Toussaint (Campbell) is the leader of the Gamma Rays and Julian's girlfriend.

SCHOOL SPIRIT

Cast: Jay Scorpio*, Tom Nolan, Elizabeth Foxx, Larry Linville, Daniele Arnaud
Director: Alan Holleb
Executive Producer: Sidney Balkin, Ken Dalton
Music by: Tom Bruner
Producer: Ashok Amritraj, Jeff Begun, Sidney Balkin, Ken Dalton
Tech Info: color/sound/90 min.   Type: Comedy Feature
Date: 1985   Origin: USA
Company: T&A, New Horizons, Amitraj, Chroma III
Distributors/Format: Cinema Group, Concorde (1/2")
Annotation: On his way to a date with sorority girl Judith Hightower (Foxx), Billy Batson (Nolan) crashes into a Mack truck and becomes a ghost. In his new state, he discovers the university president's plot to steal a $12 million endowment. Scorpio plays Professor Sylvester.

SCOUT, THE
Cast: Frank Slaten*, Albert Brooks, Brendan Fraser, Dianne Weist
Director: Michael Ritchie, Lazslo Kovacs
Executive Producer: Herbert Nanas, Jack Cummins
Music by: Bill Conti
Producer: Albert S. Ruddy, Andre Morgan, Herbert Nanas, Jack Cummins
Screenwriter: Andrew Bergman, Albert Brooks, Monica Johnson
Tech Info: color/sound/101 min.   Type: Dramatic Feature
Date: 1994   Origin: USA
Company: Fox
Distributors/Format: Fox Home Video (1/2")
Annotation: Desperate Yankee Scout Al Percolo (Brooks) will do anything to sign a new recruit. In Mexico he stumbles upon Steve Nebraska (Fraser), the greatest baseball player he has ever seen. But Steve's strange behavior soon has Al seeking psychological help for his dream recruit. Slaten plays a college umpire.

SECOND THOUGHTS
Cast: Ernie Banks*, Jesse Goins*, Craig Wasson, Lucie Arnaz, Anne Schedeen
Executive Producer: Lawrence Turman
Music by: Henry Mancini
Producer: David Foster, Lawrence Turman, Lawrence Turman
Screenwriter: Steve Brown
Storywriter: Steve Brown, Terry Louise Fisher
Tech Info: color/sound/98 min.   Type: Dramatic Feature
Date: 1983   Origin: USA
Company: EMI
Distributors/Format: Universal Home Video (1/2")
Annotation: Amy (Arnaz) is a lawyer who divorces her husband and lives with a hippie, Will (Wasson), by whom she becomes pregnant and who takes drastic measures to prevent her from having an abortion. Goins plays a security guard and Banks appears uncredited.

SECRET SOUNDS SCREAMING: THE SEXUAL ABUSE OF CHILDREN
Director: Ayoka Chenzira*
Tech Info: color/sound/30 min.   Type: Documentary Short
Date: 1986   Origin: USA
Studio: Independent
Distributors/Format: Third World Newsreel (1/2"), Women Make Movies, Inc. (16mm; 1/2")
Archives/Format: IUB - BFC/A (1/2")
Annotation: Chenzira's film about the sexual abuse of children comes out of her experiences working in a hospital and meeting a child with gonorrhea of the throat and mouth.

SEE NO EVIL, HEAR NO EVIL
Cast: Richard Pryor*, Tonya Pinkins*, Gene Wilder, Anthony Zerbe, Joan Severance, Kevin Spacey, Kristen Childs, Hardy Rawles
Director: Arthur Hiller
Music by: Stewart Copeland
Producer: Earl Barret, Arne Sultan, Marvin Worth, Burtt Harris
Screenwriter: Gene Wilder, Earl Barret, Arne Sultan, Andrew Kurtzman, Elliot Sultan

Storywriter: Earl Barret, Arne Sultan, Marvin Worth
Tech Info: color/sound/103 min.   Type: Comedy Feature
Date: 1984   Origin: USA
Company: Columbia, TriStar
Distributors/Format: RCA/Columbia Pictures Home Video (1/2")
Annotation: Wally (Pryor) is blind, Dave (Wilder) is deaf. Their comic adventures begin when Wally, pretending to see, applies for a job at Dave's store. When the two "witness" the murder of a racketeer, they end up being the prime suspects and eventually wanted fugitives. Leslie (Pinkins) is Wally's sister who helps them out along the way.

SEEMS LIKE OLD TIMES

Cast: Robert Guillaume*, Fay Hauser*, T.K. Carter*, Chevy Chase, Charles Grodin, Goldie Hawn
Director: Jay Sandrich
Executive Producer: Roger M. Rothstein
Music Performer: Marvin Hamlisch
Music by: Marvin Hamlisch
Producer: Ray Stark, Roger M. Rothstein
Screenwriter: Neil Simon
Tech Info: color/sound/101 min.   Type: Comedy Feature
Date: 1980   Origin: USA
Company: Ray Stark Production
Distributors/Format: Columbia Pictures Home Video (1/2")
Annotation: Chester (Carter), a thief, whose lawyer Glenda Parks (Hawn) has reformed him by employment, now serves as her chauffer, butler, and maintenance man. Before a dinner party Glenda is having for the governor, the Deputy District Attorney (Guillaume) and his wife Anne (Hauser), Chester gets drunk. Nick (Chase), Glenda's ex-husband who is wanted for armed robbery, not only serves the dinner but becomes the center of the comedy romance.

SENDER, THE

Cast: Al Matthews*, Kathryn Harrold, Shirley Knight, Zeljko Ivanek
Director: Robert Christian*
Music by: Trevor Jones
Producer: Edward S. Feldman
Screenwriter: Thomas Baum
Tech Info: color/sound/91 min.   Type: Dramatic Feature
Date: 1982   Origin: Great Britain
Company: Paramount
Distributors/Format: Paramount Home Video (1/2")
Annotation: An unidentified 20-year-old who has attempted suicide (Ivanek) is sent to a psychiatric hospital where it's discovered he can transmit his nightmares into the minds of others. Matthews plays a Vietnam veteran.

SERMONS AND SACRED PICTURES

Director: Lynne Sachs
Speaker: Rev. L.O. Taylor*
Tech Info: mixed/sound/29 min.   Type: Documentary Short

Date: 1991　Origin: USA
Company: Center for Southern Folklore
Distributors/Format: Center for Southern Folklore (35mm; 16mm)
Annotation: Reverend L.O. Taylor, a black Baptist minister from Memphis, was also a filmmaker, capturing images of black American life in the 1930s and 1940s. Sachs' documentary combines commentary on his life with clips and photographs from Taylor's work.

SERPENT AND THE RAINBOW, THE

Cast: Zakes Mokae*, Cathy Tyson*, Theresa Merritt*, Paul Winfield*, Conrad Roberts*, Brent Jennings*, Aleta Mitchell*, Bill Pullman
Director: Wes Craven
Executive Producer: Rob Cohen, Keith Barish
Music by: Brad Fiedel
Producer: Rob Cohen, Keith Barish, David Ladd, Doug Claybourne
Screenwriter: Richard Maxwell, A.R. Simon
Storywriter: Wade Davis
Tech Info: color/sound/98 min.　　　Type: Dramatic Feature
Date: 1988　Origin: USA
Company: Universal
Distributors/Format: MCA Home Video (1/2")
Annotation: Anthropologist Dennis Alan (Pullman) travels to Haiti to do research on a mysterious drug which causes paralysis. He is joined in his work by Dr. Marielle Duchamp (Tyson). Their research leads them into confrontations with black magic and voodoo priests like Lucien Celine (Winfield), a politician and night club owner, and the captain of the secret police, Petraud (Mokae). Roberts plays Christophe, a victim of the drug.

SERVING TWO MASTERS

Cast: Cliff McMullen*, Charles J. Johnson*, Victor Lawson*, Mshela Makogba*, James Knight*, Phillips Folayan*, Mybe Cham*, Demetrius Jackson*, Osekunjo Ogunfiditimi*, Olatide Ogunfiditimi*, Jeffrey Williamson, Nick Olcott
Director: Edward Timothy Lewis*
Producer: Edward Timothy Lewis*
Screenwriter: Edward Timothy Lewis*
Tech Info: bw/sound/53 min.　　　Type: Dramatic Feature
Date: 1987　Origin: USA
Studio: Independent
Distributors/Format: Edward T. Lewis Film Library (16mm)
Annotation: Father Matthew is a homeless Episcopal priest; Cliff Jackson is a black executive on the fast track with the difficult responsibility of defending his company's policy of doing business with South Africa during apartheid. A chance encounter between two old friends creates the dramatic conflict.

SESAME STREET PRESENTS: FOLLOW THAT BIRD

Cast: Alaina Reed*, Roscoe Orman*, Jim Henson, Frank Oz, Paul Bartel, Sandra Bernhard, Carroll Spinney
Director: Ken Kwapis
Executive Producer: Joan Ganz Cooney
Music by: Van Dyke Parks
Producer: Tony Garnett, Joan Ganz Cooney
Screenwriter: Tony Geiss, Judy Freudberg

Tech Info: color/sound/88 min.   Type: Comedy Feature
Date: 1985   Origin: USA
Company: Children's Television Workshop, World Film, Warner
Distributors/Format: Warner Bros. Home Video, Inc. (1/2")
Annotation: Big Bird (Spinney) is taken away from Sesame Street to be with birds of his kind. The Sesame Street gang tries to find him. Orman plays Gordon and Reed plays Olivia.

SEVEN SONGS FOR MALCOLM X
Director: John Akomfrah
Producer: Black Audio Film Collective
Speaker: Spike Lee*, Betty Shabazz*
Tech Info: color/sound/52 min.   Type: Documentary Feature
Date: 1993   Origin: Great Britain
Studio: Independent
Distributors/Format: First Run/Icarus Films (16mm)
Annotation: Akomfrah's film pays homage to slain Muslim leader Malcolm X.

SEVENTH COIN, THE
Cast: Whitman Mayo*, Peter O'Toole, Ally Walker, John Rhys-Davies, Alexandra Powers, Navin Chowdhry
Director: Droff Soref
Music by: Misha Segal
Producer: Lee Nelson, Omri Maron
Screenwriter: Droff Soref
Tech Info: color/sound/92 min.   Type: Dramatic Feature
Date: 1993   Origin: USA
Company: Orbit Entertainment
Distributors/Format: Hemdale Home Video (1/2")
Annotation: A deranged archaeologist, Emil Saber (O'Toole), seeks the seventh coin of King Herod to complete his collection. Mayo plays Julius Washington, coin shop owner in Jerusalem, who relates the bloody history of Herod's seven coins to Ronnie (Powers), the niece of Police Captain Galil (Rhys-Davis).

SEVENTH SIGN, THE
Cast: Akosua Busia*, Michael Biehn, Jurgen Prochnow, Demi Moore
Director: Carl Schultz
Executive Producer: Paul R. Gurian
Music by: Jack Nitzsche
Producer: Ted Field, Robert Cort, Paul R. Gurian
Screenwriter: Ellen Green, Cliff Green
Tech Info: color/sound/97 min.   Type: Dramatic Feature
Date: 1988   Origin: USA
Company: TriStar, ML Delphi Premiere, Interscope
Distributors/Format: TriStar Pictures Inc. (1/2")
Annotation: The new occupant of Abby Quinn's (Moore) garage apartment turns out to be Christ who's hoping to steal the soul of her unborn child, break the seventh sign and bring on the Apocalypse. Busia plays Penny.

SEVERED TIES

Cast: Garrett Morris*, Elke Sommer, Oliver Reed, Billy Morrisette, Johnny Legend
Director: Damon Santostefano, Richard Roberts
Executive Producer: Steven Jacobs, Norman Jacobs
Music by: Daniel Licht
Producer: Christopher Webster, Steven Jacobs, Norman Jacobs
Screenwriter: John Nystrom, Henry Dominic
Storywriter: David Casci, Damon Santostefano
Tech Info: color/sound/96 min.   Type: Comedy Feature
Date: 1992   Origin: USA
Company: Fangoria Films
Distributors/Format: Columbia/TriStar Home Video (1/2")
Annotation: Juvenile genius Harrison (Morrisette) steals a vial of organ regrowth serum and has the opportunity to use it when he severs his arm in the robbery. Harrison heads underground with his discovery where he meets Stripes (Morris), a peg-legged derelict, and his band of homeless amputees.

SGT. PEPPER'S LONELY HEARTS CLUB BAND

Cast: Billy Preston*, Papa Juggs *, Donald Pleasence, Dianne Steinberg, Steve Martin, Peter Frampton, Frankie Howard
Director: Michael Schultz*
Music Performer: Billy Preston*, Earth Wind and Fire*, Papa Juggs *, Peter Frampton, Alice Cooper, Aerosmith , Sgt. Pepper's Lonely Hearts Club Band
Music by: George Martin, John Lennon
Producer: Robert Stigwood
Storywriter: Henry Edwards
Tech Info: color/sound/96 min.   Type: Musical Feature
Date: 1978   Origin: USA
Company: Universal
Distributors/Format: MCA Videocassette, Inc. (35mm, 1/2")
Annotation: Michael Schultz directs the Bee Gees and Peter Frampton as Sgt. Pepper's Lonely Heart Club Band who, as they skyrocket to fame, must do battle against the mean Mr. Mustard (Howard). Earth, Wind, and Fire perform "Got To Get You Into My Life."

SHADOW'S SONG

Producer: Lynn Hershman
Tech Info: bw/sound/33 min.   Type: Documentary Feature
Date: 1990   Origin: USA
Studio: Independent
Company: Desire Incorporated
Distributors/Format: Lynn Hershman (1/2")
Archives/Format: IUB - BFC/A (1/2")
Annotation: A black man and a white woman, both terminally ill, discuss their feelings about death. Suffering from a brain tumor, Henry encourages those who suffer and fear death. Knowing the time of his death, he celebrates it with friends, singing his last song about crossing over to the other side.

SHAKEDOWN

Alternate: Blue Jean Cop
Cast: Antonio Fargas*, Richard Brooks*, Darryl Edwards*, Harold Perrineau Jr.*, Peter Weller, Sam Elliott, Vondie Curtis-Hall
Director: James Glickenhaus
Executive Producer: Leonard Shapiro, Alan Solomon
Music by: Jonathan Elias
Producer: J. Boyce Harman Jr., Leonard Shapiro, Alan Solomon
Screenwriter: James Glickenhaus
Tech Info: color/sound/105 min.   Type: Dramatic Feature
Date: 1988   Origin: USA
Company: Shapiro-Glickenhaus
Distributors/Format: Universal Home Video (1/2")
Annotation: Roland Dalton (Weller), a veteran of the Public Defender's office, joins forces with Richie Marks (Elliot), an honest narcotics detective to root out corruption in the New York Police Department. Fargas plays Nicky Carr; Perrineau is Tommie and Hall is the Speaker's Voice.

SHAKES THE CLOWN

Cast: La Wanda Page*, Bobcat Goldthwait, Julie Brown, Bruce Baum, Steve Bean
Director: Bobcat Goldthwait
Executive Producer: Miles A. Copeland III, Harold Welb, Barry Krost
Music by: Tom Scott
Producer: Miles A. Copeland III, Paul Colichman, Harold Welb, Barry Krost, Ann Luly-Goldthwait
Screenwriter: Bobcat Goldthwait
Tech Info: color/sound/86 min.   Type: Comedy Feature
Date: 1992   Origin: USA
Company: IRS Media
Distributors/Format: IRS Releasing (16mm)
Annotation: Writer, director, Goldthwait plays Shakes the Clown, resident of Mythical Palookaville--an all clown town. He drinks, brawls and generally disrupts the town with his antics. The cast is full of veteran comedians, including Page as a female clown barfly.

SHAQUILLE O'NEAL: LARGER THAN LIFE

Executive Producer: Don Sperling
Producer: Don Sperling, Robert Santrarcasie
Screenwriter: Larry Weltzman
Speaker: Shaquille O'Neal*
Tech Info: color/sound/55 min.   Type: Documentary Feature
Date: 1994   Origin: USA
Company: NBA Entertainment, Fox
Distributors/Format: Fox Home Video (1/2")
Annotation: With exclusive NBA footage, this video takes you inside the Shaq legend like no one has before. Follow Shaq as he rises from high school days in San Antonio to his spectacular college career at LSU to his extraordinary entrance into the NBA.

SHARKEY'S MACHINE
Cast: Bernie Casey*, Burt Reynolds, Richard Libertini, Vittorio Gassman, Charles Durning, Rachel Ward, Kathleen Turner, Brian Keith
Director: Burt Reynolds
Storywriter: William Diehl
Tech Info: color/sound/122 min.   Type: Dramatic Feature
Date: 1981   Origin: USA
Company: Orion
Distributors/Format: Orion Home Video (1/2")
Annotation: Reynolds stars and directs this detective action adventure. Casey co-stars as Reynold's partner who is somewhat reluctant to engage in dangerous endeavors to uncover a gangster kingpin (Gassman).

SHAWSHANK REDEMPTION
Cast: Morgan Freeman*, James Whitmore, Clancy Brown, Tim Robbins, Bob Gunton, William Sadler, Gil Bellows
Director: Roger Deakins, Frank Darabont
Executive Producer: Liz Glotzer, David Lester
Music by: Thomas Newman
Producer: Liz Glotzer, David Lester, Niki Martin
Screenwriter: Frank Darabont
Tech Info: color/sound/142 min.   Type: Dramatic Feature
Date: 1994   Origin: USA
Company: Castle Rock Entertainment
Distributors/Format: Columbia Pictures Home Video (1/2"), Facets Multimedia, Inc. (1/2"), Films Inc. (1/2")
Archives/Format: IUB - BFC/A (1/2")
Annotation: Andy Dufresne (Robbins) is convicted of his wife's murder and sent to Shawshank Prison for life. The seasoned convicts, headed by Red (Freeman), make bets he won't last, but Andy does well. Forming an unlikely friendship with Red, Andy proves his resourcefulness, winning favors from the warden. As the years go by, Andy and Red never give up the dream of freedom.

SHE DON'T FADE
Cast: Cheryl Dunye*
Director: Cheryl Dunye*
Tech Info: bw/sound/24 min.   Type: Experimental Short
Date: 1991   Origin: USA
Studio: Independent
Distributors/Format: Third World Newsreel (1/2")
Annotation: Shae Clark, played by director Dunye, is a black lesbian who is gossipy about her sexuality and "new approach" to women.

SHE'S GOTTA HAVE IT
Cast: Spike Lee*, Joie Lee*, Bill Lee*, Tracy Camilla Johns*, John Canada Terrell*, Raye Dowell*, Tommy Hicks*, S. Epatha Merkerson*, Reginald Hudlin*, Ernest Dickerson*
Director: Spike Lee*
Producer: Shelton J. Lee*
Screenwriter: Spike Lee*
Tech Info: mixed/sound/84 min.   Type: Comedy Feature

Date: 1986   Origin: USA
Company: Island Pictures, 40 Acres and a Mule Film Works
Distributors/Format: CBS/Fox Home Video (1/2"), Facets Multimedia, Inc. (1/2")
Archives/Format: IUB - BFC/A (1/2")
Annotation: Lee's first crossover film is the story of Nola Darling (Johns), a young African American professional woman with her entourage of three men: Mars (Lee), Greer (Terrell), and Jamie (Hicks). She's willing to share her time with all three but they object. The film is the story of a "sexually liberated" woman from a man's perspective. Dickerson is the cinematographer.

SHEENA
Cast: Trevor Thomas*, Elizabeth of Toro *, Clifton Jones*, France Zobda*, Sylvester Williams*, Oliver Litondo*, Tom Mwangi*, Tanya Roberts, Ted Wass
Director: John Guillerman
Music by: Richard Hartley
Producer: Paul Aratow
Screenwriter: Lorenzo Semple Jr., David Newman
Storywriter: David Newman, Leslie Stevens
Tech Info: color/sound/117 min.   Type: Dramatic Feature
Date: 1984   Origin: USA
Company: Delphi II, Columbia
Distributors/Format: RCA/Columbia Pictures Home Video (1/2")
Annotation: A Kenyan Shaman (Elizabeth of Toro) has a vision that the King of her country (Jones) is in danger, but he is killed before she can speak to him. The Shaman is imprisoned by the Prince (Thomas) and his Countess Zanda (Zorda) who are conspiring to sell the bush region where the Shaman lives to white contractors.

SHELLY DUVALL'S ROCK N' RHYMELAND
Cast: Bobby Brown*, Little Richard (Penniman) *, Shelley Duvall, Cyndi Lauper
Music Performer: Bobby Brown*, Little Richard (Penniman) *, Cyndi Lauper
Tech Info: color/sound/77 min.   Type: Musical Feature
Date: 1990   Origin: USA
Annotation: Shelly Duvall and friends go on a musical journey through Rhymeland in search of Mother Goose and find an assortment of stars along the way.

SHINING, THE
Cast: Scatman Crothers*, Tony Burton*, Jack Nicholson, Shelley Duvall, Danny Lloyd
Director: Stanley Kubrick
Executive Producer: Jan Harlan
Music Performer: Bela Bartok, Herbert Von Karajan
Producer: Jan Harlan, Stanley Kubrick
Screenwriter: Diane Johnson, Stanley Kubrick
Tech Info: color/sound/120 min.   Type: Dramatic Feature
Date: 1980   Origin: USA
Company: Producer Circle Company
Distributors/Format: Warner Bros. Home Video, Inc. (1/2")
Annotation: Dick Halloran (Crothers) has the "Shining" (E.S.P.) and shares his psychic powers with Danny Torrence (Lloyd), the young son of Jack (Nicholson) and Wendy Torrence (Duvall). Both Dick and Danny sense the evil that dominates the Overlook Hotel where Jack and Wendy are hired as caretakers. Larry Durkin (Burton) is the owner of an auto shop who rents Dick a snowcat to reach the isolated

Hotel.

SHIPLEY STREET
Director: Jacqueline A. Frazier*
Producer: Jacqueline A. Frazier*
Screenwriter: Jacqueline A. Frazier*
Storywriter: Jacqueline A. Frazier*
Tech Info: color/sound/30 min.   Type: Dramatic Short
Date: 1981   Origin: USA
Studio: Independent
Annotation: The story focuses on the father-daughter relationship in a black working-class family in the atmosphere of a big city. The father, Dan Wilson, and daughter, Lana, have difficulties dealing with discrimination in the workplace and school environment.

SHOCK TO THE SYSTEM, A
Cast: Samuel L. Jackson*, Elizabeth McGovern, Michael Caine, Swoozie Kurtz, Will Patton, Peter Reigert
Director: Jan Egleson
Executive Producer: Leslie Morgan
Music by: Gary Chang
Producer: Patrick McCormick, Leslie Morgan
Screenwriter: Andrew Klavan
Tech Info: color/sound/91 min.   Type: Comedy Feature
Date: 1990   Origin: USA
Company: Corsair Pictures
Annotation: Graham Marshall (Caine) is a mild-mannered executive who goes insane and decides to show how bloodthirsty he can be when he is passed over for a deserved promotion. Jackson appears as Ulysses.

SHOCKER
Cast: Richard Brooks*, Sam Scarber*, Mitch Pileggi, John Tesh, Heather Langenkamp
Director: Wes Craven
Executive Producer: Wes Craven, Shep Gordon
Music by: William Goldstein
Producer: Wes Craven, Marianne Maddalena, Bob Engelman, Shep Gordon, Barin Kumar, Peter Foster
Screenwriter: Wes Craven
Tech Info: color/sound/110 min.   Type: Dramatic Feature
Date: 1989   Origin: USA
Company: Alive
Distributors/Format: Universal Home Video (1/2")
Annotation: Horace Pinker (Pileggi) a psychotic TV repairman murders whole families, including his own--except for his son Jonathan. Jonathan (Berg) who is later adopted by Police Lieutenant Parker (Murphy) and is a high school football star, is helped by his best friend Rhino (Brooks), the coach (Scarber) and other teammates, in destroying Pinker who becomes an electrified video villain instead of an electrocuted one.

SHOOT TO KILL

Alternate: Deadly Pursuit
Cast: Sidney Poitier*, Blu Mankuma*, Tom Berenger, Kirstie Alley
Director: Roger Spottiswoode
Executive Producer: Philip Rogers
Music by: John Scott
Producer: , Ron Silverman, Philip Rogers
Screenwriter: Harv Zimmel, Michael Burton,
Storywriter: Harv Zimmel
Tech Info: color/sound/106 min.   Type: Dramatic Feature
Date: 1988   Origin: USA
Company: Silver Screen Partners III, Touchstone
Distributors/Format: Buena Vista Home Video (1/2")
Annotation: FBI agent Warren Stantin (Poitier) is forced to go into the wilds of the
Pacific Northwest on the trail of an escaped murderer. He employs the aid of an
expert tracker (Berenger) whose girlfriend (Alley) is leading a hiking expedition,
among whose members is the murderer. The film marks the return of Poitier to the
screen after a ten year absence.

SHOPPING BAG SPIRITS AND FREEWAY FETISHES: REFLECTIONS ON RITUAL SPACE

Director: Barbara McCullough*
Speaker: Kamaau Da'oud*, David Hammons*, Betye Saar*, Houston Conwill*,
Kinshasha Conwill*, N'Senga Nengudi*, K. Curtis Lyle*, Ojenke *, Kenneth Severin*,
Freedom 'n Expression *
Tech Info: color/sound/60 min.   Type: Experimental Feature
Date: 1980   Origin: USA
Studio: Independent
Distributors/Format: Third World Newsreel (1/2")
Annotation: McCullough investigates the use of ritual in the work of artists using
different media. This experimental documentary features: Hammons, Saar, the
Conwills, Nengudi, Lyle, Da'oud, Severin and Freedom 'n Expression.

SHORT CIRCUIT

Cast: Steve Guttenberg, Ally Sheedy
Director: John Badham
Music Performer: El DeBarge *
Producer: David Foster
Screenwriter: S.S. Wilson
Tech Info: color/sound/98 min.   Type: Comedy Feature
Date: 1986   Origin: USA
Company: Producers Series Organization
Distributors/Format: TriStar Pictures Inc. (1/2")
Annotation: The film concerns a government-developed robot that acquires human
qualities and is consequently viewed as defective. Stephanie Speck (Sheedy) and
Newton (Guttenberg) attempt to save "No. 5" from destruction by the defense
department. El DeBarge performs the film's theme song "Who's Johnny" which
became a Top 40 hit.

SHRUNKEN HEADS
Cast: Julius Harris*, Meg Foster, Aeryk Egan, Bo Sharon, Darris Love, Becky Herbst
Director: Richard Elfman
Executive Producer: Debra Dion
Music by: Richard Band, Danny Elfman
Producer: Charles Band, Debra Dion
Screenwriter: Matthew Bright
Tech Info: color/sound/86 min.   Type: Dramatic Feature
Date: 1994   Origin: USA
Company: Full Moon Entertainment
Distributors/Format: Full Moon Entertainment (1/2")
Annotation: Adolescent buddies Tommy (Egan), Bill (Sharon), and Freddy (Love) are murdered when they run afoul of the mob. But Mr. Sumatra (Harris), a news vendor/voodoo sorcerer, turns them into crime fighting floating shrunken heads, which revenge themselves of their murderers.

SID AND NANCY
Cast: Sy Richardson*, Chloe Webb, Gary Oldman, Drew Schofield, David Hayman
Director: Alex Cox
Music by: Pray for Rain , The Pogues
Producer: Eric Fellner
Screenwriter: Alex Cox, Abbe Wool
Tech Info: color/sound/111 min.   Type: Dramatic Feature
Date: 1986   Origin: Great Britain
Company: Zenith, Initial
Distributors/Format: Goldwyn Home Video (1/2")
Annotation: Sid Vicious (Oldman), the bass player for the Sex Pistols, meets Nancy Spungen (Webb), an American junkie. They fall in love, but drugs shorten their lives. Richardson plays a caseworker.

SIDEWALK STORIES
Cast: Eric Payne*, Trula Hoosier*, Charles Lane*, Darnell Williams*, Nicole Alysia*, Sandye Wilson*, George Riddick*, Henry Steen*, Joe Solomon*, Jomo Wilson*, Tom Hoover*, Goma Sellman*
Director: Charles Lane*
Executive Producer: Howard M. Brickner, Vicki Lebenbaum
Music by: Henry Gaffney
Producer: Charles Lane*, Howard M. Brickner, Vicki Lebenbaum
Screenwriter: Charles Lane*
Storywriter: Charles Lane*
Tech Info: bw/97 min.   Type: Comedy Feature
Date: 1989   Origin: USA
Studio: Independent
Distributors/Format: Island Home Video (1/2")
Annotation: Lane stars as a Greenwich Village street artist who takes on an unexpected role and new responsibilities when he rescues a foundling (Alysia) in distress and attracts the affection of a shop owner (Sandye Wilson). It is the homeless who finally break the silence that has prevailed throughout the film.

SILENCE OF THE LAMBS
Cast: Frankie Faison*, Kasi Lemmons*, Ted Levine, Scott Glenn, Jodie Foster, Anthony Hopkins
Director: Jonathan Demme
Producer: Edward Saxon, Kenneth Utt, Ron Bozman
Screenwriter: Ted Tally
Storywriter: Thomas Harris
Tech Info: color/sound/118 min.   Type: Dramatic Feature
Date: 1991   Origin: USA
Company: Orion
Distributors/Format: Orion Home Video (1/2")
Annotation: FBI trainee Clarice Starling (Foster) seeks the help of psychopath Hannibal "The Cannibal" Lecter (Hopkins) in order to track down a serial killer, Buffalo Bill (Levine). Friend and co-trainee Ardelia Mapp (Lemmons) helps Clarice trace Buffalo Bill's whereabouts, and warns her when Lecter escapes. Barney (Faison) is an orderly at the maximum security prison where Lecter is held. *Grace Blake is associate producer.

SILK DREAMS
Director: Huck Botko, Jeffrey Levin, Elia Lyssy, Daniel Scwartz
Speaker: Michael "The Silk" Olajide*
Tech Info: mixed/sound/52 min.   Type: Documentary Feature
Date: 1993   Origin: USA
Studio: Independent
Company: Swillysota Productions
Annotation: Shedding light on the billion dollar fight industry, the film chronicles the struggles of Michael "The Silk" Olajide, whose eloquence defies the boxing stereotype.

SILKWOOD
Cast: Bill Cobbs*, Craig T. Nelson, Meryl Streep, Kurt Russell, Cher
Director: Mike Nichols
Executive Producer: Buzz Hirsch, Larry Cano
Music by: Georges Delerue
Producer: Michael Hausman, Mike Nichols, Buzz Hirsch, Larry Cano
Screenwriter: Nora Ephron, Alice Arlen
Tech Info: color/sound/131 min.   Type: Dramatic Feature
Date: 1983   Origin: USA
Company: Fox
Distributors/Format: Fox Home Video (1/2")
Annotation: Kerr-McGee plant worker Karen Silkwood (Streep) works to expose the company's poor safety standards but dies in a suspicious car accident before she can tell her story. Cobbs plays the man in the lunchroom

SILVERADO
Cast: Danny Glover*, Joe Seneca*, Lynn Whitfield*, Kevin Costner, Kevin Kline, Scott Glenn, Jeff Goldblum, Rosanna Arquette
Director: Lawrence Kasdan
Executive Producer: Mark Kasdan, Charles Okun
Music Performer: Bruce Broughton
Music by: Bruce Broughton

Producer: Lawrence Kasdan, Mark Kasdan, Charles Okun
Screenwriter: Lawrence Kasdan, Mark Kasdan
Tech Info: color/sound/132 min.   Type: Dramatic Feature
Date: 1985   Origin: USA
Company: Columbia
Distributors/Format: Columbia Pictures Home Video (1/2")
Annotation: A group of cowboys try to clean up a corrupt town. One of them, Malachi (Glover) is refused service in a racist restaurant. Malachi's father Ezra (Seneca) is a local landowner whose property is taken away by corrupt town leadership. When Ezra is murdered, Malachi confronts Silverado corruption. Whitfield plays Rae, Malachi's sister, a Silverado prostitute.

SING

Cast: Patti Labelle*, Cuba Gooding Jr.*, Jason Blicker*, Peter Dobson, Lorraine Bracco
Director: Richard Baskin
Executive Producer: Wolfgang Glattes
Music by: Jay Gruska
Producer: Wolfgang Glattes, Craig Zadan
Screenwriter: Dean Pitchford
Tech Info: color/sound/98 min.   Type: Musical Feature
Date: 1989   Origin: USA
Company: TriStar
Distributors/Format: TriStar Pictures Inc. (1/2")
Annotation: Brooklyn high school students perform in a song-and-dance competition. LaBelle plays Mrs. DeVere and Gooding is Stan.

SINGLES

Cast: Bill Smillie*, Xavier McDaniel*, Sandra Grant*, Kyra Sedgwick, Campbell Scott, Bridget Fonda, Sheila Kelley
Director: Cameron Crowe
Executive Producer: Art Linson
Music by: Paul Westerberg
Producer: Art Linson, Richard Hashimoto, Cameron Crowe
Screenwriter: Cameron Crowe
Tech Info: color/sound/99 min.   Type: Comedy Feature
Date: 1992   Origin: USA
Company: Warner Bros.
Distributors/Format: Warner Bros. Home Video, Inc. (1/2")
Annotation: A collection of twenty-something singles (Fonda, Scott, Dillon, Sedgwick) try to find love and meaningful relationships in Seattle. McDaniel plays himself in a brief segment; Grant is a waitress at the Sea Merchant.

SISTER ACT

Cast: Bill Nunn*, Whoopi Goldberg*, Jenifer Lewis*, Harvey Keitel, Maggie Smith, Mary Wickes
Director: Emile Ardolino, Adam Greensberg
Executive Producer: Scott Rudin
Music by: Dan Carlin Jr.
Producer: Scott Rudin, Teri Schwartz
Screenwriter: Joseph Howard
Tech Info: color/sound   Type: Comedy Feature

Date: 1992   Origin: USA
Company: Touchstone
Distributors/Format: Touchstone Home Video (1/2")
Annotation: A Las Vegas lounge singer (Goldberg) is forced to hide out in a convent after witnessing a murder. She becomes the choir director and leads them to rave reviews. Nunn plays the police officer who puts her in protective custody in the convent.

SISTER ACT 2: BACK IN THE HABIT

Cast: Whoopi Goldberg*, Jenifer Lewis*, James Coburn, Maggie Smith,
Director: Bill Duke*, Oliver Wood
Executive Producer: Lawrence Mark, Mario Iscovich
Music by: Miles Goodman
Producer: Scott Rudin, Lawrence Mark, Dawn Steel, Mario Iscovich
Screenwriter: Jim Orr
Storywriter: Judy Ann Mason, James Cruickshank
Tech Info: color/sound/107 min.   Type: Comedy Feature
Date: 1993   Origin: USA
Company: Touchstone
Annotation: Goldberg returns in this sequel and goes undercover as Sister Mary Clarence at a troubled inner-city school.

SISTER, SISTER

Cast: Robert Hooks*, Diahann Carroll*, Irene Cara*, Rosalind Cash*, Dick Anthony Williams*, Paul Winfield*, Alvin Childress*, Christopher St. John
Director: John Barry
Executive Producer: Irv Wilson
Music Performer: Bobby Jones and the New Life Singers*
Music by: Alex North
Producer: John Barry, Irv Wilson
Storywriter: Maya Angelou*
Tech Info: color/sound/135 min.   Type: Television Feature
Date: 1982   Origin: USA
Company: Fox
Annotation: The uneasy reunion of three sisters Caroline, Sissy, Freida (Carroll, Cara, Cash) that opens old family wounds. Winfield plays Freida's first love; Hooks, her ex-husband; St. John, her son, and Williams is Richard the Minister with whom Caroline has an affair.

SISTERS IN THE LIFE: FIRST LOVE

Director: Yvonne Welbon*
Tech Info: color/sound/30 min.   Type: Experimental Short
Date: 1993   Origin: USA
Studio: Independent
Distributors/Format: Third World Newsreel (1/2")
Annotation: A thirty-something black lesbian reflects on falling for her best friend in junior high school.

SIX DEGREES OF SEPARATION
Cast: Will Smith*, Stockard Channing, Donald Sutherland, Mary Beth Hurt, Bruce Davison, Ian McKellen
Director: Fred Schepisi, Ian Baker
Executive Producer: Ric Kidney
Music by: Jerry Goldsmith
Producer: Fred Schepisi, Arnon Milchan, Ric Kidney
Screenwriter: John Guare
Storywriter: John Guare
Tech Info: color/sound/112 min.   Type: Comedy Feature
Date: 1993   Origin: USA
Company: MGM, United Artists
Distributors/Format: MGM/UA Home Video (1/2")
Annotation: When Manhattan art dealers Ouisa (Channing) and Flan Kittredge (Sutherland) open their door to a young man who has been stabbed and mugged in Central Park, their world is changed forever. Paul (Smith) enchants his hosts with talks of being the son of Sidney Poitier, impresses them with his gourmet cooking and even offers them small roles in his father's movie version of CATS.

SKATETOWN U.S.A.
Cast: Flip Wilson*, Scott Baio, Greg Bradford, Patrick Swayze, Ruth Buzzi, Ron Palillo
Director: William A. Levey
Executive Producer: Peter E. Strauss
Music by: Miles Goodman
Producer: William A. Levey, Lorin Dreyfuss, Peter E. Strauss
Screenwriter: Nick Castle
Storywriter: Nick Castle, William A. Levey, Lorin Dreyfuss
Tech Info: color/sound/98 min.   Type: Comedy Feature
Date: 1979   Origin: USA
Company: Rastar
Distributors/Format: Columbia Pictures (16mm)
Annotation: Stars of 70s sitcoms play roller-disco dancers. Wilson plays Harvey Ross.

SKI PATROL
Cast: T.K. Carter*, Roger Rose, Yvette Nipar, Leslie Jordan, Paul Feig
Director: Richard Correll
Executive Producer: Paul Maslansky
Music by: Bruce Miller
Producer: Paul Maslansky, Phillip B. Goldfine, Donald L. West
Screenwriter: Steven Long Mitchell, Craig W. Van Sickle
Storywriter: Steven Long Mitchell, Craig W. Van Sickle, Wink Roberts
Tech Info: color/sound/91 min.   Type: Comedy Feature
Date: 1990   Origin: USA
Company: Epic, Sarlui-Diamant, Paul Maslansky
Distributors/Format: Triumph Releasing (16mm)
Annotation: In order to celebrate Snow Peaks ski lodge's 40th anniversary, a bumbling ski patrol must get certified and save their lodge from saboteurs. Carter plays Iceman.

SKIN DEEP

Cast: Sheryl Lee Ralph*, John Ritter, Vincent Gardenia, Alyson Reed, Joel Brooks
Director: Blake Edwards
Executive Producer: Joe Roth, James G. Robinson
Music by: Tom Bocci
Producer: Joe Roth, James G. Robinson, Tony Adams
Screenwriter: Blake Edwards
Tech Info: color/sound/102 min.   Type: Comedy Feature
Date: 1989   Origin: USA
Company: BECO, Morgan Creek
Distributors/Format: Fox Home Video (1/2")
Annotation: Zach Hutton (Ritter), an award-winning writer in a creative slump, attempts to win back his estranged wife Alex (Reed). Ralph plays a receptionist.

SKINHEADS--THE SECOND COMING OF HATE

Cast: Duane Davis*, Jadili Johnson*, Clark Corkum*, Chuck Conners, Barbara Bain, Jason Culp, Brian Brophy
Director: Greydon Clark
Music by: Dan Slider
Producer: Greydon Clark
Screenwriter: Greydon Clark, David Reskin
Tech Info: color/sound/93 min.   Type: Dramatic Feature
Date: 1990   Origin: USA
Company: Amazing Movies
Distributors/Format: Greydon Clark (16mm)
Annotation: After assaulting the Jewish proprietor of a convenience store and doing battle with an African American street gang, neo-Nazis skinheads rape and murder everyone in a backwoods diner. Tiny (Davis) and Paul (Corkum) are both murder victims.

SKY IS GRAY, THE

Series: The American Short Story Collection
Cast: James Bond III*, Olivia Cole*, Cleavon Little*, Margaret Avery*, Clinton Derricks-Carroll*, Susan French*, Hal Williams*
Director: Stan Lathan*
Executive Producer: Robert Geller
Producer: Whitney Green, Robert Geller
Screenwriter: Charles Fuller*
Storywriter: Ernest Gaines*
Tech Info: color/sound/46 min.   Type: Dramatic Short
Date: 1980   Origin: USA
Company: Monterey
Distributors/Format: Fries Home Video (1/2"), Filmic Archives (1/2")
Archives/Format: IUB - BFC/A; IUB - AV (16mm; 16mm)
Annotation: James (Bond) and his mother Olivia (Cole) live in the quarters and work in the fields on River Lake plantation in Louisiana. They leave the quarters for a trip to town because James needs to see the dentist. It is a day of learning and growth for the young boy.

SLEEP NOW
Director: Pamela Jennings*
Tech Info: bw/sound/6 min.   Type: Experimental Short
Date: 1991   Origin: USA
Studio: Independent
Distributors/Format: Third World Newsreel (1/2")
Annotation: This video poem from Jennings' "American Song Cycle Series" is based on Samuel Barber's musical adaptation of a poem by James Joyce.

SLIVER
Cast: CCH Pounder*, Keene Curtis*, Tom Berenger, Sharon Stone, William Baldwin
Director: Vilmos Zsigmond, Phillip Noyce
Executive Producer: Joe Eszterhas, Howard W. Koch Jr.
Music by: Howard Shore
Producer: Joe Eszterhas, Robert Evans, Howard W. Koch Jr., William J. MacDonald
Screenwriter: Joe Eszterhas
Tech Info: color/sound/106 min.   Type: Adaptation
Date: 1993   Origin: USA
Company: Paramount
Distributors/Format: Paramount Home Video (1/2")
Annotation: A young woman (Stone) moves into an apartment in one of New York's luxurious "Sliver" buildings. She believes she has found the perfect home but from the moment she moves in, someone is watching her, a voyeur who learns her most intimate secrets. Pounder plays Lt. Victoria Hendrix and Curtis is Gus Hale.

SLOW BURN
Cast: Ivan Rogers*, Anthony James*, William Smith, Scott Anderson, Mellissa J. Conroy
Director: John Eyres
Executive Producer: Michael Mazo
Music by: Alan Gray
Producer: John Eyres, Michael Mazo
Screenwriter: Steven Lister
Tech Info: color/sound/90 min.   Type: Dramatic Feature
Date: 1986   Origin: USA
Company: MCA
Distributors/Format: Arena Home Video (1/2")
Annotation: A reporter turns detective to find the son of a successful artist who was abandoned years earlier.

SLUGGER'S WIFE, THE
Alternate: Neil Simon's The Slugger Wife
Cast: Lynn Whitfield*, Rebecca De Mornay, Martin Ritt, Michael O'Keefe, Randy Quaid
Director: Hal Ashby
Executive Producer: Margaret Booth
Music by: Patrick Williams
Producer: Ray Stark, Margaret Booth
Screenwriter: Neil Simon
Tech Info: color/sound/105 min.   Type: Comedy Feature

Date: 1985   Origin: USA
Company: Columbia
Distributors/Format: Columbia Pictures Home Video (1/2")
Annotation: Slugger Darryl Palmer (O'Keefe) can only play baseball when his rock and roll wife (De Mornay) is in the stands. However, she longs to get back to her music. Whitfield plays Tina Alvarado.

SMALL CIRCLE OF FRIENDS, A

Cast: Harry Caesar*, Jameson Parker, Karen Allen, Brad Davis
Director: Rob Cohen
Music by: Jim Steinman, Steven Morgoshes
Producer: Tim Zinnemann
Screenwriter: Ezra Sacks
Tech Info: color/sound/113 min.   Type: Dramatic Feature
Date: 1980   Origin: USA
Company: United Artists
Distributors/Format: United Artists Home Video (1/2")
Annotation: Two best friends fall for Jessica (Allen). Although she sleeps with one, she ends up living with the other in an "open" relationship. Caesar plays Jimmy, the Cook.

SMALL TIME

Cast: Richard Barboza*, Jane Ciampa Williams*, Carolyn Kenebrew*, Bernard Lunon*, David Rodriguez*
Director: Norman Loftis
Music by: Arnold Bieber
Producer: Norman Loftis
Screenwriter: Norman Loftis
Tech Info: bw/sound/88 min.   Type: Dramatic Feature
Date: 1991   Origin: USA
Company: Norman Loftis Films
Distributors/Format: Xenon Entertainment Group (1/2"), Panorama Entertainment Corporation (16mm)
Annotation: Chronicling the life of career mugger Vince Williams (Barboza) and his three man posse "Black Flag," the film documents Vince's journey to prison on a murder charge, his humiliation at the hands of police, his abusive relationship with his drug- addicted girlfriend (Kenebrew), and his first homosexual encounter. Williams plays Vince's mother; Lunon, his father; Kenebrew appears as Vicki and Rodriguez as little Vince.

SMOKE

Cast: Giancarlo Esposito*, Forest Whitaker*, Clarice Taylor*, Malik Yoba*, Harold Perrineau Jr.*, Michelle Hurst*, Ericka Gimpel*, Reglas Gilson*, Walter T. Mead*, Harvey Keitel, William Hurt, Ashley Judd
Director: Wayne Wang
Music by: Rachel Portman
Producer: Greg Johnson, Peter Newman, Kengo Horikoshi, Hisami Kuroiwa
Storywriter: Paul Auster
Tech Info: mixed/sound/112 min.   Type: Dramatic Feature

Date: 1994   Origin: USA
Company: Miramax
Distributors/Format: Miramax Home Video (1/2")
Annotation: Auggie Wren (Keitel) runs a tobacco shop in Brooklyn which assorted characters, like Tommy (Esposito) and writer Paul Benjamin (Hurt) frequent. When Paul is saved from a traffic accident by young Thomas Cole (Perrineau) who calls himself Rashid, a relationship between the two develops. Whitaker plays Thomas' absent father, whom he tracks down.

SNEAKERS
Cast: Sidney Poitier*, Robert Redford, Mary McDonnell, David Strathairn, Ben Kingsley, River Phoenix
Director: Phil Alden Robinson, John Lindley
Executive Producer: Lindsley Parsons Jr.
Music Performer: Branford Marsalis*
Music by: James Horner
Producer: Walter Parkes, Lawrence Lasker, Lindsley Parsons Jr.
Screenwriter: Phil Alden Robinson, Lawrence Lasker, Walter Parks
Tech Info: color/sound/125 min.   Type: Dramatic Feature
Date: 1992   Origin: USA
Company: Universal
Annotation: Poitier is a former CIA employee who is a renegade hacker with others who are routinely hired to test security systems. They're called "sneakers," but they're blackmailed by government agents into carrying out a covert operation, tracking down an elusive black box.

SO FINE
Cast: Tyra Farrell*, Jack Warden, Richard Kiel, Ryan O'Neal, Mariangela Melato, Fred Gwynne
Director: Andrew Bergman
Music by: Ennio Morricone
Producer: Mike Lobell
Screenwriter: Andrew Bergman
Tech Info: color/sound/91 min.   Type: Comedy Feature
Date: 1981   Origin: USA
Company: Warner Bros.
Distributors/Format: Warner Bros. Home Video, Inc. (1/2")
Annotation: Bobby (O'Neal), finds himself involved with the wife of the loan shark who is threatening his father. Farrell plays a receptionist.

SOAPDISH
Cast: Whoopi Goldberg*, Kevin Kline, Sally Field, Robert Downey Jr., Cathy Moriarty
Director: Michael Hoffman
Music Performer: Alan Silvestri
Music by: Alan Silvestri
Producer: Aaron Spelling, Alan Greisman, Victoria White, Joel Freeman
Screenwriter: Andrew Bergman, Robert Harling
Storywriter: Robert Harling
Tech Info: color/sound/92 min.   Type: Comedy Feature

Date: 1991   Origin: USA
Company: Aaron Spelling, Alan Greisman Production
Distributors/Format: Paramount Home Video (1/2")
Annotation: Rose Schwartz (Goldberg) is the writer for the soap opera "As the Sun Sets," starring Celeste (Field), with whom she is best friends. Rose does everything she can to keep Celeste in the show against the producer's wishes. In the end, it is Rose who reveals that Montana (Moriarty), Celeste's rival, is really a man.

SOJOURNER TRUTH

Series: Black Americans of Achievement Video Collection
Director: Rhonda Fabian, Jerry Baber, Keith Smith
Executive Producer: Andrew Schlessinger
Narrator: Michael Logan
Producer: Rhonda Fabian, Jerry Baber, Andrew Schlessinger
Tech Info: mixed/sound/30 min.   Type: Documentary Short
Date: 1992   Origin: USA
Studio: Independent
Company: Schelessinger Video Productions
Distributors/Format: Filmic Archives (1/2")
Annotation: Black historians and others comment on the life of Sojourner Truth, who was born a slave in New York State, freed by law in 1827, and went on to become a preacher and supporter of women's rights and anti-slavery.

SOLAR CRISIS

Cast: Dorian Harewood*, Eric James*, Carmen Twillie*, Charlton Heston, Peter Boyle, Jack Palance
Director: Richard C. Sarafian
Executive Producer: Furuoka Hideto, Takehito Sadamura, Takeshi Kawata
Music by: Maurice Jarre
Producer: Richard Edlund, James Nelson, Tsuneyuki Morishima, Furuoka Hideto, Takehito Sadamura, Takeshi Kawata
Screenwriter: Joe Gannon, Ted Sarafian
Tech Info: color/sound/118 min.   Type: Dramatic Feature
Date: 1993   Origin: Japan
Company: Boss Films, Japan America Picture Corp., et al.
Distributors/Format: Vidmark Entertainment Home Video (1/2")
Annotation: In this sci-fi adventure set in 2058, space captain Steve Kelso (Matheson) and his right hand man, Commander Berg (Harewood) must battle various forces to launch a bomb which will save the Earth from solar waves. James plays Louisiana, one of the crewmen on the spaceship; Twillie is a Salvation Army band singer.

SOLDIER'S STORY, A

Cast: Denzel Washington*, Adolph Caesar*, Larry Riley*, Arthur/Art Evans*, William Allen Young*, Howard E. Rollins Jr.*, Dennis Lipscomb
Director: Norman Jewison
Executive Producer: Charles Schultz
Music Performer: Herbie Hancock*
Music by: Herbie Hancock*
Producer: Patrick Palmer, Norman Jewison, Charles Schultz, Ronald L. Schwartz
Screenwriter: Charles Fuller*
Storywriter: Charles Fuller*

Tech Info: color/sound/102 min.   Type: Dramatic Feature
Date: 1984   Origin: USA
Company: Columbia-Delphi Productions
Distributors/Format: RCA/Columbia Pictures Home Video (1/2")
Archives/Format: IUB - BFC/A; IUB - AAAMC (1/2"; 1/2")
Annotation: Near the end of World War II, a proud black Army attorney (Rollins) is
sent to Fort Neal, Louisiana, to investigate the murder of Master Sgt. Waters
(Caesar), a vicious, bitter man who despised his own black roots. Washington,
Evans and Young play enlisted men in Water's company.

SOME KIND OF HERO
Cast: Richard Pryor*, Olivia Cole*, Margot Kidder, Lynne Moody, David Adams
Director: Michael Pressman
Executive Producer: Robert Boris
Music Performer: Patrick Williams
Music by: Patrick Williams
Producer: Robert Boris, Howard W. Koch
Screenwriter: James Kirkwood, Robert Boris
Storywriter: James Kirkwood
Tech Info: color/sound/95 min.   Type: Dramatic Feature
Date: 1982   Origin: USA
Company: Howard Koch Production
Distributors/Format: Paramount Home Video (1/2"), Sound Unlimited Home Video
(1/2")
Annotation: Eddy Keller (Pryor) is a P.O.W. who, after six years of confinement in
Hanoi, returns home to find his wife (Moody) living with another man. Because his
mother (Cole) has had a stroke and can no longer speak, she needs money to stay
in the nursing home. Eddy rises to the challenge.

SOME PEOPLE
Cast: Mary M. Easter*
Director: Linda Kuusisto
Producer: Mary M. Easter*
Screenwriter: Mary M. Easter*
Tech Info: color/sound/19 min.   Type: Experimental Short
Date: 1988   Origin: USA
Distributors/Format: Intermedia Arts Minnesota (3/4"; 1/2")
Annotation: The film interweaves dance and narrative vignettes, exploring the lives of
African Americans living on the fringes of society. Their stories are told through
movement, monologues, and song. Easter not only serves as writer and producer,
but also as choreographer and performer with a cast of five.

SOMETHING WICKED THIS WAY COMES
Cast: Pam Grier*, Jonathan Pryce, Royal Dano, Jason Robards, Diane Ladd, Vidal
Peterson, Shawn Carson
Director: Jack Clayton
Music by: James Horner
Producer: Peter Vincent Douglas
Screenwriter: Ray Bradbury
Storywriter: Ray Bradbury
Tech Info: color/sound/95 min.   Type: Dramatic Feature

Date: 1983   Origin: USA
Company: Walt Disney, Bryna
Distributors/Format: Walt Disney (16mm)
Archives/Format: IUB - BFC/A (16mm)
Annotation: When a mysterious traveling carnival comes to town, two young boys, Will (Peterson) and Jim (Carson) are terrorized by an evil Mr. Dark (Pryce) and his instrument of madness and temptation, a beautiful yet horrific Dust Witch (Grier).

SOMMERSBY
Cast: James Earl Jones*, Clarice Taylor*, Frankie Faison*, Richard Gere, Jodie Foster, Bill Pullman, Lanny Flaherty
Director: Jon Amiel, Phillippe Bousselot
Executive Producer: Richard Gere, Maggie Wilde
Music by: Danny Elfman
Producer: Richard Gere, Arnon Milchan, Maggie Wilde, Steven Reuther, Mary McLaglen
Screenwriter: Nicholas Meyer, Sarah Kernochan
Storywriter: Nicholas Meyer, Anthony Shaffer
Tech Info: color/sound/114 min.   Type: Dramatic Feature
Date: 1993   Origin: USA
Company: New Regency Films, Warner Bros.
Distributors/Format: Warner Bros. Home Video, Inc. (1/2")
Annotation: Jack Sommersby (Gere) returns home two years after the Civil War has ended and seven years after he left. Everyone notices that he's changed, but nobody's sure if he is really Sommersby. Jones is featured as Judge Issacs and Faison appears as Joseph.

SOPHISTICATED GENTS
Cast: Bernie Casey*, Ja'net DuBois*, Mario Van Peebles*, Albert Hall*, Roosevelt "Rosey" Grier*, Robert Hooks*, Beah Richards*, Alfre Woodard*, Ron O'Neal*, Rosalind Cash*, Robert Earl Jones*, Dick Anthony Williams*, Paul Winfield*, Denise Nicholas*, Melvin Van Peebles*, Thalmus Rasulala*, Raymond St. Jacques*, Sonny Jim Gaines*, Joanna Miles*, Janet MacLachlan*, Marlene Warfield*, Stymie Beard*, Bibi Besch, Harry Guardino
Director: Harry Falk
Executive Producer: Daniel Wilson
Music by: Benny Golson
Producer: Fran Sears, Daniel Wilson
Screenwriter: Melvin Van Peebles*
Storywriter: John Alfred Williams*
Tech Info: color/sound/240 min.   Type: Television Miniseries
Date: 1981   Origin: USA
Company: Daniel Wilson Productions; NBC
Distributors/Format: Xenon Entertainment Group (1/2")
Annotation: Nine boyhood friends reunite after 25 years to honor an old coach who helped guide them through their early years. They find they must confront the contrast between their present lives as black men in American society and their innocent boyhood years.

SOUL MAN

Cast: James Earl Jones*, Rae Dawn Chong*, Felix Nelson*, Jonathan "Fudge" Leonard*, Betty Cole*, Wolfe Perry*, C. Thomas Howell
Director: Steve Miner
Music Performer: Isaac Hayes*, Sam Moore*, Muddy Waters*, Lou Reed
Music by: Isaac Hayes*, Tom Scott
Producer: Steve Tesich
Screenwriter: Carol Black
Storywriter: Carol Black
Tech Info: color/sound/101 min.   Type: Comedy Feature
Date: 1986   Origin: USA
Company: Steve Miner Films, Balcor Film Investors
Distributors/Format: Balcor Film Investors (1/2"), New World Home Video (1/2")
Archives/Format: IUB - BFC/A (1/2")
Annotation: When Mark Watson's (Howell) parents refuse to pay his way through Harvard Law School, Mark lies about his race in order to get a minority scholarship. As a "black" student he learns more than he expected, especially from his uncompromising law professor (Jones) and the girl he falls in love with, Sarah (Chong). Leon (Perry) is a black student who is exploited as the star player of an intramural white basketball team.

SOUNDS OF NEW YORK, THE

Director: William Freda Jr.
Narrator: Citizen Kafka
Producer: William Freda Jr., Howard Grossman
Speaker: Ben Vereen*
Tech Info: color/sound/60 min.   Type: Documentary Feature
Date: 1990   Origin: USA
Studio: Independent
Company: Bill Freda, Inc.
Annotation: The film is a colorful portrait of street musicians in New York City, where many kinds of music can be heard on street corners, in parks, and even in the subway. Musicians offer comments on the pleasures and problems of performing in the streets.

SOUTH BEACH

Cast: Vanity *, Isabel Sanford*, Fred Williamson*, Gary Busey, Sam Jones, Peter Fonda
Director: Fred Williamson*
Executive Producer: Steve Adelstein, David Chackler, George Barnes
Producer: Fred Williamson*, Krishna Shah, Steve Adelstein, David Chackler, George Barnes
Tech Info: color/sound/93 min.   Type: Dramatic Feature
Date: 1993   Origin: USA
Company: Po'Boy Productions, Greenwich Films
Distributors/Format: Prism Entertainment (1/2")
Annotation: Jennifer (Vanity), a Miami phone sex operator, turns to her ex-husband Mack Derringer (Williamson) when a threatening caller becomes violent. Sanford appears in an uncredited role.

SOUTH BRONX HEROES

Cast: Mario Van Peebles*, Megan Van Peebles*, Melissa Esposito*, Brendan Ward
Director: William Szarka
Executive Producer: Phil Mercogliano
Music by: Al Zima, Mitch Herzog
Producer: William Szarka, Phil Mercogliano
Screenwriter: William Szarka, Don Shiffrin
Tech Info: color/sound/85 min.　　　Type: Dramatic Feature
Date: 1985　Origin: USA
Company: Zebra
Distributors/Format: Continental Film Inc. (1/2")
Annotation: Tony (Mario Van Peebles), a young ex-con just out of prison, arrives in the South Bronx to find himself surrounded by knife and gun wielding gangs. Along with his sister Chrissie (Megan Van Peebles) and a pair of orphaned runaways (Ward and Esposito), he devises a plan to put the foster parents of the orphaned runaways behind bars.

SOUTH CENTRAL

Cast: Starletta DuPois*, Carl Lumbly*, Glenn Plummer*, Christian Coleman*, Lexie D. Bigham*, Bryon Keith Mimms*, LaRita Shelby*, Vincent Dupree*, Ivory Ocean
Director: Steve Anderson, Charlie Lieberman
Executive Producer: Oliver Stone
Music by: Tim Truman
Producer: Oliver Stone, Janet Yang
Storywriter: Donald Bakee*
Tech Info: color/sound/99 min.　　　Type: Dramatic Feature
Date: 1992　Origin: USA
Company: Warner Bros.
Distributors/Format: Warner Bros. Home Video, Inc. (1/2")
Annotation: Gang member Bobby Johnson (Plummer) has been in jail for ten years. When he gets out, he tries to reclaim his ten-year-old son Jimmy (Christian) and save him from the streets. Lumbly plays the convict who inspires Bobby to change when he's in jail.

SOUTHERN COMFORT

Cast: T.K. Carter*, Powers Boothe, Fred Ward, Keith Carradine, Franklyn Seales
Director: Walter Hill
Executive Producer: William J. Immerman
Music by: Ry Cooder
Producer: David Giler, William J. Immerman
Screenwriter: Walter Hill, David Giler, Michael Kane
Tech Info: color/sound/100 min.　　　Type: Dramatic Feature
Date: 1981　Origin: USA
Company: Phoenix, Cinema Group
Distributors/Format: Fox Home Video (1/2")
Annotation: A group of National Guardsmen on maneuvers in the swamps of Louisiana enrage Cajun backwoodsmen by borrowing their canoes. A bloody battle ensues. Carter plays Cribbs.

SPACE FOR WOMEN
Director: William Greaves*
Narrator: Richardo Montalban
Producer: William Greaves*
Screenwriter: William Greaves*
Storywriter: William Greaves*
Tech Info: color/sound/28 min.   Type: Documentary Short
Date: 1981   Origin: USA
Studio: Independent
Company: William Greaves* Production & NASA
Annotation: Greaves' film focuses on brief interviews with multi-ethnic women who are presently employed in NASA's STS (Space Transportation System), better known as the Space Shuttle.

SPACE RAGE
Cast: Harold Sylvester*, Wolfe Perry*, Michael Pare, Richard Farnsworth, John Laughlin
Director: Peter McCarthy, Conrad E. Palmisano
Music by: Billy Ferrick, Zander Schloss
Producer: Morton Reed, Eric Barrett
Screenwriter: Jim Lenahan
Storywriter: Morton Reed
Tech Info: color/sound/77 min.   Type: Dramatic Feature
Date: 1987   Origin: USA
Company: Vestron
Distributors/Format: Vestron Home Video (1/2")
Annotation: After foiling a bank robbery, Grange (Pare) is banished to a penal colony on another planet where he meets Walker (Laughlin) and the Colonel (Farnsworth). Grange tries to escape but Walker and the Colonel team up to stop him. Sylvester plays Max Bryson and Perry is Billy Boy.

SPACEBALLS
Cast: Michael Winslow*, Tim Russ*, John Candy, Rick Moranis, Mel Brooks, Bill Pullman, Daphne Zuniga, Dick Van Patten
Director: Mel Brooks
Music by: John Morris
Producer: Mel Brooks
Screenwriter: Mel Brooks, Thomas Meehan, Ronny Graham
Tech Info: color/sound/96 min.   Type: Comedy Feature
Date: 1987   Origin: USA
Company: MGM, Brookfilms
Distributors/Format: MGM/UA Home Video (1/2")
Annotation: In this spoof of the STAR WARS films, Princess Vespa (Zuniga) daughter of King Roland (Van Patten), is kidnapped by Dark Helmet (Moranis). Space adventurer Lone Starr (Pullman) and his sidekick, Barf the Mawg (Candy) are assigned to retrieve Vespa. Winslow plays a radar technician.

SPACEHUNTER: ADVENTURES IN THE FORBIDDEN ZONE
Alternate: Road Gangs
Cast: Ernie Hudson*, Michael Ironside, Molly Ringwald, Peter E. Strauss, Andrea Marcovicci
Director: Lamont Johnson
Executive Producer: Ivan Reitman
Music by: Elmer Bernstein
Producer: Ivan Reitman, Don Carmody, Andre Link, John Dunning
Screenwriter: Len Blum, Dan Goldberg, David Preston, Edith Rey
Storywriter: Stewart Harding, Jean LaFleur
Tech Info: color/sound/90 min.   Type: Dramatic Feature
Date: 1983   Origin: USA
Company: Columbia
Distributors/Format: Columbia Pictures (16mm)
Annotation: Wolff (Strauss), a mercenary salvage-ship captain, teams up with Niki (Ringwald) and Washington (Hudson) in a search for three stranded girls whose ship crashed on Terra Eleven.

SPEECHLESS
Cast: Ernie Hudson*, Geena Davis, Christopher Reeves, Michael Keaton, Bonnie Bedelia, Charles Martin Smith
Director: Ron Underwood
Executive Producer: Harry Colomby
Music by: Marc Shaiman
Producer: Geena Davis, Harry Colomby, Renny Harlin
Screenwriter: Robert King
Tech Info: color/sound/98 min.   Type: Comedy Feature
Date: 1994   Origin: USA
Company: MGM, Forge
Distributors/Format: MGM Home Video (1/2")
Annotation: Kevin Vallick (Keaton) and Julia Mann (Davis) are speechwriters for opposing senatorial candidates who find themselves falling in love despite their political differences. Hudson is featured as Ventura.

SPEED
Cast: Joe Morton*, Dennis Hopper, Keanu Reeves, Sandra Bullock, Jeff Daniels
Director: Jan DeBont, Andrzej Bartkowiak
Executive Producer: Ian Bryce
Music by: Mark Mancina
Producer: Mark Gordon, Ian Bryce
Screenwriter: Graham Yost
Tech Info: color/sound/115 min.   Type: Dramatic Feature
Date: 1994   Origin: USA
Company: Fox
Distributors/Format: Films Inc. (1/2"), Fox Home Video (1/2")
Annotation: Jack Traven (Reeves), a Los Angeles Police Department SWAT team specialist, is sent to diffuse a bomb that a vengeful extortionist (Hopper) has planted on a bus. But until he does, he must keep the bus speeding through the streets of Los Angeles at more than 50 miles-per-hour or the bomb will explode. Morton plays a police chief.

SPEED ZONE
Cast: Shari Belafonte Harper*, Michael Spinks*, John Candy, Donna Dixon, Matt Frewer
Director: Jim Drake
Executive Producer: Albert S. Ruddy, Andre Morgan
Music by: David Wheatley
Producer: Albert S. Ruddy, Murray Shostak, Andre Morgan, Vivienne Leebosh
Screenwriter: Michael Short
Tech Info: color/sound/95 min.   Type: Comedy Feature
Date: 1989   Origin: USA
Company: Entcorp
Distributors/Format: Orion Home Video (1/2")
Annotation: Margaret (Belafonte) is a member of a motley group of racers who compete against ruthless drivers who are determined to win.

SPIES LIKE US
Cast: Bernie Casey*, B.B. King*, Dan Aykroyd, Chevy Chase
Director: John Landis
Music by: Paul McCartney
Producer: Brian Crazer, George Folsey Jr.
Screenwriter: Dan Aykroyd, Lowell Ganz, Babaloo Mandel
Storywriter: Dan Aykroyd, Dave Thomas
Tech Info: color/sound/109 min.   Type: Comedy Feature
Date: 1985   Origin: USA
Company: Warner Bros.
Distributors/Format: Warner Bros. Home Video, Inc. (1/2")
Annotation: Col. Rhombus (Casey), special projects trainer, is assigned to prepare Emmett Fitz-Hume (Chase) and Austin Millbarge (Aykroyd) for the field of combat. B.B. King has a cameo role as an Ace Tomato Agent who offers two government officials a Pepsi. The Pepsi is really a top secret code line that signifies access to missile control.

SPIRIT AND TRUTH MUSIC
Director: Edward Timothy Lewis*
Producer: Edward Timothy Lewis*
Speaker: Flora Molton*, Larry Wise*
Tech Info: bw/sound/20 min.   Type: Documentary Feature
Date: 1987   Origin: USA
Studio: Independent
Distributors/Format: Edward T. Lewis Film Library (16mm)
Annotation: Flora Molton performed original and traditional spirituals on the streets of Washington, D.C., and in concerts and festivals throughout the world for more than thirty years. This documentary presents her music and the experience of Larry Wise a young harmonica player who performed with her.

SPLASH
Cast: Thomas Allen Harris*
Director: Thomas Allen Harris*
Producer: Thomas Allen Harris*
Screenwriter: Thomas Allen Harris*
Tech Info: color/sound/10 min.   Type: Experimental Short

Date: 1991   Origin: USA
Studio: Independent
Company: Evolution Productions
Distributors/Format: Third World Newsreel (1/2")
Archives/Format: IUB - BFC/A (1/2")
Annotation: Harris explores the interplay between identity, fantasy, gender, homosexual desire and pre-adolescence.

SPLIT DECISIONS

Cast: Jennifer Beals*, Gene Hackman, Craig Sheffer, Jeff Fahey, Eddie Velez
Director: David Drury
Music by: Basil Poledouris
Producer: Joe Wizan, Todd Black, Michael Borofsky
Screenwriter: David Fallon
Tech Info: color/sound/95 min.   Type: Dramatic Feature
Date: 1988   Origin: USA
Company: Wizan
Distributors/Format: New Century/Vista Film Corp (1/2")
Annotation: Eddie (Sheffer), who attends the university and hopes to train for the Olympics, must eventually rescue his older brother Ray (Fahey) who signed with a sleazy manager and fights in small-time bouts. Hackman portrays their father and Beals is Barbara, the romantic interest of one of the brothers.

SQUEEZE, THE

Cast: Rae Dawn Chong*, Michael Keaton, John Davidson, Ric Abernathy, Liane Langland
Director: Roger Young
Executive Producer: Harry Colomby, David Shamroy Hamburger
Music by: Miles Goodman
Producer: Harry Colomby, Rupert Hitzig, Michael Tannen, David Shamroy Hamburger
Screenwriter: Daniel Taplitz
Tech Info: color/sound/101 min.   Type: Dramatic Feature
Date: 1987   Origin: USA
Company: TriStar, ML Delphi Premier
Annotation: Artist Harry Berg (Keaton) receives a package from Hilda (Langland) his ex-wife containing an electromagnetic device that predicts the lottery. Gangsters are after him for the device; Rachel Dobs (Chong) is after him to pay his back alimony.

ST. ELMO'S FIRE

Cast: Anna Maria Horsford*, Emilio Estevez, Andrew McCarthy, Rob Lowe, Demi Moore, Mare Winningham
Director: Joel Schumacher
Executive Producer: Ned Tanen, Bernard Schwartz
Music by: David Foster
Producer: Lauren Shuler, Ned Tanen, Bernard Schwartz
Screenwriter: Joel Schumacher, Carl Kurlander
Tech Info: color/sound/110 min.   Type: Dramatic Feature

Date: 1985   Origin: USA
Company: Columbia
Distributors/Format: Columbia Pictures Home Video (1/2")
Annotation: Seven friends struggle to get their professional and personal lives together after graduating from Georgetown University. Horsford appears as Naomi.

ST. HELENS

Cast: Ron O'Neal*, Art Carney, Cassie Yates, David Huffman
Director: Ernest Pintoff
Music by: Goblin and Buckboard
Producer: Michael Murphy
Screenwriter: Larry Ferguson, Peter Bellwood
Tech Info: color/sound/90 min.   Type: Dramatic Feature
Date: 1981   Origin: USA
Company: Parnell
Annotation: The film follows Harry Truman (Carney), the man who refused to leave his home when Mt. St. Helens erupted in 1980. O'Neal plays a helicopter pilot.

STAKEOUT

Cast: Forest Whitaker*, Emilio Estevez, Richard Dreyfuss, Madeleine Stowe, Earl Billings, Aidan Quinn
Director: John Badham
Executive Producer: John Badham
Music by: Arthur B. Rubinstein
Producer: Cathleen Summers, John Badham, Jim Kouf
Screenwriter: Jim Kouf
Tech Info: color/sound/115 min.   Type: Dramatic Feature
Date: 1987   Origin: USA
Company: Touchstone, Silver Screen Partners III
Distributors/Format: Buena Vista Home Video (1/2")
Annotation: Chris Leece (Dreyfuss) and his partner (Estevez) on the Seattle police force are assigned to stake out the home of the former girlfriend Maria (Stowe) of fugitive "Stick" Montgomery (Quinn). Romance complicates the assignment as does Stick's return for the money and Maria. Whitaker plays Jack Pismo.

STAND ALONE

Cast: Pam Grier*, Willard Pugh*, Alan Marcus*, Charles Durning, James Keach, Bert Remsen
Director: Alan Beattie
Executive Producer: George Kondos, Daniel P. Kondos
Music by: David Campbell
Producer: Leon Williams, George Kondos, Daniel P. Kondos
Screenwriter: Roy Carlson
Tech Info: color/sound/94 min.   Type: Dramatic Feature
Date: 1985   Origin: USA
Company: Texas Star, New World
Distributors/Format: New World Home Video (1/2")
Annotation: Louis (Durning), a W.W. II veteran, witnesses a gang murder in a restaurant and is urged by his attorney Catherine (Grier) not to get involved. Louis ignores her advice and later has to arm himself against the killers. Pugh plays Detective Macombers.

STAND-IN, THE
Cast: Danny Glover*, Christa Victoria*, Joe Bellan, Jane Dornacker, Marc Hayashi, Bob Sarlatte
Director: Robert N. Zagone
Executive Producer: Gail Waldron
Music by: Don Lewis
Producer: Robert N. Zagone, Gail Waldron
Screenwriter: Robert N. Zagone, Edward Azlant
Tech Info: color/sound/87 min.   Type: Comedy Feature
Date: 1985   Origin: USA
Company: Stand, Invincible
Annotation: Danny Glover plays an independent filmmaker who accidentally kills a biker. To cover up the crime, he assumes the biker's identity.

STANLEY AND IRIS
Cast: Loretta Devine*, Jane Fonda, Swoozie Kurtz, Martha Plimpton, Robert De Niro
Director: Martin Ritt
Executive Producer: Patrick Palmer
Music by: John Williams
Producer: Patrick Palmer, Arlene Sellers, Alex Winitsky
Screenwriter: Harriet Frank Jr., Irving Ravetch
Tech Info: color/sound/104 min.   Type: Dramatic Feature
Date: 1990   Origin: USA
Company: Lantana
Distributors/Format: MGM/UA Home Video (1/2")
Annotation: Stanley (De Niro) and Iris (Fonda) are co-workers at a bakery who help each other through various personal crises, including the deaths of a parent and spouse, teenage pregnancy, and illiteracy. Devine plays Bertha.

STAR 80
Cast: Keenen Ivory Wayans*, Sheila Anderson*, Jacqueline Coleman*, Cliff Robertson, Mariel Hemingway, Eric Roberts
Director: Bob Fosse
Music by: Ralph Burns
Producer: Kenneth Utt, Wolfgang Glattes
Screenwriter: Bob Fosse
Storywriter: Teresa Carpenter
Tech Info: color/sound/102 min.   Type: Dramatic Feature
Date: 1983   Origin: USA
Company: Ladd, Warner Bros.
Distributors/Format: Warner Bros. Home Video, Inc. (1/2")
Annotation: Based on the life of Playboy Playmate Dorothy Stratten (Hemingway), the film depicts the rise to fame and the murder of the model. Anderson and Coleman play dancers and Wayans is a comic.

STAR CHAMBER, THE
Cast: Yaphet Kotto*, Dick Anthony Williams*, Hal Holbrook, Sharon Gless, Michael Douglas
Director: Peter Hyams
Music Performer: Michael Small
Music by: Michael Small
Producer: Frank Yablans

Screenwriter: Peter Hyams, Roderick Taylor
Storywriter: Roderick Taylor, William Harrison Ainsworth
Tech Info: color/sound/109 min.   Type: Dramatic Feature
Date: 1983   Origin: USA
Company: Fox
Distributors/Format: Fox Home Video (1/2")
Annotation: Detective Harry Lowes (Kotto) tries to break into the Star Chamber, a group of influential politicians and judicial system members who have taken justice into their own hands. Several other African American actors are in the cast but are not listed in the credits.

STAR TREK II: THE WRATH OF KHAN
Cast: Nichelle Nichols*, Paul Winfield*, Kirstie Alley, William Shatner, Leonard Nimoy, George Takei, Bibi Besch, Richardo Montalban, Ike Eisenmann
Director: Nicholas Meyer
Music by: James Horner
Producer: Robert Sallin
Screenwriter: Jack B. Sowards
Storywriter: Jack B. Sowards, Harve Bennett
Tech Info: color/sound/113 min.   Type: Dramatic Feature
Date: 1982   Origin: USA
Company: Paramount
Distributors/Format: Paramount Home Video (1/2")
Annotation: Khan (Montalban) kidnaps Captains Terrell (Winfield) and Chekov (Koenig) and tortures them until they attempt to kill Captain Kirk (Shatner). Terrell commits suicide rather than succumb to Khan's orders. Lt. Uhuru (Nichols), communications officer on the U.S.S. Enterprise, remains by Kirk's side.

STAR TREK III: THE SEARCH FOR SPOCK
Cast: Nichelle Nichols*, Robert Hooks*, Vince Townsend*, Conroy Gedeon*, William Shatner, Leonard Nimoy, George Takei
Director: Leonard Nimoy
Executive Producer: Gary Nardino
Music Performer: James Horner
Music by: James Horner
Producer: Harve Bennett, Gary Nardino
Screenwriter: Harve Bennett
Storywriter: Gene Roddenberry
Tech Info: color/sound/105 min.   Type: Dramatic Feature
Date: 1984   Origin: USA
Company: Harve Bennett Production
Distributors/Format: Paramount Home Video (1/2")
Annotation: Communications Officer Uhura (Nichols), a crew member aboard the starship U.S.S. Enterprise, allows other crew members to leave their post to return to Genesis for Spock (Nimoy). Uhura goes to the planet Vulcan to inform Spock's father of his son's return. Her actions countermand the orders of Starfleet Admiral Morrow (Hooks). He orders the Enterprise crew not to discuss planet Genesis and sends Federation Policeman (Gedeon) to insure their secrecy.

STAR TREK IV: THE VOYAGE HOME

Cast: Brock Peters*, Nichelle Nichols*, Madge Sinclair*, William Shatner, Leonard Nimoy, DeForest Kelley, George Takei
Director: Leonard Nimoy
Music by: Leonard Rosenman
Producer: Harve Bennett
Screenwriter: Harve Bennett, Nicholas Meyer, Steve Meerson, Peter Krikes
Storywriter: Leonard Nimoy, Harve Bennett
Tech Info: color/sound/119 min.　　　Type: Dramatic Feature
Date: 1986　　Origin: USA
Company: Paramount
Distributors/Format: Facets Multimedia, Inc. (1/2"), Paramount Home Video (1/2")
Annotation: The U.S.S. Enterprise crew is together again, this time attempting to save Earth's future by returning to its past. Nichols returns as Deck Officer Uhura. Sinclair is cast as Commander of the U.S.S. Saratoga, a fellow starfleet ship.

STAR TREK V: THE FINAL FRONTIER

Cast: Nichelle Nichols*, William Shatner, Leonard Nimoy, James Doohan, Lawrence Luckinbill
Director: William Shatner
Music by: Jerry Goldsmith
Producer: Harve Bennett
Screenwriter: David Lougherty
Storywriter: William Shatner, Harve Bennett, David Lougherty
Tech Info: color/sound/107 min.　　　Type: Dramatic Feature
Date: 1989　　Origin: USA
Company: Paramount
Distributors/Format: Facets Multimedia, Inc. (1/2"), Paramount Home Video (1/2")
Annotation: Spock's (Nimoy) half brother Sybock (Luckinbill), on his voyage to meet "God," forces the crew of the U.S.S. Enterprise to go beyond their emotional pain. Nichols returns as Lt. Uhura, the only female Deck Officer on the ship.

STAR TREK VI: THE UNDISCOVERED COUNTRY

Cast: Brock Peters*, Nichelle Nichols*, Iman *, Michael Dorn*, William Shatner, Leonard Nimoy, DeForest Kelley
Director: Nicholas Meyer
Executive Producer: Leonard Nimoy
Music by: Cliff Eidelman
Producer: Leonard Nimoy, Ralph Winter, Steven Charles-Jaffe
Screenwriter: Nicholas Meyer, Denny Martin Flinn
Storywriter: Leonard Nimoy, Lawrence Konner, Mark Rosenthal
Tech Info: color/sound/120 min.　　　Type: Dramatic Feature
Date: 1991　　Origin: USA
Company: Paramount
Distributors/Format: Facets Multimedia, Inc. (1/2"), Paramount Home Video (1/2")
Annotation: When someone aboard the U.S.S. Enterprise assassinates the Klingon ambassador, Kirk and Bones (Shatner and Kelly) are accused of the crime and expelled to a Gulag in outer space where Martia (Iman), another prisoner, helps them escape and then turns on them. Eventually the conspiracy is traced to Federation leaders, including Admiral Cartwright (Peters). Dorn appears as Kirk's defense counselor. Nichols, Nytoba Uhura.

STAR TREK: GENERATIONS
Series: Star Trek
Cast: Whoopi Goldberg*, LeVar Burton*, Michael Dorn*, William Shatner, Patrick Stewart, Jonathan Frakes, Brent Spiner
Director: David Carson
Executive Producer: Bernie Williams
Music by: Dennis McCarthy
Producer: Rick Berman, Bernie Williams
Screenwriter: Ronald D. Moore, Brannon Braga
Storywriter: Ronald D. Moore, Brannon Braga, Rick Berman
Tech Info: color/sound/118 min.   Type: Dramatic Feature
Date: 1994   Origin: USA
Company: Paramount
Distributors/Format: Facets Multimedia, Inc. (1/2"), Films Inc. (1/2"), Paramount Home Video (1/2")
Annotation: The two captains of the starship U.S.S. Enterprise, Jean-Luc Pollar (Stewart) and Kirk (Shatner) are joined in an intergalactic quest. They must join forces to save millions. Goldberg reprises her television role as Guinan.

STAR TREK: THE MOTION PICTURE
Cast: Nichelle Nichols*, William Shatner, Walter Koenig, Leonard Nimoy, DeForest Kelley, George Takei
Director: Robert Wise
Music Performer: Jerry Goldsmith
Music by: Jerry Goldsmith
Producer: Gene Roddenberry
Screenwriter: Harold Livingston
Storywriter: Alan Dean Foster
Tech Info: color/sound/130 min.   Type: Dramatic Feature
Date: 1979   Origin: USA
Company: Paramount
Distributors/Format: Paramount Home Video (1/2")
Annotation: The cast of the television series reunite for their first motion picture. Seeking out signals from distant space, the crew becomes involved with an entity that calls itself V-GER and feeds off information. Lt. Uhura (Nichols) returns as one of Captain Kirk's (Shatner) deck officers.

STARS AND BARS
Cast: Beatrice Winde*, Kent Broadhurst, Harry Dean Stanton, Daniel Day Lewis, Glenne Headly
Director: Pat O'Conner
Executive Producer: Sheldon Shrager
Music by: Stanley Myers
Producer: Sandy Lieberson, Sheldon Shrager
Screenwriter: William Boyd
Tech Info: color/sound/94 min.   Type: Comedy Feature
Date: 1988   Origin: USA
Company: Columbia
Distributors/Format: Columbia Pictures Home Video (1/2")
Annotation: Henderson Dores (Day Lewis), a proper Englishmen and 19th-century art expert, travels from New York to Georgia to purchase a rediscovered Renior

painting. Winde plays Alma-May.

STEEL

Cast: Roger E. Mosley*, Art Carney, Lee Majors, Jennifer O'Neill, George Kennedy
Director: Steve Carver
Music by: Michael Colombier
Producer: Peter S. Davies, William N. Panzer
Screenwriter: Leigh Chapman
Storywriter: Rob Ewing, Peter S. Davies, William N. Panzer
Tech Info: color/sound/102 min.   Type: Dramatic Feature
Date: 1979   Origin: USA
Company: The Steel Co., World Northal Corporation
Annotation: The film chronicles the building of a skyscraper and the obstacles faced by the construction crew, which is led by worker Mike Catton (Majors). One of Gatton's fellow workers, Lionel (Mosley), suffers the loss of a partner from a fall, but continues with the rest of the crew in order to meet deadlines.

STEELE JUSTICE

Cast: Bernie Casey*, Ronny Cox, Joe Campanella, Martin Kove, Sela Ward
Director: Robert Boris
Executive Producer: Thomas Coleman, Michael Rosenblatt
Music by: Misha Segal
Producer: Thomas Coleman, Michael Rosenblatt, John Strong
Screenwriter: Robert Boris
Tech Info: color/sound/95 min.   Type: Dramatic Feature
Date: 1987   Origin: USA
Company: Atlantic
Annotation: Vietnam vet John Steele (Kore) loses his wife and job to alcoholism . He seeks revenge when his family and a friend are murdered by a Vietnamese drug kingpin. Casey plays Reese.

STEELE'S LAW

Cast: Fred Williamson*, Phyllis Cicero*, Vinnie Gaskins*, Walter Harats*, Bo Svenson, Doran Inghram, Robin McGee, Paul Tepper
Director: Fred Williamson*
Music by: Mike Logan
Producer: Fred Williamson*, Marvin Towns
Screenwriter: Charles J. Johnson*
Tech Info: color/sound   Type: Dramatic Feature
Date: 1992   Origin: USA
Company: Po' Boy Productions
Distributors/Format: Academy Home Entertainment Video (1/2")
Annotation: Against his will, Chicago police detective John Steele (Williamson) is assigned to apprehend international hit man turned psycho serial killer John Keno (Inghram) whom Steele had sent to prison but was subsequently paroled. Keno has been hired by Dallas businessmen to assassinate the Iraqi ambassador. Rose Holly (Cicero) is Steele's love interest in Dallas; Harats plays Mojo, a "snitch," and Gaskins is Special Agent Votel.

STEPFATHER, THE
Cast: Blu Mankuma*, Terry O'Quinn, Jill Schoelen, Shelley Hack
Director: Joseph Ruben
Music by: Patrick Moraz
Producer: Jay Benson
Screenwriter: Donald E. Westlake
Storywriter: Donald E. Westlake, Carolyn Lefcourt, Brian Garfield
Tech Info: color/sound/90 min.   Type: Dramatic Feature
Date: 1987   Origin: USA
Company: ITC
Distributors/Format: New Century/Vista Film Corp (1/2")
Annotation: Jerry Blake (O'Quinn), Susan, his new wife (Hack), and Stephanie, his step-daughter (Schoelen), live a picture-perfect existence in suburbia, only Stephanie dislikes her new father and fears he'll kill them all. Mankuma plays Lt. Jack Wall.

STEPHEN KING'S SILVER BULLET
Cast: Paul Butler*, Gary Busey, Everett McGill, Corey Haim, Megan Follows
Director: Daniel Attias
Music by: Jay Chattaway
Producer: Martha Schumacher
Screenwriter: Stephen King
Tech Info: color/sound/95 min.   Type: Dramatic Feature
Date: 1985   Origin: USA
Company: DEG
Distributors/Format: Paramount (1/2")
Annotation: Little Marty Coslaw (Haim) is a disabled youngster who uses his wheelchair, nicknamed "The Silver Bullet," to ward off a murderous werewolf. Butler plays Edgar Rounds.

STEPPIN'
Director: Jerald B. Harkness*
Tech Info: color/sound/56 min.   Type: Documentary Feature
Date: 1992   Origin: USA
Studio: Independent
Distributors/Format: Cinema Guild (1/2")
Annotation: The film documents traditional step shows popular among black fraternities and sororities and their historical importance.

STEWARDESS SCHOOL
Cast: Sherman Hemsley*, Lela Rochon*, Brett Cullen, Mary Cadorette, Wendy Jo Sperber, Donald Most
Director: Ken Blancato
Music by: Robert Folk
Producer: Phil Feldman, Don McFarlane
Screenwriter: Ken Blancato
Tech Info: color/sound/84 min.   Type: Comedy Feature
Date: 1986   Origin: USA
Company: Summa
Distributors/Format: Columbia Pictures Home Video (1/2")
Annotation: Philo (Cullen) and George (Most) are thrown out of pilot's school for their juvenile antics so they decide to go to stewardess school. Rochon plays the

school instructor; Hemsley is Mr. Butterworth.

STICKY FINGERS
Cast: Danitra Vance*, Loretta Devine*, Eileen Brennan, Melanie Mayron, Helen Slater
Director: Catlin Adams
Executive Producer: Jonathan Olsberg
Music by: Gary Chang
Producer: Catlin Adams, Melanie Mayron, Jonathan Olsberg
Screenwriter: Catlin Adams, Melanie Mayron
Tech Info: color/sound/97 min.   Type: Comedy Feature
Date: 1988   Origin: USA
Company: Hightop
Distributors/Format: Spectrafilm (16mm)
Annotation: Two female musicians, Hattie (Slater) and Lolly (Mayron) are left a suitcase with a million dollars to watch for their drug dealer friend Diane (Devine). Vance plays Evanston.

STIR CRAZY
Cast: Richard Pryor*, Grand L. Bush*, Franklin Ajaye*, Georg Stanford Brown*, Cedrick Hardman*, Esther Sutherland*, Gene Wilder, Pamela Poitier
Director: Sidney Poitier*
Executive Producer: Melville Tucker
Music Performer: Tom Scott
Music by: Tom Scott
Producer: Hannah Weinstein, Melville Tucker
Screenwriter: Bruce Jay Friedman
Tech Info: color/sound/111 min.   Type: Comedy Feature
Date: 1980   Origin: USA
Company: Columbia
Distributors/Format: Columbia Pictures Home Video (1/2")
Annotation: Skip (Wilder) and Harry (Pryor), who are best friends, decide to leave the corrupt city for the West. While traveling, they are wrongly accused of a robbery and sent to prison. In the midst of a prison rodeo competition, Skip and Harry escape with the help of another prisoner (Brown).

STOKER ACE
Cast: Bubba Smith*, Burt Reynolds, Ned Beatty, Loni Anderson, Jim Nabors, John Byner
Director: Hal Needham
Music by: Al Capps
Producer: Hank Moon Jean
Screenwriter: Hal Needham, Hugh Wilson
Storywriter: William Neely, Robert K. Ottum
Tech Info: mixed/sound/96 min.   Type: Dramatic Feature
Date: 1983   Origin: USA
Company: Warner Bros.
Distributors/Format: Universal Home Video (1/2")
Annotation: When NASCAR driver Stoker Ace (Reynolds) is conned into signing a contract before reading the fine print, new owner Clyde Terkle (Beatty) and his bodyguard Arnold (Smith) force Ace to race in a chicken suit, promoting Terkle's food service.

STONY ISLAND

Alternate: My Man from Stony Island
Cast: Rae Dawn Chong*, Richard Davis*, Edward Stoney Robinson*, Gene Barge*, George Englund
Director: Andrew Davis
Music by: Gene Barge*, David Matthews
Producer: Andrew Davis, Tamar Simon Hoffs
Screenwriter: Andrew Davis, Tamar Simon Hoffs
Tech Info: color/sound/97 min.   Type: Dramatic Feature
Date: 1978   Origin: USA
Company: World, Northal
Annotation: Richie (Davis) and Kevin (Robinson), a couple of project kids from Chicago's south side, struggle to form a band. They get advice from blues man Percy Price (Barge). Chong plays Janetta.

STOP! OR MY MOM WILL SHOOT

Cast: Al Fann*, Ving Rhames*, Ella Joyce*, Estelle Getty, Sylvester Stallone, JoBeth Williams
Director: Roger Spottiswoode
Executive Producer: Joe Wizan, Todd Black
Music by: Alan Silvestri
Producer: Ivan Reitman, Joe Wizan, Michael Gross, Joe Medjuck, Todd Black
Screenwriter: William Davies, William Osbourne, Blake Snyder
Tech Info: color/sound/81 min.   Type: Comedy Feature
Date: 1992   Origin: USA
Company: Northern Lights, Wizan/Black Films, Ivan Reitman
Distributors/Format: Universal Home Video (1/2")
Annotation: When his mother Tutti (Getty) comes to town, Los Angeles policeman Joe Bomowski's (Stallone) image as a "macho cop" is compromised by her constant interference in his job and love life. Joyce plays Detective McCabe and Rhames is a "bad guy."

STORME: THE LADY OF THE JEWEL BOX

Cast: Storme De Larverie*
Director: Michelle Parkerson*
Speaker: Robin Rogers, Bobby Schiffman, Joan Nestle
Tech Info: mixed/sound/21 min.   Type: Documentary Short
Date: 1987   Origin: USA
Studio: Independent
Company: Eye of the Storm Productions, Inc.
Distributors/Format: Women Make Movies, Inc. (16mm; 1/2")
Archives/Format: IUB - BFC/A (1/2")
Annotation: Parkerson's film is a portrait of Storme De Larverie, former stage manager, M.C., and performer at the Jewel Box Revue that featured male impersonators. A favorite act on the black theater circuit in the forties, fifties, and sixties, the multiracial revue attracted interracial audiences.

STORYVILLE
Cast: Woody Strode*, Chino "Fats" Williams*, Michael Warren*, Charlotte Lewis, Joanne Whalley-Kilmer, James Spader
Director: Mark Frost
Executive Producer: John Flock, John A. Davis
Music by: Carter Burwell*
Producer: Edward R. Pressman, John Flock, David Roe, John A. Davis
Screenwriter: Lee Reynolds, Mark Frost
Tech Info: color/sound/110 min.　　Type: Dramatic Feature
Date: 1992　Origin: USA
Company: Storyville Inc., Davis Entertainment, et al.
Distributors/Format: Fox Home Video (1/2")
Annotation: Cray Fowler (Spader), a powerful Louisiana lawyer from a political family, is framed for murder by political rivals. Williams is Theotis Washington; Warren plays Nathan LeFleur; Strode plays Charlie Sumpter.

STRAIGHT OUT OF BROOKLYN
Cast: Matty Rich*, George T. Odom*, Ann D. Sanders*, Lawrence/Larry Gilliard Jr.*, Barbara Sanon*, Mark Malone*, Reana E. Drummond*, Ali Shahid Abdul Wahhab*, Joseph A. Thomas*, Dorise Black*, Booker Matthews*, J.R. Hill*, Robert N. Nash*
Director: Matty Rich*
Executive Producer: Lindsay Law, Ira Deutchman
Music Performer: Arthur Baker*, Harold Wheeler*, Force MDs *, J.C. Lodge*, Shirley Matthews*, East New York Connection*, Ken Williams*, Eric Beal*, Queen Latifah*, Daddy-O *
Producer: Matty Rich*, Lindsay Law, Allen Black, Ira Deutchman
Screenwriter: Matty Rich*
Tech Info: color/sound/91 min.　　Type: Dramatic Feature
Date: 1991　Origin: USA
Studio: Independent
Company: Samuel Goldwyn/Black In Progress Production
Distributors/Format: Samuel Goldwyn Home Video (1/2")
Archives/Format: IUB - BFC/A (1/2")
Annotation: Dennis Brown (Gilliard), tired of watching his father Ray (Odom) beat his mother Frankie (Sanders) because he cannot adequately support his family, develops a plan to get his family and friends out of Brooklyn and into the life he dreams of. However, the plan backfires when Dennis steals a drug dealer's (Wahhab) pick-up bag. Rich plays Larry Love, Dennis' co-conspiring friend; Kevin (Malone) completes the trio of Brooklyn project youths.

STRAIGHT TO HELL
Cast: Grace Jones*, Sy Richardson*, Jennifer Balgobin*, Dennis Hopper, Joe Strummer, Dick Rude, Courtney Love
Director: Alex Cox
Executive Producer: Cary Brokaw, Scott Malone
Music by: Pray for Rain , The Pogues
Producer: Eric Fellner, Cary Brokaw, Scott Malone
Screenwriter: Alex Cox, Dick Rude
Tech Info: color/sound/86 min.　　Type: Comedy Feature

Date: 1987   Origin: Great Britain
Company: Initial
Distributors/Format: Island Home Video (1/2")
Annotation: Norwood (Richardson), Willy (Rude), and Simms (Strummer) fail to kill the man they were hired to eliminate so they rob a bank instead. Their getaway car breaks down in the desert near a town ruled by coffee addicts. Jones plays Sonya and Balgobin plays Fabienne.

STRAIGHT UP RAPPIN'
Producer: Tana Ross, Freke Vuijst
Tech Info: color/sound/29 min.   Type: Documentary Short
Date: 1992   Origin: USA
Company: Green Room Productions
Distributors/Format: Filmakers Library, Inc. (16mm; 1/2")
Annotation: The documentary explores the political consciousness of New York street rappers. Children of all ages rap about the Bill of Rights, child abuse, homelessness and revolution.

STRAPPED
Cast: Bokeem Woodbine*, Fredro Starr*, Kia Joy Goodwin*, Michael Biehn
Director: Forest Whitaker*
Executive Producer: Michael Apted, Robert O'Connor, Colin Callender
Producer: Michael Apted, Robert O'Connor, Nellie Nugiel, Colin Callender
Screenwriter: Dena Kleiman*
Tech Info: color/sound/102 min.   Type: Television Feature
Date: 1993   Origin: USA
Studio: HBO Studios
Distributors/Format: HBO Home Video (1/2")
Annotation: Whitaker's directorial debut features the life Diquan (Woodbine) and his pregnant girlfriend (Goodwin). When she is sent to jail for selling drugs, Diquan becomes a "snitch" for the police in exchange for money to post her bail.

STREAMERS
Cast: Michael Wright*, David Alan Grier*, Matthew Modine, George Dzundza, Mitchell Lichtenstein, Guy Boyd
Director: Robert Altman
Executive Producer: Robert Michael Geisler, John Roberdeau
Producer: Robert Altman, Nick J. Mileti, Robert Michael Geisler, John Roberdeau
Screenwriter: David Rabe
Tech Info: color/sound/118 min.   Type: Dramatic Feature
Date: 1983   Origin: USA
Company: United Artists Classics
Distributors/Format: United Artists Home Video (1/2")
Annotation: A group of army recruits in a military barracks go from being macho to baring their souls. Grier is featured as Roger.

STREET ASYLUM
Cast: Sy Richardson*, Wings Hauser, Alex Cord, Roberta Vasquez, G. Gordon Liddy
Director: Greggory Brown
Executive Producer: Walter D. Gernert
Music by: Leonard Marcel
Producer: Walter D. Gernert, Walter D. Gernert

Screenwriter: John Powers
Storywriter: Greggory Brown
Tech Info: color/sound/94 min.   Type: Dramatic Feature
Date: 1990   Origin: USA
Company: Metropolis, Hit Films
Distributors/Format: Magnum Entertainment (1/2")
Annotation: Jim Miller (Liddy) is a sadistic Los Angeles Police Chief who implants devices into his officers' spines which turn them into ultra-violent killers. He watches the mayhem from TV monitors. Richardson plays Sgt. Tatum.

STREET FIGHTER

Cast: Grand L. Bush*, Miguel Nunez*, Raul Julia, Jean-Claude Van Damme, Wen Ming-Na
Director: Steven E. de Souza
Executive Producer: Tim Zinnemann, Jun Aida, Sasha Harari
Music by: Graeme Revell
Producer: Tim Zinnemann, Edward R. Pressman, Kenzo Tsujimoto, Jun Aida, Sasha Harari
Screenwriter: Steven E. de Souza
Tech Info: color/sound/95 min.   Type: Dramatic Feature
Date: 1994   Origin: USA
Company: Edward R. Pressman Film Corp., Galaxy, Capcom Co.
Distributors/Format: Universal Home Video (1/2")
Annotation: Col. William F. Guile (Van Damme) and his allies foil war/drug lord General Bison's (Julia) attempts to conquer the world. Bush plays Balrog.

STREET KNIGHT

Cast: Bernie Casey*, Kamar Reyes, Jeff Speakman, Christopher Neame, Lewis Van Bergen, Jennifer Gatti
Director: Albert Magnoli
Executive Producer: Yoram Globus, Christopher Pearce
Music by: David Michael Frank
Producer: Yoram Globus, Christopher Pearce, Mark DiSalle
Screenwriter: Richard Friedman, Jeff Schechter
Tech Info: color/sound/93 min.   Type: Dramatic Feature
Date: 1993   Origin: USA
Company: Street Knight Productions, Global Picture Corp
Distributors/Format: Cannon Home Video (1/2")
Annotation: Corrupt police pit black and Latino gangs against each other in an attempt to spark a gang war despite a recent truce. Casey plays Raymond.

STREET OF NO RETURN

Alternate: Sans Espoir de Retour
Cast: Bill Duke*, Keith Carradine, Valentina Vargas, Bernard Fresson, Andrea Ferreol
Director: Samuel Fuller
Executive Producer: Jacques Eric Strauss, Patrick Delauneux, Antonio DaCunha Telles
Music by: Karl-Heinz Schafer
Producer: Jacques Bral, Francois Besson, Jacques Eric Strauss, Patrick Delauneux, Antonio DaCunha Telles

Screenwriter: Samuel Fuller, Jacques Bral
Tech Info: color/sound/90 min.   Type: Dramatic Feature
Date: 1991   Origin: France, Portugal, USA
Company: Thunder Films International, et al.
Distributors/Format: President Films (16mm)
Annotation: A wealthy rock singer, Michael (Carradine) becomes an alcoholic bum after his lover's boyfriend cuts his throat and ruins his voice. Lieutenant Borel (Duke) thinks Michael may be able to help him solve the murder of a policeman and stop the violence of a fullscale race riot.

STREET SMART

Cast: Morgan Freeman*, Grace Garland*, Shari Hilton*, Erik King*, Anna Maria Horsford*, Donna Bailey*, Ernest Deveaux*, Christopher Reeves
Director: Jerry Scatzberg
Music Performer: John Amos*, Miles Davis*, Robert Irving III
Producer: Yoram Globus, Menahem Golan
Screenwriter: David Freeman
Tech Info: color/sound/97 min.   Type: Dramatic Feature
Date: 1987   Origin: USA
Company: Golan/Globus
Distributors/Format: Cannon Home Video (1/2")
Annotation: Johnathon Fisher (Reeves), a reporter trying to get a good story about prostitution, meets Leo Smalls (Freeman), a Harlem pimp who is being charged with murder. Smalls introduces Fisher to his women; Harriet (Horsford) and Darlene (Hilton); his body guard, Reggie (King); and Erin (Deveaux), a young street kid.

STREET WARS

Cast: Michelle Johnson*, Bryan O'Dell*, Alan Joseph Howe*, Terrence Hart*, Laurence Lowe*, Ken Steadman*, Jean Pace*, Eric Kohner
Director: Jamaa Fanaka*
Executive Producer: Cordell MacDonald, Clarine MacDonald
Music by: Michael Dunlap, Yves Chicha, L'Azur
Producer: Jamaa Fanaka*, Ben Caldwell*, Bryan O'Dell*, Ayanna DuLaney, Cordell MacDonald, Clarine MacDonald
Screenwriter: Jamaa Fanaka*
Tech Info: color/sound/90 min.   Type: Dramatic Feature
Date: 1994   Origin: USA
Company: Jamaa Fanaka* Productions
Distributors/Format: Medallion Entertainment (1/2")
Annotation: Charles R. Williams, Jr., a.k.a. Sugarpop, the top pilot in his class at Exeter Military Academy, has West Point aspirations, but when his big brother Frank (O'Dell), a notorious drug kingpin, is assassinated, Sugarpop reluctantly inherits a suburban crackhouse empire. Johnson plays Sugarpop's girlfriend Tina; Shecog is Frank's bodyguard Humungus; Hart is Neckbone; Lowe is Rock, Sugarpop's chief rival; and Pace plays Ma Grams, matriarch of the clan.

STREETS OF FIRE

Cast: Richard Lawson*, Stone/Stoney Jackson*, Grand L. Bush*, Robert Townsend*, Mykelti Williamson*, Lynn Thigpen*, Diane Lane, Michael Pare
Director: Walter Hill
Executive Producer: Gene Levy
Music by: Ry Cooder

Producer: Lawrence Gordon, Joel Silver, Gene Levy
Storywriter: Larry Gross, Walter Hill
Tech Info: color/sound/93 min.   Type: Dramatic Feature
Date: 1984   Origin: USA
Company: RKO, Universal Studios
Distributors/Format: MCA Home Video (1/2")
Annotation: A soldier of fortune, Tom Cody (Pare) goes after a biker gang that kidnapped his rockstar ex-girlfriend, Ellen Aim (Lane). He enlists the aid of a rock band, The Sorels, Bird (Jackson), Reggie (Bush), Lester (Townsend), B.J. (Washington) and the use of their tour bus. Cody is also befriended by a policeman, Ed Prince (Lawson), who warns him to leave town.

STREETS OF GOLD

Cast: Wesley Snipes*, Klaus Maria Brandauer, Adrian Pasdar, Lloyd Nolan, Angela Molina, Elya Baskin
Director: Joe Roth
Producer: Joe Roth
Screenwriter: Heywood Gould, Richard Price, Tom Cole
Tech Info: color/sound/92 min.   Type: Dramatic Feature
Date: 1986
Company: Fox
Distributors/Format: Fox Home Video (1/2")
Annotation: Nolan Jacob (Snipes) is a backstreet fighter who after harassing a Russian defector Alex (Brandauer) selects him as his trainer. Alex prepares Nolan to fight against his former Russian team.

STREETWALKIN'

Cast: Antonio Fargas*, Conrad Roberts*, Khandi Alexander*, Leon (credited as Leon) Robinson*, Melissa Leo, Dale Midkiff, Julie Newmar, Randall Batinkoff
Director: Joan Freeman
Music by: Matt Ender, Doug Timm
Producer: Robert Alden
Screenwriter: Robert Alden, Joan Freeman
Tech Info: color/sound/86 min.   Type: Dramatic Feature
Date: 1985   Origin: USA
Company: Rodeo
Annotation: Cookie (Leo), an innocent young girl arriving in New York with her younger brother, Tim (Batinkoff), is spotted at the Port Authority bus station by Duke (Midkiff), a pimp. Cookie is soon working for Duke and is introduced to the harsh reality of underground life. The film also features Robinson as Jason, Fargas as Finesse, Alexander plays Star. Roberts has an uncredited role.

STRICTLY BUSINESS

Alternate: Go Natalie!
Cast: Samuel L. Jackson*, Anne-Marie Johnson*, Paul Butler*, Mansoor Najeeullah*, Halle Berry*, Ellis Williams*, Tommy Davidson*, Kim Coles*, James McDaniel*, Oni Faida Lampley*, Fred Braithwaite*, Joseph C. Phillips, Sarah Stavrou, Sandra McLain
Director: Kevin Hooks*
Executive Producer: Mark Burg, Chris Zarpas
Music by: Michel Colombier

Producer: Pam Gibson*, Nelson George*, Mark Burg, Andre Harrell, Chris Zarpas
Screenwriter: Pam Gibson*, Nelson George*
Tech Info: color/sound/83 min.   Type: Comedy Feature
Date: 1991   Origin: USA
Company: Island World
Distributors/Format: Warner Bros. Home Video, Inc. (1/2")
Annotation: Successful corporate executive Wayman Tinsdale III (Phillips) enlists
the aid of mailroom employee Bobby Johnson (Davidson) in order to meet the girl of
his dreams, nightclub dancer Natalie (Berry). Tinsdale nearly loses his job, as well
as Johnson's friendship, as he pursues Natalie across New York's underground
clubs. Johnson plays Diedre; Butler and McDaniel play Leroy and Roland Halloran;
Jackson, Monroe.

STRIKING DISTANCE

Cast: Roscoe Orman*, Andre Braugher*, Bruce Willis, Sarah Jessica Parker, Dennis
Farina, Robert Pastorelli
Director: Rowdy Herrington
Executive Producer: Steven Reuther
Music by: Brad Fiedel
Producer: Arnon Milchan, Steven Reuther, Hunt Lowry, Tony Thomopoulos
Screenwriter: Rowdy Herrington, Martin Kaplan
Tech Info: color/sound/101 min.   Type: Dramatic Feature
Date: 1993   Origin: USA
Company: New Regency Films, Columbia, Milchan Productions
Distributors/Format: Columbia Pictures Home Video (1/2")
Annotation: Pittsburgh policeman Tom Hardy (Willis) is unable to track the serial
killer who torments the town. In addition, he must testify in the excessive force trial
of his partner Jimmy Detillo (Pastorelli). Braugher plays Frank Morris and Orman is
Detective Sid McClelland.

SUDDEN IMPACT

Cast: Albert Popwell*, Clint Eastwood, Sondra Locke, Paul Drake, Audrie J. Neenan,
Pat Hingle, Jack Thibeau
Director: Clint Eastwood
Music Performer: Roberta Flack*
Music by: Lalo Schifrin
Producer: Clint Eastwood
Screenwriter: Joseph Stinson
Storywriter: Earl E. Smith, Charles B. Pierce
Tech Info: color/sound/117 min.   Type: Dramatic Feature
Date: 1983   Origin: USA
Company: Warner Bros.
Distributors/Format: Warner Bros. Home Video, Inc. (1/2")
Annotation: Dirty Harry (Eastwood) becomes involved in solving a series of murders
from San Francisco to a small town upstate. Horace King (Popwell), his best friend
on the force, tries to help him out and gets killed in the process. Four black men
(actors unidentified) are stopped by Harry in their attempt to hold up his favorite
diner.

SUGAR HILL

Cast: Wesley Snipes*, Ernie Hudson*, Leslie Uggams*, Clarence Williams III*, Michael Wright*, Khandi Alexander*, Kimberly Russell*, DeVaughn Nixon*, Theresa Randle*, Vondie Curtis-Hall*, Donald Adeosun Faison*, O.L. Duke*, Dulee Hill*, Sam Gordon*, Marquise Wilson*, Lord Michael Banks*, Alex Brown*, Abe Vigoda
Director: Leon Ichaso, Bojan Rosenberg, Marc Abraham
Executive Producer: Armyan Bernstein, Marc Abraham, Tom Rosenberg
Music Performer: Terence Blanchard*
Music by: Terence Blanchard*
Producer: Armyan Bernstein, Rudy Langlais, Gregory Brown, Marc Abraham, Tom Rosenberg
Screenwriter: Barry Michael Cooper*
Tech Info: color/sound/123 min.   Type: Dramatic Feature
Date: 1994   Origin: USA
Company: Beacon Communications, South Street Entertainment
Distributors/Format: Fox Home Video (1/2")
Annotation: As children in Harlem, Roemello and Raynathan Skuggs (Snipes and Wright) see their mother (Alexander) die of an overdose and their father (Williams), a musician-turned-junkie, permanently crippled by Mafia drug boss Gus (Vigoda) thugs. They turn to the drug life themselves and prosper, but Roemello falls in love with aspiring actress Melissa (Randle), and is determined to get out of the business, much to his brother's consternation. Uggams plays Melissa's mother Doris Holly; Hudson plays Lolly, a boxer turned drug dealer.

SUMMER RENTAL

Cast: Dick Anthony Williams*, Saundra Dunson-Franks*, Tanzia Franks*, Walter Franks*, Richard Crenna, John Candy, Karen Austin
Director: Carl Reiner
Executive Producer: Bernie Brillstein
Music by: Alan Silvestri
Producer: Bernie Brillstein, George Shapiro
Screenwriter: Jeremy Stevens, Mark Reisman
Tech Info: color/sound/88 min.   Type: Comedy Feature
Date: 1985   Origin: USA
Company: Paramount
Distributors/Format: Paramount Home Video (1/2")
Annotation: Jack Chester (Candy), an overworked airline traffic controller, is told by his supervisor to take a vacation. He sets off with his wife (Austin) and three children for a summer break that gets out of control. Williams plays Dan Gardner, affluent owner of the first summer house Chester and his wife occupy by mistake. Dunson-Franks is his wife, Tanzia and Walter Franks, their children.

SUMMER SCHOOL

Cast: Kelly Jo Minter*, Duane Davis*, Kirstie Alley, Mark Harmon, Robin Thomas, Patrick Laborteaux
Director: Carl Reiner
Executive Producer: Marc Trabulas
Music by: Danny Elfman
Producer: Howard West, George Shapiro, Marc Trabulas
Screenwriter: Jeff Franklin
Storywriter: Stuart Birnbaum, David Dashev, Jeff Franklin

Tech Info: color/sound/98 min.   Type: Comedy Feature
Date: 1987   Origin: USA
Company: Paramount
Distributors/Format: Paramount (1/2")
Annotation: Freddy Shoop (Harmon) is a lazy teacher looking forward to summer vacation in Hawaii when he learns he must teach a summer school class full of misfits and clowns. Minter plays Denise Green and Davis is Jerome Watkins.

SUPER SOUL BROTHER
Cast: Joycelyn Norris*, Benny Latimore*, Wild Savage*, Addie Williams*, Peter Conrad, Lee Cross
Director: Wildman Steve *
Screenwriter: Vernon Gibbs
Tech Info: color/sound/80 min.   Type: Comedy Feature
Date: 1989   Origin: USA
Distributors/Format: Xenon Entertainment Group (1/2")
Archives/Format: IUB - BFC/A (1/2")
Annotation: Wildman Steve is targeted by a crazed doctor who concocts a potion to make him a "super soul brother." The unsuspecting Steve is led through a series of bank robberies, jewel thievery and "bad" women.

SUPER, THE
Cast: Paul Benjamin*, Carol-Jean Lewis*, LaTanya Richardson*, Paul Bates*, Kenny Blank*, Todd Monteiro*, Beatrice Winde*, Joe Pesci
Director: Rod Daniel
Producer: Charles Gordon
Screenwriter: Sam Simon
Tech Info: color/sound/86 min.   Type: Comedy Feature
Date: 1991   Origin: USA
Company: Largo Entertainment
Distributors/Format: Fox Home Video (1/2")
Annotation: Slum lord Louie Kritsky (Pesci) is confined by a court order to live in his own tenant building until he repairs all the apartments. Richardson plays the Judge who sentences him. Tito (Blank) is the young boy who unwilling befriends Kritsky. Eleanor (Lewis), Gilliam (Benjamin), and Leotha (Winde), are Kritsky's fellow tenants whose problems become his own.

SUPERMAN III
Cast: Richard Pryor*, Courtney B. Vance*, Al Matthews*, Margot Kidder, Annette O'Toole, Robert Vaughn, Christopher Reeves
Director: Richard Lester
Executive Producer: Ilya Salkind
Music Performer: Chaka Khan*, Roger Miller, Marshall Crenshaw
Music by: Giorgio Moroder, Ken Thorne
Producer: Pierre Spengler, Ilya Salkind
Screenwriter: David Newman
Tech Info: color/sound/125 min.   Type: Dramatic Feature

Date: 1983   Origin: USA
Company: Alexander Salkind
Distributors/Format: Warner Bros. Home Video, Inc. (1/2")
Annotation: Gus Gorman (Pryor), a computer operator, is recruited to help destroy coffee production in Columbia using his computer. He develops a form of kryptonite that turns Superman (Reeves) into an evil villain, but when Gus's boss tries to kill Superman, Gus recognizes his mistake. Matthews makes a brief appearance as the fire chief.

SUPERNATURALS, THE
Cast: LeVar Burton*, Nichelle Nichols*, Maxwell Caulfield, Talia Balsam
Director: Armand Mastroianni
Executive Producer: Sandy Howard, Mel Pearl, Don Levin
Music by: Robert O. Ragland
Producer: Sandy Howard, Michael Murphey, Joel Soisson, Mel Pearl, Don Levin
Screenwriter: Michael Murphey, Joel Soisson
Tech Info: color/sound/80 min.   Type: Dramatic Feature
Date: 1987   Origin: USA
Company: Republic Entertainment
Annotation: Sgt. Leona Hawkins (Nichols) leads a group of army trainees in a survival mission through the Alabama woodlands. Terrorized by unexplained murders, they discover that skeletal confederate soldiers have risen from their graves to continue fighting the Civil War. Burton is Pvt. Michael Osgood.

SURF II
Cast: Cleavon Little*, Eddie Deezen, Lyle Waggoner, Ruth Buzzi, Morgan Paull
Director: Randall Badat
Music Performer: The Untouchables , The Beach Boys
Music by: Peter Bernstein
Producer: George G. Brainstein, Ron Hamady
Screenwriter: Randall Badat
Tech Info: color/sound/96 min.   Type: Comedy Feature
Date: 1981   Origin: USA
Company: Frank D. Tolin Productions
Annotation: Little makes a special appearance in Surf II as a band leader/principal. His students are all devoted surfers, except for one evil genius who hates the surfers and invents a toxic waste soft drink, Buzzz Cola, that threatens the happy lives of the whole town.

SURF NAZIS MUST DIE
Cast: Gail Neely*, Robert Harden*, Barry Brenner, Michael Sonye
Director: Peter George
Executive Producer: Peter George
Music by: Jon McCallum
Producer: Robert Tinnell, Peter George
Screenwriter: Jon Ayre
Tech Info: color/sound/95 min.   Type: Comedy Feature

Date: 1987   Origin: USA
Company: Institute
Distributors/Format: Troma (16mm)
Annotation: After an earthquake devastates California, neo-Nazis fight for control of
the beach. When, in a racial attack, Leroy (Harden) a chief engineer is killed by the
Nazis, Eleanor (Neely), his mother, exacts revenge.

SURF NINJAS

Cast: Tone-Loc *, Leslie Nielsen, Ernie Reyes Sr., Rob Schneider, Ernie Reyes Jr.,
Nicolas Cowan
Director: Neal Israel
Executive Producer: Dan Gordon, Sara Risher, Kevin Moreton
Music by: David Kitay
Producer: Dan Gordon, Sara Risher, Kevin Moreton, Evzen Kolar
Storywriter: Dan Gordon
Tech Info: color/sound/87 min.   Type: Comedy Feature
Date: 1993   Origin: USA
Company: New Line
Distributors/Format: New Line Cinema Home Video (1/2")
Annotation: Two young brothers, Johnny (Reyes) and Adam (Cowan), are happy
surfers until they discover they're actually heirs to an island kingdom. With the help
of some allies and an ancient magic, the brothers are transformed from mere surfers
to super ninjas and are able to overcome the demented despot Colonel Chi
(Nielson). Tone-Loc plays Lieutenant Spence.

SURRENDER

Cast: Iman *, Peter Boyle, Steve Guttenberg, Michael Caine, Sally Field, Julie
Kavner
Director: Jerry Belson
Executive Producer: Yoram Globus, Menahem Golan
Music by: Michel Colombier
Producer: Yoram Globus, Aaron Spelling, Menahem Golan, Alan Greisman
Screenwriter: Jerry Belson
Tech Info: color/sound/96 min.   Type: Comedy Feature
Date: 1987   Origin: USA
Company: Cannon
Distributors/Format: Warner Bros. Home Video, Inc. (1/2")
Annotation: Daisy Morgan (Field), an artist, and Sean Stein (Caine), a novelist, fall in
love after being tied up together during a museum heist. Iman appears as Hedy.

SURVIVING THE GAME

Cast: Ice-T *, Charles S. Dutton*, Gary Busey, Rutger Hauer, F. Murray Abraham
Director: Ernest Dickerson*
Executive Producer: Kevin J. Messick
Music by: Stewart Copeland
Producer: David Permut, Kevin J. Messick
Screenwriter: Eric Bernt
Tech Info: color/sound/96 min.   Type: Dramatic Feature

Date: 1994   Origin: USA
Company: Permut Presentations
Distributors/Format: New Line Cinema (16mm; 3/4"; 1/2")
Annotation: After his family and all of his friends die unexpectedly, Jack Mason
(Ice-T) throws himself in front of a truck but is pulled away at the last minute by Cole
(Dutton) and Burns (Hauer) who hire him as a hunting guide. When he learns he's
the game, Mason figures out how to survive.

SURVIVORS

Producer: Black Coalition for AIDS Prevention*, Inner City Films
Speaker: Leslie *
Tech Info: color/sound/48 min.   Type: Documentary Short
Date: 1993   Origin: USA
Studio: Independent
Distributors/Format: Filmakers Library, Inc. (16mm; 1/2")
Annotation: The film explores the impact of AIDS on a young married black couple
and their family. When a doctor's visit reveals Leslie is HIV positive, she must deal
not only with the threat to her health, but also with the suspicions of her husband's
fidelity.

SUSPECT

Cast: Bill Cobbs*, Dennis Quaid, Myra Taylor, Cher , Liam Neeson
Director: Peter Yates
Executive Producer: John Patrick Veitch
Music by: Michael Kamen
Producer: John Patrick Veitch, Daniel A. Sherkow
Screenwriter: Eric Roth
Tech Info: color/sound/118 min.   Type: Dramatic Feature
Date: 1987   Origin: USA
Company: TriStar, ML Delphi Premier
Annotation: When deaf-mute Vietnam veteran Carl Wayne Anderson (Neeson) is
wrongly accused of murder, public defender Kathleen Riley (Cher) is helped by jurist
Eddie Sanger (Quaid) to acquit her client. Cobbs plays Arraignment Judge Franklin.

SUTURE

Cast: Dennis Haysbert*, Dina Merrill*, Mel Harris, Sab Shimino, Michael Harris
Director: David Siegel
Executive Producer: Steven Soderbergh, Michelle Halberstadt
Music by: Cary Berger
Producer: Scott McGehee, David Siegel, Steven Soderbergh, Michelle Halberstadt
Screenwriter: Scott McGehee, David Siegel
Tech Info: bw/sound/96 min.   Type: Dramatic Feature
Date: 1994   Origin: USA
Company: Suture Pictures Inc., Kino-Korsakoff
Distributors/Format: Facets Multimedia, Inc. (1/2"), Suture Pictures (16mm)
Annotation: Vincent Towers (Harris) attempts to murder his nearly identical
half-brother Clay Arlington (Haysbert) in order to fake his own death.

SUZANNE, SUZANNE
Director: Camille Billops*, James Hatch
Music Performer: Camille Billops*, Christa Victoria*
Music by: Christa Victoria*
Producer: Camille Billops*, James Hatch
Speaker: Alma Dotson*, Billie Browning*, Damon Browning*, Michael Browning*, Peter Browning*, Suzanne Browning*
Tech Info: bw/sound/30 min.   Type: Documentary Short
Date: 1982   Origin: USA
Studio: Independent
Company: Hatch-Billops Production
Distributors/Format: Third World Newsreel (1/2")
Archives/Format: IUB - BFC/A (1/2")
Annotation: Suzanne, who is subject and narrator of the film, recounts her experience with her abusive father, and with drugs. The documentary addresses the effects of violence on the entire family and their attempt to cope after the father's death.

SWEET BIRD OF YOUTH
Cast: Renee Trin-iana *, James Anderson*
Director: Zeinabu irene Davis*
Music Performer: Sweet Honey in the Rock *
Music by: Sweet Honey in the Rock *
Producer: Zeinabu irene Davis*
Tech Info: color/sound/5 min.   Type: Documentary Short
Date: 1986   Origin: USA
Company: Wimmin with a Mission Productions
Annotation: The joys and pitfalls of aging are set to music by Sweet Honey in the Rock in this music video.

SWEET LIBERTY
Cast: Lynn Thigpen*, Alan Alda, Michael Caine, Bob Hoskins, Lise Hilboldt, Michelle Pfeiffer
Director: Alan Alda
Executive Producer: Louis A. Stroller
Music by: Bruce Broughton
Producer: Martin Bregman, Louis A. Stroller
Screenwriter: Alan Alda
Tech Info: color/sound/107 min.   Type: Comedy Feature
Date: 1986   Origin: USA
Company: Universal
Distributors/Format: Universal Home Video (1/2")
Annotation: Michael Burgess (Alda), a professor at a small North Carolina college, sells a revolutionary war novel to filmmakers and is shocked at the liberties they take with his script. Thigpen plays Claire.

SWEET PERFECTION
Cast: Stone/Stoney Jackson*, Tatiana Tumbtzen*, Reggie Theus*, Anthony Norman McKay*, Catero Colbert*, Lisa Cruzat*
Director: Darryl Roberts*
Producer: Darryl Roberts*, Theresa McDade*, William McDade, Kari A. Coken

Screenwriter: Darryl Roberts*, Theresa McDade*, Ivory Ocean
Tech Info: color/sound/90 min.   Type: Dramatic Feature
Date: 1987   Origin: USA
Studio: Independent
Company: A Darryl Roberts Production
Distributors/Format: Xenon Entertainment Group (1/2")
Annotation: Jackson stars in this expose of the realities of the rich and glamourous world of black Hollywood during a "perfect model" contest. A poor social outcast attempts to break into that world.

SWEET POTATO RIDE

Cast: De Juan Guy*
Director: Kim Greene*, Camille Tucker*
Tech Info: color/sound/41 min.   Type: Docudrama
Date: 1994   Origin: USA
Studio: Independent
Distributors/Format: Carousel Films (16mm)
Annotation: The film depicts a day in the life of 10-year-old African American Jelani Williams who runs away from home to escape punishment. From his journey through the Crenshaw District neighborhood of Los Angeles, he learns to appreciate his family and home.

SWINGIN' THE BLUES: COUNT BASIE

Director: Matthew Seig
Music Performer: Count Basie and his Orchestra*, Count Basie*
Speaker: Count Basie*
Tech Info: mixed/sound/60 min.   Type: Documentary Feature
Date: 1992   Origin: USA
Studio: Independent
Distributors/Format: Facets Multimedia, Inc. (1/2")
Annotation: The film follows the musical growth of Count Basie. Songs include: "One O'Clock Jump," "Air Mail Special," and "I Left My Baby."

SYVILLA: THEY DANCE TO HER DRUM

Cast: Edwina L. Tyler*, Aaron Singer*, Dyane Harvey*, Tatim Abdul Quadr*
Director: Ayoka Chenzira*
Narrator: Ayoka Chenzira*
Producer: Ayoka Chenzira*
Speaker: Syvilla Fort*
Tech Info: bw/sound/25 min.   Type: Documentary Short
Date: 1979   Origin: USA
Studio: Independent
Distributors/Format: Third World Newsreel (1/2")
Archives/Format: IUB - BFC/A (1/2")
Annotation: The film, a tribute to dance teacher Syvilla Fort, documents her unique teaching style. Her students speak about their admiration for her excellence and firmness in instructing the fundamentals of dance.

T.A.G.: THE ASSASSINATION GAME
Cast: Michael Winslow*, Linda Hamilton, Robert Carradine, Bruce Abbott
Director: Nick Castle
Music by: Craig Safan
Producer: Peter Rosten, Dan Rosenthal
Screenwriter: Nick Castle
Tech Info: color/sound/92 min.   Type: Dramatic Feature
Date: 1982   Origin: USA
Company: New World
Annotation: Gersh (Abbott) and Susan (Hamilton) are college students engaged in a game hunting each other with rubber-tipped dart guns. When Gersh starts to take the play too seriously, Susan turns to Alex (Carradine) for help. Winslow plays Gowdy.

TAKE DOWN
Cast: Kevin Hooks*, "T" Oney Smith*, Stephen Furst, Larry Miller, Edward Herrmann, Kathleen Lloyd
Director: Keith Merrill
Music by: Merrill B. Jenson
Producer: Keith Merrill
Screenwriter: Keith Merrill, Eric Hendershot
Tech Info: color/sound/107 min.   Type: Dramatic Feature
Date: 1979   Origin: USA
Company: American Film
Distributors/Format: Buena Vista Home Video (1/2")
Annotation: High-school English teacher Ed Branish (Herrmann) is given the task of coaching the school's unsuccessful wrestling team. Hooks plays Jasper Macgruder.

TAKING CARE OF BUSINESS
Alternate: Filofax
Cast: Ken Foree*, Michele Harrell*, James Belushi, Charles Grodin, Anne DeSalvo, Loryn Locklin
Director: Arthur Hiller
Executive Producer: Paul Mazursky
Music by: Stewart Copeland
Producer: Paul Mazursky, Geoffrey Taylor
Screenwriter: Jeffrey Abrams, Jill Mazursky
Tech Info: color/sound/108 min.   Type: Comedy Feature
Date: 1990   Origin: USA
Company: Silver Screen Partners IV, Hollywood Pictures
Distributors/Format: Buena Vista Home Video (1/2")
Annotation: Jimmy Dworski (Belushi), a convict who's been let out of prison to go to a World Series game, takes over the life of Spencer Barnes (Grodin) a businessman whose filofax he found. Foree appears as J.B.

TAKING OF BEVERLY HILLS, THE
Cast: Jason Blicker*, Ken Wahl, William Prince, Matt Frewer, Harley Jane Kozak
Director: Sidney J. Furie
Executive Producer: Barry Spikings, Rick Finkelstein
Music by: Jan Hammer
Producer: Barry Spikings, Graham Henderson, Rick Finkelstein

Screenwriter: Rick Natkin, David Fuller, David J. Burke
Storywriter: Sidney J. Furie, Rick Natkin, David Fuller
Tech Info: color/sound/95 min.　　Type: Dramatic Feature
Date: 1991　Origin: USA
Company: Nelson Entertainment, David Giler Productions
Distributors/Format: Columbia Pictures (16mm)
Annotation: A group of ex-policemen try to take over a remote city by staging a phony toxic-chemical spill as a means to evacuate the city. Terry "Boomer" Hayes (Wahl) is called in to save the day. Blicker plays a policeman in several scenes and a thief in others.

TAKING THE HEAT

Cast: Lynn Whitfield*, Peter Boyle, George Segal, Tony Goldwyn, Alan Arkin
Director: Robert Stevens, Tom Mankiewicz
Executive Producer: Frederick Schneier
Music by: Patrick Williams
Producer: Neal Israel, Gary Hoffman, Frederick Schneier
Screenwriter: Dan Gordon
Storywriter: Gary Hoffman
Tech Info: color/sound/91 min.　　Type: Dramatic Feature
Date: 1993　Origin: USA
Company: Viacom, Hoffman/Isreal Productions
Distributors/Format: Fox Home Video (1/2")
Annotation: New Yorker Michael Norell (Goldwyn) is hunted by both hit men and police after he witnesses a murder committed by a crime boss (Arkin). Only a beautiful detective (Whitfield) can get him to court alive and convince him to testify.

TALENT FOR THE GAME

Cast: Felton Perry*, Jamey Sheridan, Edward James Olmos, Lorraine Bracco, Terry Kinney, Jeffery Corbett
Director: Robert M. Young
Executive Producer: David Wisnievitz
Music by: David Newman
Producer: Martin Elfand, David Wisnievitz
Screenwriter: David Himmelstein, Larry Ferguson, Tom Donnelly
Tech Info: color/sound/91 min.　　Type: Dramatic Feature
Date: 1991　Origin: USA
Company: Paramount
Distributors/Format: Paramount Home Video (1/2")
Annotation: Virgil Sweet (Olmos), a baseball player turned scout, discovers Sammy Bodeen (Corbett) in Iowa. Despite a shaky start in the major leagues, Sammy pulls through. Perry plays Fred.

TALES FROM THE DARKSIDE

Cast: Rae Dawn Chong*, Nicole Leach*, Daniel Harrison*, James Remar
Director: John Harrison
Music by: John Harrison
Producer: Richard Rubinstein
Screenwriter: Michael McDowell, George A. Romero
Tech Info: mixed/sound/93 min.　　Type: Dramatic Feature

Date: 1991   Origin: USA
Company: Paramount
Distributors/Format: Paramount Home Video (1/2")
Annotation: The film is composed of three stories. In "Lover's Vow," Chong is Carola, the mysterious woman who Preston, (Remar) happens to meet on the night he promises a gargoyle not to mention its existence. Ten years later, Carola and Preston are married with children, John (Harrison) and Margaret (Leach). Preston betrays his secret to his wife with surprising consequences.

TALKIN' DIRTY AFTER DARK

Cast: Reynaldo Rey*, Martin Lawrence*, John Witherspoon*, Phyllis Yvonne Stickney*, Yolanda King*, Tom "Tiny" Lister Jr.*, Jedda Jones*, Renee Jones*, Martin Wright-Bey*, Dwayne Kennedy*, Rodney Winfield*, Darryl Sivad*, Lance Crouther*, Mark Curry*, Def Jef *, La Wanda Page*, Toukie A. Smith*, Simply Marvelous *, Myra J. *, Misa *, Joe Torry*, James Stevens III*, Chino "Fats" Williams*
Director: Topper Carew*
Music by: Matt Ender
Producer: Topper Carew*, Patricia A. Stallone
Storywriter: Topper Carew*
Tech Info: color/sound/87 min.   Type: Comedy Feature
Date: 1991   Origin: USA
Company: New Line Cinema
Distributors/Format: Facets Multimedia, Inc. (1/2"), New Line Cinema Home Video (1/2")
Annotation: Dukie's (Witherspoon) Comedy Club is where several stand-up comedians use sex, blackmail, and money to climb the ladder of success. Terry Lumbar (Lawrence) uses Dukie's wife Ruby-Lin (Jones) to advance his career, while Dukie's hottest comedy act, Aretha (Stickney) manipulates Dukie, forcing him to desert Ruby-Lin.

TALKING TO STRANGERS

Cast: Caron Tate*, Marvin Hunter, Ken Gruz, Dennis Jordan, Bill Sanders
Director: Rob Tregenza
Producer: J.K. Eareckson
Screenwriter: Rob Tregenza
Tech Info: color/sound/92 min.   Type: Dramatic Feature
Date: 1988   Origin: USA
Company: Baltimore Film Factory
Annotation: In nine randomly ordered long takes, Jesse (Gruz), a condescending "artiste," talks to nine strangers including a homeless man, a wanna-be fashion model, and Ms. Taylor (Tate), a bank loan officer who shares her personal history with him.

TALONS OF THE EAGLE

Cast: Billy Blanks*, Jalal Merhi, James Hong, Priscilla Barnes, Eric Lee
Director: Michael Kennedy
Music by: VaRouje
Producer: Jalal Merhi
Screenwriter: J. Stephen Maunder
Tech Info: color/sound/96 min.   Type: Dramatic Feature

Date: 1992   Origin: Canada
Company: Film One Productions
Distributors/Format: MCA/Universal Home Video (1/2")
Annotation: Two New York City DEA agents Tyler Wilson (Blanks) and Michael Reed (Merhi) are trained in the lethal martial arts technique "Eagle Claw" so that they can defeat the evil drug lord Master Pan.

TANK

Cast: Dorian Harewood*, T. Renee Crutcher*, C. Thomas Howell, Shirley Jones, James Garner
Director: Marvin J. Chomsky
Music by: Lalo Schifrin
Producer: Irwin Yablans
Screenwriter: Dan Gordon
Tech Info: color/sound/113 min.   Type: Comedy Feature
Date: 1984   Origin: USA
Company: Lorimar
Distributors/Format: Universal Home Video (1/2")
Annotation: Zack (Garner), an Army officer nearing retirement, uses his personal Sherman tank to free his son who has been unjustly imprisoned. Harewood portrays Sgt. Tippet; Crutcher is Gwen Tippet.

TAP

Cast: Etta James*, Gregory Hines*, Howard "Sandman" Sims*, Bunny Briggs*, Joe Morton*, Dick Anthony Williams*, Suzzanne Douglas*, Savion Glover*, Arthur Duncan*, Harold Nicholas*, Jimmy Blyde*, Michael Goldfinger*, Jinaki *, Jane Goldberg, Dianne Walker
Director: Nick Castle
Producer: Gary Adelson, Richard Vane
Screenwriter: Nick Castle
Tech Info: color/sound/110 min.   Type: Musical Feature
Date: 1989   Origin: USA
Company: Gary Adelson Production
Distributors/Format: TriStar Pictures Inc. (1/2")
Annotation: Max Washington (Hines), a recently released convict, returns to his roots in the city to tap with his father's best friend, Little Mo (Davis). They are joined by tap dancing greats Nicholas, Sims, Duncan, Blyde, Condos, and Briggs. Max's real love is Little Mo's daughter Amy (Douglas) and her son Louis (Glover), but Max complicates the relationship with his involvement in an insurance scam with Nicki (Morton) and Francis (Williams).

TAPS

Cast: Giancarlo Esposito*, Tom Cruise, Ronny Cox, George C. Scott, Timothy Hutton
Director: Harold Becker
Producer: Stanley R. Jaffe, Howard B. Jaffe
Screenwriter: Robert Mark Kamen, Darryl Ponicsan, James Lineberger
Tech Info: color/sound/119 min.   Type: Dramatic Feature

Date: 1981   Origin: USA
Company: Fox
Distributors/Format: Fox Home Video (1/2")
Annotation: Brian Moreland (Hutton) leads his fellow students at a military academy in a revolt when the school is slated for closing. Esposito plays J.C. Pierce.

TC 2000
Cast: Billy Blanks*, Bobbie Phillips, Jalal Merhi, Bolo Yeung, Matthias Hues
Director: T.J. Scott
Music by: Varouje Hagopian
Producer: Jalal Merhi
Screenwriter: T.J. Scott
Storywriter: J. Stephen Maunder
Tech Info: color/sound/92 min.   Type: Dramatic Feature
Date: 1993   Origin: Canada
Company: Shapiro Glickenhaus Entertainment, Film One Prod.
Distributors/Format: MCA/Universal Home Video (1/2")
Annotation: Jason Storm (Blanks) fends off attackers from Surface World in the earth's 21st century.

TEACHERS
Cast: Morgan Freeman*, Virginia Capers*, Nick Nolte, Judd Hirsch, JoBeth Williams
Director: Arthur Hiller
Executive Producer: Irwin Russo
Music by: Sandy Gibson
Producer: Aaron Russo, Irwin Russo
Screenwriter: W.R. McKinney
Storywriter: Aaron Russo, Irwin Russo
Tech Info: color/sound/106 min.   Type: Comedy Feature
Date: 1984   Origin: USA
Company: MGM
Distributors/Format: United Artists Home Video (1/2")
Annotation: A recent graduate sues JFK High School for letting him leave as an illiterate. Freeman plays Lewis and Capers is the landlady.

TELEPHONE, THE
Cast: Whoopi Goldberg*, Elliot Gould, Severn Darden, John Heard, Amy Wright, Ronald J. Stallings
Director: Rip Torn
Music by: Christopher Young
Producer: Moctesuma Esparza, Robert Katz
Screenwriter: Harry Nilsson, Terry Southern
Tech Info: color/sound/82 min.   Type: Comedy Feature
Date: 1988   Origin: USA
Company: Odyssey
Distributors/Format: New World Home Video (1/2")
Annotation: Vashti Blue (Goldberg) is a struggling actress who spends her time acting out a variety of roles over the telephone.

TERMINATOR 2: JUDGMENT DAY

Cast: Joe Morton*, S. Epatha Merkerson*, DeVaughn Nixon*, Gerard Williams*, Arnold Schwarzenegger, Linda Hamilton
Director: James Cameron
Producer: B.J. Rack, James Cameron
Storywriter: James Cameron
Tech Info: color/sound   Type: Dramatic Feature
Date: 1991   Origin: USA
Company: Mario Kassar, Pacific Western, Lightstorm Entert.
Distributors/Format: Carolco (1/2")
Annotation: Miles Dyson (Morton) is a scientist at a computer lab who is working with the computer chip and arm of the terminator that Sarah Connor (Hamilton) killed ten years ago. Sarah finds Dyson and tries to kill him. The Terminator stops her and explains to Dyson that he is responsible for building independently thinking computers which will destroy the world on August 29, 1997. Dyson joins with Sarah and the Terminator to save the world.

TERMINATOR, THE

Cast: Paul Winfield*, Lance Henriksen, Michael Biehn, Arnold Schwarzenegger, Linda Hamilton
Director: James Cameron
Executive Producer: Derek Gibson, John Daly
Music by: Brad Fiedel
Producer: Gale Anne Hurd, Derek Gibson, John Daly
Screenwriter: Gale Anne Hurd, James Cameron, William Wisher Jr.
Tech Info: color/sound/108 min.   Type: Dramatic Feature
Date: 1984   Origin: USA
Company: Hemdale, Pacific Western
Distributors/Format: Orion Home Video (1/2")
Annotation: In post-nuclear Los Angeles, 2029, the Terminator (Schwarzenegger) sets out to kill Sarah Conner (Hamilton) and Kyle Reese (Biehn) her protector. Winfield plays Chief of Police Traxler.

THANK GOD IT'S FRIDAY

Cast: Donna Summer*, The Commodores *, Ray Vitle*, DeWayne Jessie*, Jeff Goldblum, Valerie Landsburg, Terri Nunn
Director: Robert Klane
Music Performer: Diana Ross*, Donna Summer*, The Commodores *, Fifth Dimension *, Thelma Houston*, Village People
Producer: Bob Cohen
Screenwriter: Barry Armyan Bernstein
Tech Info: color/sound/89 min.   Type: Musical Feature
Date: 1978   Origin: USA
Company: Motown-Casablanca
Distributors/Format: Columbia Pictures Home Video (1/2")
Annotation: Bobby Speed (Vitle), a Los Angeles club DJ, schedules The Commodores to perform. Nichole Sims (Summer) tries to see Bobby so she can break into the music business. She gets her chance with Bobby and he becomes "King of Music."

THAT RHYTHM, THOSE BLUES

Director: George T. Nierenberg
Music Performer: Ruth Brown*, Charles Brown*, Fats Domino*
Producer: George T. Nierenberg, Lindsay Fontana
Screenwriter: David G. McCullough
Speaker: Ruth Brown*, Charles Brown*, Bobby Robinson*, Eddie Williams*, Shelly Stewart*, B.B Beamon*, Reverend Al Dixon*, Jerry Wekler
Tech Info: mixed/sound/56 min.   Type: Documentary Feature
Date: 1988   Origin: USA
Studio: Independent
Company: A George T. Nierenberg Production
Archives/Format: IUB - BFC/A; IUB - AAAMC (1/2")
Annotation: Charles Brown and Ruth Brown speak of their real life experiences as black artists black-balled by the white music industry. Record producers Robinson and Wekler discuss the overnight phenomenon of Rock n' Roll's success DJs. "Diggie Doo" and "Shelley The Playboy" reiterate that there was no black marketing accessibility before 1945.

THAT WAS THEN...THIS IS NOW

Cast: Morgan Freeman*, Larry B. Scott*, Emilio Estevez, Craig Sheffer, Kim Delaney
Director: Christopher Cain
Music by: Keith Olsen, Bill Cuomo
Producer: Gary R. Lindberg, John M. Ondov
Screenwriter: Emilio Estevez
Tech Info: color/sound/102 min.   Type: Dramatic Feature
Date: 1985   Origin: USA
Company: Media Ventures, Alan Belkin
Distributors/Format: Paramount (1/2")
Annotation: When his father goes to jail for killing his mother, Mark Jennings (Estevez) goes to live with his friend Byron Douglas (Sheffer). Mark reacts badly when Byron starts to grow away from him. Scott plays Terry Jones and Freeman plays Charlie Woods.

THAT'S BLACK ENTERTAINMENT

Cast: Lena Horne*, Paul Robeson*, Nat King Cole*, Cab Calloway*, Spencer Williams*, Stepin Fetchit*,
Director: William Greaves*, G. William Jones
Executive Producer: Norm Revis Jr., David Arpin
Narrator: William Greaves*
Producer: G. William Jones, Fred T. Kuehnert, Norm Revis Jr., David Arpin
Screenwriter: G. William Jones
Tech Info: mixed/sound/60 min.   Type: Documentary Feature
Date: 1989   Origin: USA
Studio: Independent
Company: Skyline Entertainment
Distributors/Format: VCI---Video Communications Inc. (1/2")
Archives/Format: IUB - BFC/A (1/2")
Annotation: In the 1930s and 1940s, an underground film industry sprang up in the black community. Rare and historic movie footage from many forgotten films has been compiled in this tribute to treasures of black cinema.

THAT'S LIFE!

Cast: Theodore "Teddy" Wilson*, Jack Lemmon, Sally Kellerman, Robert Loggia, Julie Andrews
Director: Blake Edwards
Executive Producer: Jonathan D. Krane
Music by: Henry Mancini
Producer: Tony Adams, Jonathan D. Krane
Screenwriter: Blake Edwards, Milton Wexler
Tech Info: color/sound/102 min.   Type: Comedy Feature
Date: 1986   Origin: USA
Company: Paradise Cove, Ubilam
Distributors/Format: Columbia Pictures Home Video (1/2")
Annotation: Harvey (Lemmon) and Gillian Fairchild (Andrews) are each in crisis. Harvey's turning 60 and Gillian has had a potentially cancerous node removed from her throat. Wilson plays Corey.

THELONIOUS MONK: AMERICAN COMPOSER

Director: Matthew Seig
Music Performer: Thelonious Monk*
Speaker: Barry Harris, Randy Weston, Ben Riley, Billy Taylor
Tech Info: mixed/sound/60 min.   Type: Documentary Feature
Date: 1991   Origin: USA
Studio: Independent
Distributors/Format: Facets Multimedia, Inc. (1/2")
Annotation: The music of Monk demonstrates his groundbreaking innovation. Tunes include: "'Round Midnight," "Blue Monk," "Criss Cross," "Just a Gigolo," and others. Weston, Harris, Riley, Taylor and family members share their insights.

THELONIOUS MONK: STRAIGHT NO CHASER

Director: Charlotte Zwerin
Executive Producer: Clint Eastwood
Music Performer: Thelonious Monk*
Producer: Clint Eastwood, Bruce Ricker, Charlotte Zwerin
Speaker: Charlie Rouse*, Thelonious Monk, Jr.*, Barry Harris, Harry Colomby, Tommy Flanagan, Bob Jones
Tech Info: mixed/sound/90 min.   Type: Documentary Feature
Date: 1988   Origin: USA
Company: Warner Bros.
Distributors/Format: Warner Bros. Home Video, Inc. (1/2")
Archives/Format: IUB - BFC/A (1/2" Promotional)
Annotation: The film is a documentary of the legendary pianist. Songs include: "Evidence," "Rhythm-a-Ning--On the Bean," "'Round Midnight," "Well, You Needn't" and many more.

THEY LIVE

Cast: Sy Richardson*, Raymond St. Jacques*, Dana Bratton*, David Keith, "Rowdy" Roddy Piper, Meg Foster, George "Buck" Flower
Director: John Carpenter
Executive Producer: Shep Gordon, Andre Blay
Music by: John Carpenter, Alan Howarth
Producer: Larry Franco, Shep Gordon, Andre Blay

Screenwriter: John Carpenter
Storywriter: Ray Nelson
Tech Info: color/sound/93 min.   Type: Dramatic Feature
Date: 1988   Origin: USA
Company: Alive
Distributors/Format: Universal Pictures (16mm; 1/2")
Annotation: Transient construction worker John Nada (Piper) dons a pair of hip sunglasses and sees the world for what it really is--filled with oppressive subliminal messages and an alien upper class. St. Jacques appears as a street preacher; Richardson is a revolutionary; and Bratton plays a drug-addict.

THEY STILL CALL ME BRUCE
Cast: Robert Guillaume*, David Mendenhall, Johnny Yune, Pat Paulsen, Carl Bensen, Bethany Wright
Director: James Orr, Johnny Yune
Music by: Morton Stevens
Producer: James Orr, Johnny Yune
Screenwriter: James Orr, Johnny Yune
Tech Info: color/sound/91 min.   Type: Comedy Feature
Date: 1987   Origin: USA
Company: Ji Hee, Panda
Distributors/Format: Shapiro (1/2")
Annotation: Bruce Wan (Yune) comes to Texas to give a priceless gift to the G.I. who saved his life and on the way gets involved with mobsters, a prostitute, and a movie studio. Guillaume is featured as a Veteran's Administration officer.

THING, THE
Cast: Keith David*, T.K. Carter*, Kurt Russell
Director: John Carpenter
Executive Producer: Wilbur Stark
Music by: Ennio Morricone
Producer: David Foster, Lawrence Turman, Wilbur Stark, Jonathan Webb
Screenwriter: Bill Lancaster*
Storywriter: John W. Campbell Jr.
Tech Info: color/sound/109 min.   Type: Dramatic Feature
Date: 1982   Origin: USA
Company: Turman-Foster Company Production
Distributors/Format: MCA Home Video (1/2")
Annotation: MacReady (Russell), Nauls (Carter) and Childs (David) are part of a research team in Antarctica whose camp is attacked by an alien that takes the form of its prey. They decide to blow up the camp, but in the process, Nauls is killed by the thing. Childs and MacReady are the only survivors.

THINNEST LINE, THE
Director: Daresha Kyi*
Tech Info: color/sound/10 min.   Type: Dramatic Short
Date: 1988   Origin: USA
Studio: Independent
Distributors/Format: Women Make Movies, Inc. (16mm; 1/2")
Annotation: Kyi's film explores the jealousy, competition and love between two African American women friends.

THIS IS SPINAL TAP

Alternate: Spinal Tap
Cast: Wonderful Smith*, Gloria Gifford*, Christopher Guest, Rob Reiner, Michael McKean, Harry Shearer
Director: Rob Reiner
Executive Producer: Lindsay Doran
Music by: Christopher Guest, Rob Reiner, Michael McKean, Harry Shearer
Producer: Karen Murphy, Lindsay Doran
Screenwriter: Christopher Guest, Rob Reiner, Michael McKean, Harry Shearer
Tech Info: color/sound/82 min.   Type: Comedy Feature
Date: 1984   Origin: USA
Company: Spinal Tap
Distributors/Format: Embassy Home Video (1/2")
Annotation: "Spinal Tap," an aging British heavy metal band, is filmed by documentarian Marty DeBergi (Reiner) as they experience management woes, accusations of sexism, malfunctioning props, and promotional difficulties. Smith plays the janitor.

THREE FUGITIVES

Cast: James Earl Jones*, Sy Richardson*, Nick Nolte, Martin Short, Sarah Rowland Doroff
Director: Francis Veber
Executive Producer: Francis Veber
Music by: David McHugh
Producer: Francis Veber, Lauren Shuler Donner
Screenwriter: Francis Veber
Tech Info: color/sound/96 min.   Type: Comedy Feature
Date: 1989   Origin: USA
Company: Touchstone, Silver Screen Partners IV
Distributors/Format: Buena Vista Home Video (1/2")
Annotation: Daniel Lewis (Nolte), an ex-convict, is taken hostage by would-be bank robber Ned Perry (Short) who is trying to steal money to send his daughter to school. Jones plays Detective Dugan and Richardson plays Tucker.

THROW MOMMA FROM THE TRAIN

Cast: Branford Marsalis*, Oprah Winfrey*, Danny Devito, Billy Crystal, Anne Ramsey
Director: Danny Devito
Executive Producer: Arne Schmidt
Music by: David Newman
Producer: Larry Brezner, Arne Schmidt
Screenwriter: Stu Silver
Tech Info: color/sound/88 min.   Type: Concert Feature
Date: 1987   Origin: USA
Company: Orion
Distributors/Format: Orion Home Video (1/2")
Annotation: Owen Lift (DeVito) and Larry Donner (Crystal) plan to "swap" murders--Owen will kill Larry's ex-wife and Larry will kill Owen's mother. Marsalis plays Lester and Winfrey plays herself.

THURGOOD MARSHALL: PORTRAIT OF AN AMERICAN HERO
Director: Marvin Hunter
Music Performer: Danny Ayers
Music by: Michael Hearden*, Frank Menzies
Producer: Wayne C. Sharpe*
Storywriter: Wayne C. Sharpe*, Dexter H. Reed, Jesse W. Martin
Tech Info: mixed/sound/28 min.   Type: Documentary Short
Date: 1985   Origin: USA
Company: Columbia
Distributors/Format: WETA Educational Activities (1/2")
Annotation: Using newsreel footage, photos, and interviews with friends and colleagues, this production traces Thurgood Marshall's life from childhood in Baltimore, through his years in college and his law practice.

TIGER SHARK
Cast: Mike Stone, John Quade, Pamela Bryant
Director: Emett Alston
Storywriter: Ivan Rogers*
Tech Info: color/sound/99 min.   Type: Dramatic Feature
Date: 1989   Origin: USA
Company: Chappell
Annotation: Rogers' film is an action story about a martial arts expert who, with an old friend, sets out to rescue his kidnapped girlfriend.

TIGHTROPE
Cast: Janet MacLachlan*, Valerie Thibodeaux*, Clint Eastwood, Genevieve Bujold, Dan Hedaya, Regina Richardson
Director: Richard Tuggle
Music by: Lennie Niehaus
Producer: Clint Eastwood, Fritz Manes
Screenwriter: Richard Tuggle
Tech Info: color/sound/114 min.   Type: Dramatic Feature
Date: 1984   Origin: USA
Company: Malpaso
Distributors/Format: Warner Bros. Home Video, Inc. (1/2")
Annotation: Wes Block (Eastwood), a New Orleans police detective, is on the trail of a killer with a penchant for murdering prostitutes and women who work in massage parlors. MacLachlan plays Dr. Yarlofsky and Thibodeaux is a hooker.

TIM BURTON'S THE NIGHTMARE BEFORE CHRISTMAS
Cast: Ken Page*, Chris Sarandon, Danny Elfman, Catherine O'Hara
Director: Henry Selick
Music by: Danny Elfman
Producer: Tim Burton, Denise DiNovi
Screenwriter: Caroline Thompson
Storywriter: Tim Burton
Tech Info: color/sound/75 min.   Type: Animated Feature

Date: 1993   Origin: USA
Company: Skellington Productions, Touchstone
Distributors/Format: Buena Vista Home Video (1/2")
Annotation: The Pumpkin King of Halloweenland, tires of his holiday and decides to do Christmas this year. After kidnapping Santa and delivering disturbing presents to kids, Jack realizes his mistake. Page provides the voice of Oogie Boogie, the malevolent underworld figure who tries to keep Santa even after Jack returns to release him.

TIME BOMB
Cast: Billy Blanks*, Raymond St. Jacques*, Michael Biehn, Patsy Kensit, Ray "Boom Boom" Mancini
Director: Avi Nesher
Music by: Patrick Leonard
Producer: Raffaella DeLaurentiis
Screenwriter: Avi Nesher
Tech Info: color/sound/96 min.   Type: Dramatic Feature
Date: 1991   Origin: USA
Company: Raffaella Productions, Dino DeLaurentiis Comm.
Distributors/Format: MGM-Pathe (16mm)
Annotation: Eddie Kay (Biehn), a mild-mannered watchmaker, finds himself running into a burning building to rescue a child. This triggers inexplicable flashbacks that, with the help of psychologist Nolmar (Kensit), reveal Eddy's past as a secret subject of CIA brain experiments. When a gang of killers comes after Eddy, Detective Sanchez (St. Jacques) doesn't believe it's anything more than a robbery. Blanks plays Mr. Brown.

TIME HAS COME, THE (1964-1966)
Series: Eyes On The Prize II
Director: Madison Davis Lacey Jr.*, James A. DeVinney
Executive Producer: Henry Hampton*
Music by: Bernice Johnson Reagon*
Narrator: Julian Bond*
Producer: Henry Hampton*, Madison Davis Lacey Jr.*, James A. DeVinney
Screenwriter: Madison Davis Lacey Jr.*, James A. DeVinney
Speaker: Alex Haley*, Harry Belafonte*, Muhammad Ali*, Ossie Davis*, Stokely Carmichael*, James Meredith*, Sonia Sanchez*, Malcolm X *, John Lewis*, Floyd McKissick*, Elijah Muhammad*, Louis Lomax*, Louis Farrakhan*, Willie Ricks*, Mike Wallace
Tech Info: mixed/sound/54 min.   Type: Television Documentary
Date: 1989   Origin: USA
Company: Blackside, Inc.
Distributors/Format: PBS Video (16mm; 1/2")
Archives/Format: IUB - AAAMC (1/2")
Annotation: This segment chronicles the rise of Malcolm X as a leader of the Nation of Islam, his eventual suspension from the group, and his assassination. Malcolm's philosophy inspires Student Nonviolent Coordinating Committee (SNCC) to organize and call for "Black Power" in Mississippi in 1966.

TIME RUNNER
Cast: Rae Dawn Chong*, Mark Hamill, Brion James, Gordon Tipple
Director: Michael Mazo
Music by: Braun Farmon, Robert Smart
Producer: Lloyd A. Simandl, John Curtis
Screenwriter: Greg Derochie, Ron Tarrant, Ian Bray, Christopher Hyde
Storywriter: John Curtis, Greg Derochie
Tech Info: color/sound/90 min.   Type: Dramatic Feature
Date: 1993   Origin: USA
Company: North American Pictures, Excalibur Pictures
Distributors/Format: New Line Cinema Home Video (1/2")
Annotation: During an alien invasion, Michael Raynor (Hamill) gets sucked into a time warp and finds himself on earth 30 years earlier where he's hunted by the same humanoid aliens that he was fighting before. Chong plays Karen, an alien who decides to help Raynor escape.

TIME WALKER
Cast: Austin Stoker*, Shari Belafonte Harper*, Gerard Prendergast*, Ben Murphy, Nina Axelrod, Kevin Brophy
Director: Tom Kennedy
Executive Producer: Robert Shaheen
Music by: Richard Band
Producer: Dimitri Villard, Jason Williams, Robert Shaheen
Screenwriter: Karen Levitt, Tom Friedman
Tech Info: color/sound/83 min.   Type: Dramatic Feature
Date: 1982   Origin: USA
Company: Villard, Wescom
Distributors/Format: New World Home Video (1/2")
Annotation: Belafonte plays Linda in this science fiction film which revolves around resurrected alien creatures who killed King Tut centuries ago.

TIMES SQUARE
Cast: Anna Maria Horsford*, Tiger Haynes*, Tim Curry, Trini Alvarado, Robin Johnson, Peter Coffield
Director: Alan Moyle
Executive Producer: Kevin McCormick, John Nicolella
Producer: Robert Stigwood, Kevin McCormick, John Nicolella, Jacob Brackman
Screenwriter: Jacob Brackman
Storywriter: Alan Moyle, Leanne Unger
Tech Info: color/sound/111 min.   Type: Dramatic Feature
Date: 1980   Origin: USA
Company: Butterfly Valley, RSO
Distributors/Format: AFD (1/2")
Annotation: Pamela Pearl (Alvarado) and Nicky Marotta (Johnson) are teenage girls who try to live on their own near Times Square, eventually becoming musicians. Haynes appears as Andy; Horsford plays Rosie Washington.

TINY AND RUBY: HELL DIVIN' WOMEN

Music Performer: International Sweethearts of Rhythm
Producer: Andrea Weiss*, Greta Schiller
Speaker: Ruby Lucas*, Ernestine "Tiny" Davis*
Tech Info: color/sound/30 min.   Type: Documentary Short
Date: 1988   Origin: USA
Company: Jezebel Productions
Annotation: Jazz trumpeter Ernestine "Tiny" Davis and her friend and partner of over
forty years, drummer Ruby Lucas (a.k.a. Renee Phelan) are profiled.

TO FREE THEIR MINDS

Director: William Greaves*
Producer: William Greaves*
Storywriter: William Greaves*
Tech Info: color/sound/34 min.   Type: Documentary Feature
Date: 1980   Origin: USA
Company: William Greaves* Productions
Distributors/Format: Williams Greaves Productions, Inc. (16mm)
Annotation: Greaves' film, shot candid-camera on location throughout the southern
U.S., deals with the importance of sensitivity and excellence when teaching across
racial lines.

TO LIVE AND DIE IN L.A.

Cast: Gregg Dandridge*, Willem Dafoe, Debra Feuer, William Peterson, John
Pankow
Director: William Friedkin
Executive Producer: Samuel Schulman
Music by: Wang Chung
Producer: Irving H. Levin, Samuel Schulman
Screenwriter: William Friedkin, Gerald Petievich
Tech Info: color/sound/116 min.   Type: Dramatic Feature
Date: 1985   Origin: USA
Company: New Century, SLM
Distributors/Format: MGM/UA Home Video (1/2")
Annotation: Secret service agent Richard Chance (Peterson) seeks his partner's
killer. Dandridge is one of the prison assailants.

TO LOVE, HONOR AND OBEY

Director: Christine Choy, Marlene Dunn
Tech Info: color/sound/55 min.   Type: Documentary Feature
Date: 1980   Origin: USA
Studio: Independent
Distributors/Format: Third World Newsreel (1/2")
Annotation: The film focuses on battered wives and includes an in-depth discussion
of child abuse. It explores the social, psychological, and cultural factors that
contribute to violence against women.

TO SLEEP WITH ANGER

Cast: Danny Glover*, Sheryl Lee Ralph*, Richard Brooks*, Mary Alice*, Reina King*, Vonetta McGee*, Sy Richardson*, Julius Harris*, Wonderful Smith*, Carl Lumbly*, Paul Butler*, DeVaughn Nixon*, Cory Curtis*, Paula Bellamy*, Ethel Ayler*, DeForest Coven*, Davis Roberts*
Director: Charles Burnett*, Peter Medak
Executive Producer: Danny Glover*, Harris E. Tulchin
Music Performer: Sister Rosette Tharpe*, Bobby Blue Bland*, Little Milton Campbell*, Jimmy Witherspoon*, Ethel Agier*, Z.Z. Hill*, Pat Johnson, Stephen James Taylor, Romon Flores, Willie Ornelas, Jim Lancefield, Dave Loeb, Sid Page, Charles Veal, Jennifer Johnson, Carol Castillo, Hershel Wise, Larry Corbett, Dane Little
Producer: Danny Glover*, Darin Scott*, Caldecot Chubb, Thomas S. Byrnes, Harris E. Tulchin
Screenwriter: Charles Burnett*
Tech Info: color/sound/95 min.   Type: Dramatic Feature
Date: 1990   Origin: USA
Company: Edward R. Pressman Film Corp., SVS Films, Inc.
Distributors/Format: Facets Multimedia, Inc. (1/2")
Archives/Format: IUB - BFC/A (1/2")
Annotation: Harry Mention (Glover) shows up unexpectedly one day at the home in Los Angeles of his old friend Gideon (Butler) and Gideon's wife (Alice). Harry's presence intensifies conflicts already present in the family, e.g. between Baby Brother (Brooks) and Junior (Lumbley) that have to be resolved. Ralph plays Linda, Baby Brother's wife; McGee is Pat, Junior's wife.

TOKYO POP

Cast: Gina Belafonte*, Carrie Hamilton, Yutaka Tadokoro, Taiji Tonoyama, Masumi Harukawa
Director: Fran Rubel Kuzui
Executive Producer: Kaz Kuzui, Jonathan Olsberg
Music by: Alan Brewer
Producer: Kaz Kuzui, Kaz Kuzui, Joel Tuber, Jonathan Olsberg
Screenwriter: Fran Rubel Kuzui, Lynn Grossman
Storywriter: Fran Rubel Kuzui
Tech Info: color/sound/97 min.   Type: Comedy Feature
Date: 1988   Origin: Japan
Company: Spectrafilm
Annotation: Reed (Hamilton), a rock singer in New York, decides to visit Tokyo where she teams up with a struggling Japanese band. Belafonte plays Holly.

TONGUES UNTIED

Cast: Steve Langley*, Christopher Prince*, Ron Simmons*, Michael Bell*, Bernard Branner*, Ben Callet*, Gerald Davis*, Kenneth R. Dixon*
Director: Marlon T. Riggs*
Producer: Marlon T. Riggs*, Ron Simmons*
Screenwriter: Joseph Beam*
Speaker: Marlon T. Riggs*, Essex Hemphill*, Larry Duckett*, Wayson Jones*, Gideon Ferebee*, Steve Langley*, Christopher Prince*, Brian Freeman*, A. J. Honey*, Darnell Stephens-Durio
Tech Info: color/sound/55 min.   Type: Experimental Feature

Date: 1989   Origin: USA
Company: Signifyin' Productions
Distributors/Format: Frameline Distribution (1/2"), Signifyin' Works (1/2")
Archives/Format: IUB - BFC/A (1/2")
Annotation: Riggs captures the dilemma faced by black gay men with dual loyalties and identity conflicts regarding being black and being gay. The film uses poetry, anecdote, historical footage, and dramatic re-enactments to explore such concerns as racism, homophobia, crack and AIDS.

TONI MORRISON

Series: Profile of a Writer
Director: Alan Benson
Producer: Alan Benson
Speaker: Toni Morrison*, Guy Gregory*, Bonnie Greer*
Tech Info: mixed/sound/52 min.   Type: Documentary Feature
Date: 1987   Origin: USA
Studio: Independent
Company: Home Vision and RM Arts
Distributors/Format: Facets Multimedia, Inc. (1/2"), Filmic Archives (1/2")
Archives/Format: IUB - AAAMC (1/2")
Annotation: Author Toni Morrison provides insight into the making of "Beloved," Morrison's story of motherhood, slavery, and reincarnation. The film includes oral interpretations from the novel by Gregory and Greer along with Morrison's own explication of how she envisioned "Beloved."

TOO SCARED TO SCREAM

Cast: Rony Clanton*, Leon Isaac Kennedy*, Anne Archer, Mike Conners, Ian McShane
Director: Tony Lo Bianco
Executive Producer: Ken Norris
Music by: George Garvarentz
Producer: Mike Conners, Ken Norris
Screenwriter: Neal Barbera, Glenn Leopold
Tech Info: color/sound/104 min.   Type: Dramatic Feature
Date: 1985   Origin: USA
Company: Doorman
Distributors/Format: Movie Store Home Video (1/2")
Annotation: A maniac doorman (McShane) menaces an upscale Manhattan apartment building. Kennedy is Frank and Clanton plays Barker.

TOOTSIE

Cast: Lynn Thigpen*, Dustin Hoffman, Dabney Coleman, Teri Garr, Jessica Lange
Director: Sydney Pollack
Executive Producer: Charles Evans
Music by: Dave Grusin
Producer: Sydney Pollack, Dick Richards, Charles Evans
Screenwriter: Elaine May, Larry Gelbart, Murray Schisgal
Storywriter: Larry Gelbart, Don McGuire
Tech Info: color/sound/116 min.   Type: Comedy Feature

Date: 1982 Origin: USA
Company: Columbia
Distributors/Format: Columbia Pictures Home Video (1/2")
Annotation: Michael Dorsey (Hoffman) dresses as a woman to land a role on a soap opera. He fools his co-stars but his girlfriend (Garr) suspects he's having an affair. Dorsey (a.k.a. Tootsie) although lusted after by his male co-star, falls for Julie (Lange). Thigpen plays Jo.

TORCH SONG TRILOGY

Cast: Ken Page*, Matthew Broderick, Anne Bancroft, Harvey Fierstein, Brian Kerwin, Eddie Castrodad
Director: Paul Bogart
Executive Producer: Ronald K. Fierstein
Music by: Peter Matz
Producer: Howard Gottfried, Ronald K. Fierstein
Screenwriter: Harvey Fierstein
Storywriter: Harvey Fierstein
Tech Info: color/sound/120 min.   Type: Dramatic Feature
Date: 1988 Origin: USA
Company: Howard Gottfried-Ronald K. Fierstein
Distributors/Format: New Line Cinema Home Video (1/2")
Annotation: Female impersonator Arnold Beckoff (Fierstein) has a full life with two love interests (Kerwin and Broderick), a domineering mother (Bancroft) and a teenage boy (Castrodad) who is in need of a substitute father figure. Page is featured as Murray.

TORTURE OF MOTHERS, THE

Series: International Treasures Collection
Cast: Ruby Dee*, Novella Nelson*, Starletta DuPois*, Clarice Taylor*, Juanita Clark*, W. Geoffrey King*, Jimmy Taylor*, Britt Williams*, Ronald Barnes*, Ronald Buchanan*, Kenneth Green*, Louise Stubbs
Director: Woodie King Jr.*
Narrator: Adolph Caesar*
Producer: Woodie King Jr.*
Screenwriter: Woodie King Jr.*, Truman Nelson
Storywriter: Truman Nelson
Tech Info: color/sound/60 min.   Type: Docudrama
Date: 1980 Origin: USA
Studio: Independent
Company: Essenay Entertainment
Distributors/Format: Nat'l Black Touring Circuit, Inc. (1/2")
Archives/Format: IUB - BFC/A (1/2")
Annotation: King deals with police brutality, poverty, narcotics, crime and murder in Harlem, in the summer of 1964 as he chronicles the harassment and eventual indictment and conviction of six black youths for the stabbing murder of a woman. The horrors of the trial and descriptions of social unrest are told from the perspective of the boys' mothers.

TOTAL RECALL

Cast: Mel Johnson*, Rachel Ticotin, Arnold Schwarzenegger, Sharon Stone
Director: Paul Verhoeven
Executive Producer: Mario Kassar, Andrew Vajna
Music by: Jerry Goldsmith
Producer: Buzz Feitshans, Ronald Shusett, Mario Kassar, Andrew Vajna
Screenwriter: Dan O'Bannon, Ronald Shusett
Storywriter: Phillip K. Dick
Tech Info: color/sound/113 min.   Type: Dramatic Feature
Date: 1990   Origin: USA
Company: Carolco
Distributors/Format: Carolco Home Video (1/2"), TriStar Pictures Inc. (1/2")
Annotation: Benny (Johnson) is a futuristic Mars mutant and underground cab driver who befriends the confused Quaid (Schwarzenegger) on his quest for identity. But Quaid soon comes to realize that Benny is part of a mysterious bureaucratic trap designed to destroy him.

TOUCHED BY LOVE

Alternate: To Elvis with Love
Cast: John Amos*, Diane Lane, Deborah Raffin, Christina Raines
Music by: John Barry
Producer: Michael Viner
Screenwriter: Hester Anderson
Storywriter: Lena Canada
Tech Info: color/sound/97 min.   Type: Dramatic Feature
Date: 1979   Origin: USA
Company: Dove Productions
Distributors/Format: Columbia Pictures (16mm)
Annotation: The efforts of a dedicated nurse's aide help a young girl stricken with cerebral palsy to overcome her handicap and find an outlet for her suppressed emotions. Amos plays Tony.

TOUGH ENOUGH

Cast: Stan Shaw*, Pam Grier*, Cloryce Miller*, Ernest Lee Smith*, Dennis Quaid
Director: Richard Fleischer
Music Performer: Michael Lloyd, Steve Wax
Producer: William F. Gilmore
Screenwriter: John Leone
Tech Info: color/sound/107 min.   Type: Dramatic Feature
Date: 1982   Origin: USA
Company: American Cinema Productions
Distributors/Format: Fox Home Video (1/2")
Annotation: P.T. Coolidge (Shaw) is a boxer fighting in the Toughman Contest in Forth Worth Texas. He loses because the judge does not want him to fight Art (Quaid) who eventually wins. P.T. and his wife Myra (Grier) befriend Art and the three travel to Detroit so that Art can compete in the National Competition. Art must fight Truman Wall (Smith), the best fighter in the contest.

TOUGH GUYS

Cast: Corkey Ford*, Kirk Douglas, Charles Durning, Burt Lancaster, Dana Carvey, Alexis Smith
Director: Jeff Kanew
Music by: James Newton Howard*
Producer: Joe Wizan
Screenwriter: James Cruickshank, James Orr
Tech Info: color/sound/102 min.   Type: Comedy Feature
Date: 1986   Origin: USA
Company: Silver Screen Partners II, Bryna, Touchstone
Distributors/Format: Buena Vista Home Video (1/2")
Annotation: Harry Doyle (Lancaster) and Archie Long (Douglas), two aging train robbers just released from prison, decide to go back to crime when they find life on the outside degrading. Ford appears as a gang leader.

TOUGH GUYS DON'T DANCE

Cast: Clarence Williams III*, Isabella Rossellini, Ryan O'Neal, Debra Sandlund
Director: Norman Mailer
Executive Producer: Francis Ford Coppola, Tom Luddy
Music by: Angelo Badalamenti
Producer: Yoram Globus, Francis Ford Coppola, Menahem Golan, Tom Luddy
Screenwriter: Norman Mailer
Tech Info: color/sound/108 min.   Type: Dramatic Feature
Date: 1987   Origin: USA
Company: Golan-Globus
Distributors/Format: Cannon Home Video (1/2")
Annotation: Tim Madden (O'Neal), finding himself divorced and a failed writer, marries pseudo-Southern belle Patty Lareine (Sandlund). When Tim finds a decapitated head in his drug cache, his life gets increasingly complicated. Williams plays Bolo.

TOUGHER THAN LEATHER

Cast: Run-D.M.C. *, Richard Edson, Jenny Lumet, Beastie Boys
Director: Rick Rubin
Music Performer: Run-D.M.C. *, Public Enemy *, Rick James*, Beastie Boys
Producer: George Jackson*, Doug McHenry*, Vincent Giordano
Screenwriter: Ric Menello, Rick Rubin
Tech Info: color/sound/93 min.   Type: Musical Feature
Date: 1988   Origin: USA
Company: Def American Pictures
Distributors/Format: New Line Cinema Home Video (1/2")
Annotation: Trouble is near when Run-DMC and The Beastie Boys are signed by a small-time music booking agency whose real purpose is to launder drug money.

TOY SOLDIERS

Cast: Cleavon Little*, Willard Pugh*, Ron Ross*, Jason Miller, Rodolfo DeAnda, Terri Garber
Director: David Fisher
Executive Producer: Darrell Hallenbeck
Music by: Leland Bond
Producer: David Fisher, Darrell Hallenbeck

Screenwriter: David Fisher, Walter Fox
Tech Info: color/sound/85 min.   Type: Dramatic Feature
Date: 1983   Origin: USA
Company: New World Pictures
Distributors/Format: New World Home Video (1/2")
Annotation: Buck (Little) is a Vietnam veteran who helps friends ("toy soldiers") rescue Americans held captive in Central America. Buck and his friends sabotage an attempt to get three million dollars ransom for the hostages. Pugh plays Ace and Hatman (Ross) is a butler who is one of the toy soldiers.

TOY SOLDIERS
Cast: Louis Gossett Jr.*, Denise Gordy*, Sean Astin, Andrew Divoff, Denholm Elliott, Christopher Northup
Director: Daniel Petrie Jr.
Executive Producer: Mark Burg, Chris Zarpas
Music by: Robert Folk
Producer: Mark Burg, Chris Zarpas, Patricia Herskovic, Jack E. Freedman, Wayne S. Williams
Screenwriter: Daniel Petrie Jr., David Koepp
Tech Info: color/sound/112 min.   Type: Dramatic Feature
Date: 1991   Origin: USA
Company: Island Pictures, Wayne Williams Productions, et al
Distributors/Format: TriStar Pictures Inc. (1/2")
Annotation: Gossett plays Parker, Dean of Regis, an Eastern prep school where the students are held hostage by a Latin American terrorist whose drug-kingpin father has been kidnapped by the U.S. Gordy has an uncredited role.

TOY, THE
Cast: Richard Pryor*, Annazette Chase*, Victor Romero Evans*, Virginia Capers*, Tony King*, B.J. Hooper*, Robert Costley*, Juan Coleman*, Robert Earle*, Valerian Smith*, Jackie Gleason, Teresa Ganzel, Wilfred Hyde-White, Ned Beatty
Director: Richard Donner
Music Performer: Patrick Williams
Music by: Patrick Williams
Producer: Phil Feldman
Screenwriter: Carol Sobieski
Storywriter: Francis Veber
Tech Info: color/sound/102 min.   Type: Comedy Feature
Date: 1982   Origin: USA
Company: Rastar
Distributors/Format: Columbia Pictures Home Video (1/2")
Annotation: Jack (Pryor) is sent to work for Ruby Dee Simpson (Capers) head maid for U.S. Bates (Gleason). After being fired by her, Jack is hired by Bates' son (Schwartz) to be "his toy" while he is home on vacation. Jack agrees to the job to save his house from being auctioned by Gettran (Hooper), who works for the bank. Jack's wife Angela (Chase) and good friend Clifford (King) are part of a Klan watch which leads them to the Bates' house.

TOYS
Cast: L.L. Cool J. *, Michael Gambon*, Robin Williams, Robin Wright, Joan Cusack, Donald O'Conner
Director: Barry Levinson
Music by: Hans Zimmer, Trevor Horn
Producer: Mark Johnson, Barry Levinson
Screenwriter: Barry Levinson, Valerie Curtin
Tech Info: color/sound/110 min.   Type: Dramatic Feature
Date: 1992   Origin: USA
Company: Baltimore Pictures, Fox
Distributors/Format: Fox Home Video (1/2")
Annotation: After the death of toymaker Kenneth Zevo (O'Conner), the toy factory is entrusted to The General (Gambon), who runs the place like an army, with the help of his son Patrick (L.L. Cool J.). Zevo's kids Leslie (Williams) and Gwen (Wright) try to return the factory to its previous fun state.

TRADING PLACES
Cast: Eddie Murphy*, Robert Earl Jones*, Gloria Foster*, Michelle Weeks*, Dan Aykroyd, Jamie Lee Curtis, Ralph Bellamy, Don Ameche
Director: John Landis
Executive Producer: George Folsey Jr.
Music Performer: Elmer Bernstein
Music by: Elmer Bernstein
Producer: Aaron Russo, George Folsey Jr.
Screenwriter: Timothy Harris, Herschel Weingrod
Tech Info: color/sound/118 min.   Type: Comedy Feature
Date: 1983   Origin: USA
Company: Gulf & Western, Paramount
Distributors/Format: Paramount Home Video (1/2")
Archives/Format: IUB - BFC/A (1/2")
Annotation: Billy Ray Valentine (Murphy) outwits the millionaire Duke brothers (Bellamy and Ameche) who bet each other $1.00 that they can, by putting Valentine into their wealthy young broker's (Ackroyd) place, prove (or disprove) that heredity triumphs over environment.

TRANSFORMERS: THE MOVIE, THE
Cast: Scatman Crothers*, Robert Stack, Orson Welles
Director: Nelson Shin, Kozo Morishita
Music by: Vince DiCola
Producer: Joe Bacal, Tom Griffin
Screenwriter: Ron Friedman, Flint Dille
Tech Info: color/sound/86 min.   Type: Animated Feature
Date: 1986   Origin: USA
Company: Sunbow, Marvel
Distributors/Format: DEG (16mm)
Annotation: In 2005, Transformers battle the Decepticons with help from earthly creatures known as Autobots. Crothers provides the voice of Jazz.

TRAXX

Cast: Willard Pugh*, John Hancock*, Priscilla Barnes, Shadoe Stevens
Director: Jerome Gary
Music by: Jay Gruska
Producer: Gary De Vore, Richard McWhorter
Screenwriter: Gary Devore
Tech Info: color/sound/84 min.　　　Type: Comedy Feature
Date: 1988　Origin: USA
Company: DEG
Annotation: Traxx (Stevens), a former state trooper turned mercenary, helps clean up sleazy hangouts in Hadleyville, Texas. Pugh plays Deeter.

TRESPASS

Alternate: The Looters
Cast: Joe Seneca*, Arthur/Art Evans*, Glenn Plummer*, Stone/Stoney Jackson*, Ice-T *, Devoreaux White*, Tom "Tiny" Lister Jr.*, Ice Cube *, John Toles-Bey*, Tico Wells*, Bruce A. Young*, T.E. Russell*, Bryon Minns*, Bill Paxton, William Sadler
Director: Walter Hill
Executive Producer: Robert Zemeckis, Bob Gale
Music by: Ry Cooder
Producer: Robert Zemeckis, Bob Gale, Michael S. Glick, Neil Canton
Screenwriter: Robert Zemeckis, Bob Gale
Tech Info: color/sound/101 min.　　　Type: Dramatic Feature
Date: 1992　Origin: USA
Company: Universal
Distributors/Format: Facets Multimedia, Inc. (1/2")
Annotation: Two Arkansas fire fighters stumble upon a map which leads to hidden gold stashed in an abandoned East St. Louis tenement. But while looking for the money, they watch a drug related murder. Now, they are trapped in an urban nightmare. Ice-T and Ice Cube are pitted against each other in a complicated plot that uses a rap soundtrack, video, and much gratuitous violence.

TRIBUTE TO JACKIE ROBINSON, A

Director: William Greaves*
Producer: William Greaves*
Tech Info: mixed/sound/18 min.　　　Type: Documentary Short
Date: 1990　Origin: USA
Company: William Greaves* Production
Distributors/Format: Jackie Robinson Foundation (1/2")
Annotation: Greaves' film uses archival footage of Robinson's life, focussing on his breaking the color bar when he became the first black player in the major league, and on his achievements in later life as businessman and civil rights activist.

TROUBLE BEHIND

Series: African American Perspectives
Director: Robbie Henson
Narrator: Robbie Henson
Producer: Robbie Henson
Tech Info: color/sound/56 min.　　　Type: Documentary Feature

Date: 1990   Origin: USA
Studio: Independent
Distributors/Format: California Newsreel (1/2")
Annotation: The film explores present day racism in Corbin, Kentucky. It is discussed in the context of a race riot in the town of Corbin (October 31, 1919) that drove all of the black residents out of town.

TROUBLE IN MIND

Cast: Albert Hall*, George Kirby*, Joe Morton*, Kris Kristofferson, Keith Carradine, Genevieve Bujold
Director: Alan Rudolph
Music Performer: Marianne Faithful*
Producer: Carolyn Pfeiffer, David Blocker
Screenwriter: Alan Rudolph
Tech Info: color/sound/111 min.   Type: Dramatic Feature
Date: 1985   Origin: USA
Studio: Independent
Company: Alive Films, Inc.
Distributors/Format: Charter Entertainment (1/2")
Annotation: George Kirby plays Lieutenant Gunther of the local police force who allows Hawk (Kristofferson), a murderer just out of prison, to dabble in the criminal underworld of Rain City. This results in his becoming acquainted with organized crime figures like Solo (Morton) and Leo (Hall).

TRUE BLOOD

Cast: Ken Foree*, Jeff Fahey, Sherilyn Fenn, Billy Drago, James Tolkan, Chad Lowe
Director: Frank Kerr
Music by: Scott Roewe
Producer: Peter Maris
Screenwriter: Frank Kerr
Tech Info: color/sound/97 min.   Type: Dramatic Feature
Date: 1989   Origin: USA
Company: Maris
Distributors/Format: Fries Home Video (1/2")
Annotation: Ray Trueblood (Fahey) is framed for a murder committed by Spider Masters (Drago), the leader of a rival gang, and flees New York. Ten years later, he returns to find his brother a member of Spider's gang, and he attempts to get him to quit. Foree portrays Charlie.

TRUE IDENTITY

Cast: James Earl Jones*, Lenny Henry*, Anne-Marie Johnson*, Ruth Brown*, Melvin Van Peebles*, Charles Lane*, Frank Langella, Peggy Lipton
Director: Charles Lane*
Executive Producer: Howard Rosenman, Sandy Gallin
Music by: Marc Marder
Producer: Howard Rosenman, Sandy Gallin, Teri Schwartz, Carol Baum
Storywriter: Andy Breckman
Tech Info: color/sound/92 min.   Type: Comedy Feature

Date: 1991   Origin: USA
Company: Sandollar Productions, Touchstone
Distributors/Format: Buena Vista Home Video (1/2"), Touchstone Home Video (1/2")
Archives/Format: IUB - BFC/A (1/2")
Annotation: When a jetliner seems about to crash, a businessman, Leland
Carver/Frank Luchino (Langella), reveals his secret mobster past to fast-talking
actor Miles Pope (Henry), but when the plane lands safely, Miles must assume
various identities to elude Luchino's hit men. Lane plays Duane, special effects
artist who creates a new identity for Miles; Johnson is Kristi, Miles' love interest.
Van Peebles plays a taxi driver; Brown is Martha, and Jones plays himself.

TRUE ROMANCE
Cast: Samuel L. Jackson*, Paul Bates*, Dennis Hopper, Christian Slater, Patricia
Arquette, Gary Oldman
Director: Tony Scott
Executive Producer: Bob Weinstein, Harvey Weinstein, James G. Robinson, Gary
Barber, Stanley Margolis
Music by: Hans Zimmer
Producer: Bob Weinstein, Harvey Weinstein, Steve Perry, James G. Robinson, Gary
Barber, Samuel Hadida, Bill Unger, Stanley Margolis
Screenwriter: Quentin Tarantino
Tech Info: color/sound/119 min.   Type: Dramatic Feature
Date: 1993   Origin: USA
Company: True Romance Productions, Morgan Creek, Davis Film
Distributors/Format: Warner Bros. Home Video, Inc. (1/2")
Annotation: In an attempt to rescue Alabama Whitman (Arquette) from her pimp
(Oldman), Clarence Worley (Slater) not only kills him, but accidentally picks up a
suitcase of cocaine instead of Alabama's suitcase. Mobsters then pursue them to
retrieve the drugs. Jackson plays "Big Don"; Bates is Marty.

TRUE STORY OF GLORY CONTINUES, THE
Cast: Raymond St. Jacques*
Director: Ben Burtt
Music by: Charles Davis*
Narrator: Morgan Freeman*
Producer: Ray Hebeck Jr.
Screenwriter: Ray Hebeck Jr.
Tech Info: color/sound/45 min.   Type: Documentary Short
Date: 1991   Origin: USA
Company: TriStar
Distributors/Format: RCA/Columbia Pictures Home Video (1/2"), Filmic Archives
(1/2")
Annotation: Soldiers of the 54th Massachusetts Regiment, the first black fighting unit
of the American Civil War, are portrayed through period drawings, sketches,
paintings and photos and additional footage from the motion picture GLORY.

TRUMPETISTICALLY, CLORA BRYANT
Director: Zeinabu irene Davis*
Executive Producer: Commissioned by the Women's Building, L.A.
Music Performer: Clora Bryant*
Music by: Clora Bryant*
Producer: Zeinabu irene Davis*, Commissioned by the Women's Building, L.A.

Speaker: Clora Bryant*, John "Dizzy" Gillespie*, La June Bell*, Devri *, Betty O'Hara
Tech Info: color/sound/5 min.   Type: Documentary Short
Date: 1989   Origin: USA
Company: Wimmin with a Mission Productions
Archives/Format: IUB - BFC/A (1/2")
Annotation: Davis draws a brief portrait of a black woman trumpet player, Clora
Bryant who has been playing for over 45 years.

TUFF TURF

Cast: Arthur/Art Evans*, Donald Fullilove*, Paul Mones, James Spader, Kim
Richards
Director: Fritz Kiersch
Music by: Jonathan Elias
Producer: Donald P. Borchers
Screenwriter: Jette Rinck, Murray Michaels
Storywriter: Greg Collins O'Neal
Tech Info: color/sound/112 min.   Type: Dramatic Feature
Date: 1985   Origin: USA
Company: New World
Annotation: Morgan Hiller (Spader) is a formerly rich kid from Connecticut whose
financially ruined family must move to Los Angeles, where he gets into trouble with a
local gang. Evans appears as a security guard.

TWILIGHT ZONE: THE MOVIE

Cast: Scatman Crothers*, Dan Aykroyd, Vic Morrow, Albert Brooks, John Lithgow,
Kathleen Quinlan
Director: Steven Spielberg, John Landis, George Miller, Joe Dante
Executive Producer: Frank Marshall
Music Performer: Jerry Goldsmith
Music by: Jerry Goldsmith
Producer: Steven Spielberg, John Landis, Frank Marshall
Screenwriter: George Clayton Johnson, Richard Matheson, Josh Rogan
Storywriter: Richard Matheson, Jerome Bixby
Tech Info: color/sound/101 min.   Type: Dramatic Feature
Date: 1983   Origin: USA
Company: Warner Bros.
Annotation: Crothers plays Mr. Bloom, who revitalizes a retirement home and
teaches its inhabitants about the true meaning of eternal youth. This story is one of
three Twilight Zone television remakes included in this four-part anthology.

TWILIGHT'S LAST GLEAMING

Cast: Roscoe Lee Browne*, Paul Winfield*, Joe Eszterhas, Charles Durning, Burt
Lancaster, Richard Widmark, Melvyn Douglas, Joseph Cotten
Director: Robert Aldrich
Producer: Geria
Screenwriter: Robert M. Cohen, Edward Heubsch
Storywriter: Walter Wanger
Tech Info: color/sound/144 min.   Type: Dramatic Feature

Date: 1978   Origin: USA
Company: Lorimar, Bavaria, Geria
Annotation: Winfield plays Willis Powell, a former death row inmate who is now part of a terrorist gang attempting to take over an Air Force base with nuclear capability in order to blackmail a corrupt president. Brown plays James Forrest.

TWIST

Director: Ron Mann
Executive Producer: Don Haig
Music Performer: Isley Brothers *, Smokey Robinson*, Hank Ballard
Producer: Don Haig, Ron Mann
Speaker: Chubby Checker*, Isley Brothers *, Smokey Robinson*, Hank Ballard
Tech Info: mixed/sound/78 min.   Type: Documentary Feature
Date: 1992   Origin: Canada
Company: Triton Pictures
Distributors/Format: October Films (16mm; 35mm)
Annotation: The film documents the evolution of rock and roll. It features interviews with and performances by Checker, Ballard, Robinson and the Isley Brothers.

TWISTER

Cast: Charlaine Woodard*, Harry Dean Stanton, Suzy Amis, Crispin Glover
Director: Michael Almereyda
Executive Producer: Dan Ireland, William J. Quigley
Music by: Hans Zimmer
Producer: Dan Ireland, William J. Quigley, Wieland Schulz-Keil
Screenwriter: Michael Almereyda
Tech Info: color/sound/94 min.   Type: Comedy Feature
Date: 1989   Origin: USA
Company: Wieland Schulz-Keil
Distributors/Format: Vestron Home Video (1/2")
Annotation: A tornado strikes the home of Eugene Cleveland (Stanton), where he lives with his strange extended family. Woodard plays Lola.

TWO DOLLARS AND A DREAM

Alternate: The Story of Madame C.J. Walker
Director: Stanley Nelson*
Narrator: Jill Nelson*
Producer: Stanley Nelson*, Deborah Bolling*
Storywriter: Lou Potter*
Tech Info: color/sound/56 min.   Type: Documentary Feature
Date: 1986   Origin: USA
Studio: Independent
Company: Stanley Nelson & Associates
Distributors/Format: Filmakers Library, Inc. (16mm; 1/2")
Archives/Format: IUB - BFC/A (1/2")
Annotation: Using on-camera interviews with members of her company, franchise operators, friends and acquaintances, and archival footage, Nelson documents the life of Madame C.J. Walker, the first woman in America to start from nothing and build a million dollar business. The film explores the remarkable progress of Walker's business (hair and skin care products for black women) under her hand and its subsequent decline toward the end of her daughter A'Lelia's life.

TWO OF A KIND
Cast: Ernie Hudson*, Sheila Frazier*, Scatman Crothers*, Charles Durning, John Travolta, Olivia Newton-John
Director: John Herzfeld
Music by: Patrick Williams
Producer: Joe Wizan, Roger M. Rothstein
Screenwriter: John Herzfeld
Tech Info: color/sound/87 min.   Type: Dramatic Feature
Date: 1983   Origin: USA
Company: Fox
Distributors/Format: Fox Home Video (1/2")
Annotation: Angered over the moral failings of humankind, God decides to destroy the world but angels convince him to give people another chance. Crothers play Earl and Hudson is Detective Staggs.

TWO SOCIETIES (1965-68)
Series: Eyes On The Prize II
Director: Sam Pollard*, Shelia Bernard
Executive Producer: Henry Hampton*
Narrator: Julian Bond*
Producer: Henry Hampton*, Sam Pollard*, Shelia Bernard
Speaker: Roger Wilkins*, Jessie Jackson*, Andrew Young*, Nancy Jefferson*, Clory Bryant*, Linda Bryant Hall*, Minnie Dunlap*, Albert Raby*, Helen Kelly*, Ron Scott*, Grant Friley*, Robert Lucas*, Chester Robinson*, Herb Boyd*, Arthur Johnson*, Albert Cleage*, Edward Vaughan*, Albert Wilson*, John Conyers*, Lyndon B. Johnson, Ed Washington, John McDermott, Richard Daley, Rosemary Porter, Richard Strichartz, Eleanor Josaitis, George Romney, Cyrus Vance, Howard Holland
Tech Info: mixed/sound/60 min.   Type: Television Documentary
Date: 1989   Origin: USA
Company: Blackside, Inc.
Distributors/Format: PBS Video (16mm; 1/2")
Archives/Format: IUB - AAAMC (1/2")
Annotation: In this segment, Martin Luther King Jr. leads marches in Chicago, attempting to bring about desegregation in public housing. In Detroit, Los Angeles, Newark, Miami, and many other American cities, police oppression sparks the black community's anger, resulting in the transformation of city streets into war zones.

ULTERIOR MOTIVES
Cast: Tyra Ferrell*, Thomas Ian Griffith, Mary Page Keller, Hayward Nishioka, Ellen Crawford
Director: James Becket
Executive Producer: Taro Tanabe
Music by: Parmer Fuller
Producer: Thomas Ian Griffith, J. Max Kirishima, Taro Tanabe
Screenwriter: James Becket
Storywriter: Thomas Ian Griffith, James Becket
Tech Info: color/sound   Type: Dramatic Feature

Date: 1993   Origin: USA
Company: ELK Productions Inc.
Distributors/Format: Imperial Entertainment Home Video (1/2")
Annotation: Reporter Erica Boswell (Keller) and Private Investigator Jack Blaylock (Griffith) must handle industrial espionage, governmental cover-up and treachery on many levels to break a story. Ferrell appears as a receptionist.

UNCLE JOE SHANNON
Cast: Jason Bernard*, Madge Sinclair*, Burt Young, Doug McKeon
Director: Joseph C. Hanwright
Executive Producer: Gene Kirkwood
Music Performer: Maynard Ferguson*
Music by: Bill Conti
Producer: Robert Chartoff, Irwin Winkler, Gene Kirkwood
Screenwriter: Burt Young
Tech Info: color/sound/108 min.   Type: Dramatic Feature
Date: 1978   Origin: USA
Company: United Artists
Distributors/Format: United Artists Home Video (1/2")
Annotation: Joe Shannon (Young) hits rock bottom as a struggling musician. Ferguson plays the trumpet solos. Sinclair stars as Margaret and Bernard plays "Goose."

UNCOMMON VALOR
Cast: Harold Sylvester*, Gene Hackman, Randall "Tex" Cobb, Patrick Swayze, Tim Thomerson, Robert Stack, Fred Ward, Reb Brown
Director: Ted Kotcheff
Music by: James Horner
Producer: John Milius, Buzz Feitshans
Screenwriter: Joe Gayton
Tech Info: color/sound/105 min.   Type: Dramatic Feature
Date: 1983   Origin: USA
Company: Paramount
Distributors/Format: Paramount Home Video (1/2")
Annotation: Johnson (Sylvester) is a retired army pilot recruited to rescue Colonel Rhodes's (Hackman) son from a Cambodian, Prisoner of War camp during the Vietnam war.

UNDER SIEGE
Cast: Bernie Casey*, David McKnight*, Duane Davis*, Gary Busey, Steven Seagal, Tommy Lee Jones, Erika Eleniak
Director: Andrew Davis
Executive Producer: J.F. Lawton*, Gary Goldstein
Music by: Gary Chang
Producer: J.F. Lawton*, Steven Seagal, Arnon Milchan, Steven Reuther, Gary Goldstein
Screenwriter: J.F. Lawton*, John Mason, Michael Rae
Tech Info: color/sound/100 min.   Type: Dramatic Feature

Date: 1992   Origin: USA
Company: Le Studio Canal Plus, Alcor Films, Regency Ent.
Distributors/Format: Warner Bros. Home Video, Inc. (1/2")
Annotation: A former Navy SEAL, Casey Ryback (Seagal) has been demoted to a
cook on board the U.S.S. Missouri. A band of renegade CIA operatives posing as
caterers plot to take over the ship, but Ryback stops them. Casey plays
Commander Harris and McKnight plays Flicker.

UNDER THE CHERRY MOON

Cast: Prince (Rogers Nelson) *, Jerome Benton*, Francesca Annis, Steven Berkoff,
Emmanuelle Sallet, Alexandra Stewart, Kristin Scott Thomas
Director: Prince (Rogers Nelson) *
Music Performer: Prince (Rogers Nelson) *, Prince and the Revolution
Music by: Prince (Rogers Nelson) *, Prince and the Revolution
Producer: Robert Cavallo, Joseph Ruffalo, Steven Fargnoli
Screenwriter: Becky Johnston
Tech Info: bw/sound/100 min.   Type: Musical Feature
Date: 1986   Origin: USA
Company: Warner Bros.
Annotation: Prince falls in love with a wealthy French society girl (Thomas) whose
father (Berkoff) does everything possible to keep them apart.

UNDER THE GUNN

Cast: Vanessa Williams*, Steven Williams*, Rockne Tarkington*, Sam Jones, John
Russell, Nick Cassavetes
Director: James Shardellati
Executive Producer: Steven Shotz
Producer: Warren Stein, Steven Shotz
Screenwriter: James Devney, James Shardellati, Almer John Davis
Storywriter: James Devney
Tech Info: color/sound/90 min.   Type: Dramatic Feature
Date: 1988   Origin: USA
Studio: Independent
Company: Marquis Pictures
Distributors/Format: Magnum Entertainment (1/2")
Annotation: Braxton (Jones) is helping Lt. Gallagher (Steven Williams), a police
officer tracking Simon Stone (Russell), an illegal arms salesman, when he meets
Stone's lawyer, Samantha Richards (Vanessa Williams). Stone's hit man Leon
(Tarkington) attempts to kill Braxton. Romance develops when the failed murder
attempt puts Braxton and Richards on the run.

UNDERCOVER BLUES

Cast: Obba Babatunde*, Jenifer Lewis*, Dennis Quaid, Tom Arnold, Kathleen
Turner, Larry Miller, Fiona Shaw, Stanley Tucci, Park Overall
Director: Herbert Ross, Donald Thorin
Executive Producer: Andrew Bergman, Herbert Ross
Music by: David Newman
Producer: Andrew Bergman, Herbert Ross, Mike Lobell
Screenwriter: Ian Abrams
Tech Info: color/sound/90 min.   Type: Comedy Feature

Date: 1993   Origin: USA
Company: MGM
Distributors/Format: MGM Home Video (1/2")
Annotation: Jeff and Jane Blue (Quaid and Turner) are espionage agents who are persuaded to save the world from a corrupt Czech arms embezzler. In the process they come under scrutiny by two bumbling New Orleans policemen, Sawyer (Babatunde) and Halsey (Miller).

UNFORGIVEN
Cast: Morgan Freeman*, Clint Eastwood, Richard Harris, Gene Hackman, Jaimz Woolvett ·
Director: Clint Eastwood
Executive Producer: David Valdes
Music by: Lennie Niehaus
Producer: Clint Eastwood, David Valdes
Screenwriter: David Peoples
Tech Info: color/sound/130 min.   Type: Dramatic Feature
Date: 1992   Origin: USA
Company: Malpaso Productions, Warner Bros.
Distributors/Format: Warner Bros. Home Video, Inc. (1/2")
Annotation: William Munny (Eastwood) and his old partner Ned Logan (Freeman) are convinced to go on a job as gunmen one more time. When Logan is tortured and murdered after deciding he no longer has the stomach for killing, Munny returns to the town to avenge his friend's death.

UNINVITED, THE
Cast: Austin Stoker*, George Kennedy, Clu Gulager, Alex Cord, Toni Hudson, Shari Shattuck
Director: Greydon Clark
Music by: Dan Slider
Producer: Greydon Clark
Screenwriter: Greydon Clark
Tech Info: color/sound/89 min.   Type: Dramatic Feature
Date: 1988   Origin: USA
Company: Heritage
Annotation: Financier Walter Graham (Cord) plans his escape from the law and invites two vacationing co-eds to join him on his remote beach. They bring a stray cat which escaped from a government lab and is infected with a parasitic disease. Stoker plays the Caribbean officer.

UNIVERSAL SOLDIER
Cast: Duane Davis*, Tom "Tiny" Lister Jr.*, Tico Wells*, Dolph Lundgren, Jean-Claude Van Damme, Ally Walker
Director: Roland Emmerich
Executive Producer: Mario Kassar
Music by: Christophe Franke
Producer: Joel B. Michaels, Mario Kassar, Craig Baumgarten, Alan Shapiro
Screenwriter: Dean Devlin, Richard Rothstein, Christopher Leitch
Tech Info: color/sound/98 min.   Type: Dramatic Feature

Date: 1992   Origin: USA
Company: Universal Soldier Inc., IndieProd Company, et al.
Distributors/Format: TriStar Pictures Inc. (1/2")
Annotation: Soldiers Luc Devreux (Van Damme) and Andrew Scott (Lundgren) argue and kill each other in Vietnam. Their bodies are frozen so scientists can turn them into bionic supersoldiers. Wells plays Garth; Lister is GR55; and Davis plays a policeman.

UNLAWFUL ENTRY

Cast: Roger E. Mosley*, Kurt Russell, Ray Liotta, Madeleine Stowe, Ken Lerner
Director: Jonathan Kaplan, Jamie Anderson
Music by: James Horner
Producer: Charles Gordon
Screenwriter: Lewis Colick
Storywriter: Lewis Colick, George Putnam, John Katchmer
Tech Info: color/sound/107 min.   Type: Dramatic Feature
Date: 1992   Origin: USA
Company: JVC Entertainment
Distributors/Format: Fox Home Video (1/2")
Annotation: A suspense thriller about policeman Pete Davis (Liotta) who becomes ominously involved in the lives of Michael (Russell) and Karen (Stowe) Carr, a young couple, after their house is burglarized. Roy Cole (Mosley) is Pete Davis's partner.

UNMARRIED WOMAN, AN

Cast: Novella Nelson*, Jill Clayburgh, Michael Murphy, Alan Bates, Pat Quinn
Director: Paul Mazursky
Music by: Bill Conti
Producer: Paul Mazursky, Tony Ray
Screenwriter: Paul Mazursky
Tech Info: color/sound/124 min.   Type: Dramatic Feature
Date: 1978   Origin: USA
Company: Fox
Distributors/Format: Fox Home Video (1/2")
Annotation: Erica (Clayburgh), a happily married woman for 15 years, is surprised when her husband Martin (Murphy) leaves her for a Bloomingdale's shop girl. Erica picks up the pieces of her life and becomes an independent woman who lives life on her own terms. Nelson plays Jean.

UNNATURAL CAUSES

Cast: Alfre Woodard*, Patti Labelle*, John Ritter
Director: Lamont Johnson
Producer: Blue Andre
Screenwriter: John Sayles
Storywriter: Martin M. Goldstein, Stephan Doran, Robert Jacobs
Tech Info: color/sound/96 min.   Type: Dramatic Feature
Date: 1986   Origin: USA
Studio: Independent
Distributors/Format: New Star Video (1/2")
Annotation: Vietnam veteran Frank Coleman (Ritter) and U.S. Veterans Administration counselor Maude De Victor (Woodard) fight for benefits to veterans with illnesses caused by Agent Orange.

UNSPOKEN CONVERSATION
Director: Iman Hammeen*
Tech Info: color/sound/24 min.   Type: Experimental Short
Date: 1987   Origin: USA
Studio: Independent
Distributors/Format: Third World Newsreel (1/2")
Annotation: The film depicts a young black women's reflections on identity and desire outside of her family's expectations.

UP AGAINST THE WALL
Cast: Catero Colbert*, Ron O'Neal*, Marla Gibbs*, Stone/Stoney Jackson*, Oscar Brown Jr.*, De Mann*, L. Scott Caldwell*, Zuindi Colbert*, Salli Richardson*
Director: Ron O'Neal*
Executive Producer: Dr. Jawanza Kunjufu*
Music Performer: Theodis Rodger*
Music by: Theodis Rodger*
Producer: Dr. Jawanza Kunjufu*, Chuck Colbert*, Zuindi Colbert*
Screenwriter: Dr. Jawanza Kunjufu*, Chuck Colbert*, Songodina Ifatunji*, Emma Young
Tech Info: color/sound/102 min.   Type: Dramatic Feature
Date: 1991   Origin: USA
Studio: Independent
Company: African American Images, I Am Entertainment
Distributors/Format: BMG Home Video (1/2")
Annotation: Sean Bradley (Colbert) is a promising track star who always wanted to know about his father. In his struggle toward maturity, he learns that his best friend's father (O'Neal) is also his own. Gibbs is Sean's mother.

UP THE ACADEMY
Alternate: Mad Magazine's Up the Academy
Cast: Antonio Fargas*, Ralph Macchio, Ron Liebman, Wendell Brown, Tom Citera, J. Hutchinson
Director: Robert Downey
Executive Producer: Bernie Brillstein
Music by: Jody Taylor Worth
Producer: Bernie Brillstein, Marvin Worth, Danton Rissner
Screenwriter: Tom Patchett, Jay Tarses
Tech Info: color/sound/96 min.   Type: Comedy Feature
Date: 1980   Origin: USA
Company: Warner Bros.
Distributors/Format: Warner Bros. Home Video, Inc. (1/2")
Annotation: A group of teenagers struggle with the tyrannical rule of the Major (Liebman) who runs the military academy at which they are enrolled. Fargas appears as Coach.

UP THE CREEK
Cast: Jesse Goins*, Tim Matheson, Stephen Furst, Jennifer Runyon, Dan Monahan, Sandy Helberg
Director: Robert Butler
Executive Producer: Samuel Z. Arkoff, Louis S. Arkoff
Music by: William Goldstein

Producer: Samuel Z. Arkoff, Michael L. Metzer, Fred Baum, Louis S. Arkoff
Screenwriter: Jim Kouf
Storywriter: Jim Kouf, Jeff Sherman, Douglas Grossman
Tech Info: color/sound/95 min.   Type: Comedy Feature
Date: 1984   Origin: USA
Company: Arkoff
Distributors/Format: Orion Home Video (1/2")
Annotation: Bob McGraw (Matheson) leads a team from Lepetomane University in a college river raft race where anything goes. Goins appears as Brown.

URBAN CROSSFIRE

Cast: Courtney B. Vance*, Mario Van Peebles*, Morris Chestnut*, Laurie Morrison*, Michael P. Boatman*, Kenny Leon*, Damien Pooser*, Ray Sharkey, Peter Boyle
Director: Dick Lowry
Executive Producer: Kenneth Kaufman, Tom Patchett
Producer: Ann Kindburg, Dick Lowry, Kenneth Kaufman, Tom Patchett
Screenwriter: T.S. Cook
Tech Info: color/sound/95 min.   Type: Dramatic Feature
Date: 1994   Origin: USA
Company: Patchett-Kauffman Productions, et al.
Distributors/Format: New Horizons Home Video (1/2")
Annotation: Brooklyn policemen (Van Peebles and Boatman) fight to restore order after the murder of a black Brooklyn police officer. Terror and mayhem are caused by drug lord Justis (Vance), foot soldier Raheem (Leon) and the backslider reformed ex-convict Carl (Chestnut). Morrison is uncredited.

USED CARS

Cast: Frank McKae*, Kurt Russell, Gerrit Graham, Deborah Harmon, Jack Warden
Director: Robert Zemeckis
Executive Producer: Steven Spielberg, John Milius
Music Performer: Patrick Williams, Bobby Bare
Music by: Patrick Williams, Norman Gimbel
Producer: Bob Gale, Steven Spielberg, John Milius
Screenwriter: Robert Zemeckis, Bob Gale
Tech Info: color/sound/113 min.   Type: Comedy Feature
Date: 1980   Origin: USA
Company: Columbia
Distributors/Format: RCA/Columbia Pictures Home Video (1/2")
Annotation: Rudy Russo (Russell) tries to keep his used car lot in business when it is threatened by a newer neighboring competition. Friends Jeff (Graham), and Jim (McRae) the lot's mechanic, aid in Russo's elaborately competitive advertising tactics.

VAMP

Cast: Grace Jones*, Paunita Nichols*, Chris Makepeace, Robert Rusler, Gedde Watanabe, Sandy Baron, Dedee Pfeiffer
Director: Richard Wenk
Music Performer: Jonathan Elias
Producer: Donald P. Borchers
Screenwriter: Richard Wenk
Storywriter: Richard Wenk, Donald P. Borchers
Tech Info: color/sound/93 min.   Type: Dramatic Feature

Date: 1986   Origin: USA
Company: Donald P. Borchers, Balcor Film Investors
Distributors/Format: New World Pictures (1/2")
Annotation: A group of teenagers, lost in the city, go to a restaurant and ask Maven (Nichols) for help. She tells them about a dance club where they meet Katrina (Jones) and Vic (Baron), who turn out to be vampires.

VAMPIRE'S KISS
Cast: Jennifer Beals*, Kasi Lemmons*, Maria Conchita Alonso, Nicolas Cage
Director: Robert Bierman
Executive Producer: Derek Gibson, John Daly
Music by: Colin Towns
Producer: Derek Gibson, John Daly, Barry Shils, Barbara Zitwer
Screenwriter: Joseph Minion
Tech Info: color/sound/105 min.   Type: Comedy Feature
Date: 1989   Origin: USA
Company: Hemdale
Distributors/Format: Hemdale Home Video (1/2")
Annotation: Peter Loew (Cage) is a self-centered literary agent whose life changes after he is bitten by an exotic looking woman named Rachel (Beals). Loew then must try to figure out if in fact he has become a vampire.

VARNETTE'S WORLD: A STUDY OF A YOUNG ARTIST
Director: Carroll Parrott Blue*
Music by: Benny Yee*, Rickey Kelly*
Narrator: Varnette Honeywood*
Producer: Carroll Parrott Blue*
Screenwriter: Carroll Parrott Blue*
Tech Info: color/sound/26 min.   Type: Documentary Short
Date: 1979   Origin: USA
Company: WNET-TV
Distributors/Format: Carroll Blue Film Library (16mm)
Annotation: Through African American painter Varnette Honeywood, Blue's film addresses problems that many aspiring artists face when trying to establish and maintain themselves as professionals in the art world.

VERDICT, THE
Cast: Joe Seneca*, Milo O'Shea, James Mason, Paul Newman, Jack Warden, Charlotte Rampling
Director: Sidney Lumet
Music Performer: Johnny Mandel
Music by: Johnny Mandel
Producer: David Brown, Richard D. Zanuck
Screenwriter: David Mamet
Storywriter: Barry Reed
Tech Info: color/sound/128 min.   Type: Dramatic Feature
Date: 1982   Origin: USA
Company: Zanuck/Brown Production
Distributors/Format: Fox Home Video (1/2")
Annotation: Dr. Thompson (Seneca), a 74 year old medical doctor is called to be a witness in a case of negligence toward a coma patient by two doctors who did not look at her chart. Thompson examines the patient and testifies that her coma was

caused by lack of oxygen to her brain as the result of cardiac arrest.

VICE SQUAD

Cast: Grand L. Bush*, Stack Pierce*, Marilyn Coleman*, Beverly Todd*, Maurice Emmanuel*, Cyndi James-Reese*, Gary Swanson, Wings Hauser
Director: Gary A. Sherman
Executive Producer: Sandy Howard, Frank Capra Jr., Robert Rehme
Producer: Sandy Howard, Brian Frankish, Frank Capra Jr., Robert Rehme
Screenwriter: Sandy Howard, Kenneth Peters, Robert Vincent O'Neil
Tech Info: color/sound/97 min.   Type: Dramatic Feature
Date: 1982   Origin: USA
Company: Avco, Embassy, Dynamic Films
Distributors/Format: Embassy Home Video (1/2")
Annotation: When a psychopathic murderer stalks Hollywood prostitutes, the police department attempts to trap him. Williams (Todd) and Edwards (Emmanuel) are both policemen on the trail of the killer. James-Reese appears as a prostitute; Bush as a pimp; Coleman a babysitter for one of the prostitutes; Pierce a garage owner who allows the psycho to go free.

VICE VERSA

Cast: Gloria Gifford*, Judge Reinhold, Swoozie Kurtz, Fred Savage, Corinne Bohrer
Director: Brian Gilbert
Executive Producer: Alan Ladd Jr.
Music by: David Shire
Producer: Dick Clement, Ian La Frenais, Alan Ladd Jr.
Screenwriter: Dick Clement, Ian La Frenais
Tech Info: color/sound/98 min.   Type: Comedy Feature
Date: 1988   Origin: USA
Company: Columbia
Distributors/Format: Columbia Pictures Home Video (1/2")
Annotation: A jeweled skull causes department store executive Marshall Seymour (Reinhold) to switch bodies with his son Charlie (Savage). Gifford portrays Marcie.

VIEW TO A KILL, A

Cast: Grace Jones*, Roger Moore, Christopher Walken
Director: John Glen
Producer: Albert R. Broccoli, Michael Wilson
Screenwriter: Richard Maibaum, Michael Wilson
Tech Info: color/sound/131 min.   Type: Dramatic Feature
Date: 1985   Origin: USA
Studio: Independent
Annotation: Jones is agent May Day in this James Bond series. Walken plays Max Zorin who has an earthquake scheme to gain control of the world computer market and 007 (Moore) must stop him. Jones is Zorin's playmate and Bond's adversary.

VIGILANTE

Alternate: Street Gang
Cast: Woody Strode*, Fred Williamson*, Robert Forster, Rutanya Alda
Executive Producer: Jerry Masucci, John Packard, Kenneth Pavia
Music by: Jay Chattaway
Producer: Jerry Masucci, William Lustig, Andrew Garroni, John Packard, Kenneth Pavia

Tech Info: color/sound/90 min.   Type: Dramatic Feature
Date: 1983   Origin: USA
Company: Magnum, Artists Releasing
Distributors/Format: Film Ventures (1/2")
Annotation: Factory worker Eddie (Forster) refuses to join a vigilante group formed by his co-worker Nick (Williamson) until his son is killed by a Puerto Rican gang. Strode plays Rake, a prisoner whom Eddie encounters when he is thrown into jail.

VIOLENT BREED, THE
Cast: Woody Strode*, Henry Silva, Harrison Muller, Carole Andre, Debora Keith
Director: Fernando DiLeo
Music by: Paolo Rustichelli
Producer: Ettore Spagnuolo
Screenwriter: Fernando DiLeo, Nino Marino
Tech Info: color/sound/91 min.   Type: Dramatic Feature
Date: 1986   Origin: Italy
Company: Visione, Cannon
Distributors/Format: MGM/UA Home Video (1/2")
Annotation: Paolo (Strode), Kirk (Silva), and Mike (Muller) are three commandos who launch a mission into Southeast Asia to rescue refugee children. At a crucial moment, Paolo betrays his comrades.

VISION QUEST
Cast: Forest Whitaker*, Harold Sylvester*, Matthew Modine, Linda Fiorentino, Michael Schoeffling
Director: Harold Becker
Executive Producer: Adam Fields, Sam Weston
Music by: Tangerine Dream
Producer: Peter Guber, Jon Peters, Adam Fields, Sam Weston
Screenwriter: Darryl Ponicsan
Tech Info: color/sound/107 min.   Type: Dramatic Feature
Date: 1985   Origin: USA
Company: Guber, Peters
Distributors/Format: Warner Bros. Home Video, Inc. (1/2")
Annotation: Louden Swain (Modine), a high school wrestler, is determined to lose his virginity and 20 pounds, the latter so that he can compete against the state champion. A number of people are a part of his "vision quest" including Tanneran (Sylvester) and Bulldozer (Whitaker).

VISIONS OF LIGHT: THE ART OF CINEMATOGRAPHY
Director: Stuart Samuels, Arnold Glassman, Todd McCarthy
Executive Producer: Terry Lawler, Yoshiki Nishimura
Producer: Stuart Samuels, Terry Lawler, Yoshiki Nishimura
Screenwriter: Todd McCarthy
Speaker: Ernest Dickerson*, Michael Chapman, Lazslo Kovacs, John Alonzo, John Bailey, Nestor Almendros
Tech Info: color/sound/90 min.   Type: Documentary Feature

Date: 1993   Origin: Japan
Company: American Film Institute, Nippon Hosa Kyotai, JBC
Distributors/Format: American Film Institute (16mm; 1/2")
Annotation: Many film professionals, including Dickerson, are interviewed in this
documentary film about American cinematographers.

VISIONS OF THE SPIRIT: A PORTRAIT OF ALICE WALKER
Series: America: A Cultural Mosiac
Music by: Rachel Bagby*
Narrator: Alice Walker*
Producer: Elena Featherson
Speaker: Quincy Jones*, Whoopi Goldberg*, Danny Glover*, Oprah Winfrey*,
Akosua Busia*, Barbara Christian*, Ruth Walter-Hood*, Birda Reynolds Simmons*,
Mini Lou Walker*, Rebecca Walker*, Robert Allen*, Steven Spielberg, Michael Riva
Tech Info: color/sound/58 min.   Type: Documentary Feature
Date: 1989   Origin: USA
Studio: Independent
Company: Raiden Productions, Reel Directions
Distributors/Format: Women Make Movies, Inc. (16mm; 1/2")
Archives/Format: IUB - BFC/A (1/2")
Annotation: Alice Walker narrates the struggles black women writers encounter to
attain recognition and success. It emphasizes her vision and encouragement to
other women writers.

VOICES OF THE GODS
Director: Alfred Santana*
Tech Info: color/sound/60 min.   Type: Documentary Feature
Date: 1985   Origin: USA
Studio: Independent
Distributors/Format: Third World Newsreel (1/2")
Annotation: This documentary captures the legacy of ancient African religions
practiced in the United States. It provides viewers with insight into the practices and
beliefs of the Akan and Yoruba religions and illustrates how mass media has been
used to ridicule and denigrate these belief systems. The director studies an
Egungun ancestral communion ceremony in a Yoruba village in Sheldon, South
Carolina.

VOLUNTEERS
Cast: Ji-Tu Cumbuka*, Tom Hanks, Tim Thomerson, John Candy, Clyde Kusatsu,
Gedde Watanabe
Director: Nicholas Meyer
Music by: James Horner
Producer: Walter Parkes, Richard Shepherd
Screenwriter: David Isaacs, Ken Levine
Storywriter: Keith Critchlow
Tech Info: color/sound/106 min.   Type: Comedy Feature
Date: 1985   Origin: USA
Company: HBO, Silver Screen
Distributors/Format: TriStar Pictures Inc. (1/2")
Annotation: Rich kid Lawrence Bourne III (Hanks) runs up huge gambling debts that
his father refuses to pay. To avoid the thugs who are after him, Bourne boards a
plane full of Peace Corps volunteers on their way to Thailand. Cumbuka plays

Cicero.

VOODOO DAWN

Cast: Theresa Merritt*, Tony Todd*, Raymond St. Jacques*, Bill/Billy Williams*, Gina Gershon, John Russo
Director: Steven Fierberg
Executive Producer: Bernard E. Goldberg
Music by: Taj *
Producer: Steven Mackler, Bernard E. Goldberg
Screenwriter: John Russo, Thomas Rendon, Jeffrey Delman, Evan Dunsky
Tech Info: color/sound/83 min.   Type: Dramatic Feature
Date: 1991   Origin: USA
Company: Steven Mackler Production
Distributors/Format: Academy Home Entertainment Video (1/2")
Annotation: Voodoo sorcerer Makoute (Todd) is constructing an all-powerful "voodoo man" from body parts of his victims with the help of his zombie slaves. A couple of New York college students including Miles (Williams), stumble into voodoo territory and seek refuge in a nearby community of Haitian farmworkers led by Claude (St. Jacques). Merrit plays Madame Daslay and Gershon plays Tina, a field hand.

WALK ON WHITE NAILS

Cast: Craig Wallace*, Candice A. Crawford*, Cameron Fletcher, Sandra Anderson
Director: Alonzo Crawford*
Producer: Alonzo Crawford*
Screenwriter: Alonzo Crawford*
Tech Info: bw/sound/104 min.   Type: Dramatic Feature
Date: 1991   Origin: USA
Company: Vigilant Cinema Productions
Distributors/Format: Vigilant Cinema Productions (16mm)
Annotation: Crawford's film addresses the effects of racism on the lives of two ordinary Americans, Rosemary, a white businesswoman, and Gabriel, a black dentist. Both are searching for a meaningful relationship, but they are influenced almost unwittingly by America's slave past.

WALKER

Cast: Sy Richardson*, Ed Harris, Rene Auberjonois, Richard Masur, Keith Szarabajka
Director: Alex Cox
Executive Producer: Edward R. Pressman
Music by: Joe Strummer
Producer: Edward R. Pressman, Lorenzo O'Brien, Angel Flores Marini
Screenwriter: Rudy Wurlitzer
Tech Info: color/sound/95 min.   Type: Dramatic Feature
Date: 1987   Origin: USA
Company: Edward R. Pressman, Incine
Distributors/Format: Northern Dist. Partners, Universal (16mm)
Annotation: Based on facts about U.S. involvement in Nicaragua, the film follows the career of William Walker (Harris) who decides to bring his brand of democracy to Central America. Richardson plays Capt. Hornsby.

WALKING DEAD, THE
Cast: Joe Morton*, Allen Payne*, Eddie Griffin*
Director: Preston A. Whitmore*
Screenwriter: Preston A. Whitmore*
Tech Info: color/sound/90 min.   Type: Dramatic Feature
Date: 1994   Origin: USA
Company: Savoy Pictures
Distributors/Format: Films Inc. (1/2")
Annotation: The Vietnam experience is seen through the eyes of four courageous African American marines.

WANDERERS, THE
Cast: Samm-Art Williams*, Val Avery*, Michael Wright*, Ken Wahl, Karen Allen, John Friedrich
Director: Philip Kaufman
Executive Producer: Richard R. St. Johns
Producer: Richard R. St. Johns, Martin Ransohoff
Screenwriter: Philip Kaufman, Rose Kaufman
Tech Info: color/sound/113 min.   Type: Dramatic Feature
Date: 1979   Origin: USA
Company: Orion
Distributors/Format: Orion Home Video (1/2")
Annotation: The film presents a series of vignettes about a gang of Italian American teenagers living in the Bronx, in the sixties, and their experiences, including encounters with a rival gang, the Fordham Baldies. Avery plays Mr. Sharp; Wright plays Clinton; and Williams plays Roger.

WANTED: DEAD OR ALIVE
Cast: Robert Guillaume*, Gene Simmons, Rutger Hauer
Director: Gary Sherman
Executive Producer: Authur Sarkissian
Music Performer: Joseph Renzetti
Music by: Joseph Renzetti
Producer: Robert C. Peters, Authur Sarkissian
Screenwriter: Michael Patrick Goodman, Brian Taggert
Tech Info: color/sound/104 min.   Type: Dramatic Feature
Date: 1986   Origin: USA
Company: Arthur Sarkissian, New World, Belcor Film Invest.
Distributors/Format: New World Home Video (1/2")
Annotation: Phillmore Walker (Guillaume) is a federal agent who enlists Nick Randall (Hauer) to help catch a Middle Eastern terrorist loose in Los Angeles. Walker is unaware that his bureau is using Randall as bait to catch the criminal, but when he figures out the plot, he and Randall join forces to get the terrorist.

WAR OF THE ROSES, THE
Cast: Danitra Vance*, Danny Devito, Marriane Sagebrecht, Kathleen Turner, Sean Astin, Michael Douglas
Director: Danny Devito
Executive Producer: Doug Claybourne, Polly Platt
Music by: David Newman
Producer: Arnon Milchan, Doug Claybourne, James L. Brooks, Polly Platt

Screenwriter: Michael Leeson
Tech Info: color/sound/116 min.   Type: Comedy Feature
Date: 1989   Origin: USA
Company: Gracie
Distributors/Format: Fox Home Video (1/2")
Annotation: Barbara Rose (Turner) hates everything about Oliver (Douglas), her
husband of 17 years. Oliver still loves Barbara, but he loves their house more so
when divorce proceedings start, the house becomes their battleground. Vance plays
a manicurist trainee.

WAR, THE

Cast: LaToya Chisholm*, Kevin Costner, Elijah Wood, Mare Winningham, Lexi
Randall
Director: Jon Avnet, Geoffrey Simpson
Executive Producer: Todd Baker, Eric Eisner
Music by: Thomas Newman
Producer: Jon Avnet, Jordan Kerner, Todd Baker, Eric Eisner
Screenwriter: Kathy McWorter
Tech Info: color/sound/126 min.   Type: Dramatic Feature
Date: 1994   Origin: USA
Company: MCA, Universal
Distributors/Format: MCA/Universal Home Video (1/2")
Annotation: In Mississippi, the summer of 1970, Stu (Wood) and Lidia Simmons
(Randall) are determined to build the ultimate treehouse with the help of their
friends. Their father Stephen (Costner), a newly returned Vietnam veteran, has
equally high hopes to rebuild his life and fulfill his family's dreams. Chisholm plays
Elvadine.

WARNING SIGN

Cast: Yaphet Kotto*, Meshach Taylor*, Sam Waterston, Richard Dysart, Kathleen
Quinlan
Director: Hal Barwood
Executive Producer: Matthew Robbins
Music by: Craig Safan
Producer: Matthew Robbins, Jim Bloom
Screenwriter: Matthew Robbins, Hal Barwood
Tech Info: color/sound/100 min.   Type: Dramatic Feature
Date: 1985   Origin: USA
Company: Fox
Distributors/Format: Fox Home Video (1/2")
Annotation: Cal (Waterston) and Joanie Morse (Quinlan) work at BioTek, a company
supposedly developing a strain of corn that will grow in salt water but is actually
creating a bacterium for germ warfare. The town turns to zombies when the germ is
accidentally released. Kotto plays Maj. Connolly; Taylor is a video technician

WARRIOR MARKS

Series: Global Feminism: On the Road to Beijing
Director: Pratiba Parmar
Executive Producer: Alice Walker*
Speaker: Alice Walker*, Pratiba Parmar
Tech Info: color/sound/54 min.   Type: Documentary Feature

Date: 1993   Origin: Africa
Distributors/Format: Women Make Movies, Inc. (16mm; 1/2")
Archives/Format: IUB - BFC/A (1/2")
Annotation: The film probes some of the cultural and political complexities surrounding the issue of female genital mutilation. It includes interviews with women who are concerned with and affected by female genital mutilation.

WARRIORS OF THE WASTELAND

Cast: Timothy Brent*, Thomas Moore*, Fred Williamson*, Jerry Jones, George Eastman, Anna Kanakis
Director: Enzo Girolaini
Music by: Chris Reese
Producer: Fabrizio DeAngelis
Screenwriter: Tito Carpi, Enzo Girolaini
Storywriter: Tito Carpi
Tech Info: color/sound/92 min.   Type: Dramatic Feature
Date: 1983   Origin: USA
Company: Deaf International Film S.C.L. Production
Distributors/Format: New Line Cinema Home Video (1/2")
Annotation: The deadly archer Nadir (Williamson) teams up with a warrior named Scorpion (Brent) in order to defeat an evil post-holocaust terrorist group, The Templers.

WARRIORS, THE

Cast: David Harris*, Dorsey Wright*, Roger Hill*, Lynn Thigpen*, James Remar, Michael Beck, Brian Tyler, Terry Michos
Director: Walter Hill
Music Performer: Barry Devorzon
Music by: Barry Devorzon
Producer: Lawrence Gordon
Screenwriter: David Shaber, Walter Hill
Storywriter: Sol Yurick
Tech Info: color/sound/94 min.   Type: Dramatic Feature
Date: 1979   Origin: USA
Company: A Gulf & Western Company
Distributors/Format: Paramount Home Video (1/2")
Annotation: Cochise (Harris) is the warlord of the Warriors gang from Coney Island. He taught his group the tactics of survival in the city. The group soon finds out that survival in the city depends on toughness. Hill plays Cyrus; Wright plays Cleon and Thigpen is a New York D.J.

WATCHERS III

Cast: Daryl Roach*, Wings Hauser, Gregory Scott Cummings, John K. Linton
Director: Jeremy Stanford
Executive Producer: Roger Corman
Music by: Nigel Holton
Producer: Roger Corman, Luis Llosa
Screenwriter: Michael Palmer
Tech Info: color/sound/80 min.   Type: Dramatic Feature

Date: 1994   Origin: USA
Company: Concorde-New Horizons Corp.
Distributors/Format: New Horizons Home Video (1/2")
Annotation: Jailed Delta Force veteran (Hauser) is released from Leavenworth prison by covert military personnel under false pretensions. With fellow convicts (Cummins, Roach and Linton) he helicopters into Central America only to discover they must battle a humanoid monster and his former co-workers from U.S. military intelligence.

WATER RITUAL #1: AN URBAN RITE OF PURIFICATION
Director: Barbara McCullough*
Producer: Barbara McCullough*
Screenwriter: Barbara McCullough*
Tech Info: bw/sound/4 min.   Type: Experimental Short
Date: 1990   Origin: USA
Studio: Independent
Distributors/Format: Third World Newsreel (1/2")
Archives/Format: IUB - BFC/A (1/2")
Annotation: McCullough uses aspects of African and Afro-Caribbean ritual as modern artifacts in this abstract expressionistic work.

WATERDANCE, THE
Cast: Wesley Snipes*, Starletta DuPois*, Fay Hauser*, Badja Djola*, Andrea Young*, William Forsythe, Eric Stoltz, Elizabeth Pena, Helen Hunt
Director: Neal Jiminez, Michael Steinberg, Mark Plummer
Executive Producer: Guy Riedel
Music by: Michael Convertino
Producer: Gale Anne Hurd, Marie Cantin, Guy Riedel
Screenwriter: Neal Jiminez
Tech Info: color/sound/106 min.   Type: Dramatic Feature
Date: 1992   Origin: USA
Company: No Frills Films, JBW
Distributors/Format: Samuel Goldwyn Home Video (1/2")
Annotation: Snipes plays Raymond, a ladies' man who loses his family when he loses his mobility. He and two other wheelchair bound buddies, Garcia (Stoltz) and Bloss (Forsythe), try to deal with their disability in a physical rehabilitation center. They take on the hospital bureaucracy, make a forbidden field trip and learn to fight wheelchair wars.

WE LOVE YOU LIKE A ROCK--THE DIXIE HUMMINGBIRDS
Director: Ashley James, Ray Allen
Music Performer: The Dixie Hummingbirds *
Speaker: The Dixie Hummingbirds *
Tech Info: mixed/sound/77 min.   Type: Documentary Feature
Date: 1994   Origin: USA
Annotation: For nearly 70 years, the Dixie Hummingbirds have been one of the most important groups in gospel and a major influence in the development of American pop music and Rhythm and Blues.

WE SHALL OVERCOME: THE SONG THAT MOVED A NATION
Series: America: A Cultural Mosaic
Director: Jim Brown*
Music Performer: Taj Mahal *, Joan Baez, Pete Seeger, Freedom Singers
Musical Performers:
Narrator: Harry Belafonte*
Producer: Jim Brown*, Ginger Brown, Harold Leventhal, George Stoney
Speaker: Desmond Tutu*
Tech Info: color/sound/58 min.   Type: Documentary Feature
Date: 1989   Origin: USA
Company: Ginger Group
Distributors/Format: California Newsreel (1/2"), Modern Educational Video
Network/Churchill Films (1/2")
Archives/Format: IUB - AAAMC ()
Annotation: Tracing the transformation of the title song from an old slave spiritual to
the anthem of the civil rights movement, the film chronicles its effect on human
rights movements in the United States and in other parts of the world, using
historical footage and personal recollections.

WEEDS
Cast: Ernie Hudson*, Felton Perry*, Sam Waymon*, Gerald Orange*, John
Toles-Bey*, Nick Nolte, William Forsythe, J.J. Johnson, Rita Taggart
Director: John Hancock*
Executive Producer: Mel Pearl, Billy Cross
Music by: Angelo Badalamenti
Producer: Mel Pearl, Bill Badalato, Billy Cross
Screenwriter: John Hancock*, Dorothy Tristan
Tech Info: color/sound/115 min.   Type: Dramatic Feature
Date: 1987   Origin: USA
Company: Kingsgate
Distributors/Format: DEG (16mm)
Annotation: Sentenced to life without parole, Lee Umstetter (Nolte) turns to books
and to writing for distraction. Lee gets permission to cast his play with inmates
including Navarro (Toles-Bey), Bagdad (Hudson), and musicians (Waymon is at the
keyboard). A newspaper critic sees the performance and arranges to have the play
staged on Broadway and to get Lee released. Perry is the associate warden and
Orange appears in an uncredited role.

WEEKEND AT BERNIE'S II
Cast: Novella Nelson*, Stack Pierce*, Troy Beyer*, Andrew McCarthy, Jonathan
Silverman, Terry Kiser
Director: Robert Klane
Executive Producer: Angiolo Stella
Producer: Victor Drai, Joseph Perez, Angiolo Stella
Screenwriter: Robert Klane
Tech Info: color/sound/89 min.   Type: Comedy Feature
Date: 1993   Origin: USA
Company: Victor Drai Productions, Artimm
Distributors/Format: TriStar Pictures Inc. (1/2")
Annotation: Larry Wilson (McCarthy) and Richard Parker (Silverman) discover a
safety deposit box key among Bernie Lomax's (Kiser) possessions. Thinking that it

will unlock the dead man's fortune, the two head to St. Thomas and are pursued by the mob which hires Mobu (Nelson), a voodoo queen, to animate dead Bernie for guidance. Beyer plays Claudia who is romanced by Larry; Pierce is Claudia's physician father.

WEEKEND PASS
Cast: Chip McAllister*, Theodore "Teddy" Wilson*, Grand L. Bush*, Valerie McIntosh*, D.W. Brown, Peter Ellenstein, Patrick Hauser, Pamela G. Kay, Hilary Shapiro
Director: Lawrence Bassoff
Music by: John Baer
Producer: Marilyn J. Tenser
Screenwriter: Lawrence Bassoff
Tech Info: color/sound/92 min.   Type: Comedy Feature
Date: 1984   Origin: USA
Studio: Independent
Company: Crown International Pictures
Annotation: Four sailors leave their San Diego station for a weekend of fun in Los Angeles and meet suitable female counterparts. Bunker Hill (McAllister), an ex-gang member turned clean-cut type, is one of the sailors. He gets involved in a fight with Bertram (Bush) over ex-girlfriend Etta (McIntosh).

WEEKEND WARRIORS
Cast: Randal Patrick*, Lloyd Bridges, Vic Tayback, Chris Lemmon, Daniel Greene
Director: Bert Convy
Executive Producer: Bert Convy, Stan Fimberg
Music by: Perry Botkin
Producer: Hannah Hempstead, Bert Convy, Stan Fimberg
Screenwriter: Bruce Belland, Roy M. Rogosin
Tech Info: color/sound/85 min.   Type: Comedy Feature
Date: 1986   Origin: USA
Company: Movie Store
Annotation: A bunch of film industry employees enlist in the National Guard to avoid the draft. After being threatened with active duty, Vince Tucker (Lemmon), a struggling screenwriter, stages a Hollywood extravaganza to impress visiting dignitaries. Patrick plays Kramer.

WEIRD SCIENCE
Cast: Chino "Fats" Williams*, Vince Monroe Townsend Jr.*, Jennifer Balgobin*, D'Mitch Davis*, Anthony Michael Hall, Ilan Mitchell-Smith, Kelly Le Brock
Director: John Hughes
Music by: Ira Newborn
Producer: Joel Silver
Screenwriter: John Hughes
Tech Info: color/sound/94 min.   Type: Comedy Feature
Date: 1985   Origin: USA
Company: Hughes, Silver
Distributors/Format: Universal Home Video (1/2")
Annotation: Gary (Hall) and Wyatt (Mitchell-Smith), high school freshmen, devise a computer program that will create the perfect woman (Le Brock). Townsend and Williams are bar patrons; Davis is the bartender; and Balgobin is the biker girl.

WELCOME TO OBLIVION
Cast: Meshach Taylor*, Dack Rambo, Clare Beresford, Mark Bringelson, Orlando Sacha
Director: Augusto Tamayo, Kevin Tent
Executive Producer: Roger Corman
Music by: Kevin Klingler
Producer: Roger Corman, Luis Llosa
Screenwriter: Len Jenkin, Dan Kleinman
Tech Info: color/sound/80 min.   Type: Dramatic Feature
Date: 1992   Origin: USA
Company: Concorde, Iguana Films
Distributors/Format: Concorde Home Video (1/2")
Annotation: Kenner (Rambo) goes to Oblivion, a radioactive wasteland, to secure mining rights. He's ambushed by Bishop (Sacha), Oblivion's cruel dictator, and forced into slavery with genetic mutant nomads called "Mutties." Kenner organizes a Muttie rebellion. Elijah (Taylor) is a turncoat who's been secretly reporting to Bishop.

WHAT COULD YOU DO WITH A NICKEL?
Director: Jeffrey Kleinman, Cara DeVito
Narrator: Barbara Montgomery*
Producer: Jeffrey Kleinman
Tech Info: color/sound/26 min.   Type: Documentary Short
Date: 1982   Origin: USA
Studio: Independent
Distributors/Format: First Run/Icarus Films (16mm)
Annotation: In October 1977, 200 African American and Hispanic housekeepers in the South Bronx went on strike in an attempt to form the first legally recognized domestic workers union in the United States. Even though they were unsuccessful, they provided the impetus for over 6000 housekeepers in New York City to be become organized.

WHAT IS A LINE?
Director: Shari Frilot*
Producer: Shari Frilot*
Screenwriter: Shari Frilot*
Tech Info: color/sound/10 min.   Type: Experimental Short
Date: 1994   Origin: USA
Studio: Independent
Distributors/Format: Third World Newsreel (1/2")
Annotation: Weaving the narrative of a jilted lover with footage of a train in motion, Frilot's video explores the physical, emotional and psychological convolutions jilted lovers go through.

WHAT'S LOVE GOT TO DO WITH IT
Alternate: Tina: What's Love Got to Do with It
Cast: Laurence/Larry Fishburne*, Cora Lee Day*, Khandi Alexander*, Angela Bassett*, Vanessa Bell Calloway*, Jenifer Lewis*, Richard Timothy Jones*
Director: Brian Gibson, Jamie Anderson
Executive Producer: Rogie Davies, Mario Iscovich
Music Performer: Tina Turner*, The Kings of Rhythm*

Music by: Stanley Clarke*
Producer: Rogie Davies, Mario Iscovich, Doug Chapin, Barry Krost
Screenwriter: Kate Lanier
Tech Info: color/sound/118 min.   Type: Dramatic Feature
Date: 1993   Origin: USA
Company: Touchstone
Distributors/Format: Touchstone Home Video (1/2")
Annotation: The turbulent relationship of Ike (Fishburne) and Tina Turner (Bassett) a.k.a. Anna Mae Bullock, eventually forces Tina to leave and find the confidence to pursue her life and career without her husband. Lewis plays Anna Mae's mother; Stickney, her sister Aline; Day, Grandma Georgina.

WHEN A MAN LOVES A WOMAN
Cast: LaTanya Richardson*, Tina Majorino, Andy Garcia, Meg Ryan
Director: Luis Mandoki
Executive Producer: Ronald Bass, Simon Maslow, Al Franken
Music by: Zbigniew Preisner
Producer: Jordan Kerner, Ronald Bass, Jon Avnet, Simon Maslow, Al Franken
Screenwriter: Ronald Bass, Al Franken
Tech Info: color/sound/125 min.   Type: Dramatic Feature
Date: 1994   Origin: USA
Company: Touchstone
Distributors/Format: Buena Vista Home Video (1/2")
Annotation: Alice Green (Ryan) is an alcoholic whose drinking is tearing apart her family. Her husband Michael (Garcia) takes her to a rehab clinic, but the stress of Alice's recovery leads to the couple's separation. Richardson plays Dr. Gina Mendez.

WHEN HARRY MET SALLY...
Cast: Gretchen F. Palmer*, Billy Crystal, Bruno Kirby, Carrie Fisher, Meg Ryan
Director: Rob Reiner
Music by: Marc Shaiman, Harry Connick Jr.
Producer: Steve Nicolaides, Rob Reiner, Andrew Scheinman, Jeffrey Stott
Screenwriter: Nora Ephron
Tech Info: color/sound/96 min.   Type: Comedy Feature
Date: 1989   Origin: USA
Company: Castle Rock, Nelson
Distributors/Format: Columbia Pictures Home Video (1/2")
Annotation: Harry (Crystal) and Sally (Ryan) do a post-graduation ride share from Chicago to New York which begins an unusual and slowly developing friendship/romance. Palmer plays the stewardess who witnesses the second beginning of their relationship.

WHERE DID YOU GET THAT WOMAN?
Director: Loretta Smith
Speaker: Joan Williams*
Tech Info: color/sound/28 min.   Type: Documentary Short

Date: 1983   Origin: USA
Studio: Independent
Distributors/Format: Filmakers Library, Inc. (16mm; 1/2")
Annotation: The film is a portrait of 77-year old African American Joan Williams, a washroom attendant. Using archival photographs, it documents her odyssey from an Oklahoma farm to the wartime factories of Chicago, and finally the powder room of a nightclub.

WHERE DREAMS COME TRUE
Director: William Greaves*
Narrator: Richardo Montalban
Producer: William Greaves*
Storywriter: William Greaves*
Tech Info: color/sound/28 min.   Type: Documentary Short
Date: 1979   Origin: USA
Studio: Independent
Company: The Administration
Distributors/Format: Flashback Home Video (1/2")
Annotation: The film explores career opportunities for minorities and women at NASA, describing what NASA looks for in its prospective employees.

WHERE THE DAY TAKES YOU
Cast: Will Smith*, Sean Astin, Rikki Lake, Lara Flynn Boyle, Peter Dobson
Tech Info: color/sound/107 min.   Type: Dramatic Feature
Date: 1992   Origin: USA
Company: Columbia, TriStar
Distributors/Format: Columbia/TriStar Home Video (1/2")
Annotation: Smith plays Manny, a teenage runaway trying to survive on the streets of Los Angeles in this unvarnished tale about homeless youth.

WHITE DOG
Alternate: Trained to Kill
Cast: Paul Winfield*, Kristy McNichol, Burl Ives, Jameson Parker
Director: Samuel Fuller
Screenwriter: Curtis Hanson, Samuel Fuller
Storywriter: Romain Gary
Tech Info: color/sound/90 min.   Type: Dramatic Feature
Date: 1981   Origin: USA
Company: Paramount
Distributors/Format: Paramount (1/2")
Annotation: Animal trainer Keys (Winfield) tries to recondition a beautiful white stray dog that has been trained to kill Blacks.

WHITE GIRL, THE
Cast: George Kirby*, Troy Beyer*, Taimak *, Tony Brown*, O.L. Duke*, Michael Spinks*, Teresa Yvon Farley*, Dianne B. Shaw*, Sherry Williams*, J.D. Lewis*, Nathan Garrett Jr.*, Torey Drinker*, Petronia Paley, Donald Craig
Director: Tony Brown*
Executive Producer: Sheryl Cannady
Music by: George Porter Martin, Tony Vigna
Producer: Sheryl Cannady, Jim Cannady
Screenwriter: Tony Brown*

Tech Info: color/sound/94 min.   Type: Dramatic Feature
Date: 1988   Origin: USA
Company: Tony Brown* Productions
Distributors/Format: Tony Brown Productions (1/2")
Annotation: Kim (Beyer) is an intelligent, motivated, and beautiful high school student who becomes a cocaine addict when she goes to college. Bob (Taimak) helps her get off drugs but Kim's new roommate Vanessa (Farley) tempts her again. Shaw plays Debbie and Duke plays Nicky.

WHITE KNIGHTS

Cast: Gregory Hines*, Geraldine Page, Mikhail Baryshnikov, Helen Mirren, Jerzy Skolimowsky, Isabella Rossellini
Director: Taylor Hackford
Music by: Michel Colombier
Producer: Taylor Hackford, William F. Gilmore
Screenwriter: James Goldman, Eric Hughes
Storywriter: James Goldman
Tech Info: color/sound/135 min.   Type: Dramatic Feature
Date: 1985   Origin: USA
Company: New Visions
Distributors/Format: RCA/Columbia Pictures Home Video (1/2")
Archives/Format: IUB - BFC/A (16mm)
Annotation: Raymond Greenwood (Hines), a black ex-patriot living in Siberia, and his wife Darya (Rossellini) take in Russian ex-defector Nikolai (Baryschnikov), a famous dancer. Greenwood is promised better living conditions if he gets Nikolai back into dancing shape. Together they plan an escape.

WHITE LIE

Cast: Bill Nunn*, Gregory Hines*, Annette O'Toole
Director: Bill Condon
Executive Producer: Alan Barnette
Producer: Alan Barnette, Oscar L. Costo
Screenwriter: Nevin Schreiner
Storywriter: Samuel Charters
Tech Info: color/sound/93 min.   Type: Dramatic Feature
Date: 1991   Origin: USA
Company: MCA, Universal
Distributors/Format: MCA/Universal Home Video (1/2")
Annotation: Hines plays Len Madison, Jr., press secretary to a New York mayor who accidentally uncovers a mystery about his own father's murder. Helen Lester (O'Toole), a doctor whose mother was a rape victim in the southern town he returns to, becomes Len's love interest. The film is based on the novel, "Louisiana Black" by Samuel Charters.

WHITE MEN CAN'T JUMP

Cast: Kadeem Hardison*, Wesley Snipes*, Reynaldo Rey*, Tyra Ferrell*, Bill Henderson*, Nigel Miguel*, Cylk Cozart*, Duane Martin*, Marques Johnson*, Lanei Chapman*, Sonny Craver*, Jon Hendricks*, Reggie Leon*, David Roberson*, Ernest Harden Jr.*, Donald Fullilove*, Rosie Perez, Sarah Stavrou, Woody Harrelson
Director: Ron Shelton, Russel Boyd
Executive Producer: Michele Rappaport
Music by: Bennie Wallace

Producer: Michele Rappaport, David Lester, Don Miller
Screenwriter: Ron Shelton
Tech Info: color/sound/115 min.   Type: Comedy Feature
Date: 1992   Origin: USA
Company: Finger Roll Inc, Fox
Distributors/Format: Fox Home Video (1/2")
Annotation: Billy Hoyle (Harrelson) and Sidney Deane (Snipes) are two basketball hustlers conning their way across Los Angeles playing their special brand of game. Farrell plays Rhonda, Sidney's wife.

WHITE OF THE EYE

Cast: Arthur/Art Evans*, David Keith, Cathy Moriarty, Michael Greene, Alan Rosenberg
Director: Donald Cammell
Music by: Nick Mason, Rick Fenn
Producer: Cassian Elwes, Brad Wyman
Screenwriter: Donald Cammell, China Cammell
Tech Info: color/sound/111 min.   Type: Dramatic Feature
Date: 1988   Origin: Great Britain
Company: Cannon
Distributors/Format: Cinema Group, Concorde (1/2")
Annotation: Detective Charles Mendoza (Evans) comes to suspect either Paul (Keith) or Joan White (Moriarty), a seemingly typical suburban husband and wife, of being a brutal serial killer.

WHITE SANDS

Cast: Samuel L. Jackson*, Willem Dafoe, Mickey Rourke, Mimi Rogers, Mary Elizabeth Mastrantonio
Director: Roger Donaldson
Executive Producer: James G. Robinson, David Nicksay, Gary Barber
Music by: Patrick O'Hearn
Producer: James G. Robinson, Scott Rudin, William Sackheim, David Nicksay, Gary Barber
Screenwriter: Daniel Pyne
Tech Info: color/sound/101 min.   Type: Dramatic Feature
Date: 1992   Origin: USA
Company: Morgan Creek
Distributors/Format: Warner Bros. Home Video, Inc. (1/2")
Annotation: Ray Dolezal (Dafoe) is a sheriff in New Mexico who runs into problems when he attempts to investigate the murder of an F.B.I. agent. Jackson is Greg Meeker, an F.B.I. agent who is anxious to retrieve the $1/2 million in cash that the murdered agent was carrying.

WHO LIVES, WHO DIES

Alternate: Rationing Health Care
Director: Roger Weisberg
Narrator: James Earl Jones*
Producer: Roger Weisberg
Storywriter: Roger Weisberg
Tech Info: color/sound/58 min.   Type: Documentary Feature

Date: 1987   Origin: USA
Studio: Independent
Company: Public Policies Productions
Annotation: The film raises the issue of the way we ration medical care spending priorities that determine who lives and who dies.

WHO'S IN CONTROL?
Director: Portia Cobb*
Producer: Deep Dish TV
Tech Info: color/sound/30 min.   Type: Documentary Short
Date: 1994   Origin: USA
Studio: Independent
Company: Third World Newsreel
Distributors/Format: Third World Newsreel (1/2")
Annotation: Leading black women healthcare professionals and individuals analyze how the health care system can better serve communities of color, and define reproductive rights.

WHO'S THAT GIRL
Cast: Albert Popwell*, Glenn Plummer*, Gerald Orange*, John McMartin, Madonna , Griffin Dunne, Haviland Morris
Director: James Foley
Executive Producer: Peter Guber, Jon Peters, Roger Birnbaum
Music by: Patrick Leonard, Stephen Bray
Producer: Peter Guber, Jon Peters, Bernard Williams, Roger Birnbaum, Rosilyn Heller
Screenwriter: Ken Finkleman, Andrew Smith
Storywriter: Andrew Smith
Tech Info: color/sound/94 min.   Type: Comedy Feature
Date: 1987   Origin: USA
Company: Warner Bros.
Distributors/Format: Warner Bros. Home Video, Inc. (1/2")
Annotation: After serving four years for a murder she didn't commit, Nikki Finn (Madonna) plans to hunt down the person who set her up. Popwell plays the parole chairman; Orange is the drunk in a Harlem hallway; and Plummer is a kid in Harlem.

WHO'S THE MAN?
Cast: Badja Djola*, Queen Latifah*, Ice-T *, T. Money *, Ed Lover*, Monie Love*, Jim Moody*, Dr. Dre *, Yolanda ("Yo-Yo") Whitaker*, Bernie Mac*, Busta Rhymez *, Maggie Rush*, Leaders of the New School *, Cheryl "Salt" James*, Andre B. Blake*, Todd I. *, Bowlegged Lou *, Bill Bellamy*, Fab 5 Freddy *, KRS-One *, Bushwick Bill *, Denis Leary, Karen Duffy
Director: Ted Demme, Adam Kimmel
Executive Producer: Suzanne DePasse*
Music Performer: Ed Lover*, Dr. Dre *
Music by: Michael Wolff*, Nic tenBroek*
Producer: Suzanne DePasse*, Maynell Thomas*, Charles Stettler
Screenwriter: Seth Greenland
Storywriter: Ed Lover*, Dr. Dre *, Seth Greenland
Tech Info: color/sound/85 min.   Type: Comedy Feature

Date: 1993   Origin: USA
Company: Katja Motion Picture Corp, DePasse Ent., et al.
Distributors/Format: Columbia/TriStar Pictures (35mm; 1/2"), New Line Cinema
Home Video (1/2")
Annotation: Dre and Lover are two bumbling barbers turned reluctant New York
policemen who become heroes when they clean up the streets of Harlem. Moody
plays Nick, their boss at the barbershop; Lionel (Djola) is Nick's best friend.
Numerous rappers make cameo appearances.

WHOLLY MOSES

Cast: Richard Pryor*, Tanya Boyd*, Julius Harris*, John Houseman, Dudley Moore,
Madeline Kahn
Director: Gary Weiss
Music Performer: Patrick Williams
Music by: Patrick Williams
Producer: Bernie Casey*, Freddie Fields
Screenwriter: Guy Thomas
Tech Info: color/sound/109 min.   Type: Comedy Feature
Date: 1980   Origin: USA
Company: Columbia
Distributors/Format: Columbia Pictures Home Video (1/2")
Annotation: Egyptian Princess (Boyd) finds a baby floating in a basket and names
him Moses. Herschel (Moore) was also floating in a basket but wound up with
sculptors. Convinced he is the chosen one, Herschel confronts another Pharaoh
(Pryor), who shows how superior his Gods are with magic and beliefs.

WHOOPEE BOYS, THE

Cast: Marsha Warfield*, Michael O'Keefe, Paul Rodriguez, Andy Bumatai, Carole
Shelley, Denholm Elliott, Lucinda Jenney
Director: John Byrum
Executive Producer: David Obst, Steve Zacharias, Jeff Buhai
Music by: Jack Nitzsche
Producer: David Obst, Steve Zacharias, Jeff Buhai, Peter MacGregor-Scott, Adam
Fields
Screenwriter: David Obst, Steve Zacharias, Jeff Buhai
Tech Info: color/sound/88 min.   Type: Comedy Feature
Date: 1986   Origin: USA
Company: Adam Fields, David Obst
Distributors/Format: Paramount Home Video (1/2")
Annotation: Jake (O'Keefe) and Barney (Rodriguez) are two New York hustlers who
ply their trade in Palm Beach for the winter. Jake meets Olivia (Jenney), an heiress,
and tries to collect her fortune. Warfield plays Officer White.

WHORE

Cast: Antonio Fargas*, Theresa Russell, Benjamin Mouton
Director: Ken Russell
Producer: Dan Ireland, Ronaldo Vasconcellos
Screenwriter: Ken Russell, Deborah Dalton
Storywriter: David Hines
Tech Info: color/sound/80 min.   Type: Dramatic Feature

Date: 1991   Origin: USA
Company: Cheap Date Inc., Trimark Pictures
Distributors/Format: Vidmark Entertainment Home Video (1/2")
Annotation: Russell plays Liz, a prostitute, whose only sounding board, besides television, is Rasta (Fargas), who lives on the streets. He advises Liz to reconsider the motives of her pimp and later rescues her from being battered to death.

WHOSE LIFE IS IT ANYWAY?
Cast: Mel Stewart*, Bob Balaban, Richard Dreyfuss, Christine Lahti, J.J. Johnston, John Cassavetes
Director: John Badham
Executive Producer: Ray Cooney, Martin C. Schute
Music by: Arthur B. Rubinstein
Producer: Lawrence P. Bachmann, Ray Cooney, Martin C. Schute
Screenwriter: Brian Clark, Reginald Rose
Storywriter: Brian Clark
Tech Info: color/sound/119 min.   Type: Dramatic Feature
Date: 1981   Origin: USA
Company: MGM-UA
Distributors/Format: MGM/UA Home Video (1/2")
Annotation: Ken Harrison (Dreyfuss), a happily married sculptor, is left a quadriplegic after a car accident and seeks permission from the court to be removed from life support. Stewart plays Dr. Barr.

WIDE SARGASSO SEA
Cast: Paul Campbell*, Denise Thompson*, Kayarsha "Diane" Russell*, Claudia Robinson*, James Earl*, Rowena King*, Audbrey Pilatus*, Ancile Gloudin*, Aisha King*, Anika Gordon*, Elfreida Reid*, Bobby Smith*, Tamika Grant*
Director: John Duigan
Executive Producer: Sara Risher
Music by: Stewart Copeland
Producer: Sara Risher, Jan Sharp
Screenwriter: John Duigan, Jan Sharp, Carole Angier, Shelagh Delaney, Bronwyn Murray
Tech Info: color/sound/100 min.   Type: Dramatic Feature
Date: 1993   Origin: USA
Company: Sargasso Productions Ltd.
Distributors/Format: Fine Line Home Video (1/2")
Annotation: In this "prequel" to JANE EYRE, Rochester (Parker) courts Antoinette Cosway (Lombard), and her property, but has misgivings when he learns her mother went mad. Robinson plays Christophene, a voodoo practitioner who raised Antoinette; Nelson (Gloudin), Myra (Aisha King), Hilda (Gordon) and Rose (Reid) are servants on Antoinette's Jamaican plantation. Rowena King is Amelie, a seductive housemaid; Campbell plays young Bull and Thompson is the Black Woman.

WILD ORCHID 2: TWO SHADES OF BLUE
Cast: Merry Clayton*, Sekou Bunch*, Tom Skerritt, Robert Davi, Nina Siemaszko
Director: Zalman King
Executive Producer: Mark Damon
Music by: George Clinton*
Producer: Mark Damon, David Saunders, Rafael Eisenman
Screenwriter: Zalman King, Patricia Louisiana Knop

Tech Info: color/sound/107 min.   Type: Dramatic Feature
Date: 1992   Origin: USA
Company: Blue Movie Blue Inc., Vision pdg
Distributors/Format: Triumph Releasing (16mm)
Annotation: Blue (Siemaszko), a southern California teenager, slips into prostitution to get her heroin-addicted father out of trouble. Clayton is a gospel singer.

WILD PAIR, THE

Alternate: Devil's Odds
Cast: Bubba Smith*, Raymond St. Jacques*, Lela Rochon*, Beau Bridges, Angelique De Windt
Director: Beau Bridges
Executive Producer: Helen Sarlui-Tucker
Music by: John Debney
Producer: Paul Mason, Randall Torno, Helen Sarlui-Tucker
Screenwriter: John Crowther, Joseph Gunn
Storywriter: Joseph Gunn
Tech Info: color/sound/88 min.   Type: Dramatic Feature
Date: 1987   Origin: USA
Company: Sarlui, Diamant
Distributors/Format: Trans World Entertainment (1/2")
Annotation: Benny Avalon (Smith) is a local policeman who works with ghetto kids; Joe Jennings (Bridges) is an FBI agent attempting to catch drug dealer Ivory (St. Jacques). They are teamed together unwillingly, and each refuses to trust the other until the drug dealers get violent.

WILD WOMEN DON'T HAVE THE BLUES

Director: Christine Dall
Music Performer: Ethel Waters*
Producer: Carole Van Valkenburgh, Christine Dall
Tech Info: color/sound/58 min.   Type: Documentary Feature
Date: 1989   Origin: USA
Company: Calliope Film Resources, Inc.
Distributors/Format: California Newsreel (1/2")
Annotation: Through historic performances and recordings, the film captures the spirit of pioneering blueswomen Bessie Smith, Ma Rainey, Ethel Waters, Alberta Hunter and Ida Cox.

WILDCATS

Cast: Wesley Snipes*, Nipsey Russell*, Tab Thacker*, L.L. Cool J. *, Mykelti Williamson*, Dap Sugar Willie*, Gwen McGee*, Goldie Hawn, James Keach, Swoozie Kurtz,
Director: Michael Ritchie
Music Performer: Hawk Wolinski, James Newton Howard
Music by: James Newton Howard*, Hawk Wolinski
Producer: Anthea Sylbert
Screenwriter: Ezra Sacks
Tech Info: color/sound/107 min.   Type: Comedy Feature

Date: 1986   Origin: USA
Company: Hawn, Sylbert
Distributors/Format: Warner Bros. Home Video, Inc. (1/2")
Annotation: Molly McGrathy's (Hawn) lifelong dream becomes a nightmare when she gets the chance to coach football in a ghetto high school. Team members include sex-crazed Trumain (Snipes), an extortioner named Finch (Thacker), and a gentle boy nicknamed Peanut. The principal is Ben Edwards (Russell). Judge Jordan (Wallace) rules on McGrathy's child custody hearing and her team appears as character witnesses.

WILLIE AND PHIL

Cast: Robert Townsend*, Laurence/Larry Fishburne*, Cynthia McPherson*, Hubert J. Edwards*, Margot Kidder, Ray Sharkey, Michael Ontkean
Director: Paul Mazursky
Music by: Georges Delerue, Claude Bolling
Producer: Paul Mazursky, Tony Ray
Screenwriter: Paul Mazursky
Tech Info: color/sound/116 min.   Type: Dramatic Feature
Date: 1980   Origin: USA
Company: Fox
Distributors/Format: Fox Home Video (1/2")
Annotation: Willie (Ontkean) and Phil (Sharkey) are best friends who don't let their mutual attraction for Jeannette (Kidder) come between them. Fishburne plays Wilson; Edwards appears as the black kid; and Townsend and McPherson have uncredited roles.

WINAN'S RETURN, THE

Music Performer: The Winans*, Teddy Riley*, Aaron Hall*, Damien Hall*
Tech Info: color/sound/81 min.   Type: Concert Feature
Date: 1990   Origin: USA
Company: Selah Records
Annotation: This Gospel concert features various musical artists.

WINANS, THE: LIVE IN CONCERT

Cast: The Winans *, Vanessa Bell Armstrong*
Director: Dennis Rosenblatt
Producer: Reuben Cannon*, Barry Hankerson
Tech Info: color/sound/88 min.   Type: Concert Feature
Date: 1987   Origin: USA
Company: Cannon
Distributors/Format: Xenon Entertainment Group (1/2")
Archives/Format: IUB - AAAMC (1/2")
Annotation: A spectacular performance by one of America's top-selling gospel groups. Guest appearance by Vanessa Bell Armstrong.

WIRED

Cast: Billy Preston*, Ray Sharkey, Patti D'Arbanville, J.T. Walsh, Michael Chiklis
Director: Larry Peerce
Executive Producer: P. Michael Smith, Paul Carran
Music by: Basil Poledouris, Michael Ruff
Producer: Edward S. Feldman, Charles R. Meeker, P. Michael Smith, Paul Carran
Screenwriter: Earl Mac Rauch

Tech Info: color/sound/110 min.   Type: Dramatic Feature
Date: 1989   Origin: USA
Company: F/M, Lion Screen
Distributors/Format: Taurus Home Video (1/2")
Annotation: John Belushi (Chiklis) is escorted by cabbie Angel Velasquez (Sharkey) through scenes of his drug-addicted life. Preston plays himself. The film is based on Bob Woodward's book on Belushi.

WISECRACKS
Director: Gail Singer
Executive Producer: Rina Fraticelli, Ginny Stikeman, Susan Cavan
Music by: Maribeth Solomon
Producer: Gail Singer, Signe Johannson, Rina Fraticelli, Ginny Stikeman, Susan Cavan
Speaker: Whoopi Goldberg*, Kim Wayans*, Hattie McDaniel*, Phyllis Diller, Jenny Jones, Geri Jewell, Faking it Three , Ellen DeGeneres
Tech Info: color/sound/91 min.   Type: Documentary Feature
Date: 1992   Origin: Canada
Company: Zinger Films, National Film Board of Canada
Distributors/Format: Alliance Releasing (16mm)
Annotation: Goldberg, Wayans, and McDaniel are included in this documentary on female comediennes from the early days of film and TV to today's stand-up comedy.

WITHOUT YOU, I'M NOTHING
Cast: Ken Foree*, Arnold McCuller*, Ludie Washington*, Roxanne Reese*, Vonte Sweet*, Sandra Bernhard, John Doe
Director: John Boskovich
Music Performer: Ashford & Simpson *, Prince (Rogers Nelson) *, Nina Simone*, Ice Cube *, Kenneth Gamble*, Leon Huff*, Dr. Dre *, M.C. Ren *
Music by: Patrice Rushen*, Morgan Ames*
Producer: Jonathan D. Krane
Screenwriter: Sandra Bernhard, John Boskovich
Tech Info: color/sound/89 min.   Type: Comedy Feature
Date: 1990   Origin: USA
Company: Jonathan D. Krane-Nicolas Roeg
Annotation: Bernhard's "performance" movie is filmed at a nightclub populated by middle class Blacks. Foree plays Emcee; Reese and Washington are hecklers; McCuller is a back-up singer; Sweet's role is uncredited.

WITNESS
Cast: Danny Glover*, Harrison Ford, Kelly McGillis
Director: Peter Weir
Producer: Edward S. Feldman
Screenwriter: Earl Kelley, William Kelley
Storywriter: William Kelley, Pamela Wallace, Earl Wallace
Tech Info: color/sound/112 min.   Type: Dramatic Feature
Date: 1985   Origin: USA
Company: Paramount
Distributors/Format: Paramount Home Video (1/2")
Annotation: When a young Amish woman and her son get caught up in the murder of an undercover narcotics agent, their savior turns out to be hardened Philadelphia detective John Book (Ford). Glover has a minor role as a policeman.

WIZ, THE

Cast: Diana Ross*, Richard Pryor*, Lena Horne*, Mabel King*, Michael Jackson*, Theresa Merritt*, Nipsey Russell*, Thelma Carpenter*, Ted Ross*
Director: Sidney Lumet
Executive Producer: Ken Harper
Music Performer: Luther Vandross*
Music by: Quincy Jones*
Producer: Rob Cohen, Ken Harper
Screenwriter: Joel Schumacher
Storywriter: William F. Brown
Tech Info: color/sound/133 min.   Type: Musical Feature
Date: 1978   Origin: USA
Company: Motown
Distributors/Format: MCA Home Video (1/2")
Archives/Format: IUB - BFC/A (1/2")
Annotation: Dorothy (Diana Ross), Scarecrow (Jackson), Tin Man (Russell), and Lion (Ted Ross) all go in search of their heart's desires only to find they had them all along. Pryor plays the fraudulent Wiz and Horne appears as the Good Witch of the South in this remake of THE WIZARD OF OZ from an African American perspective.

WIZARD, THE

Cast: Frank McRae*, Christian Slater, Fred Savage, Luke Edwards
Director: Todd Holland
Executive Producer: Lindsley Parsons Jr.
Music by: J. Peter Robinson*
Producer: Lindsley Parsons Jr., David Chisholm, Ken Topolsky
Screenwriter: David Chisholm
Tech Info: color/sound/97 min.   Type: Comedy Feature
Date: 1989   Origin: USA
Company: Finnegan-Pinchuk
Distributors/Format: Universal Home Video (1/2")
Annotation: Corey Woods (Savage) kidnaps his younger brother Jimmy (Edwards) from a children's home and together they set off on a cross-country trek pursued by their parents. Jimmy is a "wizard" at video games. The children enlist the help of Spanky (McRae), a mildly retarded truck driver, who helps them raise money and drives them to the national video championships held in Los Angeles.

WOLFEN

Cast: Gregory Hines*, Reginald Veljohnson*, Albert Finney, Diane Venora
Director: Michael Wadleigh
Producer: Rupert Hitzig
Screenwriter: David Eyre, Michael Wadleigh
Storywriter: Whitley Streiber
Tech Info: color/sound/115 min.   Type: Dramatic Feature
Date: 1981   Origin: USA
Company: Orion
Distributors/Format: Warner Bros. Home Video, Inc. (1/2")
Annotation: When New York is terrorized by several murders, the police are at a loss. Dewey Wilson (Finney) studies the death wounds and concludes their origins to that of a wolf. He and Police Officer Whittington (Hines) attempt to sequester the

supernatural Wolfen. Veljohnson appears briefly as a morgue attendant.

WOMEN IN WAR: VOICES FROM THE FRONT LINE PART 2
Executive Producer: Diana Meehan, Pat Mitchell
Producer: Diana Meehan, Pat Mitchell, Mary Muldoon
Speaker: Kimi Gray*
Tech Info: color/sound/48 min.   Type: Documentary Feature
Date: 1990   Origin: USA
Company: Pat Mitchell Productions
Annotation: Focusing on war-torn areas of the world, this two-part program profiles women living with the day-to-day tragedy of war.

WOMEN OF BREWSTER PLACE, THE
Cast: Oprah Winfrey*, Jackee Harry*, Robin Givens*, Paula Kelly*, Moses Gunn*, Lonette McKee*, Lynn Whitfield*, Paul Winfield*, Eugene Lee*, Clark Johnson*, Bebe Drake-Massey*, Cicely Tyson*, Glenn Plummer*, Geoffrey Thorne*, Douglas Turner Ward*, Roxanne Reese*, Joe Eszterhas
Director: Donna Deitch
Music by: David Shire
Narrator: Oprah Winfrey*
Producer: Reuben Cannon*, Patricia K. Meyer
Screenwriter: Karen Hall*
Storywriter: Gloria Naylor*
Tech Info: color/sound/180 min.   Type: Television Feature
Date: 1988   Origin: USA
Studio: Independent
Company: Harpo Inc. in Association w/King Phoenix Entertain
Distributors/Format: J2 Communications (1/2")
Annotation: Rejected by her father when she became pregnant, Mattie Michael (Winfrey) moves to Brewster Place where she eventually becomes a role model to the other women who live there. She rallies both men and women on the street to break down the wall that literally and symbolically restricts them to the dead-end street. The film was adapted from the novel of the same title by Gloria Naylor.

WORK EXPERIENCE
Cast: Lenny Henry*, Kathy Burke, John Normington, Neil Pearson
Director: James Hendrie
Producer: Mary Bell
Storywriter: James Hendrie
Tech Info: color/sound/11 min.   Type: Experimental Short
Date: 1989   Origin: USA
Company: Filmwest Associates Limited
Annotation: Terrence Weller (Henry) can't get a job because he has no experience, so he uses an unusual method to get some.

WORKING GIRL
Cast: Melanie Griffith, Harrison Ford, Sigourney Weaver, Suzanne Shepherd
Director: Mike Nichols
Music by: Carly Simon
Producer: Douglas Wick
Screenwriter: Kevin Wade
Tech Info: color/sound/114 min.   Type: Dramatic Feature

Date: 1988   Origin: USA
Company: Fox
Distributors/Format: Fox Home Video (1/2")
Annotation: Working Girl Tess McGill (Griffith) takes over her boss's (Weaver) office and boyfriend (Ford) on her way to the top of the corporate ladder. Shepherd has a minor role as a receptionist for an executive firm.

WORLD ACCORDING TO JOHN COLTRANE, THE

Director: Toby Byron, Robert Palmer
Music Performer: John Coltrane*
Speaker: Alice Coltrane*
Tech Info: mixed/sound/60 min.   Type: Documentary Feature
Date: 1991   Origin: USA
Studio: Independent
Distributors/Format: Facets Multimedia, Inc. (1/2")
Annotation: Extensive performance footage of songs like "My Favorite Things" and "Naima" capture this musician in unexpected moments of musical intimacy. Made in full cooperation with Alice Coltrane, the film explores Coltrane's life and art.

WORLD SAXOPHONE QUARTET, THE

Director: Barbara McCullough*
Tech Info: color/sound/5 min.   Type: Experimental Short
Date: 1992   Origin: USA
Studio: Independent
Distributors/Format: Third World Newsreel (1/2")
Archives/Format: IUB - BFC/A (1/2")
Annotation: McCullough's video presents an innovative quartet of jazz saxophonists, Bluiet, Lake, Hemphill, and Murray, both in concert and conversation.

WRONG GUYS, THE

Cast: Ernie Hudson*, Franklin Ajaye*, Carole White, Richard Belzer, Richard Lewis, Louie Anderson
Director: Danny Bilson
Executive Producer: Lawrence Gordon
Music by: Joseph Conlan
Producer: Lawrence Gordon, Charles Gordon, Ronald E. Frazier
Screenwriter: Danny Bilson, Paul DeMeo
Tech Info: color/sound/86 min.   Type: Comedy Feature
Date: 1988   Origin: USA
Company: New World
Distributors/Format: New World Home Video (1/2")
Annotation: Five stand-up comics, all former members of a Cub Scout den, set out on a camping trip together, but their plans are spoiled when they encounter several unpleasant surprises. Ajaye plays Franklyn and Hudson is Dawson.

WRONG IS RIGHT

Alternate: Man with the Deadly Lens, The
Cast: Rosalind Cash*, Dean Stockwell, Sean Connery, Leslie Nielson, John Saxon, Katharine Ross
Director: Patrick Duncan, Richard Brooks
Producer: Patrick Duncan, Richard Brooks
Screenwriter: Patrick Duncan

Storywriter: Charles McCarry
Tech Info: color/sound/117 min.   Type: Dramatic Feature
Date: 1982   Origin: USA
Company: Rastar
Distributors/Format: RCA/Columbia Pictures Home Video (1/2")
Annotation: The Vice President of the United States, Mrs. Ford (Cash), is one of the many public officials involved in the media frenzied presidential campaign that leads international affairs to the brink of World War III.

YEAR OF THE DRAGON

Cast: Gerald Orange*, Mickey Rourke, John Lone, Ariane , Leonard Termo
Director: Michael Cimino
Music by: David Mansfield
Producer: Dino de Laurentis
Screenwriter: Oliver Stone, Michael Cimino
Tech Info: color/sound/134 min.   Type: Dramatic Feature
Date: 1985   Origin: USA
Company: DEG
Distributors/Format: MGM/UA Home Video (1/2")
Annotation: Stanley White (Rourke), a Vietnam veteran and a decorated New York City police officer, is assigned to control Chinatown's gang problem. Orange plays Bear Siku.

YOU GOT TO MOVE

Alternate: Stories of Change in the South
Director: Veronica Selver, Lucy Phenix
Producer: Veronica Selver, Lucy Phenix
Tech Info: color/sound/87 min.   Type: Documentary Feature
Date: 1985   Origin: USA
Company: Highlander Education and Research Center
Distributors/Format: First Run/Icarus Films (16mm)
Annotation: The film illustrates various efforts at social community organizations to effect change including civil rights education projects and citizen's actions against toxic waste dumping and strip mining in Kentucky and Tennessee.

YOU GOTTA PAY THE BAND: THE LIFE OF ABBEY LINCOLN

Cast: Abbey Lincoln*
Executive Producer: Andre P. Espinet
Producer: Geena Davis, Andre P. Espinet
Tech Info: color/sound/58 min.   Type: Concert Feature
Date: 1991   Origin: USA
Studio: Independent
Annotation: The film is a concert and recording session featuring jazz vocalist Abbey Lincoln.

YOUNG AMERICANS, THE

Cast: Thandie Newton*, Nigel Clauzel*, Harvey Keitel, Viggo Mortensen, Iain Glen, Craig Kelly
Director: Danny Cannon
Executive Producer: Ronna B. Wallace, Philippe Maigret, Richard Gladstein
Music by: David Arnold
Producer: Paul Trijbits, Alison Owen, Ronna B. Wallace, Philippe Maigret, Richard

Gladstein
Screenwriter: Danny Cannon, David Hilton
Tech Info: color/sound/108 min.   Type: Dramatic Feature
Date: 1994   Origin: Great Britain
Company: The Young Americans Ltd., et al.
Distributors/Format: LIVE Home Video (1/2")
Annotation: American DEA agent John Harris (Keitel) investigates the heroin trade in the London underworld. He targets Chris (Kelly) and Lionel (Clauzel) as possible sources of information. Newton plays Rachel Stevens, Lionel's sister and Chris's girlfriend.

YOUNG DOCTORS IN LOVE

Cast: Mr. T. *, Esther Sutherland*, Harry Dean Stanton, Michael McKean, Sean Young
Director: Garry Marshall
Executive Producer: Garry Marshall
Music by: Maurice Jarre
Producer: Jerry Bruckheimer, Garry Marshall
Screenwriter: Michael Elias, Rich Eustis
Tech Info: color/sound/95 min.   Type: Comedy Feature
Date: 1982   Origin: USA
Company: ABC
Distributors/Format: Fox Home Video (1/2")
Annotation: Romance, intrigue, and comedy surround a group of medical interns in a big-city hospital. Sutherland is Nurse Willa Mae and Mr. T. has a cameo role.

YOUNG WARRIORS, THE

Alternate: The Graduates of Malibu High
Cast: Richard Roundtree*, Mike Norris, James Van Patten, Dick Shawn, Ernest Borgnine
Director: Lawrence D. Foldes
Music Performer: Rob Walsh
Music by: Rob Walsh
Producer: Lawrence D. Foldes, Russell W. Colgin, Victoria Paige Meyerink
Screenwriter: Lawrence D. Foldes, Russell W. Colgin
Tech Info: color/sound/104 min.   Type: Dramatic Feature
Date: 1983   Origin: USA
Company: Star Cinema Productions, Cannon
Distributors/Format: Cannon Home Video (1/2")
Annotation: Sgt. John Austin (Roundtree), homicide detective, is the partner of Lt. Bob Corrigan (Borgnine) whose son Kevin (Van Patten) forms a vigilante group to avenge the rape and murder of his sister.

YOUNGBLOOD

Cast: Lawrence-Hilton Jacobs*, Arthur/Art Evans*, Ralph Farquhar*, Maurice Sneed*, Bryan O'Dell*, Tony Allen*, David Pendleton*, Lionel Smith*, Ren Woods, Vince Cannon, Sheila Wills
Director: Noel Nosseck
Music by: War *
Producer: Nick Grillo, Alan Riche
Screenwriter: Paul Carter Harrison

Tech Info: color/sound/90 min.   Type: Dramatic Feature
Date: 1978   Origin: USA
Company: Aion
Distributors/Format: AIP Home Video (1/2")
Annotation: Rommel (Jacobs) returns from Vietnam to the Los Angeles ghetto where
he educates Youngblood (O'Dell) about gang life. When a gang member dies of an
overdose, they go after the pushers: Corelli (Cannon) and Youngblood's brother
Reggie (Pendleton). Allen plays Hustler; Evans is Junkie; Farquhar plays Geronimo;
Smith plays Chaka; Sneed is Skeeter-Jeeter.

YOUR CHILDREN COME BACK TO YOU
Director: Alile Sharon Larkin*
Producer: Alile Sharon Larkin*
Screenwriter: Alile Sharon Larkin*
Storywriter: Alile Sharon Larkin*
Tech Info: bw/sound/27 min.   Type: Dramatic Short
Date: 1979   Origin: USA
Studio: Independent
Distributors/Format: Women Make Movies, Inc. (16mm; 1/2")
Annotation: Larkin's film centers around a young girl, Tovi, who is pressured by her
Aunt Chris to accept a European lifestyle. Tovi instead chooses her mother and her
African heritage.

ZAJOTA AND THE BOOGIE SPIRIT
Director: Ayoka Chenzira*, Ayoka Chenzira*
Music Performer: Mino Cinelu*, Miles Davis*, Sting
Music by: Mino Cinelu*
Producer: Ayoka Chenzira*
Screenwriter: Ayoka Chenzira*
Speaker: Carol-Jean Lewis*, Thomas Osha Pinnock*
Tech Info: mixed/sound/20 min.   Type: Animated Short
Date: 1990   Origin: USA
Studio: Independent
Company: Crossgrain Pictures
Distributors/Format: Filmakers Library, Inc. (16mm; 1/2"), Red Carnelian
Films/Video (16mm; 1/2")
Archives/Format: IUB - BFC/A (1/2")
Annotation: An animated history of African peoples (Zajota) forced from their
homeland into their diasporic journey to the New World. The "Boogie Spirit" helps
the Zajota use the power and rituals of their dance and music to survive. Voice-over
narration is by Carol Jean Lewis.

ZAPPED
Cast: Scatman Crothers*, Willie Aames*, Felice Schachter*, La Wanda Page*,
Heather Thomas, Robert Mandan, Irwin Keyes
Director: Robert J. Rosenthal
Executive Producer: Howard Schuster, Fran Schuster
Music Performer: Charles Fox*
Music by: Charles Fox*
Producer: Jeffrey D. Apple, Howard Schuster, Fran Schuster
Screenwriter: Bruce Rubin, Robert J. Rosenthal
Tech Info: color/sound/98 min.   Type: Comedy Feature

Date: 1982   Origin: USA
Company: Apple/Rose Productions, Thunder, Embassy Pictures
Distributors/Format: Embassy Home Video (1/2")
Annotation: Dexter Jones (Crothers) is the coach of the high school baseball team. He inhales second-hand marijuana smoke and hallucinates about meeting Albert Einstein, but his fantasy is destroyed by his wife (Page).

ZEBRAHEAD

Cast: Paul Butler*, N'Bushe Wright*, DeShonn Castle*, Martin Priest*, Ron Johnson*, Ray Sharkey, Michael Rapaport, Candy Ann Brown
Director: Maryse Alberti, Anthony Drazan
Executive Producer: Oliver Stone, Janet Young
Music by: Taj Mahal *
Producer: Oliver Stone, Jeff Dowd, Charles Mitchell, William Willett, Janet Young
Tech Info: color/sound/102 min.   Type: Dramatic Feature
Date: 1992   Origin: USA
Company: Columbia/TriStar
Distributors/Format: Columbia/TriStar Pictures (35mm; 1/2"), Facets Multimedia, Inc. (1/2")
Archives/Format: IUB - BFC/A (1/2")
Annotation: Two young men Dee Wimms (Castle) and Zack Glass (Rapaport) dare to cross the color line and form a friendship in racially torn Detroit high school. Wright plays Nikki, Dee's cousin and Zack's love interest; Brown plays Nikki's mother.

ZELLY AND ME

Cast: Joe Morton*, Isabella Rossellini, Alexandra Johnes, Julia Beals Williams, Glynis Johns
Director: Tina Rathborne
Executive Producer: Elliott Dewitt, Tina Rathborne
Music by: Pino Donaggio
Producer: Tony Mark, Sue Jet, Elliott Dewitt, Tina Rathborne
Screenwriter: Tina Rathborne
Tech Info: color/sound/87 min.   Type: Dramatic Feature
Date: 1988   Origin: USA
Company: Cypress
Distributors/Format: Columbia Pictures Home Video (1/2")
Annotation: Eight-year-old Phoebe (Johnes) goes to live with Co-Co, her Grandmother (Johns), after her parents die in a plane crash. "Zelly" (Rossellini) is the creative nanny whom Phoebe adores and her Grandmother envies. Morton plays Earl, the gardener; Williams plays Lee, the house maid.

ZOO GANG, THE

Cast: Ben Vereen*, Jackie Haley*, Masequa Myers*, Jason Gedrick, , Tiffany Helm
Director: John Watson, Pen Densham
Music by: Patrick Gleason
Producer: John Watson, Pen Densham
Screenwriter: John Watson, Pen Densham
Storywriter: John Watson, Pen Densham, Stuart Birnbaum, David Dashen
Tech Info: color/sound/96 min.   Type: Dramatic Feature

Date: 1984   Origin: USA
Company: Insight Group
Distributors/Format: New World Home Video (1/2")
Annotation: When a local recreation club "The Zoo" is threatened by a family of bullies, Zoo members become irate and enlist the aid of a drunken, former wrestling champ, James "The Winch" Winchester (Vereen). Myers is a nurse who brings him back to health.

ZORA IS MY NAME!
Cast: Paula Kelly*, Ruby Dee*, Louis Gossett Jr.*, Flip Wilson*, Beah Richards*, Lynn Whitfield*, Count Stovall*, Oscar Brown Jr.*, Roger E. Mosley*
Director: Neema Barnett*
Executive Producer: Samuel J. Paul
Music by: Olu Dara*
Producer: Iris Merlis, Samuel J. Paul
Storywriter: Ann Wallace*
Tech Info: color/sound/90 min.   Type: Television Feature
Date: 1989   Origin: USA
Studio: PBS American Playhouse
Company: Emmalyn II Productions Company
Distributors/Format: Pacific Arts Video Records (1/2")
Annotation: Barnett dramatizes the life of Zora Neale Hurston writer, folklorist and anthropologist.

Aames, Willie
    Cut and Run, 1986
    Paradise, 1982
    Scavenger Hunt, 1979
    Zapped, 1982
Abascal, Paul
    Predator 2, 1990
Abbott, Diahnne
    Jo Jo Dancer, Your Life is Calling, 1986
Abdul Quadr, Tatim
    Syvilla: They Dance to Her Drum, 1979
Abdul Wahhab, Ali Shahid
    Straight Out of Brooklyn, 1991
Abdul-Jabbar, Kareem
    Airplane!, 1980
    D2: The Mighty Ducks, 1994
    Fish that Saved Pittsburgh, The, 1979
    Fletch, 1985
Abdurrahman, Umar
    Daughters of the Dust, 1991
Abraham, Ayisha
    Heaven, Earth & Hell, 1994
Adams, Brandon
    D2: The Mighty Ducks, 1994
    Ghost in the Machine, 1993
    Mighty Ducks, The, 1992
    People under the Stairs, The, 1991
    Sandlot, The, 1993
Adell, Ilunga
    Pass/Fail, 1978
Adrian, Bob
    Jungle Fever, 1991
African Students, Congress of South
    Witness to Apartheid, 1986
Ailey, Alvin
    Ailey Dances, 1982
Ajaye, Franklin
    Burbs, The, 1989
    Convoy, 1978
    Fraternity Vacation, 1985
    Get Crazy, 1983
    Hollywood Shuffle, 1987
    Hysterical, 1983

Ajaye, Franklin
  Jazz Singer, The, 1980
  Stir Crazy, 1980
  Wrong Guys, The, 1988
Alan-Williams, Gregory
  Above the Law, 1988
  In the Line of Fire, 1993
Aldango, Brown
  Allan Quartermain and the Lost City of Gold, 1986
  Police Academy 4: Citizens on Patrol, 1987
Aldridge, Leah
  House Party, 1990
Alexander, Erika
  Long Walk Home, The, 1991
Alexander, Khandi
  CB4: The Movie, 1993
  House Party 3, 1994
  Maid to Order, 1987
  Menace II Society, 1993
  Poetic Justice, 1993
  Streetwalkin', 1985
  Sugar Hill, 1994
  What's Love Got to Do with It, 1993
Ali, Muhammad
  Body and Soul, 1981
  Doin' Time, 1986
  Freedom Road, 1978
Ali, Veronica
  Freedom Road, 1978
Alice, Mary
  Awakenings, 1990
  Beat Street, 1984
  Bonfire of the Vanities, 1990
  He Who Walks Alone, 1978
  Inkwell, 1994
  Killing Floor, The, 1984
  To Sleep with Anger, 1990
Allen, Billie
  Losing Ground, 1982
Allen, Debbie
  Fame, 1980
  Fish that Saved Pittsburgh, The, 1979
  Jo Jo Dancer, Your Life is Calling, 1986

Allen, Debbie
    Ragtime, 1981
Allen, Eugene
    Cosmic Slop: The First Commandant, 1994
    House Party, 1990
    House Party 2: The Pajama Jam, 1991
Allen, Gavin
    Runaway, 1989
Allen, George
    Livin' Large!, 1991
Allen, Harry
    Public Enemy: Tour of a Black Planet, 1991
Allen, Jim
    Amazing Grace and Chuck, 1987
Allen, Tony
    Youngblood, 1978
Allen, Tyrees
    Riverbend, 1990
Alysia, Nicole
    Sidewalk Stories, 1989
American Dance Theater, Alvin Ailey
    Ailey Dances, 1982
    Dance Black America, 1985
Amos, John
    American Flyers, 1985
    Beastmaster, The, 1982
    Coming to America, 1988
    Die Hard 2: Die Harder, 1990
    Lock Up, 1990
    Mac, 1992
    Mardi Gras for the Devil, 1993
    Ricochet, 1991
    Touched by Love, 1979
Anderson, Adisa
    Daughters of the Dust, 1991
Anderson, Dallas
    Mighty Quinn, The, 1989
Anderson, James
    Sweet Bird of Youth, 1986
Anderson, Jeffrey
    Marked for Death, 1990

Anderson, John
Ashes and Embers, 1985
Anderson, Mamie Louise
Jungle Fever, 1991
Anderson, Michael
Different Image, A, 1982
Anderson, Pershing P.
Doctor Detroit, 1983
Anderson, Sheila
Star 80, 1983
Anderson, Sylvia
First Family, 1980
Angela, Sharon
Fly by Night, 1994
Angelou, Maya
Poetic Justice, 1993
There Are No Children Here, 1993
Another Bad Creation
Meteor Man, The, 1993
Anthony, Paul
Cosmic Slop: The First Commandant, 1994
House Party, 1990
House Party 2: The Pajama Jam, 1991
Applegate, Phyllis
Jagged Edge, 1985
Aranha, Ray
Drop Squad, 1994
Armstrong, R.G.
Ghettoblaster, 1989
Where the Buffalo Roam, 1980
Arnold, Tichina
Brewster's Millions, 1985
How I Got into College, 1989
Little Shop of Horrors, 1986
Arrindell, Lisa
Livin' Large!, 1991
One Good Cop, 1991
Ashford, Nick
New Jack City, 1991
Athens, Rooney King
Freedom Road, 1978

Atkins, Curtis
  Jungle Fever, 1991
Attaway, Ruth
  Being There, 1980
Aurelius, Neville
  Displaced Person, 1985
Austin, Michael Harris
  Fly by Night, 1994
Avery, Harrison
  Livin' Large!, 1991
Avery, James
  8 Million Ways to Die, 1986
  Appointment with Fear, 1985
  Beastmaster 2: Through the Portal of Time, 1992
  Fletch, 1985
  License to Drive, 1988
  Little Miss Millions, 1994
  Nightflyers, 1987
  Shout, The, 1991
  Stoogemania, 1986
  Stuntman, The, 1980
  Three for the Road, 1987
Avery, Margaret
  Color Purple, The, 1985
  Fish that Saved Pittsburgh, The, 1979
  Heat Wave, 1990
  Mardi Gras for the Devil, 1993
  Return of Superfly, The, 1990
  Riverbend, 1990
  Sky Is Gray, The, 1980
Avery, Val
  Messenger, The, 1986
  Wanderers, The, 1979
Ayler, Ethel
  To Sleep with Anger, 1990
B. Fine
  Cosmic Slop: The First Commandant, 1994
  House Party, 1990
  House Party 2: The Pajama Jam, 1991
Babatunde, Obba
  Dead Again, 1991
  Importance of Being Ernest, The, 1992
  Married to the Mob, 1988

Babatunde, Obba
    Miami Blues, 1990
    Philadelphia, 1993
    Undercover Blues, 1993
Bagley, Ross Elliot
    Little Rascals, The, 1994
Bailey, Donna
    Street Smart, 1987
Baker, Josephine
    Josephine Baker, 1984
Baker, Shaun
    Grand Canyon, 1991
    House Party, 1990
Balgobin, Jennifer
    Straight to Hell, 1987
    Weird Science, 1985
Banks, Aaron
    Fist of Fear, Touch of Death, 1985
Banks, Ernie
    Jimmy Hollywood, 1994
    Pastime, 1991
    Second Thoughts, 1983
Banks, Lord Michael
    Sugar Hill, 1994
Banks, Tyra
    Higher Learning, 1994
Bar Band
    Another 48 Hours, 1990
Barbara O
    Back Inside Herself, 1984
    Daughters of the Dust, 1991
    Freedom Road, 1978
    Powerful Thang, A, 1991
Barboza, Richard
    Small Time, 1991
Barefield, Eric
    Bad Boys, 1982
Barge, Gene
    Stony Island, 1978
Barnes, Adilah
    Basic Instinct, 1992

Barnes, Cheryl
   Hair, 1979
Barnes, Ronald
   Torture of Mothers, The, 1980
Barnett, Charles
   Beer, 1986
   Charlie Barnett's Terms of Enrollment, 1986
   D.C. Cab, 1984
   My Man Adam, 1986
   Nobody's Fool, 1986
Barrell, Terri
   Eubie, 1981
Barrows, Spencer
   Since Lisa..., 1994
Basie, Count
   Last of the Blue Devils, The, 1980
Bass, Suzi
   Fried Green Tomatoes, 1991
Bassett, Angela
   Boyz n the Hood, 1991
   City of Hope, 1991
   Critters 4, 1992
   F/X, 1986
   Innocent Blood, 1992
   Jacksons: An American Dream, The, 1992
   Malcolm X, 1992
   What's Love Got to Do with It, 1993
Bates, Paul
   Bonfire of the Vanities, 1990
   Crazy People, 1990
   Exterminator II, 1984
   Gun in Betty Lou's Handbag, The, 1992
   Hannah and Her Sisters, 1986
   Hot Pursuit, 1987
   Jennifer Eight, 1992
   Just Like in the Movies, 1992
   Mr. Wonderful, 1993
   Super, The, 1991
   True Romance, 1993
Battle, Hinton
   Foreign Student, 1994

Beach, Michael
    Abyss, The, 1989
    Cadence, 1990
    End of the Line, 1988
    Late for Dinner, 1991
    Lean on Me, 1989
    One False Move, 1991
Beals, Jennifer
    Blood and Concrete - A Love Story, 1991
    Bride, The, 1985
    Caro Diario, 1994
    Club Extinction, 1990
    Day of Atonement, 1993
    Dead on Sight, 1994
    Flashdance, 1983
    In the Soup, 1992
    Mrs. Parker and the Vicious Circle, 1994
    Split Decisions, 1988
    Vampire's Kiss, 1989
Beard, Stymie
    Sophisticated Gents, 1981
Beaubian, Susan
    Naked Gun, The: From the Files of Police Squad, 1988
Beauvais, Garcelle
    Manhunter, 1986
Belafonte, Gina
    Beat Street, 1984
    Bright Lights, Big City, 1988
    Tokyo Pop, 1988
Belafonte, Harry
    Drei Lieder, 1983
Belafonte Harper, Shari
    If You Could See what I Hear, 1981
    Murder by Numbers, 1990
    Speed Zone, 1989
    Time Walker, 1982
Belgrave, Cynthia
    Meteor Man, The, 1993
Bell, Darryl M.
    School Daze, 1988

Bell, George Anthony
    House Party 2: The Pajama Jam, 1991
Bell, John
    Little Man Tate, 1991
Bell, Michael
    Tongues Untied, 1989
Bell, Robert Anthony
    One False Move, 1991
Bell, Ronnie
    My Brother's Wedding, 1983
Bell, Vanessa
    Coming to America, 1988
Bell Armstrong, Vanessa
    Winans, The: Live in Concert, 1987
Bellamy, Bill
    Who's the Man?, 1993
Bellamy, Paula
    To Sleep with Anger, 1990
Belling, Kylie
    Fringe Dwellers, The, 1986
Benjamin, Paul
    Escape from Alcatraz, 1979
    I Know Why the Caged Bird Sings, 1978
    Nuts, 1987
    Super, The, 1991
Bennett, Fran
    Blind Tom: The Story of Thomas Bethune, 1987
Benson, Michon
    Jason's Lyric, 1994
Benton, Jerome
    Grafitti Bridge, 1990
    Under the Cherry Moon, 1986
Berclaz, Lath
    M.C. Lyte: Lyte Years, 1991
Bernard, Jason
    Bird, 1988
    Blue Thunder, 1983
    Children of Times Square, 1986
    Cosmic Slop: Space Traders, 1994
    Def by Temptation, 1990
    No Way Out, 1987
    Paint it Black, 1990
    Uncle Joe Shannon, 1978

Bernard, Jason
  Wargames, 1983
Berry, Bertice
  Cosmic Slop: Space Traders, 1994
Berry, Chuck
  American Hot Wax, 1978
  Chuck Berry: Hail! Hail! Rock 'n' Roll!, 1987
  National Lampoon's Class Reunion, 1982
Berry, Darien
  Juice, 1992
Berry, Halle
  Boomerang, 1992
  Father Hood, 1993
  Flintstones, The, 1994
  Jungle Fever, 1991
  Last Boy Scout, The, 1991
  Losing Isaiah, 1994
  Program, The, 1993
  Queen, 1993
  Strictly Business, 1991
Bethea, Melvin
  Jungle Fever, 1991
Beyer, Troy
  Five Heartbeats, The, 1991
  Rooftops, 1989
  Weekend at Bernie's II, 1993
  White Girl, The, 1988
Bigham, Lexie D.
  South Central, 1992
Biscoe, Donna
  Drop Squad, 1994
Black, Clinton
  Legacy of Marcus Garvey, 1988
Black, Dorise
  Straight Out of Brooklyn, 1991
Black Gospel Choir
  Leap of Faith, 1992
Blackwell, Evelyn
  Ashes and Embers, 1985
Blacque, Taurean
  Deepstar Six, 1989
  Hunter, The, 1980
  Rocky II, 1979

Blake, Andre B.
   Who's the Man?, 1993
Blalock, Norman
   Ashes and Embers, 1985
Bland, Michael
   D.C. Cab, 1984
Blank, Kenny
   Super, The, 1991
Blanks, Billy
   Back in Action, 1994
   Bloodfist, 1989
   King of Kickboxers, The, 1991
   Last Boy Scout, The, 1991
   Lionheart, 1991
   Talons of the Eagle, 1992
   TC 2000, 1993
   Time Bomb, 1991
Blicker, Jason
   American Boyfriends, 1989
   Sing, 1989
   Taking of Beverly Hills, The, 1991
Blow, Kurtis
   Knights of the City, 1985
   Krush Groove, 1985
Blow, Peggy
   Penitentiary II, 1982
Blues Band, Rhythm Rockers
   Performed Word, The, 1982
Blunt, Augie
   Ghost, 1990
Blyde, Jimmy
   Tap, 1989
Boatman, Michael P.
   Hamburger Hill, 1987
   Running on Empty, 1988
   Urban Crossfire, 1994
Bodison, Wolfgang
   Few Good Men, A, 1992
   Little Big League, 1994
Boggs, Gail
   And God Created Woman, 1988
   Curly Sue, 1991
   Ghost, 1990

Bolling, Gary
    Losing Ground, 1982
Bomb, James
    Public Enemy: Tour of a Black Planet, 1991
Bond, Cynthia
    Def by Temptation, 1990
Bond, Paula
    Caged in Paradiso, 1990
Bond III, James
    Def by Temptation, 1990
    Fish that Saved Pittsburgh, The, 1979
    Go Tell it on the Mountain, 1984
    School Daze, 1988
    Sky Is Gray, The, 1980
Bonet, Lisa
    Angel Heart, 1987
    Bank Robber, 1993
    Dead Connection, 1994
    New Eden, 1994
Bonet, Nai
    Nocturna, 1979
Bonnel, Vivian
    Ghost, 1990
Bowlegged Lou
    Cosmic Slop: The First Commandant, 1994
    House Party, 1990
    House Party 2: The Pajama Jam, 1991
    Who's the Man?, 1993
Boyd, Tanya
    Disappearance of Christina, The, 1994
    Jo Jo Dancer, Your Life is Calling, 1986
    Wholly Moses, 1980
Bradley, Kathleen
    Perfume, 1990
Braithwaite, Fred
    Strictly Business, 1991
Branch, Philip
    Foreign Student, 1994
Branner, Bernard
    Tongues Untied, 1989

Bratton, Dana
    They Live, 1988
Braugher, Andre
    Glory, 1989
    Striking Distance, 1993
Breland, Mark
    Lords of Discipline, The, 1983
Brent, Timothy
    Warriors of the Wasteland, 1983
Brice, Ron
    Fly by Night, 1994
Bridges, Todd
    Homeboys, 1992
Briggs, Bunny
    No Maps on My Taps, 1979
    Tap, 1989
Brister, B.L.
    One False Move, 1991
Brooks, Avery
    Half Slave, Half Free, 1984
    Uncle Tom's Cabin, 1987
Brooks, Richard
    84 Charlie Mopic, 1989
    Badge of the Assassin, 1985
    Saxo, 1988,
    Shakedown, 1988
    Shocker, 1989
    To Sleep with Anger, 1990
Brooks, Yvette
    Jungle Fever, 1991
    Since Lisa..., 1994
Broom, Maria
    Clara's Heart, 1988
Bropleh, Dagbe Nagbe
    Filmstatement, 1982
Brothers, Carla
    Five Heartbeats, The, 1991
Brown, Alex
    Sugar Hill, 1994
Brown, Alfredine
    D.C. Cab, 1984

Brown, Alonzo
  Action Jackson, 1988
Brown, Bobby
  Ghostbusters II, 1989
  Shelly Duvall's Rock N' Rhymeland, 1990
Brown, Carlos
  North Dallas Forty, 1979
  Remember My Name, 1978
Brown, Charnele
  Drop Squad, 1994
  How U Like Me Now, 1992
Brown, Christopher K.
  Grand Canyon, 1991
  K2, 1992
  Lionheart, 1991
Brown, Curtis
  Game, The, 1990
Brown, Darren
  Clarence and Angel, 1981
Brown, Georg Stanford
  Ava's Magical Adventure, 1994
  House Party 2: The Pajama Jam, 1991
  Our Olympic Hero: Jesse Owens Story, The, 1984
  Stir Crazy, 1980
Brown, Gerard
  Livin' Large!, 1991
Brown, Gibran
  Marvin and Tige, 1983
Brown, James
  Blues Brothers, The, 1980
  Courage of Rin Tin Tin, 1983
  Doctor Detroit, 1983
  Rocky IV, 1985
Brown, Jim
  Crack House, 1989
  Divine Enforcer, The, 1991
  Fingers, 1978
  I'm Gonna Git You Sucka, 1988
  L.A. Heat, 1988
  L.A. Vice, 1989
  One Down, Two to Go, 1983
  Twisted Justice, 1990

Brown, Ollie E.
    Blame it on the Night, 1984
Brown, Roger Aaron
    Alien Nation, 1988
    China Moon, 1994
    Don't Cry, It's Only Thunder, 1982
    Downtown, 1990
    Meet the Applegates, 1991
    Moon Over Parador, 1988
    Near Dark, 1987
    Robocop II, 1990
Brown, Ruth
    Hairspray, 1987
    True Identity, 1991
Brown, Sharon
    Chorus Line, A, 1985
    Dozens, The, 1981
    For Keeps, 1988
Brown, Tony
    White Girl, The, 1988
Brown, Wren T.
    Importance of Being Ernest, The, 1992
Brown Jr., Oscar
    Up Against the Wall, 1991
    Zora Is My Name!, 1989
Browne, Roscoe Lee
    Jumpin' Jack Flash, 1986
    Legal Eagles, 1986
    Mambo Kings, The, 1992
    Moon 44, 1991
    Naked in New York, 1994
    Nothing Personal, 1980
    Oliver & Company, 1988
    Twilight's Last Gleaming, 1978
    Unknown Powers, 1980
Bruce, Cheryl Lynn
    Music Box, 1989
Bruce, Michael
    Different Image, A, 1982
Buchanan, Ronald
    Torture of Mothers, The, 1980

Buggerrilla, Bodacious
    Black Images from the Screen, 1978
Bunch, Sekou
    Wild Orchid 2: Two Shades of Blue, 1992
Burch, Matthew
    Hot Stuff, 1979
Burge, Gregg
    Chorus Line, A, 1985
Burkhalter Elementary
    Performed Word, The, 1982
Burmester, Leo
    Fly by Night, 1994
    Passion Fish, 1993
Burnett, Angela
    Bless Their Little Hearts, 1983
Burnett, Kimberly
    Bless Their Little Hearts, 1983
Burnett, Ronald
    Bless Their Little Hearts, 1983
Burnette, Clement
    Foreign Student, 1994
Burrall, Alex
    Jacksons: An American Dream, The, 1992
Burton, Jeff
    Black Mama, 1988
Burton, LeVar
    Guyana Tragedy: The Jim Jones Story, 1983
    Hunter, The, 1980
    Star Trek: Generations, 1994
    Supernaturals, The, 1987
    Whispers on the Wind, 1990
Burton, Tony
    Armed and Dangerous, 1986
    Assault on Precinct 13, 1981
    Hook, 1991
    House Party 2: The Pajama Jam, 1991
    Inside Moves, 1980
    Mission of Justice, 1992
    Rocky II, 1979
    Rocky III, 1982
    Rocky IV, 1985
    Rocky V, 1990
    Shining, The, 1980

Bush, Grand L.
    Backtrack, 1992
    Brewster's Millions, 1985
    Chasers, 1994
    Colors, 1988
    Die Hard, 1988
    Exoricist III: The Legion, 1990
    First Power, The, 1990
    Freejack, 1992
    Hollywood Shuffle, 1987
    Maniac Cop 3: Badge of Silence, 1993
    Night Shift, 1982
    Stir Crazy, 1980
    Street Fighter, 1994
    Streets of Fire, 1984
    Vice Squad, 1982
    Weekend Pass, 1984
Bushwick Bill
    Who's the Man?, 1993
Busia, Akosua
    Ashanti, 1979
    Badge of the Assassin, 1985
    Brother Future, 1991
    Color Purple, The, 1985
    Crossroads, 1986
    Final Terror, The, 1983
    Low Blow, 1986
    Native Son, 1986
    Saxo, 1988
    Seventh Sign, The, 1988
Busta Rhymez
    Higher Learning, 1994
    Who's the Man?, 1993
Butler, Paul
    Compromising Positions, 1985
    Glengarry Glen Ross, 1992
    Homocide, 1991
    Renegades, 1989
    Romeo is Bleeding, 1994
    Rookie, The, 1990
    Stephen King's Silver Bullet, 1985
    Strictly Business, 1991
    To Sleep with Anger, 1990

Butler, Paul
  ZebraHead, 1992
Bynum, David
  Bride of Re-Animator, The, 1991
Byrde, Edye
  Doc Hollywood, 1991
  Moscow on the Hudson, 1984
  Rappin', 1985
Bythewood, Reggie Rock
  Brother from Another Planet, The, 1984
  Exterminator II, 1984
Bywaters, Yvonne
  Angel Heart, 1987
CA Community Choir, James Cleveland's South.
  Blues Brothers, The, 1980
Caesar, Adolph
  Club Paradise, 1986
  Color Purple, The, 1985
  Fist of Fear, Touch of Death, 1985
  Fortune Dane, 1986
  Soldier's Story, A, 1984
Caesar, Harry
  Bird on a Wire, 1990
  Breakin' 2: Electric Boogaloo, 1984
  City Heat, 1984
  Eddie and the Cruisers, 1983
  End, The, 1978
  Escape Artist, The, 1982
  Ghettoblaster, 1989
  Hot to Trot, 1988
  Offspring, The, 1987
  Retribution, 1988
  Roadside Prophets, 1992
  Small Circle of Friends, A, 1980
Caesar, Shirley
  Gospel, 1987
Caldwell, L. Scott
  Up Against the Wall, 1991
Calhoun, Monica
  Bagdad Cafe, 1987

Callet, Ben
  Tongues Untied, 1989
Calloway, Cab
  Blues Brothers, The, 1980
  That's Black Entertainment, 1989
Calloway, Chris
  Importance of Being Ernest, The, 1992
Calloway, Vanessa Bell
  Bebe's Kids, 1992
  Inkwell, 1994
  Stompin' at the Savoy, 1992
  What's Love Got to Do with It, 1993
Camara, Hasinatu
  Sankofa, 1994
Cambridge, Ed
  Bill and Ted's Bogus Journey, 1991
Campbell, G. Smokey
  Bagdad Cafe, 1987
  Prayer of the Rollerboys, 1992
Campbell, Naomi
  Cool As Ice, 1991
  Night We Never Met, The, 1993
Campbell, Paul
  Wide Sargasso Sea, 1993
Campbell, Tevin
  Grafitti Bridge, 1990
Campbell, Tisha
  Another 48 Hours, 1990
  Boomerang, 1992
  House Party, 1990
  House Party 2: The Pajama Jam, 1991
  House Party 3, 1994
  Little Shop of Horrors, 1986
  Rooftops, 1989
  School Daze, 1988
Capers, Virginia
  Backfire, 1989
  Beethoven's 2nd, 1993
  Ferris Bueller's Day Off, 1986
  Howard the Duck, 1986
  North Avenue Irregulars, The, 1979
  Original Intent, 1992
  Teachers, 1984

Capers, Virginia
  Toy, The, 1982
Cara, Irene
  Busted Up, 1986
  Caged in Paradiso, 1990
  Certain Fury, 1985
  City Heat, 1984
  D.C. Cab, 1984
  Fame, 1980
  For Us, the Living, 1984
  Guyana Tragedy: The Jim Jones Story, 1983
  Happily Ever After, 1993
  Sister, Sister, 1982
Carpenter, Thelma
  Cotton Club, The, 1984
  Wiz, The, 1978
Carpenter, Willie C.
  Chair, The, 1991
  Double Trouble, 1992
  Family Business, 1989
  Grand Canyon, 1991
  Hard Target, 1993
Carroll, Diahann
  Five Heartbeats, The, 1991
  I Know Why the Caged Bird Sings, 1978
  Sister, Sister, 1982
Carroll, Rocky
  Born on the Fourth of July, 1989
  Chase, The, 1994
  Fathers and Sons, 1992
  Prelude to a Kiss, 1992
Carry III, Julius J.
  Last Dragon, The, 1985
  Man with One Red Shoe, The, 1985
Carson, Lisa
  Jason's Lyric, 1994
Carson, Terence "T.C."
  Livin' Large!, 1991
Carter, Alice
  Dangerous Heart, 1994
  Gross Anatomy, 1989
  House Party 2: The Pajama Jam, 1991

Carter, Fran
   Drop Squad, 1994
Carter, Malick
   Penitentiary II, 1982
Carter, Maryce
   Clara's Heart, 1988
Carter, Nell
   Ain't Misbehavin, 1982
   Back Roads, 1981
   Bebe's Kids, 1992
   Hair, 1979
   Modern Problems, 1981
Carter, Omar
   Fly by Night, 1994
Carter, T.K.
   Amazon Women on the Moon, 1987
   Doctor Detroit, 1983
   He's My Girl, 1987
   Rage in Harlem, A, 1991
   Runaway Train, 1985
   Seed of Innocence, 1980
   Seems Like Old Times, 1980
   Ski Patrol, 1990
   Southern Comfort, 1981
   Thing, The, 1982
Carter, Terry
   Battlestar Gallactica, 1979
Casey, Bernie
   Another 48 Hours, 1990
   Backfire, 1989
   Bill and Ted's Excellent Adventure, 1989
   Cemetery Club, The, 1993
   Chains of Gold, 1992
   I'm Gonna Git You Sucka, 1988
   Never Say Never Again, 1983
   Once Upon A Time When We Were Colored, 1994
   Rent-A-Cop, 1988
   Revenge of the Nerds, 1984
   Sharkey's Machine, 1981
   Sophisticated Gents, 1981
   Spies Like Us, 1985
   Steele Justice, 1987
   Street Knight, 1993

Casey, Bernie
  Under Siege, 1992
Casey, D. Ben
  Space Camp, 1986
Casey, Kenneth
  Mighty Quinn, The, 1989
Cash, Rosalind
  Adventures of Buckaroo Banzai: Across the 8th Dimension, The, 1984
  Class of Miss Mac Michael, The, 1978
  Go Tell it on the Mountain, 1984
  Just an Overnight Guest, 1983
  Offspring, The, 1987
  Sister, Sister, 1982
  Sophisticated Gents, 1981
  Wrong Is Right, 1982
Castle, DeShonn
  ZebraHead, 1992
Cele, Baby
  Voices of Sarafina, 1988
Cenen
  Mother's Hands, 1992
Chalk, Al
  American Hot Wax, 1978
Cham, Mybe
  Serving Two Masters, 1987
Chamberlain, Wilt
  Conan the Destroyer, 1984
Chambers, Michael Boogaloo Shrimp
  Breakin', 1984
  Breakin' 2: Electric Boogaloo, 1984
Chapman, Lanei
  Importance of Being Ernest, The, 1992
  White Men Can't Jump, 1992
Chappelle, Dave
  Robin Hood: Men in Tights, 1993
Charles, Ray
  Blues Brothers, The, 1980
  Limit Up, 1990
  Love Affair, 1994
Chase, Annazette
  Toy, The, 1982

Chatman, Floyd
  Getting Over, 1981
  Penitentiary, 1979
Chavers, Arabella
  Pass/Fail, 1978
Chavis, Tracy Lee
  Posse, 1993
Cheadle, Don
  Colors, 1988
  Hamburger Hill, 1987
  Meteor Man, The, 1993
  Moving Violations, 1985
  Roadside Prophets, 1992
Chenier, Clifton
  Clifton Chenier, 1978
Chenzira, Ayoka
  Colour, 1983
Cherry, Eugene
  Bless Their Little Hearts, 1983
Chery, Marc
  Cycles, 1989
Chesher, Lydell W.
  Ricochet, 1991
Chestnut, Morris
  Boyz n the Hood, 1991
  Inkwell, 1994
  Urban Crossfire, 1994
Childress, Alvin
  Main Event, The, 1979
  Sister, Sister, 1982
Chisholm, LaToya
  War, The, 1994
Chong, Rae Dawn
  Amazon, 1991
  American Flyers, 1985
  Badge of the Assassin, 1985
  Beat Street, 1984
  Boca, 1994
  Borrower, The, 1991
  Cheech and Chong: Corsican Brothers, 1984
  Choose Me, 1984
  City Limits, 1985
  Color Purple, The, 1985

Chong, Rae Dawn
    Commando, 1985
    Common Bonds, 1992
    Denial, 1991
    Far Out Man, 1990
    Father and Son: Dangerous Relations, 1993
    Fear City, 1984
    Krush Groove, 1985
    Loon, 1989
    Principal, The, 1987
    Quest for Fire, 1981
    Running Out of Luck, 1986
    Soul Man, 1986
    Squeeze, The, 1987
    Stony Island, 1978
    Tales from the Darkside, 1991
    Time Runner, 1993
Chong, Robbi
    Cheech and Chong: Corsican Brothers, 1984
    Jimmy Hollywood, 1994
Christian, Robert
    ...And Justice for All, 1979
    Bustin' Loose, 1981
    Prince of the City, 1981
    Roll of Thunder, Hear My Cry, 1986
Christine, Wanda
    Clara's Heart, 1988
    Folks!, 1992
    Mary Thomas Story, The, 1987
Chuck D.
    Public Enemy: Tour of a Black Planet, 1991
Churchill, Candace
    Mother's Hands, 1992
Cicero, Phyllis
    Steele's Law, 1992
Cintron, Monique
    Fast Forward, 1985
Clanton, Rony
    Def by Temptation, 1990
    Hangin' with the Homeboys, 1991
    Night of the Juggler, 1980
    Rappin', 1985
    Return of Superfly, The, 1990

Clanton, Rony
    Too Scared to Scream, 1985
Clark, Damon
    Game, The, 1990
Clark, Juanita
    Torture of Mothers, The, 1980
Clark, Marlene
    Baron, The, 1987
Clarke, Hope
    Into the Night, 1985
Clarke, Michael
    Filmstatement, 1982
Clarke, Node
    Baron, The, 1987
Clauzel, Nigel
    Young Americans, The, 1994
Claxton, Mary
    Maid to Order, 1987
Clayton, Kevin
    Maid to Order, 1987
Clayton, Merry
    Blame it on the Night, 1984
    Wild Orchid 2: Two Shades of Blue, 1992
Clementson, Christine
    Scenes from the New World, 1994
Cleveland, Reverend James
    Gospel, 1987
Cliff, Jimmy
    Bongo Man, 1981
    Club Paradise, 1986
Clinton, George
    Apple, The, 1980
    Grafitti Bridge, 1990
    House Party, 1990
Cobb Sr., Dr. Charles
    Ashes and Embers, 1985
Cobbs, Bill
    Bodyguard, The, 1992
    Brother from Another Planet, The, 1984
    Color of Money, The, 1986
    Compromising Positions, 1985
    Dominick and Eugene, 1988
    Exiled in America, 1992

Cobbs, Bill
    Five Corners, 1988
    Hard Way, The, 1991
    January Man, The, 1989
    New Jack City, 1991
    People under the Stairs, The, 1991
    Roadside Prophets, 1992
    Silkwood, 1983
    Suspect, 1987
Colbert, Catero
    Perfect Model, The, 1989
    Sweet Perfection, 1987
    Up Against the Wall, 1991
Colbert, Pat
    Hysterical, 1983
    Leonard Part 6, 1987
Colbert, Zuindi
    Up Against the Wall, 1991
Cole, Betty
    Soul Man, 1986
Cole, Nat King
    That's Black Entertainment, 1989
Cole, Olivia
    Big Shots, 1987
    Coming Home, 1978
    Go Tell it on the Mountain, 1984
    Sky Is Gray, The, 1980
    Some Kind of Hero, 1982
Coleman, Christian
    South Central, 1992
Coleman, Danielle
    Jungle Fever, 1991
Coleman, Gary
    Jimmy the Kid, 1982
    Kid with the 200 I.Q., The, 1982
    Kid with the Broken Halo, The, 1981
    On the Right Track, 1981
Coleman, Jacqueline
    Star 80, 1983
Coleman, Juan
    Toy, The, 1982

Coleman, Marilyn
    Menace II Society, 1993
    Meteor Man, The, 1993
    Remember My Name, 1978
    Vice Squad, 1982
Coleman, Tony
    Heart and Souls, 1993
Coles, Kim
    Strictly Business, 1991
Collins, Richard O'Shon
    African Story Magic, 1992
Collins, Rickey
    Once Upon a Forest, 1993
Collins, Tyler
    Rage in Harlem, A, 1991
Collins Jr., Wayne
    Bebe's Kids, 1992
Colyar, Michael
    Closer, The, 1991
    Hot Shots! Part Deux, 1993
    House Party 3, 1994
    Johnny Be Good, 1988
    Poetic Justice, 1993
Converse, Frank
    Brother Future, 1991
Cook, Sharon
    Juice, 1992
Cook, Victor L.
    Hangin' with the Homeboys, 1991
Cooper, Kristoffer
    Cool Runnings, 1993
Corbett, Linita
    Foreign Student, 1994
Corkum, Clark
    Skinheads--the Second Coming of Hate, 1990
Cosby, Bill
    Bill Cosby's Picture Pages, 1988
    Bill Cosby--Himself, 1981
    Bill Cosby: 49, 1987
    California Suite, 1978
    Devil and Max Devlin, The, 1981
    Earth Day Special, The, 1990
    Ghost Dad, 1990

Cosby, Bill
   Leonard Part 6, 1987
   Meteor Man, The, 1993
   Reading Readiness - Volume 5, 1988
Costley, Robert
   Toy, The, 1982
Cothran Jr., John
   Class of 1999 II: The Substitute, 1994
   Opportunity Knocks, 1990
   Ricochet, 1991
Coufos, Paul
   Busted Up, 1986
Coughlin, Sarah Katie
   Hollywood Shuffle, 1987
Coven, DeForest
   To Sleep with Anger, 1990
Cox, E'Lon
   Jo Jo Dancer, Your Life is Calling, 1986
Cox, Etta
   Cemetery Club, The, 1993
Cox, Tony
   Rockula, 1990
Cozart, Cylk
   Blue Chips, 1994
   Fire Birds, 1990
   Heaven is a Playground, 1992
   Hot Shots!, 1991
   Love Affair, 1994
   School Daze, 1988
   White Men Can't Jump, 1992
Crable, Debra
   How U Like Me Now, 1992
Craver, Sonny
   White Men Can't Jump, 1992
Crawford, Candice A.
   Walk on White Nails, 1991
Crothers, Scatman
   Bronco Billy, 1980
   Cheap Detective, The, 1978
   Deadly Eyes, 1982
   Journey of Natty Gann, The, 1985
   Mean Dog Blues, 1978
   Scavenger Hunt, 1979

Crothers, Scatman
    Shining, The, 1980
    Transformers: The Movie, The, 1986
    Twilight Zone: The Movie, 1983
    Two of a Kind, 1983
    Zapped, 1982
Crouther, Lance
    Talkin' Dirty after Dark, 1991
Crumes, Oliver
    Madonna: Truth or Dare, 1991
Crutcher, T. Renee
    Tank, 1984
Cruz, Celia
    Mambo Kings, The, 1992
Cruzat, Lisa
    Perfect Model, The, 1989
    Sweet Perfection, 1987
Cumbuka, Ji-Tu
    Bachelor Party, 1984
    Brewster's Millions, 1985
    Midnight Edition, 1994
    Out of Bounds, 1986
    Outrageous Fortune, 1987
    Volunteers, 1985
Cummings, Sandy
    Messenger, The, 1986
Cundieff, Rusty
    3:15, The Moment of Truth, 1986
    Fear of a Black Hat, 1994
    Hollywood Shuffle, 1987
    School Daze, 1988
Cunningham, Christine
    Freedom Station, The, 1988
Curry, Mark
    Talkin' Dirty after Dark, 1991
Curry, Rahsaan
    Hair, 1979
Curtis, Cory
    Deep Cover, 1992
    To Sleep with Anger, 1990

Curtis, Keene
    Sliver, 1993
Curtis-Hall, Vondie
    Dead Man's Revenge, 1994
    Drop Squad, 1994
    Falling Down, 1993
    Heat Wave, 1990
    Mambo Kings, The, 1992
    Mystery Train, 1989
    One Good Cop, 1991
    Passion Fish, 1993
    Shakedown, 1988
    Sugar Hill, 1994
Curtle, Averell
    Jungle Fever, 1991
Curvey, Troy
    Lock Up, 1990
D-Knowledge
    Higher Learning, 1994
Da'oud, Kamaau
    Life is a Saxophone, 1985
Daise, Ron
    Daughters of the Dust, 1991
Dance Company, Charles Moore
    Dance Black America, 1985
Dandridge, Gregg
    Grand Canyon, 1991
    To Live and Die in L.A., 1985
Dane, Dana
    M.C. Lyte: Lyte Years, 1991
Daniels, John R.
    Getting Over, 1981
Darton, Marlin
    Harley Davidson and the Marlboro Man, 1991
Dash, Stacey
    Black Water, 1994
    Enemy Territory, 1987
    Mo' Money, 1992
    Moving, 1988
    Renaissance Man, 1994

Datcher, Alex
  Netherworld, 1992
  Passenger 57, 1992
  Rage and Honor, 1993
Daughtry, Rev. Herbert
  Mo' Better Blues, 1990
David, Keith
  Always, 1989
  Article 99, 1992
  Marked for Death, 1990
  Men at Work, 1990
  Platoon, 1986
  Road House, 1989
  Thing, The, 1982
Davidson, Jaye
  Crying Game, The, 1992
  Stargate, 1994
Davidson, Tommy
  Strictly Business, 1991
Davis, Cathy
  Best of Times, The, 1986
  Guy from Harlem, The, 1989
Davis, D'Mitch
  Weird Science, 1985
Davis, Duane
  Beetlejuice, 1988
  Diggstown, 1992
  How I Got into College, 1989
  Little Big League, 1994
  Necessary Roughness, 1991
  Past Tense, 1994
  Program, The, 1993
  Skinheads--the Second Coming of Hate, 1990
  Summer School, 1987
  Under Siege, 1992
  Universal Soldier, 1992
Davis, Gerald
  Tongues Untied, 1989
Davis, Guy
  Beat Street, 1984
  Def by Temptation, 1990
  Krush Groove, 1985

Davis, James S.
  Powerful Thang, A, 1991
Davis, Lloyd
  Jury of Her Peers, A, 1994
Davis, Nancy Cheryll
  Perfume, 1990
Davis, Ossie
  Avenging Angel, 1985
  Benjamin Banneker: The Man who Loved the Stars, 1981
  Client, The, 1994
  Do the Right Thing, 1989
  Freedom Man, 1989
  Gladiator, 1992
  Grumpy Old Men, 1993
  Harry and Son, 1984
  Hot Stuff, 1979
  House of God, The, 1984
  Joe Versus the Volcano, 1990
  Jungle Fever, 1991
  King, 1978
  School Daze, 1988
Davis, Paula
  D.C. Cab, 1984
Davis, Ralnardo
  Mississippi Burning, 1988
Davis, Richard
  Stony Island, 1978
Davis, Steven Keith
  Grand Canyon, 1991
Davis, Zeinabu irene
  Cycles, 1989
Davis Jr., Sammy
  Cannonball Run II, 1983
  Cannonball Run, The, 1981
  Moon Over Parador, 1988
Davis Jr., Stanley
  Fast Times at Ridgemont High, 1982
Davis-Hill, Gloria
  Jury of Her Peers, A, 1994
Dawn, Marpessa
  'Round Midnight, 1986

Dawson, Kamala
    Lightning Jack, 1994
Day, Cora Lee
    Odds & Ends: A New-Age Amazon Fable, 1993
    What's Love Got to Do with It, 1993
Day, Morris
    Adventures of Ford Fairlane, The, 1990
    Grafitti Bridge, 1990
    Purple Rain, 1984
De Larverie, Storme
    Storme: The Lady of the Jewel Box, 1987
Dean, Allison
    Cool As Ice, 1991
    Ruby in Paradise, 1993
Dee, Ruby
    Cat People, 1982
    Cop and a Half, 1993
    Do the Right Thing, 1989
    Go Tell it on the Mountain, 1984
    I Know Why the Caged Bird Sings, 1978
    Jungle Fever, 1991
    Love at Large, 1990
    Torture of Mothers, The, 1980
    Whispers on the Wind, 1990
    Zora Is My Name!, 1989
Deezer D.
    Cool As Ice, 1991
Def Jef
    Talkin' Dirty after Dark, 1991
DeHart, Wayne
    Jason's Lyric, 1994
Delegall, Bob
    Pizza Man, 1991
Delgado, Kim
    Badge of the Assassin, 1985
Delory, Donna
    Madonna: Truth or Dare, 1991
Dennis, Winston
    Commitments, The, 1992
Derricks, Cleavant
    Moscow on the Hudson, 1984
    Off Beat, 1986

Derricks-Carroll, Clinton
    Sky Is Gray, The, 1980
Deshields, Andre
    Ain't Misbehavin, 1982
Deveaux, Ernest
    Street Smart, 1987
Devine, Loretta
    Little Nikita, 1988
    Livin' Large!, 1991
    Stanley and Iris, 1990
    Sticky Fingers, 1988
DeWalt, Destinee
    Grand Canyon, 1991
Diamond, T.C.
    Earth Girls Are Easy, 1988
Diamond, Keith
    Awakenings, 1990
Dickerson, Ernest
    She's Gotta Have It, 1986
Diddley, Bo
    Rockula, 1990
Diezel, Pop
    Public Enemy: Tour of a Black Planet, 1991
Dillard, Victoria
    Deep Cover, 1992
    Ricochet, 1991
Dillon, Pat
    Sitting in Limbo, 1986
Dixon, Jeff
    Dark Exodus, 1985
Dixon, Kennedy
    Freedom Road, 1978
Dixon, Kenneth R.
    Tongues Untied, 1989
DJ Scratch
    Fly by Night, 1994
Djola, Badja
    Innocent Man, An, 1989
    Lightship, The, 1986
    Main Event, The, 1979
    Mississippi Burning, 1988
    Night Shift, 1982
    Penitentiary, 1979

Djola, Badja
  Rage in Harlem, A, 1991
  Waterdance, The, 1992
  Who's the Man?, 1993
Dlamini, Dumisani
  Sarafina!, 1992
Dobson, Tamara
  Chained Heat, 1983
Don, Bigga
  House Party 3, 1994
Donegan, Pamela
  Speeding Up Time, 1985
Donielle, Nicole
  Kiss Grandmama Goodbye, 1991
Doolkery, Leslie
  Eubie, 1981
DoQui, Leslie
  Original Intent, 1992
DoQui, Robert
  Carny, 1980
  Diplomatic Immunity, 1991
  Fast Forward, 1985
  I'm Dancing as Fast as I Can, 1982
  Original Intent, 1992
  Robocop, 1987
  Robocop II, 1990
  Robocop III, 1993
Dorn, Michael
  Jagged Edge, 1985
  Star Trek VI: The Undiscovered Country, 1991
  Star Trek: Generations, 1994
Dorsett, Tony
  Necessary Roughness, 1991
Dosreis, Asia
  Meteor Man, The, 1993
Dotson, Anthonia
  Rage in Harlem, A, 1991
Dotten, Irv
  Boomerang, 1992
Doug, Doug E.
  Class Act, 1992
  Cool Runnings, 1993
  Dr. Giggles, 1992

Doug, Doug E.
    Hangin' with the Homeboys, 1991
    Jungle Fever, 1991
Douglas, Suzzanne
    I'll Do Anything, 1994
    Inkwell, 1994
    Jason's Lyric, 1994
    Tap, 1989
Dowell, Raye
    She's Gotta Have It, 1986
    Slaves of New York, 1989
Dr. Dre
    Juice, 1992
    Who's the Man?, 1993
Drake, Bebe
    Jason's Lyric, 1994
Drake-Massey, Bebe
    Bebe's Kids, 1992
    Boomerang, 1992
    First Monday in October, 1981
    House Party, 1990
    Jo Jo Dancer, Your Life is Calling, 1986
    Last Married Couple in America, The, 1980
    Oh God! Book II, 1980
    Women of Brewster Place, The, 1988
Drew, The
    Public Enemy: Tour of a Black Planet, 1991
Drinker, Torey
    White Girl, The, 1988
Driver, John M.
    I Know Why the Caged Bird Sings, 1978
Drummond, Reana E.
    Straight Out of Brooklyn, 1991
Duah, Alexandra
    Sankofa, 1994
DuBois, Ja'net
    Heart Condition, 1990
    I'm Gonna Git You Sucka, 1988
    Sophisticated Gents, 1981
DuBois, Nicole
    Interview with the Vampire, 1994

Duke, Bill
    Action Jackson, 1988
    American Gigolo, 1980
    Bird on a Wire, 1990
    Commando, 1985
    Menace II Society, 1993
    No Man's Land, 1987
    Predator, 1987
    Street of No Return, 1991
Duke, O.L.
    Malcolm X, 1992
    Return of Superfly, The, 1990
    Sugar Hill, 1994
    White Girl, The, 1988
Duncan, Arthur
    Tap, 1989
Dunn, Kevin
    Mississippi Burning, 1988
Dunne, Murphy
    Bad Manners, 1984
    Going Berserk, 1983
    Hero and the Terror, 1988
    Loose Shoes, 1980
    Paternity, 1981
Dunson-Franks, Saundra
    Summer Rental, 1985
Dunston, Geraldine
    Dark Exodus, 1985
    Daughters of the Dust, 1991
Dunye, Cheryl
    She Don't Fade, 1991
DuPois, Starletta
    Convicts, 1991
    Dark Exodus, 1985
    Hollywood Shuffle, 1987
    Odd Jobs, 1986
    Pee Wee's Big Adventure, 1985
    Raisin in the Sun, A, 1989
    South Central, 1992
    Torture of Mothers, The, 1980
    Waterdance, The, 1992

Dupree, Vincent
  South Central, 1992
Dursey, Rose
  Over the Top, 1987
Dutton, Charles S.
  Alien 3, 1992
  Crocodile Dundee 2, 1988
  Distinguished Gentleman, The, 1992
  Foreign Student, 1994
  Low Down Dirty Shame, 1994
  Menace II Society, 1993
  Mississippi Masala, 1991
  Rudy, 1993
  Runaway, 1989
  Surviving the Game, 1994
Earl, James
  Wide Sargasso Sea, 1993
Earle, Robert
  Toy, The, 1982
Easter, Mary M.
  Some People, 1988
Eastmond, Mark "Whiz"
  House Party 2: The Pajama Jam, 1991
Eaton, Paul
  Killing Floor, The, 1984
Edmonson, Michael Mark
  Predator 2, 1990
Edwards, Darryl
  Brother from Another Planet, The, 1984
  City of Hope, 1991
  Power, 1986
  Shakedown, 1988
Edwards, David
  House Party 3, 1994
Edwards, Faith
  Power of One, The, 1992
Edwards, Hubert J.
  Willie and Phil, 1980
Eek-A-Mouse
  New Jack City, 1991

Elam, Greg
  Hear No Evil, 1993
Elizabeth of Toro
  Sheena, 1984
Ellis, Dave
  Mighty Quinn, The, 1989
Elmore, Kenny
  Filmstatement, 1982
Emmanuel, Maurice
  Vice Squad, 1982
English, Alex
  Amazing Grace and Chuck, 1987
Ennis, Anthony
  Chameleon Street, 1992
Epps, Omar
  Daybreak, 1993
  Higher Learning, 1994
  Juice, 1992
  Major League II, 1994
  Program, The, 1993
Errol, Leon
  Joe's Bed-Stuy Barbershop: We Cut Heads, 1983
Erving, Julius
  Fish that Saved Pittsburgh, The, 1979
Esposito, Giancarlo
  Amos and Andrew, 1993
  Bob Roberts, 1992
  Cotton Club, The, 1984
  Desperately Seeking Susan, 1985
  Do the Right Thing, 1989
  Fresh, 1994
  Go Tell it on the Mountain, 1984
  Harley Davidson and the Marlboro Man, 1991
  King of New York, 1990
  Maximum Overdrive, 1986
  Mo' Better Blues, 1990
  Night on Earth, 1992
  Running, 1979
  School Daze, 1988
  Smoke, 1994
  Sweet Lorraine, 1987
  Taps, 1981

Esposito, Melissa
    South Bronx Heroes, 1985
Etienne, Roger
    I'm Dancing as Fast as I Can, 1982
Evans, Arthur/Art
    CB4: The Movie, 1993
    Die Hard 2: Die Harder, 1990
    Downtown, 1990
    Half Slave, Half Free, 1984
    I Know Why the Caged Bird Sings, 1978
    Into the Night, 1985
    Jo Jo Dancer, Your Life is Calling, 1986
    Main Event, The, 1979
    Mighty Quinn, The, 1989
    National Lampoon's Class Reunion, 1982
    Native Son, 1986
    Ruthless People, 1986
    School Daze, 1988
    Soldier's Story, A, 1984
    Trespass, 1992
    Tuff Turf, 1985
    White of the Eye, 1988
    Youngblood, 1978
Evans, Ella Mae
    Downtown, 1990
Evans, Victor Romero
    Marked for Death, 1990
    Toy, The, 1982
Ewing, Patrick
    Exoricist III: The Legion, 1990
Fab 5 Freddy
    Juice, 1992
    New Jack City, 1991
    Who's the Man?, 1993
Faircloth, Jim
    Sankofa, 1994
Faison, Donald Adeosun
    Juice, 1992
    Sugar Hill, 1994
Faison, Frankie
    Betsy's Wedding, 1990
    C.H.U.D., 1984
    Cat People, 1982

Faison, Frankie
City of Hope, 1991
Exterminator II, 1984
Hanky-Panky, 1982
Manhunter, 1986
Maximum Overdrive, 1986
Mississippi Burning, 1988
Money for Nothing, 1993
Money Pit, The, 1986
Silence of the Lambs, 1991
Sommersby, 1993
Faizon
Fear of a Black Hat, 1994
Fakir, Amina
Chameleon Street, 1992
Falana, Lola
Burning Cross, The, 1990
Fann, Al
Crossroads, 1986
Frankie and Johnny, 1991
Naked Gun 2 1/2: The Smell of Fear, 1991
Parasite, 1982
Return to Horror High, 1987
Stop! or My Mom Will Shoot, 1992
Fargas, Antonio
Borrower, The, 1991
Firestarter, 1984
Howling VI--The Freaks, 1991
I'm Gonna Git You Sucka, 1988
Night of the Sharks, 1990
Pretty Baby, 1978
Shakedown, 1988
Streetwalkin', 1985
Up the Academy, 1980
Whore, 1991
Farid, Zaid
Killing Floor, The, 1984
Farley, George
Baron, The, 1987
Farley, Teresa Yvon
Bright Lights, Big City, 1988
White Girl, The, 1988

Farquhar, Ralph
  Youngblood, 1978
Farrakhan, Malik
  Daughters of the Dust, 1991
Farrell, Tyra
  Poetic Justice, 1993
  So Fine, 1981
Farris Jr., Sterling
  Jimmy Hollywood, 1994
Fatona, Andrea
  Heaven, Earth & Hell, 1994
Faulkner, Stephanie
  Ghetto Revenge, 1988
Fava, Tina
  Far Out Man, 1990
Fegan, Roy
  Five Heartbeats, The, 1991
  Hollywood Shuffle, 1987
  House Party 3, 1994
  Meteor Man, The, 1993
Ferguson, Bianca
  Gifted, The, 1994
Ferguson, Jessie
  Blind Tom: The Story of Thomas Bethune, 1987
Ferguson, Lou
  Raisin in the Sun, A, 1989
Ferlatte, Diana
  African Story Magic, 1992
Ferrell, Tyra
  Boyz n the Hood, 1991
  Equinox, 1993
  Jungle Fever, 1991
  Mighty Quinn, The, 1989
  Ulterior Motives, 1993
  White Men Can't Jump, 1992
Fetchit, Stepin
  That's Black Entertainment, 1989
Feyijinmi, Akim
  Powerful Thang, A, 1991
Feyitinmi Sinki, Asha
  Powerful Thang, A, 1991

Fields, Chip
    Blue Collar, 1978
Finn, Terry
    Bill and Ted's Bogus Journey, 1991
Fishburne, Laurence/Larry
    Apocalypse Now, 1979
    Band of the Hand, 1986
    Boyz n the Hood, 1991
    Cadence, 1990
    Class Action, 1991
    Cotton Club, The, 1984
    Death Wish II, 1982
    Decoration Day, 199
    Deep Cover, 1992
    Gardens of Stone, 1987
    Higher Learning, 1994
    King of New York, 1990
    Nightmare on Elm Street 3: Dream Warriors, A, 1987
    Quicksilver, 1986
    Red Heat, 1988
    Rumble Fish, 1983
    School Daze, 1988
    Searching for Bobby Fischer, 1993
    What's Love Got to Do with It, 1993
    Willie and Phil, 1980
Five Blind Boys
    Hallelujah!: A Gospel Celebration, 1991
Flagg, Darron
    Bagdad Cafe, 1987
Flav, Flavor
    New Jack City, 1991
    Public Enemy: Tour of a Black Planet, 1991
Flewellen, Kathy
    Ashes and Embers, 1985
Flewellen, Uwezo
    Ashes and Embers, 1985
Folayan, Phillips
    Serving Two Masters, 1987
Ford, Corkey
    Platoon, 1986
    Tough Guys, 1986

Ford, Val
    Dead Man Out, 1988
Foree, Ken
    Dawn of the Dead, 1979
    Diplomatic Immunity, 1991
    Down the Drain, 1990
    From Beyond, 1986
    Hangfire, 1991
    Jo Jo Dancer, Your Life is Calling, 1986
    Knightriders, 1981
    Leatherface: The Texas Chainsaw Massacre III, 1990
    Night of the Warrior, 1991
    Phantom of the Mall: Eric's Revenge, 1989
    Taking Care of Business, 1990
    True Blood, 1989
    Without You, I'm Nothing, 1990
Foster, Frances
    Crooklyn, 1994
    Enemy Territory, 1987
    Malcolm X, 1992
Foster, Gloria
    City of Hope, 1991
    Leonard Part 6, 1987
    Trading Places, 1983
Fox, Crystal
    Drop Squad, 1994
Foxx, Redd
    Harlem Nights, 1989
    More Video in Plain Brown Wrapper Dirty Dirty Joke, 1984
    Red Foxx in Plain Brown Wrapper, 1983
Francis, Staci
    Bonfire of the Vanities, 1990
Franciscus, Tony
    Livin' Large!, 1991
Franklin, Aretha
    Blues Brothers, The, 1980
Franklin, Don
    Fast Forward, 1985
Franks, Saundra
    Glory, 1989

Franks, Tanzia
    Summer Rental, 1985
Franks, Walter
    Summer Rental, 1985
Frazier, Joe
    Ghost Fever, 1987
    Home of Angels, 1994
Frazier, Sheila
    California Suite, 1978
    Lazarus Syndrome, The, 1979
    Two of a Kind, 1983
Frederick, Tiger
    New Jack City, 1991
Freeman, Damita Jo
    Man with One Red Shoe, The, 1985
    Private Benjamin, 1980
    Ratboy, 1986
Freeman, K. Todd
    Grand Canyon, 1991
Freeman, Messiri
    Flintstones, The, 1994
Freeman, Morgan
    Bonfire of the Vanities, 1990
    Brubaker, 1980
    Clean and Sober, 1989
    Death of a Prophet, 1981
    Driving Miss Daisy, 1989
    Earth Day Special, The, 1990
    Eyewitness, 1981
    Glory, 1989
    Johnny Handsome, 1989
    Lean on Me, 1989
    Marie, 1985
    Power of One, The, 1992
    Resting Place, 1986
    Robin Hood: Prince of Thieves, 1991
    Roll of Thunder, Hear My Cry, 1986
    Shawshank Redemption, 1994
    Street Smart, 1987
    Teachers, 1984
    That Was Then...This is Now, 1985
    Unforgiven, 1992

Freeman Jr., Al
  Booker T. Washington: The Life & the Legacy, 1982
  Malcolm X, 1992
  Once Upon A Time When We Were Colored, 1994
Freeze, Luv
  House Party 3, 1994
French, Antonia
  Exterminator, The, 1982
French, Susan
  Sky Is Gray, The, 1980
Fresh Prince
  Earth Day Special, The, 1990
Fuller, Arthur
  Perfume, 1990
Fullilove, Donald
  Back to the Future, 1985
  Tuff Turf, 1985
  White Men Can't Jump, 1992
Fulton, Patricia
  Guy from Harlem, The, 1989
Fulton-Ross, Gale
  Life is a Saxophone, 1985
G-Wiz, Gary
  Public Enemy: Tour of a Black Planet, 1991
Gable, John Clark
  Bad Jim, 1989
Gaines, James E.
  Malcolm X, 1992
Gaines, Rosie
  D.C. Cab, 1984
Gaines, Sonny Jim
  Distinguished Gentleman, The, 1992
  I Know Why the Caged Bird Sings, 1978
  Sophisticated Gents, 1981
Gamble, Val
  House Party, 1990
Gambon, Michael
  Toys, 1992
Gampu, Ken
  Enemy Unseen, 1991
  Wild Geese, The, 1978

Gantt, Leland
    Presumed Innocent, 1990
Gardner, Daniel
    House Party 3, 1994
    How U Like Me Now, 1992
Garland, Grace
    Juice, 1992
    Street Smart, 1987
Garrett Jr., Nathan
    White Girl, The, 1988
Gaskins, Vinnie
    Steele's Law, 1992
Gatewood, Olivia
    Jason's Lyric, 1994
Gauthier, Desiree
    Personal Best, 1982
Gavaza, Angela
    Cry Freedom, 1987
Gedeon, Conroy
    Big Trouble, 1986
    Star Trek III: The Search for Spock, 1984
Generation, Special
    M.C. Hammer: Please Hammer Don't Hurt 'Em, 1990
Gentry, Minnie
    Bad Lieutenant, 1992
    Brother from Another Planet, The, 1984
    Def by Temptation, 1990
Gentry, Renee
    Getting Over, 1981
Gentry-Lord, Renee
    Perfume, 1990
Gerrard, Christopher Michael
    Fly by Night, 1994
Ghanaba, Kofi
    Sankofa, 1994
Gibbs, Fabian
    Sitting in Limbo, 1986
Gibbs, Marla
    Meteor Man, The, 1993
    Up Against the Wall, 1991

Gibbs, Nigel
    Ghost in the Machine, 1993
Gibbs, Norman Alexander
    Airplane!, 1980
Gibson, Barbara
    Mississippi Burning, 1988
Gifford, Gloria
    California Suite, 1978
    D.C. Cab, 1984
    Going Berserk, 1983
    Halloween II, 1981
    This is Spinal Tap, 1984
    Vice Versa, 1988
Giles, Gilbert
    Black & White, 1991
Gillespie, John "Dizzy"
    Call of the Jitterbug, The, 1988
Gilliam, Stu
    Meteor Man, The, 1993
Gilliard Jr., Lawrence/Larry
    Fly by Night, 1994
    Straight Out of Brooklyn, 1991
Gilson, Reglas
    Smoke, 1994
Gilstrap, James
    Karate Kid Part II, The, 1986
    Naked Gun 2 1/2: The Smell of Fear, 1991
Gilyard Jr., Clarence
    Die Hard, 1988
Gimpel, Ericka
    Smoke, 1994
Gismond, Anthony
    Mandinga, 1984
Givens, Robin
    Blankman, 1994
    Boomerang, 1992
    Foreign Student, 1994
    Rage in Harlem, A, 1991
    Women of Brewster Place, The, 1988
Gloudin, Ancile
    Wide Sargasso Sea, 1993

Glover, Corey
 Platoon, 1986
Glover, Danny
 Angels in the Outfield, 1994
 Bat 21, 1988
 Birdy, 1984
 Bopha!, 1992
 Chu Chu and the Philly Flash, 1981
 Color Purple, The, 1985
 Dead Man Out, 1988
 Escape from Alcatraz, 1979
 Flight of the Intruder, 1991
 Grand Canyon, 1991
 Iceman, 1984
 Lethal Weapon, 1987
 Lethal Weapon 2, 1989
 Lethal Weapon 3, 1992
 Out, 1982
 Places in the Heart, 1984
 Predator 2, 1990
 Pure Luck, 1991
 Queen, 1993
 Rage in Harlem, A, 1991
 Raisin in the Sun, A, 1989
 Saint of Fort Washington, The, 1992
 Silverado, 1985
 Stand-In, The, 1985
 To Sleep with Anger, 1990
 Witness, 1985
Glover, Savion
 Tap, 1989
Glover, William
 Oliver & Company, 1988
Gobert, Dedrick D.
 Boyz n the Hood, 1991
Godfrey, Lynnie
 Eubie, 1981
Godfrey, Patrick
 Black & White, 1991
Goins, Jesse
 Jekyll and Hyde...Together Again, 1982
 Robocop, 1987
 Second Thoughts, 1983

Goins, Jesse
    Up the Creek, 1984
    Wargames, 1983
Goldberg, Whoopi
    Best of Comic Relief '90, 1990
    Burglar, 1987
    Clara's Heart, 1988
    Color Purple, The, 1985
    Comic Relief, 1990
    Corrina, Corrina, 1994
    Fatal Beauty, 1987
    Ghost, 1990
    Homer & Eddie, 1990
    House Party 2: The Pajama Jam, 1991
    Jumpin' Jack Flash, 1986
    Lion King, The, 1994
    Little Rascals, The, 1994
    Long Walk Home, The, 1991
    Made in America, 1993
    Naked in New York, 1994
    National Lampoon's Loaded Weapon I, 1993
    Pagemaster, The, 1994
    Player, The, 1992
    Sarafina!, 1992
    Sister Act, 1992
    Sister Act 2: Back in the Habit, 1993
    Soapdish, 1991
    Star Trek: Generations, 1994
    Telephone, The, 1988
    Whoopi Goldberg, 1985
Golden II, Norman D.
    Cop and a Half, 1993
    There Are No Children Here, 1993
Goldfinger, Michael
    Tap, 1989
Good, Constance
    I Know Why the Caged Bird Sings, 1978
Gooding, Barbara
    Bonfire of the Vanities, 1990
Gooding Jr., Cuba
    Boyz n the Hood, 1991
    Daybreak, 1993
    Few Good Men, A, 1992

Gooding Jr., Cuba
    Gladiator, 1992
    Judgement Night, 1993
    Lightning Jack, 1994
    Losing Isaiah, 1994
    Sing, 1989
Goodwin, Kia Joy
    Strapped, 1993
Gordon, Anika
    Wide Sargasso Sea, 1993
Gordon, Dexter
    'Round Midnight, 1986
    Awakenings, 1990
Gordon, Julius
    D.P., 1987
    Displaced Person, 1985
Gordon, Sam
    Sugar Hill, 1994
Gordy, Denise
    D.C. Cab, 1984
    My Man Adam, 1986
    Reform School Girls, 1986
    Toy Soldiers, 1991
Gore, George
    Juice, 1992
Goshop, Ronald
    Mighty Quinn, The, 1989
Gossett, Cyndi
    Odds & Ends: A New-Age Amazon Fable, 1993
Gossett Jr., Louis
    Aces: Iron Eagle III, 1992
    Blue Chips, 1994
    Cover-Up, 1991
    Diggstown, 1992
    Enemy Mine, 1985
    Father and Son: Dangerous Relations, 1993
    Father Clement's Story, 1987
    Finders Keepers, 1984
    Firewalker, 1986
    Good Man in Africa, A, 1994
    Guardian, The, 1984
    He Who Walks Alone, 1978
    Iron Eagle, 1986

Gossett Jr., Louis
  Iron Eagle II, 1988
  Jaws III, 1983
  Josephine Baker Story, The, 1991
  Lazarus Syndrome, The, 1979
  Officer and a Gentleman, An, 1982
  Principal, The, 1987
  Punisher, The, 1989
  River Niger, The, 1978
  Straight Up, 1988
  Toy Soldiers, 1991
  Zora Is My Name!, 1989
Graff, Todd
  Five Corners, 1988
  Fly by Night, 1994
  Opportunity Knocks, 1990
Graham, Stretch
  American Game, The, 1979
Grant, Leon W.
  Beat Street, 1984
  Krush Groove, 1985
  Playing for Keeps, 1986
Grant, Sandra
  Singles, 1992
Grant, Sarina
  Backtrack, 1992
  Doppelganger, 1993
  Jimmy the Kid, 1982
Grant, Tamika
  Wide Sargasso Sea, 1993
Green, Chuck
  Dance Black America, 1985
  No Maps on My Taps, 1979
Green, Jason
  Killing Floor, The, 1984
Green, Kenneth
  Torture of Mothers, The, 1980
Green, Redge
  Boyz n the Hood, 1991
Green, Rhetta
  Half Slave, Half Free, 1984

Green, Wanya
    Heart and Souls, 1993
Greene, Jonell
    Bebe's Kids, 1992
Grier, David Alan
    Beer, 1986
    Blankman, 1994
    Boomerang, 1992
    From the Hip, 1987
    In the Army Now, 1994
    Loose Cannons, 1990
    Me and Him, 1990
    Streamers, 1983
Grier, Pam
    Above the Law, 1988
    Allnighter, The, 1987
    Badge of the Assassin, 1985
    Bill and Ted's Bogus Journey, 1991
    Class of 1999, 1990
    Fort Apache the Bronx, 1981
    On the Edge, 1985
    Package, The, 1989
    Posse, 1993
    Something Wicked this Way Comes, 1983
    Stand Alone, 1985
    Tough Enough, 1982
Grier, Roosevelt "Rosey"
    Black Brigade, 1989
    Glove, The, 1980
    Gong Show Movie, The, 1980
    Rabbit Test, 1978
    Sophisticated Gents, 1981
Griffin, Eddie
    Coneheads, 1993
    Dice Rules, 1991
    Jason's Lyric, 1994
    Meteor Man, The, 1993
    Walking Dead, The, 1994
Griffin, Ellis
    Bless Their Little Hearts, 1983

Griffith, Lynn
  Perfume, 1990
Grosvenor, Verta Mae
  Daughters of the Dust, 1991
Guilchard, Bruce
  Purple Hearts, 1984
Guillaume, Robert
  Cosmic Slop: Space Traders, 1994
  Death Warrant, 1990
  Kid with the 200 I.Q., The, 1982
  Kid with the Broken Halo, The, 1981
  Lean on Me, 1989
  Lion King, The, 1994
  Meteor Man, The, 1993
  Prince Jack, 1985
  Seems Like Old Times, 1980
  They Still Call Me Bruce, 1987
  Wanted: Dead or Alive, 1986
Guillory, Bennet
  Maid to Order, 1987
Gumbel, Bryant
  Hard Way, The, 1991
Gumede, Patricia
  Cry Freedom, 1987
Gunn, Bill
  Losing Ground, 1982
Gunn, Moses
  Amityville II: The Possession, 1982
  Black Brigade, 1989
  Brother Future, 1991
  Certain Fury, 1985
  Firestarter, 1984
  Heartbreak Ridge, 1986
  Killing Floor, The, 1984
  Leonard Part 6, 1987
  Luckiest Man in the World, The, 1989
  Neverending Story, The, 1984
  Ninth Configuration, The, 1980
  Ragtime, 1981
  Remember My Name, 1978
  Resurrections: Paul Robeson, 1990
  Women of Brewster Place, The, 1988

Guy, De Juan
    Sweet Potato Ride, 1994
Guy, Jasmine
    Harlem Nights, 1989
    Queen, 1993
    Runaway, 1989
    School Daze, 1988
    Stompin' at the Savoy, 1992
H'Ollier, Davina
    M.C. Hammer: Please Hammer Don't Hurt 'Em, 1990
Habersham, Richard
    Long Walk Home, The, 1991
Haley, Jackie
    Zoo Gang, The, 1984
Hall, Aaron
    New Jack City, 1991
Hall, Albert
    Apocalypse Now, 1979
    Betrayed, 1988
    Fabulous Baker Boys, The, 1989
    Malcolm X, 1992
    Music Box, 1989
    Rookie of the Year, 1993
    Sophisticated Gents, 1981
    Trouble in Mind, 1985
Hall, Angela
    Bob Roberts, 1992
Hall, Anthony C.
    Blue Chips, 1994
Hall, Arsenio
    Amazon Women on the Moon, 1987
    Blankman, 1994
    Comic Relief, 1990
    Coming to America, 1988
    Harlem Nights, 1989
Hall, Damien
    New Jack City, 1991
Hall, J.D.
    Perfume, 1990
Hall, Kevin Peter
    Big Top Pee-Wee, 1988
    Harry and the Hendersons, 1987
    Highway to Hell, 1992

Hall, Kevin Peter
  Monster in the Closet, 1987
  Predator, 1987
  Predator 2, 1990
Hall, Nathaniel "Afrika"
  Livin' Large!, 1991
Hall, Willie
  Blues Brothers, The, 1980
Hamidou, Adama
  Adama, the Fulani Magician, 1981
Hammond, John
  Blue and the Gray, The, 1982
Hampton, Chasiti
  Heart and Souls, 1993
Hancock, Herbie
  'Round Midnight, 1986
Hancock, John
  Bonfire of the Vanities, 1990
  City Heat, 1984
  Collision Course, 1992
  Crossroads, 1986
  First Family, 1980
  Traxx, 1988
Hanson, Tammy
  Another You, 1991
  Boyz n the Hood, 1991
Harats, Walter
  Steele's Law, 1992
Hardaway, Anfernee "Penny"
  Blue Chips, 1994
Harden, Robert
  Surf Nazis Must Die, 1987
Harden Jr., Ernest
  White Men Can't Jump, 1992
Hardison, Kadeem
  Beat Street, 1984
  Def by Temptation, 1990
  Gunmen, 1994
  M.C. Lyte: Lyte Years, 1991
  Rappin', 1985
  Renaissance Man, 1994
  School Daze, 1988
  White Men Can't Jump, 1992

Hardman, Cedrick
    Stir Crazy, 1980
Hardman, Nate
    Bless Their Little Hearts, 1983
Harewood, Dorian
    Against All Odds, 1984
    Falcon and the Snowman, The, 1984
    Full Metal Jacket, 1987
    Gray Lady Down, 1978
    Looker, 1981
    Our Olympic Hero: Jesse Owens Story, The, 1984
    Pacific Heights, 1990
    Solar Crisis, 1993
    Tank, 1984
Harison, Susan Denise
    Jerk, The, 1979
Harkness, Sam
    American Hot Wax, 1978
Harley, Rufus
    Eddie and the Cruisers, 1983
Harper, Angel
    Clara's Heart, 1988
    Once Upon a Forest, 1993
Harrell, Michele
    American Summer, An, 1991
    Exterminator, The, 1982
    Taking Care of Business, 1990
Harrington, Cheryl Francis
    Perfume, 1990
Harris, David
    Badge of the Assassin, 1985
    Purple Hearts, 1984
    Warriors, The, 1979
Harris, Idina
    Juice, 1992
Harris, Ishmael
    Moving, 1988
Harris, Julius
    Blue and the Gray, The, 1982
    Darkman, 1990
    First Family, 1980
    Going Berserk, 1983
    Gorp, 1980

Harris, Julius
    Harley Davidson and the Marlboro Man, 1991
    Hollywood Vice Squad, 1986
    Prayer of the Rollerboys, 1992
    Shrunken Heads, 1994
    To Sleep with Anger, 1990
    Wholly Moses, 1980
Harris, Niki
    Madonna: Truth or Dare, 1991
Harris, Niles
    Jerk, The, 1979
Harris, Raphael
    Moving, 1988
Harris, Robin
    House Party, 1990
    House Party 2: The Pajama Jam, 1991
    Mo' Better Blues, 1990
Harris, Shawn
    Jerk, The, 1979
Harris, Thomas Allen
    Heaven, Earth & Hell, 1994
    Splash, 1991
Harris, Wynetta
    One More Saturday Night, 1986
Harris, Wynton
    One More Saturday Night, 1986
Harris, Zelda
    Crooklyn, 1994
Harris Jr., Wendell B.
    Chameleon Street, 1992
Harrison, Daniel
    Tales from the Darkside, 1991
Harry, Jackee
    Ladybugs, 1992
    Women of Brewster Place, The, 1988
Hart, Laverne
    New Jack City, 1991
Hart, Terrence
    Street Wars, 1994
Harvey, Dyane
    Syvilla: They Dance to Her Drum, 1979

Hassan, Afua Amowa
Filmstatement, 1982
Hauser, Fay
Jimmy the Kid, 1982
Jo Jo Dancer, Your Life is Calling, 1986
Marvin and Tige, 1983
Seems Like Old Times, 1980
Waterdance, The, 1992
Hawkins, Loye
Guy from Harlem, The, 1989
Hawkins, Screamin' Jay
American Hot Wax, 1978
Mystery Train, 1989
Hawkins, Walter
Gospel, 1987
Hawkins, Yvette
Colour, 1983
Hayes, Deryl
Breaking Point, 1994
Cadence, 1990
Hayes, Isaac
CounterForce, 1987
Deadly Exposure, 1993
Escape from New York, 1981
Guilty As Charged, 1991
I'm Gonna Git You Sucka, 1988
It Could Happen to You, 1994
Once Upon A Time When We Were Colored, 1994
Posse, 1993
Prime Target, 1991
Robin Hood: Men in Tights, 1993
Hayes, Sylvester
Importance of Being Ernest, The, 1992
Haynes, Tiger
Apprentice to Murder, 1988
Enemy Territory, 1987
Moscow on the Hudson, 1984
Ratboy, 1986
Times Square, 1980
Haysbert, Dennis
Love Field, 1992
Major League, 1989
Major League II, 1994

Haysbert, Dennis
    Mr. Baseball, 1992
    Navy Seals, 1990
    Queen, 1993
    Suture, 1994
Hayward, Carmen
    Perfume, 1990
Headley, Shari
    Coming to America, 1988
Healy, Dorian
    For Queen and Country, 1989
Hebert, Kimberly
    Lady Day at Emerson's Bar & Grill, 1994
Hemsley, Sherman
    Club Fed, 1991
    Ghost Fever, 1987
    Home of Angels, 1994
    Love at First Bite, 1979
    Mr. Nanny, 1993
    Stewardess School, 1986
Henderson, Bill
    Adventures of Buckaroo Banzai: Across the 8th Dimension, The, 1984
    City Slickers, 1991
    Inside Moves, 1980
    Murphy's Law, 1986
    No Holds Barred, 1989
    White Men Can't Jump, 1992
Henderson, Luther
    Ain't Misbehavin, 1982
Henderson, Stephen
    Raisin in the Sun, A, 1989
Hendricks, Jon
    Foreign Student, 1994
    White Men Can't Jump, 1992
Henry, Lenny
    True Identity, 1991
    Work Experience, 1989
Herron, Cindy
    Juice, 1992
Hicks, Jonathan P.
    Boomerang, 1992

Hicks, Kevin
    Cool As Ice, 1991
Hicks, Tommy
    Daughters of the Dust, 1991
    Death of a Prophet, 1981
    Delusion, 1991
    Fatal Instinct, 1992
    Meteor Man, The, 1993
    She's Gotta Have It, 1986
Higgins, Billy
    Life is a Saxophone, 1985
Hightower, Linda
    Personal Best, 1982
Hill, Dulee
    Sugar Hill, 1994
Hill, Gilbert R.
    Beverly Hills Cop, 1984
    Beverly Hills Cops III, 1994
Hill, J.R.
    Straight Out of Brooklyn, 1991
Hill, Michael E.
    D.C. Cab, 1984
Hill, Roger
    Warriors, The, 1979
Hill, Tiffany
    Just an Overnight Guest, 1983
Hilton, Shari
    Street Smart, 1987
Hilton-Jacobs, Lawrence
    Jacksons: An American Dream, The, 1992
    L.A. Heat, 1988
    Youngblood, 1978
Hines, Damon
    Adventures of Buckaroo Banzai: Across the 8th Dimension, The, 1984
    Lethal Weapon, 1987
    Lethal Weapon 2, 1989
Hines, Gregory
    Cotton Club, The, 1984
    Dead Air, 1994
    Deal of the Century, 1983
    Eubie, 1981
    Eve of Destruction, 1991
    History of the World, Part 1, 1981

Hines, Gregory
 Muppets Take Manhattan, The, 1984
 Off Limits, 1988
 Rage in Harlem, A, 1991
 Renaissance Man, 1994
 Running Scared, 1986
 Tap, 1989
 White Knights, 1985
 White Lie, 1991
 Wolfen, 1981
Hines, Maurice
 Cotton Club, The, 1984
 Eubie, 1981
Hines III, Desi Arnez
 Boyz n the Hood, 1991
 House Party, 1990
Ho Frat Hoo!!
 M.C. Hammer: Please Hammer Don't Hurt 'Em, 1990
Hoag, Ben
 Straight Up, 1988
Holder, Geoffrey
 Annie, 1981
 Boomerang, 1992
Holliday, Kene
 Badge of the Assassin, 1985
 Philadelphia Experiment, The, 1984
Hollis, Tommy
 Malcolm X, 1992
Holloway, Tom
 Filmstatement, 1982
Holly, Ellen
 School Daze, 1988
Holman, Lola
 Colour, 1983
Holmes, Jessie
 My Brother's Wedding, 1983
Holmes, Niko Denise
 Jerk, The, 1979
Holyfield, Evander
 Blood Savage, 1990
 Necessary Roughness, 1991

Honey, D.J.
   Born in Flames, 1983
Hooker, John Lee
   Blues Brothers, The, 1980
Hooks, Kevin
   Innerspace, 1987
   Take Down, 1979
Hooks, Robert
   Black Brigade, 1989
   Fast Walking, 1982
   Heat Wave, 1990
   Passenger 57, 1992
   Posse, 1993
   Sister, Sister, 1982
   Sophisticated Gents, 1981
   Star Trek III: The Search for Spock, 1984
   Words by Heart, 1984
Hooper, B.J.
   Toy, The, 1982
Hoosier, Trula
   Daughters of the Dust, 1991
   Sidewalk Stories, 1989
Hoover, Tom
   Sidewalk Stories, 1989
Hopkins, Jermaine
   Juice, 1992
   Lean on Me, 1989
Hopkins, Linda
   Go Tell it on the Mountain, 1984
Horne, Lena
   That's Black Entertainment, 1989
   Wiz, The, 1978
Horsford, Anna Maria
   Almost Perfect Affair, An, 1979
   Class, 1983
   Crackers, 1984
   Heartburn, 1986
   Mr. Jones, 1993
   Permanent Wave, 1986
   Presumed Innocent, 1990
   St. Elmo's Fire, 1985
   Street Smart, 1987
   Times Square, 1980

Horton, Walter
 Blues Brothers, The, 1980
House, Harold
 Dark Exodus, 1985
Houston, Thelma
 And God Created Woman, 1988
Houston, Whitney
 Bodyguard, The, 1992
Howe, Alan Joseph
 Street Wars, 1994
Hubert-Whitten, Janet
 New Eden, 1994
Hudlin, Reginald
 Boomerang, 1992
 Posse, 1993
 She's Gotta Have It, 1986
Hudlin, Warrington
 Boomerang, 1992
 Posse, 1993
Hudson, Ernie
 Airheads, 1994
 Collision Course, 1992
 Cowboy Way, The, 1994
 Crow, The, 1994
 Ghostbusters, 1984
 Ghostbusters II, 1989
 Going Berserk, 1983
 Hand that Rocks the Cradle, The, 1992
 Heart and Souls, 1993
 In the Army Now, 1994
 Joy of Sex, 1984
 Leviathan, 1989
 Main Event, The, 1979
 No Escape, 1994
 Penitentiary II, 1982
 Spacehunter: Adventures in the Forbidden Zone, 1983
 Speechless, 1994
 Sugar Hill, 1994
 Two of a Kind, 1983
 Weeds, 1987
 Wild Palms, 1993
 Wrong Guys, The, 1988

Hughes, Prince
  Naked Gun, The: From the Files of Police Squad, 1988
Hunter, Kevin
  One False Move, 1991
Huntsberry, Howard
  La Bamba, 1987
Hurst, Michelle
  Smoke, 1994
Huston, Marques
  Bebe's Kids, 1992
Hutcherson, Bobby
  'Round Midnight, 1986
Hutchinson, Sean
  Jason's Lyric, 1994
Hyatt, Charles
  Cool Runnings, 1993
Ice Cube
  Boyz n the Hood, 1991
  CB4: The Movie, 1993
  Higher Learning, 1994
  Trespass, 1992
Ice-T
  Breakin', 1984
  Breakin' 2: Electric Boogaloo, 1984
  CB4: The Movie, 1993
  Ice-T: OG, Original Gangster, 1991
  New Jack City, 1991
  Rappin', 1985
  Ricochet, 1991
  Surviving the Game, 1994
  Trespass, 1992
  Who's the Man?, 1993
Iman
  Exit to Eden, 1994
  House Party 2: The Pajama Jam, 1991
  L.A. Story, 1991
  No Way Out, 1987
  Star Trek VI: The Undiscovered Country, 1991
  Surrender, 1987
Immature
  House Party 3, 1994

Infinity
    Performed Word, The, 1982
Ingram, Donna
    Eubie, 1981
Ingram, Stephanie
    Cycles, 1989
Ingram-Young, Donna
    Moscow on the Hudson, 1984
Isaacs, Barbara
    Importance of Being Ernest, The, 1992
Jabaar, Kareem Abdul
    Deadly Eyes, 1982
    Game of Death, 1979
Jackson, Baha
    Boyz n the Hood, 1991
Jackson, Christopher
    National Lampoon's Vacation, 1983
    Police Academy 2: Their First Assignment, 1985
Jackson, Darryl Munyungo
    Cycles, 1989
Jackson, David
    Eubie, 1981
Jackson, Debra Jo
    Black & White, 1991
Jackson, Demetrius
    Serving Two Masters, 1987
Jackson, Donniece
    Getting Over, 1981
Jackson, Freddie
    King of New York, 1990
Jackson, George
    Fear of a Black Hat, 1994
Jackson, Jackie
    Say Amen, Somebody, 1982
Jackson, Janet
    Poetic Justice, 1993
Jackson, Kathryn
    Black Mama, 1988
Jackson, Leon
    Dance Black America, 1985

Jackson, Leonard
    Baron, The, 1987
    Boomerang, 1992
    Brother from Another Planet, The, 1984
    Rage in Harlem, A, 1991
Jackson, Luther
    Blues Brothers, The, 1980
Jackson, Michael
    Wiz, The, 1978
Jackson, Reggie
    Naked Gun, The: From the Files of Police Squad, 1988
Jackson, Rosemarie
    Fear of a Black Hat, 1994
    Hangin' with the Homeboys, 1991
Jackson, Samuel L.
    Amos and Andrew, 1993
    Betsy's Wedding, 1990
    Dead Man Out, 1988
    Def by Temptation, 1990
    Die Hard with a Vengeance, 1994
    Fathers and Sons, 1992
    Fresh, 1994
    Goodfellas, 1990
    Johnny Suede, 1992
    Juice, 1992
    Jumpin' at the Boneyard, 1992
    Jungle Fever, 1991
    Jurassic Park, 1993
    Kiss of Death, 1994
    Losing Isaiah, 1994
    Menace II Society, 1993
    Meteor Man, The, 1993
    Mob Justice, 1991
    National Lampoon's Loaded Weapon I, 1993
    New Age, The, 1994
    Patriot Games, 1992
    Pulp Fiction, 1994
    Return of Superfly, The, 1990
    Shock to the System, A, 1990
    Strictly Business, 1991
    True Romance, 1993
    White Sands, 1992

Jackson, Stone/Stoney
   Angel 4: Undercover, 1994
   Blind Vision, 1992
   By the Sword, 1994
   Jocks, 1987
   Knights of the City, 1985
   Mortuary Academy, 1992
   Perfect Model, The, 1989
   Streets of Fire, 1984
   Sweet Perfection, 1987
   Trespass, 1992
   Up Against the Wall, 1991
Jackson, Tyrone
   Ashanti, 1979
   Over the Top, 1987
Jackson II, Jermaine
   Jacksons: An American Dream, The, 1992
Jacobs, Lawrence-Hilton
   Jacksons: An American Dream, The, 1992
   L.A. Heat, 1988
   Youngblood, 1978
Jacobs, Olu
   Ashanti, 1979
   Baby...Secret of the Lost Legend, 1985
   Dogs of War, The, 1980
   Lethal Weapon 2, 1989
   Pirates, 1986
Jade
   Inkwell, 1994
James, Anthony
   Slow Burn, 1986
James, Cheryl "Salt"
   Who's the Man?, 1993
James, Don
   Hamburger Hill, 1987
James, Donald
   Bad Boys, 1982
James, Eric
   Solar Crisis, 1993
James, Etta
   Chuck Berry: Hail! Hail! Rock 'n' Roll!, 1987
   Tap, 1989

James, Hawthorne
    Five Heartbeats, The, 1991
James 1, Brother
    Public Enemy: Tour of a Black Planet, 1991
James-Reese, Cyndi
    Vice Squad, 1982
Jaxon, Cepheus
    Penitentiary II, 1982
Jazz Dancers, Mama Lu Parks
    Dance Black America, 1985
Jazzy Jay
    Beat Street, 1984
Jeeks, John
    Powerful Thang, A, 1991
Jeffers, Juliette
    Odds & Ends: A New-Age Amazon Fable, 1993
Jefferson, Robert
    African-American Perspective, An, 1989
Jefferson, Shannon
    Perfume, 1990
Jefferson, Shy
    Perfume, 1990
Jelks, John
    Dark Exodus, 1985
    Magic Love, 1993
Jelks, Vaughn Tyree
    Blind Tom: The Story of Thomas Bethune, 1987
    Blue City, 1986
Jenkins, Janice
    Clarence and Angel, 1981
Jenkins, Larry "Flash"
    Armed and Dangerous, 1986
    Body Double, 1984
    Ferris Bueller's Day Off, 1986
    Prison, 1988
Jenkins, Larry Fischer
    Fletch, 1985
Jennings, Brent
    Another 48 Hours, 1990
    Nervous Ticks, 1993
    Serpent and the Rainbow, The, 1988

Jennings, Dominique
    Die Hard 2: Die Harder, 1990
Jerido, Ebony
    Just Another Girl on the I.R.T., 1993
Jessie, DeWayne
    D.C. Cab, 1984
    Thank God It's Friday, 1978
    Where the Buffalo Roam, 1980
Jinaki
    Tap, 1989
Jo-Ann, Ebony
    Fly by Night, 1994
Joe, Prince I.
    Marked for Death, 1990
Johns, Tracy Camilla
    New Jack City, 1991
    She's Gotta Have It, 1986
Johnson, Adrienne-Joi
    Double Trouble, 1992
    Dying Young, 1991
    House Party, 1990
    Inkwell, 1994
    School Daze, 1988
Johnson, Anne-Marie
    Five Heartbeats, The, 1991
    Hollywood Shuffle, 1987
    I'm Gonna Git You Sucka, 1988
    Robot Jox, 1990
    Strictly Business, 1991
    True Identity, 1991
Johnson, Anthony S.
    House Party 3, 1994
Johnson, Ariyan
    Just Another Girl on the I.R.T., 1993
Johnson, Arnold
    Five Heartbeats, The, 1991
    Menace II Society, 1993
Johnson, Beverly
    Ashanti, 1979
    Baron, The, 1987

Johnson, Cassandra
    Gifted, The, 1994
Johnson, Charles J.
    Serving Two Masters, 1987
Johnson, Clark
    Iron Eagle II, 1988
    Women of Brewster Place, The, 1988
Johnson, Craigus R.
    Hollywood Shuffle, 1987
Johnson, Dasanea
    Heart Condition, 1990
Johnson, Doris Owanda
    Cycles, 1989
Johnson, Howard
    Eddie and the Cruisers, 1983
Johnson, Jadili
    Skinheads--the Second Coming of Hate, 1990
Johnson, Jamarr
    Killing Floor, The, 1984
Johnson, Jesse
    Blues Brothers, The, 1980
Johnson, John
    Perfume, 1990
Johnson, Jonquaette
    Heart Condition, 1990
Johnson, Louis
    Dance Black America, 1985
Johnson, Luther "Guitar Jr."
    Blues Brothers, The, 1980
Johnson, Marques
    Blue Chips, 1994
    White Men Can't Jump, 1992
Johnson, Mel
    Total Recall, 1990
Johnson, Micaeh
    Killing Floor, The, 1984
Johnson, Michelle
    Driving Me Crazy, 1991
    Genuine Risk, 1991
    Street Wars, 1994
    Till Murder Do Us Part, 1994

Johnson, Reggie
  Blues Brothers, The, 1980
  Platoon, 1986
Johnson, Ron
  ZebraHead, 1992
Johnson, Rynel
  New Jack City, 1991
Johnson, Shauntae
  Heart Condition, 1990
Johnson, Tony T.
  Downtown, 1990
Johnson Jr., Mel
  Eubie, 1981
Jones, Alicia N.
  Blue Chips, 1994
Jones, Beryl
  Police Academy 5: Assignment Miami Beach, 1988
Jones, Clifton
  Sheena, 1984
Jones, Duane
  Beat Street, 1984
  Losing Ground, 1982
Jones, Ed "Too Tall"
  Double McGuffin, The, 1979
  Necessary Roughness, 1991
Jones, Grace
  Boomerang, 1992
  Conan the Destroyer, 1984
  Deadly Vengeance, 1985
  Straight to Hell, 1987
  Vamp, 1986
  View to a Kill, A, 1985
Jones, James Earl
  Allan Quartermain and the Lost City of Gold, 1986
  Blood Tide, 1982
  By Dawn's Early Light, 1990
  City Limits, 1985
  Clear and Present Danger, 1994
  Coming to America, 1988
  Conan the Barbarian, 1981
  Convicts, 1991
  Empire Strikes Back, The, 1980
  Field of Dreams, 1989

Jones, James Earl
   Gardens of Stone, 1987
   Grim Prairie Tales, 1990
   Guyana Tragedy: The Jim Jones Story, 1983
   Heat Wave, 1990
   Hunt for Red October, The, 1990
   Lion King, The, 1994
   Matewan, 1987
   Meteor Man, The, 1993
   Naked Gun 33 1/3: The Final Insult, 1994
   Patriot Games, 1992
   Return of the Jedi, 1983
   River Niger, The, 1978
   Sandlot, The, 1993
   Sommersby, 1993
   Soul Man, 1986
   Three Fugitives, 1989
   True Identity, 1991
Jones, Jedda
   Cosmic Slop: Space Traders, 1994
   Talkin' Dirty after Dark, 1991
Jones, Jill
   Grafitti Bridge, 1990
Jones, John Steven
   Bad Lieutenant, 1992
Jones, Lauren
   Juice, 1992
Jones, Makini Gena
   Back Inside Herself, 1984
Jones, Oran "Juice"
   Juice, 1992
Jones, Quincy
   Earth Day Special, The, 1990
Jones, Renee
   Talkin' Dirty after Dark, 1991
Jones, Richard Timothy
   Renaissance Man, 1994
   What's Love Got to Do with It, 1993
Jones, Robert Earl
   Maniac Cop 2, 1991
   Sophisticated Gents, 1981
   Trading Places, 1983

Jordan, Stanley
Blind Date, 1987
Killing Floor, The, 1984
Joy, Christopher
Cheech and Chong: Up in Smoke, 1980
Joyce, Ella
Stop! or My Mom Will Shoot, 1992
Joyner, Kimble
Raisin in the Sun, A, 1989
Joyner, Mario
Hangin' with the Homeboys, 1991
Joyner, Tom
Don't Cry, It's Only Thunder, 1982
Judd, Robert
Crossroads, 1986
Judge, D. Christopher
House Party 2: The Pajama Jam, 1991
Judge, Douglas
Cadence, 1990
Kain, Khalil
Juice, 1992
Renaissance Man, 1994
Kane, Big Daddy
Meteor Man, The, 1993
Posse, 1993
Katon, Rosanne
Illusions, 1983
Lunch Wagon, 1981
Kelly, Jim
Black Eliminator, 1978
Necessary Roughness, 1991
One Down, Two to Go, 1983
Kelly, Paula
Bank Robber, 1993
Drop Squad, 1994
Jo Jo Dancer, Your Life is Calling, 1986
Women of Brewster Place, The, 1988
Zora Is My Name!, 1989
Kelly, Tonya
Inkwell, 1994

Kemp, Robert
    Ashes and Embers, 1985
Kemper, Dennis
    My Brother's Wedding, 1983
Kenebrew, Carolyn
    Small Time, 1991
Kennedy, Dwayne
    Talkin' Dirty after Dark, 1991
Kennedy, Flo
    Born in Flames, 1983
Kennedy, Jayne
    Body and Soul, 1981
    Fighting Mad, 1979
Kennedy, Jihmi
    Glory, 1989
Kennedy, Jonelle
    How U Like Me Now, 1992
Kennedy, Leon Isaac
    Body and Soul, 1981
    Fighting Mad, 1979
    Hollywood Vice Squad, 1986
    Knights of the City, 1985
    Penitentiary, 1979
    Penitentiary II, 1982
    Penitentiary III, 1987
    Too Scared to Scream, 1985
Kerner, Norberto
    Losing Ground, 1982
Kersey, Yvonne
    Homeboyz II: Crack City, 1993
Khan, Chaka
    Blues Brothers, The, 1980
Khumalo, Leleti
    Sarafina!, 1992
    Voices of Sarafina, 1988
Kid Capri
    Fly by Night, 1994
Kiley Jr., Richard David
    Chameleon Street, 1992
Killum, Guy
    Crossroads, 1986

Kilpatrick, Lincoln
    Prison, 1988
Kimble, Bo
    Heaven is a Playground, 1992
Kimbro, Art
    Beverly Hills Cop, 1984
    Killing Floor, The, 1984
King, Aisha
    Wide Sargasso Sea, 1993
King, B.B.
    Amazon Women on the Moon, 1987
    Heart and Souls, 1993
    Spies Like Us, 1985
King, Bernard
    Fast Break, 1979
King, Don
    Head Office, 1985
    Last Fight, The, 1983
King, Erik
    Joey Breaker, 1993
    Street Smart, 1987
King, Henry
    Grand Canyon, 1991
King, Mabel
    Getting Over, 1981
    Gong Show Movie, The, 1980
    Jerk, The, 1979
    Wiz, The, 1978
King, Meta
    Boyz n the Hood, 1991
King, Pernell
    Extra Change, 1987
King, Regina
    Boyz n the Hood, 1991
    Higher Learning, 1994
    Poetic Justice, 1993
King, Reina
    Maid to Order, 1987
    To Sleep with Anger, 1990
King, Rowena
    Wide Sargasso Sea, 1993

King, Tony
  Big Score, The, 1983
  Toy, The, 1982
King, W. Geoffrey
  Torture of Mothers, The, 1980
King, Yolanda
  Death of a Prophet, 1981
  Talkin' Dirty after Dark, 1991
King of Chill
  M.C. Lyte: Lyte Years, 1991
Kirby, George
  Trouble in Mind, 1985
  White Girl, The, 1988
Kirk, Keith
  Riverbend, 1990
Kirklin, Phyllis
  One False Move, 1991
Kirkwood, Craig
  Cosmic Slop: Space Traders, 1994
Kitt, Eartha
  Boomerang, 1992
  Erik the Viking, 1989
  Fatal Instinct, 1993
Knight, Ernest
  Bless Their Little Hearts, 1983
Knight, James
  Serving Two Masters, 1987
Knight-Pulliam, Keshia
  Last Dragon, The, 1985
  Polly!, 1989
Knowles, William
  Lady Day at Emerson's Bar & Grill, 1994
Knox, Elyse
  Joe's Bed-Stuy Barbershop: We Cut Heads, 1983
Komolafe, Dadisi Wells
  Life is a Saxophone, 1985
Konte, Alhaji Bai
  Alhaji Bai Konte, 1978
Kool Herc
  Beat Street, 1984

Kotero, Apollonia
  Black Magic Woman, 1991
  Purple Rain, 1984
Kotto, Yaphet
  Alien, 1979
  Almost Blue, 1993
  Badge of the Assassin, 1985
  Blue Collar, 1978
  Brubaker, 1980
  Fighting Back, 1982
  Freddy's Dead: The Final Nightmare, 1991
  Hangfire, 1991
  Midnight Run, 1988
  Star Chamber, The, 1983
  Warning Sign, 1985
Kroc
  M.C. Lyte: Lyte Years, 1991
KRS-One
  Who's the Man?, 1993
Krunch
  Public Enemy: Tour of a Black Planet, 1991
Kubheka, Nomadlozi
  Power of One, The, 1992
Kunene, Sipho
  Sarafina!, 1992
Kyi, Daresha
  Land Where My Fathers Died, 1991
Kyme
  School Daze, 1988
L.L. Cool J.
  Hard Way, The, 1991
  Toys, 1992
  Wildcats, 1986
La Noire, Rosetta
  Brewster's Millions, 1985
  Moscow on the Hudson, 1984
Labelle, Patti
  Sing, 1989
  Unnatural Causes, 1986
LaMarre, Jean
  Malcolm X, 1992

Lampley, Oni Faida
    Strictly Business, 1991
Lane, Charles
    Posse, 1993
    Sidewalk Stories, 1989
    True Identity, 1991
Lane, Mark
    There Are No Children Here, 1993
Laneuville, Eric
    Fear of a Black Hat, 1994
Lange, Ted
    Glitch, 1989
    Perfume, 1990
Langley, Steve
    Tongues Untied, 1989
Langston Smyrl, David
    Langston Hughes: The Dream Keeper, 1988
LaSalle, Eriq
    Coming to America, 1988
    Drop Squad, 1994
    Jacob's Ladder, 1990
    Rappin', 1985
Latifah, Queen
    House Party 2: The Pajama Jam, 1991
    Juice, 1992
    Jungle Fever, 1991
    My Life, 1993
    Who's the Man?, 1993
Latimore, Benny
    Super Soul Brother, 1989
Lawrence, Darius
    Blind Tom: The Story of Thomas Bethune, 1987
Lawrence, Mark Christopher
    Fear of a Black Hat, 1994
Lawrence, Martin
    Boomerang, 1992
    Do the Right Thing, 1989
    House Party, 1990
    House Party 2: The Pajama Jam, 1991
    Talkin' Dirty after Dark, 1991

Lawrence, Scott
  Doppelganger, 1993
Lawson, Richard
  Main Event, The, 1979
  Streets of Fire, 1984
Lawson, Victor
  Serving Two Masters, 1987
Leach, Nicole
  Tales from the Darkside, 1991
Leaders of the New School
  Who's the Man?, 1993
League, Janet
  Half Slave, Half Free, 1984
Leake, Damien
  Killing Floor, The, 1984
Lee, Bill
  She's Gotta Have It, 1986
Lee, Cinque
  Mystery Train, 1989
Lee, Eugene
  Women of Brewster Place, The, 1988
Lee, Joie
  Do the Right Thing, 1989
  Fathers and Sons, 1992
  Mo' Better Blues, 1990
  School Daze, 1988
  She's Gotta Have It, 1986
Lee, Kieron
  Stargate, 1994
Lee, Spike
  Crooklyn, 1994
  Do the Right Thing, 1989
  Drop Squad, 1994
  Jungle Fever, 1991
  Malcolm X, 1992
  Mo' Better Blues, 1990
  School Daze, 1988
  She's Gotta Have It, 1986
Lee Day, Cora
  Daughters of the Dust, 1991

Leggett, Doris
  Bonfire of the Vanities, 1990
Lehman, Lillian
  Body of Evidence, 1993
  Defending Your Life, 1991
Lemmons, Kasi
  Candyman, 1992
  Drop Squad, 1994
  Fear of a Black Hat, 1994
  Five Heartbeats, The, 1991
  Hard Target, 1993
  School Daze, 1988
  Silence of the Lambs, 1991
  Vampire's Kiss, 1989
Lemon, Meadowlark
  Fish that Saved Pittsburgh, The, 1979
Lennix, Harry J.
  Bob Roberts, 1992
  Five Heartbeats, The, 1991
Lennon, David
  Downtown, 1990
Leon, Kenny
  Urban Crossfire, 1994
Leon, Reggie
  White Men Can't Jump, 1992
Leonard, Jonathan "Fudge"
  Soul Man, 1986
Leroy & Skillet
  Petey Wheatstraw, 1978
Leslie, Angela
  Chameleon Street, 1992
Levingston, Javar David
  Heart and Souls, 1993
Levy, Jacquelyn
  Odds & Ends: A New-Age Amazon Fable, 1993
Lewis, Carl
  Dirty Laundry, 1987
Lewis, Carol-Jean
  Colour, 1983
  Super, The, 1991

Lewis, Dawnn
    I'm Gonna Git You Sucka, 1988
Lewis, Derek
    Hot Shot, 1987
Lewis, Emmanuel
    Lost in London, 1985
Lewis, J.D.
    White Girl, The, 1988
Lewis, Jenifer
    Corrina, Corrina, 1994
    Meteor Man, The, 1993
    Poetic Justice, 1993
    Renaissance Man, 1994
    Sister Act, 1992
    Sister Act 2: Back in the Habit, 1993
    Undercover Blues, 1993
    What's Love Got to Do with It, 1993
Lewis, Joe
    Jaguar Lives!, 1979
Lewis, Phill
    Aces: Iron Eagle III, 1992
    Brother Future, 1991
    City Slickers, 1991
Lewis, Rawle D.
    Cool Runnings, 1993
Lifford, Tina
    Grand Canyon, 1991
Lighty, Harold
    Foreign Student, 1994
Lincoln, Abbey
    You Gotta Pay the Band: The Life of Abbey Lincoln, 1991
Lindo, Delroy
    Bound by Honor, 1993
    Crooklyn, 1994
    Malcolm X, 1992
    Mr. Jones, 1993
Lister Jr., Tom "Tiny"
    8 Million Ways to Die, 1986
    Blue City, 1986
    Driving Me Crazy, 1991
    Extreme Prejudice, 1987
    No Holds Barred, 1989
    Posse, 1993

Lister Jr., Tom "Tiny"
  Prison, 1988
  Runaway Train, 1985
  Talkin' Dirty after Dark, 1991
  Trespass, 1992
  Universal Soldier, 1992
Litondo, Oliver
  Sheena, 1984
Little, Cleavon
  Fletch Lives, 1989
  FM, 1978
  Gig, The, 1985
  Jimmy the Kid, 1982
  Murder by Numbers, 1990
  Scavenger Hunt, 1979
  Sky Is Gray, The, 1980
  Surf II, 1981
  Toy Soldiers, 1983
Little Richard (Penniman)
  Down and Out in Beverly Hills, 1986
  Last Action Hero, 1993
  Pickle, The, 1993
  Shelly Duvall's Rock N' Rhymeland, 1990
Lloyd, James
  Mississippi Burning, 1988
Lockhart, Calvin
  Baltimore Bullet, The, 1980
  Baron, The, 1987
  Predator 2, 1990
Logan, George
  Cosmic Slop: The First Commandant, 1994
Lois
  Canta for Our Sisters, 1987
Long, Althea
  Daughters of the Dust, 1991
Long, Lanier
  M.C. Lyte: Lyte Years, 1991
Long, Nia
  Boyz n the Hood, 1991
  Made in America, 1993

Love, Darlene
   Lethal Weapon, 1987
   Lethal Weapon 2, 1989
Love, Faison
   Bebe's Kids, 1992
Love, Monie
   Who's the Man?, 1993
Love, Mother
   Mr. Nanny, 1993
Love, Victor
   Heaven is a Playground, 1992
   Native Son, 1986
Lover, Ed
   M.C. Lyte: Lyte Years, 1991
   Who's the Man?, 1993
Lowe, Laurence
   Street Wars, 1994
Lowery, Marcella
   New Jack City, 1991
Lumbly, Carl
   Adventures of Buckaroo Banzai: Across the 8th Dimension, The, 1984
   Brother Future, 1991
   Pacific Heights, 1990
   South Central, 1992
   To Sleep with Anger, 1990
Lunon, Bernard
   Small Time, 1991
Lynch, Jimmy
   Avenging Disco Godfather, 1986
   Petey Wheatstraw, 1978
Lynn Bruce, Cheryl
   Daughters of the Dust, 1991
M.C. Eight
   Menace II Society, 1993
M.C. Hammer
   Hammer Time, 1990
   Last Action Hero, 1993
   M.C. Hammer: Please Hammer Don't Hurt 'Em, 1990
M.C. Lyte
   Fly by Night, 1994

Mac, Bernie
    Above the Rim, 1994
    House Party 3, 1994
    Mo' Money, 1992
    Who's the Man?, 1993
Macauley, Bertina
    Cool Runnings, 1993
Macbeth, Robert
    Langston Hughes: The Dream Keeper, 1988
    Moscow on the Hudson, 1984
MacFarlane, Cassie
    Burning an Illusion, 1981
Mack, Candace
    Downtown, 1990
Mack, Joe
    M.C. Hammer: Please Hammer Don't Hurt 'Em, 1990
MacLachlan, Janet
    Big Shots, 1987
    Boy Who Could Fly, The, 1986
    Heart and Souls, 1993
    Roll of Thunder, Hear My Cry, 1986
    Sophisticated Gents, 1981
    Tightrope, 1984
Mad Man Jay
    M.C. Lyte: Lyte Years, 1991
Mahmud-Bey, Sheik
    Bonfire of the Vanities, 1990
Mahoney, Louis
    Final Conflict, The, 1981
Maina, Charles Gitonga
    Air Up There, The, 1994
Makeba, Miriam
    Sarafina!, 1992
Makogba, Mshela
    Serving Two Masters, 1987
Mallory, Troy
    American Boyfriends, 1989
Malone, Mark
    Dead of Winter, 1987
    Straight Out of Brooklyn, 1991

Malone, Patrick
    Bonfire of the Vanities, 1990
    Grand Canyon, 1991
    Original Intent, 1992
Mamanzi, Cecil Zilla
    Power of One, The, 1992
Mangwarara, Winston
    Power of One, The, 1992
Mankuma, Blu
    Another Stakeout, 1993
    Bingo, 1991
    Bird on a Wire, 1990
    Breaking Point, 1994
    Cadence, 1990
    Finders Keepers, 1984
    Girl who Spelled Freedom, The, 1985
    Immediate Family, 1989
    K2, 1992
    Knight Moves, 1993
    Look Who's Talking, 1989
    Malone, 1987
    Russia House, The, 1990
    Shoot to Kill, 1988
    Stepfather, The, 1987
Mann, De
    Up Against the Wall, 1991
Manning, Don Charles
    Colour, 1983
Mapp, James
    Life Stinks, 1991
Marchand, Mitchell
    Fathers and Sons, 1992
Marcus, Alan
    Stand Alone, 1985
Marley, Cedella
    Joey Breaker, 1993
    Mighty Quinn, The, 1989
Marlin, Lynn
    Perfume, 1990
Marsalis, Branford
    School Daze, 1988
    Throw Momma from the Train, 1987

Marshall, Joi
  Inkwell, 1994
Marshall, Larry
  Baron, The, 1987
  Cotton Club, The, 1984
  Roadie, 1980
  She-Devil, 1989
Marshall, William
  Amazon Women on the Moon, 1987
  Maverick, 1994
Martin, Christopher
  Class Act, 1992
  House Party, 1990
  House Party 2: The Pajama Jam, 1991
  House Party 3, 1994
Martin, D'Urville
  Big Score, The, 1983
  Blind Rage, 1978
Martin, Duane
  Above the Rim, 1994
  Inkwell, 1994
  White Men Can't Jump, 1992
Martin, Harvey
  Amazing Grace and Chuck, 1987
Martin, Helen
  Beverly Hills Cops III, 1994
  Doc Hollywood, 1991
  Hollywood Shuffle, 1987
  House Party 2: The Pajama Jam, 1991
  Night Angel, 1990
  Rage in Harlem, A, 1991
  Raisin in the Sun, A, 1989
  Repo Man, 1983
Martin, Kelli M.
  Jacksons: An American Dream, The, 1992
Marton, Andrew
  Into the Night, 1985
Masenda, Tonderai
  Power of One, The, 1992
Master T.
  M.C. Lyte: Lyte Years, 1991

Matshikiza, John
    Cry Freedom, 1987
    Dust, 1985
    Dust Devil, 1993
Matthew, Pat
    Colour, 1983
Matthews, Al
    Aliens, 1986
    Final Conflict, The, 1981
    Funny Money, 1983
    Riders of the Storm, 1988
    Rough Cut, 1980
    Sender, The, 1982
    Stormy Monday, 1988
    Superman III, 1983
    Yanks, 1979
Matthews, Booker
    Straight Out of Brooklyn, 1991
May, Randolph
    Jungle Fever, 1991
Mayo, Tobar
    In Your Face, 1990
    Schizoid, 1980
Mayo, Whitman
    Boyz n the Hood, 1991
    D.C. Cab, 1984
    Main Event, The, 1979
    Seventh Coin, The, 1993
McAllister, Chip
    Weekend Pass, 1984
McBride, Chi
    Cosmic Slop: Tang, 1994
McBride, Lannie Spann
    Mississippi Burning, 1988
McCann, Dorothy
    Blue Chips, 1994
McCarthy, Kendall
    Heart Condition, 1990
McClain, Saundra
    Mr. and Mrs. Bridge, 1990

McClendon, Ernestine
    Homer & Eddie, 1990
McClure, Gordon
    Mo' Money, 1992
McCrary, Darius
    Big Shots, 1987
    Mississippi Burning, 1988
McCrary, Donovan
    Boyz n the Hood, 1991
McCrary, Maria
    Big Shots, 1987
McCray, Special K
    Poetic Justice, 1993
McCuller, Arnold
    American Hot Wax, 1978
    Without You, I'm Nothing, 1990
McDaniel, James
    Malcolm X, 1992
    Strictly Business, 1991
McDaniel, Xavier
    Singles, 1992
McDonald, Marie
    Mighty Quinn, The, 1989
McDonald, Rushion
    Jason's Lyric, 1994
McFadden, Stephanie
    Love Field, 1992
McGee, Bobby
    Meteor Man, The, 1993
McGee, Cindy
    Fast Forward, 1985
McGee, Gwen
    Wildcats, 1986
McGee, Paula
    Chameleon Street, 1992
McGee, Vonetta
    Brother Future, 1991
    Repo Man, 1983
    To Sleep with Anger, 1990
McGhee, Brownie
    Angel Heart, 1987
    Jerk, The, 1979

McGuire, Saundra
  Space Camp, 1986
McHenry, Doug
  Fear of a Black Hat, 1994
McIntosh, Valerie
  Weekend Pass, 1984
McK, Misha
  He's My Girl, 1987
McKae, Frank
  Used Cars, 1980
McKay, Anthony Norman
  Perfect Model, The, 1989
  Sweet Perfection, 1987
McKee, Lonette
  'Round Midnight, 1986
  Brewster's Millions, 1985
  Cotton Club, The, 1984
  Cuba, 1979
  Gardens of Stone, 1987
  Illusions, 1983
  Jungle Fever, 1991
  Malcolm X, 1992
  Women of Brewster Place, The, 1988
McKinzie, Virginia
  Colour, 1983
McKnight, David
  Hollywood Shuffle, 1987
  Pizza Man, 1991
  Under Siege, 1992
McLaughlin, Tony
  Perfume, 1990
McLean, Shawn
  Bad Lieutenant, 1992
McMillian, Jay
  Half Slave, Half Free, 1984
McMullen, Cliff
  Foreign Student, 1994
  Serving Two Masters, 1987
McPherson, Cynthia
  Clarence and Angel, 1981
  Oliver's Story, 1978
  Willie and Phil, 1980

McQueen, Armelia
    Action Jackson, 1988
    Ain't Misbehavin, 1982
    Ghost, 1990
    No Holds Barred, 1989
McQueen, Butterfly
    Adventures of Huckleberry Finn, The, 1985
    Mosquito Coast, The, 1986
    Polly!, 1989
McRae, Carmen
    Jo Jo Dancer, Your Life is Calling, 1986
McRae, Frank
    1941, 1979
    48 Hours, 1983
    Batteries Not Included, 1987
    Cannery Row, 1982
    End, The, 1978
    Farewell to the King, 1989
    Last Action Hero, 1993
    Licence to Kill, 1989
    Lightning Jack, 1994
    Lock Up, 1990
    National Lampoon's Loaded Weapon I, 1993
    National Lampoon's Vacation, 1983
    Norma Rae, 1979
    Paradise Alley, 1978
    Red Dawn, 1984
    Rocky II, 1979
    Wizard, The, 1989
McShann, Jay
    Last of the Blue Devils, The, 1980
Mead, Walter T.
    Smoke, 1994
Meals, Sylvia
    Rocky II, 1979
    Rocky IV, 1985
Means, Angela
    House Party 3, 1994
Medley, Nick
    Sankofa, 1994

Mekeba, Miriam
    Voices of Sarafina, 1988
Merkerson, S. Epatha
    Jacob's Ladder, 1990
    Loose Cannons, 1990
    Navy Seals, 1990
    She's Gotta Have It, 1986
    Terminator 2: Judgment Day, 1991
Merrill, Dina
    Suture, 1994
Merritt, Theresa
    Best Little Whorehouse in Texas, The, 1982
    Great Santini, The, 1979
    Serpent and the Rainbow, The, 1988
    Voodoo Dawn, 1991
    Wiz, The, 1978
Miaba, Pat
    Voices of Sarafina, 1988
Michele, Michael
    New Jack City, 1991
Miguel, Nigel
    Air Up There, The, 1994
    Heaven is a Playground, 1992
    White Men Can't Jump, 1992
Mike, Brother
    Public Enemy: Tour of a Black Planet, 1991
Mike, Louise
    Clarence and Angel, 1981
Miles, Joanna
    Sophisticated Gents, 1981
Miller, Cloryce
    Tough Enough, 1982
Miller, Stephanie
    Happy Birthday to Me, 1981
    Hog Wild, 1980
Mimms, Bryon Keith
    South Central, 1992
Minns, Bryon
    Jacob's Ladder, 1990
    Trespass, 1992

Minter, Kelly Jo
    Cosmic Slop: The First Commandant, 1994
    House Party, 1990
    New Jack City, 1991
    People under the Stairs, The, 1991
    Summer School, 1987
Misa
    Talkin' Dirty after Dark, 1991
Mitchell, Aleta
    Serpent and the Rainbow, The, 1988
Mitchell, Britney
    Blue Chips, 1994
Mitchell, Calvin
    Mighty Quinn, The, 1989
Mitchell, Daryl "Chill"
    Cosmic Slop: The First Commandant, 1994
    Fly by Night, 1994
    House Party, 1990
    House Party 2: The Pajama Jam, 1991
Mitchell, Don
    Perfume, 1990
Mitchell, Scoey
    Jo Jo Dancer, Your Life is Calling, 1986
Mogotalane, Thomas
    Burden, The, 1989
Mokae, Zakes
    Body Parts, 1991
    Cry Freedom, 1987
    Dad, 1989
    Doctor, The, 1991
    Dry White Season, A, 1990
    Dust Devil, 1993
    Gross Anatomy, 1989
    Island, The, 1980
    Master Harold and the Boys, 1984
    Rage in Harlem, A, 1991
    Serpent and the Rainbow, The, 1988
    Slaughter of the Innocents, 1994
Monteiro, Todd
    Super, The, 1991

Montgomery, Barbara
    Booker T. Washington: The Life & the Legacy, 1982
    Moscow on the Hudson, 1984
Montgomery, Reggie
    Hangin' with the Homeboys, 1991
Moody, Jim
    Bad Boys, 1982
    D.C. Cab, 1984
    Day of Atonement, 1993
    Last Dragon, The, 1985
    Personal Best, 1982
    Who's the Man?, 1993
Moody, Sephton
    Penitentiary II, 1982
Moore, Burleigh
    Jason's Lyric, 1994
Moore, Juanita
    Paternity, 1981
Moore, Kaycee
    Bless Their Little Hearts, 1983
    Daughters of the Dust, 1991
Moore, Khari
    Filmstatement, 1982
Moore, Lorraine
    Bonfire of the Vanities, 1990
Moore, Melba
    All Dogs Go to Heaven, 1989
    Def by Temptation, 1990
    Hair, 1979
Moore, Perry
    Inkwell, 1994
Moore, Rudy Ray
    Avenging Disco Godfather, 1986
    Petey Wheatstraw, 1978
Moore, Thomas
    Escape from the Bronx, 1985
    Great White, The, 1982
    Warriors of the Wasteland, 1983
Morales, Mark
    Knights of the City, 1985

Moret, Peter
    Perfume, 1990
Morgan, Debbi
    Our Olympic Hero: Jesse Owens Story, The, 1984
Morris, Alex
    Riverbend, 1990
Morris, Garrett
    Almost Blue, 1993
    Census Taker, The, 1984
    Children of the Night, 1992
    Coneheads, 1993
    Critical Condition, 1986
    How to Beat the High Cost of Living, 1980
    Motorama, 1993
    Severed Ties, 1992
Morrison, Laurie
    Another 48 Hours, 1990
    Don't Tell Mom the Babysitter's Dead, 1991
    Urban Crossfire, 1994
Morton, Joe
    ...And Justice for All, 1979
    Brother from Another Planet, The, 1984
    City of Hope, 1991
    Crossroads, 1986
    Forever Young, 1992
    Good Mother, The, 1988
    In the Hands of the Enemy, 1994
    Inkwell, 1994
    Speed, 1994
    Tap, 1989
    Terminator 2: Judgment Day, 1991
    Trouble in Mind, 1985
    Walking Dead, The, 1994
    Zelly and Me, 1988
Mosley, Roger E.
    Heart Condition, 1990
    I Know Why the Caged Bird Sings, 1978
    Steel, 1979
    Unlawful Entry, 1992
    Zora Is My Name!, 1989

Mosley, Tony
    Grafitti Bridge, 1990
Moss, Hanna D.
    Class Action, 1991
Mothupi, Collin
    Cheetah, 1989
Moyo, Alois
    Power of One, The, 1992
Mr. T.
    D.C. Cab, 1984
    Penitentiary II, 1982
    Rocky III, 1982
    Young Doctors in Love, 1982
Mthoba, James
    Sarafina!, 1992
Muhammad, El-Shah
    Jungle Fever, 1991
Murphy, Charles Q.
    CB4: The Movie, 1993
    Harlem Nights, 1989
    Jungle Fever, 1991
    Mo' Better Blues, 1990
Murphy, Eddie
    48 Hours, 1983
    Another 48 Hours, 1990
    Best Defense, 1984
    Best of Saturday Night Live - Eddie Murphy, The, 1989
    Beverly Hills Cop, 1984
    Beverly Hills Cop II, 1987
    Beverly Hills Cops III, 1994
    Boomerang, 1992
    Coming to America, 1988
    Distinguished Gentleman, The, 1992
    Golden Child, The, 1986
    Harlem Nights, 1989
    Joe Piscopo, 1984
    Trading Places, 1983
Murphy, Matt
    Blues Brothers, The, 1980
Muse, Clarence
    Black Stallion, The, 1979

Mutabaruka
  Sankofa, 1994
Mutombo, Ili
  Air Up There, The, 1994
Mwangi, Tom
  Sheena, 1984
Myers, Masequa
  Zoo Gang, The, 1984
Myra J.
  24 Hours to Midnight, 1992
  Bebe's Kids, 1992
  Cosmic Slop: Space Traders, 1994
  Talkin' Dirty after Dark, 1991
Myrie, Pauline Stone
  Cool Runnings, 1993
Mzuri
  Sankofa, 1994
N'Daiye, Dialy
  Stargate, 1994
Najeeullah, Mansoor
  Chorus Line, A, 1985
  Death of a Prophet, 1981
  Scent of a Woman, 1992
  Strictly Business, 1991
Narcisse, Jarrett
  Angel Heart, 1987
Nash, Robert N.
  Straight Out of Brooklyn, 1991
Nealy, Frances
  My Brother's Wedding, 1983
Neely, Gail
  Doctor, The, 1991
  Million Dollar Mystery, 1987
  Naked Gun 2 1/2: The Smell of Fear, 1991
  Rich Girl, 1991
  Surf Nazis Must Die, 1987
Nehm, Kristina
  Fringe Dwellers, The, 1986
Nelson, Felix
  Blue City, 1986
  Soul Man, 1986

Nelson, Friday
    Freedom Station, The, 1988
Nelson, Marilyn
    Jungle Fever, 1991
Nelson, Novella
    Bonfire of the Vanities, 1990
    Cotton Club, The, 1984
    Flamingo Kid, The, 1984
    Green Card, 1990
    Orphans, 1987
    Privilege, 1991
    Seduction of Joe Tynan, The, 1979
    Torture of Mothers, The, 1980
    Unmarried Woman, An, 1978
    Weekend at Bernie's II, 1993
Nelson, Patriece
    Crooklyn, 1994
Nelson, Sean
    Fresh, 1994
Nene, Nomse
    Country Lovers, City Lovers, 1982
Nesbitt, Michael L.
    Consenting Adults, 1992
Neville, Arthel
    Jimmy Hollywood, 1994
New Edition,
    Krush Groove, 1985
Newborn III, Phineas
    Breakin', 1984
    Girls Just Want to Have Fun, 1985
Newton, Thandie
    Flirting, 1992
    Interview with the Vampire, 1994
    Young Americans, The, 1994
Ngema, Mbongeni
    Sarafina!, 1992
    Voices of Sarafina, 1988
Nicholas, Denise
    Capricorn One, 1978
    Ghost Dad, 1990
    Sophisticated Gents, 1981

Nicholas, Harold
    Five Heartbeats, The, 1991
    Tap, 1989
Nicholas-Hill, Denise
    Marvin and Tige, 1983
Nichols, Nichelle
    Star Trek II: The Wrath of Khan, 1982
    Star Trek III: The Search for Spock, 1984
    Star Trek IV: The Voyage Home, 1986
    Star Trek V: The Final Frontier, 1989
    Star Trek VI: The Undiscovered Country, 1991
    Star Trek: The Motion Picture, 1979
    Supernaturals, The, 1987
Nichols, Paunita
    Angel 3: The Final Chapter, 1988
    Deep Cover, 1992
    Scoring, 1979
    Vamp, 1986
Nixau
    Gods Must Be Crazy, The, 1984
Nixon, DeVaughn
    Bebe's Kids, 1992
    Bodyguard, The, 1992
    Rapture, The, 1991
    Sugar Hill, 1994
    Terminator 2: Judgment Day, 1991
    To Sleep with Anger, 1990
Norman, Maidie
    In the Hands of the Enemy, 1994
Norris, Joycelyn
    Super Soul Brother, 1989
Norwood Jr., Willie
    Enemy Within, The, 1994
Ntshinga, Thoko
    Dry White Season, A, 1990
Ntshona, Winston
    Air Up There, The, 1994
    Ashanti, 1979
    Dogs of War, The, 1980
    Dry White Season, A, 1990
    Marigolds in August, 1984
    Over the Top, 1987
    Power of One, The, 1992

Ntshona, Winston
Wild Geese, The, 1978
Ntsinyi, Sam
Enemy Unseen, 1991
Nunez, Miguel
Action Jackson, 1988
Joy of Sex, 1984
Street Fighter, 1994
Nunn, Bill
Dangerous Heart, 1994
Def by Temptation, 1990
Do the Right Thing, 1989
Last Seduction, The, 1994
Mo' Better Blues, 1990
National Lampoon's Loaded Weapon I, 1993
New Jack City, 1991
Regarding Henry, 1991
Save Me, 1994
School Daze, 1988
Sister Act, 1992
White Lie, 1991
Nuru-Jeter, Amini
Extra Change, 1987
O'Bryant, Tasha
Rage in Harlem, A, 1991
O'Dell, Bryan
Street Wars, 1994
Youngblood, 1978
O'Neal, Ron
Death House, 1992
Final Countdown, The, 1980
Freedom Road, 1978
Guyana Tragedy: The Jim Jones Story, 1983
Hero and the Terror, 1988
Red Dawn, 1984
Sophisticated Gents, 1981
St. Helens, 1981
Up Against the Wall, 1991
O'Neal, Shaquille
Blue Chips, 1994

Odom, George T.
 Straight Out of Brooklyn, 1991
Ogunfiditimi, Olatide
 Serving Two Masters, 1987
Ogunfiditimi, Osekunjo
 Serving Two Masters, 1987
Ogunlano, Oyafunmike
 Sankofa, 1994
Olajuwon, Hakeem
 Heaven is a Playground, 1992
Olivier, Mandisa
 Different Image, A, 1982
Ologboni, Tejumala
 African Story Magic, 1992
Omeze, Tita
 Earth Girls Are Easy, 1988
 For the Boys, 1991
Omilani, Afemo
 Drop Squad, 1994
 Money Pit, The, 1986
 Sankofa, 1994
One Effect, One Cause
 M.C. Hammer: Please Hammer Don't Hurt 'Em, 1990
Orange, Gerald
 Angel Heart, 1987
 Sudden Death, 1985
 Weeds, 1987
 Who's that Girl, 1987
 Year of the Dragon, 1985
Oree, Enjolik
 Fried Green Tomatoes, 1991
Orman, Roscoe
 F/X, 1986
 Langston Hughes: The Dream Keeper, 1988
 Sesame Street Presents: Follow that Bird, 1985
 Striking Distance, 1993
Ortiz, Church
 Defiance, 1980
 Hero at Large, 1980
 Police Academy 2: Their First Assignment, 1985

Osumare, Halifu
Dance Black America, 1985
Otis, Otis O.
CB4: The Movie, 1993
Owiti, Miriam
Air Up There, The, 1994
Pace, Jean
Street Wars, 1994
Page, Ken
Ain't Misbehavin, 1982
I'll Do Anything, 1994
Robocop, 1987
Tim Burton's the Nightmare Before Christmas, 1993
Torch Song Trilogy, 1988
Page, La Wanda
Mausoleum, 1983
Shakes the Clown, 1992
Talkin' Dirty after Dark, 1991
Zapped, 1982
Palmer, Gretchen F.
Chopper Chicks in Zombietown, 1991
Crossroads, 1986
Fast Forward, 1985
Red Heat, 1988
When Harry Met Sally..., 1989
Palmer, Kathleen Murphy
Bonfire of the Vanities, 1990
Papa Juggs
SGT. Pepper's Lonely Hearts Club Band, 1978
Paris, Freddie
Flirting, 1992
Parker, Paula Jai
Cosmic Slop: Tang, 1994
Parker Jr., Ray
Charlie Barnett's Terms of Enrollment, 1986
Complex World, 1992
Enemy Territory, 1987
Parris, Maxwell
Sankofa, 1994
Parris, Stephen
Black & White, 1991

Parson, Ron O.I.
    Raisin in the Sun, A, 1989
Parsons, Karyn
    Class Act, 1992
Patrick, Randal
    Dead Aim, 1990
    Fast Food, 1989
    Funland, 1987
    Livin' Large!, 1991
    Project X, 1987
    Till Murder Do Us Part, 1994
    Weekend Warriors, 1986
Patterson, Chuck
    Five Heartbeats, The, 1991
Payne, Allen
    CB4: The Movie, 1993
    Jason's Lyric, 1994
    New Jack City, 1991
    Rooftops, 1989
    Walking Dead, The, 1994
Payne, Eric
    Drop Squad, 1994
    Juice, 1992
    Return of Superfly, The, 1990
    School Daze, 1988
    Sidewalk Stories, 1989
Peacock, Natasha
    Crossroads, 1986
Peeples, Nia
    Deepstar Six, 1989
Pendleton, David
    Youngblood, 1978
Perrineau Jr., Harold
    Shakedown, 1988
    Smoke, 1994
Perry, Felton
    Checking Out, 1989
    Dumb and Dumber, 1994
    Mean Dog Blues, 1978
    Perfume, 1990
    Puppet Master 4, 1993
    Relentless III, 1993
    Robocop, 1987

Perry, Felton
  Robocop II, 1990
  Robocop III, 1993
  Running Scared, 1986
  Talent for the Game, 1991
  Weeds, 1987
Perry, Wolfe
  Soul Man, 1986
  Space Rage, 1987
Perryman, Al
  Dance Black America, 1985
Persaud, Stephen
  Mona Lisa, 1986
Peters, Brock
  Adventures of Huck Finn, 1980
  Alligator II: The Mutation, 1991
  Cosmic Slop: Space Traders, 1994
  Importance of Being Ernest, The, 1992
  Star Trek IV: The Voyage Home, 1986
  Star Trek VI: The Undiscovered Country, 1991
Petty, Qiana
  Blue Chips, 1994
Phillip C.
  D.C. Cab, 1984
Phillips, Lashondra
  Fried Green Tomatoes, 1991
Pickens Jr., James
  Jimmy Hollywood, 1994
Pierce, Stack
  24 Hours to Midnight, 1992
  Enemy Unseen, 1991
  Killpoint, 1984
  Low Blow, 1986
  Patriot, The, 1986
  Rage in Harlem, A, 1991
  Vice Squad, 1982
  Wargames, 1983
  Weekend at Bernie's II, 1993
Pierce, Wendell
  Rage in Harlem, A, 1991

Pierott, Lawrence
  Bless Their Little Hearts, 1983
Pilatus, Audbrey
  Wide Sargasso Sea, 1993
Pinkett, Jada
  Freedom Station, The, 1988
  Inkwell, 1994
  Jason's Lyric, 1994
  Low Down Dirty Shame, 1994
  Menace II Society, 1993
Pinkins, Tonya
  Above the Rim, 1994
  See No Evil, Hear No Evil, 1984
Pitts, Ron
  Hot Shots! Part Deux, 1993
Platt, Victoria Gabriella
  'Round Midnight, 1986
  Alma's Rainbow, 1993
Plowden, Melvin
  Rappin', 1985
Plummer, Glenn
  Colors, 1988
  Dangerous Game, 1993
  Downtown, 1990
  Frankie and Johnny, 1991
  Funny Farm, 1988
  Heat Wave, 1990
  In the Hands of the Enemy, 1994
  Menace II Society, 1993
  Pastime, 1991
  South Central, 1992
  Trespass, 1992
  Who's that Girl, 1987
  Women of Brewster Place, The, 1988
Poindexter, Bernice
  Mississippi Burning, 1988
Pointdexter, Robert
  Foreign Student, 1994
Poitier, Sidney
  Little Nikita, 1988
  Shoot to Kill, 1988
  Sneakers, 1992

Pollard, Thommy
Penitentiary, 1979
Poole, Roy
Betsy, The, 1978
Brubaker, 1980
End of August, The, 1982
Roll of Thunder, Hear My Cry, 1986
Stranger is Watching, A, 1982
Pooser, Damien
Urban Crossfire, 1994
Popwell, Albert
Sudden Impact, 1983
Who's that Girl, 1987
Positive K
M.C. Lyte: Lyte Years, 1991
Pounder, CCH
Bagdad Cafe, 1987
Benny & Joon, 1990
Disappearance of Christina, The, 1994
Go Tell it on the Mountain, 1984
I'm Dancing as Fast as I Can, 1982
Importance of Being Ernest, The, 1992
Postcards from the Edge, 1990
Prizzi's Honor, 1985
Resting Place, 1986
Robocop III, 1993
Sliver, 1993
Powell, Nicole
Drop Squad, 1994
Powers, Ben
Man Who Loved Women, The, 1983
Things Are Tough All Over, 1982
Prendergast, Gerard
Time Walker, 1982
Prendergast, James
Moscow on the Hudson, 1984
Prendergast, Sharon Marley
Mighty Quinn, The, 1989
Preston, Billy
Blame it on the Night, 1984
SGT. Pepper's Lonely Hearts Club Band, 1978
Wired, 1989

Preston, J.A.
    Body Heat, 1981
    Captain Ron, 1992
    Few Good Men, A, 1992
    Fire Birds, 1990
    Gifted, The, 1994
    Narrow Margin, 1990
    Real Life, 1979
Pride, Dion
    Double McGuffin, The, 1979
Priest, Martin
    ZebraHead, 1992
Prince, Christopher
    Tongues Untied, 1989
Prince (Rogers Nelson)
    Grafitti Bridge, 1990
    Purple Rain, 1984
    Under the Cherry Moon, 1986
Pryor, Richard
    Another You, 1991
    Black Brigade, 1989
    Blue Collar, 1978
    Brewster's Millions, 1985
    Bustin' Loose, 1981
    California Suite, 1978
    Critical Condition, 1986
    Harlem Nights, 1989
    In God We Trust, 1980
    Jo Jo Dancer, Your Life is Calling, 1986
    Moving, 1988
    Muppet Movie, The, 1979
    Richard Pryor: Live in Concert, 1979
    Richard Pryor: Live on the Sunset Strip, 1982
    See No Evil, Hear No Evil, 1984
    Some Kind of Hero, 1982
    Stir Crazy, 1980
    Superman III, 1983
    Toy, The, 1982
    Wholly Moses, 1980
    Wiz, The, 1978

Pugh, Willard
  Color Purple, The, 1985
  Guyver, The, 1992
  Hills Have Eyes II, The, 1985
  Made in Heaven, 1987
  Moving Violations, 1985
  Native Son, 1986
  Puppet Master 5: The Final Chapter, 1994
  Rage in Harlem, A, 1991
  Robocop II, 1990
  Stand Alone, 1985
  Toy Soldiers, 1983
  Traxx, 1988
Purdee, Nathan
  Return of Superfly, The, 1990
Pyant, Danene
  Killpoint, 1984
Ralph, Michael
  Drop Squad, 1994
  Malcolm X, 1992
  Marked for Death, 1990
  Scenes from the New World, 1994
Ralph, Sheryl Lee
  Distinguished Gentleman, The, 1992
  Flintstones, The, 1994
  Mighty Quinn, The, 1989
  Mistress, 1992
  Oliver & Company, 1988
  Skin Deep, 1989
  To Sleep with Anger, 1990
Ramsey, Marion
  Police Academy, 1984
  Police Academy 2: Their First Assignment, 1985
  Police Academy 3: Back in Training, 1990
  Police Academy 4: Citizens on Patrol, 1987
  Police Academy 5: Assignment Miami Beach, 1988
  Police Academy 6: City Under Siege, 1989
Randle, Asheamu Earl
  Jason's Lyric, 1994
Randle, Kenneth
  Jason's Lyric, 1994

Randle, Theresa
    Beverly Hills Cops III, 1994
    Five Heartbeats, The, 1991
    Guardian, The, 1990
    Heart Condition, 1990
    Jungle Fever, 1991
    King of New York, 1990
    Malcolm X, 1992
    Near Dark, 1987
    Sugar Hill, 1994
Rankins, George
    Hear No Evil, 1993
Rashad, Phylicia
    Once Upon A Time When We Were Colored, 1994
    Polly!, 1989
    Uncle Tom's Cabin, 1987
Rasulala, Thalmus
    Above the Law, 1988
    New Jack City, 1991
    Package, The, 1989
    Sophisticated Gents, 1981
Raveling, George
    Blue Chips, 1994
Raven-Symone
    Little Rascals, The, 1994
Ray, Aldo
    Black Eliminator, 1978
    Glove, The, 1980
Ray, Gene Anthony
    Fame, 1980
Ray, Ola
    Night Shift, 1982
Rayford, Ernest
    Killing Floor, The, 1984
Reading, Bertice
    Little Shop of Horrors, 1986
    Moon in the Gutter, 1983
Reaves-Phillips, Sandra
    'Round Midnight, 1986
    Lean on Me, 1989

Redd, Veronica
  Blue and the Gray, The, 1982
  Clean and Sober, 1989
  Five Heartbeats, The, 1991
Redmond, Markus
  Inkwell, 1994
Reed, Alaina
  Eubie, 1981
  Sesame Street Presents: Follow that Bird, 1985
Reed, Di
  Inkwell, 1994
Reed, Don
  Fear of a Black Hat, 1994
  Hollywood Shuffle, 1987
Reed, Jeffrey
  Predator 2, 1990
Reed, Kesha
  Flatliners, 1990
Reed, Lady
  Petey Wheatstraw, 1978
Reed, Mary
  Black Mama, 1988
Reed, Tanya
  Exit to Eden, 1994
Reed, Tracy
  Running Scared, 1986
Reese, Della
  Distinguished Gentleman, The, 1992
  Harlem Nights, 1989
Reese, Roxanne
  Without You, I'm Nothing, 1990
  Women of Brewster Place, The, 1988
Reeves, Dianne
  Drei Lieder, 1983
Reid, Christopher
  Best of Comic Relief '90, 1990
  Class Act, 1992
  House Party, 1990
  House Party 2: The Pajama Jam, 1991
  House Party 3, 1994

Reid, Elfreida
    Wide Sargasso Sea, 1993
Reid, Tim
    Fourth War, The, 1990
Renee Trin-iana
    Sweet Bird of Youth, 1986
Reuben, Gloria
    Immediate Family, 1989
Rey, Reynaldo
    Bebe's Kids, 1992
    Far Out Man, 1990
    House Party 3, 1994
    More Video in Plain Brown Wrapper Dirty Dirty Joke, 1984
    Rage in Harlem, A, 1991
    Talkin' Dirty after Dark, 1991
    White Men Can't Jump, 1992
Rhames, Ving
    Bound by Honor, 1993
    Casualties of War, 1989
    Drop Squad, 1994
    Flight of the Intruder, 1991
    Go Tell it on the Mountain, 1984
    Homocide, 1991
    Jacob's Ladder, 1990
    Kiss of Death, 1994
    Long Walk Home, The, 1991
    People under the Stairs, The, 1991
    Pulp Fiction, 1994
    Saint of Fort Washington, The, 1992
    Stop! or My Mom Will Shoot, 1992
Rhodis, Cuong
    Powerful Thang, A, 1991
Rhondu
    Public Enemy: Tour of a Black Planet, 1991
Rice, Jerry
    Necessary Roughness, 1991
Rich, Matty
    Straight Out of Brooklyn, 1991
Richards, Beah
    Big Shots, 1987
    Drugstore Cowboy, 1989
    Homer & Eddie, 1990
    Sophisticated Gents, 1981

Richards, Beah
   Zora Is My Name!, 1989
Richards, Michelle Lamar
   Cosmic Slop: Space Traders, 1994
Richardson, LaTanya
   Hangin' with the Homeboys, 1991
   Juice, 1992
   Losing Isaiah, 1994
   Malcolm X, 1992
   Super, The, 1991
   When a Man Loves a Woman, 1994
Richardson, Salli
   How U Like Me Now, 1992
   Low Down Dirty Shame, 1994
   Mo' Money, 1992
   Posse, 1993
   Prelude to a Kiss, 1992
   Up Against the Wall, 1991
Richardson, Sy
   Backtrack, 1992
   Colors, 1988
   Dead Man Walking, 1988
   Eye of the Stranger, 1993
   Floundering, 1994
   Kinjite: Forbidden Subjects, 1989
   Men at Work, 1990
   My Brother's Wedding, 1983
   Mystery Train, 1989
   Nocturna, 1979
   Repo Man, 1983
   Ring of Fire II: Blood and Steel, 1993
   Sid and Nancy, 1986
   Straight to Hell, 1987
   Street Asylum, 1990
   They Live, 1988
   Three Fugitives, 1989
   To Sleep with Anger, 1990
   Walker, 1987
Richmond, Deon
   Enemy Territory, 1987

Riddick, George
  Sidewalk Stories, 1989
Riley, Larry
  Crackers, 1984
  Last Time Out, 1994
  Long Gone, 1988
  Soldier's Story, A, 1984
Riley, Teddy
  New Jack City, 1991
Ringgold, Faith
  Privilege, 1991
Roach, Daryl
  CIA II Target: Alexa, 1994
  Importance of Being Ernest, The, 1992
  Legal Tender, 1991
  Pee Wee's Big Adventure, 1985
  Space Camp, 1986
  Watchers III, 1994
Roach, Max
  Ice Pirates, The, 1984
  Sit Down and Listen: The Story of Max Roach, 1984
Roberson, David
  White Men Can't Jump, 1992
Roberto, Alonzo
  Perfume, 1990
Roberts, Conrad
  Firepower, 1979
  Green Card, 1990
  Hard Way, The, 1991
  Mosquito Coast, The, 1986
  Serpent and the Rainbow, The, 1988
  Streetwalkin', 1985
Roberts, Darryl
  How U Like Me Now, 1992
  Perfect Model, The, 1989
Roberts, Davis
  Chattanooga Choo Choo, 1984
  Honky Tonk Freeway, 1981
  To Sleep with Anger, 1990
Robeson, Paul
  Midnight Ramble, 1994
  Paul Robeson: A Tribute to an Artist, 1979
  That's Black Entertainment, 1989

Robinson, Bill "Bojangles"
No Maps on My Taps, 1979
Robinson, Bumper
Enemy Mine, 1985
Robinson, Claudia
Wide Sargasso Sea, 1993
Robinson, Darren
Knights of the City, 1985
Robinson, Edward Stoney
Stony Island, 1978
Robinson, Ertha D.
Daughters of the Dust, 1991
Malcolm X, 1992
School Daze, 1988
Robinson, Holly
Howard the Duck, 1986
Jacksons: An American Dream, The, 1992
Robinson, Leon (credited as Leon)
All the Right Moves, 1983
Band of the Hand, 1986
Cliffhanger, 1993
Colors, 1988
Cool Runnings, 1993
Five Heartbeats, The, 1991
Flamingo Kid, The, 1984
Once Upon A Time When We Were Colored, 1994
Streetwalkin', 1985
Robinson, Marc
Downtown, 1990
Robinson, Scott Anthony
Jungle Fever, 1991
Robinson, Smokey
Knights of the City, 1985
Robinson, Stuart K.
Death Wish II, 1982
Rochon, Lela
Boomerang, 1992
Harlem Nights, 1989
Stewardess School, 1986
Wild Pair, The, 1987

Rock, Chris
    Beverly Hills Cop II, 1987
    Boomerang, 1992
    CB4: The Movie, 1993
    I'm Gonna Git You Sucka, 1988
    New Jack City, 1991
Rodgers, Alva
    Daughters of the Dust, 1991
    School Daze, 1988
Rodgers, Alysia
    Boyz n the Hood, 1991
    Class Act, 1992
Rodriguez, David
    Small Time, 1991
Rodriguez, Percy
    Brainwaves, 1983
    Invisible Strangler, 1984
Roger, Brother
    Public Enemy: Tour of a Black Planet, 1991
Rogers, Ingrid
    Carlito's Way, 1993
Rogers, Ivan
    Escape from...Survival Zone, 1992
    Slow Burn, 1986
Roker, Roxie
    Cosmic Slop: Space Traders, 1994
Rolle, Esther
    Driving Miss Daisy, 1989
    House of Cards, 1993
    I Know Why the Caged Bird Sings, 1978
    Mighty Quinn, The, 1989
    Raisin in the Sun, A, 1989
Rollins Jr., Howard E.
    Children of Times Square, 1986
    For Us, the Living, 1984
    House of God, The, 1984
    On the Block, 1991
    Ragtime, 1981
    Soldier's Story, A, 1984
Romero, Victor
    Burning an Illusion, 1981

Ross, Diana
    Wiz, The, 1978
Ross, Ricco
    Amazing Grace and Chuck, 1987
    Displaced Person, 1985
Ross, Richard
    Game, The, 1990
Ross, Ron
    Toy Soldiers, 1983
Ross, Ted
    Police Academy, 1984
    Wiz, The, 1978
Roundtree, Richard
    Angel 3: The Final Chapter, 1988
    Bad Jim, 1989
    Big Score, The, 1983
    City Heat, 1984
    Crack House, 1989
    Escape to Athena, 1979
    Game for Vultures, 1979
    Inchon, 1981
    Jocks, 1987
    Just an Overnight Guest, 1983
    Killpoint, 1984
    Night Visitor, 1990
    Once Upon A Time When We Were Colored, 1994
    One Down, Two to Go, 1983
    Q, 1982
    Sins of the Night, 1993
    Young Warriors, The, 1983
Rowell, Victoria
    Distinguished Gentleman, The, 1992
    Dumb and Dumber, 1994
    Leonard Part 6, 1987
Royal, Cornell
    Daughters of the Dust, 1991
Rucker, A.
    Different Image, A, 1982
Rucker, Bo
    Cross Creek, 1983

Ruffin, Lark
    Roll of Thunder, Hear My Cry, 1986
Run-D.M.C.
    Krush Groove, 1985
    Tougher Than Leather, 1988
RuPaul
    Crooklyn, 1994
Rush, Maggie
    Drop Squad, 1994
    Juice, 1992
    Who's the Man?, 1993
Rush, Robert Lee
    Bad Boys, 1982
    Dressed to Kill, 1980
    Enemy Territory, 1987
Russ, Tim
    Bird, 1988
    Crossroads, 1986
    Dead Connection, 1994
    Eve of Destruction, 1991
    Fire with Fire, 1986
    Mr. Saturday Night, 1992
    Night Eyes 2, 1992
    Spaceballs, 1987
Russell, Kayarsha "Diane"
    Wide Sargasso Sea, 1993
Russell, Kimberly
    Ghost Dad, 1990
    Hangin' with the Homeboys, 1991
    Sugar Hill, 1994
Russell, Nipsey
    Car 54, Where Are You?, 1994
    Dream One, 1984
    Posse, 1993
    Wildcats, 1986
    Wiz, The, 1978
Russell, T.E.
    Trespass, 1992
Ryder, Carl
    Public Enemy: Tour of a Black Planet, 1991

Sadler, Eric "Vietnam"
  Public Enemy: Tour of a Black Planet, 1991
Sams, Deon
  Grand Canyon, 1991
Sams, Jeffery
  Fly by Night, 1994
Sanders, Ann D.
  Straight Out of Brooklyn, 1991
Sanders, Brad
  Bebe's Kids, 1992
  Brewster's Millions, 1985
  Fear of a Black Hat, 1994
  Hollywood Shuffle, 1987
Sanford, Isabel
  Desperate Moves, 1986
  Love at First Bite, 1979
  South Beach, 1993
Sanon, Barbara
  Straight Out of Brooklyn, 1991
Sans, Tommy
  Another Kind of Music, 1978
Sanyika, Dadisi
  Life is a Saxophone, 1985
Satterfield, Jeanne
  Born in Flames, 1983
Savage, Jimmy Lee
  Sankofa, 1994
Savage, Wild
  Super Soul Brother, 1989
Saxon-Federalla, Margot
  Different Image, A, 1982
Scarber, Sam
  Against All Odds, 1984
  Borrower, The, 1991
  My Man Adam, 1986
  Over the Top, 1987
  Shocker, 1989
Schachter, Felice
  Zapped, 1982
Scorpio, Jay
  Arachnophobia, 1990
  Emanon, 1987
  School Spirit, 1985

Scott, Kimberly
    Abyss, The, 1989
    Client, The, 1994
    Downtown, 1990
    Falling Down, 1993
    Flatliners, 1990
Scott, Larry B.
    Another Stakeout, 1993
    Children of Times Square, 1986
    Extreme Prejudice, 1987
    Fear of a Black Hat, 1994
    Iron Eagle, 1986
    Revenge of the Nerds, 1984
    Revenge of the Nerds II: Nerds in Paradise, 1987
    Space Camp, 1986
    That Was Then...This is Now, 1985
Scott, Seret
    Losing Ground, 1982
    Pretty Baby, 1978
Seacer Jr., Levi
    Grafitti Bridge, 1990
Sekka, Johnny
    Ashanti, 1979
    Charlie Chan and the Curse of the Dragon Queen, 1981
    Hanky-Panky, 1982
Sellman, Goma
    Sidewalk Stories, 1989
Seneca, Joe
    Big Shots, 1987
    Crossroads, 1986
    Evil that Men Do, The, 1984
    Half Slave, Half Free, 1984
    Kramer vs. Kramer, 1979
    Malcolm X, 1992
    Mississippi Masala, 1991
    Saint of Fort Washington, The, 1992
    School Daze, 1988
    Silverado, 1985
    Trespass, 1992
    Verdict, The, 1982

Severe, Peggy
    Angel Heart, 1987
Shabaka,
    Fear of a Black Hat, 1994
Shakur, Tupac
    Above the Rim, 1994
    Juice, 1992
    Poetic Justice, 1993
Shannon-Burnett, Gaye
    My Brother's Wedding, 1983
Shaw, Dianne B.
    One More Saturday Night, 1986
    White Girl, The, 1988
Shaw, G. Tito
    Petey Wheatstraw, 1978
Shaw, Jannine
    Jury of Her Peers, A, 1994
Shaw, Stan
    Body of Evidence, 1993
    Boys in Company C, The, 1978
    Busted Up, 1986
    D.P., 1987
    Displaced Person, 1985
    Fried Green Tomatoes, 1991
    Great Santini, The, 1979
    Harlem Nights, 1989
    Runaway, 1984
    Tough Enough, 1982
Shaw, Vanessa
    Game, The, 1990
Sheila E.
    Adventures of Ford Fairlane, The, 1990
    Krush Groove, 1985
Shelby, LaRita
    South Central, 1992
Shocklee, Hank
    Public Enemy: Tour of a Black Planet, 1991
Shocklee, Keith
    Public Enemy: Tour of a Black Planet, 1991
Silas, Everett
    My Brother's Wedding, 1983

Sills, Paula
    One Down, Two to Go, 1983
Silver, Kim
    Maid to Order, 1987
Silver, Tracy
    Fast Forward, 1985
Simeon, Josette
    Cry Freedom, 1987
Simmons, Ron
    Tongues Untied, 1989
Simmons, Russell
    Krush Groove, 1985
Simon, Denise
    Perfect Model, The, 1989
Simply Marvelous
    House Party 3, 1994
    Talkin' Dirty after Dark, 1991
Simpson, O.J.
    Burning Cross, The, 1990
    Capricorn One, 1978
    CIA--Code Name Alexa, 1993
    Firepower, 1979
    Hambone and Hillie, 1984
    Naked Gun 2 1/2: The Smell of Fear, 1991
    Naked Gun 33 1/3: The Final Insult, 1994
    Naked Gun, The: From the Files of Police Squad, 1988
Sims, Howard "Sandman"
    Harlem Nights, 1989
    No Maps on My Taps, 1979
    Tap, 1989
Sinbad
    Coneheads, 1993
    Houseguest, 1994
    M.C. Lyte: Lyte Years, 1991
    Meteor Man, The, 1993
    Necessary Roughness, 1991
Sinclair, Madge
    Coming to America, 1988
    Convoy, 1978
    End of Innocence, The, 1991
    Guyana Tragedy: The Jim Jones Story, 1983
    I Know Why the Caged Bird Sings, 1978
    Lion King, The, 1994

Sinclair, Madge
    Star Trek IV: The Voyage Home, 1986
    Uncle Joe Shannon, 1978
Singer, Aaron
    Syvilla: They Dance to Her Drum, 1979
Singleton, Sam
    Death of a Prophet, 1981
Sisco, Richard
    Beat Street, 1984
Sister Souljah
    Public Enemy: Tour of a Black Planet, 1991
Sithole, Mabutho "Kid"
    Air Up There, The, 1994
Sithole, Nonhlanhla
    Sarafina!, 1992
Sivad, Darryl
    Talkin' Dirty after Dark, 1991
Slaten, Frank
    Brewster's Millions, 1985
    Johnny Dangerously, 1984
    Scout, The, 1994
Slyde, Jimmy
    'Round Midnight, 1986
Smillie, Bill
    Die Hard 2: Die Harder, 1990
    Housekeeping, 1987
    Philadelphia Experiment, The, 1984
    Piranha, 1978
    Singles, 1992
    When Time Ran Out, 1980
Smith, "T" Oney
    Take Down, 1979
Smith, Anna Deavere
    Philadelphia, 1993
Smith, Billy
    Say Amen, Somebody, 1982
Smith, Bobby
    Wide Sargasso Sea, 1993
Smith, Bubba
    Black Moon Rising, 1986
    Gremlins 2: The New Batch, 1990
    Holy Matrimony, 1994
    Police Academy 2: Their First Assignment, 1985

Smith, Bubba
Police Academy 3: Back in Training, 1990
Police Academy 5: Assignment Miami Beach, 1988
Police Academy 6: City Under Siege, 1989
Stoker Ace, 1983
Wild Pair, The, 1987
Smith, Ebonie
Cosmic Slop: Space Traders, 1994
Lethal Weapon, 1987
Lethal Weapon 2, 1989
Smith, Ernest Lee
Tough Enough, 1982
Smith, Evan Lionel
Mo' Money, 1992
Smith, Forry
Black Cobra III: The Manila Connection, 1990
Dragon: The Bruce Lee Story, 1993
Smith, J.W.
Crossroads, 1986
D.C. Cab, 1984
Deal of the Century, 1983
In Your Face, 1990
Johnny Handsome, 1989
K-9, 1989
Let's Get Harry, 1987
Outrageous Fortune, 1987
Smith, Juney
Good Morning Vietnam, 1987
Smith, Lionel
Youngblood, 1978
Smith, Lisette
Permanent Wave, 1986
Smith, Mary Alice
Krush Groove, 1985
Smith, Queenie
End, The, 1978
Smith, Roger Guenveur
Cosmic Slop: Space Traders, 1994
Deep Cover, 1992
King of New York, 1990
Poetic Justice, 1993

Smith, Tony
    Perfect Model, The, 1989
Smith, Toukie A.
    I Like it Like That, 1994
    Me and Him, 1990
    Talkin' Dirty after Dark, 1991
Smith, Valerian
    Toy, The, 1982
Smith, Will
    Imagemaker, The, 1986
    Made in America, 1993
    Six Degrees of Separation, 1993
    Where the Day Takes You, 1992
Smith, Willie "Big Eyes"
    Blues Brothers, The, 1980
Smith, Wonderful
    This is Spinal Tap, 1984
    To Sleep with Anger, 1990
Smith, Wynonna
    Cotton Club, The, 1984
Smith Jr., John Walton
    Higher Learning, 1994
Smollett, JoJo
    City of Hope, 1991
Sneed, Julie
    M.C. Hammer: Please Hammer Don't Hurt 'Em, 1990
Sneed, Maurice
    Braker, 1985
    Hysterical, 1983
    Lunch Wagon, 1981
    Main Event, The, 1979
    Mr. Mom, 1983
    Youngblood, 1978
Snipes, Wesley
    Boiling Point, 1993
    Demolition Man, 1993
    Drop Zone, 1994
    Jungle Fever, 1991
    King of New York, 1990
    Major League, 1989
    Mo' Better Blues, 1990
    New Jack City, 1991
    Passenger 57, 1992

Snipes, Wesley
    Rising Sun, 1993
    Streets of Gold, 1986
    Sugar Hill, 1994
    Waterdance, The, 1992
    White Men Can't Jump, 1992
    Wildcats, 1986
Solomon, Joe
    Sidewalk Stories, 1989
Solomon, Jonathan
    Hangin' with the Homeboys, 1991
Soremekun, Kai
    Back in Action, 1994
Soul Gee
    House Party 3, 1994
Soulfood
    Fly by Night, 1994
Spears, Hazel
    Penitentiary, 1979
Special Ed
    Fly by Night, 1994
Speed, Carol
    Avenging Disco Godfather, 1986
Speights, Leslie
    Different Image, A, 1982
    Gobots: Battle of the Rock Lords, 1986
    One Dark Night, 1983
Spinks, Jimmy/James
    Big Score, The, 1983
    Big Shots, 1987
    Damien--Omen II, 1978
    Doctor Detroit, 1983
    Hunter, The, 1980
    Killing Floor, The, 1984
    Messenger, The, 1986
    Mo' Money, 1992
    Rage in Harlem, A, 1991
    Straight Talk, 1992
Spinks, Michael
    Speed Zone, 1989
    White Girl, The, 1988

St. Jacques, Raymond
    Born Again, 1978
    Cuba Crossing, 1980
    Evil that Men Do, The, 1984
    Glory, 1989
    Sophisticated Gents, 1981
    They Live, 1988
    Time Bomb, 1991
    True Story of Glory Continues, The, 1991
    Voodoo Dawn, 1991
    Wild Pair, The, 1987
St. La Mount, Dea
    Hunter, The, 1980
Staples, Mavis
    Grafitti Bridge, 1990
Staples, Roebuck "Pops"
    True Stories, 1986
Starr, Arlena
    Livin' Large!, 1991
Starr, Fredro
    Strapped, 1993
Starr, Maurice
    American Hot Wax, 1978
    Chair, The, 1991
Steadman, Ken
    Street Wars, 1994
Steele, Jevetta
    Corrina, Corrina, 1994
Steen, Henry
    Sidewalk Stories, 1989
Stevens, D.
    Langston Hughes: The Dream Keeper, 1988
Stevens III, James
    Talkin' Dirty after Dark, 1991
Stewart, Byron
    How U Like Me Now, 1992
Stewart, Harry
    Cadence, 1990
Stewart, Mel
    Bride of Re-Animator, The, 1991
    Dead Heat, 1988
    Kid with the 200 I.Q., The, 1982
    Made in America, 1993

Stewart, Mel
    Whose Life is it Anyway?, 1981
Stewart, Tonea
    Body Snatchers, 1994
    Livin' Large!, 1991
Stickney, Phyllis Yvonne
    Inkwell, 1994
    Jungle Fever, 1991
    Malcolm X, 1992
    New Jack City, 1991
    Talkin' Dirty after Dark, 1991
Stickney, Timothy
    Return of Superfly, The, 1990
Stoker, Austin
    Assault on Precinct 13, 1981
    Time Walker, 1982
    Uninvited, The, 1988
Stovall, Count
    Booker T. Washington: The Life & the Legacy, 1982
    Zora Is My Name!, 1989
Strode, Woody
    Angkor-Cambodia Express, 1981
    Black Stallion Returns, The, 1983
    Cuba Crossing, 1980
    Final Executioner, The, 1986
    Jaguar Lives!, 1979
    Jungle Warriors, 1984
    Lust in the Dust, 1985
    Ravagers, The, 1979
    Storyville, 1992
    Vigilante, 1983
    Violent Breed, The, 1986
Stuart, Brian Paul
    Homeboyz II: Crack City, 1993
Stubbs, Levi
    Little Shop of Horrors, 1986
Summer, Donna
    Thank God It's Friday, 1978
Summerour, Lisa
    Enemy Within, The, 1994

Sutherland, Esther
  Stir Crazy, 1980
  Young Doctors in Love, 1982
Swann, Lynn
  Last Boy Scout, The, 1991
  Program, The, 1993
Sweat, Keith
  New Jack City, 1991
Sweeny, Aurelia
  Getting Over, 1981
Sweet, Vonte
  Gladiator, 1992
  Menace II Society, 1993
  Predator 2, 1990
  Without You, I'm Nothing, 1990
Sylvers, Jeremy
  Child's Play 3, 1991
Sylvester, Harold
  Corrina, Corrina, 1994
  Fast Break, 1979
  Hit List, 1990
  Innerspace, 1987
  Inside Moves, 1980
  Officer and a Gentleman, An, 1982
  Space Rage, 1987
  Uncommon Valor, 1983
  Vision Quest, 1985
T. Money
  Public Enemy: Tour of a Black Planet, 1991
  Who's the Man?, 1993
Taimak
  Last Dragon, The, 1985
  White Girl, The, 1988
Taj Mahal
  Bill and Ted's Bogus Journey, 1991
Tarkington, Rockne
  Under the Gunn, 1988
Tarver, Catherine
  Daughters of the Dust, 1991
Tate, Caron
  Prime Risk, 1985
  Talking to Strangers, 1988

Tate, Lahmard
  Jason's Lyric, 1994
Tate, Larenz
  Inkwell, 1994
  Menace II Society, 1993
Tate, Vanessa
  Riverbend, 1990
Tatum, Bill
  Born in Flames, 1983
Taylor, Anita
  Student Bodies, 1981
Taylor, Clarice
  Nothing Lasts Forever, 1984
  Smoke, 1994
  Sommersby, 1993
  Torture of Mothers, The, 1980
Taylor, Femi
  Flirting, 1992
Taylor, Jimmy
  Torture of Mothers, The, 1980
Taylor, Kirk
  Return of Superfly, The, 1990
Taylor, Melvin Howard
  Perfume, 1990
Taylor, Meshach
  Allnighter, The, 1987
  Beast Within, The, 1982
  Class Act, 1992
  Damien--Omen II, 1978
  Explorers, 1985
  From the Hip, 1987
  House of Games, 1987
  Mannequin, 1987
  Mannequin 2: On the Move, 1991
  One More Saturday Night, 1986
  Warning Sign, 1985
  Welcome to Oblivion, 1992
Taylor, Regina
  Lean on Me, 1989
Taylor, Robert
  Beat Street, 1984
  Krush Groove, 1985

Taylor, Ron
    Heart Condition, 1990
    Rage in Harlem, A, 1991
Taylor, Wally
    Mystique, 1981
    Peacemaker, 1990
    Rocky III, 1982
Teek, Angela
    Hollywood Shuffle, 1987
Tennon, Julius
    Riverbend, 1990
Terminator X
    Public Enemy: Tour of a Black Planet, 1991
Terrell, John Canada
    Boomerang, 1992
    Def by Temptation, 1990
    Elliot Fauman, Ph.D., 1990
    Five Heartbeats, The, 1991
    Recruits, 1986
    Return of Superfly, The, 1990
    Rooftops, 1989
    She's Gotta Have It, 1986
Terry, Sonny
    Jerk, The, 1979
Thacker, Tab
    City Heat, 1984
    Police Academy 4: Citizens on Patrol, 1987
    Police Academy 5: Assignment Miami Beach, 1988
    Wildcats, 1986
The Bucket Dance Company
    Dance Black America, 1985
The Clark Sisters
    Gospel, 1987
The Commodores
    Thank God It's Friday, 1978
The Fat Boys
    Disorderlies, 1987
    Krush Groove, 1985
The Hawkins Family
    Gospel, 1987

The Jazzy Jumpers
  Dance Black America, 1985
The Magnificent Force
  Dance Black America, 1985
The Mighty Clouds of Joy
  Gospel, 1987
The Time
  Grafitti Bridge, 1990
The Winans
  Winans, The: Live in Concert, 1987
Theus, Reggie
  Perfect Model, The, 1989
  Sweet Perfection, 1987
Thibodeaux, Valerie
  Tightrope, 1984
Thigpen, Kevin
  Just Another Girl on the I.R.T., 1993
  PCU, 1994
Thigpen, Lynn
  Article 99, 1992
  Blankman, 1994
  Bob Roberts, 1992
  Impulse, 1990
  Lean on Me, 1989
  Naked in New York, 1994
  Paper, The, 1994
  Running on Empty, 1988
  Streets of Fire, 1984
  Sweet Liberty, 1986
  Tootsie, 1982
  Warriors, The, 1979
Thomas, Ernest
  Malcolm X, 1992
Thomas, Joseph A.
  Straight Out of Brooklyn, 1991
Thomas, Philip Michael
  Charlie Barnett's Terms of Enrollment, 1986
Thomas, Rufus
  Mystery Train, 1989
Thomas, Tressa
  Five Heartbeats, The, 1991

Thomas, Trevor
  Sheena, 1984
Thompson, Andrea
  Colour, 1983
Thompson, Denise
  Wide Sargasso Sea, 1993
Thompson, Wesley
  L.A. Story, 1991
Thorne, Geoffrey
  Women of Brewster Place, The, 1988
Thrash, Winston
  Speeding Up Time, 1985
Thys, Michael
  Gods Must Be Crazy, The, 1984
Tierney, Maura
  Fly by Night, 1994
Tighe, Kevin
  K-9, 1989
Timbers, Veronica
  Jungle Fever, 1991
Titus, Dennis
  Mighty Quinn, The, 1989
TLC
  House Party 3, 1994
Todd, Beverly
  Clara's Heart, 1988
  Happy Hour, 1987
  Homework, 1982
  Ladies Club, The, 1986
  Lean on Me, 1989
  Moving, 1988
  Vice Squad, 1982
Todd, Joy
  Moscow on the Hudson, 1984
Todd, Tony
  Candyman, 1992
  Crow, The, 1994
  Enemy Territory, 1987
  Lean on Me, 1989
  Night of the Living Dead, 1990
  Voodoo Dawn, 1991

Todd I.
  Who's the Man?, 1993
Toles-Bey, John
  Angie, 1994
  Cadence, 1990
  Rage in Harlem, A, 1991
  Trespass, 1992
  Weeds, 1987
Tone-Loc
  Ace Ventura: Pet Detective, 1994
  Adventures of Ford Fairlane, The, 1990
  Bebe's Kids, 1992
  Blank Check, 1994
  Car 54, Where Are You?, 1994
  Ferngully: The Last Rainforest, 1992
  Poetic Justice, 1993
  Posse, 1993
  Surf Ninjas, 1993
Torry, Joe
  House Party 3, 1994
  Poetic Justice, 1993
  Talkin' Dirty after Dark, 1991
Torture
  M.C. Hammer: Please Hammer Don't Hurt 'Em, 1990
Toussaint, Lorraine
  Breaking In, 1989
  Hudson Hawk, 1991
  Mother's Boys, 1994
  Point of No Return, 1993
Townsend, Robert
  American Flyers, 1985
  Five Heartbeats, The, 1991
  Hollywood Shuffle, 1987
  Meteor Man, The, 1993
  Mighty Quinn, The, 1989
  Odd Jobs, 1986
  Ratboy, 1986
  Streets of Fire, 1984
  Willie and Phil, 1980
Townsend, Vince
  Messenger, The, 1986
  Star Trek III: The Search for Spock, 1984

Townsend Jr., Edward Jay
    City of Hope, 1991
Townsend Jr., Vince Monroe
    Maid to Order, 1987
    Weird Science, 1985
Treach (Anthony Criss)
    Jason's Lyric, 1994
Trupin, Gabriel
    Madonna: Truth or Dare, 1991
Tubman, Harriet
    Harriet Tubman, 1992
Tucker, Chris
    House Party 3, 1994
Tullis Jr., Dan
    CIA--Code Name Alexa, 1993
    Extreme Prejudice, 1987
    First Power, The, 1990
    Private Wars, 1993
Tumbtzen, Tatiana
    Perfect Model, The, 1989
    Sweet Perfection, 1987
Turman, Glynn
    Deep Cover, 1992
    Gremlins, 1984
    Inkwell, 1994
    Out of Bounds, 1986
    Penitentiary II, 1982
    River Niger, The, 1978
Turner, Arnold
    Perfume, 1990
Turner, Tina
    Last Action Hero, 1993
    Mad Max beyond Thunderdome, 1985
Turner, Tyrin
    Menace II Society, 1993
Turpin, Bahni
    Daughters of the Dust, 1991
    Rain without Thunder, 1993
    Saint of Fort Washington, The, 1992
Twala, Mary
    Sarafina!, 1992

Twillie, Carmen
    Solar Crisis, 1993
Tyler, Edwina L.
    Powerful Thang, A, 1991
    Syvilla: They Dance to Her Drum, 1979
Tyler, Gamy L.
    Pass/Fail, 1978
Tyson, Cathy
    Mona Lisa, 1986
    Serpent and the Rainbow, The, 1988
Tyson, Cicely
    Bustin' Loose, 1981
    Concorde, The--Airport '79, 1979
    Fried Green Tomatoes, 1991
    Heat Wave, 1990
    King, 1978
    Samaritan: The Mitch Snyder Story, 1986
    Woman Called Moses, A, 1989
    Women of Brewster Place, The, 1988
Uggams, Leslie
    Sizzle, 1981
    Sugar Hill, 1994
Underwood, Blair
    Father and Son: Dangerous Relations, 1993
    Heat Wave, 1990
    Krush Groove, 1985
    Posse, 1993
Urban Bush Women
    Praise House, 1991
Uwampa, Nadine
    Dust, 1985
Van Peebles, Mario
    3:15, The Moment of Truth, 1986
    Cotton Club, The, 1984
    Exterminator II, 1984
    Gunmen, 1994
    Heartbreak Ridge, 1986
    Highlander III: The Sorcerer, 1994
    Hot Shot, 1987
    Identity Crisis, 1991
    Jaws: The Revenge, 1987
    Last Resort, 1985
    New Jack City, 1991

Van Peebles, Mario
    Posse, 1993
    Rappin', 1985
    Sophisticated Gents, 1981
    South Bronx Heroes, 1985
    Stompin' at the Savoy, 1992
    Urban Crossfire, 1994
Van Peebles, Megan
    South Bronx Heroes, 1985
Van Peebles, Melvin
    Boomerang, 1992
    Jaws: The Revenge, 1987
    Posse, 1993
    Sophisticated Gents, 1981
    True Identity, 1991
Vance, Courtney B.
    Adventures of Huck Finn, 1993
    Beyond the Law, 1994
    Hamburger Hill, 1987
    Holy Matrimony, 1994
    Hunt for Red October, The, 1990
    Superman III, 1983
    Urban Crossfire, 1994
Vance, Danitra
    Hangin' with the Homeboys, 1991
    Jumpin' at the Boneyard, 1992
    Limit Up, 1990
    Little Man Tate, 1991
    Sticky Fingers, 1988
    War of the Roses, The, 1989
Vandross, Luther
    Meteor Man, The, 1993
Vanity
    52 Pick-Up, 1986
    Action Jackson, 1988
    Deadly Illusion, 1987
    Last Dragon, The, 1985
    Never Too Young to Die, 1986
    South Beach, 1993
Vaughan, Paris
    Buffy the Vampire Slayer, 1992
    Heat Wave, 1990
    Pretty Smart, 1987

Veljohnson, Reginald
 Die Hard, 1988
 Die Hard 2: Die Harder, 1990
 Posse, 1993
 Wolfen, 1981
Verduzco, Adam
 New Eden, 1994
Vereen, Ben
 All that Jazz, 1979
 Buy & Cell, 1989
 Lost in London, 1985
 Once Upon a Forest, 1993
 Pippin': His Life and Times, 1981
 Zoo Gang, The, 1984
Verreds, Rita
 Marked for Death, 1990
Victor, Akia
 Inkwell, 1994
Victoria, Christa
 Stand-In, The, 1985
Vite, Ray
 Cheech and Chong: Up in Smoke, 1980
Vitle, Ray
 Thank God It's Friday, 1978
Vu-Ann, Eric
 Sheltering Sky, The, 1990
Vyent, Louise
 Boomerang, 1992
Walcott III, Noel L.
 Marked for Death, 1990
Walker, Ann
 Cosmic Slop: Space Traders, 1994
Walker, Denis
 Fringe Dwellers, The, 1986
Walker, Herschel
 Necessary Roughness, 1991
Walker, Jimmy/Jimmie
 Airplane!, 1980
 Concorde, The--Airport '79, 1979
 Doin' Time, 1986
 Guyver, The, 1992
 Home Alone 2: Lost in New York, 1992
 Rabbit Test, 1978

Walker, Lou
    Mississippi Burning, 1988
Wallace, Basil
    Grand Canyon, 1991
    Marked for Death, 1990
    Rapid Fire, 1992
Wallace, Craig
    Walk on White Nails, 1991
Wallace, George
    Bebe's Kids, 1992
    Cosmic Slop: Space Traders, 1994
    Punchline, 1988
    Rage in Harlem, A, 1991
Wand, Magic
    Messenger, The, 1986
Ward, Alonzo
    Jaws III, 1983
Ward, Douglas Turner
    Go Tell it on the Mountain, 1984
    Women of Brewster Place, The, 1988
Ward, Francis
    Another 48 Hours, 1990
Ward, Richard
    Brubaker, 1980
    Jerk, The, 1979
Warfield, Marlene
    How I Got into College, 1989
    Jo Jo Dancer, Your Life is Calling, 1986
    Sophisticated Gents, 1981
Warfield, Marsha
    Comic Relief, 1990
    D.C. Cab, 1984
    Mask, 1985
    Whoopee Boys, The, 1986
Warner, Malcolm-Jamaal
    Father Clement's Story, 1987
Warren, Kai-Lynne
    Daughters of the Dust, 1991
Warren, Michael
    Fast Break, 1979
    Heaven is a Playground, 1992
    Stompin' at the Savoy, 1992
    Storyville, 1992

Warwick, Dionne
  Rent-A-Cop, 1988
Washington, Denzel
  Carbon Copy, 1981
  Cry Freedom, 1987
  For Queen and Country, 1989
  Glory, 1989
  Heart Condition, 1990
  Malcolm X, 1992
  Mighty Quinn, The, 1989
  Mississippi Masala, 1991
  Mo' Better Blues, 1990
  Much Ado about Nothing, 1993
  Pelican Brief, The, 1993
  Philadelphia, 1993
  Power, 1986
  Ricochet, 1991
  Soldier's Story, A, 1984
Washington, Isaiah
  Crooklyn, 1994
  Land Where My Fathers Died, 1991
Washington, Jerard
  Just Another Girl on the I.R.T., 1993
Washington, Joe
  Livin' Large!, 1991
Washington, Ludie
  Hollywood Shuffle, 1987
  Jo Jo Dancer, Your Life is Calling, 1986
  Without You, I'm Nothing, 1990
Washington, Lula
  Life is a Saxophone, 1985
Washington, Mavis
  Fast Break, 1979
Waterman, Juanita
  Cry Freedom, 1987
Waters Jr., Harry
  Back to the Future, 1985
Watkins, Craig
  Powerful Thang, A, 1991
Watson, Doc
  Petey Wheatstraw, 1978

Watson Jr., James A.
    Airplane II, 1983
    Goldengirl, 1979
Watts, Charles
    Raisin in the Sun, A, 1989
Watts, Mary
    Kiss Grandmama Goodbye, 1991
Wayans, Almayvonne
    Mo' Money, 1992
Wayans, Cara Mia
    Blankman, 1994
Wayans, Damon
    Beverly Hills Cop, 1984
    Blankman, 1994
    Colors, 1988
    Earth Girls Are Easy, 1988
    Hollywood Shuffle, 1987
    Last Action Hero, 1993
    Last Boy Scout, The, 1991
    Mo' Money, 1992
    Punchline, 1988
    Roxanne, 1987
Wayans, Keenen Ivory
    Hollywood Shuffle, 1987
    I'm Gonna Git You Sucka, 1988
    Low Down Dirty Shame, 1994
    Star 80, 1983
Wayans, Kim
    Floundering, 1994
    Hollywood Shuffle, 1987
    Low Down Dirty Shame, 1994
Wayans, Marlon
    Above the Rim, 1994
    Mo' Money, 1992
Wayans, Michael
    Blankman, 1994
Waymon, Sam
    Weeds, 1987
Weathers, Carl
    Action Jackson, 1988
    Braker, 1985
    Death Hunt, 1981
    Force 10 from Navarone, 1978

Weathers, Carl
  Fortune Dane, 1986
  Predator, 1987
  Rocky II, 1979
  Rocky III, 1982
  Rocky IV, 1985
Weaver, Jason
  Long Walk Home, The, 1991
Weaver, Rose
  Poetic Justice, 1993
Webb, Michelle
  M.C. Lyte: Lyte Years, 1991
Webb, Veronica
  Jungle Fever, 1991
Weeks, Alan
  Brighton Beach Memoirs, 1986
Weeks, Michelle
  Little Shop of Horrors, 1986
  Trading Places, 1983
Weldon, Ann
  Importance of Being Ernest, The, 1992
Wells, Adrian
  Space Camp, 1986
Wells, Tico
  Drop Squad, 1994
  Five Heartbeats, The, 1991
  Return of Superfly, The, 1990
  Trespass, 1992
  Universal Soldier, 1992
Wesley, John
  Little Rascals, The, 1994
  Moving, 1988
West, Jim
  Bob Roberts, 1992
West, Latanya
  Odds & Ends: A New-Age Amazon Fable, 1993
Weston-Moran, Kim
  Alma's Rainbow, 1993
Wheeler, Ed
  Drop Squad, 1994

Whitaker, Damon
  Bird, 1988
Whitaker, Duane
  Leatherface: The Texas Chainsaw Massacre III, 1990
  Puppet Master 5: The Final Chapter, 1994
Whitaker, Forest
  Article 99, 1992
  Bank Robber, 1993
  Bird, 1988
  Blown Away, 1994
  Body Snatchers, 1994
  Color of Money, The, 1986
  Consenting Adults, 1992
  Criminal Justice, 1990
  Crying Game, The, 1992
  Diary of a Hitman, 1991
  Downtown, 1990
  Enemy Within, The, 1994
  Fast Times at Ridgemont High, 1982
  Good Morning Vietnam, 1987
  Jason's Lyric, 1994
  Johnny Handsome, 1989
  Platoon, 1986
  Rage in Harlem, A, 1991
  Ready to Wear, 1994
  Smoke, 1994
  Stakeout, 1987
  Vision Quest, 1985
Whitaker, Len
  Assault on Precinct 13, 1981
Whitaker, Yolanda ("Yo-Yo")
  Boyz n the Hood, 1991
  Who's the Man?, 1993
White, Al
  Airplane II, 1983
  Airplane!, 1980
White, Devoreaux
  Blues Brothers, The, 1980
  Die Hard, 1988
  Places in the Heart, 1984
  Trespass, 1992

White, Karen Malina
    Lean on Me, 1989
White, Kevin C.
    Betrayed, 1988
    Music Box, 1989
White, Randy
    Necessary Roughness, 1991
White, Slappy
    Mr. Saturday Night, 1992
White, Steve
    Adventures of Ford Fairlane, The, 1990
White, Suzanna
    Jungle Fever, 1991
White, Wilbur "HiFi"
    Penitentiary, 1979
Whitefield, Raymond
    How U Like Me Now, 1992
Whitemore, Clarence
    Jason's Lyric, 1994
Whitfield, Lynn
    Dead Aim, 1990
    Doctor Detroit, 1983
    In the Army Now, 1994
    Jaws: The Revenge, 1987
    Josephine Baker Story, The, 1991
    Silverado, 1985
    Slugger's Wife, The, 1985
    Stompin' at the Savoy, 1992
    Taking the Heat, 1993
    Women of Brewster Place, The, 1988
    Zora Is My Name!, 1989
Whitfield, Vantile
    Ashes and Embers, 1985
Whitman, Eloise
    Livin' Large!, 1991
Wiggins, Alfred
    Program, The, 1993
Wiggins, Barry
    Ashes and Embers, 1985
Wilborn, Carlton
    Grief, 1993
    Madonna: Truth or Dare, 1991

Wildman Steve
    Petey Wheatstraw, 1978
Wilkes, Dawn
    Since Lisa..., 1994
Williams, Addie
    Super Soul Brother, 1989
Williams, Bill/Billy
    Drop Squad, 1994
    Game, The, 1990
    Voodoo Dawn, 1991
Williams, Billy Dee
    Alien Intruder, 1993
    Batman, 1989
    Black Brigade, 1989
    Deadly Illusion, 1987
    Driving Me Crazy, 1991
    Empire Strikes Back, The, 1980
    Fear City, 1984
    Jacksons: An American Dream, The, 1992
    Marvin and Tige, 1983
    Nighthawks, 1981
    Number One with a Bullet, 1987
    Return of the Jedi, 1983
    Shooting Stars, The, 1985
Williams, Britt
    Torture of Mothers, The, 1980
Williams, Carlton
    Crooklyn, 1994
Williams, Chino "Fats"
    Action Jackson, 1988
    Bebe's Kids, 1992
    Cosmic Slop: The First Commandant, 1994
    Hot to Trot, 1988
    Road House, 1989
    Storyville, 1992
    Swing Shift, 1984
    Talkin' Dirty after Dark, 1991
    Weird Science, 1985
Williams, Christopher
    New Jack City, 1991

Williams, Cynda
    Mo' Better Blues, 1990
    One False Move, 1991
Williams, Darnell
    How U Like Me Now, 1992
    Sidewalk Stories, 1989
    Stompin' at the Savoy, 1992
Williams, Dick Anthony
    Almost Perfect Affair, An, 1979
    Gardens of Stone, 1987
    Gifted, The, 1994
    Jerk, The, 1979
    Mo' Better Blues, 1990
    Rapture, The, 1991
    Sister, Sister, 1982
    Sophisticated Gents, 1981
    Star Chamber, The, 1983
    Summer Rental, 1985
    Tap, 1989
Williams, Ellis
    Hangin' with the Homeboys, 1991
    Music Box, 1989
    Strictly Business, 1991
Williams, Ellwoodson
    Clarence and Angel, 1981
Williams, Eyan
    Outrageous Fortune, 1987
Williams, Gerard
    Predator 2, 1990
    Terminator 2: Judgment Day, 1991
Williams, Hal
    Escape Artist, The, 1982
    Hardcore, 1979
    On the Nickel, 1980
    Private Benjamin, 1980
    Rookie, The, 1990
    Sky Is Gray, The, 1980
Williams, Irma
    Cosmic Slop: The First Commandant, 1994
Williams, Jane Ciampa
    Small Time, 1991

Williams, Kenya
  Odds & Ends: A New-Age Amazon Fable, 1993
Williams, Laura
  Downtown, 1990
  Magic Love, 1993
Williams, Olivia Frances
  Jerk, The, 1979
  Mannequin, 1987
Williams, Samm-Art
  Adventures of Huckleberry Finn, The, 1985
  Baron, The, 1987
  Blood Simple, 1984
  Hot Resort, 1985
  Night of the Juggler, 1980
  Rage in Harlem, A, 1991
  Wanderers, The, 1979
Williams, Sherry
  White Girl, The, 1988
Williams, Spencer
  That's Black Entertainment, 1989
Williams, Steven
  Blues Brothers, The, 1980
  Under the Gunn, 1988
Williams, Sylvester
  Sheena, 1984
Williams, Terrence
  Life Stinks, 1991
Williams, Vanessa
  Another You, 1991
  Candyman, 1992
  Drop Squad, 1994
  Harley Davidson and the Marlboro Man, 1991
  Jacksons: An American Dream, The, 1992
  New Jack City, 1991
  Pick-Up Artist, The, 1987
  Stompin' at the Savoy, 1992
  Under the Gunn, 1988
Williams III, Clarence
  52 Pick-Up, 1986
  Deep Cover, 1992
  Father and Son: Dangerous Relations, 1993
  I'm Gonna Git You Sucka, 1988
  Maniac Cop 2, 1991

Williams III, Clarence
    My Heroes Have Always Been Cowboys, 1991
    Purple Rain, 1984
    Sugar Hill, 1994
    Tough Guys Don't Dance, 1987
Williamson, Fred
    1990: The Bronx Warriors, 1983
    Big Score, The, 1983
    Black Cobra, 1986
    Black Cobra II, 1989
    Black Cobra III: The Manila Connection, 1990
    Blind Rage, 1978
    Counterfeit Commandos, 1978
    Delta Force Commando 2, 1991
    Fist of Fear, Touch of Death, 1985
    Foxtrap, 1985
    Last Fight, The, 1983
    Messenger, The, 1986
    New Barbarians, The, 1983
    One Down, Two to Go, 1983
    South Beach, 1993
    Steele's Law, 1992
    Vigilante, 1983
    Warriors of the Wasteland, 1983
Williamson, Mykelti
    First Power, The, 1990
    Forrest Gump, 1994
    Number One with a Bullet, 1987
    Streets of Fire, 1984
    Wildcats, 1986
Willie, Dap Sugar
    Wildcats, 1986
Wilson, Cal
    Perfume, 1990
Wilson, Dwouane
    Exterminator, The, 1982
Wilson, Flip
    Fish that Saved Pittsburgh, The, 1979
    Skatetown U.S.A., 1979
    Zora Is My Name!, 1989

Wilson, Jomo
    Sidewalk Stories, 1989
Wilson, Marquise
    Sugar Hill, 1994
Wilson, Nancy
    Big Score, The, 1983
Wilson, Reno
    Cosmic Slop: Tang, 1994
Wilson, Sandye
    Sidewalk Stories, 1989
Wilson, Theodore "Teddy"
    Carny, 1980
    Fine Mess, A, 1986
    Genuine Risk, 1991
    Hunter, The, 1980
    Life Stinks, 1991
    Maid to Order, 1987
    Run for the Roses, 1978
    That's Life!, 1986
    Weekend Pass, 1984
Wilson, Thomas F.
    Action Jackson, 1988
    April Fool's Day, 1986
Wilson, Tyrone
    Privilege, 1991
Wilson, Yvette
    Blankman, 1994
    House Party 3, 1994
Wimberly, Roderic
    Go Tell it on the Mountain, 1984
Wimbley, Damon
    Knights of the City, 1985
Winbush, Troy
    Principal, The, 1987
Winde, Beatrice
    From the Hip, 1987
    Hide in Plain Sight, 1980
    It Could Happen to You, 1994
    Oliver's Story, 1978
    Rich Kids, 1979
    Stars and Bars, 1988
    Super, The, 1991

Winfield, Paul
  Big Shots, 1987
  Blue and the Gray, The, 1982
  Blue City, 1986
  Carbon Copy, 1981
  Cliffhanger, 1993
  Death Before Dishonor, 1987
  Dennis the Menace, 1993
  For Us, the Living, 1984
  Go Tell it on the Mountain, 1984
  King, 1978
  Mike's Murder, 1984
  On the Run, 1983
  Presumed Innocent, 1990
  Serpent and the Rainbow, The, 1988
  Sister, Sister, 1982
  Sophisticated Gents, 1981
  Star Trek II: The Wrath of Khan, 1982
  Terminator, The, 1984
  Twilight's Last Gleaming, 1978
  White Dog, 1981
  Women of Brewster Place, The, 1988
Winfield, Rodney
  Bebe's Kids, 1992
  Talkin' Dirty after Dark, 1991
Winfrey, Oprah
  Color Purple, The, 1985
  Native Son, 1986
  There Are No Children Here, 1993
  Throw Momma from the Train, 1987
  Women of Brewster Place, The, 1988
Winkler, Mel
  Convicts, 1991
  Doc Hollywood, 1991
Winslow, Michael
  Alphabet City, 1984
  Buy & Cell, 1989
  Cheech and Chong's Nice Dreams, 1981
  Far Out Man, 1990
  Grandview, U.S.A., 1984
  Lovelines, 1984
  Police Academy, 1984
  Police Academy 2: Their First Assignment, 1985

Winslow, Michael
    Police Academy 3: Back in Training, 1990
    Police Academy 4: Citizens on Patrol, 1987
    Police Academy 5: Assignment Miami Beach, 1988
    Police Academy 6: City Under Siege, 1989
    Spaceballs, 1987
    Starchaser: The Legend of Orin, 1985
    T.A.G.: The Assassination Game, 1982
Winston, Hattie
    Beverly Hills Cops III, 1994
    Clara's Heart, 1988
Winston, McKinley
    Homeboyz II: Crack City, 1993
Wisdom, Bob
    Cosmic Slop: The First Commandant, 1994
Witherspoon, John
    Bebe's Kids, 1992
    Boomerang, 1992
    Cosmic Slop: The First Commandant, 1994
    Fatal Instinct, 1993
    Five Heartbeats, The, 1991
    Hollywood Shuffle, 1987
    House Party, 1990
    Jazz Singer, The, 1980
    Killer Tomatoes Strike Back, 1991
    Meteor Man, The, 1993
    Talkin' Dirty after Dark, 1991
Wolfe, Traci
    Lethal Weapon, 1987
    Lethal Weapon 2, 1989
Womack, Cecil D.
    Shout, The, 1991
Womack, Donovan
    Penitentiary, 1979
    Penitentiary II, 1982
Womack, Linda M.
    Shout, The, 1991
Woodard, Alfre
    Blue Chips, 1994
    Bopha!, 1992
    Crooklyn, 1994
    Cross Creek, 1983
    Extremities, 1986

Woodard, Alfre
  Freedom Road, 1978
  Go Tell it on the Mountain, 1984
  Grand Canyon, 1991
  Gun in Betty Lou's Handbag, The, 1992
  Health, 1980
  Heart and Souls, 1993
  Killing Floor, The, 1984
  Mary Thomas Story, The, 1987
  Miss Firecracker, 1989
  Passion Fish, 1993
  Remember My Name, 1978
  Rich in Love, 1993
  Sophisticated Gents, 1981
  Unnatural Causes, 1986
  Words by Heart, 1984
Woodard, Charlaine
  Ain't Misbehavin, 1982
  Angie, 1994
  Crackers, 1984
  Me and Him, 1990
  Meteor Man, The, 1993
  Twister, 1989
Woodard, Jimmy
  House Party 3, 1994
Woodbine, Bokeem
  Jason's Lyric, 1994
  Strapped, 1993
Woods, Kevin Jamal
  Little Rascals, The, 1994
Woods, Maurice
  Booker T. Washington: The Life & the Legacy, 1982
Wright, Dorsey
  Hair, 1979
  Hotel New Hampshire, 1984
  Warriors, The, 1979
Wright, Eugenia
  Cadence, 1990
  Penitentiary II, 1982
  Perfume, 1990

Wright, Jeffrey
Jumpin' at the Boneyard, 1992
Wright, Linda Thomas
Colour, 1983
Wright, Michael
Five Heartbeats, The, 1991
Principal, The, 1987
Streamers, 1983
Sugar Hill, 1994
Wanderers, The, 1979
Wright, N'Bushe
Fresh, 1994
ZebraHead, 1992
Wright, Samuel E.
Bird, 1988
Me and Him, 1990
Wright, Thomas Lee
City of Hope, 1991
Exterminator II, 1984
Marked for Death, 1990
Wright-Bey, Martin
Talkin' Dirty after Dark, 1991
Wryte, Eboni
Petey Wheatstraw, 1978
Wynn, Brenda Joyce
Dozens, The, 1981
Wynter, Angela
Burning an Illusion, 1981
Yancey, Kim
Raisin in the Sun, A, 1989
Yoba, Malik
Cool Runnings, 1993
Smoke, 1994
Young, Andrea
Waterdance, The, 1992
Young, Billie Jean
Mississippi Burning, 1988
Young, Bruce A.
Trespass, 1992
Young, Cedric
Big Shots, 1987
Home Alone 2: Lost in New York, 1992

Young, William Allen
    Jagged Edge, 1985
    Lock Up, 1990
    Sins, 1990
    Soldier's Story, A, 1984
Young III, Clarence
    Kiss Grandmama Goodbye, 1991
Zobda, France
    Sheena, 1984
Zuehlke, Joshua
    Amazing Grace and Chuck, 1987

Abod, Jennifer
    I Am Your Sister, 1991
Addison, Anita
    Savannah, 1989
    There Are No Children Here, 1993
Ajalon, Jamika
    Intro to Cultural Skit-Zo-Frenia, 1993
Allen, Debbie
    Polly!, 1989
Bagwell, Orlando
    Life is a Saxophone, 1985
    Malcolm X: Make it Plain, 1993
    Racism 101, 1988
Barnett, Neema
    Zora Is My Name!, 1989
Billops, Camille
    Finding Christa, 1991
    KKK Boutique Ain't Just Rednecks, The, 1994
    Older Women and Love, 1987
    Suzanne, Suzanne, 1982
Blue, Carroll Parrott
    Conversations with Roy DeCarava, 1983
    Kindred Spirits: Nigerian Artists, 1992
    Varnette's World: A Study of a Young Artist, 1979
Bond III, James
    Def by Temptation, 1990
Boulware, Domino
    Family Across the Sea, 1990
Bourne, St. Clair
    Black and the Green, The, 1982
    In Motion: Amiri Baraka, 1982
    Langston Hughes: The Dream Keeper, 1988
    Making "Do the Right Thing", 1988
Bowser, Pearl
    Midnight Ramble, 1994
Brown, Curtis
    Game, The, 1990
Brown, Georg Stanford
    Father and Son: Dangerous Relations, 1993
Brown, Jim
    We Shall Overcome: The Song that Moved a Nation, 1989

Brown, Tony
    White Girl, The, 1988
Burke, Joanne
    Mary Lou Williams: Music on My Mind, 1990
Burnett, Charles
    My Brother's Wedding, 1983
    To Sleep with Anger, 1990
Calhoun, Rochelle
    Lady Day at Emerson's Bar & Grill, 1994
Campanella Jr., Roy
    Brother Future, 1991
    Impressions of Joyce, 1979
    Pass/Fail, 1978
    Passion and Memory, 1986
    Thieves, The, 1979
Carew, Topper
    Talkin' Dirty after Dark, 1991
Carpenter, Shari
    Since Lisa..., 1994
Chenzira, Ayoka
    Alma's Rainbow, 1993
    Five Out of Five, 1987
    Hair Piece: A Film for Nappy-Headed People, 1984
    Love Potion, 1993
    Lure and the Lore, The, 1989
    MOTV (My Own TV), 1993
    Pull Your Head to the Moon: Stories of Creole Women, 1992
    Secret Sounds Screaming: The Sexual Abuse of Children, 1986
    Syvilla: They Dance to Her Drum, 1979
    Zajota and the Boogie Spirit, 1990
Chisholm, Cheryl
    On Becoming a Woman: Mothers and Daughters Talking Together, 1987
Christian, Robert
    Sender, The, 1982
Clay, Carl
    Babies Making Babies, 1990
    Radio, 1981
Cobb, Portia
    Drive by Shoot, 1993
    Who's in Control?, 1994

Cokes, Tony
    Fade to Black, 1991
Collins, Kathleen
    Cruz Brothers and Miss Malloy, The, 1980
    Losing Ground, 1982
Cosby, Bill
    Bill Cosby--Himself, 1981
Cosby, Camille O.
    Bill Cosby: 49, 1987
Coustaut, Carmen
    Extra Change, 1987
Cram, Bestor
    Midnight Ramble, 1994
Crawford, Alonzo
    Dirt, Ground, Earth, and Land, 1983
    Walk on White Nails, 1991
Crenshaw, Michelle
    Skin Deep, 1984
Crossley, Callie
    Bridge to Freedom (1965) - Episode 6, 1986
    No Easy Walk (1962-66) - Episode 4, 1986
Cundieff, Rusty
    Fear of a Black Hat, 1994
Dash, Julie
    Breaking the Silence: On Reproductive Rights, 1987
    Daughters of the Dust, 1991
    Illusions, 1983
    Lost in the Night, 1992
    Praise House, 1991
    Preventing Cancer, 1987
    Relatives, 1990
Davis, Edgar Patterson
    Jury of Her Peers, A, 1994
Davis, Scott Hilton
    Freedom Station, The, 1988
Davis, Zeinabu irene
    Canta for Our Sisters, 1987
    Crocodile Conspiracy, 1986
    Cycles, 1989
    Filmstatement, 1982
    Kneegrays in Russia, 1990
    Period Piece, A, 1991
    Powerful Thang, A, 1991

Davis, Zeinabu irene
    Recreating Black Women's Media Image, 1983
    Sweet Bird of Youth, 1986
    Trumpetistically, Clora Bryant, 1989
Dickerson, Ernest
    Juice, 1992
    Surviving the Game, 1994
Duke, Bill
    Bounty Hunter, The, 1989
    Cemetery Club, The, 1993
    Deep Cover, 1992
    Killing Floor, The, 1984
    Rage in Harlem, A, 1991
    Raisin in the Sun, A, 1989
    Sister Act 2: Back in the Habit, 1993
Dunye, Cheryl
    Janine, 1990
    Potluck and the Passion, The, 1993
    She Don't Fade, 1991
Fanaka, Jamaa
    Penitentiary, 1979
    Penitentiary II, 1982
    Penitentiary III, 1987
    Street Wars, 1994
Ford, Abraham
    Burkina Faso: Land of the People of Dignity, 1988
    Lois Mailou Jones: Fifty Years of Painting, 1983
Franklin, Carl
    One False Move, 1991
Franklin, Oliver
    Alhaji Bai Konte, 1978
Frazier, Jacqueline A.
    Shipley Street, 1981
Freeman, Monica J.
    Children's Art Carnival--Learning through the Arts, 1979
Freeman, Morgan
    Bopha!, 1992
Frilot, Shari
    Cosmic Demonstration of Sexuality, A, 1992
    What is a Line?, 1994

Gardner, Robert
   Clarence and Angel, 1981
   King James Version, 1988
Gerima, Haile
   After Winter: Sterling Brown, 1985
   Ashes and Embers, 1985
   Sankofa, 1994
   Wilmington 10--USA 10,000, The, 1978
Gibson, Linda
   Flag, 1989
Gilbert, Charlene
   Kitchen Blues, The, 1994
Gilliam, Leah
   Now Pretend, 1992
Golden, Donna
   Doing What it Takes, 1990
Goodman, Karen Sloe
   If She Grows Up Gay, 1983
Greaves, William
   Beyond the Forest, 1985
   Black Power in America: Myth or Reality?, 1986
   Booker T. Washington: The Life & the Legacy, 1982
   Deep North, The, 1989
   Fighter for Freedom, 1985
   Frederick Douglass: An American Life, 1984
   Golden Goa, 1985
   Ida B. Wells: A Passion for Justice, 1989
   Opportunities in Criminal Justice, 1978
   Plan for All Seasons, A, 1983
   Resurrections: Paul Robeson, 1990
   Space for Women, 1981
   That's Black Entertainment, 1989
   To Free Their Minds, 1980
   Tribute to Jackie Robinson, A, 1990
   Where Dreams Come True, 1979
Greene, Kim
   Sweet Potato Ride, 1994
Griffin, Ada
   Can't Jail the Revolution & Break the Walls Down, 1991
Hammeen, Iman
   Unspoken Conversation, 1987

Hancock, John
    Weeds, 1987
Harkness, Jerald B.
    Facing the Facade, 1994
    Steppin', 1992
Harris, Leslie
    Just Another Girl on the I.R.T., 1993
Harris, Thomas Allen
    Black Body, 1992
    Heaven, Earth & Hell, 1994
    Splash, 1991
Harris Jr., Wendell B.
    Chameleon Street, 1992
Holland, Randy
    Fire this Time, The, 1994
Hooks, Kevin
    Heat Wave, 1990
    Passenger 57, 1992
    Strictly Business, 1991
Hope, Melanie
    Bird in the Hand, 1992
Hudlin, Reginald
    Boomerang, 1992
    Cosmic Slop: Space Traders, 1994
    House Party, 1990
Hudlin, Warrington
    Capoeira of Brazil, 1980
    Colour, 1983
    Cosmic Slop: The First Commandant, 1994
Hughes, Albert
    Menace II Society, 1993
Hughes, Allen
    Menace II Society, 1993
Ice-T
    Ice-T: OG, Original Gangster, 1991
Jackson, George
    House Party 2: The Pajama Jam, 1991
Jackson, Muriel
    Maids: A Documentary, The, 1985
Jamal, Sati
    Homecomin', 1980

Jefferson, Roland S.
Perfume, 1990
Jennings, Pamela
Sleep Now, 1991
Johnson, David C.
Drop Squad, 1994
Johnston, Heather
Scenes from the New World, 1994
Jones, Art
Know Your Enemy, 1990
Knowledge Reigns Supreme, 1991
Media Assassin, 1989
Juaibe, Vincent
Kwanzaa: The Gathering of a People, 1982
Katsiane, Jared
amBushed, 1993
Khaliq, Obiodum
Kwanzaa: The Gathering of a People, 1982
King, Hugh
Black and Blue, 1987
King Jr., Woodie
Black Theatre Movement: From A Raisin in the Sun to the Present, 1978
Black Theatre: The Making of a Movement, 1978
Death of a Prophet, 1981
Torture of Mothers, The, 1980
Kyi, Daresha
Land Where My Fathers Died, 1991
Thinnest Line, The, 1988
Lacey Jr., Madison Davis
Back to the Movement (1979-mid 1980s), 1989
Time Has Come, The (1964-1966), 1989
Lane, Charles
Sidewalk Stories, 1989
True Identity, 1991
Lange, Ted
Othello, 1989
Larkin, Alile Sharon
Different Image, A, 1982
Miss Fluci Moses, 1987
Your Children Come Back to You, 1979

Lathan, Stan
    Beat Street, 1984
    Celebration of Life: A Tribute to the Life of Martin Luther King, Jr., 1984
    Color of Friendship, The, 1981
    Go Tell it on the Mountain, 1984
    Not in Vain: A Tribute to Martin Luther King, Jr., 1981
    Sky Is Gray, The, 1980
    Uncle Tom's Cabin, 1987
Lee, Spike
    Answer, The, 1980
    Crooklyn, 1994
    Do the Right Thing, 1989
    Joe's Bed-Stuy Barbershop: We Cut Heads, 1983
    Jungle Fever, 1991
    Malcolm X, 1992
    Mo' Better Blues, 1990
    Sarah, 1981
    School Daze, 1988
    She's Gotta Have It, 1986
Lee, William
    Edge of Tolerance, 1991
    William Lee Mad As Hell, 1990
Lewis, Edward Timothy
    Serving Two Masters, 1987
    Spirit and Truth Music, 1987
Life, Reggie
    Carnival '78, 1978
Martin, Darnell
    I Like it Like That, 1994
Massiah, Louis J.
    Bombing of Osage Avenue, The, 1986
    Power! (1966-68), 1989
Mayson, Michael
    Billy Turner's Secret, 1990
McCullough, Barbara
    Fragments, 1980
    Horace Tapscott, 1984
    Shopping Bag Spirits and Freeway Fetishes: Reflections on Ritual Space, 1980
    Water Ritual #1: An Urban Rite of Purification, 1990
    World Saxophone Quartet, The, 1992

McDaniel, Matthew
   Birth of a Nation: 4*29*1992, 1993
McHenry, Doug
   House Party 2: The Pajama Jam, 1991
   Jason's Lyric, 1994
Mekuria, Salem
   As I Remember It: A Portrait of Dorothy West, 1991
Miles, William
   Black Stars in Orbit, 1989
   I Remember Harlem: The Depression Years, 1930-1940, 1980
   I Remember Harlem: The Early Years (1600-1930), 1980
   I Remember Harlem: Toward a New Day, 1965-1980, 1980
   I Remember Harlem: Toward Freedom, 1940-1965, 1980
Moss, Carlton
   Gift of the Black Folk, The, 1978
Moss, Richard Dean
   Adventures in Assimilation, 1992
Murphy, Eddie
   Harlem Nights, 1989
Nelson, Stanley
   Two Dollars and a Dream, 1986
Noble, Gil
   Amazing Grace, An, 1978
O'Neal, Ron
   Up Against the Wall, 1991
Oglesby, Caleb
   Reflections, 1987
Parkerson, Michelle
   ...but then, She's Betty Carter, 1980
   Gotta Make this Journey: Sweet Honey in the Rock, 1983
   Odds & Ends: A New-Age Amazon Fable, 1993
   Storme: The Lady of the Jewel Box, 1987
Parks, Gordon
   Gordon Parks' Visions, 1986
   Half Slave, Half Free, 1984
Phipps, Cyrille
   Black Women, Sexual Politics & the Revolution, 1991
   Our House: Gays and Lesbians in the Hood, 1993
Poitier, Sidney
   Fast Forward, 1985
   Ghost Dad, 1990
   Hanky-Panky, 1982
   Stir Crazy, 1980

Pollard, Sam
    Ain't Gonna Shuffle No More (1964-1972), 1989
    Portrait of Max, 1988
    Two Societies (1965-68), 1989
Prince (Rogers Nelson)
    Grafitti Bridge, 1990
    Prince: Sign O' the Times, 1987
    Under the Cherry Moon, 1986
Pryor, Richard
    Jo Jo Dancer, Your Life is Calling, 1986
    Richard Pryor: Here and Now, 1983
Ragusa, Kym
    Demarcations, 1992
Reedus, Narcel
    Fight, The, 1993
Reid, Tim
    Once Upon A Time When We Were Colored, 1994
Rich, Matty
    Inkwell, 1994
    Straight Out of Brooklyn, 1991
Riggs, Marlon T.
    Affirmations, 1990
    Anthem, 1991
    Color Adjustment, 1991
    Ethnic Notions, 1986
    Long Train Running: The Story of the Oakland Blues, 1983
    No Regret (Non, Je Ne Regrette Rien), 1992
    Tongues Untied, 1989
Roberts, Darryl
    How U Like Me Now, 1992
    Perfect Model, The, 1989
    Sweet Perfection, 1987
Robinson, Debra J.
    I Be Done Was Is, 1984
Roquemore, Cliff
    Petey Wheatstraw, 1978
Royals, Demetria
    Mama's Pushcart, 1988
Sandler, Kathe
    Question of Color, A, 1992
    Remembering Thelma, 1981

Santana, Alfred
  Voices of the Gods, 1985
Schultz, Chiz
  Leslie, 1988
Schultz, Michael
  Carbon Copy, 1981
  Disorderlies, 1987
  Earth, Wind and Fire in Concert, 1982
  Krush Groove, 1985
  Last Dragon, The, 1985
  Livin' Large!, 1991
  Scavenger Hunt, 1979
  SGT. Pepper's Lonely Hearts Club Band, 1978
Shabazz, Menelik
  Blood Ah Goh Run!, 1982
  Burning an Illusion, 1981
Sharp, Saundra
  Back Inside Herself, 1984
  Life is a Saxophone, 1985
  Picking Tribes, 1988
Shearer, Jacqueline
  Keys to the Kingdom, The (1974-1980), 1989
  Massachusetts 54th Colored Infantry, The, 1991
  Promised Land, The (1967-68), 1989
Singleton, John
  Boyz n the Hood, 1991
  Higher Learning, 1994
  Poetic Justice, 1993
Smith, Juney
  Nation, The, 1992
Smith, Vejan Lee
  Mother's Hands, 1992
Speight, Alonzo
  Deft Changes: An Improvised Experience, 1991
  People United, The, 1985
Suggs, Dawn
  Chasing the Moon, 1991
  I Never Danced the Way Girls Were Supposed To, 1992
Sullivan, Kevin Rodney
  Cosmic Slop: Tang, 1994

Taylor, Jocelyn
    Frankie & Jocie, 1994
Taylor, Ron
    Eddie Murphy Delirious, 1983
Thompson, Hugh
    Get a Job, 1978
Tollin, Michael
    Hardwood Dreams, 1993
Townsend, Robert
    Eddie Murphy Raw, 1987
    Five Heartbeats, The, 1991
    Hollywood Shuffle, 1987
    Meteor Man, The, 1993
Tucker, Camille
    Sweet Potato Ride, 1994
Tyehimba, Kenyatta
    Can't Jail the Revolution & Break the Walls Down, 1991
Van Peebles, Mario
    New Jack City, 1991
    Posse, 1993
Van Peebles, Melvin
    Funky Beat, 1986
    Identity Crisis, 1991
Ward Jr., Cal
    Rally or If Beale Street Couldn't Talk, The, 1994
Warner, Malcolm-Jamaal
    Playing it Safe: Truth about HIV, AIDS and You, The, 1992
Watson, Kim
    Reflections, 1987
Wayans, Keenen Ivory
    I'm Gonna Git You Sucka, 1988
    Low Down Dirty Shame, 1994
Webb, Floyd
    Flesh, Metal, Wood, 1982
Welbon, Yvonne
    Cinematic Jazz of Julie Dash, The, 1992
    Monique, 1990
    Sisters in the Life: First Love, 1993
Whitaker, Forest
    Strapped, 1993

White, Iverson
    Dark Exodus, 1985
    Magic Love, 1993
Whitmore, Preston A.
    Walking Dead, The, 1994
Wildman Steve
    Super Soul Brother, 1989
Williams, Lamar
    Black and Blue, 1987
Williams, Marco
    From Harlem to Harvard, 1982
    In Search of Our Fathers, 1992
Williamson, Fred
    Big Score, The, 1983
    Black Cobra II, 1989
    Black Cobra III: The Manila Connection, 1990
    Fist of Fear, Touch of Death, 1985
    Foxtrap, 1985
    Last Fight, The, 1983
    Messenger, The, 1986
    One Down, Two to Go, 1983
    South Beach, 1993
    Steele's Law, 1992
Woodberry, Billy
    Bless Their Little Hearts, 1983
Woods, Fronza
    Fannie's Film, 1981
    Killing Time, 1979
Woodson, Jacqueline
    Among Good Christian Peoples, 1991
Woolery, Reginald
    38th Parallel, 1992
    Converse, 1992
    Thirty-Eighth Parallel, 1992

Airth, Miskit
  Amazing Grace, An, 1978
Ali, Malik B.
  Henry: Portrait of a Serial Killer, 1989
Ali, Waleed B.
  Henry: Portrait of a Serial Killer, 1989
Avery, Byllye
  On Becoming a Woman: Mothers and Daughters Talking Together, 1987
Blake, Grace
  School Daze, 1988
Bond III, James
  Def by Temptation, 1990
Bonet, Nai
  Nocturna, 1979
Bourne, St. Clair
  Portrait of Max, 1988
  Question of Color, A, 1992
Brown, Jim
  Richard Pryor: Here and Now, 1983
Campbell, Luther
  Rap's Most Wanted, 1991
Cosby, Camille O.
  Bill Cosby: 49, 1987
Cosby Jr., William (Bill) H.
  Bill Cosby--Himself, 1981
Craig, Carl
  Hollywood Shuffle, 1987
DePasse, Suzanne
  Class Act, 1992
  Jacksons: An American Dream, The, 1992
  Who's the Man?, 1993
Fuller, Naima
  Black Music in America: The 70's, 1979
Glover, Danny
  To Sleep with Anger, 1990
Godwin, Laurna
  Minorities in Journalism: Making a Difference, 1989
Gordy Jr., Berry
  Last Dragon, The, 1985
Greaves, William
  Bustin' Loose, 1981

Guillaume, Robert
    Kid with the 200 I.Q., The, 1982
Haddock, Mabel
    Mandela, 1986
Hall, Arsenio
    Bopha!, 1992
    Playing it Safe: Truth about HIV, AIDS and You, The, 1992
Hampton, Henry
    Ain't Gonna Shuffle No More (1964-1972), 1989
    Ain't Scared of Your Jails (1960-61) - Episode 3, 1986
    Awakenings (1954-56) - Episode 1, 1986
    Back to the Movement (1979-mid 1980s), 1989
    Bridge to Freedom (1965) - Episode 6, 1986
    Fighting Back (1957-62), Episode 2, 1986
    Keys to the Kingdom, The (1974-1980), 1989
    Mississippi: Is this America? - Episode 5, 1986
    Nation of Law?, A (1968-1971), 1989
    No Easy Walk (1962-66) - Episode 4, 1986
    Power! (1966-68), 1989
    Promised Land, The (1967-68), 1989
    Time Has Come, The (1964-1966), 1989
    Two Societies (1965-68), 1989
Harris, Helen B.
    Chameleon Street, 1992
Harris, Leslie
    Just Another Girl on the I.R.T., 1993
Hudlin, Reginald
    Bebe's Kids, 1992
Hudlin, Warrington
    Bebe's Kids, 1992
Ice-T
    Ice-T: OG, Original Gangster, 1991
Jackson, George
    House Party 3, 1994
    Krush Groove, 1985
Jefferson, Roland S.
    Perfume, 1990
Jones, Clarence
    Fly by Night, 1994
Jones, Quincy
    Color Purple, The, 1985

Kunjufu, Dr. Jawanza
  Up Against the Wall, 1991
Lawton, J.F.
  Under Siege, 1992
Lee, Spike
  Drop Squad, 1994
M.C. Hammer
  M.C. Hammer: Please Hammer Don't Hurt 'Em, 1990
Malone, Adrian
  Nigerian Art: Kindred Spirits, 1990
Mays, M.D., James
  Perfume, 1990
McDade, Theresa
  Perfect Model, The, 1989
McHenry, Doug
  House Party 3, 1994
Murphy, Eddie
  Best of Saturday Night Live - Eddie Murphy, The, 1989
Roberts, Darryl
  Perfect Model, The, 1989
Schultz, Michael
  Krush Groove, 1985
Shannon-Burnett, Gaye
  My Brother's Wedding, 1983
Townsend, Robert
  Five Heartbeats, The, 1991
Walker, Alice
  Warrior Marks, 1993
Wayans, Damon
  Blankman, 1994
  Mo' Money, 1992
White, Steve
  Adventures of Huck Finn, 1993
  Meet the Applegates, 1991
Williamson, Fred
  Messenger, The, 1986

2 Live Crew
    Boyz n the Hood, 1991
    Hangin' with the Homeboys, 1991
A-Zaya Acappella Band
    Hear No Evil, 1993
Abel, Milton
    Mr. and Mrs. Bridge, 1990
Afanasieff, Walter
    Licence to Kill, 1989
Agier, Ethel
    To Sleep with Anger, 1990
Al B. Sure
    Boyz n the Hood, 1991
Alexander, Gregory
    Hollywood Shuffle, 1987
Amos, John
    Street Smart, 1987
Another Bad Creation
    Meteor Man, The, 1993
Armstrong, Howard "Louie Bluie"
    Louie Bluie, 1985
Armstrong, Louis
    Maxine Sullivan: Love to Be in Love, 1990
    Satchmo, 1989
Ashford & Simpson
    Without You, I'm Nothing, 1990
Atlanta Bliss
    Prince: Sign O' the Times, 1987
Baker, Anita
    Anita Baker - One Night of Rapture, 1987
Baker, Arthur
    Straight Out of Brooklyn, 1991
Banton, Buju
    Darker Side of Black, 1993
Basie, Count
    Swingin' the Blues: Count Basie, 1992
Beal, Eric
    Straight Out of Brooklyn, 1991
Belafonte, Harry
    Drei Lieder, 1983

Benton, Brook
    Rhythm and Blues Part 2, 1982
Big Daddy Kane
    Meteor Man, The, 1993
Billops, Camille
    Suzanne, Suzanne, 1982
Blanchard, Terence
    Mo' Better Blues, 1990
    Sugar Hill, 1994
Bland, Bobby Blue
    To Sleep with Anger, 1990
Bland, Michael
    Grafitti Bridge, 1990
Blow, Kurtis
    Krush Groove, 1985
Boogie Boys
    Enemy Territory, 1987
Boyer, Greg
    PCU, 1994
Boys Choir of Harlem
    Jungle Fever, 1991
Brown, Bobby
    Ghostbusters II, 1989
    Shelly Duvall's Rock N' Rhymeland, 1990
Brown, Charles
    That Rhythm, Those Blues, 1988
Brown, James
    Black Women, Sexual Politics & the Revolution, 1991
    Doctor Detroit, 1983
    Jacob's Ladder, 1990
    James Brown Live in Concert, 1979
    Nation Erupts, The (Part 1 & 2), 1992
    Rocky IV, 1985
    Soul I, 1983
Brown, Ruth
    Hairspray, 1987
    Rhythm and Blues Part 1, 1982
    That Rhythm, Those Blues, 1988
Bryant, Clora
    Kneegrays in Russia, 1990
    Trumpetistically, Clora Bryant, 1989

Bus Boys
    Eddie Murphy Delirious, 1983
Butler, Jerry
    Soul II, 1983
Byas, Don
    Celebrating Bird: The Triumph of Charlie Parker, 1987
Caesar, Shirley
    Gospel, 1987
Calloway, Cab
    Call of the Jitterbug, The, 1988
    Minnie the Moocher & Many Many More, 1981
Campbell, Little Milton
    To Sleep with Anger, 1990
Cara, Irene
    All Dogs Go to Heaven, 1989
    City Heat, 1984
    D.C. Cab, 1984
    Flashdance, 1983
Carter, Betty
    ...but then, She's Betty Carter, 1980
Carter, Ron
    'Round Midnight, 1986
Chambers, Jimmy
    Ashanti, 1979
Chambers, Paul
    John Coltrane: The Coltrane Legacy, 1985
Charles, Ray
    Evening with Ray Charles, An, 1981
Cherry, Ed
    Langston Hughes: The Dream Keeper, 1988
Cinelu, Mino
    Zajota and the Boogie Spirit, 1990
Cleveland, Reverend James
    Gospel, 1987
Cliff, Jimmy
    Marked for Death, 1990
Clinton, George
    Cheech and Chong: Still Smokin', 1983
    PCU, 1994
Cochron, Lee
    Say Amen, Somebody, 1982

Cole, Nat King
  Nat King Cole - Unforgettable, 1989
Coltrane, John
  John Coltrane: The Coltrane Legacy, 1985
  Nation Erupts, The (Part 1 & 2), 1992
  World According to John Coltrane, The, 1991
Connection, East New York
  Straight Out of Brooklyn, 1991
Cook, Sam
  Cadence, 1990
Cooper, Gary
  PCU, 1994
Cosby, Bill
  Bill Cosby--Himself, 1981
Cowan, Bennie
  PCU, 1994
Cray, Robert
  Chuck Berry: Hail! Hail! Rock 'n' Roll!, 1987
Creole, Kid
  Against All Odds, 1984
Crothers, Scatman
  Rhythm and Blues Part 1, 1982
  Rhythm and Blues Part 2, 1982
Daddy-O
  Straight Out of Brooklyn, 1991
Dara, Olu
  Langston Hughes: The Dream Keeper, 1988
Daring, Mason
  Brother from Another Planet, The, 1984
Davis, Eddie "Lockjaw"
  Bill Cosby: 49, 1987
Davis, Mary Bond
  Soul I, 1983
Davis, Miles
  Converse, 1992
  John Coltrane: The Coltrane Legacy, 1985
  Street Smart, 1987
  Toni Morrison: A Writer in America, 1987
  Zajota and the Boogie Spirit, 1990
Davis, Ray
  PCU, 1994

Davis, Tyrone
  Soul I, 1983
Dee, Papa
  Predator 2, 1990
Dehn, Mura
  In a Jazz Way: A Portrait of Mura Dehn, 1985
Devoe, Bell Biv
  Black Women, Sexual Politics & the Revolution, 1991
Diddley, Bo
  Rockula, 1990
Dolphy, Eric
  John Coltrane: The Coltrane Legacy, 1985
Domino, Fats
  That Rhythm, Those Blues, 1988
Don, Bigga
  House Party 3, 1994
Dorsey, Thomas A.
  Say Amen, Somebody, 1982
Dr. Dre
  Who's the Man?, 1993
  Without You, I'm Nothing, 1990
Dr. Fink
  Prince: Sign O' the Times, 1987
Drinkard, Nicholas
  Cissy Houston: Sweet Inspiration, 1987
Drinkard Moss, Ann
  Cissy Houston: Sweet Inspiration, 1987
Duke Ellington Band
  Memories of Duke, 1984
Eccles, Clancy
  Reggae Sunsplash II, 1979
Eckstine, Billy
  Rhythm and Blues Part 1, 1982
Edison, Harry "Sweets"
  Celebrating Bird: The Triumph of Charlie Parker, 1987
El DeBarge
  Short Circuit, 1986
Ellington, Duke
  Duke Ellington: Reminiscing in Tempo, 1991
  Memories of Duke, 1984

Faithful, Marianne
  Trouble in Mind, 1985
Fantastic Duo
  Beat Street, 1984
Fat Boys
  Fat Boys on Video--Brrr, Watch 'Em, 1986
Fats Waller
  Ain't Misbehavin, 1982
Fava, Tina
  Rocky IV, 1985
Fegan, Roy
  Hollywood Shuffle, 1987
Ferguson, Maynard
  Uncle Joe Shannon, 1978
Fifth Dimension
  Thank God It's Friday, 1978
Fire, Earth Wind and
  SGT. Pepper's Lonely Hearts Club Band, 1978
Flack, Roberta
  Bustin' Loose, 1981
  Sudden Impact, 1983
Florida Mass Choir
  Florida Mass Choir, The: Now I See, 1990
Force MDs
  Straight Out of Brooklyn, 1991
Ford Smith, Willie Mae
  Say Amen, Somebody, 1982
Fox, Charles
  Zapped, 1982
Franklin, Aretha
  Cissy Houston: Sweet Inspiration, 1987
  Jumpin' Jack Flash, 1986
Franti, Michael
  Darker Side of Black, 1993
Gaillard, Sam
  Rhythm and Blues Part 2, 1982
Gaines, Rosie
  Grafitti Bridge, 1990
Gale, Eric
  One False Move, 1991

Gamble, Kenneth
    Without You, I'm Nothing, 1990
Gardner, Stu
    Bill Cosby--Himself, 1981
    Bill Cosby: 49, 1987
Garrison, Jimmy
    John Coltrane: The Coltrane Legacy, 1985
Gaye, Marvin
    Jacob's Ladder, 1990
Georgia Mass Choir
    Georgia Mass Choir, 1989
Gillespie, John "Dizzy"
    Celebrating Bird: The Triumph of Charlie Parker, 1987
    Dizzy Gillespie: Jazz in America, 1980
Gordon, Dexter
    'Round Midnight, 1986
    Dexter Gordon Quartet, 1979
Grandmaster Melle Mel
    Beat Street, 1984
Green, Al
    Gospel According to Al Green, 1984
Hall, Aaron
    Winan's Return, The, 1990
Hall, Damien
    Winan's Return, The, 1990
Hancock, Herbie
    Colors, 1988
    Harlem Nights, 1989
    Soldier's Story, A, 1984
Hawkins, Walter
    Gospel, 1987
Hayes, Isaac
    Soul Man, 1986
Hendrix, Jimi
    Adventures of Ford Fairlane, The, 1990
    Jimi Hendrix: Experience, 1992
Heron, Gil Scott
    Baron, The, 1987
Hi Five
    Boyz n the Hood, 1991

Higgins, Billy
 'Round Midnight, 1986
Hill, Z.Z.
 To Sleep with Anger, 1990
Hines, Earl
 Call of the Jitterbug, The, 1988
Hooker, John Lee
 Blues Brothers, The, 1980
Houston, Cissy
 Cissy Houston: Sweet Inspiration, 1987
Houston, Thelma
 Thank God It's Friday, 1978
Houston, Whitney
 Cissy Houston: Sweet Inspiration, 1987
Howard, James Newton
 Marked for Death, 1990
Hubbard, Freddie
 'Round Midnight, 1986
Huff, Leon
 Without You, I'm Nothing, 1990
Hyman, Phyllis
 School Daze, 1988
Ice Cube
 Boyz n the Hood, 1991
 Darker Side of Black, 1993
 Nation Erupts, The (Part 1 & 2), 1992
 Rap, Race & Equality, 1994
 Without You, I'm Nothing, 1990
Ice-T
 Breakin', 1984
 Breakin' 2: Electric Boogaloo, 1984
 Nation Erupts, The (Part 1 & 2), 1992
 Rap, Race & Equality, 1994
 Ricochet, 1991
Isley Brothers
 Twist, 1992
Jackson, Freddie
 All Dogs Go to Heaven, 1989
 Def by Temptation, 1990
Jackson, Janet
 Place of Rage, A, 1991

Jackson, Mahalia
　　Mississippi Burning, 1988
　　Say Amen, Somebody, 1982
James, Rick
　　Tougher Than Leather, 1988
Jarreau, Al
　　Breakin', 1984
　　City Heat, 1984
Jenkins, Ella
　　Free at Last, 1990
Johnson Reagon, Bernice
　　Martin Luther King Commemorative Collection, 1993
Jones, Rev. Arthur T.
　　Florida Mass Choir, The:　Now I See, 1990
Jordan, Louis
　　Rhythm and Blues Part 1, 1982
Jordan, Stanley
　　Blind Date, 1987
Jordon, Sheila
　　Clarence and Angel, 1981
Kabbabie, Louis
　　PCU, 1994
Kahn, Chaka
　　I Never Danced the Way Girls Were Supposed To, 1992
Kelly, Wynton
　　John Coltrane:　The Coltrane Legacy, 1985
Khan, Chaka
　　Superman III, 1983
King, Ben E.
　　Soul I, 1983
Knight, Gladys
　　Licence to Kill, 1989
　　Rocky IV, 1985
　　Soul II, 1983
Komolafe, Dadisi Wells
　　Life is a Saxophone, 1985
Kool Moe Dee
　　Boyz n the Hood, 1991
　　Far Out Man, 1990
L.L. Cool J.
　　Black Women, Sexual Politics & the Revolution, 1991
　　Hard Way, The, 1991

Labelle, Patti
   Licence to Kill, 1989
Lakeside
   Powerful Thang, A, 1991
Latifah, Queen
   Straight Out of Brooklyn, 1991
Lavender Light,
   Among Good Christian Peoples, 1991
Lesbian and Gay Gospel, Choir
   Among Good Christian Peoples, 1991
Lewis, Tracy
   PCU, 1994
Lil' Louis & The World
   I Never Danced the Way Girls Were Supposed To, 1992
Little Richard (Penniman)
   Big Shots, 1987
   Shelly Duvall's Rock N' Rhymeland, 1990
Lodge, J.C.
   Straight Out of Brooklyn, 1991
Logan, John "Juke"
   Crossroads, 1986
Loose Ends
   Playing for Keeps, 1986
Love, Monie
   Boyz n the Hood, 1991
   Darker Side of Black, 1993
Lover, Ed
   Who's the Man?, 1993
Lymon, Frankie
   I Promise to Remember, 1983
Lynne, Gloria
   Rhythm and Blues Part 1, 1982
M.C. Hammer
   Addams Family, The, 1991
   Hammer Time, 1990
   M.C. Hammer: Please Hammer Don't Hurt 'Em, 1990
M.C. Ren
   Without You, I'm Nothing, 1990
Marley, Bob
   Bob Marley: Legend, 1984
   Reggae Sunsplash II, 1979

Marsalis, Branford
　　Mo' Better Blues, 1990
　　Sneakers, 1992
Martin, Sallie
　　Say Amen, Somebody, 1982
Matthews, Shirley
　　Straight Out of Brooklyn, 1991
McCarthy, Kendall
　　Eddie Murphy Delirious, 1983
McKee, Lonette
　　'Round Midnight, 1986
McKnight, Dewayne
　　PCU, 1994
Meeks, Charles
　　One False Move, 1991
Mel, Grandmaster Melle
　　Beat Street, 1984
Milburn, Amos
　　Rhythm and Blues Part 1, 1982
Milton, Darrin
　　Kneegrays in Russia, 1990
Milton, Kevin
　　Kneegrays in Russia, 1990
Mingus, Charles
　　Celebrating Bird: The Triumph of Charlie Parker, 1987
　　Stations of the Elevated, 1980
Mississippi Mass Choir
　　Mississippi Mass Choir, The, 1989
Monk, Thelonious
　　Celebrating Bird: The Triumph of Charlie Parker, 1987
　　Thelonious Monk: American Composer, 1991
　　Thelonious Monk: Straight No Chaser, 1988
Monroe, Allen
　　Mr. and Mrs. Bridge, 1990
Moore, Melba
　　Def by Temptation, 1990
Moore, Sam
　　Rhythm and Blues Part 2, 1982
　　Soul Man, 1986
Mosson, Cardell
　　PCU, 1994

Mtume, James
 Native Son, 1986
Mutabaruka
 H-2 Worker, 1990
N.Y.City Breakers
 Beat Street, 1984
Najee
 Def by Temptation, 1990
Naughty by Nature
 Meteor Man, The, 1993
 Rap, Race & Equality, 1994
Nelson, Novella
 Langston Hughes: The Dream Keeper, 1988
Neville Brothers
 City of Hope, 1991
 Place of Rage, A, 1991
New Edition,
 Krush Groove, 1985
New Life Singers, Bobby Jones and the
 Sister, Sister, 1982
Nightingale, Maxine
 Soul I, 1983
Norman, Jessye
 Jessye Norman, Singer, 1991
O'Neal, Eddie and Edgar
 Say Amen, Somebody, 1982
O'Neal, Shaquille
 Shaq Diesel the Music Videos, 1994
Owens, Jimmy
 Conversations with Roy DeCarava, 1983
Papa Juggs
 Marked for Death, 1990
 SGT. Pepper's Lonely Hearts Club Band, 1978
Parker, Charlie
 Celebrating Bird: The Triumph of Charlie Parker, 1987
Parker Jr., Ray
 Ghostbusters, 1984
 Ghostbusters II, 1989
 Mississippi Burning, 1988
Payne, Freda
 Soul II, 1983

Payne, Williams Michael
    PCU, 1994
Pendergrass, Teddy
    Choose Me, 1984
Perkins, Charles
    Mr. and Mrs. Bridge, 1990
Phillip C.
    Grafitti Bridge, 1990
Pikes, Charles
    Say Amen, Somebody, 1982
Poets, The Last
    Black Women, Sexual Politics & the Revolution, 1991
Pointer Sisters
    Ricochet, 1991
Preston, Billy
    Rhythm and Blues Part 1, 1982
    SGT. Pepper's Lonely Hearts Club Band, 1978
Pride, Dion
    Double McGuffin, The, 1979
Prince (Rogers Nelson)
    Batman, 1989
    Grafitti Bridge, 1990
    Nation Erupts, The (Part 1 & 2), 1992
    Place of Rage, A, 1991
    Prince: Sign O' the Times, 1987
    Purple Rain, 1984
    Under the Cherry Moon, 1986
    Without You, I'm Nothing, 1990
Procope, Russell
    Memories of Duke, 1984
Public Enemy
    Black Women, Sexual Politics & the Revolution, 1991
    Nation Erupts, The (Part 1 & 2), 1992
    Public Enemy: Tour of a Black Planet, 1991
    Tougher Than Leather, 1988
Ranks, Shabba
    Black Women, Sexual Politics & the Revolution, 1991
    Darker Side of Black, 1993
    Marked for Death, 1990
    Rocky IV, 1985

Reaves-Phillips, Sandra
    'Round Midnight, 1986
Reeves, Dianne
    Drei Lieder, 1983
Reid, Christopher
    House Party, 1990
Reid, Rufus
    Dexter Gordon Quartet, 1979
Riley, Teddy
    Winan's Return, The, 1990
Ritchie, Lionel
    Endless Love, 1981
Roach, Max
    Death of a Prophet, 1981
    Langston Hughes: The Dream Keeper, 1988
Robinson, Paul
    Nina Simone, 1985
Robinson, Smokey
    Twist, 1992
Rock Steady Crew
    Beat Street, 1984
Rodger, Theodis
    Up Against the Wall, 1991
Rodgers, Nile
    Alphabet City, 1984
Ross, Diana
    Thank God It's Friday, 1978
Ross, Richard
    Mr. and Mrs. Bridge, 1990
Rufus
    Powerful Thang, A, 1991
Run-D.M.C.
    Boyz n the Hood, 1991
    Ghostbusters II, 1989
    Krush Groove, 1985
    Tougher Than Leather, 1988
Scott, Lee G.
    Say Amen, Somebody, 1982
Seacer Jr., Levi
    Prince: Sign O' the Times, 1987

Shango
  Beat Street, 1984
Sheer Delight
  Rhythm and Blues Part 1, 1982
Sheila E.
  Adventures of Ford Fairlane, The, 1990
  Krush Groove, 1985
  Prince: Sign O' the Times, 1987
Shider, Gary
  PCU, 1994
Simone, Nina
  Nina Simone, 1985
  Without You, I'm Nothing, 1990
Sister Sledge
  Playing for Keeps, 1986
Sledge, Percy
  Soul II, 1983
Smith, Bertha
  Say Amen, Somebody, 1982
Smith, O.C.
  Rhythm and Blues Part 2, 1982
Snap
  Hangin' with the Homeboys, 1991
Solomon, Timothy "Poppin' Pete"
  Breakin', 1984
Soul Gee
  House Party 3, 1994
Spear, Burning
  Reggae Sunsplash II, 1979
Staple Singers
  Place of Rage, A, 1991
Staples, Mavis
  Grafitti Bridge, 1990
Stewart, Harry
  Cadence, 1990
Summer, Donna
  Thank God It's Friday, 1978
Sutton, Brenda
  One False Move, 1991
Sutton, Michael
  One False Move, 1991

Sweet Honey in the Rock
    Gotta Make this Journey: Sweet Honey in the Rock, 1983
    Sweet Bird of Youth, 1986
System, The
    Beat Street, 1984
Taj Mahal
    We Shall Overcome: The Song that Moved a Nation, 1989
Terminator X
    Livin' Large!, 1991
Terry, Sonny
    Crossroads, 1986
Tharpe, Sister Rosette
    To Sleep with Anger, 1990
The Angels of Mercy
    Leap of Faith, 1992
The Bus Boys
    48 Hours, 1983
The Clark Sisters
    Gospel, 1987
The Commodores
    Thank God It's Friday, 1978
The Dixie Hummingbirds
    We Love You Like A Rock--The Dixie Hummingbirds, 1994
The Furious Five
    Beat Street, 1984
The Get Fresh Crew, Dougie Fresh and
    Ghostbusters II, 1989
The Hawkins Family
    Gospel, 1987
The Kings of Rhythm,
    What's Love Got to Do with It, 1993
The Mighty Clouds of Joy
    Gospel, 1987
The Ohio Players
    Powerful Thang, A, 1991
The Soul Sonic Force, African Bambataa and
    Beat Street, 1984
The Teenagers
    I Promise to Remember, 1983
The Treacherous Three
    Beat Street, 1984

The Wailers
    Reggae Sunsplash II, 1979
Third World
    Reggae Sunsplash II, 1979
Thomas, Carla
    Soul II, 1983
Thomas, Greg
    PCU, 1994
Thomas, Rufus
    Soul II, 1983
Thompson, Lucky
    Celebrating Bird: The Triumph of Charlie Parker, 1987
Tindall, Nichole
    PCU, 1994
Tone-Loc
    Marked for Death, 1990
Tony! Toni! Tone!
    Boyz n the Hood, 1991
Tosh, Peter
    Marked for Death, 1990
    Peter Tosh Live, 1984
    Reggae Sunsplash II, 1979
Turner, Reverend Julian
    One False Move, 1991
Turner, Tina
    What's Love Got to Do with It, 1993
Tyner, McCoy
    John Coltrane: The Coltrane Legacy, 1985
US Girls
    Beat Street, 1984
Vandross, Luther
    Luther Vandross Live at Wembley, 1989
    Meteor Man, The, 1993
    Wiz, The, 1978
Vanity
    Action Jackson, 1988
Vaughan, Sarah
    Sarah Vaughan: The Divine One, 1991
Victoria, Christa
    Finding Christa, 1991
    Suzanne, Suzanne, 1982

Waddoud, Abdul
    Langston Hughes: The Dream Keeper, 1988
Waits, Frederick
    Deft Changes: An Improvised Experience, 1991
Walden, Narada Michael
    Licence to Kill, 1989
Walker, T-Bone
    Hangin' with the Homeboys, 1991
War
    Cheech and Chong: Up in Smoke, 1980
Ward, Val
    Onliest One Alive, The, 1989
Waters, Ethel
    Wild Women Don't Have the Blues, 1989
Waters, Muddy
    Soul Man, 1986
Webb, Chick
    Call of the Jitterbug, The, 1988
Webb, Floyd
    Flesh, Metal, Wood, 1982
Webster, Ben
    Ben Webster: The Brute and the Beautiful, 1992
Wells, Mary
    Rhythm and Blues Part 2, 1982
Wheeler, Harold
    Straight Out of Brooklyn, 1991
Whitfield, Mark
    Deft Changes: An Improvised Experience, 1991
Whodini
    Funky Beat, 1986
Wilkerson Jr., Edward
    Flesh, Metal, Wood, 1982
Williams, Cootie
    Memories of Duke, 1984
Williams, Ken
    Straight Out of Brooklyn, 1991
Winans, The
    Winan's Return, The, 1990
Winslow, Michael
    Police Academy 4: Citizens on Patrol, 1987

Witherspoon, Jimmy
    To Sleep with Anger, 1990
Wonder, Stevie
    Jungle Fever, 1991
Woods, Belita
    PCU, 1994
Workman, Reggie
    John Coltrane: The Coltrane Legacy, 1985
Zapp
    Powerful Thang, A, 1991

Abod, Jennifer
    I Am Your Sister, 1991
AIDS Prevention, Black Coalition for
    Survivors, 1993
Ajalon, Jamika
    Intro to Cultural Skit-Zo-Frenia, 1993
Bagwell, Orlando
    Ain't Scared of Your Jails (1960-61) - Episode 3, 1986
    Mississippi: Is this America? - Episode 5, 1986
    Racism 101, 1988
    Roots of Resistance: A Story of the Underground Railroad, 1989
    Running with Jesse, 1989
Belafonte, Harry
    Beat Street, 1984
Berry, Chuck
    Chuck Berry: Hail! Hail! Rock 'n' Roll!, 1987
Billops, Camille
    Finding Christa, 1991
    Older Women and Love, 1987
    Suzanne, Suzanne, 1982
Black Spectrum Theater
    Babies Making Babies, 1990
Blue, Carroll Parrott
    Conversations with Roy DeCarava, 1983
    Nigerian Art: Kindred Spirits, 1990
    Varnette's World: A Study of a Young Artist, 1979
Bolling, Deborah
    Public Enemy: Tour of a Black Planet, 1991
    Two Dollars and a Dream, 1986
Bourne, St. Clair
    Black and the Green, The, 1982
    In Motion: Amiri Baraka, 1982
    Making "Do the Right Thing", 1988
Brown, Curtis
    Game, The, 1990
Brown, Jim
    We Shall Overcome: The Song that Moved a Nation, 1989
Brown, Reginald
    Homecomin', 1980
Brown, Tony
    Black History Documentaries, 1994
    Highlights of America's Black Eagles, 1985

Burnett, Charles
    My Brother's Wedding, 1983
Burnett, Ewan
    Rap, Race & Equality, 1994
Caldwell, Ben
    Street Wars, 1994
Calloway, Shirley M.
    Perfume, 1990
Campanella Jr., Roy
    Impressions of Joyce, 1979
    Pass/Fail, 1978
    Passion and Memory, 1986
    Thieves, The, 1979
Campbell, Luther
    Rap's Most Wanted, 1991
Cannon, Reuben
    Winans, The: Live in Concert, 1987
    Women of Brewster Place, The, 1988
Carew, Topper
    D.C. Cab, 1984
    Talkin' Dirty after Dark, 1991
Casey, Bernie
    Wholly Moses, 1980
Chenzira, Ayoka
    Alma's Rainbow, 1993
    Hair Piece: A Film for Nappy-Headed People, 1984
    Love Potion, 1993
    Lure and the Lore, The, 1989
    MOTV (My Own TV), 1993
    Syvilla: They Dance to Her Drum, 1979
    Zajota and the Boogie Spirit, 1990
Chisholm, Cheryl
    On Becoming a Woman: Mothers and Daughters Talking Together, 1987
Clark-Lewis, Elizabeth
    Freedom Bags, 1980
Cobb, Charles
    Chasing the Basketball Dream, 1984
Cokes, Tony
    Fade to Black, 1991
Colbert, Chuck
    Up Against the Wall, 1991

Colbert, Zuindi
Up Against the Wall, 1991
Cole, Maria
Nat King Cole - Unforgettable, 1989
Collins, Kathleen
Cruz Brothers and Miss Malloy, The, 1980
Losing Ground, 1982
Cosby, Bill
Leonard Part 6, 1987
Counter, S. Allen
I Shall Moulder before I Shall Be Taken, 1978
Cox, Bette
Blind Tom: The Story of Thomas Bethune, 1987
Craig, Carl
House Party 3, 1994
I'm Gonna Git You Sucka, 1988
Cram, Bestor
Midnight Ramble, 1994
Crawford, Alonzo
Walk on White Nails, 1991
Crossley, Callie
Bridge to Freedom (1965) - Episode 6, 1986
No Easy Walk (1962-66) - Episode 4, 1986
Daniels, John R.
Getting Over, 1981
Dash, Julie
Daughters of the Dust, 1991
Illusions, 1983
Preventing Cancer, 1987
Relatives, 1990
Davis, Bridgett
Creative Detours, 1992
Davis, Edgar Patterson
Jury of Her Peers, A, 1994
Davis, Ossie
Second American Revolution, 1984
Davis, Richard
Cadence, 1990
Common Bonds, 1992
Davis, Scott Hilton
Freedom Station, The, 1988

Davis, Zeinabu irene
  Canta for Our Sisters, 1987
  Cycles, 1989
  Filmstatement, 1982
  Kneegrays in Russia, 1990
  Powerful Thang, A, 1991
  Sweet Bird of Youth, 1986
  Trumpetistically, Clora Bryant, 1989
Driskell, David
  Gift of the Black Folk, The, 1978
  Hidden Heritage: The Roots of Black American Painting, 1990
Dunye, Cheryl
  Janine, 1990
Easter, Mary M.
  Some People, 1988
Elliott, Dolores
  Portrait of Max, 1988
Fanaka, Jamaa
  Penitentiary, 1979
  Penitentiary II, 1982
  Penitentiary III, 1987
  Street Wars, 1994
Ford, Abraham
  Lois Mailou Jones: Fifty Years of Painting, 1983
Franklin, Oliver
  Alhaji Bai Konte, 1978
Frazier, Jacqueline A.
  Shipley Street, 1981
Frilot, Shari
  Cosmic Demonstration of Sexuality, A, 1992
  What is a Line?, 1994
Gardner, Robert
  Clarence and Angel, 1981
George, Nelson
  CB4: The Movie, 1993
  Def by Temptation, 1990
  Strictly Business, 1991
Gerima, Haile
  After Winter: Sterling Brown, 1985
  Ashes and Embers, 1985
  Sankofa, 1994

Gerima, Shirikiana Aina
Sankofa, 1994
Gibson, Pam
Strictly Business, 1991
Gifford, David
From Harlem to Harvard, 1982
Godwin, Laurna
Minorities in Journalism: Making a Difference, 1989
Goggin Jr., Regis J.
African-American Perspective, An, 1989
Goldberg, Whoopi
Laugh, A Tear, A, 1990
Golden, Donna
Nation Erupts, The (Part 1 & 2), 1992
Our House: Gays and Lesbians in the Hood, 1993
Gray, Ronald K.
Losing Ground, 1982
Greaves, William
Beyond the Forest, 1985
Black Power in America: Myth or Reality?, 1986
Booker T. Washington: The Life & the Legacy, 1982
Deep North, The, 1989
Fighter for Freedom, 1985
Frederick Douglass: An American Life, 1984
Golden Goa, 1985
Ida B. Wells: A Passion for Justice, 1989
Opportunities in Criminal Justice, 1978
Plan for All Seasons, A, 1983
Resurrections: Paul Robeson, 1990
Space for Women, 1981
To Free Their Minds, 1980
Tribute to Jackie Robinson, A, 1990
Where Dreams Come True, 1979
Harris, Thomas Allen
Splash, 1991
Higgins, Billy
Heaven is a Playground, 1992
Hudlin, Warrington
Boomerang, 1992
Capoeira of Brazil, 1980
Colour, 1983
House Party, 1990

Hughes, Albert
    Menace II Society, 1993
Hughes, Allen
    Menace II Society, 1993
Jackson, Billy
    Booker T. Washington: The Life & the Legacy, 1982
    Didn't We Ramble On: The Black Marching Band, 1989
Jackson, George
    Disorderlies, 1987
    House Party 2: The Pajama Jam, 1991
    Jason's Lyric, 1994
    New Jack City, 1991
    Tougher Than Leather, 1988
Jafa, Arthur
    Daughters of the Dust, 1991
Jamal, Sati
    Homecomin', 1980
Johnson, Deborah
    Doc Hollywood, 1991
Johnson, Ernest
    Cosmic Slop: Space Traders, 1994
    Cosmic Slop: Tang, 1994
    Cosmic Slop: The First Commandant, 1994
Johnston, Heather
    Scenes from the New World, 1994
Jones, Art
    Nation Erupts, The (Part 1 & 2), 1992
Kennedy, Leon Isaac
    Knights of the City, 1985
    Penitentiary III, 1987
King Jr., Woodie
    Black Theatre Movement: From A Raisin in the Sun to the Present, 1978
    Black Theatre: The Making of a Movement, 1978
    Death of a Prophet, 1981
    Torture of Mothers, The, 1980
Kino, Arsenal
    Bongo Man, 1981
Kuzwayo, Ellen
    Tsiamelo, A Place of Goodness, 1983
Kyi, Daresha
    Land Where My Fathers Died, 1991

Lacey Jr., Madison Davis
Back to the Movement (1979-mid 1980s), 1989
Time Has Come, The (1964-1966), 1989
Lane, Charles
Alma's Rainbow, 1993
Sidewalk Stories, 1989
Laneuville, Eric
Brother Future, 1991
Larkin, Alile Sharon
Different Image, A, 1982
Miss Fluci Moses, 1987
Your Children Come Back to You, 1979
Lee, Shelton J.
She's Gotta Have It, 1986
Lee, Spike
Answer, The, 1980
Crooklyn, 1994
Do the Right Thing, 1989
Joe's Bed-Stuy Barbershop: We Cut Heads, 1983
Jungle Fever, 1991
Malcolm X, 1992
Mo' Better Blues, 1990
Sarah, 1981
School Daze, 1988
Lewis, Edward Timothy
Serving Two Masters, 1987
Spirit and Truth Music, 1987
Life, Reggie
Carnival '78, 1978
Markin, Carole
From Harlem to Harvard, 1982
Massiah, Louis J.
Bombing of Osage Avenue, The, 1986
Nation of Law?, A (1968-1971), 1989
Power! (1966-68), 1989
McCullough, Barbara
Water Ritual #1: An Urban Rite of Purification, 1990
McDade, Theresa
Sweet Perfection, 1987
McDaniel, Matthew
Birth of a Nation: 4*29*1992, 1993

McHenry, Doug
    House Party 2: The Pajama Jam, 1991
    Jason's Lyric, 1994
    Krush Groove, 1985
    New Jack City, 1991
    Tougher Than Leather, 1988
Medina, Benny
    Above the Rim, 1994
Miles, William
    Black Champions, 1986
    Black Stars in Orbit, 1989
    Black West, The, 1994
    Different Drummer: Blacks in the Military, The, 1983
    I Remember Harlem: The Depression Years, 1930-1940, 1980
    I Remember Harlem: The Early Years (1600-1930), 1980
    I Remember Harlem: Toward a New Day, 1965-1980, 1980
    I Remember Harlem: Toward Freedom, 1940-1965, 1980
    James Baldwin: The Price of the Ticket, 1988
    Liberators: Fighting on Two Fronts in World War II, 1992
    Paul Robeson: Man of Conscience, 1987
    Positively Black, 1983
    Preaching the Word, 1987
Miller, Dian R.
    Dark End of the Street, The, 1981
Moore, Rudy Ray
    Avenging Disco Godfather, 1986
Morris, Wayne
    Brother Future, 1991
Murphy, Eddie
    Another 48 Hours, 1990
    Eddie Murphy Delirious, 1983
Nelson, Stanley
    Freedom Bags, 1980
    Two Dollars and a Dream, 1986
O'Dell, Bryan
    Street Wars, 1994
O'Reilly, Aida Talka
    African Story Magic, 1992
Owens, Brent
    Bronx: A Cry for Help, The, 1989

Parkerson, Michelle
...but then, She's Betty Carter, 1980
Gotta Make this Journey: Sweet Honey in the Rock, 1983
Phipps, Cyrille
Black Women, Sexual Politics & the Revolution, 1991
Our House: Gays and Lesbians in the Hood, 1993
Respect Is Due, 1992
Pollard, Sam
Portrait of Max, 1988
Two Societies (1965-68), 1989
Pryor, Richard
Bustin' Loose, 1981
Jo Jo Dancer, Your Life is Calling, 1986
Richard Pryor: Live on the Sunset Strip, 1982
Reid, Tim
Once Upon A Time When We Were Colored, 1994
Rich, Matty
Straight Out of Brooklyn, 1991
Riggs, Marlon T.
Affirmations, 1990
Anthem, 1991
Color Adjustment, 1991
Ethnic Notions, 1986
Long Train Running: The Story of the Oakland Blues, 1983
No Regret (Non, Je Ne Regrette Rien), 1992
Tongues Untied, 1989
Roberts, Darryl
How U Like Me Now, 1992
Perfect Model, The, 1989
Sweet Perfection, 1987
Robeson, Susan
Don't Believe the Hype: The Politics of Rap, 1991
Robinson, Butch
Drop Squad, 1994
Robinson, Debra J.
I Be Done Was Is, 1984
Kiss Grandmama Goodbye, 1991
Sandler, Kathe
Remembering Thelma, 1981
Schultz, Chiz
Baron, The, 1987
Leslie, 1988
Raisin in the Sun, A, 1989

Schultz, Gloria
    Earth, Wind and Fire in Concert, 1982
Schultz, Michael
    Disorderlies, 1987
    Earth, Wind and Fire in Concert, 1982
Scott, Darin
    Fear of a Black Hat, 1994
    Menace II Society, 1993
    Offspring, The, 1987
    To Sleep with Anger, 1990
Scott, Ron
    Commissioned in Concert, 1989
Shabazz, Menelik
    Blood Ah Goh Run!, 1982
Shannon-Burnett, Gaye
    My Brother's Wedding, 1983
Sharp, Saundra
    Back Inside Herself, 1984
Sharpe, Wayne C.
    Thurgood Marshall: Portrait of an American Hero, 1985
Shearer, Jacqueline
    Keys to the Kingdom, The (1974-1980), 1989
    Massachusetts 54th Colored Infantry, The, 1991
    Promised Land, The (1967-68), 1989
Simmons, Ron
    Tongues Untied, 1989
Singleton, John
    Higher Learning, 1994
    Poetic Justice, 1993
Skaggs, Calvin
    Fly by Night, 1994
    Go Tell it on the Mountain, 1984
Smith, Juney
    Nation, The, 1992
Smith, Yvonne
    Adam Clayton Powell, 1989
Speight, Alonzo
    People United, The, 1985
Thomas, Maynell
    Class Act, 1992
    Who's the Man?, 1993

Thomas, Pamela A.
  Midnight Ramble, 1994
Thompson, Hugh
  Get a Job, 1978
Townsend, Robert
  Hollywood Shuffle, 1987
Tsimatsima, Blanche
  Tsiamelo, A Place of Goodness, 1983
Van Peebles, Melvin
  Identity Crisis, 1991
Wallace, Latressa
  Black Wallstreet, 1991
Waters, Robert E.
  Fighting Mad, 1979
Watson, Earl
  House Party, 1990
Wayans, Keenen Ivory
  Eddie Murphy Raw, 1987
Weathersby, Cassius Vernon
  D.C. Cab, 1984
  Getting Over, 1981
  Pacific Inferno, 1985
Webb, Floyd
  Flesh, Metal, Wood, 1982
Weiss, Andrea
  Tiny and Ruby: Hell Divin' Women, 1988
White, Iverson
  Dark Exodus, 1985
  Magic Love, 1993
White, Maurice
  Earth, Wind and Fire in Concert, 1982
Williams, Marco
  From Harlem to Harvard, 1982
  In Search of Our Fathers, 1992
Williams, Tyger
  Menace II Society, 1993
Williamson, Fred
  One Down, Two to Go, 1983
  South Beach, 1993
  Steele's Law, 1992

Wilson, Annette
    Black Wallstreet, 1991
Winfield, Paul
    Force 10 from Navarone, 1978
Women's Interart Center
    Fannie's Film, 1981
    Killing Time, 1979
Woodberry, Billy
    Bless Their Little Hearts, 1983
Woods, Fronza
    Fannie's Film, 1981
    Killing Time, 1979
Woodson, Jacqueline
    Among Good Christian Peoples, 1991

Angelou, Maya
  I Know Why the Caged Bird Sings, 1978
Bambara, Toni Cade
  Bombing of Osage Avenue, The, 1986
Barefield, Eric
  Little Nikita, 1988
Beam, Joseph
  Tongues Untied, 1989
Billops, Camille
  Finding Christa, 1991
Blue, Carroll Parrott
  Conversations with Roy DeCarava, 1983
  Varnette's World: A Study of a Young Artist, 1979
Bond III, James
  Def by Temptation, 1990
Bourne, St. Clair
  Making "Do the Right Thing", 1988
Brown, Curtis
  Game, The, 1990
Brown, Gerard
  Juice, 1992
Brown, Reginald
  Homecomin', 1980
Brown, Tony
  White Girl, The, 1988
Bufford, Takashi
  House Party 3, 1994
Burnett, Charles
  Bless Their Little Hearts, 1983
  My Brother's Wedding, 1983
  To Sleep with Anger, 1990
Campanella Jr., Roy
  Impressions of Joyce, 1979
  Pass/Fail, 1978
  Passion and Memory, 1986
  Thieves, The, 1979
Chenzira, Ayoka
  Alma's Rainbow, 1993
  Hair Piece: A Film for Nappy-Headed People, 1984
  Pull Your Head to the Moon: Stories of Creole Women, 1992
  Zajota and the Boogie Spirit, 1990

Christian, Barbara
    Gloria Naylor, 1992
Clay, Carl
    Babies Making Babies, 1990
    Radio, 1981
Cokes, Tony
    Fade to Black, 1991
Colbert, Chuck
    Up Against the Wall, 1991
Collins, Kathleen
    Losing Ground, 1982
Coombs, Orde
    Black Music in America: The 70's, 1979
Cooper, Barry Michael
    Above the Rim, 1994
    New Jack City, 1991
    Sugar Hill, 1994
Cosby, Bill
    Bill Cosby--Himself, 1981
    Bill Cosby: 49, 1987
Coustaut, Carmen
    Extra Change, 1987
Crawford, Alonzo
    Walk on White Nails, 1991
Crossley, Callie
    Bridge to Freedom (1965) - Episode 6, 1986
    No Easy Walk (1962-66) - Episode 4, 1986
Cundieff, Rusty
    Fear of a Black Hat, 1994
    House Party 2: The Pajama Jam, 1991
Dash, Julie
    Daughters of the Dust, 1991
    Illusions, 1983
Davis, Edgar Patterson
    Jury of Her Peers, A, 1994
Davis, Ossie
    Second American Revolution, 1984
Davis, Scott Hilton
    Freedom Station, The, 1988
Davis, Zeinabu irene
    Filmstatement, 1982
    Powerful Thang, A, 1991

Dickerson, Ernest
  Juice, 1992
Easter, Mary M.
  Some People, 1988
Elder, Lonne
  Runaway, 1989
Ellis, Trey
  Cosmic Slop: Space Traders, 1994
  Inkwell, 1994
Fanaka, Jamaa
  Penitentiary, 1979
  Penitentiary II, 1982
  Penitentiary III, 1987
  Street Wars, 1994
Farquhar, Ralph
  Krush Groove, 1985
Ford, Abraham
  Burkina Faso: Land of the People of Dignity, 1988
  Lois Mailou Jones: Fifty Years of Painting, 1983
Frazier, Jacqueline A.
  Shipley Street, 1981
Frilot, Shari
  Cosmic Demonstration of Sexuality, A, 1992
  What is a Line?, 1994
Fuller, Charles
  Sky Is Gray, The, 1980
  Soldier's Story, A, 1984
George, Nelson
  Strictly Business, 1991
Gerima, Haile
  Ashes and Embers, 1985
  Sankofa, 1994
Gibson, Pam
  Strictly Business, 1991
Graff, Todd
  Angie, 1994
  Fly by Night, 1994
Greaves, William
  Beyond the Forest, 1985
  Black Power in America: Myth or Reality?, 1986
  Deep North, The, 1989
  Fighter for Freedom, 1985
  Frederick Douglass: An American Life, 1984

Greaves, William
    Golden Goa, 1985
    Ida B. Wells: A Passion for Justice, 1989
    Opportunities in Criminal Justice, 1978
    Plan for All Seasons, A, 1983
    Resurrections: Paul Robeson, 1990
    Space for Women, 1981
Hall, Karen
    Women of Brewster Place, The, 1988
Hancock, John
    Weeds, 1987
Harris, Leslie
    Just Another Girl on the I.R.T., 1993
Harris, Luke Charles
    Question of Color, A, 1992
Harris, Thomas Allen
    Splash, 1991
Harris Jr., Wendell B.
    Chameleon Street, 1992
Hickman, Gail Morgan
    Big Score, The, 1983
    Murphy's Law, 1986
    Number One with a Bullet, 1987
Hudlin, Reginald
    Bebe's Kids, 1992
    House Party, 1990
Hudlin, Warrington
    Capoeira of Brazil, 1980
    Cosmic Slop: The First Commandant, 1994
Ifatunji, Songodina
    Up Against the Wall, 1991
Jamal, Sati
    Homecomin', 1980
James, Donald
    Little Nikita, 1988
Jefferson, Roland S.
    Perfume, 1990
Johnson, Charles J.
    Steele's Law, 1992
Johnson, David C.
    Drop Squad, 1994

Johnston, Heather
    Scenes from the New World, 1994
Kennedy, Leon Isaac
    Body and Soul, 1981
    Knights of the City, 1985
King Jr., Woodie
    Death of a Prophet, 1981
    Torture of Mothers, The, 1980
Kleiman, Dena
    Strapped, 1993
Kunjufu, Dr. Jawanza
    Up Against the Wall, 1991
Lacey Jr., Madison Davis
    Back to the Movement (1979-mid 1980s), 1989
    Time Has Come, The (1964-1966), 1989
Lancaster, Bill
    Thing, The, 1982
Lane, Charles
    Sidewalk Stories, 1989
Larkin, Alile Sharon
    Different Image, A, 1982
    Your Children Come Back to You, 1979
Lawton, J.F.
    Blankman, 1994
    Mistress, 1992
    Under Siege, 1992
Lee, Cinque
    Crooklyn, 1994
Lee, Joie
    Crooklyn, 1994
Lee, Leslie
    Go Tell it on the Mountain, 1984
    Killing Floor, The, 1984
    Langston Hughes: The Dream Keeper, 1988
Lee, Spike
    Answer, The, 1980
    Crooklyn, 1994
    Jungle Fever, 1991
    Malcolm X, 1992
    Mo' Better Blues, 1990
    School Daze, 1988
    She's Gotta Have It, 1986

Lewis, Edward Timothy
  Serving Two Masters, 1987
M.C. Hammer
  M.C. Hammer: Please Hammer Don't Hurt 'Em, 1990
Malone, Mark
  Dead of Winter, 1987
Martin, Darnell
  I Like it Like That, 1994
Massiah, Louis J.
  Nation of Law?, A (1968-1971), 1989
  Power! (1966-68), 1989
McCullough, Barbara
  Water Ritual #1: An Urban Rite of Purification, 1990
McDade, Theresa
  Perfect Model, The, 1989
  Sweet Perfection, 1987
Moss, Carlton
  Gift of the Black Folk, The, 1978
Murphy, Eddie
  Beverly Hills Cop II, 1987
  Eddie Murphy Raw, 1987
  Harlem Nights, 1989
Ngema, Mbongeni
  Sarafina!, 1992
Nickens, Daryl G.
  House Party 2: The Pajama Jam, 1991
Olmert, Michael
  Nigerian Art: Kindred Spirits, 1990
Parkerson, Michelle
  ...but then, She's Betty Carter, 1980
  Odds & Ends: A New-Age Amazon Fable, 1993
Parks, Gordon
  Gordon Parks' Visions, 1986
Patrick, Randal
  Fast Food, 1989
Payne, William Mosley
  Livin' Large!, 1991
Pinnock, Thomas Osha
  MOTV (My Own TV), 1993
Pollard, Sam
  Ain't Gonna Shuffle No More (1964-1972), 1989

Potter, Lou
  Booker T. Washington: The Life & the Legacy, 1982
  Fighter for Freedom, 1985
  Frederick Douglass: An American Life, 1984
  Half Slave, Half Free, 1984
  In Motion: Amiri Baraka, 1982
  Liberators: Fighting on Two Fronts in World War II, 1992
Prince (Rogers Nelson)
  Grafitti Bridge, 1990
Pryor, Richard
  Jo Jo Dancer, Your Life is Calling, 1986
  Richard Pryor: Here and Now, 1983
  Richard Pryor: Live on the Sunset Strip, 1982
Qualles, Paris
  Inkwell, 1994
Reed, Ishmael
  James Baldwin: The Price of the Ticket, 1988
Rich, Matty
  Straight Out of Brooklyn, 1991
Richardson, Sy
  Posse, 1993
Riggs, Marlon T.
  Affirmations, 1990
Roberts, Darryl
  How U Like Me Now, 1992
  Perfect Model, The, 1989
  Sweet Perfection, 1987
Robertson, Lanie
  Lady Day at Emerson's Bar & Grill, 1994
Robinson, Butch
  Drop Squad, 1994
Roquemore, Cliff
  Petey Wheatstraw, 1978
Saldaan McClintock, Derrick
  Diary of a Young Soul Rebel, 1991
Sandler, Kathe
  Question of Color, A, 1992
  Remembering Thelma, 1981
Scott, Darin
  Offspring, The, 1987

Shabazz, Menelik
    Burning an Illusion, 1981
Shearer, Jacqueline
    Keys to the Kingdom, The (1974-1980), 1989
    Promised Land, The (1967-68), 1989
Singleton, John
    Boyz n the Hood, 1991
    Higher Learning, 1994
    Poetic Justice, 1993
Smith, Vejan Lee
    Mother's Hands, 1992
Smith Jr., Bobby L.
    Jason's Lyric, 1994
Sosa, George
    Nation Erupts, The (Part 1 & 2), 1992
Speight, Alonzo
    People United, The, 1985
Steele, Shelby
    Seven Days in Bensonhurst, 1990
Suggs, Dawn
    I Never Danced the Way Girls Were Supposed To, 1992
Taylor, Clyde
    Midnight Ramble, 1994
Taylor, David
    Drop Squad, 1994
    Get Crazy, 1983
    Hanky-Panky, 1982
    Lightship, The, 1986
Thomas, Theodore
    Roots of Resistance: A Story of the Underground Railroad, 1989
Thompson, Hugh
    Get a Job, 1978
Thompson, John
    Scavenger Hunt, 1979
Toles-Bey, John
    Rage in Harlem, A, 1991
Toney, David
    House Party 3, 1994
Townsend, Robert
    Five Heartbeats, The, 1991
    Hollywood Shuffle, 1987

Van Peebles, Mario
    Identity Crisis, 1991
Van Peebles, Melvin
    Sophisticated Gents, 1981
Wayans, Damon
    Blankman, 1994
    Mo' Money, 1992
Wayans, Keenen Ivory
    Eddie Murphy Raw, 1987
    Five Heartbeats, The, 1991
    Hollywood Shuffle, 1987
    I'm Gonna Git You Sucka, 1988
    Low Down Dirty Shame, 1994
Webb, Floyd
    Flesh, Metal, Wood, 1982
Wesley, Richard
    Fast Forward, 1985
    Native Son, 1986
White, Iverson
    Dark Exodus, 1985
    Magic Love, 1993
Whitmore, Preston A.
    Walking Dead, The, 1994
Williams, Marco
    In Search of Our Fathers, 1992
Williams, Samm-Art
    Half Slave, Half Free, 1984
Williams, Tyger
    Menace II Society, 1993
Williamson, Fred
    Fist of Fear, Touch of Death, 1985
    Last Fight, The, 1983
Women's Interart Center
    Killing Time, 1979
Woods, Fronza
    Killing Time, 1979
Wright, Thomas Lee
    New Jack City, 1991

20th Century-Fox
2121 Avenue of the Stars #200
Los Angeles, CA 90067
(310)277-2221

3-D Productions
2215 Headland Dr.
East Point, GA 30344
(404)305-0045

A Sharp Show
P.O. Box 75796 Sanford Stat.
Los Angeles, CA 90075

A Wing and a Prayer Films
252 Greene Ave. #4A
Brooklyn, NY 11238
(702)243-5117

Abraham Ford
717 Calvert Lane
Ft. Washington, MD 20744
(301)292-6196

Alexandra Juhasz
(215)925-7734

American Federation of Arts (Films/4)
41 East 65 Street
New York, NY 10021
(212)988-7700

American Zoetrope
3400 Riverside Drive
Suite 600
Burbank, CA 91505
(818)557-3707

Appalshop
306 Madison St.
Whitesburg, KY 41858
(606)633-0108

Audio Brandon Films, Inc.
34 MacQuesten Parkway So.
Mount Vernon, NY 10550
(914)664-5051

Audio Brandon Video Catalog
1144 Wilmette Avenue
Wilmette, IL 60091

B-Down Filmworks
616 Windcliff Dr.
Marietta, GA 30067
(800)463-696

Barr Films
12801 Schabarum Ave.
P.O. Box 7878
Irwindale, CA 91706
(818)338-7878

Best Films
108 New South Road
Hicksville, NY 11801
(516)931-6969

BFA Educational Media
468 Park Ave, South
New York, NY 10016
(212)684-5910

Big Productions
2237 Parker Street
Berkeley, CA 94704
(510)843-2447

Billy Woodberry
1607 S. Shenandoah
Los Angeles, CA 90035
(310)205-0929

Britannica Films
310 S. Michigan Ave.
Chicago, IL 60604
(312)347-7900

British Film Institute
21 Stephen St.
London W1P 1PL, UK

Budget Video
1534 N. Highland

Hollywood, CA 90028
(213)466-2431

Cal Ward Jr.
(312)274-4927

California Newsreel
149 9th St.
Suite 420
San Francisco, CA 94103
(213)874-4107

Camden Entertainment Group
468 N. Camden Dr. 2nd Floor
Beverly Hills, CA 90210
(310)285-1712

Caravan Pictures
3000 W. Olympic Blvd.
Bldg 5
Santa Monica, CA 90404

Carol Mayes
(213)368-4690

Carolco
8800 Sunset Blvd
Los Angeles, CA 90069
(310)859-8800

Carousel Films
260 5th Ave.
Room 405
New York, NY 10001
(212)683-1660

Carroll Blue Film Library
Transit Media/AFI
P.O. Box 315
Franklin Lakes, NJ 07417
(201)891-8240

Castle Hill Home Video
1414 Sixth Avenue
New York, NY 10019

Castle Rock Entertainment
335 N. Maple Dr. #135
Beverly Hills, CA 90210
(310)285-2300

CBS/Fox
1330 Avenue of the Americas
5th Floor
New York, NY 10019
(212)373-4800

Center for Southern Folklore
130 Beale Street
Memphis, TN 38103
(901)525-3655

Chamba Mediaworks, Inc.
310 Water St.
Guilford, CT 06437
(203)453-9943

Charles Burnett Production
4534 S. Presidio Dr.
Los Angeles, CA 90008
(213)295-8396

Cherel Ito
106 Bedford St., #4E
New York, NY 10014
(212)691-2524

Chimpanzee Productions
9500 Gilman Drive
#0327
La Jolla, CA 92093
(619)534-8651

Cinema Guild
1697 Broadway
Suite 506
New York, NY 10019
(212)246-5522

Clarity Educational Productions, Inc.
22-D Hollywood Ave.
Ho-Ho-Kus, NJ 07423
(800)343-5540

Clementine Films
1041 N. Formosa Ave.
Bldg. #312
West Hollywood, CA 90046

Columbia/TriStar Home Video
Sony Pictures Plaza
10202 W. Washington Blvd.
Culver City, CA 90232
(310)280-7799

Columbia/TriStar Pictures
Sony Pictures Plaza
10202 W. Washington Blvd.
Culver City, CA 90232
(310)280-7799

Digital Domain
300 Ron Ave.
Venice, CA 90291

Direct Cinema Limited
P.O. Box 10003
Santa Monica, CA 90410

Discovery Channel
7700 Wisconsin Ave.
Bethesda, MD 20814

Disney Channel, The
(818)569-7538

Don't Believe the Hype
708 North 1st St.
#512
Minneapolis, MN 55401
(612)340-9316

Dularon, Inc.
P.O. Box 2121
Muskogee, OK 74402
(918)682-6268

Educational Video Network
1401 19th St.
Huntsville, TX 77340
(409)295-5767

Edward T. Lewis Film Library
22-D Hollywood Avenue
Hohokus, NJ 07423
(800)343-5540

Electronic Arts Intermix
536 Broadway, 9th floor
New York, NY 10012

Elkins Entertainment/Showtime
8306 Wilshire Blvd.
Suite 438
Beverly Hills, CA 90211
(310)285-0700

Empress Productions
8335 Topanga Canyon Blvd.
#123
West Hills, CA 91304
(818)886-9358

Evergreen
228 West Houston
New York, NY 10014
(212)691-7362

Facets Multimedia, Inc.
1517 W. Fullerton Avenue
Chicago, IL 60614
(800)331-6197

Fifth Day Films
(213)664-5938

Filmakers Library, Inc.
124 East 40th Street
New York, NY 10016
(212)808-4980

Filmic Archives
The Cinema Center
Botsford, CT 06404
(800)366-1920

Films for the Humanities
P.O. Box 2053

Princeton, NJ 08543
(800)257-5126

Films Inc.
5547 North Ravenswood Avenue
Chicago, IL 60640
(800)323-4222

First Run/Icarus Films
153 Waverly Place
6ht Floor
New York, NY 10014
(800)876-1710

Frameline Distribution
346 9th St.
San Francisco, CA 94103
(415)703-8650

Gabriel Films
457 Washington St.
New York, NY 10013
(212)941-6200

Garret Williams
(213)250-8898

Golconda Media
2 College St.
Suite 213
Toronto, Ont. Canada
(416)232-0321

Gumbo Film Group
P.O. Box 22565
Seattle, WA 98122
(206)328-8618

Harpo Productions/ABC
110 N. Carpenter
Chicago, IL 60607
(312)633-0806

Harpo Studios
1058 West Washington Blvd
Chicago, IL 60607
(312)633-1000

Hyde Park Productions
2707 Spencers Tr.
Marietta, GA 30062

Icarus Films
200 Park Ave., South
Suite 1319
New York, NY 10003
(212)674-3375

Image Film & Video Center
75 Bennett Street, NW
Suite N-1
Atlanta, GA 30309
(404)352-4225

Indiana University
Media Resources
Franklin Hall 0001
Bloomington, IN 47405
(812)855-2921

Indy 317-464-9405
(317)464-9405

Intellimation
P.O. Box 1922
Santa Barbara, CA 93116
(800)532-6327

Iris Films
63 W. 83 St.
New York, NY 10024
(212)721-6400

Island Pictures
8920 Sunset Blvd.
2nd Floor
Los Angeles, CA 90069
(310)276-4500

ITVS
(612)225-9035

Kathe Sandler
(212)864-4343

Kindred Spirit Productions
322 W. 14th St.
#3C
New York, NY 10014
(212)802-7247

Kino International Corp.
333 W. 39th St.
Suite 503
New York, NY 10018
(800)562-3330

KJM3
274 Madison Avenue
Suite 601
New York, NY 10016

Landmark Films Inc.
3450 Slade Run Drive
Falls Church, VA 22042

Major Video Concepts, Inc.
7998 Georgetown Road
Indianapolis, IN 46268
(800)365-0150

Mandeville Films
500 S. Buena Vista St.
Burbank, CA 91521
(818)560-1000

MCA Distributing Corp
70 Universal City Plaza
Universal City, CA 91608
(818)777-1000

Media Education Foundation
26 Center Street
Northampton, MA 01060
(800)659-6882

Media Home Entertainment, Inc.
7510 W. 6th St.
Suite 1032
Los Angeles, CA 90014
(213)236-1336

Metropolis Pictures
P.O. Box 0791
New York, NY 10024
(212)928-2156

MGM
2500 Broadway
Santa Monica, CA 90404
(310)449-3000

Miles Educational Film Production, Inc.
356 W. 58th St.
Suite C648
New York, NY 10019
(212)560-6916

Miramax Films
375 Greenwich Street
New York, NY 10013

Miramax Home Video
375 Greenwich Street
New York, NY 10013

Monica Freeman
(404)438-9497

Movie Unlimited
(800)668-4344

MPI Home Video
16101 S. 108th Ave.
Orland Park, IL 60462
(800)323-0442

Mypheduh Films, Inc.
48 Q Street NE
Washington, DC 20002
(202)529-0220

National Black Women's Health Project
1237 Ralph David Abernathy
Boulevard, S.W.
Atlanta, GA 30310
(404)758-9590

National Film Board of Canada
1251 Avenue of the Americas
16th Floor
New York, NY 10020
(212)596-1770

National Geographic Society Educational Films
P.O.Box 98019
Washington, DC 20090
(800)368-2728

New Day Films
22-D Hollywood Ave
Hohokus, NJ 07423
(201)652-6590

New Line Cinema
853 Broadway
New York, NY 10003
(800)221-5150

New Yorker Films
16 West 61st St.
New York, NY 10023
(212)247-6110

Octillion Entertainment
609 Westmoreland Ave.
Los Angeles, CA 90005
(213)480-3220

October Films
65 Bleecker Street
Second Floor
New York, NY 10012
(800)628-6237

Oracy Productions
P.O. Box 71083
Milwaukee, WI 53211
(414)264-0913

Our Film Works
(312)764-6170

Paramount
5451 Marathon St.

Hollywood, CA 90038
(213)462-0700

Paramount/HBO
1100 Avenue of the Americas
New York, NY 10036
(212)512-1431

PBS Video
1320 Braddock Place
Alexandria, VA 22314
(800)344-3337

Peak Productions/TriStar
10202 W. Washington Blvd.
Lean Bldg. 220
Culver City, CA 90232
(310)280-8894

Penn State University
Special Services Building
1127 Fox Hill Road
University Park, PA 16803
(814)865-6314

Penny Broke Productions
7550 Zombar Avenue #1
Van Nuys, CA 91404

Persuasion Productions
740A 14th St. #183
San Francisco, CA 94114
(415)995-4667

Phoenix Film and Video
468 Park Avenue South
New York, NY 10016
(212)684-5910

Phoenix/BFA Films & Video
468 Park Ave., South
New York, NY 10016
(212)684-5910

Pictorial Histories
713 So. 3rd st. W

Missoula, MT 59801

Proud To Be...
1235-E East Blvd
Suite 209
Charlotte, NC 28203
(704)523-2227

Purdue University Public Affairs Video Archives
Purdue University
West Lafayette, IN

Red Carnelian Films/Video
300 West 55th
Suite 10V
New York, NY 10019
(718)622-5092

Reel Images
The Cinema Center
Botsford, CT 06404

Ryanmac Productions
14622 Ventura Blvd.
#1016
Sherman Oaks, CA 91403
(818)501-3351

Scribe Video Center
1342 Cypress St.
Philadelphia, PA 19107
(215)763-1903

Shari Carpenter
(212)281-5926

Signifyin' Works
2600 10th Street
Suite 106
Berkeley, CA 94710

Speak Films
5455 Wilshire Blvd.
Suite 1614
Los Angeles, CA 90036
(818)560-1000

Swank Motion Pictures, Inc.
350 Vanderbilt Motor Parkway
Hauppauge, NY 11787
(800)876-3344

Tanya Hart Communications
5548 Green Oak Dr.
Los Angeles, CA 90068
(213)461-0695

Ted Lyde
(818)905-7004

Third World Newsreel
335 West 38th Street
5th Floor
New York, NY 10018
(212)947-9277

Tied to the Tracks Films
951A Dolores St.
San Francisco, CA 94110

Tim Reid Productions
1640 So. Sepulveda Blvd. #311
Los Angeles, CA 90025
(310)231-3400

Tony Brown Productions
1501 Broadway
Suite 2014
New York, NY 10036
(212)575-0876

Touchstone Pictures
Pier 62 W. 23rd St.
Hudson River #328
New York, NY 10011
(212)691-0006

Triumph-Realty
3870 Crenshaw Blvd.
#219
Los Angeles, CA 90008
(213)295-2012

Turner Original Productions
1050 Techwood Dr. NW
Atlanta, GA 30318
(404)885-4440

U.C.E. Pictures/Blessed, Inc.
9420 Reseda Blvd. #430
Northridge, CA 91324
(818)360-0888

United Artists
2500 Broadway St.
Santa Monica, CA 90404
(310)449-3000

United Artists Home Video
729 Seventh Ave.
New York, NY 10019
(212)575-4715

United Image Entertainment
1640 South Sepulveda Blvd.
Suite 311
West Los Angeles, CA 90025

Universal Pictures
100 Universal City Plaza
Universal City, CA 91608
(818)777-1000

University of Illinois Film/Video Center
1325 S. Oak St.
Champaign, IL 61820
(217)333-0950

University of Michigan
144 Lane Hall
Ann Arbor, MI 48109
(313)764-0350

Vigilant Cinema Productions
219 S. Street, N.W.
Washington, DC 20001
(202)332-7848

W.E.B. Du Bois Film Project
1507 North 16th Street

Philadelphia, PA 19121
(215)763-1900

Walt Disney
500 Buena Vista
Burbank, CA 91521
(818)560-1000

Warner Bros. Studio
4000 Warner Blvd.
Burbank, CA 91522
(818)954-6000

Wayne State University
159 Purdy Library
Detroit, MI 48202
(313)577-1980

WETA Educational Activities
Box 2626
Washington, DC 20013
(703)998-2821

Williams Greaves Productions, Inc.
230 W. 55th St., Broadway
New York, NY 10019
(212)246-7221

Women Make Movies, Inc.
462 Broadway 5th Floor
New York, NY 10013
(212)925-0606

Xenon Entertainment Group
1440 Ninth Street
Santa Monica, CA 90401
(800)829-1913

Academy of Motion Picture Arts & Sciences
Margaret Harris Library
333 S. La Cienega Boulevard
Beverly Hills, CA 90211
(310)247-3020

Archive of African American Music & Culture
Department of Afro-American Studies
Smith Research Center, Suite 180-81
2805 E. 10th Street
Indiana University
Bloomington, IN   47408
(812)855-8547

Black Film Center/Archive
Department of Afro-American Studies
Smith Research Center, Suite 180-81
2805 E. 10th Street
Indiana University
Bloomington, IN 47408
(812)855-6041

Center for Southern Folklore
130 Beale Street
Memphis, TN 38103
(901)525-3655

George Eastman House
900 East Avenue
Rochester, NY 14607
(716)271-3361

Library of Congress
Motion Picture Division
Madison Building
Washington, D.C. 20540
(202)707-8572

Museum of Modern Art (MoMA)
11 W. 53rd Street
New York, NY 10019
(212)708-9605

National Archive Records Administration
Motion Picture Branch
8601 Adelphi Road
College Park, MD 20740
(301)713-7060

New York Public Library
Donnell Library Center
20 W. 53rd Street
New York, NY 10019
(212)621-0618

Performing Arts Research Center at Lincoln Center
111 Amsterdam Avenue
New York, NY 10023
(212)870-1659

Schomburg Center for Research in Black Culture
515 Malcolm X Boulevard
New York, NY 10037
(212)491-2200

UCLA Film and Television Archive
1438 Melnitz Hall
405 Hilgard Avenue
Los Angeles, CA 90024
(310)206-5388

University of Southern California Cinema/TV Library
Edward L. Doheny Memorial Library
University Park
Los Angeles, CA 90089
(213)740-2344

Wisconsin Center for Film and Theatre Research
University of Wisconsin-Madison
407 State Historical Society
816 State Street
Madison, WI 53706
(608)264-6466

Books

Articles on Blacks in Film and Television, ca. 1965-ca. 1990. Felix Winston, project manager. Los Angeles, California: Institute of Research, 1965, 1990.

Blackfilm, a Critical Retrospective. Los Angeles: Gem Publishing Co., 1987.

Blackframes: Critical Perspectives on Black Independent Cinema. Mybe B. Cham, Claire Andrade-Watkins, James A. Snead, et.al. contributing writers. Cambridge, Massachusetts: MIT Press, 1988.

Blacks and Film, 1894-present: Popular Culture as Socio/Ideological Barometer and Consciously Commercial Work as Acts of Renegade Art. New Haven, Connecticut: William Reese Company, 1985.

Bernardi, Daniel, ed. The Birth of Whiteness: Race and the Emergence of United States Cinema. New Jersey: Rutgers University Press, 1996.

Bobo, Jacqueline. Black Women as Cultural Readers. New York: Columbia University Press, 1995.

Bogle, Donald. Toms, Coons, Mulattoes, Mammies, and Bucks. New York: Viking Press, 1973.

Cripps, Thomas. Black Film as Genre. Bloomington: Indiana University Press, 1978.

_____. Making Movies Black: The Hollywood Message Movie from World War II to the Civil Rights Era. New York: Oxford University Press, 1993.

_____. Slow Fade to Black: The Negro in American Film, 1900-1942. New York: Oxford University Press, 1977.

Diawara, Manthia. Black American Cinema. New York: Routledge, 1993.

Dyson, Michael E. Making Malcolm: The Myth and Meaning of Malcolm X. New York: Oxford University Press, 1995.

Guerrero, Edward. Framing Blackness: The African American Image in Film. Philadelphia: Temple University Press, 1993.

Harris, Erich L. African American Screenwriters Now: Conversations with Hollywood's Black Pack. California: Silman-James Press, 1996.

Hill, George H. <u>Blacks in Hollywood: Five Favorable Years in Film & Television 1987-1991</u>. Los Angeles: Daystar Publishing, 1992.

Kisch, John and Edward Mapp. <u>A Separate Cinema: Fifty Years of Black-Cast Posters</u>. New York: Farrar, Straus, and Giroux, 1992.

Klotman, Phyllis R. <u>Screenplays of the African American Experience</u>. Bloomington: Indiana University Press, 1991.

Landay, Eileen. <u>Black Film Stars</u>. New York: Drake Publishers, 1973.

Leab, Daniel. <u>From Sambo to Superspade: The Black Experience in Motion Pictures</u>. Boston: Houghton Mifflin, 1976.

Lee, Spike. <u>Spike Lee's Gotta have It: Inside Guerrilla Filmmaking</u>. New York: Simon & Schuster, 1987.

Lee, Spike, et. al. <u>Five for Five: The Films of Spike Lee</u>. New York: Stewart, Tabori & Chang, 1991.

Lee, Spike with Lisa Jones. <u>Do the Right Thing: A Spike Lee Joint</u>. New York: Fireside, 1989.

_____. <u>Mo' Better Blues</u>. New York: Simon & Schuster, 1990.

_____. <u>Uplift the Race: The Construction of School Daze</u>. New York: Simon & Schuster, 1988.

Lee, Spike with Ralph Wiley. <u>By Any Means Necessary: The Trials and Tribulations of the Making of Malcolm X</u>. New York: Hyperion, 1992.

Mapp, Edward. <u>Blacks in American Films: Today and Yesterday</u>. Metuchen, New Jersey: The Scarecrow Press, 1972.

Martin, Michael T. <u>Cinemas of the Black Diaspora: Diversity, Dependence, and Oppositionality</u>. Detroit: Wayne State University Press, 1995.

Maynard, Richard, ed. <u>The Black Man on Film: Racial Stereotyping</u>. Rochelle Park, New Jersey: Hayden Book Co., Inc., 1974.

Murray, James. <u>To Find an Image: Black Films From Uncle Tom to Superfly</u>. New York: Bobbs-Merrill, 1973.

Nesteby, James R. <u>Black Images in American Films, 1896-1954: The Interplay Between Civil Rights and Film Culture</u>. Washington, D.C.: University Press of America, 1982.

Noble, Peter. The Negro in Films. London: Skelton Robinson, 1948: reprinted New York: Arno Press, 1970.

Null, Gary. Black Hollywood: The Negro in Motion Pictures. Secaucus, New Jersey: The Citadel Press, 1974.

Parish, James R. Today's Black Hollywood. New York: Windsor Publishing Corp., 1996.

Patterson, Lindsay, ed. Black Films and Film-makers: A Comprehensive Anthology from Stereotype to Superhero. New York: Dodd Mead, 1975.

Pines, Jim. Blacks in Cinema: The Changing Image. London: Cassell and Collier Macmillan, 1974.

Pines, Jim. Blacks in Film: A Survey of Racial Themes and Images in the American Film. London: Studio Vista, 1975.

Reckley, Sr., Ralph, et. al. Images of the Black Male in Literature and Film: Essays in Criticism. Baltimore?: Middle Atlantic Writers Association Press, 1994.

Reid, Mark. Redefining Black Film. Berkeley: University of California Press, 1993.

Rhines, Jesse A. Black Film, White Money. New Brunswick: Rutgers University Press, 1996.

Ross, Karen. Black and White Media: Black Images in Popular Film and Television. Cambridge, Massachusetts: Polity Press, 1996.

Dissertations

Anderson, Lisa M. Icons, Myths and Reflections: Images of African American Women in American Theatre and Film. Thesis--University of Washington, 1995.

Ashton, Charlotte R. The Changing Image of Blacks in American Film: 1944-1973. Thesis--Princeton, University, 1981.

Birtha, Rachel R. Pluralistic Perspectives on the Black-Directed, Black-Oriented Feature Film: A Study of Content. Thesis--University of Minnesota, 1977.

Bobo, Jacqueline. Articulation and Hegemony: Black Women's Response to the Film The Color Purple. Thesis--University of Oregon, 1989.

Carter, Eleanor Y. <u>African American History in Literature and Film</u>. Thesis--
John Hopkins University, 1994.

Diakite, Madubuko. <u>Film, Culture, and the Black Filmmaker: A Study of
Functional Relationships and Parallel Developments</u>. New York: Arno
Press, 1980. (Dissertation)

Gibson, Gloria J. <u>The Cultural Significance of Music to the Black
Independent Filmmaker</u>. Thesis--Indiana University, 1987.

Jackson, Elizabeth K. <u>Contemporary Black Film, Television and Video
Makers: A Survey: Analysis of Procedures</u>. Thesis--Northwestern
University, 1989.

Jones, Joyce L. <u>The Image of Black Women in Film</u>. Thesis--Marquette
University, 1977.

Reid, Renee D. <u>The Black Image: The Portrayal of Blacks in Film and the
Influence of Television on Black Social Behavior</u>. Thesis--Harvard
University, 1982.

Segal, Michael S. <u>Film and Knowledge: A Case of Blacks in American Film</u>.
Thesis--UCLA, 1983.

Seward, Adrienne L. <u>Early Black Film and Folk Tradition: An Interpretive
Analysis of the Use of Folklore in Selected All-Black Cast Feature Films</u>.
Thesis--Indiana University, 1985.

Vaughn, Jennifer. <u>The Representation of Black Masculinity in American Film</u>.
Thesis--University of Rhode Island, 1993.

Filmographies and Bibliographies

<u>Black and Minority Film Resources in Metropolitan Washington</u>. Washington,
D.C.: Media Associates, 1980.

<u>Black and Third Cinema: Film and Television Bibliography</u>. London: Black
Film Institute, 1991.

Givanni, June. <u>Black Film and Video List</u>. London: BFI Education, 1992.

Gray, John. <u>Blacks in Film and Television: A Pan-African Bibliography of
Films, Filmmakers, and Performers</u>. New York: Greenwood Press, 1990.

Klotman, Phyllis R. <u>Frame by Frame--A Black Filmography</u>. Bloomington:
Indiana University Press, 1979.

Marcelline, Ashley. Ashley Marcelline's Black Film & Video Guide. Thornhill, Ontario: Black Cinema Network, 1994.

Meeker, Davis. Jazz in the Movies: A Guide to Jazz Musicians 1917-1977. New Rochelle: Arlington House Publications. (First published in London, 1977.)

Parish, James R. with George Hill. Black Action Films: Plots, Critiques, Casts and Credits for 235 Theatrical and Made-for-Television Releases. Jefferson, N.C.: McFarland, 1989.

Powers, Anne. Blacks in American Movies: A Selected Bibliography. Metuchen, New Jersey: The Scarecrow Press, 1974.

Sampson, Henry T. Blacks in Black and White: A Source Book on Black Films, (1904-1950). Metuchen, New Jersey: Scarecrow Press, 1977, 1995.

Sharp, Saundra. Black History Film List: 150 Films and Where to Find Them. Los Angeles, California: Poets Pay Rent, Too, 1989.

Monographs

In Touch with the Spirit: Black Religious and Musical Expression in American Cinema. Phyllis Klotman and Gloria Gibson-Hudson, conveners. Bloomington: Indiana University Press, 1994.

Periodicals

Black Camera. The newsletter of Black Film Center/Archive. Bloomington: Indiana University Printing.
Black Film Review. Washington, D.C.
Black Talent News, Los Angeles, California
Cineaste. New York
Ebony. Chicago, Illinois
Essence. New York
Jump Cut. New York
Independent, The. New York

Main Distributor Sources

Variety's Video Directory Plus. New York: R.R. Bowker, 1986-(Quarterly); CD-ROM.

Video Source Book, The. Syosset, N.Y.: National Video Clearinghouse, 1979-(Annual); Detroit, Mi, Gale Research, Inc., 1989-(Annual).

Bowker's Complete Video Directory. New York: R.R. Bowker, c1990-(Annual); CD-ROM; New Providence, NJ, 1992-(Annual).

Feature Films

Winners:

Actor in a Leading Role [Prior to 1976 {49th} Awards, this category was known as "Best Actor."]
Sidney Poitier in Lilies of the Field; Rainbow Productions, United Artists. {"Homer Smith"}; 1963.

Actor in a Supporting Role
Louis Gossett, Jr. in An Officer and a Gentleman, Lorimar Production in association with Martin Elfand; Paramount. {"Sgt. Emil Foley"};1982.
Denzel Washington in Glory, Tri-Star Pictures Production; Tri-Star. {"Trip"}; 1989.

Actress in a Supporting Role
Hattie McDaniel in Gone with the Wind, Selznick International Pictures; Metro-Goldwyn-Mayer. ("Mammy"}; 1939.
Whoopi Goldberg in Ghost, Howard W. Koch Production; Paramount. {"Oda Mae Brown"}; 1990.

Music - Scoring
Prince for Purple Rain, Purple Films Company Production; Warner Bros.; 1984.
Herbie Hancock for 'Round Midnight, Irwin Winkler Production; Warner Bros.; 1986.

Music - Score
Isaac Hayes for "Theme from Shaft" from Shaft, Shaft Productions, Ltd.; Metro-Goldwyn-Mayer; music and lyrics by; 1971.
Irene Cara, et al, for "Flashdance...What a Feeling" from Flashdance, Polygram Pictures Production; Paramount; lyrics by; 1983.
Stevie Wonder for "I Just Called to Say I Love You" from The Woman in Red, Woman in Red Production; Orion; music and lyric by; 1984.
Lionel Richie for "Say You, Say Me" from White Nights, New Visions Production; Columbia; music and lyrics by; 1985.

Nominees:

Actor in a Leading Role
Sidney Poitier in The Defiant Ones, Stanley Kramer Productions; United Artists. {"Noah Cullen"}; 1958.
James Earl Jones in The Great White Hope, Lawrence Turman Films Productions; 20th Century-Fox. {Jack Jefferson"}; 1970.

Paul Winfield in <u>Sounder</u>, Radnitz/Mattel Productions; 20th Century-Fox. {Nathan Lee Morgan}; 1972.

Morgan Freeman in <u>Driving Miss Daisy</u>, Zanuck Company Production; Warner Bros. {"Hoke Colburn"}; 1989.

Denzel Washington in <u>Malcolm X</u>, By Any Means Necessary Cinema Production; Warner Bros. {"Malcolm X"}; 1992.

Laurence Fishburne in <u>What's Love Got to Do with It</u>, Touchstone Pictures Production; Buena Vista. {"Ike Turner"}; 1993.

Morgan Freeman in <u>The Shawshank Redemption</u>, Castle Rock Entertainment Production; Columbia. {"Red"}; 1994.

Actor in a Supporting Role

Howard E. Rollins, Jr. in <u>Ragtime</u>, Ragtime Production; Paramount. {Coalhouse Walker, Jr."}; 1981.

Adolph Caesar in <u>A Soldier's Story</u>, Caldix Films Production; Columbia. {Sgt. Waters"}; 1984.

Morgan Freeman in <u>Street Smart</u>, Cannon Films Production; Cannon Releasing. {"Fast Black"}; 1987.

Denzel Washington in <u>Cry Freedom</u>, Marble Arch Production; Universal. {"Steve Biko"}; 1987.

Jaye Davidson in <u>The Crying Game</u>, Palace Pictures Production; Miramax Films. {"Dil"}; 1992. [Black British Actor.]

Samuel L. Jackson in <u>Pulp Fiction</u>, A Band Apart/Jersey Film Production; Miramax Films. {"Jules Winnfield"}; 1994.

Actress in a Leading Role

Dorothy Dandridge in <u>Carmen Jones</u>, Otto Preminger Productions; 20th Century-Fox. {"Carmen Jones"}; 1954.

Diana Ross in <u>Lady Sings the Blues</u>, Motown-Weston-Furie Production; Paramount. {"Billie Holiday"}; 1972.

Cicely Tyson in <u>Sounder</u>, Radnitz/Mattel Productions; 20th Century-Fox. {"Rebecca Morgan"}; 1972.

Diahann Carroll in <u>Claudine</u>, Third World Cinema Productions in association with Joyce Selznick and Tina Pine; 20th Century-Fox. {"Claudine"}; 1974.

Whoopi Goldberg in <u>The Color Purple</u>, Warner Bros. Production; Warner Bros. {"Celie"}; 1985.

Angela Bassett in <u>What's Love Got to Do with It</u>, Touchstone Pictures Production; Buena Vista. {"Tina Turner"}; 1993.

Actress in a Supporting Role

Juanita Moore in <u>Imitation of Life (1959)</u>, Universal-International. {"Annie Johnson"}; 1959.

Beah Richards in <u>Guess Who's Coming to Dinner</u>, Columbia. {"Mrs. Prentice"}; 1967.

Alfre Woodard in <u>Cross Creek</u>, Robert B. Radnitz/Martin Ritt/Thorn EMI Films Production; Universal. {"Geechee"}; 1983.

Margaret Avery in <u>The Color Purple</u>, Warner Bros. Production; Warner Bros.
{"Shug Avery"}; 1985.
Oprah Winfrey in <u>The Color Purple</u>, Warner Bros. Production; Warner Bros.
{"Sofia"}; 1985.

Best Picture:
Quincy Jones, Producer, et al, for <u>The Color Purple</u>, Warner Bros.
Production; Warner Bros.; 1985.

Costume Design:
Ruth Carter for <u>Malcolm X</u>, By Any Means Necessary Cinema Production;
Warner Bros.; 1992.

Directing:
John Singleton for <u>Boyz n the Hood</u>, Columbia Pictures Production;
Columbia; 1991.

Documentary:
Callie Crossley [and James A. DeVinney], Producers for <u>Eyes on the Prize:
America's Civil Rights Years/Bridge to Freedom 1965</u>, Blackside Inc.
Production; 1987.
William Miles [and Nina Rosenblum], Producers for <u>Liberators: Fighting on
Two Fronts in World War II</u>, Miles Educational Film Productions, Inc.
Production; 1992.

Music - Scoring:
Duke Ellington for <u>Paris Blues</u>, Pennebaker Production; United Artists; 1961.
Quincy Jones for <u>In Cold Blood</u>, Pax Enterprises Production; Columbia; 1967.
Isaac Hayes for <u>Shaft</u>, Shaft Productions, Ltd.; Metro-Goldwyn-Mayer; 1971.
Quincy Jones for <u>The Wiz</u>, Motown/Universal Pictures Production; Universal;
1978.
Quincy Jones, Andrae Crouch, et al, for <u>The Color Purple</u>, Warner Bros.
Production; Warner Bros.; 1985.
Jonas Gwangwa, et al, for <u>Cry Freedom</u>, Marble Arch Production; Universal;
1987. [Black South African.]

Music - Song:
Quincy Jones for "The Eyes of Love" from <u>Banning</u>, Universal; music by;
1967.
Quincy Jones for "For Love of Ivy" from <u>For Love of Ivy</u>, American
Broadcasting Companies-Palomar Pictures International Production;
Cinerama; music by; 1968.
Lionel Richie for "Endless Love" from <u>Endless Love</u>, Polygram/Universal
Pictures/ Keith Barish/Dyson Lovell Production; Universal; music and lyrics
by; 1981.
Ray Parker, Jr. for "Ghostbusters" from <u>Ghostbusters</u>, Columbia Pictures

Production; Columbia; music and lyrics by; 1984.

Quincy Jones, et al, for "Miss Celie's Blues (Sister)" from <u>The Color Purple</u>, Warner Bros. Production; Warner Bros.; music by; 1985.

Quincy Jones, Lionel Richie, et al, "Miss Celie's Blues (Sister)" from <u>The Color Purple</u>, Warner Bros. Production; Warner Bros.; lyrics by; 1985.

Jonas Gwangwa, et al, for "Cry Freedom" from <u>Cry Freedom</u>, Marble Arch Production; Universal; music and lyrics by; 1987. [Black South African.]

Lamont Dozier for "Two Hearts" from <u>Buster</u>, N.F.H. Production; Hemdale Releasing; music by; 1988.

Janet Jackson, James Harris III and Terry Lewis for "Again" from <u>Poetic Justice</u>, Columbia Pictures Production; Columbia; music and lyrics by, 1993.

James Ingram, et al, for "The Day I Fell in Love" from <u>Beethoven's 2nd</u>, Universal Pictures Production; Universal; music and lyrics by; 1993.

James Ingram, et al, for "Look What Love Has Done" from <u>Junior</u>, Northern Lights Entertainment Production; Universal; music and lyrics by; 1994.

Screenwriting:

Lonne Elder, III for <u>Sounder</u>, Radnitz/Mattel Productions; 20th Century-Fox; 1972.

Suzanne de Passe, et al, for <u>Lady Sings the Blues</u>, Motown-Weston-Furie Production; Paramount; 1972.

Charles Fuller for <u>A Soldier's Story</u>, Caldix Films Production; Columbia; 1984.

Spike Lee for <u>Do the Right Thing</u>, Forty Acres and a Mule Filmworks Production; Universal; 1989.

John Singleton for <u>Boyz n the Hood</u>, Columbia Pictures Production; Columbia; 1991.

Short Films - Live Action:

David M. Massey for <u>Last Breeze of Summer</u>, The American Film Institute; 1991.

Dianne Houston, et al, for <u>Tuesday Morning Ride</u>, Chantcleer Films; 1995.

Special Awards:

Quincy Jones. Jean Hersholt Humanitarian Award; 1994.

Phyllis R. Klotman is Professor of Afro-American Studies and American and Film Studies, and Founding Director of the Black Film Center/Archive at Indiana University. She has published five books and over 30 articles and essays on African American literature and film, including Frame by Frame: A Black Filmography and Screenplays of the African American Experience.

Gloria J. Gibson, Associate Professor of Afro-American Studies, is Assistant Director of the Black Film Center/Archives and Director of the Archive of Traditional Music. She has published numerous articles in the area of black cinema and specifically black women's cinema.